DELAWARE CODE ANNOTATED

REVISED 1974

2021 Interim Supplement #1

Prepared Under the Supervision of
the Delaware Code Revisors

DANIEL F. WOLCOTT, JR. and JAMES P. SHARP

by

the Editorial Staff of the Publishers

Supplementing the 2020 Cumulative Supplement

Including Legislation Enacted
Through 83 Del. Laws, c. 208,
by the 151st General Assembly,
as effective on January 1, 2022

MICHIE ™

COPYRIGHT © 2021
BY
STATE OF DELAWARE

*For information regarding the Delaware Code Annotated, please consult the
User's Guide appearing in Volume 1 of the Code.*

ISBN 978-0-327-10880-1

"MICHIE" is a trademark of Reed Elsevier
Properties, Inc., used under license

(Pub. 41402)

PREFACE

This Supplement to the Delaware Code follows the plan and scope of previous Supplements and is to be used in conjunction with the 2020 Cumulative Supplement.

This Supplement updates the Delaware Code and its 2020 Cumulative Supplement by including all signed Session Laws of a general and permanent nature enacted through 83 Del. Laws, c. 208 of the 2021 Regular Session of the 151st General Assembly, whether or not specifically amendatory of the Code, with the exception of amendatory legislation to Titles 12, 14, 15 and 18, which legislation is contained in the appropriate 2021 Replacement Volumes. A second 2021 Interim Supplement, containing all material in this publication plus updates related to the remainder of those Session Laws enacted after 83 Del. Laws, c. 208 in the 2021 Regular and Special Sessions of the 151st General Assembly, will be provided in early 2022.

Pursuant to 1 Del. C. § 211, in some cases, the Revisors have made changes in phraseology, arrangement and designation of text matter to correct grammatical or typographical errors or to conform with the style of the Code, but without change in substance.

Additionally, 70 Del. Laws, c. 186, amended 1 Del. C. § 211 by adding a subsection (c) which reads: "The Revisors shall gender neutralize or otherwise insure that a sole masculine or feminine designation never occurs unless it could only apply to one gender." Accordingly, statutes affected by legislation passed during the 2019 Regular Session of the 150th General Assembly have been rephrased in accordance with 1 Del. C. § 211(c) to render the language gender neutral.

This Supplement updates the Delaware Code annotations by including notes taken from Delaware cases appearing in the following sources:

Atlantic Reporter, 3d Series
Supreme Court Reporter
Federal Reporter, Third Series
Federal Supplement
Federal Rules Decisions
Bankruptcy Reporter

User information, comments, and questions.

Visit the website at http://www.lexisnexis.com for an on-line bookstore, technical support, customer support and other company information.

For further information or assistance, please call us toll-free at (800) 833-9844 or email us at Customer.Support@LexisNexis.com.

December 2021   MICHIE

TABLE OF CONTENTS OF THE CODE

TITLE 11

CRIMES AND CRIMINAL PROCEDURE

PART I

DELAWARE CRIMINAL CODE

PART II

CRIMINAL PROCEDURE GENERALLY

PART IV

PRISONS AND PRISONERS

PART V

LAW-ENFORCEMENT ADMINISTRATION

TITLE 13

DOMESTIC RELATIONS

TITLE 16

HEALTH AND SAFETY

PART I

LOCAL BOARDS OF HEALTH; HEALTH PROGRAMS

PART II

REGULATORY PROVISIONS CONCERNING PUBLIC HEALTH

PART III

VITAL STATISTICS

PART IV

FOOD AND DRUGS

PART V

MENTAL HEALTH

PART VI

SAFETY

PART XI

DELAWARE HEALTH CARE COMMISSION

PART XIII

DELAWARE HEALTH INFORMATION NETWORK

TITLE 25

PROPERTY

PART II

MORTGAGES AND OTHER LIENS

PART III

RESIDENTIAL LANDLORD-TENANT CODE

PART VI

MANUFACTURED HOME COMMUNITIES

PART VII

COMMON INTERESTS AND OWNERSHIP OF REAL ESTATE

TITLE 26

PUBLIC UTILITIES

TITLE 30

STATE TAXES

PART I

GENERAL PROVISIONS; STATE TAX AGENCIES; PROCEDURE AND ENFORCEMENT

PART II

INCOME, INHERITANCE AND ESTATE TAXES

PART III

OCCUPATIONAL AND BUSINESS LICENSES AND TAXES

PART IV

COMMODITY TAXES

TITLE 31

WELFARE

PART I

IN GENERAL

DELAWARE CODE ANNOTATED

CONSTITUTION
OF THE
UNITED STATES OF AMERICA

AMENDMENTS TO
CONSTITUTION OF UNITED STATES

AMENDMENT IV.

NOTES TO DECISIONS

II. REASONABILITY GENERALLY.

Reasonable suspicion. — Defendant's detention was reasonable, did not constitute a violation of constitutional rights and allowed for the lawful protective search of defendant's person for weapons because: (1) it was reasonable for an officer to suspect that an informant's tip was credible and that defendant was armed or engaged in criminal activity; (2) according to the tip, an individual reportedly possessed a weapon in a crowded convenience store; and (3) defendant reacted to a lawful inquiry in a way that could be interpreted as aggressive. Diggs v. State, 2021 Del. LEXIS 241 (Del. July 27, 2021).

III. WARRANTS.

Cell phones. — Search warrant affidavit properly described how detectives knew, based on wiretap information, that defendant was in possession of a cell phone used to communicate with a codefendant about suspected enterprise business; the Magistrate could reasonably infer from defendant's involvement with the enterprise that defendant's cell phone and enterprise-related evidence would likely be present at defendant's house and in defendant's car. Anderson v. State, 249 A.3d 785 (Del. 2021).

A general warrant to search defendant's smartphones violated defendant's rights under U.S. Const. amend. 4, Del. Const. art. I, § 6 and the particularity requirement in 11 Del. C. § 2306 because: (1) the general warrant was unlimited in time and scope; (2) the smartphone evidence was critical to the State's case and defendant's convictions; and (3) its admission was not harmless error beyond a reasonable doubt. Taylor v. State, 2021 Del. LEXIS 279 (Del. Sept. 8, 2021).

AMENDMENT V.

NOTES TO DECISIONS

III. DOUBLE JEOPARDY.

Thus when judge declared mistrial defendant was not placed in jeopardy. — In the absence of a verdict of not guilty of first-degree rape by the prior jury, double jeopardy did not bar defendant's retrial for that charge because there was no judgment of acquittal or final resolution of the charges by the jury where a mistrial was declared; there was never even any announcement that the jury was unanimously against defendant's guilt as to the offense. Benson v. State, 242 A.3d 1085 (Del. 2020).

AMENDMENT VI.

NOTES TO DECISIONS

II. SPEEDY TRIAL BY JURY.

And certain factors considered. — Barker v. Wingo, 407 U.S. 514, 92 S. Ct. 2182, 31 L. Ed. 2d 101 (1972) factors did not weigh in favor of finding a violation of defendant's right to a speedy trial because: (1) although more than a year had passed between defendant's arrest and first trial date, the delays were not solely attributable to the State; (2) defendant had not objected to the continuances of the trial date, or raised speedy trial rights, in the proceedings below; and (3) defendant had not shown that the delays prejudiced the defense. Benson v. State, 242 A.3d 1085 (Del. 2020).

Unless the length of delay is determined to be presumptively prejudicial, it is not necessary to consider the additional Barker v. Wingo, 407 U.S. 514, 92 S. Ct. 2182, 31 L. Ed. 2d 101 (1972) factors of the reason for delay, the defendant's assertion of the right to a speedy trial, and the prejudice to the defendant; the court considered additional Barker factors because there was more than 1 year between defendant's arrest and first trial. Benson v. State, 242 A.3d 1085 (Del. 2020).

V. CONFRONT WITNESSES.

Right of cross-examination not violated. — Trial court did not violate defendant's confrontation rights in a trial for home invasion and other charges by limiting the cross-examination of a subtenant of an apartment about drug paraphernalia found in the subtenant's room; the evidence was speculative and minor in importance compared to other evidence of guilt such as a weapon, shell casings, defendant's access to apartment keys and the identification of defendant as the intruder. Appiah v. State, 244 A.3d 681 (Del. 2020).

VII. ASSISTANCE OF COUNSEL.

Right of self-representation. — Defendant's claim, that the trial court's denial of a request for new counsel violated defendant's right to self-representation, was without merit; trial court was well within its discretion to deny the request during trial when the same request had been thoroughly considered a week before trial. Appiah v. State, 244 A.3d 681 (Del. 2020).

AMENDMENT VIII.

NOTES TO DECISIONS

III. CRUEL AND UNUSUAL PUNISHMENT.

Conditions of confinement. — Defendant lacked standing to assert a claim seeking release from incarceration due to the COVID-19 pandemic; the motion indicated only that defendant suffered from several health issues, but did not identify any specific health issues that would leave defendant uniquely susceptible to COVID-19. State v. Desmond, — A.3d —, 2020 Del. Super. LEXIS 3020 (Del. Super. Ct. Oct. 21, 2020).

CONSTITUTION
OF THE
STATE OF DELAWARE
ADOPTED 1897
AS AMENDED

ARTICLE I
BILL OF RIGHTS

§ 3. Free and equal elections.

NOTES TO DECISIONS

Vote by mail. — Operation of Delaware vote-by-mail statutes, 15 Del. C. § 5601 et seq. (now repealed), and the sending out vote-by-mail ballots or counting any ballots returned pursuant to the statutes were not to be permanently enjoined; the Delaware Legislature, in the face of an epidemic of airborne disease, and in light of the health emergency declared by the Governor of Delaware, made a determination that vote-by-mail was necessary for the continued operation of governmental functions and that it was impracticable to address this problem otherwise. Republican State Comm. v. State, 250 A.3d 911 (Del. Ch. 2020).

The vote-by-mail statutes utilized in the 2020 general election (15 Del. C. §§ 5601 to 5621, now repealed) were not unconstitutional on their face in light of their election-day ballot deadline because: (1) the General Assembly chose to apply the deadline already pertaining to absentee ballots (15 Del. C. § 5508) to those statutes; and (2) plaintiffs failed to demonstrate that the deadline was so burdensome on its face as to deprive voters of a constitutional exercise of the right to vote in a free and equal election. League of Women Voters of Del., Inc. v. State Dep't of Elections, 250 A.3d 922 (Del. Ch. 2020).

Statutory election-day ballot deadlines in the vote-by-mail statutes (15 Del. C. §§ 5601 to 5621, now repealed) and the statute setting the time for return of absentee ballots (15 Del. C. § 5508) were constitutional as applied to the 2020 general election; nothing in the record showed that voters availing themselves of the expanded right to mail ballots would be burdened beyond the usual requirement that they post their ballots at least a few days prior to the deadline. League of Women Voters of Del., Inc. v. State Dep't of Elections, 250 A.3d 922 (Del. Ch. 2020).

§ 4. Trial by jury.

NOTES TO DECISIONS

Waiver of jury trial. — Defendant's motion to strike the complaint's jury trial demand, on the ground that the jury trial waiver in the parties' purchase agreement extended to all related transactions and agreements, was denied because: (1) the waiver was expressly limited to the purchase agreement in question; and (2) the plaintiffs' claims were all asserted under a separate agreement. Tekni-Plex, Inc. v. LLFlex, LLC, — A.3d —, 2021 Del. Super. LEXIS 334 (Del. Super. Ct. Apr. 22, 2021).

§ 6. Searches and seizures.

NOTES TO DECISIONS

I. GENERAL CONSIDERATIONS.

Inmate's telephone calls. — Superior Court did not err in denying defendant's motion to exclude prison phone calls because the State had substantial governmental interest in preventing witness tampering; Superior court did not abuse its discretion in denying defendant's motion for continuance because there was evidence that counsel knew of prison phone calls, but did not request their production. Saavedra v. State, 225 A.3d 364 (Del. 2020).

II. UNREASONABLE SEARCHES.

A. IN GENERAL.

Exigent circumstances. — Defendant's detention was reasonable, did not constitute a violation of constitutional rights and allowed for the lawful protective search of defendant's person for weapons because: (1) it was reasonable for an officer to suspect that an informant's tip was credible and that defendant was armed or engaged in criminal activity; (2) according to the tip, an individual reportedly possessed a weapon in a crowded convenience store; and (3) defendant reacted to a lawful inquiry in a way that could be interpreted as aggressive. Diggs v. State, 2021 Del. LEXIS 241 (Del. July 27, 2021).

Search of automobile. — Defendant's motion to suppress was denied in part because from the 4 corners of the probable cause affidavit, the police had probable cause to believe that defendant's residence had evidence of the unlawful sexual intercourse at issue; the affidavit included the victim's description of the sexual assault and established a logical nexus between the items sought and defendant's vehicle and residence. State v. King, — A.3d —, 2021 Del. Super. LEXIS 48 (Del. Super. Ct. Jan. 21, 2021).

IV. PROBABLE CAUSE.

When probable cause justifies search warrant. — Police officers had probable cause to obtain a search warrant for a residence because: (1) the officers' possession of 5 capiases for defendant's arrest gave them the right to enter defendant's bedroom; (2) the officers were permitted to observe any contraband in plain view while in defendant's bedroom making a lawful arrest; and (3) a confidential informant indicated that defendant lived in and sold crack cocaine at the place the police sought to search.

State v. Lovett, — A.3d —, 2020 Del. Super. LEXIS 2817 (Del. Super. Ct. Oct. 2, 2020).

Probable cause based on informant's information. — Sufficient probable cause existed to support the issuance of a search warrant where: (1) the affidavit indicated that the affiants' training, experience and participation in past drug investigations allowed the affiant to tie certain recovered items to drug dealing activity; (2) the white powdery residue from the plastic baggies field tested positive for cocaine; and (3) the affiant provided notes of physical surveillance performed. State v. Peart, — A.3d —, 2021 Del. Super. LEXIS 243 (Del. Super. Ct. Mar. 25, 2021).

Probable cause maturing out of trash search. — Police department was not required to obtain a warrant prior to conducting a search of the contents of defendant's garbage can because: (1) the trash can was outside the curtilage of defendant's residence; (2) defendant failed to take any steps to protect the garbage from public view once the receptacle was placed at the end of the driveway for the purposes of trash collection; and (3) given those facts, defendant did not have a reasonable expectation of privacy in the trash can. State v. Peart, — A.3d —, 2021 Del. Super. LEXIS 243 (Del. Super. Ct. Mar. 25, 2021).

Probable cause maturing out of justification of stop of automobile. — Defendant's motion to suppress was granted because: (1) an odor or presence of marijuana was misstated and did not exist; (2) the arrival of 5 additional police officers who positioned themselves in a manner consistent with preparing for a search, (despite any evidence that a search was likely necessary) was inappropriate; and (3) police overstated the prevalence of "blunt spray" and failed to use normal police procedure and recordkeeping. State v. Cornelius, — A.3d —, 2021 Del. Super. LEXIS 501 (Del. Super. Ct. July 8, 2021).

Driving under the influence case. — Defendant was not entitled to suppress evidence from a preliminary breath test (PBT) because: (1) the officer's odor-eyes-speech observations did not involve coercion; (2) all of the field tests, except for the alphabet test, were refused by defendant and not part of the officer's determination of probable cause; (3) the alphabet test was executed entirely voluntarily; and (4) no coercion was employed against the defendant to force him to submit to the PBT. State v. Street, — A.3d —, 2020 Del. Super. LEXIS 2791 (Del. Super. Ct. Sept. 17, 2020).

DNA testing. — Warrant for defendant's DNA was not supported by probable cause because the affidavit in question failed to establish a sufficient nexus between defendant's DNA and evidence of a crime; specifically, the affidavit failed to describe the likelihood of recovering DNA from the evidence seized versus merely speculating that there was reason to believe defendant's DNA would be found on a gun and/or ammunition. State v. Lovett, — A.3d —, 2020 Del. Super. LEXIS 2817 (Del. Super. Ct. Oct. 2, 2020).

Cell phones. — Defendant's motion to suppress a cell phone as evidence was denied because warrants were supported by probable cause where: (1) a magistrate presented with the affidavit in question could reasonably have found a basis to believe that data reflecting defendant's location during a shooting would be on the cell phone; and (2) the affidavits supported the magistrate's determination that there was a nexus between the murder and defendant's cell phone. State v. Wilson, — A.3d —, 2021 Del. Super. LEXIS 84 (Del. Super. Ct. Jan. 29, 2021).

Search warrant affidavit properly described how detectives knew, based on wiretap information, that defendant was in possession of a cell phone used to communicate with a codefendant about suspected enterprise business; the Magistrate could reasonably infer from defendant's involvement with the enterprise that defendant's cell phone and enterprise-related evidence would likely be present at defendant's house and in defendant's car. Anderson v. State, 249 A.3d 785 (Del. 2021).

A general warrant to search defendant's smartphones violated defendant's rights under U.S. Const. amend. 4, Del. Const. art. I, § 6 and the particularity requirement in 11 Del. C. § 2306 because: (1) the general warrant was unlimited in time and scope; (2) the smartphone evidence was critical to the State's case and defendant's convictions; and (3) its admission was not harmless error beyond a reasonable doubt. Taylor v. State, 2021 Del. LEXIS 279 (Del. Sept. 8, 2021).

§ 7. Procedural rights in criminal prosecutions; jury trial; self-incrimination; deprivation of life, liberty or property.

NOTES TO DECISIONS

Analysis

VI.   Speedy and Public Trial.
VIII. Right Against Self-Incrimination.

VI. SPEEDY AND PUBLIC TRIAL.

Speedy and public trial. — Defendant's motion to dismiss and/or reduce bail was denied because the delay at issue in defendant's case was not attributable to the State, but rather to the judicial emergency arising from the COVID-19 pandemic impacting the scheduling of criminal trials. State v. Rosas, — A.3d —, 2021 Del. Super. LEXIS 197 (Del. Super. Ct. Mar. 10, 2021).

Court denied defendant's motion to dismiss for lack of speedy trial because: (1) the decision to take emergency health measures to limit the spread of the COVID-19 did not weigh against the State; (2) the continued inability to hold trials in a way that did not put the public, the parties, court staff and counsel at serious risk was a good-faith and reasonable justification

for delay; and (3), the court was not convinced that defendant's pretrial detention was unduly oppressive or that the defendant's anxiety was disproportionate because of COVID-19. State v. Rodriguez, — A.3d —, 2021 Del. Super. LEXIS 270 (Del. Super. Ct. Mar. 30, 2021).

VIII. RIGHT AGAINST SELF-INCRIMINATION.

Routine booking questions. — Statements made by defendant after initially declining to make a statement to the police were suppressed because: (1) an officer made conversation with defendant about what other people had said about defendant's living situation, rather than simply following the formal booking process; and (2) the officer failed to inform defendant of Miranda rights before engaging in further conversation with defendant about potentially incriminating information. State v. Lovett, — A.3d —, 2020 Del. Super. LEXIS 2817 (Del. Super. Ct. Oct. 2, 2020).

§ 8. Prosecution by indictment or information; double jeopardy; just compensation for property.

NOTES TO DECISIONS

II. DOUBLE JEOPARDY.

Multiple prosecutions and sentences for different acts permitted. — Defendant's racketeering and drug convictions were affirmed because: (1) defendant's first-degree conspiracy and racketeering convictions did not

violate double jeopardy where the offenses of racketeering and first-degree conspiracy each required proof of facts not necessary to complete the other; and (2) the facts so found could support separate convictions and punishments. White v. State, 243 A.3d 381 (Del. 2020).

§ 11. Excessive bail or fines; cruel punishments; health of prisoners.

NOTES TO DECISIONS

I. EXCESSIVE BAIL.

Speedy trial delays. — Defendant's motion to dismiss and/or reduce bail was denied because the speedy trial delay at issue in defendant's case was not attributable to the State, but rather to the judicial emergency arising from the COVID-19 pandemic impacting the scheduling of criminal trials. State v. Rosas, — A.3d —, 2021 Del. Super. LEXIS 197 (Del. Super. Ct. Mar. 10, 2021).

§ 12. Right to bail; access to accused.

Cross references.
Determining the amount of bail, § 2107 of Title 11.

§ 18. Prohibition against quartering soldiers in homes.

Section 18. No soldier shall in time of peace be quartered in any house without the consent of the owner; nor in time of war but by a civil magistrate, in manner to be prescribed by law.

Cross references.
This section is being reprinted to correct an error in the bound volume, substituting "nor" for "not."

§ 20. Right to keep and bear arms.

NOTES TO DECISIONS

Public safety interest. — Where probable cause existed for a gun owner to be involuntarily committed (although later discharged), the Commissioner did not err in entering an order mandating relinquishment of firearms because: (1) there was sufficient evidence the owner had a mental condition and was a danger to that owner's self and others; (2) the relinquishment order was a necessary result of a finding of probable cause; and (3) the State's objective of reducing gun violence and preventing suicide was significant, substantial, important and met an intermediate level of constitutional scrutiny (despite placing a substantial burden on the right to bear arms). State v. Smith, — A.3d —, 2020 Del. Super. LEXIS 2953 (Del. Super. Ct. Aug. 18, 2020).

§ 21. Equal Rights.

Equality of rights under the law shall not be denied or abridged on account of race, color, national origin, or sex.

History.
81 Del. Laws, c. 373, § 2; 82 Del. Laws, c. 1, § 2; 82 Del. Laws, c. 287, § 1; 83 Del. Laws, c. 1, § 1.

Revisor's note.
The proposed amendment to the Constitution, initially approved as Chapter 287 of 82 Del. Laws on June 25, 2020, was finally approved as Section 1 of Chapter 1 of 83 Del. Laws on Jan. 28, 2021.

Effect of amendments.
82 Del. Laws, c. 287, effective June 25, 2020, and 83 Del. Laws, c. 1, effective Jan. 28, 2021, added "race, color, national origin, or".

ARTICLE II
LEGISLATURE

§ 15. Compensation, expenses and allowances of members.

Section 15. The President of the Senate and members of the General Assembly shall receive an annual salary and an annual expense allowance for transportation and such other necessary and proper purposes as the General Assembly shall by law provide. Funds appropriated hereunder shall be paid out of the Treasury of the State.

History.
30 Del. Laws, c. 15; 46 Del. Laws, c. 322; 47 Del. Laws, c. 13; 51 Del. Laws, c. 270; 52 Del. Laws, c. 1; 55 Del. Laws, c. 1; 56 Del. Laws, c. 19; 59 Del. Laws, c. 447; 60 Del. Laws, c. 48; 60 Del. Laws, c. 52.

Revisor's note.
This section is being reprinted to correct a history error in the bound volume.

§ 25. Laws permitting zoning ordinances and use of land.

Section 25. The General Assembly may enact laws under which municipalities and the County of Sussex and the County of Kent and the County of New Castle may adopt zoning ordinances, laws or rules limiting and restricting to specified districts and regulating therein buildings and structures according to their construction and the nature and extent of their use, as well as the use to be made of land in such districts for other than agricultural purposes; and the exercise of such authority shall be deemed to be within the police power of the State.

History.
35 Del. Laws, c. 1; 36 Del. Laws, c. 1; 47 Del. Laws, c. 323; 48 Del. Laws, c. 79; 54 Del. Laws, c. 368; 54 Del. Laws, c. 369; 55 Del. Laws, c. 7; 55 Del. Laws, c. 8.

Revisor's note.
This section is being reprinted to correct a history error in the bound volume.

ARTICLE III
EXECUTIVE

§ 22. Election and term of office of certain county officers; commission.

Section 22. The terms of office of Clerks of the Peace, Registers of Wills, Recorders, and Sheriffs shall be 4 years. These officers shall be chosen by the qualified electors of the respective counties at general elections, and be commissioned by the Governor.

History.
57 Del. Laws, c. 291; 58 Del. Laws, c. 110; 64 Del. Laws, c. 178; 65 Del. Laws, c. 235; 66 Del. Laws, c. 342; 67 Del. Laws, c. 96; 72 Del. Laws, c. 357, § 1; 73 Del. Laws, c. 98, § 1; 74 Del. Laws, c. 299, § 12; 75 Del. Laws, c. 53, § 1.

Revisor's note.
This section is being reprinted to correct a history error in the bound volume.

ARTICLE IV
JUDICIARY

§ 2. Justices of Supreme Court and other State Judges; qualifications; residence; precedence.

Section 2. There shall be five Justices of the Supreme Court who shall be citizens of the State and learned in the law. One of them shall be the Chief Justice who shall be designated as such by his or her appointment and who when present shall preside at all sittings of the Court. In the absence of the Chief Justice the Justice present who is senior in length of service shall preside. If it is otherwise impossible to determine seniority among the Justices, they shall determine it by lot and certify accordingly to the Governor.

In addition to members of the Supreme Court there shall be other State Judges, who shall be citizens of the State and learned in the law. They shall include: (1) the Chancellor and the Vice-Chancellors; (2) The President Judge and the Judges of the Superior Court, three of whom shall be Resident Judges and one of whom shall after appointment reside in each county of the State; (3) the Chief Judge and the Judges of the Family Court; (4) the Chief Judge and Judges of the Court of Common Pleas, one of whom after appointment shall reside in each county of the State; and (5) the Chief Magistrate of the Justice of the Peace Court.

There shall also be such number of additional Vice-Chancellors, and Judges as may hereinafter be provided for by Act of the General Assembly. Each of such Vice-Chancellors, and Judges shall be citizens of the State and learned in the law.

If it is otherwise impossible to determine seniority of service among the Vice-Chancellors, or among the said Judges, they shall determine it by lot respectively and certify accordingly to the Governor.

The tenure and status of the Justices of the Supreme Court and State Judges as shall have been appointed as provided for by the Constitution or by Act of the General Assembly prior to the time this amended Article IV of this Constitution becomes effective shall in no wise be affected.

History.

47 Del. Laws, c. 177; 48 Del. Laws, c. 109; 53 Del. Laws, c. 301; 60 Del. Laws, c. 540; 61 Del. Laws, c. 533; 71 Del. Laws, c. 379, § 31; 72 Del. Laws, c. 136, § 31; 74 Del. Laws, c. 299, §§ 2, 16; 75 Del. Laws, c. 53, § 1; 75 Del. Laws, c. 137, § 2; 76 Del. Laws, c. 11, § 1; 76 Del. Laws, c. 416, § 1; 77 Del. Laws, c. 433, § 1.

Revisor's note.

This section is being reprinted to correct a history error in the bound volume and cumulative supplement.

§ 3. Appointment of judges; terms of office; vacancies; political representation; confirmation of appointment.

NOTES TO DECISIONS

Constitutionality. — Plaintiff (a Delaware lawyer and political independent) did not have standing to challenge a Delaware constitutional provision, Del. Const. art. IV, § 3, that required appointments to Delaware's major courts to reflect a partisan balance; plaintiff did not show the necessary injury in fact, because plaintiff did not prove readiness and ability to apply for appointment at the time of commencement of the action (were plaintiff not barred because of lack of political affiliation with a major political party). Carney v. Adams, — U.S. —, 141 S. Ct. 493, 208 L. Ed. 2d 305 (U.S. 2020).

ARTICLE V
ELECTIONS

§ 1. Time and manner of holding general election.

NOTES TO DECISIONS

Vote by mail. — Operation of Delaware vote-by-mail statutes, 15 Del. C. § 5601 et seq. (now repealed), and the sending out vote-by-mail ballots or counting any ballots returned pursuant to the statutes were not to be permanently enjoined; the Delaware Legislature, in the face of an epidemic of airborne disease, and in light of the health emergency declared by the Governor of Delaware, made a determination that vote-by-mail was necessary for the continued operation of governmental functions and that it was impracticable to address this problem otherwise. Republican State Comm. v. State, 250 A.3d 911 (Del. Ch. 2020).

The vote-by-mail statutes utilized in the 2020 general election (15 Del. C. §§ 5601 to 5621, now repealed) were not unconstitutional on their face in light of their election-day ballot deadline because: (1) the General Assembly chose to apply the deadline already pertaining to absentee ballots (15 Del. C. § 5508) to those statutes; and (2) plaintiffs failed to demonstrate that the deadline was so burdensome on its face as to deprive voters of a constitutional exercise of the right to vote in a free and equal election. League of Women Voters of Del., Inc. v. State Dep't of Elections, 250 A.3d 922 (Del. Ch. 2020).

Statutory election-day ballot deadlines in the vote-by-mail statutes (15 Del. C. §§ 5601 to 5621, now repealed) and the statute setting the time for return of absentee ballots (15 Del. C. § 5508) were constitutional as applied to the 2020 general election; nothing in the record showed that voters availing themselves of the expanded right to mail ballots would be burdened beyond the usual requirement that they post their ballots at least a few days prior to the deadline. League of Women Voters of Del., Inc. v. State Dep't of Elections, 250 A.3d 922 (Del. Ch. 2020).

§ 2. Qualifications for voting; members of the Armed Services of the United States stationed within State; persons disqualified; forfeiture of right.

NOTES TO DECISIONS

Vote by mail. — The vote-by-mail statutes utilized in the 2020 general election (15 Del. C. §§ 5601 to 5621, now repealed) were not unconstitutional on their face in light of their election-day ballot deadline because: (1) the General Assembly chose to apply the deadline already pertaining to absentee ballots (15 Del. C. § 5508) to those statutes; and (2) plaintiffs failed to demonstrate that the deadline was so burdensome on its face as to deprive voters of a constitutional exercise of the right to vote in a free and equal election. League of Women Voters of Del., Inc. v. State Dep't of Elections, 250 A.3d 922 (Del. Ch. 2020).

Statutory election-day ballot deadlines in the vote-by-mail statutes (15 Del. C. §§ 5601 to 5621, now repealed) and the statute setting the time for return of absentee ballots (15 Del. C. § 5508) were constitutional as applied to the 2020 general election; nothing in the record showed that voters availing themselves of the expanded right to mail ballots would be burdened beyond the usual requirement that they post their ballots at least a few days prior to the deadline. League of Women Voters of Del., Inc. v. State Dep't of Elections, 250 A.3d 922 (Del. Ch. 2020).

§ 4A. General laws for absentee voting.

NOTES TO DECISIONS

Vote by mail. — Operation of Delaware vote-by-mail statutes, 15 Del. C. § 5601 et seq. (now repealed), and the sending out vote-by-mail ballots or counting any ballots returned pursuant to the statutes were not to be permanently enjoined; the Delaware Legislature, in the face of an epidemic of airborne disease, and in light of the health emergency declared by the Governor of Delaware, made a determination that vote-by-mail was necessary for the continued operation of governmental functions and that it was impracticable to address this problem otherwise. Republican State Comm. v. State, 250 A.3d 911 (Del. Ch. 2020).

(PROPOSED AMENDMENT)

§ 4A. General laws for absentee voting.

NOTES TO DECISIONS

Vote by mail. — Operation of Delaware vote-by-mail statutes, 15 Del. C. § 5601 et seq. (now repealed), and the sending out vote-by-mail ballots or counting any ballots returned pursuant to the statutes were not to be permanently enjoined; the Delaware Legislature, in the face of an epidemic of airborne disease, and in light of the health emergency declared by the Governor of Delaware, made a determination that vote-by-mail was necessary for the continued operation of governmental functions and that it was impracticable to address this problem otherwise. Republican State Comm. v. State, 250 A.3d 911 (Del. Ch. 2020).

ARTICLE VIII
REVENUE AND TAXATION

§ 1. Uniformity of taxes; collection under general laws; exemption for public welfare purposes.

NOTES TO DECISIONS

I. UNIFORMITY.

Net operating loss limitations. — Delaware Division of Revenue's policy under 30 Del. C. § 1903, of limiting separate-company net operating loss (NOL) to the consolidated NOL deduction of the federal consolidated group of which the taxpayer was a member, violated the state uniformity clause; it treated Delaware corporate taxpayers differently depending on whether they filed their federal returns as consolidated groups or separate corporations. Verisign, Inc. v. Dir. of Revenue, — A.3d —, 2020 Del. Super. LEXIS 3011 (Del. Super. Ct. Dec. 17, 2020).

ARTICLE XVI
AMENDMENTS AND CONVENTIONS

(PROPOSED AMENDMENT)

§ 1. Proposal and concurrence of Constitution amendments in General Assembly; procedure.

Section 1. Any amendment or amendments to this Constitution may be proposed in the Senate or House of Representatives; and if the same shall be agreed to by two-thirds of all the members elected to each House, such proposed amendment or amendments shall be entered on their journals, with the yeas and nays taken thereon, and such proposed amendment or amendments must be disseminated to the public not more than 120 days before the next general election and not less than 90 days before the next general election as provided for by an act of the General Assembly; and if in the General Assembly next after the said election such proposed amendment or amendments shall upon yea and nay vote be agreed to by two thirds of all the members elected to each House, the same shall thereupon become part of the Constitution.

History.
83 Del. Laws, c. 147, § 1.

Revisor's note.
An amendment to this section of the Constitution set out above was initially approved as Section 1 of Chapter 147 of 83 Del. Laws on June 29, 2021.

Effect of amendments.
83 Del. Laws, c. 147, effective June 29, 2021, added "and concurrence" in the section heading; hyphenated "two-thirds", deleted "the Secretary of State shall cause" following "thereon, and" and substituted "must be disseminated to the public not more than 120 days before the next general election and not less than 90 days" for "to be published three months" and "as provided for by an act of the General Assembly" for "in at least three newspapers in each county in which such newspapers shall be published".

ARTICLE XVII
CONTINUITY OF GOVERNMENTAL OPERATIONS

§ 1. Continuity of state and local governmental operations in periods of emergency.

NOTES TO DECISIONS

Vote by mail. — Operation of Delaware vote-by-mail statutes, 15 Del. C. § 5601 et seq. (now repealed), and the sending out vote-by-mail ballots or counting any ballots returned pursuant to the statutes were not to be permanently enjoined; the Delaware Legislature, in the face of an epidemic of airborne disease, and in light of the health emergency declared by the Governor of Delaware, made a determination that vote-by-mail was necessary for the continued operation of governmental functions and that it was impracticable to address this problem otherwise. Republican State Comm. v. State, 250 A.3d 911 (Del. Ch. 2020).

DELAWARE CODE ANNOTATED

TITLE 1
GENERAL PROVISIONS

Chapter
5. Legal Holidays, §§ 501 to 502.

CHAPTER 5
LEGAL HOLIDAYS

Sec.
501. Designation

§ 501. Designation

(a) The following days shall be legal holidays in this State:

(1) January 1, known as New Year's Day.

(2) The third Monday in January, known as Martin Luther King, Jr. Day.

(3) Good Friday.

(4) June 19, known as Juneteenth.

(5) July 4, known as Independence Day.

(6) The first Monday in September, known as Labor Day.

(7) November 11, known as Veterans Day.

(8) The fourth Thursday in November, known as Thanksgiving Day.

(9) The Friday following Thanksgiving Day.

(10) December 25, known as Christmas.

(11) Saturdays.

(12) The day of the General Election as it biennially occurs; and

(13) In Sussex County, Return Day, the second day after the General Election, after 12:00 Noon.

(b) If any of the legal holidays fall on Sunday, the Monday following shall be a legal holiday. If any of the legal holidays other than Saturday fall on Saturday, the Friday preceding shall be a legal holiday.

(c) The last Monday in May shall be the legal holiday, known as Memorial Day, in the State.

(d) Veterans Day shall be a legal holiday for all public school students and the employees of public districts and charter schools. If Veterans Day falls on a Sunday, the following Monday shall be a legal holiday. If Veterans Day falls on a Saturday, the preceding Friday shall be a legal holiday.

(e) The Director of the Office of Management and Budget shall promulgate policies and procedures to implement 2 floating holidays.

History.

11 Del. Laws, c. 195; 12 Del. Laws, c. 14; 15 Del. Laws, c. 192; 18 Del. Laws, c. 697; 19 Del. Laws, c. 694; 20 Del. Laws, cc. 67, 511; 22 Del. Laws, cc. 164, 165, 391; 26 Del. Laws, c. 182; Code 1915, §§ 2841, 2841A to 2841D; 28 Del. Laws, c. 214; 30 Del. Laws, c. 193; 34 Del. Laws, c. 190, § 1; 34 Del. Laws, c. 191, § 1; 36 Del. Laws, c. 247; 37 Del. Laws, c. 233, § 1; 40 Del. Laws, c. 207; Code 1935, § 3321; 43 Del. Laws, c. 202, § 1; 43 Del. Laws, c. 203, § 1; 47 Del. Laws, c. 40, § 1; 47 Del. Laws, c. 143, § 1; 47 Del. Laws, c. 247, § 1; 48 Del. Laws, c. 49, § 1; 1 Del. C. 1953, § 501; 52 Del. Laws, c. 83; 53 Del. Laws, c. 23, § 1; 54 Del. Laws, c. 308; 55 Del. Laws, c. 28, § 1; 57 Del. Laws, c. 14; 59 Del. Laws, c. 268, § 1; 60 Del. Laws, c. 602, § 1; 60 Del. Laws, c. 634, § 1; 64 Del. Laws, c. 451, § 1; 65 Del. Laws, c. 62, § 1; 66 Del. Laws, c. 330, §§ 1, 2; 67 Del. Laws, c. 19, §§ 1, 2; 67 Del. Laws, c. 22, §§ 1, 2; 72 Del. Laws, c. 105, § 1; 74 Del. Laws, c. 319, § 1; 76 Del. Laws, c. 113,

§ 1; 77 Del. Laws, c. 84, § 56; 77 Del. Laws, c. 328, § 28; 83 Del. Laws, c. 37, § 1.

Effect of amendments.

83 Del. Laws, c. 37, effective June 3, 2021,

substituted "Veterans" for Veterans'" in the first paragraph of (a) and wherever it appeared in (c).

TITLE 2
TRANSPORTATION

Part
II. Transportation Department

PART II
TRANSPORTATION DEPARTMENT

CHAPTER 13
DELAWARE TRANSPORTATION AUTHORITY

§ 1335. Maintaining adequate supplies of road materials [Operation of this statute was suspended by 83 Del. Laws, c. 56, § 114].

(a) *Legislative findings.* — The General Assembly finds that the interests of the State are not well served when its ability to obtain a ready supply and competitive prices for critical materials used in its transportation projects, such as asphalt and concrete, is impeded due to the consolidation of ownership of facilities for the processing and/or manufacture of such materials in specific geographic areas. This situation has arisen in Kent and Sussex Counties, and may potentially occur in New Castle County. Therefore, the General Assembly determines that the State should be empowered to enter into appropriate arrangements to reduce the impacts of these consolidations.

(b) Any provision of the Delaware Code notwithstanding, the Department of Transportation is hereby authorized and directed to develop and implement a program to obtain a ready supply of critical road-building materials, including but not limited to asphalt and/or concrete, for its highway construction and reconstruction projects. This program may include the acquisition of land, raw materials, and equipment to operate facilities for the processing and manufacture of road materials. The Department may also contract with private entities for the operation of such facilities, pursuant to Chapter 69 of Title 29.

(c) The provisions of §§ 1309, 1319, 1321, and 1329 of this title shall apply to the Department's actions pursuant to this section, including any contractual arrangements for these facilities, as if conducted under the auspices of the Delaware Transportation Authority, except that during its planning process the Department shall meet and confer with the land use officials in the county in which such facilities will be located, to obtain their comments on the proposal.

(d) Notwithstanding subsection (c) of this section, the authorities granted to the Department in aforementioned section, the Department shall not contract for any additional capacity with a private firm or firms without first securing the approval of the State Representative and Senator in whose legislative districts the proposed road materials facility would be located.

History.

74 Del. Laws, c. 308, § 109; 76 Del. Laws, c. 288, § 101; 77 Del. Laws, c. 87, § 92; 77 Del. Laws, c. 329, § 100; 78 Del. Laws, c. 76, § 103; 78 Del. Laws, c. 292, § 88; 79 Del. Laws, c. 79, § 98; 79 Del. Laws, c. 292, § 106; 80 Del. Laws, c. 78, § 106; 80 Del. Laws, c. 299, § 96; 81 Del. Laws, c. 59, § 97; 81 Del. Laws, c. 303, § 100; 82 Del. Laws, c. 86, § 96; 82 Del. Laws, c. 244, § 103; 83 Del. Laws, c. 56, § 114.

Revisor's note.

Section 101 of 76 Del. Laws, c. 288, effective July 1, 2008; 77 Del. Laws, c. 87, § 92, effective July 1, 2009; 77 Del. Laws, c. 329, § 100, effective July 1, 2010 (by virtue of § 139 of that act); 78 Del. Laws, c. 76, § 103, effective July 1, 2011 (by virtue of § 147 of that act); 78 Del. Laws, c. 292, § 88, effective July 1, 2012 (by virtue of § 135); 79 Del. Laws, c. 79, § 98, effective July 1, 2013 (by virtue of § 145 of that act); 79 Del. Laws, c. 292, § 106, effective July 1, 2014 (by virtue of § 161 of that act); 80 Del. Laws, c. 78, § 106, effective July 1, 2015 (by virtue of § 159 of the act); 80 Del. Laws, c. 299, § 96, effective July 1, 2016 (by virtue of § 158 of that act); 81 Del. Laws, c. 59, § 97, effective July 3, 2017 (by virtue of § 163 of that act); 81 Del. Laws, c. 303, § 100, effective July 1, 2018 (by virtue of § 137 of the act); 82 Del. Laws, c. 86, § 96, effective July 1, 2019 (by virtue of § 163 of that act); 82 Del. Laws, c. 244, § 103, effective July 1, 2020 (by virtue of § 167 of that act); and 83 Del. Laws, c. 56, § 114, effective June 30, 2021 (by virtue of § 178 of that act), provided: "Supplies of Road Materials. 74 Del. Laws, c. 308 § 109 is suspended until such time as the Department of Transportation shall suggest its re-institution and such suspension has been overridden by an Act of the General Assembly."

CHAPTER 14

TRANSPORTATION TRUST FUND

Sec.
1417. Budget of Authority.

§ 1417. Budget of Authority.

The expenditures of the Authority from the Transportation Trust Fund, including expenditures required to be made by resolutions or trust agreements made or to be made by the Authority, shall be approved annually by the General Assembly. The obligations under any such resolution or trust agreement shall be met solely from motor fuel taxes, motor vehicle document fees, motor vehicle registration fees, motor carrier road use taxes and registration fees, the moneys transferred or disbursed to the Transportation Trust Fund under § 307 of Title 21, receipts and revenues derived from the Delaware Turnpike and any other receipts and revenues of the Authority pledged and assigned to the holders of bonds of the Authority. The budget for capital and operating expenditures of the Authority payable from the Transportation Trust Fund shall be presented annually by the Authority to the General Assembly. If the General Assembly does not approve the operating budget of the Authority before July 1 for the year such budget is submitted, the operating budget, as submitted to the General Assembly, shall be deemed adopted by the Authority until such time as the budget is approved by the General Assembly, provided that the operating expenditures of the Authority shall not exceed similar expenditures of the Authority for the year before the budget year by more than a factor equal to the Consumer Price Index as defined in § 1320(f) of this title. Any obligations incurred by the Authority under an operating budget deemed adopted by the Authority shall be binding on the Authority. Failure by the General Assembly to approve the capital or operating budget of the Authority shall not affect or impair the obligation of the Authority to meet its obligations to holders of outstanding bonds. The provisions of Chapter 84 of Title 29, including the establishment of priorities for spending state funds, shall apply to available money and bonding capacity in the Transportation Trust Fund for highway projects. The Authority's annual budget as prepared and approved shall reflect that a significant objective of this chapter is to achieve adequate funding and predictable implementation of the Department of Transportation's Capital Transportation Program and other needs of the transportation system.

History.
66 Del. Laws, c. 87, § 1; 66 Del. Laws, c. 360, § 49; 67 Del. Laws, c. 46, § 54; 67 Del. Laws, c. 285, § 56(i); 83 Del. Laws, c. 37, § 31.

Effect of amendments.
83 Del. Laws, c. 37, effective June 3, 2021, substituted "under" for "pursuant to" preceding "§ 307" in the second sentence and in the fifth sentence, "before" for "prior to" twice in the third sentence and "Transportation" for "Improvement" preceding "Program" in the final sentence.

CHAPTER 19
TRANSPORTATION NETWORKS

Sec.
1901. Definitions.

§ 1901. Definitions.

As used in this chapter:

(1) "Digital network" means any online-enabled technology application service, website or system offered or utilized by a transportation network company that enables the prearrangement of rides with transportation network company drivers.

(2) "Personal vehicle" means a vehicle that is used by a transportation network company driver and is:

    a. Owned, leased or otherwise authorized for use by the transportation network company driver; and

    b. Not a taxicab, limousine, or public carrier as defined in Chapter 18 of this title.

(3) "Prearranged ride" means the provision of transportation by a TNC driver to a rider, beginning when a TNC driver accepts a ride requested by a rider through a digital network controlled by a transportation network company, continuing while the TNC driver transports a requesting rider, and ending when the last rider departs from the personal vehicle. A prearranged ride does not include:

    a. Transportation provided using a taxicab, limousine, or other public carrier pursuant to Chapter 18 of this title; or

    b. A shared expense carpool or vanpool arrangement; or

    c. A regional transportation provider.

(4) "Protective hairstyle" includes braids, locks, and twists.

(5) "Race" includes traits historically associated with race, including hair texture and a protective hairstyle.

(6) "Transportation network company" or "TNC" means a corporation, partnership, sole proprietorship, or other entity that is licensed pursuant to this chapter and operating in Delaware that uses a digital network to connect transportation network company riders to transportation network company drivers who provide prearranged rides. A transportation network company shall not be deemed to control, direct or manage the personal vehicles or transportation network company drivers that connect to its digital network, except where agreed to by written contract. "Transportation network company" does not include a transportation broker arranging nonemergency medical transportation for Medicaid or Medicare members pursuant to a contract with the State or a managed-care organization.

(7) "Transportation network company driver" or "TNC driver" means an individual who:

    a. Receives connections to potential passengers and related services from a transportation network company in exchange for payment of a fee to the transportation network company; and

    b. Uses a personal vehicle to offer or provide a prearranged ride to riders upon connection through a digital network controlled by a transportation network company in return for compensation or payment of a fee.

(8) "Transportation network company rider" or "rider" means an individual or persons who use a transportation network company's digital network to connect with a transportation network company driver who provides prearranged rides to the rider in the TNC driver's personal vehicle between points chosen by the rider.

History.

80 Del. Laws, c. 374, § 1; 83 Del. Laws, c. 13, § 1.

added present (4) and (5) and redesignated the remaining paragraphs accordingly.

Effect of amendments.

83 Del. Laws, c. 13, effective April 13, 2021,

CHAPTER 20
PUBLIC-PRIVATE INITIATIVES PROGRAM IN TRANSPORTATION

Sec.
2003. Projects.

§ 2003. Projects.

(a) *Project.* — Subject to subsection (c) of this section, the Secretary may entertain and solicit proposals from, and may negotiate and enter into agreements with, private entities or consortia thereof, for projects using in whole or in part private sources of financing involving (i) all or a portion of the study, planning, design, construction, leasing, financing, operation and maintenance of transportation systems, or (ii) the repair, and/or expansion, leasing, financing, operation and maintenance of existing transportation systems, or any combination of the foregoing.

(b) *Eligibility.* — The Secretary may entertain and solicit proposals from any source whatsoever; provided however, that the Secretary shall only enter into agreements regarding a transportation project that has been specifically authorized by the General Assembly, and that such authorization includes all material terms of the proposed project, including without limitation any terms concerning repayment of debt or capital to or for the benefit of any private entity; further provided (i) which has been authorized by the Delaware General Assembly (except that no agreement may be entered into which compels (A) direct or indirect expenditures or loans on the part of the State in excess of the total sum which may be appropriated by the Delaware General Assembly as the State's financial participation with respect to said transportation system or; (B) credit enhancements which pledge the full faith and credit of the State); and/or (ii) for which the General Assembly has provided specific or categorical funding authorization for purposes of implementing this chapter; and (iii) which is consistent with § 8419(2)(a) of Title 29, applicable provisions of the Department's long range transportation plan, any applicable recommendations developed by the Cabinet Committee on State Planning pursuant to Chapter 91 of Title 29, and applicable provisions of the Federal Clean Air Act [42 U.S.C. § 1857 et seq. and 42 U.S.C. § 7551].

(c) *Proposals.* — (1) The Secretary shall solicit proposals through a request for proposals pursuant to Chapter 69, Title 29, accompanied by material explaining of the Public-Private Initiatives Program enacted hereunder and describing the selection process and criteria. The Secretary may identify in these requests for proposals specific systems, corridors or routes for improvement.

(2) Alternatively, potential projects may be identified and proposed by any potential contracting party. Such unsolicited proposals will also be

accepted provided they satisfy the criteria outlined in accordance with this chapter. In the event that an unsolicited proposal is deemed in compliance with this chapter and accepted for review, the Secretary shall publicly announce, not less than once a week for 2 consecutive weeks in a newspaper published or circulated in each county of the State, the acceptance of the unsolicited proposal along with a detailed description of the unsolicited proposal, and shall provide 60 days within which other interested parties may submit proposals relating to the same subject. Notwithstanding any other provisions of this Code to the contrary, all proposals made pursuant to this chapter may provide for the design-build mode of infrastructure development;

(3) Proprietary information contained in proposals not selected for projects and records of negotiations in progress shall be exempt from public disclosure.

(d) *Fees authorized.* — To offset a portion of the costs of initiating this program and reviewing proposals received for projects under this chapter, the Department is authorized to assess a non-refundable Proposal Review Fee for each proposal not to exceed $50,000.

(e) *Selection and approval.* — (1) The projects shall be selected by a project committee, chaired by the Secretary, consisting of the Secretary, the Director of Financial Management and Budget, the Chief Engineer of the Department of Transportation, and up to 4 other persons to be appointed by the Secretary. The projects shall be selected without regard to the provisions of Chapter 69 of Title 29.

Each proposal shall be weighed on its own merits and ranked according to the selection criteria stipulated in the request for proposals, provided that upon receipt of all proposals the project committee may group similar types of project proposals together for purposes of evaluation and selection, and provided further that the proposals selected by such committee from any such group of proposals must be those with the highest ranking within that group, and provided further that such committee may elect not to select any proposals from an established group of proposals, and provided further that as to similar proposals or proposals that are mutually exclusive so that the undertaking of 1 would preclude the need, desirability, or ability of undertaking the other, only the proposal with the highest ranking among such proposals shall be selected, and, subject to approval as set forth above, proceed to negotiations. Each of the agreements shall be negotiated individually as a stand-alone project.

(2) Each selected project must be subsequently approved, within 45 days of its selection, by both (i) the directly affected metropolitan planning organization or organizations and (ii) the Council on Transportation established under § 8409 of Title 29 or its successor, in that order. If a directly affected metropolitan planning organization approves a selected project, it shall be deemed to have given its approval to amend the Transportation Improvement Program to include such project. If the Council on Transportation approves a selected project, it shall be deemed to have given its approval to amend the State Capital Improvement Program to include such project. Approval for each selected project by the affected metropolitan planning organization and the Council on Transportation shall be based solely upon the project's compatibility with State and regional transportation plans, compliance with applicable laws and regulations, and fiscal impact upon the State Capital Improvement Program or regional Transportation Improvement Program. If either organization disapproves a project, it shall set forth in writing its reasons for doing so.

If neither approval nor disapproval is granted within 45 days after the proposal was delivered to any affected metropolitan planning organization or the Council on Transportation, the proposal shall be deemed approved by those organizations. Moreover, in the event that a project is disapproved as provided above, the Department may resubmit the plan or revise version thereof no sooner than 60 days after notification that the plan has been disapproved by either party.

(3) The Secretary shall promptly notify the Co-chairs of the Joint Bond Bill Committee of the Delaware General Assembly when a project has been duly selected by the project committee. After the Co-chairs' receipt of such notice, the Co-chairs shall meet and either approve or reject the project. Upon their approval of the project, it shall be deemed as an amendment to the Capital Improvements Program for the fiscal year in which the approval is granted.

(f) *Compliance.* — Except as otherwise expressly provided in this chapter, all projects must comply with all applicable rules and statutes in existence at the time the agreement is entered into, including but not limited to this title, § 711 of Title 19, § 6960 of Title 29 and 49 C.F.R. Part 21, provided that the provisions of Chapter 69 of Title 29 other than § 6960 of Title 29 thereof shall not be applicable to the projects regardless of the use of State funds. Compliance with § 6960 of Title 29, or in the alternative, federal prevailing wage laws, shall be required without regard to the source of funds for a project. Each agreement may provide for protection for the contracting party from future discretionary regulatory changes which would substantially or materially change the terms and conditions or financial assumptions of the agreement.

(g) *Financing.* — (1) The Department is authorized, notwithstanding any other provision of this Code, to (i) use any federal, state or other funds, including without limitation funds obtained from or through the Delaware Transportation Authority, any loans from the Public-Private Initiatives Program Revolving Loan Fund established in § 2912 of this title and federal transportation funds, to finance, secure, guarantee, service project debt or repay project costs; and (ii) do such things as necessary and desirable to maximize the funding and financing of such projects, provided that private capital participation in the total capital cost for each project shall be negotiated with the other terms of the agreement. Notwithstanding other provisions of this chapter, the amount of such participation shall be taken into account in determining the negotiated rate of return on the investment in the project. In addition, the projected total percentage of public capital investment, as well as the limits of the Department's financial liability for the project, shall be expressly disclosed in the agreement.

(2) The Department, either directly or through a designated party, may apply for, receive and accept from any federal agency or any other governmental body grants or financial support of whatever nature for any purpose described in this chapter. The Department may transfer or lend the proceeds of any such grant, or utilize such proceeds available for credit enhancement, to public agencies or contracting parties, on terms and conditions complying with applicable federal and state law.

History.
70 Del. Laws, c. 280, § 1; 71 Del. Laws, c. 150, § 78; 72 Del. Laws, c. 164, § 1; 74 Del. Laws, c. 69, §§ 82, 86-92; 83 Del. Laws, c. 37, § 32.

Effect of amendments.
83 Del. Laws, c. 37, effective June 3, 2021, in (e)(2), substituted "under" for "pursuant to" in the first sentence, "State Capital Improvement" for "Capital Improvements" in the third sen-

tence, and "the" for "such" preceding "proposal" in two places in the penultimate sentence.

CHAPTER 21
COMPLETE COMMUNITY ENTERPRISE DISTRICT

§ 2102. Definitions.

As used in this chapter:

(1) "Complete Community Enterprise District" or "District" means an area of a municipality or county, or both, that meets the criteria set forth in §§ 2103 and 2104 of this title.

(2) "Department" means the Department of Transportation.

(3) "Farebox recovery ratio" means the fraction of a transit system's operating expenses which are met by the fares paid by passengers.

(4) "Level of service" means a qualitative measure describing operational conditions within a traffic stream based on service measures such as speed and travel time, freedom to maneuver, traffic interruptions, comfort, and convenience.

(5) "Parcel of land" means any quantity of land capable of being described with such definiteness that its locations and boundaries may be established and which is designated by its owner or developer as land to be used or developed as a unit or which has been used or developed as a unit.

(6) "Project" means any State-funded capital-related improvement or addition to the State's transportation infrastructure, including transit systems, facilities, stations and equipment, sidewalks, multi-use paths, protected bicycle lanes, and bicycle boulevards.

History.
80 Del. Laws, c. 224, § 1; 83 Del. Laws, c. 38, § 1.

deleted former (4) and redesignated the remaining paragraphs accordingly.

Effect of amendments.
83 Del. Laws, c. 38, effective June 3, 2021,

§ 2103. District designation.

(a) Any municipality, county, or municipality-county partnership may enter into an agreement with the Department to create a Complete Community Enterprise District.

(b)(1) A municipality, county, or municipality-county partnership and the Department must agree on the boundaries of the District and must create a master development plan for the District that must subsequently be reviewed through the preliminary land use services process under Chapter 92 of Title 29 and adopted into the municipality's, county's, or municipality-county partnership's comprehensive plan.

(2) The master development plan required by paragraph (b)(1) of this section must, upon creation of the District, include enhanced mass transit routes in the District and maximize the use of walking and bicycling by residents and employees.

(3) The master development plan required by paragraph (b)(1) of this section may include the following:

a. A mix of parcels of land zoned for residential, commercial, light industrial, or institutional uses.

b. A guide for the specific design of the physical form, public spaces, and amenities of the District so that transit, walking, and cycling are safe and comfortable modes of travel for all the residents of the District.

   c. An agreement on level of service requirements specific to the District.

(c) Once a master development plan has been created, the Department shall conduct a transportation planning study to evaluate existing and proposed future conditions in and around the District boundaries agreed to under this section. The study shall determine the effects of creating the District and identify the projects needed within the District to implement the policies defined in § 2105 of this title and the projects needed outside the District to meet the highway capacity and quality of service standards of the Department and the county or municipality in which the District is located. The Department shall publish this study on its website at least 10 business days prior to any hearing required under § 2662, §4962, or §6962 of Title 9 or § 312 of Title 22.

History.
   80 Del. Laws, c. 224, § 1; 83 Del. Laws, c. 38, § 2.

Effect of amendments.
   83 Del. Laws, c. 38, effective June 3, 2021, in (2), added "upon creation of the District" and substituted "and maximize the use of walking and bicycling by residents and employees" for "upon its creation".

§ 2104. District requirements.

A Complete Community Enterprise District must meet all of the following requirements:
   (1) Be contiguous.
   (2) Be no more than 9 square miles in area.
   (3) Be a compact shape that is not a linear corridor.
   (4) Be zoned and otherwise regulated such that the District may be developed at a density that is high enough to enable frequent transit service to the residents of the District.
   (5) Exempt all development on all parcels of land included in the District from any municipal or county requirements for the provision of off-street parking.
   (6) Contain more total area zoned for residential use than is zoned for commercial or other uses. Each parcel of land within the District must be zoned to maximize the use of transit, walking, and bicycling by residents and employees.
   (7) Consist of more than 1 parcel and part of at least 1 parcel must be within a ½ mile of any of the following:
      a. An existing bus or rail stop where passengers can board and alight.
      b. A planned or existing bus or rail station.
   (8) Include adjacent neighborhoods within a ½ mile of a bus or rail stop or planned or existing bus or rail station.
   (9) Be part of a master development plan for the District that maximizes the use of transit, walking, and bicycling by residents and employees, as required under § 2103(b)(2) of this title.

History.
   80 Del. Laws, c. 224, § 1; 83 Del. Laws, c. 38, § 3.

Effect of amendments.
   83 Del. Laws, c. 38, effective June 3, 2021, in (2), added "no" and deleted "than 1 square mile but less" following "more"; substituted "that is not a linear corridor" for "with an isoperimetric quotient of at least 0.7" in (3); substituted "Each parcel of land within the District must be zones to maximize the use of transit, walking, and bicycling by residents and employees" for "No parcel of land included in the District may be zoned commercial regional"; and added (7), (8) and (9).

TITLE 3
AGRICULTURE

Part
I. Department of Agriculture
II. Regulatory Provisions
VI. Domestic and Foreign Animals, Birds, Reptiles and Insects

PART I
DEPARTMENT OF AGRICULTURE

CHAPTER 9
DELAWARE AGRICULTURAL LANDS PRESERVATION ACT

SUBCHAPTER II
AGRICULTURAL PRESERVATION DISTRICTS

§ 909. District restrictions.

(a) The farmlands and forestlands included in an Agricultural Preservation District are subject to the following restrictions:

(1) No rezoning or major subdivision of the real property shall be allowed;

(2) Activities conducted on the real property shall be limited to agricultural and related uses, and residential use of the real property shall be limited as follows:

a. No more than 1 acre of land for each 20 acres of usable land owned in a District or an expansion of a District, to a maximum of 10 acres, shall be allowed for dwelling housing; and

b. The dwelling housing shall be limited to residential use of the owner, relatives of the owner and persons providing permanent and seasonal farm labor services; provided however, that the Foundation may, pursuant to regulations adopted after notice and public hearing, allow, from the effective date of an initial District Agreement, no more than a total of 3 dwellings or dwelling lots located in the Agriculture Preservation District to be transferred from an owner or relatives of an owner to any other person, subject to the following limitations and requirements:

1. The owner or relative of an owner seeking to make the transfer shall establish that a hardship condition exists, as defined pursuant to Foundation regulations, and obtain Foundation approval;

2. The dwelling or dwelling lot, after transfer, shall be used only for residential purposes;

3. The transferred property shall not qualify for District benefits or benefits of easement conveyance established under this chapter; and

4. If a preservation easement has been acquired by the Foundation on the real property subject to transfer, the owner or relatives of the owner shall, as a condition of Foundation approval, pay to the Foundation an amount equal to 25 percent of the then current fair market value of the land subject to transfer; and

c. Any transfer of real property in a District or an expansion of a District to another person shall be preceded by the execution by the transferee of a document, in recordable form and as prescribed by the Foundation, which sets forth the acreage allowed for dwelling housing and the restrictions which apply to the real property under this chapter and the regulations of the Foundation.

(3) The restrictions shall be deemed covenants which run with and bind the lands in the District for a period of 10 years or any extended period from the date of placement of the lands in the District.

(4) For any new District or expansion of a District approved after August 23, 2004, the provisions of paragraph (a)(2)b. of this section shall be replaced by the following restrictions:

a. With respect to the acreage allowed for dwelling housing pursuant to paragraph (a)(2)a. of this section, there shall be a limit of 3 dwelling houses for residential use placed on the allowable acreage at 3 locations designated by the owner, unless there exists more than 3 dwelling houses on the real property at the time of approval of the new district or expansion of a District, in which case the allowable acreage shall be allocated to the existing dwelling houses and no additional dwelling houses shall be allowed.

b. The dwelling housing utilized pursuant to paragraph (a)(4)a. of this section, above, for residential use shall not be restricted to owners, relatives of owners or persons providing permanent and seasonal farm labor services, and any person shall be entitled to use the dwelling housing for residential purposes.

c. The owners of real property in any District or expansion of a District, which District is in existence on August 23, 2004, shall be entitled to be released from the restrictions of paragraph (a)(2)b. of this section, provided such owner executes an amendment to their District Agreement in a form designated and acceptable to the Foundation, subjecting the real property to the restrictions set forth in paragraphs (a)(1), (a)(2)a., (a)(4)a. and (a)(4)b. of this section. If an owner of real property in any District or expansion of a District has before August 23, 2004, conveyed a preservation easement to the Foundation, such owner shall be entitled to be released from the restrictions of paragraph (a)(2)b. of this section as contained in the preservation easement, provided the owner executes an amendment to the preservation easement in a form designated and acceptable to the Foundation subjecting the real property to the restrictions set forth in paragraphs (a)(1), (a)(2)a., (a)(4)a. and (a)(4)b. of this section.

(5) The following uses shall be deemed "related uses" for purposes of paragraph (a)(2) of this section:

a. A farm market or roadside stand shall be allowed provided the products offered for sale are grown or produced on the property included within the District and such farm market or roadside stand complies with § 2601(b)(5), § 4901(b)(5), or § 6902(b)(5) of Title 9.

b. Hayrides, horseback riding, guided tours, and petting zoos shall be allowed, provided that said activities are limited to no more than

50 persons on the premises at a time. Notwithstanding the foregoing, educational tours and agricultural demonstration events shall not be subject to the 50-person limitation.

c. Horse stabling and training and caring for horses is permitted; provided however, quasi-public horse events such as polo fields and horse shows, shall not be permitted.

d. Hunting, trapping, and fishing shall be allowed provided said activities are limited to private noncommercial activities and do not adversely affect the agricultural use of the property.

e. Spray irrigation designed to replenish soil nutrients and improve the quality of the soil is allowed provided that the spray effluent is treated pursuant to the best available treatment technology, is disposed of on property utilized for the production of conventional cash crops, and all storage and treatment of the effluent disposed of on the District property takes place on property other than District property.

f. Easements, licenses and other property interests for utility, telecommunications, and access uses are allowed provided that:

1. The property subject to the easement, license or other property interest is limited to only the area necessary to accommodate the utility, telecommunications or access use;

2. The area affected by the use is located so as to minimize, to the maximum extent practicable, the impact on farming activities and operations;

3. No commercial advertising or commercial activities unrelated to the utility, telecommunications or access use shall be conducted on the area of the utility, telecommunications or access use;

4. Any document used to grant an easement, license or other property interest shall limit the activities to utility, telecommunications or access uses and shall contain the prohibitions of commercial advertising or commercial activities unrelated to the permitted use; and

5. The written approval of the Foundation shall be obtained in accordance with the rules and regulations of the Foundation.

g. Farm structures in existence at the time of approval of a District or expansion of a District that are no longer used in farming operations may be used for the enclosed storage of property belonging to others.

h. A restricted landing area utilized for the personal use of the owner or tenant of the owner is permitted provided that said use does not require any rezoning of the property or conditional use allowing for commercial use. As used herein, "restricted landing area" means any area of land, water or both which is used for the landing and takeoff of aircraft.

i. A "bed and breakfast" may be operated in any allowed dwelling located on the property.

j. A daycare center for the care of no more than 5 children under the age of 16 shall be allowed in any allowed dwelling located on the property.

k. Farm structures in existence at the time of approval of a District or expansion of a District that are no longer used in farming operations, and any related temporary ancillary structure used in conjunction with the existing farm structures, may be used for public and private gatherings, such as weddings, parties, conferences, fund-raising ceremonies and other similar events, provided that all of the following requirements are satisfied:

1. The property with improvements on which the allowed activities are conducted must be owned by the person subject to the District Agreement or preservation easement.

2. The area on which the allowed activities are conducted cannot be subdivided from the agricultural lands.

3.A. The area on which the allowed activities are conducted must be limited, to the extent feasible, to avoid impacts on current and beneficial agricultural use of the agricultural lands. Farmland that is in current and beneficial agricultural use may be used for events under this paragraph (a)(5)k.3.A. if all of the following apply:

I. One acre or less of land is used.

II. An area of land equal or greater to the amount in paragraph (a)(5)k.3.A.I. of this section is converted to active beneficial agricultural use.

B. The exterior dimensions of the existing farm structures may be increased in size as follows:

I. By no more than 50% of the footprint area of the existing farm structure at the time the structure became part of a District.

II. A canopy attached to the allowed farm structure may not exceed more than 30% of the farm structure's footprint area.

4. The person seeking to conduct activities allowed under this paragraph (a)(5)k. shall submit to the Foundation Board, in advance and on an application form provided by the Foundation, a detailed description and plan of the proposed activities.

5. The application shall have been approved by the Foundation, subject to such terms and conditions deemed necessary and desirable to protect the agricultural value of the property, which terms and conditions shall be subject to the enforcement provisions set forth in § 920(a) of this title.

6. The person seeking to conduct activities allowed under this subsection shall have agreed, in writing, to comply with the terms and conditions set forth in the Foundation Board's approval.

l. Annual and semi-annual events related to agricultural commodities and agricultural enterprises during the growing season, and other annual and semi-annual events during the nonprimary growing season, subject to case by case review and approval by the Foundation Board, and if approved subject to such terms and conditions imposed to protect the agricultural value of the property, which terms and conditions shall be subject to the enforcement provisions set forth in § 920(a) of this title.

m. A private restricted landing area used for agricultural spraying and applications, including spraying and applications conducted under government sponsored programs, subject to the written approval of the Foundation Board.

(b) Farmlands and/or forestlands included in an Agricultural Preservation District shall be released from such District at the expiration of 10 years from the date such lands are initially placed in the District if the owner of the farmlands and/or forestlands provides written notification to the Foundation of intent to withdraw such lands from the District at least 6 months prior to the expiration of the referenced 10-year period; otherwise, such lands shall remain in the District for additional 5-year periods until such time that the owner provides prior to the expiration date of any such additional period at least 6 months prior written notice to the Foundation of intent to withdraw the lands from the District.

(c) In event of a purchase of an agricultural lands preservation easement by the Foundation, the restrictions set forth in subsection (a) of this section shall become permanent and subject to release only under § 917 of this title, or in the case of the restrictions set forth in paragraph (a)(2)b. of this section, under paragraph (a)(4)c. of this section.

History.

68 Del. Laws, c. 118, § 2; 71 Del. Laws, c. 257, § 1; 74 Del. Laws, c. 423, §§ 1, 2; 80 Del. Laws, c. 233, § 1; 80 Del. Laws, c. 344, § 1; 81 Del. Laws, c. 441, § 1; 83 Del. Laws, c. 26, § 1.

Effect of amendments.

83 Del. Laws, c. 26, effective June 3, 2021, substituted "are" for "shall be" in the introductory paragraph of (a); rewrote (a)(5)k.3.

PART II

REGULATORY PROVISIONS

CHAPTER 13
NURSERIES AND NURSERY STOCK

§ 1301. Definitions.

The following words shall, for purposes of this chapter, be defined as follows:

(1) "Agent" — any person who performs services for another person under an express or implied agreement. A person may be an agent without receiving compensation for services.

(2) "Agriculture" — the production of plants and animals useful to man, including all forms of farm products and farm production.

(3) "Broker" — any person who negotiates the purchase or sale of any material. A broker may or may not handle either the material which is involved or the proceeds of a sale.

(4) "Certificate" — a document authorized or prepared by an authorized federal or state regulatory official that affirms, declares, or verifies that a plant or other regulated article meets phytosanitary (quarantine), nursery inspection, pest freedom, plant registration or certification, or other legal requirements. Such documents are known by their purpose of issuance: phytosanitary certificate [for the purpose of verifying compliance with phytosanitary (quarantine) requirements]; nursery stock certificate (for the purpose of verifying compliance with nursery inspection and pest freedom standards); registration or certification tags, seals (for the purpose of verifying compliance with registration or certification requirements); etc.

(5) "Certification" — the act by the Department of affirming, declaring, or verifying compliance with phytosanitary (quarantine), nursery inspection, pest freedom, plant registration or certification, or any other set of legal requirements.

(6) "Chain store" — any business with 1 or more retail outlets that sells plants, plant material or nursery stock, and that are owned by a common parent business entity.

(7) "Commission merchant" — any person, who receives on consignment or solicits any material from a licensee, producer or his or her agent or accepts material in trust for purposes of sale and sells or resells any material on commission or for a fee.

(8) "Consignee" — any person to whom any plant, nursery stock, horticultural product, etc. is shipped for handling, sale, resale, or other purpose.

(9) "Consignor" — any person who ships or delivers to a consignee any plant, nursery stock, horticultural product, etc. for handling, planting, sale, resale, or any other purpose.

(10) "Dangerously injurious plant pest" — a plant pest that constitutes a significant threat to the agricultural, forest or horticultural interests of this State, or the State's general environmental quality.

(11) "Dealer" — any person who obtains title to, or possession, control, or delivery of, any plant, plant material or nursery stock, from a producer for the purpose of resale.

(12) "Department" — the State of Delaware Department of Agriculture and includes, but is not limited to, its officers, inspectors, employees, agents or representatives.

(13) "Florist(s)" — includes, but is not limited to, a person(s) or business(es) engaged in the production or sale, wholesale or retail of plants, plant materials or nursery stock for temporary, semi-permanent, seasonal or permanent, indoor or outdoor use.

(14) "Garden Center" — includes, but is not limited to, a business establishment engaged in the year round, retail sale of plants, plant material or nursery stock from a specific, permanent sales location.

(15) "Greenhouse" — includes, but is not limited to, an establishment or business engaged in the production of plants, plant material or nursery stock within a climate controlled structure, for distribution beyond on-site or personal use.

(16) "Grower" — includes but is not limited to, any person who raises, grows or propagates, for profit or other reasons, outdoors or indoors, any horticultural product, nursery stock, or plant.

(17) "Horticultural product" — those products stated in Group 18 of the United States Department of Labor Standard Industrial Classification Manual which are grown under cover or outdoors, including bulbs, flowers, shrubbery, florist greens, fruit stock, floral products, nursery stock, ornamental plants, potted plants, roses, seed, Christmas trees, fruits, food crops grown in greenhouses, vegetables, and horticultural specialties not otherwise specified.

(18) "Hold order" — an order or notice written by the Department to the owner(s) or person(s) in charge or in possession of a premises, plant, conveyance or article infested or infected with or exposed to infestation or infection of dangerously injurious plant pest(s), making it unlawful to move the aforementioned article(s) unless treated in accordance with the Department's prescribed procedures.

(19) "Infected" — a plant that has been determined by the Department to be contaminated with an infectious, transmissible or contagious pest or so exposed to the aforementioned that contamination can reasonably be expected to exist. This includes disease conditions, regardless of their mode of transmission or any disorder of plants which manifest symptoms

which, after investigation are determined by a federal or state pest prevention agency, to be characteristic of an infectious, transmissible, or contagious disease.

(20) "Infested" — a plant that has been determined by the Department to be contaminated by a dangerously injurious plant pest, or so exposed to the aforementioned that contamination can reasonably be expected to exist.

(21) "Landscaper(s)" — includes but is not limited to, any person(s) who keeps at a premises, or procures for transplantation, nursery stock for installation on the property of another person.

(22) "Mail-order merchant(s)" — includes but is not limited to, any person, dealer, or producer who sells or markets, wholesale or retail, any of its orders or business by drop shipment, catalog, telemarketing, telephone, mail-order or other indirect means.

(23) "Mark" — the Department shall affix, for purposes of identification or separation, a conspicuous official indicator to, on, around, or near, plants or plant material, known or suspected to be, infected or infested with a dangerously injurious plant pest. This includes, but is not limited to, paint, markers, tags, seals, stickers, tape, signs or placards.

(24) "Move" — to ship, offer for shipment, receive for transport, carry or, in any manner whatsoever, convey or relocate a regulated plant, plant material or nursery stock, from one place to another.

(25) "Nursery" — any location where nursery stock is grown, propagated, stored, or sold; or any location from which nursery stock is distributed direct to a customer. (See "Sales location")

(26) "Nursery industry license" — a document issued by the Department authorizing a person(s) to engage in a nursery or nursery related business at a particular location under a specified business name.

(27) "Nursery stock" — any plant for planting, propagation, or ornamentation, including:

    a. All plants, trees, shrubs, vines, perennials grafts, cuttings, buds, clones, and seedlings that may be sold for propagation, whether cultivated or wild, and all viable parts of these plants.

    b. Any other plant or plant part, including cut Christmas trees or any nonhardy plant or plant part, including annuals, bedding plants, and vegetable plants.

(28) "Owner(s)" — includes, but is not limited to, the person, persons, family, group, firm, association, business, company, incorporated entity or organization with the legal right of possession, proprietorship of, or responsibility for the property or place where any of the regulated articles as defined in this chapter are to be found, or person(s) who is in possession of, in proprietorship of, or has responsibility for the regulated articles.

(29) "Person(s)" — includes, but is not limited to, individual, family, firm, association, group, business, company, incorporated entity or organization.

(30) "Pre-clearance" — an agreement between quarantine officials of exporting and importing states to pass plants, plant material, etc., through quarantine by allowing the exporting state to inspect the plants pre-shipment, rather than the importing state inspecting the shipment upon arrival.

(31) "Pest" — includes any biotic agent (any living agent capable of reproducing itself) that is known to cause damage or harm to agriculture or the environment.

(32) "Plant" — includes, but is not limited to, any part of a plant, tree, aquatic plant, plant material, shrub, vine, fruit, rhizome, vegetable, seed,

bulb, stolon, tuber, corm, pip, cutting, scion, bud, graft, or fruit pit, including:

    a. Agricultural commodities: plant materials including any horticultural product.

    b. Nursery stock.

    c. Non-cultivated or feral plants, gathered from the environment.

    d. Plants produced by tissue culture, cloning or from stem cell cultures or other prepared media culture.

(33) "Plant pest" — includes, but is not limited to, any pest of plants, agricultural commodities, horticultural products, nursery stock, or non-cultivated plants. This includes, but is not limited to, insects, snails, nematodes, fungi, viruses, bacterium, microorganisms, mycoplasma like organisms, weeds, plants or parasitic higher plants.

(34) "Producer" — includes, but is not limited to, any person who raises, grows or propagates, for profit or other reasons, outdoors or indoors, any horticultural product, nursery stock, or plant.

(35) "Quarantine" — a legal instrument duly imposed or enacted by the Department as a means for mitigating pest risk. These actions include, but are not limited to, confinement or restriction of entry, movement, shipment or transportation of plants known or suspected to be infected or infested with some dangerously injurious plant pests.

(36) "Roadside market" — includes, but is not limited to a business engaged in the retail sale of plants, plant material or nursery stock on a seasonal basis and which may operate from a specific sales location or multiple mobile locations.

(37) "Registration" — the official recording of a growing location, person, plant, sales location or any other thing or place as one that has met specified requirements and therefore eligible for a particular activity, operation or purpose.

(38) "Sales location" — every location from which nursery stock is delivered directly to a customer.

(39) "Secretary" — the Secretary of the State of Delaware Department of Agriculture or his or her designee.

(40) "Sell" — includes offer for sale, expose for sale, possess for sale, exchange, barter or trade.

(41) "Shipment" — any article or thing which is, may be, or has been transported or conveyed from one place to another.

History.

65 Del. Laws, c. 491, § 1; 68 Del. Laws, c. 329, §§ 1, 2; 70 Del. Laws, c. 332, § 1; 83 Del. Laws, c. 33, § 1.

Effect of amendments.

83 Del. Laws, c. 33, effective June 3, 2021, deleted "but not limited to" from the end of the introductory paragraph of (27); substituted "cuttings, buds, clones, and seedlings" for "cuttings and buds" in (27)a.; and in (27)b., deleted "but not limited to" preceding "annuals" and added a comma following the first instance of "plants".

CHAPTER 17

COMMERCIAL FEEDS

§ 1701. Title.

This chapter shall be known as the "Delaware Commercial Feed Law of 2021."

History.
3 Del. C. 1953, § 1701; 56 Del. Laws, c. 69; 83 Del. Laws, c. 98, § 1.

Effect of amendments.
83 Del. Laws, c. 98, effective July 30, 2021, substituted "2021" for "1967".

§ 1702. Enforcing agency.

This chapter shall be administered by the Department of Agriculture of this State, hereinafter referred to as the "Department."

History.
3 Del. C. 1953, § 1702; 56 Del. Laws, c. 69; 57 Del. Laws, c. 764, § 8; 83 Del. Laws, c. 98, § 1.

Effect of amendments.
83 Del. Laws, c. 98, effective July 30, 2021, reenacted this section without change.

§ 1703. Definitions of words and terms.

When used in this chapter:

(1) "Brand name" means any word, name, symbol or device, or any combination thereof, identifying the commercial feed of a distributor or registrant and distinguishing it from that of others.

(2) "Commercial feed" means all materials or combination of materials which are distributed for the use as feed or for mixing in feed, for animals and cultured aquatic stock other than man except:

    a. Unmixed or unprocessed whole seeds and meals made directly from the entire seed;

    b. Unground hay, straw, stover, silage, cobs, husks, and hulls when not mixed with other materials;

    c. Individual chemical compounds when not mixed with other materials.

(3) "Contract feeder" means a person who, as an independent contractor, feeds commercial feed to animals pursuant to a contract whereby such commercial feed is supplied, furnished or otherwise provided to such person and whereby such person's remuneration is determined all or in part by feed consumption, mortality, profits, or amount or quality of product.

(4) "Customer-formula feed" means a mixture of commercial feeds or materials each batch of which mixture is mixed according to the specific instructions of the final purchaser, or contract feeder.

(5) "Distribute" means to offer for sale, sell, or barter, commercial feed or customer-formula feed; or to supply, furnish or otherwise provide commercial feed or customer-formula feed to a contract feeder.

(6) "Distributor" means any person who distributes pursuant to paragraph (5) of this section.

(7) "Drug" means any article intended for use in the diagnosis, cure, mitigation, treatment, or prevention of disease in animals other than humans; and articles other than commercial feed intended to affect the structure or any function of the animal body.

(8) "Feed ingredient" means each of the constituent materials making up a commercial feed.

(9) "Label" means a display of written, printed or graphic matter upon or affixed to the container in which a commercial feed is distributed, or on the invoice or delivery slip with which a commercial feed or customer-formula feed is distributed.

(10) "Manufacture" means to grind, mix, or blend, or further process a commercial or customer-formula feed for distribution.

(11) "Medicated feed" means any feed which contains drug ingredients

intended or presented for the cure, mitigation, treatment, or prevention of diseases of animals other than man or which contains drug ingredients intended to affect the structure or any function of the body of animals other than humans.

(12) "Mineral feed" means a commercial feed intended to supply primarily mineral elements or inorganic nutrients.

(13) "Official sample" means any sample of feed taken by the Department or its agent and designated as "official" by the Department.

(14) "Percent" or "percentage" means percentage by weight.

(15) "Person" means an individual, partnership, corporation, association, and other entities.

(16) "Pet" means dog or cat.

(17) "Pet food" means any commercial feed prepared and distributed for consumption by pets.

(18) "Product name" means the name of the commercial feed which identifies it as to kind, class or specific use and distinguishes it from all other products bearing the same brand name.

(19) "Quantity statement" means the net weight (mass), liquid measure, or count.

(20) "Sell" or "sale" includes exchange.

(21) "Specialty pet" means any animal normally maintained in a household, such as, but not limited to, rodents, ornamental birds, ornamental fish, reptiles, and amphibians, ferrets, hedgehogs, marsupials, and rabbits not raised for food or fur.

(22) "Specialty pet food" means any commercial feed prepared and distributed for consumption by specialty pets.

(23) "Supplement" means a feed used with another to improve the nutritive balance or performance of the total.

(24) "Ton" means a net weight of 2,000 pounds avoirdupois.

History.
3 Del. C. 1953, § 1703; 56 Del. Laws, c. 69; 69 Del. Laws, c. 103, § 6; 70 Del. Laws, c. 186, § 1; 83 Del. Laws, c. 98, § 1; 83 Del. Laws, c. 177, § 1.

Effect of amendments.
83 Del. Laws, c. 98, effective July 30, 2021, redesignated the existing definitions to appear in alphabetical order, adding present (7), (10), (11), (16), (17), (19), (21)-(23); substituted periods for semicolons at the end of present (1), (2)c., (4)-(6), (8), (9), (12)-(15), (18), (20) and (24); added "or registrant" in present (1); added "or combination of materials" in the introduc-

tory paragraph of present (2); added a comma following "husks" in present (2)b. and following "sell" in present (5); substituted "or" for "and/or" in present (4); substituted "paragraph (5)" for "subdivision (2)" in present (6); substituted "commercial feed" for "substance or mixture of substances designed or" in present (12); rewrote present (15); and added "and distinguishes it from all other products bearing the same brand name" in present (18).

83 Del. Laws, c. 177, effective September 15, 2021, attempted to make a change already enacted by 83 Del. Laws, c. 98, effective July 30, 2021.

§ 1704. Registration.

(a) Each commercial feed, such as animal food, pet food, specialty pet food, supplements, or medicated feed shall be registered before being distributed in this State; provided, however, that customer-formula feeds are exempt from registration. The application for registration shall be submitted on forms furnished by the Department, and shall also be accompanied by a label or other printed matter describing the product. Upon approval by the Department, a copy of the registration shall be furnished to the applicant. All registrations expire on December 31 of each year. The application shall include the information required by § 1705(a)(2), (3), (4), and (5) of this title. The Department may permit on the registration the alternative listing of ingredients of comparable feeding value, provided that the label for each package shall state the specific ingredients which are in such package.

(b) A distributor shall not be required to register any commercial feed product which is already registered under this chapter by another person, provided that the label does not differ in any respect.

(c) Changes in the guarantee of either chemical or ingredient composition of a registered commercial feed may be permitted provided there is satisfactory evidence that such changes would not result in a lowering of the feeding value of the product for the purpose for which designed.

(d) The Department may refuse registration of any application not in compliance with this chapter and may cancel any registration subsequently found not to be in compliance with any provision of this chapter; provided, however, that no registration shall be refused or cancelled until the registrant shall have been given the opportunity to be heard before the Department and to amend his or her application in order to comply with the requirements of this chapter.

History.
3 Del. C. 1953, § 1704; 56 Del. Laws, c. 69; 57 Del. Laws, c. 764, § 8; 70 Del. Laws, c. 186, § 1; 83 Del. Laws, c. 98, § 1.

Effect of amendments.
83 Del. Laws, c. 98, effective July 30, 2021, in (a), added "such as animal food, pet food, specialty pet food, supplements, or medicated feed" in the first sentence, and substituted "§ 1705(a)(2), (3), (4), and (5)" for "paragraphs (2), (3), (4), and (5) of subsection (a) of § 1705"; in (b), deleted "brand of" preceding "commercial", and added "product" and "provided that the label does not differ in any respect"; and, in (d), added "the" preceding "opportunity" and added "or her".

§ 1705. Labeling.

(a) Any commercial feed distributed in this State shall be accompanied by a legible label bearing the following information:

(1) The quantity statement;

(2) The product name and brand name, if any, under which the commercial feed is distributed;

(3) The guaranteed analysis of the commercial feed, listing the minimum percentage of crude protein, minimum percentage of crude fat, and maximum percentage of crude fiber. For all mineral feeds and for those commercial feeds containing a level of added mineral ingredients established by regulation, the list shall include the following, if added: Minimum and maximum percentages of calcium (Ca), minimum percentage of phosphorus (P), minimum percentage of iodine (I), and minimum percentage of salt (NaCl). Other substances or elements, determinable by laboratory methods, may be guaranteed by permission of the Department. When any items are guaranteed, they shall be subject to inspection and analysis in accordance with the methods and regulations that may be prescribed by the Department. The Department may by regulation designate certain commercial feeds which need not be labeled to show guarantees for crude protein, crude fat, and crude fiber;

(4) The common or usual name of each ingredient used in the manufacture of the commercial feed, except as the Department may, by regulation, permit the use of a collective term for a group of ingredients all of which perform the same function. An ingredient statement is not required for single standardized ingredient feeds which are officially defined;

(5) The name and principal mailing address of the manufacturer or person responsible for distributing the commercial feed.

(6) If a drug containing product is used, the label, invoice, delivery slip, or other shipping document must contain the following:

　　a. Directions for safe and effective use;

　　b. The purpose of the medication (claim statement); and

c. The established name of each active drug ingredient and the level of each drug used in the final mixture.

(b) When a commercial feed is distributed in this State in bags or other containers, the label shall be placed on or affixed to the container; when a commercial feed is distributed in bulk, the label shall accompany delivery and be furnished to the purchaser at the time of delivery.

(c) A customer-formula feed shall be accompanied by an invoice, label, delivery slip, or other shipping document bearing the following information:

(1) Name and address of the mixer;

(2) Name and address of the purchaser;

(3) Date of sale;

(4) The product name and brand name, if any, and number of pounds of each registered commercial feed used in the mixture and the name and number of pounds of each other feed ingredient added;

(5) If a drug containing product is used:

a. Directions for safe and effective use;

b. The purpose of the medication (claim statement);

c. The established name of each active drug ingredient and the level of each drug used in the final mixture.

(d) [Repealed.]

History.

3 Del. C. 1953, § 1705; 56 Del. Laws, c. 69; 57 Del. Laws, c. 764, § 8; 83 Del. Laws, c. 98, § 1.

Effect of amendments.

83 Del. Laws, c. 98, effective July 30, 2021, substituted "quantity statement" for "net weight" in (a)(1); added a comma following "fat" in the final sentence of (a)(3) and following "bulk" in (b); in (a)(5), added "mailing" and "manufacturer or"; added (a)(6); rewrote the introductory paragraph of (c); added (c)(5) and made a related stylistic change; and repealed (d).

§ 1706. Registration fees.

(a) For each commercial feed distributed in this State an annual registration fee must be paid to the Department as follows:

(1) For all commercial feed other than pet food, the registration fee is $23 per each product of each brand; provided, however, that the customer-formula feeds are exempt if the registration fee is paid on the commercial feeds which they contain.

(2) Following the effective date of this statute, for each pet food the registration fee is $50 per each product of each brand in year 1, $75 for each product of each brand in year 2, and $100 per each product of each brand in each subsequent year; provided, however that for a pet food manufactured by a nonprofit the registration fee is $23 for each product of each brand.

(b) All registration fees collected under paragraph (a)(1) of this section are to be transferred to the State Treasurer and paid into the General Fund of the State.

(c) The total of the registration fees collected under paragraph (a)(2) of this section is to be distributed as follows:

(1) $25 from each fee to the General Fund.

(2) The cost of developing and maintaining the technology to implement the requirements of this subsection to the Department of Agriculture.

(3) The remaining balance to the Spay/Neuter Fund created by Chapter 30F of Title 16.

a. The Office of Animal Welfare must prepare an annual report on the use of the fees under this paragraph for the Spay/Neuter Fund.

b. This annual report must be provided to the Secretary of Agriculture, the Secretary of Health and Social Services, the Chair of the

Senate Agriculture Committee, the Chair of the Senate Health and Social Services Committee, the Chair of the House of Representatives Agriculture Committee, and the Chair of the House of Representatives Health and Human Development Committee.

History.
3 Del. C. 1953, § 1706; 56 Del. Laws, c. 69; 57 Del. Laws, c. 764, § 8; 67 Del. Laws, c. 260, § 1; 83 Del. Laws, c. 98, § 1; 83 Del. Laws, c. 177, § 1.

Effect of amendments.
83 Del. Laws, c. 98, effective July 30, 2021, added "each product of each" in (a).

83 Del. Laws, c. 177, effective September 15, 2021, rewrote (a); substituted "collected under paragraph (a)(1) of this section are to" for "shall" in (b); and added (c).

§ 1707. Adulteration.

No person shall distribute an adulterated feed. A commercial feed or customer-formula feed shall be deemed to be adulterated:

(1) If any poisonous, deleterious or nonnutritive ingredient has been added in sufficient amount to render it injurious to health when fed in accordance with directions for use on the label;

(2) If any valuable constituent has been, in whole or in part, omitted or abstracted therefrom or any less valuable substance substituted therefor;

(3) If its composition or quality falls below or differs from that which it is purported or is represented to possess by its labeling;

(4) If it contains added hulls, screenings, straw, cobs or other high fiber material unless the name of each such material is stated on the label;

(5) If it contains viable weed seeds in amounts exceeding the limits which the Department shall establish by rule or regulation;

(6) If it contains any added poisonous, deleterious, non-nutritive substance, food or color additive, or new animal drug which is unsafe within the meaning of the Federal Food, Drug, and Cosmetic Act [21 U.S.C. § 301 et seq.];

(7) If it consists in whole or part of any filthy, putrid, or decomposed substance, or if it is otherwise unfit for feed;

(8) If it has been prepared, packed, or held under unsanitary conditions whereby it may have become contaminated with filth, or whereby it may have been rendered injurious to health.

History.
3 Del. C. 1953, § 1707; 56 Del. Laws, c. 69; 57 Del. Laws, c. 764, § 8; 83 Del. Laws, c. 98, § 1.

Effect of amendments.
83 Del. Laws, c. 98, effective July 30, 2021,

added a comma following "been" and following "part" in (2); added (6)-(8) and made a related stylistic change.

§ 1708. Misbranding.

No person shall distribute misbranded feed. A commercial feed or customer-formula feed shall be deemed to be misbranded:

(1) If its labeling is false or misleading in any particular;

(2) If it is distributed under the name of another feed;

(3) If it is not labeled as required in § 1705 of this title and in regulations prescribed under this chapter;

(4) If it purports to be or is represented as a commercial feed, or if it purports to contain or is represented as containing a commercial feed ingredient, unless such commercial feed or feed ingredient conforms to the definition of identity, if any, prescribed by regulation of the Department; in the adopting of such regulations the Department shall give due regard to commonly accepted definitions such as those issued by the Association of American Feed Control Officials;

(5) If any word, statement, or other information required by or under authority of this chapter to appear on the label or labeling is not prominently placed thereon with such conspicuousness (as compared with other words, statements, designs, or devices, in the labeling) and in such terms as to render it likely to be read and understood by the ordinary individual under the customary conditions of purchase and use.

History.
3 Del. C. 1953, § 1708; 56 Del. Laws, c. 69; 57 Del. Laws, c. 764, § 8; 83 Del. Laws, c. 98, § 1.

Effect of amendments.
83 Del. Laws, c. 98, effective July 30, 2021, in (4), substituted "commercial feed" for "feed ingredient" following "represented as a", and added "commercial" following "containing a" and "commercial feed or" following "unless such".

§ 1709. Inspections; sampling; analysis.

(a) The Department, individually or through its authorized agent, shall sample, inspect, make analyses of, and test commercial feeds and customer-formula feeds distributed within this State at such time and place, and to such an extent as it may deem necessary to determine whether such feeds are in compliance with this chapter. The Department, individually or through its agent, may enter upon any public or private premises including any vehicle of transport during regular business hours in order to have access to commercial feeds and customer-formula feeds and to records relating to their distribution and storage.

(b) The methods of sampling and analysis shall be those adopted by the Association of Official Agricultural Chemists International. In cases not covered by such methods, or in cases where methods are available in which improved applicability has been demonstrated, the Secretary may adopt such appropriate methods from other sources.

(c) The Department, in determining for administrative purposes whether a commercial feed is deficient in any component, shall be guided solely by the "official sample" as defined in § 1703 of this title and obtained and analyzed as provided for in subsection (b) of this section.

(d) When the inspection and analysis of an official sample indicates a commercial feed has been adulterated or misbranded, the results of analysis shall be forwarded by the Department to the distributor and the purchaser. Within 30 days of a request, the Department shall furnish to the distributor a portion of the samples concerned.

History.
3 Del. C. 1953, § 1709; 56 Del. Laws, c. 69; 57 Del. Laws, c. 764, § 8; 83 Del. Laws, c. 98, § 1.

Effect of amendments.
83 Del. Laws, c. 98, effective July 30, 2021, added "and storage" in the final sentence of (a); in (b), in the first sentence, deleted "Department from sources such as the Journal of the" preceding "Association" and added "International" and added the second sentence; and in (c), placed "official sample" in quotes and deleted "subdivision (14) of" preceding "§ 1703".

§ 1710. Regulations.

The Department shall enforce this chapter, and after due publicity and due public hearing may promulgate and adopt such reasonable regulations as may be necessary in order to secure the efficient administration of this chapter. Publicity concerning the public hearing shall be reasonably calculated to give interested parties adequate notice and adequate opportunity to be heard.

History.
3 Del. C. 1953, § 1710; 56 Del. Laws, c. 69; 57 Del. Laws, c. 764, § 8; 83 Del. Laws, c. 98, § 1.

Effect of amendments.
83 Del. Laws, c. 98, effective July 30, 2021, reenacted this section without change.

§ 1711. Detained commercial feeds; "withdrawal from distribution" orders; condemnation and confiscation.

(a) When the Department or its authorized agent has reasonable cause to believe any lot of commercial feed is being distributed in violation of this chapter or of any of the regulations promulgated under this chapter, it may issue and enforce a written or printed "withdrawal from distribution" order, warning the distributor not to dispose of the lot of feed in any manner until written permission is given by the Department or the Court. The Department shall release any lot of commercial feeds so withdrawn when such distributor has complied with this chapter and the regulations issued hereunder. If compliance is not obtained within 30 days, the Department may begin, or upon request of the distributor shall begin, proceedings for condemnation.

(b) Any lot of commercial feed not in compliance with this chapter or regulations promulgated hereunder shall be subject to seizure on complaint of the Department to a court of competent jurisdiction in the area in which said commercial feed is located. In the event the court finds the said commercial feed to be in violation of this chapter or regulations promulgated hereunder and orders the condemnation of said commercial feed, the same shall be disposed of in any manner consistent with the quality of the commercial feed and the laws of the State; provided, that in no instance shall the disposition of said commercial feed be ordered by the court without first giving the claimant an opportunity to apply to the court for release of said commercial feed or for permission to process or relabel said commercial feed to bring it into compliance with this chapter.

History.

3 Del. C. 1953, § 1711; 56 Del. Laws, c. 69; 57 Del. Laws, c. 764, § 8; 83 Del. Laws, c. 98, § 1.

Effect of amendments.

83 Del. Laws, c. 98, effective July 30, 2021, reenacted this section without change.

§ 1712. Penalties.

(a) Any person convicted of violating any of the provisions of this chapter or any regulations hereunder or the rules and regulations issued thereunder, or who shall impede, obstruct, hinder or otherwise prevent or attempt to prevent the Department or its duly authorized agent in performing duties prescribed by this chapter or regulations issued hereunder, shall be fined not more than $250 for the first violation, and not less than $500 for each subsequent violation. In all prosecutions under this chapter involving the composition of a lot of commercial feed, a certified copy of the official analysis signed by the Department shall be accepted as prima facie evidence of the composition.

(b) Nothing in this chapter shall be construed as requiring the Department or its representative to report for prosecution or for the institution of seizure proceedings as a result of minor violations of this chapter where the public interest will be best served by a suitable notice of warning in writing.

(c) When any violation of this chapter is reported to the Attorney General, he or she shall cause appropriate proceedings to be instituted and prosecuted in a court of competent jurisdiction without delay. Before the Department reports a violation for prosecution, an opportunity shall be given the distributor to present his or her views to the Department.

(d) The Department may apply for and the court may grant a temporary or permanent injunction restraining any person from violating or continuing to violate this chapter or any rule or regulation promulgated thereunder notwithstanding the existence of other remedies at law. Any injunction shall be issued without bond.

(e) Any person adversely affected by an act, order or ruling made pursuant to this chapter may within 45 days thereafter, bring an action in the Superior Court in the county where the enforcement official has his or her office, for a new trial of the issues bearing upon such chapter, order or ruling, and upon such trial the Court may issue and enforce such orders, judgments or decrees as the Court may deem proper, just and equitable.

History.
3 Del. C. 1953, § 1712; 56 Del. Laws, c. 69; 57 Del. Laws, c. 764, § 8; 70 Del. Laws, c. 186, § 1; 83 Del. Laws, c. 98, § 1.

Effect of amendments.
83 Del. Laws, c. 98, effective July 30, 2021, substituted ""$250" and "$500" for "$50" in (a); and added "or her" in (e).

§ 1713. Publications.

The Department shall publish at least semiannually, in such form as it may deem proper, a report of the results of the analyses of official samples of commercial feeds sold within this State as compared with the analyses guaranteed in the registration and on the label.

History.
3 Del. C. 1953, § 1713; 56 Del. Laws, c. 69; 57 Del. Laws, c. 764, § 8; 83 Del. Laws, c. 98, § 1.

Effect of amendments.
83 Del. Laws, c. 98, effective July 30, 2021, reenacted this section without change.

§ 1714. Cooperation with other entities.

The Department may cooperate and enter into agreements with governmental agencies of this State, other states, agencies of the federal government, and private associations in order to carry out the purpose and provisions of this chapter.

History.
83 Del. Laws, c. 98, § 1.

Revisor's note.
This section became effective upon the signature of the Governor on July 30, 2021.

CHAPTER 21

COMMERCIAL FERTILIZERS AND SOIL CONDITIONERS

Revision of chapter.
83 Del. Laws, c. 140, § 1, effective Sept. 10, 2021, revised this chapter by substituting present §§ 2101 to 2123 of this title for former §§ 2102 to 2122 of this title. No detailed expla- nation of the changes made by the 2021 act has been attempted, but, where appropriate, the historical citations to former sections have been added to corresponding sections in the revised chapter.

§ 2101. Title.

This chapter shall be known as the Delaware Commercial Fertilizer and Soil Conditioner Law of 2021.

History.
3 Del. C. 1953, § 2101; 58 Del. Laws, c. 157; 83 Del. Laws, c. 140, § 1.

§ 2102. Enforcing agency.

This chapter shall be administered by the State Department of Agriculture of the State, hereinafter referred to as the Department.

History.
3 Del. C. 1953, § 2102; 58 Del. Laws, c. 157;
83 Del. Laws, c. 140, § 1.

§ 2103. Definitions of words and terms.

When used in this chapter:

(1) The term "brand" means a term, design, or trademark used in connection with 1 or several grades of commercial fertilizer.

(2) The term "commercial fertilizer" means any substance containing 1 or more recognized plant nutrient(s) which is used for its plant nutrient content and which is designed for use or claimed to have value in promoting plant growth, except unmanipulated animal and vegetable manures, marl, lime, limestone, wood ashes and other products exempted by regulation of the Secretary;

a. A "fertilizer material" is a commercial fertilizer which either:

1. Contains important quantities of no more than 1 of the primary plant nutrients (nitrogen, phosphate and potash), or

2. Has 85% or more of its plant nutrient content present in the form of a single chemical compound, or

3. Is derived from a plant or animal residue or by-product or a natural material deposit which has been processed in such a way that its content of primary plant nutrients has not been materially changed except by purification and concentration;

b. A "mixed fertilizer" is a commercial fertilizer containing any combination of mixture of fertilizer materials;

c. A "specialty fertilizer" is a commercial fertilizer distributed primarily for nonfarm use, such as home gardens, lawns, shrubbery, flowers, golf courses, municipal parks, cemeteries, greenhouses and nurseries;

d. A "bulk fertilizer" is a commercial fertilizer distributed in a nonpackaged form.

(3) The term "custom blend" means a fertilizer blended according to specifications provided to a blender in a soil test nutrient recommendation or to meet the specific consumer (end user) request(s) prior to blending.

(4) The term "deficiency" means the amount of nutrient found by analysis less than that guaranteed which may result from a lack of nutrient ingredients or from lack of uniformity.

(5) The term "Department" means State Department of Agriculture.

(6) The term "distributor" means any person who imports, consigns, manufactures, produces, compounds, mixes or blends commercial fertilizer, or soil conditioner, or who offers for sale, sells, barters or otherwise supplies commercial fertilizer or soil conditioner in this State.

(7) The term "grade" means the percentage of total nitrogen, available phosphate, and soluble potash stated in whole numbers in the same terms, order and percentages as in the guaranteed analysis. Provided, however, that specialty fertilizers may be guaranteed in fractional units of less than 1% of total nitrogen, available phosphate, and soluble potash; provided, further, that fertilizer materials, bone meal, manures, and similar materials may be guaranteed in fractional units.

(8) The term "guaranteed analysis" shall mean the minimum percentage of plant nutrients claimed in the following order and form:

a. Total Nitrogen (N) — percent
Available Phosphate (P2O5) — percent
Soluble Potash (K2O) — percent

b. For unacidulated mineral phosphatic materials and basic slag, bone, tankage and other organic phosphate materials, the total phosphate and/or degree of fineness may also be guaranteed;

c. Guarantees for plant nutrients other than nitrogen, phosphorus and potassium may be permitted or required by regulation of the Secretary. The guarantees for such other nutrients shall be expressed in the form of the element. The sources of such other nutrients (oxides, salt, chelates, etc.) may be required to be stated on the application for registration and may be included on the label. Other beneficial substances or compounds, determinable by laboratory methods, also may be guaranteed by permission of the Secretary and with the advice of the director of the agricultural experiment station. When any plant nutrients or other substances or compounds are guaranteed, they shall be subject to inspection and analysis in accord with the methods and regulations prescribed by the Secretary;

d. Potential basicity or acidity expressed in terms of calcium carbonate equivalent in multiples of 100 pounds per ton, when required by regulation;

(9) The term "investigational allowance" means an allowance for variations inherent in the taking, preparation and analysis of an official sample of fertilizer.

(10) The term "label" means the display of all written, printed or graphic matter upon the immediate container or statement accompanying a commercial fertilizer or soil conditioner.

(11) The term "labeling" means any advertising, promotional or promotion of any fertilizer or soil conditioner including, but not limited to, all written, printed, graphic or electronic communication used in promoting the sale of such fertilizer or soil conditioner.

(12) The term "official sample" means any sample of commercial fertilizer or soil conditioner taken by the Secretary or the Secretary's agent and designated as "official" by the Secretary.

(13) The term "open formula" means mixed fertilizer labeled so as to show in addition to requirements of § 2105 of this title the name and grade of materials and the quantity of each used per ton in compounding or mixing.

(14) The term "percent" or "percentage" means the percentage by weight.

(15) The term "person" includes individual, partnership, association, firm and corporation.

(16) The term "registrant" means the person who registers commercial fertilizer or soil conditioner under this chapter.

(17) The term "Secretary" means the Secretary of the State Department of Agriculture or the Secretary's duly authorized delegates.

(18) The term "soil conditioner" means any substance or mixture of substances, including any plant biostimulant, imported, manufactured, prepared or sold for manurial soil-enriching or soil-corrective purposes or intended to be used for promoting or stimulating the growth of plants, increasing the productivity of plants, improving the quality of crops, or producing any chemical, biochemical, biological or physical change in the soil, except commercial fertilizer as defined in this chapter, unmanipulated animal and vegetable manures, and agricultural liming materials.

(19) The term "ton" means a net weight of 2,000 pounds avoirdupois.

History. 70 Del. Laws, c. 186, § 1; 83 Del. Laws, c. 140,
3 Del. C. 1953, § 2103; 58 Del. Laws, c. 157; § 1.

§ 2104. Registration.

(a) Each brand and grade of commercial fertilizer shall be registered before being distributed in this State. The application for registration shall be submitted to the Department on a form furnished by the Department, and shall be accompanied by a fee of $1.15 per each grade of each brand, except those fertilizers sold in packages of 10 pounds or less shall be registered at a fee of $40 per each grade of each brand. Upon approval by the Department, a copy of the registration shall be furnished to the applicant. All registrations expire on December 31 of each year. The application shall include the following information:

(1) The net weight;

(2) The brand and grade;

(3) The guaranteed analysis;

(4) The name and address of the registrant.

(b) Each soil conditioner before being distributed in the State will be registered. The application for this registration will include a label or facsimile thereof for said material, and the Department may require proof to substantiate claims made for the material.

(c) Notwithstanding subsections (a) and (b) of this section, a distributor shall not be required to register any commercial fertilizer or soil conditioner which is already registered under this chapter by another person, providing the label does not differ in any respect.

(d) Also, notwithstanding any other provision of this section, a distributor shall not be required to register custom blends of commercial fertilizer or soil conditioner, but shall be required to register his firm at a fee of $100 for each individual facility distributing custom blends in the state and to label such fertilizer as provided in § 2105(b) of this title. All registrations expire on December 31 of each year.

(e) All amendments to the terms of registration or application therefor are subject to fees specified in subsection (a) of this section and § 2106 of this title.

History. 67 Del. Laws, c. 260, § 1; 83 Del. Laws, c. 140,
3 Del. C. 1953, § 2104; 58 Del. Laws, c. 157; § 1.

§ 2105. Labels.

(a) Any commercial fertilizer distributed in this State in containers shall have placed on or affixed to the container a label setting forth in clearly legible and conspicuous form the information required by § 2104(a)(1)-(4) of this title. In case of bulk shipments, this information in written or printed form shall accompany delivery and be supplied to the purchaser at the time of delivery.

(b) A commercial fertilizer formulated according to the open formula method according to specifications furnished by a consumer prior to mixing shall be labeled to show the net weight, guaranteed analysis of each ingredient, and the name and address of the distributor; and after mixing, the guaranteed analysis on the label is to be determined by percentage of weight of a ton the same as is defined under "grade" in § 2103 of this title.

History.
3 Del. C. 1953, § 2105; 58 Del. Laws, c. 157;
83 Del. Laws, c. 140, § 1.

§ 2106. Inspection fees and tonnage reports.

(a) There shall be paid to the Department for all commercial fertilizers or soil conditioners distributed in this State to nonregistrants an inspection fee at the rate of 10 cents per ton;

(1) Not less than 15 cents per ton effective January 1, 2022;

(2) Not less than 20 cents per ton effective January 1, 2023;

(3) Not less than 25 cents per ton effective January 1, 2024;

provided that sales to manufacturers or exchanges between them are hereby exempted. Fees so collected shall be paid to the Department, which shall deposit the same in the General Fund an appropriated special fund account in the Department.

On individual packages of commercial fertilizer or soil conditioners containing 10 pounds or less, there shall be paid, in lieu of the annual registration fee of $1.15 per each grade of each brand and the inspection fee, an annual registration fee and inspection fee of $40 for each grade of each brand of fertilizer and soil conditioners sold or distributed. Where a person sells commercial fertilizer or soil conditioners in packages of 10 pounds or less and in packages over 10 pounds, this annual registration and inspection fee of $40 shall apply only to that portion sold in packages of 10 pounds or less, and that portion sold in packages over 10 pounds shall be subject to the same inspection fee as provided in this chapter.

(b) Every person who distributes a commercial fertilizer or soil conditioner in this State shall file with the Department on forms furnished by the Department a semiannual statement for the periods ending December 31, and June 30, setting forth the number of net tons of each commercial fertilizer or soil conditioner distributed in this State during that period. The report shall be due on or before the last day of the month following the close of each period and with such statement the inspection fee shall be filed according to the rate set forth in subsection (a) of this section.

If the tonnage report is not filed and the payment of inspection fee is not made within 30 days after the end of each period, a surcharge amounting to 10 percent (minimum $10) per month of the amount shall be assessed against the registrant, and the Department shall have a lien against the registrant for the amount owed, including surcharge.

(c) When more than 1 person is involved in the distribution of a commercial fertilizer or soil conditioner, the last person who has the fertilizer or soil conditioner registered and who distributes to a nonregistrant (dealer or consumer) is responsible for reporting the tonnage and paying the inspection fee, unless the report and payment have already been submitted by a prior distributor of a fertilizer or soil conditioner.

(d) No information furnished the Department under this section shall be disclosed publicly in such a way as to divulge confidential information about the business operation of anyone.

(e) Fees so collected shall be used for the payment of the costs of inspection, sampling and analysis, and other expenses necessary for the administration of this chapter

History.
3 Del. C. 1953, § 2106; 58 Del. Laws, c. 157; 83 Del. Laws, c. 140, § 1.

§ 2107. Inspection; sampling; analysis.

(a) It shall be the duty of the Secretary to sample, inspect, and test commercial fertilizers or soil conditioners distributed within this State at any time and place and to such an extent as he may deem necessary to determine whether such commercial fertilizers or soil conditioners are in compliance with the provisions of this chapter. The Secretary, individually or through the Secretary's agent, is authorized to enter upon any public or private premises or carriers during regular business hours in order to have access to commercial fertilizers or soil conditioners subject to the provisions of this chapter and the rules and regulations pertaining thereto, and to the records relating to their distribution; provided, however, that the action of the Secretary or his or her agent hereunder shall be with the consent of the person having control over the property in which such fertilizer or soil conditioner is kept, and if without such consent, then the Secretary or his or her agent is to obtain a valid search warrant therefor, specifying the premises to be searched and the purpose of the search, and setting forth probable cause.

(b) The methods of analysis and sampling shall be those adopted by the Association of Official Analytical Chemists International. In cases not covered by such methods, or in cases where methods are available in which improved applicability has been demonstrated, the Secretary may adopt such appropriate methods from other sources.

(c) The Secretary, in determining for administrative purposes whether any commercial fertilizer is deficient in plant food, shall be guided solely by the "official sample" as defined in § 2103 of this title, and obtained and analyzed as provided for in subsection (b) of this section.

(d) The results of official analysis of commercial fertilizers or soil conditioners and portions of official samples shall be distributed by the Secretary as provided in the regulations.

History.
3 Del. C. 1953, § 2107; 58 Del. Laws, c. 157; 70 Del. Laws, c. 186, § 1; 83 Del. Laws, c. 140, § 1.

§ 2108. Plant food deficiency.

(a) If analysis shows that a commercial fertilizer is deficient in 1 or more of its guaranteed primary plant foods (NPK) beyond the "investigational allowances" as established by published regulation, or if the overall index value of the fertilizer is below the level established by regulation, a penalty of 2.3 times the commercial value (as defined in § 2109 of this title) of such deficiency(s) shall be assessed. When a fertilizer is subject to a penalty under both, the larger penalty payment shall apply.

(b) Deficiencies beyond the investigational allowances as established by regulation as provided in subsection (a) of this section in any other constituent(s) covered under § 2103(8)b., c., and d. of this title, which the registrant is required to or may guarantee, shall be evaluated and penalties prescribed therefor by the Secretary by published regulation.

(c) All penalties assessed under this section shall be paid to the consumer of the lot of commercial fertilizer represented by the sample analyzed within 3 months after the date of notice from the Secretary to the registrant, receipts taken therefor and promptly forwarded to the Secretary. If said consumers cannot be found, the amount of the penalty shall be paid to the Department which shall deposit same in the General Fund.

(d) A deficiency in an official sample of mixed fertilizer resulting from nonuniformity is not distinguishable from a deficiency due to actual plant nutrient shortage and is properly subject to official action.

History.
3 Del. C. 1953, § 2108; 58 Del. Laws, c. 157; 67 Del. Laws, c. 260, § 1; 83 Del. Laws, c. 140, § 1.

§ 2109. Commercial value.

For the purpose of determining the commercial values to be applied under the provisions of § 2108 of this title, the Secretary shall determine and publish annually the values per unit of nitrogen, available phosphate, and soluble potash in commercial fertilizers in this State. The values so determined and published shall be used in determining and assessing penalties.

History.
3 Del. C. 1953, § 2109; 58 Del. Laws, c. 157;
83 Del. Laws, c. 140, § 1.

§ 2110. Misbranding.

No person shall distribute misbranded fertilizer or soil conditioner. A commercial fertilizer or soil conditioner shall be deemed to be misbranded:

(1) If its labeling is false or misleading in any particular;

(2) If it is distributed under the name of another fertilizer product or soil conditioner;

(3) If it is not labeled as required in § 2105 of this title and in accordance with regulations prescribed under this chapter;

(4) If it purports to be or is represented as a commercial fertilizer or soil conditioner or is represented as containing a plant nutrient or commercial fertilizer or soil conditioner, unless such plant nutrient or commercial fertilizer or soil conditioner conforms to the definition of identity, if any, prescribed by regulation of the Secretary; in the adopting of such regulations the Secretary shall give due regard to commonly accepted definitions and official fertilizer or soil conditioner terms such as those issued by the Association of American Plant Food Control Officials.

History.
3 Del. C. 1953, § 2110; 58 Del. Laws, c. 157;
83 Del. Laws, c. 140, § 1.

§ 2111. Adulteration.

No person shall distribute an adulterated fertilizer product or soil conditioner. A commercial fertilizer or soil conditioner shall be deemed to be adulterated:

(1) If it contains any deleterious or harmful ingredient in sufficient amount to render it injurious to beneficial plant life, animals, humans, aquatic life, soil, or water when applied in accordance with directions for use on the label, or if adequate warning statements or directions for use which may be necessary to protect plant life, animals, humans, aquatic life, soil, or water are not shown upon the label;

(2) If its composition falls below or differs from that which it is purported to possess by its labeling;

(3) If it contains unwanted crop seed or weed seed.

History.
3 Del. C. 1953, § 2111; 58 Del. Laws, c. 157;
83 Del. Laws, c. 140, § 1.

§ 2112. Publications.

The Secretary shall publish at least annually and in such forms as the Secretary may deem proper:

(1) Information concerning the distribution of commercial fertilizers and soil conditioners;

(2) Results of analyses based on official samples of commercial fertilizers distributed within the State as compared with the analyses guaranteed under §§ 2104 and 2105 of this title.

History.   70 Del. Laws, c. 186, § 1; 83 Del. Laws, c. 140,
3 Del. C. 1953, § 2112; 58 Del. Laws, c. 157;   § 1.

§ 2113. Rules and regulations.

The Secretary may prescribe and enforce such rules and regulations relating to investigational allowances, definitions, records, and the distribution of commercial fertilizers and soil conditioners as may be necessary to carry into effect the full intent and meaning of this chapter. All regulations promulgated pursuant to this chapter shall be published and made available to all citizens.

The Department of Agriculture may adopt any policies and regulations necessary to permit the registration and distribution of plant biostimulants when the use, registration, or distribution of plant biostimulants is permitted by the Association of American Plant Food Control Officials.

History.
3 Del. C. 1953, § 2113; 58 Del. Laws, c. 157;
83 Del. Laws, c. 140, § 1.

§ 2114. Fertilizer and soil conditioner short in weight.

If any commercial fertilizer or soil conditioner in the possession of the consumer is found by the Secretary to be short in weight, the registrant of said commercial fertilizer or soil conditioner shall within 30 days after official notice from the Secretary pay to the consumer a penalty equal to 4 times the value of the actual shortage.

History.
3 Del. C. 1953, § 2114; 58 Del. Laws, c. 157;
83 Del. Laws, c. 140, § 1.

§ 2115. Cancellation of registrations.

The Department may cancel the registration of any brand of commercial fertilizer or soil conditioner or refuse to register any brand of commercial fertilizer or soil conditioner as herein provided, upon satisfactory evidence that the registrant has used fraudulent or deceptive practices in the evasions or attempted evasions of this chapter or any rules and regulations promulgated thereunder; provided that no registration shall be revoked or refused until the registrant shall have been given the opportunity to appear for a hearing by the Secretary.

History.
3 Del. C. 1953, § 2115; 58 Del. Laws, c. 157;
83 Del. Laws, c. 140, § 1.

§ 2116. "Stop sale" orders.

The Secretary may issue and enforce a written or printed "stop sale, use or removal" order to the owner or custodian of any lots of commercial fertilizer or soil conditioner to hold such commercial fertilizer or soil conditioner at a designated place when the Secretary finds that it is being offered or exposed for sale in violation of any of the provisions of this chapter, until the law has been complied with and said commercial fertilizer or soil conditioner is released in writing by the Secretary, or said violation has been otherwise legally disposed of by written authority. The Secretary shall release the commercial fertilizer or soil conditioner so withdrawn when the requirements of this chapter have been complied with and all costs and expenses incurred in connection with the withdrawal have been paid.

History.
3 Del. C. 1953, § 2116; 58 Del. Laws, c. 157;
83 Del. Laws, c. 140, § 1.

§ 2117. Seizure, condemnation, and sale.

Any lot of commercial fertilizer or soil conditioner not in compliance with the provisions of this chapter shall be subject to seizure on complaint of the Secretary to a court of competent jurisdiction in the county in which said commercial fertilizer or soil conditioner is located. In the event 1 court finds the said commercial fertilizer or soil conditioner to be in violation of this chapter and orders the condemnation of said commercial fertilizer or soil conditioner, it shall be disposed of in any manner consistent with the quality of the commercial fertilizer or soil conditioner and the laws of the State. Provided that in no instance shall the disposition of said commercial fertilizer or soil conditioner be ordered by the court without first giving the claimant an opportunity to apply to the court for release of said commercial fertilizer or soil conditioner or for permission to process or relabel said commercial fertilizer or soil conditioner to bring it into compliance with this chapter.

History.
3 Del. C. 1953, § 2117; 58 Del. Laws, c. 157; 83 Del. Laws, c. 140, § 1.

§ 2118. Violations.

(a) If it shall appear from the examination of any commercial fertilizer or soil conditioner that any of the provisions of this chapter or the rules and published regulations issued thereunder have been violated, the Secretary shall cause notice of the violations to be given to the registrant, distributor, or possessor from whom said sample was taken, and any person so notified shall be given opportunity to be heard under such rules and regulations as may be prescribed by the Secretary. If it appears after such hearing, either in the presence or absence of the person so notified, that any of the provisions of this chapter or rules and regulations issued thereunder have been violated, the Secretary may certify the fact to the Attorney General.

(b) Any person convicted of violating any provision of this chapter or the rules and regulations issued thereunder shall be punished in the discretion of the Superior Court, which shall have exclusive original jurisdiction over offenses under this chapter.

(c) Nothing in this chapter shall be construed as requiring the Secretary or his representative to report for prosecution or for the institution of seizure proceedings as a result of minor violations of this chapter when the Secretary believes that the public interests will be best served by a suitable notice of warning in writing.

(d) It shall be the duty of the Attorney General to whom any violation is reported to cause appropriate proceedings to be instituted and prosecuted in a court of competent jurisdiction without delay.

(e) The Secretary is hereby authorized to apply for and the Court of Chancery is authorized to grant a temporary or permanent injunction restraining any person from violating or continuing to violate any of the provisions of this chapter or any rule or regulation promulgated under this chapter notwithstanding the existence of other remedies at law. Injunctions shall be issued without bond.

History.
3 Del. C. 1953, § 2118; 58 Del. Laws, c. 157; 70 Del. Laws, c. 186, § 1; 83 Del. Laws, c. 140, § 1.

§ 2119. Hearing required.

If, after notification by the Secretary of the Department's order penalizing any person under §§ 2108 and 2114 of this title, denying registration under § 2104 of this title, or cancelling registration under § 2115 of this title, any aggrieved person shall so demand in writing, the Secretary shall hold a hearing. At such hearing a record shall be kept of all evidence and testimony, which shall be under oath, and of the Secretary's findings and decisions. Based on the evidence presented and the law set forth in this chapter, as well as regulations adopted pursuant thereto, the Secretary shall affirm, revoke or modify the Department's original order.

History.
3 Del. C. 1953, § 2119; 58 Del. Laws, c. 157;
83 Del. Laws, c. 140, § 1.

§ 2120. Appeals.

Nothing in this chapter shall be construed to prohibit appeals to a court of competent jurisdiction by persons aggrieved by a decision of the Secretary under § 2119 of this title. Such an appeal shall be on the record and confined to a determination as to whether the Secretary abused his or her discretion, provided that no appeal shall stay an order by the Department.

History.
3 Del. C. 1953, § 2120; 58 Del. Laws, c. 157;   70 Del. Laws, c. 186, § 1; 83 Del. Laws, c. 140, § 1.

§ 2121. Exchanges between manufacturers.

Nothing in this chapter shall be construed to restrict or avoid sales or exchanges of commercial fertilizers or soil conditioners to each other by importers, manufacturers, or manipulators who mix fertilizer materials for sale or as preventing the free and unrestricted shipments of commercial fertilizer or soil conditioners to manufacturers or manipulators who have registered their brands as required by the provisions of this chapter.

History.
3 Del. C. 1953, § 2121; 58 Del. Laws, c. 157;
83 Del. Laws, c. 140, § 1.

§ 2122. Delegation of duties.

All authority vested in the State Secretary of Agriculture by virtue of the provisions of this chapter may with like force and effect be executed by such employees of the Department of Agriculture as may be designated for said purpose.

History.
3 Del. C. 1953, § 2122; 58 Del. Laws, c. 157;
83 Del. Laws, c. 140, § 1.

§ 2123. Cooperation with other entities.

The Department may cooperate and enter into agreements with governmental agencies of this State, other states, and agencies of the federal government in order to carry out the purpose and provisions of this chapter.

History.
83 Del. Laws, c. 140, § 1.

CHAPTER 29

INVASIVE PLANTS [EFFECTIVE JULY 1, 2022].

Revisor's note.
Section 2 of 83 Del. Laws, c. 8, provided: "This act takes effect on July 1, 2022."

§ 2901. Purpose [Effective July 1, 2022].

The purpose of this chapter is to prohibit invasive plant species at their point of sale or delivery into this State.

History.
83 Del. Laws, c. 8, § 1.

§ 2902. Definitions [Effective July 1, 2022].

As used in this chapter:

(1) "Invasive plant" means any living part, cultivar, variety, species, or subspecies not native to Delaware identified by the Secretary as having the potential to do all of the following:

    a. Result in widespread dispersal and establishment.

    b. Out-compete other species in the same area.

    c. Exhibit rapid growth or high seed or propagule productions.

    d. Become established in natural areas in the State.

(2) "Secretary" means the Secretary of the Delaware Department of Agriculture.

History.
83 Del. Laws, c. 8, § 1.

§ 2903. Restrictions on invasive plants [Effective July 1, 2022].

(a) No person may import, export, buy, sell, transport, distribute, or propagate any viable portion, including seeds, of an invasive plant in this State, unless the Secretary provides prior written approval under subsection (b) of this section.

(b) The Secretary may provide written approval for a person to conduct an activity prohibited under subsection (a) of this section if the purpose of the activity is for any of the following:

(1) Disposal.

(2) Control.

(3) Research or education.

(4) Export for the purpose of disposal, control, research, or education.

History.
83 Del. Laws, c. 8, § 1.

§ 2904. Regulations; designation of plants [Effective July 1, 2022].

(a) The Secretary may promulgate and adopt regulations deemed necessary to carry out the purposes of this chapter.

(b) The Secretary shall maintain a list of invasive plants, known as the "Invasive Plant List".

(1) The Secretary shall maintain the Invasive Plant List with the advice of the Delaware Native Species Commission, so long as the Delaware Native Species Commission exists.

(2) The Secretary may make the alterations to the Invasive Plant List under Chapter 101 of Title 29.

(c) The Invasive Plant list must include, at a minimum, all of the following:

(1) Multiflora rose (Rosa multiflora).

(2) Japanese honeysuckle (Lonicera japonica).

(3) Oriental bittersweet (Celastrus orbiculatus).

(4) Japanese stilt grass (Microstegium vimineum).

(5) Japanese knotweed (Fallopia japonica).

(6) Autumn olive (Elaeagnus umbellata).

(7) Norway maple (Acer platanoides).

(8) European reed (Phragmites australis subsp. australis).

(9) Hydrilla (Hydrilla verticillata).

(10) Morrow's honeysuckle (Lonicera morrowii).

(11) Mile-a-minute weed (Persicaria perfoliata).

(12) Yam-leaved Clematis (Clematis terniflora).

(13) European Privet (Ligustrum vulgare).
(14) European Sweetflag (Acorus calamus).
(15) Wineberry (Rubus phoenicolasius).
(16) Japanese barberry (Berberis thunbergii).
(17) Lesser periwinkle (Vinca minor).
(18) Garlic mustard (Alliaria petiolata).
(19) Winged euonymus (Euonymus alatus).
(20) Porcelain berry (Ampelopsis glandulosa).
(21) Callery pear (Pyrus calleryana).
(22) Marsh Dewflower (Murdannia keisak).
(23) Lesser celandine (Ficaria verna).
(24) Purple loosestrife (Lythrum salicaria).
(25) Amur honeysuckle (Lonicera maackii).
(26) Tartarian honeysuckle (Lonicera tatarica).
(27) Tree of heaven (Ailanthus altissima).
(28) Spotted knapweed (Centaurea stoebe subsp. micranthos).
(29) Creeping water primrose (Ludwigia peploides subsp. glabrescens).
(30) Water hyacinth (Eichhornia crassipes).
(31) Parrot-feather (Myriophyllum aquaticum).
(32) English ivy (Hedrix helix).
(33) Orange daylily (Hemerocallis fulva).
(34) Yellow flag iris (Iris pseudoacorus).
(35) Creeping Jenny (Lysimachia nummularia).
(36) Japanese pachysandra (Pachysandra terminalis).
(37) Chinese wisteria (Wisteria sinensis).

(d) The Secretary shall maintain a watch list of potentially invasive plants.

(1) The Secretary shall maintain the watch list of potentially invasive plants with the advice of the Delaware Native Species Commission, so long as the Delaware Native Species Commission exists.

(2) A plant on the watch list of potentially invasive plants may only be sold or offered for sale at a retail or wholesale outlet if the plant has a tag or label that identifies the plant as being potentially invasive.

History.
83 Del. Laws, c. 8, § 1.

§ 2905. Acceptance of grants [Effective July 1, 2022].

The Department of Agriculture and the Department of Natural Resources and Environmental Control may accept, use, or expand a gift, grant, aid, or loan that may be available from any source, public or private, for the purposes of carrying out the provisions of this chapter.

History.
83 Del. Laws, c. 8, § 1.

§ 2906. Violations [Effective July 1, 2022].

(a) A person who violates this chapter is subject to a civil penalty of not less than $50 and not more than $500 for each proven occurrence.

(b) Before imposing a penalty under subsection (a) of this section, the Secretary must offer the person advice on compliance with this chapter and an administrative hearing under § 2907 of this title.

(c) The Secretary must send a person who violates this chapter a written notice of the violation. The written notice of a violation must contain information regarding the opportunity for an administrative hearing under § 2907 of this title.

(d)(1) A person who violates this chapter may enter into a written agreement with the Secretary, specifying terms and conditions for compliance with this chapter.

(2) A person who is in compliance with all of the terms and conditions of a written agreement under paragraph (d)(1) of this section is not in violation of this chapter.

(e) All civil penalties collected under this section are payable to the Delaware Department of Agriculture and must be used for enforcement of this chapter.

History.
83 Del. Laws, c. 8, § 1.

§ 2907. Hearing procedure; appeals [Effective July 1, 2022].

(a) The Secretary, or the Secretary's designee shall conduct all administrative proceedings under this chapter.

(b) A person accused of violating this chapter has the right to appear personally, to be represented by counsel, and to submit evidence and witnesses in defense of the charges.

(c) The Secretary or the Secretary's designee shall make and preserve a full record of the proceeding. A transcript of the record may be purchased upon payment to the Department of Agriculture of the cost of preparing such a transcript.

(d) The Secretary or the Secretary's designee shall issue a decision in writing to the person accused of violating this chapter within 30 days of the conclusion of the hearing.

(e) The decision by the Secretary or the Secretary's designee is appealable to the Superior Court within 30 days of the date the decision is mailed.

(f) Written notice of an appeal under subsection (e) of this section, must state the grounds for the appeal and be served on the Secretary.

History.
83 Del. Laws, c. 8, § 1.

PART VI

DOMESTIC AND FOREIGN ANIMALS, BIRDS, REPTILES AND INSECTS

Chapter
82. Rabies Control in Animal and Human Populations, §§ 8201 to 8225.

CHAPTER 82

RABIES CONTROL IN ANIMAL AND HUMAN POPULATIONS

SUBCHAPTER I
RABIES CONTROL IN ANIMAL AND HUMAN POPULATIONS

§ 8202. Definitions.

(a) "Animal" means any species of mammal, not including humans.

(b) "Animal exposed to rabies" means a domestic animal that has been bitten or scratched so that the skin has been broken by a rabid animal or a suspected rabid animal, or that has had contamination of an open scratch or wound, eye or mucous membrane with saliva or other potentially infectious material such as neural tissue. The Department shall be the primary agency to manage such exposures.

(c) "Animal welfare officer" means a person employed by the Department of Health and Social Services or Department of Agriculture or a municipality as an enforcement officer.

(d) "Bite" means any penetration of the skin by the teeth.

(e) "Cat" means Felis catus.

(f) "Compendium" means the most current version of The Compendium of Animal Rabies Prevention and Control prepared by the National Association of State Public Health Veterinarians.

(g) "Control and observation" and "controlled and observed" means that the animal is under the owner's control and is being observed for clinical signs of infection with rabies virus.

(h) "Department" means the Department of Agriculture, or officially designated agent thereof.

(i) "Division" means the Division of Public Health, or officially designated agent thereof.

(j) "Dog" means Canis familiaris.

(k) "Exotic" means not native to or generally found in Delaware. An exotic animal is ecologically foreign to Delaware.

(l) "Human exposed to rabies" means a human that has been bitten or scratched by a rabid animal or suspected rabid animal, or that has had contamination of an open scratch or wound, eye, or mucous membrane with saliva or other potentially infectious material such as neural tissue. The Division is the primary agency to manage such exposures.

(m) "Kennel" means any place wherein dogs are kept for the purposes of breeding, training, sale, or show.

(n) "Owner" means any person, firm, partnership, association, or corporation keeping, harboring, or with legal responsibility for a cat, dog, or other animal.

(o) "Person" means any individual, business, partnership, firm, joint stock company, corporation, association, trust, estate, or other legal entity.

(p) "Rabid animal" means any animal confirmed rabid through laboratory testing.

(q) "Rabies" means, in human and animal, an acute viral disease of the central nervous system, caused by a rhabdovirus, also known as hydrophobia or Lyssa, usually transmitted to man through the injection of saliva by an animal bite.

(r) "Rabies vector species" means the wild animal species in the state of Delaware that most commonly carry and transmit the rabies virus to other animals, including bat, racoon, skunk fox, groundhog, or feral cat.

(s) "Strict quarantine" means confinement, under restraint by leash, closed gage, or paddock, on the private premises of the owner or at another location specified by the Department or Division, of an animal in such a manner whereby there exists no opportunity for contact with other animals or humans, excepting one person, 18 years of age or older, who cares for that animal.

(t) "Scratch" means a mark or injury caused by the claws or nails of an animal.

(u) "Suspected rabid animal" means a mammal (domestic or wildlife) exhibiting clinical signs of infection with rabies (abnormal behavior with neurologic impairment) and any bat, racoon, skunk, fox, groundhog, or feral cat.

History.
66 Del. Laws, c. 247, § 1; 68 Del. Laws, c. 285, § 1; 75 Del. Laws, c. 326, § 1; 80 Del. Laws, c. 248, § 2; 83 Del. Laws, c. 32, § 1.

Effect of amendments.
83 Del. Laws, c. 32, effective June 3, 2021, substituted "'Animal' means" for "The term 'animal' shall mean" in (a); added (b), (g), (k), (*l*), (p) and (r)–(u), and redesignated the remaining and intervening paragraphs accordingly; in present (c), substituted "'Animal welfare officer' means" for "The term 'animal welfare officer' shall mean"; in present (d), substituted "'Bite' means" for "The term 'bite' shall mean"; in present (e), substituted "'Cat' means" for "The tern 'cat' shall mean"; rewrote present (f); substituted "'Department' means" for "The term 'Department of Agriculture' shall mean" and added "of Agriculture" in present (h); substituted "'Division' means" for "The term 'Division of Public Health' shall mean" and added "of Public Health" in present (i); in present (j), substituted "'Dog' means" for "The term 'dog' shall mean"; in present (m), substituted "'Kennel' means" for "The term 'kennel' shall mean" and added a comma following "sale"; rewrote present (n); in present (o), substituted "'Person' means" for "The term 'person' shall mean" and added a comma following "estate"; and in (q), substituted "'Rabies' means" for "The term 'rabies' shall mean" and "human" for "man".

§ 8203. Reporting of rabies.

Any medical practitioner, hospital, veterinarian, or other person having knowledge of the following situations shall report the facts within 12 hours by telephone, email, fax, or in person as follows:

(1) Any suspected or confirmed case of human rabies to the Division.

(2) Any suspected or confirmed case of animal rabies to the Department.

(3) Any human known or suspected of having been exposed to rabies to the Division.

(4) Any animal known or suspected of having been exposed to rabies to the Department.

History.
66 Del. Laws, c. 247, § 1; 75 Del. Laws, c. 326, § 1; 83 Del. Laws, c. 32, § 2.

Effect of amendments.
83 Del. Laws, c. 32, effective June 3, 2021, in the introductory paragraph, added a comma following "veterinarian" and substituted "within 12 hours by telephone, email, fax, or in person as follows" for "to the Division of Public Health"; in (1), added "to the Division"; in (2), substituted "suspected or confirmed case of animal rabies to the Department" for "animal known to have a or suspected of having been exposed to rabies"; added (3) and (4).

§ 8204. Rabies vaccination required for dogs, cats, and ferrets; anti-rabies clinics.

(a) *Vaccination of dogs.* — (1) Any person owning a dog 6 months of age or older in this State shall have that dog vaccinated against rabies by a licensed veterinarian; exemption from vaccination against rabies may be permitted if a licensed veterinarian has examined the animal and based on the veterinarian's professional judgment, has certified in writing that at the time, vaccination would endanger the animal's health because of its infirmity, disability, illness, or other medical considerations and a titer test, in the case of these medical exemptions, may be administered to assist in determining the need for the vaccination. The owner of the dog will receive a copy of the rabies vaccination certificate legibly signed by the licensed veterinarian. The owner of the dog will be responsible for keeping a valid rabies vaccination certificate or exemption certificate in their possession for inspection by an animal control officer, the Department, or the Division, if deemed necessary. Certification that the animal is exempt from vaccination shall be valid for a period of 1 year from the date of the issuance of the certificate of exemption, after which time the animal shall be re-examined by a licensed veterinarian and vaccinated against rabies or a new certificate of exemption shall be issued to the animal's owner.

(2) Upon request by an animal welfare officer, the Department, or the Division, all owners of kennels, excluding licensed boarding kennels, shall present immediately a valid rabies vaccination certificate or exemption certificate, signed by a licensed veterinarian, for each dog 6 months of age or older owned by the kennel. Kennel owners will be specifically responsible for keeping all vaccination certificates for all dogs owned or kept at their premise until at least 12 months after the effective expiration date of the vaccination or exemption. If a dog is sold or traded, then the valid vaccination certificate or exemption certificate shall be given to the new owner of the dog. If no valid certificate is given to the new owner, the new owner shall have the dog vaccinated and be issued a valid vaccination certificate or examined and be issued an exemption certificate. Certification that the animal is exempt from vaccination shall be valid for a period of 1 year from the date of the issuance of the certificate of exemption, after which time the animal shall be re-examined by a licensed veterinarian and vaccinated against rabies or a new certificate of exemption shall be issued to the animal's owner.

(b) *Vaccination of cats.* — Any person owning a cat 6 months of age or older in this State shall have the cat vaccinated against rabies by a licensed veterinarian; exemption from vaccination against rabies may be permitted if a licensed veterinarian has examined the animal and based on the veterinarian's professional judgment has certified in writing that at the time, vaccination would endanger the animal's health because of its infirmity, disability, illness, or other medical considerations and a titer test, in the case of these medical exemptions, may be administered to assist in determining the need for the vaccination. The owner of the cat will be responsible for keeping a valid rabies vaccination certificate or exemption certificate in their possession for inspection by an animal welfare officer, the Department, or the Division. Certification that the animal is exempt from vaccination shall be valid for a period of 1 year from the date of the issuance of the certificate of exemption, after which time the animal shall be re-examined by a licensed veterinarian and vaccinated against rabies or a new certificate of exemption shall be issued to the animal's owner.

(c) *Vaccination of ferrets.* — Any person owning a ferret 6 months of age or older in this State shall have the ferret vaccinated against rabies by a licensed veterinarian; exemption from vaccination against rabies may be permitted if a licensed veterinarian has examined the animal and based on the veterinarian's professional judgment has certified in writing that at the time, vaccination would endanger the animal's health because of its infirmity, disability, illness, or other medical considerations and a titer test, in the case of these medical exemptions, may be administered to assist in determining the need for the vaccination. The owner of the ferret is responsible for keeping a valid rabies vaccination certificate or exemption certificate in that owner's possession for inspection by an animal welfare officer, the Department, or the Division. Certification that the animal is exempt from vaccination shall be valid for a period of 1 year from the date of the issuance of the certificate of exemption, after which time the animal shall be re-examined by a licensed veterinarian and vaccinated against rabies or a new certificate of exemption shall be issued to the animal's owner.

(d) Any animal that receives a certificate of exemption under this section must be treated as unvaccinated in case of potential rabies exposure.

(e) Any form necessary to implement this section shall be designed by the Department of Agriculture and made available to licensed veterinarians.

(f) *Duties of veterinarian.* — (1) Each licensed veterinarian may select a rabies vaccine of their choice and use procedures for administering it consistent with the recommendations of the Veterinary Biologics Division of the U.S. Department of Agriculture which licenses that vaccine.

(2) A rabies vaccination certificate will be promptly issued to the owner of each dog, cat, or ferret vaccinated against rabies. The licensed veterinarian administering the vaccine shall complete the certificate specifying accurately the manufacturer's specifications of the duration of immunity of the rabies vaccination used and the date the animal shall be revaccinated in accordance with the specific criteria of the Compendium or as mandated by Delaware state law. The licensed veterinarian shall sign the certificate in a legible manner. The certificate shall also include the veterinarian's address, telephone number, and state license number. Veterinarians shall maintain copies of these certificates for a minimum of 12 months after the effective expiration date of the vaccination.

(g) *Public antirabies clinics.* — The Compendium will serve as a basis for the procedures and practices used in public antirabies clinics. The Department or the licensed veterinarian selected to administer the vaccine at the public antirabies clinic will be consulted on the specific rabies vaccine or vaccines that shall be used at those clinics. All administrative procedures and personnel, excluding veterinary staffing, will be approved by the State Veterinarian. The responsible organization conducting the public antirabies clinic will be responsible for maintaining copies of these certificates for a minimum of 12 months after the effective expiration date of the vaccination.

(h) *Penalty.* — Any person who violates any provision of this section shall be fined $25. No penalty imposed by this section shall be suspended.

History.

66 Del. Laws, c. 247, § 1; 70 Del. Laws, c. 186, § 1; 75 Del. Laws, c. 309, § 1; 75 Del. Laws, c. 326, § 1; 78 Del. Laws, c. 323, § 1; 80 Del. Laws, c. 248, § 3; 82 Del. Laws, c. 262, § 1; 83 Del. Laws, c. 32, § 3.

Effect of amendments.

83 Del. Laws, c. 32, effective June 3, 2021, in (a)(1), added "licensed" preceding the first instance of "veterinarian" in the first sentence and in the second sentence, in the third sentence, substituted "Department" for "Department of Agriculture" and "Division" for "Division of Public Health"; in the first sentence of (a)(2), substituted "Department" for "Department of Agriculture", deleted "of Public Health" following "Division" and added "licensed" preceding "veterinarian"; in the second sentence of (b), substituted "their" for "his or her"; and in the second sentences of (b) and (c), substituted "Department, or the Division" for "the Department of Natural Resources and Environmental Control, the Department of Agriculture, or the Division of Public Health"; added added "licensed" in the first sentence of (c), second and third sentences of (f)(2) and the second sentence of (g); in (f)(1), substituted "their" for "his"; in the first sentence of (f)(2), substituted "dog, cat, or ferret" for "dog or cat", and added a comma following "number" in the penultimate sentence; and in the second sentence of (g), deleted "of Agriculture" following "Department".

§ 8205. Prohibition of vaccination of certain animals for rabies.

(a) No licensed veterinarian or other person may vaccinate a native wild mammal, native wild animal hybrid, exotic mammal, or exotic mammal hybrid with a rabies vaccine not intended for use in that animal, except when specifically approved by the Department.

(b) Anyone violating this section shall be fined not less than $50 nor more than $250.

History.
66 Del. Laws, c. 247, § 1; 68 Del. Laws, c. 285, § 2; 75 Del. Laws, c. 326, § 1; 83 Del. Laws, c. 32, § 4.

Effect of amendments.
83 Del. Laws, c. 32, effective June 3, 2021, in

(a), added "native" twice, deleted "animal" following the first instance of "wild", substituted "hybrid, exotic mammal, or exotic mammal hybrid" for "hybrid or other animal" and "Department" for "Department of Agriculture".

§ 8206. Prohibition on the importation of certain animals.

(a) The Department may also ban importation of certain species of animals into the State, or require special permits for importation of certain species, if it is felt that these species of animals represent an unacceptable risk of rabies infection to humans and animals.

(b) Anyone violating this section shall be fined not less than $100 nor more than $500.

History.
66 Del. Laws, c. 247, § 1; 75 Del. Laws, c. 326, § 1; 83 Del. Laws, c. 32, § 5.

Effect of amendments.
83 Del. Laws, c. 32, effective June 3, 2021,

deleted "of Agriculture" following "Department" in (a).

§ 8207. Disposition of animals exposed to rabies.

(a) *Postexposure management of animals exposed to rabies must follow the guidelines set forth in the Compendium.* — The Department may make inspections as is deemed necessary to assure that the animal is properly controlled and observed or strictly quarantined, issue appropriate quarantine orders, and release the quarantine after the designated period. All costs relating to strict quarantine shall be borne by the owner of the animal. In instances where strict quarantine orders are violated, the owner shall implement alternative quarantine arrangements in consultation with the Department. Any person who violates any provision of this subsection shall be fined not less than $100 nor more than $200.

(b) *Reports of suspected rabies exposures to vaccinated dogs, cats, and ferrets by vaccinated dogs, cats, and ferrets.* — A report of suspected rabies exposure to a vaccinated dog, cat, or ferret does not require control and observation when the owner of the animal suspected of being exposed can provide proof of current rabies vaccination for the aggressor dog, cat, or ferret to the Department and attest to the truthfulness of the identity of the aggressor and documentation of the aggressor's vaccination status.

(c) *Release of quarantine following suspected rabies exposure to dogs, cats, and ferrets by dogs, cats, or ferrets.* — In the event that the owner of the animal suspected of being exposed to rabies can attest to the Department that the biting animal is alive and not displaying clinical signs of rabies at 10 days following the date of suspected exposure, the quarantine for the bitten animal can be released.

(d) *Vaccinated within 28 days of exposure.* — A dog, cat, or ferret that has received its initial vaccination against rabies within 28 days prior to the exposure or suspected exposure is considered unvaccinated for the purposes of quarantining the animal pursuant to this chapter, but not for the purpose of meeting the rabies vaccination requirement included in this chapter.

(e) *Reporting of conditions of quarantine.* — (1) The owner of a dog, cat, or ferret controlled and observed or strictly quarantined pursuant to this chapter is responsible for reporting truthful and factual information to the Department or a licensed veterinarian, if that dog, cat, or ferret shows marked behavior changes, escapes, sickens, or dies during the quarantine period. If the quarantined animal dies, escapes, or for any other reason is not available to complete the quarantine period, the owner shall notify the Department by telephone within 12 hours and complete a signed, notarized affidavit stating the reason for the animal's unavailability to complete the quarantine period. This affidavit must be submitted to the Department within 7 days of the animal's disappearance or death.

(2) Any veterinarian, approved kennel, or other person having knowledge of a controlled and observed or strictly quarantined dog, cat, or ferret which shows marked behavior changes, escapes, sickens, or dies shall report the facts to the Department by telephone within 12 hours.

(3) Any person failing to comply with the provisions of this subsection shall be fined not less than $50 nor more than $200.

(f) *Disposition during quarantine.* — A dog, cat, or ferret under strict quarantine may not be moved from the place of quarantine, destroyed, given away, or otherwise disposed of without the written permission of the Department. Any person failing to comply with the provisions of this subsection shall be fined not less than $50 nor more than $200.

(g) *Surrender of dogs, cats, or ferrets for quarantine.* — A person may not fail or refuse to surrender any dog, cat, or ferret for control and observation, strict quarantine, or destruction as required in this section when demand is made by written order of the Department or Division.

History.
66 Del. Laws, c. 247, § 1; 75 Del. Laws, c. 309, §§ 2, 3; 75 Del. Laws, c. 326, § 1; 83 Del. Laws, c. 32, § 6.

Effect of amendments.
83 Del. Laws, c. 32, effective June 3, 2021, rewrote (a) through (d); and added (e) through (g).

§ 8208. Responsibility and liability of owner of dog, cat, or ferret for quarantine when dog, cat, or ferret is known or suspected to have exposed a human being to rabies.

(a) *Quarantine at time of exposure.* — The owner of any dog, cat, or ferret that is known or suspected to have exposed a human being to rabies shall place the dog, cat, or ferret under a strict quarantine for a period of at least 10 days commencing at the time of the exposure. Any person who fails to comply with this subsection shall be fined not less than $25 nor more than $100.

(1) If the owner of the dog, cat, or ferret can provide proof of a currently valid rabies vaccination, that dog, cat, or ferret may be placed under a strict quarantine on the premises of the owner or custodian.

(2) If the owner of the dog, cat, or ferret cannot provide proof of a currently valid rabies vaccination, that dog, cat, or ferret must be quarantined by a veterinarian, kennel, or other facility approved by the Department. The cost of quarantine in this instance is to be borne by the owner of the dog, cat, or ferret.

(3) If the owner of that dog, cat, or ferret cannot show proof of a valid rabies vaccination, the quarantine period shall be extended beyond the 10 days until such time that the dog, cat, or ferret has been examined by a licensed veterinarian and a rabies vaccine has been administered to that dog, cat, or ferret by a licensed veterinarian. The dog, cat, or ferret must not be vaccinated during the initial 10-day strict quarantine period.

(4) In cases where the behavioral disposition of the dog, cat, or ferret poses a public health danger which renders quarantine of the animal unsafe for its caregivers, the Division, in consultation with the Department and the attending veterinarian, may elect to forego the 10 day strict

quarantine and euthanize the patient and submit the brain for rabies testing.

(b) *Quarantine after notice of exposure.* — An owner who fails to place under strict quarantine any dog, cat, or ferret that exposes a human being to rabies after being notified that the exposure occurred and of the quarantine requirements must quarantine the dog, cat, or ferret in an approved place and manner. An owner failing to quarantine the dog, cat, or ferret shall be fined not less than $100 nor more than $200.

(c) *Reporting of conditions of quarantine.* — (1) The owner of a dog, cat or ferret quarantined pursuant to this chapter is responsible for reporting the facts by telephone to the Division or a licensed veterinarian, if that dog, cat, or ferret shows marked behavior changes, escapes, sickens, or dies during the quarantine period. If the quarantined animal dies, escapes or for any other reason is not available to complete the quarantine period, the owner shall immediately notify the Division by telephone within 12 hours, to be followed by a signed, notarized affidavit stating the reason for the animal's unavailability to complete the quarantine period. This affidavit must be submitted within 7 days of the animal's disappearance or death to the Division.

(2) Any veterinarian, approved kennel or other person having knowledge of a quarantined dog, cat or ferret which shows marked behavior changes, escapes, sickens, or dies shall report the facts to the Division by telephone within 12 hours.

(3) Any person failing to comply with the provisions of this subsection shall be fined not less than $50 nor more than $200.

(d) *Disposition during quarantine.* — A dog, cat, or ferret under quarantine may not be moved from the place of quarantine, killed, given away, or otherwise disposed of without the written permission of the Division of Public Health or Department of Agriculture.

(e) *Surrender of dogs, cats, or ferrets for quarantine.* — A person may not fail or refuse to surrender any dog, cat or ferret for quarantine or destruction as required in this section when demand is made by written order of the Department of Agriculture or Division.

(f) *Law-enforcement canines.* — Notwithstanding any other provision of this chapter, a police dog from any recognized law-enforcement agency is not subject to being quarantined after biting any person, if such bite occurred while the dog was being used for a law-enforcement purpose and the dog is current on its rabies vaccination. The law-enforcement agency shall notify the Division by telephone if the dog shows marked behavior changes, escapes, sickens, or dies.

History.
66 Del. Laws, c. 247, § 1; 68 Del. Laws, c. 285, § 3; 75 Del. Laws, c. 309, §§ 4-6; 75 Del. Laws, c. 326, § 1; 83 Del. Laws, c. 32, § 7.

Effect of amendments.
83 Del. Laws, c. 32, effective June 3, 2021, in the section heading, twice inserted a comma following "cat", and substituted "is known or suspected to have exposed" for "exposes"; rewrote (a) through (e); and added (f).

§ 8209. Disposition and quarantine of animal other than dog, cat, or ferret which exposes a human being to rabies.

(a) *Destruction or quarantine.* — When an animal, other than a dog, cat, or ferret, exposes a human being to rabies, the Division or the Department may require the destruction of the animal for rabies testing, or the quarantine of the animal in an approved place and manner.

(b) *Surrender of animal.* — A person may not fail or refuse to surrender said animal for quarantine or destruction as required in this section when demand is made by written order of the Department or the Division.

(c) *Report of behavior changes, escapes, etc.* — Any person having knowledge of an animal, quarantined under the provisions of this section, which shows marked behavior changes, escapes, sickens, or dies, shall report the facts to the Department by telephone.

(d) *Penalty.* — Any person interfering with the provisions of this section shall be fined not less than $100 nor more than $200.

History.
66 Del. Laws, c. 247, § 1; 75 Del. Laws, c. 309, § 7; 75 Del. Laws, c. 326, § 1; 83 Del. Laws, c. 32, § 8.

Effect of amendments.
83 Del. Laws, c. 32, effective June 3, 2021, in section heading and in (a), added a comma following "cat"; in (a), deleted "Public Health"

following "Division" and "of Agriculture" following "Department"; in (b), deleted "of Agriculture" following "Department" and "of Public Health" following "Division"; in (c), added a comma following "sickens" and deleted "of Agriculture" following "Department" and added "by telephone".

§ 8210. Submission of animal for rabies testing and examination during quarantine.

(a) When an animal is destroyed for the purposes of rabies testing, every effort shall be made to keep the head and brain intact and unfrozen for transfer to the Division of Public Health Laboratory within 72 hours. Precautions shall be taken to avoid exposure to humans during all stages of specimen preparation and transport to the Division of Public Health Laboratory. The Division will review requests for rabies laboratory testing of rabies vector species in cases with a potential human exposure and will test samples if the rabies vector species is available and in adequate condition for valid results. The Division is responsible for ensuring that the destroyed animal is transported safely, and for notifying the submitting party of the rabies testing results.

(b) The Division or the Department may order the owner of an animal which is suspected of having exposed a human being to rabies to have the animal examined by a licensed veterinarian at any time during the quarantine period. The cost of the veterinary examination and any other associated cost shall be borne by the owner of the biting animal which is suspected of having exposed the human being to rabies. Any animal determined by a licensed veterinarian or the Department to be inhumanely suffering may be destroyed in a humane manner and the head promptly submitted to the Division of Public Health Laboratory for rabies testing.

(c) Notwithstanding any other provision of this chapter, the Department or the Division may issue a written order that an animal suspected of exposing a human being to rabies or having bitten a person and that animal having not been immunized with a vaccine specifically approved for use in that species and administered by a licensed veterinarian, shall be destroyed in a humane manner for laboratory examination for rabies, if it is determined that the animal is not being quarantined adequately or that there are other reasons which make it necessary for the preservation of human health.

(d) A person may not fail or refuse to surrender the remains of an animal for the purposes of rabies testing when a written order is made by the Division or the Department.

(e) *Penalty.* — Any person interfering with the provisions of this section shall be fined not less than $100 nor more than $300.

History.
66 Del. Laws, c. 247, § 1; 68 Del. Laws, c. 285, § 4; 75 Del. Laws, c. 326, § 1; 83 Del. Laws, c. 32, § 9.

Effect of amendments.
83 Del. Laws, c. 32, effective June 3, 2021, in (a), in the first sentence added "for transfer to the Division of Public Health Laboratory

within 72 hours" and substituted "all states of specimen preparation and transport" for "destruction and until transported", added the penultimate sentence, and substituted "is" for "of Public Health shall be" in the final sentence; in (b), in the first sentence, deleted "of Public Health" following "Division" and "of Agriculture" following "Department", added "veterinary" in the second sentence, and in the third sentence, added "or" following "veterinarian, deleted "of Agriculture or the Department of Natural Resources and Environmental Control" following "Department" and substituted "destroyed" for "killed"; in (c), deleted "the Department of Natural Resources and Environmental Control" following "chapter", "of Agriculture" following "Department", "of Public Health" following "Division", added "licensed" preceding "veterinarian", and substituted "destroyed" for "killed"; and added (d) and (e).

§ 8211. Joint regulatory powers of Department of Natural Resources and Environmental Control, Department of Agriculture, Department of Health and Social Services, Division of Public Health; quarantine and areawide emergencies.

(a) *Regulations.* — The Department of Natural Resources and Environmental Control, Department of Agriculture, Department of Health and Social Services, and Division of Public Health are hereby delegated the power to adopt joint regulations signed by all 3 Department Secretaries setting forth procedures regulating the conduct of practitioners of human health, human health services, animal health services and animal control agencies for the purpose of fulfilling or carrying out the purpose and intent of this chapter.

(b) *Areawide quarantine.* — If rabies is known to exist within an area, the Division, in conjunction with the Department of Natural Resources and Environmental Control and the Department may establish a rabies quarantine and shall define the boundaries or the quarantine area and specify the animal or animals subject to quarantine. All these animals within the quarantine area and subject to the quarantine restrictions shall be kept in strict upon the premises of the owner at all times until the quarantine is terminated. An animal, subject to the quarantine, may not be brought into the quarantine area or taken out of the quarantine area without written permission.

(c) *Areawide rabies emergency.* — The Director of the Division may declare an areawide rabies emergency and shall define the boundaries of the area and place specified animals under quarantine. By doing so, the Director of the Division authorizes the Department of Natural Resources and Environmental Control, its agents and state and local police officers to destroy on sight any animals not in compliance with quarantine orders.

(d) [Repealed.]

History.
66 Del. Laws, c. 247, § 1; 75 Del. Laws, c. 326, § 1; 83 Del. Laws, c. 32, § 10.

Effect of amendments.
83 Del. Laws, c. 32, effective June 3, 2021, added "Department of Health and Social Services" in the section heading and in (a); deleted "of Public Health" following "Division" in the first sentence of (b) and the first and last sentences of (c); in (b), deleted "of Agriculture" following "Department" in the first sentence and "confinement" following "strict" in the second sentence of (b); and repealed (d).

§ 8212. Enforcement.

The provisions of this chapter may be enforced by any authorized employee or agent of the Departments of Agriculture, Natural Resources and Environmental Control or Health and Social Services.

History.
66 Del. Laws, c. 247, § 1; 75 Del. Laws, c. 326, § 1; 83 Del. Laws, c. 32, § 11.

Effect of amendments.
83 Del. Laws, c. 32, effective June 3, 2021, substituted "Services" for "Service".

PART X
HORSE RACING

CHAPTER 101
HORSE RACING
SUBCHAPTER I
DELAWARE THOROUGHBRED RACING COMMISSION

§ 10103. Powers, duties and jurisdiction.

NOTES TO DECISIONS

Disciplinary duties.

Horse trainer's argument was not considered to be substantial where the trainer's interests were far more likely harmed by widespread dissemination of a video showing the trainer flipping a horse by prodding it with a rake than by the Delaware Thoroughbred Racing Commission's relatively short suspension; given that the trainer was already 30 days into a 60-day suspension, it was difficult to perceive what more harm would be visited upon the trainer by an additional 30-day suspension. Cobb v. Del. Thoroughbred Racing Comm'n, — A.3d —, 2021 Del. Super. LEXIS 549 (Del. Super. Ct. Aug. 17, 2021).

TITLE 4
ALCOHOLIC LIQUORS

CHAPTER 1
GENERAL PROVISIONS

§ 101. Definitions.

As used in this title, in addition to their usual meaning:

(1) "Alcohol" means ethyl alcohol produced by the distillation of any fermented liquid, whether rectified or diluted with water or not, whatever may be the origin thereof, and includes synthetic ethyl alcohol, but it does not mean ethyl alcohol, diluted or not, that has been denatured or otherwise rendered unfit for beverage purposes.

(2) "Alcoholic liquor" or "alcoholic liquors" include the 5 varieties of liquor defined in this section (alcohol, spirits, wine, beer and alcoholic cider) as well as every liquid or solid, patented or not, containing alcohol, spirits, wine, beer or alcoholic cider and capable of being consumed by a human being, and any liquid or solid containing more than 1 of the 5 varieties defined in this section is considered as belonging to that variety which usually has the higher percentage of alcohol. "Alcoholic liquor" or "alcoholic liquors" does not include a powdered alcoholic beverage. Notwithstanding any other definition in this chapter, "alcoholic liquor" does not include solids and confections that contain 2% or less alcohol by weight, so long as the package which contains the product or any menu or other medium noticing the product for sale, if the product contains between ½ of 1% alcohol by volume and 2% alcohol by weight, is labeled with the word "alcoholic," the phrase "contains alcohol," or some other indication that the product contains alcohol.

(3) "Appeals Commission" shall mean 3 persons, 1 from each County, appointed by the Governor with the advice and consent of a majority of the Senate.

(4) "Barrel", when used as a container for beer, means such container having a capacity of 31 United States standard gallons of 231 cubic inches.

(5) "Beer" means any beverage containing more than ½ of 1% of ethyl alcohol by volume, obtained by the alcoholic fermentation of any infusion or decoction of barley malt and hops in water and includes, among other things, ale, porter, stout and other malt or brewed liquors.

(6) "Beer garden" means a defined, outdoor establishment not less than 10,000 contiguous square feet, which is open to the public for at least 5 consecutive months. A beer garden must employ a daily average of not less than 25 full-time employees. A beer garden may sell beer, wine, and spirits by the glass or beer by the bottle, for consumption on any portion of the licensed premises. The sale of food is not required for licensure, but is permitted. The boundaries of a beer garden must be enclosed with a barrier no less than 42 inches high from the floor elevation, constructed of wood, concrete, plastic, rope, or wrought iron fencing, or other approved material. A beer garden must have a physical structure, which may be

permanent or removable, and must be substantial. A "substantial physical structure" shall mean equipment and structures costing no less than $250,000 at the time of acquisition. A beer garden license may not be used by an existing liquor license holder to expand the size or nature of the licensed establishment.

(7) "Bottle" means any vessel that is corked, capped or stopped or arranged so to be and intended to contain or to convey liquids.

(8) "Bottle club" means an establishment operated for profit or pecuniary gain where customers of the establishment enter on the premises for the purpose of consuming alcoholic liquors that are brought onto the premises by the customers, consumed on the premises by the customers, and removed by the customers when the customers depart.

(9) "Cabaret" means an establishment where patrons are entertained by performers who dance, sing, play instruments or perform other legal acts for entertainment, but not to include a dinner theater, and where such entertainment may be performed during or after service or dinner, and where a minor, as defined in § 708 of this title, is to be denied admission to or permission to remain on premises after 9:00 p.m. (official eastern time) unless accompanied by a parent or by a legal guardian.

(10) "Caterer" means any proprietorship, partnership or corporation engaged in the business of providing food and beverages at social gatherings such as weddings, dinners, benefits, banquets or other similar events for consideration on a regular basis and duly licensed by the State as caterers with at least 60% of its gross receipts resulting from the sale of food.

(11) Without regard to its usual meaning, and by way of limitation, "alcoholic cider" means any fermented beverage made from apples, containing more than ½ of 1% but not more than 7% of ethyl alcohol by volume. For purposes of this title, alcoholic cider shall be treated as within the definition of "wine" unless the specific language of a particular section indicates a contrary intent.

(12) "Club" means a corporation or association created by competent authority, which is the owner, lessee or occupant of premises operated solely for objects of national, social, patriotic, political or athletic nature, or the like, whether or not for pecuniary gain, and the property as well as the advantages of which belong to or are enjoyed by the stockholders or by the members of such corporation or association. A public golf course, open to all members of the public, whether privately or publicly owned, whose primary purpose is the operation of a golf course shall be included within meanings of this definition. Members of the public, utilizing the golf facility, shall be considered guests of the club.

(13) "Commissioner" means the person appointed by the Governor and confirmed by the Senate who serves as the Alcoholic Beverage Control Commissioner for the State.

(14) "Concert hall" shall mean an indoor facility used to host live entertainment that is owned, leased, under easement, and/or operated by any person and that has capacity for at least 600 patrons for any single event. In order for a facility to be licensed as a concert hall, the facility shall host a minimum of 250 live music events in any biennial licensing period. A facility meeting this definition may license the entire building, including patio, with the concert hall license.

(15) "Cooking wine" means a wine that is no more than 20% alcohol by volume and includes no less than 1.5% salt that is intended for cooking and not for beverage consumption.

(16) "Denatured alcohol" means ethyl alcohol or liquors containing ethyl alcohol to which substances or ingredients have been added to render the ethyl alcohol or liquors unfit for beverage purposes.

(17) "Disorderly house" means house, or reputed house, of prostitution, ill-fame or assignation.

(18) "Distillery", "winery" and "brewery" mean not only the premises whereon alcohol or spirits is distilled or rectified, wine is fermented or beer is brewed, but, in addition, the person owning, representing or in charge of such premises and the operations conducted thereon, including the blending and bottling or other handling and preparation of alcoholic liquor in any form.

(19) "Division" means "Division of Alcohol and Tobacco Enforcement."

(20) "Establishment" means any place located physically in this State where alcoholic liquor of 1 or more varieties is stored, sold or used by authority of any law of this State, including a hotel, restaurant, tavern, beer garden, or club as defined in this section, or where alcoholic liquor of 1 or more varieties is manufactured by virtue of any law of this State.

(21) "Fermented beverage" means any product similar to beer, including sake and seltzer, containing ½ of 1% or more of alcohol by volume, brewed from substitutes for malt, including rice, grain, bran, glucose, sugar and molasses.

(22) "Gathering of persons" or "gathering" means a banquet, picnic, bazaar, fair or similar private gathering or similar public gathering where food or drink are sold, served or dispensed by nonprofit organizations such as churches, colleges and universities, volunteer fire companies, political parties or other similar nonprofit groups having a common civic, social, educational or religious purpose, or where entrance tickets are sold or entrance fees are required by those nonprofit organizations.

(23) "Hotel" means any establishment, provided with special space and accommodation, where, in consideration of payment, food and lodging are habitually furnished to travelers.

(24) "Import" means the transporting or ordering or arranging for the transportation or shipment of alcoholic liquor into the State whether by a resident of the State or otherwise.

(25) "Importer" means the person transporting or ordering, authorizing or arranging the transportation or shipment of alcoholic liquors into this State, whether the person is a resident or citizen of this State or not, said person being permitted to sell said alcoholic liquors only to those persons licensed to resell alcoholic liquors; provided, however, that nothing contained in this definition shall be construed as prohibiting an importer from selling such alcoholic liquors to either an active owner of that business for that person's use and not for resale or to a full-time, bona fide employee of that business for that person's use and not for resale; and provided further, that nothing contained in this definition shall be construed as prohibiting an importer from selling beer in "half-barrel" or "quarter-barrel" containers to the holders of a personal license. The Commissioner may enact such rules regulating the sale of alcoholic liquor to active owners and employees of licensed importers as it deems necessary.

(26) "License" means any license or permit to manufacture, to sell, to purchase, to transport, to import or to possess alcoholic liquor authorized or issued by the Commissioner under the provisions of Chapter 5 of this title.

(27) "Manufacture" means distill, rectify, ferment, brew, make, mix, concoct or process any substance or substances capable of producing a

beverage containing more than ½ of 1% of alcohol by volume and includes blending, bottling or other preparation for sale.

(28) "Manufacturer" means any person engaged in the manufacture of any alcoholic liquor and among others includes a distiller, a rectifier, a wine maker, a brewer, and includes a bottler or one who prepares alcoholic liquor for sale.

(29) "Mead" means an alcoholic beverage that is naturally fermented (not distilled or frozen) wherein the major source of fermentable sugars comes from honey.

(30) "Member of a club" means an individual who, whether as a charter member or admitted in accordance with the rules or the bylaws of the club, has become a member thereof, who maintains membership by the payment of dues in the manner established by the rules or bylaws, and whose name and address is entered on the list of members supplied to the Commissioner at the time of the application for a license under Chapter 5 of this title, or, if admitted thereafter, within 8 days after admission and payment of dues, if such dues are required. The Commissioner is authorized to extend the meaning of the words "member of a club" to include those who are granted temporary membership or membership of less than 1 year in accordance with a rule or bylaw of the club approved by the Commissioner. "Member of a club" which is a multiple activity club means a person who, pursuant to the charter, bylaws or rules of the club, is a member in good standing of such club, and whose name and address is supplied in writing to the Commissioner by the club within 8 days after admission to membership, or who holds a temporary membership in such club, pursuant to a charter provision, or bylaw or rule approved by the Commissioner.

(31) "Motorsports speedway" shall mean a motorsports speedway (including any contiguous land when being used in connection with its events) that is owned, leased, under easement, and/or operated by any person and having a seating capacity of at least 5,000 seats. A motorsports speedway may operate under its own license while using the premises of a license holder at a horse racetrack, but only to the extent that neither license holder uses the same portion of the premises at the same time and no commingling of inventory occurs. The converse of this shall also apply to a license holder at a horse racetrack using the premises of a motorsports speedway.

(32) "Movie theater" shall mean an indoor facility used to host showings of motion pictures and that has a capacity of at least 500 patrons for any single movie showing or for showing of multiple movies in separate theaters at the same time. In order for a facility to be licensed as a movie theater, the facility shall host a minimum of 250 movie showings in any calendar year and shall be open at least 5 days a week.

(33) "Multiple activity club" is a club as to which, in the determination of the Commissioner, the service of spirits, wine or beer is not the principal activity in the premises of the club as established by the following:

    a. Gross revenue of the club from the sale of spirits, wine and beer does not exceed 40% of its total annual revenue including dues, fees and assessments, and either

    b. Meals are served by the club at regular hours on at least 6 days of the week,

    c. The club has a physical facility, regularly used by members of the club, which is devoted primarily to activities other than the sale or consumption of spirits, wine or beer, or

d. A public golf course, as defined in paragraph (12) of this section, may be licensed as a multiple activity club, however, is not subject to the requirements as set forth in paragraph (33)c. of this section.

(34) "Multi-purpose sports facility" shall mean a stadium, featuring sporting events where admission fees are charged to the public and having a seating capacity of at least 2,500 seats, and excludes stadia which are operated and maintained by educational institutions, including, but not limited to, high schools, colleges or universities.

(35) "Off-site caterer" means any proprietorship, partnership or corporation engaged in the business of providing food and beverages at social gatherings, such as weddings, dinners, benefits, banquets or other similar events, that are held off the site of the caterer's business for consideration and on a regular basis. An off-site caterer must be duly licensed by the State under Title 30 as a caterer, with at least 60% of its gross receipts resulting from the sale of food.

(36) "Person" includes an individual, a partnership, a corporation, a club or any other association of individuals.

(37) "Powdered alcoholic beverage" means any powders or crystals that, after being mixed with sugar, water, or any other nonalcoholic materials, ferments or otherwise becomes a wine, beer, or other alcoholic beverage.

(38) "Preparation" means any medicine (patented or proprietary); any mixture containing drugs or mineral substances; any perfume, lotion, tincture, varnish, dressing, fluid extract or essence, vinegar, cream, ointment or salve; any distillate or decoction, whether or not containing other substances in solution or suspension, that contains ethyl alcohol or any alcoholic liquor to any amount exceeding ½ of 1% by volume.

(39) "Residence" means the place occupied by a person as a domicile or otherwise, either permanently or temporarily, and includes not only the premises occupied, but also every annex or dependency thereof held under the same title as the premises occupied.

(40) "Restaurant" means any establishment which is regularly used and kept open principally for the purpose of serving complete meals to persons for consideration and which has seating at tables for 12 or more persons and suitable kitchen facilities connected therewith for cooking an assortment of foods under the charge of a chef or cook.

(41) "Retailer" means the person permitted to sell alcoholic liquors in a store in the State, not for consumption on the premises.

(42) "Sale" means every act of selling as defined in this section.

(43) "Sell" means: solicit or receive an order for; keep or expose for sale; deliver for value or in any other way than purely gratuitously; keep with intent to sell; keep or transport in contravention of this title; traffic in; or for any valuable consideration, promised or obtained, directly or indirectly, or under any pretext or by any means whatsoever, procure or allow to be procured for any other person, to carry alcoholic liquors on one's person or to transport with one and with intent to sell the same, but not in any establishment where the sale thereof is allowed.

(44) "Spirits" means any beverage containing more than ½ of 1% of ethyl alcohol by volume mixed with water and other substances in solution, and includes, among other things, brandy, rum, whiskey and gin.

(45) "Spirits, wine and beer tasting" means the consumption of spirits, wine and beer for the purpose of sampling for prospective purchase only. The quantity of any individual spirit, wine and beer sampled is not to exceed 1 ounce for wine and beer and ½ ounce for spirits.

(46) "Taproom" means an establishment provided with special space and accommodations and operated primarily for the sale by the glass and

for consumption on the premises of alcoholic liquors with the sale of food as a secondary object as distinguished from a restaurant where the sale of food is the primary object.

(47) "Tavern" means any establishment with special space and accommodation for sale of beer and wine as defined in this section to be sold to each customer in single servings.

(48) "Temporary large event" means a public or private gathering of more than 1,000 people where food or drink are sold, served or dispensed and which requires an entrance ticket or entrance fee to attend, including but not limited to a: music festival; car show; auction; convention or rally.

(49) "Temporary large event promoter" means the person arranging or promoting the temporary large event.

(50) "Traveler" means an individual guest or customer of a hotel, restaurant or tavern.

(51) "Vehicle" means any means of transportation by land, by water or by air, and includes everything made use of in any way whatsoever for such transportation.

(52) "Whoever", when used in reference to any offender under this title, includes every person who acts individually or by permission or agreement for any other person, and includes also such other person.

(53) "Wine" means any beverage containing more than ½ of 1% ethyl alcohol by volume obtained by the fermentation of the natural contents of fruits, vegetables or other products and other vinous liquors, and also includes such beverages when fortified by the addition of alcohol or spirits as defined in this section.

History.

38 Del. Laws, c. 18, §§ 3, 4; Code 1935, §§ 6132, 6133(12); 45 Del. Laws, c. 263, § 1; 4 Del. C. 1953, § 101; 50 Del. Laws, c. 300, § 1; 51 Del. Laws, c. 239; 56 Del. Laws, c. 335, §§ 1, 2; 59 Del. Laws, c. 107, §§ 1-3, 71; 59 Del. Laws, c. 128, § 1; 60 Del. Laws, c. 466, §§ 1, 2; 63 Del. Laws, c. 397, § 1; 64 Del. Laws, c. 437, § 1; 65 Del. Laws, c. 50, §§ 1-3; 65 Del. Laws, c. 283, § 1; 67 Del. Laws, c. 48, § 1; 67 Del. Laws, c. 109, § 1; 69 Del. Laws, c. 6, § 1; 69 Del. Laws, c. 18, § 1; 70 Del. Laws, c. 186, § 1; 70 Del. Laws, c. 353, § 1; 70 Del. Laws, c. 559, §§ 1-4; 71 Del. Laws, c. 210, § 1; 71 Del. Laws, c. 302, §§ 1, 2; 72 Del. Laws, c. 486, §§ 1-4; 73 Del. Laws, c. 244, § 1; 73 Del. Laws, c. 393, § 1; 74 Del. Laws, c. 250, § 1; 76 Del. Laws, c. 32, § 6; 77 Del. Laws, c. 339, § 1; 78 Del. Laws, c. 220, § 1; 79 Del. Laws, c. 6, § 1; 79 Del. Laws, c. 229, § 1; 79 Del. Laws, c. 308, § 1; 80 Del. Laws, c. 4, § 1; 80 Del. Laws, c. 109, § 1; 81 Del. Laws, c. 15, § 1; 81 Del. Laws, c. 69, § 1; 81 Del. Laws, c. 100, § 1; 81 Del. Laws, c. 372, § 1; 82 Del. Laws, c. 4, § 1; 83 Del. Laws, c. 36, § 1; 83 Del. Laws, c. 152, § 1; 83 Del. Laws, c. 207, § 1.

Effect of amendments.

83 Del. Laws, c. 36, effective June 3, 2021, added (20) and redesignated remaining paragraphs accordingly.

83 Del. Laws, c. 152, effective September 15, 2021, added present (8) and redesignated the remaining paragraphs accordingly; and in present (33)d., substituted "(12)" for "(11)" and "(33)c." for "(31)c."

83 Del. Laws, c. 207, effective Sept. 17, 2021, in (47), deleted "by the glass and for consumption on the premises" following "sale" and added "and wine" and "to be sold to each customer in single servings".

CHAPTER 5

LICENSES AND TAXES

SUBCHAPTER II
PURCHASE, SALE AND DISPENSING

§ 512. Licenses [Effective until Mar. 31, 2022].

(a) Any person, who is the owner or lessee, or who is recognized by the Commissioner as being in charge of a hotel, beer garden, motel, taproom, restaurant, motorsports speedway, concert hall, horse racetrack, multi-purpose sports facility, club or multiple activity club, may apply to the Commissioner for a license to purchase spirits, beer, or wine from an importer and to receive, keep and sell such spirits, beer, or wine either by the glass or by the bottle for consumption on any portion of the premises approved by the Commissioner for that purpose. Such a license entitles a club to sell such spirits, wine, or beer only to members of that club. A multiple activity club which holds such a license may apply for an additional license to sell such spirits, wine, or beer to any person who is a guest of such club or of a member of such club who is duly registered in accordance with a bylaw or rule of such club, approved by the Commissioner, provided that if the Commissioner determines that any applicant is not a multiple activity club, as defined in § 101 of this title, the application shall be denied. There shall be no age restrictions on persons permitted on the premises of a licensed multiple activity club.

(1) Notwithstanding any law, regulation, or rule to the contrary, any restaurant, brewpub, tavern, or taproom, or other entity with a valid on-premise license issued pursuant to Chapter 5, subchapter II of this title may sell alcoholic beverages in transactions for take-out, curbside, or drive through service.

(2) All alcoholic beverages sold for off-premise consumption under this subsection must:

a. Be sold in containers that are securely closed; and

b. Not exceed 3 750 ML bottles of wine, 1 case of beer, and 1 liter of spirits per customer per day.

(b)(1) The license issued to a horse racetrack or multi-purpose sports facility pursuant to this section shall continue to be valid whether or not a race meet or sporting event is in progress.

(2) Subject to the provisions, restrictions and prohibitions of this title, the Commissioner may allow a horse racetrack to brew beer on its premises under all of the following conditions and restrictions:

a. The brewing facility must be situated on the premises of, or be physically a part of, the horse racetrack.

b. The brewing facility must not brew more than 4,000 barrels of beer in any calendar year.

c. In addition to other permitted sales, the horse racetrack may sell at the licensed premises beer manufactured on the licensed premises for on-premises consumption.

d. In addition to other permitted sales, the horse racetrack may sell at the licensed premises beer manufactured on the licensed premises for consumption off of the premises if the beer is sold in a growler.

e. The horse racetrack may sell beer manufactured on licensed premises in labeled barrels, bottles, or other closed containers to wholesalers licensed under this title for delivery by them to persons inside or outside this State.

f. The horse racetrack is prohibited from owning, operating, or being affiliated with any importer of alcoholic liquor, either in or without this State.

g. The Commissioner may make and publish such rules and regulations with respect to the assessment and payment of the tax on beer, under § 581 of this title, as the Commissioner deems proper, and all such rules and regulations that are not inconsistent with this title shall have the force and effect of law.

(3) The issuance of a horse racetrack license that permits the manufacture and sale of beer for off-premises consumption are exempt from the distance requirements for establishments licensed or to be licensed under § 543(d) of this title, and such requirements do not affect the granting of a horse racetrack license.

(c) Any person operating a dinner theater presenting public performances featuring live actors in dramatic or musical productions may apply to the Commissioner for a license to keep and sell alcoholic liquor to patrons for consumption on the premises served at such performances, and for consumption on the premises during intermissions, subject to such rules and regulations as may be promulgated by the Delaware Alcoholic Beverage Control Commissioner, provided that the licensee does not serve alcohol unaccompanied by a meal at more than 10 performances during the calendar year.

(d) Any person who has purchased a bottle of alcoholic liquor other than beer from a premises licensed for the sale and consumption on the premises where sold licensed under this title, and who has partially consumed the contents of such bottle on the licensed premises, may, if the bottle is capped, remove it from the licensed premises for the purpose of consumption off the licensed premises.

(e) Any person receiving a license under this section shall be permitted to charge a cover charge at any time live entertainment is actually being provided by the licensee, provided that any licensee charging a cover charge shall prominently display the fact that a cover charge is being made, both at the entrance to the premises and on the menu if one is used on the premises.

(f) Any person operating a bowling alley or movie theater may apply to the Commissioner for a license to keep and sell alcoholic liquor to patrons for consumption on the premises only. A license for a movie theater shall allow for consumption by patrons within the theater or theaters where movies are being shown. A movie theater which obtains a license must sell alcoholic liquors at a separate bar or location away from other food and drink, may only sell 1 alcoholic beverage at a time per age-verified patron and may only serve 2 alcoholic beverages per patron per movie showing. Movie theater managers and employees involved in serving alcohol must complete alcohol service training as prescribed by the Commissioner.

(g)(1) A caterer may apply to the Commissioner for a license to purchase alcoholic liquors from an importer and to receive, keep and sell such alcoholic liquors either by the glass or by the bottle, for consumption on any portion of the premises approved by the Commissioner for that purpose.

(2) An off-site caterer may apply to the Commissioner for a license to purchase alcoholic liquors from an importer and to receive, keep, transport and sell such alcoholic liquors either by the glass or by the bottle for consumption on any portion of off-site premises approved by the Commissioner for that purpose. Transporting of alcoholic liquors by an off-site caterer must be done in accordance with the Commissioner's rules.

(h) Notwithstanding any provision of this title to the contrary, motorsports speedways may permit patrons to bring inside with them alcoholic beverages regulated under this title for their own personal consumption, provided that they have a lawful ticket for admission to the facility and are of the lawful age to consume alcoholic beverages. The motorsports speedway may restrict the portions of the facility that patrons may act in accord with this section. Notwithstanding any provision of this title to the contrary, a motorsports speedway is not required to maintain a license required pursuant to § 554 of this title in order to permit patrons to bring inside with them alcoholic beverages regulated under this title for their own personal consumption.

(i) A certificated air passenger carrier maintaining and operating a warehouse storage facility in the State may apply to the Commissioner for a license to purchase alcoholic liquors from an importer and to receive at the carrier's warehouse or airport facility, keep at the carrier's warehouse or airport facility, transport to the carrier's airport facility, and sell such alcoholic liquor to its passengers for consumption on its aircraft only.

(j) An establishment licensed as a restaurant shall not be required to use the word "restaurant" in its tradename, menus, advertisements or signage unless the Commissioner specifically finds that the public may be confused as to its status as a restaurant.

(k) Any person who holds a valid restaurant license issued by the Commissioner may deny a minor, as defined in § 708 of this title, admission to or permission to remain on the premises after 9:00 p.m. (official Eastern time) unless accompanied by a parent or by a legal guardian.

History.
38 Del. Laws, c. 18, § 17; Code 1935, § 6146; 4 Del. C. 1953, § 512; 55 Del. Laws, c. 283, § 1; 56 Del. Laws, c. 335, § 3; 57 Del. Laws, c. 189; 57 Del. Laws, c. 447; 58 Del. Laws, c. 199; 59 Del. Laws, c. 107, § 17A; 59 Del. Laws, c. 590, §§ 2, 4; 60 Del. Laws, c. 466, §§ 3, 9; 64 Del. Laws, c. 434, §§ 1, 2; 67 Del. Laws, c. 109, §§ 8-10; 69 Del. Laws, c. 6, § 2; 71 Del. Laws, c. 42, § 1; 71 Del. Laws, c. 182, § 1; 71 Del. Laws, c. 210, § 2; 71 Del. Laws, c. 472, § 1; 72 Del. Laws, c. 486, § 9; 73 Del. Laws, c. 244, §§ 2-6; 73 Del. Laws, c. 393, § 2; 75 Del. Laws, c. 246, § 1; 78 Del. Laws, c. 220, § 2; 79 Del. Laws, c. 308, § 2; 80 Del. Laws, c. 109, § 2; 81 Del. Laws, c. 69, § 2; 81 Del. Laws, c. 254, § 1; 82 Del. Laws, c. 4, § 2; 82 Del. Laws, c. 99, § 3; 82 Del. Laws, c. 117, § 1; 82 Del. Laws, c. 141, § 1;

82 Del. Laws, c. 247, §§ 2, 5; 82 Del. Laws, c. 279, § 1; 83 Del. Laws, c. 9, § 2.

Revisor's note.
Section 5 of 83 Del. Laws, c. 9, provided: "This act expires on March 31, 2022, unless otherwise extended by a subsequent act of the General Assembly."

Effect of amendments.
83 Del. Laws, c. 9, effective Mar. 23, 2021, designated the second undesignated paragraph of (a) as (a)(1), deleted "if the alcoholic beverages for off-premise consumption are in containers which are securely closed" from the end and extending its expiration date to Mar. 31, 2022, by operation of § 5 of that act; and added (a)(2), which also expired effective Mar. 31, 2022, by operation of § 5 of that act.

§ 512. Licenses [Effective Mar. 31, 2022].

(a) Any person, who is the owner or lessee, or who is recognized by the Commissioner as being in charge of a hotel, beer garden, motel, taproom, restaurant, motorsports speedway, concert hall, horse racetrack, multi-purpose sports facility, club or multiple activity club, may apply to the Commissioner for a license to purchase spirits, beer, or wine from an importer and to receive, keep and sell such spirits, beer, or wine either by the glass or by the bottle for consumption on any portion of the premises approved by the Commissioner for that purpose. Such a license entitles a club to sell such spirits, wine, or beer only to members of that club. A multiple activity club which holds such a license may apply for an additional license to sell such spirits, wine, or beer to any person who is a guest of such club or of a member of such club who is duly registered in accordance with a bylaw or rule of such club, approved by the Commissioner, provided that if the Commissioner determines that any applicant is not a multiple activity club, as defined in § 101 of this title, the application shall be denied. There shall be no age restrictions on persons permitted on the premises of a licensed multiple activity club.

    (1)-(2) [Repealed.]

  (b)(1) The license issued to a horse racetrack or multi-purpose sports facility pursuant to this section shall continue to be valid whether or not a race meet or sporting event is in progress.

    (2) Subject to the provisions, restrictions and prohibitions of this title, the Commissioner may allow a horse racetrack to brew beer on its premises under all of the following conditions and restrictions:

      a. The brewing facility must be situated on the premises of, or be physically a part of, the horse racetrack.

      b. The brewing facility must not brew more than 4,000 barrels of beer in any calendar year.

      c. In addition to other permitted sales, the horse racetrack may sell at the licensed premises beer manufactured on the licensed premises for on-premises consumption.

      d. In addition to other permitted sales, the horse racetrack may sell at the licensed premises beer manufactured on the licensed premises for consumption off of the premises if the beer is sold in a growler.

      e. The horse racetrack may sell beer manufactured on licensed premises in labeled barrels, bottles, or other closed containers to wholesalers licensed under this title for delivery by them to persons inside or outside this State.

      f. The horse racetrack is prohibited from owning, operating, or being affiliated with any importer of alcoholic liquor, either in or without this State.

      g. The Commissioner may make and publish such rules and regulations with respect to the assessment and payment of the tax on beer, under § 581 of this title, as the Commissioner deems proper, and all such rules and regulations that are not inconsistent with this title shall have the force and effect of law.

    (3) The issuance of a horse racetrack license that permits the manufacture and sale of beer for off-premises consumption are exempt from the distance requirements for establishments licensed or to be licensed under § 543(d) of this title, and such requirements do not affect the granting of a horse racetrack license.

  (c) Any person operating a dinner theater presenting public performances featuring live actors in dramatic or musical productions may apply to the Commissioner for a license to keep and sell alcoholic liquor to patrons for consumption on the premises served at such performances, and for consumption on the premises during intermissions, subject to such rules and regulations as may be promulgated by the Delaware Alcoholic Beverage Control Commissioner, provided that the licensee does not serve alcohol unaccompanied by a meal at more than 10 performances during the calendar year.

(d) Any person who has purchased a bottle of alcoholic liquor other than beer from a premises licensed for the sale and consumption on the premises where sold licensed under this title, and who has partially consumed the contents of such bottle on the licensed premises, may, if the bottle is capped, remove it from the licensed premises for the purpose of consumption off the licensed premises.

(e) Any person receiving a license under this section shall be permitted to charge a cover charge at any time live entertainment is actually being provided by the licensee, provided that any licensee charging a cover charge shall prominently display the fact that a cover charge is being made, both at the entrance to the premises and on the menu if one is used on the premises.

(f) Any person operating a bowling alley or movie theater may apply to the Commissioner for a license to keep and sell alcoholic liquor to patrons for consumption on the premises only. A license for a movie theater shall allow for consumption by patrons within the theater or theaters where movies are being shown. A movie theater which obtains a license must sell alcoholic liquors at a separate bar or location away from other food and drink, may only sell 1 alcoholic beverage at a time per age-verified patron and may only serve 2 alcoholic beverages per patron per movie showing. Movie theater managers and employees involved in serving alcohol must complete alcohol service training as prescribed by the Commissioner.

(g)(1) A caterer may apply to the Commissioner for a license to purchase alcoholic liquors from an importer and to receive, keep and sell such alcoholic liquors either by the glass or by the bottle, for consumption on any portion of the premises approved by the Commissioner for that purpose.

(2) An off-site caterer may apply to the Commissioner for a license to purchase alcoholic liquors from an importer and to receive, keep, transport and sell such alcoholic liquors either by the glass or by the bottle for consumption on any portion of off-site premises approved by the Commissioner for that purpose. Transporting of alcoholic liquors by an off-site caterer must be done in accordance with the Commissioner's rules.

(h) Notwithstanding any provision of this title to the contrary, motorsports speedways may permit patrons to bring inside with them alcoholic beverages regulated under this title for their own personal consumption, provided that they have a lawful ticket for admission to the facility and are of the lawful age to consume alcoholic beverages. The motorsports speedway may restrict the portions of the facility that patrons may act in accord with this section. Notwithstanding any provision of this title to the contrary, a motorsports speedway is not required to maintain a license required pursuant to § 554 of this title in order to permit patrons to bring inside with them alcoholic beverages regulated under this title for their own personal consumption.

(i) A certificated air passenger carrier maintaining and operating a warehouse storage facility in the State may apply to the Commissioner for a license to purchase alcoholic liquors from an importer and to receive at the carrier's warehouse or airport facility, keep at the carrier's warehouse or airport facility, transport to the carrier's airport facility, and sell such alcoholic liquor to its passengers for consumption on its aircraft only.

(j) An establishment licensed as a restaurant shall not be required to use the word "restaurant" in its tradename, menus, advertisements or signage unless the Commissioner specifically finds that the public may be confused as to its status as a restaurant.

(k) Any person who holds a valid restaurant license issued by the Commissioner may deny a minor, as defined in § 708 of this title, admission to or permission to remain on the premises after 9:00 p.m. (official Eastern time) unless accompanied by a parent or by a legal guardian.

History.
38 Del. Laws, c. 18, § 17; Code 1935, § 6146; 4 Del. C. 1953, § 512; 55 Del. Laws, c. 283, § 1; 56 Del. Laws, c. 335, § 3; 57 Del. Laws, c. 189; 57 Del. Laws, c. 447; 58 Del. Laws, c. 199; 59 Del. Laws, c. 107, § 17A; 59 Del. Laws, c. 590, §§ 2, 4; 60 Del. Laws, c. 466, §§ 3, 9; 64 Del. Laws, c. 434, §§ 1, 2; 67 Del. Laws, c. 109, §§ 8-10; 69 Del. Laws, c. 6, § 2; 71 Del. Laws, c. 42, § 1; 71 Del. Laws, c. 182, § 1; 71 Del. Laws, c. 210, § 2; 71 Del. Laws, c. 472, § 1; 72 Del. Laws, c. 486, § 9; 73 Del. Laws, c. 244, §§ 2-6; 73 Del. Laws, c. 393, § 2; 75 Del. Laws, c. 246, § 1; 78 Del. Laws, c. 220, § 2; 79 Del. Laws, c. 308, § 2; 80 Del. Laws, c. 109, § 2; 81 Del. Laws, c. 69, § 2; 81 Del. Laws, c. 254, § 1; 82 Del. Laws, c. 4, § 2; 82 Del. Laws, c. 99, § 3; 82 Del. Laws, c. 117, § 1; 82 Del. Laws, c. 141, § 1; 82 Del. Laws, c. 247, §§ 2, 5; 82 Del. Laws, c. 279, § 1; 83 Del. Laws, c. 9, § 2; 83 Del. Laws, c. 9, § 5.

Revisor's note.
Section 5 of 83 Del. Laws, c. 9, provided: "This act expires on March 31, 2022, unless otherwise extended by a subsequent act of the General Assembly."

Effect of amendments.
83 Del. Laws, c. 9, effective Mar. 23, 2021, designated the second undesignated paragraph of (a) as (a)(1), deleted "if the alcoholic beverages for off-premise consumption are in containers which are securely closed" from the end and extending its expiration date to Mar. 31, 2022, by operation of § 5 of that act; and added (a)(2), which also expired effective Mar. 31, 2022, by operation of § 5 of that act.

§ 512B. Brewery-pubs.

(a) Subject to the provisions, restrictions and prohibitions of this title, the Commissioner may grant a brewery-pub license to each qualified applicant therefor. No person shall own or operate a brewery-pub unless licensed to do so by the Commissioner. For purposes of this section, a "brewery-pub" shall be an establishment in which beer, cider, mead and/or fermented beverages are manufactured on the premises of the licensed establishment, limited to restaurants owned or leased by the brewery-pub applicant.

(b) The following conditions and restrictions shall apply to the holder of each brewery-pub license:

(1) It must be situated on the premises of, or be physically a part of, a restaurant;

(2) It may brew, bottle, and sell beer at no more than 3 licensed establishments, provided that each such licensed establishment qualifies as a separate brewery-pub under this section;

(3) It shall brew no more than 4,000 barrels of beer in any calendar year;

(4) It may sell beer manufactured on licensed premises in labeled barrels, bottles, or other closed containers to wholesalers licensed under this title for delivery by them to persons inside or outside this State;

(5) It may sell at the licensed premises beer manufactured on the licensed premises at retail for consumption off the premises;

(6) It may sell at the licensed premises beer manufactured on the licensed premises for on-premises consumption;

(7) It shall be prohibited from owning, operating or being affiliated with any importer of alcoholic liquor, either in or without this State; and

(8) The provisions of § 506 of this title to the contrary notwithstanding, it shall be permitted to have an interest in, be affiliated with, operate, or own another supplier or manufacturer located outside the State and have an interest in a farm winery, microbrewery, and/or craft distillery licensed under this chapter and actually located in this State, provided that the total domestic sales of beer of all affiliated suppliers or manufacturers shall not exceed 6 million barrels in a calendar year.

(c) It shall be unlawful for a person to operate a brewery-pub if:

(1) The restaurant portion of the licensed establishment fails to offer complete meals for consideration to patrons or fails to operate as a bona fide restaurant as defined by Commissioner rules or this title;

(2) The license is denied, cancelled, suspended or revoked for any of the grounds contained in § 543 or § 561 of this title;

(3) The business is transferred to a different location.

(d) This section shall not prohibit the granting of a restaurant license to sell alcoholic liquors, for on-premises consumption, as provided in § 512 of this title.

(e) The Commissioner may make and publish such rules and regulations with respect to the assessment and payment of the tax on beer, as contained in § 581 of this title, as it deems proper, and all such rules and regulations that are not inconsistent with this title shall have the force and effect of law.

(f) Notwithstanding any other provision of this title to the contrary, the holder of a brewery-pub license may also make, bottle and sell an alcoholic liquor that is fermented or distilled on the premises, subject to the following conditions and restrictions:

(1) All of the conditions and restrictions relating to beer set forth in subsection (b) of this section; and

(2) Alcoholic liquor that is fermented or distilled on the premises shall be taxed in accordance with § 581 of this title.

(g) The provisions of § 546 of this title to the contrary notwithstanding, the sale for off-premises consumption at up to a combined total of 3 licensees licensed under this section or 2 licensees licensed under this section and a microbrewery licensed pursuant to § 512C of this title all owned or controlled by the same person shall be permitted.

History.

68 Del. Laws, c. 205, § 1; 70 Del. Laws, c. 469, §§ 1, 2; 71 Del. Laws, c. 83, § 1; 72 Del. Laws, c. 486, § 9; 73 Del. Laws, c. 225, § 1; 77 Del. Laws, c. 432, §§ 4, 5; 79 Del. Laws, c. 157, § 1; 82 Del. Laws, c. 22, § 1; 82 Del. Laws, c. 141, § 2; 83 Del. Laws, c. 36, § 2.

Effect of amendments.

83 Del. Laws, c. 36, effective June 3, 2021, substituted "cider, mead, and/or fermented beverages are" for "is" in the second sentence of (a).

§ 512C. Microbreweries; license; alternating premises.

(a) Upon proper application and subject to the applicable provisions, restrictions, and prohibitions under this title, the Commissioner may grant a license to any of the following:

(1) A person who is the owner or lessee of a microbrewery to manufacture and sell beer, fermented beverages, mead, and cider.

(2) A person who owns a tenant microbrewery under subsection (i) of this section.

(b) For purposes of this section,

(1) "Alternating premises" means the portion of a microbrewery's premises that is used at different times by 2 or more microbreweries to manufacture beer, mead, or cider.

(2) "Host microbrewery" means the microbrewery that owns the brewing equipment in an alternating premises.

(3) "Microbrewery" means a single establishment in which beer, fermented beverages, mead, or cider is manufactured and which is operated by the licensee under this section.

(4) "Tenant microbrewery" means the microbrewery that does not own, but uses, the brewing equipment in an alternating premises.

(c) Notwithstanding any provision of this title to the contrary, a microbrewery license allows the licensee to do all of the following:

(1) To manufacture and sell on the licensed premises beer, fermented beverages, mead, or cider or a combination thereof, but the licensee may not manufacture or sell more than the maximum amount permitted by

federal regulations to qualify for a "reduced rate of tax for certain brewers" under 27 C.F.R., Part 25, § 25.152(a)(2).

(2) To manufacture on the licensed premises beer, fermented beverages, mead, or cider for persons, other than the licensee, licensed under this title or for persons outside this State.

(3) To sell beer, fermented beverages, mead, and cider manufactured on the licensed premises in labeled barrels, bottles or other closed containers to importers licensed under this title for delivery by them to persons inside or outside the State.

(4) To sell at the licensed premises beer, fermented beverages, mead, and cider manufactured on the licensed premises for consumption on or off the licensed premises. The amount of beer, fermented beverages, mead, and cider sold for off-premises consumption is limited to a maximum of 5 cases per day to each retail customer.

(5) To purchase and store product from a Delaware licensed importer or retailer licensed under § 516 of this title, and sell the product to its retail customers for consumption on the premises where sold so long as the product is manufactured by an entity that holds a Delaware license under § 512A, § 512B, § 512C, or § 512E of this title or the manufacturer, as determined by the Commissioner, would qualify for a license under 1 or more of these sections if the manufacturer were physically located in the State.

(6) The provisions of § 506 of this title to the contrary notwithstanding, to be permitted to have an interest in, be affiliated with, operate, or own another supplier or manufacturer located outside the State and have an interest in a farm winery, brewery-pub, or craft distillery licensed under this chapter and actually located in this State, provided that the total domestic sales of beer of all affiliated suppliers or manufacturers does not exceed 6 million barrels in a calendar year.

(d) It is unlawful for a person to operate a microbrewery if any of the following apply:

(1) The license is denied, canceled, suspended, or revoked for any of the grounds under § 543 or § 561 of this title.

(2) The establishment is moved to a location other than the licensed premises.

(3) The licensee owns, operates, or is affiliated with any importer of alcoholic liquor either in or without this State.

(e) A microbrewery licensee is exempt from the distance requirements for establishments licensed or to be licensed under § 543(d) of this title, and such requirements may not affect the granting of a microbrewery license.

(f) All beer, fermented beverages, mead, and cider sold by a microbrewery licensee for off-premise consumption must be in containers that are securely sealed and have an attached label setting forth the information required under this title, Commissioner rules, and laws of the State.

(g) Any microbrewery or brewery licensed by the Commissioner to manufacture beer, fermented beverages, mead, or cider in this State may provide samples of the beer, fermented beverages, mead, or cider manufactured at the licensed premises in a manner approved by the Commissioner.

(h) Notwithstanding § 546 of this title, a microbrewery may sell a product that the microbrewery manufactures for off-premises consumption at a licensee licensed under this section and at up to 2 brewery-pubs licensed under § 512B of this title that are all owned or controlled by the same person.

(i)(1) The requirements to grant a license to a tenant microbrewery must include all of the following:

a. An agreement with a host microbrewery that allows the tenant microbrewery to use the host microbrewery's brewing equipment for specified periods of time to manufacture beer, mead, or cider. The compensation to the host microbrewery under an agreement may not be based upon the profit of the tenant microbrewery and is subject to the approval of the Commissioner.

b. The host microbrewery and the tenant microbrewery must have the approval of the Federal Trade and Tax Bureau ("TTB"), or its successor, to operate as an alternating premises.

c. The tenant microbrewery must retain title to all of the tenant microbrewery's raw materials, except for water.

d. The tenant microbrewery must act as the brewer of the beer, mead, or cider.

e. Upon completion of the manufacturing process, the tenant microbrewery shall remove all product from the alternating premises and transport the product to a location approved by the Commissioner for the tenant microbrewery to store and sell for on or off premises consumption. A tenant microbrewery may satisfy the requirement under this paragraph (i)(1)e. by leasing space from the host microbrewery but the tenant microbrewery may only store the tenant microbrewery's brands in the leased space.

(2) The Commissioner may suspend or revoke the license of the tenant microbrewery upon the termination of the agreement between the host microbrewery and the tenant microbrewery.

(3) The Commissioner may suspend all licenses at the alternating premises if the TTB suspends the approval of the host or tenant microbrewery, The Commissioner must provide reasons for and conditions of a suspension under this paragraph (i)(3).

History.

69 Del. Laws, c. 361, § 1; 71 Del. Laws, c. 211, §§ 1-3; 72 Del. Laws, c. 486, § 9; 76 Del. Laws, c. 32, §§ 1-5; 77 Del. Laws, c. 432, §§ 1-3; 79 Del. Laws, c. 157, § 1; 81 Del. Laws, c. 261, § 1; 82 Del. Laws, c. 22, § 1; 82 Del. Laws, c. 141, § 3; 83 Del. Laws, c. 36, § 3; 83 Del. Laws, c. 168, § 1.

Effect of amendments.

83 Del. Laws, c. 36, effective June 3, 2021, added "fermented beverages" throughout the section.

83 Del. Laws, c. 168, effective September 15, 2021, substituted "Microbreweries; license; alternating premises" for "Microbrewery" in the section heading; rewrote (a) and (b); substituted "allows the licensee to do all of the following" for "shall allow the licensee" in the introductory paragraph of (c); added a comma following "mead" wherever it appears in (c)(1)-(4) and (f), following "§ 512C" in (c)(5), following "suspended" in (d)(1), following "operates" in (d)(3) and following "rules" in (f)"; substituted a period for a semicolon at the end (c)(1)-(4) and (d)(1), for "; and" at the end of (c)(5) and

for "; or" at the end of (d)(2); in (c)(1), substituted "may" for "shall" and "under 27 C.F.R., Part 25, § 25.152(a)(2)" for "as currently found in the 27 C.F.R., Part 25, § 25.152(a)(2) or as hereafter amended"; substituted "is" for "shall be" in the second sentence of (c)(4), in the introductory paragraph of (d) and in (e); in (c)(5), substituted "the" for "said" following "sell", "under" for "pursuant to" preceding "§ 512A", and substituted "1 or more of these" for "said" and "the manufacturer" for "it" following "sections if"; in (c)(6), substituted "or" for "and/or" preceding "craft" and "does" for "shall" preceding "not exceed"; added "any of the following apply" in the introductory paragraph of (d); substituted "under" for "contained in" in (d)(1) and for "as contained in" in (e); substituted "may" for "shall" in (e); in (f), substituted "must" for "shall", "that" for "which" following "containers", added "an" preceding "attached" and deleted "thereto a" thereafter, and substituted 'the' for "such" preceding "information" and "under" for "by"; substituted "the licensed" for "said" in (g); rewrote (h); and added (i).

§ 513. Sale of beer and wine for consumption on premises of tavern.

(a) Any person in charge of a tavern may apply to the Commissioner for a license to purchase from an importer and to receive, keep, and sell beer and wine, if such beverages are consumed on the premises where sold.

(b), (c) [Repealed.]

History.

38 Del. Laws, c. 18, § 17; Code 1935, § 6146; 4 Del. C. 1953, § 513; 54 Del. Laws, c. 377, § 1; 67 Del. Laws, c. 109, § 11; 69 Del. Laws, c. 6, § 3; 72 Del. Laws, c. 486, § 9; 73 Del. Laws, c. 244, §§ 7, 8; 82 Del. Laws, c. 4, § 3; 83 Del. Laws, c. 207, § 2.

Effect of amendments.

83 Del. Laws, c. 207, effective Sept. 17, 2021, inserted "and wine" in the section heading and (a); and in (a), added a comma following "keep" and substituted "beverages are" for "beer is".

§ 515. Sale to members of club and multiple activity club.

(a) A club or multiple activity club may apply to the Commissioner for a license to purchase spirits, wine, or beer and to sell the spirits, wine, or beer to a member of the club.

(b)(1) A bottle club is not a club.

(2) [Repealed.]

History.

38 Del. Laws, c. 18, § 17; Code 1935, § 6146; 4 Del. C. 1953, § 515; 56 Del. Laws, c. 335, § 4; 59 Del. Laws, c. 107, §§ 19, 20; 63 Del. Laws, c. 232, § 1; 67 Del. Laws, c. 109, § 12; 67 Del. Laws, c. 122, § 1; 72 Del. Laws, c. 486, § 9; 81 Del. Laws, c. 69, § 1; 83 Del. Laws, c. 152, § 2.

Effect of amendments.

83 Del. Laws, c. 152, effective Sept. 15, 2021,

deleted "'bottle club' defined" from the end of the section heading; in (a), added a comma following "wine" in two places and substituted "the" for "such" preceding each of the second occurrences of "spirits" and "club"; rewrote (b)(1); and repealed (b)(2).

§ 515A. Licenses for bottle clubs.

(a) Except as provided in this section, it is unlawful to operate a bottle club for profit or pecuniary gain.

(b) The Commissioner may, upon application, grant a license to the owner, lessor, or person in charge of the premises to operate a bottle club in accordance with this chapter.

(c) The Commissioner may only grant a bottle club license to the following:

(1) A person doing business in an establishment meeting the standards of a restaurant. The license permits the establishment to operate as a bottle club on every day of the week and on holidays, except between the hours of 2:00 a.m. and 9:00 a.m. during which time alcoholic liquors may not be consumed on the premises of the establishment.

(2) A person renting premises to customers for holding weddings or other social gatherings where there is adequate food, as determined by the Commissioner, provided by the customer or a caterer. The license permits the establishment to operate as a bottle club on every day of the week and on holidays, except between the hours of 2:00 a.m. and 9:00 a.m. during which time alcoholic liquors may not be consumed on the premises of the establishment. If a bottle club licensed under this paragraph (c)(2) has a function that utilizes an off-site caterer, all alcohol must be provided by the off-site caterer.

History.

63 Del. Laws, c. 232, § 2; 67 Del. Laws, c. 122, § 2; 72 Del. Laws, c. 486, § 9; 83 Del. Laws, c. 152, § 3.

Effect of amendments.

83 Del. Laws, c. 152, effective September 15, 2021, deleted the quotation marks surrounding

"bottle clubs" in the section heading; in (a), substituted "is" for "shall be" preceding "unlawful", added "a bottle club" preceding "for profit" and deleted "a 'bottle club'" from the end; in (b), added a comma following "lessor" and deleted the quotation marks surrounding "bottle club"; and rewrote (c).

§ 524. Notice of application [Effective until Mar. 31, 2022].

(a) An application for a new license to purchase for resale, for transfer of an existing license, or for a substantive change to a license or licensed premise shall be filed with the Commissioner's office.

(b) Upon filing of an application for a new license to purchase for resale or for a substantive change to a license or licensed premise the applicant shall cause notice to be advertised in at least 2 different newspapers circulated in the community in which the applicant will operate if the application is approved for 3 issues. One of the newspapers must be a "local newspaper," as determined by the Commissioner either through rules or on a case by case basis. If the newspaper is a daily newspaper, the first publication shall be made within 3 days of the filing of the application and the third publishing shall occur within 10 days of filing the application. If the newspaper is a weekly publication, the first publication shall be made within 8 days of filing the application and the third publishing shall occur within 22 days of filing the application.

(c) Within 3 days of filing of an application for a new license to purchase for resale or for a substantive change to a license or licensed premise a notice shall be mailed by certified mail or first class mail as evidenced by a certificate of mailing postage-pre-paid to the following entities, individuals or groups of individuals:

(1) Except as provided in paragraph (c)(2) of this section, all property owners within 200 feet from any point on the property boundary line of the premises to which the license is to apply;

(2) All property owners within 1,000 feet from any point on the property boundary line of the premises to which the license is to apply if the premises is located within $^1/_4$ of a mile of a riverfront, beachfront or other open water, or if the applicant intends to include space for outside dining, outside entertainment or the outside service or consumption of alcoholic beverages;

(3) The governing body of any incorporated areas within 1 mile from any point on the property boundary line of the premises to which the license is to apply.

(d) The notices referred to in subsections (b) and (c) of this section shall provide such information as determined by the Commissioner either through duly adopted rules or on a case by case basis. The following notice will, in addition to the aforesaid Commissioner approved notice, satisfy this notice provision:

"[Name of applicant] has on [Date of application] applied with the Alcoholic Beverage Control ("Commissioner") for [Nature of application] for a premises located at [Location of the premises, including street and city]. Persons who are against this application should provide written notice of their objections to the Commissioner. For the Commissioner to be required to hold a hearing to consider additional input from persons against the application, the Commissioner must receive one or more documents containing a total of at least 10 signatures of residents or property owners located within 1 mile of the premises or in any incorporated areas located within 1 mile of the premises. The protest(s) must be filed with the Alcoholic Beverage Control Commissioner at the 3rd Floor, Carvel State Office Building, 820 North French Street, Wilmington, DE 19801. The protest(s) must be received by the Commissioner's office on or before [state a date at least 30 days after the application is filed]. Failure to file such a protest may result in the Commissioner considering the application without further notice, input or hearing. If you have questions regarding this matter please contact the Commissioner's Office."

(e) The term "substantive change" referenced in this section shall mean any of the following:

(1) Any permanent change that will increase the square footage of the licensed premises;

(2) Any temporary change that will last longer than 60 days and result in an increase of the square footage of the licensed premises;

(3) Any change that would require a variance of the Commissioner's rules or suspension thereof and results in:

    a. Live entertainment on a licensed patio;

    b. External speakers or amplifiers on a licensed patio; or

    c. Wet bar on a licensed patio;

(4) Any change in the floor plan of a restaurant licensee which would increase the number of bar seats or increase the area utilized for entertainment; or

(5) Any additional circumstance that the Commissioner determines is a substantive change.

(f) Notwithstanding subsection (e) of this section or any other law, rule, or regulation to the contrary, "substantive change" does not mean any of the following:

(1) An expansion of outdoor seating for serving of food and drinks that as of March 31, 2021, satisfied/meets all of the requirements of paragraph A.2. of the Nineteenth Modification of Governor Carney's State of Emergency Declaration effective May 22, 2020, even if the State of Emergency Due to Public Health Threat is no longer in effect.

(2) An expansion of outdoor seating for serving of food and drinks after March 31, 2021, that meets all of the following requirements:

    a. A plan approved by the appropriate political subdivision that does all of the following:

        1. Considers local traffic patterns and parking capacity needs, but may extend the boundaries of seating beyond current property boundaries under the discretion of the appropriate political subdivision and applicable property owners on all local right of ways.

        2. Does not intrude upon the State's right of way, unless approved by the Delaware Department of Transportation in writing.

        3. Maintains current access, unless approved by Delaware Department of Transportation in writing.

        4. Maintains proper access to the property for all emergency services.

        5. Abides by the current Declaration of State of Emergency Due to Public Health Threat and its modification requirements relating to food and drink establishments unless the State of Emergency is no longer in effect.

        6. Complies with the Americans with Disabilities Act [42 U.S.C. § 12101 et seq.].

        7. Adheres to all local noise ordinances.

        8. Allows for the proper control over the distribution of alcoholic beverages.

        9. Does not result in total outdoor seating capacity that exceeds the indoor seating capacity that the food or drink establishment was authorized to have prior to the Declaration of the State of Emergency Due to Public Health on March 12, 2020.

    b. Approval by the Office of Alcohol Beverage Control regarding the service of alcohol on premises.

(g) Any plan approved by or submitted to the appropriate political subdivision and the Office of Alcohol Beverage Control pursuant to subsection (f) of this section may allow for the service of alcoholic beverages without the requirement to serve food.

(h) Any plan submitted to the appropriate political subdivision and the Office of Alcohol Beverage Control pursuant to subsection (f) of this section that meets all of the requirements of paragraph (f)(2) of this section should not be denied approval absent exceptional circumstances.

History.

38 Del. Laws, c. 18, § 18; Code 1935, § 6147; 43 Del. Laws, c. 275, § 1; 44 Del. Laws, c. 205, § 1; 46 Del. Laws, c. 222, § 1; 4 Del. C. 1953, § 524; 59 Del. Laws, c. 107, §§ 29, 30; 67 Del. Laws, c. 118, §§ 1, 2; 70 Del. Laws, c. 186, § 1; 71 Del. Laws, c. 435, § 1; 72 Del. Laws, c. 221, §§ 2-4; 72 Del. Laws, c. 486, § 9; 73 Del. Laws, c. 136, § 1; 74 Del. Laws, c. 242, § 1; 82 Del. Laws, c. 247, §§ 3, 5; 83 Del. Laws, c. 9, § 3.

Revisor's note.

Section 5 of 83 Del. Laws, c. 9, provided:

"This act expires on March 31, 2022, unless otherwise extended by a subsequent act of the General Assembly."

Effect of amendments.

83 Del. Laws, c. 9, effective Mar. 23, 2021, rewrote (f); and added (g) and (h). Subsections (f)-(h) expired by operation of § 5 of that act, effective Mar. 31, 2022.

§ 524. Notice of application [Effective Mar. 31, 2022].

(a) An application for a new license to purchase for resale, for transfer of an existing license, or for a substantive change to a license or licensed premise shall be filed with the Commissioner's office.

(b) Upon filing of an application for a new license to purchase for resale or for a substantive change to a license or licensed premise the applicant shall cause notice to be advertised in at least 2 different newspapers circulated in the community in which the applicant will operate if the application is approved for 3 issues. One of the newspapers must be a "local newspaper," as determined by the Commissioner either through rules or on a case by case basis. If the newspaper is a daily newspaper, the first publication shall be made within 3 days of the filing of the application and the third publishing shall occur within 10 days of filing the application. If the newspaper is a weekly publication, the first publication shall be made within 8 days of filing the application and the third publishing shall occur within 22 days of filing the application.

(c) Within 3 days of filing of an application for a new license to purchase for resale or for a substantive change to a license or licensed premise a notice shall be mailed by certified mail or first class mail as evidenced by a certificate of mailing postage-pre-paid to the following entities, individuals or groups of individuals:

 (1) Except as provided in paragraph (c)(2) of this section, all property owners within 200 feet from any point on the property boundary line of the premises to which the license is to apply;

 (2) All property owners within 1,000 feet from any point on the property boundary line of the premises to which the license is to apply if the premises is located within $\frac{1}{4}$ of a mile of a riverfront, beachfront or other open water, or if the applicant intends to include space for outside dining, outside entertainment or the outside service or consumption of alcoholic beverages;

 (3) The governing body of any incorporated areas within 1 mile from any point on the property boundary line of the premises to which the license is to apply.

(d) The notices referred to in subsections (b) and (c) of this section shall provide such information as determined by the Commissioner either through duly adopted rules or on a case by case basis. The following notice will, in addition to the aforesaid Commissioner approved notice, satisfy this notice provision:

"[Name of applicant] has on [Date of application] applied with the Alcoholic Beverage Control ("Commissioner") for [Nature of application] for a premises located at [Location of the premises, including street and city]. Persons who are against this application should provide written notice of their objections to the Commissioner. For the Commissioner to be required to hold a hearing to consider additional input from persons against the application, the Commissioner must receive one or more documents containing a total of at least 10 signatures of residents or property owners located within 1 mile of the premises or in any incorporated areas located within 1 mile of the premises. The protest(s) must be filed with the Alcoholic Beverage Control Commissioner at the 3rd Floor, Carvel State Office Building, 820 North French Street, Wilmington, DE 19801. The protest(s) must be received by the Commissioner's office on or before [state a date at least 30 days after the application is filed]. Failure to file such a protest may result in the Commissioner considering the application without further notice, input or hearing. If you have questions regarding this matter please contact the Commissioner's Office."

(e) The term "substantive change" referenced in this section shall mean any of the following:

(1) Any permanent change that will increase the square footage of the licensed premises;

(2) Any temporary change that will last longer than 60 days and result in an increase of the square footage of the licensed premises;

(3) Any change that would require a variance of the Commissioner's rules or suspension thereof and results in:

a. Live entertainment on a licensed patio;

b. External speakers or amplifiers on a licensed patio; or

c. Wet bar on a licensed patio;

(4) Any change in the floor plan of a restaurant licensee which would increase the number of bar seats or increase the area utilized for entertainment; or

(5) Any additional circumstance that the Commissioner determines is a substantive change.

(f)-(h) [Repealed.]

History.
38 Del. Laws, c. 18, § 18; Code 1935, § 6147; 43 Del. Laws, c. 275, § 1; 44 Del. Laws, c. 205, § 1; 46 Del. Laws, c. 222, § 1; 4 Del. C. 1953, § 524; 59 Del. Laws, c. 107, §§ 29, 30; 67 Del. Laws, c. 118, §§ 1, 2; 70 Del. Laws, c. 186, § 1; 71 Del. Laws, c. 435, § 1; 72 Del. Laws, c. 221, §§ 2-4; 72 Del. Laws, c. 486, § 9; 73 Del. Laws, c. 136, § 1; 74 Del. Laws, c. 242, § 1; 82 Del. Laws, c. 247, §§ 3, 5; 83 Del. Laws, c. 9, § 3; 83 Del. Laws, c. 9, § 5.

Revisor's note.
Section 5 of 83 Del. Laws, c. 9, provided: "This act expires on March 31, 2022, unless otherwise extended by a subsequent act of the General Assembly."

Effect of amendments.
83 Del. Laws, c. 9, effective Mar. 23, 2021, rewrote (f); and added (g) and (h). Subsections (f)-(h) expired by operation of § 5 of that act, effective Mar. 31, 2022.

SUBCHAPTER III

DETERMINATION OF APPLICATIONS

§ 541. Procedural requirements governing Commissioner's action; hearing; appeal.

NOTES TO DECISIONS

Function of Superior Court. — In an action concerning approval of a package retail liquor store, the appeal had to be dismissed; appellants could only file an appeal with Supe-

rior Court after a decision had been made by   A.3d —, 2020 Del. Super. LEXIS 2820 (Del.
the Appeals Commission. Adorno v. Cordrey, —   Super. Ct. Oct. 1, 2020).

§ 543. Grounds for refusal of license; transfer or extension of premises [Effective until Mar. 31, 2022].

(a) The Commissioner shall refuse to grant a license to be used in any county or subdivision thereof, if contrary to any prohibitory law then in force, in such county or subdivision thereof.

(b) The Commissioner may refuse to license an applicant if the Commissioner has substantial evidence that would reasonably support a belief that:

(1) Except for restaurants, there are sufficient licensed premises in the locality; or the granting of a license in the locality stated in the application is not otherwise demanded by public interest or convenience;

(2) The applicant is an importer of alcoholic liquors and has not furnished an acceptable bond for the purpose of assuring tax payments;

(3) The applicant appears to be financially irresponsible;

(4) The applicant has been provided with funds by, or has any forbidden connection with, a manufacturer, supplier or importer of alcoholic liquors;

(5) The applicant has made false statements to the Commissioner;

(6) The applicant has been convicted of violating any of the liquor laws of this State, or has been convicted and imprisoned for a crime;

(7) The applicant or any of the applicant's directors or officers, or any of the applicant's shareholders who hold more than 10% of the outstanding issued shares has been convicted of violating any of the prohibited acts defined in Chapter 47 of Title 16, the Uniform Controlled Substances Act, or its functional equivalent under the laws of the United States, any state or territory or any other country, including, but not limited to, the illegal manufacture, delivery, trafficking, possession or consumption of any controlled or noncontrolled substance, or the delivery or possession of illegal drug paraphernalia or illegal hypodermic syringes or needles, or the conspiracy, solicitation or other attempt to engage in such illegal activities;

(8) As to a restaurant applicant, the applicant has failed to designate a substantial portion of the premises' floor space, as determined by the Commissioner, to be used for the storage, preparation, service and consumption of complete meals;

(9) As to a restaurant applicant, the applicant's projected or actual receipts from the sale of complete meals fails to represent a substantial portion of the establishment's total gross receipts as determined by the Commissioner, provided that gross receipts received as payments from the State Lottery Office shall not be included by the Commissioner in his or her determination;

(10) As to a restaurant applicant, the applicant's proposed premises or any proposed extension of the premises of an existing licensed restaurant is protested in accordance with the provisions contained in § 541(b) of this title or any applicable Commissioner rule, and the Commissioner finds that substantial evidence exists to conclude that the establishment's primary purpose will be the serving of alcoholic liquor to patrons. In reaching its decision, the Commissioner shall consider factors including, but not limited to, the number and sizes of bars in the establishment, the establishment's floor plan, an approximate percentage of the projected revenue to be derived from the sale of alcoholic liquor as compared to the

percentage of revenue to be derived from the sale of complete meals, the establishment's seating capacity, storage and preparation area for food service, and the number of service employees employed, or to be employed, in the establishment and their functions.

(11) A substantial objection to the granting of the license has been presented by the community within which the license is to operate, or that the granting of such license is otherwise not in the public interest. For the purposes of this subsection, the term "substantial objection" shall include:

a. Any objection, or group of objections, presented to the Commissioner either individually or as a group, by persons who reside within the election district where the license is to operate and all contiguous election districts, sufficient to give the Commissioner reason to believe that a majority of the residents of the community within which the license is to operate oppose the issuance of the license; or

b. Any objection, or group of objections, presented to the Commissioner either individually or as a group, the content of which gives the Commissioner reason to believe the quality of life of the community within which the license is to operate will be adversely affected by the granting of the license.

(c) The Commissioner may refuse to grant a license to sell alcoholic liquor to any new establishment to be located in the vicinity of a church, school or college. The Commissioner may issue a license to any establishment located in the vicinity of a church, school or college when such establishment has been located in a place prior to the time any church, school or college may thereafter be located in the vicinity of such establishment.

(d) The Commissioner shall refuse to grant a license for the sale of alcoholic liquor by any store or establishment for consumption off the premises, when there is an existing licensed establishment of similar type within ½ mile by accessible public road or street in any incorporated city or town, or within 3 miles by accessible public road or street in any unincorporated or rural area measured in driving distance both ways between the existing and proposed establishments. This subsection does not apply to any of the following:

(1) An existing license or to the sale, transfer of ownership, or renewal of an existing license.

(2) A club licensed to sell off the premises where sold, farm winery, brewery-pub, microbrewery, or craft distillery.

(3) A licensee who desires to move the location of the license to a location within 500 feet thereof by accessible public road or street. However, a licensee located in a shopping center or shopping mall may move the location of the license any distance within the same shopping center or shopping mall, whether such center or mall consist of 1 or more than 1 separate buildings.

(4) An applicant for an off premises license whose license location meets 1 of the following:

a. Is between 1800 feet and ½ mile from an existing license of similar type in any incorporated city or town, if the applicant can provide a report, determined reliable by the Commissioner after written input from the Division that indicates either of the following:

1. A minimum yearly increase of 1% in the population of individuals 21 years old or older over the past 3 consecutive years measured from the month before the submission of the application.

2. A minimum increase of 3% in the population of individuals 21 years old or older in the past year measured from the month

before the submission of the application within a distance of ½ mile from the borders of the property where the applicant seeks licensure.

b. Is between 1½ miles and 3 miles from an existing license of similar type in any unincorporated or rural area if the applicant can provide a report, determined reliable by the Commissioner after written input from the Division that indicates either of the following:

1. A minimum yearly increase of 1% in the population of individuals 21 years old or older over the past 3 consecutive years measured from the month before the submission of the application.

2. A minimum increase of 3% in the population of individuals 21 years old or older in the past year measured from the month before the submission of the application within a distance of 1½ miles from the borders of the property where the applicant seeks licensure.

(e) The Commissioner may grant a licensee whose license was valid on December 31, 2019, and who desires to move the location of the license due to the destruction of the building, loss of lease, diversion of highway traffic pattern, or similar reason beyond the control of the licensee a new license if the application satisfies this subsection; subsection (d) of this section, as in effect before January 1, 2020; and all other requirements under this title.

(f)(1) The Commissioner shall refuse to grant a license to sell alcoholic liquor to any restaurant or eating place located on or a part of the Delaware Turnpike.

(2) The Commissioner shall refuse to grant a license to sell alcoholic liquor to any new store located in an unincorporated area on or along any state highway listed in § 701(d) of Title 21 within 1½ miles of a Department of Motor Vehicles' facility on or along the same state highway.

(g) The Commissioner shall not grant a new license of any type and shall not grant an extension of premises of an existing license of any type unless the application for said new license or for said extension is accompanied by a Certificate of Compliance from the appropriate political subdivision showing:

(1) That the premises where the license is to be used are properly zoned for the applicant's intended use; and

(2) That all necessary permits have been approved; and

(3) That the applicant has complied with all other applicable licensing requirements of the appropriate political subdivision.

This subsection shall not apply to any application for a temporary extension of premises as authorized by Commissioner rule; provided, that any such application has not been objected to by the appropriate political subdivision which shall be provided with notice of the application by the applicant within 7 days of the date the application is filed with the Commissioner.

This subsection shall not apply to any extension of premises of an existing license granted by the Commissioner pursuant to § 524(f) even if the State of Emergency is no longer in effect.

(h) Any existing restaurant which was licensed by the State to permit the sale of alcoholic beverages and which was in compliance with applicable state, county or municipal laws and regulations as of June 14, 1991 shall be permitted to continue to operate in the same manner as it was operating on said date so long as said license is in effect, notwithstanding any ordinance or other restriction subsequently enacted by a municipal corporation.

(i) The Commissioner shall refuse to grant a license for the sale of alcoholic liquor by any taproom or tavern establishment when there is an existing licensed establishment of similar type within 1200 feet by accessible public road or street in any incorporated city or town, or within ⁹⁄₁₀ of a mile by accessible public road or street in any unincorporated or rural area measured in driving distance both ways between the existing and proposed establishments. This subsection does not apply to any of the following:

(1) An existing license or to the sale, transfer of ownership, or renewal of an existing license.

(2) A licensee who desires to move the location of the license to a location within 500 feet thereof by accessible public road or street. However, a licensee located in a shopping center or shopping mall may move the location of the license any distance within the same shopping center or shopping mall, whether the center or mall consists of 1 or more separate buildings.

History.

38 Del. Laws, c. 18, §§ 22, 24; Code 1935, §§ 6151, 6153; 4 Del. C. 1953, § 543; 54 Del. Laws, c. 324; 54 Del. Laws, c. 377, § 2; 55 Del. Laws, c. 116, § 1; 55 Del. Laws, c. 283, § 2; 55 Del. Laws, c. 342, §§ 1, 2; 55 Del. Laws, c. 446; 56 Del. Laws, c. 34; 57 Del. Laws, c. 708; 58 Del. Laws, c. 542; 59 Del. Laws, c. 107, §§ 34-37; 61 Del. Laws, c. 145, § 1; 63 Del. Laws, c. 373, § 1; 64 Del. Laws, c. 430, § 1; 66 Del. Laws, c. 178, § 1; 67 Del. Laws, c. 109, § 15; 68 Del. Laws, c. 44, §§ 1, 2; 69 Del. Laws, c. 338, § 1; 70 Del. Laws, c. 186, § 1; 71 Del. Laws, c. 435, §§ 4, 5; 72 Del. Laws, c. 157, § 1; 72 Del. Laws, c. 486, § 9; 78 Del. Laws, c. 285, § 21; 82 Del. Laws, c. 98, § 1; 82 Del. Laws, c. 247, §§ 3, 5; 83 Del. Laws, c. 9, § 3; 83 Del. Laws, c. 56, § 106; 83 Del. Laws, c. 176, § 1.

Revisor's note.

Section 5 of 83 Del. Laws, c. 9, provided:

"This act expires on March 31, 2022, unless otherwise extended by a subsequent act of the General Assembly."

Section 178 of 83 Del. Laws, c. 56, provided: "This act shall take effect in accordance with the provisions of state law." The act became effective upon the signature of the Governor on June 30, 2021.

Effect of amendments.

83 Del. Laws, c. 9, effective Mar. 23, 2021, added the final undesignated paragraph of (g). The amendment expired by operation of § 5 of that act, effective Mar. 31, 2022.

83 Del. Laws, c. 56, effective June 30, 2021, added (f)(2).

83 Del. Laws, c. 176, effective Sept. 15, 2021, deleted "taproom" following "liquor" in the introductory paragraph of (d); deleted "or taproom" following "premises" in (d)(4); and added (i).

§ 543. Grounds for refusal of license; transfer or extension of premises [Effective Mar. 31, 2022].

(a) The Commissioner shall refuse to grant a license to be used in any county or subdivision thereof, if contrary to any prohibitory law then in force, in such county or subdivision thereof.

(b) The Commissioner may refuse to license an applicant if the Commissioner has substantial evidence that would reasonably support a belief that:

(1) Except for restaurants, there are sufficient licensed premises in the locality; or the granting of a license in the locality stated in the application is not otherwise demanded by public interest or convenience;

(2) The applicant is an importer of alcoholic liquors and has not furnished an acceptable bond for the purpose of assuring tax payments;

(3) The applicant appears to be financially irresponsible;

(4) The applicant has been provided with funds by, or has any forbidden connection with, a manufacturer, supplier or importer of alcoholic liquors;

(5) The applicant has made false statements to the Commissioner;

(6) The applicant has been convicted of violating any of the liquor laws of this State, or has been convicted and imprisoned for a crime;

(7) The applicant or any of the applicant's directors or officers, or any of the applicant's shareholders who hold more than 10% of the outstanding issued shares has been convicted of violating any of the prohibited acts defined in Chapter 47 of Title 16, the Uniform Controlled Substances Act, or its functional equivalent under the laws of the United States, any state or territory or any other country, including, but not limited to, the illegal

manufacture, delivery, trafficking, possession or consumption of any controlled or noncontrolled substance, or the delivery or possession of illegal drug paraphernalia or illegal hypodermic syringes or needles, or the conspiracy, solicitation or other attempt to engage in such illegal activities;

(8) As to a restaurant applicant, the applicant has failed to designate a substantial portion of the premises' floor space, as determined by the Commissioner, to be used for the storage, preparation, service and consumption of complete meals;

(9) As to a restaurant applicant, the applicant's projected or actual receipts from the sale of complete meals fails to represent a substantial portion of the establishment's total gross receipts as determined by the Commissioner, provided that gross receipts received as payments from the State Lottery Office shall not be included by the Commissioner in his or her determination;

(10) As to a restaurant applicant, the applicant's proposed premises or any proposed extension of the premises of an existing licensed restaurant is protested in accordance with the provisions contained in § 541(b) of this title or any applicable Commissioner rule, and the Commissioner finds that substantial evidence exists to conclude that the establishment's primary purpose will be the serving of alcoholic liquor to patrons. In reaching its decision, the Commissioner shall consider factors including, but not limited to, the number and sizes of bars in the establishment, the establishment's floor plan, an approximate percentage of the projected revenue to be derived from the sale of alcoholic liquor as compared to the percentage of revenue to be derived from the sale of complete meals, the establishment's seating capacity, storage and preparation area for food service, and the number of service employees employed, or to be employed, in the establishment and their functions.

(11) A substantial objection to the granting of the license has been presented by the community within which the license is to operate, or that the granting of such license is otherwise not in the public interest. For the purposes of this subsection, the term "substantial objection" shall include:

     a. Any objection, or group of objections, presented to the Commissioner either individually or as a group, by persons who reside within the election district where the license is to operate and all contiguous election districts, sufficient to give the Commissioner reason to believe that a majority of the residents of the community within which the license is to operate oppose the issuance of the license; or

     b. Any objection, or group of objections, presented to the Commissioner either individually or as a group, the content of which gives the Commissioner reason to believe the quality of life of the community within which the license is to operate will be adversely affected by the granting of the license.

(c) The Commissioner may refuse to grant a license to sell alcoholic liquor to any new establishment to be located in the vicinity of a church, school or college. The Commissioner may issue a license to any establishment located in the vicinity of a church, school or college when such establishment has been located in a place prior to the time any church, school or college may thereafter be located in the vicinity of such establishment.

(d) The Commissioner shall refuse to grant a license for the sale of alcoholic liquor by any store, or establishment for consumption off the premises, when there is an existing licensed establishment of similar type within ½ mile by accessible public road or street in any incorporated city or town, or within 3 miles by accessible public road or street in any unincorporated or rural area measured in driving distance both ways between the existing and proposed establishments. This subsection does not apply to any of the following:

(1) An existing license or to the sale, transfer of ownership, or renewal of an existing license.

(2) A club licensed to sell off the premises where sold, farm winery, brewery-pub, microbrewery, or craft distillery.

(3) A licensee who desires to move the location of the license to a location within 500 feet thereof by accessible public road or street. However, a licensee located in a shopping center or shopping mall may move the location of the license any distance within the same shopping center or shopping mall, whether such center or mall consist of 1 or more than 1 separate buildings.

(4) An applicant for an off premises license whose license location meets 1 of the following:

a. Is between 1800 feet and ½ mile from an existing license of similar type in any incorporated city or town, if the applicant can provide a report, determined reliable by the Commissioner after written input from the Division that indicates either of the following:

1. A minimum yearly increase of 1% in the population of individuals 21 years old or older over the past 3 consecutive years measured from the month before the submission of the application.

2. A minimum increase of 3% in the population of individuals 21 years old or older in the past year measured from the month before the submission of the application within a distance of ½ mile from the borders of the property where the applicant seeks licensure.

b. Is between 1½ miles and 3 miles from an existing license of similar type in any unincorporated or rural area if the applicant can provide a report, determined reliable by the Commissioner after written input from the Division that indicates either of the following:

1. A minimum yearly increase of 1% in the population of individuals 21 years old or older over the past 3 consecutive years measured from the month before the submission of the application.

2. A minimum increase of 3% in the population of individuals 21 years old or older in the past year measured from the month before the submission of the application within a distance of 1½ miles from the borders of the property where the applicant seeks licensure.

(e) The Commissioner may grant a licensee whose license was valid on December 31, 2019, and who desires to move the location of the license due to the destruction of the building, loss of lease, diversion of highway traffic pattern, or similar reason beyond the control of the licensee a new license if the application satisfies this subsection; subsection (d) of this section, as in effect before January 1, 2020; and all other requirements under this title.

(f)(1) The Commissioner shall refuse to grant a license to sell alcoholic liquor to any restaurant or eating place located on or a part of the Delaware Turnpike.

(2) The Commissioner shall refuse to grant a license to sell alcoholic liquor to any new store located in an unincorporated area on or along any state highway listed in § 701(d) of Title 21 within 1½ miles of a Department of Motor Vehicles' facility on or along the same state highway.

(g) The Commissioner shall not grant a new license of any type and shall not grant an extension of premises of an existing license of any type unless the application for said new license or for said extension is accompanied by a Certificate of Compliance from the appropriate political subdivision showing:

(1) That the premises where the license is to be used are properly zoned for the applicant's intended use; and

(2) That all necessary permits have been approved; and

(3) That the applicant has complied with all other applicable licensing requirements of the appropriate political subdivision.

This subsection shall not apply to any application for a temporary extension of premises as authorized by Commissioner rule; provided, that any such application has not been objected to by the appropriate political subdivision which shall be provided with notice of the application by the applicant within 7 days of the date the application is filed with the Commissioner.

(h) Any existing restaurant which was licensed by the State to permit the sale of alcoholic beverages and which was in compliance with applicable state, county or municipal laws and regulations as of June 14, 1991 shall be permitted to continue to operate in the same manner as it was operating on said date so long as said license is in effect, notwithstanding any ordinance or other restriction subsequently enacted by a municipal corporation.

(i) The Commissioner shall refuse to grant a license for the sale of alcoholic liquor by any taproom or tavern establishment when there is an existing licensed establishment of similar type within 1200 feet by accessible public road or street in any incorporated city or town, or within 9/10 of a mile by accessible public road or street in any unincorporated or rural area measured in driving distance both ways between the existing and proposed establishments. This subsection does not apply to any of the following:

(1) An existing license or to the sale, transfer of ownership, or renewal of an existing license.

(2) A licensee who desires to move the location of the license to a location within 500 feet thereof by accessible public road or street. However, a licensee located in a shopping center or shopping mall may move the location of the license any distance within the same shopping center or shopping mall, whether the center or mall consists of 1 or more separate buildings.

History.

38 Del. Laws, c. 18, §§ 22, 24; Code 1935, §§ 6151, 6153; 4 Del. C. 1953, § 543; 54 Del. Laws, c. 324; 54 Del. Laws, c. 377, § 2; 55 Del. Laws, c. 116, § 1; 55 Del. Laws, c. 283, § 2; 55 Del. Laws, c. 342, §§ 1, 2; 55 Del. Laws, c. 446; 56 Del. Laws, c. 34; 57 Del. Laws, c. 708; 58 Del. Laws, c. 542; 59 Del. Laws, c. 107, §§ 34-37; 61 Del. Laws, c. 145, § 1; 63 Del. Laws, c. 373, § 1; 64 Del. Laws, c. 430, § 1; 66 Del. Laws, c. 178, § 1; 67 Del. Laws, c. 109, § 15; 68 Del. Laws, c. 44, §§ 1, 2; 69 Del. Laws, c. 338, § 1; 70 Del. Laws, c. 186, § 1; 71 Del. Laws, c. 435, §§ 4, 5; 72 Del. Laws, c. 157, § 1; 72 Del. Laws, c. 486, § 9; 78 Del. Laws, c. 285, § 21; 82 Del. Laws, c. 98, § 1; 82 Del. Laws, c. 247, §§ 3, 5; 83 Del. Laws, c. 9, § 3; 83 Del. Laws, c. 56, § 106; 83 Del. Laws, c. 176, § 1; 83 Del. Laws, c. 9, § 5.

Revisor's note.

Section 5 of 83 Del. Laws, c. 9, provided:

"This act expires on March 31, 2022, unless otherwise extended by a subsequent act of the General Assembly."

Section 178 of 83 Del. Laws, c. 56, provided: "This act shall take effect in accordance with the provisions of state law." The act became effective upon the signature of the Governor on June 30, 2021.

Effect of amendments.

83 Del. Laws, c. 9, effective Mar. 23, 2021, added the final undesignated paragraph of (g). The amendment expired by operation of § 5 of that act, effective Mar. 31, 2022.

83 Del. Laws, c. 56, effective June 30, 2021, added (f)(2).

83 Del. Laws, c. 176, effective Sept. 15, 2021, deleted "taproom" following "liquor" in the introductory paragraph of (d); deleted "or taproom" following "premises" in (d)(4); and added (i).

SUBCHAPTER V
CANCELLATION OR SUSPENSION
OF LICENSE

§ 561. Grounds for cancellation or suspension [Effective until Mar. 31, 2022].

(a) The Commissioner may cancel every license made use of on behalf of any person other than the one to whom or on behalf of whom it has been issued.

(b) The Commissioner may suspend any license and/or fine any licensee for the sale of alcoholic liquors if it has reasonable grounds to believe that the licensee has committed any of the following violations, or may cancel any license for the sale of alcoholic liquors for the following violations, if repeated and continuous:

(1) The licensee has violated any provision of this title or any regulation of the Commissioner pursuant hereto;

(2) The licensee has made any false representation or statement to the Commissioner in order to induce or prevent action by the Commissioner;

(3) The licensee is not maintaining an acceptable bond, if said bond is required;

(4) The licensee is acting as an agent of a manufacturer of alcoholic liquor or has borrowed money or accepted gratuities from such a manufacturer or any agent thereof;

(5) The licensee maintains a noisy, lewd, disorderly, or unsanitary establishment or has been supplying impure or otherwise deleterious beverages or food;

(6) The licensee is in the habit of using dangerous or narcotic drugs, or is in the habit of using alcoholic beverages to excess;

(7) The licensee has sold alcoholic liquor in contravention of § 708 of this title;

(8) The licensee has in the licensee's possession on the licensee's licensed premises or has sold or offered for sale any alcoholic beverages not purchased or sold pursuant to this title;

(9) The licensee has misrepresented any alcoholic liquor sold by the licensee as purchased through the Commissioner or has in the licensee's possession, or has used any wrappers, labels, corks, caps, stamps or bottles not purchased from or through the Commissioner which are deceptively similar to those used by the Commissioner;

(10) The licensee has since the granting of the licensee's license been convicted of a felony or has been convicted of violating any of the liquor laws of this State, general or local, including the provisions of this title;

(11) The licensee has admitted guilt or has been adjudged guilty of violations of local, municipal, county or State regulations, ordinances or codes related to the operation of a licensed premises;

(12) There is any other reason which in the opinion of the Commissioner based on public convenience or necessity warrants cancelling or suspending the license;

(13) The licensee or a representative thereof has disciplined, threatened or otherwise penalized any person for refusing to violate or aiding the enforcement of the provisions of this title or the rules of the Commissioner.

(c) The Commissioner shall not cancel or suspend any license for the sale of alcoholic liquors or impose any fine for an alleged violation of § 708 or § 904 of this title where the licensee or its employee has made a reasonable effort to determine the age of a purchaser of alcoholic liquors. For purposes of this subsection, a licensee or its employee shall be deemed to have made a reasonable effort to determine the age of a purchaser if, prior to any sale of alcoholic liquors, the licensee or its employee requires the purchaser to display identification, with a photograph of the purchaser thereon affixed, which sets forth information that would lead a reasonable man to believe the purchaser to be 21 years of age or older.

(d) Any of the grounds for refusal of a license as provided for in § 543 of this title shall also be adequate grounds for suspension of a license.

(e) The Commissioner may cancel any retail license if it has reasonable grounds to believe that the license was granted in violation of § 546(b) of this title, or any rule enacted pursuant to § 546(d) of this title.

(f) If the Commissioner receives notice from the appropriate political subdivision that any Certificate of Compliance issued to satisfy an applicant's duty under § 543(g) of this title has been suspended, then the Commissioner shall suspend any license or extension of an existing license granted in reliance on such Certificate of Compliance until such time as the Commissioner receives notice from the appropriate political subdivision that such Certificate has been reinstated. If the Commissioner receives notice from the appropriate political subdivision that any Certificate of Compliance issued to satisfy an applicant's duty under § 543(g) of this title has been canceled, then the Commissioner shall revoke any license or extension of an existing license granted in reliance on such Certificate of Compliance.

(g) The Commissioner may suspend any license for the sale of alcoholic liquors held by any taproom or restaurant or fine any licensee holding such a license if it has reasonable grounds to believe that the licensee has operated, caused the operation of or permitted the operation of any stationary source of sound in such a manner as to create an operative average sound level which is equal to or greater than 65 dBA, but less than 75 dBA, when measured at any location 100 feet or more from the licensed premises' real property boundary. The Commissioner shall suspend any license for the sale of alcoholic liquors held by any taproom or restaurant and fine any licensee holding such a license if it has reasonable grounds to believe that the licensee has operated, caused the operation of or permitted the operation of any stationary source of sound in such a manner as to create an operative average sound level which is equal to or greater than 75 dBA when measured at any location 100 feet or more from the real property boundary of the licensed premises. For the purpose of this section, "operative average sound level" means the energy average of the A-weighted sound pressure level during the business hours of operation of the licensed premises. The operative average sound level may be determined by an average of not less than 3 individual decibel readings taken not less than 10 minutes apart and taken from the same location. Provided however, that nothing in this subsection shall apply within the boundaries of any municipality.

(h)(1) Notwithstanding any law, regulation, or rule to the contrary, the Commissioner may temporarily suspend any license if the Commissioner has reasonable grounds to believe that the public's safety is at risk and that the licensee has violated the provisions of any of the following:

a. Declaration of State of Emergency Due to Public Health Threat or any State of Emergency's Modification requirements relating to food and drink establishments unless the State of Emergency is no longer in effect.

b. Title 4.

(2) The temporary suspension shall be until the Commissioner no longer has reasonable grounds to believe that the public's safety is at risk, but can be no longer than 20 days unless otherwise provided herein.

(3) At the time of the temporary suspension, the Commissioner shall provide the licensee with notice of a hearing, which shall be held by electronic, telephonic or remote means, within 20 days of the issuance of the temporary suspension.

(4) If a licensee fails to attend such hearing, the Commissioner may continue the temporary suspension. If the temporary suspension is continued, a licensee may request the Commissioner to hold another hearing which shall be provided by electronic, telephone, or remote means within 20 days of the licensee's request.

(5) After a hearing, the Commissioner may do any of the following:

a. Continue the temporary suspension until a public hearing is scheduled in accordance with § 562 of this title if the commissioner believes that the public safety will be at risk if the temporary suspension is lifted.

b. Lift the suspension if the Commissioner believes that lifting the temporary suspension will not result in a risk to public safety.

c. Impose appropriate conditions or fines on the licensee.

d. Take whatever action the Commissioner believes is necessary and appropriate in order to ensure that the public safety will not be at risk by the licensee. Except the Commissioner may not cancel or revoke a license unless pursuant to § 562 of this title.

History.
38 Del. Laws, c. 18, § 29; Code 1935, § 6158; 41 Del. Laws, c. 246, § 1; 4 Del. C. 1953, § 561; 55 Del. Laws, c. 296, § 1; 57 Del. Laws, c. 416; 59 Del. Laws, c. 107, §§ 43-48; 59 Del. Laws, c. 590, § 7; 61 Del. Laws, c. 493, § 1; 67 Del. Laws, c. 109, § 17; 68 Del. Laws, c. 130, § 1; 68 Del. Laws, c. 376, § 2; 70 Del. Laws, c. 186, § 1; 71 Del. Laws, c. 435, §§ 6, 7; 72 Del. Laws, c. 486, § 9; 74 Del. Laws, c. 154, § 1; 75 Del. Laws, c. 417, § 2; 82 Del. Laws, c. 247, §§ 4, 5; 83 Del. Laws, c. 9, § 4.

Revisor's note.
Section 5 of 83 Del. Laws, c. 9, provided: "This act expires on March 31, 2022, unless otherwise extended by a subsequent act of the General Assembly."

Effect of amendments.
83 Del. Laws, c. 9, effective Mar. 23, 2021, rewrote (h). Subsection (h) expired by operation of § 5 of that act, effective Mar. 31, 2022.

§ 561. Grounds for cancellation or suspension [Effective Mar. 31, 2022].

(a) The Commissioner may cancel every license made use of on behalf of any person other than the one to whom or on behalf of whom it has been issued.

(b) The Commissioner may suspend any license and/or fine any licensee for the sale of alcoholic liquors if it has reasonable grounds to believe that the licensee has committed any of the following violations, or may cancel any license for the sale of alcoholic liquors for the following violations, if repeated and continuous:

(1) The licensee has violated any provision of this title or any regulation of the Commissioner pursuant hereto;

(2) The licensee has made any false representation or statement to the Commissioner in order to induce or prevent action by the Commissioner;

(3) The licensee is not maintaining an acceptable bond, if said bond is required;

(4) The licensee is acting as an agent of a manufacturer of alcoholic liquor or has borrowed money or accepted gratuities from such a manufacturer or any agent thereof;

(5) The licensee maintains a noisy, lewd, disorderly, or unsanitary establishment or has been supplying impure or otherwise deleterious beverages or food;

(6) The licensee is in the habit of using dangerous or narcotic drugs, or is in the habit of using alcoholic beverages to excess;

(7) The licensee has sold alcoholic liquor in contravention of § 708 of this title;

(8) The licensee has in the licensee's possession on the licensee's licensed premises or has sold or offered for sale any alcoholic beverages not purchased or sold pursuant to this title;

(9) The licensee has misrepresented any alcoholic liquor sold by the licensee as purchased through the Commissioner or has in the licensee's possession, or has used any wrappers, labels, corks, caps, stamps or bottles not purchased from or through the Commissioner which are deceptively similar to those used by the Commissioner;

(10) The licensee has since the granting of the licensee's license been convicted of a felony or has been convicted of violating any of the liquor laws of this State, general or local, including the provisions of this title;

(11) The licensee has admitted guilt or has been adjudged guilty of violations of local, municipal, county or State regulations, ordinances or codes related to the operation of a licensed premises;

(12) There is any other reason which in the opinion of the Commissioner based on public convenience or necessity warrants cancelling or suspending the license;

(13) The licensee or a representative thereof has disciplined, threatened or otherwise penalized any person for refusing to violate or aiding the enforcement of the provisions of this title or the rules of the Commissioner.

(c) The Commissioner shall not cancel or suspend any license for the sale of alcoholic liquors or impose any fine for an alleged violation of § 708 or § 904 of this title where the licensee or its employee has made a reasonable effort to determine the age of a purchaser of alcoholic liquors. For purposes of this subsection, a licensee or its employee shall be deemed to have made a reasonable effort to determine the age of a purchaser if, prior to any sale of alcoholic liquors, the licensee or its employee requires the purchaser to display identification, with a photograph of the purchaser thereon affixed, which sets forth information that would lead a reasonable man to believe the purchaser to be 21 years of age or older.

(d) Any of the grounds for refusal of a license as provided for in § 543 of this title shall also be adequate grounds for suspension of a license.

(e) The Commissioner may cancel any retail license if it has reasonable grounds to believe that the license was granted in violation of § 546(b) of this title, or any rule enacted pursuant to § 546(d) of this title.

(f) If the Commissioner receives notice from the appropriate political subdivision that any Certificate of Compliance issued to satisfy an applicant's duty under § 543(g) of this title has been suspended, then the Commissioner shall suspend any license or extension of an existing license granted in reliance on such Certificate of Compliance until such time as the Commissioner receives notice from the appropriate political subdivision that such Certificate has been reinstated. If the Commissioner receives notice from the appropriate political subdivision that any Certificate of Compliance issued to satisfy an applicant's duty under § 543(g) of this title has been canceled, then the Commissioner shall revoke any license or extension of an existing license granted in reliance on such Certificate of Compliance.

(g) The Commissioner may suspend any license for the sale of alcoholic liquors held by any taproom or restaurant or fine any licensee holding such a license if it has reasonable grounds to believe that the licensee has operated, caused the operation of or permitted the operation of any stationary source of sound in such a manner as to create an operative average sound level which is equal to or greater than 65 dBA, but less than 75 dBA, when measured at any location 100 feet or more from the licensed premises' real property boundary. The Commissioner shall suspend any license for the sale of alcoholic liquors held by any taproom or restaurant and fine any licensee holding such a license if it has reasonable grounds to believe that the licensee has operated, caused the operation of or permitted the operation of any stationary source of sound in such a manner as to create an operative average sound level which is equal to or greater than 75 dBA when measured at any location 100 feet or more from the real property boundary of the licensed premises. For the purpose of this section, "operative average sound level" means the energy average of the A-weighted sound pressure level during the business hours of operation of the licensed premises. The operative average sound level may be determined by an average of not less than 3 individual decibel readings taken not less than 10 minutes apart and taken from the same location. Provided however, that nothing in this subsection shall apply within the boundaries of any municipality.

(h) [Repealed.]

History.
  38 Del. Laws, c. 18, § 29; Code 1935, § 6158; 41 Del. Laws, c. 246, § 1; 4 Del. C. 1953, § 561; 55 Del. Laws, c. 296, § 1; 57 Del. Laws, c. 416; 59 Del. Laws, c. 107, §§ 43-48; 59 Del. Laws, c. 590, § 7; 61 Del. Laws, c. 493, § 1; 67 Del. Laws, c. 109, § 17; 68 Del. Laws, c. 130, § 1; 68 Del. Laws, c. 376, § 2; 70 Del. Laws, c. 186, § 1; 71 Del. Laws, c. 435, §§ 6, 7; 72 Del. Laws, c. 486, § 9; 74 Del. Laws, c. 154, § 1; 75 Del. Laws, c. 417, § 2; 82 Del. Laws, c. 247, §§ 4, 5; 83 Del. Laws, c. 9, § 4; 83 Del. Laws, c. 9, § 5.

Revisor's note.
  Section 5 of 83 Del. Laws, c. 9, provided: "This act expires on March 31, 2022, unless otherwise extended by a subsequent act of the General Assembly."

Effect of amendments.
  83 Del. Laws, c. 9, effective Mar. 23, 2021, rewrote (h). Subsection (h) expired by operation of § 5 of that act, effective Mar. 31, 2022.

§ 562. Public hearing and right of appeal [Effective until Mar. 31, 2022].

(a) No license shall be cancelled or suspended, or any licensee fined:

(1) Until the licensee has been given a public hearing by the Commissioner at which time the licensee shall be entitled to legal representation and to present witnesses; and

(2) Unless the ground therefor shall be established by clear and convincing evidence.

A full and complete record shall be kept of all proceedings incident to such hearing. All testimony shall be recorded but need not be transcribed unless an order of the Commissioner is appealed to the Superior Court as set forth in subsection (c) of this section.

(b) Any order of the Commissioner relative to suspension or cancellation of a license, or a fine imposed against a licensee shall become final 10 days after the licensee receives notice thereof, unless within 10 days of the date of the postmark on the Commissioner's decision a written appeal is filed in the Superior Court. No bond shall be required for filing such appeal.

(c) The appeal shall state the grounds upon which a review is sought. After the appeal is filed, service shall be made by the Sheriff upon the Commissioner. The Commissioner shall certify and file with the court all documents and papers and a transcript of all testimony taken in the matter, together with the Commissioner's findings therein as soon as practicable but in no event later than 20 calendar days from the date of service of the appeal. The Superior Court's review of an appeal shall be on the record and the Superior Court shall take into account the experience and specialized competence of the agency and the purpose under which the agency acted. Further, the Superior Court's review, in the absence of fraud, shall be limited to whether the agency's decision is supported by substantial evidence on the record and is free from legal error.

(d) An appeal without bond may be taken from the decision of the Superior Court to the Supreme Court of this State in the same manner as is provided in civil cases. Upon the final determination of judicial proceedings, the Commissioner shall enter an order in accordance with such determination, or shall take such further or other action as the Court may order. A petition for judicial review shall act as a supersedeas.

(e) The public hearing required in subsection (a) of this section may be by electronic, telephone, or remote means.

History.
38 Del. Laws, c. 18, § 29; Code 1935, § 6158; 47 Del. Laws, c. 119, § 1; 4 Del. C. 1953, § 562; 55 Del. Laws, c. 296, § 2; 59 Del. Laws, c. 107, §§ 49, 50; 72 Del. Laws, c. 486, §§ 9, 19, 20; 78 Del. Laws, c. 384, § 3; 82 Del. Laws, c. 247, §§ 4, 5; 83 Del. Laws, c. 9, § 4.

Revisor's note.
Section 5 of 83 Del. Laws, c. 9, provided:

"This act expires on March 31, 2022, unless otherwise extended by a subsequent act of the General Assembly."

Effect of amendments.
82 Del. Laws, c. 247, effective July 16, 2020, added (e). The amendment expired Mar. 31, 2022, by operation of § 5 of that act, as amended by 83 Del. Laws, c. 9, §§ 4 and 5, effective Mar. 23, 2021.

§ 562. Public hearing and right of appeal [Effective Mar. 31, 2022].

(a) No license shall be cancelled or suspended, or any licensee fined:

(1) Until the licensee has been given a public hearing by the Commissioner at which time the licensee shall be entitled to legal representation and to present witnesses; and

(2) Unless the ground therefor shall be established by clear and convincing evidence.

A full and complete record shall be kept of all proceedings incident to such hearing. All testimony shall be recorded but need not be transcribed unless an order of the Commissioner is appealed to the Superior Court as set forth in subsection (c) of this section.

(b) Any order of the Commissioner relative to suspension or cancellation of a license, or a fine imposed against a licensee shall become final 10 days after the licensee receives notice thereof, unless within 10 days of the date of the postmark on the Commissioner's decision a written appeal is filed in the Superior Court. No bond shall be required for filing such appeal.

(c) The appeal shall state the grounds upon which a review is sought. After the appeal is filed, service shall be made by the Sheriff upon the Commissioner. The Commissioner shall certify and file with the court all documents and papers and a transcript of all testimony taken in the matter, together with the Commissioner's findings therein as soon as practicable but in no event later than 20 calendar days from the date of service of the appeal. The Superior Court's review of an appeal shall be on the record and the Superior Court shall take into account the experience and specialized competence of the agency and the purpose under which the agency acted. Further, the Superior Court's review, in the absence of fraud, shall be limited to whether the agency's decision is supported by substantial evidence on the record and is free from legal error.

(d) An appeal without bond may be taken from the decision of the Superior Court to the Supreme Court of this State in the same manner as is provided in civil cases. Upon the final determination of judicial proceedings, the Commissioner shall enter an order in accordance with such determination, or shall take such further or other action as the Court may order. A petition for judicial review shall act as a supersedeas.

(e) [Repealed.]

History.
38 Del. Laws, c. 18, § 29; Code 1935, § 6158; 47 Del. Laws, c. 119, § 1; 4 Del. C. 1953, § 562; 55 Del. Laws, c. 296, § 2; 59 Del. Laws, c. 107, §§ 49, 50; 72 Del. Laws, c. 486, §§ 9, 19, 20; 78 Del. Laws, c. 384, § 3; 82 Del. Laws, c. 247, §§ 4, 5; 83 Del. Laws, c. 9, § 4; 83 Del. Laws, c. 9, § 5.

Revisor's note.
Section 5 of 83 Del. Laws, c. 9, provided:

"This act expires on March 31, 2022, unless otherwise extended by a subsequent act of the General Assembly."

Effect of amendments.
82 Del. Laws, c. 247, effective July 16, 2020, added (e). The amendment expired Mar. 31, 2022, by operation of § 5 of that act, as amended by 83 Del. Laws, c. 9, §§ 4 and 5, effective Mar. 23, 2021.

SUBCHAPTER VII

TAXES

§ 581. Rates of tax [For application of this section, see 81 Del. Laws, c. 54, § 2].

(a) All persons required to be licensed under this title as an importer shall pay a tax upon the sale of alcoholic beverages to any person who purchases alcohol from an importer in this State at the rates set forth in subsection (d) of this section.

(b) All persons licensed under this title to manufacture alcoholic beverages shall pay a tax on all alcoholic beverages sold to customers in this State at the rates set forth in subsection (d) of this section. This subsection shall not apply to sales to customers who are:

(1) Importers of alcoholic beverages subject to licensing under this title;

(2) Distributors of alcoholic beverages licensed by a state other than Delaware where the alcoholic beverages are sold for resale in such other state; or

(3) In the case of sales of beer, an instrumentality of the United States Armed Forces.

(c) Except as provided in subsection (a) or (b) of this section, any person who imports alcoholic beverages for consumption in this State shall pay to the Department of Finance the tax on such imports at the rates set forth in subsection (d) of this section.

(d) The tax payable under this section shall be as follows:

(1) For each barrel of beer or fermented beverage, $8.15.

(2) For each gallon of cider, $.27.

(3) For each gallon of wine, $1.63.

(4) For each gallon of spirits containing 25 % or less of ethyl alcohol by volume, $3.00.

(5) For each gallon of spirits containing more than 25 % ethyl alcohol by volume, $4.50.

(6) For each gallon of alcohol per gallon of ethyl alcohol contained, $8.15, except that the tax of $8.15 shall not apply to the purchase of alcohol by pharmacists, physicians, dentists, veterinarians, wholesale druggists or manufacturing plants where the alcohol is used in scientific work, for the manufacture of pharmaceutical products, or for use in the manufacture or compounding of preparations unfit for beverage purposes.

(e) The Commissioner shall make and publish such rules and regulations with respect to the collection and payment of the taxes imposed by this section as it deems proper, and all such rules and regulations that are not inconsistent with the provisions of this title shall have the force and effect of law.

(f) For the months of August 2019 and July 2020, all persons required to be licensed under this title as an importer shall be entitled to a nonrefundable credit against the tax on alcoholic beverages imposed pursuant to subsection (a) of this section in an amount equal to ½ of the tax previously paid on such importer's alcoholic liquor floor stock or inventory resting in the State on July 31, 2019, as reported in accordance with commission rules. Any amounts of credit not used by virtue of the preceding sentence may be carried forward and used against future tax imposed by this section. A person required to be licensed under this title as an importer shall not be entitled to the credit permitted pursuant to this subsection if such person fails to report such person's alcoholic liquor floor stock or inventory resting in the State on July 31, 2019, on a timely-filed report.

History.

38 Del. Laws, c. 18, § 16; Code 1935, § 6145; 43 Del. Laws, c. 274, § 1; 4 Del. C. 1953, § 581; 49 Del. Laws, c. 342, § 13; 53 Del. Laws, c. 106; 57 Del. Laws, c. 136, § 30; 57 Del. Laws, c. 741, § 27C; 58 Del. Laws, c. 294, §§ 1, 2; 58 Del. Laws, c. 584, § 1; 62 Del. Laws, c. 113, § 1; 67 Del. Laws, c. 258, § 1; 68 Del. Laws, c. 107, §§ 3, 4; 70 Del. Laws, c. 488, §§ 1, 2, 5; 70 Del. Laws, c. 559, §§ 5, 6; 71 Del. Laws, c. 211, § 5; 72 Del. Laws, c. 486, § 9; 78 Del. Laws, c. 251, § 3; 81 Del. Laws, c. 54, § 1; 82 Del. Laws, c. 68, § 1; 83 Del. Laws, c. 36, § 4.

Effect of amendments.

83 Del. Laws, c. 36, effective June 3, 2021, added "or fermented beverage" in (d)(1).

CHAPTER 7
REGULATORY PROVISIONS

§ 709. Prohibition of sales and delivery at certain times [Effective until meeting the contingency in 82 Del. Laws, c. 193, § 5].

(a) No entity licensed pursuant to § 501 of this title or importer shall sell or deliver alcoholic liquor on Sundays, Thanksgiving, Easter or Christmas or at hours other than those prescribed by the rules or regulations of the Commissioner, except as subsection (f) of this section may apply. An importer may receive and process orders on any day, including Sundays and holidays.

(b) No holder of a license for the sale of alcoholic liquors for off-premises consumption shall sell or deliver the same on Thanksgiving, Easter or Christmas or between the hours of 1:00 a.m. and 9:00 a.m. on Mondays through Saturdays, except as subsection (f) of this section may apply, and on Sundays before 10:00 a.m. or after 8:00 p.m. Any municipality with a population of 50,000 or more may limit sales within the boundaries of the municipality pursuant to this subsection to a maximum of 4 hours on Sundays as established by ordinance of the municipality. The closing hours for days of the week other than Sunday may be made earlier in any municipality having a population of 50,000 or more persons, by ordinance of the municipal corporation; provided however, that such ordinance be consistent with the Delaware state and federal constitutions as well as treat all businesses fairly. During the months of October through December a holder of a license for the sale of alcoholic liquor for off-premises consumption shall be permitted to have sales take place beginning at 8:00 a.m. on Fridays through Saturdays.

(c) No holder of a license for the sale of alcoholic liquor for on-premises consumption shall sell the same between the hours of 1:00 a.m. and 9:00 a.m. The closing hour may be made earlier in any municipality by ordinance of the municipal corporation. The sale of alcoholic liquors by a licensee for consumption on the premises where sold shall be permitted on every day of the year; provided, that no licensee shall be required to be open to sell alcoholic liquors on Sundays, Thanksgiving, Easter or Christmas.

(d) Any holder of a license to sell alcoholic liquor, for either on-premises consumption or off-premises consumption, who wishes to sell alcoholic liquors on Sundays, except a gathering license, shall pay a biennial license fee of $500 for the issuance of a special license to serve alcoholic liquors on Sundays, which shall be in addition to any other license fees which may be required of the licensee. If a licensee holds a license to sell for on-premises consumption and off-premises consumption it shall only be required to purchase 1 special license if it wishes to serve alcoholic liquors on Sunday.

(e) In the municipalities and other political subdivisions of this State where daylight saving time is observed, whether authorized by law or by custom, daylight saving time shall apply to the hours mentioned in this section for the period during which daylight saving time exists.

(f) Importers or holders of a license for the sale of spirits, wines or beer may deliver beer on Sundays in motor vehicles equipped with permanently-installed devices for the refrigeration and dispensing of beer to licensed gatherings only; provided, however, that such licensee shall have first given notice of such delivery to the Commissioner.

(g), (h) [Repealed.]

History.
38 Del. Laws, c. 18, § 33; Code 1935, § 6162; 42 Del. Laws, c. 194, § 1; 43 Del. Laws, c. 277, § 1; 45 Del. Laws, c. 260, § 1; 45 Del. Laws, c. 265, § 1; 4 Del. C. 1953, § 717; 55 Del. Laws, c. 311, § 1; 56 Del. Laws, c. 265, § 1; 57 Del. Laws, c. 352, §§ 1, 2; 58 Del. Laws, c. 146, § 1; 59 Del. Laws, c. 107, §§ 57, 58; 59 Del. Laws, c. 115, § 1; 60 Del. Laws, c. 466, §§ 7, 8; 62 Del. Laws, c. 381, §§ 1-3; 65 Del. Laws, c. 156, § 1; 67 Del. Laws, c. 109, §§ 19, 21; 68 Del. Laws, c. 107, § 5; 69 Del. Laws, c. 6, § 5; 69 Del. Laws, c. 384, §§ 1, 2; 70 Del. Laws, c. 186, § 1; 70 Del. Laws, c. 248, § 1; 71 Del. Laws, c. 109, § 1; 72 Del. Laws, c. 486, § 11; 73 Del. Laws, c. 244, § 10; 74 Del. Laws, c. 29, § 1; 74 Del. Laws, c. 141, §§ 1-3; 74 Del. Laws, c. 146, § 1; 74 Del. Laws, c. 202, § 1; 74 Del. Laws, c. 259, §§ 1, 2; 76 Del. Laws, c. 237, §§ 1-3; 77 Del. Laws, c. 72, § 3; 80 Del. Laws, c. 62, § 1; 80 Del. Laws, c. 382, § 1; 81 Del. Laws, c. 62, § 1; 83 Del. Laws, c. 108, § 1.

Effect of amendments.
83 Del. Laws, c. 108, effective July 30, 2021, added "and delivery" in the section heading; and added the final sentence in (a).

§ 709. Prohibition of sales and delivery at certain times [Effective upon meeting the contingency in 82 Del. Laws, c. 193, § 5].

(a) No entity licensed pursuant to § 501 of this title or importer shall sell or deliver alcoholic liquor on Sundays, Thanksgiving, Easter or Christmas or at hours other than those prescribed by the rules or regulations of the Commissioner, except as subsection (f) of this section may apply. An importer may receive and process orders on any day, including Sundays and holidays.

(b) No holder of a license for the sale of alcoholic liquors for off-premises consumption shall sell or deliver the same on Thanksgiving, Easter or Christmas or between the hours of 1:00 a.m. and 9:00 a.m. on Mondays through Saturdays, except as subsection (f) of this section may apply, and on Sundays before 10:00 a.m. or after 8:00 p.m. Any municipality with a population of 50,000 or more may limit sales within the boundaries of the municipality pursuant to this subsection to a maximum of 4 hours on Sundays as established by ordinance of the municipality. The closing hours for days of the week other than Sunday may be made earlier in any municipality having a population of 50,000 or more persons, by ordinance of the municipal corporation; provided however, that such ordinance be consistent with the Delaware state and federal constitutions as well as treat all businesses fairly. During the months of October through December a holder of a license for the sale of alcoholic liquor for off-premises consumption shall be permitted to have sales take place beginning at 8:00 a.m. on Fridays through Saturdays.

(c) No holder of a license for the sale of alcoholic liquor for on-premises consumption shall sell the same between the hours of 1:00 a.m. and 9:00 a.m. The closing hour may be made earlier in any municipality by ordinance of the municipal corporation. The sale of alcoholic liquors by a licensee for consumption on the premises where sold shall be permitted on every day of the year;

provided, that no licensee shall be required to be open to sell alcoholic liquors on Sundays, Thanksgiving, Easter or Christmas.

(d) Any holder of a license to sell alcoholic liquor, for either on-premises consumption or off-premises consumption, who wishes to sell alcoholic liquors on Sundays, except a gathering license, shall pay a biennial license fee of $500 for the issuance of a special license to serve alcoholic liquors on Sundays, which shall be in addition to any other license fees which may be required of the licensee. If a licensee holds a license to sell for on-premises consumption and off-premises consumption it shall only be required to purchase 1 special license if it wishes to serve alcoholic liquors on Sunday.

(e) [Repealed.]

(f) Importers or holders of a license for the sale of spirits, wines or beer may deliver beer on Sundays in motor vehicles equipped with permanently-installed devices for the refrigeration and dispensing of beer to licensed gatherings only; provided, however, that such licensee shall have first given notice of such delivery to the Commissioner.

(g), (h) [Repealed.]

History.

38 Del. Laws, c. 18, § 33; Code 1935, § 6162; 42 Del. Laws, c. 194, § 1; 43 Del. Laws, c. 277, § 1; 45 Del. Laws, c. 260, § 1; 45 Del. Laws, c. 265, § 1; 4 Del. C. 1953, § 717; 55 Del. Laws, c. 311, § 1; 56 Del. Laws, c. 265, § 1; 57 Del. Laws, c. 352, §§ 1, 2; 58 Del. Laws, c. 146, § 1; 59 Del. Laws, c. 107, §§ 57, 58; 59 Del. Laws, c. 115, § 1; 60 Del. Laws, c. 466, §§ 7, 8; 62 Del. Laws, c. 381, §§ 1-3; 65 Del. Laws, c. 156, § 1; 67 Del. Laws, c. 109, §§ 19, 21; 68 Del. Laws, c. 107, § 5; 69 Del. Laws, c. 6, § 5; 69 Del. Laws, c. 384, §§ 1, 2; 70 Del. Laws, c. 186, § 1; 70 Del. Laws, c. 248, § 1; 71 Del. Laws, c. 109, § 1; 72 Del. Laws, c. 486, § 11; 73 Del. Laws, c. 244, § 10; 74 Del. Laws, c. 29, § 1; 74 Del. Laws, c. 141, §§ 1-3; 74 Del. Laws, c. 146, § 1; 74 Del. Laws, c. 202, § 1; 74 Del. Laws, c. 259, §§ 1, 2; 76 Del. Laws, c. 237, §§ 1-3; 77 Del. Laws, c. 72, § 3; 80 Del. Laws, c. 62, § 1; 80 Del. Laws, c. 382, § 1; 81 Del. Laws, c. 62, § 1; 83 Del. Laws, c. 108, § 1; 82 Del. Laws, c. 193, §§ 3, 5.

Effect of amendments.

83 Del. Laws, c. 108, effective July 30, 2021, added "and delivery" in the section heading; and added the final sentence in (a).

CHAPTER 9
CRIMINAL OFFENSES AND PENALTIES

Sec.
904. Offenses concerning certain persons.

§ 904. Offenses concerning certain persons.

(a)(1) Whoever sells any alcoholic liquor to any person who has not reached the age of 21 years, or sells to any person of more than such age any alcoholic liquor knowing that such alcoholic liquor is bought for a person who is less than 21 years of age and is to be drunk by the latter, shall, in addition to the payment of costs, be fined not less than $250 nor more than $500 and, on failure to pay such fine and costs, shall be imprisoned for 30 days.

(2) In any prosecution for an offense under this subsection, it shall be an affirmative defense that the individual, who has not reached the age of 21 years, presented to the accused identification, with a photograph of such individual affixed thereon, which identification sets forth information which would lead a reasonable person to believe such individual was 21 years of age or older.

(b) Any person under the age of 21 years who knowingly makes false statement to any person engaged in the sale of alcoholic liquor for the purpose of obtaining the same and to the effect that he is 21 years of age or older, shall, in addition to the payment of costs, be fined for the first offense, not less than $100 nor more than $500, and on failure to pay such fine and costs, shall be imprisoned for 30 days, and for each subsequent like offense, shall be fined not less than $500 nor more than $1,000, and on failure to pay such fine and costs shall be imprisoned for 60 days.

(c) Whoever purchases, buys or gives alcoholic liquor for or to a person under the age of 21 years or knowingly allows a person under his or her supervision and under the age of 21 years to consume alcoholic liquor shall, in addition to the payment of costs, be fined for the first offense, not less than $100 nor more than $500, and may be ordered by the court to perform community service for a period of 40 hours in such form and on such terms as the court shall deem appropriate under the circumstances and may be imprisoned for not more than 30 days; and for each subsequent like offense, shall be fined not less than $500 nor more than $1,000 and may be ordered by the court to perform community service for a period of 80 hours in such form and on such terms as the court shall deem appropriate under the circumstances and may be imprisoned for not more than 60 days. This subsection shall not apply to religious services or members of the same family within the private home of any of said members.

(d) Except as provided in subsection (n) of this section, whoever, being the holder of a license to operate a tavern or taproom, admits or permits to remain in such tavern or taproom any individual under the age of 21 years, shall be fined not more than $100.

(e) Except as provided in subsection (n) of this section, whoever, being under the age of 21 years, enters or remains in a tavern, taproom or package store, or while therein possesses at any time alcoholic liquors, shall be fined $50.

(f)(1) Whoever, being under the age of 21 years, has alcoholic liquor in his or her possession at any time, or consumes or is found to have consumed alcoholic liquor, shall be fined $100 for the first violation and not less than $200 nor more than $500 for each subsequent violation.

(2) Notwithstanding paragraph (f)(1) of this section, whoever commits a violation of this subsection must be assessed a civil penalty for a first violation or a second violation. Information concerning this civil offense may not appear on an individual's certified criminal record.

(3) Whoever commits a third or subsequent violation of this subsection is guilty of an unclassified misdemeanor.

(4) This section does not apply to the possession or consumption of alcoholic liquor in connection with any religious service or by members of the same family within the private home of any of said members.

(5) A peace officer having reasonable grounds to believe that a juvenile has committed an offense under this subsection may issue the juvenile a civil citation in lieu of a civil penalty.

(g) Nothing in this section shall prevent the employment of a person, 16 years of age or older, in clubs with authorized dining facilities, hotels, racetracks and restaurants licensed under this title where such employment has been authorized by permit issued by the Commission, provided that such a person shall not be involved in the sale or service of alcoholic liquor.

(h) Nothing in this section shall prevent the employment of a person 18 years of age or older to serve alcoholic liquor to patrons of establishments licensed under this title for the on-premises sale and consumption of alcoholic liquor, excepting taverns and taprooms.

(i) Nothing in this section shall prevent the employment of a person, 16 years of age or older, in a catering business serving liquors, provided that such person shall not be engaged in the sale or service of alcoholic liquor.

(j) Nothing in this section shall prevent the employment of a person, 16 years of age or older, in a bowling alley licensed to serve alcoholic beverages, provided that such person shall not be engaged in the sale or service of alcoholic liquor.

(k) Justices of the peace shall have original jurisdiction to hear, try, and finally determine alleged violations of this section.

(*l*) Nothing in this section shall prevent a licensed importer from employing a person who is 18, 19 or 20 years of age to:

(1) Work in an office, warehouse or other facility used by the importer in the operation of its business;

(2) Make or assist in deliveries of alcoholic liquors to licensed establishments in this State;

(3) Transport or assist in the transporting of alcoholic liquors to or from the importer's warehouse.

Such person may enter any licensed establishment in this State for the purpose of making or assisting the delivery of alcoholic liquors thereto or for any purpose related to such delivery.

No such person shall be employed by a licensed importer as a salesperson or sales representative.

(m) Nothing in this section shall prevent the employment in a store by a retailer of anyone who has reached the age of 18 years, under such conditions as the Commission may by rule prescribe; provided, however, that no such minor shall sell or serve alcoholic liquors.

(n) Nothing in this section shall prohibit or prevent persons under the age of 21 years from entering or remaining in a premises licensed as a tavern or taproom for the purpose of a social event, including, but not limited to, events exclusively for persons under the age of 21 years, provided that the premises licensed as a taproom or tavern is closed for business (including any Sunday); and provided further, that during any such social event, no alcoholic liquor shall be sold, furnished or given to any person at any time before, during or after the social event. All alcoholic liquor must be either removed from the licensed premises or placed under lock and key at all times during the social event and any time before or after the social event when persons under the age of 21 years are present on the licensed premises.

(o) Any person who was convicted of a first offense under subsections (e) and (f) of this section or the same offense under any county or municipal code, ordinance, or regulation and who was under the age of 21 at the time of the offense may, upon reaching the age of 21, apply for an expungement of the record of the conviction and any indicia of arrest to the court in which the person was convicted. For violations of subsection (e) or (f) of this section, an order granting such expungement shall issue upon proof that the person has reached the age of 21, unless the person has failed to comply with the sentencing order or the person has another charge under this section, or under the same offense under any county or municipal code, ordinance, or regulation, which remains outstanding. Upon issuance of the order of expungement, the records of the conviction and any indicia of arrest shall be dealt with in accordance with the procedures specified in subchapter VII of Chapter 43 of Title 11. Nothing in this section prohibits the Family Court from expunging a record of conviction as otherwise provided by law. The application for or granting of a pardon under §§ 4361 through 4364 of Title 11 does not prohibit an expungement under this section. All sentencing orders for violations of this section by persons under the age of 21 at the time of the offense shall state that the record of the conviction may be expunged upon reaching the age of 21 and thereafter. The civil filing fee shall apply to applications for expungement plus a $100 fee payable to the State Bureau of Identification for administrative costs.

(p) [Expired.]

History.

38 Del. Laws, c. 18, §§ 46, 50; Code 1935, §§ 6174, 6178; 41 Del. Laws, c. 253, §§ 1, 2; 45 Del. Laws, c. 263, § 1; 47 Del. Laws, c. 150, § 1; 4 Del. C. 1953, § 904; 53 Del. Laws, c. 390, §§ 1, 2; 54 Del. Laws, c. 295; 55 Del. Laws, c. 300; 55 Del. Laws, c. 335; 58 Del. Laws, c. 201; 58 Del. Laws, c. 239, § 46; 58 Del. Laws, c. 511, §§ 2-7; 59 Del. Laws, c. 234, § 1; 59 Del. Laws, c. 297, §§ 1-3; 61 Del. Laws, c. 448, § 1; 61 Del. Laws, c. 493, § 3; 61 Del. Laws, c. 511, §§ 1-3; 63 Del. Laws, c. 95, § 1; 64 Del. Laws, c. 216, §§ 3, 4; 64 Del. Laws, c. 435, § 1; 67 Del. Laws, c. 425, § 1; 68 Del. Laws, c. 242, § 1; 70 Del. Laws, c. 123, § 1; 70 Del. Laws, c. 186, § 1; 70 Del. Laws, c. 558, §§ 1-3; 72 Del. Laws, c. 134, § 1; 72 Del. Laws, c. 348, § 1; 72 Del. Laws, c. 349, § 1; 72 Del. Laws, c. 350, § 1; 74 Del. Laws, c. 237, §§ 1, 2; 75 Del. Laws, c. 255, § 2; 75 Del. Laws, c. 265, § 1; 81 Del. Laws, c. 338, § 1; 82 Del. Laws, c. 83, § 11; 82 Del. Laws, c. 143, § 1; 83 Del. Laws, c. 37, § 2; 83 Del. Laws, c. 198, § 1.

Effect of amendments.

83 Del. Laws, c. 37, effective June 3, 2021, rewrote (f).

83 Del. Laws, c. 198, effective Sept. 17, 2021, added (f)(5).

TITLE 5
BANKING
PART IV
OTHER BUSINESSES UNDER JURISDICTION OF STATE BANKING DEPARTMENT

CHAPTER 22
LICENSED LENDERS
SUBCHAPTER I
LICENSING

§ 2202. License required.

RESEARCH REFERENCES AND PRACTICE AIDS

Delaware Law Reviews.
First State or Follower?: Marijuana in Delaware, 26 Widener L. Rev. 21 (2020).

TITLE 6
COMMERCE AND TRADE

Subtitle
II. Other Laws Relating to Commerce and Trade

SUBTITLE I
UNIFORM COMMERCIAL CODE
ARTICLE 2
SALES
PART 7
REMEDIES

§ 2-725. Statute of limitations in contracts for sale.

NOTES TO DECISIONS

Analysis

Time limitations.
— Expiration.

Time limitations.

— Expiration.

Plaintiff's breach of warranty claim was time-barred because the claim accrued on the date of plaintiff's pelvic mesh implantation surgery on September 12, 2012, while the 4-year statute of limitations expired on September 12, 2016; plaintiff had filed suit on October 23, 2020. Hagan v. Boston Sci. Corp., 2021 Del. Super. LEXIS 397 (Del. Super. Ct. May 12, 2021).

In plaintiff's product liability action, alleging injuries after receiving surgery to implant a pelvic mesh device manufactured by defendant, the claims were time-barred by the statute of limitations under 6 Del. C. § 2-725 and Iowa Code Ann. § 614.1(4) because: (1) plaintiff waited more than 5 years to bring the action; (2) plaintiff's personal injury claims accrued in either 2005 (following the first revision surgery) or in 2008 (following a public notice of defects associated with pelvic mesh devices issues by FDA); and (3) as a result, the statute of limitations in 10 Del. C. § 8119 expired before the lawsuit was filed in 2020. Bredberg v. Boston Sci. Corp., 2021 Del. Super. LEXIS 449 (Del. Super. Ct. June 2, 2021).

SUBTITLE II

OTHER LAWS RELATING TO COMMERCE AND TRADE

CHAPTER 12A

UNIFORM ELECTRONIC TRANSACTIONS ACT

§ 12A-103. Scope.

(a) Except as otherwise provided in subsection (b) of this section, this chapter applies to electronic records and electronic signatures relating to a transaction.

(b) This chapter does not apply to a transaction to the extent it is governed by:

(1) A law governing the creation and execution of wills or codicils;

(2) The Uniform Commercial Code other than Sections 1-107 [see now Section 1-306] and 1-206 [former version of Section 1-206, to which this reference referred, has been repealed], Article 2, and Article 2A;

(3) The Uniform Computer Information Transactions Act;

(4) The General Corporation Law of the State [§§ 101 to 398 of Title 8], the Delaware Professional Service Corporation Act [§ 601 et seq. of Title 8], the Delaware Revised Uniform Partnership Act [§ 15-101 et seq. of this title], the Delaware Revised Uniform Limited Partnership Act [§ 17-101 et seq. of this title], the Delaware Limited Liability Company Act [§ 18-101 et seq. of this title], the Delaware Uniform Partnership Law and the Delaware Statutory Trust Act [§ 3801 et seq. of Title 12];

(5) The Corporation Law for State Banks and Trust Companies, Credit Card Institutions and the Corporation Law for State Savings Banks in Chapters 7, 15 and 16, respectively, of Title 5.

(c) This chapter applies to an electronic record or electronic signature otherwise excluded from the application of this chapter under subsection (b) of this section to the extent it is governed by a law other than those specified in subsection (b) of this section.

(d) A transaction subject to this chapter is also subject to other applicable substantive law.

History.

72 Del. Laws, c. 457, § 1; 73 Del. Laws, c. 329, § 9; 83 Del. Laws, c. 69, § 1.

Effect of amendments.

83 Del. Laws, c. 69, effective June 30, 2021, substituted "or codicils" for "codicils, or testamentary trusts" in (b)(1).

CHAPTER 13

FRAUDULENT TRANSFERS

§ 1301. Definitions.

NOTES TO DECISIONS

Claims.

In a breach of contract and fraud case brought by a banking administrative agent against a loan obligation portfolio, the fraudulent transfer claim survived dismissal because: (1) plaintiff properly pleaded a transfer of funds; (2) plaintiff sufficiently alleged the port-folio was insolvent; and (3) sufficient constructive fraudulent transfer elements were also alleged, including insolvency and that the portfolio had not received fair consideration for the transfers. CIBC Bank USA v. JH Portfolio Debt Equities, LLC, — A.3d —, 2021 Del. Super. LEXIS 451 (Del. Super. Ct. June 2, 2021).

§ 1302. Insolvency.

NOTES TO DECISIONS

Analysis

Payment.
— Debts.

Payment.

— Debts.

In a breach of contract and fraud case brought by a banking administrative agent against a loan obligation portfolio, the fraudulent transfer claim survived dismissal because: (1) plaintiff properly pleaded a transfer of funds; (2) plaintiff sufficiently alleged the port-folio was insolvent; and (3) sufficient constructive fraudulent transfer elements were also alleged, including insolvency and that the portfolio had not received fair consideration for the transfers. CIBC Bank USA v. JH Portfolio Debt Equities, LLC, — A.3d —, 2021 Del. Super. LEXIS 451 (Del. Super. Ct. June 2, 2021).

§ 1304. Transfers fraudulent as to present and future creditors.

NOTES TO DECISIONS

Analysis

Pleadings.
— Sufficiency.

Pleadings.

— Sufficiency.

Defendants were entitled to dismissal of Chapter 7 bankruptcy trustee's constructive fraud claims under Delaware's Uniform Fraudulent Transfer Act (6 Del. C. § 1301 et seq.) for failure to state a claim because the trustee did not adequately allege lack of reasonably equivalent value; however, other constructive fraud claims survived because the trustee did not fail to plead lack of reasonably equivalent value and debtors' insolvency for those claims. Miller v. Fallas (In re J & M Sales, Inc.), — B.R. —, 2021 Bankr. LEXIS 2268 (Bankr. D. Del. Aug. 20, 2021).

Defendants were entitled to dismissal of Chapter 7 bankruptcy trustee's actual fraud claims under Delaware's Uniform Fraudulent Transfer Act (6 Del. C. § 1301 et seq.) and 11 U.S.C. § 548; the facts alleged were insufficient to support the conclusion that an acquisition and subsequent payments were intended to hinder, delay or defraud the debtors' creditors. Miller v. Fallas (In re J & M Sales, Inc.), — B.R. —, 2021 Bankr. LEXIS 2268 (Bankr. D. Del. Aug. 20, 2021).

§ 1305. Transfers fraudulent as to present creditors.

NOTES TO DECISIONS

Analysis

Pleadings.
— Sufficiency.

Pleadings.

— Sufficiency.

In a breach of contract and fraud case brought by a banking administrative agent against a loan obligation portfolio, the fraudulent transfer claim survived dismissal because: (1) plaintiff properly pleaded a transfer of funds; (2) plaintiff sufficiently alleged the port-folio was insolvent; and (3) sufficient constructive fraudulent transfer elements were also alleged, including insolvency and that the portfolio had not received fair consideration for the transfers. CIBC Bank USA v. JH Portfolio Debt Equities, LLC, — A.3d —, 2021 Del. Super. LEXIS 451 (Del. Super. Ct. June 2, 2021).

§ 1307. Remedies of creditors.

NOTES TO DECISIONS

Analysis

Applicability.
— Insurance.

Applicability.

— Insurance.

Insurer's uninsurability defense was inapplicable under Delaware law because: (1) the investment funds validly nominated Delaware as the jurisdiction of the "law most favorable" to them in their insurance policy's conflict of law provision; (2) under 6 Del. C. § 2708, Delaware law was a presumptively valid, significant, material and reasonable choice of law; and (3) the anti-fraudulent conveyance statute in Delaware (6 Del. C. § 1307) did not render insuring against clawback claims for which restitution or disgorgement might be exacted contrary to state public policy. Sycamore Partners Mgmt., L.P. v. Endurance Am. Ins. Co., — A.3d —, 2021 Del. Super. LEXIS 182 (Del. Super. Ct. Feb. 26, 2021).

§ 1308. Defenses, liability and protection of transferee.

NOTES TO DECISIONS

Avoidance.

Plaintiffs were not entitled to summary judgment on defendant's fraudulent transfer claim because defendant presented evidence creating a material fact in dispute as to whether plaintiff A was insolvent when it transferred certain assets, namely: a statement by the court in an opinion; a statement by the creditor in defendant's request for admissions; plaintiff A's consideration of bankruptcy; plaintiff A's financial statements; and plaintiff A's inability to pay its obligations. Humanigen, Inc. v. Savant Neglected Diseases, LLC, — A.3d —, 2021 Del. Super. LEXIS 503 (Del. Super. Ct. July 9, 2021).

Creditor was entitled to summary judgment on defendant's fraudulent transfer claim because: (1) the creditor had not received any benefit; (2) the spoils from future judgments were far from certain and not quantifiable; and (3) the creditor was not a beneficiary. Humanigen, Inc. v. Savant Neglected Diseases, LLC, — A.3d —, 2021 Del. Super. LEXIS 503 (Del. Super. Ct. July 9, 2021).

§ 1309. Extinguishment of cause of action.

NOTES TO DECISIONS

Time limitations.

Several of the funds' constructive fraudulent transfer claims were timely so long as 1 of their creditors was entitled, as of the petition date, to assert a claim against the defendants under the fraudulent transfer laws of Delaware and New York. Zohar CDO 2003-1, Ltd. v. Patriarch Partners, LLC, 631 B.R. 133 (Bankr. D. Del. 2021).

Defendants were entitled to dismissal of Chapter 7 bankruptcy trustee's constructive fraud claims under Delaware's Uniform Fraudulent Transfer Act (6 Del. C. § 1301 et seq.), where such claims sought to recover transfers that occurred more than 4 years before the petition date, because such claims were time-barred under 6 Del. C. § 1309; however such claims were not time-barred under 11 U.S.C. § 548. Miller v. Fallas (In re J & M Sales, Inc.), — B.R. —, 2021 Bankr. LEXIS 2268 (Bankr. D. Del. Aug. 20, 2021).

CHAPTER 15

DELAWARE REVISED UNIFORM PARTNERSHIP ACT

SUBCHAPTER I

GENERAL PROVISIONS

§ 15-103. Effect of partnership agreement; nonwaivable provisions.

(a) Except as otherwise provided in subsection (b) of this section, relations among the partners and between the partners and the partnership are governed by the partnership agreement. To the extent the partnership agreement does not otherwise provide, this chapter governs relations among the partners and between the partners and the partnership.

(b) The partnership agreement may not:

(1) Vary the rights and duties under § 15-105 of this title except to eliminate the duty to provide copies of statements to all of the partners;

(2) Restrict a partner's rights to obtain information as provided in § 15-403 of this title, except as permitted by § 15-403(f) of this title;

(3) Eliminate the implied contractual covenant of good faith and fair dealing;

(4) Vary the power to dissociate as a partner under § 15-602(a) of this title, except to require the notice under § 15-601(1) of this title to be in writing;

(5) Vary the right of a court to expel a partner in the events specified in § 15-601(5) of this title;

(6) Vary the requirement to wind up the partnership business in cases specified in § 15-801(4), (5) or (6) of this title;

(7) Vary the law applicable to a limited liability partnership under § 15-106(b) of this title; or

(8) Vary the denial of partnership power to issue a certificate of partnership interest in bearer form under § 15-503(h) of this title.

(c) Notwithstanding anything to the contrary contained in this section, §§ 15-201(a), 15-203 and 15-501 of this title may be modified only to the extent provided in a statement of partnership existence or a statement of qualification and in a partnership agreement. Unless otherwise provided in a partnership agreement, the provisions of this chapter apply to a partnership that has a statement of partnership existence or a statement of qualification and a partnership agreement that has modified §§ 15-201(a), 15-203 and 15-501 of this title.

(d) It is the policy of this chapter to give maximum effect to the principle of freedom of contract and to the enforceability of partnership agreements.

(e) A partner or other person shall not be liable to a partnership or to another partner or to another person that is a party to or is otherwise bound by a partnership agreement for breach of fiduciary duty for the partner's or other person's good faith reliance on the provisions of the partnership agreement.

(f) A partnership agreement may provide for the limitation or elimination of any and all liabilities for breach of contract and breach of duties (including fiduciary duties) of a partner or other person to a partnership or to another partner or to another person that is a party to or is otherwise bound by a partnership agreement; provided, that a partnership agreement may not limit or eliminate liability for any act or omission that constitutes a bad faith violation of the implied contractual covenant of good faith and fair dealing.

History.
72 Del. Laws, c. 151, § 1; 72 Del. Laws, c. 390, §§ 1-3; 73 Del. Laws, c. 85, § 4; 74 Del. Laws, c. 266, §§ 2-4; 76 Del. Laws, c. 106, § 3; 77 Del. Laws, c. 59, § 2; 83 Del. Laws, c. 62, § 1.

Revisor's note.
Section 2 of 83 Del. Laws, c. 62, provided:

"This act shall become effective August 1, 2021."

Effect of amendments.
83 Del. Laws, c. 62, effective Aug. 1, 2021, added the final sentence in (c).

SUBCHAPTER II
NATURE OF PARTNERSHIP

§ 15-202. Formation of partnership; powers.

(a) Except as otherwise provided in subsection (b) of this section, the association of 2 or more persons (i) to carry on as co-owners a business for profit forms a partnership, whether or not the persons intend to form a partnership, and (ii) to carry on any purpose or activity not for profit, forms a partnership when the persons intend to form a partnership. A limited liability partnership is for all purposes a partnership.

(b) Subject to § 15-1206 of this title, an association formed under a statute other than (i) this chapter, (ii) a predecessor statute or (iii) a comparable statute of another jurisdiction, is not a partnership under this chapter.

(c) In determining whether a partnership is formed under § 15-202(a)(i) of this title, the following rules apply:

    (1) Joint tenancy, tenancy in common, tenancy by the entireties, joint property, common property or part ownership does not by itself establish a partnership, even if the co-owners share profits made by the use of the property.

    (2) The sharing of gross returns does not by itself establish a partnership, even if the persons sharing them have a joint or common right or interest in property from which the returns are derived.

    (3) A person who receives a share of the profits of a business is presumed to be a partner in the business, unless the profits were received in payment:

        (i) Of a debt by installments or otherwise;

        (ii) For services as an independent contractor or of wages or other compensation to an employee;

        (iii) Of rent;

        (iv) Of an annuity or other retirement or health benefit to a beneficiary, representative or designee of a deceased or retired partner;

        (v) Of interest or other charge on a loan, even if the amount of payment varies with the profits of the business, including a direct or indirect present or future ownership of the collateral, or rights to income, proceeds or increase in value derived from the collateral; or

        (vi) For the sale of the goodwill of a business or other property by installments or otherwise.

(d) A partnership shall possess and may exercise all the powers and privileges granted by this chapter or by any other law or by its partnership agreement, together with any powers incidental thereto, including such powers and privileges as are necessary or convenient to the conduct, promotion or attainment of the business, purposes or activities of the partnership.

(e) Notwithstanding any provision of this chapter to the contrary, without limiting the general powers enumerated in subsection (d) of this section, a partnership shall, subject to such standards and restrictions, if any, as are set forth in its partnership agreement, have the power and authority to make contracts of guaranty and suretyship and enter into interest rate, basis, currency, hedge or other swap agreements or cap, floor, put, call, option, exchange or collar agreements, derivative agreements, or other agreements similar to any of the foregoing.

(f) A partnership has the power and authority to grant, hold or exercise a power of attorney, including an irrevocable power of attorney.

(g) Any act or transaction that may be taken by or in respect of a partnership under this chapter or a partnership agreement, but that is void or voidable when taken, may be ratified (or the failure to comply with any requirements of the partnership agreement making such act or transaction void or voidable may be waived) by the partners or other persons whose approval would be required under the partnership agreement (i) for such act or transaction to be validly taken, or (ii) to amend the partnership agreement in a manner that would permit such act or transaction to be validly taken, in each case at the time of such ratification or waiver; provided, that if the void or voidable act or transaction was the issuance or assignment of any partnership interests, the partnership interests purportedly issued or assigned shall be deemed not to have been issued or assigned for purposes of determining whether the void or voidable act or transaction was ratified or waived pursuant to this subsection. Any act or transaction ratified, or with respect to which the failure to comply with any requirements of the partnership agreement is waived, pursuant to this subsection shall be deemed validly taken at the time of such act or transaction. If an amendment to the partnership agreement to permit any such act or transaction to be validly taken would require notice to any partners or other persons under the partnership agreement and the ratification or waiver of such act or transaction is effectuated pursuant to this subsection by the partners or other persons whose approval would be required to amend the partnership agreement, notice of such ratification or waiver shall be given following such ratification or waiver to the partners or other persons who would have been entitled to notice of such an amendment and who have not otherwise received notice of, or participated in, such ratification or waiver. The provisions of this subsection shall not be construed to limit the accomplishment of a ratification or waiver of a void or voidable act by other means permitted by law. Upon application of the partnership which is formed under the laws of the State of Delaware or doing business in the State of Delaware, any partner of such a partnership or any person claiming to be substantially and adversely affected by a ratification or waiver pursuant to this subsection (excluding any harm that would have resulted if such act or transaction had been valid when taken), the Court of Chancery may hear and determine the validity and effectiveness of the ratification of, or waiver with respect to, any void or voidable act or transaction effectuated pursuant to this subsection, and in any such application, the partnership shall be named as a party, and no other party need be joined in order for the Court to adjudicate the validity and effectiveness of the ratification or waiver, and the Court may make such order respecting further or other notice of such application as it deems proper under these circumstances; provided, that nothing herein limits or affects the right to serve process in any other manner now or hereafter provided by law, and this sentence is an extension of and not a limitation upon the right otherwise existing of service of legal process upon nonresidents.

History.
72 Del. Laws, c. 151, § 1; 72 Del. Laws, c. 390, § 12; 73 Del. Laws, c. 296, § 5; 77 Del. Laws, c. 289, § 8; 80 Del. Laws, c. 43, § 2; 83 Del. Laws, c. 62, § 2.

Revisor's note.
Section 2 of 83 Del. Laws, c. 62, provided:

"This act shall become effective August 1, 2021."

Effect of amendments.
83 Del. Laws, c. 62, effective Aug. 1, 2021, added (g).

SUBCHAPTER IV
RELATIONS OF PARTNERS TO EACH OTHER AND TO PARTNERSHIP

§ 15-401. Partner's rights and duties.

(a) Each partner is deemed to have an account that is:

(1) Credited with an amount equal to the money plus the value of any other property, net of the amount of any liabilities, the partner contributes to the partnership and the partner's share of the partnership profits; and

(2) Charged with an amount equal to the money plus the value of any other property, net of the amount of any liabilities, distributed by the partnership to the partner and the partner's share of the partnership losses.

(b) Each partner is entitled to an equal share of the partnership profits and is chargeable with a share of the partnership losses in proportion to the partner's share of the profits.

(c) In addition to indemnification under § 15-110 of this title, a partnership shall reimburse a partner for payments made and indemnify a partner for liabilities incurred by the partner in the ordinary course of the business of the partnership or for the preservation of its business or property; however, no person shall be required as a consequence of any such indemnification to make any payment to the extent that the payment is inconsistent with § 15-306(b) or (c) of this title.

(d) A partnership shall reimburse a partner for an advance to the partnership beyond the amount of capital the partner agreed to contribute.

(e) A payment or advance made by a partner which gives rise to a partnership obligation under subsection (c) or (d) of this section constitutes a loan to the partnership which accrues interest from the date of the payment or advance.

(f) Each partner has equal rights in the management and conduct of the partnership business and affairs.

(g) A partner may use or possess partnership property only on behalf of the partnership.

(h) A partner is not entitled to remuneration for services performed for the partnership, except for reasonable compensation for services rendered in winding up the partnership.

(i) A person may become a partner only with the consent of all of the partners.

(j) A difference arising as to a matter in the ordinary course of business of a partnership may be decided by a majority of the partners. An act outside the ordinary course of business of a partnership may be undertaken only with the consent of all of the partners.

(k) This section does not affect the obligations of a partnership to other persons under § 15-301 of this title.

(l) A partner has the power and authority to delegate to 1 or more other persons any or all of the partner's rights, powers and duties to manage and control the business and affairs of the partnership, which delegation may be made irrespective of whether the partner has a conflict of interest with respect to the matter as to which its rights, powers or duties are being delegated, and the person or persons to whom any such rights, powers or duties are being delegated shall not be deemed conflicted solely by reason of the conflict of interest of the partner. Any such delegation may be to agents, officers and employees of the partner or the partnership, and by a management agreement or other agreement with, or otherwise to, other persons, including a committee of 1 or more persons. Such delegation by a partner shall be irrevocable if it states that it is irrevocable. Such delegation by a partner shall not cause the partner to cease to be a partner of the partnership or cause the person to whom any such rights, powers and duties have been delegated to be a partner of the partnership. No other provision of this chapter or other law shall be construed to restrict a partner's power and authority to delegate any or all of its rights, powers and duties to manage and control the business and affairs of the partnership.

(m) A partner shall have no preemptive right to subscribe to any additional issue of partnership interests or another interest in a partnership.

History.
72 Del. Laws, c. 151, § 1; 73 Del. Laws, c. 296, §§ 7, 8; 80 Del. Laws, c. 43, §§ 3, 4; 81 Del. Laws, c. 87, § 2; 83 Del. Laws, c. 62, § 3.

Revisor's note.
Section 2 of 83 Del. Laws, c. 62, provided: "This act shall become effective August 1, 2021."

Effect of amendments.
83 Del. Laws, c. 62, effective Aug. 1, 2021, in (l), added "which delegation ... conflict of interest of the partner" to the end of the first sentence, "including a committee of 1 or more persons" in the second sentence and "or other law" in the final sentence.

§ 15-403. Partner's rights and duties with respect to information.

(a) Each partner and the partnership shall provide partners, former partners and the legal representative of a deceased partner or partner under a legal disability and their agents and attorneys, access to the books and records of the partnership and other information concerning the partnership's business and affairs (in the case of former partners, only with respect to the period during which they were partners) upon reasonable demand, for any purpose reasonably related to the partner's interest as a partner in the partnership. The right of access shall include access to:

(1) True and full information regarding the status of the business and financial condition of the partnership;

(2) Promptly after becoming available, a copy of the partnership's federal, state and local income tax returns for each year;

(3) A current list of the name and last known business, residence or mailing address of each partner;

(4) A copy of any statement and written partnership agreement and all amendments thereto, together with executed copies of any written powers of attorney pursuant to which the statement or the partnership agreement and any amendments thereto have been executed;

(5) True and full information regarding the amount of cash and a description and statement of the agreed value of any other property or services contributed by each partner and which each partner has agreed to contribute in the future, and the date on which each partner became a partner; and

(6) Other information regarding the affairs of the partnership as is just and reasonable.

The right of access includes the right to examine and make extracts from books and records and other information concerning the partnership's business and affairs. The partnership agreement may provide for, and in the absence of such provision in the partnership agreement, the partnership or the partner from whom access is sought may impose, reasonable standards (including standards governing what information (including books, records and other documents) is to be furnished at what time and location and at whose expense) with respect to exercise of the right of access.

(b) A partnership agreement may provide that the partnership shall have the right to keep confidential from partners for such period of time as the partnership deems reasonable, any information which the partnership reasonably believes to be in the nature of trade secrets or other information the disclosure of which the partnership in good faith believes is not in the best interest of the partnership or could damage the partnership or its business or affairs or which the partnership is required by law or by agreement with a third party to keep confidential.

(c) A partnership and its partners may maintain the books and records and other information concerning the partnership in other than paper form, including on, by means of, or in the form of any information storage device, method, or 1 or more electronic networks or databases (including 1 or more distributed electronic networks or databases), if such form is capable of conversion into paper form within a reasonable time.

(d) Any demand by a partner or by a partner's attorney or other agent under this section shall be in writing and shall state the purpose of such demand. In every instance where an attorney or other agent shall be the person who seeks a right of access to the information described in subsection (a) of this section, the demand shall be accompanied by a power of attorney or such other writing which authorizes the attorney or other agent to so act on behalf of the partner.

(e) Any action to enforce any right arising under this section shall be brought in the Court of Chancery. If the partnership or a partner refuses to permit access as described in subsection (a) of this section or does not reply to a demand that has been made within 5 business days (or such shorter or longer period of time as is provided for in a partnership agreement but not longer than 30 business days) after the demand has been made, the demanding partner, former partner, or legal representative of a deceased partner or partner under a legal disability may apply to the Court of Chancery for an order to compel such disclosure. The Court of Chancery is hereby vested with exclusive jurisdiction to determine whether or not the person making the demand is entitled to the books and records or other information concerning the partnership's business and affairs sought. The Court of Chancery may summarily order the partnership or partner to permit the demanding partner, former partner or legal representative of a deceased partner or partner under a legal disability and their agents and attorneys to provide access to the information described in subsection (a) of this section and to make copies or extracts therefrom; or the Court of Chancery may summarily order the partnership or partner to furnish to the demanding partner, former partner or legal representative of a deceased partner or partner under a legal disability and their agents and attorneys the information described in subsection (a) of this section on the condition that the partner, former partner or legal representative of a deceased partner or partner under a legal disability first pay to the partnership or to the partner from whom access is sought the reasonable cost of obtaining and furnishing such information and on such other conditions as the Court of Chancery deems appropriate. When a demanding partner, former partner or legal representative of a deceased partner or partner under a legal disability seeks to obtain access to information described in subsection (a) of this section, the demanding partner, former partner or legal representative of a deceased partner or partner under a legal disability shall first establish (1) that the demanding partner, former partner or legal representative of a deceased partner or partner under a legal disability has complied with the provisions of this section respecting the form and manner of making demand for obtaining access to such information and (2) that the information the demanding partner, former partner or legal representative of a deceased partner or partner under a legal disability seeks is reasonably related to the partner's interest as a partner in the partnership. The Court of Chancery may, in its discretion, prescribe any limitations or conditions with reference to the access to information, or award such other or further relief as the Court of Chancery may deem just and proper. The Court of Chancery may order books, records and other documents, pertinent extracts therefrom, or duly authenticated copies thereof, to be brought within the State of Delaware and kept in the State of Delaware upon such terms and conditions as the order may prescribe.

(f) If a partner is entitled to obtain information under this chapter or a partnership agreement for a purpose reasonably related to the partner's interest as a partner or other stated purpose, the partner's right shall be to obtain such information as is necessary and essential to achieving that purpose. The rights of a partner to obtain information as provided in this section may be expanded or restricted in an original partnership agreement or in any subsequent amendment approved or adopted by all of the partners or in compliance with any applicable requirements of the partnership agreement.

History.

72 Del. Laws, c. 151, § 1; 73 Del. Laws, c. 85, § 9; 77 Del. Laws, c. 289, §§ 9, 10; 79 Del. Laws, c. 301, § 1; 82 Del. Laws, c. 47, § 5; 82 Del. Laws, c. 257, § 5; 83 Del. Laws, c. 62, § 4.

Revisor's note.

Section 2 of 83 Del. Laws, c. 62, provided: "This act shall become effective August 1, 2021."

Effect of amendments.

83 Del. Laws, c. 62, effective Aug. 1, 2021, substituted "(including books, records and other documents)" for "and documents are" in the second sentence of the final paragraph of (a); substituted "records and other documents" for "documents and records" in the final sentence of (e); and, in (f), added the first sentence and "expanded or" in the second sentence.

CHAPTER 17
LIMITED PARTNERSHIPS

SUBCHAPTER I
GENERAL PROVISIONS

§ 17-106. Nature of business permitted; powers.

(a) A limited partnership may carry on any lawful business, purpose or activity, whether or not for profit, with the exception of the business of banking as defined in § 126 of Title 8.

(b) A limited partnership shall possess and may exercise all the powers and privileges granted by this chapter or by any other law or by its partnership agreement, together with any powers incidental thereto, including such powers and privileges as are necessary or convenient to the conduct, promotion or attainment of the business, purposes or activities of the limited partnership.

(c) Notwithstanding any provision of this chapter to the contrary, without limiting the general powers enumerated in subsection (b) of this section above, a limited partnership shall, subject to such standards and restrictions, if any, as are set forth in its partnership agreement, have the power and authority to make contracts of guaranty and suretyship and enter into interest rate, basis, currency, hedge or other swap agreements or cap, floor, put, call, option, exchange or collar agreements, derivative agreements or other agreements similar to any of the foregoing.

(d) Unless otherwise provided in a partnership agreement, a limited partnership has the power and authority to grant, hold or exercise a power of attorney, including an irrevocable power of attorney.

(e) Any act or transaction that may be taken by or in respect of a limited partnership under this chapter or a limited partnership agreement, but that is void or voidable when taken, may be ratified (or the failure to comply with any requirements of the partnership agreement making such act or transaction void or voidable may be waived) by the partners or other persons whose approval would be required under the partnership agreement (i) for such act or transaction to be validly taken, or (ii) to amend the partnership agreement in a manner that would permit such act or transaction to be validly taken, in each case at the time of such ratification or waiver; provided, that if the void or voidable act or transaction was the issuance or assignment of any partnership interests, the partnership interests purportedly issued or assigned shall be deemed not to have been issued or assigned for purposes of determining whether the void or voidable act or transaction was ratified or waived pursuant to this subsection. Any act or transaction ratified, or with respect to which the failure to comply with any requirements of the partnership agreement is waived, pursuant to this subsection shall be deemed validly taken at the time of such act or transaction. If an amendment to the partnership agreement to permit any such act or transaction to be validly taken would require notice to any partners or other persons under the partnership agreement and the ratification or waiver of such act or transaction is effectuated pursuant to this subsection by the partners or other persons whose approval would be required to amend the partnership agreement, notice of such ratification or waiver shall be given following such ratification or waiver to the partners or other persons who would have been entitled to notice of such an amendment and who have not otherwise received notice of, or participated in, such ratification or waiver. The provisions of this subsection shall not be construed to limit the accomplishment of a ratification or waiver of a void or voidable act by other means permitted by law. Upon application of the limited partnership, any partner or any person claiming to be substantially and adversely affected by a ratification or waiver pursuant to this subsection (excluding any harm that would have resulted if such act or transaction had been valid when taken), the Court of Chancery may hear and determine the validity and effectiveness of the ratification of, or waiver with respect to, any void or voidable act or transaction effectuated pursuant to this subsection, and in any such application, the limited partnership shall be named as a party and service of the application upon the registered agent of the limited partnership shall be deemed to be service upon the limited partnership, and no other party need be joined in order for the Court to adjudicate the validity and effectiveness of the ratification or waiver, and the Court may make such order respecting further or other notice of such application as it deems proper under these circumstances; provided, that nothing herein limits or affects the right to serve process in any other manner now or hereafter provided by law, and this sentence is an extension of and not a limitation upon the right otherwise existing of service of legal process upon nonresidents.

History.

6 Del. C. 1953, § 1703; 59 Del. Laws, c. 105, § 1; 63 Del. Laws, c. 420, § 1; 65 Del. Laws, c. 188, § 1; 70 Del. Laws, c. 78, § 2; 71 Del. Laws, c. 78, § 4; 72 Del. Laws, c. 128, § 1; 73 Del. Laws, c. 297, § 2; 75 Del. Laws, c. 31, § 2; 77 Del. Laws, c. 288, § 3; 83 Del. Laws, c. 63, § 1.

Revisor's note.

Section 10 of 83 Del. Laws, c. 63, provided: "This act shall become effective August 1, 2021."

Effect of amendments.

83 Del. Laws, c. 63, effective Aug. 1, 2021, added (e).

SUBCHAPTER II

FORMATION; CERTIFICATE OF LIMITED PARTNERSHIP

§ 17-220. Division of a limited partnership.

(a) As used in this section and §§ 17-203 and 17-301 of this title:

(1) "Dividing partnership" means the domestic limited partnership that is effecting a division in the manner provided in this section.

(2) "Division" means the division of a dividing partnership into two or more domestic limited partnerships in accordance with this section.

(3) "Division contact" means, in connection with any division, a natural person who is a Delaware resident, any division partnership in such division or any other domestic limited partnership or other business entity as defined in § 17-211 of this title formed or organized under the laws of the State of Delaware, which division contact shall maintain a copy of the plan of division for a period of 6 years from the effective date of the division and shall comply with paragraph (g)(3) of this section.

(4) "Division partnership" means a surviving partnership, if any, and each resulting partnership.

(5) "Organizational documents" means the certificate of limited partnership and partnership agreement of a domestic limited partnership.

(6) "Resulting partnership" means a domestic limited partnership formed as a consequence of a division.

(7) "Surviving partnership" means a dividing partnership that survives the division.

(b) Pursuant to a plan of division, any domestic limited partnership may, in the manner provided in this section, be divided into 2 or more domestic limited partnerships. The division of a domestic limited partnership in accordance with this section and, if applicable, the resulting cessation of the existence of the dividing partnership pursuant to a certificate of division shall not be deemed to affect the personal liability of any person (including any general partner of the dividing partnership) incurred prior to such division with respect to matters arising prior to such division, nor shall it be deemed to affect the validity or enforceability of any obligations or liabilities of the dividing partnership incurred prior to such division; provided, that the obligations and liabilities of the dividing partnership shall be allocated to and vested in, and valid and enforceable obligations of, such division partnership or partnerships to which such obligations and liabilities have been allocated pursuant to the plan of division, as provided in subsection (*l*) of this section. Each resulting partnership in a division shall be formed in compliance with the requirements of this chapter and subsection (i) of this section.

(c) If the partnership agreement of the dividing partnership specifies the manner of adopting a plan of division, the plan of division shall be adopted as specified in the partnership agreement. If the partnership agreement of the dividing partnership does not specify the manner of adopting a plan of division and does not prohibit a division of the limited partnership, the plan of division shall be adopted in the same manner as is specified in the partnership agreement for authorizing a merger or consolidation that involves the limited partnership as a constituent party to the merger or consolidation. If the partnership agreement of the dividing partnership does not specify the manner of adopting a plan of division or authorizing a merger or consolidation that involves the limited partnership as a constituent party and does not prohibit a division of the limited partnership, the adoption of a plan of division shall be authorized by the approval:

(1) By all general partners of the dividing partnership; and

(2) Limited partners who own more than 50% of the then current percentage or other interest in the profits of the dividing partnership owned by all of the limited partners of the dividing partnership.

In any event, the adoption of a plan of division also shall require the approval of any person who, 'at the effective date or time of the division, shall be a general partner of any division partnership. Notwithstanding prior approval, a plan of division may be terminated or amended pursuant to a provision for such termination or amendment contained in the plan of division.

(d) Unless otherwise provided in a plan of division, the division of a domestic limited partnership pursuant to this section shall not require such limited partnership to wind up its affairs under § 17-803 of this title or pay its liabilities and distribute its assets under § 17-804 of this title, and the division shall not constitute a dissolution of such limited partnership.

(e) In connection with a division under this section, rights or securities of, or interests in, the dividing partnership may be exchanged for or converted into cash, property, rights or securities of, or interests in, the surviving partnership or any resulting partnership or, in addition to or in lieu thereof, may be exchanged for or converted into cash, property, rights or securities of, or interests in, a domestic limited partnership or any other business entity which is not a division partnership or may be canceled or remain outstanding (if the dividing partnership is a surviving partnership).

(f) A plan of division adopted in accordance with subsection (c) of this section:

(1) May effect any amendment to the partnership agreement of the dividing partnership if it is a surviving partnership in the division; or

(2) May effect the adoption of a new partnership agreement for the dividing partnership if it is a surviving partnership in the division; and

(3) Shall effect the adoption of a partnership agreement for each resulting partnership.

Any amendment to a partnership agreement or adoption of a new partnership agreement for the dividing partnership, if it is a surviving partnership in the division, or adoption of a partnership agreement for each resulting partnership made pursuant to the foregoing sentence shall be effective at the effective time or date of the division. Any amendment to a partnership agreement or adoption of a new partnership agreement for the dividing partnership, if it is a surviving partnership in the division, shall be effective notwithstanding any provision in the partnership agreement of the dividing partnership relating to amendment or adoption of a new partnership agreement, other than a provision that by its terms applies to an amendment to the partnership agreement or the adoption of a new partnership agreement, in either case, in connection with a division, merger or consolidation.

(g) If a domestic limited partnership is dividing under this section, the dividing partnership shall adopt a plan of division which shall set forth:

(1) The terms and conditions of the division, including:

a. Any conversion or exchange of the partnership interests of the dividing partnership into or for partnership interests or other securities or obligations of any division partnership or cash, property or rights or securities or obligations of or interests in any other business entity or domestic limited partnership which is not a division partnership, or that the partnership interests of the dividing partnership shall remain outstanding or be canceled, or any combination of the foregoing; and

    b. The allocation of assets, property, rights, series, debts, liabilities and duties of the dividing partnership among the division partnerships;

(2) The name of each resulting partnership and, if the dividing partnership will survive the division, the name of the surviving partnership;

(3) The name and business address of a division contact which shall have custody of a copy of the plan of division. The division contact, or any successor division contact, shall serve for a period of 6 years following the effective date of the division. During such 6 year period the division contact shall provide, without cost, to any creditor of the dividing partnership, within 30 days following the division contact's receipt of a written request from any creditor of the dividing partnership, the name and business address of the division partnership to which the claim of such creditor was allocated pursuant to the plan of division; and

(4) Any other matters that the dividing partnership determines to include therein.

(h) If a domestic limited partnership divides under this section, the dividing partnership shall file a certificate of division executed by at least 1 general partner of the dividing partnership on behalf of such dividing partnership in the office of the Secretary of State in accordance with § 17-204 of this title, and a certificate of limited partnership that complies with § 17-201 of this title for each resulting partnership executed by all general partners of such resulting partnership in accordance with § 17-204 of this title. The certificate of division shall state:

(1) The name of the dividing partnership and, if it has been changed, the name under which its certificate of limited partnership was originally filed and whether the dividing partnership is a surviving partnership;

(2) The date of filing of the dividing partnership's original certificate of limited partnership with the Secretary of State;

(3) The name of each division partnership;

(4) The name and business address of the division contact required by paragraph (g)(3) of this section;

(5) The future effective date or time (which shall be a date or time certain) of the division if it is not to be effective upon the filing of the certificate of division;

(6) That the division has been approved in accordance with this section;

(7) That the plan of division is on file at a place of business of such division partnership as is specified therein, and shall state the address thereof;

(8) That a copy of the plan of division will be furnished by such division partnership as is specified therein, on request and without cost, to any partner of the dividing partnership; and

(9) Any other information the dividing partnership determines to include therein.

(i) The certificate of division and each certificate of limited partnership for each resulting partnership required by subsection (h) of this section shall be filed simultaneously in the office of the Secretary of State and, if such certificates are not to become effective upon their filing as permitted by § 17-206(b) of this title, then each such certificate shall provide for the same effective date or time in accordance with § 17-206(b) of this title. Concurrently with the effective date or time of a division, the partnership agreement of each resulting partnership shall become effective.

(j) A certificate of division shall act as a certificate of cancellation for a dividing partnership which is not a surviving partnership.

(k) A partnership agreement may provide that a domestic limited partnership shall not have the power to divide as set forth in this section.

(*l*) Upon the division of a domestic limited partnership becoming effective:

(1) The dividing partnership shall be divided into the distinct and independent resulting partnerships named in the plan of division, and, if the dividing partnership is not a surviving partnership, the existence of the dividing partnership shall cease.

(2) For all purposes of the laws of the State of Delaware, all of the rights, privileges and powers, and all the property, real, personal and mixed, of the dividing partnership and all debts due on whatever account to it, as well as all other things and other causes of action belonging to it, shall without further action be allocated to and vested in the applicable division partnership in such a manner and basis and with such effect as is specified in the plan of division, and the title to any real property or interest therein allocated to and vested in any division partnership shall not revert or be in any way impaired by reason of the division.

(3) Each division partnership shall, from and after effectiveness of the certificate of division, be liable as a separate and distinct domestic limited partnership for such debts, liabilities and duties of the dividing partnership as are allocated to such division partnership pursuant to the plan of division in the manner and on the basis provided in paragraph (g)(1)b. of this section.

(4) Each of the debts, liabilities and duties of the dividing partnership shall without further action be allocated to and be the debts, liabilities and duties of such division partnership as is specified in the plan of division as having such debts, liabilities and duties allocated to it, in such a manner and basis and with such effect as is specified in the plan of division, and no other division partnership shall be liable therefor, so long as the plan of division does not constitute a fraudulent transfer under applicable law, and all liens upon any property of the dividing partnership shall be preserved unimpaired, and all debts, liabilities and duties of the dividing partnership shall remain attached to the division partnership to which such debts, liabilities and duties have been allocated in the plan of division, and may be enforced against such division partnership to the same extent as if said debts, liabilities and duties had originally been incurred or contracted by it in its capacity as a domestic limited partnership.

(5) In the event that any allocation of assets, debts, liabilities and duties to division partnerships in accordance with a plan of division is determined by a court of competent jurisdiction to constitute a fraudulent transfer, each division partnership shall be jointly and severally liable on account of such fraudulent transfer notwithstanding the allocations made in the plan of division; provided, however, the validity and effectiveness of the division are not otherwise affected thereby.

(6) Debts and liabilities of the dividing partnership that are not allocated by the plan of division shall be the joint and several debts and liabilities of all of the division partnerships.

(7) It shall not be necessary for a plan of division to list each individual asset, property, right, series, debt, liability or duty of the dividing partnership to be allocated to a division partnership so long as the assets, property, rights, series, debts, liabilities or duties so allocated are reasonably identified by any method where the identity of such assets, property, rights, series, debts, liabilities or duties is objectively determinable.

(8) The rights, privileges, powers and interests in property of the dividing partnership that have been allocated to a division partnership, as well as the debts, liabilities and duties of the dividing partnership that have been allocated to such division partnership pursuant to a plan of division, shall remain vested in each such division partnership and shall not be deemed, as a result of the division, to have been assigned or transferred to such division partnership for any purpose of the laws of the State of Delaware.

(9) Any action or proceeding pending against a dividing partnership may be continued against the surviving partnership as if the division did not occur, but subject to paragraph (*l*)(4) of this section, and against any resulting partnership to which the asset, property, right, series, debt, liability or duty associated with such action or proceeding was allocated pursuant to the plan of division by adding or substituting such resulting partnership as a party in the action or proceeding. Any action or proceeding pending against a general partner of a dividing partnership may be continued against such general partner as if the division did not occur and against the general partner of any resulting partnership to which the asset, property, right, series, debt, liability or duty associated with such action or proceeding was allocated pursuant to the plan of division by adding or substituting such general partner as a party in the action or proceeding.

(m) In applying the provisions of this chapter on distributions, a direct or indirect allocation of property or liabilities in a division is not deemed a distribution for purposes of this chapter.

(n) The provisions of this section shall not be construed to limit the means of accomplishing a division by any other means provided for in a partnership agreement or other agreement or as otherwise permitted by this chapter or as otherwise permitted by law.

(o) All limited partnerships formed on or after August 1, 2019, shall be governed by this section. All limited partnerships formed prior to August 1, 2019, shall be governed by this section; provided, that if the dividing partnership is a party to any written contract, indenture or other agreement entered into prior to August 1, 2019, that, by its terms, restricts, conditions or prohibits the consummation of a merger or consolidation by the dividing partnership with or into another party, or the transfer of assets by the dividing partnership to another party, then such restriction, condition or prohibition shall be deemed to apply to a division as if it were a merger, consolidation or transfer of assets, as applicable.

History.

82 Del. Laws, c. 46, § 17; 82 Del. Laws, c. 258, § 8; 83 Del. Laws, c. 63, § 2.

Revisor's note.

Section 10 of 83 Del. Laws, c. 63, provided: "This act shall become effective August 1, 2021."

Effect of amendments.

83 Del. Laws, c. 63, effective Aug. 1, 2021, substituted "§§ 17-203 and 17-301 of this title" for "§§ 17-203, 17-301 and 17-1203" in the introductory paragraph of (a).

SUBCHAPTER III

LIMITED PARTNERS

§ 17-305. Access to and confidentiality of information; records.

(a) Each limited partner, in person or by attorney or other agent, has the right, subject to such reasonable standards (including standards governing what information (including books, records and other documents) is to be furnished, at what time and location and at whose expense) as may be set forth in the partnership agreement or otherwise established by the general partners, to obtain from the general partners from time to time upon reasonable demand for any purpose reasonably related to the limited partner's interest as a limited partner:

(1) True and full information regarding the status of the business and financial condition of the limited partnership;

(2) Promptly after becoming available, a copy of the limited partnership's federal, state and local income tax returns for each year;

(3) A current list of the name and last known business, residence or mailing address of each partner;

(4) A copy of any written partnership agreement and certificate of limited partnership and all amendments thereto, together with executed copies of any written powers of attorney pursuant to which the partnership agreement and any certificate and all amendments thereto have been executed;

(5) True and full information regarding the amount of cash and a description and statement of the agreed value of any other property or services contributed by each partner and which each partner has agreed to contribute in the future, and the date on which each became a partner; and

(6) Other information regarding the affairs of the limited partnership as is just and reasonable.

(b) A general partner shall have the right to keep confidential from limited partners for such period of time as the general partner deems reasonable, any information which the general partner reasonably believes to be in the nature of trade secrets or other information the disclosure of which the general partner in good faith believes is not in the best interest of the limited partnership or could damage the limited partnership or its business or which the limited partnership is required by law or by agreement with a third party to keep confidential.

(c) A limited partnership may maintain its books, records and other documents in other than paper form, including on, by means of, or in the form of any information storage device, method, or 1 or more electronic networks or databases (including 1 or more distributed electronic networks or databases), if such form is capable of conversion into paper form within a reasonable time.

(d) Any demand under this section shall be in writing and shall state the purpose of such demand. In every instance where an attorney or other agent shall be the person who seeks the right to obtain the information described in subsection (a) of this section, the demand shall be accompanied by a power of attorney or such other writing which authorizes the attorney or other agent to so act on behalf of the limited partner.

(e) Any action to enforce any right arising under this section shall be brought in the Court of Chancery. If a general partner refuses to permit a limited partner, or attorney or other agent acting for the limited partner, to obtain from the general partner the information described in subsection (a) of this section or does not reply to the demand that has been made within 5 business days (or such shorter or longer period of time as is provided for in a partnership agreement but not longer than 30 business days) after the demand has been made, the limited partner may apply to the Court of Chancery for an order to compel such disclosure. The Court of Chancery is hereby vested with exclusive jurisdiction to determine whether or not the person seeking such information is entitled to the information sought. The Court of Chancery may summarily order the general partner to permit the limited partner to obtain the information described in subsection (a) of this section and to make copies or abstracts therefrom, or the Court of Chancery may summarily order the general partner to furnish to the limited partner the information described in subsection (a) of this section on the condition that the limited partner first pay to the limited partnership the reasonable cost of obtaining and furnishing such information and on such other conditions as the Court of Chancery deems appropriate. When a limited partner seeks to obtain the information described in subsection (a) of this section, the limited partner shall first establish: (1) that the limited partner has complied with the provisions of this section respecting the form and manner of making demand for obtaining such information, and (2) that the information the limited partner seeks is reasonably related to the limited partner's interest as a limited partner. The Court of Chancery may, in its discretion, prescribe any limitations or conditions with reference to the obtaining of information, or award such other or further relief as the Court of Chancery may deem just and proper. The Court of Chancery may order books, records and other documents, pertinent extracts therefrom, or duly authenticated copies thereof, to be brought within the State of Delaware and kept in the State of Delaware upon such terms and conditions as the order may prescribe.

(f) If a limited partner is entitled to obtain information under this chapter or a partnership agreement for a purpose reasonably related to the limited partner's interest as a limited partner or other stated purpose, the limited partner's right shall be to obtain such information as is necessary and essential to achieving that purpose. The rights of a limited partner to obtain information as provided in this section may be expanded or restricted in an original partnership agreement or in any subsequent amendment approved or adopted by all of the partners or in compliance with any applicable requirements of the partnership agreement. The provisions of this subsection shall not be construed to limit the ability to expand or restrict the rights of a limited partner to obtain information by any other means permitted by law.

(g) A limited partnership shall maintain a current record that identifies the name and last known business, residence, or mailing address of each partner.

History.
6 Del. C. 1953, § 1710; 59 Del. Laws, c. 105, § 1; 63 Del. Laws, c. 420, § 1; 65 Del. Laws, c. 188, § 1; 66 Del. Laws, c. 316, § 35; 70 Del. Laws, c. 362, § 15; 73 Del. Laws, c. 73, § 20; 77 Del. Laws, c. 288, §§ 22, 23; 79 Del. Laws, c. 326, § 3; 81 Del. Laws, c. 356, § 5; 82 Del. Laws, c. 258, § 12; 83 Del. Laws, c. 63, § 3.

Revisor's note.
Section 10 of 83 Del. Laws, c. 63, provided: "This act shall become effective August 1, 2021."

Effect of amendments.
83 Del. Laws, c. 63, effective Aug. 1, 2021, substituted "(including books, records and other documents) is" for "and documents are" inn the introductory paragraph of (a); in (c), added "books" and "and other documents"; substituted "records and other documents" for "documents and records" in the final sentence of (e); and, in (f), added the first sentence and "expanded or" in the second sentence, and in the third sentence substituted "expand or restrict" for "impose restrictions on" and "by law" for "under this chapter".

SUBCHAPTER IV
GENERAL PARTNERS

§ 17-403. General powers and liabilities.

(a) Except as provided in this chapter or in the partnership agreement, a general partner of a limited partnership has the rights and powers and is subject to the restrictions of a partner in a partnership that is governed by the Delaware Uniform Partnership Law in effect on July 11, 1999 (6 Del. C. § 1501 et seq.).

(b) Except as provided in this chapter, a general partner of a limited partnership has the liabilities of a partner in a partnership that is governed by the Delaware Uniform Partnership Law in effect on July 11, 1999 (6 Del. C. § 1501 et seq.) to persons other than the partnership and the other partners. Except as provided in this chapter or in the partnership agreement, a general partner of a limited partnership has the liabilities of a partner in a partnership that is governed by the Delaware Uniform Partnership Law in effect on July 11, 1999 (6 Del. C. § 1501 et seq.) to the partnership and to the other partners.

(c) Unless otherwise provided in the partnership agreement, a general partner of a limited partnership has the power and authority to delegate to 1 or more other persons any or all of the general partner's rights, powers and duties to manage and control the business and affairs of the limited partnership, which delegation may be made irrespective of whether the general partner has a conflict of interest with respect to the matter as to which its rights, powers or duties are being delegated, and the person or persons to whom any such rights, powers or duties are being delegated shall not be deemed conflicted solely by reason of the conflict of interest of the general partner. Any such delegation may be to agents, officers, and employees of the general partner or the limited partnership and by a management agreement or another agreement with, or otherwise to, other persons, including a committee of 1 or more persons. Unless otherwise provided in the partnership agreement, such delegation by a general partner of a limited partnership shall be irrevocable if it states that it is irrevocable. Unless otherwise provided in the partnership agreement, such delegation by a general partner of a limited partnership shall not cause the general partner to cease to be a general partner of the limited partnership or cause the person to whom any such rights, powers and duties have been delegated to be a general partner of the limited partnership. No other provision of this chapter or other law shall be construed to restrict a general partner's power and authority to delegate any or all of its rights, powers, and duties to manage and control the business and affairs of the limited partnership.

(d) A judgment creditor of a general partner of a limited partnership may not levy execution against the assets of the general partner to satisfy a judgment based on a claim against the limited partnership unless:

(1) A judgment based on the same claim has been obtained against the limited partnership and a writ of execution on the judgment has been returned unsatisfied in whole or in part;

(2) The limited partnership is a debtor in bankruptcy;

(3) The general partner has agreed that the creditor need not exhaust the assets of the limited partnership;

(4) A court grants permission to the judgment creditor to levy execution against the assets of the general partner based on a finding that the assets of the limited partnership that are subject to execution are clearly insufficient to satisfy the judgment, that exhaustion of the assets of the limited partnership is excessively burdensome, or that the grant of permission is an appropriate exercise of the court's equitable powers; or

(5) Liability is imposed on the general partner by law or contract independent of the existence of the limited partnership.

History.

6 Del. C. 1953, § 1709; 59 Del. Laws, c. 105, § 1; 63 Del. Laws, c. 420, § 1; 65 Del. Laws, c. 188, § 1; 69 Del. Laws, c. 258, § 34; 71 Del. Laws, c. 78, § 36; 73 Del. Laws, c. 73, §§ 22, 23; 73 Del. Laws, c. 297, § 9; 80 Del. Laws, c. 44, § 9; 81 Del. Laws, c. 88, § 14; 83 Del. Laws, c. 63, § 4.

Revisor's note.

Section 10 of 83 Del. Laws, c. 63, provided:

"This act shall become effective August 1, 2021."

Effect of amendments.

83 Del. Laws, c. 63, effective Aug. 1, 2021, added "which delegation ... conflict of interest of the general partner" in the first sentence, "including a committee of 1 or more persons" in the second sentence and "or other law" in the final sentence.

SUBCHAPTER X
DERIVATIVE ACTIONS

§ 17-1001. Right to bring action.

NOTES TO DECISIONS

Analysis

Demand.
— Excused.

Demand.

— Excused.

Plaintiff successfully pleaded demand futility as to a general partner (GP) because the amended complaint alleged particularized facts that the GP, acting through the board, violated its contractual duty to the company by consciously failing to oversee its mission-critical objective of maintaining pipeline integrity; as a result, the GP faced a substantial likelihood of liability for breaching its contractual duty in the limited partnership agreement. Inter-Marketing Group United States v. Armstrong, — A.3d —, 2020 Del. Ch. LEXIS 391 (Del. Ch. Jan. 31, 2020).

While plaintiff did not pursue a books and records investigation before filing its amended complaint, dismissal based on lack of demand was not warranted because plaintiff had access to a fully developed criminal trial record involving the same oil spill at issue in the derivative litigation; that record, as utilized by plaintiff, contained sufficient evidence to survive a motion to dismiss. Inter-Marketing Group United States v. Armstrong, — A.3d —, 2020 Del. Ch. LEXIS 391 (Del. Ch. Jan. 31, 2020).

§ 17-1003. Complaint.

NOTES TO DECISIONS

Analysis

Demand.
— Excused.

Demand.

— Excused.

Plaintiffs stated a claim for breach of fiduciary duty against defendants where: (1) the complaint alleged that defendants created an entity to which they directed more than $4 million from reinsurance funds and manufacturer rebates which should have gone to dealerships (and ultimately to the partnerships); (2) 2 partners participated in at least 1 of defendant's alleged controller's self-dealing transactions. Lipman v. GPB Capital Holdings LLC, — A.3d —, 2020 Del. Ch. LEXIS 340 (Del. Ch. Nov. 18, 2020).

SUBCHAPTER XII
STATUTORY PUBLIC BENEFIT LIMITED PARTNERSHIPS

§ 17-1201 Law applicable to statutory public benefit limited partnerships; how formed.

This subchapter applies to all statutory public benefit limited partnerships, as defined in § 17-1202(a) of this title. If a limited partnership is formed as or elects to become a statutory public benefit limited partnership in the manner prescribed in this section, it shall be subject in all respects to the provisions of this chapter, except to the extent this subchapter imposes additional or different requirements, in which case such additional or different requirements shall apply, and notwithstanding § 17-1101 of this title or any other provision of this title, such additional or different requirements imposed by this subchapter may not be altered in the partnership agreement. If a limited partnership is not formed as a statutory public benefit limited partnership, it may become a statutory public benefit limited partnership in the manner specified in its partnership agreement or by amending its partnership agreement and certificate of limited partnership to comply with the requirements of this subchapter.

History.

82 Del. Laws, c. 46, § 30; 83 Del. Laws, c. 63, § 5.

Revisor's note.

Section 10 of 83 Del. Laws, c. 63, provided: "This act shall become effective August 1, 2021."

Effect of amendments.

83 Del. Laws, c. 63, effective Aug. 1, 2021, substituted "§ 17-1202(a)" for "§ 17-1202" in the first sentence; in the second sentence inserted "is formed as or", deleted "under this subchapter" preceding "in the manner", substituted "section" for "subchapter" and added the second and third occurrences of "additional or different"; and added the final sentence.

§ 17-1202 Statutory public benefit limited partnership defined; contents of certificate of limited partnership and partnership agreement.

(a) A "statutory public benefit limited partnership" is a for-profit limited partnership formed under and subject to the requirements of this chapter that is intended to produce a public benefit or public benefits and to operate in a responsible and sustainable manner. To that end, a statutory public benefit limited partnership shall be managed in a manner that balances the partners' pecuniary interests, the best interests of those materially affected by the limited partnership's conduct, and the public benefit or public benefits set forth in its partnership agreement and in its certificate of limited partnership. A statutory public benefit limited partnership shall state in its partnership agreement and in the heading of its certificate of limited partnership that it is a statutory public benefit limited partnership and shall set forth in its partnership agreement and in its certificate of limited partnership 1 or more specific public benefits to be promoted by the limited partnership. In the event of any inconsistency between the public benefit or benefits to be promoted by the limited partnership as set forth in its partnership agreement and in its certificate of limited partnership, the partnership agreement shall control as among the partners and other persons who are party to or otherwise bound by the partnership agreement. A general partner who becomes aware that the specific public benefit or benefits to be promoted by the limited partnership as set forth in its partnership agreement are inaccurately set forth in its certificate of limited partnership, shall promptly amend the certificate of limited partnership. Any provision in the partnership agreement or certificate of limited partnership of a statutory public benefit limited partnership that is inconsistent with this subchapter shall not be effective to the extent of such inconsistency.

(b) "Public benefit" means a positive effect (or reduction of negative effects) on 1 or more categories of persons, entities, communities or interests (other than partners in their capacities as partners) including, but not limited to, effects of an artistic, charitable, cultural, economic, educational, environmental, literary, medical, religious, scientific or technological nature. "Public benefit provisions" means the provisions of a partnership agreement contemplated by this subchapter.

History.

82 Del. Laws, c. 46, § 30; 83 Del. Laws, c. 63, § 6.

Revisor's note.

Section 10 of 83 Del. Laws, c. 63, provided:

"This act shall become effective August 1, 2021."

Effect of amendments.

83 Del. Laws, c. 63, effective Aug. 1, 2021, rewrote (a).

§ 17-1203. Certain amendments and mergers; votes required

History.

82 Del. Laws, c. 46, § 30; repealed by 83 Del. Laws, c. 63, § 7, effective Aug. 1, 2021.

Revisor's note.

Section 10 of 83 Del. Laws, c. 63, provided:

"This act shall become effective August 1, 2021."

§ 17-1204 Duties of general partners or other persons.

(a) The general partners or other persons with authority to manage or direct the business and affairs of a statutory public benefit limited partnership shall manage or direct the business and affairs of the statutory public benefit limited partnership in a manner that balances the pecuniary interests of the partners, the best interests of those materially affected by the limited partnership's conduct, and the specific public benefit or public benefits set forth in its partnership agreement and certificate of limited partnership. Unless otherwise provided in a partnership agreement, no general partner or other person with authority to manage or direct the business and affairs of the statutory public benefit limited partnership shall have any liability for monetary damages for the failure to manage or direct the business and affairs of the statutory public benefit limited partnership as provided in this subsection.

(b) A general partner of a statutory public benefit limited partnership or any other person with authority to manage or direct the business and affairs of the statutory public benefit limited partnership shall not, by virtue of the public benefit provisions or § 17-1202(a) of this title, have any duty to any person on account of any interest of such person in the public benefit or public benefits set forth in its partnership agreement and certificate of limited partnership or on account of any interest materially affected by the limited partnership's conduct and, with respect to a decision implicating the balance requirement in subsection (a) of this section, will be deemed to satisfy such person's fiduciary duties to limited partners and the limited partnership if such person's decision is both informed and disinterested and not such that no person of ordinary, sound judgment would approve.

History.
82 Del. Laws, c. 46, § 30; 83 Del. Laws, c. 63, § 8.

Revisor's note.
Section 10 of 83 Del. Laws, c. 63, provided: "This act shall become effective August 1, 2021."

Effect of amendments.
83 Del. Laws, c. 63, effective Aug. 1, 2021, added "partnership agreement and" in the first sentence of (a) and in (b).

§ 17-1205 Periodic statements and third-party certification.

A statutory public benefit limited partnership shall no less than biennially provide its limited partners with a statement as to the limited partnership's promotion of the public benefit or public benefits set forth in its partnership agreement and certificate of limited partnership and as to the best interests of those materially affected by the limited partnership's conduct. The statement shall include:

(1) The objectives that have been established to promote such public benefit or public benefits and interests;

(2) The standards that have been adopted to measure the limited partnership's progress in promoting such public benefit or public benefits and interests;

(3) Objective factual information based on those standards regarding the limited partnership's success in meeting the objectives for promoting such public benefit or public benefits and interests; and

(4) An assessment of the limited partnership's success in meeting the objectives and promoting such public benefit or public benefits and interests.

History.
 82 Del. Laws, c. 46, § 30; 83 Del. Laws, c. 63, § 9.

Revisor's note.
 Section 10 of 83 Del. Laws, c. 63, provided: "This act shall become effective August 1, 2021."

Effect of amendments.
 83 Del. Laws, c. 63, effective Aug. 1, 2021, added "partnership agreement and" in the first sentence of the introductory paragraph.

CHAPTER 18

LIMITED LIABILITY COMPANY ACT

SUBCHAPTER I

GENERAL PROVISIONS

§ 18-101. Definitions.

NOTES TO DECISIONS

Managers.
 Defendant was a member and manager of the subject limited liability company; the certificate of formation identified defendant as a member and provided that management was vested in the members. Robinson v. Darbeau, — A.3d —, 2021 Del. Ch. LEXIS 36 (Del. Ch. Mar. 1, 2021).
 Sufficient evidence supported the finding that the parties impliedly agreed to a limited liability company (LLC) agreement because: (1) defendant operated the LLC alongside plaintiff, who, along with the LLC, referred to defendant as a "co-owner" and "co-director" in countless situations and presented defendant as a co-equal to clients and the public; and (2) defendant contributed to the LLC's operations, performing various administrative tasks, and contributed financially to the LLC. Robinson v. Darbeau, — A.3d —, 2021 Del. Ch. LEXIS 36 (Del. Ch. Mar. 1, 2021).

§ 18-106. Nature of business permitted; powers.

 (a) A limited liability company may carry on any lawful business, purpose or activity, whether or not for profit, with the exception of the business of banking as defined in § 126 of Title 8.

 (b) A limited liability company shall possess and may exercise all the powers and privileges granted by this chapter or by any other law or by its limited liability company agreement, together with any powers incidental thereto, including such powers and privileges as are necessary or convenient to the conduct, promotion or attainment of the business, purposes or activities of the limited liability company.

 (c) Notwithstanding any provision of this chapter to the contrary, without limiting the general powers enumerated in subsection (b) of this section, a limited liability company shall, subject to such standards and restrictions, if any, as are set forth in its limited liability company agreement, have the power and authority to make contracts of guaranty and suretyship and enter into interest rate, basis, currency, hedge or other swap agreements or cap, floor, put, call, option, exchange or collar agreements, derivative agreements, or other agreements similar to any of the foregoing.

(d) Unless otherwise provided in a limited liability company agreement, a limited liability company has the power and authority to grant, hold or exercise a power of attorney, including an irrevocable power of attorney.

(e) Any act or transaction that may be taken by or in respect of a limited liability company under this chapter or a limited liability company agreement, but that is void or voidable when taken, may be ratified (or the failure to comply with any requirements of the limited liability company agreement making such act or transaction void or voidable may be waived) by the members, managers or other persons whose approval would be required under the limited liability company agreement:

(1) For such act or transaction to be validly taken; or

(2) To amend the limited liability company agreement in a manner that would permit such act or transaction to be validly taken, in each case at the time of such ratification or waiver;

provided, that if the void or voidable act or transaction was the issuance or assignment of any limited liability company interests, the limited liability company interests purportedly issued or assigned shall be deemed not to have been issued or assigned for purposes of determining whether the void or voidable act or transaction was ratified or waived pursuant to this subsection. Any act or transaction ratified, or with respect to which the failure to comply with any requirements of the limited liability company agreement is waived, pursuant to this subsection shall be deemed validly taken at the time of such act or transaction. If an amendment to the limited liability company agreement to permit any such act or transaction to be validly taken would require notice to any members, managers or other persons under the limited liability company agreement and the ratification or waiver of such act or transaction is effectuated pursuant to this subsection by the members, managers or other persons whose approval would be required to amend the limited liability company agreement, notice of such ratification or waiver shall be given following such ratification or waiver to the members, managers or other persons who would have been entitled to notice of such an amendment and who have not otherwise received notice of, or participated in, such ratification or waiver. The provisions of this subsection shall not be construed to limit the accomplishment of a ratification or waiver of a void or voidable act by other means permitted by law. Upon application of the limited liability company, any member, any manager or any person claiming to be substantially and adversely affected by a ratification or waiver pursuant to this subsection (excluding any harm that would have resulted if such act or transaction had been valid when taken), the Court of Chancery may hear and determine the validity and effectiveness of the ratification of, or waiver with respect to, any void or voidable act or transaction effectuated pursuant to this subsection, and in any such application, the limited liability company shall be named as a party and service of the application upon the registered agent of the limited liability company shall be deemed to be service upon the limited liability company, and no other party need be joined in order for the Court to adjudicate the validity and effectiveness of the ratification or waiver, and the Court may make such order respecting further or other notice of such application as it deems proper under these circumstances; provided, that nothing herein limits or affects the right to serve process in any other manner now or hereafter provided by law, and this sentence is an extension of and not a limitation upon the right otherwise existing of service of legal process upon nonresidents.

History.

68 Del. Laws, c. 434, § 1; 71 Del. Laws, c. 77, § 5; 72 Del. Laws, c. 129, § 2; 73 Del. Laws, c. 295, § 3; 75 Del. Laws, c. 51, § 2; 77 Del. Laws, c. 287, § 3; 83 Del. Laws, c. 61, § 1.

Revisor's note.

Section 10 of 83 Del. Laws, c. 61, provided:

"This act shall become effective August 1, 2021."

Effect of amendments.

83 Del. Laws, c. 61, effective Aug. 1, 2021, added (e).

§ 18-108. Indemnification.

NOTES TO DECISIONS

Advancement.

Limited liability company agreement unambiguously provided that the company was required to advance the reasonable attorneys' fees and expenses plaintiffs incurred in defending certain claims because: (1) plaintiffs were covered persons under the agreement's broad advancement and indemnification provisions; (2) Delaware had a strong public policy in favor of indemnification and advancement; and (3) the first-party/third-party claim distinction did not apply. Int'l Rail Partners LLC v. Am. Rail Partners, LLC, — A.3d —, 2020 Del. Ch. LEXIS 345 (Del. Ch. Nov. 24, 2020).

In an action by a rail company against its management company and others for alleged mismanagement and self-dealing, the rail company was not entitled to an interlocutory appeal from a lower court order that permitted advancement of attorney fees and costs to defendants because: (1) there were no exceptional circumstances; and (2) the potential benefits of interlocutory review did not outweigh the inefficiency, disruption and probable costs caused by an interlocutory appeal. Am. Rail Partners, LLC v. Int'l Rail Partners, LLC, 245 A.3d 517 (Del. 2021).

§ 18-109. Service of process on managers and liquidating trustees.

NOTES TO DECISIONS

Analysis

Jurisdiction.
— Consent.
— Personal.

Jurisdiction.

— Consent.

Delaware courts had personal jurisdiction over a manager of limited liability companies; the manager impliedly consented to being sued in a Delaware court regarding the companies' civil suits when the manager personally engaging in the fraudulent conduct alleged by plaintiff with regard to misrepresentation made to a developer. R. Keating & Sons, Inc. v. Chiselcreek Dev., LLC, — A.3d —, 2020 Del. Super. LEXIS 2868 (Del. Super. Ct. Oct. 30, 2020).

— Personal.

In an action by an investment consulting group against a fund manager and its founding partner for breach of contract and enforcement of a nondisclosure agreement, the court lacked jurisdiction over the partner because the part-

ner had not engaged in sufficient conduct to constitute transacting business in the State; further, jurisdiction was lacking because the only claim brought against the partner was for fraud in connection with an oral agreement with a third party, not a corporate governance or internal affairs claim. Endowment Research Grp., LLC v. Wildcat Venture Partners, LLC, — A.3d —, 2021 Del. Ch. LEXIS 42 (Del. Ch. Mar. 5, 2021).

In an action by oil-purchasing businesses against a founder and others allegedly involved in a secret side-business scheme, the court lacked personal jurisdiction under 10 Del. C. § 3104 over the founder because the complaint did not tether the formation of any Delaware entity to the secret side business; the LLC consent statute (6 Del. C. § 18–109) did not support personal jurisdiction because the founder was not the formal manager, acting manager or a material participant in the LLC's management. Lone Pine Res., LP v. Dickey, 2021 Del. Ch. LEXIS 114 (Del. Ch. June 7, 2021).

§ 18-110. Contested matters relating to managers; contested votes.

NOTES TO DECISIONS

Analysis

Authority.
Removal.

Authority.

Denying a motion to maintain did not irreparably or substantially harm a limited liability company (LLC) in any forthcoming appeal of the determination of a declaratory judgment claim as to the LLC's rightful management; the

LLC would necessarily remain as the nominal defendant if the purported manager decided to appeal a conclusion that the claim under this statute was waived. Lynch v. Gonzalez, — A.3d —, 2020 Del. Ch. LEXIS 296 (Del. Ch. Sept. 22, 2020).

Plaintiff was found to have complied with the unambiguous terms of a limited liability corporation's (LLC's) operating agreement in an action to obtain a declaratory judgment that plaintiff had lawfully altered an LLC's governance structure by acquiring sufficient equity in the LLC to justify its designation of a seventh governor to the board of governors; plaintiff's written notice of its transfers of LLC units would have been effective by the date plaintiff was eligible to have the unit transfers recognized by the LLC. Pearl City Elevator, Inc. v. Gieseke, — A.3d —, 2021 Del. Ch. LEXIS 54 (Del. Ch. Mar. 23, 2021).

Because 6 Del. C. §§ 18-110 and 18-802 applied only to Delaware limited liability companies (LLCs), an LLC's conversion to a Puerto Rican entity deprived the court of jurisdiction to declare the LLC's proper managers and to order judicial dissolution. In re Coinmint, LLC, 2021 Del. Ch. LEXIS 172 (Del. Ch. May 10, 2021).

Removal.

Occurrence of an event of default under a limited liability company (LLC) agreement by the LLC's failure to remove a construction lien in a timely manner, and the written notice that a member of the LLC provided to the managing member of the LLC in an attempt to remove the managing member, satisfied the removal requirements of the LLC agreement; accordingly, pursuant to the LLC agreement, the member was to assume the status of managing member. Jernigan Capital Operating Co., LLC v. Storage Partners of KOP, LLC, — A.3d —, 2020 Del. Ch. LEXIS 380 (Del. Ch. Dec. 31, 2020).

Plaintiffs sufficiently pleaded a claim for a declaration that plaintiff's removal as a manager was not valid; the complaint alleged that, in retaliation for plaintiff's initial complaint in the instant matter, defendants orchestrated a scheme to remove plaintiff as a manager involving a secretive process where the chief operating officer tricked the Series D unitholders into executing written consents by misrepresenting plaintiff's support among the other unitholders. DG BF, LLC v. Ray, — A.3d —, 2021 Del. Ch. LEXIS 37 (Del. Ch. Mar. 1, 2021).

SUBCHAPTER II
FORMATION; CERTIFICATE OF FORMATION

§ 18-217. Division of a limited liability company.

(a) As used in this section and §§ 18-203 and 18-301 of this title:

(1) "Dividing company" means the domestic limited liability company that is effecting a division in the manner provided in this section.

(2) "Division" means the division of a dividing company into 2 or more domestic limited liability companies in accordance with this section.

(3) "Division company" means a surviving company, if any, and each resulting company.

(4) "Division contact" means, in connection with any division, a natural person who is a Delaware resident, any division company in such division or any other domestic limited liability company or other business entity as defined in § 18-209 of this title formed or organized under the laws of the State of Delaware, which division contact shall maintain a copy of the plan of division for a period of 6 years from the effective date of the division and shall comply with paragraph (g)(3) of this section.

(5) "Organizational documents" means the certificate of formation and limited liability company agreement of a domestic limited liability company.

(6) "Resulting company" means a domestic limited liability company formed as a consequence of a division.

(7) "Surviving company" means a dividing company that survives the division.

(b) Pursuant to a plan of division, any domestic limited liability company may, in the manner provided in this section, be divided into 2 or more domestic limited liability companies. The division of a domestic limited liability company in accordance with this section and, if applicable, the resulting cessation of the existence of the dividing company pursuant to a certificate of division shall not be deemed to affect the personal liability of any person incurred prior to such division with respect to matters arising prior to such division, nor shall it be deemed to affect the validity or enforceability of any obligations or liabilities of the dividing company incurred prior to such division; provided, that the obligations and liabilities of the dividing company shall be allocated to and vested in, and valid and enforceable obligations of, such division company or companies to which such obligations and liabilities have been allocated pursuant to the plan of division, as provided in subsection (*l*) of this section. Each resulting company in a division shall be formed in compliance with the requirements of this chapter and subsection (i) of this section.

(c) If the limited liability company agreement of the dividing company specifies the manner of adopting a plan of division, the plan of division shall be adopted as specified in the limited liability company agreement. If the limited liability company agreement of the dividing company does not specify the manner of adopting a plan of division and does not prohibit a division of the limited liability company, the plan of division shall be adopted in the same manner as is specified in the limited liability company agreement for authorizing a merger or consolidation that involves the limited liability company as a constituent party to the merger or consolidation. If the limited liability company agreement of the dividing company does not specify the manner of adopting a plan of division or authorizing a merger or consolidation that involves the limited liability company as a constituent party and does not prohibit a division of the limited liability company, the adoption of a plan of division shall be authorized by the approval by members who own more than 50 percent of the then current percentage or other interest in the profits of the dividing company owned by all of the members. Notwithstanding prior approval, a plan of division may be terminated or amended pursuant to a provision for such termination or amendment contained in the plan of division.

(d) Unless otherwise provided in a plan of division, the division of a domestic limited liability company pursuant to this section shall not require such limited liability company to wind up its affairs under § 18-803 of this title or pay its liabilities and distribute its assets under § 18-804 of this title, and the division shall not constitute a dissolution of such limited liability company.

(e) In connection with a division under this section, rights or securities of, or interests in, the dividing company may be exchanged for or converted into cash, property, rights or securities of, or interests in, the surviving company or any resulting company or, in addition to or in lieu thereof, may be exchanged for or converted into cash, property, rights or securities of, or interests in, a domestic limited liability company or any other business entity which is not a division company or may be canceled or remain outstanding (if the dividing company is a surviving company).

(f) A plan of division adopted in accordance with subsection (c) of this section:

(1) May effect any amendment to the limited liability company agreement of the dividing company if it is a surviving company in the division; or

(2) May effect the adoption of a new limited liability company agreement for the dividing company if it is a surviving company in the division; and

(3) Shall effect the adoption of a limited liability company agreement for each resulting company.

Any amendment to a limited liability company agreement or adoption of a new limited liability company agreement for the dividing company, if it is a surviving company in the division, or adoption of a limited liability company agreement for each resulting company made pursuant to the foregoing sentence shall be effective at the effective time or date of the division. Any amendment to a limited liability company agreement or adoption of a limited liability company agreement for the dividing company, if it is a surviving company in the division, shall be effective notwithstanding any provision in the limited liability company agreement of the dividing company relating to amendment or adoption of a new limited liability company agreement, other than a provision that by its terms applies to an amendment to the limited liability company agreement or the adoption of a new limited liability company agreement, in either case, in connection with a division, merger or consolidation.

(g) If a domestic limited liability company is dividing under this section, the dividing company shall adopt a plan of division which shall set forth:

(1) The terms and conditions of the division, including:

a. Any conversion or exchange of the limited liability company interests of the dividing company into or for limited liability company interests or other securities or obligations of any division company or cash, property or rights or securities or obligations of or interests in any other business entity or domestic limited liability company which is not a division company, or that the limited liability company interests of the dividing company shall remain outstanding or be canceled, or any combination of the foregoing; and

b. The allocation of assets, property, rights, series, debts, liabilities and duties of the dividing company among the division companies;

(2) The name of each resulting company and, if the dividing company will survive the division, the name of the surviving company;

(3) The name and business address of a division contact which shall have custody of a copy of the plan of division. The division contact, or any successor division contact, shall serve for a period of 6 years following the effective date of the division. During such 6-year period the division contact shall provide, without cost, to any creditor of the dividing company, within 30 days following the division contact's receipt of a written request from any creditor of the dividing company, the name and business address of the division company to which the claim of such creditor was allocated pursuant to the plan of division; and

(4) Any other matters that the dividing company determines to include therein.

(h) If a domestic limited liability company divides under this section, the dividing company shall file a certificate of division executed by 1 or more authorized persons on behalf of such dividing company in the office of the Secretary of State in accordance with § 18-204 of this title and a certificate of formation that complies with § 18-201 of this title for each resulting company executed by 1 or more authorized persons in accordance with § 18-204 of this title. The certificate of division shall state:

(1) The name of the dividing company and, if it has been changed, the name under which its certificate of formation was originally filed and whether the dividing company is a surviving company;

(2) The date of filing of the dividing company's original certificate of formation with the Secretary of State;

(3) The name of each division company;

(4) The name and business address of the division contact required by paragraph (g)(3) of this section;

(5) The future effective date or time (which shall be a date or time certain) of the division if it is not to be effective upon the filing of the certificate of division;

(6) That the division has been approved in accordance with this section;

(7) That the plan of division is on file at a place of business of such division company as is specified therein, and shall state the address thereof;

(8) That a copy of the plan of division will be furnished by such division company as is specified therein, on request and without cost, to any member of the dividing company; and

(9) Any other information the dividing company determines to include therein.

(i) The certificate of division and each certificate of formation for each resulting company required by subsection (h) of this section shall be filed simultaneously in the office of the Secretary of State and, if such certificates are not to become effective upon their filing as permitted by § 18-206(b) of this title, then each such certificate shall provide for the same effective date or time in accordance with § 18-206(b) of this title. Concurrently with the effective date or time of a division, the limited liability company agreement of each resulting company shall become effective.

(j) A certificate of division shall act as a certificate of cancellation for a dividing company which is not a surviving company.

(k) A limited liability company agreement may provide that a domestic limited liability company shall not have the power to divide as set forth in this section.

(*l*) Upon the division of a domestic limited liability company becoming effective:

(1) The dividing company shall be divided into the distinct and independent resulting companies named in the plan of division, and, if the dividing company is not a surviving company, the existence of the dividing company shall cease.

(2) For all purposes of the laws of the State of Delaware, all of the rights, privileges and powers, and all the property, real, personal and mixed, of the dividing company and all debts due on whatever account to it, as well as all other things and other causes of action belonging to it, shall without further action be allocated to and vested in the applicable division company in such a manner and basis and with such effect as is specified in the plan of division, and the title to any real property or interest therein allocated to and vested in any division company shall not revert or be in any way impaired by reason of the division.

(3) Each division company shall, from and after effectiveness of the certificate of division, be liable as a separate and distinct domestic limited liability company for such debts, liabilities and duties of the dividing company as are allocated to such division company pursuant to the plan of division in the manner and on the basis provided in paragraph (g)(1)b. of this section.

(4) Each of the debts, liabilities and duties of the dividing company shall without further action be allocated to and be the debts, liabilities and duties of such division company as is specified in the plan of division as having such debts, liabilities and duties allocated to it, in such a manner and basis and with such effect as is specified in the plan of division, and no other division company shall be liable therefor, so long as the plan of division does not constitute a fraudulent transfer under applicable law, and all liens upon any property of the dividing company shall be preserved unimpaired, and all debts, liabilities and duties of the dividing company shall remain attached to the division company to which such debts, liabilities and duties have been allocated in the plan of division, and may be enforced against such division company to the same extent as if said debts, liabilities and duties had originally been incurred or contracted by it in its capacity as a domestic limited liability company.

(5) In the event that any allocation of assets, debts, liabilities and duties to division companies in accordance with a plan of division is

determined by a court of competent jurisdiction to constitute a fraudulent transfer, each division company shall be jointly and severally liable on account of such fraudulent transfer notwithstanding the allocations made in the plan of division; provided, however, the validity and effectiveness of the division are not otherwise affected thereby.

(6) Debts and liabilities of the dividing company that are not allocated by the plan of division shall be the joint and several debts and liabilities of all of the division companies.

(7) It shall not be necessary for a plan of division to list each individual asset, property, right, series, debt, liability or duty of the dividing company to be allocated to a division company so long as the assets, property, rights, series, debts, liabilities or duties so allocated are reasonably identified by any method where the identity of such assets, property, rights, series, debts, liabilities or duties is objectively determinable.

(8) The rights, privileges, powers and interests in property of the dividing company that have been allocated to a division company, as well as the debts, liabilities and duties of the dividing company that have been allocated to such division company pursuant to a plan of division, shall remain vested in each such division company and shall not be deemed, as a result of the division, to have been assigned or transferred to such division company for any purpose of the laws of the State of Delaware.

(9) Any action or proceeding pending against a dividing company may be continued against the surviving company as if the division did not occur, but subject to paragraph (*l*)(4) of this section, and against any resulting company to which the asset, property, right, series, debt, liability or duty associated with such action or proceeding was allocated pursuant to the plan of division by adding or substituting such resulting company as a party in the action or proceeding.

(m) In applying the provisions of this chapter on distributions, a direct or indirect allocation of property or liabilities in a division is not deemed a distribution for purposes of this chapter.

(n) The provisions of this section shall not be construed to limit the means of accomplishing a division by any other means provided for in a limited liability company agreement or other agreement or as otherwise permitted by this chapter or as otherwise permitted by law.

(o) All limited liability companies formed on or after August 1, 2018, shall be governed by this section. All limited liability companies formed prior to August 1, 2018, shall be governed by this section; provided, that if the dividing company is a party to any written contract, indenture or other agreement entered into prior to August 1, 2018, that, by its terms, restricts, conditions or prohibits the consummation of a merger or consolidation by the dividing company with or into another party, or the transfer of assets by the dividing company to another party, then such restriction, condition or prohibition shall be deemed to apply to a division as if it were a merger, consolidation or transfer of assets, as applicable.

History.

81 Del. Laws, c. 357, § 20; 82 Del. Laws, c. 48, § 8; 82 Del. Laws, c. 259, § 8; 83 Del. Laws, c. 61, § 2.

Revisor's note.

Section 10 of 83 Del. Laws, c. 61, provided: "This act shall become effective August 1, 2021."

Effect of amendments.

83 Del. Laws, c. 61, effective Aug. 1, 2021, substituted "§§ 18-203, and 18-301 of this title" for "§§ 18-203, 18-301 and 18-1203" in the introductory paragraph of (a).

SUBCHAPTER III
MEMBERS

§ 18-301. Admission of members.

NOTES TO DECISIONS

Certificate of formation.
Defendant was a member and manager of the subject limited liability company; the certificate of formation identified defendant as a member and provided that management was vested in the members. Robinson v. Darbeau, — A.3d —, 2021 Del. Ch. LEXIS 36 (Del. Ch. Mar. 1, 2021).

§ 18-304. Events of bankruptcy.

NOTES TO DECISIONS

Assignment.
A limited liability partnership membership interest, other than economic interest, terminated when the member filed a personal bankruptcy petition; bankruptcy law does not preempt the 6 Del. C. § 18-304 directive that a member of a limited liability company is divested of the right to participate in management upon filing for personal bankruptcy while becoming an assignee with economic rights under 6 Del. C. § 18-702. Zachman v. Real Time Cloud Servs. LLC, 251 A.3d 115 (Del. 2021).

§ 18-305. Access to and confidentiality of information; records.

(a) Each member of a limited liability company, in person or by attorney or other agent, has the right, subject to such reasonable standards (including standards governing what information (including books, records and other documents) is to be furnished at what time and location and at whose expense) as may be set forth in a limited liability company agreement or otherwise established by the manager or, if there is no manager, then by the members, to obtain from the limited liability company from time to time upon reasonable demand for any purpose reasonably related to the member's interest as a member of the limited liability company:

(1) True and full information regarding the status of the business and financial condition of the limited liability company;

(2) Promptly after becoming available, a copy of the limited liability company's federal, state and local income tax returns for each year;

(3) A current list of the name and last known business, residence or mailing address of each member and manager;

(4) A copy of any written limited liability company agreement and certificate of formation and all amendments thereto, together with executed copies of any written powers of attorney pursuant to which the limited liability company agreement and any certificate and all amendments thereto have been executed;

(5) True and full information regarding the amount of cash and a description and statement of the agreed value of any other property or services contributed by each member and which each member has agreed to contribute in the future, and the date on which each became a member; and

(6) Other information regarding the affairs of the limited liability company as is just and reasonable.

(b) Each manager shall have the right to examine all of the information described in subsection (a) of this section for a purpose reasonably related to the position of manager.

(c) The manager of a limited liability company shall have the right to keep confidential from the members, for such period of time as the manager deems reasonable, any information which the manager reasonably believes to be in the nature of trade secrets or other information the disclosure of which the manager in good faith believes is not in the best interest of the limited liability company or could damage the limited liability company or its business or which the limited liability company is required by law or by agreement with a third party to keep confidential.

(d) A limited liability company may maintain its books, records and other documents in other than paper form, including on, by means of, or in the form of any information storage device, method, or 1 or more electronic networks or databases (including 1 or more distributed electronic networks or databases), if such form is capable of conversion into paper form within a reasonable time.

(e) Any demand under this section shall be in writing and shall state the purpose of such demand. In every instance where an attorney or other agent shall be the person who seeks the right to obtain the information described in subsection (a) of this section, the demand shall be accompanied by a power of attorney or such other writing which authorizes the attorney or other agent to so act on behalf of the member.

(f) Any action to enforce any right arising under this section shall be brought in the Court of Chancery. If the limited liability company refuses to permit a member, or attorney or other agent acting for the member, to obtain or a manager to examine the information described in subsection (a) of this section or does not reply to the demand that has been made within 5 business days (or such shorter or longer period of time as is provided for in a limited liability company agreement but not longer than 30 business days) after the demand has been made, the demanding member or manager may apply to the Court of Chancery for an order to compel such disclosure. The Court of Chancery is hereby vested with exclusive jurisdiction to determine whether or not the person seeking such information is entitled to the information sought. The Court of Chancery may summarily order the limited liability company to permit the demanding member to obtain or manager to examine the information described in subsection (a) of this section and to make copies or abstracts therefrom, or the Court of Chancery may summarily order the limited liability company to furnish to the demanding member or manager the information described in subsection (a) of this section on the condition that the demanding member or manager first pay to the limited liability company the reasonable cost of obtaining and furnishing such information and on such other conditions as the Court of Chancery deems appropriate. When a demanding member seeks to obtain or a manager seeks to examine the information described in subsection (a) of this section, the demanding member or manager shall first establish:

> (1) That the demanding member or manager has complied with the provisions of this section respecting the form and manner of making demand for obtaining or examining of such information, and

> (2) That the information the demanding member or manager seeks is reasonably related to the member's interest as a member or the manager's position as a manager, as the case may be.

The Court of Chancery may, in its discretion, prescribe any limitations or conditions with reference to the obtaining or examining of information, or award such other or further relief as the Court of Chancery may deem just and proper. The Court of Chancery may order books, records and other documents, pertinent extracts therefrom, or duly authenticated copies thereof, to be brought within the State of Delaware and kept in the State of Delaware upon such terms and conditions as the order may prescribe.

(g) If a member is entitled to obtain information under this chapter or a limited liability company agreement for a purpose reasonably related to the member's interest as a member or other stated purpose, the member's right shall be to obtain such information as is necessary and essential to achieving that purpose. The rights of a member or manager to obtain or examine information as provided in this section may be expanded or restricted in an original limited liability company agreement or in any subsequent amendment approved or adopted by all of the members or in compliance with any applicable requirements of the limited liability company agreement. The provisions of this subsection shall not be construed to limit the ability to expand or restrict the rights of a member or manager to obtain or examine information by any other means permitted by law.

(h) A limited liability company shall maintain a current record that identifies the name and last known business, residence or mailing address of each member and manager.

History.
68 Del. Laws, c. 434, § 1; 70 Del. Laws, c. 186, § 1; 70 Del. Laws, c. 360, § 12; 73 Del. Laws, c. 83, § 15; 77 Del. Laws, c. 287, §§ 21, 22; 79 Del. Laws, c. 302, § 3; 81 Del. Laws, c. 357, § 26; 82 Del. Laws, c. 259, § 12; 83 Del. Laws, c. 61, § 3.

Revisor's note.
Section 10 of 83 Del. Laws, c. 61, provided: "This act shall become effective August 1, 2021."

Effect of amendments.
83 Del. Laws, c. 61, effective Aug. 1, 2021, in the introductory paragraph of (a), substituted "(including books, records and other documents) is" for "and documents are"; in (d), added "books" and "and other documents"; substituted "records and other documents" for "documents and records" in the last sentence of the final paragraph of (f); and, in (g), added the first sentence, added "or examine" in the second and third sentences, added "expanded or" in the second sentence, and in the third sentence substituted "expand or restrict" for "impose restrictions on" and "by law" for "under this chapter".

NOTES TO DECISIONS

Analysis

Discovery.
Scope.

Discovery.
Where a company was ordered in a final judgment to produce certain books and records for inspection by the shareholder, that company was not entitled to relief from the judgment because: (1) the company failed to demonstrate that allegedly newly discovered evidence could not have been, in the exercise of reasonable diligence, discovered for use at the trial; and (2) the company was not entitled to relief based on fraud because its cursory argument did not come close to showing the type of egregious conduct necessary to reopen a final judgment for fraud. Riker v. Teucrium Trading, LLC, — A.3d —, 2021 Del. Ch. LEXIS 87 (Del. Ch. May 3, 2021).

Scope.
Plaintiff (a stockholder and member of LLCs) was entitled to access to specific corporate books and records for the purpose of inspection, rather than their production; the inspection orders had to deploy "rifled precision," because the stockholder/member's right of inspection did not have an unlimited scope and had to be limited to documents that were necessary, essential and sufficient to the purpose. Ferris v. Ferris Props., — A.3d —, 2020 Del. Ch. LEXIS 334 (Del. Ch. Nov. 12, 2020).

Chancery Court acted within its discretion when it denied the broad requests of a member of a limited liability company for all communications between parties and lists of transactions because: (1) the requests were improperly broad; (2) they called for the company to create documents that did not exist or sought documents unrelated to the member's proper purpose; (3) the Court did not deny any request simply due to it being informal records which were being sought; and (4) the Court did not limit any records to which access was granted solely to formal records. Durham v. Grapetree, 246 A.3d 566 (Del. 2021).

SUBCHAPTER IV
MANAGERS

§ 18-407. Delegation of rights and powers to manage.

Unless otherwise provided in the limited liability company agreement, a member or manager of a limited liability company has the power and authority to delegate to 1 or more other persons any or all of the member's or manager's, as the case may be, rights, powers and duties to manage and control the business and affairs of the limited liability company, which delegation may be made irrespective of whether the member or manager has a conflict of interest with respect to the matter as to which its rights, powers or duties are being delegated, and the person or persons to whom any such rights, powers or duties are being delegated shall not be deemed conflicted solely by reason of the conflict of interest of the member or manager. Any such delegation may be to agents, officers and employees of a member or manager or the limited liability company, and by a management agreement or another agreement with, or otherwise to, other persons, including a committee of 1 or more persons. Unless otherwise provided in the limited liability company agreement, such delegation by a member or manager shall be irrevocable if it states that it is irrevocable. Unless otherwise provided in the limited liability company agreement, such delegation by a member or manager of a limited liability company shall not cause the member or manager to cease to be a member or manager, as the case may be, of the limited liability company or cause the person to whom any such rights, powers and duties have been delegated to be a member or manager, as the case may be, of the limited liability company. No other provision of this chapter or other law shall be construed to restrict a member's or manager's power and authority to delegate any or all of its rights, powers and duties to manage and control the business and affairs of the limited liability company.

History.
69 Del. Laws, c. 260, § 25; 71 Del. Laws, c. 77, § 28; 73 Del. Laws, c. 295, § 8; 80 Del. Laws, c. 45, § 7; 81 Del. Laws, c. 89, § 11; 83 Del. Laws, c. 61, § 4.

Revisor's note.
Section 10 of 83 Del. Laws, c. 61, provided: "This act shall become effective August 1, 2021."

Effect of amendments.
83 Del. Laws, c. 61, effective Aug. 1, 2021, added "which delegation ... conflict of interest of the member or manager" in the first sentence, "including a committee of 1 or more persons" in the second sentence and "or other law" in the final sentence.

SUBCHAPTER VI

DISTRIBUTIONS AND RESIGNATION

§ 18-602. Resignation of manager.

NOTES TO DECISIONS

Notice.
Dismissal of claims against a limited liability company was appropriate in an action brought by a founding and former member of the company, regarding the effect of the member's resignation efforts, because the motion fell short of demonstrating that the member could not recover under any reasonably conceivable set of circumstances; the company sought to hold the member to a resignation notice and contended that it was not conditional. Moscowitz v. Theory Entm't LLC, — A.3d —, 2020 Del. Ch. LEXIS 324 (Del. Ch. Oct. 28, 2020).

§ 18-603. Resignation of member.

NOTES TO DECISIONS

Implied agreements.
Purported resignation provision in an implied limited liability company (LLC) agreement, which only required the other member/manager draft and sign a resolution removing the other member, did not have the effect of removing defendant as a member or manager of the LLC; the court found defendant's testimony, explaining that plaintiff's entire narrative was fabricated and that defendant only learned of the existence of the resolution through litigation between the parties, more credible. Robinson v. Darbeau, — A.3d —, 2021 Del. Ch. LEXIS 36 (Del. Ch. Mar. 1, 2021).

SUBCHAPTER VII
ASSIGNMENT OF LIMITED LIABILITY COMPANY INTERESTS

§ 18-701. Nature of limited liability company interest.

NOTES TO DECISIONS

Ownership.

Creditors did not violate the automatic stay in bankruptcy with their foreclosure sales of real property in which the debtor's solely-owned Delaware limited liability company al-legedly had an interest; the debtor, as a member, had no interest in specific property of the company. Sobayo v. Nguyen (In re Sobayo), — B.R. —, 2021 Bankr. LEXIS 1610 (B.A.P. 9th Cir. June 9, 2021).

§ 18-702. Assignment of limited liability company interest.

NOTES TO DECISIONS

Bankruptcy.

A limited liability partnership membership interest, other than economic interest, terminated when the member filed a personal bankruptcy petition; bankruptcy law does not preempt the 6 Del. C. § 18-304 directive that a member of a limited liability company is divested of the right to participate in management upon filing for personal bankruptcy while becoming an assignee with economic rights under 6 Del. C. § 18-702. Zachman v. Real Time Cloud Servs. LLC, 251 A.3d 115 (Del. 2021).

§ 18-703. Member's limited liability company interest subject to charging order.

NOTES TO DECISIONS

Charging orders.

In an action (by former shareholders of a corporation dissenting to a merger) to enforce a judgment by the appraisal judgment creditors, the dissenting former shareholders stated a claim for outsider reverse veil-piercing because: (1) they properly pleaded claim for an exceptional circumstance in order to avoid fraud and injustice.; (2) the charging order did not prohibit the claim; and (3) although the reverse veil-piercing was appropriate, the claim for unjust enrichment (ostensibly utilized as a separate means to reach LLC assets subject to the charging order) was prevented under the charging order's provisions against the use of equitable claims and remedies (such as unjust enrichment). Manichaean Capital, LLC v. Exela Techs., Inc., 251 A.3d 694, 2021 Del. Ch. LEXIS 100 (Del. Ch. 2021).

SUBCHAPTER VIII
DISSOLUTION

§ 18-802. Judicial dissolution.

NOTES TO DECISIONS

Analysis

Dissolution.
— Warranted.
Jurisdiction.
— Personal.
Motion to dismiss.

Dissolution.

— Warranted.

Although defendant contrived the circumstances giving rise to deadlock, dissolution of the limited liability company (LLC) was warranted because: (1) defendant proved that the parties had an irreconcilable disagreement concerning plaintiff's continuing management of the LLC; (2) the deadlock, therefore, was genuine and sufficient; and (3) defendant's breach of the obligation to replicate plaintiff's right to equal distributions was not a basis to invalidate the dissolution. Mehra v. Teller, — A.3d —, 2021 Del. Ch. LEXIS 16 (Del. Ch. Jan. 29, 2021).

Parties' joint venture was dissolved by the court after it found that 1 party had breached a noncompetition provision once it was acquired by a competitor because: (1) the company was deadlocked at the board and member level; (2) the company had no remaining business, as it had no employees, officers, CEO, product, customers or revenue; (3) it lacked cash or a prospect for obtaining financing; and (4) it was no longer reasonably practicable for the company to carry on its business. Symbiont.Io, Inc v. Ipreo Holdings, LLC, — A.3d —, 2021 Del. Ch. LEXIS 174 (Del. Ch. Aug. 13, 2021).

Jurisdiction.

— Personal.

Because 6 Del. C. §§ 18-110 and 18-802 applied only to Delaware limited liability companies (LLCs), an LLC's conversion to a Puerto Rican entity deprived the court of jurisdiction to declare the LLC's proper managers and to order judicial dissolution. In re Coinmint, LLC, 2021 Del. Ch. LEXIS 172 (Del. Ch. May 10, 2021).

Motion to dismiss.
Petitioner sufficiently pleaded a claim for judicial dissolution of a limited liability company (LLC) because: (1) the parties' alleged inability to break their deadlock made plain the deadlock procedure's shortcomings, as the procedure did not mandate a price, pricing formula or a closing timeline during which either member could buy out the other; (2) it was alleged that the LLC was hemorrhaging cash, defaulting on loans and unable to appoint key management personnel; and (3) the LLC's languishing financial condition favored dissolution. Seokoh, Inc. v. Lard-PT, LLC, — A.3d —, 2021 Del. Ch. LEXIS 62 (Del. Ch. Mar. 30, 2021).

§ 18-805. Trustees or receivers for limited liability companies; appointment; powers; duties.

NOTES TO DECISIONS

Standard of review.
In the absence of a standard of review in the order appointing a receiver, neither 6 Del. C. § 18-805 nor Ch. Ct. R. 148-168 provide a standard for judging actions taken by a lawfully appointed receiver; it was permissible for Chancery Court to hold a de novo hearing on exceptions to a receiver's determinations as to claims and accounts, giving deference to discretionary business decisions permitted under an LLC agreement which relied in good faith upon reasonably reliable records and other sources of information. In re Dissolution of Jeffco Mgmt., LLC, — A.3d —, 2021 Del. Ch. LEXIS 13 (Del. Ch. Jan. 28, 2021).

SUBCHAPTER X
DERIVATIVE ACTIONS

§ 18-1001. Right to bring action.

NOTES TO DECISIONS

Standing.
Plaintiff lacked standing to pursue its derivative claims because it was no longer a member of an LLC (nor was it when it litigation was initiated); under 6 Del. C. § 18-1001, only members (or assignees) could bring derivative claims on behalf of a Delaware LLC. Clifford Paper, Inc. v. WPP Investors, LLC, 2021 Del. Ch. LEXIS 109 (Del. Ch. June 1, 2021).

§ 18-1003. Complaint.

NOTES TO DECISIONS

Adequacy.
New York trial court properly denied controlling members' motion to dismiss a minority member's complaint to recover damages for breach of fiduciary duty, misappropriation of corporate opportunity and civil conspiracy under Delaware law; the complaint pled with particularity that the controlling members were interested in the challenged transactions, such that demand was excused as futile. Joseph v. Rassi, 197 A.D.3d 1156, 151 N.Y.S.3d 369 (N.Y. App. Div. 2d Dep't 2021).

SUBCHAPTER XI
MISCELLANEOUS

§ 18-1101. Construction and application of chapter and limited liability company agreement.

NOTES TO DECISIONS

Analysis

Exculpatory clause.
Fiduciary duty.

Exculpatory clause.
Plaintiffs failed to sufficiently plead claims for breaches of fiduciary duty involving tortious interference with contract and intentional interference with existing or prospective business relations; the limited liability company's operating agreement exculpated the managers from the monetary liability plaintiffs sought for their alleged breaches. DG BF, LLC v. Ray, — A.3d —, 2021 Del. Ch. LEXIS 37 (Del. Ch. Mar. 1, 2021).

Fiduciary duty.
Plaintiff failed to sufficiently plead a breach of fiduciary duty claim because: (1) subject limited liability company agreements waived

traditional fiduciary duties and supplanted them with contractual standards of conduct; and (2) plaintiff neglected to plead breaches of contractual standards. Smith v. Scott, — A.3d —, 2021 Del. Ch. LEXIS 76 (Del. Ch. Apr. 23, 2021).

Joint venture's motion to dismiss breach of fiduciary duty claims was denied; the complaint contained a well-pleaded allegation that the individual in question committed acts for self-interested reasons (among other things, for self-enrichment and to facilitate insurance

fraud). In re Cadira Grp. Holdings, LLC Litig., — A.3d —, 2021 Del. Ch. LEXIS 151 (Del. Ch. July 12, 2021).

Two company managers were held personally liable for their breaches of fiduciary duty, because the relevant limitation-of-liability clause did not apply; their conduct was intentional and resulted in each gaining a financial benefit to which they were not entitled through their respective LLCs. Stone & Paper Inv'rs, LLC v. Blanch, 2021 Del. Ch. LEXIS 167 (Del. Ch. July 30, 2021).

§ 18-1104. Cases not provided for in this chapter.

NOTES TO DECISIONS

Fiduciary duty.

Plaintiff sufficiently pleaded a breach of loyalty claim against defendant because: (1) the complaint described an orchestrated series of self-interested actions by defendants, taken to the detriment of the company and plaintiff; (2) such allegations included that defendants took

2 sources of company assets (adjacent land and $700,000 in which plaintiff had a stake); and (3) nothing in the limited liability company's operating agreement explicitly absolved defendant manager of any fiduciary breach. Largo Legacy Grp., LLC v. Charles, — A.3d —, 2021 Del. Ch. LEXIS 140 (Del. Ch. June 30, 2021).

SUBCHAPTER XII
STATUTORY PUBLIC BENEFIT LIMITED LIABILITY COMPANIES

§ 18-1201. Law applicable to statutory public benefit limited liability companies; how formed.

This subchapter applies to all statutory public benefit limited liability companies, as defined in § 18-1202(a) of this title. If a limited liability company is formed as or elects to become a statutory public benefit limited liability company in the manner prescribed in this section, it shall be subject in all respects to the provisions of this chapter, except to the extent this subchapter imposes additional or different requirements, in which case such additional or different requirements shall apply, and notwithstanding § 18-1101 of this title or any other provision of this title, such additional or different requirements imposed by this subchapter may not be altered in the limited liability company agreement. If a limited liability company is not formed as a statutory public benefit limited liability company, it may become a statutory public benefit limited liability company in the manner specified in its limited liability company agreement or by amending its limited liability company agreement and certificate of formation to comply with the requirements of this subchapter.

History.

81 Del. Laws, c. 357, § 34; 83 Del. Laws, c. 61, § 5.

Revisor's note.

Section 10 of 83 Del. Laws, c. 61, provided: "This act shall become effective August 1, 2021."

Effect of amendments.

83 Del. Laws, c. 61, effective Aug. 1, 2021,

substituted "§ 18-1202(a)" for "§ 18-1202" in the first sentence; in the second sentence, added "is formed as or", deleted "under this subchapter" preceding "in the manner", substituted "section" for "subchapter" and added the second and third occurrences of "additional or different"; and added the final sentence.

§ 18-1202. Statutory public benefit limited liability company defined; contents of certificate of formation and limited liability company agreement.

(a) A "statutory public benefit limited liability company" is a for-profit limited liability company formed under and subject to the requirements of this chapter that is intended to produce a public benefit or public benefits and to operate in a responsible and sustainable manner. To that end, a statutory public benefit limited liability company shall be managed in a manner that balances the members' pecuniary interests, the best interests of those materially affected by the limited liability company's conduct, and the public benefit or public benefits set forth in its limited liability company agreement and in its certificate of formation. A statutory public benefit limited liability company shall state in its limited liability company agreement and in the heading of its certificate of formation that it is a statutory public benefit limited liability company and shall set forth in its limited liability company agreement and in its certificate of formation 1 or more specific public benefits to be promoted by the limited liability company. In the event of any inconsistency between the public benefit or benefits to be promoted by the limited liability company as set forth in its limited liability company agreement and in its certificate of formation, the limited liability company agreement shall control as among the members, the managers and other persons who are party to or otherwise bound by the liability company agreement. A manager of a statutory public benefit limited liability company or, if there is no manager, then any member of a statutory public benefit limited liability company who becomes aware that the specific public benefit or benefits to be promoted by the limited liability company as set forth in its limited liability company agreement are inaccurately set forth in its certificate of formation, shall promptly amend the certificate of formation. Any provision in the limited liability company agreement or certificate of formation of a statutory public benefit limited liability company that is inconsistent with this subchapter shall not be effective to the extent of such inconsistency.

(b) "Public benefit" means a positive effect (or reduction of negative effects) on 1 or more categories of persons, entities, communities or interests (other than members in their capacities as members) including, but not limited to, effects of an artistic, charitable, cultural, economic, educational, environmental, literary, medical, religious, scientific or technological nature. "Public benefit provisions" means the provisions of a limited liability company agreement contemplated by this subchapter.

History.
81 Del. Laws, c. 357, § 34; 83 Del. Laws, c. 61, § 6.

Revisor's note.
Section 10 of 83 Del. Laws, c. 61, provided:

"This act shall become effective August 1, 2021."

Effect of amendments.
83 Del. Laws, c. 61, effective Aug. 1, 2021, rewrote (a).

§ 18-1203. Certain amendments and mergers; votes required.

History.
81 Del. Laws, c. 357, § 34; repealed by 83 Del. Laws, c. 61, § 7, effective Aug. 1, 2021.

Revisor's note.
Section 10 of 83 Del. Laws, c. 61, provided:

"This act shall become effective August 1, 2021."

§ 18-1204. Duties of members or managers.

(a) The members or managers or other persons with authority to manage or direct the business and affairs of a statutory public benefit limited liability company shall manage or direct the business and affairs of the statutory public benefit limited liability company in a manner that balances the pecuniary interests of the members, the best interests of those materially affected by the limited liability company's conduct, and the specific public benefit or public benefits set forth in its limited liability company agreement and certificate of formation. Unless otherwise provided in a limited liability company agreement, no member, manager or other person with authority to manage or direct the business and affairs of the statutory public benefit limited liability company shall have any liability for monetary damages for the failure to manage or direct the business and affairs of the statutory public benefit limited liability company as provided in this subsection.

(b) A member or manager of a statutory public benefit limited liability company or any other person with authority to manage or direct the business and affairs of the statutory public benefit limited liability company shall not, by virtue of the public benefit provisions or § 18-1202(a) of this title, have any duty to any person on account of any interest of such person in the public benefit or public benefits set forth in its limited liability company agreement and certificate of formation or on account of any interest materially affected by the limited liability company's conduct and, with respect to a decision implicating the balance requirement in subsection (a) of this section, will be deemed to satisfy such person's fiduciary duties to members and the limited liability company if such person's decision is both informed and disinterested and not such that no person of ordinary, sound judgment would approve.

History.
81 Del. Laws, c. 357, § 34; 83 Del. Laws, c. 61, § 8.

Revisor's note.
Section 10 of 83 Del. Laws, c. 61, provided: "This act shall become effective August 1, 2021."

Effect of amendments.
83 Del. Laws, c. 61, effective Aug. 1, 2021, added "limited liability company agreement and" in the first sentence of (a) and in (b).

§ 18-1205. Periodic statements and third-party certification.

A statutory public benefit limited liability company shall no less than biennially provide its members with a statement as to the limited liability company's promotion of the public benefit or public benefits set forth in its limited liability company agreement and certificate of formation and as to the best interests of those materially affected by the limited liability company's conduct. The statement shall include:

(1) The objectives that have been established to promote such public benefit or public benefits and interests;

(2) The standards that have been adopted to measure the limited liability company's progress in promoting such public benefit or public benefits and interests;

(3) Objective factual information based on those standards regarding the limited liability company's success in meeting the objectives for promoting such public benefit or public benefits and interests; and

(4) An assessment of the limited liability company's success in meeting the objectives and promoting such public benefit or public benefits and interests.

History.
81 Del. Laws, c. 357, § 34; 83 Del. Laws, c. 61, § 9.

Revisor's note.
Section 10 of 83 Del. Laws, c. 61, provided: "This act shall become effective August 1, 2021."

Effect of amendments.
83 Del. Laws, c. 61, effective Aug. 1, 2021, added "limited liability company agreement and" in the first sentence of the introductory paragraph.

CHAPTER 20
TRADE SECRETS

§ 2001. Definitions.

NOTES TO DECISIONS

Misappropriation.

Defendant was not entitled to summary judgment on plaintiff's Delaware Uniform Trade Secrets Act (6 Del. C. § 2001 et seq.) claim; a reasonable fact-finder could conclude that the optimized process for operating plaintiff's plant-based manufacturing system as a whole, the optimized process of applying it to specific proteins, and the proprietary methods and know-how for optimizing each step of the process collectively constituted trade secrets worthy of statutory protection and were not readily ascertainable. Inc. v. Fraunhofer USA, Inc., 2020 Del. Ch. LEXIS 297 (September 25, 2020).

Former employee's acceptance of a position with a competitor in a different business segment did not support preliminary injunctive relief; misappropriation claims under the Defend Trade Secrets Act (18 U.S.C. § 1831 et seq.), the Minnesota Uniform Trade Secrets Act (Minn. Stat. § 325C.01 et seq.) and the Delaware Uniform Trade Secrets Act (6 Del. C. § 2001 et seq.)were unlikely to succeed because there was neither evidence of misappropriation nor meeting of the high bar for inevitable disclosure. United Healthcare Servs. v. Louro, — F. Supp. 3d —, 2021 U.S. Dist. LEXIS 27333 (D. Minn. Feb. 12, 2021).

§ 2006. Statute of limitations.

NOTES TO DECISIONS

Time limitations.

Successor company's claims of unlawful accessing and disclosing of its trade secrets after expiration of an access agreement were time-barred where the claim accrued when defendant allegedly falsely certified compliance with confidentiality and nonuse obligations or when

the successor should have discovered the facts underlying its claims; those dates were more than 3 years before the complaint was filed. Ocimum Biosolutions (India) Ltd. v. LG Corp., 2021 U.S. Dist. LEXIS 45742 (D. Del. Mar. 11, 2021).

§ 2007. Effect on other law.

NOTES TO DECISIONS

Analysis

Claims.
— Displacement.
Preemption.

Claims.

— Displacement.

Delaware's Uniform Trade Secrets Act (6 Del. C. § 2001 et seq.) displaced plaintiff's conversion claim; the basis of the conversion claim was the same as plaintiff's misappropriation claim, namely that defendant misappropriated plaintiff's trade secrets by using or proposing to

use plaintiff's technology without plaintiff's authorization. Inc. v. Fraunhofer USA, Inc., 2020 Del. Ch. LEXIS 297 (September 25, 2020).

Preemption.

Delaware's Uniform Trade Secret Act (6 Del. C. § 2001 et seq.) preempted plaintiff's unjust enrichment claim; the unjust enrichment claim rested on the same facts as plaintiff's trade secrets claim, which encompassed the restitutionary elements and purposes of plaintiff's common law unjust enrichment claim. Inc. v. Message Sys., 2021 Del. Ch. LEXIS 11 (January 22, 2021).

CHAPTER 23
INTEREST

§ 2301. Legal rate; loans insured by Federal Housing Administration.

NOTES TO DECISIONS

Analysis

Interest.
— Prejudgment.

Interest.

— Prejudgment.

Because a prevailing party's damages in a

contractual dispute flowed from legal and not equitable claims, the court awarded simple and not compound interest. Optical Air Data Sys., LLC v. L-3 Communs. Corp., — A.3d —, 2021 Del. Super. LEXIS 113 (Del. Super. Ct. Feb. 8, 2021).

CHAPTER 25
PROHIBITED TRADE PRACTICES

SUBCHAPTER II
CONSUMER FRAUD

§ 2511. Definitions.

As used in this subchapter, unless the context otherwise requires:

(1) "Advertisement" means the attempt by publication, dissemination, solicitation or circulation to induce, directly or indirectly, any person to enter into any obligation or acquire any title or interest in, any merchandise.

(2) "Examination" means inspection, study or copying.

(3) "Lease" means any lease, offer to lease or attempt to lease any merchandise for any consideration.

(4) "Local telephone directory" means a telephone classified advertising directory or the business section of a telephone directory that is distributed free of charge to some or all telephone subscribers in a local area.

(5) "Local telephone number" means a telephone number that has the 3-number prefix(es) used by the telephone service company(ies) for telephones physically located within the area covered by the local telephone directory in which the number is listed. The term does not include long distance numbers or toll or toll free numbers listed in a local telephone directory.

(6) "Merchandise" means any objects, wares, goods, commodities, intangibles, real estate or services.

(7) "Person" means an individual, corporation, government, or governmental subdivision or agency, statutory trust, business trust, estate, trust, partnership, unincorporated association, 2 or more of any of the foregoing having a joint or common interest, or any other legal or commercial entity.

(8) "Sale" means any sale, offer for sale or attempt to sell any merchandise for any consideration.

(9) "Unfair practice" means any act or practice that causes or is likely to cause substantial injury to consumers which is not reasonably avoidable by consumers themselves and not outweighed by countervailing benefits to consumers or to competition. In determining whether an act or practice is unfair, violations of public policy as established by law, regulation, or judicial decision applicable in this State may be considered as evidence of substantial injury.

History.

6 Del. C. 1953, § 2511; 55 Del. Laws, c. 46; 71 Del. Laws, c. 420, §§ 2, 3; 71 Del. Laws, c. 470, § 11; 73 Del. Laws, c. 329, § 35; 83 Del. Laws, c. 85, § 1.

Effect of amendments.

83 Del. Laws, c. 85, effective July 23, 2021, added (9).

NOTES TO DECISIONS

Applicability.

In a trust's action against a life insurer and its parent company following payment of the policy surrender value instead of the death benefit, the court granted defendants' motion for summary judgment, finding that there was no breach where the insured had tendered the policy's surrender value because the policy's clear terms redefined the death benefit as the surrender value upon the insured reaching the age of 100 (an event which did occur, as the insured had reached the age of 100 prior to death); the trust was not entitled to summary judgment on its claim for a violation of Delaware Consumer Fraud Act (6 Del. C. § 2511 et seq.) or the Unfair Practices in the Insurance Business statutes (18 Del. C. § 2301 et seq.), because neither provided a private right of action against insurance companies. Olga J. Nowak Irrevocable Trust v. Voya Fin., Inc., — A.3d —, 2020 Del. Super. LEXIS 2977 (Del. Super. Ct. Nov. 30, 2020), aff'd, 256 A.3d 207 (Del. 2021).

§ 2512. Purpose; construction.

NOTES TO DECISIONS

Comparison with other law.

In a trust's action against a life insurer and its parent company following payment of the policy surrender value instead of the death benefit, the court granted defendants' motion for summary judgment, finding that there was no breach where the insured had tendered the policy's surrender value because the policy's clear terms redefined the death benefit as the surrender value upon the insured reaching the age of 100 (an event which did occur, as the insured had reached the age of 100 prior to death); the trust was not entitled to summary judgment on its claim for a violation of Delaware Consumer Fraud Act (6 Del. C. § 2511 et seq.) or the Unfair Practices in the Insurance Business statutes (18 Del. C. § 2301 et seq.), because neither provided a private right of action against insurance companies. Olga J. Nowak Irrevocable Trust v. Voya Fin., Inc., — A.3d —, 2020 Del. Super. LEXIS 2977 (Del. Super. Ct. Nov. 30, 2020), aff'd, 256 A.3d 207 (Del. 2021).

§ 2513. Unlawful practice.

(a) The act, use, or employment by any person of any deception, fraud, false pretense, false promise, misrepresentation, unfair practice, or the concealment, suppression, or omission of any material fact with intent that others rely upon such concealment, suppression, or omission, in connection with the sale, lease, receipt, or advertisement of any merchandise, whether or not any person has in fact been misled, deceived, or damaged thereby, is an unlawful practice. It shall also be an unlawful practice to misrepresent the geographic location of a business or supplier which raises or sells flowers and/or ornamental plants by any of the following:

(1) Listing a local telephone number in a local telephone directory if:

a. Calls to the telephone number are routinely forwarded or otherwise transferred to a business location that is outside the calling area covered by the local telephone directory other than to counties contiguous to this State; and

b. The listing fails to identify the locality and state of the supplier's business; or

(2) Listing a fictitious business name or an assumed business name in a local telephone directory if:

a. The name misrepresents the supplier's geographic location; and

b. The listing fails to identify the locality and state of the supplier's business.

(b) This section shall not apply:

(1) To the owner or publisher of newspapers, magazines, publications or printed matter wherein such advertisement appears, or to the owner or operator of a radio or television station which disseminates such advertisement when the owner, publisher or operator has no knowledge of the intent, design or purpose of the advertiser; or

(2) To any advertisement or merchandising practice which is subject to and complies with the rules and regulations, of and the statutes administered by, the Federal Trade Commission; or

(3) To matters subject to the jurisdiction of the Public Service Commission, or of the Insurance Commissioner of this State, except for matters covered by § 1014 of Title 26, but only as they relate to community-owned energy generating facilities.

History.

6 Del. C. 1953, § 2513; 55 Del. Laws, c. 46; 69 Del. Laws, c. 203, § 23; 71 Del. Laws, c. 420, § 1; 71 Del. Laws, c. 470, §§ 12, 13; 83 Del. Laws, c. 85, § 2; 83 Del. Laws, c. 178, § 5.

Effect of amendments.

83 Del. Laws, c. 85, effective July 23, 2021, in the introductory paragraph of (a), added "unfair practice" and "receipt" in the first sentence and "any of the following" in the second sentence.

83 Del. Laws, c. 178, effective September 17, 2021, added the exception in (b)(3).

NOTES TO DECISIONS

Analysis

Failure to state a claim.
Insurance.

Failure to state a claim.

Plaintiffs sufficiently pleaded a claim under the Delaware Consumer Fraud Act (6 Del. C. § 2511 et seq.) because: (1) plaintiffs' fraudulent inducement claim was not barred by the economic loss doctrine; (2) the Act was parallel to common law, but with fewer proof requirements; and (3) the Act was a legislative creation, whereas the economic loss doctrine was judicially created. R. Keating & Sons, Inc. v. Chiselcreek Dev., LLC, — A.3d —, 2020 Del. Super. LEXIS 2868 (Del. Super. Ct. Oct. 30, 2020).

Insurance.

In a trust's action against a life insurer and its parent company following payment of the policy surrender value instead of the death benefit, the court granted defendants' motion for summary judgment, finding that there was no breach where the insured had tendered the policy's surrender value because the policy's clear terms redefined the death benefit as the surrender value upon the insured reaching the age of 100 (an event which did occur, as the insured had reached the age of 100 prior to death); the trust was not entitled to summary judgment on its claim for a violation of Delaware Consumer Fraud Act (6 Del. C. § 2511 et seq.) or the Unfair Practices in the Insurance Business statutes (18 Del. C. § 2301 et seq.), because neither provided a private right of action against insurance companies. Olga J. Nowak Irrevocable Trust v. Voya Fin., Inc., — A.3d —, 2020 Del. Super. LEXIS 2977 (Del. Super. Ct. Nov. 30, 2020), aff'd, 256 A.3d 207 (Del. 2021).

§ 2525. Private cause of action; savings clause for private claims against persons who acquired property by unlawful practices.

NOTES TO DECISIONS

Standing.

In a trust's action against a life insurer and its parent company following payment of the policy surrender value instead of the death benefit, the court granted defendants' motion for summary judgment, finding that there was no breach where the insured had tendered the policy's surrender value because the policy's clear terms redefined the death benefit as the surrender value upon the insured reaching the age of 100 (an event which did occur, as the insured had reached the age of 100 prior to death); the trust was not entitled to summary judgment on its claim for a violation of Delaware Consumer Fraud Act (6 Del. C. § 2511 et seq.) or the Unfair Practices in the Insurance Business statutes (18 Del. C. § 2301 et seq.), because neither provided a private right of action against insurance companies. Olga J. Nowak Irrevocable Trust v. Voya Fin., Inc., — A.3d —, 2020 Del. Super. LEXIS 2977 (Del. Super. Ct. Nov. 30, 2020), aff'd, 256 A.3d 207 (Del. 2021).

SUBCHAPTER VII

BUYER PROPERTY PROTECTION ACT

§ 2572. Disclosure of material defects.

NOTES TO DECISIONS

Analysis

Contract.
— Breach.
Damages.
Disclosure.
— Inadequate.
Material defect.
Violation.
— Failure to establish.

Contract.

— Breach.

Plaintiff's breach of contract claim, based in part on the Delaware Buyer Protection Act (6 Del. C. § 2574 et seq.) was not barred by the doctrine of merger by deed or this statute; the merger doctrine only applied to questions of title, quantity and land use, and neither applied to claims under the Act nor breach of contract claims. Mullins v. Ascetta, — A.3d —, 2021 Del. Super. LEXIS 102 (Del. Super. Ct. Feb. 3, 2021).

Damages.

There was no testimony that all listed work was reasonable, necessary and related to breach because: (1) expert testimony was required and lacking; and (2) except for 1 item, plaintiffs had not proven a costs-of-repair case. Mullin v. Ascetta, — A.3d —, 2021 Del. Super. LEXIS 596 (Del. Super. Ct. Sept. 20, 2021).

Plaintiffs' claim for diminution in value was based on facts that either were not considered or not related to any action on defendants' part; any award for diminution in value based only on those items for which defendants were responsible would be speculative and improper. Mullin v. Ascetta, — A.3d —, 2021 Del. Super. LEXIS 596 (Del. Super. Ct. Sept. 20, 2021).

Where plaintiffs would have to move out of their house while work was being done, related to a material defect that was not disclosed or covered by the homeowner's warranty, the court found a 5-month period would be an appropriate times-pan for the work; the court awarded $8,500 for alternative housing costs and $10,644 for moving expenses associated with same. Mullin v. Ascetta, — A.3d —, 2021 Del. Super. LEXIS 596 (Del. Super. Ct. Sept. 20, 2021).

Disclosure.

— Inadequate.

Plaintiffs had proven by a preponderance of the evidence that there was a material defect in a roof that should have been disclosed on the seller's disclosure by defendants but was not; testimony of defendants' home inspector was not credible, as the trial court found the inspec-

tion was at best incomplete and cast serious doubt on its credibility. Mullin v. Ascetta, — A.3d —, 2021 Del. Super. LEXIS 596 (Del. Super. Ct. Sept. 20, 2021).

While defendants might (or might not) have known what the defect was that caused floors to squeak, the excessive and continued squeaking of the floors was well known to the sellers; that issue should have been disclosed. Mullin v. Ascetta, — A.3d —, 2021 Del. Super. LEXIS 596 (Del. Super. Ct. Sept. 20, 2021).

Material defect.

As to a plumbing drain that was improperly added to the drain-line cleanout, even if it were added after the house was purchased by the buyers, there was neither evidence that the issue caused any problem after repair work was completed nor any evidence that it was a material defect; on those facts, there was no duty of disclosure. Mullin v. Ascetta, — A.3d —, 2021 Del. Super. LEXIS 596 (Del. Super. Ct. Sept. 20, 2021).

Even if there had been a prior issue requiring the placement of soffits after purchase by the buyers, there was no evidence that there was any continuing problem from that issue after the soffits were installed or that it was a material defect; as a result, there was no duty of disclosure. Mullin v. Ascetta, — A.3d —, 2021 Del. Super. LEXIS 596 (Del. Super. Ct. Sept. 20, 2021).

Violation.

— Failure to establish.

Defendants had no duty to disclose that of which they had no knowledge, including alleged issues with walls, venting and a light. Mullin v. Ascetta, — A.3d —, 2021 Del. Super. LEXIS 596 (Del. Super. Ct. Sept. 20, 2021).

§ 2574. Other inspections or warranties.

NOTES TO DECISIONS

Breach of contract.

Plaintiff's breach of contract claim, based in part on the Delaware Buyer Protection Act (6 Del. C. § 2574 et seq.) was not barred by the doctrine of merger by deed or this statute; the merger doctrine only applied to questions of

title, quantity and land use, and neither applied to claims under the Act nor breach of contract claims. Mullins v. Ascetta, — A.3d —, 2021 Del. Super. LEXIS 102 (Del. Super. Ct. Feb. 3, 2021).

CHAPTER 27

CONTRACTS

SUBCHAPTER I
GENERAL PROVISIONS

§ 2708. Choice of law.

Analysis

Agreement.
— Certainty.
Relationships.
— Material.

Agreement.

— Certainty.

Insurer's uninsurability defense was inapplicable under Delaware law because: (1) the investment funds validly nominated Delaware as the jurisdiction of the "law most favorable" to them in their insurance policy's conflict of law provision; (2) under 6 Del. C. § 2708, Delaware law was a presumptively valid, significant, material and reasonable choice of law; and (3) the anti-fraudulent conveyance statute in Delaware (6 Del. C. § 1307) did not render insuring against clawback claims for which restitution or disgorgement might be exacted contrary to state public policy. Sycamore Partners Mgmt., L.P. v. Endurance Am. Ins. Co., — A.3d —, 2021 Del. Super. LEXIS 182 (Del. Super. Ct. Feb. 26, 2021).

Relationships.

— Material.

General choice-of-law provision in a stock purchase agreement, applying Delaware law, did not require dismissal of plaintiff's California Corporate Securities Law of 1968 (Cal. Corp. Code § 25000 et seq.) claim because: (1) California law applied to part of plaintiff's allegations of fraud; (2) California possessed a materially greater interest in the application of the securities act than Delaware; and (3) any waiver by plaintiff of its right to assert a claim under the securities act would have been contrary to California's public policies. Swipe Acquisition Corp. v. Krauss, — A.3d —, 2021 Del. Ch. LEXIS 14 (Del. Ch. Jan. 28, 2021).

SUBCHAPTER IV
CONSUMER CONTRACTS

§ 2731. Definitions.

As used in this subchapter:

(1) "Automatic renewal provision" means a provision under which a contract is renewed for a specified period of more than 1 month if the renewal causes the contract to be in effect more than 12 months after the day of the initiation of the contract and such renewal is effective unless the consumer gives notice to the seller of the consumer's intention to terminate the contract.

(2) "Clearly and conspicuously" means either that printed disclosures must be in larger type than the surrounding text, or in contrasting type, font, or color to the surrounding text of the same size, or set off from the surrounding text of the same size by symbols or other marks, or by way of a recorded audio disclosure, in a manner that clearly calls attention to the language.

(3) "Consumer" means an individual who purchases or leases merchandise primarily for personal, family or household purposes.

(4) "Contract" means any contract for the sale of merchandise or any lease.

(5) "Lease" means any lease, offer to lease or attempt to lease any merchandise.

(6) "Merchandise" means any objects, wares, goods, commodities, intangibles, real estate or services, other than insurance.

(7) "Person" means an individual, corporation, government or governmental subdivision or agency, statutory trust, business trust, estate, trust, partnership, unincorporated association, 2 or more of any of the foregoing having a joint or common interest or any other legal or commercial entity.

(8) "Sale" means any sale, offer for sale or attempt to sell any merchandise for cash or credit.

(9) "Seller" means any person engaged in commerce that sells, leases, or offers to sell or lease any merchandise to a consumer.

History.
66 Del. Laws, c. 276, § 1; 73 Del. Laws, c. 329, § 38; 83 Del. Laws, c. 115, § 1.

added present (1), (2), (4) and (9) and redesignated the remaining and intervening paragraphs accordingly.

Effect of amendments.
83 Del. Laws, c. 115, effective Jan. 1, 2022,

§ 2732. Deceptive practices in consumer contracts.

In a contract for the sale or lease of merchandise to a consumer, a person engages in a deceptive practice when that person knowingly or recklessly:

(1) Distorts or obscures the terms, conditions or meaning of the contract or creates a likelihood of confusion or misunderstanding by the use of unintelligible words, phrases or sentences; or

(2) Omits information required by law to be disclosed in contracts with a consumer; or

(3) Violates § 2734 of this title; or

(4) With respect to a contract that automatically renews and without regard to the duration of such renewal period, fails to provide a cost-effective, timely, and easy to use mechanism for cancellation. A consumer who enters into a contract online shall be permitted to cancel the contract online.

History.
66 Del. Laws, c. 276, § 1; 70 Del. Laws, c. 186, § 1; 83 Del. Laws, c. 115, § 1.

added (3) and (4) and made related stylistic changes.

Effect of amendments.
83 Del. Laws, c. 115, effective Jan. 1, 2022,

§ 2733. Guidelines.

The following are factors that a court may consider in determining whether a contract complies with this subchapter:

(1) Whether cross-references are confusing.

(2) Whether sentences are unreasonably long or complex.

(3) Whether sentences contain double negatives and exceptions to exceptions.

(4) Whether sentences and sections are in a confusing or illogical order.

(5) Whether it contains words with obsolete meanings or words that differ in their legal meaning from their ordinary meaning.

(6) Whether conditions, exceptions to the main provision of the agreement and protection for consumers or restrictions of consumers' right are given equal prominence with the main provision.

History.
66 Del. Laws, c. 276, § 1; 83 Del. Laws, c. 115, § 1.

Effect of amendments.
83 Del. Laws, c. 115, effective Jan. 1, 2022, reenacted the section without change.

§ 2734. Contracts with automatic renewal provisions.

(a) Any seller that sells, leases, or offers to sell or lease any merchandise to a consumer pursuant to a contract that contains an automatic renewal provision shall disclose the terms of the automatic renewal provision clearly and conspicuously at the time the contract is entered into.

(b) Any seller that sells or leases any merchandise to a consumer pursuant to a contract that is renewed for a specified period of more than 1 month if the renewal causes the contract to be in effect more than 12 months after the day of the initiation of the contract, shall notify the consumer of each upcoming extension of the contract no less than 30 days and no more than 60 days before the cancellation deadline pursuant to the automatic renewal provision. Such notification shall disclose clearly and conspicuously:

    (1) That unless the consumer cancels the contract, the contract will automatically renew;

    (2) The date by which the consumer must cancel the contract to avoid automatic renewal;

    (3) The procedures the consumer must follow to cancel the contract; and

    (4) How the consumer may obtain details of the automatic renewal provision, whether by contacting the seller at a specified telephone number or address, by providing a copy of the provision, by providing access to the contract, or by any other appropriate method.

(c) A seller that fails to comply with the requirements of this section is in violation of this subchapter unless the seller demonstrates that:

    (1) As part of the seller's routine business practice, the seller has both:

        a. Established and implemented written procedures to comply with this section; and

        b. Enforces compliance with such procedures;

    (2) Any failure to comply with this subchapter is the result of error; and

    (3) As part of the seller's routine business practice, where an error has caused the failure to comply with this subchapter, the unearned portion of the contract subject to the automatic renewal provision is refunded as of the date on which the seller is notified of the error or becomes aware of the error, whichever is earlier.

(d) This section does not apply to:

    (1) Matters subject to the jurisdiction of the Public Service Commission.

    (2) Matters subject to the jurisdiction of the Insurance Commissioner of this State.

    (3) Matters subject to the jurisdiction of the Federal Communications Commission.

    (4) Leases subject to the Residential Landlord-Tenant Code, Chapters 51 through 59 of Title 25, or the Manufactured Homes and Manufactured Home Communities Act, Chapter 70 of Title 25.

History.
83 Del. Laws, c. 115, § 1.

Revisor's note.
  This section became effective on Jan. 1, 2022, by operation of 6 Del. C. § 2737(c).

Section 1 of 83 Del. Laws, c. 115, made effective Jan. 1, 2022, by 6 Del. C. § 2737(c) in that act, transferred former § 2734 of this title, concerning remedies, to present § 2735 of this title.

§ 2735. Remedies.

(a) Any person who engages in a deceptive practice governed by this subchapter shall be liable to a consumer in an amount equal to treble the amount of actual damages proved, plus reasonable attorneys' fees.

(b) A consumer likely to be damaged by a deceptive practice governed by this subchapter may be granted an injunction against it under the principles of equity and on terms the court considers reasonable.

(c) With respect to any contract containing an automatic renewal provision that is renewed in violation of § 2734 of this title, such contract is voidable by the consumer.

    (1) The consumer shall void the automatic renewal contract using any method that would have been sufficient to cancel the contract prior to its renewal.

    (2) A consumer who voids a contract pursuant to this subsection shall not be liable for any costs, fees, or expenses associated with the contract that accrue after the date on which the consumer voided the contract. The seller may retain a prorated fraction of any prepaid fees or costs based on

the time since the renewal was executed and the time remaining in the renewal period. The seller shall refund any remaining prepaid fees or costs to the consumer within 30 days.

History.
66 Del. Laws, c. 276, § 1; 83 Del. Laws, c. 115, § 1.

Revisor's note.
Section 1 of 83 Del. Laws, c. 115, made effective Jan. 1, 2022, by 6 Del. C. § 2737(c) in that act, transferred the former version of this

section, concerning application, to present § 2736 of this title and renumbered former § 2734 of this title as this section.

Effect of amendments.
83 Del. Laws, c. 115, effective Jan. 1, 2022, added (c).

NOTES TO DECISIONS

Analysis
Arbitration.
Misrepresentations.

Arbitration.
In light of the presumption favoring arbitration, the parties' arbitration agreement was not unconscionable, even though it limited the buyer's remedies of recovering attorney's fees if the buyer prevailed on the buyer's consumer war-

ranty claims against a car dealer. Elia v. Hertrich Family of Auto. Dealerships, Inc., 2013 Del. Super. LEXIS 554 (Del. Super. Ct. Dec. 13, 2013), aff'd, 103 A.3d 514 (Del. 2014).

Misrepresentations.
Consumer fraud and deceptive practices claims arising from faulty and incomplete home renovations failed; no misrepresentations were shown. Conaway v. New Hope Tile, LLC, 2017 Del. C.P. LEXIS 30 (Del. C.P. May 31, 2017).

§ 2736. Application.

This subchapter shall not apply to contracts in which the total contract price or the total amount financed exceeds $50,000, or to any contract entered into with or acquired by a banking organization or building and loan association as defined by Chapters 1 and 17, respectively, of Title 5 or to any public utility tariff on file with the Delaware Public Service Commission pursuant to Chapter 7 [repealed] of Title 26.

History.
66 Del. Laws, c. 276, § 1; 83 Del. Laws, c. 115, § 1.

Revisor's note.
Chapter 7 of Title 26, referred to in this section, was repealed by 59 Del. Laws, c. 393, §§ 6-14, and c. 397, § 1, effective June 28, 1974. For present provisions as to public carriers, see Chapter 18 of Title 2.

Effect of amendments.
Section 1 of 83 Del. Laws, c. 115, made effective Jan. 1, 2022, by 6 Del. C. § 2737(c) in that act, transferred the former version of this section, concerning enforcement, to present § 2737 of this title and renumbered former § 2735 of this title as this section.

NOTES TO DECISIONS

Analysis
Construction with other law.
Contract.
— Price.

Construction with other law.
Consumers' claim that satellite television providers and the providers' employee violated the Consumer Contracts Act, 6 Del. C. § 2731 et seq., when installing service at the consumers' home, was excluded because the claim depended on an alleged violation of the Home Solicitation Sales Act, 6 Del. C. § 4401 et seq., which was not applicable where the consumer

requested home installation. Erhart v. DirecTV, Inc., 2012 Del. Super. LEXIS 283 (Del. Super. Ct. June 20, 2012).

Contract.

— Price.
Owner could not sustain counterclaim against a mechanics' lien claimant for violation of this section where the contract price exceeded $50,000; if the "Extras Pages" were not incorporated into the contract, there was no remedy under the act. Ewing v. Bice, 2001 Del. Super. LEXIS 278 (Del. Super. Ct. July 25, 2001).

§ 2737. Enforcement.

(a)(1) Before bringing an action with respect to the automatic renewal of any contract containing an automatic renewal provision that is renewed in violation of § 2734 of this title, the consumer must provide the seller with notice of the violation and a request to cancel the extension of the contract. The consumer shall send the notice by:

  a. Email;

  b. Mail; or

  c. Any other method the business wants to offer.

 (2) If within 30 days of the consumer sending the notice, the seller:

  a. Cures the violation;

  b. Provides the consumer with a written statement that the alleged violations have been cured and that no further violations of that kind shall occur; and

  c. Sends a copy of such statement to the Director of Consumer Protection of the Department of Justice,

then no action shall be initiated under this chapter by the consumer against the seller for the cured violation of § 2734 of this title.

 (3) Nothing in this section shall preclude investigation or enforcement action by the Attorney General for violations of this chapter.

 (b) In addition to any remedies a consumer may have at law or in equity, a violation of this subchapter shall be deemed an unlawful practice under § 2513 of this title and a violation of subchapter II of Chapter 25 of this title.

 (c) The automatic renewal provisions of this subchapter shall become effective January 1, 2022.

History.

66 Del. Laws, c. 276, § 1; 69 Del. Laws, c. 291, § 98(a); 77 Del. Laws, c. 282, § 18; 83 Del. Laws, c. 115, § 1.

Revisor's note.

Section 1 of 83 Del. Laws, c. 115, made effective Jan. 1, 2022, by subsection (c) of this section in that act, renumbered former § 2736 of this title as this section.

Effect of amendments.

83 Del. Laws, c. 115, effective Jan. 1, 2022, redesignated the former section text as (a) and (b), substantially rewriting those subsections; and added (c).

CHAPTER 35
BUILDING CONSTRUCTION PAYMENTS

§ 3502. Payments to contractor impressed with trust.

NOTES TO DECISIONS

Contractors.

Plaintiffs sufficiently pleaded a conversion claim because the complaint alleged that defendants committed a violation when they used funds from plaintiffs and the bank to pay unrelated debts instead of paying the subcontractors; defendants had allegedly divested or misappropriated funds held in trust in violation of this statute. R. Keating & Sons, Inc. v. Chiselcreek Dev., LLC, — A.3d —, 2020 Del. Super. LEXIS 2868 (Del. Super. Ct. Oct. 30, 2020).

§ 3503. Use or application of money received by contractor.

NOTES TO DECISIONS

Misappropriation.

Plaintiffs sufficiently pleaded a conversion claim because the complaint alleged that defendants committed a violation when they used funds from plaintiffs and the bank to pay unrelated debts instead of paying the subcontractors; defendants had allegedly divested or misappropriated funds held in trust in violation of this statute. R. Keating & Sons, Inc. v. Chiselcreek Dev., LLC, — A.3d —, 2020 Del. Super. LEXIS 2868 (Del. Super. Ct. Oct. 30, 2020).

CHAPTER 45
EQUAL ACCOMMODATIONS

§ 4501. Purpose and construction.

This chapter is intended to prevent, in places of public accommodations, practices of discrimination against any person because of race, age, marital status, creed, religion, color, sex, disability, sexual orientation, gender identity, or national origin. This chapter shall be liberally construed to the end that the rights herein provided for all people, without regard to race, age, marital status, creed, religion, color, sex, disability, sexual orientation, gender identity, or national origin, may be effectively safeguarded. Furthermore, in defining the scope or extent of any duty imposed by this chapter, higher or more comprehensive obligations established by otherwise applicable federal, state, or local enactments may be considered.

History.

6 Del. C. 1953, § 4502; 54 Del. Laws, c. 181, § 1; 58 Del. Laws, c. 133, § 1; 58 Del. Laws, c. 386, § 1; 65 Del. Laws, c. 377, § 1; 70 Del. Laws, c. 350, § 1; 75 Del. Laws, c. 356, § 8; 77 Del. Laws, c. 90, § 1; 79 Del. Laws, c. 47, § 1; 79 Del. Laws, c. 371, § 4; 81 Del. Laws, c. 440, § 1; 83 Del. Laws, c. 74, § 1.

Revisor's note.

Section 5 of 83 Del. Laws, c. 74, provided: "This act is known as 'The Religious Freedom for All Act'."

Effect of amendments.

83 Del. Laws, c. 74, effective June 30, 2021, added "religion" in the first two sentences.

§ 4502. Definitions.

For purposes of this chapter:

(1) "Automatic door" shall mean a door equipped with a power-operated mechanism and controls that open and close the door automatically upon receipt of a momentary actuating signal. The switch that begins the automatic cycle may be a photoelectric device, floor mat, or manual switch.

(2) "Chairperson" means the Chairperson of the State Human Relations Commission.

(3) "Commission" means the State Human Relations Commission.

(4) "Complainant" means the person who files a complaint under § 4508 of this title.

(5) "Conciliation" means the attempted resolution of issues raised by a complaint, or by the investigation of such complaint, through informal negotiations.

(6) "Conciliation agreement" means a written agreement setting forth the resolution of the issues in conciliation.

(7) "Disability" means any condition or characteristic that renders a person a person with a disability as defined in this section.

(8) "Discriminatory public accommodations practice" means an act that is unlawful under this chapter.

(9) "Division" means the Division of Human Relations.

(10) "Gender identity" means a gender-related identity, appearance, expression or behavior of a person, regardless of the person's assigned sex at birth.

(11) "Has a record of such impairment" means has a history of, or has been misclassified as having, a mental or physical impairment that substantially limits 1 or more major life activities.

(12) "Is regarded as having an impairment" means an individual that establishes that the individual subjected to an action prohibited under this chapter because of an actual or perceived physical or mental impairment whether or not the impairment limits or is perceived to limit a major life activity.

(13) "Major life activities" includes caring for oneself, performing manual tasks, seeing, hearing, eating, sleeping, walking, standing, lifting,

bending, speaking, breathing, learning, reading, concentrating, thinking, communicating, and working. "Major life activities" also includes the operation of a major bodily function, including functions of the immune system, normal cell growth, digestive, bowel, bladder, neurological brain, respiratory, circulatory, endocrine, and reproductive functions. Such impairment does not include impairments that are transitory and minor.

(14) "Marital status" means the legal relationship of parties as determined by the laws of marriage applicable to them or the absence of such a legal relationship.

(15) "Panel" means a group of 3 or more Commissioners appointed by the Chairperson to perform any task authorized by this chapter.

(16) "Panel chair" means that Commissioner serving on a panel who is designated by the Chairperson to serve as the Chairperson of the panel.

(17) "Person with a disability" means any person who satisfies any 1 of the following:

    a. Has a physical or mental impairment which substantially limits 1 or more major life activities.

    b. Has a record of such impairment.

    c. Is regarded as having such an impairment.

(18) "Place of public accommodation" means any establishment which caters to or offers goods or services or facilities to, or solicits patronage from, the general public. This definition includes state agencies, local government agencies, and state-funded agencies performing public functions. This definition includes hotels and motels catering to the transient public, but it does not apply to the sale or rental of houses, housing units, apartments, rooming houses, or other dwellings, nor to tourist homes with less than 10 rental units catering to the transient public.

(19) "Protective hairstyle" includes braids, locks, and twists.

(20) "Race" includes traits historically associated with race, including hair texture and a protective hairstyle.

(21) "Religion" includes all aspects of religious observance and practice, as well as belief.

(22) "Respondent" means a person who is alleged to have committed a discriminatory public accommodations practice.

(23) "Service animal" means a dog individually trained to do work or perform tasks for the benefit of a person with a disability, including a physical, sensory, psychiatric, intellectual, or other mental disability.

(24) "Sexual orientation" includes heterosexuality, homosexuality, or bisexuality.

(25) "Special Administration Fund" means the Fund created pursuant to § 3005 of Title 31 .

(26) "Transitory impairment" means an impairment with an actual or expected duration of 6 months or less.

History.

6 Del. C. 1953, § 4501; 54 Del. Laws, c. 181, § 1; 66 Del. Laws, c. 68, § 1; 70 Del. Laws, c. 350, § 1; 75 Del. Laws, c. 356, §§ 9, 11, 26, 28; 77 Del. Laws, c. 90, § 2; 77 Del. Laws, c. 346, § 1; 79 Del. Laws, c. 47, §§ 2, 3; 79 Del. Laws, c. 371, § 5; 81 Del. Laws, c. 440, § 2; 83 Del. Laws, c. 13, § 2; 83 Del. Laws, c. 74, § 2; 83 Del. Laws, c. 195, § 1.

Revisor's note.

Section 5 of 83 Del. Laws, c. 74, provided: "This act is known as 'The Religious Freedom for All Act'."

Effect of amendments.

83 Del. Laws, c. 13, effective April 13, 2021, added present (15) and (16) and redesignated the remaining paragraphs accordingly.

83 Del. Laws, c. 74, effective June 30, 2021, substituted "For purposes of" for "As used in" in the introductory paragraph; and added present (17) and redesignated the remaining paragraphs accordingly.

83 Del. Laws, c. 195, effective September 17, 2021, rewrote (7); deleted the second sentence in (10); and added present (11)-(13), (17), (24) and (26) and redesignated the remaining and intervening paragraphs accordingly.

§ 4503. Persons entitled to protection.

All persons within the jurisdiction of this State are entitled to the full and equal accommodations, facilities, advantages and privileges of any place of public accommodation regardless of the race, age, marital status, creed, religion, color, sex, handicap, sexual orientation, gender identity, or national origin of such persons.

History.

6 Del. C. 1953, § 4503; 54 Del. Laws, c. 181, § 1; 58 Del. Laws, c. 133, § 1; 58 Del. Laws, c. 386, § 1; 65 Del. Laws, c. 377, § 2; 70 Del. Laws, c. 350, § 1; 77 Del. Laws, c. 90, § 3; 79 Del. Laws, c. 47, § 4; 83 Del. Laws, c. 74, § 3.

Revisor's note.

Section 5 of 83 Del. Laws, c. 74, provided:

"This act is known as 'The Religious Freedom for All Act'."

Effect of amendments.

83 Del. Laws, c. 74, effective June 30, 2021, added "religion".

§ 4504. Unlawful practices.

(a)(1)a. No person being the owner, lessee, proprietor, manager, director, supervisor, superintendent, agent, or employee of any place of public accommodation, may directly or indirectly refuse, withhold from, or deny to any person, on account of race, age, marital status, creed, religion, color, sex, disability, sexual orientation, gender identity, or national origin, any of the accommodations, facilities, advantages, or privileges thereof.

b. A person who does not allow parking by a holder of a special license plate or permit for persons with disabilities as allowed under § 2134 through § 2135 of Title 21 is engaged in an unlawful practice under this chapter.

(2) A place of public accommodation may provide reasonable accommodations based on gender identity in areas of facilities where disrobing is likely, such as locker rooms or other changing facilities, which reasonable accommodations may include a separate or private place for the use of persons whose gender-related identity, appearance or expression is different from their assigned sex at birth, provided that such reasonable accommodations are not inconsistent with the gender-related identity of such persons.

(3) A place of public accommodation must permit service animals as follows:

a. An individual with a disability accompanied by a service animal in any place of public accommodation.

b. An individual training a service animal to be used by persons with disabilities accompanied by a service animal in any place of public accommodation.

(b)(1) No person, being the owner, lessee, proprietor, manager, superintendent, agent, or employee of any place of public accommodation, shall directly or indirectly publish, issue, circulate, post, or display any written, typewritten, mimeographed, printed, television, Internet, or radio communications notice or advertisement to the effect that any of the accommodations, facilities, advantages, and privileges of any place of public accommodation shall be refused, withheld from or denied to any person on account of race, age, marital status, creed, religion, color, sex, disability, sexual orientation, gender identity, or national origin, or that the patronage or custom thereat of any person belonging to or purporting to be appearing to be of any particular race, age, marital status, creed, religion, color, sex, disability, sexual orientation, gender identity, or national origin is unlawful, objectionable, or not acceptable, desired, accommodated, or solicited, or that the patronage of persons of any particular race, age, marital status, creed, religion, color, sex, disability, sexual orientation, gender identity, or national origin is preferred or is particularly welcomed, desired, or solicited.

(2) A sign that prohibits parking by a holder of a special license plate or permit for persons with disabilities as allowed under § 2134 through § 2135 of Title 21 is a violation under paragraph (b)(1) of this section.

(c) It shall be unlawful to assist, induce, incite or coerce another person to commit any discriminatory public accommodations practice prohibited by subsection (a) or (b) of this section.

(d) *Requirements for newly constructed places of public accommodation.* — All buildings which are constructed after January 1, 2011, and intended for use as places of public accommodation (as defined in § 4502 of this title), must be equipped with an automatic door or calling device at each entrance that is intended to be a main entrance accessible by members of the general public. For purposes of this subsection, a calling device shall mean any device that allows a person with a disability to request assistance with entry meeting the following minimum specifications:

(1) The device must provide a recognizable signal inside the place of public accommodation;

(2) The device must be capable of being operated using only 1 hand or limb;

(3) The device must have at least 1 sign next to it which identifies the device and how to use it; and

(4) The device must be capable of being operated in accordance with all requirements of the Americans with Disabilities Act [42 U.S.C. § 12101 et seq.] Accessibility Guidelines.

(e) Nothing in this section shall be interpreted as an abrogation of any requirements otherwise imposed by applicable federal or state laws or regulations.

(f) A person, being the owner, lessee, proprietor, manager, director, supervisor, superintendent, agent, or employee of any place of public accommodation, may not engage in an act or practice that is unlawful under subsections (a) through (d) of this section against an individual because the individual has done 1 of the following:

(1) Opposed an act or practice that is unlawful under subsections (a) through (d) of this section.

(2) Made a charge, testified, assisted, or participated in any manner in an investigation, proceeding, or hearing to enforce subsections (a) through (d) of this section.

History.

6 Del. C. 1953, § 4504; 54 Del. Laws, c. 181, § 1; 58 Del. Laws, c. 133, § 1; 58 Del. Laws, c. 386, § 1; 65 Del. Laws, c. 377, § 3; 66 Del. Laws, c. 68, § 1; 70 Del. Laws, c. 350, § 1; 75 Del. Laws, c. 356, §§ 10, 28; 77 Del. Laws, c. 90, § 4; 77 Del. Laws, c. 346, §§ 2, 4; 79 Del. Laws, c. 47, § 5; 81 Del. Laws, c. 440, § 3; 82 Del. Laws, c. 209, § 1; 83 Del. Laws, c. 74, § 4; 83 Del. Laws, c. 160, § 1.

Revisor's note.

Section 5 of 83 Del. Laws, c. 74, provided: "This act is known as 'The Religious Freedom for All Act'."

Effect of amendments.

83 Del. Laws, c. 74, effective June 30, 2021, added "religion" in (a)(1) and in three places in (b); and, in (b), added a comma following "agent", following "post" and following "gender identity" in three places, and added "television, Internet".

83 Del. Laws, c. 160, effective Sept. 15, 2021, added (a)(1)b.; in (b)(1), added a comma following "advantages", "accommodated" and "desired"; and added (b)(2).

CHAPTER 46
FAIR HOUSING ACT

§ 4602. Definitions.

As used in this chapter:

(1) "Age" — For the purpose of defining what is a discriminatory housing practice, "age" means any age 18 years or older.

(2) "Aggrieved persons" includes any person who:

    a. Claims to have been injured, directly or indirectly, by a discriminatory housing practice;

    b. Believes that such person will be injured, directly or indirectly, by a discriminatory housing practice that is about to occur; or

    c. Is associated with a person having a protected status under this chapter and claims to have been injured, directly or indirectly, as a result of a discriminatory housing practice against such person having the protected status.

(3) "Chairperson" means the Chairperson of the State Human Relations Commission.

(4) "Commission" means the State Human Relations Commission.

(5) "Complainant" means the person (including the Commission) who files a complaint under § 4610 of this title.

(6) "Conciliation" means the attempted resolution of issues raised by a complaint, or by the investigation of such complaint, through informal negotiations involving the aggrieved person, the respondent and the Commission.

(7) "Conciliation agreement" means a written agreement setting forth the resolution of the issues in conciliation.

(8) "Court" means the Superior Court of the State unless otherwise designated.

(9) "Covered multifamily dwellings" means:

    a. Buildings consisting of 4 or more dwelling units if such buildings have 1 or more elevators; and

    b. Ground floor dwelling units in other buildings consisting of 4 or more dwelling units.

(10) "Disability" means as defined in § 4502 of this title.

(11) "Discriminatory housing practice" means an act that is unlawful under § 4603, § 4604, § 4605, § 4606 or § 4618 of this title.

(12) "Division" means the Division of Human Relations.

(13) "Dwelling" means any building, structure or portion thereof which is occupied as, or designed or intended for occupancy as, a residence by 1 or more families, together with any land which is offered for sale, rent or exchange therewith and also means any vacant land which is offered for sale, lease or exchange for the construction or location thereon of any such building, structure or portion thereof. "Dwelling" also includes the public and common use areas associated therewith.

(14) "Familial status" means: one or more individuals who have not attained the age of 18 years being domiciled with:

    a. A parent or another person having legal custody of such individual or individuals; or

    b. The designee of such parent or other person having such custody, with the written permission of such parent or other person; or

    c. Any person who is pregnant or is in the process of securing legal custody of any individual who has not attained the age of 18 years.

(15) "Family" includes a single individual.

(16) "Gender identity" means a gender-related identity, appearance, expression or behavior of a person, regardless of the person's assigned sex at birth.

(17) "Housing for older persons" means housing:

    a. Provided under any state or federal program that the Commission determines is specifically designed and operated to assist elderly persons;

    b. Intended for, and solely occupied by, persons 62 years of age or older; or

    c. Intended and operated for occupancy by at least 1 person 55 years of age or older per unit. In determining whether housing qualifies as housing for older persons under this subsection, the Commission shall develop regulations which shall require at least the following factors:

        1. That at least 80 percent of the units are occupied by at least 1 person 55 years of age or older per unit; and

        2. The publication of, and adherence to, policies and procedures which demonstrate an intent by the owner or manager to provide housing for persons 55 years of age or older.

(18) "Marital status" means the legal relationship of parties as determined by the laws of marriage applicable to them or the absence of such a legal relationship.

(19) "Panel" means 3 or more Commissioners appointed by the Chair to perform any act authorized under this chapter.

(20) "Panel Chair": that Commissioner designated by the Commission Chair to preside at case hearings, and, further, to perform such other duties as may be specified by applicable laws and regulations.

(21) "Person" includes 1 or more individuals, corporations, partnerships, associations, labor organizations, legal representatives, mutual companies, joint-stock companies, trusts, unincorporated organizations, trustees, trustees in bankruptcy in cases under Title 11 of the United States Code, receivers, fiduciaries and land use commissions or boards.

(22) "Protective hairstyle" includes braids, locks, and twists.

(23) "Race" includes traits historically associated with race, including hair texture and a protective hairstyle.

(24) "Residential real estate-related transaction" means any of the following:

    a. The making, brokering or purchasing of loans or providing other financial assistance:

        1. For purchasing, constructing, improving, repairing or maintaining a dwelling; or

        2. Secured by residential real estate; or

    b. The selling, brokering or appraising of residential real property.

(25) "Respondent" means:

    a. The person or other entity accused in a complaint of an unfair housing practice; and

    b. Any other person or entity identified in the course of investigation and notified as required with respect to respondents so identified under § 4610(a)(2)a. of this title.

(26) "Sexual orientation" includes heterosexuality, homosexuality, or bisexuality.

(27) "Source of income" means any lawful source of money paid directly, indirectly, or on behalf of a renter or buyer of housing including:

a. Income derived from any lawful profession or occupation;

b. Income or rental payments derived from any government or private assistance, grant, or loan program.

(28) "Special Administration Fund" means the Fund established and maintained pursuant to § 3005 of Title 31.

(29) "To rent" includes to lease, to sublease, to assign a lease, to let and otherwise to grant, continue or renew for a consideration the right to occupy premises not owned by the occupant.

(30) "To sell" or "sale" includes a sale, gift, exchange or other means of conveyance.

History.

6 Del. C. 1953, § 4601; 57 Del. Laws, c. 32, § 1; 62 Del. Laws, c. 330, § 2; 68 Del. Laws, c. 311, § 1; 75 Del. Laws, c. 356, §§ 21-23, 27; 77 Del. Laws, c. 90, § 6; 79 Del. Laws, c. 47, §§ 7, 8; 80 Del. Laws, c. 355, § 2; 83 Del. Laws, c. 13, § 3; 83 Del. Laws, c. 195, § 2.

Effect of amendments.

83 Del. Laws, c. 13, effective April 13, 2021, added present (22) and (23) and redesignated the remaining paragraphs accordingly.

83 Del. Laws, c. 195, effective September 17, 2021, rewrote (10), which included the deletion of former (10)a.-c.; deleted the former final sentence in (16); and substituted "includes" for "exclusively means" in (26)

CHAPTER 49A
AUTO REPAIR FRAUD PREVENTION

§ 4902A. Definitions.

For the purposes of this chapter, the following definitions shall apply:

(1) "Airbag" means a motor vehicle inflatable occupant restraint system device that is part of a supplemental restraint system.

(2) "Automotive repair facility" means any person who performs auto repair work on a motor vehicle for financial profit.

(3) "Auto repair work" means performing or attempting to perform repairs and/or maintenance on a motor vehicle for financial profit.

(4) "Counterfeit supplemental restraint system component" means a replacement supplemental restraint system component, including, but not limited to, an airbag, that displays a mark identical to, or substantially similar to, the genuine mark of a motor vehicle manufacturer or a supplier of parts to the manufacturer of a motor vehicle without authorization from that manufacturer or supplier, respectively.

(5) "Motor vehicle" is as defined by § 101(40) of Title 21.

(6) "Nonfunctional airbag" means a replacement airbag that meets any of the following criteria:

a. The airbag was previously deployed or damaged;

b. The airbag has an electric fault that is detected by the vehicle's airbag diagnostic systems when the installation procedure is completed and the vehicle is returned to the customer who requested the work to be performed or when ownership is intended to be transferred;

c. The airbag includes a part or object, including a supplemental restraint system component, that is installed in a motor vehicle to mislead the owner or operator of the motor vehicle into believing that a functional airbag has been installed; or

d. The airbag is subject to the prohibitions of 49 U.S.C. § 30120(j).

(7) "Pattern of violations" means 3 or more violations within a 1-year period.

(8) "Person" includes an individual, corporation, statutory trust, business trust, estate, trust, partnership, association, 2 or more persons having a joint or common interest or any other legal or commercial entity.

(9) "Supplemental restraint system" means a passive inflatable motor vehicle occupant crash protection system designed for use in conjunction with a seat belt as defined in 49 CFR 571.209. A supplemental restraint system includes 1 or more airbags and all components required to ensure that an airbag works as designed by the vehicle manufacturer including both of the following:

   a. The airbag operates as designed in the event of a crash; and

   b. The airbag is designed to meet federal motor vehicle safety standards for the specific make, model, and year of the vehicle in which it is or will be installed.

History.

70 Del. Laws, c. 428, § 2; 73 Del. Laws, c. 329, § 39; 83 Del. Laws, c. 205, § 1.

Effect of amendments.

83 Del. Laws, c. 205, effective September 17,

2021, added present (1), (4), (6) and (9) and redesignated the remaining and intervening paragraphs accordingly; and substituted "§ 101(40) of Title 21" for "21 § 101(35)" in present (5).

§ 4903A. Unlawful practices.

(a) Deception, fraud, false pretense, false promise, misrepresentation or the concealment, suppression or omission of any material fact with the intent that others rely upon such concealment, suppression or omission of any material fact in connection with auto repair work by any automotive repair facility, whether or not any person has in fact been misled, deceived or damaged thereby, or the act, use or employment by any auto repair facility of a deceptive trade practice in connection with auto repair work shall constitute an unlawful practice.

(b) Acts or practices by an automotive repair facility prohibited by subsection (a) of this section shall include but are not limited to:

   (1) Refusing to return a customer's motor vehicle because the customer refused to pay for unauthorized auto repair work in violation of § 4907A of this title;

   (2) Misrepresenting that auto repair work has been made to a motor vehicle;

   (3) Misrepresenting that auto repair work is necessary to a motor vehicle repair;

   (4) Misrepresenting that the motor vehicle is in a dangerous condition or that the customer's continued use of the vehicle may be harmful or cause significant damage to the vehicle;

   (5) Misrepresenting that the motor vehicle will or will not pass state inspection requirements or is not otherwise in compliance with state or federal requirements in connection with soliciting auto repair work;

   (6) Performing unauthorized auto repair work in connection with a misrepresentation;

   (7) Installing or reinstalling in a motor vehicle any object in lieu of an operative air bag including a counterfeit supplemental restraint system component or a nonfunctional airbag;

   (8) Selling, installing or reinstalling any device that causes the vehicle's diagnostic systems to fail to warn when the vehicle is equipped with a counterfeit supplemental restraint system component, nonfunctional airbag, or when no airbag is installed.

   (9) Fraudulently altering any customer contract, estimate, invoice or other document;

(10) Fraudulently misusing a customer's credit card; or

(11) Engaging in a pattern of violations of § 4904A, § 4905A, § 4906A or § 4907A of this title or violating § 4904A, § 4905A, § 4906A or § 4907A of this title with the intent to hinder the discovery of practices or acts prohibited by this section.

(c) A person shall not knowingly manufacture, import, distribute, sell, or offer for sale any device intended to replace a supplemental restraint system component in any motor vehicle if the device is a counterfeit supplemental restraint system component, a nonfunctional airbag, or a device that causes a vehicle to fail to meet federal motor vehicle safety standards as provided in 49 CFR 571.208.

History.
70 Del. Laws, c. 428, § 2; 74 Del. Laws, c. 277, § 1; 83 Del. Laws, c. 205, § 2.

2021, rewrote (b)(7); added present (b)(8) and redesignated the remaining paragraphs in (b) accordingly; and added (c).

Effect of amendments.
83 Del. Laws, c. 205, effective September 17,

§ 4907A. Unauthorized repairs.

An automotive repair facility may not charge a customer for repairs not originally authorized or requested by the customer, or a person the auto repair facility reasonably believes is acting on the customer's behalf, unless the automotive repair facility receives written or oral permission from the customer in conformance with this chapter. To the extent a charge does not exceed an estimate by 20% or $50, whichever is less, no cause of action pursuant to § 4909A(c) of this title shall accrue. Nothing in this section shall preclude enforcement pursuant to § 4903A(b)(6) and (10) of this title.

History.
70 Del. Laws, c. 428, § 2; 83 Del. Laws, c. 205, § 2.

Laws, c. 205, § 2, effective Sept. 17, 2021, "(10)" was substituted for "(9)" in the final sentence.

Revisor's note.
Based upon changes contained in 83 Del.

TITLE 7
CONSERVATION

PART I
GAME, WILDLIFE AND DOGS

CHAPTER 1
PROTECTED WILDLIFE

§ 102. Powers and duties.

NOTES TO DECISIONS

Regulatory authority.

Hunters could use semi-automatic rifles for deer hunting, pursuant to 7 Del. C. § 704(g), so long as they followed all statutory restrictions regarding the types of sights, ammunition and number of cartridges allowed; the Department of Natural Resources and Environmental Control exceeded its statutory authority by prohibiting semi-automatic rifles within its hunting guide. Del. State Sportsmen's Ass'n v. Garvin, — A.3d —, 2020 Del. Super. LEXIS 2927 (Del. Super. Ct. Nov. 18, 2020).

CHAPTER 5
LICENSES

SUBCHAPTER I

HUNTING, TRAPPING AND FISHING LICENSES, TAGS, AND STAMPS; PUBLIC LANDS USE FEES

§ 521. Public lands use fees; blind site permit; conservation access pass [Effective July 1, 2022].

(a) Whoever utilizes a blind site on public lands managed by the Division of Fish and Wildlife and included in the Division's lottery program for the purposes of hunting waterfowl or deer shall pay an annual blind site permit fee of $20. This fee is hereby waived for hunters participating in Division of Fish and Wildlife designated youth hunting days.

(b) Notwithstanding paragraph (b)(1) of this section, a conservation access pass that serves as a permit is required for any registered motor vehicle as defined in Title 21 used to access public lands owned or managed by the Division of Fish and Wildlife for any, as determined by the Department, allowable activity. Such pass shall be displayed by the motor vehicle operator on or within said vehicle in a manner as specified by the Department. Such pass shall be assigned and limited to a single, specified registered motor vehicle, and may be transferred to another registered motor vehicle of same ownership for a fee of $10 paid to the Department.

    (1) A conservation access pass shall not be required to access:

        a. The Michael Castle Trail and those associated direct access roads and parking areas designated by the Department within the C&D Canal Conservation Area.

        b. Those fishing or boating access areas, educational facilities, or shooting range facilities designated by the Department.

        c. Applicable lands leased from the Department, provided access is for the purpose for which such lands are leased.

        d. Other areas designated by the Department.

    (2) An annual conservation access pass shall be issued free of charge with resident and nonresident general hunting licenses, resident and nonresident hunting guide licenses, and nonresident 3-day small game hunting licenses.

    (3) The following conservation access pass fees shall be paid to the Department or its duly authorized agents:

        a. $32.50 for a resident annual pass.

        b. $10 for a resident 3-day pass valid for 3 consecutive days.

        c. $65 for a nonresident annual pass.

        d. $20 for a nonresident 3-day pass valid for 3 consecutive days.

        e. A Delaware resident who is 65 years of age or older may pay a 1-time fee of $65, which will permit the resident access to any public lands permitted under this section for the lifetime of the resident provided the applicant provides proof of age at the time such application is made.

  (c) All funds received from the purchase of conservation access passes shall be deposited and administered in accordance with §§ 105 and 107 of this title solely for wildlife-associated user access facilities and projects on and the management and maintenance of subject public lands.

History.
  76 Del. Laws, c. 72, § 10; 76 Del. Laws, c. 188, § 1; 78 Del. Laws, c. 83, § 1; 80 Del. Laws, c. 333, § 6; 83 Del. Laws, c. 191, § 1.

Revisor's note.
  Section 2 of 83 Del. Laws, c. 191, provided: "This act takes effect July 1, 2022."

Effect of amendments.
  83 Del. Laws, c. 191, effective July 1, 2022, made a minor stylistic change in (3)d.; and added (3)e.

CHAPTER 7
REGULATIONS AND PROHIBITIONS CONCERNING GAME AND FISH
SUBCHAPTER I
GENERAL PROVISIONS

§ 704. Prohibited hunting and trapping devices and methods; confiscation of devices; primitive weapon season.

NOTES TO DECISIONS

Analysis

Regulations.
Semi-automatic weapons.

Regulations.
  If the legislature intended for the term "rifle" to be limited to specific types of rifles, it would have defined the types of rifles, just as it did for

handguns in 7 Del. C. § 704(g) and as it did for shotguns in 7 Del. C. § 711.; 7 Del. C. § 711 (which applies to shotguns, not rifles) only restricts the use of automatic-loading or hand-operated repeating shotguns that hold more than 3 shells at 1 time in the magazine and chamber combined and does not prohibit all automatic-loading or hand-operated repeating shotguns. Del. State Sportsmen's Ass'n v. Garvin, — A.3d —, 2020 Del. Super. LEXIS 2927 (Del. Super. Ct. Nov. 18, 2020).

Semi-automatic weapons.
Hunters could use semi-automatic rifles for deer hunting, pursuant to 7 Del. C. § 704(g), so long as they followed all statutory restrictions regarding the types of sights, ammunition and

number of cartridges; the Department of Natural Resources and Environmental Control exceeded its statutory authority by prohibiting semi-automatic rifles within its hunting guide. Del. State Sportsmen's Ass'n v. Garvin, — A.3d —, 2020 Del. Super. LEXIS 2927 (Del. Super. Ct. Nov. 18, 2020).

§ 711. Hunting with automatic-loading gun prohibited; penalty.

NOTES TO DECISIONS

Regulations.
Hunters could use semi-automatic rifles for deer hunting, pursuant to 7 Del. C. § 704(g), so long as they followed all statutory restrictions regarding the types of sights, ammunition and number of cartridges allowed; 7 Del. C. § 711 (which applies to shotguns, not rifles) only restricts the use of automatic-loading or hand-

operated repeating shotguns that hold more than 3 shells at 1 time in the magazine and chamber combined and does not prohibit all automatic-loading or hand-operated repeating shotguns. Del. State Sportsmen's Ass'n v. Garvin, — A.3d —, 2020 Del. Super. LEXIS 2927 (Del. Super. Ct. Nov. 18, 2020).

CHAPTER 9

FINFISHING IN TIDAL WATERS

§ 903. Department of Natural Resources and Environmental Control; authority; permits; regulations.

(a) The Department shall administer and enforce the laws and regulations of the State relating to finfishing in the tidal waters of the State.

(b) The Department shall have the authority to cooperate and assist departments, agencies and offices of the State and other states, local governments and the federal government in the management and conservation of finfishery resources.

(c) The Department may issue permits to scientific and/or educational institutions, or employees thereof, allowing said party or parties to be at a specific location, at a specific time, and to use equipment to fish for, or use methods to take finfish, where said equipment, method, location or time would otherwise be illegal under this chapter or any regulation promulgated pursuant to this chapter.

(d) [Repealed.]

(e) The Department, in accordance with the procedures under subchapters I and II of the Administrative Procedures Act (Chapter 101 of Title 29), has the authority to promulgate regulations, which shall have the force and effect of law, to enhance the conservation and management of coastal finfisheries, including the biological and socioeconomic aspects of coastal finfisheries. Any regulation pertaining to fishing for food fish shall require a statement addressing whether or not said regulation will have a significant impact upon the conservation of the fishery in question. Except where otherwise provided in this section, such regulations shall be consistent with this chapter, and may only include, and encompass, the following areas:

    (1)a. Add legal fishing equipment or methods to fish for bait fish in addition to the provisions of § 908 of this title.

      b. Closed and/or open areas to fish for bait fish according to the provisions of § 909 of this title.

      c. Add legal fishing equipment or methods to fish for food fish in addition to § 910 of this title.

d. Restrict fishing within areas designated as striped bass spawning areas according to § 930 of this title; provided that any restriction on fishing is consistent with fishing restrictions imposed by other states adjoining designated striped bass spawning areas located in Delaware.

e. Closed or open areas within Rehoboth Bay and its tributaries, Indian River and Indian River Bay and their tributaries, Little Assawoman Bay and its tributaries, Big Assawoman Bay and its tributaries, Nanticoke River and its tributaries and all tributaries entering the Delaware River and Delaware Bay to fishing with gill nets for food fish.

f. Restrict the mesh size of recreational drift gill nets that may be fished for American shad in the Delaware River.

g. Regulate and/or restrict the type of fishing gear or methods which may be used within the geographical boundaries of permitted artificial reef sites within the Delaware Bay and within Delaware's territorial sea (defined as 0 to 3 miles seaward of Delaware's ocean coastline).

(2)a. The Department may promulgate such other regulations concerning a species of finfish that spend part or all of their life cycle within the tidal waters of the State; provided that such regulations are consistent with a fisheries management plan or rule promulgated pursuant to or adopted by the Atlantic States Marine Fisheries Commission, the Atlantic Coastal Fisheries Cooperative Management Act [16 U.S.C. § 5101 et seq.], the Mid-Atlantic Fishery Management Council, or the National Marine Fisheries Service for the protection and conservation of said species of finfish. Such regulations may include management measures, as described herein, that are necessary to implement the fisheries management plan or rule.

1. Notwithstanding this subsection and Chapter 101 of Title 29, the Department may promulgate regulations to adopt a specified management measure for finfish subject to this chapter by issuance of an order signed by the Secretary of the Department where the management measure is specified in 1 or more of the following, and adopting the specific management measure ensures compliance or maintains consistency with 1 or more of the following:

A. A fisheries management plan or rule established pursuant to or by the Atlantic States Marine Fisheries Commission, as set forth in §§ 1501 through 1504 of this title and the Atlantic Coastal Fisheries Cooperative Management Act, 16 U.S.C. § 5104(b).

B. A fisheries management plan or rule established pursuant to or by the Mid-Atlantic Fishery Management Council.

C. A fisheries management plan or rule established pursuant to or by the National Marine Fisheries Service.

2. Whenever the Department promulgates a regulation to adopt a specified management measure pursuant to paragraph (e)(2)a.1. of this section, the Department shall do all of the following:

A. Publish on its website a public notice with a copy of the Secretary's order and regulation that implement the specified management measure. The regulation will become effective

48 hours after the Department publishes on its website the public notice required by this paragraph.

B. File the Secretary's order and regulation that implement the specified management measure in the next issue of the Delaware Register of Regulations.

3. Any regulations or management measures promulgated under paragraph (e)(2)a.1. of this section must be consistent with the original specified management measure promulgated pursuant to or adopted by the Atlantic States Marine Fisheries Commission, the Atlantic Coastal Fisheries Cooperative Management Act [16 U.S.C. § 5101 et seq.], the Mid-Atlantic Fishery Management Council, or the National Marine Fisheries Service.

4. Restrictions on the areas from which a species may be taken; and

5. Restrictions on the mesh sizes of nets from which a species may be taken.

b. Management measures may include the following:

1. Minimum and/or maximum size limits of a species according to § 929 of this title.

2. Restrictions on the quantities of a species that may be taken.

3. Restrictions on the periods of time that a species may be taken.

4. Restrictions on the areas from which a species may be taken.

5. Restrictions on the mesh sizes of nets from which a species may be taken.

6. Restrictions on the fishing equipment or methods to fish for a species.

c. In lieu of a fisheries management plan for any species of finfish, the Department, in conjunction with the State of New Jersey's Department of Environmental Protection, may develop a fisheries management plan for said species and promulgate interim regulations concerning said species of finfish within the Delaware River and Delaware Bay; provided that the State of New Jersey's Department of Environmental Protection adopts substantially similar interim regulations. Said interim regulations, in Delaware, shall become effective on the date substantially similar regulations become effective in the State of New Jersey.

1. These interim regulations may include the following management measures:

A. Minimum and/or maximum size limits of a species that may be taken and possessed.

B. Restrictions on the quantities of a species that may be taken.

C. Restrictions on the periods of time that a species may be taken.

D. Restrictions on the areas from which a species may be taken.

E. Restrictions on the mesh sizes of nets from which a species may be taken.

F. Restrictions on the fishing equipment or methods to fish for a species.

2. Upon the acceptance by the Department of a fisheries management plan for a species of finfish adopted pursuant to

paragraph (e)(2)a. of this section, all interim regulations adopted pursuant to this paragraph (e)(2)c. pertaining to the management of said species shall become void once the Department promulgates new regulations implementing the applicable fisheries management plan.

d. Any regulation adopted pursuant to paragraphs (e)(2)a. and (e)(2)c. of this section shall be consistent with the management principles for development of fisheries management plans or rules as set forth under § 901 of this title.

(3) The Department may promulgate such other regulations concerning any species of finfish or marine mammal that spend part or all of their life cycle within the tidal waters of the State; provided, that such regulations are consistent with management plans approved by the U.S. Secretary of Commerce for the protection and conservation of said finfish or marine mammal.

(f) The Department shall have the authority to issue permits or carry out any other administrative procedure provided for under this chapter, including but not limited to, permits, licenses and applications.

(g) The passage and approval of this subsection shall repeal those provisions contained in § 929 of this title that conflict with any Department regulation only if and when the Department promulgates any regulation contrary to said section of this chapter.

(h) The Department shall have the authority to adopt emergency regulations involving finfish subject to this chapter in accordance with the procedures set forth in the Administrative Procedures Act § 10119 of Title 29.

(i) The Department is authorized to collect pertinent data with respect to fisheries, including, but not limited to, information regarding the type and quantity of fish or weight thereof, areas in which fishing was conducted and time of fishing. The information collected by or reported to the Department shall be confidential and shall not be disclosed in a manner or form that permits identification of any person or vessel, except when required by court order.

(j) The Department shall have the authority to issue a permit to a person for the artificial propagation, aquaculture and possession of finfish which otherwise would be illegal in this State provided that all finfish removed from the tidal waters under the jurisdiction of this State for obtaining eggs or sperm are to be released immediately or disposed of in a manner specified in the permit.

History.

64 Del. Laws, c. 251, § 1; 64 Del. Laws, c. 279, § 1; 65 Del. Laws, c. 192, § 1; 65 Del. Laws, c. 408, § 1; 68 Del. Laws, c. 199, § 2; 70 Del. Laws, c. 186, § 1; 71 Del. Laws, c. 72, § 1; 76 Del. Laws, c. 71, § 13; 77 Del. Laws, c. 239, § 1; 82 Del. Laws, c. 125, § 1; 83 Del. Laws, c. 37, § 3.

Effect of amendments.

83 Del. Laws, c. 37, effective June 3, 2021, in the first sentence of the introductory paragraph of (e), added a comma following "Department" and substituted "under subchapters I and II of the Administrative Procedures Act (Chapter 101 of Title 29)" for "set forth in the Administrative Procedures Act, §§ 10101 through 10119 of Title 29, shall have".

PART V

PUBLIC LANDS, PARKS AND MEMORIALS

Chapter
47. State Parks, §§ 4701 to 4738.

CHAPTER 47

STATE PARKS

Subchapter I. General Provisions

Sec.
4701. Powers and duties [For applicability of

this section, see 83 Del. Laws, c. 182, § 2].

SUBCHAPTER I

GENERAL PROVISIONS

§ 4701. Powers and duties [For applicability of this section, see 83 Del. Laws, c. 182, § 2].

(a) The Department of Natural Resources and Environmental Control may do all of the following:

(1) Select and acquire by gift, devise, bequest, purchase, and through the exercise of the power of eminent domain, such lands as are desirable to be utilized chiefly for recreation, and to develop and maintain such areas.

(2) Expend for such acquisition, development, and maintenance, such funds as are appropriated for such purposes, or received as earnings from the operation of such areas, or received from any other source.

(3) Employ such administrative and technical assistance as is, in the opinion of the Department, necessary in order to plan, develop, and maintain the areas which it administers.

(4) Make and enforce regulations relating to the protection, care, and use of the areas it administers.

(5)a. Establish and collect such user charges, which shall approximate and reasonably reflect all costs necessary to defray the expenses of the Department for the use of the facilities and services it provides in areas it administers. The Department shall, in addition, establish and impose a schedule of fees for entrance to state parks and for surf fishing vehicles and snowmobiles on said lands, with the concurrence and approval of the General Assembly. The Secretary of the Department of Natural Resources and Environmental Control shall establish the period and areas on which park fees and user charges shall be imposed. The Secretary shall annually prepare a schedule of park entrance and surf fishing vehicle and snowmobile fees under this section and submit the same as part of the Department's annual operating budget proposal. All of the fees collected under this section shall be deposited in the General Fund of this State and designated solely for park operations and maintenance; provided, however, that no fee shall be imposed on any recognized veteran's service organization for the use of any state park or portion thereof for purposes of patriotic or memorial services, provided that advance written notification of not less than 15 days is given to the agency and does not conflict with other previously scheduled activities within the park.

b.1. Delaware residents who are 62 years of age or older and who own a motor vehicle validly registered in Delaware may pay an annual fee of not less than ½ of the annual fee established for Delaware residents under paragraph (a)(5)a. of this section for each such registered motor vehicle which shall permit such vehicle entrance to any state park or recreation area during the calendar year for which the fee was paid. Persons who are 62 years of age or older and who own a motor vehicle validly registered in another state may pay an annual fee of not less than ½ of the annual fee established for out-of-state registered vehicles under paragraph (a)(5)a. of this section for each such registered motor vehicle which shall permit the vehicle entrance to any state park or recreation area during the calendar year for which the fee was paid. Each applicant under this paragraph shall furnish proof of age, vehicle ownership, and vehicle registration at the time such application is made. Annual permits issued under this paragraph will be valid for any day excluding holidays. No annual permit issued under this paragraph will be honored on any day unless the owner of the vehicle for which such permit is issued is the operator of the vehicle at the time of entrance to the state park or recreation area to which admission is sought. All the fees collected under the authority of this section shall be deposited in the General Fund, and designated solely for park operations and maintenance.

2. A Delaware resident who is 65 years of age or older may pay a 1-time fee of $45, which will permit the resident to enter any state park or recreation area for the lifetime of the resident, so long as the resident is the operator of or a passenger in a Delaware-registered vehicle at the time of entrance to the state park or recreation area to which admission is sought. An applicant for a lifetime permit must furnish proof of age and Delaware residency at the time application for the permit is made. All fees collected under the authority of this paragraph must be deposited in the General Fund and designated solely for park operations and maintenance.

c. Delaware residents who are disabled, and who hold a valid and current Gold Access Passport Card, as issued by the National Park Service of the United States Department of the Interior, shall be exempted from the annual or daily entrance fees required by this section.

d. Any resident who has served honorably for 90 or more consecutive days on active duty in the armed forces of the United States, including service as member of the Delaware National Guard, in military actions in Southwest Asia associated with Operation Iraqi Freedom or Operation Enduring Freedom may, for the first 12 months following the date the resident was honorably discharged or removed from active status, receive a pass granting the resident free admission to any state park in this State without charge.

e. Any resident, who does not qualify for free admission under paragraph (a)(5)d. of this section, who has honorably served or is honorably serving in the armed forces of the United States, including service as a member of the Delaware National Guard, and who owns a motor vehicle validly registered in Delaware may pay an annual fee of ½ of the annual fee established for Delaware residents under

paragraph (a)(5)a. of this section for each such registered motor
vehicle which shall permit such vehicle entrance to any state park or
recreation area during the calendar year for which the fee was paid.
Each applicant under this paragraph shall furnish proof of service in
the armed forces of the United States, vehicle ownership, and vehicle
registration at the time such application is made. All the fees collected
under the authority of this paragraph shall be designated solely for
park operations and maintenance.

f. A resident who is an active Delaware volunteer firefighter, an
active Delaware volunteer emergency medical technician (EMT), or a
life-member of a Delaware volunteer fire department is entitled to
receive annually, without charge, either a surf fishing vehicle permit
or an annual permit to enter state parks and recreation areas. A
firefighter, EMT, or life-member who volunteers in Delaware but lives
out of state is entitled to receive annually, at the Delaware resident
rate, either a surf fishing vehicle permit or an annual permit to enter
state parks and recreation areas.

1. "Active Delaware volunteer firefighter" means a person who
is a member of a Delaware volunteer fire department and who
responds to at least 20% of the department's annual alarms or
crew calls as a nonpaid firefighter.

2. "Active volunteer emergency medical technician" or "EMT"
means a person who is a member of a Delaware volunteer fire
department or a Delaware volunteer ambulance company and
who responds to at least 20% of the department's or company's
annual emergency medical service calls as a nonpaid EMT,
EMT-C, or EMT-P, as described in § 9701(11), (12), and (13)
respectively of Title 16.

3. "Life-member of a Delaware volunteer fire department"
means a person who is a member of a Delaware volunteer fire
department and who has been awarded life membership status by
that department.

4. To qualify without charge for a surf fishing vehicle permit or
annual permit to enter state parks and recreation areas under
this paragraph, the firefighter, EMT, or life-member must submit
annually to the Department an original letter on official fire
department or ambulance company letterhead, signed by the fire
department's or ambulance company's president and authenticated by the president of the Delaware Volunteer Firefighter's
Association. The letter must explain how the person qualifies for
a surf fishing vehicle permit or annual permit to enter state parks
and recreation areas under this paragraph.

5. One surf fishing vehicle permit or annual permit to enter
state parks and recreation areas may be issued annually to a
vehicle registered to the qualifying active Delaware Volunteer
Firefighter, active emergency medical technician (EMT), or life
member in accordance with procedures established by the Department.

g.1. The Department is authorized to administer a program for the
issuance of numbered surf fishing and state park specialty vehicle
plates. A state park specialty vehicle plate shall serve as an
annual permit. The Department will establish fees, rules, and
regulations for the purchase, replacement, transfer, renewal,
nonrenewal, and forfeiture of such plates managed through this

voluntary program. The Department may charge a fee for surf fishing and state park specialty vehicle plates not to exceed $500 per plate or may auction surf fishing and state park specialty plates under paragraph (a)(5)g.2. of this section in which case the amount charged shall be based upon interest and demand for such plates as determined by auction.

2. The Secretary is hereby authorized to establish, implement, and manage an auction program to sell surf fishing and state park specialty vehicle plates as provided for in paragraph (a)(5)g.1. of this section. Any auction of such vehicle plates shall be conducted in accordance with accepted auction practices and shall require valid vehicle registration as proof of eligibility, limit individuals to acquiring 1 vehicle plate per licensed vehicle, and ensure that the highest bid from an eligible individual is the successful bid. Vehicle plates numbered 1 through 200 shall be limited to vehicles registered in Delaware.

(6) Make on its own motion or in cooperation with other agencies of the State, studies of the recreational facilities now available in the State, and of the recreational needs of the State, and determine what areas not now available for public recreation should be acquired.

(7) Enter into agreements with proper persons or corporations for periods not to exceed 25 years for operation of services on the areas it administers.

(8) Employ and fix the salaries of such personnel as it deems proper for the enforcement of its rules and regulations. Enforcement personnel may arrest with a warrant for any violation of the Department of Natural Resources and Environmental Control rules and regulations, or without a warrant for any such violation committed in their presence. Enforcement personnel, with respect to the enforcement of the Department of Natural Resources and Environmental Control rules and regulations, shall have all the powers of investigation, detention, and arrest conferred by law on peace officers or constables.

(9) Grant, with the written approval of the Cabinet Committee on State Planning Issues, easements, for either private or public purpose over or under any public lands which it administers, for the purpose of transmission lines, such as: Telephone and telegraph lines, electric power lines, gas pipelines, and water and sewage pipelines and appurtenances. The term of any such easement together with the amount of any fee charged therefor shall be determined by the Department of Natural Resources and Environmental Control acting with approval of the Cabinet Committee on State Planning Issues, and any funds received for the grant of such easements shall be deposited by the Department of Natural Resources and Environmental Control with the State Treasurer.

(10) Select and obtain, by lease or agreement with the owners thereof and upon such terms and conditions as the Department of Natural Resources and Environmental Control, with the approval of the Cabinet Committee on State Planning Issues, shall determine, such lands as the Department of Natural Resources and Environmental Control deems appropriate and desirable for park and recreation use and purposes, and to improve, develop, operate, and maintain such lands for such purposes. The Department of Natural Resources and Environmental Control may only exercise the powers granted in this paragraph by lease or agreement entered into with the federal government or with a municipality, agency, or political subdivision of this State.

(11) Enter into an agreement with the Barcroft Company of Lewes, Delaware, for a period not to exceed 25 years, for the use of land presently leased to Barcroft, as well as an adjoining triangular-shaped property containing approximately .76 of an acre; provided, however, that the funds received from such agreement shall be appropriated to the Department of Natural Resources and Environmental Control to be used to rebuild and maintain, for the use of the public, a fishing pier located in the breakwater at Cape Henlopen State Park.

(12) Employ and fix the salaries of such personnel to be known as "seasonal patrol officers" who shall assist the Department of Natural Resources and Environmental Control's park rangers and other peace officers employed under § 8003(13) of Title 29 to enforce the Division of Parks and Recreation's rules and regulations. The Director of the Division of Parks and Recreation, or the Director's designee, shall establish qualifications and provide training as deemed necessary and desirable for seasonal patrol officers.

a. Except as otherwise provided in paragraph (a)(12)c. of this section, seasonal patrol officers have the power to do all of the following:

1. Issue civil summonses for civil violations.

2. Issue summonses for class D environmental violations, except for violations concerning persons actively engaged in surf fishing.

3. Issue written and verbal warnings.

4. Report any observed or suspected illegal activity to a park ranger or other peace officer.

b. Summonses and warnings issued by a seasonal patrol officer under paragraph (a)(12)a. of this section have the same force and effect as summonses and warnings issued by a park ranger or other peace officer under § 8003A of Title 29.

c. The Director of the Division of Parks and Recreation or authorized designee shall establish a policy pertaining to seasonal patrol officers that specifies the class D environmental violations and the civil violations for which seasonal patrol officers may issue summonses pursuant to paragraphs (a)(12)a.1. and (a)(12)a.2.

(b) The Department of Natural Resources and Environmental Control may establish state parks on any or all portions of state lands in Sussex County bordering on the Atlantic Ocean which have been or may hereafter be acquired and may administer them directly.

(c) The Department of Natural Resources and Environmental Control shall plan, develop and maintain all areas entrusted to its administration as to preserve in every reasonable degree the scenic, historic, scientific, prehistoric and wildlife values of such areas.

(d) All state parks and other areas acquired primarily for recreational use shall, from the date of their establishment as such, come under the jurisdiction of the Department of Natural Resources and Environmental Control and shall be closed to hunting, except in areas designated by the Department of Natural Resources and Environmental Control for such purpose.

(e) The Department of Natural Resources and Environmental Control shall establish an advance reservation system to allow disabled persons to reserve accessible campsites for the disabled at state parks.

History.
41 Del. Laws, c. 259, § 2; 7 Del. C. 1953, c. 4703; 53 Del. Laws, c. 111; 56 Del. Laws, c. 86; 56 Del. Laws, c. 102; 56 Del. Laws, c. 407; 57 Del. Laws, c. 578; 57 Del. Laws, c. 734; 57 Del. Laws, c. 739, § 124; 60 Del. Laws, c. 243, § 1; 61 Del. Laws, c. 299, § 1; 61 Del. Laws, c. 389, §§ 1-4; 62 Del. Laws, c. 1, § 1; 62 Del. Laws, c.

44, §§ 1, 2; 63 Del. Laws, c. 191, § 4(i); 66 Del. Laws, c. 138, § 1; 68 Del. Laws, c. 86, §§ 1, 2; 69 Del. Laws, c. 85, § 1; 72 Del. Laws, c. 260, § 1; 72 Del. Laws, c. 381, § 1; 74 Del. Laws, c. 290, § 1; 74 Del. Laws, c. 291, § 2; 78 Del. Laws, c. 266, § 13; 78 Del. Laws, c. 300, § 1; 78 Del. Laws, c. 362, § 1; 79 Del. Laws, c. 30, § 1; 79 Del. Laws, c. 443, § 1; 82 Del. Laws, c. 140, § 1; 83 Del. Laws, c. 182, § 1.

Revisor's note.

Section 2 of 83 Del. Laws, c. 182, provided: "This act applies beginning with the 2021 an-nual state park and recreation area permit seasons."

Effect of amendments.

83 Del. Laws, c. 182, effective September 17, 2021, added "either" in each of the two sen-tences in the introductory paragraph of (a)(5)f.; added "or an annual permit to enter state parks and recreation areas" in each of the two sen-tences in the introductory paragraph of (a)(5)f. and (a)(5)f.4. and once in (a)(5)f.5.; and substi-tuted "or" for "and/or" in (a)(5)f.1.

PART VI

ARCHAEOLOGICAL AND GEOLOGICAL RESOURCES

Chapter
54. Unmarked Human Burials and Human Skeletal Remains, §§ 5401 to 5411.

CHAPTER 54

UNMARKED HUMAN BURIALS AND HUMAN SKELETAL REMAINS

Revision of chapter.

83 Del. Laws, c. 142, § 1, effective Sept. 10, 2021, revised this chapter by substituting pres-ent §§ 5401 to 5411 of this title for former §§ 5401 to 5410 of this title. No detailed expla-nation of the changes made by the 2021 act has been attempted, but, where appropriate, the historical citations to former sections have been added to corresponding sections in the revised chapter.

§ 5401. Purpose.

The purposes of this chapter are:

(1) To help provide adequate protection for unmarked human burials and human skeletal remains found anywhere within the State, including subaqueous lands, but excluding those found anywhere on federal land.

(2) To provide adequate protection for unmarked human burials and human skeletal remains not within the jurisdiction of the Medical Exam-iner that are encountered during archaeological excavation, construction, or other ground disturbing activities.

(3) To provide for adequate skeletal analysis of remains removed or excavated from unmarked human burials.

(4) To provide for the dignified and respectful reinterment or other disposition of Native American, African American, and all other skeletal remains, including those of enslaved individuals and individuals of undetermined cultural affiliation.

History.

66 Del. Laws, c. 38, § 1; 75 Del. Laws, c. 153, §§ 4, 5; 83 Del. Laws, c. 142, § 1.

§ 5402. Definitions.

As used in this chapter:

(1) "Committee" means a body of stakeholders that inform the treatment and disposition of unmarked human burials and skeletal remains:

a. When burials or remains are determined to be Native American, the Committee shall be chaired by the Director or the Director's designee, and consist of the Chief of the Nanticoke Indian Tribe and the Chief of the Lenape Indian Tribe of Delaware, or the Chiefs' designees, 2 members appointed by each Chief, the Director of the Division of Historical and Cultural Affairs of the Department of State or the Director's designee, 1 member appointed by the Director, and a ninth member from the private sector appointed by the Governor. Governor's appointee shall serve 1-year, renewable terms. This is a standing committee.

b. When burials or remains are determined to be other than Native American, an ad hoc committee shall be formed. The committee shall include individuals well suited to ensure treatment and disposition of the human burial and skeletal remains furthers the goal of providing for the dignified and respectful reinterment or other disposition including recognition of the special consideration for African Americans, including enslaved persons, and for persons of undetermined cultural affiliation. The Committee shall be chaired by the Director or the Director's designee, and consist of 1 member of the private sector appointed by the Governor who shall serve 1-year renewable terms and 7 members appointed by the Director, representing interested parties, which may include any of the following:

1. Known or presumed lineal descendants.

2. Individuals or organizations with a likely cultural affiliation to the remains.

3. The landowner.

4. A professional archaeologist.

5. An historian or person of similar expertise.

(2) "Director" means the Director of the Division of Historical and Cultural Affairs, Department of State.

(3) "Human skeletal remains" or "remains" means any part of the body of a deceased human being in any stage of decomposition.

(4) "Lineal descendant" means any individual tracing their ancestry directly or by proven kinship.

(5) "Medical Examiner" means as defined in Chapter 47 of Title 29.

(6) "Person" means an individual, corporation, partnership, trust, institution, association, or any other private entity or any officer or employee, agent, department, or instrumentality of the United States or of any state or political subdivision thereof.

(7) "Professional archaeologist" means a person having all of the following qualifications:

a. A graduate degree in archaeology, anthropology, history, or another related field with a specialization in archaeology.

b. A minimum of 1 year's experience in conducting basic archaeological field research, including the excavation and removal of human skeletal remains.

c. Has designed and executed an archaeological study and presented written results and interpretations of such study.

(8) "Proven kinship" means the relationship among individuals that exists because of genetic descent, which includes racial descent.

(9) "Skeletal analyst" means any individual having all of the following qualifications:

a. A graduate degree in a field involving the study of the human skeleton such as skeletal biology, forensic osteology, or other relevant aspects of physical anthropology or medicine.

b. A minimum of 1 year's experience in conducting laboratory reconstruction and analysis of skeletal remains, including the differentiation of the physical characteristics denoting cultural or biological affinity.

c. Has designed and executed a skeletal analysis and presented the written results and interpretations of such analysis.

(10) "Unmarked human burial" means any interment of human skeletal remains for which there exists no grave marker or any other historical documentation providing information as to the identity of the deceased.

History.
66 Del. Laws, c. 38, § 1; 75 Del. Laws, c. 153, § 4; 83 Del. Laws, c. 142, § 1.

§ 5403. Avoidance, protection, and preservation of remains.

All persons are encouraged to undertake due diligence to identify, demarcate, and preserve in situ, unmarked human burials to avoid encountering skeletal remains; and to share information with the Division of Historical and Cultural Affairs, including reports or studies undertaken for these purposes.

History.
83 Del. Laws, c. 142, § 1.

§ 5404. Discovery of remains and notification of authorities.

(a) Any person knowing or having reasonable grounds to believe that unmarked human burials or human skeletal remains are being encountered shall notify immediately the Medical Examiner or the Director.

(b) When any person encounters unmarked burials or human skeletal remains as a result of construction, agricultural, or any other ground-disturbing activities, the person shall cease the ground-disturbing activity immediately upon discovery and notify the Medical Examiner or the Director of the discovery.

(c) Human burials or human skeletal remains which are encountered by a professional archaeologist as a result of survey or excavations must be reported to the Director. Excavation and other activities may resume after written approval is provided by the Director. The treatment, analysis, and disposition of the remains shall conform to the provisions of this chapter.

(d) The Director shall notify the Chief Medical Examiner of any reported human skeletal remains discovered by a professional archaeologist.

History.
66 Del. Laws, c. 38, § 1; 75 Del. Laws, c. 153, § 4; 83 Del. Laws, c. 142, § 1.

§ 5405. Jurisdiction over remains.

(a) Subsequent to notification of the discovery of an unmarked human burial or human skeletal remains, the Medical Examiner shall certify in writing to the Director, as soon as possible, whether the remains come under the Medical Examiner's jurisdiction.

(b) If the Medical Examiner determines that the remains come under the Medical Examiner's jurisdiction, the Medical Examiner will immediately proceed with an investigation pursuant to Chapter 47 of Title 29.

(c) All those remains determined to be not within the jurisdiction of the Medical Examiner shall be within the jurisdiction of the Director.

History.
66 Del. Laws, c. 38, § 1; 70 Del. Laws, c. 186, § 1; 75 Del. Laws, c. 153, § 4; 83 Del. Laws, c. 142, § 1.

§ 5406. Archaeological investigation of human skeletal remains.

All excavations not under the jurisdiction of the Medical Examiner shall be either conducted by, or under the supervision of, a professional archaeologist and shall be subject to permission from the landowner. All permissible excavations shall be conducted in accordance with the regulations promulgated for this chapter.

History.
66 Del. Laws, c. 38, § 1; 75 Del. Laws, c. 153, § 4; 83 Del. Laws, c. 142, § 1.

§ 5407. Consultation, analysis, and disposition.

(a) The Director shall notify the Committee of all skeletal remains determined to be Native American within 5 days of learning of the discovery of human burials or skeletal remains pursuant to § 5404 of this title. The Director shall provide the Committee with a written plan for the proposed treatment and ultimate disposition of the skeletal remains within 60 days of making the notification.

(b) For all non-Native American burials or skeletal remains, the director shall begin forming the Committee within 5 days of learning of the discovery pursuant to § 5404 of this title. The Director shall publish notice of all discoveries of human skeletal remains other than Native American on the Division's website, and at least once per week for 2 successive weeks in a newspaper of general circulation in the county where the burials or skeletal remains were situated, in an effort to determine the identity or lineal descendants or both of the deceased. Lineal descendants shall have 30 days after the last published notice to notify the Director of their ancestry or proven kinship to the skeletal remains. Within 60 days of the end of the notification period the Director shall convene the Committee to develop a written plan for treatment and disposition of human skeletal remains. Treatment and ultimate disposition of the skeletal remains shall be subject to the written permission of the lineal descendants or shall be determined by the Director if no lineal descendant is identified.

(c) All skeletal analysis conducted pursuant to this chapter shall be undertaken only by a skeletal analyst.

(d) Any previously excavated skeletal remains of Native Americans of the State which are on display or remain uncovered as of June 5, 1987, shall be reinterred within 1 year. Treatment and disposition of all Native American remains discovered after enactment shall be determined by the Committee or, if direct descent can be determined, by a lineal descendant. In any event, Native American skeletal remains discovered after enactment shall be reinterred within 90 days unless an extension or other disposition is granted by the Committee.

(e) All reasonable efforts shall be made to maintain burials and skeletal remains in situ if that is the consensus of the Committee. Any person which is responsible, either directly or indirectly, for the unearthing of human remains deemed to be under the jurisdiction of the Division of Historical and Cultural Affairs shall be responsible for the cost of research to determine the identity, delineation of the burial ground, excavation, and reinterment, and providing a suitable marker for those remains.

History.
66 Del. Laws, c. 38, § 1; 68 Del. Laws, c. 290, § 84; 75 Del. Laws, c. 153, §§ 4, 7; 83 Del. Laws, c. 142, § 1.

§ 5408. Prohibited acts.

No person, unless acting pursuant to Chapter 47 of Title 29, shall:

(1) Knowingly acquire any human skeletal remains removed from unmarked burials in Delaware, except in accordance with this title.

(2) Knowingly sell any human skeletal remains acquired from unmarked burials in Delaware.

(3) Knowingly exhibit human skeletal remains.

(4) Knowingly fail to notify the Medical Examiner or the Director of a discovery of unmarked human burials or skeletal remains pursuant to § 5404 of this title.

History.
66 Del. Laws, c. 38, § 1; 75 Del. Laws, c. 153, § 4; 83 Del. Laws, c. 142, § 1.

§ 5409. Exceptions.

(a) Human skeletal remains acquired from commercial biological supply houses or through medical means are not subject to this chapter.

(b) Human skeletal remains determined to be within the jurisdiction of the Medical Examiner are not subject to the prohibitions contained in this chapter.

(c) Human skeletal remains acquired through archaeological excavations under the supervision of a professional archaeologist are not subject to the prohibitions as provided in § 5408(1) of this title.

(d) Remains discovered within the known boundaries of a marked cemetery under the purview of the Department of Health and Social Services pursuant to Chapter 79A of Title 29 are not subject to this chapter.

History.
66 Del. Laws, c. 38, § 1; 75 Del. Laws, c. 153, §§ 4, 8; 83 Del. Laws, c. 142, § 1.

§ 5410. Criminal penalties.

Any person who violates § 5408 of this title shall upon conviction be sentenced to pay a fine of not less than $1,000 nor more than $10,000 or be imprisoned not more than 2 years or both. The Superior Court shall have jurisdiction of offenses under this chapter.

History.
66 Del. Laws, c. 38, § 1; 75 Del. Laws, c. 153, §§ 4, 6, 9; 83 Del. Laws, c. 142, § 1.

§ 5411. Rules, regulations, standards, and guidelines.

The Division of Historical and Cultural Affairs may, with the approval of the Department of State, formulate and adopt such rules, regulations, standards, and guidelines as it considers necessary for the effective execution of its purposes under this chapter.

History.
75 Del. Laws, c. 153, § 10; 83 Del. Laws, c. 142, § 1.

PART VII
NATURAL RESOURCES

CHAPTER 60
ENVIRONMENTAL CONTROL
SUBCHAPTER II
POWERS AND DUTIES OF SECRETARY AND DEPARTMENT

§ 6003. Permit — Required.

NOTES TO DECISIONS

Analysis

Penalties.
Permits.
— Requirement proper.

Penalties.

Superior Court erred by overturning Environmental Appeals Board's determination that no penalty should be assessed against appellees for transporting solid waste from a transfer station without a permit. Del. Solid Waste Auth. v. Del. Dep't of Nat. Res. & Envtl. Control, 250 A.3d 94 (Del. 2021).

Permits.

— Requirement proper.

In a case in which appellee was found to have transported solid waste from a transfer station without a valid permit, the Delaware Supreme Court held that the Superior Court and the Environmental Appeals Board erred by holding unlawful a condition requiring that all valid transporters have valid permits to transport solid waste; the condition accords with duly promulgated regulations and is therefore lawful. Del. Solid Waste Auth. v. Del. Dep't of Nat. Res. & Envtl. Control, 250 A.3d 94 (Del. 2021).

§ 6008. Appeals to Board.

NOTES TO DECISIONS

Analysis

Evidence.
— Hearing.
Permits.
— Scope.

Evidence.

— Hearing.

7 Del. C § 6008's plain language does not support applying less deference to the enforcement decisions of the Secretary of the Department of Natural Resources and Environmental Control where the Environmental Appeals Board holds the initial evidentiary hearing. Del. Solid Waste Auth. v. Del. Dep't of Nat. Res. & Envtl. Control, 250 A.3d 94 (Del. 2021).

Permits.

— Scope.

The 2014 revised version of 7 Del. Admin. Code § 7101-6.3.1.14.1 did not apply to a permit application for wastewater treatment facility construction where that application was more properly characterized as an amendment to an existing 2013 wastewater treatment facility construction permit; neither a hydrogeologic suitability report, nor a surface water assessment report, were required to secure changes to a 2013 permit. Keep Our Wells Clean v. Del. Dep't of Natural Res. & Envtl. Control, 243 A.3d 441 (Del. 2020).

Opinions of the Attorney General.

FOIA Petition Regarding the Environmental Appeals Board, see No. 20-IB23, October 13, 2020.

TITLE 8
CORPORATIONS

Chapter
1. General Corporation Law, §§ 101 to 398.

CHAPTER 1
GENERAL CORPORATION LAW

SUBCHAPTER I
FORMATION

§ 102. Contents of certificate of incorporation.

NOTES TO DECISIONS

Analysis

Board of directors.
— Exculpation.
— — Bad faith.
— — Clauses in charters.
— — Duty of loyalty.
Limitation of liability.
— Directors.
— — Provisions to shield.
Stockholders.

Board of directors.

— Exculpation.

— — Bad faith.

Derivative action, alleging that directors breached fiduciary duties by pursuing reclassification of shares, had to be dismissed because: (1) no presuit demand was made; (2) the complaint failed to plead facts suggesting a majority of directors acted in bad faith, were not exculpated or could not exercise disinterested and independent judgment regarding a demand; (3) futility was evaluated on a director-by-director basis; and (4) the board did not have a new majority and had some conflicted directors. UFCW & Participating Food Indus. Empls Tri-State Pension Fund v. Zuckerberg, 250 A.3d 862 (Del. Ch. 2020), aff'd, — A.3d —, 2021 Del. LEXIS 298 (Del. 2021).

— — Clauses in charters.

After a 2-step merger, a stockholder failed to sufficiently plead that the directors breached their duties of loyalty because: (1) the corporation's certificate of incorporation contained an exculpatory provision that barred any claims for monetary damages against a director for duty of care violations; and (2) the mere threat of a proxy contest did not render the directors conflicted. Rudd v. Brown, — A.3d —, 2020 Del. Ch. LEXIS 288 (Del. Ch. Sept. 11, 2020).

— — Duty of loyalty.

Defendant was not entitled to exculpation of a claim for money damages, to the extent de-

fendant acted in the capacity of a director, because the complaint pleaded a claim for breach of the duty of loyalty; to the extent that defendant acted as CEO, which appeared to have been defendant's primary role in the sale process, exculpation was not available. Firefighters' Pension Sys. v. Presidio, Inc., 251 A.3d 212 (Del. Ch. 2021).

Shareholder failed to state a nonexculpated breach of fiduciary duty claim arising from a merger; the shareholder failed to sufficiently allege either that significant shareholders were conflicted controllers or that the corporation's chief executive officer lacked independence from the acquiring company. Flannery v. Genomic Health, Inc., — A.3d —, 2021 Del. Ch. LEXIS 175 (Del. Ch. Aug. 16, 2021).

Limitation of liability.

— Directors.

— — Provisions to shield.

Derivative action, alleging that directors breached fiduciary duties by pursuing reclassification of shares, had to be dismissed because: (1) no presuit demand was made; (2) the complaint failed to plead facts suggesting a majority of directors acted in bad faith, were not exculpated or could not exercise disinterested and independent judgment regarding a demand; (3) futility was evaluated on a director-by-director basis; and (4) the board did not have a new majority and had some conflicted directors. UFCW & Participating Food Indus. Empls Tri-State Pension Fund v. Zuckerberg, 250 A.3d 862 (Del. Ch. 2020), aff'd, — A.3d —, 2021 Del. LEXIS 298 (Del. 2021).

Stockholders.

Common stockholders are not prohibited from agreeing to an ex ante waiver of mandatory appraisal rights, consistent with the statutory flexibility provided to corporations and the strong public policy favoring private ordering; thus, sophisticated and informed stockholders represented by counsel validly agreed in a stockholders agreement to refrain from exercising their appraisal rights in exchange for valu-able consideration. Manti Holdings, LLC v. Authentix Acquisition Co., 2021 Del. LEXIS 286 (September 13, 2021).

§ 109. Bylaws.

Stockholders.

Common stockholders are not prohibited from agreeing to an ex ante waiver of mandatory appraisal rights, consistent with the statutory flexibility provided to corporations and the strong public policy favoring private ordering; thus, sophisticated and informed stockholders represented by counsel validly agreed in a stockholders agreement to refrain from exercising their appraisal rights in exchange for valu-able consideration. Manti Holdings, LLC v. Authentix Acquisition Co., 2021 Del. LEXIS 286 (September 13, 2021).

§ 111. Jurisdiction to interpret, apply, enforce or determine the validity of corporate instruments and provisions of this title. [For application of this section, see 80 Del. Laws, c. 265, § 17].

Subject matter jurisdiction.

Chancery Court had subject matter jurisdiction over plaintiffs' claim seeking a declaratory judgment that defendants were not entitled to indemnification under a merger agreement; the merger agreement fell within the scope of agreements giving rise to the Court's exercise of subject matter jurisdiction under this statute and addressed the merger of 2 Delaware corporations. Legent Grp., LLC v. Axos Fin., Inc., — A.3d —, 2021 Del. Ch. LEXIS 3 (Del. Ch. Jan. 8, 2021).

SUBCHAPTER II
POWERS

§ 122. Specific powers.

Property rights.

Corporation could enforce a provision of a stockholders agreement in which common stockholders agreed to refrain from exercising appraisal rights; there is no statutory bar against corporations entering into stockholders agreements, an action which is within the power to make contracts. Manti Holdings, LLC v. Authentix Acquisition Co., — A.3d —, 2021 Del. LEXIS 286 (Del. Sept. 13, 2021).

SUBCHAPTER IV
DIRECTORS AND OFFICERS

§ 141. Board of directors; powers; number, qualifications, terms and quorum; committees; classes of directors; nonstock corporations; reliance upon books; action without meeting; removal.

Analysis

II. Officers.
   B. Powers and Duties.
Directors.
— Duty of loyalty.
— — Breach.
— Resignation.
IV. Stockholders.
Procedure for redress.
— Derivative suit.
— — Ripeness.

II. OFFICERS.
   B. POWERS AND DUTIES.

Directors.

— Duty of loyalty.

— — Breach.

Issuance of a mandatory injunction requiring redemption of a stockholder rights plan that was intended to insulate corporate management from activists trying to influence the control of a corporation, or a so-called poison pill, was appropriate; the directors of the corporation breached the fiduciary duties when adopting the plan and failed to show that the plan fell within the range of reasonable responses. In re Williams Cos. Stockholder Litig., — A.3d —, 2021 Del. Ch. LEXIS 34 (Del. Ch. Feb. 26, 2021).

Derivative plaintiffs owed fiduciary duties to the company and all stockholders because a claim pursued in arbitration on the company's behalf was a corporate asset, resulted in an award that belonged to the company and left the company's board with authority over the award after it became a final judgment; allegations that the derivative plaintiffs wrongfully withheld the award, causing financial harm by forcing the company to take unfavorable loans, stated a claim for breach of the fiduciary duty of loyalty. OptimisCorp v. Atkins, 2021 Del. Ch. LEXIS 153 (July 15, 2021).

— Resignation.

Director who also served as a consultant had not manifested an intent to resign because: (1) the director's failure to respond to communications, and to attend at least 3 board meetings, was probably due to the director's poor health, and (2) a statement the director made to another consultant, that the director's health would no longer allow the director to serve the corporation and asking that the consultant recommend potential future clients, likely referred to the director's need to step back from consulting work. Villette v. MondoBrain, Inc., — A.3d —, 2020 Del. Ch. LEXIS 375 (Del. Ch. Dec. 29, 2020).

IV. STOCKHOLDERS.

Procedure for redress.

— Derivative suit.

— — Ripeness.

Derivative action, alleging that directors breached fiduciary duties by pursuing reclassification of shares, had to be dismissed because: (1) no presuit demand was made; (2) the complaint failed to plead facts suggesting a majority of directors acted in bad faith, were not exculpated or could not exercise disinterested and independent judgment regarding a demand; (3) futility was evaluated on a director-by-director basis; and (4) the board did not have a new majority and had some conflicted directors. UFCW & Participating Food Indus. Empls Tri-State Pension Fund v. Zuckerberg, 250 A.3d 862 (Del. Ch. 2020), aff'd, — A.3d —, 2021 Del. LEXIS 298 (Del. 2021).

§ 145. Indemnification of officers, directors, employees and agents; insurance.

NOTES TO DECISIONS

Analysis

Advancement.
— Right to advancement.

Advancement.

— Right to advancement.

Corporate director possessed an enforceable advancement right against a corporation for indemnifiable litigation expenses relating to the director's status as director of the company; the director's indemnification agreement (as evidenced by metadata for the director's signature page) was signed on April 20, 2018, and was therefore valid. Perryman v. Stimwave Techs., Inc., — A.3d —, 2020 Del. Ch. LEXIS 363 (Del. Ch. Dec. 9, 2020).

SUBCHAPTER V

STOCK AND DIVIDENDS

§ 151. Classes and series of stock; redemption; rights.

NOTES TO DECISIONS

Stockholders.

Provision of a stockholders agreement in which common stockholders agreed to refrain from exercising appraisal rights was not a stock restriction under this section; the provision imposed personal obligations on stockholders, rather than restricting stock rights. Manti Holdings, LLC v. Authentix Acquisition Co., 2021 Del. LEXIS 286 (September 13, 2021).

§ 157. Rights and options respecting stock.

NOTES TO DECISIONS

Board of directors.

Breach-of-contract claim, alleging that a company had not kept a promise to grant equity in exchange for services, survived a motion to dismiss because: (1) the complaint alleged that the stock grant was evidenced by a string of emails approved by the members of the board of directors; and (2) although cases suggest that a mere exchange of emails will not suffice, the issue was better reviewed on a full record to determine whether there was in evidence an unambiguous written instrument approved by the board members. Hoffman v. Thras, — F. Supp. 3d —, 2021 U.S. Dist. LEXIS 89598 (D. Mass. May 10, 2021).

§ 160. Corporation's powers respecting ownership, voting, etc., of its own stock; rights of stock called for redemption.

(a) Every corporation may purchase, redeem, receive, take or otherwise acquire, own and hold, sell, lend, exchange, transfer or otherwise dispose of, pledge, use and otherwise deal in and with its own shares; provided, however, that no corporation shall:

(1) Purchase or redeem its own shares of capital stock for cash or other property when the capital of the corporation is impaired or when such purchase or redemption would cause any impairment of the capital of the corporation, except that a corporation other than a nonstock corporation may purchase or redeem out of capital any of its own shares which are entitled upon any distribution of its assets, whether by dividend or in liquidation, to a preference over another class or series of its stock, or, if no shares entitled to such a preference are outstanding, any of its own shares, if such shares will be retired upon their acquisition and the capital of the corporation reduced in accordance with §§ 243 and 244 of this title. Nothing in this subsection shall invalidate or otherwise affect a note, debenture or other obligation of a corporation given by it as consideration for its acquisition by purchase, redemption or exchange of its shares of stock if at the time such note, debenture or obligation was delivered by the corporation its capital was not then impaired or did not thereby become impaired;

(2) Purchase, for more than the price at which they may then be redeemed, any of its shares which are redeemable at the option of the corporation; or

(3)a. In the case of a corporation other than a nonstock corporation, redeem any of its shares, unless their redemption is authorized by § 151(b) of this title and then only in accordance with such section and the certificate of incorporation, or

b. In the case of a nonstock corporation, redeem any of its membership interests, unless their redemption is authorized by the certificate of incorporation and then only in accordance with the certificate of incorporation.

(b) Nothing in this section limits or affects a corporation's right to resell any of its shares theretofore purchased or redeemed out of surplus and which have not been retired, for such consideration as shall be fixed by the board of directors.

(c) Shares of a corporation's capital stock shall neither be entitled to vote nor be counted for quorum purposes if such shares belong to:

(1) The corporation;

(2) Another corporation, if a majority of the shares entitled to vote in the election of directors of such other corporation is held, directly or indirectly; or

(3) Any other entity, if a majority of the voting power of such other entity is held, directly or indirectly, by the corporation or if such other entity is otherwise controlled, directly or indirectly, by the corporation.

Nothing in this section shall be construed as limiting the right of any corporation to vote stock, including but not limited to its own stock, held by it in a fiduciary capacity.

(d) Shares which have been called for redemption shall not be deemed to be outstanding shares for the purpose of voting or determining the total number of shares entitled to vote on any matter on and after the date on which notice of redemption has been sent to holders thereof and a sum sufficient to redeem such shares has been irrevocably deposited or set aside to pay the redemption price to the holders of the shares upon surrender of certificates therefor.

History.

8 Del. C. 1953, § 160; 56 Del. Laws, c. 50; 57 Del. Laws, c. 649, § 1; 59 Del. Laws, c. 106, § 3; 59 Del. Laws, c. 437, § 9; 70 Del. Laws, c. 349, § 3; 77 Del. Laws, c. 253, §§ 16, 17; 82 Del. Laws, c. 45, § 5; 83 Del. Laws, c. 60, § 1.

Revisor's note.

Section 2 of 83 Del. Laws, c. 60, provided:

"Section 1 of this act shall be effective on August 1, 2021."

Effect of amendments.

83 Del. Laws. c. 60, effective Aug. 1, 2021, rewrote (c).

SUBCHAPTER VI
STOCK TRANSFERS

§ 203. Business combinations with interested stockholders.

NOTES TO DECISIONS

Agreement to acquire or hold stock.

Shareholder of a corporation that was acquired in a merger failed to state a claim for violation of this section because the acquiring company was not an interested stockholder prior to approval of the merger; it was not reasonable to read the proxy in such a way as to say that a group of significant shareholders had fully and unconditionally agreed to vote their shares in favor. Flannery v. Genomic Health, Inc., — A.3d —, 2021 Del. Ch. LEXIS 175 (Del. Ch. Aug. 16, 2021).

SUBCHAPTER VII
MEETINGS, ELECTIONS, VOTING AND NOTICE

§ 218. Voting trusts and other voting agreements.

NOTES TO DECISIONS

Voting agreements.

Corporation could enforce a provision of a stockholders agreement in which common stockholders agreed to refrain from exercising appraisal rights; this section does not bar corporations from entering into stockholders agreements, which is within the power to make contracts. Manti Holdings, LLC v. Authentix Acquisition Co., 2021 Del. LEXIS 286 (September 13, 2021).

§ 220. Inspection of books and records.

NOTES TO DECISIONS

Analysis

Complaint.
Demand for inspection.
— Prerequisites.
Discovery.
Entitlement to inspection.
— Demonstrated.
— Not demonstrated.
Proceedings under section.
— Attorneys' fees.
— Demand futility.
— Mootness.
Purpose of inspection.
— Evidence.
— Found proper.
— Not found.
— Standard of review.
Right to inspection.
— Discretion of court.
— Limited.
— Time limitations.

Complaint.

For purposes of a motion to dismiss, a shareholder's agreement that the entire production of materials under this section would be incorporated by reference in any filing by the shareholder did not give defendants carte blanche to cite to any such document for any purpose; defendants could not rely on the documents for the sake of rewriting the complaint in favor of their own version of events. Flannery v. Genomic Health, Inc., — A.3d —, 2021 Del. Ch. LEXIS 175 (Del. Ch. Aug. 16, 2021).

Demand for inspection.

— Prerequisites.

In an action to inspect defendant company's books and records, a plaintiff was entitled to inspect nonprivileged documents relating to the company investigations of officers and directors engaged in improper accounting practices relating to servicing costs and liabilities, and internal documents submitted to the board relating to those servicing costs and liabilities. Jacob v. Bloom Energy Corp., — A.3d —, 2021 Del. Ch. LEXIS 32 (Del. Ch. Feb. 25, 2021).

Discovery.

Defendant was required to produce information regarding document collection, as well as the search and review process, in a books and records action because: (1) the request sought standard information; and (2) plaintiff was entitled to a formal, verified response. Dolan v.

Jobu Holdings, LLC, — A.3d —, 2021 Del. Ch. LEXIS 30 (Del. Ch. Feb. 17, 2021).

Entitlement to inspection.

— Demonstrated.

In an action in which stockholders sought to inspect books and records of company, judgment was entered for stockholders; there was no prejudice to the company in producing all categories of information deemed necessary and essential to all stockholders. Pettry v. Gilead Scis., Inc., — A.3d —, 2020 Del. Ch. LEXIS 347 (Del. Ch. Nov. 24, 2020).

Requested nonprivileged electronic communications concerning the existence of available alternatives to the 2019 settlement or the board's negotiations with the Federal Trade Commission were necessary and essential to plaintiff's proper purpose because: (1) plaintiff did not forfeit its statutory inspection rights by candidly describing the strength of its potential claims; and (2) the documents already produced were of little probative value to plaintiff's investigatory purpose. Employees' Ret. Sys. of R.I. v. Facebook, Inc., — A.3d —, 2021 Del. Ch. LEXIS 27 (Del. Ch. Feb. 10, 2021).

— Not demonstrated.

Plaintiff was not entitled to production of attorney-client privileged and work product documents (including unredacted copies of board minutes and certain privileged electronic communications) because plaintiff had not seen the responsive, nonprivileged electronic communications that defendant was withholding; as such, plaintiff could not demonstrate that the privileged information it sought was unavailable elsewhere. Employees' Ret. Sys. of R.I. v. Facebook, Inc., — A.3d —, 2021 Del. Ch. LEXIS 27 (Del. Ch. Feb. 10, 2021).

Proceedings under section.

— Attorneys' fees.

When a corporation paid the legal fees incurred in connection with a company's response to a books and records demand, the payment reflected services rendered by counsel to the corporation while the corporation wound down its obligations with respect to the action (e.g., prevailing party costs, etc.); the majority shareholder's claim for reimbursement of legal expenses, therefore, failed for want of proof. In re Happy Child World, Inc., — A.3d —, 2020 Del. Ch. LEXIS 302 (Del. Ch. Sept. 29, 2020).

— Demand futility.

While plaintiff did not pursue a books and records investigation before filing its amended complaint, dismissal based on lack of demand was not warranted because plaintiff had access to a fully developed criminal trial record involving the same oil spill at issue in the derivative litigation; that record, as utilized by plaintiff, contained sufficient evidence to survive a motion to dismiss. Inter-Marketing Group United States v. Armstrong, — A.3d —, 2020 Del. Ch. LEXIS 391 (Del. Ch. Jan. 31, 2020).

— Mootness.

Plaintiff's books and records inspection action was moot because: (1) plaintiff was no longer a stockholder of defendant corporation by reason of defendant's merger and no longer had standing to commence or to maintain an action derivatively on behalf of defendant; and (2) plaintiff's only purpose for the action was an issue that did not survive accomplishment of the merger. Grimes v. DSC Communs. Corp., 1998 Del. Ch. LEXIS 253 (Del. Ch. Nov. 6, 1998).

Purpose of inspection.

— Evidence.

In an action to inspect defendant company's books and records, the company was justified in rejecting a plaintiff's demand for inspection; plaintiff's demand was not accompanied by satisfactory documentary evidence demonstrating that plaintiff was a stockholder at a point proximate to the date of the demand. Jacob v. Bloom Energy Corp., — A.3d —, 2021 Del. Ch. LEXIS 32 (Del. Ch. Feb. 25, 2021).

— Found proper.

Stockholder's request to investigate possible breaches of fiduciary duty was a proper purpose for a books and records inspection demand; the evidence established a credible basis to suspect that the directors might have favored the interests of certain directors, or their affiliates, over the company's interests in rejecting a term sheet. Alexandria Venture Invs., LLC v. Verseau Therapeutics, Inc., — A.3d —, 2020 Del. Ch. LEXIS 367 (Del. Ch. Dec. 18, 2020).

— Not found.

Stockholder failed to state a proper purpose for a books and records inspection demand regarding the appointment of a board observer to the board; the board's forward-looking statements that the observer would become a director if additional approvals were secured, even coupled with the observer's belief that the observer was a director, did not create an inference that board members acted out of self-interest, in bad faith or in breach of fiduciary duty. Alexandria Venture Invs., LLC v. Verseau Therapeutics, Inc., — A.3d —, 2020 Del. Ch. LEXIS 367 (Del. Ch. Dec. 18, 2020).

Stockholder failed to state a proper purpose for a books and records inspection demand concerning a director's role in hiring decisions or recommendations because: (1) the stockholder did not present evidence that the director received or would receive improper benefits from the hiring of former employees from the director's former place of employment; and (2) there was no evidence to reasonably infer that the hiring decisions were not aligned with the interests of the company or its stockholders. Alexandria Venture Invs., LLC v. Verseau Therapeutics, Inc., — A.3d —, 2020 Del. Ch. LEXIS 367 (Del. Ch. Dec. 18, 2020).

Stockholder failed to state a proper purpose for a books and records inspection regarding the evaluation of whether a director might have been motivated by self-interest in the director's consideration of "other company business;" the stockholder did not explain what "other company business" entailed and did not even hint as to the director having engaged in any wrongdoing. Alexandria Venture Invs., LLC v. Verseau Therapeutics, Inc., — A.3d —, 2020 Del. Ch. LEXIS 367 (Del. Ch. Dec. 18, 2020).

— Standard of review.
In an action ordering appellant to produce certain books and records to appellees, a "credible basis" test was the standard by which investigative inspections were to be judged; the court should defer consideration of defenses not directly bearing on stockholder's inspection rights. AmerisourceBergen Corp. v. Leb. Cty. Employees' Ret. Fund, 243 A.3d 417 (Del. 2020).

Right to inspection.

— Discretion of court.
Plaintiff was entitled to inspect some categories of books and records sought in a demand for inspection; defendant was to produce, or make available for inspection, documents sufficient to identify board committees or subcommittees responsible for oversight and monitoring of an investigation as defined in the demand. Gross v. Biogen Inc., — A.3d —, 2021 Del. Ch. LEXIS 66 (Del. Ch. Apr. 14, 2021).

— Limited.
Plaintiff (a stockholder and member of LLCs) was entitled to access to specific corporate books and records for the purpose of inspection, rather than their production; the inspection orders had to deploy "rifled precision," because the stockholder/member's right of inspection did not have an unlimited scope and had to be limited to documents that were necessary, essential and sufficient to the purpose. Ferris v. Ferris Props., — A.3d —, 2020 Del. Ch. LEXIS 334 (Del. Ch. Nov. 12, 2020).

— Time limitations.
Dismissal of the stockholders' complaint, regarding a demand to inspect a company's books and records, was appropriate because: (1) the company had not affirmatively refused the stockholders' demand; (2) the stockholders' complaint to compel inspection was filed before the statutory 5-business-day response period had lapsed; and (3) Chancery Court was without jurisdiction in the stockholders' prematurely-filed complaint. Mad Investors Grmd, LLC v. GR Cos., Inc., — A.3d —, 2020 Del. Ch. LEXIS 323 (Del. Ch. Oct. 28, 2020).

§ 225. Contested election of directors; proceedings to determine validity.

NOTES TO DECISIONS

Analysis

Jurisdiction.
— Equity.
Notice.

Jurisdiction.

— Equity.
Court of Chancery did not err by exercising its equitable powers to grant relief for a de facto breach of a voting agreement because: (1) the Court granted equitable relief for the harm flowing from appellants' breach of their equitable duties as directors; and (2) this claim involved facts separate from a breach of con-

tract claim. Bäcker v. Palisades Growth Capital II, L.P., 246 A.3d 81 (Del. 2021).

Notice.
Nominees were properly appointed to the board because the certificate of incorporation and the bylaws, when read together, authorized the sole common stockholder to act by written consent to appoint 2 directors to the board at any time and without notice; in the context of the written consent, the stockholder was not required to provide 60 days' notice prior to the appointment of the nominees because they were not appointed at a meeting of stockholders. Goldberg v. Bruck, 2021 Del. Ch. LEXIS 126 (Del. Ch. June 23, 2021).

§ 227. Powers of Court in elections of directors.

NOTES TO DECISIONS

Removal of directors.
Defendant was validly removed as a director of plaintiff at a special meeting of stockholders on July 31, 2018; the 2 stockholders voting to

remove defendant owned a majority of plaintiff's outstanding common stock on that date. Simple Global, Inc. v. Banasik, — A.3d —, 2021 Del. Ch. LEXIS 129 (Del. Ch. June 24, 2021).

§ 228. Consent of stockholders or members in lieu of meeting [For application of section, see 81 Del. Laws, c. 86, § 40]

NOTES TO DECISIONS

Applicability.
Nominees were properly appointed to the board because the certificate of incorporation and the bylaws, when read together, authorized the sole common stockholder to act by written

consent to appoint 2 directors to the board at any time and without notice; in the context of the written consent, the stockholder was not required to provide 60 days' notice prior to the appointment of the nominees because they were not appointed at a meeting of stockholders. Goldberg v. Bruck, 2021 Del. Ch. LEXIS 126 (Del. Ch. June 23, 2021).

SUBCHAPTER IX
MERGER, CONSOLIDATION OR CONVERSION

§ 259. Status, rights, liabilities, of constituent and surviving or resulting corporations following merger or consolidation.

RESEARCH REFERENCES AND PRACTICE AIDS

Delaware Law Reviews.
M&A Advisor Misconduct: A Wrong Without a Remedy?, 45 Del. J. Corp. L. 177 (2021).

§ 262. Appraisal rights [For application of this section, see § 17; 82 Del. Laws, c. 45, § 23; and 82 Del. Laws, c. 256, § 24].

NOTES TO DECISIONS

Analysis

Appraisal proceeding.
— Costs.
Fair value of shares.
— Measure of recovery.
Interest.
— Discretion of court.
Standard of review.

Appraisal proceeding.

— Costs.

For the purpose of determining insurance coverage for costs associated with an appraisal action, appraisal actions (including any breaches of fiduciary duty claimed in support of a call for appraisal) are not proceedings that adjudicate wrongdoing; appraisal actions do not involve "violations" of any law or rule and thus do not fall within the definition of a "securities claim." In re Solera Ins. Coverage Appeals, 240 A.3d 1121 (Del. 2020).

For the purpose of determining insurance coverage for costs associated with an appraisal action, appraisal proceedings are neutral in nature; an appraisal proceeding seeks a statutory determination of fair value that does not require a finding of wrongdoing. In re Solera Ins. Coverage Appeals, 240 A.3d 1121 (Del. 2020).

Insurers' motion to dismiss was granted because: (1) even if the appraisal demands were a "claim" under the relevant insurance policies, the appraisal action was not for an act that occurred before the run-off date; (2) without the merger's execution, no appraisal right existed; and (3) if the merger had not closed, none of the dissenting stockholders who submitted appraisal demands would have had standing to pursue appraisal. Jarden v. Ace Am. Ins. Co., 2021 Del. Super. LEXIS 534 (July 30, 2021).

Common stockholders are not prohibited from agreeing to an ex ante waiver of mandatory appraisal rights, consistent with the statutory flexibility provided to corporations and the strong public policy favoring private ordering; thus, sophisticated and informed stockholders represented by counsel validly agreed in a stockholders agreement to refrain from exercising their appraisal rights in exchange for valuable consideration. Manti Holdings, LLC v. Authentix Acquisition Co., 2021 Del. LEXIS 286 (September 13, 2021).

Fair value of shares.

— Measure of recovery.

Following a squeeze-out merger of a corporation by a majority shareholder, the minority shareholders were entitled to an appraisal award; because the shareholders had all breached their fiduciary duties to the corporation, the court subtracted the shareholders' liabilities to the corporation from their pro rata interest in the corporation's fair value (including its litigation assets), as this method effectively adjusted their equity-based appraisal award in proportion to their personal liabilities to the corporation. In re Happy Child World, Inc., — A.3d —, 2020 Del. Ch. LEXIS 302 (Del. Ch. Sept. 29, 2020).

Interest.

— Discretion of court.

Prejudgment interest was rightfully awarded to former owners because: (1) the method of calculating the appraisal award incorporated into the company's fair value its litigation assets while avoiding double-recovery; and (2) the entirety of the final appraisal award reflected money that the former owners were deprived from accessing throughout the litigation. Happy Child World, Inc., — A.3d —, 2020 Del. Ch. LEXIS 362 (Del. Ch. Dec. 9, 2020).

Standard of review.

In an appraisal action brought by petitioners who owned shares of common stock in a company acquired through a reverse triangular merger, the Court of Chancery held that the fair value of the stock was $23.60 per share because: (1) the deal price was the most reliable evidence of value at the time the merger agreement was signed; (2) the operative reality changed between signing of the merger agreement and closing when the federal Tax Cuts and Jobs Act of 2017 (P.L. 115–97) became law; and (3) the reduced corporate tax rate, from 35% to 21%, necessitated an upward adjust-

ment to the deal-price-less-synergies metric. In re Appraisal of Regal Entm't Grp., 2021 Del. Ch. LEXIS 93 (Del. Ch. May 13, 2021).

SUBCHAPTER X

SALE OF ASSETS, DISSOLUTION AND WINDING UP

§ 271. Sale, lease or exchange of assets; consideration; procedure.

NOTES TO DECISIONS

Analysis

Applicability.
— All or substantially all of the assets.
— — Quantitative and qualitative considerations.

Applicability.

— All or substantially all of the assets.

— — Quantitative and qualitative considerations.

Omnibus agreement did not require stock-

holder approval; because 8 Del. C. § 271 did not cover the worst case transaction for plaintiff, a foreclosure involving all of its assets, it logically did not apply to a lesser included alternative that provided greater benefits to plaintiff and its stockholders. Stream TV Networks, Inc. v. SeeCubic, Inc., 250 A.3d 1016 (Del. Ch. 2020).

§ 279. Trustees or receivers for dissolved corporations; appointment; powers; duties.

NOTES TO DECISIONS

Analysis

Applicability.
Appointment of trustee or receiver.
— Discretion of court.

Applicability.

In a dispute involving deed restrictions for a residential community developed by a corporation, the Chancery Master found that the right to enforce the deed restrictions was "property" within the meaning of 8 Del. C. § 279; although contingent, it still had potential value to the holder. Civic Ass'n of Surrey Park v. Riegel, — A.3d —, 2021 Del. Ch. LEXIS 194 (Del. Ch. June 2, 2021).

Appointment of trustee or receiver.

— Discretion of court.

In a dispute involving deed restrictions for a

residential community developed by a corporation, the Chancery Master concluded that appointment of a receiver for the corporation on a pretrial motion with a disputed factual record would be inappropriate; there was a live dispute regarding distribution by the corporation where the community's civic association pleading claimed that the corporation's right to enforce had passed to the association's predecessor-in-interest, while homeowners disagreed with the association's averment. Civic Ass'n of Surrey Park v. Riegel, — A.3d —, 2021 Del. Ch. LEXIS 194 (Del. Ch. June 2, 2021).

§ 280. Notice to claimants; filing of claims.

NOTES TO DECISIONS

Analysis

Security.
— Sufficiency.

Security.

— Sufficiency.

Dissolving company seeking to make an interim distribution to its shareholders pursuant to 8 Del. C. §§ 280 and 281 could reserve $250

million for unknown claims because: (1) the company had sold its operating business 3 years earlier to a buyer who had assumed responsibility for claims relating to that business; (2) Canadian litigation over privacy breach claims was unpredictable; and (3) a reserve of $1.05 billion Canadian was ordered before an interim distribution was authorized. In re Altaba, Inc., 241 A.3d 768 (Del. Ch. 2020).

§ 281. Payment and distribution to claimants and stockholders.

NOTES TO DECISIONS

Analysis

Reasonable provision for claims.
— Reserve for contingent claims.

Reasonable provision for claims.

— Reserve for contingent claims.
   Dissolving company seeking to make an interim distribution to its shareholders pursuant to 8 Del. C. §§ 280 and 281 could reserve $250 million for unknown claims because: (1) the company had sold its operating business 3 years earlier to a buyer who had assumed responsibility for claims relating to that business; (2) Canadian litigation over privacy breach claims was unpredictable; and (3) a reserve of $1.05 billion Canadian was ordered before an interim distribution was authorized. In re Altaba, Inc., 241 A.3d 768 (Del. Ch. 2020).

§ 282. Liability of stockholders of dissolved corporations.

NOTES TO DECISIONS

Reserve for contingent claims.
   Dissolving company seeking to make an interim distribution to its shareholders pursuant to 8 Del. C. §§ 280 and 281 could reserve $250 million for unknown claims because: (1) the company had sold its operating business 3 years earlier to a buyer who had assumed responsibility for claims relating to that business; (2) Canadian litigation over privacy breach claims was unpredictable; and (3) a reserve of $1.05 billion Canadian was ordered before an interim distribution was authorized. In re Altaba, Inc., 241 A.3d 768 (Del. Ch. 2020).

SUBCHAPTER XV
PUBLIC BENEFIT CORPORATIONS

§ 361. Law applicable to public benefit corporations; how formed.

RESEARCH REFERENCES AND PRACTICE AIDS

Delaware Law Reviews.
   Benefit Corporations: The End Of Share- holder Primacy in the Takeover Context?, 45 Del. J. Corp. L. 279 (2021).

§ 362. Public benefit corporation defined; contents of certificate of incorporation.

RESEARCH REFERENCES AND PRACTICE AIDS

Delaware Law Reviews.
   Benefit Corporations: The End Of Share- holder Primacy in the Takeover Context?, 45 Del. J. Corp. L. 279 (2021).

§ 365. Duties of directors.

RESEARCH REFERENCES AND PRACTICE AIDS

Delaware Law Reviews.
   Benefit Corporations: The End Of Share- holder Primacy in the Takeover Context?, 45 Del. J. Corp. L. 279 (2021).

§ 366. Periodic statements and third-party certification.

RESEARCH REFERENCES AND PRACTICE AIDS

Delaware Law Reviews.
   Benefit Corporations: The End Of Share- holder Primacy in the Takeover Context?, 45 Del. J. Corp. L. 279 (2021).

TITLE 9
COUNTIES

PART I
PROVISIONS AFFECTING ALL COUNTIES

CHAPTER 3
COUNTY GOVERNMENTS GENERALLY

SUBCHAPTER II
COUNTY GOVERNMENTS

§ 349. Public advertising and notices.

Notwithstanding any provision to the contrary, public advertising and notices by any county in the State of any nature may include use of the State's electronic procurement advertising system required by § 6902(10) of Title 29 or other website allowing for the electronic posting of local government bid opportunities, and the website designed pursuant to §§ 10004(e)(5), 10115(b) and 10124(1) of Title 29.

History.
78 Del. Laws, c. 288, § 9; 82 Del. Laws, c. 36, § 1; 83 Del. Laws, c. 65, § 2.

Laws, c. 65, § 1, effective June 30, 2021, "§§ 10004(e)(5)" was substituted for "§§ 10004(e)(4)".

Revisor's note.
Based upon changes contained in 83 Del.

PART II
NEW CASTLE COUNTY

CHAPTER 11
COUNTY EXECUTIVE AND COUNTY COUNCIL

SUBCHAPTER I
POWERS OF THE GOVERNMENT
OF NEW CASTLE COUNTY

§ 1101. General powers.

NOTES TO DECISIONS

Governmental powers.

Failure to exhaust administrative remedies rendered claims in a sewer service dispute premature; the property owner had not re- quested a sewer capacity determination for a development proposal upon which the county, exercising its statutory powers, could act. Glen Allen Farm, LLC v. New Castle Cty., — A.3d —, 2020 Del. Ch. LEXIS 301 (Del. Ch. Sept. 29, 2020).

§ 1101A. Definitions [Effective until July 1, 2022].

For purposes of this chapter, beginning for the fiscal year 2023 budget:

(1) "Chief Financial Officer" means the Chief Financial Officer of New Castle County or a designee.

(2) "Fire protection" means the prevention and extinguishment of fires; maintenance of apparatus and equipment, including ambulances, rescue trucks, aerial, or platform trucks and rescue boats; provision of basic life support; and operation of stations.

(3)a. "Local service function" or "LSF" means a local governmental service, or a group of closely allied governmental services, that is all of the following:

1. A service for which, New Castle County or any municipality, as distinguished from the State, has a primary responsibility for provision and financing, under the Constitution, Code, or judicial decision.

2. Performed or financially supported by New Castle County and by at least 1 municipality, in whole or in part, instead of New Castle County.

3. Funded by New Castle County, in whole or in part, through property tax revenue.

b. "Local service function" or "LSF" may include any of the following:

1. Planning and zoning, including subdivision regulations.

2. Adoption and enforcement of ordinances for the protection of persons and property from hazards in the use, occupancy, condition, alteration, maintenance, repair, sanitation, removal, and demolition of buildings, structures, and appurtenant grounds; the operation of equipment; and outdoor signs, including codes and regulations for any of the following:

A. Zoning.

B. Building.

C. Plumbing.

D. Property maintenance.

3. Programs for redevelopment, affordable housing, and urban renewal.

4. Parks and park related activities and recreational programs.

5. Police protection.

6. Fire protection.

7. 9-1-1 communications.

8. Animal control.

9. Public works, including maintenance and operation of sanitary and storm sewers, drainage systems, sewage disposal facilities, and refuse disposal facilities, including trash and garbage collection disposal.

10. Lighting of streets, roads, alleys, and other public places.

11. Maintenance and operation of the water supply system.

12. Library system.

(4) "Municipality" means a municipal corporation located within New Castle County and incorporated by an act of the General Assembly.

(5) "New Castle County service percentage" means the degree to which New Castle County provides a local service function within a municipality, determined by subtracting the degree to which a municipality provides the local service function from 100%. The New Castle County service percentage in the unincorporated area equals 100%.

History.
83 Del. Laws, c. 7, § 1.

Revisor's note.
Section 11 of 83 Del. Laws, c. 7, provided: "Sections 1 through 4 of this act are effective immediately." The act was signed by the Governor on Feb. 23, 2021.

Section 13 of 83 Del. Laws, c. 7, provided: "Section 10 of this act is effective July 1, 2022."

Effect of amendments.
83 Del. Laws, c. 7, effective July 1, 2022, rewrote the section.

§ 1101A. Definitions [Effective July 1, 2022].

For purposes of this chapter:

(1) "Chief Financial Officer" means the Chief Financial Officer of New Castle County or a designee.

(2) "Fire protection" means the prevention and extinguishment of fires; maintenance of apparatus and equipment, including ambulances, rescue

trucks, aerial, or platform trucks and rescue boats; provision of basic life support; and operation of stations.

(3)a. "Local service function" or "LSF" means a local governmental service, or a group of closely allied governmental services, that is all of the following:

1. A service for which, New Castle County or any municipality, as distinguished from the State, has a primary responsibility for provision and financing, under the Constitution, Code, or judicial decision.

2. Performed or financially supported by New Castle County and by at least 1 municipality, in whole or in part, instead of New Castle County.

3. Funded by New Castle County, in whole or in part, through property tax revenue.

b. "Local service function" or "LSF" may include any of the following:

1. Planning and zoning, including subdivision regulations.

2. Adoption and enforcement of ordinances for the protection of persons and property from hazards in the use, occupancy, condition, alteration, maintenance, repair, sanitation, removal, and demolition of buildings, structures, and appurtenant grounds; the operation of equipment; and outdoor signs, including codes and regulations for any of the following:

A. Zoning.

B. Building.

C. Plumbing.

D. Property maintenance.

3. Programs for redevelopment, affordable housing, and urban renewal.

4. Parks and park related activities and recreational programs.

5. Police protection.

6. Fire protection.

7. 9-1-1 communications.

8. Animal control.

9. Public works, including maintenance and operation of sanitary and storm sewers, drainage systems, sewage disposal facilities, and refuse disposal facilities, including trash and garbage collection disposal.

10. Lighting of streets, roads, alleys, and other public places.

11. Maintenance and operation of the water supply system.

12. Library system.

(4) "Municipality" means a municipal corporation located within New Castle County and incorporated by an act of the General Assembly.

(5) "New Castle County service percentage" means the degree to which New Castle County provides a local service function within a municipality, determined by subtracting the degree to which a municipality provides the local service function from 100%. The New Castle County service percentage in the unincorporated area equals 100%.

History.
83 Del. Laws, c. 7, § 1; 83 Del. Laws, c. 7, § 10.

Revisor's note.
Section 11 of 83 Del. Laws, c. 7, provided: "Sections 1 through 4 of this act are effective

immediately." The act was signed by the Governor on Feb. 23, 2021.

Section 13 of 83 Del. Laws, c. 7, provided: "Section 10 of this act is effective July 1, 2022."

Effect of amendments.

83 Del. Laws, c. 7, effective July 1, 2022, rewrote the section.

§ 1102. Local service functions; subcategories; responsibility for performance [Effective July 1, 2022].

(a) New Castle County may divide a local service function into subcategories on forms used under § 1128 of this title. A subcategory of a local service function constitutes a local service function.

(b) The responsibility for all or part of a local service function in a municipality is established as set forth under the approved budget enacted for fiscal year 2023 under § 1155 of this title, or by the later of any of the following:

(1) A municipality provides timely notice of a change in degree of performance of a local service function to New Castle County under § 1127(d)(2) of this title.

(2) New Castle County and a municipality enact ordinances transferring responsibility for performance of a local service function under subsection (c) of this section.

(3) A service performed by a municipality is classified as a local service function under subsection (d) of this section.

(4) A new local service function is established under § 1128 of this title.

(c)(1) Responsibility for the performance or funding of a local service function may be transferred between New Castle County and a municipality by concurring affirmative action in the form of an ordinance enacted by the County Council of New Castle County and of the governing body of the municipality.

(2) The ordinances transferring a local service function under paragraph (c)(1) of this section must state all of the following:

a. The nature of the local service function transferred.

b. The effective date of the transfer.

c. The manner in which affected employees engaged in the performance of the local service function will be transferred, reassigned, or otherwise treated.

d. The manner in which real property, facilities, equipment, or other personal property required in the exercise of the local service function will be transferred, sold, or otherwise treated.

e. The method of financing to be used in the exercise of the local service function received.

f. Other legal, financial, and administrative arrangements necessary to effect transfer of the local service function in an orderly and equitable manner.

(d)(1) If a municipality is performing a service that is included in the New Castle County general operating budget, the municipality may request that the service be classified as a local service function in the next fiscal year by providing a notice to New Castle County by August 1 that states all of the following:

a. The service that is included in the New Castle County general operating budget.

b. The degree of performance.

c. The date municipality began performing the service.

(2) New Castle County may request, and the municipality must provide, additional information that may reasonably be needed to determine the degree of performance of the service by the municipality.

(3) By November 1, New Castle County shall notify the municipality of New Castle County's determination regarding the municipality's request under paragraph (d)(1) of this section.

(4) If a municipality is unable to reach agreement with New Castle County regarding the municipality's request under paragraph (d)(1) of this section, the municipality may demand arbitration under the procedure in § 1128(d) of this title.

(e) [Repealed.]

History.
9 Del. C. 1953, § 1102; 55 Del. Laws, c. 85, § 1; 71 Del. Laws, c. 401, § 15; 82 Del. Laws, c. 233, § 1; 83 Del. Laws, c. 7, § 10.

Revisor's note.
Section 13 of 83 Del. Laws, c. 7, provided: "Section 10 of this act is effective July 1, 2022."

Effect of amendments.
83 Del. Laws, c. 7, effective July 1, 2022, in the section heading substituted "Local service" for "Transfer of" and added "subcategories; responsibility for performance"; and rewrote the section.

SUBCHAPTER II
COUNTY EXECUTIVE

§ 1120. Power to appoint Chief Administrative Officer and Department Directors.

(a) The County Executive shall appoint a Chief Administrative Officer who shall serve at the pleasure of the County Executive. The Chief Administrative Officer shall be qualified by education, training and experience for the duties to be performed.

(b) The County Executive, with the advice and consent of the County Council, shall appoint the General Manager of Land Use, the General Manager of Special Services, the General Manager of Community Services, the Chief Procurement Officer, the Chief Financial Officer, the Chief Human Resources Officer, the County Attorney, as well as the heads of any subsequently created departments, who shall each serve at the pleasure of the County Executive.

(c) Notwithstanding any other provision of state or county law, on February 9, 2005, any persons then serving in any of the positions enumerated in this section shall cease to be classified service members of the New Castle County Merit System, but may thereafter continue to serve at the pleasure of the County Executive.

History.
9 Del. C. 1953, § 1120; 55 Del. Laws, c. 85, § 1; 59 Del. Laws, c. 336, § 1; 71 Del. Laws, c. 401, § 17; 75 Del. Laws, c. 9, § 1; 83 Del. Laws, c. 132, § 1.

Effect of amendments.
83 Del. Laws, c. 132, effective Sept. 10, 2021, added "the County Attorney" in (b).

SUBCHAPTER III
BUDGETING

Revision of subchapter.
Section 2 of 83 Del. Laws, c. 7, effective Feb. 23, 2021, added subpart I of this subchapter, comprising §§ 1125 through 1128 of this title; and § 4 of the act designated §§ 1131 through 1138 of this title as subpart II of this subchapter. Section 11 of 83 Del. Laws, c. 7, provided: "Sections 1 through 4 of this act are effective immediately." The act was signed by the Governor on Feb. 23, 2021.

SUBPART I
LOCAL SERVICE FUNCTIONS

Revision of subchapter.
See same catchline following the subchapter III heading of this chapter.

§ 1125. Local service functions; New Castle County property tax rates in municipalities [Effective until July 1, 2022].

(a) Beginning for the fiscal year 2023 budget, in determining the New Castle County property tax rate for real property in a municipality, New Castle County shall consider the degree that a local service function is fully or partially performed or financially supported by the municipality instead of New Castle County under §§ 1102 and 1128 of this title.

(b) Beginning for the fiscal year 2023 budget, New Castle County shall establish a property tax rate for real property in a municipality based on the degree of any local service function fully or partially performed or financially supported by the municipality instead of New Castle County under §§ 1102 and 1128 of this title.

(c) A property tax rate for real property in a municipality does not have to be either of the following:

(1) The same as a property tax rate for property located in other municipalities or in the unincorporated area of New Castle County.

(2) The same as a property tax rate set in a prior year.

(d) New Castle County may divide a local service function into subcategories on forms used under § 1128 of this title. A subcategory of a local service function constitutes a local service function.

History.
83 Del. Laws, c. 7, § 3.

Revisor's note.
Section 13 of 83 Del. Laws, c. 7, provided: "Section 10 of this act is effective July 1, 2022."

Effect of amendments.
83 Del. Laws, c. 7, effective July 1, 2022, in (a) and (b), deleted "Beginning for the fiscal year 2023 budget" from the beginning and substituted "§ 1102" for "§§ 1102 and 1128"; and repealed (d).

§ 1125. Local service functions; New Castle County property tax rates in municipalities [Effective July 1, 2022].

(a) In determining the New Castle County property tax rate for real property in a municipality, New Castle County shall consider the degree that a local service function is fully or partially performed or financially supported by the municipality instead of New Castle County under § 1102 of this title.

(b) New Castle County shall establish a property tax rate for real property in a municipality based on the degree of any local service function fully or partially performed or financially supported by the municipality instead of New Castle County under § 1102 of this title.

(c) A property tax rate for real property in a municipality does not have to be either of the following:

(1) The same as a property tax rate for property located in other municipalities or in the unincorporated area of New Castle County.

(2) The same as a property tax rate set in a prior year.

(d) [Repealed.]

History.
83 Del. Laws, c. 7, § 3; 83 Del. Laws, c. 7, § 10.

Revisor's note.
Section 13 of 83 Del. Laws, c. 7, provided: "Section 10 of this act is effective July 1, 2022."

Effect of amendments.
83 Del. Laws, c. 7, effective July 1, 2022, in (a) and (b), deleted "Beginning for the fiscal year 2023 budget" from the beginning and substituted "§ 1102" for "§§ 1102 and 1128"; and repealed (d).

§ 1126. Local service functions; calculation of net county LSF cost and individual LSF tax rates [Effective until July 1, 2022].

(a) Beginning for the fiscal year 2023 budget, New Castle County shall calculate the net county LSF cost for each local service function. The "net county LSF cost" equals the amount in the New Castle County budget for the local service function for the next fiscal year. The "net county LSF cost" is the amount of direct and indirect costs applicable to that local service function, and excludes service charges, grants, or other revenue or funds that New Castle County directly attributes or otherwise apportions to that local service function.

(b) Except as provided for fire protection under subsection (c) of this section, beginning for the fiscal year 2023 budget, New Castle County shall convert the net county LSF cost for each local service function into a real property tax rate for each municipality and the unincorporated area by calculating each of the following for each municipality and the unincorporated area:

(1) The "share of New Castle County assessment", which equals the taxable assessed value of all real property within a municipality or the unincorporated area divided by the aggregate taxable assessed value for all real property in the County.

(2) The "New Castle County service percentage" for a municipality, as determined under §§ 1102 and 1128 of this title.

(3) The "weighted service share", which equals a municipality's or the unincorporated area's share of New Castle County assessment multiplied by the municipality's or the unincorporated area's New Castle County service percentage.

(4) The "total weighted service amount", which equals the sum of all weighted service shares.

(5) The "final service weight", which equals a municipality's or the unincorporated area's weighted service share divided by the total weighted service amount.

(6) The "apportioned net LSF cost", which equals the municipality's or the unincorporated area's final service weight multiplied by the net county LSF cost.

(7) The "individual LSF tax rate", which equals the municipality's or the unincorporated area's apportioned net LSF cost divided by the taxable assessed value of all real property in the respective municipality or the unincorporated area, adjusted to reflect New Castle County's estimated level of cash receipts.

(c) For fire protection that is partially financially supported but not directly provided by New Castle County and that is also partially financially supported but not directly provided by a municipality, New Castle County shall convert the net county LSF cost into a real property tax rate for each municipality under § 1102(e) of this title.

(d) New Castle County shall adopt policies and procedures to implement this section.

History.
83 Del. Laws, c. 7, § 3.

Revisor's note.
Section 13 of 83 Del. Laws, c. 7, provided: "Section 10 of this act is effective July 1, 2022."

Effect of amendments.
83 Del. Laws, c. 7, effective July 1, 2022,

deleted "beginning for the fiscal year 2023 budget" from the beginning of the first sentence in (a) and preceding "New Castle County" in the introductory paragraph of (b); substituted "§ 1102" for "§§ 1102 and 1128" in (b)(2); and rewrote (c).

§ 1126. Local service functions; calculation of net county LSF cost and individual LSF tax rates [Effective July 1, 2022].

(a) New Castle County shall calculate the net county LSF cost for each local service function. The "net county LSF cost" equals the amount in the New Castle County budget for the local service function for the next fiscal year. The "net county LSF cost" is the amount of direct and indirect costs applicable to that local service function, and excludes service charges, grants, or other revenue or funds that New Castle County directly attributes or otherwise apportions to that local service function.

(b) Except as provided for fire protection under subsection (c) of this section, New Castle County shall convert the net county LSF cost for each local service function into a real property tax rate for each municipality and the unincorporated area by calculating each of the following for each municipality and the unincorporated area:

(1) The "share of New Castle County assessment", which equals the taxable assessed value of all real property within a municipality or the unincorporated area divided by the aggregate taxable assessed value for all real property in the County.

(2) The "New Castle County service percentage" for a municipality, as determined under § 1102 of this title.

(3) The "weighted service share", which equals a municipality's or the unincorporated area's share of New Castle County assessment multiplied by the municipality's or the unincorporated area's New Castle County service percentage.

(4) The "total weighted service amount", which equals the sum of all weighted service shares.

(5) The "final service weight", which equals a municipality's or the unincorporated area's weighted service share divided by the total weighted service amount.

(6) The "apportioned net LSF cost", which equals the municipality's or the unincorporated area's final service weight multiplied by the net county LSF cost.

(7) The "individual LSF tax rate", which equals the municipality's or the unincorporated area's apportioned net LSF cost divided by the taxable assessed value of all real property in the respective municipality or the unincorporated area, adjusted to reflect New Castle County's estimated level of cash receipts.

(c) For fire protection that is partially financially supported but not directly provided by New Castle County and that is also partially financially supported but not directly provided by a municipality, New Castle County shall convert the net county LSF cost into a real property tax rate for each municipality and the unincorporated area that does not directly provide fire protection by calculating all of the following for each municipality and the unincorporated area:

(1) The "service area share", which equals the taxable assessed value of real property within the municipality or the unincorporated area not directly providing fire protection divided by the sum of the taxable assessed value for all real property in the unincorporated area and all municipalities not directly providing fire protection.

(2) The "apportioned gross amount", which equals the service area share multiplied by the net county LSF cost for fire protection.

(3) The "net New Castle County fire protection cost", which is New Castle County's contribution of funds or in-kind services to volunteer fire companies within New Castle County, increased by indirect costs applicable to fire protection and decreased by service charges, grants, or other revenue that New Castle County directly attributes or otherwise apportions to fire protection.

(4) The "credit percentage", which equals the municipality's actual direct contribution of funds or in-kind contributions of goods or services to a volunteer fire company in the previous year, divided by the municipali-

ty's apportioned gross amount. The "credit percentage" may not exceed 100%. The "credit percentage" is 0% for the unincorporated area.

(5) The "New Castle County fire protection percentage", which equals 100% minus the municipality's credit percentage. The "New Castle County fire protection percentage" for the unincorporated area is 100%.

(6) The "weighted service share", which equals the municipality's or the unincorporated area's service area share multiplied by the municipality's or the unincorporated area's New Castle County fire protection percentage.

(7) The "total weighted service amount", which equals the sum of the weighted service shares.

(8) The "final service weight", which equals the municipality's or the unincorporated area's weighted service share divided by the total weighted service amount.

(9) The "apportioned net LSF cost", which equals the final service weight multiplied by the net county LSF cost for fire protection.

(10) The "individual fire protection tax rate" which equals the municipality's or the unincorporated area's apportioned net fire protection cost divided by the taxable assessed value of real property in the respective municipality or the unincorporated area, adjusted to reflect New Castle County's estimated level of cash receipts.

(d) New Castle County shall adopt policies and procedures to implement this section.

History.
83 Del. Laws, c. 7, § 3; 83 Del. Laws, c. 7, § 10.

Revisor's note.
Section 13 of 83 Del. Laws, c. 7, provided: "Section 10 of this act is effective July 1, 2022."

Effect of amendments.
83 Del. Laws, c. 7, effective July 1, 2022, deleted "beginning for the fiscal year 2023 budget" from the beginning of the first sentence in (a) and preceding "New Castle County" in the introductory paragraph of (b); substituted "§ 1102" for "§§ 1102 and 1128" in (b)(2); and rewrote (c).

§ 1127. Local service functions; change in degree of performance; notice requirements [Effective July 1, 2022].

(a) By August 1 of each year, a municipality shall provide notice to New Castle County if the municipality intends to begin performing, stop performing, or change the degree of performance of a local service function, other than fire protection, during New Castle County's fiscal year beginning the following July 1.

(b) In the notice under subsection (a) of this section, the municipality shall state with specificity which of the following modifications the municipality intends to make to its performance of the local service function:

(1) Initiating performance.

(2) Ceasing performance.

(3) Changing the degree of performance.

(c) New Castle County may request, and the municipality must provide, additional information that may reasonably be needed to understand the municipality's proposed modification.

(d)(1) A municipality must initiate or cease performance of a local service function under § 1102(c) of this title.

(2) A municipality may change the degree of performance of a local service function that the municipality already performs by providing notice to New Castle County under subsection (a) of this section.

History.
83 Del. Laws, c. 7, § 10.

Revisor's note.
Section 13 of 83 Del. Laws, c. 7, provided:
"Section 10 of this act is effective July 1, 2022."

§ 1128. Local service functions; determining the New Castle County service percentage and credit percentage; transition year [Effective until July 1, 2022].

(a)(1) New Castle County will develop the forms and instructions for municipalities to request that New Castle County recognize the New Castle County service percentage for a local service function or direct contribution of funds or in-kind contribution of goods and services to a volunteer fire company. New Castle County will hold meetings to discuss the draft forms and instructions with municipalities before the forms and instructions become final.

(2) By January 31, 2021, New Castle County shall provide to each municipality the forms and instructions under paragraph (a)(3) of this section to submit the municipality's request that New Castle County recognize the following:

a. The New Castle County service percentage for a local service function is less than 100% based on the municipality's performance or partial performance of the local service function.

b. In the case of fire protection that a municipality does not provide directly, the municipality's direct contribution of funds or in-kind contribution of goods and services to a volunteer fire company.

(3) New Castle County shall provide a copy of each of the following:

a. New Castle County's budget for the current fiscal year.

b. A standardized form listing each local service function and the documentation necessary to support a request that New Castle County recognize the degree to which the municipality performs or financially supports a local service function instead of New Castle County.

c. Contact information for appropriate representatives that a municipality may contact to discuss relevant financial information of New Castle County and the municipality, and the scope and nature of services provided by both entities.

(b)(1) By March 1, 2021, a municipality shall submit its application and supporting documentation to New Castle County if the municipality is requesting that New Castle County recognize a New Castle County service percentage less than 100% for any local service function based on the municipality's degree of performance of the local service function.

(2) By September 1, 2021, a municipality shall submit its application and supporting documentation to New Castle County if the municipality is requesting that New Castle County recognize the municipality's contribution of funds or in-kind contributions of goods and services to a volunteer fire company.

(3) New Castle County may request, and the municipality must provide, additional information that may reasonably be needed to determine the degree of performance of local service functions provided by the municipality.

(c)(1) By July 1, 2021, New Castle County shall notify each municipality of New Castle County's determination regarding the New Castle County service percentage for each local service function other than fire protection. A disagreement regarding New Castle County's calculations under this paragraph (c)(1) is subject to negotiation between New Castle County and the municipality.

(2) By October 1, 2021, New Castle County shall notify each municipality of New Castle County's determination regarding the dollar amount of direct and in-kind donations that the County will recognize to calculate the individual fire protection rate. A disagreement regarding New Castle County's calculations under this paragraph (c)(2) is subject to negotiation between New Castle County and the municipality.

(d)(1)a. By September 1, 2021, a municipality that is unable to reach agreement with New Castle County regarding the New Castle County service percentage for a local service function under paragraph (c)(1) of this section may provide notice to New Castle County demanding arbitration which includes the municipality's designated member of the arbitration panel under paragraph (d)(2) of this section. If the municipality does not provide such notice by September 1, 2021, New Castle County's determination is final and may not be appealed.

b. By November 1, 2021, a municipality that is unable to reach agreement with New Castle County regarding the New Castle County individual fire protection tax rate under paragraph (c)(2) of this section may provide notice to New Castle County demanding arbitration that includes the municipality's designated member of the arbitration panel under paragraph (d)(3) of this section. If the municipality does not provide such notice by November 1, 2021, New Castle County's determination is final and may not be appealed.

(2) If arbitration is demanded under paragraph (d)(1)a. of this section, an arbitration panel will be created which is comprised of 3 members, selected as follows:

a. The municipality's designee.

b. By September 10, 2021, the County Executive shall designate a member.

c. By September 20, 2021, the arbitration panel designees of the County Executive and the municipality shall jointly select the third member. If the 2 arbitration panel designees cannot agree on the selection of the third member by September 20, 2021, the third arbitration panel member is the Chair of the New Castle County Financial Advisory Council or the Chair's designee.

d. The arbitration hearing must occur by December 15, 2021. At the hearing, New Castle County and the municipality may present testimony, evidence, and oral argument as to the matters in dispute.

(3) If arbitration is demanded under paragraph (d)(1)b. of this section, an arbitration panel will be created which is comprised of 3 members, selected as follows:

a. The municipality's designee.

b. By November 10, 2021, the County Executive shall designate a member.

c. By November 20, 2021, the arbitration panel designees of the County Executive and the municipality shall jointly select the third member. If the 2 arbitration panel designees cannot agree on the selection of the third member by November 20, 2021, the third arbitration panel member is the Chair of the New Castle County Financial Advisory Council or the Chair's designee.

d. The arbitration hearing must occur by December 15, 2021. At the hearing, New Castle County and the municipality may present testimony, evidence, and oral argument as to the matters in dispute.

(4) An arbitration panel may establish rules for the arbitration hearing, including information required to be produced by a party and deadlines for the submission of evidence.

(5) An arbitration panel shall issue its decision by January 31, 2022. An arbitration panel's decision is binding and may not be appealed.

(e) Notwithstanding subsections (a) through (d) and (f) of this section, either of the following may occur:

(1) New Castle County and a municipality may enter into an agreement setting different terms or timing for negotiations, calculations, or approval of the New Castle County service percentages.

(2) New Castle County may determine New Castle County service percentages for a municipality that does not make a request in the manner required under this section. New Castle County's determination under this paragraph (e)(2) is final, may not be appealed, and is not subject to arbitration under subsection (d) of this section.

(f) New Castle County shall adopt policies and procedures to implement this section.

(g) This section applies beginning for the fiscal year 2023 budget.

History.
83 Del. Laws, c. 7, § 3.

Revisor's note.
Section 13 of 83 Del. Laws, c. 7, provided: "Section 10 of this act is effective July 1, 2022."

Effect of amendments.
83 Del. Laws, c. 7, effective July 1, 2022, deleted "transition year" following "percentage" in the section heading and rewrote the section.

§ 1128. Local service functions; determining the New Castle County service percentage and credit percentage [Effective July 1, 2022].

(a)(1) [Repealed.]

(2) By July 1 of each year, New Castle County shall provide to each municipality the forms and instructions under paragraph (a)(3) of this section to submit the municipality's request that New Castle County recognize the following:

a. The New Castle County service percentage for a local service function is less than 100% based on the municipality's performance or partial performance of the local service function.

b. In the case of fire protection that a municipality does not provide directly, the municipality's direct contribution of funds or in-kind contribution of goods and services to a volunteer fire company.

(3) New Castle County shall provide a copy of each of the following:

a. New Castle County's budget for the current fiscal year.

b. A standardized form listing each local service function and the documentation necessary to support a request that New Castle County recognize the degree to which the municipality performs or financially supports a local service function instead of New Castle County.

c. Contact information for appropriate representatives that a municipality may contact to discuss relevant financial information of New Castle County and the municipality, and the scope and nature of services provided by both entities.

(b)(1) By September 1 of each year, a municipality shall submit its application and supporting documentation to New Castle County if the municipality is requesting that New Castle County recognize either of the following:

a. New Castle County service percentage less than 100% for any local service function based on the municipality's degree of performance of the local service function.

    b. In the case of fire protection that a municipality does not provide directly, the municipality's contribution of funds or in-kind contributions of goods and services to a volunteer fire company.

    (2) New Castle County may request, and the municipality must provide, additional information that may reasonably be needed to determine the degree of performance of local service functions provided by the municipality.

(c)(1) By November 1 of each year, New Castle County shall notify each municipality of New Castle County's determination regarding the New Castle County service percentage for each local service function and the dollar amount of direct and in-kind donations that the County will recognize to calculate the individual fire protection rate. A disagreement regarding New Castle County's determination under this paragraph (c)(1) is subject to negotiation between New Castle County and the municipality.

    (2) [Repealed.]

(d)(1)a. By December 1 of each year, a municipality that is unable to reach agreement with New Castle County regarding the New Castle County service percentage for a local service function or individual fire protection tax rate under paragraph (c)(1) of this section may provide notice to New Castle County demanding arbitration that includes the municipality's designated member of the arbitration panel under paragraph (d)(2) of this section. If the municipality does not provide such notice by by December 1, New Castle County's determination is final and may not be appealed.

    b. [Repealed.]

    (2) If arbitration is demanded under paragraph (d)(1)a. of this section, an arbitration panel will be created which is comprised of 3 members, selected as follows:

    a. The municipality's designee.

    b. By December 10, the County Executive shall designate a member.

    c. By December 20, the arbitration panel designees of the County Executive and the municipality shall jointly select the third member. If the 2 arbitration panel designees cannot agree on the selection of the third member by December 20, the third arbitration panel member is the Chair of the New Castle County Financial Advisory Council or the Chair's designee.

    d. The arbitration panel may establish rules for the arbitration hearing, including information required to be produced by a party and deadlines for the submission of evidence.

    (3) The arbitration hearing must occur by January 31. At the hearing, New Castle County and the municipality may present testimony, evidence, and oral argument as to the matters in dispute.

    (4) [Repealed.]

    (5) An arbitration panel shall issue its decision by February 15. An arbitration panel's decision is binding and may not be appealed.

(e) Notwithstanding subsections (a) through (d) and (f) of this section, either of the following may occur:

    (1) New Castle County and a municipality may enter into an agreement setting different terms or timing for negotiations, calculations, or approval of the New Castle County service percentages.

    (2) New Castle County may determine New Castle County service percentages for a municipality that does not make a request in the manner

required under this section. New Castle County's determination under this paragraph (e)(2) is final, may not be appealed, and is not subject to arbitration under subsection (d) of this section.

(f) New Castle County shall adopt policies and procedures to implement this section.

(g) [Repealed.]

History.
83 Del. Laws, c. 7, § 3; 83 Del. Laws, c. 7, § 10.

Revisor's note.
Section 13 of 83 Del. Laws, c. 7, provided: "Section 10 of this act is effective July 1, 2022."

Effect of amendments.
83 Del. Laws, c. 7, effective July 1, 2022, deleted "transition year" following "percentage" in the section heading and rewrote the section.

§ 1129. Local service functions; Local Service Function Review Committee.

(a) New Castle County shall create the Local Service Function Review Committee ("Committee") for the purpose of conducting an annual review of this subpart of this subchapter. The Committee must complete the review no later than August 3.

(b) The Local Service Function Review Committee is comprised of the following representatives:

(1) The Chief Financial Officer, or a designee, who serves as chair.

(2) One member of County Council, selected by the County Council.

(3) Two members from municipal governments in New Castle County appointed by the County Council from a list of names provided by the Delaware League of Local Governments.

(4) One member who is a resident of New Castle County and who owns real property in the unincorporated area of New Castle County, appointed by the County Council.

(c)(1) The chair of the Committee must provide the Committee with administrative support, including the preparation and distribution of meeting notices, agendas, minutes, correspondence, and reports.

(2)a. A quorum of the Committee is a majority of its members.

b. Official action by the Committee requires the approval of a quorum of the Committee.

c. The Committee may adopt rules necessary for its operation and may create working subcommittees.

d. The chair of the Committee may invite individuals with relevant expertise to participate in the Committee's discussions.

(d)(1) The Committee shall include all of the following in the annual review under subsection (a):

a. The calculation procedure under § 1126 of this title.

b. The New Castle County service percentage or credit percentage process under § 1128 of this title.

c. Changes to the service functions that are eligible for an individual LSF tax rate under § 1128 of this title.

(2) The Committee's review must include a specific topic under paragraph (d)(1) of this section that is requested by a municipality before June 1 of the current year.

(e) The Local Service Function Review Committee must provide an annual report containing a summary of the review conducted under this section and any recommendations for improvements to all members of the County Council, each municipality in New Castle County, all members of the General Assembly who represent New Castle County, and the Division of Research by September 15 of each year.

History.
83 Del. Laws, c. 7, § 9.

Revisor's note.
Section 12 of 83 Del. Laws, c. 7, provided:

"Sections 5 through 9 of this act are effective January 1, 2022."

SUBPART II
BUDGETING

Revision of subchapter.
See same catchline following the subchapter III heading of this chapter.

§ 1131. Separate budgeting for local service functions performed by the County.

(a) The Chief Administrative Officer and the County Executive, in the preparation of the annual operating budget, shall divide and segregate in a separate budget, entitled Local Service Function Budget, all appropriations for the performance or funding of local service functions by New Castle County within the municipalities and the unincorporated area. The Chief Administrative Officer and the County Executive, in the preparation of the Local Service Function Budget, shall specify separately the total appropriation required for the performance or funding of each local service function by New Castle County.

(b) The County Executive shall submit to the County Council a proposed revenue ordinance which will achieve sufficient revenues to balance the total operating budget, including the Local Service Function Budget. The County Executive in the preparation of the proposed revenue ordinance may not, and the County Council and the County Executive in the enactment of the annual revenue ordinance may not, impose ad valorem taxation on real property within any municipality to pay the cost of New Castle County's performance or funding of any local service function in excess of the individual LSF tax rate or individual fire protection rate.

(c) The County Executive's proposed budget presented to the County Council shall include tables providing all of the following information:

(1) The calculation of the proposed individual LSF tax rate and individual fire protection tax rate for each local service function for each municipality and the unincorporated area.

(2) The proposed aggregate of the individual LSF tax rates and individual fire protection tax rates for each municipality and the unincorporated area.

(d) New Castle County may also impose ad valorem taxation on real property within any municipality as follows:

(1) In any instance where a municipality initiates the performance of a local service function without the consent of New Castle County under § 1102 of this title.

(2) For the cost of operation by the County of park and recreational facilities which are not local in nature and which serve the metropolitan area.

(3) To any municipality not expending funds in the previous fiscal year for the given local service function or not adequately performing the local service function.

(e) The Chief Administrative Officer and the County Executive, in the preparation of the annual operating budget, shall divide and segregate in a separate budget entitled General Operating Budget all appropriations not properly allocable to the Local Service Function Budget or other operating budget fund. The County Council, in estimating the revenues which will be necessary for the payment of these appropriations, shall include the estimated revenues to be derived from county-wide ad valorem taxation of real property.

(f) The County Executive in the preparation of the proposed revenue ordinance, and the County Council and the County Executive in the enactment of the annual revenue ordinance, shall uniformly impose ad valorem taxation on real property within the County to pay the cost of the General Operating Budget.

History.
9 Del. C. 1953, § 1131; 55 Del. Laws, c. 85, § 1; 71 Del. Laws, c. 401, §§ 15, 21-24; 83 Del. Laws, c. 7, § 4; 83 Del. Laws, c. 7, § 5.

Revisor's note.
Section 12 of 83 Del. Laws, c. 7, provided: "Sections 5 through 9 of this act are effective January 1, 2022."

Effect of amendments.
83 Del. Laws, c. 7, effective Jan. 1, 2022, deleted "outside the limits of municipalities" from the end of the section heading, rewrote (a);

rewrote the final sentence of (b); rewrote former (c) as present (c) and (d), redesignating the remaining subsections accordingly; rewrote the introductory paragraph of present (d); rewrote present (d)(1); in present (d)(2), substituted "For" for "To" and substituted a period for "; and" at the end; in present (d)(3), added the first occurrence of "function" and the second occurrence of "local service"; and, in present (e), substituted "appropriations" for "expenditures" in the first and second sentences and added a comma following "Council" in the second sentence.

§ 1132. Preparation of the annual operating budget; distribution of budget requests; completed forms; preliminary budget; preliminary budget hearings; operating budget; distribution of operating budget.

(a) The Chief Administrative Officer shall annually, not later than January 1, distribute budget request forms to the County Council and for each office, department, board, or agency which is receiving or seeking to receive an appropriation from the County Council payable from any operating fund of the County.

(b) County Council and the heads of all offices, departments, boards or agencies shall enter upon the budget request forms requests for appropriations for the ensuing year and such supporting information as the Chief Administrative Officer shall have specified. The Chief Administrative Officer shall establish deadlines for the presentation of completed forms by such time and in such manner as necessary for the timely preparation and presentation of the annual operating budget.

(c) The Chief Administrative Officer shall prepare a preliminary budget for the consideration of the County Executive. The preliminary budget shall include all budget requests, the recommendations of the Chief Administrative Officer with respect to each request, an estimate of the receipts from each source of revenue, and a statement of the total estimated income and the total recommended expenditures for each operating fund.

(d) The County Executive shall review the preliminary budget and may hold hearings thereupon at which the head of all offices, departments or boards may be given an opportunity to be heard with respect to their requests. The Chief Administrative Officer shall thereupon prepare the operating budget as directed by the County Executive. The operating budget shall be presented to the County Council by the County Executive, together with a budget message outlining the County Executive's reasons for the requested appropriations, and shall be accompanied by proposed revenue and operating budget ordinances to give effect to the budget as presented. If the estimated revenue from existing sources is deemed by the County Executive to be insufficient to balance the budget, the County Executive shall recommend revenues sufficient to achieve a balanced budget.

(e) The proposed ordinance for the operating budget shall provide appropriations in a lump sum under the following classes for each office, department, or board to which appropriations are made:

(1) Personal services of officers and employees;

(2) Contractual services;

(3) Training;

(4) Communications and utilities;

(5) Materials and supplies;

(6) Equipment;

(7) Grants and fixed charges;

(8) Debt services;

(9) Such other general classes as the County Executive or the County Council may annually establish.

(f) The operating budget and the proposed revenue and operating budget ordinances shall be submitted to the County Council not later than April 1. Sufficient copies of the operating budget shall be supplied by the County Executive to the Clerk of the County Council for distribution to members of the County Council and to interested citizens.

History.
9 Del. C. 1953, § 1132; 55 Del. Laws, c. 85, § 1; 70 Del. Laws, c. 186, § 1; 71 Del. Laws, c. 401, §§ 15, 25-27; 83 Del. Laws, c. 7, § 4.

§ 1133. Administration and enforcement of the operating budget ordinance; adoption of operating budget; allocations and allotments; approval of allocations and allotments; revisions.

(a) The adoption of the operating budget ordinance is an appropriation of the sum specified in the budget for the purpose and from the funds indicated. The appropriation is valid only for the year for which it is made, and any part of an appropriation which is not encumbered or expended lapses at the end of the year.

(b) Following the adoption of the operating budget ordinance, the Chief Administrative Officer shall determine, with the approval of the County Executive, such allocation or allotment procedures as deemed appropriate for a proper administration of the budget. The head of each office, department, or board shall submit to the Chief Administrative Officer such work programs and requests for allocations and allotments as deemed appropriate for the most efficient and effective operation of each office, department or board.

(c) The approval of such allocations and allotments, in the amounts submitted or in amended amounts approved by the County Executive, shall constitute budgetary allocations and allotments which shall be binding upon such office, department, or board, and the Department of Administration shall not approve nor issue any requisition, purchase order, voucher, or check that is not in accordance with such allocation or allotment.

(d) The allocations and allotments provided in this section may be altered at the direction of the County Executive. The County Executive shall direct appropriate revisions in allocations and allotments to keep expenditures within the revenues received or anticipated.

History.
9 Del. C. 1953, § 1133; 55 Del. Laws, c. 85, § 1; 70 Del. Laws, c. 186, § 1; 71 Del. Laws, c. 401, §§ 28-31; 83 Del. Laws, c. 7, § 4; 83 Del. Laws, c. 7, § 5.

Revisor's note.
Section 12 of 83 Del. Laws, c. 7, provided: "Sections 5 through 9 of this act are effective January 1, 2022."

Effect of amendments.
83 Del. Laws, c. 7, effective Jan. 1, 2022, in (a), in the first sentence, substituted "is" for "shall constitute" and, in the second sentence, substituted "The appropriation is" "Such appropriation shall be considered", added "it is" preceding "made" and substituted "an" for "such" and "lapses" for "shall lapse".

§ 1134. Preparation of the capital program and the capital budget; preparation by Chief Administrative Officer; recommendation by County Executive; action by County Council.

(a) The Chief Administrative Officer shall annually prepare a capital program and a capital budget under the direction of the County Executive. In the course of the preparation of the capital program, the Chief Administrative Officer shall confer with the Department of Land Use to ascertain that the proposed capital program is in accordance with the comprehensive development plan prepared by the Department of Land Use.

(b) No later than April 1 of each year, the County Executive shall recommend to the County Council, a capital program for the ensuing 6 years and a capital budget for the ensuing year. Not later than the date that the program is submitted to County Council, the County Executive shall submit the capital program to the Department of Land Use for its review and recommendations to County Council. The County Executive shall also submit the capital program to the Planning Board for the sole purpose of determining if it is in accordance with the comprehensive development plan.

(c) The proposed capital program, and the proposed capital budget, must have the content and be in the form necessary to enable the County Council to take action as required under § 1159 of this title.

(d)(1) The County Executive, in the preparation of the capital budget, may not include in the revenue estimates any estimated revenues to be derived from ad valorem taxation of real property within a municipality for any capital appropriation including debt service which is related to the performance or funding by the County of a local service function in excess of the individual LSF tax rate or individual fire protection rate for that local service function.

(2) The County Council, in the adoption of the capital budget by ordinance, may not impose ad valorem taxation on real property within a municipality for the payment of the cost of any capital appropriation, including debt service, which is related to the performance or funding by the County of a local service function in excess of the individual LSF tax rate or individual fire protection rate for that local service function.

(3) The provisions of this subsection are not applicable to capital appropriations, including debt service, for the acquisition by the County of park and recreational facilities which are not local in nature and which serve the metropolitan area.

(e) The County Executive and the County Council, in the adoption of a capital budget by ordinance, shall uniformly impose ad valorem taxation on real property within the County for the payment of the cost of any capital appropriation, including debt service, except for costs related to the performance or funding by the County of a local service function in excess of the individual LSF tax rate or individual fire protection rate for that local service function.

History.

9 Del. C. 1953, § 1134; 55 Del. Laws, c. 85, § 1; 71 Del. Laws, c. 401, §§ 15, 32-34; 83 Del. Laws, c. 7, § 4; 83 Del. Laws, c. 7, § 5.

Revisor's note.

Section 12 of 83 Del. Laws, c. 7, provided: "Sections 5 through 9 of this act are effective January 1, 2022."

Effect of amendments.

83 Del. Laws, c. 7, effective Jan. 1, 2022, substituted "the capital program" for "it" in the second and third sentences of (b); rewrote (c); in (d), designated the first through third sentences as (d)(1)-(3), respectively; in (d)(1) and (d)(2), substituted "may" for "shall", "appropriation" for "expenditure" and "in excess of the individual LSF tax rate or individual fire protection rate for that local service function" for "which is performed by the municipality for its own residents and for which the cost is paid out of municipal revenues", and added "or funding"; in (d)(3), substituted "are" for "shall" preceding

"subsection" and "appropriations" for "expenditures"; and rewrote (e).

§ 1135. Administration of the capital budget.

The Chief Administrative Officer, under the supervision of the County Executive, shall be responsible for the administration of the capital budget as adopted by ordinance. The Chief Administrative Officer shall cause each office, department or board to take necessary action to provide for the prompt and efficient execution of the capital budget.

History.
9 Del. C. 1953, § 1135; 55 Del. Laws, c. 85,
§ 1; 71 Del. Laws, c. 401, § 35; 83 Del. Laws, c. 7, § 4.

§ 1136. Fiscal year.

The fiscal year of the County shall commence on July 1 of each year and conclude upon June 30 of the following year.

History.
9 Del. C. 1953, § 1136; 55 Del. Laws, c. 85,
§ 1; 83 Del. Laws, c. 7, § 4.

§ 1137. Encumbrance defined.

For the purpose of this subchapter, the term "encumbrance" shall mean a commitment for expenditure of an appropriation evidenced by a valid purchase order, similar document or process for the acquisition of supplies, material, work or services.

History.
9 Del. C. 1953, § 1137; 55 Del. Laws, c. 85,
§ 1; 71 Del. Laws, c. 401, § 36; 83 Del. Laws, c. 7, § 4.

§ 1138. Budgets for grants.

The County Council may accept federal, state, and private grant funds. The Chief Administrative Officer shall submit to the County Council a budget, which shall not be part of the General Operating Budget or of the Capital Budget, for the expenditure of each such grant. Approval of such a budget shall constitute an appropriation of the sum specified therein for the purpose indicated. Such appropriation shall be considered valid until the funds are expended. The Chief Administrative Officer under the supervision of the County Executive shall be responsible for the administration of grant budgets.

History.
60 Del. Laws, c. 219, § 1; 71 Del. Laws, c.
401, §§ 15, 37; 83 Del. Laws, c. 7, § 4.

SUBCHAPTER IV
COUNTY COUNCIL

§ 1155. Consideration and adoption of the annual operating budget ordinance.

(a) The County Council, upon receipt of the operating budget, shall immediately publish a notice in a newspaper of general circulation in the County, setting forth all of the following:

(1) A summary of the estimated revenues and appropriations.

(2) The detail of recommended new sources of revenue or increased rates of existing taxes, licenses, fees, or other revenue.

(3) The website address where a copy of the budget may be located and identification of the pages of the budget on which a listing of all individual LSF tax rates and individual fire protection tax rates for each municipality may be found.

(4) That copies of the budget are available upon request at the office of the Clerk of County Council.

(5) The date, time, and place at which the County Council will commence its public hearings upon the proposed budget, which may not be less than 10 days after the date of publication of such notice.

(b) The County Council, upon conclusion of its public hearings but not later than June 1, shall enact the operating budget ordinance. The County Council may increase, decrease, or delete any item of appropriation recommended by the County Executive, and may add new items of appropriation.

(c) No amendment to the operating budget ordinance shall increase the aggregate of authorized appropriations to an amount greater than the estimate of revenue for the corresponding period.

(d)(1) The County Council, in the adoption of the annual operating budget ordinance, shall divide and segregate in a separate budget, entitled Local Service Function Budget, all appropriations for the performance or funding of local service functions by New Castle County within the municipalities and unincorporated area.

(2) The County Council, in estimating the revenues for the payment of the cost of each such local service function, may not include in the estimate any estimated revenues to be derived from ad valorem taxation of real property within any municipality. related to the performance or funding by the County of a local service function in excess of the individual LSF tax rate or individual fire protection rate for that local service function.

(e) New Castle County may also impose ad valorem taxation on real property within any municipality as follows:

(1) In any instance where a municipality initiates the performance of a local service function without the consent of New Castle County under § 1102 of this title.

(2) For the cost of operation by the County of park and recreational facilities which are not local in nature and which serve the metropolitan area.

(3) To any municipality not expending funds in the previous fiscal year for the given local service function or not adequately performing the local service function.

(f) County Council, in the adoption of the annual operating budget ordinance, shall divide and segregate in a separate budget, entitled General Operating Budget, all appropriations not properly allocated to the Local Service Function Budget or other operating budget funds. County Council, in estimating the revenues necessary for the payment of these appropriations, shall include the estimated revenue to be derived from county-wide ad valorem taxation of real property.

History.
9 Del. C. 1953, § 1155; 55 Del. Laws, c. 85, § 1; 71 Del. Laws, c. 401, §§ 15, 43-45; 83 Del. Laws, c. 7, § 6.

Revisor's note.
Section 12 of 83 Del. Laws, c. 7, provided: "Sections 5 through 9 of this act are effective January 1, 2022."

Effect of amendments.
83 Del. Laws, c. 7, effective Jan. 1, 2022, added "all of the following" in the introductory paragraph of (a); substituted "appropriations." for "expenditures;" in (a)(1); added a comma following "fees" in (a)(2); substituted a period for a semicolon at the end (a)(2) and present (a)(4); added present (a)(3) and redesignated the remaining paragraphs in (a) accordingly; added "upon request" in present (a)(4); and substituted "may" for "shall" in (a)(5); substituted "appropriations" for "expenditures" in (c) and in the first and second sentences of present (f); rewrote (d), designating the first and second sentences of the former introductory paragraph as present (d)(1) and (2), respectively, and deleting the former final sentence of the introductory paragraph; added the introductory paragraph of present (e), redesignating former (d)(1) and (2) as present (e)(1) and (2) and added (e)(3); rewrote present (e)(1); substituted "For" for "To" in present (e)(2); and redesignated former (e) as present (f).

§ 1158. Budget of revenues.

(a) The County Council, at the meeting at which the annual operating budget ordinance is adopted, and within the limits of its power and subject to other provisions of this title, shall ordain such taxes and other revenue measures as will yield sufficient revenue, which, together with any available surplus, will balance the budget.

(b) The County Council shall estimate revenues only upon the basis of the cash receipts anticipated for the fiscal year.

(c) The County Executive shall certify the estimated yield from each item of revenue and of the amounts of surplus to be used in the balancing of the budget to the County Council.

(d) The annual operating budget ordinance is not effective until the County Council has adopted revenue measures which, together with the available surplus, are in the opinion of the County Executive, estimated to yield sums at least sufficient to balance the proposed appropriations. The Office of Finance may not approve any expenditure under any portion of an annual operating budget ordinance until such balancing shall have been provided.

(e) County Council, in the enactment of the annual revenue ordinance or other revenue measures, may not impose ad valorem taxation on real property within any municipality to pay the cost of New Castle County's performance or funding of any local service function in excess of the individual LSF tax rate or individual fire protection rate for that local service function.

(f) New Castle County may also impose ad valorem taxation on real property within any municipality as follows:

(1) In any instance where a municipality initiates the performance of a local service function without the consent of New Castle County under § 1102 of this title.

(2) For the cost of operation by the County of park and recreational facilities which are not local in nature and which serve the metropolitan area.

(3) To any municipality not expending funds in the previous fiscal year for the given local service function or not adequately performing the local service function.

(g) County Council, in the enactment of the annual revenue ordinance or in the enactment of other revenue measures, shall uniformly impose ad valorem taxation on real property within the County and pay the cost of the General Operating Budget.

History.
9 Del. C. 1953, § 1158; 55 Del. Laws, c. 85, § 1; 71 Del. Laws, c. 401, §§ 15, 46-49; 83 Del. Laws, c. 7, § 6.

Revisor's note.
Section 12 of 83 Del. Laws, c. 7, provided: "Sections 5 through 9 of this act are effective January 1, 2022."

Effect of amendments.
83 Del. Laws, c. 7, effective Jan. 1, 2022, in (b), substituted "The County shall estimate revenues" for "Revenues shall be estimated"; in (c), added "County Executive shall certify the" and deleted "shall be certified" following "bud-get" and "by the County Executive" from the end; in (d), in the first sentence substituted "is not" for "shall not become", "has" for "shall have" preceding "adopted", "are" for "shall" following "surplus" and "appropriations" for "expenditures" at the end, and deleted "be" following "Executive", and substituted "may" for "shall" in the second sentence; in (e), rewrote the first sentence, added the second sentence, deleted the former final sentence, and redesignated former (e)(1) and (2) as present (f)(1) and (2), rewriting present (f)(1) and substituted "For" for "To" in present (f)(2); added the introductory paragraph of present (f) and (f)(3); and redesignated former (f) as present (g).

§ 1159. Capital program and capital budget.

(a) County Council shall adopt a capital program and adopt a capital budget before, or at the same meeting as, it adopts the annual operating budget.

(b) The capital program shall detail all permanent physical improvements, including the acquisition of real estate, that are planned to be financed, in whole or in part, from funds that are, or may become, subject to control or appropriation by the County Council during each of the ensuing 6 years. For each separate project there shall be shown the amount and the source of money that has been expended or encumbered, or is to be expended or encumbered before the next fiscal year, and also the amount and the sources of money planned to be expended during each of the ensuing 6 years.

(c) The County Council may not amend the capital program as submitted to it by the County Executive, until it has received from the County Executive recommendations with respect to the proposed amendment. The County Council is not bound by the County Executive's recommendations and may act without them if they are not received within 15 days from the date they are requested.

(d) The Capital Budget Ordinance shall show the total capital appropriations.

(e) Amendments to the Capital Budget Ordinance must conform to the pertinent portions of the capital program in its original or amended form.

(f)(1) The County Council, in the adoption of the Capital Budget Ordinance, may not include in the revenue estimates, any estimated revenues to be derived from ad valorem taxation of real property within a municipality for any capital appropriation, including debt service, which is related to the performance or funding by the County of a local service function in excess of the individual LSF tax rate or individual fire protection rate for that local service function.

(2) The County Council, in the adoption of the Capital Budget Ordinance, may not impose ad valorem taxation on real property within a municipality for the payment of the cost of any capital appropriation, including debt service, which is related to the performance or funding by the County of a local service function in excess of the individual LSF tax rate or individual fire protection rate for that local service function.

(3) New Castle County may also impose ad valorem taxation on real property within any municipality as follows:

a. In any instance where a municipality initiates the performance of a local service function without the consent of New Castle County under § 1102 of this title.

b. For capital appropriations, including debt service, for the acquisition by the County of park and recreational facilities which are not local in nature and which serve the metropolitan area.

c. To any municipality not expending funds in the previous fiscal year for the given local service function or not adequately performing the local service function.

(g) The County Council, in the adoption of a capital budget by ordinance, shall uniformly impose ad valorem taxation on real property within the County for the payment of the cost of any capital appropriation, including debt service, which is not related to the performance or funding by the County of a local service function in excess of the individual LSF tax rate or individual fire protection rate for the local service function.

History.
9 Del. C. 1953, § 1159; 55 Del. Laws, c. 85, § 1; 71 Del. Laws, c. 401, §§ 15, 50, 51-54; 83 Del. Laws, c. 7, § 6.

Revisor's note.
Section 12 of 83 Del. Laws, c. 7, provided: "Sections 5 through 9 of this act are effective January 1, 2022."

Effect of amendments.
83 Del. Laws, c. 7, effective Jan. 1, 2022, in the second sentence of (c), substituted "is not" for "shall not be" and "the County Executive's" for "such"; and rewrote (f) and (g).

§ 1160. Unrestricted use of present revenues.

History.
9 Del. C. 1953, § 1160; 55 Del. Laws, c. 85, § 1; repealed by 83 Del. Laws, c. 7, § 6, effective Jan. 1, 2022.

SUBCHAPTER V

GENERAL PROVISIONS

§ 1183. Prohibitions and penalties.

(a) The following prohibitions apply:

(1) A person may not be appointed to, or removed from, or in any way favored or discriminated against with respect to, any county position, or appointive county administrative office, because of race, or color, or national origin, political or religious opinions or affiliations, sex, sexual orientation, or gender identity. For purposes of this subsection:

a. "Protective hairstyle" includes braids, locks, and twists.

b. "Race" includes traits historically associated with race, including hair texture and a protective hairstyle.

(2) A person may not, wilfully or corruptly, make any false statement, certificate, mark, rating, or report in regard to any test, certification or appointment under the personnel provisions of this chapter, or in any manner commit or attempt to commit any fraud preventing the impartial execution of the personnel provisions or of the rules and regulations made under this chapter.

(3) A person who seeks appointment or promotion with respect to any county position or appointive county administrative office may not, directly or indirectly, give, render, or pay any money, service, or other valuable thing to any person for, or in connection with, that person's test, appointment, proposed appointment, promotion, or proposed promotion.

(b) Any person who by himself or herself or with others wilfully or corruptly violates this section shall be fined not more than $500, or imprisoned for not more than 1 year, or both. Any person convicted under this section shall be ineligible, for a period of 5 years thereafter, to hold any county office or position and, if that person is an officer or employee of the County, that person shall immediately forfeit his or her office or position. The Superior Court shall have exclusive original jurisdiction over offenses under this section.

History.
9 Del. C. 1953, § 1183; 55 Del. Laws, c. 85, § 1; 70 Del. Laws, c. 186, § 1; 77 Del. Laws, c. 90, § 12; 79 Del. Laws, c. 47, § 14; 83 Del. Laws, c. 13, § 4.

Effect of amendments.
83 Del. Laws, c. 13, effective April 13, 2021, substituted "apply" for "shall be applicable" in the introductory paragraph of (a); rewrote (a)(1); in (a)(2), substituted "A person may not" for "No person shall" and a period for a semicolon at the end; added a comma following "rating" in (a)(2) and following "render", "service" and the second occurrence of "promotion" in (a)(3); and in (a)(3), substituted "A" for "No" and "may not" for "shall".

CHAPTER 13

COUNTY DEPARTMENTS

SUBCHAPTER III
DEPARTMENT OF SPECIAL SERVICES

§ 1341. Functions.

NOTES TO DECISIONS

Sanitary sewers.

Failure to exhaust administrative remedies rendered claims in a sewer service dispute premature; the property owner had not requested a sewer capacity determination for a development proposal upon which the county, exercising its statutory powers, could act. Glen Allen Farm, LLC v. New Castle Cty., —A.3d —, 2020 Del. Ch. LEXIS 301 (Del. Ch. Sept. 29, 2020).

SUBCHAPTER V
DEPARTMENT OF ADMINISTRATION

§ 1392. Appointment of County Attorney.

The County Attorney shall be appointed by the County Executive with the advice and consent of the New Castle County Council. The County Attorney shall serve at the pleasure of the County Executive.

History.

9 Del. C. 1953, § 1442; 55 Del. Laws, c. 85, § 2; 71 Del. Laws, c. 401, § 59; 83 Del. Laws, c. 132, § 2.

Effect of amendments.

83 Del. Laws, c. 132, effective Sept. 10, 2021, added "with the advice and consent of the New Castle County Council" in the first sentence.

CHAPTER 15
GOVERNMENT OF NEW CASTLE COUNTY

SUBCHAPTER II
POWERS AND DUTIES

§ 1521. Enumeration of certain specific powers.

NOTES TO DECISIONS

Sanitary sewers.

Failure to exhaust administrative remedies rendered claims in a sewer service dispute premature; the property owner had not requested a sewer capacity determination for a development proposal upon which the county, exercising its statutory powers, could act. Glen Allen Farm, LLC v. New Castle Cty., —A.3d —, 2020 Del. Ch. LEXIS 301 (Del. Ch. Sept. 29, 2020).

CHAPTER 25
BUILDING CODE

Sec.
2515. Exceptions.

§ 2515. Exceptions.

This chapter does not apply to any of the following:

(1) A building or structure devoted to agricultural use as defined in Chapter 26 of this title.

(2) A property, building, or structure located within a municipality unless New Castle County has any responsibility for the local service function under § 1102 of this title.

History.

44 Del. Laws, c. 84, § 17; 45 Del. Laws, c. 111, § 1; 16 Del. C. 1953, § 8317; 53 Del. Laws, c. 348, § 3; 58 Del. Laws, c. 277; 75 Del. Laws, c. 85, § 5; 83 Del. Laws, c. 7, § 7.

Revisor's note.

Section 12 of 83 Del. Laws, c. 7, provided: "Sections 5 through 9 of this act are effective January 1, 2022."

Effect of amendments.
83 Del. Laws, c. 7, effective Jan. 1, 2022, rewrote the section.

CHAPTER 26
ZONING
SUBCHAPTER I
GENERAL PROVISIONS

§ 2602. Zoning plan and regulations.

NOTES TO DECISIONS

Sanitary sewers.
Failure to exhaust administrative remedies rendered claims in a sewer service dispute premature; the property owner had not requested a sewer capacity determination for a development proposal upon which the county, exercising its statutory powers, could act. Glen Allen Farm, LLC v. New Castle Cty., — A.3d —, 2020 Del. Ch. LEXIS 301 (Del. Ch. Sept. 29, 2020).

SUBCHAPTER II
THE QUALITY OF LIFE ACT

§ 2652. Definitions.

NOTES TO DECISIONS

Comprehensive plan.
Grant of summary judgment to the county was affirmed because the regulation of New Castle County's Unified Development Code, that golf courses could not satisfy community area open space requirements, continued to apply to appellant's parcel (which was subject to restrictive covenants limiting use of the parcel to that of an 18-hole golf course); the adoption of the updated county comprehensive development plan was not intended to change any existing development regulations or change the power of the restrictive covenant. Pike Creek Rec. Servs., LLC v. New Castle Cty., — A.3d —, 2021 Del. LEXIS 255 (Del. Aug. 5, 2021).

CHAPTER 29
PROPERTY MAINTENANCE

Sec.
2910. Exceptions.

§ 2910. Exceptions.

This chapter does not apply to a property, building, or structure located within a municipality unless New Castle County has any responsibility for the local service function under § 1102 of this title.

History.
75 Del. Laws, c. 212, § 6; 83 Del. Laws, c. 7, § 8.

Revisor's note.
Section 12 of 83 Del. Laws, c. 7, provided:

"Sections 5 through 9 of this act are effective January 1, 2022."

Effect of amendments.
83 Del. Laws, c. 7, effective Jan. 1, 2022, rewrote the section.

CHAPTER 34
STORMWATER MANAGEMENT

Revisor's note.

Section 2 of 83 Del. Laws, c. 133, provided: "This act is effective immediately and implemented as follows:

"(1) The Clerk of New Castle County Council shall provide notice, published in the Register of Regulations, that the ordinance required under § 3402(a) of Title 9 has been adopted by county government and the date this ordinance was adopted.

"(2) The implementation date is the date the ordinance required under § 3402(a) of Title 9 was adopted, as provided under paragraph (1)." The act became effective upon the signature of the Governor on Sept. 10, 2021, however implementation information is not yet available.

§ 3401. Definitions.

For purposes of this chapter:

(1) "Stormwater maintenance district" means an area in New Castle County, created under this chapter, that has ascertainable boundaries and provides efficient and economical stormwater maintenance.

(2) "Stormwater management" means a system of vegetative, structural, and other measures that does all of the following:

a. For water quantity control, controls the volume and rate of stormwater runoff which may be caused by land disturbing activities or activities upon the land.

b. For water quality control, controls adverse effects on water quality that may be caused by land disturbing activities or activities upon the land.

History.
83 Del. Laws, c. 133, § 1.

§ 3402. Establishing a stormwater maintenance district.

(a) County government shall adopt an ordinance implementing this chapter, that provides the procedures and criteria for the establishment and operation of stormwater maintenance districts.

(b) *Subdivisions and land developments approved after [the implementation date of this chapter].* — Any new subdivision or land development in any unincorporated area in New Castle County that is approved after [the implementation date of this chapter], shall establish a stormwater maintenance district, as required by the ordinance adopted under subsection (a) of this section, as a condition of plan approval. Fees for the district must not be incurred until the subdivision or land development is complete and the stormwater infrastructure is approved by the appropriate regulating agency.

(c) *Subdivisions and land developments established before [the implementation date of this chapter].* — Any subdivision or land development established before [the implementation date of this chapter], in any unincorporated area in New Castle County contained within ascertainable boundaries, may petition county government under the ordinance adopted under subsection (a) of this section to declare the area a stormwater maintenance district.

(d) The county government may establish a stormwater maintenance district within an incorporated area of the County under subsection (a) of this section, but only with the concurrence of the local governing body.

History.
83 Del. Laws, c. 133, § 1.

§ 3403. Public hearing.

(a) Upon receipt of a petition under § 3402(c) of this title from an existing subdivision or land development, the county government shall hold a public hearing on the petition. The notice of the public hearing must be published at least once in a newspaper published within New Castle County. The notice must be published between 10 and 21 days before the public hearing and must contain all of the following:

(1) A description of the boundaries of the proposed stormwater maintenance district.

(2) A statement that the county government will hold a hearing to consider whether or not to create the proposed district.

(3) A statement that in the event the county government decides to create the proposed stormwater maintenance district, the county government will assess the unit costs of stormwater maintenance against each unit of real property within the stormwater maintenance district.

(b) Any new subdivision or land development required to establish a stormwater maintenance district under § 3402 of this title is also subject to all hearing procedures and all requirements for a proposed plan as established under the New Castle County Code.

History.
83 Del. Laws, c. 133, § 1.

§ 3404. Creation of stormwater maintenance district.

(a) If the county government determines, after the public hearing required under § 3403 of this title, that it is in the public interest to establish the proposed stormwater maintenance district under the ordinance adopted under § 3402(a) of this title, county government shall adopt an ordinance establishing the stormwater maintenance district.

(b) Except as provided under the ordinance adopted under § 3402(a) of this title, the establishment of a stormwater maintenance district and the resulting infrastructure maintenance managed by New Castle County takes precedence over any homeowner obligation for stormwater management included in declarations of restrictions or similar development agreements. Any common open space or infrastructure within a community not maintained as part of a stormwater maintenance district remains the responsibility of the homeowners.

History.
83 Del. Laws, c. 133, § 1.

§ 3405. Agreements for stormwater maintenance authorized.

The county government may enter into an agreement with the New Castle Conservation District or other government, nonprofit, or for-profit agency or organization to maintain the stormwater infrastructure of each stormwater maintenance district.

History.
83 Del. Laws, c. 133, § 1.

§ 3406. Award of contracts.

Either county government or the New Castle Conservation District may enter into contracts for maintenance of stormwater infrastructure that cannot be completed by existing staff. All contracts entered under this section must follow applicable state and local laws and policies.

History.
83 Del. Laws, c. 133, § 1.

§ 3407. Levy and collection of stormwater maintenance fee.

(a) In order to fund the annual and long-term costs for each stormwater maintenance district, the county government shall establish a fee structure for each district and divide the annual cost, plus a pro rata administrative cost as determined by the county government, by the total number of applicable units within the stormwater maintenance district to arrive at the annual unit cost. The annual unit cost shall be assessed against each unit located within the boundaries of the stormwater maintenance district. No parcel of real estate may be exempt from paying its annual unit cost. The established fee structure does not need to be uniform among districts.

(b) County government shall levy and collect the annual unit cost assessed against each unit in a stormwater maintenance district at the same time and in the same manner as other New Castle County taxes and the annual unit cost is a lien on real property the same as other New Castle County taxes. The county government shall include this fee on tax bills under the heading "stormwater maintenance fee."

History.
83 Del. Laws, c. 133, § 1.

§ 3408. Administration of funds.

All amounts collected under this chapter shall be paid into a fund of New Castle County as provided under the ordinance adopted under § 3402(a) of this title and all payments for stormwater maintenance shall be paid out of this fund. Should New Castle County fail in any 1 year to collect all of the fees in the stormwater maintenance district necessary to pay the price for stormwater maintenance in any year, the county government may pay the deficit out of this fund pending enforcement of the lien. The county government may make payments out of this fund in anticipation of collection of the stormwater maintenance fee.

History.
83 Del. Laws, c. 133, § 1.

§ 3409. Continuation and termination of contracts; consolidation of stormwater maintenance districts.

The county government may determine not to continue stormwater maintenance for any stormwater maintenance district at the expiration of any agreement entered into under this chapter. The county government may, without further public hearings, consolidate 2 or more stormwater maintenance districts into a single district.

History.
83 Del. Laws, c. 133, § 1.

§ 3410. Annual budgeting.

(a) The annual amounts required for stormwater maintenance under this chapter must be included in the annual budget under separate headings for each stormwater maintenance district. County expenditures related to stormwater maintenance districts will be available for public review on the county government website.

(b) After levying the stormwater maintenance fee, the county government shall deliver a separate fee collection warrant, together with a list of charges in each stormwater maintenance district, to the County Chief Financial Officer and shall command that the County Chief Financial Officer collect from the persons named in the list their stormwater maintenance fee and its amount.

(c) Should a stormwater maintenance district be formed after the commencement of any fiscal year, the county government shall include an amount sufficient to reimburse the general fund for the expenditure during the last fiscal year in the next annual budget, as well as an amount sufficient to pay the cost for the coming fiscal year.

History.
  83 Del. Laws, c. 133, § 1.

PART III
KENT COUNTY

CHAPTER 41
GOVERNMENT OF KENT COUNTY

SUBCHAPTER I
GENERAL PROVISIONS

§ 4108. County Administrator.

(a) *Appointment; qualifications; compensation.* — The county government shall appoint a County Administrator by the affirmative vote of a majority of the members of the county government, for a term not exceeding 4 years, and fix the Administrator's compensation. The County Administrator shall be appointed solely on the basis of the Administrator's executive and administrative qualifications. At the time of the Administrator's contractual starting date the Administrator must be a resident of Kent County, and, during the Administrator's tenure of office, the Administrator shall at all times reside within Kent County.

(b) *Removal from office.* — The county government may remove the County Administrator from office before the expiration of the Administrator's term, but only in accordance with the following procedures:

(1) By affirmative vote of a majority of all the members of the county government upon adoption of a preliminary resolution which shall state the reason for the removal. A copy of the preliminary resolution shall be delivered promptly to the County Administrator.

(2) Within 10 days after a copy of the preliminary resolution is delivered to the County Administrator, the Administrator may file with the county government a written request for a public hearing. This hearing shall be held at a special county government meeting not later than 30 days after the request is filed. The County Administrator may file with the county government a written reply not later than 5 days prior to the hearing. The County Administrator shall be permitted to appear in person at the hearing in lieu of a full written reply to the charges made and may present the Administrator's case with witnesses as the circumstances may require.

(3) The county government may adopt a final resolution of removal, which may be made effective immediately, by affirmative vote of a majority of all the members at any time after 10 days from the date when a copy of the preliminary resolution was delivered to the Administrator, if the Administrator has not requested a hearing.

(c) *Acting county administrator.* — The county government may designate a qualified acting county administrative officer to exercise the powers and perform the duties of the County Administrator during the latter's absence or disability.

(d) *Powers and duties.* — The County Administrator is the chief administrative officer of the County. The County Administrator shall attend the meetings of the county government and be responsible to the county government for the proper administration of all the affairs of the County which the county government has authority to control. Under the direction of the county government, the County Administrator has the following powers and duties, except as otherwise provided by this chapter, law, or governing personnel regulations:

(1) The County Administrator shall appoint and, when the Administrator deems it necessary, suspend or remove any county employees and appointive administrative officers with the exception of the Director of Finance. The Administrator may authorize any administrative officer who is subject to the Administrator's direction and supervision to exercise these powers with respect to subordinates in that officer's department, office or agency.

(2) The County Administrator shall direct and supervise the administration of all departments, offices and agencies of the County.

(3) The County Administrator has the right to take part in discussion at all county government meetings but may not vote.

(4) The County Administrator shall see that all laws, provisions of this chapter, and acts of the county government, subject to enforcement by the County Administrator or by officers subject to the Administrator's direction and supervision, are faithfully executed.

(5) The County Administrator shall prepare and submit a proposed annual budget and capital program to the county government, with the Administrator's recommendations and shall execute the budget as finally adopted.

(6) The County Administrator shall make reports, at least once monthly, to the county government in regard to matters of administration, and keep the county government fully advised as to the financial condition of the county government.

(7) The County Administrator shall submit to the county government and make available to the public a complete report on the finances and administrative activities of the County within 60 days after the end of each fiscal year.

(8) The County Administrator shall familiarize himself or herself in detail with the affairs of all officers, departments, boards, and agencies and make recommendations and reports to the county government at such times as the government may direct. The County Administrator may order an audit of any office or agency at any time by the independent auditor engaged by the county government.

(9) The County Administrator shall perform such other duties as are specified in this chapter or as may be required by the county government.

History.
83 Del. Laws, c. 144, § 1; 70 Del. Laws, c. 186, § 1.

Revisor's Notes
This section became effective upon the signature of the Governor on Sept. 10, 2021.

SUBCHAPTER II
POWERS AND DUTIES

§ 4112. Employment by county officers of a chief deputy and clerks.

History.
31 Del. Laws, c. 13, § 16; 32 Del. Laws, c. 67, § 1; Code 1935, § 1191; 44 Del. Laws, c. 100, § 2; 9 Del. C. 1953, § 4112; 51 Del. Laws, c.

103, § 1; repealed by 83 Del. Laws, c. 144, § 3, effective Sept. 10, 2021.

§ 4117. County Engineer and other employees; appointment and duties.

(a) The County Administrator may appoint a County Engineer for such term, and at such compensation as the Administrator deems proper. The County Engineer shall be responsible for and have general supervision over all public engineering work in the County including, but not limited to, the construction of sanitary sewers, trunk lines, sewerage disposal plants, sanitary sewer systems in general and maintenance thereof, drainage, construction, lighting service and other projects of a public nature.

(b) The County Administrator may employ, for such periods and for such compensation as the Administrator deems proper, such draftsmen, rodmen, and assistants as, in its opinion, are necessary to carry on such public work.

History.
9 Del. C. 1953, § 4117; 56 Del. Laws, c. 103, § 2; 83 Del. Laws, c. 144, § 3.

Effect of amendments.
83 Del. Laws, c. 144, effective Sept. 10, 2021,

substituted "County Administrator" for "county government" and "the Administrator" for "it" in the first sentence of (a) and in (b).

CHAPTER 50
COUNTY ENGINEER AND OTHER EMPLOYEES

§ 5001. Appointment of County Engineer; draftsmen; rodmen and assistants.

History.
9 Del. C. 1953, § 5001; 55 Del. Laws, c. 217;

repealed by 83 Del. Laws, c. 144, § 2, effective Sept. 10, 2021.

PART IV
SUSSEX COUNTY

CHAPTER 70
COUNTY GOVERNMENT AND COUNTY ADMINISTRATORS

§ 7002. County government.

NOTES TO DECISIONS

Opinions of the Attorney General.
FOIA Petition Regarding Sussex County, see No. 21-IB14, June 30, 2021.

PART VI
COUNTY OFFICERS

Chapter
96. Recorders, §§ 9601 to 9628.

CHAPTER 96
RECORDERS

Sec.
9605. Recordation of instruments.

§ 9605. Recordation of instruments.

(a) Each recorder shall record, within a reasonable time, deeds, indentures, letters of attorney relating to land, mortgages, releases of lien of mortgages, leases, releases, assignments, conditional sales and leases of railroad and railway equipment and rolling stock, oaths of office, plots and descriptions, appointments of deputy registers of wills, certificates of commissioners and agreements of owners bounding and marking lands, petitions and orders for sheriffs' deeds and all instruments authorized or directed by law to be recorded or lodged by the recorder of deeds. The recorder shall forthwith make a proper note of the same in the indices.

(b)(1) A recorder may not knowingly record or receive for filing any contract, mortgage, lease, deed or conveyance, or any other indenture or agreement affecting real property that contains any promise, covenant, or restriction that limits, restrains, prohibits, or otherwise provides against the sale, gift, transfer, assignment, conveyance, ownership, lease, rental, use, or occupancy of real property to or by any person because of race, color, creed, religion, sex, sexual orientation, gender identity, disability, age, marital status, familial status, source of income, national origin, or ancestry. For purposes of this paragraph (b)(1):

a. "Protective hairstyle" includes braids, locks, and twists.

b. "Race" includes traits historically associated with race, including hair texture and a protective hairstyle.

(2) Paragraph (b)(1) of this section does not prohibit a recorder from recording or receiving for filing any contract, mortgage, lease, deed or conveyance, or any other indenture or agreement affecting real property that contains a provision that is permitted by the exceptions to the Delaware Fair Housing Act under §§ 4603A and 4607 of Title 6.

(c) For the purpose of this chapter and this section, any reference in any section of this chapter to the recordation of any document or instrument in books or volumes shall not prohibit the recorder from causing the instrument to be preserved for examination or reproduction by means of any archival filming or storage process approved by the Delaware State Archivist and Records Administrator. The recorder shall be authorized to determine which records shall be available in book form or only in photographic or electronic form.

(d) No recorder shall accept for recording any deed or other instrument purporting to convey title to real estate unless and until the Recorder has first received an affidavit of residence and gain in the form in subsection (e) of this section; provided however, that the Recorder may accept for recording any such deed or other such instrument purporting to convey title to real estate without first receiving such an affidavit of residence and gain if the transaction or instrument is one of those transactions or instruments exempted from the definition of "document" for the purposes of imposition of the realty transfer tax in § 5401(1) of Title 30. The Recorder of New Castle County may delegate this duty to another county department with the consent of the County Executive.

(e) The form to be used in making such affidavit of residence and gain shall be separately made available by each recorder and such form shall require information and authorization from, by or on behalf of the seller, to the extent such information is known to the person making the affidavit; provided however, that if the seller is a Delaware resident or a corporation domiciled in Delaware, it shall be necessary only to so state on the affidavit of residence and gain or any other affidavit provided by the recorder for this purpose:

(1) An adequate description of the seller, including name, residence, address, taxpayer identification number and principal place of business as appropriate.

(2) Whether or not the seller is a nonresident individual, nonresident estate, nonresident trust or nonresident partner, as such terms are defined in Chapter 11 of Title 30, or, if the seller is a corporation, whether or not it is a foreign corporation.

(3) The actual consideration received by the seller and whether or not the seller had a gain on the sale of real estate to which title is purporting to be conveyed.

(4) Within such affidavit the seller shall also authorize the Division of Revenue or such other appropriate state agency as may be designated to obtain any appropriate or necessary federal income tax forms, including their attached schedules or other attachments, and any other related papers filed by such seller which relate solely to the said real estate to which title is purported to be conveyed by the deed or instrument being recorded.

(f) The recorder shall not accept for recordation any deed or other instrument affecting real property unless the deed or other instrument contains thereon in a conspicuous place the county tax assessment parcel identification number of the parcel or parcels affected. In all cases where the affected parcel was just created by subdivision, the number of the parcel which was subdivided shall be identified and the number of the newly created parcel or parcels shall be listed, if available. In cases where the affected parcel was just created by the combining of separate parcels, the number of the parcels that were combined shall be identified. The number or numbers of the newly created parcel or parcels shall be listed, if available.

(g) The recorder shall be authorized to issue regulations concerning the format and size of instruments to be accepted for recordation including, but not limited to the map scale, type size, paper size, margins and requirements for open areas within an instrument to assure that the document is in a form proper for micrographic or electronic reproduction. The recorder may require that, for any instrument presented that does not comply with the regulations or that is not otherwise in a form acceptable for micrographic reproduction, a typed statement be attached and made a part of the document stating the kind of instrument, the date, the parties to the instrument, a description of the property and any other pertinent data necessary to allow the instrument to be microfilmed.

(h) The recorder of deeds shall not accept for recordation any deed or other instrument affecting real property unless the deed or other instrument contains the words "prepared by" followed by the name and address of the person who drafted or prepared the deed or other instrument for recording. The information required by this subsection shall appear on the first page of the instrument to be recorded.

(i) The Recorder of Deeds for Kent County shall not accept for recording any deed or other instrument purporting to convey title to real estate until the recorder has received payment of all state and municipal realty transfer tax due on the transfer, with the exception of the City of Dover realty transfer tax; provided however, that any municipality which has imposed a realty transfer tax may continue to collect such tax upon written notification to the recorder of such election. The Recorder of Deeds for Kent County shall accept any Class C recordings for manufactured homes, but only if the Kent County government, by ordinance, first authorizes and defines Class C grading within Kent County.

(j) The county recorders of deeds shall not record military service discharge documents. The county recorders of deeds shall transfer all recorded military service discharge documents to the Delaware Commission of Veterans Affairs, the State's Repository pursuant to § 8721 of Title 29. The Delaware Commission of Veterans Affairs shall maintain all certificates of release or discharge from active military service or similar discharge documents as defined.

History.

Code 1915, § 1374; 31 Del. Laws, c. 16, § 1; Code 1935, § 1546; 45 Del. Laws, c. 132, §§ 1, 3; 45 Del. Laws, c. 258, § 1; 46 Del. Laws, c. 43, §§ 1, 3; 47 Del. Laws, c. 29, §§ 1, 3; 9 Del. C. 1953, § 9605; 49 Del. Laws, c. 246, § 1; 50 Del. Laws, c. 509, § 1; 56 Del. Laws, c. 99, §§ 1, 2; 57 Del. Laws, c. 82, §§ 1, 2; 59 Del. Laws, c. 84, §§ 1, 2; 60 Del. Laws, c. 234, § 1; 60 Del. Laws, c. 277, § 1; 67 Del. Laws, c. 178, § 1; 67 Del. Laws, c. 179, § 1; 67 Del. Laws, c. 261, § 16; 67 Del. Laws, c. 319, § 1; 69 Del. Laws, c. 145, § 1; 70 Del. Laws, c. 186, § 1; 70 Del. Laws, c. 587, § 38; 72 Del. Laws, c. 382, § 1; 75 Del. Laws, c. 235, §§ 1, 2; 77 Del. Laws, c. 120, § 1; 81 Del. Laws, c. 409, § 2; 83 Del. Laws, c. 13, § 5.

Effect of amendments.

83 Del. Laws, c. 13, effective Apr. 13, 2021, added the final sentence in the introductory paragraph of (b)(1) and added (b)(1)a. and (b)(1)b.

TITLE 10
COURTS AND JUDICIAL PROCEDURE

Part
I. Organization, Powers, Jurisdiction and Operation of Courts
III. Procedure
IV. Special Proceedings
V. Limitation of Actions
VII. Justices of the Peace

PART I

ORGANIZATION, POWERS, JURISDICTION AND OPERATION OF COURTS

Chapter
9. The Family Court of the State of Delaware, §§ 901 to 1077.

CHAPTER 3
COURT OF CHANCERY
SUBCHAPTER III
GENERAL JURISDICTION AND POWERS

§ 342. Adequate remedy in other courts.

NOTES TO DECISIONS

Injunction.
Chancery Court lacked subject matter jurisdiction to hear a telecommunications company's claim for a building permit injunction to compel the city to follow the law because the company failed to plead any reasonable apprehension of future harm that would make the declaratory judgment an inadequate or incomplete remedy; in any event, the building permit injunction sounded in mandamus. Crown Castle Fiber LLC v. City of Wilmington, 2021 Del. Ch. LEXIS 147 (Del. Ch. July 8, 2021).

Chancery Court lacked subject matter jurisdiction to hear a telecommunications company's claim for an injunction ordering the city to negotiate with the company in good faith; the company's declaratory judgment provided it with an adequate remedy at law, namely (if the company's view of the law was confirmed) that the need for a license agreement in the first instance would be obviated. Crown Castle Fiber LLC v. City of Wilmington, 2021 Del. Ch. LEXIS 147 (Del. Ch. July 8, 2021).

§ 348. Disputes involving deed covenants or restrictions.

NOTES TO DECISIONS

Analysis

Attorneys' fees.
Evidence.

Attorneys' fees.
Where a homeowners' association obtained a default judgment against a homeowner whose deck violated deed restrictions, the Master in Chancery recommended denial of the homeowner's motion to set aside the judgment; the association was not entitled to attorney fees because it did not prevail at trial, but was entitled to costs as the prevailing party in the default action presided over by the Master. Keen-Wik Ass'n v. Campisi, — A.3d —, 2020 Del. Ch. LEXIS 322 (Del. Ch. Oct. 19, 2020).

Evidence.
In an action by a homeowners' association to enforce deed restrictions related to a house addition, there was insufficient evidence to determine whether the association's architectural committee (AC) concluded a roof color was not a "soft tone" (which were automatically acceptable) or whether the AC reasonably applied a standard regarding structure harmony with surroundings and adjacent or neighboring properties. Wild Quail Golf & Country Club Homeowners' Ass'n v. Babbitt, 2021 Del. Ch. LEXIS 112 (Del. Ch. June 3, 2021).

CHAPTER 5

SUPERIOR COURT

SUBCHAPTER IV

PROCEDURE

§ 564. Mandamus.

NOTES TO DECISIONS

Analysis

Mandamus.
— Denied.

Mandamus.

— Denied.

Prisoner's petition to correct a constitutional cruel and unusual punishment violation, arising out of concern of contracting the COVID-19 virus, was improper because: (1) the prisoner failed to state a claim upon which relief could be granted; (2) the remedy for a violation of constitutional rights was not through a writ of mandamus, but rather through a 42 U.S.C. § 1983 action in the United States District Court; and (3) the prisoner's claim that contracting COVID-19 was an inevitability did not entitle the prisoner to be released. Beeks v. Jennings, 2021 Del. Super. LEXIS 459 (Del. Super. Ct. June 8, 2021).

CHAPTER 9

THE FAMILY COURT OF THE STATE OF DELAWARE

SUBCHAPTER I

ORGANIZATION, ADMINISTRATION AND OPERATION

§ 915. Commissioners; appointment; duties; review.

NOTES TO DECISIONS

Analysis

Review.
— Scope.

Review.

— Scope.

Family Court found no error in a Commissioner's decision to attribute a self-employed father earning $22 per hour at the time of the hearing with income of $125,000 per year where: (1) the father had turned down a job earning $60,000-$70,000 after having been laid off from a supervisor position where he had earned approximately $145,000 annually; (2) the father had been earning $125,000 per year prior to promotion to supervisor; (3) the father did not continue to look for appropriate employment once he started doing hourly work just 3 months after losing his job; (4) there was no testimony suggesting that the parties' incomes were ever comparable; and (5) using the father's income before the father became a supervisor was the most reasonable alternative in the absence of other evidence of reasonable income in the father's field. L.C. v. J.C., — A.3d —, 2020 Del. Fam. Ct. LEXIS 42 (Del. Fam. Ct. Oct. 5, 2020).

SUBCHAPTER II
JURISDICTION AND POWERS

§ 928. Extended jurisdiction — Juvenile delinquency.

NOTES TO DECISIONS

Other institutional confinement.
Respondent minor was given credit for time served because the residential alternative to detention (RAD) facility at which he had been housed met the definition of "other institutional confinement;" the RAD was a staff-secured fa- cility which had placed the respondent under 24-hour supervision and provided treatment which was rehabilitative in nature. State v. M.D., — A.3d —, 2020 Del. Fam. Ct. LEXIS 26 (Del. Fam. Ct. May 21, 2020).

SUBCHAPTER III
PROCEDURE
PART A
PROCEEDINGS IN THE INTEREST OF A CHILD

§ 1004A. Juvenile Offender Civil Citation Program.

(a) There is hereby established a juvenile offender civil citation option to provide a civil alternative to arrest and criminal prosecution for eligible youth who have committed minor misdemeanor acts of delinquency as set forth herein. The Juvenile Offender Civil Citation Program shall be coordinated by a statewide Civil Citation Coordinator within the Division of Youth Rehabilitative Services and shall include assessment and intervention services that a juvenile voluntarily agrees to complete in lieu of formal arrest and prosecution.

(b)(1) Referral to the Juvenile Offender Civil Citation Program shall be initiated by a peace officer through the issuance of a civil citation. Any peace officer having reasonable grounds to believe that a juvenile has committed or attempted to commit a misdemeanor act of delinquency may issue the juvenile a civil citation. The issuance of a civil citation shall be at the discretion of the peace officer and limited to qualified juvenile offenders. Participation in the Juvenile Offender Civil Citation Program is voluntary on the part of the juvenile offender and requires parental consent. Referral to the Juvenile Offender Civil Citation Program shall be made with the consent of the victim if one exists.

(2) An act of delinquency classified as a misdemeanor is eligible for disposition pursuant to a civil citation, except any Title 21 misdemeanor, unlawful sexual contact in violation of § 767 of Title 11, and unlawful imprisonment second degree in violation of § 781 of Title 11. A juvenile is also eligible for disposition pursuant to a civil citation based on a referral under § 904 of Title 4 or § 4764 of Title 16.

(3) For purposes of this section, a "qualified juvenile offender" means a juvenile who meets both of the following:

a. No prior adjudication of delinquency.

b. No prior referral to the Juvenile Offender Civil Citation or any other diversion program unless more than 1 year has elapsed since the first referral and the prior referral was for a different offense.

(c) A civil citation shall be initiated by entering all required information into the Law Enforcement Investigative Support System (LEISS) to include a description of the misdemeanor offense believed to have been committed; contact information for the designated civil citation community providers; notification that the juvenile must contact the identified civil citation community provider within 7 business days to schedule their intake and initial assessment; and a warning that failure to contact the identified civil citation community provider may result in the juvenile's arrest and the commencement of delinquency proceedings as otherwise provided in this subchapter.

(d) At the time of issuance of a civil citation by the peace officer, the peace officer shall advise the juvenile that the juvenile has the option to refuse the civil citation and instead be taken into custody and subject to arrest and prosecution as otherwise provided in this subchapter. Upon issuance of a civil citation, the peace officer shall submit the civil citation through LEISS to the Civil Citation Coordinator.

(e) A juvenile issued a civil citation shall contact the identified civil citation community provider within 7 business days or as otherwise directed in the civil citation and thereafter report to the identified provider to which the juvenile is referred.

(f)(1) Providers shall assess referred juveniles using an approved risk assessment tool and may recommend the juvenile to participate in counseling, treatment, community service or other interventions appropriate to the needs of the juvenile as identified by the assessment.

(2) For purposes of Chapter 86 of Title 11, a civil citation community provider is all of the following:

a. Engaged in the rehabilitation of accused persons in the administration of criminal justice.

b. An authorized user, if qualified under the minimum requirements established under § 8608 of Title 11.

c. An authorized agency, if qualified under §§ 8610 and 8611 of Title 11.

(g) Upon completion of all terms and conditions of the Juvenile Offender Civil Citation Program, the juvenile shall be discharged successfully without arrest.

(h) If the juvenile fails to comply with any requirements of the Juvenile Offender Civil Citation Program, including any assessments or required services, or otherwise violates any terms or conditions imposed by the identified provider, the juvenile shall be unsuccessfully discharged from the Juvenile Offender Civil Citation Program. The Civil Citation Coordinator shall advise the referring peace officer of a juvenile's unsuccessful termination from the program. A peace officer, upon receiving notice that a juvenile to whom they have issued a civil citation has been unsuccessfully discharged from the Juvenile Offender Civil Citation Program, shall be authorized to arrest the juvenile and proceed as otherwise provided in this subchapter.

(i) Participation in the Juvenile Offender Civil Citation Program shall not, with respect to a subsequent arrest, serve to disqualify or otherwise preclude a juvenile from participating in any diversion program at the discretion of the Attorney General.

(j) Notwithstanding anything in this section to the contrary, those juveniles referred to the Juvenile Civil Citation Program under § 904 of Title 4 or § 4764 of Title 16 may not be arrested for refusal to participate in the program or violating terms and conditions of the program.

History.
80 Del. Laws, c. 412, § 1; 81 Del. Laws, c. 198, § 1; 81 Del. Laws, c. 233, § 1; 81 Del. Laws, c. 452, § 1; 83 Del. Laws, c. 198, § 3.

Effect of amendments.
83 Del. Laws, c. 198, effective Sept. 17, 2021, added the final sentence in (b)(2); and added (j).

§ 1007. Disposition of child pending adjudication; payment for care.

(a) Pending adjudication no child alleged to be delinquent may be placed in secure detention operated, or contracted, by the Department of Services for Children, Youth and Their Families unless the Court determines that no means less restrictive of the child's liberty gives reasonable assurance that the child will attend the adjudicatory hearing and:

(1) The child is a fugitive from another jurisdiction on a delinquency petition; or

(2) The child is charged with an offense, which, if committed by an adult would constitute a felony, including offenses contained within this title, Title 11, and Chapter 47 of Title 16, the Uniform Controlled Substance Act; or

(3) The child is charged with an offense, which, if committed by an adult would constitute a class A misdemeanor, provided that offense involved violence, a sexual offense, unlawful imprisonment, or a weapons offense; or

(4) The child has, in the past, failed to appear at a delinquency hearing and circumstances indicate the child will likely fail to appear for further proceedings, or, absent a prior history of failure to appear, circumstances demonstrate a substantial probability that the child will fail to appear at a subsequent hearing; or

(5) The child is alleged to be intimidating 1 or more witnesses or otherwise unlawfully interfering with the administration of justice; or

(6) The child has escaped from a secure or nonsecure detention facility, or has demonstrated a pattern of repeated failure to comply with court-ordered placement pursuant to a delinquency petition in an out-of-home residential or foster care setting; or

(7) The child has incurred new charges while a resident, as a result of a prior delinquency petition, of a nonsecure detention facility, out-of-home residential or foster care setting and the parent, guardian, custodian or facility refuses to take custody of the child; or

(8) The child has breached a condition of release; or,

(9) Having been released pending adjudication on prior charges for which the child could have been detained, the child is alleged to have committed additional changes on which the child would not normally be permissibly held in secure detention under this section.

(b) Prior to making a decision of secure detention pending adjudication the Court shall consider and, where appropriate, employ any of the following alternatives:

(1) Release on the child's own recognizance;

(2) Release to parents, guardian, custodian or other willing member of the child's family acceptable to the Court;

(3) Release on bail, with or without conditions;

(4) Release with imposition of restrictions on activities, associations, movements and residence reasonably related to securing the appearance of the child at the next hearing;

(5) Release to a nonsecure detention alternative developed by the Department of Services for Children, Youth and Their Families such as home detention, daily monitoring, intensive home base services with supervision, foster placement, or a nonsecure residential setting.

(c) If the Court places a child in secure detention pending adjudication, the Court shall state in writing the basis for its detention determination pursuant to subsection (a) of this section and the reasons for not employing any of the secure detention alternatives under subsection (b) of this section. In the event that a risk assessment instrument has been completed for the child for the pending offense, with the resulting presumptive disposition being to release the child, or hold the child in a nonsecure detention facility, the Court shall further state in writing the basis for overriding that presumption.

(d) If a child aged 16 or older has been ordered by a court to be held in secure detention pending trial in Superior Court and is found to be nonamenable to

Family Court pursuant to §§ 1010 and 1011 of this title, the Department of Services for Children, Youth and Their Families may file a motion in Superior Court to place the child in a secure detention facility other than a facility operated by the Department of Services for Children, Youth and Their Families because the Department's secure detention facilities are at or beyond capacity or the child poses a security risk to self or other youth served by the Department of Services for Children, Youth and Their Families in the facilities it operates. If a motion is filed, Superior Court shall conduct an evidentiary hearing unless the parties reach an agreement to a secure detention for the child.

(1) After an evidentiary hearing, the Superior Court may order the child to be placed in a secure detention facility not operated by the Department of Services for Children, Youth and Their Families if the Court finds by clear and convincing evidence that the Department of Services for Children, Youth and Their Families' secure detention facilities are at or beyond capacity and the child's safety or health is at risk by remaining at a facility operated by the Department of Services for Children, Youth and Their Families. If the Court makes such a finding, the Department of Services for Children, Youth and Their Families shall provide the Court with a status on the capacity of the Department of Services for Children, Youth and Their Families' secured detention facilities at least weekly and no child may be held in a secured detention facility for adults for more than 60 days.

(2) After an evidentiary hearing, the Superior Court may order the child to be placed in a secure detention facility not operated by the Department of Services for Children, Youth and Their Families if the Court finds by clear and convincing evidence that the child is a danger to self or other youth served by the Department of Services for Children, Youth and Their Families in the facilities it operates and the child's needs would be better served at a facility not operated by the Department of Services for Children, Youth and Their Families.

(e) If a child has been placed in secure detention pending adjudication on a commitment from the Justice of the Peace Court, an initial hearing to determine the appropriateness of detention and to review conditions of release shall be held the next day the Family Court is in session.

(f) A detention review with counsel shall be heard within 14 days of the initial detention hearing and if detention is continued, detention review hearings shall be held thereafter at intervals not to exceed 30 days.

(g) When a juvenile is detained pending adjudication the adjudicatory hearing shall be held no later than 30 days from the date of detention. If no adjudicatory hearing is held within 30 days, upon motion by a juvenile, the Family Court shall within 72 hours fix a date for the adjudicatory hearing unless it grants a continuance of the hearing for good cause shown.

(h) Pending adjudication the Court may release a child alleged to be dependent or neglected to the custodian; or, where the welfare of the child appears to require such action, place the child in the care of the Department of Services for Children, Youth and Their Families or any suitable person or agency; provided, however, that if the child is placed with someone other than a relative, the Family Court may require an evaluation and report from the Department of Services for Children, Youth and Their Families.

(i) In any instance in which a person responsible for the custody and care of a child refuses to take custody pending adjudication of that child, the Family Court may order the person legally liable therefore to pay for the child's care during the period of placement outside the person's own home.

(j) Pending adjudication, the Court may defer proceedings pending further investigation, medical or other examination, or where the interest of a child will thereby be served.

(k) For purposes of subsections (a)-(c) of this section above, the term "the Court" shall mean both the Justice of the Peace Court and the Family Court. In all other subsections the term shall mean the Family Court only.

History.

10 Del. C. 1953, § 936; 58 Del. Laws, c. 114, § 1; 64 Del. Laws, c. 108, §§ 6, 20; 67 Del. Laws, c. 390, § 1; 67 Del. Laws, c. 391, § 1; 69 Del. Laws, c. 335, § 1; 70 Del. Laws, c. 186, § 1; 77 Del. Laws, c. 375, § 1; 79 Del. Laws, c. 24, § 1; 81 Del. Laws, c. 308, § 1; 83 Del. Laws, c. 40, § 1.

Revisor's note.

Section 3 of 83 Del. Laws, c. 40, provided: "This act shall take effect on January 1, 2022."

Effect of amendments.

83 Del. Laws, c. 40, effective Jan. 1, 2022, added "or contracted" in the introductory paragraph of (a); added present (d); redesignated the remaining paragraphs accordingly; and added "Family" preceding "Court" in present (g) and preceding the second appearance of "Court" in (h).

§ 1011. Transfer of cases from Superior Court to Family Court.

(a) In any case in which the Superior Court has jurisdiction over a child, the Attorney General may transfer the case to the Family Court for trial and disposition if, in the Attorney General's opinion, the interests of justice would be best served.

(b) Upon application of the defendant in any case where the Superior Court has original jurisdiction over a child, the Court may transfer the case to the Family Court for trial and disposition if, in the opinion of the Court, the interests of justice would be best served by such transfer. Before ordering any such transfer, the Superior Court shall hold a hearing at which it may consider evidence as to the following factors and such other factors which, in the judgment of the Court are deemed relevant:

(1) The nature of the present offense and the extent and nature of the defendant's prior record, if any;

(2) The nature of past treatment and rehabilitative efforts and the nature of the defendant's response thereto, if any; and

(3) Whether the interests of society and the defendant would be best served by trial in the Family Court or in the Superior Court.

(c)(1) The hearing described in subsection (b) of this section shall be held by the Superior Court only upon timely application of the defendant. Such application shall be deemed timely if made within 60 days of arraignment. The Court may enlarge said time period for good cause.

(2) The hearing shall be held by the Superior Court as soon after such application is made as is practicable. Within 90 days of the arraignment, the Superior Court shall announce its decision as to whether the case is to be transferred to the Family Court; however, the Court's failure to do so shall not be considered as providing a basis for transferring the case to the Family Court, for dismissing the charges, or for providing any other form of relief.

(d) In the event the case is transferred by the Superior Court under this section, the case shall proceed as if it had been initially brought in the Family Court, and the Family Court shall have jurisdiction of the case, anything to the contrary in this chapter notwithstanding.

(e) Notwithstanding any provision of this section or title to the contrary, the Superior Court shall retain jurisdiction over any case involving a child where the child has previously been declared to be nonamenable to the rehabilitative processes of the Family Court pursuant to § 1010 of this title, or where the child has previously been the subject of a denied application for transfer pursuant to this section, or where the child has previously been convicted as an adult of any felony as set forth in Title 11 or 16.

History.

10 Del. C. 1953, § 939; 58 Del. Laws, c. 116, § 2; 69 Del. Laws, c. 335, § 1; 70 Del. Laws, c. 263, § 2; 70 Del. Laws, c. 186, § 1; 70 Del. Laws, c. 598, §§ 4, 5; 73 Del. Laws, c. 408, § 1; 83 Del. Laws, c. 40, § 1.

Revisor's note.

Section 3 of 83 Del. Laws, c. 40, provided: "This act shall take effect on January 1, 2022."

Effect of amendments.

83 Del. Laws, c. 40, effective Jan. 1, 2022, in (c)(1), substituted "60" for "30" in the second sentence, deleted the former third and fourth sentences, and added the final sentence.

NOTES TO DECISIONS

Analysis

Transfer.
— Denied.
— Granted.

Transfer.

— Denied.

Transfer of defendant juvenile's charges to Family Court was not warranted because: (1) the evidence against defendant for the offense of theft of a motor vehicle was strong; (2) defendant's past criminal record was varied and lengthy; (3) defendant failed to comply with community supervision; and (4) defendant's violent behavior had escalated despite multiple rehabilitative efforts and services. State v. Dunn, — A.3d —, 2021 Del. Super. LEXIS 472 (Del. Super. Ct. June 15, 2021), transferred, — A.3d —, 2021 Del. Super. LEXIS 513 (Del. Super. Ct. 2021).

In actions involving murder, weapons offenses and other related crimes, the factors under 10 Del. C. § 1011 weighed against transferring defendant's case to Family Court because: (1) there was a fair likelihood of conviction given the totality of the evidence presented; (2) the charges were violent and serious; (3) defendant had previously been adjudicated delinquent for multiple charges (including 4 felonies), (4) defendant had not responded well to prior treatment efforts; and (5) there was no evidence defendant would be serviced differently if returned to Family Court. State v. Charles, — A.3d —, 2021 Del. Super. LEXIS 554 (Del. Super. Ct. Aug. 6, 2021).

— Granted.

Superior Court granted defendant's motion to transfer charges to the Family Court, where the State did not establish proof positive or presumption that defendant used, displayed or discharged a firearm during the commission of the felonies for which defendant was charged; as to the remaining charges, the enumerated factors weighed in favor of transfer. State v. Ackridge, — A.3d —, 2021 Del. Super. LEXIS 29 (Del. Super. Ct. Jan. 12, 2021).

Juvenile was amenable to the rehabilitative process of the Family Court because: (1) although the evidence of the present offense was strong, and the juvenile's behavior with a codefendant demonstrated a conscious decision to steal a vehicle while at least 1 of the offenders possessed and fired a firearm (resulting in the shooting of an innocent person), the juvenile had only 1 prior adjudication for a misdemeanor; (2) the juvenile's criminal history was only 1-year old; (3) the juvenile had responded well to past treatment; and (4) it was in the juvenile's best interest, as well as society's, to allow the juvenile an opportunity to take advantage of what services may be of benefit and available through Family Court. State v. Dunn, — A.3d —, 2021 Del. Super. LEXIS 513 (Del. Super. Ct. July 20, 2021).

Where defendant juvenile was charged with 2 counts of first-degree robbery and related weapons counts for offenses committed when defendant was 14, the Superior Court granted a motion to transfer the case to the Family Court under 10 Del. C. § 1011 because defendant was in need of treatment for relationships, mental health and family support; because the State did not provide any evidence the same needs could be met in the adult system, it was in defendant's best interest as well (as society's) to allow defendant an opportunity to take advantage of any beneficial services available through the Family Court. State v. Mays-Robinson, 2021 Del. Super. LEXIS 553 (Del. Super. Ct. Aug. 18, 2021).

Under 10 Del. C. § 1011(b), defendant's burden was met where the factors weighed in favor of transfer; at 17 years of age, there was time for Level IV or V placement with community supervision that may be available as defendant transitioned into adulthood. State v. Vazquez, — A.3d —, 2021 Del. Super. LEXIS 583 (Del. Super. Ct. Sept. 7, 2021).

PART B
ADULT CRIMINAL PROCEEDINGS

§ 1024. First offenders domestic violence diversion program.

(a) For the purposes of this section, "domestic violence" means any act or acts committed by an adult against another person who falls into the protected class defined in § 1041(2)b. of this title, which constitute any of the following criminal offenses under Title 11:

(1) Offensive touching (§ 601).

(2) Menacing (§ 602).

(3) Reckless endangering in the second degree (§ 603).

(4) Assault in the third degree (§ 611).

(5) Terroristic threatening (§ 621).

(6) Vehicular assault in the second degree (former § 628).

(7) Sexual harassment (§ 763).

(8) Unlawful sexual contact in the third degree (§ 767).

(9) Unlawful imprisonment in the second degree (§ 781).

(10) Coercion (§ 791).

(11) Reckless burning or exploding (§ 804).

(12) Criminal mischief classified as a misdemeanor (§ 811).

(13) Criminal trespass in the first, second, or third degree (§§ 821, 822, 823).

(14) Harassment (§ 1311).

(15) Aggravated harassment (former § 1312).

(b) Those acts of domestic violence for which an offender may elect to apply for first offender status under this rule shall be limited to the following criminal offenses under Title 11:

(1) Offensive touching (§ 601).

(2) Menacing (§ 602).

(3) Assault in the third degree (§ 611).

(4) Terroristic threatening (§ 621).

(5) Sexual harassment (§ 763).

(6) Criminal mischief classified as a misdemeanor (§ 811).

(7) Criminal trespass in the first, second, or third degree (§§ 821, 822, 823).

(8) Criminal contempt of a domestic violence protective order or lethal violence protective order (§ 1271A).

(9) Harassment (§ 1311).

(10) Aggravated harassment (former § 1312).

(c) Any adult who meets all of the following may qualify for first offense election:

(1) Has not been convicted of a violent felony or any domestic violence offense under Title 11 listed in subsection (a) of this section, or under any statute of the United States or of any state thereof including the District of Columbia relating to a violent felony or acts of domestic violence substantially similar to those criminal offenses listed in subsection (a) of this section.

(2) Has not previously been afforded first offender treatment or other diversion programs for domestic violence violence.

(3) Has been charged with a domestic violence offense listed in subsection (b) of this section section.

(4) [Repealed.]

(d) Any person qualifying under subsection (c) of this section as a first offender and who elects to apply under this section shall admit to the offense by entering a plea of guilty, as a first offender. The court, without entering a judgment of guilt and with the consent of the accused and the State, may defer further proceedings and shall place the offender on probation for a period of 1 year upon terms and conditions of which shall include:

(1) Enrollment with a Delaware Domestic Violence Coordinating Council certified domestic violence treatment provider for the purposes of evaluation and such treatment as the evaluation counselor deems necessary necessary.

(2) Satisfactory completion of the Delaware Domestic Violence Coordinating Council certified treatment program program.

(3) Evaluation for alcohol and other drug abuse, and successful completion of a course of treatment as may be indicated by the evaluation evaluation.

(4) Restitution, where appropriate, to the victim victim.

(5) No unlawful contact with the victim during the period of probation probation.

(6) Other such terms and conditions as the Court may impose.

(e) If a term or condition of probation is violated, including failure to appear for evaluation at an assigned evaluating agency, the offender shall be brought before the Court, or if the offender fails to appear before the Court, in either case, upon a determination by the Court that the terms have been violated, the Court shall enter an adjudication of guilty and proceed as otherwise provided under Title 11.

(f) Upon fulfillment of the terms and conditions of probation, including, but not limited to, satisfactory completion of courses of instruction and/or programs of counseling/rehabilitation, and payment of all costs and fees, the court shall discharge the person and dismiss the proceedings against the offender and shall simultaneously therewith submit to the Attorney General a report thereof which shall be retained by the Attorney General for use in future proceedings, if required.

(g) Discharge and dismissal under this section shall be without adjudication of guilt and is not a conviction for purposes of this section or for purposes of disqualification or disabilities imposed by law upon conviction of a crime, except the additional penalties imposed for second or subsequent offenses under Title 11.

(h) Any person who elects to apply for first offender status shall by said application be deemed to have waived the right to a speedy trial and further agrees to pay the cost of prosecution as a condition. If a person elects not to apply for first offender status or if the application is not accepted, the matter shall be promptly scheduled for trial.

(i) There may be only 1 discharge and dismissal under this section with respect to any person.

History.
69 Del. Laws, c. 157, § 1; 69 Del. Laws, c. 335, § 1; 70 Del. Laws, c. 186, § 1; 80 Del. Laws, c. 360, § 1; 83 Del. Laws, c. 112, § 1.

Effect of amendments.
83 Del. Laws, c. 112, effective Aug. 4, 2021, rewrote (a) and (b); added "who meets all of the following may qualify for first offense election" in the introductory paragraph of (c); substituted a period for a semicolon at the end of (c)(1), (c)(2), (d)(1)-(d)(4) and for "; and" at the end of (c)(3) and (d)(5); repealed (c)(4); in the introductory paragraph of (d), deleted "At the time of arraignment" at the beginning of the first sentence, and in the second sentence added "and the State" and deleted "but not limited" following "include".

PART D

PROTECTION FROM ABUSE PROCEEDINGS

§ 1041. Definitions.

NOTES TO DECISIONS

Analysis

Abuse.
— Burden of proof.

Abuse.

— Burden of proof.
Wife's petition for a protection from abuse was properly granted because: (1) she established that the husband had engaged in a course of alarming or distressing conduct in a manner likely to cause fear or emotional distress or to provoke a violent or disorderly response; (2) the husband incorrectly claimed that the Commissioner and Family Court ig-

nored the wife's role in the parties' fights; (3) while the Commissioner found the wife had instigated and engaged in some of the disputes, the husband's reactions were found to be disproportionate; and (4) the Family Court did not abuse its discretion in accepting those findings and according weight to the Commissioner's assessment of witness credibility. Collins v. Collins, 243 A.3d 440 (Del. 2020).

§ 1043. Ex parte orders and emergency hearings.

NOTES TO DECISIONS

Due process.

Wife's petition for a protection from abuse was properly granted because: (1) she established that the husband had engaged in a course of alarming or distressing conduct in a manner likely to cause fear or emotional distress or to provoke a violent or disorderly response; (2) the husband incorrectly claimed that the Commissioner and Family Court ignored the wife's role in the parties' fights; (3) while the Commissioner found the wife had instigated and engaged in some of the disputes, the husband's reactions were found to be disproportionate; and (4) the Family Court did not abuse its discretion in accepting those findings and according weight to the Commissioner's assessment of witness credibility. Collins v. Collins, 243 A.3d 440 (Del. 2020).

PART E

INTERSTATE ENFORCEMENT OF DOMESTIC VIOLENCE PROTECTION ORDERS

§ 1049B. Judicial enforcement of order.

NOTES TO DECISIONS

Validity of foreign order.

Denial of a protected individual's request to register a foreign protection order from Maryland was appropriate; the order was not valid, as the respondent had not been given an opportunity to be heard before the Maryland tribunal issuing the order. J.C. v. M.K., — A.3d —, 2021 Del. Fam. Ct. LEXIS 1 (Del. Fam. Ct. Jan. 22, 2021).

PART H

MISCELLANEOUS

§ 1065. Obtaining personal jurisdiction.

(a) Jurisdiction is acquired over a party in any civil action by transmitting to the party a copy of the summons and the petition or complaint (the papers) by any of the following methods:

(1) By personal service.

(2) By leaving a copy at the party's dwelling house or usual place of abode with some person of suitable age and discretion residing there.

(3) By any form of mail.

(4) In the manner prescribed by court rule.

(5) In the manner directed by the Court, including publication in print or on a legal notices website established by the Court, if other methods of service have failed or are deemed to have been inadequate.

(b) If a party to whom papers have been transmitted by ordinary mail shall fail to appear in the action and there shall be no reliable proof that such party has received notice thereof, then the Court shall order that further effort be made to provide notice to that party which may include notice by certified or registered mail, or by any other method for providing notice specified in subsection (a) of this section above.

(c) Jurisdiction shall be acquired over a minor by any of the above methods directed to the minor and to the minor's parent, custodian or guardian.

(d) If, for any particular action, another statute or rule adopted pursuant to statute prescribes a method or methods for acquiring jurisdiction over a party, then jurisdiction shall be acquired thereby.

(e) It is not necessary to transmit papers or otherwise provide notice to a party who has entered an appearance in the action.

83 Del. Laws, c. 96, § 1.

Effect of amendments.

83 Del. Laws, c. 96, effective July 30, 2021, substituted "is" for "shall be" in the introduc-

tory paragraph of (a); substituted a period for "; or" at the end of (a)(1)-(4); and added "in print or on a legal notices website established by the Court" in (a)(5).

CHAPTER 19
GENERAL PROVISIONS APPLICABLE TO COURTS AND JUDGES
SUBCHAPTER I
COURTS AND JUDGES

§ 1902. Removal of actions from courts lacking jurisdiction.

NOTES TO DECISIONS

Analysis

Applicability.
Elections.
Remedies.
Transfer.

Applicability.

Transfer of plaintiff's breach of contract action was not warranted because: (1) Chancery Court had subject matter jurisdiction; (2) plaintiff's request for specific performance was a genuine appeal to equity; (3) it was within Chancery Court's discretion to exercise its ancillary jurisdiction over the remainder of plaintiff's claims under the cleanup doctrine; and (4) defendant did not have a right to a jury trial on its counterclaims. FirstString Research, Inc. v. JSS Med. Research Inc., 2021 Del. Ch. LEXIS 104 (Del. Ch. May 28, 2021).

Elections.

Plaintiffs were not required to transfer their fraudulent misrepresentation claims from the Chancery Court under this statute because any election to transfer was the choice of the affected party; plaintiffs had the ability to bring the action in the Superior Court any time before the statute of limitations ran. Nieves v. Insight Bldg. Co., LLC, 2021 Del. Super. LEXIS 419 (Del. Super. Ct. May 19, 2021).

Remedies.

Chancery Court lacked subject matter juris-

diction over plaintiff's claim for a tax refund return, warranting transfer to the Superior Court at plaintiff's election; money damages in the amount of the tax refund (less any set-offs as determined by the Superior Court), coupled with a declaration that defendant had to pay within 10 days of the judgment, would more than suffice to provide as complete, practical, and efficient a remedy as could be provided by Chancery Court. Epic/Freedom, LLC v. Aveanna Healthcare, LLC, — A.3d —, 2021 Del. Ch. LEXIS 51 (Del. Ch. Mar. 19, 2021), transferred, —A.3d —, 2021 Del. Super. LEXIS 526 (Del. Super. Ct. 2021).

Transfer.

Superior Court allowed a trust's motion to transfer under 10 Del. C. § 1902 because: (1) the written notice of election to transfer did not invoke that Court's jurisdiction while jurisdiction lay with the Supreme Court; (2) accepting the filing of the notice did not vest the Court with jurisdiction to transfer reformation counts while jurisdiction was elsewhere; (3) it simply allowed the trust the opportunity to comply with the 60-day limitation in 10 Del. C. § 1902; and (4) granting the trust's motion to transfer fulfilled the statutory direction to liberally construe 10 Del. C. § 1902 to permit and facilitate transfers. Olga J. Nowak Irrevocable Trust v. Voya Fin., Inc., — A.3d —, 2021 Del. Super. LEXIS 557 (Del. Super. Ct. Aug. 20, 2021).

CHAPTER 20
JUDICIAL EMERGENCY ACT

§ 2004. Authority of Chief Justice to declare a judicial emergency; contents of order; duration of order.

NOTES TO DECISIONS

Health emergencies.

Court denied defendant's motion to dismiss for lack of speedy trial because: (1) the decision to take emergency health measures to limit the spread of the COVID-19 did not weigh against

the State; (2) the continued inability to hold trials in a way that did not put the public, the parties, court staff and counsel at serious risk was a good-faith and reasonable justification for delay; and (3) the court was not convinced that defendant's pretrial detention was unduly oppressive or that the defendant's anxiety was disproportionate because of COVID-19. State v. Rodriguez, — A.3d —, 2021 Del. Super. LEXIS 270 (Del. Super. Ct. Mar. 30, 2021).

PART III

PROCEDURE

CHAPTER 31

PROCESS; COMMENCEMENT OF ACTIONS

§ 3104. Personal jurisdiction by acts of nonresidents.

NOTES TO DECISIONS

Analysis

Conspiracy.
Course of conduct.
Jurisdiction.
— Personal.
— — Not satisfied.
— Transactional.
Minimum contacts.
— Analysis.
— Requirements.
Nexus.
Service of process.
— Foreign.

Conspiracy.

Turks and Caicos entity and a Panamanian entity were not subject to personal jurisdiction under the conspiracy theory; while the judgment creditor alleged that the entities were engaged in a conspiracy to prevent the creditor from recovering on a judgment, by fraudulently transferring an ownership interest between the entities, it was not reasonably conceivable that any substantial act or substantial effect in furtherance of the conspiracy occurred in Delaware. Deutsche Bank AG v. Devon Park Bioventures, L.P., — A.3d —, 2021 Del. Ch. LEXIS 139 (Del. Ch. June 30, 2021).

Course of conduct.

In an action by an investment consulting group against a fund manager and its founding partner for breach of contract and enforcement of a nondisclosure agreement, the court lacked jurisdiction over the partner because the partner had not engaged in sufficient conduct to constitute transacting business in the State; further, jurisdiction was lacking because the only claim brought against the partner was for fraud in connection with an oral agreement with a third party, not a corporate governance or internal affairs claim. Endowment Research Grp., LLC v. Wildcat Venture Partners, LLC, — A.3d —, 2021 Del. Ch. LEXIS 42 (Del. Ch. Mar. 5, 2021).

Jurisdiction.

— Personal.

— — Not satisfied.

Insured was unable to establish specific personal jurisdiction over an insurer pursuant to Delaware's long-arm statute (10 Del. C. § 3104) because the contractual obligation to pay the insured, when the tortfeasor was unavailable or unable to pay, arose in the forum where the contract was negotiated and executed (which, in this case, was North Carolina). Eaton v. Allstate Prop. & Cas. Ins. Co., 2021 Del. Super. LEXIS 562 (Del. Super. Ct. Apr. 28, 2021).

— Transactional.

In a breach of contract and fraud case brought by a banking administrative agent against a loan obligation portfolio, joint venture entities and lenders, the court had jurisdiction over the portfolio because the contracts were business transactions in Delaware; exercising personal jurisdiction comported with due process. CIBC Bank USA v. JH Portfolio Debt Equities, LLC, 2021 Del. Super. LEXIS 451 (Del. Super. Ct. June 2, 2021).

Minimum contacts.

— Analysis.

There was no basis for exercising personal jurisdiction over a Connecticut company under the following circumstances: (1) a Delaware corporation accepted hazardous waste from the company's Kentucky-based facility; (2) the waste was shipped from Kentucky to an LLC's Missouri-based facility, where it was detonated; (3) the Delaware corporation invoiced the company for the removal from the corporation's Pennsylvania headquarters with instruction to send payment there; and (4) the company derived perhaps 0.1% of its annual sales revenue from Delawareans. Green Am. Recycling, LLC v. Clean Earth, Inc., — A.3d —, 2021 Del. Super. LEXIS 446 (Del. Super. Ct. June 1, 2021).

In an action by oil-purchasing businesses against a founder and others allegedly involved in a secret side-business scheme, the court lacked personal jurisdiction under 10 Del. C. § 3104 over the founder because the complaint did not tether the formation of any Delaware entity to the secret side business; the LLC consent statute (6 Del. C. § 18–109) did not support personal jurisdiction because the founder was not the formal manager, acting manager or a material participant in the LLC's management. Lone Pine Res., LP v. Dickey, 2021 Del. Ch. LEXIS 114 (Del. Ch. June 7, 2021).

— **Requirements.**

Plaintiff was not entitled to compel service by publication because: (1) although the court issued 2 writs, only 1 service attempt was made on defendant; and (2) based on that fact, it did not appear that plaintiff made similar diligent attempts to find an alternative address for defendant for service of process. Webb v. Layton & Assocs., — A.3d —, 2020 Del. Super. LEXIS 2971 (Del. Super. Ct. Dec. 10, 2020).

Court lacked personal jurisdiction over a Turks and Caicos entity and a Panamanian entity because the only substantial action with which the entities were charged was transferring an ownership interest in a limited partnership which was itself a citizen of Delaware; as such, the entities had not subjected themselves to Delaware long-arm service and lacked sufficient minimum contacts with Delaware to satisfy due process. Deutsche Bank AG v. Devon Park Bioventures, L.P., 2021 Del. Ch. LEXIS 139 (June 30, 2021).

Plaintiffs provided a sufficient basis to exercise specific personal jurisdiction over defendant because: (1) although defendant did not directly transact business or perform work or services in Delaware, or contract to provide such services or work in Delaware, it contracted with Facebook to supply fact-checking services and stories which were disseminated by Facebook in Delaware; (2) that dissemination was done in such a manner as to allegedly cause tortious injury in Delaware; and (3) the alleged tortious injury was reasonably foreseeable by defendant. Owens v. Lead Stories, LLC, 2021 Del. Super. LEXIS 515 (July 20, 2021).

Nexus.

In an insurance coverage declaratory action brought by the insureds, the court denied the out-of-state insurers' motion to dismiss for lack of jurisdiction because Delaware permits the exercise of personal jurisdiction where there is a nexus between the claims and the nonresident's forum-related conduct; further, the exercise of jurisdiction did not offend due process because a non-Delaware insurance company that insured a corporation incorporated under the laws of Delaware could foresee the possibility of being haled into court there. Energy Transfer Equity, L.P. v. Twin City Fire Ins. Co., — A.3d —, 2020 Del. Super. LEXIS 2803 (Del. Super. Ct. Sept. 25, 2020).

Service of process.

— **Foreign.**

Plaintiffs effectively served process because: (1) plaintiffs attempted unsuccessfully to serve defendants several times at their homes, consistent with Singapore law; and (2) after persisting for some time, and without having any means of discerning defendants' current location or any indication when either would return to their residences, plaintiffs sought alternative service. Skye Mineral Inv'rs, LLC v. DXS Capital (U.S.) Ltd., — A.3d —, 2021 Del. Ch. LEXIS 152 (Del. Ch. July 15, 2021).

Because plaintiffs properly sought alternative service by court order, they did not intentionally relinquish their right to effect service under 10 Del. C. § 3104(d)(4). Skye Mineral Inv'rs, LLC v. DXS Capital (U.S.) Ltd., — A.3d —, 2021 Del. Ch. LEXIS 152 (Del. Ch. July 15, 2021).

CHAPTER 37

SURVIVAL OF ACTIONS AND CAUSES OF ACTION; WRONGFUL DEATH ACTIONS

SUBCHAPTER II

WRONGFUL DEATH ACTIONS

§ 3721. Definitions.

NOTES TO DECISIONS

Children.

Children. The term "child" does not include stepchildren under the Wrongful Death Act (10 Del. C. § 3721 et seq.), and 10 Del. C. § 3724(a) specifically, because: (1) Delaware courts had ruled that a stepparent, not standing in loco parentis to a stepchild, is barred from bringing suit under 10 Del. C. § 3724(a); and (2) the legislature had chosen to define "child" for the purposes of that Act, but did not include stepchildren in that definition. Brand v. Bayhealth Med. Ctr., Inc., — A.3d —, 2021 Del. Super. LEXIS 577 (Del. Super. Ct. Aug. 23, 2021).

§ 3724. Action for wrongful death.

NOTES TO DECISIONS

Parents.

The term "child" does not include stepchildren under the Wrongful Death Act (10 Del. C. § 3721 et seq.), and 10 Del. C. § 3724(a) specifically, because: (1) Delaware courts had ruled that a stepparent, not standing in loco parentis to a stepchild, is barred from bringing suit under 10 Del. C. § 3724(a); and (2) the legislature had chosen to define "child" in 10 Del. C. § 3721 for the purposes of that Act, but did not include stepchildren in that definition. Brand v. Bayhealth Med. Ctr., Inc., — A.3d —, 2021 Del. Super. LEXIS 577 (Del. Super. Ct. Aug. 23, 2021).

CHAPTER 39

PLEADING AND PRACTICE

§ 3901. Affidavits of defense; judgments by default on written instruments; opening judgments.

NOTES TO DECISIONS

Analysis

Applicability.
Compliance.

Applicability.

10 Del. C. § 3901's answer-by-affidavit requirement is inapplicable both to challenged and unchallenged claims until a pre-answer Super. Ct. Civ. R. 12(b) motion is resolved because: (1) motions for partial dismissal filed under Super. Ct. Civ. R. 12(b) toll the period for answering the entire complaint; and (2) a defendant does not concede or default on a complaint, as a matter of law, when moving against only some of that complaint before answering any of it or the remainder. Unbound Partners Ltd. P'ship v. Invoy Holdings Inc., 251 A.3d 1016.

Compliance.

Averments in an amended complaint, concerning the transfer of a mower from respondent to petitioner, were admitted because the amended complaint attached the contract described with the required demand for an answer by affidavit; however, respondent was late with the proffered affidavit after being granted the opportunity to file an affidavit. Doughty-McKenna Family Trust v. Doughty, — A.3d —, 2021 Del. Super. LEXIS 147 (Del. Super. Ct. Feb. 19, 2021).

CHAPTER 40

TORT CLAIMS ACT

SUBCHAPTER I

STATE TORT CLAIMS

§ 4001. Limitation on civil liability.

NOTES TO DECISIONS

Analysis

Insurance.
Sovereign immunity.

Insurance.

Lack of insurance coverage is not construed as a waiver to sovereign immunity; such an interpretation would expand the liability to which the State had agreed under Chapter 65 of Title 18 (Insurance for the Protection of the State, 18 Del. C. § 6501 et seq.) and would be inconsistent with the stated purpose of the State Tort Claims Act (10 Del. C. § 4001 et seq.) in limiting liability. Christianson v. Dart-Delaware Transit Corp., — A.3d —, 2020 Del. Super. LEXIS 2937 (Del. Super. Ct. Nov. 24, 2020).

Sovereign immunity.

Because a vehicle owner had not alleged an applicable exception to the State Tort Claims Act (10 Del. C. § 4001 et seq.), sovereign immunity barred the owner's damages claim against the State; the owner alleged neither that the State and its employees were performing a nondiscretionary duty nor that the State or its agents seized the vehicle in bad faith or with gross negligence. Betson v. State, — A.3d —, 2021 Del. Super. LEXIS 208 (Del. Super. Ct. Mar. 11, 2021).

SUBCHAPTER II
COUNTY AND MUNICIPAL TORT CLAIMS

§ 4011. Immunity from suit.

NOTES TO DECISIONS

Analysis

Defamation.
Property.
— Damages.
Torts.

Defamation.

In a defamation case, where plaintiff's pleading indicated that a statement published in a newspaper made a false accusation of criminal conduct which allegedly caused injury to plaintiff's reputation and business, defendant was entitled to immunity under the Tort Claims Act (10 Del. C. § 4001 et seq.); the statement at issue was published when defendant was County Executive and acting in the capacity of an governmental employee. Toner v. Meyer, — A.3d —, 2020 Del. Super. LEXIS 2819 (Del. Super. Ct. Oct. 1, 2020).

Property.

— Damages.

Vehicle owner's damages claim against a county was barred because the owner failed to

plead that the County and Municipal Tort Claims Act (10 Del. C. § 4010 et seq.) did not apply, or to allege that the county's actions fit within 1 of Act's exceptions; although the owner's claim arguably challenged the county's use of the owner's motor vehicle, police seizure of a vehicle did not constitute a "use of motor vehicles" within the Act's meaning. Betson v. State, — A.3d —, 2021 Del. Super. LEXIS 208 (Del. Super. Ct. Mar. 11, 2021).

Torts.

In plaintiff's action, seeking damages against a county for the alleged tortious misconduct of a land-use employee incidentally committed within a government building, the county was immune from suit because: (1) plaintiff did not meet the burden of establishing that the public building exception applied; and (2) the alleged injury was not related to the construction, operation or maintenance of any public building. Black v. New Castle Cty., 2021 Del. Super. LEXIS 588.

§ 4012. Exceptions to immunity.

NOTES TO DECISIONS

Analysis

Public building.
Scope.

Public building.

In plaintiff's action, seeking damages against a county for the alleged tortious misconduct of a land-use employee incidentally committed within a government building, the county was immune from suit because: (1) plaintiff did not meet the burden of establishing that the public building exception applied; and (2) the alleged injury was not related to the construction, operation or maintenance of any public building. Black v. New Castle Cty., 2021 Del. Super. LEXIS 588.

Scope.

Vehicle owner's damages claim against a county was barred because the owner failed to plead that the County and Municipal Tort Claims Act (10 Del. C. § 4010 et seq.) did not apply, or to allege that the county's actions fit within 1 of Act's exceptions; although the owner's claim arguably challenged the county's use of the owner's motor vehicle, police seizure of a vehicle did not constitute a "use of motor vehicles" within the Act's meaning. Betson v. State, — A.3d —, 2021 Del. Super. LEXIS 208 (Del. Super. Ct. Mar. 11, 2021).

CHAPTER 43
EVIDENCE AND WITNESSES
SUBCHAPTER III
CHAIN OF CUSTODY

§ 4331. Chain of physical custody or control.

NOTES TO DECISIONS

Authentication.

After defendant properly requested the presence at trial of the officer who seized and packaged the substances that formed the basis of defendant's convictions of aggravated posses-

sion of heroin and possession of marijuana, it was reversible error for the court to relieve the State of the burden to produce that officer and allow the testimony of a second officer who was present at the scene of defendant's apprehension in the requested officer's stead; absent the appearance of the witness identified in defendant's demand, it was error for the court to admit a forensic chemist's report and testimony regarding the items seized. Hairston v. State, 249 A.3d 375 (Del. 2021).

§ 4332. Presence of forensic toxicologist or forensic chemist at criminal proceeding; availability of chemical report to defense counsel.

NOTES TO DECISIONS

Analysis

Evidence.
— Production.

Evidence.

— Production.

After defendant properly requested the presence at trial of the officer who seized and packaged the substances that formed the basis of defendant's convictions of aggravated possession of heroin and possession of marijuana, it was reversible error for the court to relieve the State of the burden to produce that officer and allow the testimony of a second officer who was present at the scene of defendant's apprehension in the requested officer's stead; absent the appearance of the witness identified in defendant's demand, it was error for the court to admit a forensic chemist's report and testimony regarding the items seized. Hairston v. State, 249 A.3d 375 (Del. 2021).

SUBCHAPTER IV
EXPERT WITNESSES

§ 4335. Economic expert opinion on the amount of future lost wages and/or future medical expenses.

NOTES TO DECISIONS

Compliance.

Accident victim was not barred from presenting future lost earnings claims in a negligence action, when the premises owner asserted that the victim failed to secure the appropriate expert witness testimony, because the victim's burden was to provide a reasonable basis upon which a jury could estimate with a fair degree of certainty the probable loss that the victim would suffer; there was no requirement for the victim to present evidence through expert testimony of damage mitigation through alternative forms of employment. Coco v. Trolley Square Hosp., LLC, — A.3d —, 2020 Del. Super. LEXIS 2853 (Del. Super. Ct. Oct. 26, 2020).

CHAPTER 45
JURY SELECTION AND SERVICE

Sec.
4503. Definitions.

§ 4503. Definitions.

As used in this chapter:

(1) "Clerk" means the prothonotary of each county, and includes any deputy or clerk in the office of the prothonotary.

(2) "Court" means the Superior Court of the State, and includes any Judge of the Court.

(3) "Juror qualification form" means a form approved by the Court which shall elicit information relevant to the selection of jurors in accordance with this chapter.

(4) "Jury selection plan" means a written plan designed to carry out the policy and the provisions of this chapter.

(5) "Master list" means a list or an electronic system for the storage of the names of prospective jurors selected randomly from the source list.

(6) "Protective hairstyle" includes braids, locks, and twists.

(7) "Qualified jury wheel" means a device or an electronic system for the storage of the names of prospective jurors on a master list who are not disqualified from jury service.

(8) "Race" includes traits historically associated with race, including hair texture and a protective hairstyle.

(9) "Source list" means a list or an electronic system for the storage of the names on the voter registration list which may be supplemented with names from other sources to foster the policy of this chapter.

(10) "Voter registration list" means the current official record of persons registered to vote in a general election.

History.

60 Del. Laws, c. 225, § 2; 64 Del. Laws, c. 186, § 1; 66 Del. Laws, c. 5, § 1; 83 Del. Laws, c. 13, § 6.

Effect of amendments.

83 Del. Laws, c. 13, effective April 13, 2021, added present (6) and (8) and redesignated the remaining and intervening paragraphs accordingly; and substituted a period for a semicolon at the end of (1), (2), (4), (5) and present (9) and (10) and for "; and" in (3).

§ 4505. Grand jury.

RESEARCH REFERENCES AND PRACTICE AIDS

Delaware Law Reviews.

The Case for Recording the Grand Jury Process, 39 Delaware Lawyer 26 (Winter 2021).

§ 4507. Jury selection plan.

RESEARCH REFERENCES AND PRACTICE AIDS

Delaware Law Reviews.

The Case for Recording the Grand Jury Process, 39 Delaware Lawyer 26 (Winter 2021).

CHAPTER 49
EXECUTIONS

Subchapter V. Sale Under Execution

Sec.
4974. Place for public sale of real estate.

SUBCHAPTER I
SUBJECTS OF EXECUTION; EXEMPTIONS

§ 4901. Real estate.

NOTES TO DECISIONS

Sale.

In a suit involving defendant's failure to pay homeowner's association fees totalling $4,004, defendant's motion to set aside the sheriff's sale was denied and the sale of the property confirmed; considering plaintiff's 3 writs of levy, the sheriff's several attempts to enter the property, and the sheriff's unfruitful levy on defendant's vehicle, no sufficient personal estate could be found to satisfy the outstanding debt. 1960 Superfine Lane Owners Ass'n v. Haronis, — A.3d —, 2020 Del. Super. LEXIS 3051 (Del. Super. Ct. Dec. 28, 2020).

§ 4914. Exemptions in bankruptcy and insolvency.

NOTES TO DECISIONS

Real property.

Debtor's position in prior foreclosure action, in which the debtor successfully argued lack of notice of foreclosure due to not being in residence at the subject property at that time, did not estop the debtor from arguing that the property was debtor's principal residence when that debtor filed for bankruptcy; objecting bank did not meet its burden of proof to show that debtor improperly invoked the homestead exemption for real property by merely claiming debtor was not living in property on date when debtor filed bankruptcy petition, given that the debtor (although absent from the property on the petition date) maintained the property with all personal belongings intact and still intended to make the property the debtor's home in the event the debtor's medical condition improved

to a degree to allow it. In re Goldfeder, — B.R.
—, 2020 Bankr. LEXIS 3013 (Bankr. D. Del.
Oct. 26, 2020).

SUBCHAPTER V
SALE UNDER EXECUTION

§ 4974. Place for public sale of real estate.

(a) As used in this section, "public building" and "public property" mean a building or property that is open to members of the public who wish to attend a sheriff's sale. "Public building" or "public property" includes a building or property not owned by the government or a governmental entity.

(b) All sales of real estate, made by a sheriff by virtue of execution process, shall be made at any 1 of the following locations:

(1) On the premises to be sold.

(2) At the courthouse for the county in which the premises are situated.

(3) At the Sheriff's Office or the building in which the Sheriff's Office is located.

(4) At any public building or outdoors on any public property located in the county where the premises are situated.

(c) Unless otherwise directed by court order, the sheriff conducting a sale retains exclusive authority to determine the location and means for the sale of real property by virtue of execution as permitted by subsection (b) of this section.

History.
Code 1852, § 2448; 16 Del. Laws, c. 540; 17 Del. Laws, c. 622; Code 1915, § 4362; Code 1935, § 4820; 10 Del. C. 1953, § 4974; 58 Del. Laws, c. 11; 72 Del. Laws, c. 194, § 1; 73 Del. Laws, c. 437, § 1; 78 Del. Laws, c. 71, § 1; 83 Del. Laws, c. 174, § 1.

Effect of amendments.
83 Del. Laws, c. 174, effective September 15, 2021, rewrote the section.

NOTES TO DECISIONS

Public building.
Sheriff's sale did not violate 10 Del. C. § 4974, as it took place in Wilmington, the county seat of the county where the levied property was situated; the building at which the sale took place was a "public building" because it was rented by the sheriff for the purpose of holding a public sale and was open to members of the public. Wirth v. Top Bail Sur., Inc., — A.3d —, 2021 Del. Super. LEXIS 298 (Del. Super. Ct. Apr. 14, 2021).

PART IV
SPECIAL PROCEEDINGS

Chapter
71. Criminal Nuisance Abatement, §§ 7101 to 7134.

CHAPTER 57
UNIFORM ARBITRATION ACT

§ 5714. Vacating an award.

NOTES TO DECISIONS

Summary judgment.
Plaintiffs' motion for summary judgment, seeking confirmation of an arbitration award, was granted because the defendant did not: (1) demonstrate that there was a material issue of disputed fact requiring denial of the motion; or (2) satisfy the burden to present evidence from which any rational trier of fact could infer that plaintiffs engaged in fraud. Roma Landmark Theaters, LLC v. Cohen Exhibition Co. LLC, 2021 Del. Ch. LEXIS 106 (Del. Ch. May 28, 2021).

CHAPTER 63
UNIFORM CONTRIBUTION AMONG TORTFEASORS LAW

§ 6301. Definition.

NOTES TO DECISIONS

Medical malpractice.

Defendants (a medical doctor and surgery practice) in a medical negligence claim and the settling party (SP) in a separate personal injury action were not joint tortfeasors because: (1) the medical negligence claim against defendants differed legally and factually from the personal injury claim against the SP; (2) defendants and the SP owed different duties to plaintiff; and (3) the time, place and nature of the injuries allegedly caused by defendants differed from those the SP allegedly caused. Neylon v. Zabel, — A.3d —, 2020 Del. Super. LEXIS 2854 (Del. Super. Ct. Oct. 23, 2020).

§ 6304. Release of 1 joint tortfeasor.

NOTES TO DECISIONS

Analysis

Tortfeasors.
— Joint.

Tortfeasors.

— Joint.

Defendants (a medical doctor and surgery practice) in a medical negligence claim and the settling party (SP) in a separate personal injury action were not joint tortfeasors because: (1) the medical negligence claim against defendants differed legally and factually from the personal injury claim against the SP; (2) defendants and the SP owed different duties to plaintiff; and (3) the time, place and nature of the injuries allegedly caused by defendants differed from those the SP allegedly caused. Neylon v. Zabel, — A.3d —, 2020 Del. Super. LEXIS 2854 (Del. Super. Ct. Oct. 23, 2020).

CHAPTER 65
DECLARATORY JUDGMENTS

§ 6501. Power of courts; form and effect of declaration.

NOTES TO DECISIONS

Analysis

Controversy.
— Not found.
Jurisdiction.
— Subject matter.
Mergers.

Controversy.

— Not found.

Plaintiff's declaratory judgment claim, regarding certain payments under a transaction payment provision (TPP) and patent royalties provision (PRP), were not justiciable because: (1) defendant made the payment under the TPP; and (2) the disagreement over the PRP had no current significance, given that defendant did not have any royalty agreements. Goldenberg v. Immunomedics, Inc., — A.3d —, 2021 Del. Ch. LEXIS 72 (Del. Ch. Apr. 19, 2021).

Jurisdiction.

— Subject matter.

Dismissal of a foreign company's count for a declaratory judgment for lack of subject matter jurisdiction was appropriate because the Delaware Declaratory Judgment Act, 10 Del C. § 6501 et seq., did not independently confer jurisdiction on the Chancery Court of Delaware; rather, the Chancery Court would only assume jurisdiction over a claim for declaratory relief if equity would otherwise independently have jurisdiction over the controversy, without reference to the Act. Vama F.Z. Co. v. WS02, Inc., — A.3d —, 2021 Del. Ch. LEXIS 57 (Del. Ch. Mar. 29, 2021).

Superior Court lacked subject matter jurisdiction over plaintiffs' declaratory judgment claim seeking to quiet title because: (1) the examination of extrinsic evidence was necessary to determine both plaintiffs' and defendants' claims of ownership; and (2) the Court of Chancery had exclusive jurisdiction over the matter. Cook v. Deep Hole Creek Assocs., — A.3d —, 2021 Del. Super. LEXIS 339 (Del. Super. Ct. Apr. 21, 2021).

Mergers.

Plaintiff failed to sufficiently plead a declaratory judgment claim, concerning interpretation of a merger agreement, because there was only 1 way to read the merger agreement regarding a second contract; that reading provided that the earnout's 6-year trigger applied only to a single renewal. Obsidian Fin. Grp., LLC v. Identity Theft Guard Sols., Inc., — A.3d —, 2021 Del. Ch. LEXIS 74 (Del. Ch. Apr. 22, 2021).

§ 6502. Power to construe.

NOTES TO DECISIONS

Mergers.
Plaintiff failed to sufficiently plead a declaratory judgment claim, concerning interpretation of a merger agreement, because there was only 1 way to read the merger agreement regarding a second contract; that reading provided that

the earnout's 6-year trigger applied only to a single renewal. Obsidian Fin. Grp., LLC v. Identity Theft Guard Sols., Inc., — A.3d —, 2021 Del. Ch. LEXIS 74 (Del. Ch. Apr. 22, 2021).

§ 6503. Construction of contract before or after breach.

NOTES TO DECISIONS

Ripeness.
Dismissal of a shopping center owner's complaint against a property owner's association was appropriate because: (1) the association abandoned a proposed amendment to the declaration of covenants, conditions, and restrictions as to raising the payments which the owner paid toward the common expenses; (2) given that the proposed amendment was never

acted upon, the owner could not demonstrate any contractual breach; and (3) due to the resolution abandoning the amendment, the owner could not demonstrate any probability of a future breach. Vill. of Five Points Ventures, LLC v. Vill. of Five Points Prop. Owners Ass'n, — A.3d —, 2020 Del. Ch. LEXIS 335 (Del. Ch. Nov. 13, 2020).

§ 6511. Parties.

NOTES TO DECISIONS

Standing.
Limited liability company (LLC) could not prosecute a declaratory judgment claim as to the parties' respective ownership stakes in the LLC because the LLC did not have standing as a proper party with a real and affected interest in the claim; the LLC had no rights relevant to

any declaration of ownership, was not the beneficiary of any declaratory relief in the action and would not suffer any cognizable harm from the purported private transfer between the parties. Lynch v. Gonzalez, — A.3d —, 2020 Del. Ch. LEXIS 296 (Del. Ch. Sept. 22, 2020).

§ 6512. Purpose and construction of chapter.

NOTES TO DECISIONS

Applicability.
Movants were not entitled to judgment on the pleadings when the movants petitioned for declaratory judgments, and litigation between the parties was pending in 2 different courts and jurisdictions, because: (1) the movants' requests were overly broad, overripe and did

not speak to an active controversy; and (2) the movants were responsible for a split in the litigation involving the parties between the different courts and jurisdictions. Markusic v. Blum, 2021 Del. Ch. LEXIS 119 (Del. Ch. June 16, 2021).

CHAPTER 71
CRIMINAL NUISANCE ABATEMENT

Sec.
7123. Admissibility of evidence to prove criminal nuisance.

§ 7123. Admissibility of evidence to prove criminal nuisance.

(a) In any action involving any criminal nuisance, evidence of the general reputation of the place or an admission or finding of guilty of any person under the criminal laws at any such place is admissible for the purpose of proving the existence of said criminal nuisance and is prima facie evidence of such criminal nuisance and of knowledge of and of acquiescence and participation therein on the part of the person charged with maintaining said criminal nuisance.

(b) In any action brought pursuant to this chapter, any evidence of any prior efforts or lack of efforts by the defendant to abate the criminal nuisance shall be admissible, and shall be considered by the court in its decision as to what, if any, remedies or penalties shall be imposed.

(c) Where a criminal prosecution or juvenile delinquency proceeding results in a criminal conviction or adjudication of delinquency, such conviction or adjudication shall create a rebuttable presumption that the criminal nuisance occurred. Any evidence or testimony admitted in the criminal or juvenile proceedings, including transcripts or a court reporter's notes of the transcripts of the adult or juvenile criminal proceedings, whether or not they have been transcribed, may be admitted in the civil action brought pursuant to this chapter.

(d) In the event that the evidence or records of a criminal proceeding which did not result in a conviction or adjudication of delinquency have been sealed in accordance with § 10002(o) of Title 29, § 4322(a) of Title 11, and §§ [former] 1001 [now repealed], 1002 and 1063 of this title, the Court, in a civil action brought pursuant to this chapter may, notwithstanding any other provision of this chapter, order such evidence or records to be unsealed if the Court finds that such evidence or records would be relevant to the fair disposition of the civil action.

(e) If proof of the existence of the criminal nuisance depends, in whole or in part, upon the affidavits or testimony of witnesses who are not peace officers, the Court may upon a showing of prior threats of violence or acts of violence by any defendant or any other person, issue orders to protect those witnesses including, but not limited to, the nondisclosure of the name, address or any other information which may identify those witnesses.

(f) A law-enforcement agency may make available to any person or entity seeking to secure compliance with this chapter any police report, or edited portion thereof, or forensic laboratory report, or edited portion thereof, concerning the alleged criminal nuisance on or within the premises involved. A law-enforcement agency may also make any officer or officers available to testify as a fact or expert witness in a civil action brought pursuant to this chapter. The agency shall not disclose such information where, in the agency's opinion, such disclosure would jeopardize an investigation, prosecution or other proceeding, or where such disclosure would violate any federal or state statute.

History.

72 Del. Laws, c. 484, § 1; 76 Del. Laws, c. 158, § 19; 78 Del. Laws, c. 161, §§ 28-32; 78 Del. Laws, c. 382, § 1; 83 Del. Laws, c. 65, § 1.

Laws, c. 65, § 1, effective June 30, 2021, "§ 10002(o)" was substituted for "§ 10002(*l*)" in (d).

Revisor's note.

Based upon changes contained in 83 Del.

PART V

LIMITATION OF ACTIONS

CHAPTER 81

PERSONAL ACTIONS

§ 8106. Actions subject to 3-year limitation.

NOTES TO DECISIONS

Analysis

Agreement.
— Seal.
Contract.
— Continuous.
— Employment.
Fiduciary duty.
Fraud.
— Concealment.
— Discovery.
Laches.
Malpractice.
— Legal.
Notice.
Partnerships.
Property.
— Construction.
Tolling.

Agreement.

— Seal.

Buyers' rescission claims based in contract were time-barred under the 3-year statute of limitations because: (1) the word "sealed" was not attached to the signature line of the agreements; and (2) the "(s)" which was preprinted on the form and beside the individual sellers' signatures was neither a corporate seal nor was it sufficient to render the agreements under seal with regards to the individual sellers' signatures. Sweetwater Point, LLC v. Kee, — A.3d —, 2020 Del. Super. LEXIS 2882 (Del. Super. Ct. Nov. 5, 2020).

Contract.

— Continuous.

Continuing contract 'or continuing breach doctrine did not apply to plaintiff's claim for breach of the parties' settlement agreement, rendering plaintiff's claim time barred, because: (1) plaintiff could have alleged a claim within 3 years of defendant's clear refusal to satisfy plaintiff's request to cooperate in other litigation; and (2) plaintiff's subsequent and repeated efforts did not trigger the continuing claim or continuing breach doctrine. Donald M. Durkin Contr., Inc. v. City of Newark, — A.3d —, 2020 Del. Super. LEXIS 2811 (Del. Super. Ct. Sept. 29, 2020).

Claims of breach of contract and breach of the duty of good faith and fair dealing were not barred by Delaware's 3-year statute of limitations, 10 Del. C. § 8106, because the parties had a continuous contract with defendant which defendant had continuously breached. Youngman v. Yucaipa Am. All. Fund I, L.P. (In re ASHINC Corp.), 2021 Bankr. LEXIS 1178 (May 4, 2021).

— Employment.

Trial court properly held that the former employee's breach of contract claim was not barred by the 3-year statute of limitations because: (1) the court found that the contract was executed on March 21, 2016; (2) the former employer

breached the contract sometime after that date by failing to pay the amount owed; and (3) the employee filed suit on March 21, 2019. Adams v. Harmon, — A.3d —, 2021 Del. Super. LEXIS 355 (Del. Super. Ct. Apr. 28, 2021).

Fiduciary duty.

Plaintiff's breach of fiduciary duty claim was timely; plaintiff's claim did not accrue until 2017, when defendant refused to reimburse the company for predevelopment expenses. Largo Legacy Grp., LLC v. Charles, 2021 Del. Ch. LEXIS 140 (Del. Ch. June 30, 2021).

Fraud.

— Concealment.

Fraudulent concealment inquiry barred dismissal of plaintiff's complaint based on the 3-year statute of limitations; defendant's reporting of usual and customary prices (exclusive of prescription savings card discounts on forms reporting pharmaceutical transactions) were affirmative acts that concealed information from plaintiff, who alleged that defendant had the requisite knowledge and intent to report inflated usual and customary prices. Envolve Pharm. Sols., Inc. v. Rite Aid Hdqtrs. Corp., — A.3d —, 2021 Del. Super. LEXIS 41 (Del. Super. Ct. Jan. 15, 2021).

— Discovery.

Plaintiffs' fraud claims were not barred by the statute of limitations because plaintiffs were first placed on notice in 2016 that defendants had not paid the subcontractors (despite having received all disbursements for the work completed); plaintiffs thereafter obtained a builder information sheet from the bank in October of 2017 and discovered that the developer's statements were false. R. Keating & Sons, Inc. v. Chiselcreek Dev., LLC, — A.3d —, 2020 Del. Super. LEXIS 2868 (Del. Super. Ct. Oct. 30, 2020).

Laches.

Laches barred validly removed director/defendant's challenge to the transfer of defendant's stock under a private loan contract (PLC) because: (1) the transfer of shares under the PLC occurred on March 21, 2014; (2) under the analogous statute of limitations, defendant was required to assert a challenge to the transfer of shares under the PLC no later than March 21, 2017; (3) defendant did not assert a challenge to the share transfer under the PLC until filing counterclaims on April 1, 2019. Simple Global, Inc. v. Banasik, 2021 Del. Ch. LEXIS 129 (Del. Ch. June 24, 2021).

Malpractice.

— Legal.

Legal malpractice action against an attorney and a law firm was not time-barred because it had been filed exactly 3 years from the date that the trial in the underlying matter concluded (which was exactly the last day that it could have been filed within the limitations period); dismissal of the claim against the individual attorney was not warranted because amendment of the complaint to correct the spelling of that attorney's name did not create a new cause of action. Zohra v. Norman Law Firm, — A.3d —, 2021 Del. Super. LEXIS 126 (Del. Super. Ct. Feb. 12, 2021).

Notice.

In an action involving claims for property damage, the claims were time-barred because: (1) defendant identified several concerns with plaintiffs' property and recommended that they perform further inspection in their 2011 reports; (2) plaintiffs were therefore on inquiry notice of their claims in 2011; and (3) plaintiffs would have likely discovered the issues identified in a 2018 building moisture survey if they had followed defendant's recommendations. Nalda v. Green Valley Home Insps., LLC, — A.3d —, 2021 Del. Super. LEXIS 563 (Del. Super. Ct. Aug. 24, 2021).

Partnerships.

In a dispute regarding payout to a separated limited partner under a separation agreement, complaint's recounting of the partner's breach of the implied covenant of good faith and fair dealing stated a claim for payment within a reasonable time; issues of fact remained as to when the statute of limitations began to run. Thomas v. Headlands Tech Principal Holdings, L.P., — A.3d —, 2020 Del. Super. LEXIS 2832 (Del. Super. Ct. Sept. 22, 2020).

Property.

— Construction.

Homeowners' negligence action against a builder was time-barred; the homeowners sent a letter to the builder complaining of significant water intrusion in the basement of the property in 2011, but the homeowners did not file their complaint within 3 years of becoming aware of the issue. Altenbauch v. Benchmark Builders, Inc., — A.3d —, 2021 Del. Super. LEXIS 272 (Del. Super. Ct. Mar. 26, 2021).

Tolling.

Successor company's breach of contract claims were time-barred where they were based on conduct that occurred more than 3 years prior; moreover, the argument that the limitations period had been tolled was rejected as the complaint did not sufficiently allege fraudulent concealment or that the successor's injury was impossible to discover. Ocimum Biosolutions (India) Ltd. v. LG Corp., — F. Supp. 3d —, 2021 U.S. Dist. LEXIS 45742 (March 11, 2021).

Plaintiff pleaded sufficient facts to trigger the tolling doctrines on its breach of fiduciary duty claim because plaintiff: (1) was entitled to rely upon a company manager's competence and good faith in protecting its interests; and (2) operated under the assumption that adjacent land would be attributed its fair value when conveyed to a new entity (as contemplated by defendant's proposal) and did not learn that defendant assessed it as valueless until shortly before January 24, 2017. Largo Legacy Grp., LLC v. Charles, _ A.3d _, 2021 Del. Ch. LEXIS 140 (June 30, 2021).

§ 8111. Work, labor or personal services.

NOTES TO DECISIONS

Compensation.

Cause of action for past due commissions was governed by a 1–year statute of limitations, and barred, because: (1) plaintiff's claim arose on receipt of a February 2014 letter stating that defendants would no longer pay any commissions, (2) commissions fell under the definition of "wages;" and (3) while plaintiff denied being an employee or having been paid wages, it was indisputable that prior to termination plaintiff acquired sales for defendant and was compensated for this service by way of commissions. Hammer v. Howard, — A.3d —, 2020 Del. C.P. LEXIS 12 (Del. C.P. Oct. 15, 2020), aff'd, — A.3d —, 2021 Del. Super. LEXIS 637 (Del. Super. Ct. 2021).

§ 8119. Personal injuries.

NOTES TO DECISIONS

Analysis

Accrual.
Defamation.
Emotional distress.

Accrual.

In plaintiff's product liability action, alleging injuries after receiving surgery to implant a pelvic mesh device manufactured by defendant, the claims were time-barred by the statute of limitations under 6 Del. C. § 2-725 and Iowa Code Ann. § 614.1(4) because: (1) plaintiff waited more than 5 years to bring the action; (2) plaintiff's personal injury claims accrued in either 2005 (following the first revision surgery) or in 2008 (following a public notice of defects associated with pelvic mesh devices issues by FDA); and (3) as a result, the statute of limitations in 10 Del. C. § 8119 expired before the lawsuit was filed in 2020. Bredberg v. Boston Sci. Corp., 2021 Del. Super. LEXIS 449 (Del. Super. Ct. June 2, 2021).

Defamation.

Plaintiff's defamation claims were time barred because: (1) the defamatory statement was allegedly made in or about May 2017; (2) the 2-year statute of limitations expired in 2019; and (3) the complaint was filed on July 15, 2020. Mahoganne' Soul v. Stephens, — A.3d —, 2020 Del. Super. LEXIS 2885 (Del. Super. Ct. Nov. 10, 2020), aff'd, — A.3d —, 2021 Del. LEXIS 334 (Del. 2021).

Emotional distress.

Plaintiff's claim for intentional and negligent infliction of emotional distress was time barred because: (1) Del. Sup. Ct. Admin. Directive 7 required plaintiff to file the claim by July 1, 2020, but plaintiff filed the complaint on July 15, 2020; (2) the fact that the courthouse was closed to the public during a pandemic did not relieve plaintiff of the responsibility to file the complaint in a timely fashion; and (3) the courthouse was reopened to the public before the limitations period expired. Mahoganne' Soul v. Stephens, — A.3d —, 2020 Del. Super. LEXIS 2885 (Del. Super. Ct. Nov. 10, 2020), aff'd, — A.3d —, 2021 Del. LEXIS 334 (Del. 2021).

§ 8130. Exemption from liability for donation of prepared food.

History.

63 Del. Laws, c. 216, § 1; repealed by 83 Del. Laws, c. 196, § 1, effective Sept. 17, 2021.

PART VI

FEES AND COSTS

CHAPTER 88

PROCEEDINGS IN FORMA PAUPERIS

§ 8803. Court review.

NOTES TO DECISIONS

Analysis

Complaint.
— Frivolous.
Mandamus.

Complaint.

— Frivolous.

Plaintiff's claim, alleging that defendants misdiagnosed plaintiff with schizophrenia, was legally frivolous because: (1) plaintiff's complaint contained claims that were substantially similar to those that were earlier brought, and dismissed, in both a federal district court case and a prior state case; and (2) plaintiff failed to include an affidavit of merit when filing the instant lawsuit. Jones v. Hay, — A.3d —, 2019 Del. Super. LEXIS 5280 (Del. Super. Ct. Nov. 25, 2019), aff'd, 237 A.3d 818 (Del. 2020).

Dismissal of a litigant's complaint challenging the adoption of a Presidential Executive Order, on grounds that the complaint was legally frivolous, was appropriate; the litigant failed to state any cognizable claim concerning the Executive Order. Kelly v. Trump, 2021 Del. LEXIS 220 (Del. July 7, 2021).

Mandamus.

Inmate's petition for a writ of mandamus was dismissed as factually and legally frivolous; in requesting that the inmate's status sheet reflect 900 statutory earned good time credit, the inmate neither demonstrated a clear legal right to the request nor provided evidence to support that contention. Burris v. Superior Court, — A.3d —, 2020 Del. Super. LEXIS 2990 (Del. Super. Ct. Dec. 15, 2020), aff'd, — A.3d —, 2021 Del. LEXIS 96 (Del. 2021).

PART VII

JUSTICES OF THE PEACE

CHAPTER 95

PROCEDURE

SUBCHAPTER II
CIVIL ACTIONS FOR DEBT
TRIALS

§ 9536. Setoff or counterclaim.

(a) In every action before a justice of the peace, within the justice's jurisdiction, the defendant, if he or she has against the plaintiff any account, demand, or cause of action, cognizable before a justice of the peace, shall bring it forward and plead it as a setoff; and the justice shall enter on the docket the nature and amount of such counterclaim. Any defendant, neglecting to do so, shall, if the action against him or her be prosecuted to judgment, lose such account, demand, or cause of action, and be forever barred from recovering it.

(b) If the defendant has any account, demand, or cause of action, against the plaintiff, exceeding $25,000, the defendant may bring it forward and plead it as a setoff under subsection (a) of this section. The defendant does not, by neglecting to plead it, lose such cause of action.

(c) If the defendant pleads a setoff exceeding $25,000 and it is found on the trial that there is any sum due the defendant from the plaintiff, judgment shall be given against the plaintiff, in the defendant's favor, for such sum, provided the sum does not exceed $25,000. If the sum exceeds $25,000 that fact shall be stated on the record, and judgment shall be given for costs for the defendant, who may prosecute such cause of action in court; or the defendant may remit the excess above $25,000 and take judgment for that sum.

History.
Code 1852, §§ 2089-2091; 18 Del. Laws, c. 678, § 1; Code 1915, § 4014; 34 Del. Laws, c. 221, § 3; Code 1935, § 4500; 10 Del. C. 1953, § 9540; 55 Del. Laws, c. 297, § 5; 57 Del. Laws, c. 192, § 5; 65 Del. Laws, c. 30, § 1; 67 Del. Laws, c. 426, § 4; 69 Del. Laws, c. 425, § 4; 70 Del. Laws, c. 186, § 1; 83 Del. Laws, c. 37, § 39.

Effect of amendments.
83 Del. Laws, c. 37, effective June 3, 2021, rewrote (b) and (c).

APPEALS

§ 9571. Appeal in civil actions.

NOTES TO DECISIONS

Time limitations.
Car owner's case did not have to be dismissed for lack of jurisdiction, due to failure to comply with C.P. Ct. Civ. R. 72.3(e), because: (1) the owner timely filed a notice of appeal with the Justice of the Peace Court; (2) the owner's notice of appeal was filed on the same day that the owner filed an appeal with the Court of Common Pleas; (3) if the owner did fail to meet the requirement of C.P. Ct. Civ. R. 72.3(e), it would simply mean that the record in the Justice of the Peace Court was not stayed, not that the Court of Common Pleas lacked jurisdiction to hear the owner's appeal; and (4) C.P. Ct. Civ. R. 72.3(e) was not jurisdictional. Schneider v. Am. Car Wash, Inc., — A.3d —, 2021 Del. C.P. LEXIS 8 (Del. C.P. Mar. 11, 2021).

§ 9572. Proceedings on appeal.

(a) The appellant shall have the appellant's appeal entered in the Court of Common Pleas of the county where the judgment was given within the time and in the manner provided by the rules of that Court, and the Clerk of Court shall docket the action and issue process in accordance with the rules of the Court. When the appeal is entered, the Court of Common Pleas shall have jurisdiction and take cognizance thereof, and the pleadings and proceedings thereafter shall be as in other civil actions commenced in the Court, except as otherwise provided in this section.

(b) In the appeal each party may make demands against the other, and the Court or jury by its or their verdict may find a sum either for plaintiff, or defendant, but not for an amount exceeding $25,000, exclusive of interest and costs, unless such party has claimed more than that sum before the justice. Judgment shall be rendered accordingly.

(c) If a judgment is rendered against an appellant, or the appellant's executors or administrators, the Clerk of Court shall enter judgment against the sureties or their executors or administrators for the amount entered against the appellant, or the appellant's executors or administrators, and as a part of the same judgment. A judgment so entered shall from that date become a lien on all of the real estate of the surety in the county, in the same manner and as fully as other judgments rendered in the Court of Common Pleas are liens, and may be executed and enforced in the same way as other judgments in that Court.

(d) A surety or the surety's executors or administrators shall be entitled to the remedies provided in subchapter II of Chapter 77 of Title 18.

History.
Code 1852, §§ 2142, 2143; 11 Del. Laws, c. 225, § 2; 18 Del. Laws, c. 678, § 1; Code 1915, § 4036; 35 Del. Laws, c. 222; Code 1935, § 4523; 10 Del. C. 1953, § 9580; 55 Del. Laws, c. 297, § 7; 57 Del. Laws, c. 192, § 7; 65 Del. Laws, c. 30, § 2; 67 Del. Laws, c. 426, § 5; 68 Del. Laws, c. 53, § 5; 69 Del. Laws, c. 423, §§ 9, 10; 69 Del. Laws, c. 425, § 5; 70 Del. Laws, c. 186, § 1; 83 Del. Laws, c. 37, § 40.

Effect of amendments.
83 Del. Laws, c. 37, effective June 3, 2021, substituted "$25,000" for "$15,000" in the first sentence of (b).

ATTACHMENT

§ 9583. Issuance of writ; affidavit.

(a) A justice shall issue a writ of attachment on an affidavit made and filed by the plaintiff, or any credible person for the plaintiff, that the defendant is justly indebted to the plaintiff in a stated sum not exceeding $25,000, and any of the following apply:

(1) The defendant has absconded.

(2) The individual believes that the defendant is about to remove the defendant's person or the defendant's effects out of the State, with intent to defraud the defendant's creditors.

(3) The defendant intentionally conceals the defendant's person, so that process of summons cannot be served on the defendant.

(4) The defendant is a nonresident of the State.

(b) A justice must issue a writ of attachment if all of the following apply:

(1) The affidavit under subsection (a) of this section provides specific facts demonstrating the validity of the debt and for believing that a situation under paragraphs (a)(1) through (a)(4) of this section exists.

(2) The plaintiff provides, at the time of filing, a cash bond in the amount of $100.

(c) The cash bond under paragraph (b)(2) of this section is conditioned that if the suit is not prosecuted with effect, or if the judgment rendered in the suit is in favor of a defendant, the plaintiff will pay any and all costs which may be awarded to a defendant, together with any and all damages, not exceeding the amount of the bond, which a defendant in the suit may have sustained by reason of such attachment, the remainder, if any, to be returned to the plaintiff when judgment is rendered.

History.
Code 1852, § 2156; 18 Del. Laws, c. 678, § 1; Code 1915, § 4043; 34 Del. Laws, c. 221, § 6; Code 1935, § 4530; 10 Del. C. 1953, § 9590; 55 Del. Laws, c. 297, § 8; 57 Del. Laws, c. 192, § 8; 65 Del. Laws, c. 30, § 3; 66 Del. Laws, c. 393, § 1; 67 Del. Laws, c. 426, § 6; 69 Del. Laws, c. 425, § 6; 70 Del. Laws, c. 186, § 1; 83 Del. Laws, c. 37, § 41.

Effect of amendments.
83 Del. Laws, c. 37, effective June 3, 2021, rewrote the section.

TITLE 11
CRIMES AND CRIMINAL PROCEDURE

Part
I. Delaware Criminal Code
II. Criminal Procedure Generally
IV. Prisons and Prisoners
V. Law-Enforcement Administration

PART I
DELAWARE CRIMINAL CODE

Chapter
4. Defenses to Criminal Liability, §§ 401 to 477.
5. Specific Offenses, §§ 501 to 1474.

CHAPTER 2
GENERAL PROVISIONS CONCERNING OFFENSES

§ 207. When prosecution is barred by former prosecution for the same offense.

NOTES TO DECISIONS

New trial.

In the absence of a verdict of not guilty of first-degree rape by the prior jury, double jeopardy did not bar defendant's retrial for that charge because there was no judgment of acquittal or final resolution of the charges by the jury where a mistrial was declared; there was never even any announcement that the jury was unanimously against defendant's guilt as to the offense. Benson v. State, 242 A.3d 1085 (Del. 2020).

§ 222. General definitions.

NOTES TO DECISIONS

Dangerous instrument.

Because the specific implement employed by defendant was a corkscrew wine opener with a knife on 1 end, any confusion about whether defendant displayed the blade end of the knife or the sharp end of the corkscrew was of no moment for the purpose of analyzing defendant's culpability; display of either end would support defendant's conviction for first-degree robbery if the jury believed that defendant utilized the opener to take money. State v. Pinkston, — A.3d —, 2020 Del. Super. LEXIS 2833 (Del. Super. Ct. Oct. 9, 2020).

CHAPTER 4
DEFENSES TO CRIMINAL LIABILITY

§ 401. Mental illness or psychiatric disorder.

NOTES TO DECISIONS

Due process.

Appellant was not deprived of the right to a competency hearing because the record did not support appellant's contention that such a hearing was required; at the pretrial conference, appellant's trial counsel informed the Superior Court that appellant was rejecting the State's outstanding plea offer and stated that based on the 30 or so times counsel had spoken with the defendant (including that morning), counsel had no belief that there were presently any competency issues. Calhoun v. State, 240 A.3d 1 (Del. 2020).

§ 464. Justification — Use of force in self-protection.

(a) The use of force upon or toward another person is justifiable when the defendant reasonably believes that such force is immediately necessary for the purpose of protecting the defendant against the use of unlawful force by the other person on the present occasion.

(b) Except as otherwise provided in subsections (d) and (e) of this section, a person employing protective force may estimate the necessity thereof under the circumstances as the person reasonably believes them to be when the force is used, without retreating, surrendering possession, doing any other act which the person has no legal duty to do or abstaining from any lawful action.

(c) The use of deadly force is justifiable under this section if the defendant reasonably believes that such force is necessary to protect the defendant against death, serious physical injury, kidnapping or sexual intercourse compelled by force or threat.

(d) The use of force is not justifiable under this section to resist an arrest which the defendant knows or should know is being made by a peace officer, whether or not the arrest is lawful.

(e) The use of deadly force is not justifiable under this section if:

(1) The defendant, with the purpose of causing death or serious physical injury, provoked the use of force against the defendant in the same encounter; or

(2) The defendant knows that the necessity of using deadly force can be avoided with complete safety by retreating, by surrendering possession of a thing to a person asserting a claim of right thereto or by complying with a demand that the defendant abstain from performing an act which the defendant is not legally obligated to perform except that:

a. The defendant is not obliged to retreat in or from the defendant's dwelling; and

b. The defendant is not obliged to retreat in or from the defendant's place of work, unless the defendant was the initial aggressor; and

c. A public officer justified in using force in the performance of the officer's duties, or a person justified in using force in assisting an officer or a person justified in using force in making an arrest or preventing an escape, need not desist from efforts to perform the duty or make the arrest or prevent the escape because of resistance or threatened resistance by or on behalf of the person against whom the action is directed.

History.
11 Del. C. 1953, § 464; 58 Del. Laws, c. 497, § 1; 59 Del. Laws, c. 203, § 5; 70 Del. Laws, c. 186, § 1; 83 Del. Laws, c. 73, § 1.

Effect of amendments.
83 Del. Laws, c. 73, effective June 30, 2021, added "reasonably" in (a) through (c).

§ 465. Justification — Use of force for the protection of other persons.

(a) The use of force upon or toward the person of another is justifiable to protect a third person when:

(1) The defendant would have been justified under § 464 of this title in using such force to protect the defendant against the injury the defendant reasonably believes to be threatened to the person whom the defendant seeks to protect; and

(2) Under the circumstances as the defendant reasonably believes them to be, the person whom the defendant seeks to protect would have been justified in using such protective force; and

(3) The defendant reasonably believes that intervention is necessary for the protection of the other person.

(b) Although the defendant would have been obliged under § 464 of this title to retreat, to surrender the possession of a thing or to comply with a demand before using force in self-protection, there is no obligation to do so before using force for the protection of another person, unless the defendant knows that the defendant can thereby secure the complete safety of the other person.

(c) When the person whom the defendant seeks to protect would have been obliged under § 464 of this title to retreat, to surrender the possession of a thing or to comply with a demand if the person knew that the person could obtain complete safety by so doing, the defendant is obliged to try to cause the person to do so before using force in the person's protection if the actor knows that complete safety can be secured in that way.

(d) Neither the defendant nor the person whom the defendant seeks to protect is obliged to retreat when in the other's dwelling or place of work to any greater extent than in their own.

History.
11 Del. C. 1953, § 465; 58 Del. Laws, c. 497, § 1; 70 Del. Laws, c. 186, § 1; 83 Del. Laws, c. 73, § 2.

Effect of amendments.
83 Del. Laws, c. 73, effective June 30, 2021, added "reasonably" in (a)(1) through (a)(3).

§ 466. Justification — Use of force for the protection of property.

(a) The use of force upon or toward the person of another is justifiable when the defendant reasonably believes that such force is immediately necessary:

(1) To prevent the commission of criminal trespass or burglary in a building or upon real property in the defendant's possession or in the possession of another person for whose protection the defendant acts; or

(2) To prevent entry upon real property in the defendant's possession or in the possession of another person for whose protection the defendant acts; or

(3) To prevent theft, criminal mischief or any trespassory taking of tangible, movable property in the defendant's possession or in the possession of another person for whose protection the defendant acts.

(b) The defendant may in the circumstances named in subsection (a) of this section use such force as the defendant reasonably believes is necessary to protect the threatened property, provided that the defendant first requests the person against whom force is used to desist from interference with the property, unless the defendant reasonably believes that:

(1) Such a request would be useless; or

(2) It would be dangerous to the defendant or another person to make the request; or

(3) Substantial harm would be done to the physical condition of the property which is sought to be protected before the request could effectively be made.

(c) The use of deadly force for the protection of property is justifiable only if the defendant reasonably believes that:

(1) The person against whom the force is used is attempting to dispossess the defendant of the defendant's dwelling otherwise than under a claim of right to its possession; or

(2) The person against whom the deadly force is used is attempting to commit arson, burglary, robbery or felonious theft or property destruction and either:

a. Had employed or threatened deadly force against or in the presence of the defendant; or

b. Under the circumstances existing at the time, the defendant reasonably believed the use of force other than deadly force would expose the defendant, or another person in the defendant's presence, to the reasonable likelihood of serious physical injury.

(d) Where a person has used force for the protection of property and has not been convicted for any crime or offense connected with that use of force, such person shall not be liable for damages or be otherwise civilly liable to the one against whom such force was used.

History.
11 Del. C. 1953, § 466; 58 Del. Laws, c. 497, § 1; 62 Del. Laws, c. 266, §§ 1, 2; 70 Del. Laws, c. 186, § 1; 83 Del. Laws, c. 73, § 3.

added "reasonably" once in the introductory paragraph of (a) and (c) and in (c)(2)b. and twice in the introductory paragraph of (b).

Effect of amendments.
83 Del. Laws, c. 73, effective June 30, 2021,

§ 467. Justification — Use of force in law enforcement.

(a) The use of force upon or toward the person of another is justifiable when:

(1) The defendant is making an arrest or assisting in making an arrest and reasonably believes that such force is immediately necessary to effect the arrest; or

(2) The defendant is attempting to arrest an individual that has taken a hostage, and refused to comply with an order to release the hostage; and

a. The defendant reasonably believes that the use of force is necessary to prevent physical harm to any person taken hostage; or

b. The defendant has been ordered by an individual the defendant reasonably believes possesses superior authority or knowledge to apply the use of force.

(b) The use of force is not justifiable under this section unless:

(1) The defendant makes known the purpose of the arrest or reasonably believes that it is otherwise known or cannot reasonably be made known to the person to be arrested; and

(2) When the arrest is made under a warrant, the warrant is valid or reasonably believed by the defendant to be valid; or

(3) When the arrest is made without a warrant, the defendant reasonably believes the arrest to be lawful.

(c) The use of deadly force is justifiable under this section if all other reasonable means of apprehension have been exhausted, and:

(1) The defendant reasonably believes the arrest is for any crime involving physical injury or threat thereof, and the deadly force is directed at a vehicle to disable it for the purpose of effecting the arrest, or the defendant reasonably believes the arrest is for a felony involving physical injury or threat thereof;

(2) The defendant reasonably believes that the force employed creates no substantial risk of injury to innocent persons; and

(3) The defendant reasonably believes that there is a substantial risk that the person to be arrested will cause death or serious physical injury, or will never be captured if apprehension is delayed.

(d) The use of force to prevent the escape of an arrested person from custody is justifiable when the force could justifiably have been employed to effect the arrest under which the person is in custody, except that a guard or other person authorized to act as a peace officer is justified in using any force, including deadly force, which the person reasonably believes to be immediately necessary to prevent the escape of a person from a jail, prison or other institution for the detention of persons charged with or convicted of a crime.

(e) The use of force upon or toward the person of another is justifiable when the defendant reasonably believes that such force is immediately necessary to prevent such other person from committing suicide, inflicting serious physical injury upon the person's self or committing a crime involving or threatening physical injury, damage to or loss of property or a breach of the peace, except that the use of deadly force is not justifiable under this subsection unless:

(1) The defendant reasonably believes that there is a substantial risk that the person whom the defendant seeks to prevent from committing a crime will cause death or serious physical injury to another unless the commission of the crime is prevented and that the use of deadly force presents no substantial risk of injury to innocent persons; or

(2) The defendant reasonably believes that the use of deadly force is necessary to suppress a riot or mutiny after the rioters or mutineers have been ordered to disperse and warned, in any manner that the law may require, that such force will be used if they do not obey.

(f) The use of deadly force is justifiable under this section if the defendant is attempting to arrest an individual that has taken a hostage, and has refused to comply with an order to release the hostage; and

(1) The defendant reasonably believes that the use of force is necessary to prevent physical harm to any person taken hostage, or the defendant has been ordered by an individual the defendant reasonably believes possesses superior authority or knowledge to apply the use of force; and

(2) The defendant reasonably believes that the force employed creates no substantial risk of injury to innocent persons; and

(3) The defendant or a person of superior authority or knowledge who order the use of deadly force reasonably believes that there is a substantial risk that the person to be arrested will cause death or serious physical injury.

History.

11 Del. C. 1953, § 467; 58 Del. Laws, c. 497, § 1; 59 Del. Laws, c. 203, § 6; 70 Del. Laws, c. 186, § 1; 75 Del. Laws, c. 180, §§ 1, 2; 83 Del. Laws, c. 73, § 4.

Effect of amendments.

83 Del. Laws, c. 73, effective June 30, 2021, added "reasonably" wherever it appears in the section.

§ 468. Justification — Use of force by persons with special responsibility for care, discipline or safety of others.

The use of force upon or toward the person of another is justifiable if it is reasonable and moderate and:

(1) The defendant is the parent, guardian, foster parent, legal custodian or other person similarly responsible for the general care and supervision of a child, or a person acting at the request of a parent, guardian, foster parent, legal custodian or other responsible person, and:

a. The force is used for the purpose of safeguarding or promoting the welfare of the child, including the prevention or punishment of misconduct; and

b. The force used is intended to benefit the child, or for the special purposes listed in paragraphs (2)a., (3)a., (4)a., (5), (6) and (7) of this section. The size, age, condition of the child, location of the force and the strength and duration of the force shall be factors considered in determining whether the force used is reasonable and moderate; but

c. The force shall not be justified if it includes, but is not limited to, any of the following: Throwing the child, kicking, burning, cutting, striking with a closed fist, interfering with breathing, use of or threatened use of a deadly weapon, prolonged deprivation of sustenance or medication, or doing any other act that is likely to cause or does cause physical injury, disfigurement, mental distress, unnecessary degradation or substantial risk of serious physical injury or death; or

(2) The defendant is a teacher or a person otherwise entrusted with the care or supervision of a child for a special purpose, and:

a. The defendant reasonably believes the force used is necessary to further the special purpose, including the maintenance of reasonable discipline in a school, class or other group, and that the use of force is consistent with the welfare of the child; and

b. The degree of force, if it had been used by the parent, guardian, foster parent or legal custodian of the child, would be justifiable under paragraph (1)a. and b. of this section and not enumerated under paragraph (1)c. of this section; or

(3) The defendant is the guardian or other person similarly responsible for the general care and supervision of a person who is incompetent, and:

a. The force is used for the purpose of safeguarding or promoting the welfare of the person who is incompetent, including the prevention of misconduct, or, when such person who is incompetent is in a hospital or other institution for care and custody, for the maintenance of reasonable discipline in such institution; and

b. The force used is reasonable and moderate; the size, age, condition of the person who is incompetent, location of the force and the strength and duration of the force shall be factors considered in determining whether the force used is reasonable and moderate; and

c. The force is not enumerated under paragraph (1)c. of this section; and

d. The force is not proscribed as abuse or mistreatment under Chapter 11 of Title 16; or

(4) The defendant is a doctor or other therapist or a person assisting at the doctor's or other therapist's direction, and:

a. The force is used for the purpose of administering a recognized form of treatment which the defendant reasonably believes to be adapted to promoting the physical or mental health of the patient; and

b. The treatment is administered with the consent of the patient or, if the patient is a minor or a person who is incompetent, with the consent of a parent, guardian or other person legally competent to consent in the patient's behalf, or the treatment is administered in an emergency when the defendant reasonably believes that no one competent to consent can be consulted and that a reasonable person, wishing to safeguard the welfare of the patient, would consent; or

(5) The defendant is a warden or other authorized official of a correctional institution, or a superintendent, administrator or other authorized official of the Division of Youth Rehabilitative Service, and:

a. The defendant reasonably believes that the force used is necessary for the purpose of enforcing the lawful rules or procedures of the institution; and

b. The nature or degree of force used is not forbidden by any statute governing the administration of the institution; and

c. If deadly force is used, its use is otherwise justifiable under this Criminal Code; or

(6) The defendant is a person responsible for the safety of a vessel or an aircraft or a person acting at the responsible person's direction, and:

a. The defendant reasonably believes that the force used is necessary to prevent interference with the operation of the vessel or aircraft or obstruction of the execution of a lawful order; and

b. If deadly force is used, its use is otherwise justifiable under this Criminal Code; or

(7) The defendant is a person who is authorized or required by law to maintain order or decorum in a vehicle, train or other carrier or in a place where others are assembled, and:

a. The defendant reasonably believes that the force used is necessary for such purpose; and

b. The force used is not designed to cause or known to create a substantial risk of causing death, physical injury or extreme mental distress.

History.
11 Del. C. 1953, § 468; 58 Del. Laws, c. 497, § 1; 68 Del. Laws, c. 442, §§ 1, 2, 4; 70 Del. Laws, c. 186, § 1; 78 Del. Laws, c. 224, §§ 12, 13; 83 Del. Laws, c. 73, § 5.

Effect of amendments.
83 Del. Laws, c. 73, effective June 30, 2021, added "reasonably" in (2)a., (4)a. and b., (5)a., (6)a. and (7)a.

§ 470. Provisions generally applicable to justification.

(a) When the defendant reasonably believes that the use of force upon or toward the person of another is necessary for any of the purposes for which such relief would establish a justification under § § 462-468 of this title but the defendant is reckless or negligent in having such belief or in acquiring or failing to acquire any knowledge or belief which is material to the justifiability of the use of force, the justification afforded by those sections is unavailable in a prosecution for an offense for which recklessness or negligence, as the case may be, suffices to establish culpability.

(b) When the defendant is justified under §§ 462-468 of this title in using force upon or toward the person of another but the defendant recklessly or negligently injures or creates a risk of injury to innocent persons, the justification afforded by those sections is unavailable in a prosecution for an offense involving recklessness or negligence towards innocent persons.

History.
11 Del. C. 1953, § 469; 58 Del. Laws, c. 497, § 1; 63 Del. Laws, c. 276, § 1; 70 Del. Laws, c. 186, § 1; 83 Del. Laws, c. 73, § 6.

Effect of amendments.
83 Del. Laws, c. 73, effective June 30, 2021, added "reasonably" near the beginning of (a).

§ 471. Definitions relating to justification.

(a) "Deadly force" means force which the defendant uses with the purpose of causing or which the defendant knows creates a substantial risk of causing death or serious physical injury, including the use of a chokehold as "chokehold" is defined under § 607A of this title. Purposely firing a firearm in the direction of another person or at a vehicle in which another person is believed to be constitutes deadly force. A threat to cause death or serious bodily harm, by the production of a weapon or otherwise, so long as the defendant's purpose is limited to creating an apprehension that deadly force will be used if necessary, does not constitute deadly force.

(b) "Dwelling" means any building or structure, though movable or temporary, or a portion thereof, which is for the time being the defendant's home or place of lodging.

(c) "Force," in addition to its ordinary meaning, includes confinement.

(d) "Physical force" means force used upon or directed toward the body of another person.

(e)(1) "Reasonably believes," when applied to a defendant who is not a law-enforcement officer acting in the officer's official capacity, means holds a belief that is reasonable from the viewpoint of a reasonable person in the defendant's situation under the circumstances.

(2) "Reasonably believes," when applied to a defendant who is a law-enforcement officer acting in the officer's official capacity, means holds

a belief that is reasonable from the viewpoint of a reasonable law-enforcement officer in the defendant's situation under the circumstances.

(f) "Unlawful force" means force which is employed without the consent of the person against whom it is directed and the employment of which constitutes an offense or actionable tort or would constitute such offense or tort except for a defense (such as the absence of intent, negligence or mental capacity; duress; youth; or diplomatic status) not amounting to a privilege to use the force. Assent constitutes consent, within the meaning of this section, whether or not it otherwise is legally effective, except assent to the infliction of death or serious bodily harm.

History.
11 Del. C. 1953, § 470; 58 Del. Laws, c. 497, § 1; 63 Del. Laws, c. 276, § 1; 70 Del. Laws, c. 186, § 1; 83 Del. Laws, c. 73, § 7.

Effect of amendments.
83 Del. Laws, c. 73, effective June 30, 2021, added "including the use of a chokehold as 'chokehold' is defined under § 607A of this title" in the first sentence of (a); added (e); and redesignated former (e) as (f).

CHAPTER 5

SPECIFIC OFFENSES

SUBCHAPTER I

INCHOATE CRIMES

§ 531. Attempt to commit a crime.

NOTES TO DECISIONS

Sex offenses.
Rational juror could find defendant guilty of attempted first-degree rape because: (1) the evidence included the child's testimony regarding what defendant did, that the child was under 12 years old and that defendant was more than 18 years old; (2) multiple witnesses, including defendant, testified there was an incident involving defendant and the family; and (3) it was within the jury's discretion to accept

SUBCHAPTER II

OFFENSES AGAINST THE PERSON

SUBPART A

ASSAULTS AND RELATED OFFENSES

§ 601. Offensive touching; unclassified misdemeanor; class A misdemeanor.

NOTES TO DECISIONS

Analysis

Evidence.
— Sufficient.

Evidence.

— Sufficient.
Defendant was properly found guilty of offen-

sive touching; based on defendant's own description of events, defendant chased and grabbed the victim in an attempt to regain defendant's car keys, which the victim did not have. State v. R----- R------, — A.3d —, 2018 Del. Fam. Ct. LEXIS 60 (Del. Fam. Ct. July 31, 2018).

§ 607A. Aggravated strangulation; penalty; defenses.

(a) As used in this section:

(1) "Chokehold" means of any of the following:

a. A technique intended to restrict another person's airway, or prevent or restrict the breathing of another person.

b. A technique intended to constrict the flow of blood by applying pressure or force to the carotid artery, the jugular vein, or the side of the neck of another person.

(2) "Law-enforcement officer" means as defined in § 222 of this title.

(b) A person commits the offense of aggravated strangulation if all of the following conditions are satisfied:

(1) The person is a law-enforcement officer.

(2) The person knowingly or intentionally uses a chokehold on another person.

(3) The person is acting within the person's official capacity as a law-enforcement officer.

(c) Notwithstanding §§ 462-468 of this title to the contrary, the use of a chokehold is only justifiable when the person reasonably believes that the use of deadly force is necessary to protect the life of a civilian or a law-enforcement officer.

(d) Except as provided in paragraph (e) of this section, aggravated strangulation is a class D felony.

(e) Aggravated strangulation is a class C felony if the person caused serious physical injury or death to the other person while committing the offense.

(f) A charge under this section does not limit or preclude any other charge being brought against the person.

History.
82 Del. Laws, c. 281, § 1; 83 Del. Laws, c. 37, § 4.

Effect of amendments.
83 Del. Laws, c. 37, effective June 3, 2021, in

(f), substituted "charge" for "person charged" preceding "under" and "does" for "shall".

SUBPART B
ACTS CAUSING DEATH

§ 632. Manslaughter; class B felony.

A person is guilty of manslaughter when:
(1) The person recklessly causes the death of another person; or
(2) With intent to cause serious physical injury to another person the person causes the death of such person, employing means which would to a reasonable person in the defendant's situation, knowing the facts known to the defendant, seem likely to cause death; or
(3) The person intentionally causes the death of another person under circumstances which do not constitute murder because the person acts under the influence of extreme emotional disturbance; or
(4) [Repealed.]
(5) The person intentionally causes another person to commit suicide.
Manslaughter is a class B felony.

History.
11 Del. C. 1953, § 632; 58 Del. Laws, c. 497, § 1; 67 Del. Laws, c. 130, § 8; 70 Del. Laws, c. 186, § 1; 74 Del. Laws, c. 106, § 2; 83 Del. Laws, c. 200, § 1.

Effect of amendments.
83 Del. Laws, c. 200, effective Sept. 17, 2021, repealed (4).

NOTES TO DECISIONS

Sentence.
Defendant was not entitled to a reduction of sentence to a total of 5 years suspended, after completion of a Level V substance abuse/mental health program followed by continued treatment at Leval IV while on community supervision, because: (1) defendant had to serve no less than the concurrent minimum 2-year terms of imprisonment for manslaughter convictions; and (2) the requested reduction would violate that 2-year minimum required by 11 Del. C. § 632 and 11 Del. C. § 4205(b)(2) and (d). State v. Guseman, —A.3d —, 2021 Del. Super. LEXIS 205 (Del. Super. Ct. Mar. 10, 2021).

§ 635. Murder in the second degree; class A felony.

NOTES TO DECISIONS

Sentencing.
Superior Court did not abuse its discretion denying defendant's motion for a correction of a theoretically illegal sentence because: (1) the maximum statutory penalty for second-degree murder was life imprisonment; and (2) the Court imposed a sentence of 30 years of imprisonment, suspended after 25 years for decreasing levels of supervision. Jones v. State, 250 A.3d 76 (Del. 2021).

SUBPART C
ABORTION AND RELATED OFFENSES

§ 651. Abortion; class F felony.

History.
11 Del. C. 1953, § 651; 58 Del. Laws, c. 497, § 1; 67 Del. Laws, c. 130, § 8; 70 Del. Laws, c. 186, § 1; repealed by 83 Del. Laws, c. 200, § 1, effective Sept. 17, 2021.

§ 652. Self-abortion; class A misdemeanor.

History.
11 Del. C. 1953, § 652; 58 Del. Laws, c. 497, § 1; 67 Del. Laws, c. 130, § 8; 70 Del. Laws, c. 186, § 1; repealed by 83 Del. Laws, c. 200, § 1, effective Sept. 17, 2021.

§ 653. Issuing abortional articles; class B misdemeanor.

History.
11 Del. C. 1953, § 653; 58 Del. Laws, c. 497, § 1; 67 Del. Laws, c. 130, § 8; 70 Del. Laws, c. 186, § 1; repealed by 83 Del. Laws, c. 200, § 1, effective Sept. 17, 2021.

§ 654. "Abortion" defined.

History.
   11 Del. C. 1953, § 654; 58 Del. Laws, c. 497,

§ 1; 70 Del. Laws, c. 186, § 1; repealed by 83 Del. Laws, c. 200, § 1, effective Sept. 17, 2021.

SUBPART D
SEXUAL OFFENSES

§ 761. Definitions generally applicable to sexual offenses.

(a) "Cognitive disability" means a developmental disability that substantially impairs an individual's cognitive abilities including, but not limited to, delirium, dementia and other organic brain disorders for which there is an identifiable pathologic condition, as well as nonorganic brain disorders commonly called functional disorders. "Cognitive disability" also includes conditions of mental retardation, severe cerebral palsy, and any other condition found to be closely related to mental retardation because such condition results in the impairment of general intellectual functioning or adaptive behavior similar to that of persons who have been diagnosed with mental retardation, or such condition requires treatment and services similar to those required for persons who have been diagnosed with mental retardation.

(b) "Cunnilingus" means any oral contact with the female genitalia.

(c) "Fellatio" means any oral contact with the male genitalia.

(d) "Object" means any item, device, instrument, substance or any part of the body. It does not mean a medical instrument used by a licensed medical doctor or nurse for the purpose of diagnosis or treatment.

(e) "Position of trust, authority or supervision over a child" includes, but is not limited to:

(1) Familial, guardianship or custodial authority or supervision; or

(2) A teacher, coach, counselor, advisor, mentor or any other person providing instruction or educational services to a child or children, whether such person is compensated or acting as a volunteer; or

(3) A babysitter, child care provider, or child care aide, whether such person is compensated or acting as a volunteer; or

(4) A health professional, meaning any person who is licensed or who holds himself or herself out to be licensed or who otherwise provides professional physical or mental health services, diagnosis, treatment or counseling which shall include, but not be limited to, doctors of medicine and osteopathy, dentists, nurses, physical therapists, chiropractors, psychologists, social workers, medical technicians, mental health counselors, substance abuse counselors, marriage and family counselors or therapists and hypnotherapists, whether such person is compensated or acting as a volunteer; or

(5) Clergy, including but not limited to any minister, pastor, rabbi, lay religious leader, pastoral counselor or any other person having regular direct contact with children through affiliation with a church or religious institution, whether such person is compensated or acting as a volunteer; or

(6) Any law-enforcement officer, as that term is defined in § 222 of this title, and including any person acting as an officer or counselor at a correctional or counseling institution, facility or organization, whether such person is compensated or acting as a volunteer; or

(7) Any other person who because of that person's familial relationship, profession, employment, vocation, avocation or volunteer service has regular direct contact with a child or children and in the course thereof assumes responsibility, whether temporarily or permanently, for the care or supervision of a child or children.

(f) "Semen" means fluid produced in the male reproductive organs, which may include spermatozoa.

(g)(1) "Sexual contact" means any of the following touching, if the touching, under the circumstances as viewed by a reasonable person, is intended to be sexual in nature:

> a. Any intentional touching by the defendant of the anus, breast, buttocks, or genitalia of another person.

> b. Any intentional touching of another person with the defendant's anus, breast, buttocks, semen, or genitalia.

> c. Intentionally causing or allowing another person to touch the defendant's anus, breast, buttocks, or genitalia.

(2) "Sexual contact" includes touching when covered by clothing.

(h) "Sexual intercourse" means:

(1) Any act of physical union of the genitalia or anus of 1 person with the mouth, anus or genitalia of another person. It occurs upon any penetration, however slight. Ejaculation is not required. This offense encompasses the crimes commonly known as rape and sodomy; or

(2) Any act of cunnilingus or fellatio regardless of whether penetration occurs. Ejaculation is not required.

(i) "Sexual offense" means any offense defined by §§ 763 through 780, 783(4), 783(6), 783A(4), 783A(6), 787(b)(3), 787(b)(4), 1100A, 1108 through 1112B, 1335(a)(6), 1335(a)(7), 1352(2), and 1353(2), and 1361(b) of this title.

(j) "Sexual penetration" means:

(1) The unlawful placement of an object, as defined in subsection (d) of this section, inside the anus or vagina of another person; or

(2) The unlawful placement of the genitalia or any sexual device inside the mouth of another person.

(k) "Without consent" means:

(1) The defendant compelled the victim to submit by any act of coercion as defined in §§ 791 and 792 of this title, or by force, by gesture, or by threat of death, physical injury, pain or kidnapping to be inflicted upon the victim or a third party, or by any other means which would compel a reasonable person under the circumstances to submit. It is not required that the victim resist such force or threat to the utmost, or to resist if resistance would be futile or foolhardy, but the victim need resist only to the extent that it is reasonably necessary to make the victim's refusal to consent known to the defendant; or

(2) The defendant knew that the victim was unconscious, asleep or otherwise unaware that a sexual act was being performed; or

(3) The defendant knew that the victim suffered from a cognitive disability, mental illness or mental defect which rendered the victim incapable of appraising the nature of the sexual conduct or incapable of consenting; or

(4) Where the defendant is a health professional, as defined herein, or a minister, priest, rabbi or other member of a religious organization engaged in pastoral counseling, the commission of acts of sexual contact, sexual penetration or sexual intercourse by such person shall be deemed to be without consent of the victim where such acts are committed under the guise of providing professional diagnosis, counseling or treatment and where at the times of such acts the victim reasonably believed the acts were for medically or professionally appropriate diagnosis, counseling or treatment, such that resistance by the victim could not reasonably have been manifested. For purposes of this paragraph, "health professional" includes all individuals who are licensed or who hold themselves out to be

licensed or who otherwise provide professional physical or mental health services, diagnosis, treatment or counseling and shall include, but not be limited to, doctors of medicine and osteopathy, dentists, nurses, physical therapists, chiropractors, psychologists, social workers, medical technicians, mental health counselors, substance abuse counselors, marriage and family counselors or therapists and hypnotherapists; or

(5) The defendant had substantially impaired the victim's power to appraise or control the victim's own conduct by administering or employing without the other person's knowledge or against the other person's will, drugs, intoxicants or other means for the purpose of preventing resistance.

(*l*) A child who has not yet reached that child's sixteenth birthday is deemed unable to consent to a sexual act with a person more than 4 years older than said child. Children who have not yet reached their twelfth birthday are deemed unable to consent to a sexual act under any circumstances.

History.
11 Del. C. 1953, § 773; 58 Del. Laws, c. 497, § 1; 60 Del. Laws, c. 416, § 1; 61 Del. Laws, c. 56; 65 Del. Laws, c. 494, § 1; 66 Del. Laws, c. 269, §§ 27, 28; 69 Del. Laws, c. 44, § 1; 69 Del. Laws, c. 440, §§ 1, 2; 70 Del. Laws, c. 186, § 1; 71 Del. Laws, c. 285, §§ 3-7; 71 Del. Laws, c. 467, § 6; 72 Del. Laws, c. 109, § 1; 74 Del. Laws, c. 345, § 2; 75 Del. Laws, c. 392, § 2; 76 Del. Laws, c. 66, § 1; 77 Del. Laws, c. 150, §§ 1-3; 77 Del. Laws, c. 318, § 1; 80 Del. Laws, c. 175, § 2; 82 Del. Laws, c. 150, § 1; 83 Del. Laws, c. 37, § 5.

Effect of amendments.
83 Del. Laws, c. 37, effective June 3, 2021, rewrote (g).

NOTES TO DECISIONS

Position of trust, authority or supervision.
Evidence of the relationship between defendant and a victim was sufficient to permit a finding that the State satisfied its burden of showing that defendant stood in a position of familial authority over the victim because: (1) the victim testified that defendant was the victim's uncle; (2) the victim had known defendant all the victim's life, looked up to defendant and loved defendant; and (3) the victim confided in defendant when having problems in school or with the victim's parent. Cirwithian v. State, 252 A.3d 433 (Del. 2021).

§ 772. Rape in the second degree; class B felony.

NOTES TO DECISIONS

Appeals.
Where defendant was charged with first-degree rape and kidnapping, and pleaded guilty to second-degree rape and kidnapping, defendant was not erroneously sentenced to 20 years incarceration under 11 Del. C. § 4204(k) because: (1) although the plea agreement did not reference that statute, the record reflected that the plea was knowing, intelligent and voluntary; (2) the sentences for rape and kidnapping were appropriate and fell within the necessary statutory limits; and (3) the 11 Del. C. § 4204(k) condition was statutorily authorized. Bowden v. State, 256 A.3d 206 (Del. 2021).

§ 773. Rape in the first degree; class A felony.

NOTES TO DECISIONS

Analysis

Evidence.
— Sufficient.

Evidence.

— Sufficient.
Rational juror could find defendant guilty of attempted first-degree rape because: (1) the evidence included the child's testimony regarding what defendant did, that the child was under 12 years old and that defendant was more than 18 years old; (2) multiple witnesses, including defendant, testified there was an incident involving defendant and the family; and (3) it was within the jury's discretion to accept 1 witness' testimony and reject the conflicting testimony of other witnesses. Benson v. State, 242 A.3d 1085 (Del. 2020).

§ 778. Sexual abuse of a child by a person in a position of trust, authority or supervision in the first degree; penalties.

NOTES TO DECISIONS

Position of trust, authority or supervision.

Evidence of the relationship between defendant and a victim was sufficient to permit a finding that the State satisfied its burden of showing that defendant stood in a position of familial authority over the victim because: (1)

the victim testified that defendant was the victim's uncle; (2) the victim had known defendant all the victim's life, looked up to defendant and loved defendant; and (3) the victim confided in defendant when having problems in school or with the victim's parent. Cirwithian v. State, 252 A.3d 433 (Del. 2021).

SUBPART E
KIDNAPPING AND RELATED OFFENSES

§ 783. Kidnapping in the second degree; class C felony.

NOTES TO DECISIONS

Analysis

Offenses.
— Underlying.

Offenses.

— Underlying.

Where defendant was charged with first-degree rape and kidnapping, and pleaded guilty to second-degree rape and kidnapping, defendant was not erroneously sentenced to 20

years incarceration under 11 Del. C. § 4204(k) because: (1) although the plea agreement did not reference that statute, the record reflected that the plea was knowing, intelligent and voluntary; (2) the sentences for rape and kidnapping were appropriate and fell within the necessary statutory limits; and (3) the 11 Del. C. § 4204(k) condition was statutorily authorized. Bowden v. State, 256 A.3d 206 (Del. 2021).

§ 787. Trafficking an individual, forced labor and sexual servitude; class D felony; class C felony; class B felony; class A felony.

(a) For the purposes of this section, the following definitions shall apply:

(1) "Adult" has the meaning ascribed in § 302 of Title 1;

(2) "Coercion" means:

a. The use or threat of force against, abduction of, serious harm to, or physical restraint of an individual;

b. The use of a plan, pattern, or statement with intent to cause an individual to believe that failure to perform an act will result in the use of force against, abduction of, serious harm to, or physical restraint of an individual;

c. The abuse or threatened abuse of law or legal process;

d. Controlling or threatening to control an individual's access to a controlled substance enumerated in § 4714, § 4716, § 4718, § 4720 or § 4722 of Title 16;

e. The destruction of, taking of, or the threat to destroy or take an individual's identification document or other property;

f. Use of debt bondage;

g. The use of an individual's physical, cognitive disability or mental impairment, where such impairment has substantial adverse effects on the individual's cognitive or volitional functions; or

h. The commission of civil or criminal fraud;

(3) "Commercial sexual activity" means any sexual activity for which anything of value is given, promised to, or received by any person;

(4) "Debt bondage" means inducing an individual to provide:

a. Commercial sexual activity in payment toward or satisfaction of a real or purported debt; or

b. Labor or services in payment toward or satisfaction of a real or purported debt if:

          1. The reasonable value of the labor or services is not applied toward the liquidation of the debt; or

          2. The length of the labor or services is not limited and the nature of the labor or services is not defined;

(5) "Forced labor or services" means labor, as defined in this section, or services, as defined in this section, that are performed or provided by another person and are obtained or maintained through coercion as enumerated in paragraph (b)(1) of this section;

(6) "Human trafficking" means the commission of any of the offenses created in subsection (b) of this section;

(7) "Identification document" means a passport, driver's license, immigration document, travel document, or other government-issued identification document, including a document issued by a foreign government, whether actual or purported;

(8) "Labor or services" means activity having economic or financial value, including commercial sexual activity. Nothing in this definition should be construed to legitimize or legalize prostitution;

(9) "Maintain" means in relation to labor or services, to secure continued performance thereof, regardless of any initial agreement on the part of the victim to perform such type of service;

(10) "Minor" has the meaning ascribed in § 302 of Title 1;

(11) "Obtain" means in relation to labor or services, to secure performance thereof;

(12) "Serious harm" means harm, whether physical or nonphysical, including psychological, economic, or reputational, to an individual which would compel a reasonable individual of the same background and in the same circumstances to perform or continue to perform labor or services or sexual activity to avoid incurring the harm;

(13) "Sexual activity" means any of the sex-related acts enumerated in § 761 of this title, or in § 1342, § 1351, § 1352(1), § 1353(1), § 1354 or § 1355 of this title or sexually-explicit performances;

(14) "Sexually explicit performance" means a live public act or show, production of pornography, or the digital transfer of any of such, intended to arouse or satisfy the sexual desires or appeal to the prurient interest of viewers;

(15) "State" means a state of the United States, the District of Columbia, Puerto Rico, the United States Virgin Islands, or any territory or insular possession subject to the jurisdiction of the United States. The term includes an Indian tribe or band recognized by federal law or formally acknowledged by state; and

(16) "Victim" means a person who is subjected to the practices set forth in subsection (b) of this section or to conduct that would have constituted a violation of subsection (b) of this section had 79 Del. Laws, c. 276 been in effect when the conduct occurred, regardless of whether a perpetrator is identified, apprehended, prosecuted or convicted.

(b) *Prohibited activities.* — (1) *Trafficking an individual.* — A person is guilty of trafficking an individual if the person knowingly recruits, transports, harbors, receives, provides, obtains, isolates, maintains, advertises, solicits, or entices an individual in furtherance of forced labor in violation of paragraph (b)(2) of this section or sexual servitude in violation of paragraph (b)(3) of this section. Trafficking an individual is a class C felony unless the individual is a minor, in which case it is a class B felony.

(2) *Forced labor.* — A person is guilty of forced labor if the person knowingly uses coercion to compel an individual to provide labor or

services, except where such conduct is permissible under federal law or law of this State other than 79 Del. Laws, c. 276. Forced labor is a class C felony unless the individual is a minor, in which case it is a class B felony.

(3) *Sexual servitude.* — a. A person commits the offense of sexual servitude if the person knowingly:

1. Maintains or makes available a minor for the purpose of engaging the minor in commercial sexual activity; or

2. Uses coercion or deception to compel an adult to engage in commercial sexual activity.

b. Sexual servitude is a class C felony unless the individual is a minor, in which case it is a class B felony.

c. It is not a defense in a prosecution under paragraph (b)(3)a.1. of this section that the minor consented to engage in commercial sexual activity or that the defendant believed the minor was an adult.

(4) *Patronizing a victim of sexual servitude.* — A person is guilty of patronizing a victim of sexual servitude if the person knowingly gives, agrees to give, or offers to give anything of value so that the person may engage in commercial sexual activity with another person and the person knows that the other person is a victim of sexual servitude. Patronizing a victim of sexual servitude is a class D felony unless the victim of sexual servitude is a minor, in which case it is a class C felony. It is not a defense in a prosecution when the victim of sexual servitude is a minor that the minor consented to engage in commercial sexual activity or that the defendant believed the minor was an adult.

(5) *Trafficking of persons for use of body parts.* — A person is guilty of trafficking of persons for use of body parts when a person knowingly:

a. Recruits, entices, harbors, provides or obtains by any means, another person, intending or knowing that the person will have body parts removed for sale; or

b. Benefits, financially or by receiving anything of value, from participation in a venture which has engaged in an act described in violation of this section. Such person shall be guilty of a class A felony. Nothing contained herein shall be construed as prohibiting the donation of an organ by an individual at a licensed medical facility after giving an informed voluntary consent.

(6) *Aggravating circumstance.* — An aggravating circumstance during the commission of an offense under paragraphs (b)(1)-(3) of this section occurs when:

a. The person recruited, enticed, or obtained the victim from a shelter designed to serve victims of human trafficking, victims of domestic violence, victims of sexual assault, runaway youth, foster children, or the homeless; or

b. The person used or threatened use of force against, abduction of, serious harm to, or physical restraint of the victim.

If an aggravating circumstance occurred, the classification of the offense under paragraphs (b)(1)-(3) of this section is elevated by 1 felony grade higher than the underlying offense.

(c) *Organizational liability.* — (1) An organization may be prosecuted for an offense under this section pursuant to § 281 of this title (Criminal liability of organizations).

(2) The court may consider the severity of an organization's offense under this section and order penalties in addition to those otherwise provided for the offense, including:

a. A fine of not more than $25,000 per offense;

b. Disgorgement of profit from illegal activity in violation of this section; and

c. Debarment from state and local government contracts.

(d) *Restitution is mandatory under this section.* — (1) In addition to any other amount of loss identified, the court shall order restitution, including the greater of:

a. The gross income or value to the defendant of the victim's labor or services; or

b. The value of the victim's labor as guaranteed under the minimum wage and overtime provisions of the Fair Labor Standards Act (FLSA) (29 U.S.C. § 201 et seq.) or of Title 19, whichever is greater.

(2) The court shall order restitution under this subsection (d) even if the victim is unavailable to accept payment of restitution.

(3) If the victim is unavailable for 5 years from the date of the restitution order, the restitution ordered under this subsection (d) must be paid to the Victim Compensation Fund established under § 9016 of this title.

(e) *Forfeiture.* — (1) On motion, the court shall order a person convicted of an offense under paragraphs (b)(1)-(3) of this section to forfeit any interest in real or personal property that was used or intended to be used to commit or facilitate the commission of the offense or that constitutes or derives from proceeds that the person obtained, directly or indirectly, as a result of the offense.

(2) In any proceeding against real or personal property under this section, the owner may assert a defense, and has the burden of establishing, by a preponderance of the evidence, that the forfeiture is manifestly disproportional to the seriousness of the offense.

(3) Proceeds from the public sale or auction of property forfeited under this subsection must be distributed in the manner otherwise provided for the distribution of proceeds of judicial sales.

(f) *Admissibility of certain evidence.* — In a prosecution or civil action for damages under this section, evidence of a specific instance of the alleged victim's past sexual behavior, or reputation or opinion evidence of past sexual behavior of the alleged victim, is not admissible unless the evidence is:

(1) Admitted in accordance with §§ 3508 and 3509 of this title; or

(2) Offered by the prosecution in a criminal case to prove a pattern of trafficking by the defendant.

(g) *Special provisions regarding a minor.* — (1) A minor who has engaged in commercial sexual activity is presumed to be a neglected or abused child under § 901 et seq. of Title 10. Whenever a police officer has probable cause to believe that a minor has engaged in commercial sexual activity, the police officer shall make an immediate report to the Department of Services for Children, Youth and Their Families pursuant to § 901 et seq. of Title 16.

(2) A party to a juvenile delinquency proceeding in which a minor is charged with prostitution or loitering, or an attorney guardian ad litem or court-appointed special advocate appointed in a proceeding under § 901 et seq. of Title 10, may file a motion on behalf of a minor in a juvenile delinquency proceeding seeking to stay the juvenile delinquency proceedings. Such motion may be opposed by the Attorney General. The Family Court may consider such a motion and, in its discretion, may stay the juvenile delinquency proceeding indefinitely. Upon such motion, the Department of Services for Children, Youth and Their Families and/or the Family Court may identify and order available specialized services for the

minor that, in the opinion of the Department of Services for Children, Youth and Their Families or Family Court, are best suited to the needs of the juvenile. So long as the minor substantially complies with the requirement of services identified by the Department of Services for Children, Youth and Their Families and/or ordered by the Family Court, the Attorney General shall, upon motion, nolle prosequi the stayed charges no earlier than 1 year after the stay was imposed. Upon motion of the Attorney General that the minor has not substantially complied with the requirement of services identified by the Department of Services for Children, Youth and Their Families and/or ordered by the Family Court, the Family Court shall lift the stay for further proceedings in accordance with the regular course of such proceedings.

(h) *Defense to charge of prostitution or loitering.* — An individual charged with prostitution or loitering committed as a direct result of being a victim of human trafficking may assert as an affirmative defense that the individual is a victim of human trafficking.

(i) *Civil action.* — (1) A victim may bring a civil action against a person that commits an offense under subsection (b) of this section for compensatory damages, punitive damages, injunctive relief, and any other appropriate relief.

(2) In an action under this subsection, the court shall award a prevailing victim reasonable attorneys' fees and costs, including reasonable fees for expert witnesses.

(3) An action under this subsection must be commenced not later than 5 years after the later of the date on which the victim:

a. Was freed from the human trafficking situation; or

b. Attained 18 years of age.

(4) Damages awarded to the victim under this subsection for an item must be offset by any restitution paid to the victim pursuant to subsection (d) of this section for the same item.

(5) This subsection does not preclude any other remedy available to the victim under federal law or law of this State other than this section.

(j) *Application for pardon and petition to expunge; motion to vacate adjudication of delinquency or conviction and expungement record.* — (1) Notwithstanding any provision of Chapter 43 of this title or any other law to the contrary, a person arrested or convicted of any crime, except those deemed to be violent felonies pursuant to § 4201 of this title committed as a direct result of being a victim of human trafficking may file an application for a pardon pursuant to article VII of the Delaware Constitution and § 4361 et seq. of this title and may file a petition requesting expungement of such criminal record pursuant to § 4371 et seq. of this title.

(2) A person convicted or adjudicated delinquent of any crime, except those deemed to be violent felonies pursuant to § 4201 of this title, committed as a direct result of being a victim of human trafficking may file a motion in the court in which the adjudication of delinquency or conviction was obtained to vacate the adjudication or judgment of conviction. A motion filed under this paragraph must:

a. Be in writing;

b. Be sent to the Delaware Department of Justice;

c. [Repealed.]

d. Describe the evidence and provide copies of any official documents showing that the person is entitled to relief under this paragraph.

If the motion satisfies the foregoing requirements, the court shall hold a hearing on a motion, provided that the court may dismiss a motion without a hearing if the court finds that the motion fails to assert grounds on which relief may be granted. Official documentation of the person's status as a victim of this section, " trafficking in persons" , or "a severe form of trafficking" from a federal, state, or local government agency shall create a presumption that the person's participation in any crime, except those deemed to be violent felonies pursuant to § 4201 of this title, committed was a direct result of having been a victim of human trafficking but shall not be required for the court to grant a petition under this paragraph. If the petitioner can show to the satisfaction of the court that he or she is entitled to relief in a proceeding under this paragraph, the court shall grant the motion and, pursuant to this paragraph, enter an order vacating the adjudication of delinquency or judgment of conviction and dismissing the accusatory pleading, and may take such additional action as is appropriate in the circumstances or as justice requires.

(3) Notwithstanding any provisions of Chapter 43 of this title, Chapter 9 of Title 10, or any other law to the contrary, any person filing a motion under paragraph (j)(2) of this section in Superior Court or Family Court may also seek in that motion expungement of the criminal or juvenile record related to such conviction. If the court grants the motion to vacate the adjudication of delinquency or conviction under paragraph (j)(2) of this section and the movant also requested expungement, the court's order shall require expungement of the police and court records relating to the charge and conviction or adjudication of delinquency. Such order shall contain a statement that the expungement is ordered pursuant to this paragraph and, not withstanding any limitations to the contrary, that the provisions of § 4372(e), 4376 4377 of this title and § 1019 of Title 10 apply to such order.

(4) Notwithstanding any provision of Chapter 43 of this title or any other law to the contrary, upon granting the motion, the Court of Common Pleas shall provide Superior Court with the certified order granting the motion to vacate. Upon finding that the Court of Common Pleas entered an order under paragraph (j)(2) of this section, the Superior Court shall enter an order requiring expungement of the police and court records relating to the charge and conviction. Such order shall contain a statement that the expungement is ordered pursuant to this paragraph and, notwithstanding any limitations to the contrary, that the provisions of §§ 4372(e), 4376 and 4377 of this title apply to such order.

(k) The Human Trafficking Coordinating Council is hereby dissolved and reestablished as the Human Trafficking Interagency Coordinating Council to assume the functions of the Human Trafficking Coordinating Council and to administer and implement this chapter, and to perform such other responsibilities as may be entrusted to it by law.

(1) The Human Trafficking Interagency Coordinating Council shall consist of 24 members:

    a. Three representatives of the Judicial Branch, as appointed by the Chief Justice;

    b. A representative of the Department of Justice to be appointed by the Attorney General;

    c. A representative of the Office of Defense Services to be appointed by the Chief Defender;

    d. A representative of the law-enforcement community to be appointed by the Speaker of the Delaware House of Representatives;

e. A representative of the heath-care community to be appointed by the President Pro Tempore of the Delaware State Senate;

f. A representative of the Department of Health and Social Services to be appointed by the Secretary of the Department of Health and Social Services;

g. A representative of the Department of Labor to be appointed by the Secretary of Labor;

h. A representative of the Department of Services for the Children, Youth and Their Families to be appointed by the Secretary of the Department of Services for the Children, Youth and Their Families;

i. Four members who are advocates or persons who work with victims of human trafficking to be appointed by the Governor for a 3 year term and shall be eligible for reappointment. Members shall include representation from all 3 counties of the State.

j. The representative appointed to the Council by the Secretary of the Department of Health and Social Services shall serve as the temporary Chair of the Council to guide the initial organization of the council by setting a date, time, and place for the initial organizational meeting, and by supervising the preparation and distribution of the notice and agenda for the initial organizational meeting of the council. Members of the Council shall elect a Chair and a Vice Chair from among the members of the Council at the initial organizational meeting. Thereafter, the Chair and Vice Chair shall be elected annually from among the members.

k. A representative of the Delaware Department of Education to be appointed by the Secretary of the Department of Education.

l. A representative of the Division of Professional Regulation to be appointed by the Director of the Division of Professional Regulation.

m. Two members of the House of Representatives to be appointed by the Speaker of the House, 1 of which must be a member of the minority caucus.

n. Two members of the Senate to be appointed by the President Pro Tempore of the Senate, 1 of which must be a member of the minority caucus.

o. A representative of the Department of Transportation to be appointed by the Secretary of the Department of Transportation.

p. A representative from the Criminal Justice Council to be appointed by the Executive Director of the Criminal Justice Council.

q. A person who has been a victim of human trafficking to be appointed by the Governor for a 3 year term and shall be eligible for reappointment.

r. The Council may include a resident of any county who has prior experience in working with victims of human trafficking in a legal or advocacy capacity.

(2) The Council shall:

a. Develop a comprehensive plan to provide victims of human trafficking with services;

b. Effectuate coordination between agencies, departments and the courts with victims of human trafficking;

c. Collect and evaluate data on human trafficking in this State;

d. Promote public awareness about human trafficking, victim remedies and services, and trafficking prevention;

e. Create a public-awareness sign that contains the state and National Human Trafficking Resource Center hotline information;

f. Coordinate training on human trafficking prevention and victim services for state and local employees who may have recurring contact with victims or perpetrators; and

g. Conduct other appropriate activities.

(3) Meetings; quorum; officers; committees; procedure.

a. The Council shall meet at least 4 times per year. Thirteen members shall constitute a quorum.

b. The Chairperson shall have the duty to convene and preside over meetings of the Council and prepare an agenda for meetings. The Department of Health and Social Services shall provide the administrative support for the Council.

c. The Vice-Chair's duty shall be to act as Chair in the absence of the Chair.

d. The Council shall establish committees composed of Council members and other knowledgeable individuals, as it deems advisable, to assist in planning, policy, goal and priority recommendations and developing implementation plans to achieve the purposes of the Council.

e. The Council shall submit a written report of its activities and recommendations to the Governor, General Assembly and the Chief Justice of the Supreme Court at least once every year on or before September 15.

(*l*) *Display of public awareness sign; penalty for failure to display.* — (1) The Delaware Department of Transportation shall display a public-awareness sign required by this section in every transportation station, rest area, and welcome center in the State which is open to the public.

(2) A public awareness sign created under paragraph (k)(2)e. of this section shall be displayed at locations designated by the Council in a place that is clearly conspicuous and visible to employees. These locations shall include adult entertainment facilities, entities found to be maintaining a criminal nuisance involving prostitution under § 7104 of Title 10, job recruitment centers, hospitals, and emergency care providers. The Council shall approve a list of locations on an annual basis.

(3) The Delaware Department of Labor shall impose a fine of $300 per violation on an employer that knowingly fails to comply with paragraph (k)(2)e. of this section. The fine is the exclusive remedy for failure to comply.

(m) *Eligibility for services.* — (1) A victim of human trafficking is eligible for a benefit or service, which is available through the State and identified in the plan developed under paragraph (k)(2)a. of this section, including compensation under § 9009 of this title, regardless of immigration status.

(2) A minor engaged in commercial sexual activity is eligible for a benefit or service, which is available through the State and identified in the plan developed under paragraph (k)(2)a. of this section, regardless of immigration status.

(3) As soon as practicable after a first encounter with an individual who reasonably appears to a police officer to be a victim or a minor engaged in commercial sexual activity, the police officer shall notify the appropriate state or local agency, as identified in the plan developed under paragraph (k)(2)a. of this section, that the individual may be eligible for a benefit or service under this section.

(n) *Law-enforcement agency protocol.* — (1) On request from an individual who a police officer or prosecutor reasonably believes is a victim who is or has been subjected to a severe form of trafficking or criminal offense required for the individual to qualify for a nonimmigrant T or U visa under 8 U.S.C. § 1101(a)(15)(T), as amended from time to time, or 8 U.S.C. § 1101(a)(15)(U), as amended from time to time, or for continued presence, under 22 U.S.C. § 7105(c)(3), as amended from time to time, the police officer or prosecutor, as soon as practicable after receiving the request, shall request that a certifying official in his or her law-enforcement agency complete, sign, and give to the individual the Form I-914B or Form I-918B provided by the United States Citizenship and Immigration Services on its Internet website, and ask a federal law-enforcement officer to request continued presence.

(2) If the law-enforcement agency having responsibility under paragraph (n)(1) of this section determines that an individual does not meet the requirements for such agency to comply with paragraph (n)(1) of this section, that agency shall inform the individual of the reason and that the individual may make another request under paragraph (n)(1) of this section and submit additional evidence satisfying the requirements.

(o) Nothing contained in this section shall preclude a separate charge, conviction and sentence for any other crime set forth in this title, or in the Delaware Code.

History.
76 Del. Laws, c. 125, § 1; 70 Del. Laws, c. 186, § 1; 79 Del. Laws, c. 276, § 1; 80 Del. Laws, c. 26, § 3; 81 Del. Laws, c. 110, § 1; 81 Del. Laws, c. 174, § 1; 81 Del. Laws, c. 211, § 1; 82 Del. Laws, c. 60, § 1; 82 Del. Laws, c. 83, § 8; 83 Del. Laws, c. 44, § 1; 83 Del. Laws, c. 45, § 1.

Effect of amendments.
83 Del. Laws, c. 44, effective June 15, 2021, substituted "24" for "15" in the introductory paragraph of (k)(1); added (k)(1)l.-(k)(1)r.; and substituted "Thirteen" for "Seven" in (k)(3)a.

83 Del. Laws, c. 45, effective June 15, 2021, added "adjudication of delinquency or" in the introductory paragraph of (j), once each in the first sentence of the introductory paragraph and final sentence of the concluding paragraph of (j)(2) and following "vacate the" in the second sentence of (j)(3); in the first sentence of the introductory paragraph of (j)(2), added "or adjudicated delinquent" and "adjudication or"; and, in (j)(3), in the first sentence added "Chapter 9 of Title 10" and "or juvenile", and added "or adjudication of delinquency" in the second sentence.

SUBCHAPTER III
OFFENSES INVOLVING PROPERTY
SUBPART B
CRIMINAL TRESPASS AND BURGLARY

§ 827. Multiple offenses.

A person may be convicted both of burglary and of the offense which it was the purpose of the person's unlawful entry to commit or for an attempt to commit that offense. A person may be convicted both of home invasion burglary first degree and any of the underlying offenses designated in § 826(b) of this title.

History.
11 Del. C. 1953, § 827; 58 Del. Laws, c. 497, § 1; 70 Del. Laws, c. 186, § 1; 78 Del. Laws, c. 252, § 6; 82 Del. Laws, c. 215, § 1; 83 Del. Laws, c. 37, § 6.

Effect of amendments.
83 Del. Laws, c. 37, effective June 3, 2021, added the final sentence.

SUBPART C
ROBBERY

§ 831. Robbery in the second degree; class E or D felony.

NOTES TO DECISIONS

Analysis

Offenses.
— Lesser included.

Offenses.
— Lesser included.
Victim's inconsistencies about whether the

implement was either a corkscrew or a knife, and whether defendant put it to the victim's neck or merely threatened the victim, did not further defendant's argument that the evidence supported a second-degree robbery conviction; counsel was not ineffective in failing to request

a lesser-included offense of second-degree robbery, in that such a request would have been denied. State v. Pinkston, — A.3d —, 2020 Del. Super. LEXIS 2833 (Del. Super. Ct. Oct. 9, 2020).

§ 832. Robbery in the first degree; class B felony.

NOTES TO DECISIONS

Analysis

Deadly weapon.
— Analysis.

Deadly weapon.

— Analysis.

Because the specific implement employed by defendant was a corkscrew wine opener with a knife on 1 end, any confusion about whether

defendant displayed the blade end of the knife or the sharp end of the corkscrew was of no moment for the purpose of analyzing defendant's culpability; display of either end would support defendant's conviction for first-degree robbery if the jury believed that defendant utilized the opener to take money. State v. Pinkston, — A.3d —, 2020 Del. Super. LEXIS 2833 (Del. Super. Ct. Oct. 9, 2020).

SUBCHAPTER V

OFFENSES RELATING TO CHILDREN AND VULNERABLE ADULTS

SUBPART A

CHILD WELFARE; SEXUAL OFFENSES

§ 1100. Definitions relating to children.

NOTES TO DECISIONS

Abuse.

Court properly found that defendant committed child abuse because defendant's conduct, which included dragging and hitting a child with a closed fist, was proven to be intentional, not accidental, and caused the child to experience pain; testimony included not only that

defendant pummeled the child with defendant's fists, but that the child was in a fetal position as defendant was doing so, eventually crawling to get away from defendant. State v. D— R, — A.3d —, 2019 Del. Fam. Ct. LEXIS 70 (Del. Fam. Ct. May 15, 2019).

§ 1102. Endangering the welfare of a child; class A misdemeanor; class E or G felony.

NOTES TO DECISIONS

Appeals.

Even viewing the evidence most favorably to the State, where the predicate offense of terroristic threatening was dropped from the charges before the case was submitted to the jury, the verdict of guilty of endangering the welfare of a

child was inescapably inconsistent; therefore, the jury's verdict of guilty as to the charge of endangering the welfare of a child had to be vacated. State v. Wilkerson, — A.3d —, 2021 Del. Super. LEXIS 582 (Del. Super. Ct. Sept. 7, 2021).

SUBPART B

SALE AND DISTRIBUTION OF TOBACCO PRODUCTS

§ 1123. Liability of employer.

(a) If a sale or distribution of any tobacco product or tobacco substitute or coupon is made in violation of § 1116, § 1118, § 1119, or § 1120 of this title, the owner, proprietor, franchisee, store manager or other person in charge of the establishment where the violation occurred shall be guilty of the violation and shall be subject to the fine only if the retail licensee has received written notice of the provisions of §§ 1116 through 1121 of this title by the Department of Safety and Homeland Security. For purposes of determining the liability of a person who owns or controls franchises or business operations in multiple locations, for a second or subsequent violation of this subpart, each individual franchise or business location shall be deemed a separate establishment.

(b) Notwithstanding any other provision of this subpart, in any prosecution for a violation of § 1116, § 1118, or § 1120 of this title, the owner, proprietor, franchisee, store manager, or other person in charge of the establishment where the alleged violation occurred has an affirmative defense if the person or entity can establish that before the date of the violation, the person or entity did all of the following:

(1) Adopted and enforced a written policy against selling tobacco products or tobacco substitutes to individuals under 21 years of age.

(2) Informed its employees of the applicable laws regarding the sale of tobacco products or tobacco substitutes to individuals under 21 years of age.

(3) Required employees to sign a form indicating that they have been informed of and understand the written policy required under this subsection.

(4) Required employees to verify the age of tobacco product or tobacco substitute customers by means of photographic identification.

(5) Established and enforced disciplinary sanctions for noncompliance.

(c) The affirmative defense established in subsection (b) of this section may be used by an owner, proprietor, franchisee, store manager, or other person in charge of the establishment no more than 1 time at each location within any 36-month period.

History.
70 Del. Laws, c. 318, § 4; 72 Del. Laws, c. 69, § 1; 74 Del. Laws, c. 110, § 138; 79 Del. Laws, c. 249, § 1; 82 Del. Laws, c. 10, § 8; 83 Del. Laws, c. 37, § 7.

Effect of amendments.
83 Del. Laws, c. 37, effective June 3, 2021, in the introductory paragraph of (b), added a comma following "manager" and following the second occurrence of "violation", substituted "has" for "shall have" following "occurred", "the" for "such" following "defense if" and "before" for "prior to", and added "did all of the following"; substituted "individuals" for "persons" in (b)(1) and (2); substituted a period for a semicolon in (b)(1)-(3) and for "; and" in (b)(4); and substituted "under this subsection" for "herein" in (b)(3).

§ 1125. Unannounced inspections; reporting; enforcement.

(a) The Department of Safety and Homeland Security or its delegates shall conduct annual, random, unannounced inspections at locations where tobacco products or tobacco substitutes are sold or distributed to test and ensure compliance with and enforcement of §§ 1116 through 1120 of this title.

(b) An individual under the age of 21 may be enlisted by the Department of Safety and Homeland Security or its delegates to test compliance with and enforcement of §§ 1116 through 1120 of this title, provided however, that the individual may be used only under the direct supervision of the Department of Safety and Homeland Security, its employees or delegates and only where written parental consent has been provided for an individual under the age of 18.

(c) Participation in the inspection and enforcement activities of this section by an individual under 21 years of age shall not constitute a violation of this subpart for the individual under 21 years of age, and the individual under 21 years of age is immune from prosecution thereunder, or under any other provision of law prohibiting the purchase of these products by an individual under 21 years of age.

(d) The Department of Safety and Homeland Security shall adopt and publish guidelines for the use of individuals under 21 years of age in inspections conducted under this section.

(e) The Department of Safety and Homeland Security may enter into an agreement with any local law-enforcement agency for delegation of the inspection and enforcement activities of this section within the local law-enforcement agency's jurisdiction. The contract shall require the inspection and enforcement activities of the local law-enforcement agency to comply with this subpart and with all applicable laws.

(f) In cases where inspection and enforcement activities have been delegated to a local law-enforcement agency pursuant to this section, any inspection or enforcement by the Department of Safety and Homeland Security in the jurisdiction of the local law-enforcement agency shall be coordinated with the local law enforcement agency.

(g) The Delaware Department of Health and Social Services shall annually submit to the Secretary of the United States Department of Health and Human Services the report required by § 1926 of the federal Public Health Service Act (42 U.S.C. § 300x-26). A copy of this report shall be available to the Governor and the General Assembly.

History.
70 Del. Laws, c. 318, § 4; 74 Del. Laws, c. 110, § 138; 79 Del. Laws, c. 249, § 1; 82 Del. Laws, c. 10, § 10; 83 Del. Laws, c. 37, § 8.

Effect of amendments.
83 Del. Laws, c. 37, effective June 3, 2021, in

(a), substituted "conduct" for "shall be responsible for conducting" and "§§ 1116 through 1120" for "§§ 1116-1120 and 1124 [repealed]"; and deleted "and 1124 [repealed]" following "1120" in (b).

§ 1126. Jurisdiction.

The Justice of the Peace Court has jurisdiction over violations of this subpart, except in the instance of violations by an individual who has not attained the age of 18, in which case the Family Court has jurisdiction.

History.
70 Del. Laws, c. 318, § 4; 83 Del. Laws, c. 37, § 9.

Effect of amendments.
83 Del. Laws, c. 37, effective June 3, 2021,

substituted "Justice" for "Justices", "has" for "shall have" preceding "jurisdiction" in two places, and "an individual" for "a person".

SUBCHAPTER VI

OFFENSES AGAINST PUBLIC ADMINISTRATION

SUBPART B
ABUSE OF OFFICE

§ 1213. Definitions relating to abuse of office.

(a) The definitions under § 1209 of this title apply to §§ 1211 and 1212 of this title.

(b) As used in § 1211 of this title:

(1) "Protective hairstyle" includes braids, locks, and twists.

(2) "Race" includes traits historically associated with race, including hair texture and a protective hairstyle.

History.
11 Del. C. 1953, § 1213; 58 Del. Laws, c. 497, § 1; 83 Del. Laws, c. 13, § 7.

Effect of amendments.
83 Del. Laws, c. 13, effective April 13, 2021,

in (a), substituted "The definitions under" for "In §§ 1211 and 1212 of this title, the definitions given in" and added "apply to §§ 1211 and 1212 of this title"; and added (b).

SUBPART F
OFFENSES RELATING TO JUDICIAL AND SIMILAR PROCEEDINGS

§ 1271A. Criminal contempt of a domestic violence protective order or lethal violence protective order; class A misdemeanor; class F felony.

NOTES TO DECISIONS

Analysis

Evidence.
— Sufficient.

Evidence.

— Sufficient.

Sufficient evidence supported the jury's finding that defendant's violation of a domestic violence protective order occurred in Delaware because: (1) the victim, defendant's ex-spouse, received the offending messages while at work in Delaware; and (2) both messages were sent during ordinary work hours, establishing a substantial likelihood that defendant intended that the victim would receive them in Delaware. Cogan v. State, 247 A.3d 229 (Del. 2021).

SUBCHAPTER VII
OFFENSES AGAINST PUBLIC HEALTH, ORDER AND DECENCY

SUBPART A
RIOT, DISORDERLY CONDUCT AND RELATED OFFENSES

§ 1304. Hate crimes; class A misdemeanor, class G felony, class F felony, class E felony, class D felony, class C felony, class B felony, class A felony.

(a) Any person who commits, or attempts to commit, any crime as defined by the laws of this State, and who intentionally:

(1) Commits said crime for the purpose of interfering with the victim's free exercise or enjoyment of any right, privilege or immunity protected by the First Amendment to the United States Constitution, or commits said crime because the victim has exercised or enjoyed said rights; or

(2) Selects the victim because of the victim's race, religion, color, disability, sexual orientation, gender identity, national origin or ancestry, shall be guilty of a hate crime. For purposes of this section:

a. "Gender identity" means a gender-related identity, appearance, expression, or behavior of a person, regardless of the person's assigned sex at birth.

b. "Protective hairstyle" includes braids, locks, and twists.

c. "Race" includes traits historically associated with race, including hair texture and a protective hairstyle.

d. "Sexual orientation" means heterosexuality, bisexuality, or homosexuality.

(b) Hate crimes shall be punished as follows:

(1) If the underlying offense is a violation or unclassified misdemeanor, the hate crime shall be a class A misdemeanor;

(2) If the underlying offense is a class A, B, or C misdemeanor, the hate crime shall be a class G felony;

(3) If the underlying offense is a class C, D, E, F, or G felony, the hate crime shall be 1 grade higher than the underlying offense;

(4) If the underlying offense is a class A or B felony, the hate crime shall be the same grade as the underlying offense, and the minimum sentence of imprisonment required for the underlying offense shall be doubled.

History.

70 Del. Laws, c. 138, § 1; 70 Del. Laws, c. 186, § 1; 71 Del. Laws, c. 175, §§ 1, 2; 79 Del. Laws, c. 47, § 15; 83 Del. Laws, c. 13, § 8; 83 Del. Laws, c. 195, § 3.

Effect of amendments.

83 Del. Laws, c. 13, effective April 13, 2021, rewrote (a)(2).

83 Del. Laws, c. 195, effective September 17, 2021, attempted to make a change which could not be implemented, due to an intervening amendment of the section.

§ 1325. Cruelty to animals; class A misdemeanor; class F felony.

(a) For the purpose of this section, the following words and phrases shall include, but not be limited to, the meanings respectively ascribed to them as follows:

(1) "Abandonment" includes completely forsaking or deserting an animal originally under one's custody without making reasonable arrangements for custody of that animal to be assumed by another person.

(2) "Animal" shall not include fish, crustacea or molluska.

(3) "Cruel" includes every act or omission to act whereby unnecessary or unjustifiable physical pain or suffering is caused or permitted.

(4) "Cruel mistreatment" includes any treatment whereby unnecessary or unjustifiable physical pain or suffering is caused or permitted.

(5) "Cruel neglect" includes neglect of an animal, which is under the care and control of the neglector, whereby pain or suffering is caused to the animal or abandonment of any domesticated animal by its owner or custodian. By way of example, cruel neglect shall also include allowing an animal to live in unsanitary conditions, such as keeping an animal where the animal's own excrement is not removed from the animal's living area and/or other living conditions which are injurious to the animal's health.

(6) "Cruelty to animals" includes mistreatment of any animal or neglect of any animal under the care and control of the neglector, whereby unnecessary or unjustifiable physical pain or suffering is caused. By way of example, "cruelty to animals" includes the following: unjustifiable beating of an animal; overworking an animal; tormenting an animal; abandonment of an animal; tethering of any dog for 9 consecutive hours or more in any 24-hour period, except on any farm; tethering any dog for any amount of time if the dog is under 4 months of age or is a nursing mother while the offspring are present, except on any farm; and failure to feed properly or give proper shelter or veterinary care to an animal.

(7) "Custody" includes the responsibility for the welfare of an animal subject to one's care and control whether one owns it or not.A person who provides sterilization or care to a free-roaming cat that lacks discernible owner identification is not deemed to have "custody," "care," or "control" of the cat for purposes of this section.

(8) "Farm" means any place that meets the 2017 USDA Federal Census of Agriculture definition of farm: "any place from which $1,000 or more of agricultural products were produced and sold, or normally would have been sold, during the census year".

(9) "Person" includes any individual, partnership, corporation or association living and/or doing business in the State.

(10) "Proper feed" includes providing each animal with daily food and water of sufficient quality and quantity to prevent unnecessary or unjustifiable physical pain or suffering by the animal.

(11) "Proper shelter" includes providing each animal with adequate shelter from the weather elements as required to prevent unnecessary or unjustifiable physical pain or suffering by the animal.

(12) "Proper veterinary care" includes providing each animal with

veterinary care sufficient to prevent unnecessary or unjustifiable physical pain or suffering by the animal.

(13) "Serious injury" shall include any injury to any animal which creates a substantial risk of death, or which causes prolonged impairment of health or prolonged loss or impairment of the function of any bodily organ.

(14) "Tethering" shall include fastening or restraining with a rope, chain, cord, or similar device creating a fixed radius; tethering does not include walking a dog on a leash, regardless of the dog's age.

(b) A person is guilty of cruelty to animals when the person intentionally or recklessly:

(1) Subjects any animal to cruel mistreatment; or

(2) Subjects any animal in the person's custody to cruel neglect; or

(3) Kills or injures any animal belonging to another person without legal privilege or consent of the owner; or

(4) Cruelly or unnecessarily kills or injures any animal. This section does not apply to the killing of any animal normally or commonly raised as food for human consumption, provided that such killing is not cruel. A person acts unnecessarily if the act is not required to terminate an animal's suffering, to protect the life or property of the actor or another person or if other means of disposing of an animal exist which would not impair the health or well-being of that animal; or,

(5) Captures, detains, transports, removes or delivers any animal known to be a pet or owned or unowned companion animal, or any other animal of scientific, environmental, economic or cultural value, under false pretenses to any public or private animal shelter, veterinary clinic or other facility, or otherwise causes the same through acts of deception or misrepresentation of the circumstances and disposition of any such animal.

(6) Confines an animal unattended in a standing or parked motor vehicle in which the temperature is either so high or so low as to endanger the health or safety of the animal. A law-enforcement officer, animal welfare officer, or firefighter who has probable cause to believe that an animal is confined in a motor vehicle under conditions that are likely to cause suffering, injury, or death to the animal may use reasonable force to remove the animal left in the vehicle in violation of this provision. A person removing an animal under this section shall use reasonable means to contact the owner. If the person is unable to contact the owner, the person may take the animal to an animal shelter and must leave written notice bearing his or her name and office, and the address of the location where the animal can be claimed. This provision shall not apply to the legal transportation of horses, cattle, swine, sheep, poultry, or other agricultural animals in motor vehicles designed to transport such animals. The owner of the vehicle from which the animal is rescued and the owner of the animal rescued are not liable for injuries suffered by the person rescuing the animal.

Paragraphs (b)(1), (2) and (4) of this section are inapplicable to accepted veterinary practices and activities carried on for scientific research.

Cruelty to animals is a class A misdemeanor, unless the person intentionally kills or causes serious injury to any animal in violation of paragraph (b)(4) of this section or unless the animal is killed or seriously injured as a result of any action prohibited by paragraph (b)(5) of this section, in which case it is a class F felony.

(c) Any person convicted of a misdemeanor violation of this section shall be prohibited from owning or possessing any animal for 5 years after said conviction, except for animals grown, raised or produced within the State for resale, or for sale of a product thereof, where the person has all necessary licenses for such sale or resale, and receives at least 25 percent of the person's annual gross income from such sale or resale. Any person convicted of a second or subsequent misdemeanor violation of this section shall be prohibited from owning or possessing any animal for 5 years after said conviction without exception.

A violation of this subsection is subject to a fine in the amount of $1,000 in any court of competent jurisdiction and to forfeiture of any animal illegally owned in accordance with the provisions of § 3035F of Title 16.

(d) Any person convicted of a felony violation of this section shall be prohibited from owning or possessing any animal for 15 years after said conviction, except for animals grown, raised or produced within the State for resale, or for sale of a product thereof, where the person has all necessary licenses for such sale or resale, and receives at least 25 percent of the person's annual gross income from such sale or resale. Any person convicted of a second or subsequent felony violation of this section shall be prohibited from owning or possessing any animal for 15 years after said conviction without exception.

A violation of this subsection is subject to a fine in the amount of $5,000 in any court of competent jurisdiction and to forfeiture of any animal illegally owned in accordance with the provisions of § 3035F of Title 16.

(e) Any trained and certified animal welfare officer of the Department of Health and Social Service's Office of Animal Welfare or the Department of Agriculture may impound an animal owned or possessed in apparent violation of this section, consistent with § 3035F of Title 16.

(f) This section shall not apply to the lawful hunting or trapping of animals as provided by law.

(g) Notwithstanding any provision to the contrary, for a first offense misdemeanor violation of this section relating to animals left in motor vehicles or the tethering of dogs, a warning shall be issued.

(h) Exclusive jurisdiction of offenses under this section relating to animals left in motor vehicles or the tethering of dogs shall be in the Superior Court.

History.

11 Del. C. 1953, § 1325; 58 Del. Laws, c. 497, § 1; 62 Del. Laws, c. 71, §§ 1, 2; 63 Del. Laws, c. 260, § 1; 64 Del. Laws, c. 196, §§ 1-3; 67 Del. Laws, c. 130, § 8; 69 Del. Laws, c. 280, §§ 1, 2; 70 Del. Laws, c. 60, § 1; 70 Del. Laws, c. 186, § 1; 72 Del. Laws, c. 75, § 1; 73 Del. Laws, c. 182, §§ 1, 2; 73 Del. Laws, c. 238, §§ 1, 2; 78 Del. Laws, c. 390, §§ 1, 2; 79 Del. Laws, c. 375, § 4; 80 Del. Laws, c. 156, §§ 1, 2; 80 Del. Laws, c. 200, § 3; 80 Del. Laws, c. 248, § 2; 81 Del. Laws, c. 450, § 1; 82 Del. Laws, c. 238, § 3; 83 Del. Laws, c. 158, § 1.

Effect of amendments.

83 Del. Laws, c. 158, effective September 15, 2021, in (a)(6), substituted "example, 'cruelty to animals' includes the following" for "example this includes", made a related stylistic change, and added a comma following "period".

SUBPART E
OFFENSES INVOLVING DEADLY WEAPONS AND DANGEROUS INSTRUMENTS

§ 1442. Carrying a concealed deadly weapon; class G felony; class D felony.

NOTES TO DECISIONS

Double jeopardy.

Defendant was not entitled to a correction of sentence because: (1) 3 separate convictions and sentences for 1 episode of possessing a loaded handgun did not violate constitutional or double jeopardy protections; (2) defendant's convictions for possession of a firearm by a person prohibited (PFBPP), possession of ammunition by a person prohibited (PABPP), and carrying a concealed deadly weapon-firearm (CCDW) were proper because the elements to support a conviction for CCDW were different from those elements needed to support PFBPP and PABPP; and (3) though CCDW, PFBPP and

PABPP could be completed with a single act of handling a loaded firearm, each crime was objectively susceptible to independent commis-sion and proof. State v. Ryle, — A.3d —, 2021 Del. Super. LEXIS 452 (Del. Super. Ct. June 2, 2021).

§ 1448. Possession and purchase of deadly weapons by persons prohibited; penalties.

NOTES TO DECISIONS

Analysis

Double jeopardy.
Evidence.
— Sufficient.
Minors.
Sentence.
— Enhancement.
— Habitual offender.
— Not excessive.

Double jeopardy.

Defendant was not entitled to a correction of sentence because: (1) 3 separate convictions and sentences for 1 episode of possessing a loaded handgun did not violate constitutional or double jeopardy protections; (2) defendant's convictions for possession of a firearm by a person prohibited (PFBPP), possession of ammunition by a person prohibited (PABPP), and carrying a concealed deadly weapon-firearm (CCDW) were proper because the elements to support a conviction for CCDW were different from those elements needed to support PFBPP and PABPP; and (3) though CCDW, PFBPP and PABPP could be completed with a single act of handling a loaded firearm, each crime was objectively susceptible to independent commission and proof. State v. Ryle, — A.3d —, 2021 Del. Super. LEXIS 452 (Del. Super. Ct. June 2, 2021).

Evidence.

— Sufficient.

Where defendant had previously been convicted of a felony and pleaded guilty in federal court to knowingly possessing a firearm, these facts were sufficient to establish that defendant committed the state offense of possession of a firearm by a person prohibited; that the sentencing guidelines for the 2 offenses differed was immaterial. State v. Goodman, — A.3d —, 2021 Del. Super. LEXIS 369 (Del. Super. Ct. Apr. 29, 2021), aff'd, — A.3d —, 2021 Del. LEXIS 273 (Del. 2021).

Minors.

Respondent minor was given credit for time served because the residential alternative to detention (RAD) facility at which he had been housed met the definition of "other institutional confinement;" the RAD was a staff-secured facility which had placed the respondent under 24-hour supervision and provided treatment which was rehabilitative in nature. State v. M.D., — A.3d —, 2020 Del. Fam. Ct. LEXIS 26 (Del. Fam. Ct. May 21, 2020).

Sentence.

— Enhancement.

Superior Court properly resentenced defendant to 15 years at supervision Level V, for possession of a firearm by a person prohibited because: (1) while defendant contended that the sentencing judge erred by failing to set forth on the record reasons for deviating from the "presumptive sentence" adopted by the Sentencing Accountability Commission, the statute specifically referred to the "presumptive sentence;" (2) the presumptive sentence in defendant's case, a class C felony, was up to 30 months at Level V; and (3) the sentence imposed could be easily explained by reference to the guidelines for an aggravated sentence based upon prior criminal history. Gibson v. State, 244 A.3d 989 (Del. 2020).

— Habitual offender.

Where defendant was convicted of the violent felony of first-degree burglary in 2003, defendant's subsequent 2007 federal weapons conviction constituted an additional violent felony; having been convicted of 2 violent felonies prior to a guilty plea to manslaughter in 2018, defendant's designation as a habitual offender was legal and survived a motion to correct sentence. State v. Goodman, — A.3d —, 2021 Del. Super. LEXIS 369 (Del. Super. Ct. Apr. 29, 2021), aff'd, — A.3d —, 2021 Del. LEXIS 273 (Del. 2021).

— Not excessive.

Defendant's request for a Level V reduction under Super. Ct. Crim. R. 35(b) would violate the 10-year minimum required by 11 Del. C. § 1448(e)(1)(c); the motion was filed more than 4.5 years after defendant was sentenced, with defendant's underlying medical conditions and exposure to COVID-19 additionally not constituting extraordinary circumstances. State v. Dickerson, — A.3d —, 2021 Del. Super. LEXIS 453 (Del. Super. Ct. June 4, 2021).

PART II

CRIMINAL PROCEDURE GENERALLY

CHAPTER 19
ARREST AND COMMITMENT; FRESH PURSUIT
SUBCHAPTER I
ARREST AND COMMITMENT

§ 1902. Questioning and detaining suspects.

NOTES TO DECISIONS

Informant.

Defendant's detention was reasonable, did not constitute a violation of constitutional rights and allowed for the lawful protective search of defendant's person for weapons because: (1) it was reasonable for an officer to suspect that an informant's tip was credible and that defendant was armed or engaged in criminal activity; (2) according to the tip, an individual reportedly possessed a weapon in a crowded convenience store; and (3) defendant reacted to a lawful inquiry in a way that could be interpreted as aggressive. Diggs v. State, 2021 Del. LEXIS 241 (Del. July 27, 2021).

§ 1903. Searching questioned person for weapon.

NOTES TO DECISIONS

Analysis

Reasonable ground.
— Found.

Reasonable ground.

— Found.

Defendant's detention was reasonable, did not constitute a violation of constitutional rights and allowed for the lawful protective search of defendant's person for weapons because: (1) it was reasonable for an officer to suspect that an informant's tip was credible and that defendant was armed or engaged in criminal activity; (2) according to the tip, an individual reportedly possessed a weapon in a crowded convenience store; and (3) defendant reacted to a lawful inquiry in a way that could be interpreted as aggressive. Diggs v. State, 2021 Del. LEXIS 241 (Del. July 27, 2021).

CHAPTER 21

RELEASE OF PERSONS ACCUSED OF CRIMES

§ 2107. Determining the amount of bail [Effective until fulfillment of the contingency in 83 Del. Laws, c. 72, § 3].

(a) In determining the amount of bail to be required to be posted as surety under § 2105 of this title or to be required for a conditions of release bond not guaranteed by financial terms, the court shall not require oppressive bail but shall require such bail as reasonably will assure the reappearance of the defendant, compliance with the conditions set forth in the bond, and the safety of the community. In fixing the amount, the court shall also take into consideration the criteria set forth in § 2105(b) of this title.

(b) In any event, if a defendant is charged with an offense punishable by fine only, the amount of the bail shall not exceed double the amount of the maximum fine for each charge. When a defendant has been convicted of an offense and only a fine has been imposed as the sentence of the court, the amount of bail shall not exceed double the amount of the fine.

(c) Notwithstanding any provision of this title to the contrary, for a defendant charged with committing:

(1) Any Title 11 class A felony.

(2) Abuse of a pregnant female in the first degree, in violation of § 606 of this title.

(3) Strangulation, in violation of § 607 of this title.

(4) Assault in the second degree, in violation of § 612 of this title.

(5) Assault in the first degree, in violation of § 613 of this title.

(6) Manslaughter, in violation of § 632 of this title.

(7) Murder of a child by abuse or neglect in the second degree, in violation of § 633 of this title.

(8) Rape in the fourth degree, in violation of § 770(a)(1) or (a)(3) of this title.

(9) Rape in the third degree, in violation of § 771 of this title.

(10) Rape in the second degree, in violation of § 772 of this title.

(11) Continuous sexual abuse of a child, in violation of § 776 of this title.

(12) Sex offender unlawful sexual conduct against a child, in violation of § 777A of this title.

(13) Sexual abuse of a child by a person in a position of trust, authority or supervision in the first degree, in violation of § 778 of this title.

(14) Kidnapping in the first degree, in violation of § 783A of this title.

(15) Trafficking an individual; forced labor; sexual servitude, in violation of § 787(b)(1)–(3) of this title.

(16) Sexual servitude (victim is a minor), in violation of § 787(b)(3) of this title.

(17) Arson in the first degree, in violation of § 803 of this title.

(18) Burglary first degree, in violation of § 826 of this title.

(19) Robbery in the first degree, in violation of § 832 of this title.

(20) Child abuse in the first degree, in violation of § 1103B of this title.

(21) Sexual exploitation of a child, in violation of § 1108 of this title.

(22) Unlawful dealing in child pornography, in violation of § 1109 of this title.

(23) Sexual solicitation of a child, in violation of § 1112A(h) of this title.

(24) Promoting sexual solicitation of a child, in violation of § 1112B(g) of this title.

(25) Escape after conviction in violation of § 1253 of this title.

(26) Stalking, in violation of § 1312 of this title.

(27) Possession of a deadly weapon during commission of a felony, in violation of § 1447 of this title.

(28) Possession of a firearm during commission of a felony, in violation of § 1447A of this title.

(29) Possession of a firearm by persons prohibited, in violation of § 1448(a)(1), (a)(4), (a)(6), or (a)(7) of this title.

(30) Racketeering, in violation of § 1503 of this title.

(31) Aggravated act of intimidation, in violation of § 3533 of this title.

(32) Any violent felony as defined by § 4201(c) of this title, allegedly committed while defendant is pending adjudication on a previously charged violent felony.

(33) Any violent felony as defined by § 4201(c) of this title, allegedly committed against a petitioner with an active protection from abuse order against the defendant.

(34) Any violent felony as defined by § 4201(c) of this title, allegedly committed against a victim while the defendant is pending adjudication on

a previously charged domestic violence offense as defined by § 1041(2) of Title 10, allegedly committed against the same victim.

(35) Any domestic violence offense as defined by § 1041(2) of Title 10, allegedly committed while defendant is pending adjudication on a previously charged violent felony as defined by § 4201(c) of this title, allegedly committed against the same victim.

(36) Felony noncompliance with bond, in violation of § 2109(c)(1) or 2113(c)(1) of this title and involving a violent felony offense as defined by § 4201(c) of this title.

(37) Felony domestic violence offenses as defined by § 1041(2) of Title 10 and causing physical injury as defined by § 222(23) of this title or serious physical injury as defined by § 222(26) of this title.

(38) Drug dealing (Tier 3), in violation of § 4752 of title 16.

the presumption is that the court will set conditions of release bond guaranteed by financial terms in an amount within or above the guidelinespublished by the Delaware Sentencing Accountability Commission (SENTAC) for that offense and secured by cash only.

(d) In any case where a court sets bail pursuant to the presumption within subsection (c) of this section, a court of competent jurisdiction may, consistent with Chapter 21 of this title and court rules, review bail to consider whether bail in a different amount or with a different security is appropriate to reasonably ensure the reappearance of the defendant, compliance with the conditions set forth in the bond, and the safety of the community. The court may modify the defendant's bail in accordance with its findings and determinations at the hearing.

(e) The court shall document the reason(s) for setting bail at a particular amount and level, whether cash, secured, or unsecured, or for modifying bail under subsection (d) of this section.

(f) In any case where a court sets bail for an offense listed in subsection (c) of this section, the court shall require the defendant to relinquish any firearms in their possession.

(g) In addition to the information required in the annual report established in § 2114(i) of this title, the Criminal Justice Council shall include information of the following in the aggregate and disaggregated by race, gender, and zip code of:

(1) Rates of defendants' eligibility under subsection (c) of this section.

(2) Rates of initial detention.

(3) Rates of detention throughout the pretrial period.

(4) Average length of stay from arrest to adjudication.

History.

11 Del. C. 1953, § 2107; 56 Del. Laws, c. 231, § 1; 79 Del. Laws, c. 36, § 1; 81 Del. Laws, c. 200, § 1; 83 Del. Laws, c. 72, § 1.

Revisor's note.

Section 2 of 83 Del. Laws, c. 72, provided: "This act becomes effective 30 days after its enactment into law." This act was signed by the Governor on June 30, 2021, and became on July 30, 2021.

Section 3 of 83 Del. Laws, c. 72, provided: "This act shall expire upon the enactment of the constitutional amendment regarding bail found in Senate Bill No. 11 of the 151st General Assembly." Senate Bill No. 11 of the 151st General Assembly, initially amending Del. Const. art. I, § 12, was not acted upon in 2021, but may still become law in 2022. A second identical amendment would then have to be approved by the 152nd General Assembly in order to finally amend that section of the Delaware Constitution.

Effect of amendments.

83 Del. Laws, c. 72, effective July 30, 2021, rewrote (c) and added (d)-(g). That amendment expires upon fulfillment of the contingency in § 3 of that act.

§ 2107. Determining the amount of bail [Effective upon fulfillment of the contingency in 83 Del. Laws, c. 72, § 3].

(a) In determining the amount of bail to be required to be posted as surety under § 2105 of this title or to be required for a conditions of release bond not guaranteed by financial terms, the court shall not require oppressive bail but shall require such bail as reasonably will assure the reappearance of the defendant, compliance with the conditions set forth in the bond, and the safety of the community. In fixing the amount, the court shall also take into consideration the criteria set forth in § 2105(b) of this title.

(b) In any event, if a defendant is charged with an offense punishable by fine only, the amount of the bail shall not exceed double the amount of the maximum fine for each charge. When a defendant has been convicted of an offense and only a fine has been imposed as the sentence of the court, the amount of bail shall not exceed double the amount of the fine.

(c) Notwithstanding any provision of this title to the contrary, for a defendant charged with committing a violent felony involving a firearm or with committing a violent felony while on probation or pretrial release, the presumption is that a conditions of release bond guaranteed by financial terms secured by cash only will be set.

(d)-(g) [Repealed.]

History.

11 Del. C. 1953, § 2107; 56 Del. Laws, c. 231, § 1; 79 Del. Laws, c. 36, § 1; 81 Del. Laws, c. 200, § 1; 83 Del. Laws, c. 72, § 1; 83 Del. Laws, c. 72, §§ 1, 3.

Revisor's note.

Section 2 of 83 Del. Laws, c. 72, provided: "This act becomes effective 30 days after its enactment into law." This act was signed by the Governor on June 30, 2021, and became on July 30, 2021.

Section 3 of 83 Del. Laws, c. 72, provided: "This act shall expire upon the enactment of the constitutional amendment regarding bail found in Senate Bill No. 11 of the 151st General Assembly." Senate Bill No. 11 of the 151st General Assembly, initially amending Del. Const. art. I, § 12, was not acted upon in 2021, but may still become law in 2022. A second identical amendment would then have to be approved by the 152nd General Assembly in order to finally amend that section of the Delaware Constitution.

Effect of amendments.

83 Del. Laws, c. 72, effective July 30, 2021, rewrote (c) and added (d)-(g). That amendment expires upon fulfillment of the contingency in § 3 of that act.

CHAPTER 23

SEARCH AND SEIZURE

SUBCHAPTER I

GENERAL PROVISIONS

§ 2306. Application or complaint for search warrant.

NOTES TO DECISIONS

Analysis

Particularity.
Probable cause.
— Found.

Particularity.

A general warrant to search defendant's smartphones violated defendant's rights under U.S. Const. amend. 4, Del. Const. art. I, § 6 and the particularity requirement in 11 Del. C. § 2306 because: (1) the general warrant was unlimited in time and scope; (2) the smartphone evidence was critical to the State's case and defendant's convictions; and (3) its admission was not harmless error beyond a reasonable doubt. Taylor v. State, 2021 Del. LEXIS 279 (Del. Sept. 8, 2021).

Probable cause.

— Found.

Sufficient probable cause existed to support the issuance of a search warrant where: (1) the affidavit indicated that the affiants' training, experience and participation in past drug investigations allowed the affiant to tie certain recovered items to drug dealing activity; (2) the white powdery residue from the plastic baggies field tested positive for cocaine; and (3) the affiant provided notes of physical surveillance performed. State v. Peart, — A.3d —, 2021 Del.

Super. LEXIS 243 (Del. Super. Ct. Mar. 25, 2021).

§ 2307. Issuance; contents; execution and return of search warrants.

NOTES TO DECISIONS

Analysis

Probable cause.
— Found.

Probable cause.

— Found.

Sufficient probable cause existed to support the issuance of a search warrant where: (1) the affidavit indicated that the affiants' training, experience and participation in past drug investigations allowed the affiant to tie certain recovered items to drug dealing activity; (2) the white powdery residue from the plastic baggies field tested positive for cocaine; and (3) the affiant provided notes of physical surveillance performed. State v. Peart, — A.3d —, 2021 Del. Super. LEXIS 243 (Del. Super. Ct. Mar. 25, 2021).

§ 2311. Disposition of property validly seized.

NOTES TO DECISIONS

Analysis

Use.
— Commission of crimes.

Use.

— Commission of crimes.

Commissioner had a reasonable basis to hold that a cell phone was used in the commission of the murder for which defendant was convicted; defendant was not entitled to the lawful possession of the cell phone used to abuse the victim before the murder, to express guilt following the crime and to cover up the murder so defendant could flee before the victim's body was discovered. State v. Veal, — A.3d —, 2020 Del. Super. LEXIS 2954 (Del. Super. Ct. Dec. 4, 2020).

CHAPTER 25
EXTRADITION AND DETAINERS
SUBCHAPTER II
DETAINERS; UNIFORM AGREEMENT ON DETAINERS

§ 2540. Preamble; purpose.

NOTES TO DECISIONS

Pleas.
Defendant's postconviction relief motion was denied because contentions that defendant's rights were violated under the Uniform Agreement on Detainers (11 Del. C. § 2540 et seq.) were procedurally barred under Super. Ct. Crim. R. 61(i)(3); they implicated alleged errors or defects occurring prior to the entry of defendant's guilty plea, which were waived when the plea was entered and accepted. State v. Slaughter, — A.3d —, 2021 Del. Super. LEXIS 138 (Del. Super. Ct. Feb. 16, 2021).

CHAPTER 27
JURISDICTION AND VENUE

SUBCHAPTER I
GENERAL PROVISIONS

§ 2702. Jurisdiction of the Justice of the Peace Court of offenses contained in Chapter 5 of this title.

(a) The Justice of the Peace Court shall have original jurisdiction to hear, try and finally determine all misdemeanors created in Chapter 5 of this title, and any attempt, conspiracy or solicitation to commit such misdemeanors unless such jurisdiction is excluded by subsection (b) of this section or is otherwise excluded by law.

(b) The Justice of the Peace Court shall not have jurisdiction over the following misdemeanors created in Chapter 5 of this title:

(1) Section 601(a)(2) of this title (offensive touching with bodily fluid).

(2) Section 614 of this title (assault on a sports official);

(3) Section 625 of this title (unlawfully administering drugs);

(4) Section 627 of this title (prohibited acts as to substances releasing vapors or fumes);

(5) Section 628A of this title (vehicular assault in the second degree);

(6) Section 652 of this title (self-abortion) [repealed];

(7) Section 653 of this title (issuing abortional articles) [repealed];

(8) Section 763 of this title (sexual harassment);

(9) Section 764 of this title (indecent exposure 2nd degree);

(10) Section 765 of this title (indecent exposure 1st degree);

(11) Section 766 of this title (incest);

(12) Section 767 of this title (unlawful sexual contact 3rd degree);

(13) Section 785 of this Title (interference with custody);

(14) Section 805 of this title (cross or religious symbol burning);

(15) Section 850 of this title (use, possession, manufacture, distribution and sale of unlawful telecommunication and access devices);

(16) Section 871 of this title (falsifying business records);

(17) Section 873 of this title (tampering with public records);

(18) Section 877 of this title (offering a false instrument for filing);

(19) Section 881 of this title (bribery);

(20) Section 882 of this title (bribe receiving);

(21) Section 892 of this title (fraud in insolvency);

(22) Section 906 of this title (deceptive business practices);

(23) Section 910 of this title (debt adjusting);

(24) Section 916 of this title (home improvement fraud);

(25) Section 917 of this title (new home construction fraud);

(26) Section 918 of this title (ticket scalping)

(27) Section 921 of this title (sale of transferred recorded sounds);

(28) Section 932 of this title (unauthorized access to computer system);

(29) Section 933 of this title (theft of computer services);

(30) Section 934 of this title (interruption of computer services);

(31) Section 935 of this title (misuse of computer system information);

(32) Section 936 of this title (destruction of computer equipment);

(33) Section 937 of this title (unrequested or unauthorized electronic mail);

(34) Section 938 of this title (failure to promptly cease electronic communication upon request);

(35) Section 1101 of this title (abandonment of a child);

(36) Section 1103 of this title (child abuse in the third degree);

(37) Section 1102 of this title (endangering the welfare of a child).

(38) Section 1105 of this title (crime against a vulnerable adult);

(39) Section 1106 of this title (unlawfully dealing with a child);

(40) Section 1113 of this title (criminal nonsupport);

(41) Section 1114 of this title (body-piercing; tattooing or branding);

(42) Section 1205 of this title (giving unlawful gratuities);

(43) Section 1206 of this title (receiving unlawful gratuities);

(44) Section 1207 of this title (improper influence);

(45) Section 1211 of this title (official misconduct);

(46) Section 1212 of this title (profiteering);

(47) Section 1246 of this title (compounding a crime);

(48) Section 1249 of this title (abetting the violation of driver's license restrictions);

(49) Section 1250 of this title (offenses against law-enforcement animals);

(50) Section 1256 of this title (promoting prison contraband);

(51) Section 1260 of this title (misuse of prisoner mail);

(52) Section 1266 of this title (tampering with a juror);

(53) Section 1267 of this title (misconduct by a juror);

(54) Section 1271A of this title (criminal contempt of a domestic violence protective order);

(55) Section 1273 of this title (unlawful grand jury disclosure);

(56) Section 1304 of this title (hate crimes);

(57) Section 1327 of this title (maintaining a dangerous animal);

(58) Section 1332 of this title (abusing a corpse);

(59) Section 1333 of this title (trading in human remains and associated funerary objects);

(60) Section 1335 of this title (violation of privacy);

(61) Section 1365 of this title (obscene literature harmful to minors);

(62) Section 1366 of this title (outdoor motion picture theatres);

(63) Section 1411 of this title (unlawfully disseminating gambling information);

(64) Section 1428 of this title (maintaining an obstruction of gambling location);

(65) Section 1448A of this title (offenses related to criminal history record checks for sale of firearms);

(66) Section 1456 of this title (unsafe storage of a firearm);

(67) Section 1457 of this title (possession of a weapon in a safe school zone).

History.

11 Del. C. 1953, § 2702; 58 Del. Laws, c. 497, § 2; 59 Del. Laws, c. 203, § 33; 59 Del. Laws, c. 547, §§ 17, 18; 63 Del. Laws, c. 327, § 1; 66 Del. Laws, c. 141, § 1; 69 Del. Laws, c. 301, § 1; 71 Del. Laws, c. 240, § 2; 72 Del. Laws, c. 83, § 1; 72 Del. Laws, c. 147, § 1; 72 Del. Laws, c. 391, § 2; 73 Del. Laws, c. 31, §§ 2, 3; 73 Del. Laws, c. 36, § 1; 73 Del. Laws, c. 255, §§ 3, 4; 74 Del. Laws, c. 155, § 1; 74 Del. Laws, c. 322, §§ 2, 3; 77 Del. Laws, c. 416, § 1; 78 Del. Laws, c. 168, § 7; 78 Del. Laws, c. 406, § 4; 82 Del. Laws, c. 35, § 1; 83 Del. Laws, c. 169, § 2; 83 Del. Laws, c. 200, § 1.

Revisor's note.

Based upon changes contained in 83 Del. Laws, c. 200, effective Sept. 17, 2021, "[repealed]" was inserted in (b)(6) and (7).

CHAPTER 35
WITNESSES AND EVIDENCE
SUBCHAPTER I
GENERAL PROVISIONS

§ 3507. Use of prior statements as affirmative evidence.

NOTES TO DECISIONS

Analysis

Foundation.
— Established.
Statement.
— Admissible.

Foundation.

— Established.

State laid a proper foundation for admission of the 11-year-old victim's prior recorded statement because: (1) the State asked the victim whether the victim tried to tell the truth when speaking to people the morning of the incident, which by inference could be considered as including the children advocacy center interviewer; (2) the victim testified that the prior recorded statement was given voluntarily; and (3) defense counsel had a full and effective opportunity to cross-examine the victim. Ward v. State, 239 A.3d 389 (Del. 2020).

Statement.

— Admissible.

Superior Court properly admitted cumulative statements from witnesses because: (1) defendant waived any objection to the form of the statements by failing to preserve the issue; (2) the Court carefully considered whether the prior statement had probative value over and above the content of the witness's present testimony; (3) the Court credited material facts contained in the statements, but not contained in (and thus not cumulative of) the witness' trial testimony; and (4) the State presented comprehensive physical, video and testamentary evidence supporting the conclusion that defendant shot the victim in order to conceal a prior robbery of a drug dealer. McMullen v. State, 253 A.3d 107 (Del. 2021).

CHAPTER 39
SENTENCE, JUDGMENT, EXECUTION AND MANDATORY TESTING

SUBCHAPTER I
SENTENCE, JUDGMENT AND EXECUTION

§ 3901. Fixing term of imprisonment; credits.

NOTES TO DECISIONS

Applicability.

Application of the 2019 Amended Sentencing Act (82 Del. Laws, c. 66) to modify the terms of defendant's pre-existing sentence and to order each separate period of defendant's confinement to run (or deem those periods to have been running) concurrently was prohibited; the Act did not apply retroactively. State v. Caulk, 2021 Del. Super. LEXIS 507 (Del. Super. Ct. July 12, 2021).

Defendant's motion for a reduction of sentence, filed more than a year after defendant was sentenced, was untimely; subsequent statutory changes by the 2019 Amended Sentencing Act (82 Del. Laws, c. 66) did not constitute an extraordinary circumstance to overcome the 90-day time limitation. State v. Caulk, — A.3d —, 2021 Del. Super. LEXIS 507 (Del. Super. Ct. July 12, 2021).

CHAPTER 41
FINES, COSTS, PENALTIES AND FORFEITURES

Subchapter I. General Provisions

Sec.

4101. Payment of fines, costs and restitution upon conviction.

SUBCHAPTER I
GENERAL PROVISIONS

§ 4101. Payment of fines, costs and restitution upon conviction.

(a) On conviction upon indictment or information for any crime or offense, all the costs shall be paid by the party convicted.

(b) Immediately upon imposition by a court, including a justice of the peace, of any sentence to pay a fine, costs, restitution or all 3, the same shall be a judgment against the convicted person for the full amount of the fine, costs, restitution or all 3, assessed by the sentence. Such judgment shall be immediately executable, enforceable and/or transferable by the State or by the victim to whom such restitution is ordered in the same manner as other judgments of the court. If not paid promptly upon its imposition or in accordance with the terms of the order of the court, or immediately if so requested by the State, the clerk or Prothonotary shall cause the judgment to be entered upon the civil judgment docket of the court; provided, however, that where a stay of execution is otherwise permitted by law such a stay shall not be granted as a matter of right but only within the discretion of the court. If the court imposing any sentence to pay a fine, costs, restitution or all 3 has no civil docket for the entry of a judgment, then such court may immediately transfer such judgment to the civil judgment docket of an appropriate court, as shall be determined by the court imposing such sentence. Judgments docketed pursuant to this subsection shall be exempt from the provisions of § 4711 of Title 10 which mandate the expiration of judgments, and which require the renewal of such judgments.

(c) The provisions of this section are cumulative and shall not impair any judgment given upon any conviction.

(d) In addition to, and at the same time as, any fine, penalty or forfeiture is assessed to any criminal defendant or any child adjudicated delinquent, there shall be levied an additional penalty of $1.00 imposed and collected by the courts for crimes or offenses as defined in § 233 of this title. When a fine, penalty or forfeiture is suspended, in whole or in part, the penalty assessment shall not be suspended.

(1) Upon collection of the penalty assessment, the same shall be paid over to the prothonotary or clerk of courts, as the case may be, who shall collect the same and transmit it to the State Treasury to be deposited in a separate account for the administration of this subsection, which account shall be designated the "Videophone Fund," which is hereby created. This fund is to be administered by the Criminal Justice Council. Funds shall be utilized to cover line charges, maintenance costs and purchase and upgrade of videophone systems used by state and local agencies in the criminal justice system.

(2) For each fiscal year, if the balance in the Videophone Fund exceeds $250,000, said funds shall be transferred to the General Fund of the State of Delaware on June 30. The Criminal Justice Council shall submit a detailed spending plan for the use of the videophone funds to the Director of the Office of Management and Budget and Controller General no later than September 30 of each fiscal year. No funds shall be expended until the plan is approved by the Director of the Office of Management and Budget and the Controller General.

(3) The courts may expunge the record of any videophone assessment which remains uncollected for a period in excess of 3 years.

(e)(1) If any school teacher or administrator who holds a license or certificate under Title 14 or who is a teacher or administrator in a charter school but is exempt from licensing under § 507(c) of Title 14 or is a teacher or administrator employed by any state agency or under contract to a state agency is convicted of a violation of § 904(c) of Title 4 as a felony offense in this title, any offense in Chapter 47 of Title 16, and/or any offense in the Delaware Code that is a crime against a child, or a similar statute of another state, commonwealth or the District of Columbia, the court shall forward a copy of the conviction data to the employing school district's superintendent, school person-in-charge or state agency head.

(2) If the arrest and conviction occurs outside the State of Delaware, the teacher or administrator shall notify the superintendent, school person-in-charge or state agency head by providing copies of the conviction documents and sentence.

A teacher or administrator who fails to comply with paragraph (e)(2) of this section shall be guilty of a violation.

(f) In addition to, and at the same time as, any fine, penalty or forfeiture is assessed to any criminal or traffic defendant or any child adjudicated delinquent, there shall be levied an additional penalty of $1.00 imposed and collected by the courts for crimes or offenses as defined in § 233 of this title. When a fine, penalty or forfeiture is suspended, in whole or in part, the penalty assessment shall not be suspended.

(1) Upon collection of the penalty assessment, the same shall be paid over to the prothonotary or clerk of courts, as the case may be, who shall collect the same and transmit it to the State Treasury to be deposited in a separate account for the administration of this subsection, which account shall be designated the "DELJIS Fund", which is hereby created. The Fund is to be administered by the DELJIS Director. Funds shall be utilized to cover line charges, maintenance costs and upgrading of software and hardware that comprise the system known as the Criminal Justice Information System (CJIS) utilized by state and local law-enforcement agencies in addition to all agencies designated as "Criminal Justice Agencies".

(2) For each fiscal year, if the balance in the DELJIS Fund exceeds $250,000, said funds shall be transferred to the General Fund of the State on June 30. The DELJIS Director shall submit a detailed spending plan for the use of the DELJIS funds to the Director of the Office of Management and Budget and Controller General no later than September 30 of each fiscal year. No funds shall be expended until the plan is approved by the Director of the Office of Management and Budget and the Controller General.

(g)(1) In addition to, and at the same time as any fine, penalty or forfeiture is assessed to a criminal defendant, recipient of a civil offense, or any child adjudicated delinquent, there shall be levied an additional surcharge of 50% of the fine for the Transportation Trust Fund imposed and collected for any violations of Title 21.

(2) For fiscal years ending prior to July 1, 2008, no more than $1.5 million of the surcharge collected under this Section shall be deposited into the Transportation Trust Fund. Any amount in excess of $1.5 million collected prior to July 1, 2008, shall be deposited into the General Fund.

(3) If a fine or penalty is waived in whole or in part, the court may, in its discretion, waive up to the same percentage of the assessment.

(h) In addition to, and at the same time as, any fine or other penalty is assessed to any criminal or traffic defendant or any child adjudicated delinquent, there shall be levied an additional penalty of $15 imposed and collected by the courts for each crime and offense as defined in § 233 of this title or for any civil violation or civil penalty under this title, subchapters IV and V of Chapter 47 of Title 16, or Title 21. When a fine or other penalty is suspended in whole or in part, the penalty assessment may not be suspended, except for a violation of § 4129 of Title 21.

(1) Upon collection of the penalty assessment, the assessment must be paid over to the prothonotary or clerk of courts, as the case may be, who shall collect the same and transmit it to the State Treasury to be deposited in a separate account for the administration of this subsection, which account shall be designated the "Fund to Combat Violent Crimes," which is hereby created.

(2) One-half of the Fund, but no more than $2,125,000 per year, shall be distributed to the Department of Safety and Homeland Security for use in connection with initiatives to combat violent crime. Funds distributed to the Department of Safety and Homeland Security hereunder may be used to cover salaries, overtime and other salary costs, expenses, equipment, and supplies for state troopers and other personnel.

(3) One-half of the Fund, but no more than $2,125,000 per year, shall be distributed to local law-enforcement agencies for use in connection with initiatives to combat violent crime. Funds may be used to cover overtime, expenses, equipment and supplies, and as otherwise set forth in paragraph (h)(6) of this section.

(4) The Fund to Combat Violent Crimes Committee shall administer the moneys distributable to local law-enforcement agencies hereunder. The Committee shall be comprised of 5 members, namely the Secretary of the Department of Safety and Homeland Security, the Superintendent of the Delaware State Police, the Attorney General, the President of the Delaware Police Chiefs Council and the President of the Delaware State Lodge of the Fraternal Order of Police, or the respective designees of such members. The Secretary of the Department of Safety and Homeland Security shall be the chairperson of the Committee.

a. All local law-enforcement agencies seeking funds hereunder shall submit a yearly request for funding to the Committee. Such request shall include, without limitation:

1. A detailed description of how the requested funds will be used by the local law-enforcement agency to combat violent crime;

2. The amount of any and all funds received by said local law-enforcement agency from the Fund during the previous 5 fiscal years; and

3. The name of the local law-enforcement agency requesting said funds and the name of the individual in such agency who shall be responsible for keeping accurate records as to the use of said funds.

b. In addition, prior to receiving any funds hereunder in any fiscal year, all local law-enforcement agencies shall certify in writing to the Committee that:

1. Funds received from the Fund to Combat Violent Crimes will supplement, not supplant, any nonstate funding to local law-enforcement agencies that would otherwise be available for activities funded under this paragraph;

2. The award of any funds hereunder shall not guarantee that funding shall be available to the same extent in future fiscal years;

3. The responsibility for any future decrease in funding shall be borne by the local law-enforcement agency, not the State.

c. The Committee may require such additional information from local law-enforcement agencies, and may otherwise adopt such procedures and forms, as shall be necessary for the effective administration of this paragraph.

(5) If a majority of the Committee determines that all of the funds requested by a local law-enforcement agency will be used for purposes permitted hereunder, the Committee shall authorize payment to each local law-enforcement agency as follows:

a. Each full-time local law-enforcement agency shall receive $15,000 per year and each part-time local law-enforcement agency shall receive $7,500 per year.

b. All funds in excess of the amounts set forth above shall be distributed to local law-enforcement agencies on a pro rata basis, based upon the local law-enforcement agency's actual strength of full-time sworn officers.

(6) Local law-enforcement agencies shall not be permitted to use moneys hereunder to cover salaries or other salary costs, except overtime, unless the Committee:

a. Determines that sufficient funding is available from the Fund to Combat Violent Crimes to support such expenditures on a long-term basis; and

      b. Issues a written opinion to that effect, signed by all of the members of the Committee and provided to the Governor and the chair and co-chair of the Joint Finance Committee, no earlier than June 30, 2012.

    (7) Any funds granted to a local law-enforcement agency pursuant to paragraphs (h)(5) and (6) of this section that are not fully expended within 12 months of receipt thereof must be returned by the agency to the Fund to Combat Violent Crimes within 60 days, unless the agency has requested and has received an authorization in writing for an extension of up to 120 days by the Committee.

    (8) Notwithstanding anything to the contrary herein, no more than $4.25 million of the funds collected under this paragraph in each fiscal year shall be deposited into the Fund to Combat Violent Crimes. Any amount in excess of $4.25 million in each fiscal year shall be deposited into the General Fund.

    (9) For purposes of this section:

      a. "Full-time local law-enforcement agency" shall mean any local law-enforcement agency providing continuous, 24-hour coverage to a county or municipality.

      b. "Fund" shall mean the Fund to Combat Violent Crimes.

      c. "Initiative to combat violent crime" means any initiative, plan, proposal, operation or strategy designed to reduce the prevalence of 1 more offenses classified as a "violent felonies" pursuant to § 4201(c) of this title.

      d. "Local law-enforcement agency" means any county or municipal police department within this State, but does not include any county sheriff's office.

      e. "Part-time local law-enforcement agency" shall mean any local law-enforcement agency providing less than continuous, 24-hour coverage to a county or municipality.

(i) Prior to any fine, penalty or forfeiture being assessed a criminal defendant or any child adjudicated delinquent, the Attorney General or other prosecuting agency shall notify the court if the victim was 62 years of age or older. In addition to, and at the same time as, any fine, penalty or forfeiture is assessed to any criminal defendant or any child adjudicated delinquent, there shall be levied an additional penalty of $100 imposed and collected by the courts for crimes or offenses in Chapter 5 of Title 11 where the victim was 62 years of age or older. When a fine, penalty or forfeiture is suspended, in whole or in part, the penalty assessment under this subsection shall not be suspended.

    (1) Upon collection of the penalty assessment, the same shall be paid over to the prothonotary or clerk of courts, as the case may be, who shall collect the same and transmit it to the State Treasury to be deposited in a separate account for the administration of this subsection, which account shall be designated the "Senior Trust Fund", which is hereby created. The Fund is to be administered by the Director of the Division of Services for Aging and Adults with Physical Disabilities. The Fund shall be utilized in providing assistance for new or expanded programs on or after October 1, 2012, for the senior population. The Senior Trust Fund must be used to support the direct provision of aging services by community based service organizations.

    (2) [Repealed.]

(j) In addition to, and at the same time as any fine, penalty, or forfeiture assessed to a criminal defendant or recipient of a civil offense, there shall be levied an additional penalty of $10 imposed and collected for any violations of Title 21. When a fine, penalty, or forfeiture is suspended, in whole or in part, this penalty assessment may not be suspended, except for a violation of § 4129 of Title 21.

(1) This penalty assessment shall, for collection purposes, have first priority over all other penalty assessments created by this section and shall:

a. Have first priority after payments to the Victim Compensation Fund and restitution, consistent with § 4106(c) of this title, and the Court Security Fund, created by § 8505 of Title 10; and

b. Have priority over all other penalty assessments, costs, or fees established by an act of the General Assembly.

(2) Upon collection of this penalty assessment, the assessment must be paid over to the State Treasury to be deposited in a separate account for the administration of this subsection, which account shall be designated as the "Volunteer Ambulance Company Fund" (Fund), which is hereby created.

(3) The Fund shall be administered by the State Fire Prevention Commission. The Commission shall pay the moneys from the Fund directly to each volunteer ambulance company in this State in proportion to the number of ambulance runs by a volunteer ambulance company out of the total number of ambulance runs by all volunteer ambulance companies in this State.

(4) For the purposes of this subsection:

a. "Ambulance runs" means volunteer ambulance company responses to dispatched calls for service.

b. "Basic life support (BLS)" shall have the same meaning as set forth in § 9702 of Title 16.

c. "Volunteer ambulance company" means a nonprofit ambulance company that is certified by the State Fire Prevention Commission and is providing basic life support (BLS) services.

History.

Code 1852, §§ 2939-2941; Code 1915, § 4816; Code 1935, § 5304; 11 Del. C. 1953, § 4101; 57 Del. Laws, c. 508, §§ 1, 2; 63 Del. Laws, c. 140, § 1; 63 Del. Laws, c. 141, § 6; 70 Del. Laws, c. 461, § 1; 71 Del. Laws, c. 43, § 2; 71 Del. Laws, c. 387, § 1; 74 Del. Laws, c. 27, §§ 7, 8; 74 Del. Laws, c. 68, § 70; 75 Del. Laws, c. 88, § 21(6); 75 Del. Laws, c. 424, § 1; 76 Del. Laws, c. 77, § 1; 76 Del. Laws, c. 133, § 1; 78 Del. Laws, c. 160, § 1; 78 Del. Laws, c. 239, § 1; 79 Del. Laws, c. 436, § 1; 80 Del. Laws, c. 74, § 1; 80 Del. Laws, c. 276, §§ 1, 2; 81 Del. Laws, c. 34, § 1; 83 Del. Laws, c. 54, § 180.

Effect of amendments.

83 Del. Laws, c. 54, effective June 30, 2021, repealed (i)(2).

§ 4106. Restitution for property damage or loss.

NOTES TO DECISIONS

Analysis

Costs.
— Victim.

Costs.

— Victim.

Reimbursement to the victim for first month's rent, last month's rent, and an application fee in the total amount of $1,615 was properly recoverable as restitution from defendant; the victim had relocated due to defendant's criminal conduct and ongoing safety concerns. State v. Alvarez, — A.3d —, 2021 Del. Super. LEXIS 505 (Del. Super. Ct. July 9, 2021).

Victim's security deposit was not imposed as an item of restitution against defendant; the victim would be returned the security deposit from the lessor (unless prevented from doing so by the victim's own actions, such as by causing damage to the property or not paying rent. State v. Alvarez, — A.3d —, 2021 Del. Super. LEXIS 505 (Del. Super. Ct. July 9, 2021).

CHAPTER 42
CLASSIFICATION OF OFFENSES; SENTENCES

§ 4204. Authorized disposition of convicted offenders.

NOTES TO DECISIONS

Analysis

Appeals.
Imprisonment.
— Impermissible increase.
Sentence.
— Modification.
Standard of review.

Appeals.

Superior Court did not commit plain error in sentencing defendant; it did not fail to identify aggravating factors and did not limit itself to only incorporating the State's memorandum (given that the trial court's analysis included other relevant factors). White v. State, 243 A.3d 381 (Del. 2020).

Imprisonment.

— Impermissible increase.

Superior Court properly resentenced defendant to 15 years at supervision Level V, for possession of a firearm by a person prohibited because: (1) while defendant contended that the sentencing judge erred by failing to set forth on the record reasons for deviating from the "presumptive sentence" adopted by the Sentencing Accountability Commission, the statute specifically referred to the "presumptive sentence;" (2) the presumptive sentence in defendant's case, a class C felony, was up to 30 months at Level V; and (3) the sentence imposed could be easily explained by reference to the guidelines for an aggravated sentence based upon prior criminal history. Gibson v. State, 244 A.3d 989 (Del. 2020).

Sentence.

— Modification.

Inmate was not entitled to an order reducing a term of imprisonment because: (1) the sentence was appropriate at the time it was rendered; (2) even though the inmate's aspirations were commendable, they did not compel a reduction; and (3) the court declined to reverse imposition of the 11 Del. C. § 4204(k) condition (requiring that the sentence be served without benefit of any form of early release, good time, furlough, work release, supervised custody or any other form of reduction or diminution of sentence), as there was nothing about the condition that prohibited the inmate from any rehabilitative program or effort without benefit of sentence diminution. State v. Singleton, — A.3d —, 2020 Del. Super. LEXIS 2952 (Del. Super. Ct. Dec. 3, 2020).

Defendant's request to reduce sentence was denied because the Superior Court's original sentencing judgment was appropriate; each of the aggravators cited by the Court at the sentencing hearing, and in its sentencing order, was well-supported by the record. State v. Davis, — A.3d —, 2021 Del. Super. LEXIS 475 (Del. Super. Ct. June 15, 2021).

Where defendant was charged with first-degree rape and kidnapping, and pleaded guilty to second-degree rape and kidnapping, defendant was not erroneously sentenced to 20 years incarceration under 11 Del. C. § 4204(k) because: (1) although the plea agreement did not reference that statute, the record reflected that the plea was knowing, intelligent and voluntary; (2) the sentences for rape and kidnapping were appropriate and fell within the necessary statutory limits; and (3) the 11 Del. C. § 4204(k) condition was statutorily authorized. Bowden v. State, 256 A.3d 206 (Del. 2021).

Standard of review.

Defendant's 30-year sentence, without option of early release, was not violative of cruel and unusual punishment standards because: (1) a comparison of the crimes committed and the sentence imposed did not lead to an inference of gross disproportionality; (2) defendant was convicted of 6 felonies, with a racketeering felony carrying an up to 25 years imprisonment term; and (3) after serving a prior 14-year sentence in federal prison, defendant had opted to return to the illegal drug trade by orchestrating an expansive drug enterprise. Lloyd v. State, 249 A.3d 768 (Del. 2021).

§ 4204A. Youth convicted in Superior Court.

(a) [Repealed.]

(b) When a child who has not reached that child's eighteenth birthday is sentenced in Superior Court to a period of incarceration, such sentence shall initially be served in a juvenile facility upon imposition of the sentence and such child shall remain in the custody of or be transferred forthwith to the Division of Youth Rehabilitative Services until the child's eighteenth birthday, at which time such child shall be transferred forthwith to the Department of Correction to serve the remaining portion of said sentence.

(1) If a child has reached the child's sixteenth birthday has been sentenced in Superior Court, the Department of Services for Children, Youth and Their Families ("The Department") may file a motion in Superior Court to place the child in a secured detention facility other than a facility operated by the Department because the Department's secured detention facilities are at or beyond capacity or the child poses a security risk to self or other youth served by the Department in the facilities it operates. If a motion is filed, Superior Court shall conduct an evidentiary hearing unless the parties reach an agreement.

(2) After an evidentiary hearing, the Superior Court may order the child to be placed in a secured detention facility not operated by the Department if the Court finds by clear and convincing evidence that the Department's secured detention facilities are at or beyond capacity and the child's safety or health is at risk by remaining at a facility operated by the Department. If the Court makes such a finding, the Department shall thereafter provide the Court with a status on the capacity of the Department's secured detention facilities at least weekly, and no child may be held in a secured detention facility for adults for more than 30 days.

(3) After an evidentiary hearing, the Superior Court may order the child to be placed in a secured detention facility not operated by the Department if the Court finds by clear and convincing evidence that the child is a danger to self or other youth served by the Department in the facilities it operates and the child's needs would be better served at a facility not operated by the Department.

(c) [Repealed.]

(d)(1) Notwithstanding any provision of this title to the contrary, any offender sentenced to an aggregate term of incarceration in excess of 20 years for any offense or offenses other than murder first degree that were committed prior to the offender's eighteenth birthday shall be eligible to petition the Superior Court for sentence modification after the offender has served 20 years of the originally imposed Level V sentence.

(2) Notwithstanding any provision of this title to the contrary, any offender sentenced to a term of incarceration for murder first degree when said offense was committed prior to the offender's eighteenth birthday shall be eligible to petition the Superior Court for sentence modification after the offender has served 30 years of the originally imposed Level V sentence.

(3) Notwithstanding any provision of this subsection or title to the contrary, any offender who has petitioned the Superior Court for sentence modification pursuant to this subsection shall not be eligible to submit a second or subsequent petition until at least 5 years have elapsed since the date on which the Court ruled upon the offender's most recent petition. Further, the Superior Court shall have the discretion at the time of each sentence modification hearing to prohibit a subsequent sentence modification petition for a period of time in excess of 5 years if the Superior Court finds there to be no reasonable likelihood that the interests of justice will require another hearing within 5 years.

(4) Notwithstanding the provisions of § 4205 or § 4217 of this title, any court rule or any other provision of law to the contrary, a Superior Court Judge upon consideration of a petition filed pursuant to this subsection (d), may modify, reduce or suspend such petitioner's sentence, including any minimum or mandatory sentence, or a portion thereof, in the discretion of

the Court. Nothing in this section, however, shall require the Court to grant such a petitioner a sentence modification pursuant to this section.

(5) The Superior Court shall have the authority to promulgate appropriate rules to regulate the filing and litigation of sentence modification petitions pursuant to this paragraph.

History.
69 Del. Laws, c. 353, § 1; 70 Del. Laws, c. 186, § 1; 70 Del. Laws, c. 597, § 2; 71 Del. Laws, c. 5, §§ 2-4; 72 Del. Laws, c. 149, § 2; 79 Del. Laws, c. 37, § 4; 83 Del. Laws, c. 40, § 2.

Revisor's note.
Section 3 of 83 Del. Laws, c. 40, provided: "This act shall take effect on January 1, 2022."

Effect of amendments.
83 Del. Laws, c. 40, effective Jan. 1, 2022, deleted "Confinement of" from the beginning of the section heading; repealed (a) and (c); substituted "eighteenth" for "sixteenth" twice in (b); and added (b)(1) through (b)(3).

§ 4205. Sentence for felonies.

NOTES TO DECISIONS

Analysis

Sentence.
— Not excessive.
— — Manslaughter.

Sentence.

— Not excessive.

— — Manslaughter.
Defendant was not entitled to a reduction of sentence to a total of 5 years suspended, after completion of a Level V substance abuse/mental health program followed by continued treatment at Leval IV while on community supervision, because: (1) defendant had to serve no less than the concurrent minimum 2-year terms of imprisonment for manslaughter convictions; and (2) the requested reduction would violate that 2-year minimum required by 11 Del. C. § 632 and 11 Del. C. § 4205(b)(2) and (d). State v. Guseman, — A.3d —, 2021 Del. Super. LEXIS 205 (Del. Super. Ct. Mar. 10, 2021).

§ 4205A. Additional penalty for serious sex offenders or pedophile offenders.

NOTES TO DECISIONS

Pedophile offenders.
Because the jury found beyond a reasonable doubt that the victim was less than 14 years old, the court had no discretion other than to apply the sentencing enhancement in this section. State v. Clark, — A.3d —, 2021 Del. Super. LEXIS 68 (Del. Super. Ct. Jan. 25, 2021).

§ 4213. Arrest of persons under the influence of drugs; drug detoxification centers.

(a) For purposes of this section only, the following phrases shall have meanings respectively ascribed to them:

(1) "A person under the influence of drugs" shall mean a person whose powers of self-control have been substantially impaired because of the consumption of a drug described in Chapter 47 of Title 16.

(2) "Drug abuser" shall mean any person who compulsively and habitually uses drugs to the extent that they injure the person's health and interfere with the person's social and economic functioning.

(b) The Director of the Division of Substance Abuse and Mental Health ("Director") shall designate certain hospital, clinic, or other treatment facilities as "drug detoxification centers." The Director shall so designate such a facility only when the Director is satisfied that the facility has the medical and other staff, as well as the equipment, to diagnose and treat drug abusers as provided for in this section.

(c) Upon arrest for any crime which is not a felony under this title or Title 16, an arrestee who believes that the arrestee is under the influence of drugs as defined in subsection (a) of this section shall have the right to request immediate admission to a drug detoxification center. Upon such request, the arresting officer shall, as soon as transportation is available and as soon as conditions at the scene of the arrest permit, arrange to have the arrestee transported to the nearest available drug detoxification center.

(1) No expression of a desire to be admitted to a drug detoxification center shall be admissible in evidence in any criminal prosecution against the arrestee.

(2) Notwithstanding any provision of this Code to the contrary, no arrestee shall be heard to object in any court to failure to arraign the arrestee before a magistrate during the period of transportation to or stay in a drug detoxification center, or for a reasonable time not to exceed 24 hours after release.

(3) An arresting officer shall, when the officer suspects an arrestee of being under the influence of drugs, inform the arrestee of the rights under this section.

(4) No arrestee may revoke a request to be taken to a drug detoxification center after having made that request, and any drug detoxification center to which an arrestee is brought must consent to admission and testing of the arrestee, subject to limitations of facilities and staff.

(d) A drug detoxification center shall initially test admittees under this section to determine if they are under the influence of drugs or are drug abusers. If tests prove negative, the admittee shall be released forthwith to the custody of the arresting authorities. Any arrestee requesting admission to a drug detoxification center is deemed to consent to all medical and psychiatric tests considered necessary by the center to carry out its function under this section. The results of tests taken at a drug detoxification center or statements made by admittees under this section to drug detoxification center staff shall not be admissible as evidence in a criminal prosecution against the admittee.

(e) Admittees under this section whom the drug detoxification center determines to be drug abusers shall be asked if they wish to receive further treatment. Those consenting to further treatment shall remain until discharged by the drug detoxification center or until they wish to leave. No one admitted under this section shall be permitted to leave the drug detoxification center until the arresting police agency is notified.

(f) Upon a satisfactory showing to the court that a person is a drug abuser as defined in subsection (a) of this section and has completed treatment under this section in a manner satisfactory to the chairperson of the drug diagnostic team at the drug detoxification center to which the person was admitted, the charge of consumption or use of the drug, under Chapter 47 of Title 16, shall be dismissed.

(g) Whenever a police officer sees a person whom the officer believes to have taken drugs and needs medical treatment, the police officer may take that person into custody and arrange to have the person taken to a drug detoxification center or arrange to secure other medical help. This subsection shall apply whether or not the officer may under the circumstances lawfully arrest the person whom the officer believes to have taken drugs. No officer acting in good faith shall be subject to criminal or civil liability for any action under this subsection.

(h) To further the implementation of this section, the Director of the Division of Substance Abuse and Mental Health may prescribe regulations for the operation of drug detoxification centers and may assist such drug detoxification centers by distributing to them such funds as the General Assembly may from time to time appropriate to the Director for expenditure on their behalf.

History.

11 Del. C. 1953, § 4212A; 58 Del. Laws, c. 250, § 1; 58 Del. Laws, c. 497, § 3; 58 Del. Laws, c. 543; 70 Del. Laws, c. 186, § 1; 83 Del. Laws, c. 37, § 10.

Effect of amendments.

83 Del. Laws, c. 37, effective June 3, 2021,

replaced "Drug Abuse Control" with "Substance Abuse and Mental Health ('Director')" in the first sentence of (b) and with "Substance Abuse and Mental Health" in (h); and added a comma following "clinic" in the first sentence of (b).

§ 4214. Habitual criminal; life sentence

NOTES TO DECISIONS

Analysis

Habitual offender.
— Evidence.
— — Sufficient.
Sentence.
— Proper.

Habitual offender.

— Evidence.

— — Sufficient.

Where defendant was convicted of the violent felony of first-degree burglary in 2003, defendant's subsequent 2007 federal weapons conviction constituted an additional violent felony; having been convicted of 2 violent felonies prior to a guilty plea to manslaughter in 2018, defendant's designation as a habitual offender was legal and survived a motion to correct sentence.

State v. Goodman, — A.3d —, 2021 Del. Super. LEXIS 369 (Del. Super. Ct. Apr. 29, 2021), aff'd, — A.3d —, 2021 Del. LEXIS 273 (Del. 2021).

Sentence.

— Proper.

Defendant's 30-year sentence, without option of early release, was not violative of cruel and unusual punishment standards because: (1) a comparison of the crimes committed and the sentence imposed did not lead to an inference of gross disproportionality; (2) defendant was convicted of 6 felonies, with a racketeering felony carrying an up to 25 years imprisonment term; and (3) after serving a prior 14-year sentence in federal prison, defendant had opted to return to the illegal drug trade by orchestrating an expansive drug enterprise. Lloyd v. State, 249 A.3d 768 (Del. 2021).

§ 4217. Jurisdiction over sentence retained.

NOTES TO DECISIONS

Analysis

Discretion.
Extraordinary circumstances.
— Not established.
Medical condition.
Modification.
Substantial risk.
Time limitations.

Discretion.

Decision of whether the early release of low-risk offenders would lessen the dangers posed by COVID-19 to the general prison population was best left to the discretion of the Department of Correction; the Department may move for the modification of any prisoner's sentence for good cause under 11 Del. C. § 4217. Hernandez-Vargas v. State, 240 A.3d 2 (Del. 2020).

Extraordinary circumstances.

— Not established.

Defendant's motion for modification of sentence was time-barred because: (1) defendant was sentenced on January 24, 2020, and filed the motion on January 6, 2021, after the 90-day filing deadline in Super. Ct. Crim. R. 35(b); and (2) although defendant asserted that the prison staff's alleged mishandling of COVID-19 constituted extraordinary circumstances, the Supreme Court of Delaware considered and dismissed that argument. State v. Tann, — A.3d —, 2021 Del. Super. LEXIS 185 (Del. Super. Ct. Mar. 5, 2021).

Medical condition.

Denial of defendant's sentence modification motion was upheld because defendant's motion was repetitive and untimely; 11 Del. C. § 4217, not Super. Ct. Crim. R. 35(b), was the statutory vehicle for seeking a medical modification of sentence (such as that sought by defendant's motion indicating that his medical conditions and potential exposure to COVID-19 constituted extraordinary circumstances justifying modification of sentence). Johnson v. State, 239 A.3d 388 (Del. 2020).

Modification.

Superior Court properly denied defendant's 11 Del. C. § 4221 motion for review of sentence because defendant's contention that the Department of Correction (DOC) had not acted appropriately to contain the spread of COVID-19 within the prison system did not provide a basis for relief; if defendant's specific individual medical condition warranted sentence modification, an application by DOC under 11 Del. C. § 4217 was the proper vehicle to deliver such relief. Drummond v. State, 254 A.3d 396, 2021 Del. LEXIS 191 (Del. 2021).

Substantial risk.

Defendant continued to pose a substantial risk to the community and did not qualify for sentence modification pursuant to 11 Del. C. § 4217; especially troubling was defendant's conviction for dealing heroin, but 1 of defendant's most recent convictions. State v. Clements, — A.3d —, 2021 Del. Super. LEXIS 476 (Del. Super. Ct. June 14, 2021).

Time limitations.

Denial of appellant's motions for modification of sentence was upheld because appellant could not avoid the 90-day time period in Super. Ct. Crim. R. 35(b) by filing a placeholder motion within that period and then filing a motion with the substantive grounds for relief after the 90-day period had expired; such action was contrary to the plain language of Super. Ct. Crim. R. 35(b). Jones v. State, 251 A.3d 116 (Del. 2021).

§ 4218. Probation before judgment.

(a) Subject to the limitations set forth in this section, for a violation or misdemeanor offense under Title 4, 7, or this title, or for any violation or misdemeanor offense under Title 21 which is designated as a motor vehicle offense subject to voluntary assessment by § 709 of Title 21, or a violation of § 2702 of Title 14, or for violations of § 4166(d) of Title 21, or for violations of § 4172 of Title 21, or for a violation of a county or municipal code, or for a misdemeanor offense under § 4764, § 4771 or § 4774 of Title 16, or for a misdemeanor offense under § 4810(a) of Title 29, a court exercising criminal jurisdiction after accepting a guilty plea or nolo contendere plea may, with the consent of the defendant and the State, stay the entry of judgment, defer further proceedings, and place the defendant on "probation before judgment" subject to such reasonable terms and conditions as may be appropriate. The terms and conditions of any probation before judgment shall include the following requirements: (i) the defendant shall provide the court with that defendant's current address; (ii) the defendant shall promptly provide the court with written notice of any change of address; and (iii) the defendant shall appear if summoned at any hearing convened for the purpose of determining whether the defendant has violated or fulfilled the terms and conditions of probation before judgment. The terms and conditions may include any or all of the following:

(1) Ordering the defendant to pay a pecuniary penalty;

(2) Ordering the defendant to pay court costs to the State;

(3) Ordering the defendant to pay restitution;

(4) Ordering the defendant to perform community service;

(5) Ordering the defendant to refrain from contact with certain persons; and

(6) Ordering the defendant to conduct themselves in a specified manner.

The length of the period of probation before judgment shall be fixed by the court, but in no event shall the total period of probation before judgment exceed the maximum term of commitment provided by law for the offense or 1 year, whichever is greater.

(b) This section shall not apply to any of the following:

(1) Any Title 11 "domestic violence" offense as defined in § 1024(a) of Title 10. First offenders domestic violence diversion program.

(2) Section 900A of this title. Conditional discharge for issuing a bad check as first offense.

(3) Section 4177B of Title 21. First offenders; election in lieu of trial.

(c)(1) Notwithstanding any provision of this section to the contrary, no person shall be admitted to probation before judgment if:

　　a. The person is currently serving a sentence of incarceration, probation, parole or early release of any type imposed for another offense;

　　b. The person is charged with any offense set forth in this title, and has previously been convicted of any violent felony;

　　c. The person is charged with any offense set forth in this title, and has previously been convicted of any nonviolent felony within 10 years of the date of the commission of the alleged offense;

d. The person is charged with any offense set forth in this title, and has previously been convicted of any misdemeanor offense within 5 years of the date of the commission of the alleged offense;

e. The person is charged with any offense set forth in Title 4 or 7, and has been previously convicted of any offense set forth in Title 4 or 7 within 5 years of the date of the commission of the alleged offense;

f. The person is currently charged with any offense set forth in § 709 of Title 21, and has been previously convicted of any offense set forth in Title 21 within 5 years of the date of the commission of the alleged offense;

g. The person is currently charged with a violation of § 2702 of Title 14 and has been previously convicted of a violation of 2702 of Title 14 within 5 years of the date of the alleged offense; or

h. The person is charged with a violation of a county or municipal code provision and has previously been convicted of a violation of another county or municipal code provision within 5 years of the date of the commission of the alleged offense.

i. The person is charged with an offense involving a motor vehicle and holds a commercial driver license (CDL).

(2) For the purposes of this subsection, the following shall also constitute a previous conviction:

a. A conviction under the laws of another state, the United States, or any territory of the United States of any offense which is the same as, or equivalent to, any offense specified in paragraph (c)(1) of this section; or

b. [Repealed.]

c. Any adjudication, resolution, disposition or program set forth in § 4177B(e)(1) of Title 21.

(d) This section shall not be available to any person who has previously been admitted to probation before judgment for any offense involving the same title within 5 years of the current offense.

(e) Nothing in this section shall be construed to permit probation before judgment for a violation of a county or municipal code that would not be permitted for the corresponding state code offense.

(f) Upon a violation of a term or condition of the court's order of probation before judgment, the court may enter judgment and proceed with disposition of the person as if the person had not been placed on probation before judgment.

(g) Upon fulfillment of the terms and conditions of probation before judgment, the court shall enter an order discharging the person from probation. The burden shall be upon the defendant to demonstrate that the terms and conditions of probation have been fulfilled. The discharge is the final disposition of the matter. Discharge of a person under this section shall be without judgment of conviction and is not a conviction for purposes of any disqualification or disability imposed by law because of conviction of a crime.

(h) Notwithstanding any provision of this section to the contrary, the court shall not admit a defendant to probation before judgment nor otherwise apply any provision of this section unless the defendant first gives written consent to the court permitting any hearing or proceeding pursuant to this section to occur in the defendant's absence if:

(1) Timely notice of the hearing or proceeding is sent or delivered to the address provided by the defendant pursuant to subsection (a) of this section; and

(2) The defendant fails to appear at said proceeding.

In the event that a defendant fails to appear at any hearing or proceeding pursuant to this section, the court may proceed in the defendant's absence if it first finds that timely notice of the hearing or proceeding was sent or delivered to the address provided by the defendant pursuant to subsection (a) of this section. Nothing in this subsection shall limit the power of the court to hold a hearing to determine whether a defendant is in violation of the terms of that defendant's probation.

(i) Notwithstanding the provisions of subsection (a) of this section to the contrary, in any case in which the Delaware Department of Justice does not intend to enter its appearance, the consent of the State shall not be required prior to placing a defendant on "probation before judgment." In such cases, the defendant may be placed on probation before judgment only for charges arising from a single arrest. Notwithstanding the foregoing, except for the offenses under Title 21 to which this section applies, the Attorney General or other prosecuting authority may advise the court of aggravating circumstances in opposition to placing a defendant on "probation before judgment."

History.
72 Del. Laws, c. 126, § 1; 70 Del. Laws, c. 186, § 1; 72 Del. Laws, c. 453, §§ 1-8; 73 Del. Laws, c. 301, §§ 3, 4; 75 Del. Laws, c. 184, § 1; 75 Del. Laws, c. 364, § 2; 76 Del. Laws, c. 251, § 2; 78 Del. Laws, c. 13, § 13; 78 Del. Laws, c. 230, § 2; 80 Del. Laws, c. 238, § 1; 80 Del. Laws, c. 415, § 1; 81 Del. Laws, c. 250, § 3; 83 Del. Laws, c. 12, § 1; 83 Del. Laws, c. 112, § 2.

Effect of amendments.
83 Del. Laws, c. 12, effective April 13, 2021, added "or" at end of (c)(2)a.; repealed (c)(2)b.; added "involving the same title" in (d); and added the second sentence in (i).
83 Del. Laws, c. 112, effective Aug. 4, 2021, rewrote the introductory paragraph of (b) and (b)(1); and substituted a period for "; or" at the end of (b)(2).

§ 4220. Modification, suspension or reduction of sentence for substantial assistance.

NOTES TO DECISIONS

Ineffective assistance of counsel.
Superior Court gave sufficient consideration to appellant's allegations of professional misconduct, and properly denied a motion to modify sentence, because: (1) appellant had already filed a complaint against counsel with the Office of Disciplinary Counsel, a copy of which was attached to the motion; and (2) the Court made its own independent inquiry and determined that the allegations were unsubstantiated. McCove v. State, 238 A.3d 849 (Del. 2020).

§ 4221. Modification, deferral, suspension or reduction of sentence for serious physical illness, injury or infirmity.

NOTES TO DECISIONS

Reduction.
Trial court did not err by considering defendant's motion for sentence modification under Super. Ct. Crim. R. 35, rather than under this statute, because this statute applied only to sentences of 1 year or less; defendant's sentence exceeded 1 year. Woods v. State, 246 A.3d 567 (Del. 2021).

Superior Court properly denied defendant's 11 Del. C. § 4221 motion for review of sentence because defendant's contention that the Department of Correction (DOC) had not acted appropriately to contain the spread of COVID-19 within the prison system did not provide a basis for relief; if defendant's specific individual medical condition warranted sentence modification, an application by DOC under 11 Del. C. § 4217 was the proper vehicle to deliver such relief. Drummond v. State, 254 A.3d 396, 2021 Del. LEXIS 191 (Del. 2021).

CHAPTER 43
SENTENCING, PROBATION, PAROLE AND PARDONS

SUBCHAPTER II
PROBATION AND PAROLE SERVICES

§ 4321. Probation and parole officers.

(a) The Department and its probation and parole officers shall conduct such preparole investigations or perform such other duties under this chapter as may be ordered by the court, Parole Board or Department; provided, however, that all presentence investigations and reports for the Superior Court and the Court of Common Pleas shall be prepared as provided in § 4335 of this title.

(b)(1) The Department shall furnish to each person released under the supervision of the Department a written statement of the conditions of the person's probation or parole and shall instruct the person regarding these conditions.

(2) The officers, under the supervision of the Department, shall evaluate each person in their charge under Supervision Accountability Level II, III or IV, using an objective risk and needs assessment instrument and shall create a case plan for those persons assessed to be moderate- to high-risk that targets the need factors identified by the assessment. The Department shall make efforts to provide treatment and services responsive to the person's needs and characteristics. Use of the objective risk assessment instrument and associated case plans shall commence by December 31, 2013.

(3) The officers shall keep informed of the conduct and condition of persons in their charge, shall aid them to secure employment, shall exercise supervision over them, shall see that they are in compliance with and fulfill the conditions of their release and shall use all suitable methods to aid and encourage them to bring about improvement in their conduct and conditions and to meet their probation or parole obligations.

(4)a. A special condition of supervision may be set by orders of the court, Board of Parole or the probation and parole officer acting under the authority of the court or Board of Parole.

b. Special conditions of supervision imposed by the probation and parole officer shall be in accordance with Department procedures and may be enforced in the interim period of final review by the court or Board of Parole.

(c) The officer shall keep detailed records of their work, shall assist in the collection and dispersal of all moneys in accordance with the orders of the court and Department and shall make such reports in writing and perform such other duties which the rules and regulations of the Department require, or which the court, the Board of Parole or the Commissioner may require.

(d) Probation and parole officers shall exercise the same powers as constables under the laws of this State and may conduct searches of individuals under probation and parole supervision in accordance with Department procedures while in the performance of the lawful duties of their employment and shall execute lawful orders, warrants and other process as directed to the officer by any court, judge or Board of Parole of this State; however, a probation and parole officer shall only have such power and duties if the officer participates in and/or meets the minimum requirements of such training and education deemed necessary by the Department and Board of Examiners.

(e) Probation and parole officers may be tasked to participate in joint operations with federal authorities while in the performance of the lawful duties of their employment. Any contraband, property and/or money seized in the course of such joint operations shall be apportioned in accordance with federal distribution guidelines. Any distribution to probation and parole shall become the property of the Department of Correction, Bureau of Community Corrections. Any proceeds from the disposal of such property shall be used for the purchase of security equipment and technology necessary for the support of the employees of the Bureau.

(f) Specialized juvenile probation and parole officers, assigned to the Division of Youth Rehabilitative Services and as designated and sworn by the Secretary of the Department of Services for Children, Youth and Their Families, shall exercise the same powers as constables exercise under the laws of this State, and may conduct searches of individuals under the supervision of the Department of Services for Children, Youth and Their Families' Division of Youth Rehabilitative Services in accordance with agency procedure, while in the performance of the lawful duties of their employment, and shall execute lawful orders, warrants and other process as directed to such officer by any court or judge; however, a specialized juvenile probation and parole officer shall have such above-enumerated powers and duties only if the officer has met the minimum requirements of training and education deemed necessary by the Department of Services for Children, Youth and Their Families.

(g) The Department shall undertake an assessment of the availability of community resources to meet the treatment and rehabilitation needs of the supervised population every 3 years and endeavor to develop and support programs in accordance with identified needs. The first 3-year report shall be completed by December 31, 2013.

(h) The Department shall devise and adopt a body-worn camera policy that shall meet or exceed the standards established by the Council on Police Training by regulation.

History.
11 Del. C. 1953, § 4321; 54 Del. Laws, c. 349, § 7; 67 Del. Laws, c. 442, § 3; 70 Del. Laws, c. 186, § 1; 72 Del. Laws, c. 108, § 1; 73 Del. Laws, c. 60, § 1; 77 Del. Laws, c. 443, § 1; 78 Del. Laws, c. 392, §§ 2, 3; 79 Del. Laws, c. 283, § 1; 83 Del. Laws, c. 83, § 1.

Effect of amendments.
83 Del. Laws, c. 83, effective July 21, 2021, added (h).

§ 4322. Protection of records.

NOTES TO DECISIONS

Opinions of the Attorney General.
FOIA Petition Regarding the Delaware Department of Corrections, see No. 21-IB01, January 14, 2021.

FOIA Petition Regarding the Delaware Department of Corrections, see No. 21-IB10, May 4, 2021.

SUBCHAPTER III
PROBATION AND SENTENCING PROCEDURES

§ 4332. Conditions of probation or suspension of sentence; house arrest for offenders.

(a) The Department may adopt standards concerning the conditions of probation or suspension of sentence which the court may use in a given case. The standard conditions shall apply in the absence of any other specific or inconsistent conditions imposed by the court. The presentence report may recommend conditions to be imposed by the court. Nothing in this chapter shall limit the authority of the court to impose or modify any general or specific conditions of probation or suspension of sentence. The Department may recommend and, by order, the court may impose and may at any time order modification of any conditions of probation or suspension of sentence. Before any conditions are modified, a report by the Department shall be presented to and considered by the court. The court shall cause a copy of any order to be delivered to the Department and to the probationer.

(b) The Department may adopt standards governing any program of house arrest for offenders. The presentence report may recommend conditions to be imposed by the court. In addition to any conditions imposed by the Department or by the court, each program involving house arrest for offenders, regardless of the official or unofficial name of the program, shall include a reasonable monthly payment by each offender participating in the program, clear and consistent sanctions when a participant in the program violates any of the conditions, and the ownership or leasing of all equipment by the Department of Correction.

(c) The Department is authorized to use offender electronic monitoring systems and any new or emerging offender monitoring technology that will assist in the supervision of offenders placed on house arrest.

(d) The Department is authorized to supervise offenders on house arrest without the use of any specific electronic equipment, so long as sufficient and reasonable methods for ensuring compliance with the terms of house arrest are employed.

History.

11 Del. C. 1953, § 4333; 54 Del. Laws, c. 349, § 7; 66 Del. Laws, c. 29, § 1; 76 Del. Laws, c. 399, § 1; 83 Del. Laws, c. 35, § 1.

Effect of amendments.

83 Del. Laws, c. 35, effective June 3, 2021, deleted "nonviolent" preceding "offenders" in the section heading and in the first and second sentences in (b); and in (a), deleted "However" at the beginning of the fourth sentence, "duly entered" preceding "the court" in the fifth sentence, and deleted "such" following "any" in the penultimate and final sentences.

§ 4334. Arrest for violation of conditions; subsequent disposition.

NOTES TO DECISIONS

Analysis

Revocation.
— Authority of court.
— Proper.
Violation.

Revocation.

— Authority of court.

Once defendant committed a violation of probation (VOP), the Superior Court was authorized to impose any period of incarceration up to and including the balance of Level V time remaining on defendant's sentence; the record did not reflect, and defendant did not allege, that the VOP sentence exceeded statutory limits or the Level V time previously suspended. Wiggins v. State, 249 A.3d 105 (Del. 2021).

— Proper.

Because the 11-month sentence for defendant's violation of probation fell well within the previously suspended prison term for that charge, the Superior Court was authorized to reimpose that previously suspended prison term. State v. Wisher, — A.3d —, 2020 Del. Super. LEXIS 2808 (Del. Super. Ct. Sept. 28, 2020).

Where defendant engaged in a violation of probation (VOP), a claim that there was no Level V time remaining on the sentence was incorrect because: (1) defendant had been originally sentenced to 25 years of Level V incarceration, suspended after 12 years; (2) when released from prison, defendant still had 13 years of suspended Level V time remaining on the sentence; (3) once defendant committed a VOP, the Superior Court could impose any period of incarceration, up to and including the balance of the Level V time remaining on the sentence; and (4) the 18 months of nonsuspended Level V time did not exceed Level V time previously suspended and was within statutory limits. Cook v. State, 243 A.3d 441 (Del. 2020).

Violation.

Based on defendant's admission as to having violated probation by accessing the internet, and statements at the violation of probation (VOP) hearing concerning interactions with unconscious persons,, the trial court was within its discretion to conclude that home confinement or GPS monitoring would not suffice under the circumstances. Whittle v. State, 2021 Del. LEXIS 267 (August 12, 2021).

SUBCHAPTER VII
EXPUNGEMENT OF CRIMINAL RECORDS

§ 4373. Mandatory expungement; application through SBI.

(a) *Eligibility.* — On an appropriate request to the State Bureau of Identification under this section, the Bureau shall expunge all charges relating to a case if 1 of the following applies:

(1) The person was arrested or charged with the commission of 1 or more crimes and the case is terminated in favor of the accused.

(2) The person was convicted of 1 or more violations relating to the same case, 3 years have passed since the date of conviction, and the person has no prior or subsequent convictions.

(3) The person was convicted of 1 or more misdemeanors, or a combination of 1 or more misdemeanors and 1 or more violations, relating to the same case, 5 years have passed since the date of conviction, and the person has no prior or subsequent convictions.

(b) *Exclusions.* — In addition to the exclusions under § 4372(f) of this title, the following misdemeanor convictions are not eligible for mandatory expungement under this section:

(1) A misdemeanor crime of domestic violence. For purposes of this section, a "misdemeanor crime of domestic violence", means a misdemeanor offense that meets both of the following:

a. Was committed by any of the following:

1. A member of the victim's family, as "family" is defined under § 901 of Title 10, regardless, however, of the state of residence of the parties.

2. A former spouse of the victim.

3. A person who cohabited with the victim at the time of or within 3 years before the offense.

4. A person with a child in common with the victim.

5. A person with whom the victim had a substantive dating relationship, as defined under § 1041 of Title 10, at the time of or within 3 years before the offense.

b. Is a misdemeanor or violation under any of the following sections: § 601, § 602, § 603, § 611, § 614, § 621, § 625, § 628A, § 781, § 785, § 791, § 804, § 811, § 821, § 822, § 823, or § 1311 of this title.

(2) Offenses where the victim is a child.

(3) Offenses where the victim is a "vulnerable adult", as defined under § 1105 of this title.

(4) Any misdemeanor set forth in subparts A, B, C, or F of subchapter VI of Chapter 5 of this title.

(5) Any of the following misdemeanors:

a. Unlawfully administering drugs, under § 625 of this title, when the charged in conjunction with a sexual offense, as defined in § 761(f) of this title.

b. Sexual harassment, under § 763 of this title.

c. Indecent exposure in the second degree, under § 764 of this title.

d. Indecent exposure in the first degree, under § 765 of this title.

e. Trespassing with intent to peer or peep into a window or door of another, under § 820 of this title.

f. Organized retail crime, under § 841B of this title.

g. Home improvement fraud, under § 916 of this title.

h. New home construction fraud, under § 917 of this title.

    i. Offenses against law-enforcement animals, under § 1250 of this title.

    j. Promoting prison contraband, under § 1256 of this title.

    k. Resisting arrest, under § 1257 of this title.

    l. Use of an animal to avoid capture, under § 1257A of this title.

    m. Hate crime, under § 1304 of this title.

    n. Malicious interference with emergency communication, under § 1313 of this title.

    o. Abusing a corpse, under § 1332 of this title.

    p. Violation of privacy, under § 1335 of this title.

    q. Lewdness, under § 1341 of this title.

    r. Patronizing a prostitute, under § 1343 of this title.

    s. Permitting prostitution, under § 1355 of this title.

    t. Carrying a concealed dangerous instrument, under § 1443 of this title.

    u. Unlawfully dealing with a dangerous weapon, under § 1445 of this title.

    v. Unlawfully permitting a minor access to a firearm, under § 1456 of this title.

    w. Possession of a weapon in a Safe School and Recreation Zone, under § 1457 of this title.

(c) If more than 1 case or arrest is eligible for expungement under this section, it may be combined into a single application for expungement.

(d) The State Bureau of Identification shall promulgate procedures and forms relating to the implementation of this section.

(e) The State Bureau of Identification may promulgate reasonable regulations and a reasonable fee schedule to accomplish the purposes of this section.

(f) [Repealed.]

History.
62 Del. Laws, c. 317, § 2; 70 Del. Laws, c. 186, § 1; 72 Del. Laws, c. 150, § 6; 76 Del. Laws, c. 392, § 2; 77 Del. Laws, c. 156, § 1; 77 Del. Laws, c. 348, § 1; 77 Del. Laws, c. 416, § 1; 78 Del. Laws, c. 256, §§ 1, 2; 82 Del. Laws, c. 83, § 3; 83 Del. Laws, c. 37, § 11.

Effect of amendments.
83 Del. Laws, c. 37, effective June 3, 2021, substituted "or violation" for "offense" in (b)(1)b.

SUBCHAPTER VIII
DIMINUTION OF CONFINEMENT

§ 4381. Earned good time.

(a) Subject to the limitations set forth in subsection (b) of this section, all sentences, other than a life sentence, imposed for any offense pursuant to any provision of this title, Title 16 and/or Title 21 may be reduced by good time credit under the provisions of this subchapter and rules and regulations adopted by the Commissioner of Corrections. This provision will apply regardless of any previously imposed statutory limitations set forth in this title, Title 16 or Title 21.

(b) The awarding of good time credit set forth in subsection (a) of this section above will not apply to sentences imposed pursuant to § 4214 or § 4204(k) of this title or sentences imposed prior to the enactment of this statute.

(c) "Good time" may be earned for good behavior while in the custody of the Department of Correction when the person has not been guilty of any violation of discipline, rules of the Department or any criminal activity and has labored with diligence toward rehabilitation according to the following conditions:

    (1) During the first year of any sentence, good time may be awarded at the rate of 2 days per month beginning on the first day of confinement.

(2) After completing 365 days of any sentence, good time may be awarded at the rate of 3 days per month.

(3) No person shall be awarded more than 36 days of good time under this subsection for good behavior in any 1 year consisting of 365 calendar days actually served.

(d) "Good time" may be earned by participation in education, rehabilitation, work, or other programs as designated by the Commissioner. Good time may be awarded for satisfactory participation in approved programs at a rate of up to 10 days per calendar month. For offenders sentenced on or after August 8, 2012, up to 60 days of additional good time may be awarded for successful completion of an approved program designed to reduce recidivism.

(e) No more than a total of 180 days of "good time" may be earned in any 1 year consisting of 365 days actually served. Good time credits shall be applied such that the resulting release date is not prior to the effective completion date of the offender's approved program. For offenders serving multiple sentences, good time shall be credited to the consolidated time being served, rather than individually to each sentence.

History.

67 Del. Laws, c. 130, § 5; 74 Del. Laws, c. 346, § 2; 76 Del. Laws, c. 351, §§ 1-3; 77 Del. Laws, c. 406, § 1; 78 Del. Laws, c. 392, §§ 9, 10; 79 Del. Laws, c. 187, § 1; 83 Del. Laws, c. 82, § 2.

Effect of amendments.

83 Del. Laws, c. 82, effective July 20, 2021, substituted "10" for "5" in the second sentence of (d); and substituted "180" for "160" in the first sentence of (e).

NOTES TO DECISIONS

Mandamus.

Inmate's petition for a writ of mandamus was dismissed as factually and legally frivolous; in requesting that the inmate's status sheet reflect 900 statutory earned good time credit, the inmate neither demonstrated a clear legal right to the request nor provided evidence to support that contention. Burris v. Superior Court, — A.3d —, 2020 Del. Super. LEXIS 2990 (Del. Super. Ct. Dec. 15, 2020), aff'd, — A.3d —, 2021 Del. LEXIS 96 (Del. 2021).

SUBCHAPTER IX
HOUSE ARREST

§ 4391. Definitions.

The following words, terms and phrases, when used in this subchapter, have the meanings ascribed to them in this section, except where the context clearly indicates a different meaning:

(1) "Crime of violence" means any crime which involves the use or threat of physical force or violence against any individual. For purposes of this subchapter, no motor vehicle offense is a crime of violence where it is not a part of an additional crime.

(2) "Good standing" means that an offender participating in the house arrest program has, at the time such person entered the program and continuously thereafter, met the following qualifications:

a. No pending warrants or charges.

b. No major violations during the immediately preceding 45 days.

c. Adherence to all conditions of probation, work-release and case plans.

(3) "House arrest" or "house arrest program" means a form of intensive supervised custody in the community, including surveillance on weekends, administered by intensive supervision officers. The house arrest program shall be an individual program in which the freedom of the offender is restricted within the stable, approved place of residence of the offender or within the stable, approved place of residence of a host, parent, sibling or

child of the offender and in which specific sanctions are imposed and enforced.

(4) "Public service" means that work which is required of an offender participating in the house arrest program and shall include work which the offender is ordered to perform, without payment, for the benefit of the community, separate and apart from any paid employment which the offender may be permitted to obtain. All public service work shall be performed for designated tax-supported or tax-exempt entities which have entered into an informal agreement with the Department to administer the work performed by the offender. The words "public service" include any of the following:

a. Work on any property or building owned or leased by the State, by any county or by a municipality or by any nonprofit organization or agency or work for any program under the control or sponsorship of a charitable enterprise.

b. Work on a state, county or municipally-owned road or highway.

c. Landscaping, maintenance or service work in any state, county or municipal park or recreation areas.

d. Work in a state, county or municipal hospital or for any nonprofit health or medical center or facility.

History.

66 Del. Laws, c. 29, § 3; 83 Del. Laws, c. 35, § 2.

Effect of amendments.

83 Del. Laws, c. 35, effective June 3, 2021, deleted "shall" following "subchapter" in the introductory paragraph; substituted "means" for "shall mean" in the first sentence of (1), and in the introductory paragraph of (2), the first sentence of both (3) and the introductory paragraph of present (4); substituted a period for a semicolon at the end of (2)a., (2)b., and (4)a.-

(4)c.; in the second sentence of (3), deleted "limited to nonviolent offenders and shall be" preceding "an individual", "nonviolent" preceding "offender or" and "offender and", and added "host"; deleted definition for " 'Nonviolent offender'" and redesignated former (5) as present (4); and in the introductory paragraph of present (4), substituted "the" for "such" preceding "offender" twice in the first sentence and once in the second sentence and substituted "include" for "shall include, but are not limited to" in the third sentence..

§ 4392. Identification and selection of participants.

(a) An offender sentenced to supervision Level I, II or III is not eligible for house arrest placement unless specifically ordered by the sentencing judge, or as a result of administrative detention under § 4334(d) of this title.

(b) Any person committed to the corrections center to serve a short-term sentence for a crime shall be identified by the classification officer before or upon arrival at the corrections center if the person has not already been identified prior to transportation to the corrections center.

(c) The sentencing judge, in sentencing an offender, may impose a house arrest sentence as an alternative to imprisonment.

History.

66 Del. Laws, c. 29, § 3; 76 Del. Laws, c. 399, § 2; 78 Del. Laws, c. 392, § 13; 83 Del. Laws, c. 35, § 3.

(b), deleted "nonviolent" preceding "crime", and substituted "the" for "such" preceding the second instance of "person".

Effect of amendments.

83 Del. Laws, c. 35, effective June 3, 2021, in

§ 4393. Requirements for participation.

(a) No person shall be eligible for the house arrest program unless the person meets the following requirements:

(1) Participation shall be; voluntary.

(2) Participation shall be limited to the following types of offenders:

a. Individuals found guilty of crimes who, due to the characteristics of the crime and/or the offender's background, would not be placed on regular probation.

  b. Probation violators charged with technical or misdemeanor violations.

  c. Parole violators charged with technical or misdemeanor violations.

 (b) The supervision of offenders assigned to home confinement and the use of the electronic monitoring devices shall be restricted to the area within the geographical boundaries of the State unless otherwise determined by the Commissioner of the Department of Correction.

History.

 66 Del. Laws, c. 29, § 3; 73 Del. Laws, c. 320, § 3; 83 Del. Laws, c. 35, § 4.

Effect of amendments.

 83 Del. Laws, c. 35, effective June 3, 2021, substituted "the" for "such" preceding "person"

in the introductory paragraph of (a); substituted a period for a semicolon at the end of (a)(1), (a)(2)a. and (a)(2)b.; and in (a)(2)a., deleted "nonviolent" preceding "crimes" and "and" following "crimes".

PART IV

PRISONS AND PRISONERS

CHAPTER 65
DEPARTMENT OF CORRECTION

SUBCHAPTER II
COMMISSIONER OF CORRECTION

§ 6518. Adult Correction Healthcare Review Committee.

 (a) The Adult Correction Healthcare Review Committee (Committee) is hereby established.

 (b) For administrative and budgetary purposes, the Committee shall be placed within the Criminal Justice Council. The Criminal Justice Council shall provide fiscal oversight as determined by the Executive Director of the Criminal Justice Council. Staff of the Committee are under the authority of and subject to the oversight and supervision of the Executive Director of the Criminal Justice Council.

 (c) The Committee shall consist of 8 voting members, appointed by the Governor and confirmed by the Delaware State Senate which shall include all of the following;

  (1) A Delaware licensed physician.

  (2) A Delaware licensed psychiatrist or forensic psychologist.

  (3) A Delaware licensed psychologist.

  (4) A Delaware licensed registered nurse.

  (5) A member of the Delaware Bar.

  (6) An expert in the field of substance abuse treatment.

(7) Any additional healthcare professional who by virtue of training, education, and specialization holds expertise in correctional healthcare.

(8) An individual representing a nonprofit that is serving the families of inmates or the inmates themselves, or a local civil rights organization.

(d) The Committee shall also consist of the following 3 nonvoting ex-officio members:

(1) The Chief of the Bureau of Healthcare, Substance Abuse, and Mental Health Services.

(2) Chairperson of the House Corrections Committee.

(3) Chairperson of the Senate Corrections and Public Safety Committee.

(e) Voting members shall be appointed for a term of 3 years.

(f) No member of the committee other than those designated in subsection (d) of this section may be an employee of the Department of Correction or a contractor providing medical services under the direction of the Department of Correction.

(g) Nonvoting ex-officio members may designate another individual to attend Committee meetings. The nonvoting ex-officio members identified in paragraphs (d)(2) and (d)(3) of this section may only designate a member of their respective corrections committees.

(h) Members shall receive no salary for their service, but may be reimbursed for reasonable expenses incurred in their work for the commission.

(i) Five voting members of the Committee must be present to constitute a quorum.

(j) The Medical Society of Delaware, the Delaware Psychiatric Society, the Delaware Psychological Association, the Delaware Nurses Association, and the Delaware State Bar Association, may submit recommendations to the Governor for consideration of appointment.

(k) The chair of the Committee shall be elected annually by majority vote of the voting Committee members.

(l) The Committee serves in an advisory capacity to the Governor, the General Assembly, and the Commissioner of the Department of Correction on all matters in Delaware's adult correction system relating to the provision of inmate health-care services, the review of all inmate deaths and autopsies relating to those deaths, the construction of health-care contracts that provide inmate health-care services, and the review of all statistics relating to inmate health care.

(m) The Committee shall not be considered a public body as defined at § 10002 of Title 29.

(n) The Committee shall do all of the following:

(1) Perform advisory reviews of medical records and autopsies of inmates who have died while incarcerated.

(2) Review and monitor the quality and appropriateness of health-care services rendered in Delaware's adult correctional facilities.

(3) Review critical incident and mortality and morbidity review reports.

(4) Receive and review monthly summaries of inmate, staff, public, and other health-care related grievances and the resolutions of these grievances in order to be fully appraised of the state of health-care services in Delaware's adult correction facilities.

(5) Receive and review monthly reports of inmate hospital admissions and infectious disease diagnoses, such as hepatitis C, tuberculosis, human immunodeficiency virus (HIV), methicillin resistant staphylococcus aureus (MRSA), and meningitis, from all adult correction facilities.

(6) Have access to any and all otherwise protected health-care information relating to current and former inmates supervised by the Department of Correction notwithstanding any other statute to the contrary.

(7) Advise the Governor, the General Assembly, and the Commissioner of the Department of Correction on any other matters relating to adult inmate health care that the Committee considers reasonable and worthwhile including all of the following:

a. Assurance that all inmates receive appropriate and timely services in a safe environment.

b. Systematic monitoring of the treatment environment.

c. Assisting in the reduction of professional and general liability risks.

d. Enhancing efficient utilization of resources.

e. Assisting in credential review.

f. Enhancing the identification of continuing educational needs.

g. Facilitating the identification of strengths, weaknesses, and opportunities for improvement.

h. Facilitating the coordination and integration of information systems.

i. Assuring the resolution of identified problems.

j. Changes considered necessary by the Committee.

(8) By November 30, 2021, provide a report to the Governor, the General Assembly, and the Commissioner of the Department of Correction regarding the efficacy and appropriateness of the Department's response to COVID-19 from March 12, 2020, to March 30, 2021.

a. All of the following shall be included in the report identified in this paragraph (n)(8):

1. The total number of inmates who tested positive for COVID-19.

2. The total number of inmates at each correctional institution who tested positive for COVID-19.

3. The total number of correctional officers who tested positive for COVID-19.

4. The total number of correctional officers at each correctional institution who tested positive for COVID-19.

5. The total number of deaths of inmates and correctional officers due to COVID-19.

6. The strengths, weaknesses, and opportunities for improvement of the Department's response to COVID-19.

7. An assessment of the medical treatment provided to inmates who tested positive for COVID-19.

b. In order to discharge its obligations under this paragraph (n)(8), the Committee may do all of the following:

1. Request records of or the appearance of the Department or any contractor who provided medical services to an inmate from March 12, 2020, to March 30, 2021, relating to COVID-19.

2. Consult with any additional medical professional.

3. Engage additional staff other than the Criminal Justice Council.

c. Any individual who provides services to the Committee under this paragraph (n)(8) must abide by federal and state laws regarding privacy of protected health information. Any person aggrieved by a violation of this paragraph shall have, in additional to any other rights, a right of action in the Superior Court pursuant to subsection (t) of this section.

(o) The Committee may request the appearance of any contractor providing medical and behavioral health services to an inmate under the direction of the

Department of Correction at a Committee meeting in order to provide information to the Committee.

(p) The Committee shall refer to the appropriate licensing board grievance cases in which there is a serious deviation from the community standard of care by a health-care worker or other employee of a prison health-care contractor, if the health-care worker or other employee's profession or occupation is governed under Title 24.

(q) The Department of Correction shall forward copies of National Commission of Correctional Health Care (NCCHC) and American Correctional Association (ACA) surveys, reports, and evaluations to the Committee upon their request. Whenever a survey, evaluation, or similar act is conducted by or on behalf of NCCHC or ACA, the Committee may be contacted and be allowed to contribute to the survey, evaluation, or other activity. The transmission of documents in the possession of the Department of Correction to the Committee shall not be considered a waiver of any statutory or common law privilege.

(r) All of the following shall be provided to the Committee at the Committee's request:

(1) Autopsy reports of inmates who have died while incarcerated within the control of the Department of Safety and Homeland Security.

(2) Evaluations performed by the Delaware Psychiatric Center of an inmate within the control of the Department of Health and Social Services except those records protected by 42 C.F.R. Part 2 [42 C.F.R. § 2.1 et seq.].

(3) Inmate medical and behavioral health services records in the custody of the Department of Correction.

(4) Records of a contractor providing medical and behavioral health services to an inmate under the direction of the Department of Correction.

(s) Any document received or generated by the Committee is hereby specifically excluded from the definition of public record as set forth at § 10002 of Title 29.

(t) All Committee members must abide by federal and state laws regarding privacy of protected health information. In addition any other remedies available under federal and state law, any person aggrieved by a violation of this paragraph shall have a right of action in the Superior Court and may recover for each violation all of the following:

(1) Against any person who intentionally or recklessly violates a provision of this paragraph, damages of $5,000 or actual damages, whichever is greater.

(2) Reasonable attorneys' fees.

(3) Such other relief, including an injunction, as a court may deem appropriate.

(u) This section is intended only to provide ongoing independent review, monitoring, advice, and critique of the provision of health-care services to inmates within the custody of the Department of Correction. Accordingly, nothing in this chapter shall give rise to any right, entitlement or a private cause of action for civil damages or injunctive relief for any public or private party.

(v) The Committee shall submit a report by December 31 of each year to the Governor, the General Assembly and the Commissioner of the Department of Correction on the state of inmate health-care services in Delaware's adult correction system by delivering a copy to the Governor, and the Clerks of the House of Representatives and the Senate, and the Commissioner of the Department of Correction.

(w) Notwithstanding any provision of this section to the contrary, for 2021 and 2022, the Chairperson of the House Corrections Committee and the

Chairperson of the Senate Corrections and Public Safety Committee shall be voting members of the Committee, but cannot designate another individual to attend Committee meetings or vote.

History.

76 Del. Laws, c. 388, § 1; 78 Del. Laws, c. 382, § 1; 80 Del. Laws, c. 378, § 1; 82 Del. Laws, c. 67, § 1; 83 Del. Laws, c. 199, § 1.

Effect of amendments.

83 Del. Laws, c. 199, effective Sept. 17, 2021, in the introductory paragraph of (c), substi-

tuted "8" for "6" and inserted "all of"; substituted a period for a semicolon at the end of (c)(1)-(c)(5); added (c)(7), (c)(8), (n)(8) and (w); substituted "Healthcare, Substance Abuse, and Mental Health" for "Correctional Healthcare" in (d)(1); and substituted "Five" for "Four" in (i).

SUBCHAPTER III
BUREAUS AND DIVISIONS OF THE DEPARTMENT

§ 6520. Establishment of bureaus.

There shall be within the Department the following bureaus:

(1) A Bureau of Administrative Services.

(2) A Bureau of Healthcare, Substance Abuse, and Mental Health Services.

(3) A Bureau of Prisons.

(4) A Bureau of Community Corrections.

(5) Such other bureaus, divisions, and subdivisions, with such personnel as the Commissioner shall deem desirable.

History.

11 Del. C. 1953, § 6520; 54 Del. Laws, c. 349, § 1; 78 Del. Laws, c. 305, § 7; 83 Del. Laws, c. 34, § 1.

Effect of amendments.

83 Del. Laws, c. 34, effective June 3, 2021, rewrote section.

SUBCHAPTER VI
CLASSIFICATION AND EMPLOYMENT

§ 6532. Work by inmates.

(a) The Department may establish compulsory programs of employment, work experience and training for all physically able inmates. To the maximum extent practical, these programs shall approximate normal conditions of employment in free agriculture, industry and business, with respect to equipment, management practices and general procedures.

(b) The products of inmate labor and services may be sold and marketed to tax-supported departments and institutions and agencies of the State and its governmental subdivisions and such other employers or entities within or outside of the State, as the Department shall determine. The Department may make contractual arrangements for the use of inmate labor by other tax-supported units of government responsible for the conservation of natural resources or other public works. The Department may also assign inmates to community work projects including, but not limited to, litter control along state highways and on state beaches and trash removal from state facilities, as provided in subsection (c) of this section.

(c) Before entering into an agreement with any other state department seeking prisoner-workers in accordance with this section, the Department shall have established a pilot litter-control program in each of the 3 counties with the cooperation of the Department of Transportation. The Department of Transportation shall advise the Department as to the kinds of equipment and the costs thereof that will be required and will act at all times as the consultant to the Department in this program.

(d) Inmates shall be compensated or awarded additional good time credits, at the discretion of and at rates fixed by the Department, for labor performed, including institutional maintenance.

(e) In the event that an inmate shall labor for more than 40 hours in 1 week, said inmate shall be compensated at 1½ times the regular hourly rates paid to said inmates for such work time the inmate has labored in excess of 40 hours in 1 week.

(f) The Department shall cause to be placed into an account, payable to each inmate upon the inmate's discharge, income from the inmate's employment and any other income or benefits, accruing to or payable to, and for the benefit of said inmate, including but not limited to any worker's compensation or Social Security benefits. From the account of each inmate, the Department shall deduct, in order of the priority set forth herein, the following sums:

(1) Support payments for dependents of the inmate who are receiving public assistance during the period of incarceration, or to whom the inmate is under a court ordered obligation to provide support and restitution as may have been assessed against said inmate pursuant to court order;

(2) Court costs, fines, and such other items as may be assessed against said inmate pursuant to court order; and

(3) A proportionate share of the costs of incarceration of inmates in the facility in which said inmate is housed including but not limited to room, board, medical care, legal services, prison education, training, library services, counseling and treatment services, religious services and other programs and services as shall be provided together with an allocation of the overhead for operating such prison and the Department in accordance with a fee schedule to be established by the Department.

(g) In assigning inmates to employment, work experience, training and community work project programs in accordance with this section:

(1) Assignments to programs conducted or operated outside the physical boundaries of Department-run correctional facilities shall not be available to inmates serving time for any crime classified as a class A felony, or any crime classified as a class B felony which involves a sex offense, escape or assault.

(2) The Department is authorized to establish regulations or guidelines further restricting the participation of inmates in such programs so as to minimize potential danger to the community.

(h) The Department is authorized to revoke previously earned good time (whether such good time was earned pursuant to this section or other provisions of this title) from inmates who refuse to perform labor as required by the Department pursuant to this section. In addition, the Department may impose such other lawful disciplinary measures as it deems appropriate upon inmates refusing to perform labor as required by the Department pursuant to this section.

(i) No greater amount of labor shall be required of any inmate than the inmate's physical health and strength will reasonably permit, nor shall any inmate be placed at such labor as the institutional physician determines to be beyond the inmate's ability to perform.

(j) Inmates refusing to participate in compulsory programs of employment established by the Department pursuant to this program shall not be eligible for parole nor shall the Department apply for modification of sentence, and shall further be subject to such other disciplinary measures as the Commissioner may establish by regulation.

History.
11 Del. C. 1953, § 6532; 54 Del. Laws, c. 349,

§ 1; 62 Del. Laws, c. 96, § 1; 62 Del. Laws, c. 350, § 1; 62 Del. Laws, c. 377, §§ 1, 2; 67 Del.

Laws, c. 350, § 31; 67 Del. Laws, c. 396, § 1; 70 Del. Laws, c. 186, § 1; 77 Del. Laws, c. 327, § 230; 83 Del. Laws, c. 82, § 1.

Effect of amendments.

83 Del. Laws, c. 82, effective July 20, 2021,

substituted "or awarded additional good time credits, at the discretion of and at" for "at" in (d).

SUBCHAPTER VII
DISCIPLINE, MEDICAL CARE AND DISCHARGE

§ 6536. Medical care.

NOTES TO DECISIONS

Analysis

Medical care.
— Adequacy.

Medical care.

— Adequacy.

Defendant was not entitled to receive shipments of vitamin supplements to treat a self-diagnosed medical condition because: (1) the

text of this section did not require the Department of Correction to allow receipt of any treatment regimen chosen by the defendant; and (2) a medical professional employed by the Department had concluded that there was no medical basis for defendant to receive the relief requested. State v. Desmond, — A.3d —, 2020 Del. Super. LEXIS 3020 (Del. Super. Ct. Oct. 21, 2020).

§ 6538. Furloughs.

NOTES TO DECISIONS

Eligibility.

Denial of furlough according to 11 Del. C. § 6538(e) does not violate the ex post facto clause. Fatir v. Edwards, — A.3d —, 2021 Del. Super. LEXIS 487 (Del. Super. Ct. June 23, 2021).

Decision not to pass the recommendation, that petitioner receive a furlough, through the chain of command at the Department of Correction was warranted because: (1) when the

petitioner began the furlough recommendation process in 2019, the Department was statutorily prohibited from granting petitioner a furlough (given that the petitioner had been convicted of a class A felony); and (2) the court had no authority to compel an act which the Delaware Legislature had expressly prohibited. Fatir v. Edwards, — A.3d —, 2021 Del. Super. LEXIS 487 (Del. Super. Ct. June 23, 2021).

PART V
LAW-ENFORCEMENT ADMINISTRATION

Chapter
83. State Police, §§ 8301 to 8397.
84. Delaware Police Training Program, §§ 8401 to 8410.
84A. Body-Worn Cameras for Law-Enforcement Officers, §§ 8401A to 8402A.

CHAPTER 83
STATE POLICE

Subchapter III. Service, Disability and
Survivor's Pensions
Sec.
8351. Definitions.

SUBCHAPTER III
SERVICE, DISABILITY AND SURVIVOR'S PENSIONS

§ 8351. Definitions.

As used in this subchapter:

(1) "Board" shall mean the Board of Pension Trustees established by § 8308 of Title 29.

(2) "Compensation" shall mean all salary or wages, excluding overtime

payments and special payments for extra duties, payable to a member for service.

(3) "Credited service" shall mean, for any member:

a. Service as an employee; and

b. Equalized state service if the member elects a unified pension.

(4) "Dependent" shall mean a dependent child or dependent parent. A dependent child is a person who is unmarried and either:

a. Has not attained age 18; or

b. Has attained age 18 but not age 22 and is attending school on a full-time basis; or

c. Has attained age 18 and is permanently disabled as the result of a disability which began before the child attained age 18.

A dependent parent is the parent of a member who was receiving at least one half of the parent's support from the member at the time of the member's death.

(5) "Employee" shall mean an individual who is first employed by the State on or after July 1, 1980, on a full-time basis pursuant to an appointment as a State Police officer, as provided in § 8301 of this title.

(6) "Equalized state service" shall mean:

a. Years of service as an "employee" as defined in § 5501(f)(1) and (3) of Title 29, multiplied by 25/30, provided that the individual is not accruing nor collecting benefits under Chapter 55 of Title 29. It shall not include service for which the employee has received the withdrawal benefit provided by § 5530 of Title 29, or the refund provided by § 5523(b) of Title 29, unless such benefit or refund is first repaid with interest at a rate determined by the Board before such service may be equalized.

b. Years of service as an "employee" as defined in § 5551(5) of Title 29, multiplied by 25/30, provided that the individual is not accruing nor collecting benefits under Chapter 55A of Title 29. It shall not include service for which the employee has received the withdrawal benefit provided by § 5580 of Title 29, or the refund provided by § 5573(b) of Title 29, unless such benefit or refund is first repaid with interest at a rate determined by the Board before such service may be equalized.

c. Years of service as an "employee" as defined in § 8801(5) of this title multiplied by 25/25, provided that the individual is not accruing nor collecting benefits under Chapter 88 of this title. It shall not include service for which the employee has received the withdrawal benefit provided by § 8824 of this title, or the refund provided by § 8814(d) of this title, unless such benefit or refund is first repaid with interest at a rate determined by the Board before such service may be equalized.

(7) "Final average compensation" shall mean 1/36 of the compensation paid to an employee during any period of 36 consecutive months or any 36 months comprised of 3 periods of 12 consecutive months in the years of credited service in which the compensation was highest.

(8) "Fund" shall mean the Fund established by § 8393 of this title.

(9) "Inactive member" shall mean a member who:

a. Has terminated service;

b. Is not eligible to begin receiving a service or disability pension; and

c. Has neither applied for nor received a refund of the contributions.

(10) "Member" shall mean a person who is first hired as an employee on or after July 1, 1980, and whose compensation is not subject to the federal old-age, survivors and disability insurance tax.

(11) "Normal retirement date" shall mean the date at which a member is eligible for a service pension pursuant to § 8363(a) of this title. For a member who has received a disability benefit, the period of disability plus credited service, not to exceed 20 years, shall be used in determining normal retirement date.

(12) "Partial disability" shall mean a medically determined physical or mental impairment which renders the member unable to function as a State Police officer and which is reasonably expected to last at least 12 months.

(13) "Primary survivor" shall mean a person in the following order of priority, unless the priority is changed by the member on a form prescribed by the Board and filed with the Board at the time of the member's death:

　a. The surviving spouse; or

　b. If there is no eligible surviving spouse, a dependent child (or with the survivor's pension divided among them in equal shares, all such children, including any resulting from a pregnancy prior to the member's death); or

　c. If there is no eligible surviving spouse, or eligible dependent child, a dependent parent (or, with the survivor's pension divided between them in equal shares, both such parents).

(14) "Retired member" shall mean a member who has terminated service, other than an inactive member, who is eligible to receive a service or disability pension under this subchapter.

(15) "Total disability" shall mean a medically determined physical or mental impairment which renders the member totally unable to work in any occupation for which the member is reasonably suited by training or experience, which is reasonably expected to last at least 12 months.

History.
62 Del. Laws, c. 361, § 1; 67 Del. Laws, c. 86, § 1; 70 Del. Laws, c. 186, § 1; 77 Del. Laws, c. 167, § 1; 79 Del. Laws, c. 140, § 1; 79 Del. Laws, c. 174, § 1; 82 Del. Laws, c. 87, § 1.

Revisor's note.
Section 2g. of 83 Del. Laws, c. 55, effective June 30, 2021, provided: "This supplement [a one-time salary supplement of $1,000.00 for state employees] shall be considered within the pension definitions stated in 29 Del. C. § 5501 (c), §5501(d), §5501 (e), §5600 (3), and 11 Del. C. §8351 (2)."

This section is being reprinted to correct an error in (6)b. in the cumulative supplement.

CHAPTER 84
DELAWARE POLICE TRAINING PROGRAM

§ 8401. Definitions.

As used in this chapter:

(1) "Approved school" means a school authorized by the Council to provide a mandatory training and education for police officers as prescribed in this chapter.

(2) "Articulation agreement" means a written agreement for the transfer of academic credit.

(3) "Body-worn camera" means an electronic device that is worn by a law-enforcement officer and records audio and video data on the device itself or transmits audio and video data to another location for recording.

(4) "Council" means the Council on Police Training.

(5) "Permanent appointment" means appointment by the authority of any municipality or governmental unit in or of this State or the University of Delaware to permanent status as a police officer.

(6) "Police officer" means a sworn member of a police force or other law-enforcement agency of this State or of any county or municipality who is responsible for the prevention and the detection of crime and the enforcement of laws of this State or other governmental units within the State.

    a. For purposes of this chapter this term shall include permanent full-time law-enforcement officers of the Department of Natural Resources and Environmental Control, state fire marshals, municipal fire marshals who are graduates of a Delaware Police Academy which is accredited/authorized by the Council on Police Training, sworn members of the City of Wilmington Fire Department who have graduated from a Delaware Police Academy which is authorized/ accredited by the Council on Police Training, environmental protection officers, enforcement agents of the Department of Natural Resources and Environmental Control, agents of the State Division of Alcohol and Tobacco Enforcement, officers or agents of the State Police Drug Diversion Unit, officers or agents of the Delaware Police Sex Offender Task Force, agents employed by a state, county or municipal law-enforcement agency engaged in monitoring sex offenders, state detective or special investigator of the Department of Justice and officers of the University of Delaware Police Division, Delaware State University Police Department.

    b. For purposes of this chapter this term shall not include the following:

        1. A sheriff, regular deputy sheriff or constable.

        2. A security force for a state agency or other governmental unit; or, a seasonal, temporary or part-time law-enforcement officer of the Department of Natural Resources and Environmental Control.

        3. A person holding police power by virtue of occupying any other position or office.

        4. An animal welfare officer of the Office of Animal Welfare or the Department of Agriculture.

(7) "Seasonal appointment" means appointment for less than 6 months each year but more than 4 weeks for police duties necessitated by seasonal demands.

History.

11 Del. C. 1953, § 8401; 57 Del. Laws, c. 261; 57 Del. Laws, c. 670, § 1A; 63 Del. Laws, c. 31, § 1; 68 Del. Laws, c. 172, §§ 1, 2; 68 Del. Laws, c. 330, § 1; 72 Del. Laws, c. 367, § 2; 72 Del. Laws, c. 371, § 2; 72 Del. Laws, c. 379, § 3; 73 Del. Laws, c. 195, § 3[2]; 73 Del. Laws, c. 249, § 2; 74 Del. Laws, c. 250, § 2; 74 Del. Laws, c. 331, § 1; 76 Del. Laws, c. 43, § 2; 76 Del. Laws, c. 163, § 1; 78 Del. Laws, c. 155, § 4; 79 Del. Laws, c. 200, § 1; 80 Del. Laws, c. 200, § 5; 83 Del. Laws, c. 83, § 2.

Effect of amendments.

83 Del. Laws, c. 83, effective July 21, 2021, added present (3) and redesignated the remaining paragraphs accordingly.

§ 8402. Members of Council.

(a) The Council shall be composed of 16 members.

(b) The Council shall be composed of: a chairperson to be appointed by and to serve at the pleasure of the Governor; the Attorney General; the Superintendent of the Delaware State Police; the Chief of the City of Wilmington Police; the Chief of the New Castle County Police Department; the Chief of the

City of Dover Police Department; the Chief of the City of Newark Police Department; the Secretary of Education; the President of the Delaware League of Local Governments; the mayor of an incorporated municipality in Kent County, to be appointed by the Governor; the mayor of an incorporated municipality in Sussex County, to be appointed by the Governor; the Chairperson of the Delaware Police Chiefs' Council, Inc; the Chair of Public Safety Committee of the House of Representatives; the Chair of the Corrections and Public Safety Committee of the Senate; 2 members of the public appointed by the Governor, who shall not be law-enforcement officers or be affiliated with law enforcement. The Chairperson shall have had substantial practical experience in the field of law enforcement. Each public member's term shall be for 3 years.

History.

11 Del. C. 1953, § 8403; 57 Del. Laws, c. 261; 57 Del. Laws, c. 670, §§ 1B, 1C; 63 Del. Laws, c. 31, § 1; 65 Del. Laws, c. 492, §§ 1, 2; 68 Del. Laws, c. 49, §§ 1, 2; 70 Del. Laws, c. 186, § 1; 73 Del. Laws, c. 65, § 9; 83 Del. Laws, c. 83, § 2.

substituted "16" for "12" in (a); in (b), in the first sentence deleted "or police commissioner" following "mayor" in two places and added "the Chair of Public Safety Committee of the House ... affiliated with law enforcement", and added the final sentence.

Effect of amendments.

83 Del. Laws, c. 83, effective July 21, 2021,

§ 8403. Organization of Council.

(a) A Vice-Chairperson and a Secretary shall be elected from among the members of the Council. The Council shall hold no less than 2 regular meetings each year and may meet at such other times as it may determine. The Chairperson shall fix the time and place of such meetings in the Chair's discretion, but upon written request of any 3 members, the Chairperson shall call a meeting pursuant to the terms of such request. Nine members shall constitute a quorum. Each member of the Council may have a proxy to represent the member at Council meetings.

(b) Notwithstanding any provision of law, Council membership shall not disqualify any member from holding any other public or private employment or constitute a forfeit of such office.

(c) Council members shall receive no compensation for their services but shall be allowed their actual and necessary expenses incurred in the performance of their duties.

History.

11 Del. C. 1953, § 8404; 57 Del. Laws, c. 261; 57 Del. Laws, c. 670, § 1C; 63 Del. Laws, c. 31, § 1; 65 Del. Laws, c. 492, § 3; 68 Del. Laws, c. 49, § 3; 70 Del. Laws, c. 186, § 1; 83 Del. Laws, c. 83, § 2.

Effect of amendments.

83 Del. Laws, c. 83, effective July 21, 2021, in (a), substituted "Chair's" for "Commissioner's" in the third sentence and "Nine" for "Seven" in the fourth sentence.

§ 8404. Powers and duties.

(a) The Council may:

    (1) Establish minimum qualifications for applicants as police officers;

    (2) Establish minimum educational and training qualifications requisite to permanent appointment as a police officer;

    (3) Issue certification of completion of police officer training prescribed under this chapter;

    (4) Suspend or revoke certification in the event that an individual:

        a. Obtained a certificate by fraud or deceit;

        b. Has failed to successfully complete any in-service or advanced training required by the Council;

        c. Has been convicted of a felony, or of a misdemeanor involving moral turpitude, or of any local, state or federal criminal offense involving, but not limited to, theft, fraud, or violation of the public trust, or of any drug law;

    d. Has been found, after examination by a licensed psychologist or psychiatrist, to be psychologically or emotionally unfit to perform the duties or exercise the powers and authority of a police officer;

    e. Has received a hearing pursuant to the Police Officer's Bill of Rights, or who has knowingly and voluntarily waived that individual's right to such a hearing and:

        1. Has been discharged from employment with a law-enforcement agency for a breach of internal discipline; or

        2. Has retired or resigned prior to the entry of findings of fact concerning an alleged breach of internal discipline for which the individual could have been legitimately discharged had the individual not retired from or resigned that individual's position prior to the imposition of discipline by the employing agency.

(5) Prescribe standards for in-service or continued training of police officers, which shall include at least 2 hours every 4 years on the detection, prevention and prosecution of sexual assault for all police officers who perform uniformed patrol duties or are assigned to investigative units responsible for sex crimes, and which training shall be conducted on a staggered basis so that half of the eligible members of any law-enforcement or police organization receive said training in each 2-year period;

(6) Establish minimum educational and training qualifications for seasonal employment as a police officer;

(7) Establish certification and recertification requirements for police officer applicants who have previously been employed with permanent appointment as a police officer but have not been so employed within the 12 months prior to application;

(8) Prescribe equipment and facility standards for schools at which police training courses shall be conducted, including but not limited to existing county or municipal schools;

(9) Establish minimum training requirements, attendance requirements and standards of operations for police training schools;

(10) Prescribe minimum qualifications for instructors at such schools and certify, as qualified, or decertify such instructors to their particular courses of study;

(11) Approve and issue certificates of approval to such police training schools, to inspect such schools from time to time and to revoke for cause any approval or certificate issued to such schools;

(12) Consult and cooperate with all agencies of government, state and local, concerning the development and administration of the training and standard program and to contract with such agencies as it deems necessary to the performance of its powers and duties;

(13) Accept or receive grants or donations from any source, public or private, for the purposes of this chapter;

(14) Make such rules and regulations as may be necessary to carry out the purposes and objectives of this chapter;

(15) Provide a modification from the application of any provision of this chapter or the rules and regulations promulgated thereunder, for any police officer of a municipality if:

    a. The police officer is employed on a seasonal basis; and

    b. The municipality makes application for such modification and establishes that it will suffer a hardship if the modification is not granted;

(16) Establish an approved training program for seasonal police officers which shall be required prior to active police duty, and in addition, if the officer is to be armed, that the police officer be certified in the use of firearms at an approved police training school;

(17) Authorize articulation agreements between an approved school and an accredited institution of higher education located in the State for the provision of police officer training prescribed under this chapter;

(18) Establish the criteria to afford reciprocity to police officers certified in other states by an agency like the Council or by the federal government by waiving some or all of the minimum education and training qualifications for police officers under this chapter if they have satisfied substantially equivalent education and training;

(19) Mandate training for all persons seeking permanent or seasonal appointment as a police officer in the detection, prosecution and prevention of child sexual and physical abuse, exploitation and domestic violence, and the obligations imposed by Delaware law, including § 903 of Title 16, and federal law in the prompt reporting thereof. Such training shall be coordinated under §§ 911 and 931(b)(4) of Title 16 to ensure consistent trainings across disciplines.

(b) The Director of the Delaware State Police Training Division shall be responsible for administering the mandatory training and education for police officers program with responsibility and authority to obtain professional assistance from other police and professional organizations to accomplish the purposes and objectives of the program.

(c) The Council shall propose regulations detailing mandatory standards for the use of body-worn cameras by police officers no later than January 15, 2022, to ensure widespread and consistent use of body-worn cameras. While developing the standards, the Council shall hold a minimum of 2 public meetings to solicit input from the community on the body-worn camera regulations to ensure that victims' rights advocates, community groups, and member of the public have an opportunity to contribute to the development of the regulations. The Council shall include the Delaware State Troopers Association and the Delaware Fraternal Order of Police in discussions concerning regulations detailing mandatory standards for the use of body-worn cameras by police officers. The Council shall consult with the Department of Correction, the Department of Services for Children, Youth, and Their Families, and the Office of Defense Services in the development of the regulations. Notwithstanding anything to the contrary in Chapter 101 of Title 29, the regulations shall not come into effect until after review by the Delaware State Troopers Association and the Delaware Fraternal Order of Police and formal approval by the Council on Police Training. At a minimum, the regulations shall address standards governing body-worn cameras use, activation, electronic storage, and dissemination.

History.
11 Del. C. 1953, § 8405; 57 Del. Laws, c. 261; 57 Del. Laws, c. 670, § 1D; 63 Del. Laws, c. 31, § 1; 67 Del. Laws, c. 313, § 1; 68 Del. Laws, c. 330, §§ 2-4; 70 Del. Laws, c. 186, § 1; 74 Del. Laws, c. 331, §§ 2-4; 77 Del. Laws, c. 323, § 3; 80 Del. Laws, c. 55, § 1; 80 Del. Laws, c. 187, § 8; 83 Del. Laws, c. 83, § 2.

Effect of amendments.
83 Del. Laws, c. 83, effective July 21, 2021, added (c).

§ 8405. Mandatory training; exceptions.

(a) Except as provided in subsection (e) of this section, every municipality or other governmental unit of this State employing or intending to employ police officers shall require their attendance at an approved school. Every such municipality, other governmental unit or the University of Delaware or

Delaware State University shall require that no person be given or accept an appointment as a police officer unless such person has successfully completed the required police training and education course at an approved school.

(b) Police officers already serving under permanent appointment on July 11, 1969, shall not be compelled to meet this requirement as a condition of:

(1) Tenure;

(2) Continuing employment;

(3) Reemployment; or

(4) Employment by another police agency, provided that the period of suspended services under paragraph (b)(3) or (4) of this section does not exceed 12 months.

Failure of any such police officer to fulfill such requirements as the Council may hereafter establish by regulation shall not make the officer ineligible for promotion to which the officer might otherwise be eligible. The exemptions granted under this subsection shall not be construed to include in-service or continued training requirements which may be established by Council.

(c) All police officers and all persons seeking permanent appointment as a police officer shall undergo training to assist them in identifying symptoms of mental illness, mental disability, and/or physical disability and in responding appropriately to situations involving persons having a mental illness, mental disability, and/or physical disability. The training must include instruction concerning the interaction between police officers and minors that have a mental illness, mental disability and/or physical disability. Additionally, all police officers serving under permanent appointment as of January 1, 2007, must undertake this training by January 1, 2008.

(d) A component of training for all persons enrolled in an approved school must be a course in the detection, prosecution, and prevention of sexual assault. Such evidence-based training must be victim-centered, and trauma-informed.

(e) Nothing contained in this chapter limits the authority, power, or duties of the Secretary of the Department of Safety and Homeland Security under § 8203 of Title 29.

History.

11 Del. C. 1953, § 8406; 57 Del. Laws, c. 261; 57 Del. Laws, c. 670, § 1D; 63 Del. Laws, c. 31, § 1; 67 Del. Laws, c. 230, §§ 1, 2; 68 Del. Laws, c. 330, § 5; 70 Del. Laws, c. 186, § 1; 72 Del. Laws, c. 367, § 3; 75 Del. Laws, c. 292, § 1; 80 Del. Laws, c. 55, § 1; 83 Del. Laws, c. 37, § 12.

Effect of amendments.

83 Del. Laws, c. 37, effective June 3, 2021, substituted "subsection (e)" for "subsection (d)" in the first sentence of (a); in (d), substituted "must" for "shall" in the first and second sentences and added a comma following "prosecution" in the first sentence; and, in (e), substituted "limits" for "shall limit" and "the Department of Safety and Homeland Security under" for "Public Safety as set forth in" and added a comma following "power".

CHAPTER 84A

BODY-WORN CAMERAS FOR LAW-ENFORCEMENT OFFICERS

Revisor's note.

This Chapter became effective upon the signature of the Governor on July 21, 2021.

§ 8401A. Definitions.

For the purposes of this chapter all terms mean as defined as in § 8401 of this title.

History.
83 Del. Laws, c. 83, § 3.

§ 8402A. Body-worn camera requirements.

(a) In accordance with the regulations established in §§ 8404, 4321, and 9003 of this title, a police officer, a probation and parole officer of the Department of Correction assigned to a law-enforcement task force, and an employee of the Department of Services for Children, Youth, and Their Families designated as a special investigator or serious juvenile offender officer shall wear a body-worn camera while on duty in a role that is likely to result in interactions with the public.

(b) A police officer, a probation and parole officer of the Department of Correction assigned to a law-enforcement task force, and an employee of Department of Services for Children, Youth, and Their Families designated as a special investigator or serious juvenile offender officer required to wear a body-worn camera under subsection (a) of this section shall use the body-worn camera to record interactions with the public while on duty in accordance with the regulations established in §§ 8404, 4321, and 9003 of this title.

(c) The Department of Safety and Homeland Security, Office of Management and Budget, Department of Technology, Department of Justice, and Office of Defense Services shall work to implement a statewide body-worn camera program as funding is made available to procure body-worn cameras for law-enforcement officers where necessary, to establish a central data storage program to house body-worn camera footage, and to provide adequate personnel to administer the program.

History.
83 Del. Laws, c. 83, § 3.

PART VI

VICTIMS OF CRIMES

CHAPTER 92

LAW-ENFORCEMENT OFFICERS' BILL OF RIGHTS

§ 9200. Limitations on political activity; "law-enforcement officer" defined; rights of officers under investigation.

NOTES TO DECISIONS

Analysis

Termination.
— Due process.

Termination.

— Due process.

Court dismissed the terminated university police officer's U.S. Const. amend. 14 due process claim against a university police department because the officer had not yet completed the initial probationary period of employment and could not show a protected property inter-est under the Law Enforcement Officers' Bill of Rights (LEOBR, 11 Del. C. § 9200 et seq.); the failure to provide plaintiff with an administrative hearing did not violate LEOBR because there was a separate contractual disciplinary grievance procedure which allowed for termination of officers during their probationary period without having to adhere to the statutory procedural requirements of LEOBR. Sapienza v. Del. State Univ. Police Dep't, — A.3d —, 2021 Del. Super. LEXIS 125 (Del. Super. Ct. Feb. 10, 2021).

§ 9203. Hearing — Required on suspension or other disciplinary action.

NOTES TO DECISIONS

Due process.
Court dismissed the terminated university police officer's U.S. Const. amend. 14 due process claim against a university police depart-

ment because the officer had not yet completed the initial probationary period of employment and could not show a protected property interest under the Law Enforcement Officers' Bill of Rights (LEOBR, 11 Del. C. § 9200 et seq.); the failure to provide plaintiff with an administrative hearing did not violate LEOBR because there was a separate contractual disciplinary grievance procedure which allowed for termination of officers during their probationary period without having to adhere to the statutory procedural requirements of LEOBR. Sapienza v. Del. State Univ. Police Dep't, — A.3d —, 2021 Del. Super. LEXIS 125 (Del. Super. Ct. Feb. 10, 2021).

§ 9205. Hearing — Procedure.

NOTES TO DECISIONS

Legal counsel.

Petitioner's writ of mandamus seeking to allow a nonattorney representative at a police officer disciplinary hearing was denied because the use of the phrase "legal counsel" in 11 Del. C. § 9205(b) had legal significance; only those who are licensed to practice law in the State of Delaware may provide legal representation. Paskey v. Del. Crim. Justice Council, — A.3d —, 2021 Del. Super. LEXIS 342 (Del. Super. Ct. Apr. 20, 2021).

§ 9207. Hearing — Written decision and findings of fact to be delivered to officer.

NOTES TO DECISIONS

Constitutional claims.

Petitioner's writ of mandamus seeking to allow a nonattorney representative at a police officer disciplinary hearing was denied because the use of the phrase "legal counsel" in 11 Del. C. § 9205(b) had legal significance; only those who are licensed to practice law in the State of Delaware may provide legal representation. Paskey v. Del. Crim. Justice Council, — A.3d —, 2021 Del. Super. LEXIS 342 (Del. Super. Ct. Apr. 20, 2021).

CHAPTER 94
VICTIMS' BILL OF RIGHTS
SUBCHAPTER I
VICTIMS GENERALLY

§ 9410. Information from law-enforcement agency.

NOTES TO DECISIONS

Opinions of the Attorney General

FOIA Petition Regarding the Delaware State Police, see No. 21-IB07, March, 24, 2021.

TITLE 13
DOMESTIC RELATIONS

CHAPTER 3
HUSBAND AND WIFE; CONTRACTS AND PROPERTY RIGHTS

SUBCHAPTER II
PREMARITAL AGREEMENTS

§ 326. Enforcement.

RESEARCH REFERENCES AND PRACTICE AIDS

Delaware Law Reviews.
Divorce and Third-Party Trusts in Delaware,
17 Del. L. Rev. 1 (2021).

CHAPTER 5
DESERTION AND SUPPORT

SUBCHAPTER I
DUTY TO SUPPORT

§ 501. Duty to support minor child; duty to support child over 18 years of age.

NOTES TO DECISIONS

Duty to support child in high school. — Family Court Commissioner properly ordered the father to pay child support in the amount of $1547 monthly because: (1) the earnings of the children were meager to the point that they did not impact the child support calculation; (2) the duty to support the son, for both parents, remained while the son was 18 years old and attended high school; (3) the mother paid the rent at the room the son used in Florida, bought the food he ate and covered most of his travel to and from Delaware; and (4) the fact that the son's school was in Florida, and not Delaware, was not relevant to the calculation. J v. Division Of Child Support, 2021 Del. Fam. Ct. LEXIS 17.

RESEARCH REFERENCES AND PRACTICE AIDS

Delaware Law Reviews.
Divorce and Third-Party Trusts in Delaware,
17 Del. L. Rev. 1 (2021).

SUBCHAPTER II
CIVIL ENFORCEMENT

§ 514. Determination of amount of support.

NOTES TO DECISIONS

Factors considered in proceeding to modify support order. — Family Court Commissioner properly ordered the father to pay child support in the amount of $1547 monthly because: (1) the earnings of the children were meager to the point that they did not impact the child support calculation; (2) the duty to support the son, for both parents, remained while the son was 18 years old and attended high school; (3) the mother paid the rent at the room the son used in Florida, bought the food he ate and covered most of his travel to and from Delaware; and (4) the fact that the son's school was in Florida, and not Delaware, was not relevant to the calculation. J v. Division Of Child Support, 2021 Del. Fam. Ct. LEXIS 17.

CHAPTER 7
PARENTS AND CHILDREN

Subchapter II. Custody Proceedings

Sec.
734. Relocation.

SUBCHAPTER I
GENERAL PROVISIONS

§ 701. Rights and responsibilities of parents; guardian appointment.

NOTES TO DECISIONS

Fostering relationship between other parent and children. — Father was granted sole custody of the child because: (1) the testimony and evidence made clear that the parties had documented and serious communications problems instigated by the mother; and (2) the mother did not appear to fully understand the effects of her past behavior and found no reason the parties could not coparent effectively. L.B. v. G.L., — A.3d —, 2021 Del. Fam. Ct. LEXIS 3 (Del. Fam. Ct. Jan. 15, 2021).

Shared custody. — Court awarded the parties joint legal custody and shared residential placement of the children because: (1) best interest factors 1, 2, 3, 5, 7 and 8 were all neutral; (2) each parent played an important role in the children's lives, to the extent permitted by the other; and (3) no single factor carried more weight than another in the case. G.B. v. R.P.B., — A.3d —, 2021 Del. Fam. Ct. LEXIS 6 (Del. Fam. Ct. Apr. 27, 2021).

SUBCHAPTER II
CUSTODY PROCEEDINGS

§ 721. Commencement of proceedings; venue; notice; pleadings; attorney for child; removal from jurisdiction; considerations.

NOTES TO DECISIONS

Appointment of attorney. — Under the circumstances, which included the removal of the parties' child from the mother's care and the child's lack of contact with the father before the child's removal, the appointment of an attorney to represent the child in the custody proceeding was not error; furthermore, the child's attorney took representation of the child seriously and zealously represented the child's interests. Roberts v. Blocker, 239 A.3d 390 (Del. 2020).

§ 727. Custody.

NOTES TO DECISIONS

Prior incident of domestic violence. — Court properly granted a mother's motion to modify custody because: (1) the child was more comfortable with the mother and wished to have more time with her; (2) the mother's home was neat, clean and very welcoming; (3) the father threatened to take pills and stated that he wanted to die in front of the child; and (4) the father's history of domestic violence reflected negatively on his mental health and had negatively impacted the mother and the child. G-------- C-------- -------- -------------- v. R---P----------- ---- G---- ------N-----, — A.3d —, 2019 Del. Fam. Ct. LEXIS 72 (Del. Fam. Ct. Mar. 14, 2019).

Preference of child. — Sole legal custody was awarded to mother because: (1) the child was adamant that he had no desire to have a relationship with the father; (2) the child had lived with the mother since birth; (3) the child had a strong relationship with the mother; and (4) the father had not contacted the child for the last year. D.W. v. E.C., — A.3d —, 2020 Del. Fam. Ct. LEXIS 21 (Del. Fam. Ct. July 23, 2020).

Custody based upon more stable living environment. — Court awarded the parties joint legal custody of the children because: (1) the father was more likely to share information and keep both parents involved in decisions affecting the parties' daughters (2) the father's relatives had a fine relationship with the children when they were with the father; (3) the mental and physical health of all individuals involved favored the father; and (4) the overwhelming weight of the evidence indicated that the father was more likely than the mother to provide stability for the children in a normal environment, to ensure that they get to school on school days and to provide the children with the opportunity to develop a more normal and consistent life style. A.K. v. A.K., — A.3d —, 2020 Del. Fam. Ct. LEXIS 29 (Del. Fam. Ct. Aug. 19, 2020).

Court concluded that awarding the mother sole legal custody and primary residential placement, with no contact by the father, was in the children's best interest because: (1) the father subjected the children to physical and emotional abuse throughout their lives; and (2) contact between the children and the father would both endanger the children's physical health and significantly impair their emotional development. S.T. v. C.T., — A.3d —, 2020 Del. Fam. Ct. LEXIS 37 (Del. Fam. Ct. Oct. 20, 2020).

Upon consideration of the enumerated best interest factors, the court awarded the parties joint legal custody, and the mother primary residential placement, of the child because: (1) both parties' positions were understandable and reasonable based upon their testimony; (2) the child loved both parents and enjoyed spending time with both parents and their respective families; (3) both parties appeared to have positive relationships with the child; (4) it appeared that the child had a more stable home in the house that he shared with the mother since birth; and (5) the evidence suggested that the mother primarily handled the child's health issues. Redacted v. Redacted, — A.3d —, 2020 Del. Fam. Ct. LEXIS 43 (Del. Fam. Ct. Nov. 9, 2020).

Joint custody. — Father was awarded sole legal custody because: (1) the father was more likely to ensure respectful time with the mother; (2) the mother had exhibited retribu-tion toward the father for unknown reasons and denied him time with the children; and (3) the mother failed to address the children's healthcare needs. M.D. v. J.C., — A.3d —, 2019 Del. Fam. Ct. LEXIS 65 (Del. Fam. Ct. Dec. 23, 2019).

Mother and father were awarded joint legal custody because: (1) there was no evidence that the child was at risk of harm in the father's care; (2) both mother and father were in good physical and mental health; and (3) the mother tended to place her own best interests above child's when it came to matters involving the father. G.S. v. S.S., — A.3d —, 2020 Del. Fam. Ct. LEXIS 23 (Del. Fam. Ct. July 23, 2020).

Mother and father were awarded joint legal custody because: (1) the court did not believe that the mother would keep the father informed if she were awarded sole custody; (2) both parties appeared to have good relationships with the children; and (3) both parents provided adequate care for the children. N.G. v. D.L., — A.3d —, 2020 Del. Fam. Ct. LEXIS 22 (Del. Fam. Ct. July 31, 2020).

In a custody proceeding, the court ordered the parties to have joint legal custody, with the father having primary residential placement, because: (1) he was far more likely to facilitate a relationship between the child and the other parent; (2) the mother acted in a manner wherein she attempted to oust the father from the child's life; (3) with the exception of the maternal grandparents, all relatives lived in the Delaware area; (4) the father was in fine mental and physical health; and (5) none of the mother's statements were valid reasons in considering the child's best interest to relocate. T.A.C. v. K.S.J., — A.3d —, 2020 Del. Fam. Ct. LEXIS 30 (Del. Fam. Ct. Aug. 17, 2020).

Court awarded the parties joint legal custody and shared residential placement of the children because: (1) best interest factors 1, 2, 3, 5, 7 and 8 were all neutral; (2) each parent played an important role in the children's lives, to the extent permitted by the other; and (3) no single factor carried more weight than another in the case. G.B. v. R.P.B., — A.3d —, 2021 Del. Fam. Ct. LEXIS 6 (Del. Fam. Ct. Apr. 27, 2021).

Poor relationship between parents. — Father was granted sole custody of the child because: (1) the testimony and evidence made clear that the parties had documented and serious communications problems instigated by the mother; and (2) the mother did not appear to fully understand the effects of her past behavior and found no reason the parties could not coparent effectively. L.B. v. G.L., — A.3d —, 2021 Del. Fam. Ct. LEXIS 3 (Del. Fam. Ct. Jan. 15, 2021).

Court awarded mother sole legal custody and primary placement of the children because: (1) the children were unique and required intervention services; (2) the mother had been the primary caretaker and had provided stable housing, care and proper education for the children; (3) both parties believed that the children would prefer to primarily reside with the mother; (4) the children had not resided with the father for more than 4 years; and (5) the mother had filed for a protection from abuse order against the father 4 different times since 2015. P---- B----- v. J---- B----, — A.3d —, 2021 Del. Fam. Ct. LEXIS 5 (Del. Fam. Ct. Mar. 5, 2021).

§ 728. Residence; visitation; sanctions.

NOTES TO DECISIONS

Unsupervised visitation approved. — Expanding the mother's visitation in a gradual manner to unsupervised contact every other weekend, with future visitation to include an overnight, was in the child's best interest because: (1) the visits that occurred had been positive; (2) the mother had an adult child with a physical disability that prevented her from being away from home for long periods of time; and (3) the child wanted to get to know her siblings at the mother's home. J E. C v. R E. Y, 2020 Del. Fam. Ct. LEXIS 51 (Del. Fam. Ct. Mar. 30, 2020).

Incarcerated parent. — Court modified visitation and established a graduated schedule for the father's reintroduction because: (1) the father had been incarcerated for almost 1 year of the 5-year-old child's life; (2) the child was autistic; (3) promoting too much visitation on the child too quickly could have a negative impact on the child and his adjustment; and (4) the mother's approach better addressed the child's needs. M.R. v. C.G., — A.3d —, 2020 Del. Fam. Ct. LEXIS 38 (Del. Fam. Ct. Oct. 9, 2020).

It was in the best interest of children to have telephone contact with their father twice weekly, video contact with the father once weekly and monthly in-person contact with the children at a correctional facility because: (1) the father had a substantial and positive relationship with the parties' oldest child; (2) the victims of the father's crimes were not related to the children; (3) both the mother and the father supported visitation at the correctional facility and frequent video and telephone contact; and (4) although the father had made inappropriate comments about the mother while he was in contact with the children, and had attempted to exert coercive control over the mother (satisfying the definition of domestic abuse), best interest factors still supported visitation. D v. T, — A.3d —, 2020 Del. Fam. Ct. LEXIS 52 (Del. Fam. Ct. Sept. 3, 2020), aff'd, 256 A.3d 756 (Del. 2021).

Visitation should provide meaningful contact opportunities. — Father's testimony regarding the children's behavior immediately following visitation exchange, and the mother's testimony about the children being tired after such exchanges, demonstrated the benefit of a week on/week off schedule; an alternating weekly schedule would allow for increased meaningful contact for the children with each parent because there would be less time spent adjusting from transitions or feeling tired. L.S. v. C.C., — A.3d —, 2020 Del. Fam. Ct. LEXIS 3 (Del. Fam. Ct. Feb. 28, 2020).

Visitation modified. — Petition for visitation modification was granted because the mother did not have stable housing and failed to make responsible decisions for the children's health and safety; the children spent time in a motel while the mother was at work for not less than 8 hours, 5 days per week. M.D. v. J.C., — A.3d —, 2020 Del. Fam. Ct. LEXIS 20 (Del. Fam. Ct. June 24, 2020).

Family Court did not err by denying a father's petition to modify visitation or by granting the mother's cross-petition to increase her visitation, because: (1) the father did not prove the mother's mid-week visitation would endanger the child's physical health or significantly impair emotional development; (2) there was no basis to restrict the mother's contact with the child; (3) the best interest factors weighed in favor of granting of the mother's additional visitation with the child; and (4) therapy had aided the mother in making significant improvements in managing her anger. Tremont v. Tremont, 248 A.3d 104 (Del. 2021).

Visitation not modified. — Continued visitation with the mother pursuant to the social worker's therapeutic protocol was in the children's best interest because the social worker: (1) had seen the children for 7 years; (2) developed a protocol for visitation that considered the trauma the children experienced and their current relationship with the mother; and (3) was willing to continue to provide individual counseling for the children and reunification services for the mother. C.O. v. D.R., — A.3d —, 2020 Del. Fam. Ct. LEXIS 32 (Del. Fam. Ct. Oct. 8, 2020).

Mental health of parent. — In contentious visitation proceedings, following the father's request for unsupervised visitation or visitation in his home, the court entered an order requiring supervised visitation until a new family therapist was put in place; the court found that order to be in the child's best interests where the father had made significant improvements through family therapy, but was primarily responsible for creating the child's unhealthy relationship with her parents. W.S. v. J.M., — A.3d —, 2020 Del. Fam. Ct. LEXIS 28 (Del. Fam. Ct. Sept. 21, 2020).

Grandparent visitation. — Family Court properly denied a former stepgrandfather's petition for third-party visitation, concluding that the mother's objections to visitation were not clearly unreasonable; the court recognized the strained relationship between the mother and the former step-grandfather, which included their inability to communicate with each other and the former step-grandfather making negative comments to and about the mother. Jarvis v. Mole, 242 A.3d 574 (Del. 2020).

Award of primary placement. — Family Court did not abuse its discretion by modifying child custody to award father sole custody and primary residence of the child because: (1) the Court found that the child would not be harmed if the previous custody order was modified; and (2) the statutory best-interests factors (mental and physical health of the individuals, parents' attention to their rights/responsibilities to the child, and criminal history of the parties) supported the father having primary residence of the child and the restriction of the mother's contact with the child. Roberts v. Blocker, 239 A.3d 390 (Del. 2020).

In a custody proceeding, the court ordered the parties to have joint legal custody, with the father having primary residential placement, because: (1) he was far more likely to facilitate a relationship between the child and the other parent; (2) the mother acted in a manner wherein she attempted to oust the father from the child's life; (3) with the exception of the maternal grandparents, all relatives lived in the Delaware area; (4) the father was in fine mental and physical health; and (5) none of the mother's statements were valid reasons in considering the child's best interest to relocate. T.A.C. v. K.S.J., — A.3d —, 2020 Del. Fam. Ct. LEXIS 30 (Del. Fam. Ct. Aug. 17, 2020).

Shared custody. — Court awarded the parties joint legal custody and shared residential placement of the children because: (1) best interest factors 1, 2, 3, 5, 7 and 8 were all neutral; (2) each parent played an important role in the children's lives, to the extent permitted by the other; and (3) no single factor carried more weight than another in the case. G.B. v. R.P.B., — A.3d —, 2021 Del. Fam. Ct. LEXIS 6 (Del. Fam. Ct. Apr. 27, 2021).

§ 729. Modification of prior orders.

NOTES TO DECISIONS

Modification of custody in best interests of minor child. — Family Court did not abuse its discretion by modifying child custody to award father sole custody and primary residence of the child because: (1) the Court found that the child would not be harmed if the previous custody order was modified; and (2) the statutory best-interests factors (mental and physical health of the individuals, parents' attention to their rights/responsibilities to the child, and criminal history of the parties) supported the father having primary residence of the child and the restriction of the mother's contact with the child. Roberts v. Blocker, 239 A.3d 390 (Del. 2020).

Modification not in best interest of the child. — Continued visitation with the mother pursuant to the social worker's therapeutic protocol was in the children's best interest because the social worker: (1) had seen the children for 7 years; (2) developed a protocol for visitation that considered the trauma the children experienced and their current relationship with the mother; and (3) was willing to continue to provide individual counseling for the children and reunification services for the mother. C.O. v. D.R., — A.3d —, 2020 Del. Fam. Ct. LEXIS 32 (Del. Fam. Ct. Oct. 8, 2020).

Relationship with grandparents. — Family Court properly denied a former stepgrandfather's petition for third-party visitation, concluding that the mother's objections to visitation were not clearly unreasonable; the court recognized the strained relationship between the mother and the former step-grandfather, which included their inability to communicate with each other and the former step-grandfather making negative comments to and about the mother. M.R. v. C.G., — A.3d —, 2020 Del. Fam. Ct. LEXIS 38 (Del. Fam. Ct. Oct. 9, 2020).

Relocation of child to more stable living environment. — Court properly granted a mother's motion to modify custody because: (1) the child was more comfortable with the mother and wished to have more time with her; (2) the mother's home was neat, clean and very welcoming; (3) the father threatened to take pills and stated that he wanted to die in front of the child; and (4) the father's history of domestic violence reflected negatively on his mental health and had negatively impacted the mother and the child. G-------- C------- -------- --------------- v. R--- P----------- ---- G----- ------N-----, — A.3d —, 2019 Del. Fam. Ct. LEXIS 72 (Del. Fam. Ct. Mar. 14, 2019).

Joint custody. — Mother and father were awarded joint legal custody because: (1) the child loved each of his parents; (2) both mother and father were in good physical and mental health; and (3) both parents had complied with the original Virginia custody order. T.M. v. A.H., — A.3d —, 2019 Del. Fam. Ct. LEXIS 60 (Del. Fam. Ct. Sept. 13, 2019).

Impairment of child's health. — In contentious visitation proceedings, following the father's request for unsupervised visitation or visitation in his home, the court entered an order requiring supervised visitation until a new family therapist was put in place; the court found that order to be in the child's best interests where the father had made significant improvements through family therapy, but was primarily responsible for creating the child's unhealthy relationship with her parents. W.S. v. J.M., — A.3d —, 2020 Del. Fam. Ct. LEXIS 28 (Del. Fam. Ct. Sept. 21, 2020).

Overnight visitation. — Family Court did not err by denying a father's petition to modify visitation or by granting the mother's cross-petition to increase her visitation, because: (1) the father did not prove the mother's mid-week visitation would endanger the child's physical health or significantly impair emotional development; (2) there was no basis to restrict the mother's contact with the child; (3) the best interest factors weighed in favor of granting of the mother's additional visitation with the child; and (4) therapy had aided the mother in making significant improvements in managing her anger. Tremont v. Tremont, 248 A.3d 104 (Del. 2021).

Visitation awarded. — Expanding the mother's visitation in a gradual manner to unsupervised contact every other weekend with future visitation to include an overnight, was in the child's best interest because: (1) the visits that occurred had been positive; (2) the mother had an adult child with a physical disability that prevented her from being away from home for long periods of time; and (3) the child wanted to get to know her siblings at the mother's home. J E. C v. R E. Y, 2020 Del. Fam. Ct. LEXIS 51 (Del. Fam. Ct. Mar. 30, 2020).

§ 731. Attorneys' fees.

NOTES TO DECISIONS

Fees awarded. — Mother was required to reimburse the father $2,520 in attorneys' fees by November 30, 2020, because: (1) the rate charged, and time spent, by the father's attorney was reasonable; (2) the father's attorney was unavailable for other work during the case; (3) the father prevailed on his contempt claims; and (4) the court reduced the father's fee request by 2.4 hours in light of duplicative work. A.K. v. A.K., — A.3d —, 2020 Del. Fam. Ct. LEXIS 40 (Del. Fam. Ct. Oct. 6, 2020).

§ 734. Relocation.

When in the course of litigation involving custody or visitation, there is a proposed relocation of a child for a period of 60 days or more involving either a move outside the State of Delaware or a move that materially affects the current custodial and residential arrangement or order, the Court must consider the following factors:

(1) The nature, quality, extent of involvement, and duration of the child's relationship with the individual proposing to relocate and with the nonrelocating individual, siblings, and other significant individuals in the child's life.

(2) The age, developmental stage, needs of the child, and the likely impact the relocation will have on the child's physical, educational, and emotional development, taking into consideration any special needs of the child.

(3) The feasibility of preserving the relationship between the nonrelocating individual and the child through suitable visitation arrangements, considering the logistics and financial circumstances of the parties.

(4) The child's preference, taking into consideration the age and maturity of the child.

(5) Whether there is an established pattern of conduct of the individual seeking the relocation, either to promote or thwart the relationship of the child and the nonrelocating individual;

(6) Whether the relocation of the child will enhance the general quality of life for both the individual seeking the relocation and the child, including financial or emotional benefit or educational opportunity.

(7) The reasons of each individual for seeking or opposing the relocation.

(8) Any other factor affecting the best interest of the child.

History.
83 Del. Laws, c. 171, § 1.

Revisor's note.
This section became effective upon the signature of the Governor on Sept. 15, 2021.

CHAPTER 7A

CHILD PROTECTION FROM DOMESTIC VIOLENCE AND SEX OFFENDERS ACT

**Subchapter I. Child Protection From
Domestic Violence Act**

Sec.
703A. Definitions.

SUBCHAPTER I

CHILD PROTECTION FROM DOMESTIC VIOLENCE ACT

§ 703A. Definitions.

(a) "Domestic violence" includes but is not limited to physical or sexual abuse or threats of physical or sexual abuse and any other offense against the person committed by 1 parent against the other parent, against any child living in either parent's home, or against any other adult living in the child's home. "Domestic violence" does not include reasonable acts of self-defense by 1 parent for self-protection or in order to protect the child from abuse or threats of abuse by the other parent or other adult living in the child's home.

(b) "Perpetrator of domestic violence" means any individual who has been convicted of committing any of the following criminal offenses in the State, or any comparable offense in another jurisdiction, against the child at issue in a custody or visitation proceeding, against the other parent of the child, or against any other adult or minor child living in the home:

(1) Any felony level offense.

(2) Assault in the third degree.

(3) Reckless endangering in the second degree.

(4) Reckless burning or exploding.

(5) Unlawful imprisonment in the second degree.

(6) Unlawful sexual contact in the third degree.

(7) Criminal contempt of Family Court protective order based on an assault or other physical abuse, threat of assault or other physical abuse or any other actions placing the petitioner in immediate risk or fear of bodily harm.

(8) Child abuse in the third degree.

History.
69 Del. Laws, c. 309, § 4; 70 Del. Laws, c. 186, § 1; 76 Del. Laws, c. 174, § 3; 83 Del. Laws, c. 113, § 1.

Effect of amendments.
83 Del. Laws, c. 113, effective Aug. 4, 2021, substituted a period for a semicolon at the end of (b)(1)-(5) and for "; or" at the end of (b)(6); and added (b)(8).

§ 705A. Rebuttable presumption against custody or residence of minor child to perpetrator of domestic violence.

NOTES TO DECISIONS

Domestic violence shown. — Maternal grandparents established by clear and convincing evidence a statutory ground for the termination of the father's parental rights on the basis of unintentional abandonment, because he failed to plan adequately for the child's physical and emotional needs; the father's conviction for the mother's murder rendered him a perpetrator of domestic violence, resulting in a presumption that precluded him from having legal and physical custody of the child. Butler v. Evans, 246 A.3d 556 (Del. 2021).

§ 706A. Evidence of domestic violence.

NOTES TO DECISIONS

Domestic violence not shown. — Court awarded the parties joint legal custody and shared residential placement of the children because: (1) best interest factors 1, 2, 3, 5, 7 and 8 were all neutral; (2) each parent played an important role in the children's lives, to the extent permitted by the other; and (3) no single factor carried more weight than another in the case. G.B. v. R.P.B., — A.3d —, 2021 Del. Fam. Ct. LEXIS 6 (Del. Fam. Ct. Apr. 27, 2021).

Domestic violence shown. — Father was granted sole custody of the child because: (1) the testimony and evidence made clear that the parties had documented and serious communications problems instigated by the mother; and (2) the mother did not appear to fully understand the effects of her past behavior and found no reason the parties could not coparent effectively. L.B. v. G.L., — A.3d —, 2021 Del. Fam. Ct. LEXIS 3 (Del. Fam. Ct. Jan. 15, 2021).

CHAPTER 11

TERMINATION AND TRANSFER OF PARENTAL RIGHTS IN ADOPTION PROCEEDINGS

Sec.
1107A. Notice of hearing to terminate and transfer parental rights.

§ 1103. Grounds for termination of parental rights.

NOTES TO DECISIONS

Abandonment evidenced by conduct of parent. — Petition to terminate the mother's parental rights, based on abandonment, was granted because: (1) the mother left the child at a drug treatment facility and did not contact the Division of Family Services; (2) the mother had not manifested the ability or willingness to assume legal and physical custody of the child; (3) the mother did not have the financial resources to provide for the child; (4) the mother had no housing; (5) the mother had no resources to provide food or clothing for the child; and (6) there was no evidence that the mother cared enough for the child to provide for the child's physical or mental health, safety or general well-being. Dep't of Servs. for Children v. H.S., — A.3d —, 2020 Del. Fam. Ct. LEXIS 35 (Del. Fam. Ct. Aug. 28, 2020).

Wishes of the child. — Clear and convincing evidence supported the Family Court's finding that termination of a father's parental rights was in the child's best interests, because: (1) there was evidence of domestic violence; (2) the child wished for termination of the father's parental rights; and (3) there was no evidence that he would be able to monetarily provide for the child for any period of time before her eighteenth birthday. Butler v. Evans, 246 A.3d 556 (Del. 2021).

Substance abuse problems. — Termination of a mother's parental rights was in the child's best interests because: (1) the child

wished to live with current foster parents; (2) the child recalled being abused and subjected to domestic violence; and (3) the mother had diagnosed mental health conditions and a drug dependency that severely affected her ability to provide care for a child. Dep't of Servs. for Children v. H.S., — A.3d —, 2020 Del. Fam. Ct. LEXIS 35 (Del. Fam. Ct. Aug. 28, 2020).

Commission of a felony. — In a termination of parental rights case, where the father's background included incarceration in 1990 for aggravated assault, as well as over 8 years of incarceration for carrying a concealed firearm and attempted second-degree murder (in addition to his current incarceration), Evid. R. 404 did not prohibit consideration of the father's criminal history; the best interest analysis required that the parties' criminal history be considered. Redacted v. Redacted, 2017 Del. Fam. Ct. LEXIS 54 (Del. Fam. Ct. Nov. 1, 2017).

Incarceration of parent. — Maternal grandparents established by clear and convincing evidence a statutory ground for the termination of the father's parental rights on the basis of unintentional abandonment, because he failed to plan adequately for the child's physical and emotional needs; the father's conviction for the mother's murder rendered him a perpetrator of domestic violence, resulting in a presumption that precluded him from having legal and physical custody of the child. Butler v. Evans, 246 A.3d 556 (Del. 2021).

§ 1107. Time for hearing; preparation of social report.

NOTES TO DECISIONS

Privacy. — In a termination of parental rights case, information in a social report (re-

garding children's school names, the mother's phone number, the mother's present and past employers and the mother's high school and college) would be protected because: (1) Evid. R. 803 provided an exception to the hearsay rule as it related to reports prepared in the normal course of business as part of an investigation pursuant to authority granted by law; and (2) that exception applied to social reports prepared as part of a termination of parental rights proceeding. Redacted v. Redacted, 2017 Del. Fam. Ct. LEXIS 54 (Del. Fam. Ct. Nov. 1, 2017).

§ 1107A. Notice of hearing to terminate and transfer parental rights.

(a) Notice of the time, place and purpose of the hearing shall be served upon the parent or parents, person or persons or organization holding parental rights at the respondent's last known address or to the address recited in the petition.

(b) No such notice of hearing shall be necessary if a waiver executed by the parent or parents, person or persons or organization holding parental rights has been filed with the petition, in accordance with § 1106A(b) of this title. The Court may require notice to be served upon any other person or organization.

(c) If, at any time in a proceeding for termination of parental rights, the Court finds that an unknown father of the child may not have received notice, the Court shall determine whether he can be identified. The determination must be based on evidence that includes a review of:

(1) The information required by § 1105(a)(9) of this title;

(2) Whether the woman has filed for or received payments or promises of support, other than from a governmental agency, with respect to the child or because of her pregnancy; and

(3) Whether any individual has formally acknowledged or claimed paternity of the child.

(d) If inquiry pursuant to subsection (c) of this section identifies as the father of the child an individual who has not received notice of the proceeding, the Court shall require notice to be served upon him pursuant to this section.

(e) If, in an inquiry pursuant to this section, the woman who gave birth to the child and who is consenting to the termination of her parental rights fails to disclose the identity of a possible father or reveal his whereabouts, she must be advised by the petitioner that the proceeding for adoption may be delayed or subject to challenge if a possible father is not given notice of the proceeding and that the lack of information about the father's medical and genetic history may be detrimental to the child.

(f)(1) If the Court finds that personal service within the State cannot be accomplished upon the parent or parents, person or persons, or organization holding parental rights, the Court shall then cause notice of the time, place, and purpose of the hearing to be published in at least 1 of the following methods:

a. On a legal notices website established by the Court, for at least 3 successive weeks.

b. In a newspaper of 1 or more counties, as the Court may judge best for giving the parent or parents, or person or persons, or organization holding parental rights notice. The notice must be published once per week, for 3 successive weeks.

(2) The formal wording of a notice under this section must be approved by the Court.

(3) Publication shall also be made in the locality in which the parent or parents, person or persons, or organization holding parental rights is believed to be located if different from the county where the publication just described has been caused.

(4) The Court may, upon the petitioner's request, order that personal service and publication occur simultaneously.

(g) If any publication is ordered pursuant to subsection (f) of this section, the Court shall also order that the Clerk of the Court, at least 3 weeks prior to the hearing, send by regular and registered or certified mail to the parent or parents or person or persons or organization holding parental rights, at the address or addresses given in the petition, a copy of the same notice, or a similar notice of the time, place and purpose of the hearing.

(h) Personal service at any time prior to the hearing shall be sufficient to give jurisdiction.

(i) Notice provided pursuant to this section shall constitute conclusive evidence of service and a hearing will then proceed at the time and date set, with or without the appearance of the parent or parents, person or persons or organization so notified.

(j) The Budget Act shall provide the Department with appropriated special fund (ASF) authority in order to provide public notice of court action or actions involving minors under the Department's custody whose parents' whereabouts are unknown, per Family Court rules. Any other fees, assessments, costs or financial obligations imposed by Family Court for the issuance and service of subpoenas or summons by way of court rules, regulations or administrative procedures may not be charged to the Department. Any such costs associated with these procedures shall be the financial responsibility of Family Court.

History.
73 Del. Laws, c. 171, § 13; 70 Del. Laws, c. 186, § 1; 73 Del. Laws, c. 319, § 1; 83 Del. Laws, c. 96, § 2.

Effect of amendments.
83 Del. Laws, c. 96, effective July 30, 2021, rewrote (f).

§ 1114. Placement for adoption and post-termination placement order.

NOTES TO DECISIONS

Guardianship. — Family Court erred in interpreting 13 Del. C. § 1114 as prohibiting standard guardianship for a child whose parents' parental rights were terminated because: (1) that section reflected the preference for adoption of a child whose parents' parental rights were terminated, but also recognized that adoption may not be possible; and (2) nothing in the plain language of 13 Del. C. § 1114 prohibited a standard guardianship for a child whose parents' parental rights were terminated. Harris v. Div. of Family Servs., 251 A.3d 115 (Del. 2021).

CHAPTER 15

DIVORCE AND ANNULMENT

§ 1505. Divorce; marriage irretrievably broken and reconciliation improbable; defenses; efforts at reconciliation.

RESEARCH REFERENCES AND PRACTICE AIDS

Delaware Law Reviews.
Divorce and Third-Party Trusts in Delaware, 17 Del. L. Rev. 1 (2021).

§ 1508. Obtaining jurisdiction over respondent.

(a) After the filing of the petition, jurisdiction may be acquired over respondent in any of the following ways:

(1) By issuance of summons by the Clerk of the Family Court, and service thereof by the sheriff upon respondent, by delivering a copy of the summons, petition and any affidavit to respondent personally or by delivering copies thereof to an agent authorized by appointment or by law to receive service of process;

(2) By appearance of respondent, either personally or by executing and

filing an appearance document in a form approved by the Court, with or without issuance of summons;

(3) By appearance of counsel for respondent, with or without issuance of summons;

(4) Under a court rule not inconsistent with this section.

(b) If the petition avers that it is unlikely that jurisdiction can be acquired over respondent except by mailing and publication, or by publication only, whether respondent is a resident or a nonresident of this State, jurisdiction may be acquired over respondent by mailing and publication, or by publication only, under subsection (d) of this section.

(c) If an effort has been made unsuccessfully to obtain jurisdiction over respondent as provided in subsection (a) of this section, then jurisdiction may be acquired over respondent by mailing and publication, or by publication only, under subsection (d) of this section.

(d)(1) When service is to be made upon respondent by mailing and publication, the Clerk of the Family Court shall do all of the following:

    a. Send a copy of the summons, petition, and any affidavit to respondent by registered or certified mail, return receipt requested, to the address that petitioner had averred it is most likely that mail will be received by respondent.

    b. Cause a notice in the form that the Court approves to be published on a legal notices website established by the Court or once in a newspaper of general circulation in the county where the action is pending.

(2) If petitioner has averred that he or she knows of no address where it is most likely that mail will be received by respondent there shall be no mailing.

(3) No further notice shall be required unless the Court, deeming the circumstances exceptional, requires further notice.

(e) [Repealed.]

(f) When the petition avers that respondent is a resident of this State, the summons shall be delivered to an officer for service in the county where it appears most likely that service can be effected on respondent.

(g) The expense of mailing and publication shall be taxed as part of the costs of the case.

(h) Original process, whether an original, alias or pluries writ, is returnable 20 days after the issuance of the writ, except that the Court by rule, or by order after application for cause shown, may provide that the writ be returnable sooner or later.

History.

24 Del. Laws, c. 221, § 10; Code 1915, § 3013; Code 1935, § 3506; 43 Del. Laws, c. 205, § 1; 13 Del. C. 1953, § 1512; 58 Del. Laws, c. 349, § 10; 59 Del. Laws, c. 350, § 1; 60 Del. Laws, c. 297, §§ 6-9; 70 Del. Laws, c. 186, § 1; 83 Del. Laws, c. 96, § 3.

Effect of amendments.

83 Del. Laws, c. 96, effective July 30, 2021, rewrote (d); and repealed (e).

§ 1512. Alimony in divorce and annulment actions; award; limitations.

NOTES TO DECISIONS

Credit card payments. — Wife was not awarded alimony because of her failure to submit both corroborating evidence to support her claimed expenses and sufficient evidence to justify sharing her credit card debt with the husband as part of her expenses; the wife's excessive spending due to gambling had caused her current financial troubles, in addition to poor money management. M. M v. O. M, — A.3d —, 2020 Del. Fam. Ct. LEXIS 50 (Del. Fam. Ct. Sept. 18, 2020).

Medical condition of spouse. — Family

Court did not commit reversible error in determining a wife had a severe and incapacitating illness, supporting a claim that the wife's part-time employment was appropriate, because: (1) testimony from the wife, the wife's former boss and the wife's sister-in-law substantiated the wife's struggles with anxiety, depression and severe insomnia; and (2) the husband did not identify contrary evidence and was not entitled to a modification or termination of his alimony obligation. Fletcher v. Feutz, 246 A.3d 540 (Del. 2021).

Award of permanent alimony. — Husband was ordered to pay the wife his monthly surplus of $249 as permanent alimony because: (1) the wife did not have capacity to meet her entire monthly deficit at the time; (2) the husband was able to meet his needs at present; (3) the parties had sufficient income to support an average middle-class lifestyle; and (4) the wife's role as the primary caretaker of the parties' 5 children during the marriage prevented her from developing a separate working career. A.K. v. A.K., — A.3d —, 2021 Del. Fam. Ct. LEXIS 2 (Del. Fam. Ct. Jan. 28, 2021).

Imputed income. — While both parties appeared to have a deficit when the court considered their reported income and expenses, the husband was attributed income as a result of other adults residing in his home; therefore the husband was ordered to pay alimony to the wife, who earned considerably less, even after imputing full-time income to her based on the entry-level rate of a waitress. A v. B, — A.3d —, 2018 Del. Fam. Ct. LEXIS 64 (Del. Fam. Ct. Apr. 17, 2018).

Cohabitation as grounds for termination of alimony award. — Family Court correctly held that the former wife and her partner were not cohabiting because the couple: (1) did not contribute money to each other's mortgage or utilities or leave personal items at each other's houses; (2) asked permission to visit the other's home and spent the majority of their nonworking time apart; and (3) lacked any joint account, or shared expenses, of any kind. Fletcher v. Feutz, 246 A.3d 540 (Del. 2021).

Dependency not found. — Request for alimony and court costs was denied because the husband had the ability to earn, and according to his testimony did earn, more than his listed reasonable needs; the husband was not dependent upon the wife for support because he had a small surplus and was quite capable of supporting himself through employment. M.A.L. v. K.B., — A.3d —, 2019 Del. Fam. Ct. LEXIS 67 (Del. Fam. Ct. Sept. 4, 2019).

Court did not find that the wife was dependent upon the husband for her support because: (1) her available income was comparable to her expenses; (2) the small amount she lacked each month was minimal compared to the available assets; (3) it was a very long-term marriage where the parties accumulated significant assets over a lengthy period of time; and (4) the parties were both approaching retirement and would soon be expected to start using their retirement savings. L.S. v. C.C., — A.3d —, 2020 Del. Fam. Ct. LEXIS 3 (Del. Fam. Ct. Feb. 28, 2020).

RESEARCH REFERENCES AND PRACTICE AIDS

Delaware Law Reviews.
Divorce and Third-Party Trusts in Delaware, 17 Del. L. Rev. 1 (2021).

§ 1513. Disposition of marital property; imposition of lien; insurance policies.

NOTES TO DECISIONS

Section applies to acts prior to its effective date. — Property the parties bought before marriage, and before 13 Del. C. § 1513(b)(2) existed, was nonetheless governed by that provision; that property (held as joint tenants with rights of survivorship) was marital property to be divided with other marital property pursuant to 13 Del. C. § 1513(a), because plaintiff's vested right in ownership of the property did not extend to a vested right as to determining the treatment of that property (absent a premarital agreement regarding its treatment). M v. B, — A.3d —, 2020 Del. Fam. Ct. LEXIS 49 (Del. Fam. Ct. July 14, 2020).

Factors considered in dividing marital property. — Court found that it was equitable to divide the nonretirement and nonbusiness assets 50/50 because: (1) the parties had accumulated significant assets; (2) there was not a considerable amount of time remaining to accumulate additional assets before retirement;

and (3) while the husband had superior earning ability, his future cash flow was taken into consideration in the valuation of the sole proprietorship. L.S. v. C.C., — A.3d —, 2020 Del. Fam. Ct. LEXIS 3 (Del. Fam. Ct. Feb. 28, 2020).

Trial court found that the amounts the parties owed to each other was a wash because: (1) in total, the husband owed the wife $53,834, constituting rental income, unpaid rent and half of the husband's IRA account; and (2) the wife owed the husband $41,400 for half of the wife's pension, currently in pay status, since the date of separation. K v. K, — A.3d —, 2021 Del. Fam. Ct. LEXIS 8 (Del. Fam. Ct. Apr. 29, 2021).

Overcoming presumption of marital property. — Husband rebutted the presumption that a motorcycle and residence were marital property because the motorcycle, the residence and the mortgage were titled in the husband's name alone, indicating his intention to keep such property as his solely owned nonmarital property. P.B. v. M.W., — A.3d —, 2021 Del. Fam. Ct. LEXIS 16 (Del. Fam. Ct. Aug. 11, 2021).

Marital home. — Wife was awarded 55% of the equity in the marital home calculated from the date of refinancing because: (1) the wife's acceptance of the husband's $1,000 payment seemed to be consideration for the execution of the refinancing documentation that the husband requested the wife sign; (2) the wife had an inferior income and educational level; (3) and the court was unable to determine the value of the home at the date of separation. M. M v. O. M, — A.3d —, 2020 Del. Fam. Ct. LEXIS 50 (Del. Fam. Ct. Sept. 18, 2020).

Proceeds from personal injury suit. — Court found that it was equitable to award the wife half of the value of 2 vehicles purchased with funds from a joint account because the weekly deposits into the joint account, used by both parties during the marriage, constituted gifts to the marriage from the husband's personal injury settlement funds. P.B. v. M.W., — A.3d —, 2021 Del. Fam. Ct. LEXIS 16 (Del. Fam. Ct. Aug. 11, 2021).

RESEARCH REFERENCES AND PRACTICE AIDS

Delaware Law Reviews.
Divorce and Third-Party Trusts in Delaware, 17 Del. L. Rev. 1 (2021).

§ 1515. Attorneys' fees.

NOTES TO DECISIONS

Fees not awarded. — Wife was not entitled to attorneys' fees; other provisions of the order had remedied the financial disparity which existed at the outset of the case. L.S. v. C.C., — A.3d —, 2020 Del. Fam. Ct. LEXIS 3 (Del. Fam. Ct. Feb. 28, 2020).

Husband was not responsible for the wife's attorneys' fees because the husband did not have the requisite funds to pay the wife's and his own attorneys' fees; in addition, the wife could use her proceeds from the husband's buy-out or sale of the marital home to pay her own attorneys, fees. M. M v. O. M, — A.3d —, 2020 Del. Fam. Ct. LEXIS 50 (Del. Fam. Ct. Sept. 18, 2020).

§ 1519. Modification or termination of decree or order; termination of alimony; enforcement of alimony order.

NOTES TO DECISIONS

Showing required under agreement stipulating that alimony will cease upon wife's cohabitation. — Family Court correctly held that the former wife and her partner were not cohabiting because the couple: (1) did not contribute money to each other's mortgage or utilities or leave personal items at each other's houses; (2) asked permission to visit the other's home and spent the majority of their nonworking time apart; and (3) lacked any joint account, or shared expenses, of any kind. Fletcher v. Feutz, 246 A.3d 540 (Del. 2021).

CHAPTER 19

UNIFORM CHILD CUSTODY JURISDICTION AND ENFORCEMENT ACT

Subchapter I. General Provisions
Sec.
1908. Notice to persons outside State.

SUBCHAPTER I

GENERAL PROVISIONS

§ 1901. Short title.

NOTES TO DECISIONS

Jurisdiction standard. — Delaware (rather than Georgia) was the more convenient forum for deciding the custody of a child because: (1) the child was in Georgia for only 2 months; (2) the father lived less than 10 minutes from Delaware; (3) the mother resided in Delaware until she unilaterally moved to Georgia after the petition was served on her in Delaware, despite the father's clearly articulated objections; and (4) the mother presented false statements in Delaware concerning jurisdiction and her legal representation. T.A.C. v. K.S.J., — A.3d —, 2020 Del. Fam. Ct. LEXIS 30 (Del. Fam. Ct. Aug. 17, 2020).

§ 1908. Notice to persons outside State.

(a) Notice required for the exercise of jurisdiction when a person is outside this State may be given in a manner prescribed by the law of this State for service of process or by the law of the state in which the service is made. Notice must be given in a manner reasonably calculated to give actual notice but may be by publication in print or on a legal notices website established by the Court if other means are not effective.

(b) Proof of service may be made in the manner prescribed by the law of this State or by the law of the state in which the service is made.

(c) Notice is not required for the exercise of jurisdiction with respect to a person who submits to the jurisdiction of the court.

History.
73 Del. Laws, c. 426, § 1; 83 Del. Laws, c. 96, § 4.

Effect of amendments.
83 Del. Laws, c. 96, effective July 30, 2021, added "in print or on a legal notices website established by the Court" in the second sentence of (a).

SUBCHAPTER II
JURISDICTION

§ 1920. Initial child custody jurisdiction.

NOTES TO DECISIONS

Litigation in child's "home state" preferred. — Family Court declined to exercise jurisdiction over a custody matter because Delaware was not the "home state" of the child; the child had not resided in Delaware for the requisite 6-month period. Redacted v. Redacted, — A.3d —, 2020 Del. Fam. Ct. LEXIS 45 (Del. Fam. Ct. Jan. 24, 2020).

§ 1925. Simultaneous proceedings.

NOTES TO DECISIONS

Forum non conveniens. — Delaware Family Court yielded jurisdiction to Georgia because: (1) the mother initiated proceedings in the Georgia courts before she sought relief in Delaware; (2) a writ of habeas corpus issued by Georgia was commenced before the mother traveled to Delaware and initiated the emergency ex parte petition for custody; (3) Delaware would not be a convenient forum, as Georgia was an approximately 16-hour drive away; (4) the father had taken the child from Georgia to Delaware without the mother's permission, later refusing to turn the child over to the police department or the mother when so ordered; (5) witnesses and other evidence remained in Georgia; and (6) Delaware was not the "home state" of the child, given that the child had not resided in Delaware for the requisite 6-month period. Redacted v. Redacted, — A.3d —, 2020 Del. Fam. Ct. LEXIS 45 (Del. Fam. Ct. Jan. 24, 2020).

§ 1926. Inconvenient forum.

NOTES TO DECISIONS

Forum non conveniens. — Delaware Family Court yielded jurisdiction to Georgia because: (1) the mother initiated proceedings in the Georgia courts before she sought relief in Delaware; (2) a writ of habeas corpus issued by Georgia was commenced before the mother traveled to Delaware and initiated the emergency ex parte petition for custody; (3) Delaware would not be a convenient forum, as Georgia was an approximately 16-hour drive away; (4) the father had taken the child from Georgia to Delaware without the mother's permission, later refusing to turn the child over to the police department or the mother when so ordered; (5) witnesses and other evidence remained in Georgia; and (6) Delaware was not the "home state" of the child, given that the child had not resided in Delaware for the requisite 6-month period. Redacted v. Redacted, — A.3d —, 2020 Del. Fam. Ct. LEXIS 45 (Del. Fam. Ct. Jan. 24, 2020).

Family Court concluded that British Columbia was a more convenient forum for purposes of a custody modification petition because the children had been residing there for over 3 years; the initial petition was based upon incidents that occurred in British Columbia and actually named a number of individuals from the children's school there who would be witnesses. Redacted v. Redacted, 2021 Del. Fam. Ct. LEXIS 12 (Del. Fam. Ct. Aug. 12, 2021).

Out-of-state jurisdiction not shown. —

Delaware (rather than Georgia) was the more convenient forum for deciding the custody of a child because: (1) the child was in Georgia for only 2 months; (2) the father lived less than 10 minutes from Delaware; (3) the mother resided in Delaware until she unilaterally moved to Georgia after the petition was served on her in Delaware, despite the father's clearly articulated objections; and (4) the mother presented false statements in Delaware concerning jurisdiction and her legal representation. T.A.C. v. K.S.J., — A.3d —, 2020 Del. Fam. Ct. LEXIS 30 (Del. Fam. Ct. Aug. 17, 2020).

§ 1927. Jurisdiction declined by reason of conduct.

NOTES TO DECISIONS

Jurisdiction declined. — Delaware Family Court yielded jurisdiction to Georgia because: (1) the mother initiated proceedings in the Georgia courts before she sought relief in Delaware; (2) a writ of habeas corpus issued by Georgia was commenced before the mother traveled to Delaware and initiated the emergency ex parte petition for custody; (3) Delaware would not be a convenient forum, as Georgia was an approximately 16-hour drive away; (4) the father had taken the child from Georgia to Delaware without the mother's permission, later refusing to turn the child over to the police department or the mother when so ordered; (5) witnesses and other evidence remained in Georgia; and (6) Delaware was not the "home state" of the child, given that the child had not resided in Delaware for the requisite 6-month period. Redacted v. Redacted, — A.3d —, 2020 Del. Fam. Ct. LEXIS 45 (Del. Fam. Ct. Jan. 24, 2020).

CHAPTER 22
DIVISION OF CHILD SUPPORT SERVICES

Sec.
2208. State Directory of New Hires.

§ 2208. State Directory of New Hires.

(a) *General.* — There is hereby established within the Division of Child Support Services an automated directory (to be known as the "State Directory of New Hires") which shall contain information supplied by employers pursuant to § 1154(i) of Title 30.

(b) *Entry of information into data base.* — Within 5 business days of receipt of a report supplied by an employer pursuant to § 1156A of Title 30, information included in the report shall be entered into the data base maintained by the State Directory of New Hires.

(c) *Information comparisons.* — The State Directory of New Hires shall, directly or by contract, conduct automated comparisons of the Social Security numbers reported by employers pursuant to § 1156A of Title 30 and the Social Security numbers appearing in the records of the State case registry. When an information comparison reveals a match with respect to the Social Security number of an individual required to provide support under a support order, the State Directory of New Hires shall provide the Division of Child Support Services with the name, address and Social Security number of the employee to whom the Social Security number is assigned, the date services for remuneration were first performed by the employee, and the name, address and identifying number assigned under § 6109 of the Internal Revenue Code of 1986 (26 U.S.C. § 6109) to the employer.

(d) *Provision of information to the National Directory of New Hires.* — Within 3 business days after the date information regarding a newly hired employee is entered into the State Directory of New Hires, the State Directory of New Hires shall furnish the information to the National Directory of New Hires established pursuant to § 453(i) of Title IV, Part D, of the Social Security Act (42 U.S.C. § 653(i)). On a quarterly basis, the State Directory of New Hires shall also furnish to the National Directory of New Hires extracts of the reports required under § 303(a)(6) of the Social Security Act [42 U.S.C. § 503(a)(6)] to be made to the Secretary of Labor concerning the wages and unemployment compensation paid to individuals, by such dates, in such format, and containing such information as prescribed by federal regulation.

(e) *Uses of new hire information.* — The State Directory of New Hires shall make the specified information available to the following entities for the purposes described below.

(1) The State Directory of New Hires shall provide information derived from the comparison conducted pursuant to subsection (c) of this section to the Division of Child Support Services, which shall use the information to locate individuals for purposes of establishing paternity and establishing, modifying and enforcing child support obligations.

(2) The State Directory of New Hires shall grant access to information provided by employers pursuant to § 1156A of Title 30 to the state agency responsible for administering a program specified in 42 U.S.C. § 1320b-7(b) for purposes of verifying eligibility for the program.

(3) The State Directory of New Hires shall grant access to information provided by employers pursuant to § 1156A of Title 30 to the State Division of Unemployment Insurance for the purpose of administering the State's unemployment insurance services program and the State Division of Industrial Affairs for the purpose of administering the Workers' Compensation Program.

History.
71 Del. Laws, c. 216, § 1; 70 Del. Laws, c. 186, § 1; 78 Del. Laws, c. 311, § 1; 80 Del. Laws, c. 234, § 17; 83 Del. Laws, c. 107, § 2.

Del. Laws, c. 107, § 2, effective July 30, 2021, "(i)" was substituted for "(h)" following "§ 1154" in (a).

Revisor's note.
Based upon changes made necessary by 83

CHAPTER 23
GUARDIANSHIP OF A CHILD

SUBCHAPTER II
GENERAL PROCEDURES FOR APPOINTMENT OF GUARDIANS

§ 2322. Contents of petition.

NOTES TO DECISIONS

Dependent, neglected, or abused. — Family Court properly denied an uncle's petitions for guardianship because the uncle failed to plead any facts in his petitions suggesting that the children were dependent, neglected, or abused as pleading directives required. Harris v. Div. of Family Servs., 251 A.3d 115 (Del. 2021).

§ 2325. Hearing procedure and notice requirements.

(a) When a guardianship petition is filed, the petition shall be served upon the parent or parents, person or persons or organization holding parental rights at the respondent's last known address.

(b) If the Court finds that personal service within the State cannot be accomplished upon the parent or parents, person or persons, or organization holding parental rights, the petitioner shall cause notice to be published either on a legal notices website established by the Court or in a newspaper of general circulation in the county where the respondent is most likely to be residing.

(c) Personal service at any time prior to the hearing shall be sufficient to give jurisdiction.

(d) Notice provided pursuant to this section shall constitute conclusive evidence of service and a hearing will then proceed at the time and date set, with or without the appearance of the parent or parents, person or persons, or organization so notified.

History.
73 Del. Laws, c. 150, § 1; 76 Del. Laws, c. 95, §§ 1-3; 79 Del. Laws, c. 246, § 1; 83 Del. Laws, c. 96, § 5.

Effect of amendments.
83 Del. Laws, c. 96, effective July 30, 2021, in

(b), substituted "finds" for "shall find" and added "either on a legal notices website established by the Court or".

SUBCHAPTER III
GUARDIAN OF THE CHILD

§ 2332. Termination, modification or rescission of guardianship order.

NOTES TO DECISIONS

Termination of guardianship. — Father's petition to rescind guardianship was granted because the evidence, including 5 consecutive months of drug-free urine screens, supported that substance abuse was no longer an issue for father; the father also lived in a stable home and held steady employment. R.S. v. C.A., — A.3d —, 2020 Del. Fam. Ct. LEXIS 24 (Del. Fam. Ct. June 30, 2020).

CHAPTER 24
THIRD-PARTY VISITATION

SUBCHAPTER I
GENERAL PROVISIONS

§ 2404. Hearing procedure and notice requirements.

(a) When a petition is filed under this chapter, the Court shall set a date for a hearing on the petition, and shall cause notice of time, place and purpose of the hearing to be served as required in this section.

(b) Notice of the time, place and purpose of the hearing shall be served upon the parent or parents, guardian or guardians, person or persons, DSCYF, or licensed agency holding parental rights at the respondent's last known address or to the address received in the petition.

(c) If the Court finds that personal service within the State cannot be accomplished upon a party, the petitioner shall cause notice to be published either on a legal notices website established by the Court or in a newspaper of general circulation in the county where the respondent is most likely to be residing.

(d) Personal service at any time prior to the hearing shall be sufficient to confer jurisdiction upon the Court.

(e) Notice provided pursuant to this section shall constitute conclusive evidence of service and a hearing will then proceed at the time and date set, with or without the appearance of the parent or parents, guardian or guardians, person or persons, Department, or licensed agency holding parental rights so notified.

History.
77 Del. Laws, c. 43, § 9; 83 Del. Laws, c. 96, § 6.

Effect of amendments.
83 Del. Laws, c. 96, effective July 30, 2021, in (c), substituted "finds" for "shall find" and added "either on a legal notices website established by the Court or".

SUBCHAPTER II
THIRD-PARTY VISITATION PROCEEDINGS

§ 2410. Persons eligible to petition for third-party visitation.

NOTES TO DECISIONS

Grandparent visitation. — Family Court properly denied a former stepgrandfather's petition for third-party visitation, concluding that the mother's objections to visitation were not clearly unreasonable; the court recognized the strained relationship between the mother and the former step-grandfather, which included their inability to communicate with each other and the former step-grandfather making negative comments to and about the mother. Jarvis v. Mole, 242 A.3d 574 (Del. 2020).

§ 2412. Grounds for persons obtaining third-party visitation with a child.

NOTES TO DECISIONS

Visitation denied. — Family Court properly denied a former stepgrandfather's petition for third-party visitation, concluding that the mother's objections to visitation were not clearly unreasonable; the court recognized the strained relationship between the mother and the former step-grandfather, which included their inability to communicate with each other and the former step-grandfather making negative comments to and about the mother. Jarvis v. Mole, 242 A.3d 574 (Del. 2020).

Consistent with the parents' fundamental liberty interests to make decisions concerning the care, custody and control of the child, Family Court gave special weight to the primary residential parent's view on visitation, and to the child's best interests, in denying a grandparent's petition for third-party visitation; although the grandparent did not enjoy as much contact with the child as the grandparent would have liked to have had, the grandparent did still have some contact. Reed v. Chavez, — A.3d —, 2021 Del. LEXIS 269 (Del. Aug. 16, 2021).

CHAPTER 25
DSCYF CUSTODY

SUBCHAPTER I
GENERAL PROVISIONS

§ 2504. Hearing procedure and notice requirements.

(a) When a petition is filed under this chapter, the Court shall set a date for a hearing on the petition, and shall cause notice of time, place, and purpose of the hearing to be served as required in this section.

(b) Notice of the time, place, and purpose of the hearing shall be served upon the parent or parents, guardian or guardians, person or persons, DSCYF, or licensed agency holding parental rights at the respondent's last known address or to the address received in the petition.

(c) If the Court finds that personal service within the State cannot be accomplished upon a party, the petitioner shall cause notice to be published either on a legal notices website established by the Court or in a newspaper of general circulation in the county where the respondent is most likely to be residing.

(d) Personal service at any time prior to the hearing shall be sufficient to confer jurisdiction upon the Court.

(e) Notice provided pursuant to this section shall constitute conclusive evidence of service and a hearing will then proceed at the time and date set, with or without the appearance of the parent or parents, guardian or guardians, person or persons, DSCYF, or licensed agency holding parental rights so notified.

(f) When a petition is filed under this chapter, the Court shall appoint an attorney authorized to practice law in this State to represent the child. When appointing an attorney, the Court may also appoint a Court Appointed Special Advocate volunteer to work in conjunction with the attorney. The rights, responsibilities and duties in representing the child are set forth in § 9007A of Title 29. For the purposes of the Child Abuse Prevention and Treatment Act (42 U.S.C. § 5106a, et seq.), the attorney for the child and the Court Appointed Special Advocate volunteer, if one is appointed, shall fulfill the role of guardian ad litem for the child.

History.
77 Del. Laws, c. 43, § 10; 80 Del. Laws, c. 417, § 2; 83 Del. Laws, c. 96, § 7.

Effect of amendments.
83 Del. Laws, c. 96, effective July 30, 2021, in (c), substituted "finds" for "shall find" and added "either on a legal notices website established by the Court or".

TITLE 16
HEALTH AND SAFETY

PART I
LOCAL BOARDS OF HEALTH; HEALTH PROGRAMS

CHAPTER 1
DEPARTMENT OF HEALTH AND SOCIAL SERVICES

Subchapter IX. Healthy Mothers and Children

SUBCHAPTER IX
HEALTHY MOTHERS AND CHILDREN

§ 197. Delaware Perinatal Quality Collaborative.

(a)(1) The Delaware Perinatal Quality Collaborative ("Collaborative") is established to improve pregnancy outcomes for women and newborns by addressing all of the following:

    a. Obstetrical blood loss management.

    b. Pregnant women with substance use disorder.

    c. Infants born with neonatal abstinence syndrome.

    d. Advancing evidence-based clinical practices and processes through quality care review, audit, and continuous quality improvement.

(2) The Collaborative shall function in cooperation with the Delaware Healthy Mother and Infant Consortium.

(b) The Collaborative is comprised of the following members:

    (1) The Chair of the Delaware Healthy Mother and Infant Consortium.

    (2) The Chair of the Child Death Review Commission.

    (3) The President of the Delaware Healthcare Association.

    (4) The Chair of the Delaware Chapter of the American College of Obstetricians and Gynecologists.

    (5) The President of the Board of Directors of the Delaware Chapter of the American Academy of Pediatrics.

    (6) The President of the Board of Directors of the Delaware Chapter of the American Academy of Family Physicians.

    (7) The Chair of the Delaware Chapter of the Association of Women's Health, Obstetric and Neonatal Nurses.

(8) One member, appointed by the Governor in consultation with the Chair of the Collaborative, who is a consumer advocate for patient-centered care and is committed to and interested in reducing maternal morbidity and mortality.

(9) A licensed midwife, appointed by the Governor in consultation with the Chair of the Midwifery Advisory Council, who is a nonvoting member.

(10) Seven members, appointed by the Governor to represent both of the following:

    a. Hospitals, as defined in § 1001 of this title, that provide childbirth and delivery services.

    b. Freestanding birthing centers, as defined in § 122(3)p.1. of this title.

(c)(1) An appointed member serves at the pleasure of the appointing authority.

(2) A member who serves by virtue of position may designate another individual to serve in the member's place, at the member's pleasure.

    a. A member making a designation under this paragraph (c)(2) must provide the designation in writing to the Chair.

    b. A designee of a member who serves by virtue of position has the same duties and rights as the member who serves by virtue of position.

(d) The Governor may consider a member to have resigned if the member is absent for 3 consecutive, regular meetings.

(e)(1) The Collaborative shall annually elect a Chair and a Vice-Chair.

(2) A majority of the voting members of the Collaborative constitutes a quorum. A vacant position is not counted for quorum purposes.

(3) The approval of a majority of the voting members present at a meeting with quorum is required for the Collaborative to take official action.

(4) The Collaborative may adopt rules and by-laws necessary for its operation.

(5) The Collaborative shall meet at the call of the Chair, or as provided by by-laws adopted by the Collaborative, but must meet at least once a year.

(f)(1) Each member of the Collaborative shall comply with the provisions under Chapter 58 of Title 29.

(2) The members of the Collaborative serve without compensation. However, members may be reimbursed for reasonable and necessary expenses incident to their duties as members of the Collaborative, to the extent that funds are available.

(3) The Collaborative's expenditures must be made under Chapter 69 of Title 29.

(g) The Collaborative shall do all of the following:

(1) Maintain a core set of quality improvement projects based on best practices and interventions that have a measurable impact on health outcomes.

(2) Identify performance metrics to set statewide quality benchmarks.

(3) Support the use of real-time hospital and facility-based data to perform rapid-cycle quality improvement and advocate for real-time data at a state level.

(4) Share successes of quality improvement projects at hospitals and facilities.

(h) The Collaborative may do all of the following:

(1) Develop a responsive, real time, risk-adjusted, statewide perinatal data system.

(2) Access timely, accurate, and standardized information and utilize perinatal data to drive quality improvement initiatives.

(3) Develop a collaborative, confidential data-sharing network, including public and private obstetric and neonatal providers, insurers, and public health professionals, to support a system for peer review, bench marking, and continuous quality improvement activities for perinatal care.

(4) Conduct other activities the Collaborative considers necessary to carry out the intent of the General Assembly as expressed in this section.

(i) The Collaborative is constituted as an independent public instrumentality. For administrative and budgetary purposes only, the Collaborative is placed within the Department of Health and Social Services, Division of Public Health.

(j)(1) The Collaborative is not a public body under Chapter 100 of Title 29.

(2) The meetings of the Collaborative are closed to the public unless otherwise determined by the Chair of the Collaborative, except that the Collaborative shall hold at least 2 public meetings each year to receive comment on the general state of pregnancy outcomes for women and newborns in this State.

(3) The Collaborative shall provide an annual report to the General Assembly containing recommendations for improving pregnancy outcomes for women and newborns in this State.

(4) Any document received or generated by the Collaborative is not a public record under Chapter 100 of Title 29 and is confidential under § 1768(b) of Title 24. Notwithstanding the foregoing, documents received from the public at, agendas for, or minutes of the Collaborative's public meetings are a "public record" under Chapter 100 of Title 29, unless determined not to be "public record" under § 10002 of Title 29.

(5) The Collaborative is a peer review committee under § 1768(a) of Title 24.

History.
82 Del. Laws, c. 260, § 1; 83 Del. Laws, c. 65, § 1.

Revisor's note.
Based upon changes contained in 83 Del.

Laws, c. 65, § 1, effective June 30, 2021, in the second sentence of (j)(4), "public record" was placed in quotation marks and "(*l*)" was deleted following "§ 10002".

PART II

REGULATORY PROVISIONS CONCERNING PUBLIC HEALTH

CHAPTER 8C
SCREENING OF NEWBORN INFANTS FOR METABOLIC, HEMATOLOGIC, ENDOCRINOLOGIC, IMMUNOLOGIC, AND CERTAIN STRUCTURAL DISORDERS

§ 804C. Newborn Screening Program.

(a) The Department of Health and Social Services shall adopt rules and regulations under and pursuant to this State's Administrative Procedures Act, Chapter 101 of Title 29, to carry out the objectives of this chapter. All prior regulations and rules promulgated by the Delaware Division of Public Health in regard to the screening of newborn infants for diseases shall remain in full force and effect until amended or repealed by the Department.

(b) All hospitals, birthing centers and other birth attendants shall obtain a satisfactory specimen within 24 to 48 hours of age and shall perform, or arrange for, screening for critical congenital heart defects.

(c) The Division of Public Health shall provide results to the physician on record.

(d) The Director of the Division of Public Health, with advice from the Committee, will determine which disorders shall be on the screening panel.

(e) Blood specimens for metabolic, hematologic, endocrinologic, and immunologic disorders will be destroyed after screening and testing is complete. Screening and testing includes confirmation of any diagnosis.

(f) Records obtained from screenings will be retained by the Division of Public Health.

(g) *Fees.* — (1) (1) The Newborn Screening Program shall bill the birth facility or individual attending the birth for services provided for each newborn screened under these regulations including but not limited to, the cost of the kits for collection of specimens, the laboratory fee for analysis, and administrative costs. The amount billed will be determined by the Director of the Division of Public Health in consultation with the Advisory Committee and the program staff. The fee will be determined in July of each year based on the cost of the program. All fees collected as a result of billing are hereby appropriated to, and shall be retained by, the Newborn Screening Program to defray operating expenses associated with this chapter, operation of the Program, and programming to ensure the optimal health and development across the lifespan of the maternal and child health population.

(2) No Delaware newborn shall be denied testing for hereditary disorders because of inability of the newborn's parent or legal guardian to pay the fee.

History.

80 Del. Laws, c. 96, § 1; 83 Del. Laws, c. 167, § 1.

Effect of amendments.

83 Del. Laws, c. 167, effective September 15, 2021, substituted "regard" for "regards" in the second sentence of (a); substituted "within 24 to 48" for "prior to 72" in (b); deleted "parent or legal guardian and" preceding "physician" in (c); rewrote (e); and rewrote the final sentence of (g)(1).

§ 805C. Parental options.

(a) All newborns in Delaware shall have a satisfactory specimen taken within 24 to 48 hours of age and shall be screened for metabolic, hematologic, endocrinologic, immunologic and certain structural disorders. Parents may elect not to participate in any of the following:

(1) Screening to be performed;

(2) The blood spot to be stored following testing; and/or

(3) The results of the screen to be securely shared electronically through a health information exchange so that health-care providers can appropriately access information.

(b) The informed consent process shall assure that the parent or guardian who elects that a newborn shall not be tested understands the consequences of such a decision, including the inability to prevent developmental delay and death. Language conveying such information shall be recommended by the Committee for approval by the Division Director.

(c) There will be no research utilizing the stored blood specimens or the stored data without parental consent, except for population-based studies in which all identifying information is removed.

History.

80 Del. Laws, c. 96, § 1; 83 Del. Laws, c. 167, § 1.

Effect of amendments.

83 Del. Laws, c. 167, effective September 15, 2021, in the first sentence of the introductory paragraph of (a), substituted "within 24 to 48" for "prior to 72" and "be" for "been" preceding "screened"; and deleted "the blood spots may be used within the Division of Public Health for quality assurance or performance improvement activities including pilot studies when a new disorder is being considered for addition to the panel, or may be used by the Division of Public Health for any other purpose authorized by law" from the end of (c).

§ 806C. Confidentiality.

(a) No person may disclose or be compelled to disclose the identity of any person upon whom a blood specimen for metabolic, hematologic, endocrinologic, immunologic and certain structural disorders screen is performed, or the results of such test in a manner which permits identification of the subject of the test, except to the following person:

(1) The subject of the test or the subject's legal guardian.

(2) Any person who secures a legally effective release of test results executed by the subject of the test or the subject's legal guardian.

(3) For purposes of diagnosis, treatment or follow-up.

(4) As authorized by court order.

(5) To a medical examiner authorized to conduct an autopsy on a child or an inquest on the death of a child.

(6) Health facility staff committees or accreditation or oversight review organizations which are conducting program monitoring, program evaluation or service reviews, including the Child Death Review Commission conducting reviews pursuant to Title 31.

(7) Individuals who have access to an electronic medical record (EMR), in which the information is retained pursuant to § 1203(a)(6) of this title, or a health information exchange.

(8) Pursuant to Chapter 9 of this title as it relates to investigation of child abuse.

(b) No person to whom the results of a blood specimen for metabolic, hematologic, endocrinologic, immunologic and certain structural disorders screen have been disclosed pursuant to subsection (a) of this section shall disclose the test results to another person except as authorized by subsection (a) of this section.

(c) The provisions in this section shall not interfere with the transmission of information as may be necessary to obtain third-party payment for medical care related to a metabolic, hematologic, endocrinologic, immunologic, or certain structural disorders or with the documentation of cause of death on death certificates.

History.
80 Del. Laws, c. 96, § 1; 80 Del. Laws, c. 187, § 16; 83 Del. Laws, c. 167, § 1.

Effect of amendments.
83 Del. Laws, c. 167, effective September 15, 2021, substituted "a" for "an" preceding "blood" in (b).

CHAPTER 9
ABUSE OF CHILDREN
SUBCHAPTER I
REPORTS AND INVESTIGATIONS OF ABUSE AND NEGLECT

§ 908. Immunity from liability, and special reimbursement to safe havens for expenses related to certain babies.

NOTES TO DECISIONS

Analysis

Reports.
— Substance use.

Reports.

— Substance use.

Hospital, which made a report of prenatal substance exposure in accordance with 16 Del. C. § 903B, was entitled to immunity because: (1) the hospital contacted the Division of Family Services in good faith, based on the child's positive urine test on the date of birth; (2) both the maternity patient and child tested positive for marijuana; and (3) the fact that the patient had a prescription to use medical marijuana did not erase the hospital's immunity under 16 Del. C. § 903B. Coursey v. St. Francis Hosp., Inc., — A.3d —, 2020 Del. Super. LEXIS 2980 (Del. Super. Ct. Dec. 8, 2020).

CHAPTER 9B.
INFANTS WITH PRENATAL SUBSTANCE EXPOSURE.

§ 903B. Notification to Division; immunity from liability.

NOTES TO DECISIONS

Marijuana.

Hospital, which made a report of prenatal substance exposure in accordance with 16 Del. C. § 903B, was entitled to immunity because: (1) the hospital contacted the Division of Family Services in good faith, based on the child's positive urine test on the date of birth; (2) both the maternity patient and child tested positive for marijuana; and (3) the fact that the patient had a prescription to use medical marijuana did not erase the hospital's immunity under 16 Del. C. § 903B. Coursey v. St. Francis Hosp., Inc., — A.3d —, 2020 Del. Super. LEXIS 2980 (Del. Super. Ct. Dec. 8, 2020).

CHAPTER 10
HOSPITALS

§ 1001. "Hospital" defined [For application of this section, see 83 Del. Laws, c. 102, § 2].

(a) As used in this chapter, "hospital" means a health-care organization that has a governing body, an organized medical and professional staff, and inpatient facilities, and provides either medical diagnosis, treatment and care, nursing and related services for ill and injured patients, or rehabilitation services for the rehabilitation of ill, injured or disabled patients 24 hours per day, 7 days per week and primarily engaged in providing inpatient services.

(b) Hospitals may be further classified as:

(1) *General.* — Providing diverse patient services, diagnostic and

therapeutic, for a variety of medical conditions. A general hospital must provide on-site:

a. Diagnostic x-ray services with facilities and staff for a variety of procedures.

b. Clinical laboratory services with facilities and with anatomical pathology services regularly and conveniently available available.

c. Operating room service with facilities and staff.

d. Emergency department with facilities and staff.

(2) *Long-term care.* — Providing inpatient services for patients whose medically-complex conditions require a long hospital stay with an average length of stay of greater than 25 days.

(3) *Psychiatric.* — Providing services for the diagnosis and treatment of patients with psychiatric-related illness.

(4) *Rehabilitation.* — Providing intensive inpatient rehabilitative services for 1 or more conditions requiring rehabilitation.

(5) *Surgical.* — Providing inpatient and outpatient surgical and related services in which the anticipated duration of the patient's stay will not exceed 72 hours following admission. A surgical hospital must provide all of the following services on-site:

a. Diagnostic x-ray services with facilities and staff for a variety of procedures.

b. Clinical laboratory services with facilities and anatomical pathology services regularly and conveniently available.

c. Operating room service with facilities and staff.

d. Basic emergency care.

(c) Hospitals classified under paragraphs (b)(2) through (4) of this section shall not be required to comply with the provisions of paragraph (b)(1) of this section, but must, at a minimum, provide on-site basic emergency care services.

History.

16 Del. C. 1953, § 1021; 56 Del. Laws, c. 360; 70 Del. Laws, c. 149, § 87; 70 Del. Laws, c. 186, § 1; 80 Del. Laws, c. 404, § 1; 82 Del. Laws, c. 73, § 1; 83 Del. Laws, c. 102, § 1.

Revisor's note.

Section 2 of 83 Del. Laws, c. 102, provided that: "Nothing in this act shall be interpreted as affecting or invalidating any services provided by hospitals in Delaware prior to the effective date of this act." The act became effective upon the signature of the Governor on July 30, 2021.

Effect of amendments.

83 Del. Laws, c. 102, effective July 30, 2021, hyphenated "on-site" in the the second sentence of the introductory paragraph of (b)(1); substituted a period for a semicolon at the end of (b)(1)a. and b.; and added (b)(5) and (c).

§ 1012. Reportable events.

(a) Hospitals must report all major adverse incidents involving a patient to the Department within 10 calendar days.

(1) A major adverse incident is a patient safety event (not primarily related to the natural course of the patient's illness or underlying condition) that reaches a patient. The Department shall define "major adverse incident" and provide further clarification in regulation.

(2) Major adverse incidents must be investigated by the hospital.

(3) A summary of the hospital's investigative findings will be forwarded to the Department within a timeframe agreeable to both parties.

(b) Hospitals must notify the Department immediately of any event occurring within the hospital that jeopardizes the health or safety of patients or employees including:

(1) An unscheduled interruption for 3 or more hours of physical plant or clinical services impacting the health or safety of patients or employees.

(2) A fire, disaster or accident which results in evacuation of patients out of the hospital.

(3) An alleged or suspected crime which endangers the life or safety of patients or employees, which is also reportable to the police department, and which results in an immediate on-site investigation by the police.

(4) An alleged incident of medication diversion, as defined under § 1131 of this title.

(c) Information submitted as a major adverse incident is considered peer review information and not subject to public disclosure except as aggregate data.

History.
16 Del. C. 1953, § 1033; 56 Del. Laws, c. 360; 70 Del. Laws, c. 149, § 96; 70 Del. Laws, c. 186, § 1; 82 Del. Laws, c. 73, § 1; 83 Del. Laws, c. 22, § 11.

Amendment Notes
83 Del. Laws, c. 22, effective June 3, 2021, added (b)(4).

CHAPTER 11
LONG-TERM CARE FACILITIES AND SERVICES.

SUBCHAPTER III
ABUSE, NEGLECT, MISTREATMENT, FINANCIAL EXPLOITATION, OR MEDICATION DIVERSION OF PATIENTS OR RESIDENTS

Revisor's note.
Section 1 of 83 Del. Laws, c. 22, effective June 3, 2021, in the subchapter head, deleted "or" following "Mistreatment" and substituted "Exploitation, or Medication Diversion of Patients or Residents" for "Exploitation of Residents or Patients".

§ 1131. Definitions.

As used in this subchapter:

(1) "Abuse" means the infliction of injury, unreasonable confinement, intimidation, or punishment with resulting physical harm, pain, or mental anguish and includes all of the following:

a. *Physical abuse.* — "Physical abuse" means the unnecessary infliction of pain or injury to a patient or resident. "Physical abuse" includes hitting, kicking, punching, slapping, or pulling hair. If any act constituting physical abuse has been proven, the infliction of pain is presumed.

b. *Sexual abuse.* — "Sexual abuse" includes any sexual contact, sexual penetration, or sexual intercourse, as those terms are defined in § 761 of Title 11, with a patient or resident by an employee or volunteer working at a facility. It is not a defense that the sexual contact, sexual penetration, or sexual intercourse was consensual.

c. *Emotional abuse.* — "Emotional abuse" means the use of oral, written, or gestured language that includes disparaging and derogatory terms to patients, residents, their families, or within their hearing distance, regardless of their age, ability to comprehend, or disability. "Emotional abuse" includes the violation of resident rights and privacy through the posting of inappropriate materials on social media. "Emotional abuse" includes all of the following: ridiculing, demeaning, humiliating, or cursing at a patient or resident; punishment or deprivation; or threatening a patient or resident with physical harm.

    d. [Repealed.]

(2), (3) [Repealed.]

(4) "Facility" means all of the following:

    a. Any facility required to be licensed under this chapter.

    b. Any facility operated by or for the State which provides long-term care residential services.

    c. The Delaware Psychiatric Center and hospitals licensed by the Department under §§ 5001 and 5136 of this title.

    d. Any hospital as defined under Chapter 10 of this title. "Hospital" is included in the definition of facility only for the purposes and application of this section and § 1136 of this title.

(5) "Financial exploitation" means the illegal or improper use of a patient's or resident's resources or financial rights by another person, whether for profit or other advantage.

(6) [Repealed.]

(7) "High managerial agent" means an officer of a facility or any other agent in a position of comparable authority with respect to the formulation of the policy of the facility or the supervision in a managerial capacity of subordinate employees.

(8) "Investigation" the collection of evidence in response to an allegation of abuse, neglect, mistreatment, financial exploitation, or medication diversion of a patient or resident to determine if that patient or resident has been abused, neglected, mistreated, or financially exploited or has been the victim of medication diversion. The Department shall develop protocols for its investigations which focus on ensuring the safety and well-being of the patient or resident and which satisfy the requirements of this chapter.

(9) "Licensed independent practitioner" means a physician or an individual licensed and authorized to write medical orders under Chapter 17 or Chapter 19 of Title 24 and who is providing care for the patient or resident or is overseeing the health care provided to the resident.

(10)a. "Medication diversion" means the knowing or intentional interruption, obstruction, or alteration of the delivery or administration of a prescription drug to a patient or resident, if both of the following apply:

    1. The prescription drug was prescribed or ordered by a licensed independent practitioner for the patient or resident.

    2. The interruption, obstruction, or alteration occurred without the prescription or order of a licensed independent practitioner.

    b. "Medication diversion" does not mean conduct performed by any of the following:

    1. A licensed independent practitioner or licensed health-care professional who acted in good faith within the scope of the individual's practice or employment.

    2. An individual acting in good faith while rendering emergency care at the scene of an emergency or accident.

(11) "Mistreatment" means the inappropriate use of medications, isolation, or physical or chemical restraints on or of a patient or resident.

(12) "Neglect" means the failure to provide goods and services necessary to avoid physical harm, mental anguish, or mental illness. Neglect includes all of the following:

a. Lack of attention to physical needs of the patient or resident including toileting, bathing, meals, and safety.

b. Failure to report patient or resident health problems or changes in health problems or changes in health condition to an immediate supervisor or nurse.

c. Failure to carry out a prescribed treatment plan for a patient or resident.

d. A knowing failure to provide adequate staffing which results in a medical emergency to any patient or resident where there has been a documented history of at least 2 prior cited instances of such inadequate staffing within the past 2 years in violation of minimum maintenance of staffing levels as required by statute or regulations promulgated by the Department, all so as to evidence a wilful pattern of such neglect.

(13) "Person" means a human being and, where appropriate, a public or private corporation, an entity, an unincorporated association, a partnership, a government, or governmental instrumentality.

(14) [Repealed.]

(15) "Prescription drug" means a drug required by federal or state law or regulation to be dispensed only by a prescription, which means a lawful written or verbal order of a practitioner for a drug, including finished dosage forms and active ingredients, subject to § 503(b) of the Federal Food, Drug, and Cosmetic Act (21 U.S.C. § 353(b)).

History.

65 Del. Laws, c. 442, § 1; 70 Del. Laws, c. 222, § 3; 70 Del. Laws, c. 186, § 1; 70 Del. Laws, c. 550, § 1; 71 Del. Laws, c. 487, § 1; 72 Del. Laws, c. 120, §§ 1-4; 77 Del. Laws, c. 201, § 9; 78 Del. Laws, c. 30, § 1; 79 Del. Laws, c. 193, § 1; 80 Del. Laws, c. 404, § 1; 81 Del. Laws, c. 206, § 32; 81 Del. Laws, c. 209, §§ 2,14; 83 Del. Laws, c. 22, § 2.

Effect of amendments.

83 Del. Laws, c. 22, effective June 3, 2021, repealed (1)d.; in the first sentence in (8), deleted "or" following "mistreatment", added "or medication diversion", substituted "patient or resident" for "resident or patient" twice and added "or has been the victim of medication diversion"; added present (10).

§ 1132. Reporting requirements.

(a)(1) Any employee of a facility or person who provides services to a patient or resident on a regular or intermittent basis who has reasonable cause to believe that a patient or resident in a facility has been abused, neglected, mistreated, or financially exploited or has been the victim of medication diversion shall immediately report the abuse, neglect, mistreatment, financial exploitation, or medication diversion to the Department by oral communication. The employee or person providing services to a patient or resident shall file a written report within 48 hours after the employee or person providing services to a patient or resident first gains knowledge of the abuse, neglect, mistreatment, financial exploitation, or medication diversion.

(2) In addition to the persons required to report abuse, neglect, mistreatment, financial exploitation, or medication diversion under paragraph (a)(1) of this section, any other person, including a patient or resident, may contact the Department to report any complaint concerning the health, safety, and welfare of patients or residents.

(3) The Department shall inform a person making a report under

paragraph (a)(1) or (a)(2) of this section of the person's right to obtain information concerning the disposition of the report. The person must receive, if requested, information on the general disposition of the report at the conclusion of the investigation.

(4) If the Department does not have jurisdiction over the report, the Department shall so advise the person making the report under paragraph (a)(1) or (a)(2) of this section and shall promptly refer the person to the appropriate agency.

(b) Any person required by subsection (a) or (c) of this section to make an oral and a written report who fails to do so is to be fined not more than $1,000 or imprisoned not more than 15 days, or both.

(c) In addition to those persons subject to subsection (a) of this section, any other person shall make a report if the person has reasonable cause to believe that a patient or resident has been abused, neglected, mistreated, or financially exploited, or has been the victim of medication diversion. A report under this subsection is confidential and the reporting person cannot be compelled to do either of the following:

(1) Notify the facility, care provider, or individual implicated in the event.

(2) Provide information regarding the reported abuse, neglect, mistreatment, financial exploitation, or medication diversion to the facility, care provider, or individual implicated in the event.

(d) Any person who intentionally makes a false report under this subchapter is guilty of a class A misdemeanor.

(e) Any correspondence or other written communication from a patient or resident to the Department, the Attorney General's office, the protection and advocacy agency, or a law-enforcement agency must, if delivered to or received by a facility, be promptly forwarded, unopened, by the facility to the agency to which it is written. Violation of this subsection is punishable by a civil penalty not to exceed $1,000 per violation.

(f) Any correspondence or other written communication from the Department, the Attorney General's office, the protection and advocacy agency, or a law-enforcement agency to a patient or resident must, if delivered to or received by a facility, be promptly forwarded, unopened, by the facility to the patient or resident. Violation of this subsection is punishable by a civil penalty not to exceed $1,000 per violation.

History.
65 Del. Laws, c. 442, § 1; 70 Del. Laws, c. 186, § 1; 71 Del. Laws, c. 292, § 1; 71 Del. Laws, c. 487, §§ 3, 5, 6; 74 Del. Laws, c. 196, § 1; 77 Del. Laws, c. 201, § 10; 81 Del. Laws, c. 206, § 33; 83 Del. Laws, c. 22, § 3.

Effect of amendments.
83 Del. Laws, c. 22, effective June 3, 2021, rewrote (a)(1); and substituted "financial exploitation, or medication diversion" for "or financial exploitation" in (a)(2) and (c)(2); in (a)(2), deleted "facility" preceding "resident" and preceding "residents"; substituted "The person must" for "Such person shall" in the second sentence of (a)(3); deleted the former final sentence of (b); in the first sentence of (c),

substituted "a report" for "such a report", deleted "of a facility" following "resident", added "neglected" following "abused", deleted "neglected" following "mistreatment", added a comma and "or has been the victim of medication diversion"; in the second sentence of (c), substituted "A report under this subsection is" for "Such reports are"; deleted "or" following "mistreatment" in (c)(2); substituted "patient or resident" for "resident or patient" in (e); and in the first sentence of (f), added a comma following "agency", and substituted "patient or resident must" for "resident or patient shall", "a" for "the" following "received by" and "the patient or resident" for "such resident or patient" at the end.

NOTES TO DECISIONS

Defamation.
Plaintiff's defamation claims against a nursing home, arising out of employees' accusation that plaintiff committed abuse against a resi-

dent, were dismissed because: (1) the employees were required to report suspected abuse by 16 Del. C. § 1132(a)(1); (2) employees were protected from defamation claims by 16 Del. C.

§ 1135(a); and (3) under 24 Del. C. § 1930, nurses were protected from any liability in exercising their duty to report abuse so long as they acted in good faith. Cooper v. Cadia Pike Creek, — A.3d —, 2021 Del. Super. LEXIS 105 (Del. Super. Ct. Feb. 4, 2021).

§ 1133. Contents of reports.

The reports required under this subchapter must contain all of the following information:

(1) The name and sex of the patient orresident.

(2) The name and address of the facility in which the patient or resident resides.

(3) The age of the patient or resident, if known.

(4) The name and address of the reporter and where the reporter can be contacted.

(5) Any information relative to the nature and extent of the abuse, neglect, mistreatment, financial exploitation, or medication diversion and, if known to the reporter, any information relative to prior abuse, neglect, mistreatment, financial exploitation, or medication diversion of the patient or resident.

(6) The circumstances under which the reporter became aware of the abuse, neglect, mistreatment, financial exploitation, or medication diversion.

(7) What action, if any, was taken to treat or otherwise assist the patient or resident.

(8) Any other information which the reporter believes to be relevant in establishing the cause of the abuse, neglect, mistreatment, financial exploitation, or medication diversion.

History.
65 Del. Laws, c. 442, § 1; 70 Del. Laws, c. 186, § 1; 81 Del. Laws, c. 206, § 34; 83 Del. Laws, c. 22, § 4.

Effect of amendments.
83 Del. Laws, c. 22, effective June 3, 2021, in the introductory paragraph, substituted "must" for "shall"; in (5), added "neglect" following "abuse" two times, substituted "or medication diversion" for "or neglect", and "medication diversion of the" for "neglect of such"; in (6), added "neglect" following "abuse" and substituted "medication diversion" for "neglect"; and in (8), substituted "the abuse, neglect" for "such abuse" and "medication diversion" for "neglect".

§ 1134. State response to reports of adult abuse, neglect, mistreatment, financial exploitation, or medication diversion.

(a) The Department shall ensure that patients or residents are afforded the same rights and protections as other individuals in the State.

(b) [Repealed.]

(c) The Department shall establish and maintain a 24-hour statewide toll-free telephone report line operating at all times and capable of receiving reports of alleged abuse, neglect, mistreatment, financial exploitation, and medication diversion.

(d) On receipt of an allegation of abuse, neglect, mistreatment, financial exploitation, or medication diversion, the Department shall do all of the following:

(1) Receive and maintain reports in a computerized central data base.

(2) Acknowledge all complaints, when authorized by the person making the report. The acknowledgement shall identify other relevant remedial agencies, including the protection and advocacy agency, Office of the Long-Term Care Ombudsperson, and victim rights resource organizations.

(3) Forward complaints to the appropriate Department staff who shall determine, through the use of standard operating procedures developed by the Department, whether an investigation should be initiated to respond to the complaint. The Department shall develop the protocols for making

this determination and the protocols must give priority to ensuring the well-being and safety of patients and residents.

(4) Begin the investigation within 24 hours of receipt of any report or complaint that alleges any of the following:

a. A patient's or resident's health or safety is in imminent danger.

b. A patient or resident has died due to alleged abuse, neglect, mistreatment, or medication diversion.

c. A patient or resident has been hospitalized or received medical treatment due to alleged abuse, neglect, mistreatment, or medication diversion.

d. The existence of circumstances that could result in abuse, neglect, mistreatment, or medication diversion and that could place a patient's or resident's health or safety in imminent danger.

e. A patient or resident has been the victim of financial exploitation or risk thereof and exigent circumstances warrant an immediate response.

(5) Except in situations outlined in paragraph (d)(4) of this section, initiate and conclude an investigation within 10 days of receiving a report or complaint unless extenuating facts warrant a longer time to complete the investigation.

(6) Contact the appropriate law-enforcement agency immediately on receipt of any complaint requiring an investigation under this section and provide the police with a detailed description of the complaint received.

a. The appropriate law-enforcement agency shall conduct its investigation or provide the Department within a reasonable time an explanation detailing the reasons why it is unable to conduct the investigation.

b. The Department may defer its own investigation in these circumstances until it receives appropriate guidance from the Attorney General's Office and the relevant police agency with respect to how to proceed with its investigation thereby assuring a coordinated investigation.

c. Notwithstanding any provision of the Delaware Code to the contrary, to the extent the law-enforcement agency with jurisdiction over the case is unable to assist, the Department may request that the Delaware State Police exercise jurisdiction over the case and, upon such request, the Delaware State Police may exercise such jurisdiction.

(7) If a case is classified as an investigation under this subchapter, have the authority to secure a medical examination of a long-term care patient or resident on the consent of the patient or resident without the consent of the long-term care facility if the patient or resident has been reported to be a victim of abuse, neglect, or mistreatment, or medication diversion.

(8) When a written report of abuse, neglect, mistreatment, financial exploitation, or medication diversion is made by a person required to report under § 1132(a) of this title, the Department shall contact the person who made the report within 48 hours of the receipt of the report in order to ensure that full information has been received and to obtain any additional information, including medical records, which may be pertinent.

(9) Conduct an investigation involving all reports which, if true, would constitute a criminal offense, or an attempt to commit a criminal offense, under any of the following provisions of Title 11: § § 601, 602, 603, 604, 611, 612, 613, 621, 625, 626, 627, 631, 632, 633, 634, 635, 636, 645, 763,

764, 765, 767, 768, 769, 770, 771, 772, 773, 774, 775, 791, 841, 842, 843, 844, 845, 846, 848, 851, 861, 862 and 908.

(10) Develop protocols to ensure that it conducts its investigation in coordination with the relevant law-enforcement agency. The primary purpose of the Department's investigation must be the protection of the patient or resident.

(11) Do any of the following when investigating abuse, neglect, mistreatment, financial exploitation, or medication diversion reports:

a. Make unannounced visits to the facility, as required, to determine the nature and cause of the alleged abuse, neglect, mistreatment, financial exploitation, or medication diversion.

b. Interview available witnesses identified by any source as having personal knowledge relevant to the reported abuse, neglect, mistreatment, financial exploitation, or medication diversion.

c. Conduct interviews in private unless the witness expressly requests that the interview not be private.

d. Write an investigation report that includes all of the following:

1. The investigator's personal observations.

2. A review of the medical and all other relevant documents and records.

3. A summary of each witness statement.

4. A statement of the factual basis for the findings for each incident or problem alleged in the complaint.

(12)-(16) [Repealed.]

(17) Before the completion of an investigation, file a petition for the temporary care and protection of the patient or resident if the Department determines that immediate removal is necessary to protect the patient or resident from further abuse, neglect, mistreatment, financial exploitation, or medication diversion.

(18) On completing an investigation of a complaint, the Department shall take 1 or more of the following courses of action, as appropriate:

a. If representatives of the Department, the Attorney General's Office, or the appropriate law-enforcement agency are unable to substantiate a complaint that applicable laws or regulations have been violated, the Department, Attorney General's Office, or appropriate law-enforcement agency shall so advise the complainant and the facility, agency, or individual against which the complaint was made.

b. If Department representatives are able to substantiate a complaint that applicable laws or regulations have been violated, the Department shall take appropriate enforcement action.

1. An enforcement action may include instituting actions by the Department for injunctive relief or other relief deemed appropriate.

2. The Attorney General's Office shall provide legal advice and assist the Department to institute an enforcement action.

c. If the Department discovers a violation of federal laws or regulations or rules administered by any other government agency, the Department shall refer the matter directly to the appropriate government agency for an enforcement action.

d.-f. [Repealed.]

(19) Protect the privacy of the long-term care patient or resident and the patient's or resident's family.

a. The Department shall establish guidelines concerning the disclosure of information relating to complaints and investigations regarding abuse, neglect, mistreatment, financial exploitation, or medication diversion involving that patient or resident.

b. The Department may require persons to make written requests for access to records maintained by the Department.

c. Records maintained for investigations conducted under this section are not public records under Chapter 100 of Title 29 and the Department may only release information to persons who have a legitimate public safety need for the information and the information must be used only for the purpose for which it is released under a user agreement with the Department.

(e) The protection and advocacy agency may complement the Department's complaint resolution system through monitoring, investigation, and advocacy on behalf of facility patients or residents. In furtherance of this authority, protection and advocacy agency representatives may engage in all of the following functions:

(1) Solicit and receive oral and written reports and complaints of abuse, neglect, mistreatment, financial exploitation, or medication diversion of facility patients or residents.

(2) Access a facility.

(3) Interview patients, residents, facility staff, and agents.

(4) Inspect and copy records pertaining to the patient or resident with valid consent or as otherwise authorized by federal law.

(f) The Department may develop protocols with the protection and advocacy agency to facilitate coordination whenever both agencies have initiated an overlapping investigation.

(g) The immunities and protections under § 1135 of this title apply to persons offering reports or testimony to initiate or support protection and advocacy agency investigation or advocacy.

(h) *Appointment of special investigators; powers and duties.* — (1) The Secretary of the Department may appoint qualified persons to be special investigators.

a. The investigators hold office at the pleasure of the Secretary.

b. Any individual appointed under this section must have all of the following qualifications:

1. A minimum of 10 years experience as a police officer, as that term is defined in § 1911(a) of Title 11.

2. Significant investigatory experience while working as a police officer.

3. Be in good standing with the previous or present law-enforcement agency where the individual was or is employed.

4. Other qualifications deemed appropriate by the Secretary.

(2) Special investigators appointed under this section may conduct investigations of abuse, neglect, mistreatment, financial exploitation, or medication diversion of patients and residents of facilities and adults who are impaired as defined in § 3902 of Title 31 anywhere in this State as directed by the Department and have the power to make arrests and serve writs anywhere in this State.

a. In conducting the investigations, the special investigators have the statewide powers enumerated under § 1911 of Title 11 and other powers as conferred by law on police officers, but the powers are limited to offenses involving abuse, neglect, mistreatment, financial exploitation, or medication diversion of patients and residents of long-term care facilities and adults who are impaired anywhere in this State as directed by the Department.

b. To the extent possible, special investigators under this section may consult with the police agency having jurisdiction and the Department before making an arrest and shall do so in all cases after making the arrest.

(3) The Secretary of the Department shall fix the salary of special investigators within the appropriations made to the Department.

(4) Special investigators shall assist in the training of other Department staff.

(i) On receipt of any report under paragraph (d)(5) of this section, the law-enforcement agency having jurisdiction shall conduct a full and complete criminal investigation based on their departmental policies and shall assess probable cause and effectuate arrests when appropriate.

(1) The Attorney General's Office or other law-enforcement agency conducting the investigation shall keep the Department informed of the case status and all major decisions under memoranda of understanding between the Department and the Attorney General's Office and other relevant law-enforcement agencies entered into under subsection (j) of this section.

(2) The Attorney General's Office shall keep the Department well informed of the case status and all major decisions, including the disposition of criminal charges and the specifics of any sentencing order rendered.

(j) The Department, the Attorney General's Office, and other law-enforcement agencies shall develop memoranda of understanding under this subchapter which provide for timely notification, co-investigation, referral of cases, including automatic referral in certain cases, and ongoing coordination in order to keep each other apprised of the status of their respective investigations. The memoranda of understanding may be amended as needed.

(k) If the Department suspects or discovers information indicating the commission of violations of standards of professional conduct by facilities licensed under this chapter or by staff employed by such facilities, the Department shall immediately contact the Attorney General's Office and the relevant professional licensing board.

(l) The Department and the Attorney General's Office shall cooperate with law-enforcement agencies to develop training programs to increase the effectiveness of Department personnel, Attorney General's Office personnel, and law-enforcement officers in investigating suspected cases of abuse, neglect, mistreatment, financial exploitation, or medication diversion.

(m) If a criminal prosecution for abuse, neglect, mistreatment, financial exploitation, or medication diversion is initiated by the Attorney General's Office based on a report under this subchapter, and incarceration of the individual who is the subject of the report is ordered by the court, the Attorney General's Office shall keep the Department informed of actions taken by the court which result in the release of the individual if the Attorney General's Office is represented at the hearing.

(n) If a criminal prosecution for abuse, neglect, mistreatment, financial exploitation, or medication diversion is initiated by the Attorney General's Office against a person employed by or associated with a facility or organization required to be licensed or whose staff are required to be licensed under Delaware law, the Attorney General's Office shall notify the Department within 48 hours and the Department shall then notify the individual's employer as follows:

(1) When the individual is charged with having committed at least 1 felony offense involving an allegation of abuse, neglect, mistreatment, financial exploitation, or medication diversion.

(2) On an adjudication of guilt of the person for any misdemeanor or violation, when the offense involved abuse, neglect, mistreatment, financial exploitation, or medication diversion.

History.
65 Del. Laws, c. 442, § 1; 70 Del. Laws, c. 222, § 4; 70 Del. Laws, c. 186, § 1; 71 Del. Laws, c. 487, § 4; 72 Del. Laws, c. 3, § 4; 74 Del. Laws, c. 212, § 1; 77 Del. Laws, c. 201, §§ 11-14; 77 Del. Laws, c. 318, § 6; 78 Del. Laws, c. 179, § 164; 81 Del. Laws, c. 206, § 35; 81 Del. Laws, c. 209, §§ 3, 14; 83 Del. Laws, c. 22, § 5.

Effect of amendments.
83 Del. Laws, c. 22, effective June 3, 2021, in the section heading, (e)(1) and (*l*), substituted "financial exploitation, or medication diversion" for "or financial exploitation"; in (c), deleted "and" following "mistreatment", and substituted "exploitation, and medication diversion" for "exploitation"; rewrote (d); substituted "under" for "compiled in" in (g); rewrote (h); substituted "On" for "Upon" in the introductory paragraph of (i); substituted "Attorney General's Office" for "Department of Justice" in (i)(2); substituted "Attorney General's Office" for "Office of the Attorney General" in the first sentence of (j) and in (k); rewrote (m) and (n).

§ 1135. Immunities and other protections.

(a) A person making any oral or written report under this subchapter is not liable in any civil or criminal action by reason of the report where the report was made in good faith or under the reasonable belief that the abuse, neglect, mistreatment, financial exploitation, or medication diversion has occurred.

(b) A facility may not discharge, or in any manner discriminate or retaliate against any person, by any means whatsoever, who in good faith makes or causes to be made, a report under this subchapter, or who testifies or who is about to testify in any proceeding concerning abuse, neglect, mistreatment, financial exploitation, or medication diversion of patients or residents.

(c) Any facility which discharges, discriminates, or retaliates against a person because the person reports, testifies, or is about to testify concerning abuse, neglect, mistreatment, financial exploitation, or medication diversion of patients or residents is liable to the person for treble damages, costs, and attorney fees. If a facility discharges, demotes, or retaliates by any other means against a person after the person makes a report, testifies, or is subpoenaed to testify as a result of a report authorized under this subchapter, there is a rebuttable presumption that the facility discharged, demoted, or retaliated against the person as a result of the report or testimony.

(d) This section does not apply to any person who has engaged in the abuse, neglect, mistreatment, financial exploitation, or medication diversion of a patient or resident.

History.
65 Del. Laws, c. 442, § 1; 70 Del. Laws, c. 186, § 1; 77 Del. Laws, c. 201, §§ 15, 16; 81 Del. Laws, c. 206, § 36; 83 Del. Laws, c. 22, § 6.

Effect of amendments.
83 Del. Laws, c. 22, effective June 3, 2021, rewrote the section.

NOTES TO DECISIONS

Defamation.
Plaintiff's defamation claims against a nursing home, arising out of employees' accusation that plaintiff committed abuse against a resident, were dismissed because: (1) the employees were required to report suspected abuse by 16 Del. C. § 1132(a)(1); (2) employees were protected from defamation claims by 16 Del. C. § 1135(a); and (3) under 24 Del. C. § 1930, nurses were protected from any liability in exercising their duty to report abuse so long as they acted in good faith. Cooper v. Cadia Pike Creek, — A.3d —, 2021 Del. Super. LEXIS 105 (Del. Super. Ct. Feb. 4, 2021).

§ 1136. Violations.

(a) Any person who knowingly or recklessly abuses, mistreats, or neglects a patient or resident is guilty of a class A misdemeanor.

    (1) If the abuse involves sexual contact such person is guilty of a class G felony.

    (2) If the abuse, mistreatment, or neglect results in serious physical

injury, sexual penetration, or sexual intercourse, such person is guilty of a class C felony.

(3) If the abuse, mistreatment, or neglect results in death, then the person is guilty of a class A felony.

(b) Any person who knowingly causes medication diversion of a patient or resident,is guilty of the following:

(1) A class G felony.

(2) A class F felony, if committed by a health-care professional.

(c) Any person who knowingly commits financial exploitation of a patient's or resident's resources is guilty of the following:

(1) A class A misdemeanor if the value of the resources is less than $1,000.

(2) A class G felony if the value of the resources is $1,000 or more.

(d) Any member of the board of directors or a high managerial agent who knows that patients or residents of the facility are being abused, mistreated, neglected, or financially exploited or are the victim of medication diversion and fails to promptly take corrective action is guilty of a class A misdemeanor.

(e) Nothing in this section precludes a separate charge, conviction, and sentence for any other crime under this title or this Code.

History.
65 Del. Laws, c. 442, § 1; 72 Del. Laws, c. 120, §§ 5, 6; 78 Del. Laws, c. 30, §§ 2, 3; 79 Del. Laws, c. 193, § 2; 81 Del. Laws, c. 206, § 37; 83 Del. Laws, c. 22, § 7.

Effect of amendments.
83 Del. Laws, c. 22, effective June 3, 2021,
deleted "of a facility" following "resident" in the introductory paragraph of (a); added "or are the victim of medication diversion" in (d); and in (e), substituted "precludes" for "shall preclude" and "under this title or this Code" for "set forth in this title, or in the Delaware Code".

NOTES TO DECISIONS

Negligence per se.
Dismissal of a personal representative's negligence per se claim against a long-term nursing facility was inappropriate; the personal representative adequately pleaded violations on the part of the facility that supported findings of criminal liability sufficient to survive a motion for dismissal. Cunningham v. Kentmere Rehab. & Healthcare Ctr., Inc., — A.3d —, 2021 Del. Super. LEXIS 244 (Del. Super. Ct. Mar. 25, 2021).

§ 1137. Suspension or revocation of license for violation by licensed or registered professional.

On a finding of abuse, neglect, mistreatment, or medication diversion by a licensed or registered professional, or a licensed or registered professional's failure to report abuse, neglect, mistreatment, or medication diversion by a licensed or registered professional, the Department or the Attorney General's Office shall notify the appropriate licensing or registration board. If, after a hearing, a licensed or registered professional is found to have abused, neglected, or mistreated, or committed medication diversion against, a patient or resident or has failed to report abuse, neglect, mistreatment, or medication diversion, the appropriate board shall suspend or revoke the licensed or registered professional's license.

History.
65 Del. Laws, c. 442, § 1; 83 Del. Laws, c. 22, § 8.

Effect of amendments.
83 Del. Laws, c. 22, effective June 3, 2021, rewrote the section.

§ 1138. Suspension or revocation of license for violation by facility.

On a finding that abuse, neglect, mistreatment, financial exploitation, or medication diversion has occurred in a facility, if it is determined that a member of the board of directors or a high managerial agent knew that patients or residents were abused, neglected, mistreated, or financially exploited or the victim of medication diversion and failed to promptly take corrective action, the Department must suspend or revoke the facility's license.

History.
65 Del. Laws, c. 442, § 1; 81 Del. Laws, c. 206, § 38; 83 Del. Laws, c. 22, § 9.

Effect of amendments.
83 Del. Laws, c. 22, effective June 3, 2021, rewrote the section.

§ 1139. Treatment by spiritual means.

Nothing in this subchapter may be construed to mean that a patient or resident is abused, neglected, or mistreated, or is the victim of medication diversion, for the sole reason the patient or resident relies on, or is being furnished with, treatment by spiritual means through prayer alone in accordance with the tenets and practices of a recognized church or religious denomination, nor may anything in this subchapter be construed to authorize or require any medical care or treatment over the implied or express objection of the patient or resident.

History.
65 Del. Laws, c. 442, § 1; 70 Del. Laws, c. 186, § 1; 81 Del. Laws, c. 206, § 39; 83 Del. Laws, c. 22, § 10.

Effect of amendments.
83 Del. Laws, c. 22, effective June 3, 2021,

substituted "neglected, or mistreated, or is the victim of medication diversion" for "mistreated, or neglected", "on" for "upon" and "the" for "said" following "objection of".

CHAPTER 16

LITTER CONTROL LAW

§ 1602. Declaration of intent.

It is the intention of this chapter to end littering on public or private property, including bodies of water, as a threat to the health and safety of the citizens, fish, birds, and other animals of this State. It is also the intent of the General Assembly to single out for enhanced penalties those who dump a substantial quantity of litter in violation of this chapter.

History.
60 Del. Laws, c. 613, § 1; 82 Del. Laws, c. 167, § 1; 83 Del. Laws, c. 180, § 1.

Effect of amendments.
83 Del. Laws, c. 180, effective September 17,

2021, added "fish, birds, and animals" in the first sentence.

§ 1603. Definitions.

As used in this chapter:

(1) "Balloon" means a bag made from rubber, latex, polychloroprene, nylon, mylar, or other material which is or can be filled with air, water, or a gas, including helium, hydrogen, nitrous oxide, or oxygen.

(2) "Dumping" means the deposit of litter in a substantial quantity on public or private property.

(3) "LIEF" means the Littering Investigation and Enforcement Fund.

(4) "Litter" includes all rubbish, waste material, refuse, cans, bottles, garbage, trash, debris, dead animals, 1 to 4 balloons released at 1 time, or other discarded materials of every kind and description.

(5) "Mass release of balloons" means the intentional release of 5 or more balloons at 1 time.

(6) "Public or private property" includes the right-of-way of any road or highway; any body of water or watercourse, or the shores or beaches thereof; any park, playground, building, refuge, or conservation or recreation area; and any residential or farm properties, timberlands, or forests.

(7) "Substantial quantity" means a gross, uncompressed volume of litter equal to or greater than 32 gallons or 4.28 cubic feet, which is the capacity of a standard garbage can.

History.
  60 Del. Laws, c. 613, § 1; 82 Del. Laws, c. 167, § 2; 83 Del. Laws, c. 180, § 2.

Effect of amendments.
  83 Del. Laws, c. 180, effective September 17,

2021, added present (1) and (5) and redesignated the remaining and intervening paragraphs accordingly; and added "1 to 4 balloons released at 1 time" in present (4).

§ 1604. Unlawful activities.

(a) *Littering.* — It is unlawful for a person to deposit, throw, release, or leave, or cause or permit the depositing, placing, throwing, or leaving of litter on public or private property of this State, unless either of the following 2 conditions is met:

(1) The property is designated by the State or by any of its agencies or political subdivisions for the management of litter, and the person is authorized by the proper public authority to use the property for that purpose.

(2) Both of the following apply:

  a. The litter is placed in a litter receptacle or container installed on or at the property.

  b. The person is the owner or tenant in lawful possession of the property or has first obtained consent of the owner or tenant in lawful possession, or the act is done under the personal direction of the owner or tenant, all in a manner consistent with the public welfare.

(b) *Dumping.* — It is unlawful for a person to dump litter in substantial quantities on public or private property, except under paragraphs (a)(1) through (a)(2) of this section.

(c) *Mass release of balloons.* — It is unlawful for a person to intentionally release, or intentionally cause or permit the release of, 5 or more balloons on private or public property of this State.

(d) This section does not apply to any of the following:

(1) A balloon that is released for scientific or meteorological purposes, on behalf of a governmental agency, or under a governmental contract.

(2) A hot air balloon that is recovered after launching.

(3) A balloon that is released and remains indoors.

(4) A balloon that, for recreational purposes, is filled with water and recovered after recreation.

(5) A balloon that is unintentionally or negligently released.

History.
  60 Del. Laws, c. 613, § 1; 82 Del. Laws, c. 167, § 3; 83 Del. Laws, c. 180, § 3.

Effect of amendments.
  83 Del. Laws, c. 180, effective September 17,

2021, added "release" in the introductory paragraph of (a); substituted "(a)(2)" for "(a)(3)" in (b); and added (c) and (d).

§ 1605. Penalties; jurisdiction; voluntary assessment form [For application of this section, see 83 Del. Laws, c. 180, § 7].

(a)(1) A person found guilty of littering under § 1604(a) of this title must be punished by a fine of not less than $50 and up to 8 hours of community service for a first offense, and $75 and up to 25 hours of community service for a second offense within 2 years of the first offense. This paragraph does not apply to the intentional release of 1 to 4 balloons. The penalty for intentionally releasing 1 to 4 balloons is provided in paragraph (a)(3)a. of this section.

(2) A person found guilty of dumping under § 1604(b) of this title must be punished by a fine of not less than $500 and not less than 8 hours of community service for a first offense, and a fine of not less than $1,000 and not less than 16 hours of community service for a second offense within 2 years of the first offense. Each instance of dumping constitutes a separate offense under this chapter.

(3) Balloons.

    a. A person who is found in violation of § 1604(a) of this title by releasing 1 to 4 balloons must do the following:

        1. For a first violation, pay a civil penalty of not less than $25.

        2. For a second or subsequent violation within 2 years of a first violation, pay a civil penalty of not less than $75 and complete up to 8 hours of community service.

    b. A person who is found in violation of § 1604(c) of this title through the mass release of balloons must do the following:

        1. For a first violation, pay a civil penalty of not less than $250 and complete up to 8 hours of community service.

        2. For a second or subsequent violation, pay a civil penalty of not less than $350 and complete up to 25 hours of community service.

(4) An additional mandatory penalty of $500 must be imposed, in addition to the fine, for every first or subsequent offense, or an additional mandatory civil penalty of $500 must be imposed in addition to the civil penalty for every first or subsequent violation, if the offense or violation occurred in any of the following locations:

    a. On or along a Delaware byway, as defined in § 101 of Title 17.

    b. A State park, forestry area, or fish and wildlife area.

    c. A federal wildlife refuge.

    d. Land within the State that is administered by the United States Department of Interior, National Park Service.

(5) In addition to the penalties listed in paragraphs (a)(1) through (a)(4) of this section, the Court may require a person found guilty of violating this chapter to do 1 or both of the following:

    a. Pick up and remove from any public street, highway, public or private right-of-way, public beach, stream, bank, or public park all litter deposited or dumped on the property by anyone before the date of execution of sentence.

    b. Pay as restitution an amount determined by the Court to the Littering Investigation and Enforcement Fund. The State shall maintain the LIEF as a subaccount of the Special Law Enforcement Assistance Fund established under subchapter II of Chapter 41 of Title 11. Disbursement of LIEF funds must be authorized under the procedures established under § 4113 of Title 11, for the purpose of investigation, enforcement, and remediation of unlawful littering or dumping.

(b) The Justice of the Peace Court has jurisdiction over a violation of this chapter.

(c) The Court shall make public the names of persons convicted of violating this chapter.

(d)(1) A peace officer of this State who charges a person with littering or mass release of balloons under § 1604 of this title may, in addition to issuing a summons for the offense or violation, provide the offender with a voluntary assessment form which, when properly executed by the officer and the offender, allows the offender to dispose of the charge without the necessity of personally appearing in the Court to which the summons is returnable.

(2)a. Payments made under paragraphs (a)(1) through (a)(4) of this section must be remitted to and received by the Court to which the summons is returnable within 10 days from the date of arrest or, for the release of 1 to 4 balloons or mass release of balloons, the date of the violation, excluding Saturday and Sunday.

b. Restitution made to the LIEF under paragraph (a)(5)b. of this section must be remitted to and received by the Court ordering restitution within 10 days from the date of the order for restitution, excluding Saturday and Sunday.

(3) The fine imposed under this subsection must be the minimum fine as provided for in subsection (a) of this section, plus other costs as may be assessed by law.

(4) "Voluntary assessment form", as used in this section, means the written agreement or document signed by the violator in which the violator agrees to pay by mail the fine for the offense described in the agreement or document together with costs and penalty assessment.

History.
60 Del. Laws, c. 613, § 1; 62 Del. Laws, c. 387, §§ 1, 2; 70 Del. Laws, c. 186, § 1; 76 Del. Laws, c. 325, § 1; 77 Del. Laws, c. 350, § 3; 82 Del. Laws, c. 167, § 4; 83 Del. Laws, c. 180, § 4.

Revisor's note.
Section 7 of 83 Del. Laws, c. 180, provided: "The civil penalties under § 1605(a)(3)a., § 1605(a)(3)b., and § 1605(a)(4) of Title 16 do not apply to an individual who litters with balloons or conducts a mass release of balloons on or before April 30, 2022. For persons who are not individuals, the civil penalties under § 1605(a)(3)a., § 1605(a)(3)b., and § 1605(a)(4) of Title 16 apply in full as of the effective date of this act." The act became effective upon the signature of the Governor on Sept. 17, 2021.

Effect of amendments.
83 Del. Laws, c. 180, effective September 17, 2021, added the final sentence in (a)(1); added present (a)(3) and redesignated the remaining paragraphs accordingly; in the introductory paragraph of present (a)(4), substituted "or" for "second, and" following "every", and added "or an additional ... subsequent violation" and "or violation" preceding "occurred"; substituted "(a)(4)" for "(a)(3)" in the introductory paragraph of present (a)(5) and in (d)(2)a.; substituted "1" for "one" in the introductory paragraph of present (a)(5); substituted "of" for a comma preceding "Chapter 41" in the second sentence of (a)(5)b.; in (d)(1), added "or mass release of balloons", substituted "§ 1604" for "§ 1604(a)" and added "or violation" preceding "provide"; added "or, for the release ... date of the violation" in (d)(2)a.; and substituted "paragraph (a)(5)b." for "paragraph (a)(4)b." in (d)(2)b.

§ 1606. Prima facie evidence.

(a)(1) The throwing, depositing, dropping, releasing, or dumping of litter from a motor vehicle, boat, airplane, or other conveyance in violation of this chapter is prima facie evidence that the operator of the conveyance violated chapter.

(2) If, under paragraph (a)(1) of this section, a motor vehicle is used and the identity of the operator is not discernable, there is a rebuttable presumption that the registered owner of the motor vehicle caused or contributed to the violation.

(b) A license to operate a conveyance listed in paragraph (a)(1) of this section may be suspended for a period not to exceed 30 days together with, or in lieu of, other penalties for littering under this chapter or another law of this State. But, if littering or dumping from a conveyance listed in subsection (a) of this section is a first offense, the license may not be suspended and the sanctions provided in § 1605 of this title apply.

History.
60 Del. Laws, c. 613, § 1; 82 Del. Laws, c. 167, § 5; 83 Del. Laws, c. 180, § 5.

Effect of amendments.
83 Del. Laws, c. 180, effective September 17, 2021, added "releasing" in (a)(1).

§ 1609. Notice.

A retail or wholesale establishment that sells balloons must prominently display the following notice at the location in the establishment where balloons are sold or where payment is made:

> "The intentional release of balloons into the air is a violation of Delaware law and is subject to penalties. 16 Del. Code Ch. 16."

History.
83 Del. Laws, c. 180, § 6.

Revisor's Notes
This section became effective upon the signature of the Governor on Sept. 17, 2021.

CHAPTER 17

REFUSE AND GARBAGE

Sec.
1709. Trash containers on highways; penalty.

§ 1709. Trash containers on highways; penalty.

(a)(1) A person, by agent or otherwise, may not cause a trash container having a capacity of 2 cubic yards or greater to be placed on a highway, unless the container has all of the following:

    a. A strip of red and white, high-intensity, reflective conspicuity adhesive tape that is no less than 4 inches wide and wrapped fully around the midpoint of the container. The midpoint of the container is between the bottom of the container and the opening at the top.

    b. The name and phone number of the owner of the container, or the owner's agent, in font that is no less than 3 inches high.

(2) For purposes of this section, "highway" means a way or place open to the use of the public as a matter of right for purposes of vehicular travel and includes the entire width between the boundary lines of the way or place, including parking spaces, berms, and shoulders. "Highway" does not mean a road or driveway on grounds owned by private persons, colleges, universities, or other private institutions.

(b)(1) An owner of a container that refuses, fails, or neglects to comply with this section is subject to a civil penalty in an amount that is not less than $50 or more than $500.

(2) Any law-enforcement officer, as defined under § 9702 of this title, may enforce this section.

(3) Justice of the Peace Court has jurisdiction over violations of this section.

History.
74 Del. Laws, c. 286, § 1; 83 Del. Laws, c. 172, § 1.

Revisor's note.
Section 2 of 83 Del. Laws, c. 172, provided: "This act takes effect 90 days after its enactment into law." The act was signed by the Governor on Sept. 15, 2021, and became effective on Dec. 14, 2021.

Effect of amendments.
83 Del. Laws, c. 172, effective December 14, 2021, rewrote the section.

CHAPTER 22

SUBSTANCE ABUSE TREATMENT ACT

Sec.
2226. Distribution of fentanyl testing strips;
    immunity.

§ 2226. Distribution of fentanyl testing strips; immunity.

(a) The purpose of this section is to expand the harm reduction strategies available in Delaware to address the epidemic level of drug overdose deaths through the distribution of fentanyl testing strips. Fentanyl is a potent opioid that is increasingly being mixed into illicitly sold drugs, often without the buyer's knowledge. In 2018, fentanyl was involved in 72% of overdose deaths in Delaware. The distribution of fentanyl testing strips provides an opportunity to prevent potential overdose deaths.

(b) For purposes of this section, "person" means 1 of the following that provides aid to drug users without the expectation of monetary or other compensation from the individual aided:

(1) A lay individual.

(2) A nonprofit organization.

(c) This section does not apply to any of the following:

(1) A manufacturer or distributor of fentanyl testing strips.

(2) A pharmacy.

(3) A hospital.

(4) A medical clinic.

(5) A for profit organization.

(6) A credentialed individual.

(d) A person may distribute functional fentanyl testing strips to determine the presence of fentanyl or fentanyl-related substances.

(e) A person who provides functional fentanyl testing strips to an individual to determine the presence of fentanyl or fentanyl-related substances under this section must do so in good faith and with reasonable care.

(f) A person who provides functional fentanyl testing strips to an individual to determine the presence of fentanyl or fentanyl-related substances is not subject to civil damages in excess of the limits of any applicable insurance coverage, unless it is established that the person caused injuries or death wilfully, wantonly, or recklessly or by gross negligence.

(g) Nothing in this section is intended to waive the State's sovereign immunity or the privileges and immunities under Chapter 40 of Title 10.

History.
83 Del. Laws, c. 21, § 1.

Revisor's note.
This section became effective upon the signature of the Governor on June 3, 2021.

CHAPTER 26

CHILDHOOD LEAD POISONING PREVENTION ACT

§ 2601. Short title; definitions.

(a) This act shall be known and may be cited as the Childhood Lead Poisoning Prevention Act.

(b) For purposes of this chapter:

(1) "Elevated blood lead level" means any blood lead level determined by regulations established by the Division of Public Health to be detrimental to the health, behavioral development, or cognitive potential of a child.

(2) "Screening" means a capillary blood lead test, including where a drop of blood is taken from a finger or heel of the foot.

(3) "Testing" means a venous blood lead test where blood is drawn from a vein.

History.
69 Del. Laws, c. 310, § 1; 83 Del. Laws, c. 75, § 1.

Effect of amendments.
83 Del. Laws, c. 75, effective June 30, 2021, added "definitions" in the section heading; and added (b).

§ 2602. Physicians and health-care facilities to screen children.

(a) Every health-care provider who is the primary health-care provider for a child shall order lead poisoning screening of the child, under regulations adopted by the Division of Public Health, at or around 12 and 24 months of age.

(b) [Repealed.]

(c)(1) If screening under subsection (a) of this section determines that a child has an elevated blood lead level, the health-care provider shall order testing under regulations adopted by the Division of Public Health.

(2) A health-care provider is encouraged to use the health-care provider's clinical judgement to determine when testing should be used in lieu of screening under subsection (a) of this section.

(d) All laboratories and health-care providers involved in blood lead level analysis, including screening and testing, shall participate in a universal reporting system as established by the Division of Public Health.

(e) Nothing in this section may be construed to require any child to undergo screening or testing if the child's parent or guardian objects on the grounds that the screening or testing conflicts with the parent's or guardian's religious beliefs.

(f) [Repealed.]

History.
69 Del. Laws, c. 310, § 1; 70 Del. Laws, c. 186, § 1; 77 Del. Laws, c. 402, §§ 1, 3; 83 Del. Laws, c. 75, § 2.

Effect of amendments.
83 Del. Laws, c. 75, effective June 30, 2021, rewrote (a) and (c); repealed (b) and (f); in (d), added "and health-care providers" and "blood", and substituted "including screening and testing, shall" for "will"; and, in (e), substituted "may" for "shall", deleted "a lead blood level" following "undergo", substituted "testing if the child's" for "test whose" and "testing conflicts" for "test conflicts."

§ 2603. Screening prior to child care or school enrollment.

(a) For every child who has reached the age of 12 months, child care facilities and public and private nursery schools, preschools, and kindergartens shall require proof of screening for lead poisoning for admission or continued enrollment.

(b) Except in the case of enrollment in kindergarten, the screening under subsection (a) of this section may be done within 60 calendar days of the date of enrollment.

(c) A child's parent or guardian must provide 1 of the following:

(1) A statement from the child's primary health-care provider that the child has received a screening for lead poisoning.

(2) A certificate signed by the parent or guardian stating that the screening is contrary to the parent's or guardian's religious beliefs.

History.
69 Del. Laws, c. 310, § 1; 74 Del. Laws, c. 76, § 1; 83 Del. Laws, c. 75, § 3.

Effect of amendments.
83 Del. Laws, c. 75, effective June 30, 2021, rewrote the section.

§ 2604. Reimbursement by third-party payers.

Blood lead testing, screening, screening-related services, and diagnostic evaluations as required by § 2602 of this title are reimbursable under health insurance contracts and group and blanket health insurance under §§ 3337 and 3554 of Title 18, respectively.

History.
69 Del. Laws, c. 310, § 1; 83 Del. Laws, c. 75, § 4.

Effect of amendments.
83 Del. Laws, c. 75, effective June 30, 2021, rewrote the section.

§ 2605. Childhood Lead Poisoning Advisory Committee.

(a) The Childhood Lead Poisoning Prevention Advisory Committee is established to advise on the implementation of this chapter and to make any necessary recommendations for the implementation of this chapter or improvements of the processes to be followed by the agencies responsible for the implementation of this chapter.

(b) The Committee shall annually prepare and distribute a report to the General Assembly regarding this chapter, the intervention activities, studies of incidence, the State Blood Lead Screening Program, and monitoring and implementation of regulations promulgated under this chapter.

(c) The Committee consists of the following:

(1) The Secretary of the Department of Education.

(2) The Secretary of the Department of Health and Social Services.

(3) The Secretary of the Department of Services for Children, Youth & their Families.

(4) The Director of the Delaware State Housing Authority.

(5) The President of the Delaware Association of School Administrators.

(6) The President of the Delaware Association of Realtors.

(7) A Delaware pediatric provider, appointed by the Governor.

(8) Two members, appointed by the Governor, each from a different county.

(d) A member serving by virtue of position may appoint a designee to serve in the member's stead and at the member's pleasure.

(e) The Committee shall elect a Chair and a Vice Chair from among the Committee's members.

(f) The Committee may form advisory subcommittees, which may include individuals who are not members of the Committee, to assist the Committee in its duties.

(g) The Department of Health and Social Services shall provide staff support for the Committee.

History.
73 Del. Laws, c. 46, § 2; 70 Del. Laws, c. 186, § 1; 82 Del. Laws, c. 17, § 1; 83 Del. Laws, c. 27, § 1.

Effect of amendments.
83 Del. Laws, c. 27, effective June 3, 2021, in (a), deleted "There is hereby established", added "is established" following "Committee", deleted "the Childhood Lead Poisoning Preven- tion Act established pursuant to" following the first instance of "implementation of", substi- tuted the first instance of "this chapter" for "the program" and the second sentence for "said plan"; in (b), substituted the first instance of "this chapter" for "the Childhood Lead Poison- ing Prevention Act", and "under" for "pursuant to"; substituted "consists of the following" for "shall consist of 9 members as follows" in the

introductory paragraph of (c); added "The" to (c)(1) – (c)(6); added "A" to (c)(7); added a comma following "members" in (c)(8); in (d), substituted "A member" for "Members" and "the member's" for "their" twice; added "Com-

mittee's" in (e); in (f), substituted "may" for "shall have the power to" and "Committee" for "Commission" following "assist the"; and added (g).

§ 2606. Annual report.

The Division of Public Health shall annually, on or before January 1, provide a report on elevated blood lead levels to the General Assembly by delivering a copy of the report to the Secretary of the Senate, Chief Clerk of the House of Representatives, and the Director and Librarian of the Division of Research.

History.
83 Del. Laws, c. 75, § 5.

Revisor's note.
This section became effective upon the signature of the Governor on June 30, 2021.

CHAPTER 27
ANATOMICAL GIFTS AND STUDIES

Subchapter II. Uniform Anatomical Gift
Act
Sec.

SUBCHAPTER II
UNIFORM ANATOMICAL GIFT ACT

§ 2721. Requests for anatomical gifts.

(a)(1) At or near the time of death of any patient in a hospital, the attending physician or hospital designee shall make contact with the OPO in order to determine the suitability for organ, tissue and eye donation for any purpose specified under this chapter. This contact and the disposition shall be noted in the patient's medical record.

    (2)a. If the OPO determines that additional medical history or information is required to determine suitability for the donation, the OPO may seek additional health information on the potential anatomical donor from the Delaware Health Information Network (DHIN).

    b. If the OPO has entered into an agreement with the DHIN for access to clinical data in DHIN's possession, DHIN shall provide the OPO with timely access to medical information on the potential anatomical donor.

(b) Protocol for referral of potential anatomical donors to OPO.

    (1) The person designated by the hospital to contact the OPO shall have the following information available:

        a. Patient's name and identifier number;

        b. Patient's age;

        c. Anticipated cause of death;

        d. Past medical history; and

        e. Other pertinent medical information.

    (2)a. If the OPO determines that donation is not appropriate based on established medical criteria, this shall be noted by hospital personnel in the patient's record and no further action shall be necessary.

    b. If the OPO determines that donation may be appropriate, the OPO shall make a reasonable search of the records of the Donate Life Delaware Registry or the applicable state donor registry that it knows exists for the geographic area in which the individual resided or resides in order to ascertain whether the individual has made an anatomical gift.

c. If the referred patient has a document of gift, including registration with the Donate Life Delaware Registry, the OPO representative or the designated requestor shall attempt to notify a person listed in § 2711(c) of this title of the gift.

d. If no document of gift is known to the OPO representative or the designated requestor, 1 of these 2 individuals shall ask the persons listed in § 2711(c) of this title whether the decedent had a validly executed document of gift. If there is no evidence of an anatomical gift by the decedent, the OPO representative or the designated requestor shall notify a person listed in § 2711(c) of this title of the option to donate organs and tissues. The request for donation shall be made by the OPO representative, or the designated requester in consultation with the attending physician or the hospital designee.

(3) The person in charge of the hospital or that person's designated representative shall indicate in the medical record of the decedent:

a. Whether or not a document of gift is known to exist or whether a gift was made; and

b. The name of the person granting or refusing the gift and that person's relationship to the decedent.

(4) If the OPO determines, based upon a medical record review, that a hospitalized individual who is dead or whose death is imminent may be a prospective donor, the hospital shall, if requested by the OPO, conduct a blood or tissue test or minimally invasive examination, which is reasonably necessary to evaluate the medical suitability of a part that is or may be the subject of an anatomical gift. Specific consent to testing or examination under this paragraph (b)(4) is not required. The results of tests and examinations under this paragraph (b)(4) shall be used or disclosed only:

a. To evaluate medical suitability for donation and to facilitate the donation process; and

b. As required or permitted by law.

(5) The attending physician, in collaboration with the OPO, shall ensure that, prior to the withdrawal or withholding of any measures which are necessary to maintain the medical suitability of a part that is or may be the subject of an anatomical gift, the OPO has either:

a. Had the opportunity to advise the applicable persons set forth in § 2711(c) of this title of the option to make an anatomical gift; or

b. Ascertained that the individual expressed a known objection.

(6) Each hospital in the State shall develop and implement a protocol for referring potential anatomical donors as provided in this section. The protocol shall require that, at or near the time of the death of any patient, the hospital shall contact by telephone the OPO to determine suitability for anatomical donation of the potential donor. The protocol shall encourage discretion and sensitivity to family circumstances and beliefs in all discussions regarding donations of organs, tissue or eyes.

a. *Limitation.* — If the hospital staff advises the OPO that the hospital staff has actual knowledge that the decedent did not wish to be an anatomical donor, the gift of all or any part of the decedent's body shall not be requested.

b. *Medical record reviews.* — Death medical record reviews must be performed annually in each acute care general hospital for the sole purpose of determining anatomical donor potential at the hospital.

The hospital may perform the medical record review or may designate the OPO to conduct the review. If the hospital chooses to conduct its own review, it must do so in accordance with clinical specifications and guidelines established by the OPO. If the hospital conducts the review, the OPO must provide the necessary training to hospital personnel conducting the review. The hospital must report the results of the review to the OPO no later than 45 days following the completion of the review. If the hospital designates the OPO to conduct the review, the OPO shall provide the hospital with written assurance that the OPO shall maintain the confidentiality of patient identifying information.

c. After a donor's death, a person to whom an anatomical gift may pass under § 2712 of this title may conduct a test or examination which is reasonably necessary to evaluate the medical suitability of the body or part for its intended purpose.

d. Any examination conducted under this section may include an examination and copying of records necessary to determine the medical suitability of the part. This subsection includes medical, dental and other health-related records.

e. A hospital shall enter into agreements or affiliations with the OPO for coordination of procurement and use of anatomical gifts.

(7) A physician or technician may remove a donated part from the body of a donor that the physician or technician is qualified to remove.

(8) A revocation of a gift made under this chapter is effective only if the applicable organ procurement organization, tissue bank, eye bank, or transplant hospital knows of and can reasonably communicate the revocation to the involved physicians or technicians before an incision has been made to remove a part from the donor's body or before invasive procedures have begun to prepare the recipient.

(c) A person, including a medical examiner, that seeks to facilitate the making of an anatomical gift for the purposes of transplantation or therapy from a decedent who was not a hospital patient at the time of death shall notify the OPO at or around the time of the person's death in order to allow the OPO to evaluate the potential donation and, if applicable, coordinate the donation process.

(d) The OPO may, upon request and payment of associated fees, obtain certified copies of death records of a donor from the Delaware Department of Health and Social Services, Office of Vital Statistics.

History.

65 Del. Laws, c. 487, § 4; 70 Del. Laws, c. 186, § 1; 71 Del. Laws, c. 453, § 7; 80 Del. Laws, c. 182, § 1; 83 Del. Laws, c. 139, § 1.

Effect of amendments.

83 Del. Laws, c. 139, effective Sept. 10, 2021, added (a)(2).

CHAPTER 30E

SCHOOL ACCESS TO EMERGENCY MEDICATION ACT

Revision of chapter.

Section 1 of 83 Del. Laws, c. 122, effective Aug. 10, 2021, designated §§ 3001E to 3007E as subchapter I and added subchapter II.

Revisor's note.

Section 4 of 83 Del. Laws, c. 122, provided: "This act is effective on enactment and is implemented the earlier of the following:

"(1) One year from the date of the act's enactment.

"(2) On promulgation of final regulations under this act and the Secretary of the Department of Health and Social Services providing notice to the Registrar of Regulations, published in the Register of Regulations, that the contingency under this paragraph (2) of this section has been fulfilled." The act became effective upon the signature of the Governor on Aug. 10, 2021.

SUBCHAPTER I
SCHOOL ACCESS TO EMERGENCY MEDICATION

§ 3001E. Definitions.

For purposes of this subchapter:

(1) "Emergency medication" means a medication necessary for response to a life-threatening allergic reaction.

(2) "Licensed health-care provider" means anyone lawfully authorized to prescribe medications and treatments.

(3) "School" means an educational facility serving students in kindergarten through grade 12, and any associated pre-kindergarten program in such facility.

(4) "School nurse" means a registered nurse employed by a local education agency meeting the certification and licensure requirements of the employing agency.

(5) "Trained person" means an educator, coach or person hired or contracted by schools serving students in pre-kindergarten through grade 12 who has completed the training to administer emergency medicine to diagnosed and undiagnosed individuals.

(6) "Without an order" means that the school nurse or trained person may administer emergency medication, as further described within this subchapter, without an individual prescription from a licensed health-care provider for a person to receive the emergency medication. In lieu of a licensed health-care provider's order, i.e., an individual prescription, the Division of Public Health will issue guidance on the administration of emergency medication in the school setting. The Division of Public Health will continue to provide medical emergency standing orders for allergic reactions and anaphylaxis in previously undiagnosed individuals for use by registered nurses in public school districts and charter schools.

History.

79 Del. Laws, c. 342, § 1; 83 Del. Laws, c. 122, §§ 1, 2.

Effect of amendments.

83 Del. Laws, c. 122, effective Aug. 10, 2021, rewrote the introductory clause; and, in (6), substituted "subchapter" for "chapter" in the first sentence, in the second sentence substituted "on the" for "for" preceding "administration" and added "of" thereafter, and in the final sentence deleted "public charter school" preceding "registered nurses" and added "in public school districts and charter schools".

§ 3002E. Responsibilities of the Department of Education.

The Department of Education shall adopt rules and regulations regarding emergency medication, including but not limited to the training of trained persons and documentation thereof; and the storage, provision and administration of emergency medication and documentation thereof.

History.
79 Del. Laws, c. 342, § 1; 83 Del. Laws, c.
122, § 1.

§ 3003E. Responsibilities of the Division of Public Health.

The Division of Public Health shall provide guidance on the administration of emergency medications without an order in the school setting to undiagnosed individuals. The Division of Public Health will continue to provide medical emergency standing orders for allergic reactions and anaphylaxis in previously undiagnosed individuals for use by public/charter school registered nurses.

History.
79 Del. Laws, c. 342, § 1; 83 Del. Laws, c.
122, § 1.

§ 3004E. Responsibilities of the school.

(a) The school nurse, in consultation with the school administration, shall identify and train a sufficient number of eligible persons willing or required by position to become trained persons to administer emergency medication.

(b) The school shall maintain stock emergency medication.

History.
79 Del. Laws, c. 342, § 1; 83 Del. Laws, c.
122, § 1.

§ 3005E. Training.

(a) The Department of Education shall develop, for approval by the Division of Public Health, a training course to prepare trained persons to administer emergency medications to diagnosed and undiagnosed individuals.

(b) Except for a school nurse, an educator, coach or person hired or contracted by schools serving students in pre-kindergarten through grade 12 shall not be compelled to become a trained person, unless this is a requirement of hire or contract.

History.
79 Del. Laws, c. 342, § 1; 83 Del. Laws, c.
122, § 1.

§ 3006E. Storage of emergency medication.

(a) Emergency medication which shall be administered by the school nurse, shall be located in a secure but accessible area which is easily accessible to the school nurse.

(b) Emergency medication which shall be administered by a trained person, shall be located in a secure but accessible area, which is identified by the school as easily accessible.

History.
79 Del. Laws, c. 342, § 1; 83 Del. Laws, c.
122, § 1.

§ 3007E. Provision of limited liability protections.

Any trained person or school nurse, who, in good faith and without expectation of compensation from the person aided or treated, renders emergency care or treatment in response to an apparent allergic reaction by the use of an emergency medication shall not be liable for damages for injuries alleged to have been sustained by the aided or treated person or for damages for the death of the aided or treated person alleged to have occurred by reason of an act or omission in the rendering of such emergency care or treatment, unless it is established that such injuries or such death were caused wilfully, wantonly or by gross negligence on the part of the trained person or school nurse who rendered the emergency care or treatment by the use of an emergency medication.

History.
79 Del. Laws, c. 342, § 1; 83 Del. Laws, c. 122, § 1.

SUBCHAPTER II
ACCESS TO EPINEPHRINE AUTOINJECTORS IN INSTITUTIONS OF HIGHER EDUCATION

§ 3011E. Definitions.

For purposes of this subchapter:

(1) "Administer" means the direct application of an epinephrine auto-injector to the body of an individual.

(2) "Dispensing" means providing 1 or more epinephrine autoinjectors according to an order of a licensed health-care provider.

(3) "Epinephrine autoinjector" means a single-use device used for the automatic injection of a premeasured dose of epinephrine into the human body.

(4) "Institution of higher education" means a public or private educational institution, physically located in this State, that provides a program of education beyond the high school level and awards an associate's, bachelor's, or advanced degree.

(5) "Licensed health-care provider" means a physician or an individual licensed and authorized to write prescriptions for individuals under Title 24.

(6) "Records" means the recordings of interviews and all oral or written reports, statements, minutes, memoranda, charts, statistics, data, and other documentation generated by the State Emergency Medical Services Medical Director.

(7) "Self-administration" means the process whereby an individual gives themselves a single dose of epinephrine from a previously dispensed, properly labeled autoinjector.

History.
83 Del. Laws, c. 122, § 3.

§ 3012E. Emergency access to epinephrine autoinjectors.

The Department shall do all of the following:

(1) Promote the safe use of epinephrine autoinjectors at institutions of higher education to reduce deaths from anaphylaxis.

(2) Promulgate regulations to implement this subchapter.

History.
83 Del. Laws, c. 122, § 3.

§ 3013E. Epinephrine autoinjectors; prescribing, dispensing, storage.

(a) A licensed health-care provider may prescribe epinephrine autoinjectors in the name of an institution of higher education for use under this subchapter.

(b) A licensed health-care provider or pharmacist may dispense epinephrine autoinjectors under a prescription issued in the name of an institution of higher education.

(c) An institution of higher education may acquire and stock a supply of epinephrine autoinjectors under a prescription issued under this subchapter as follows:

(1) The epinephrine autoinjectors must be stored in a location readily accessible in an emergency.

(2) The epinephrine autoinjectors must be stored in accordance with the epinephrine autoinjector's instructions for use and any additional requirements established by the Department.

(3) An institution of higher education shall designate employees or agents who have completed the training required under § 3015E of this title to be responsible for the storage, maintenance, and general oversight of epinephrine autoinjectors acquired by the institution of higher education.

History.
83 Del. Laws, c. 122, § 3.

§ 3014E. Epinephrine autoinjectors; administration.

(a) An employee or agent of an institution of higher education, who has completed the training required under § 3015E of this title may, on the premises of or in connection with the institution of higher education, use epinephrine autoinjectors prescribed under § 3013E of this title as follows:

(1) Provide an epinephrine autoinjector to an individual who the employee, agent, or the individual believes in good faith is experiencing anaphylaxis for immediate self-administration, regardless of whether the individual has a prescription for an epinephrine autoinjector or has previously been diagnosed with an allergy.

(2) Administer an epinephrine autoinjector to any individual who the employee or agent believes in good faith is experiencing anaphylaxis, regardless of whether the individual has a prescription for an epinephrine autoinjector or has previously been diagnosed with an allergy.

(b) An individual who uses an epinephrine autoinjector under subsection (a) of this section must do all of the following:

(1) Notify the appropriate emergency medical service units as soon as possible.

(2) Report the use to the appropriate licensed physician or medical authority, if known.

History.
83 Del. Laws, c. 122, § 3.

§ 3015E. Epinephrine autoinjectors; training.

(a) An employee or agent of an institution of higher education must complete an anaphylaxis training program before providing or administering an epinephrine autoinjector made available by an institution of higher education. The training must be conducted by a nationally-recognized organization experienced in training laypersons in emergency health treatment or an entity or individual approved by the Department. Training may be conducted online or in person and, at a minimum, must cover all of the following:

(1) Techniques on how to recognize symptoms of severe allergic reactions, including anaphylaxis.

(2) Standards and procedures for the storage and administration of an epinephrine autoinjector.

(3) Risks of administering an epinephrine autoinjector that has expired or that was not stored at the proper temperature.

(4) Potential contraindications, risks, side effects, or medication reactions after appropriate use.

(5) The differences in usage, storage, and administration of an EpiPen Jr. autoinjector.

(6) What to do if an individual is at a borderline weight.

(7) Emergency follow-up procedures.

(b) The entity that conducts the training shall issue a certificate, on a form developed or approved by the Department, to each person who successfully completes the anaphylaxis training program.

(c) An individual who successfully completes an anaphylaxis training under this section may use epinephrine autoinjectors prescribed under § 3013E of this title for 2 years from the date of completion on the certificate issued under subsection (b) of this section.

History.
83 Del. Laws, c. 122, § 3.

§ 3016E. Epinephrine autoinjectors; immunity.

(a) A licensed health-care provider who prescribes or dispenses an epinephrine autoinjector to an institution of higher education under this subchapter must do so in good faith and with reasonable care. Unless it is established that the licensed health-care provider caused injuries or death as a result of unreasonable care, wilfully, wantonly, or by gross negligence, a licensed health-care provider is not subject to any of the following as a result of prescribing or dispensing an epinephrine autoinjector under this subchapter:

    (1) Disciplinary or other adverse action under the professional licensing laws of this State.

    (2) Criminal liability.

    (3) Liability for damages for injuries or death.

(b) A pharmacist who dispenses an epinephrine autoinjector to an institution of higher education under this subchapter must do so in good faith and with reasonable care. Unless it is established that the pharmacist caused injuries or death as a result of unreasonable care, wilfully, wantonly, or by gross negligence, a pharmacist is not subject to any of the following as a result of dispensing an epinephrine autoinjector under this subchapter:

    (1) Disciplinary or other adverse action under the professional licensing laws of this State.

    (2) Criminal liability.

    (3) Liability for damages for injuries or death.

(c) An institution of higher education that possesses and makes available epinephrine autoinjectors under this subchapter must do so in good faith and with reasonable care. Unless it is established that the institution of higher education caused injuries or death as a result of unreasonable care, wilfully, wantonly, or by gross negligence, an institution of higher education is not subject to any of the following as a result of possessing or making available an epinephrine autoinjector under this subchapter:

    (1) Disciplinary or other adverse action under the professional licensing laws of this State.

    (2) Criminal liability.

    (3) Liability for damages for injuries or death.

(d) An individual who administers or provides an epinephrine autoinjector under this subchapter is exempt from liability under § 6801 of this title.

History.
83 Del. Laws, c. 122, § 3.

§ 3017E. Epinephrine autoinjectors; reports.

(a) An institution of higher education that possesses and makes available epinephrine autoinjectors shall submit to the Department, on a form developed by the Department, a report of each incident that involves the administration of the institution of higher education's epinephrine autoinjector.

(b) Records of the State Emergency Medical Services Medical Director, and emergency medical services quality care review committee relating to epinephrine autoinjector reviews and audits are confidential and privileged, protected, and are not subject to discovery, subpoena, or admission into evidence in any judicial or administrative proceeding. Raw data used in any epinephrine autoinjector review or audit is not a public record under Chapter 100 of Title 29 and is confidential under § 1768(b) of Title 24.

(c) The Department shall file an annual report with the General Assembly by January 1 that provides all of the following information for the prior academic year:

(1) A summary and analysis of all reports submitted under subsection (a) of this section.

(2) The number of institutions of higher education that received epinephrine autoinjectors under this subchapter.

(3) The number of individuals trained to administer epinephrine autoinjectors under this subchapter.

History.
83 Del. Laws, c. 122, § 3.

CHAPTER 30F
ANIMAL WELFARE

SUBCHAPTER II
ANIMAL POPULATION CONTROL PROGRAM AND SPAY/NEUTER FUND

§ 3018F. Program administration.

(a) The administrator shall administer the Program and shall be responsible for:

(1) Distributing, collecting and compiling all forms, including but not limited to, veterinarian participation agreements, sterilization and immunization certifications, and creating a database there from for enforcement and accountability purposes; and

(2) Maintaining a list of participating veterinarians; and

(3) Determining eligibility; and

(4) Directing the collection of co-payments; and

(5) Obtaining the maximum number of spay/neuter/inoculation procedures available to the Program's financial parameters per calendar year.

(b) All reimbursement shall be through the administrator.

(c) The cost of administering the Pet Population Control Spay/Neuter Program may be reimbursed from the Spay/Neuter Fund.

History.
75 Del. Laws, c. 326, § 1; 76 Del. Laws, c. 284, § 5; 79 Del. Laws, c. 377, § 2; 81 Del. Laws, c. 224, § 4; 81 Del. Laws, c. 450, § 2; 83 Del. Laws, c. 177, § 2.

Effect of amendments.
83 Del. Laws, c. 177, effective September 15, 2021, rewrote (c).

SUBCHAPTER IV
GENERAL PROVISIONS CONCERNING DOGS

§ 3048F. Dogs running at large.

(a)(1) No dog, unless exempted under this section, shall be permitted to run at large outside at any time, and must be secured by means of a leash that is capable of physically restraining the movement of the dog. A dog is not at large if it is within the real property limits of its owner, or on private property with permission, or within a vehicle being driven or parked.

(2) The following dogs are exempt from the leash requirements and need only be at heel or under reasonable control of a competent person and obedient to the person's command.

a. Working dogs, which are dogs that are not merely pets but that learn and perform tasks to assist their human companions, and include dogs trained to hunt, herd, assist law enforcement or search and rescue personnel, or assist persons with disabilities, while actively engaged in performing such functions.

b. Dogs within a designated "off-leash" dog park or area, or within an area permitted by a governmental entity, including a municipality, and attended by the dog's owner or custodian.

(3) Allowing a dog to run at large is a violation. Any owner or custodian who violates this subsection shall be fined not less than $25 or more than $50 for a first violation. For each subsequent offense occurring within 12 months of a prior offense, the person shall be fined not less than $50 or more than $100. The minimum fine for a subsequent offense is not subject to suspension.

(b) [Repealed.]

(c) Whoever, being the owner, custodian, possessor, or harborer of any female dog, allows such dog to run or remain at large in this State while in heat shall be fined not less than $50 nor more than $100. For each subsequent offense occurring within 12 months of a prior offense, the owner, custodian, possessor, or harborer shall be fined not less than $100 or more than $200. The minimum fine for a subsequent offense shall not be subject to suspension. Allowing a female dog to run at large while in heat is a violation.

(d) Whoever, being the owner, custodian, possessor, or harborer of any dog that while running at large and without provocation, bites a person, shall be fined not less than $100 nor more than $500. For each subsequent offense involving the same dog, such owner, custodian, possessor, or harborer shall be fined not less than $750 or more than $1,500. The minimum fines provided for in this subsection, $100 for the first offense and $750 for each subsequent offense, shall not be subject to suspension.

(e) Upon conviction in any court of an offense under subsection (d) of this section, the court shall cause a report to be forwarded to the Department. Said report shall contain the name of the defendant, the name of the dog, the license number of the dog, the date of the offense, and the date of conviction. The Department shall maintain these reports for a period of 3 years.

History.
77 Del. Laws, c. 428, § 7; 80 Del. Laws, c. 248, § 5; 82 Del. Laws, c. 238, § 2; 83 Del. Laws, c. 158, § 2.

Effect of amendments.
83 Del. Laws, c. 158, effective September 15, 2021, rewrote (a); and repealed (b).

CHAPTER 30G

NALOXONE

§ 3001G. Administration of naloxone by public safety personnel and the Community-Based Naloxone Access Program.

(a) An individual who is public safety personnel is authorized to receive, carry, and administer the drug naloxone if the individual has completed a Department-approved training course. For purposes of this section, "public safety personnel" means as defined under § 9702 of this title.

(b) Public safety personnel who, acting in good faith and after completing a Department-approved training course, administers the drug naloxone to an individual whom the public safety personnel reasonably believes to be undergoing an opioid-related drug overdose is not liable for damages for injuries or death sustained to the individual in connection with administering the drug, unless it is established that such injuries or death were caused wilfully, wantonly, recklessly, or by gross negligence on the part of thepublic safety personnel who administered the drug.

(c) Nothing in this chapter mandates that an agency require its public safety personnel to carry or administer naloxone.

(d) Notwithstanding any other provision of law, the purchase, acquisition, possession or use of naloxone pursuant to this section shall not constitute the unlawful practice of a profession or violation of the Uniform Controlled Substances Act [§ 4701 et seq. of this title].

(e) DHSS shall create written and uniform treatment and care plans for emergency and critical patients statewide that constitute the standing orders for the administration of naloxone by public safety personnel and participants in the Community-Based Naloxone Access Program. The treatment protocol for naloxone administration under this chapter must be approved and signed by the State EMS Medical Director, or the Medical Director or the Director of the Division of Public Health, Department of Health and Social Services. A doctor prescribing naloxone who, acting in good faith, directly or by standing order, prescribes or dispenses the drug naloxone to a person who completes an approved-training program who, in the judgment of the health-care provider, is capable of administering the drug for an emergency opioid overdose, shall not be subject to disciplinary or other adverse action under any professional licensing statute, criminal liability, or liable for damages for injuries or death sustained to the individual in connection with administering the drug, unless it is established that such injuries or death were caused wilfully, wantonly, or by gross negligence on the part of the doctor who signed the standing order and protocol.

(f) DHSS is authorized to oversee the implementation and monitoring of the Public Safety Personnel and Community-Based Naloxone Access Programs.

(g) Pharmacists who dispense naloxone under this section must do so in good faith and with reasonable care. Unless it is established that the pharmacist caused injuries or death as a result of unreasonable care, wilfully, wantonly, or by gross negligence, a pharmacist is not subject to any of the following as a result of dispensing naloxone:

(1) Disciplinary or other adverse action under the professional licensing laws of this State.

(2) Criminal liability.

(3) Liability for damages for injuries or death.

(h) A lay individual who administers naloxone to an individual under the Community-Based Naloxone Access Program is rendering emergency care under § 6801 of this title.

History.
79 Del. Laws, c. 384, § 1; 81 Del. Laws, c. 83, § 1; 81 Del. Laws, c. 265, § 1; 83 Del. Laws, c. 25, § 1.

Effect of amendments.
83 Del. Laws, c. 25, effective June 3, 2021, added (h).

PART III

VITAL STATISTICS

CHAPTER 31

REGISTRATION OF BIRTHS, DEATHS, MARRIAGES, DIVORCES, ANNULMENTS AND ADOPTIONS

SUBCHAPTER I
GENERAL PROVISIONS

§ 3101. Definitions.

For purposes of this chapter:

(1) "Dead body" means a lifeless human body or such parts of such human body from the condition of which it reasonably may be concluded that death recently occurred.

(2) "Department" means the Department of Health and Social Services.

(3) "File" means the presentation of a vital record provided for in this chapter for registration by the Office of Vital Statistics.

(4) "Induced termination of pregnancy" means the purposeful interruption of an intrauterine pregnancy with the intention other than to produce a live-born infant or to remove a dead fetus and which does not result in a live birth. This definition excludes management of prolonged retention of products of conception following fetal death.

(5) "Institution" means any establishment, public or private, which provides in-patient medical, surgical or diagnostic care or treatment or nursing, custodial or domiciliary care, or to which persons are committed by law.

(6) "Live birth" means the complete expulsion or extraction from its mother of a product of human conception, irrespective of the duration of pregnancy, which after expulsion or extraction breathes or shows any other evidence of life such as beating of the heart, pulsations of the umbilical cord or definite movement of voluntary muscles, whether or not the umbilical cord has been cut or the placenta is attached. Heartbeats are to be distinguished from transient cardiac contractions; respirations are to be distinguished from fleeting respiratory efforts or gasps.

(7) "Physician" means a person authorized or licensed to practice medicine or osteopathy pursuant to the laws of this State.

(8) "Registration" means the acceptance by the Office of Vital Statistics and the incorporation of vital records provided for in this chapter into its official records.

(9) "Spontaneous fetal death" or "stillborn fetus" is defined as a spontaneous death (i.e., not an induced termination of pregnancy) prior to the complete expulsion or extraction from its mother of a product of conception. The death is indicated by the fact that after such separation, the fetus does not breathe or show any other evidence of life such as beating of the heart, pulsation of the umbilical cord or definite movement of voluntary muscles. Heartbeats are to be distinguished from transient cardiac contractions; respirations are to be distinguished from fleeting respiratory efforts or gasps.

(10) "Stillbirth" means any complete expulsion or extraction from its mother of a product of human conception that weighs 350 grams or more, or in the absence of weight, of 20 completed weeks gestation or more, resulting in other than a live birth and which is not an induced termination of pregnancy.

(11) "System of vital statistics" means the registration, collection, preservation, amendment and certification of vital records; the collection of other reports required by this chapter; and activities related thereto including the tabulation, analysis and publication of vital statistics.

(12) "Vital records" means certificates or reports of birth, death, marriage, divorce or annulment, and data related thereto.

(13) "Vital statistics" means the data derived from certificates and reports of birth, death, spontaneous fetal death, marriage, divorce or annulments, and related reports.

History.
40 Del. Laws, c. 96, §§ 1-10; Code 1935, § 806; 44 Del. Laws, c. 69, § 1; 16 Del. C. 1953, § 3124; 52 Del. Laws, c. 88, § 1; 68 Del. Laws, c. 274, § 1; 70 Del. Laws, c. 149, § 137; 70 Del. Laws, c. 378, § 1; 81 Del. Laws, c. 123, § 1; 83 Del. Laws, c. 37, § 18.

Effect of amendments.
83 Del. Laws, c. 37, effective June 3, 2021, substituted "For purposes of" for "As used in" in the introductory paragraph and "that weighs 350 grams or more" for "the weight of which is in excess of 350 grams" in (10).

SUBCHAPTER II
REGISTRATION REQUIREMENTS AND PROCEDURES

§ 3123. Registration of death.

(a) A certificate of death for each death which occurs in this State shall be filed with the Office of Vital Statistics, or as otherwise directed by the State Registrar, within 3 days after death, or as soon as possible after a death under subsections (e) and (f) of this section, and prior to final disposition of the dead body, and shall be registered if it has been completed and filed in accordance with this section.

(1) If the place of death is unknown but the dead body is found in this State, the certificate of death shall be completed and filed in accordance with this section. The place where the body is found shall be shown as the place of death. If the date of death is unknown, it may be determined by approximation.

(2) When death occurs in a moving conveyance in the United States and the body is first removed from the conveyance in this State, the death shall be registered in this State and the place where it is first removed shall be considered the place of death. When a death occurs on a moving conveyance while in international waters or airspace or in a foreign country or its airspace and the body is first removed from the conveyance in this State, the death shall be registered in this State but the certificate shall show the actual place of death insofar as can be determined.

(b) The funeral director who assumes custody of the dead body shall file the certificate of death with the Office of Vital Statistics unless an official death investigation is required. The funeral director shall obtain the personal data from the next-of-kin or best qualified person or source available and send that data to the attending physician or medical examiner for certification.

(c) When no official death investigation is required, the medical certification shall be completed, signed and returned to the funeral director within 48 hours after death, or as soon as possible after a death under subsections (e) and (f) of this section, by the attending physician; or a registered nurse or an advanced practice registered nurse (APRN) acting in accordance with § 1902(r) of Title 24. In the absence of the attending physician, the certificate may be completed and signed by the attending physician's designated physician or the chief medical officer of the institution in which death occurred if such individual has knowledge about the medical history of the case.

(d) When an official death investigation is required pursuant to § 4706(a) of Title 29, the medical examiner shall assume custody of the dead body, determine the manner and cause of death and shall complete and sign the certificate of death and shall file the certificate of death with the Office of Vital Statistics.

(e) If the cause of death cannot be determined within 48 hours after death, the attending physician or medical examiner shall file with the Office of Vital Statistics a pending certificate of death and a toxicology study shall be performed. If a cause of death cannot be determined after the toxicology study is performed, the remains and all reports or studies shall be turned over to the Division of Forensic Science for review. When the cause of death is determined a revised certificate of death shall be issued and presented to the funeral director or the funeral director's agent, who in turn shall file the certificate with the Office of Vital Statistics.

(f) When a death is presumed to have occurred within this State but the body cannot be located, a certificate of death may be prepared by the State Registrar upon receipt of a court order which shall include the finding of facts required to complete the certificate of death. Such certificate of death shall be marked "By Court Order" and shall show on its face the date of registration and shall identify the court and the date of decree.

(g) One of the following individuals shall pronounce a death:

    (1) The attending physician.

    (2) The medical examiner.

    (3) A registered nurse or an advanced practice registered nurse (APRN) acting in accordance with § 1902(r) of Title 24.

    (4) The medical control physician under § 1760(b) of Title 24.

(h) All medical certifications of death, required pursuant to subsections (c)-(e) of this section shall be electronically prepared, certified and signed by 1 of the individuals designated in subsection (g) of this section.

(i) All certificates of death shall be electronically filed with the Delaware Vital Events Registration System (DelVERS).

History.

25 Del. Laws, c. 66, § 3; 27 Del. Laws, c. 84, § 7; 27 Del. Laws, c. 85, § 13; Code 1915, § 804; 35 Del. Laws, c. 55; Code 1935, § 787; 44 Del. Laws, c. 69, § 1; 48 Del. Laws, c. 319, § 1; 16 Del. C. 1953, § 3125; 52 Del. Laws, c. 88, § 2; 68 Del. Laws, c. 274, § 1; 69 Del. Laws, c. 146, § 1; 70 Del. Laws, c. 186, § 1; 71 Del. Laws, c. 320, § 1; 79 Del. Laws, c. 265, § 14; 81 Del. Laws, c. 123, § 4; 81 Del. Laws, c. 340, § 4; 82 Del. Laws, c. 75, § 4; 82 Del. Laws, c. 268, §§ 2, 3; 83 Del. Laws, c. 10, § 1; 83 Del. Laws, c. 52, § 10; 83 Del. Laws, c. 111, § 1.

Revisor's note.

Section 3 of 82 Del. Laws, c. 268, provided: "This act expires on March 30, 2021, unless otherwise extended by a subsequent act of the General Assembly." 83 Del. Laws, c. 10, § 1, effective Mar. 30, 2021, repealed that expiration date.

Based upon changes contained in 83 Del. Laws, c. 52, § 10, made effective July 1, 2021, by § 21 of that act, "§ 1902(t)" was substituted for "§ 1902(aa)" in the first sentence of (c) and in (g)(3).

Based upon changes contained in 83 Del.

Laws, c. 111, § 1, effective Aug. 4, 2021, "§ 1902(r)" was substituted for "§ 1902(t)" in the first sentence of (c) and in (g)(3).

Effect of amendments.
82 Del. Laws, c. 268, effective July 20, 2020, added (h) and (i).

PART IV

FOOD AND DRUGS

CHAPTER 47

UNIFORM CONTROLLED SUBSTANCES ACT

SUBCHAPTER I
DEFINITIONS

§ 4701. Definitions.

As used in this chapter:

(1) "Addicted" or "addiction" shall mean dependence upon a drug in the following manner:

a. Psychological dependence upon a drug in the sense that the user lacks the ability to abstain from taking or using the drug or experiences a compulsive need to continue its use; and

b. A tolerance to the effects of the drug which leads the user to require larger and more potent doses; and

c. Such physical dependence upon the drug that the user suffers withdrawal symptoms if the user is deprived of its dosage.

(2) "Administer" means the direct application of a controlled substance, whether by injection, inhalation, ingestion or any other means to the body of a patient or research subject by:

a. A practitioner (or, in the practitioner's presence, by the practitioner's authorized agent); or

b. The patient or research subject at the direction and in the presence of the practitioner.

(3) "Administration" means the Drug Enforcement Administration, United States Department of Justice or its successor agency.

(4) "Agent" means an authorized person who acts on behalf of or at the direction of a manufacturer, distributor or dispenser. It does not include a common or contract carrier, public warehouseperson or employee of the carrier or warehouseperson.

(5) "Anabolic steroid" means any of the controlled substances defined in § 4718(f) of this title.

(6) "Benzodiazepine" means any substance or drug which contains a benzene ring fused to a 7-member diazepine ring, results in the depression of the central nervous system and is primarily intended to treat insomnia, convulsions and anxiety, and used for muscle relaxation and pre-operation treatment including alprazolam, clonazepam, diazepam, lorazepam, and temazepam.

(7) "Controlled substance" means a drug, substance or immediate precursor in Schedules I through V of subchapter II of this chapter. For purposes of the crimes set forth in subchapters IV and V of this chapter, and of forfeiture set forth in § 4784 of this title, "controlled substance" includes "designer drug", as defined in paragraph (10) of this section.

(8) "Counterfeit controlled substance" means a controlled substance which, or the container or labeling of which, without authorization, bears the trademark, trade name, or other identifying mark, imprint, number or device or any likeness thereof, of a manufacturer, distributor or dispenser other than the person who in fact manufactured, distributed or dispensed the substance.

(9) "Deliver" or "delivery" means the actual, constructive or attempted transfer from one person to another of a controlled substance, whether or not there is an agency relationship.

(10) "Designer drug" means a substance that has a chemical structure substantially similar to that of a controlled substance or that was specifically designed to or may produce an effect substantially similar to that of a controlled substance. Examples of chemical classes in which "designer drugs" are found include, but are not limited to, the following: Phenethylamines, N-substituted piperidines, morphinans, ecgonines, quinazolinones, substituted indoles, arylcycloalkylamines, cannabinoids, cathinones, and any synthetic analogue of a controlled substance. "Designer drug" does not include any substance that was manufactured, delivered or dispensed in conformance with an approved new drug application, or an exemption for investigating use within the meaning of § 505 of the Federal Food, Drug and Cosmetic Act (21 U.S.C. § 355), or that was manufactured, delivered or dispensed in conformance with a registration issued by the Attorney General of the United States within the meaning of §§ 301-304 of the Federal Controlled Substances Act (21 U.S.C. §§ 821-824).

(11) "Dispense" means to deliver a controlled substance to an ultimate user or research subject by or pursuant to the lawful order of a practitioner, including the prescribing for a legitimate medical purpose by an individual practitioner in the usual course of the practitioner's professional practice, administering, packaging, labeling or compounding necessary to prepare the substance for that delivery.

(12) "Dispenser" means a practitioner who dispenses.

(13) "Distribute" means to deliver other than by administering or dispensing a controlled substance.

(14) "Distributor" means a person who distributes.

(15) "Dose" means an amount or unit of a compound, mixture, or preparation containing a controlled substance that is separately identifiable and in a form that indicates that it is the amount or unit by which the controlled substance is separately administered to or taken by an individual. A dose includes, but is not limited to: a pill; a capsule; a tablet; or a vial.

(16) "Drug" means (i) substances recognized as drugs in the official United States Pharmacopoeia, official Homeopathic Pharmacopoeia of the United States or official National Formulary or any supplement to any of them; (ii) substances intended for use in the diagnosis, cure, mitigation, treatment or prevention of disease in man or animals; (iii) substances (other than food) intended to affect the structure or any function of the body of man or animals; and (iv) substances intended for use as a component of any article specified in clause (i), (ii) or (iii) of this paragraph. It does not include devices or their components, parts or accessories.

(17) "Drug detection animal trainer" means all persons, not classified as a practitioner, pharmacy, distributor, manufacturer or researcher, but under the classification of "Other Controlled Substance Registrants." This registrant shall have formal training and may train animals for drug detection using controlled substances listed under the registration. These registrants shall have equipment and a site appropriate for registration.

(18) "Drug paraphernalia" shall mean all equipment, products and materials of any kind which are used, intended for use or designed for use, in planting, propagating, cultivating, growing, harvesting, manufacturing, compounding, converting, producing, processing, preparing, testing, analyzing, packaging, re-packaging, storing, containing, concealing, injecting, ingesting, inhaling or otherwise introducing into the human body, a controlled substance the manufacture, delivery, possession or use of which is in violation of this chapter. The term "drug paraphernalia" includes, but is not limited to:

a. Kits used, intended for use or designed for use in planting, propagating, cultivating, growing or harvesting of any species of plant which is a controlled substance, the use, cultivation, delivery or possession of which is in violation of this chapter or from which such a controlled substance can be derived;

b. Kits used, intended for use or designed for use in manufacturing, compounding, converting, producing, processing or preparing controlled substances, the use, manufacture, delivery or possession of which is in violation of this chapter;

c. Isomerization devices used, intended for use or designed for use in increasing the potency of any species of plant which is a controlled substance, the use, manufacture, delivery or possession of which is in violation of this chapter;

d. Testing equipment used, intended for use or designed for use in identifying, or in analyzing the strength, effectiveness or purity of controlled substances, the use, manufacture, delivery or possession of which is in violation of this chapter;

e. Scales and balances used, intended for use or designed for use in weighing or measuring controlled substances, the use, manufacture, delivery or possession of which is in violation of this chapter;

f. Diluents and adulterants, such as quinine hydrochloride, mannitol, mannite, dextrose or lactose, which are used, intended for use or designed for use in cutting controlled substances, the use, manufacture, delivery or possession of which is in violation of this chapter;

g. Separation gins and sifters used, intended for use or designed for use in removing twigs and seeds from, or otherwise cleaning or refining, marijuana;

h. Blenders, bowls, containers, spoons and mixing devices used, intended for use or designed for use in compounding controlled substances, the use, manufacture, delivery or possession of which is in violation of this chapter;

   i. Capsules, balloons, envelopes and other containers used, intended for use or designed for use in packaging small quantities of controlled substances, the use, manufacture, delivery or possession of which is in violation of this chapter;

   j. Containers or other objects used, intended for use or designed for use in storing or concealing controlled substances, the use, manufacture, delivery or possession of which is in violation of this chapter;

   k. Hypodermic syringes, needles and other objects used, intended for use or designed for use in parenterally injecting controlled substances, the use, manufacture, delivery or possession of which is in violation of this chapter; and

   l. Objects used, intended for use or designed for use in ingesting, inhaling or otherwise introducing marijuana, cocaine, hashish or hashish oil into the human body such as:

      1. Metal, wooden, acrylic, glass, stone, plastic or ceramic pipes with or without screens, permanent screens, hashish heads or punctured metal bowls;

      2. Water pipes;

      3. Carburetion tubes and devices;

      4. Smoking and carburetion masks;

      5. Roach clips or objects used to hold burning material, such as a marijuana cigarette, that has become too small or too short to be held in the hand;

      6. Miniature cocaine spoons, and cocaine vials;

      7. Chamber pipes;

      8. Carburetor pipes;

      9. Electric pipes;

      10. Air-driven pipes;

      11. Chillums;

      12. Bongs; and

      13. Ice pipes or chillers.

(19) "Finished drug product" means a drug legally marketed under the Federal Food, Drug, and Cosmetic Act (21 U.S.C. § 321 et seq.) that is in finished dosage form.

(20) "Finished product" means any material, compound, mixture or preparation which contains any quantity of a controlled or noncontrolled substance.

(21) "Human growth hormone" is synonymous with the term "human chorionic gonadotropin."

(22) "Immediate precursor" means a substance which the Secretary has found to be and by rule designates as being the principal compound commonly used or produced primarily for use, and which is an immediate chemical intermediary used or likely to be used in the manufacture of a controlled substance, the control of which is necessary to prevent, curtail or limit manufacture.

(23) "Isomer" means the optical isomer, except as used in § 4714(d) of this title and § 4716(b)(4) of this title. As used in § 4714(d) of this title, the term "isomer" means the optical positional or geometric isomer. As used in § 4716(b)(4) of this title, the term "isomer" means the optical or geometric isomer.

(24) "Knowingly" means a person acts knowingly with respect to any delivery, possession, use or consumption within the meaning of this

chapter when the person knows or is aware of such delivery, possession, use or consumption. The person's knowledge may be inferred by the trier of fact from the surrounding circumstances, considering whether a reasonable person in the defendant's circumstances would have had such knowledge. A prima facie case of knowledge is established upon the introduction of some evidence of the surrounding circumstances from which a reasonable juror might infer the defendant's knowledge.

(25) "Lawful prescription or order" means a prescription or order that is issued for a legitimate medical purpose by a licensed and registered practitioner pursuant to a "patient-practitioner relationship" as defined in this section, that is not obtained by misrepresentation, fraud, forgery, deception or subterfuge, and is distributed or dispensed in conformity with § 4739 of this title.

(26) "Licensed practitioner" means any individual who is authorized by law to prescribe drugs in the course of professional practice or research in any state.

(27) "Manufacture" means the production, preparation, propagation, compounding, conversion or processing of a controlled substance, either directly or indirectly by extraction from substances of natural origin, or independently by means of chemical synthesis or by a combination of extraction and chemical synthesis and includes any packaging or repackaging of the substance or labeling or relabeling of its container except that this term does not include the preparation or compounding of a controlled substance by an individual for the individual's own use or the preparation, compounding, packaging or labeling of a controlled substance:

a. By a practitioner as an incident to the practitioner's administering or dispensing of a controlled substance in the course of the practitioner's professional practice; or

b. By a practitioner, or by the practitioner's authorized agent under the practitioner's supervision, for the purpose of, or as an incident to, research, teaching or chemical analysis and not for delivery.

(28) "Marijuana" means all parts of the plant Cannabis sativa L., whether growing or not, the seeds thereof, the resin extracted from any part of the plant, and every compound, manufacture, salt, derivative, mixture or preparation of the plant, its seeds or resin. It does not include the mature stalks of the plant, fiber produced from the stalks, oil or cake made from the seeds of the plant, or any other compound, manufacture, salt, derivative, mixture or preparation of the mature stalks (except the resin extracted therefrom), fiber, oil or cake, or the sterilized seed of the plant which is incapable of germination. Marijuana does not include products approved by the US Food and Drug Administration.

(29) "Narcotic drug" means any of the following, whether produced directly or indirectly by extraction from substances of vegetable origin, or independently by means of chemical synthesis:

a. Opium opiates, derivatives of opium and opiates, including their isomers, esters, ethers, salts and salts of isomers, esters and ethers, whenever the existence of such isomers, esters, ethers and salts is possible within the specific chemical designation. Such term does not include isoquinoline alkaloids of opium.

b. Poppy straw and concentrate of poppy straw.

c. Coca leaves, except coca leaves and extracts of coca leaves from which cocaine, ecgonine and derivatives of ecgonine or their salts have been removed.

d. Cocaine, its salts, optical and geometric isomers, and salts of isomers.

e. Ecgonine, its derivatives, their salts and salts of isomers.

f. Any compound, mixture or preparation which contains any quantity of any of the substances referred to in paragraphs (29)a. through e. of this section.

(30) "Non-benzodiazepine hypnotic" means any zaleplon, zolpidem, and any schedule II or schedule III drug, as defined by the Controlled Substances Act, 21 U.S. C. § 812(c) and 21 C.F.R. 1308, which produces effects similar to that of a benzodiazepine.

(31) "Opiate" means any substance having an addiction-forming or addiction-sustaining liability similar to morphine or being capable of conversion into a drug having addiction-forming or addiction-sustaining liability. It does not include, unless specifically designated as controlled under § 4711 of this title, the dextrorotatory isomer of 3-methoxy-n-methylmorphinan and its salts (dextromethorphan). It does include its racemic and levorotatory forms.

(32) "Opium poppy" means the plant of the species Papaver somniferum L., except its seeds.

(33) "Other controlled substance registrants" means all persons and firms, except persons or firms exempt from registration, who are not classified as pharmacies, distributors, manufacturers, practitioners or researchers. Examples of persons or firms in this classification include, but are not limited to, analytical laboratories and drug detection animal trainers, having a legitimate need to use "controlled substances" as defined in this section.

(34) "Patient-practitioner relationship" means, with respect to prescribing drugs for a patient, that the practitioner is a licensed practitioner who:

a. Has conducted at least 1 in-person medical evaluation of the patient and performed a medical history and physical examination sufficient to establish a diagnosis and to identify underlying conditions of, or contraindications to, the treatment recommended or provided; or

b. Personally knows the patient and the patient's general health status through an existing patient-practitioner relationship; or

c. Provides treatment in consultation with or upon referral of another practitioner who has an existing patient-practitioner relationship with the patient and who has agreed to supervise the patient's treatment, including follow-up care and use of the prescribed medications; or

d. Provides treatment to the patient through an on-call or cross-coverage situation for another practitioner who has an existing patient-practitioner relationship with the patient; or

e. Provides continuing medications on a short-term basis for a new patient prior to the first appointment; or

f. Provides treatment based upon admission orders for a newly hospitalized patient.

(35) "Person" means individual, corporation, government or governmental subdivision or agency, statutory trust, business trust, estate, trust, partnership or association, or any other legal entity.

(36) "Personal use quantity" shall mean 1 ounce or less of marijuana in the form of leaf marijuana. "Leaf marijuana" means the dried leaves and flowering tops of the plant cannabis sativa L.

(37) "Poppy straw" means all parts, except the seeds of the opium poppy, after mowing.

(38) "Possession," in addition to its ordinary meaning, includes location in or about the defendant's person, premises, belongings, vehicle or otherwise within the defendant's reasonable control.

(39) "Practitioner" means:

a. A physician, dentist, veterinarian, scientific investigator or other person licensed, registered or otherwise permitted to distribute, dispense, conduct research with respect to or to administer a controlled substance in the course of professional practice or research in this State.

b. A pharmacy, hospital or other institution licensed, registered, or otherwise permitted to distribute, dispense, conduct research with respect to or to administer a controlled substance in the course of its professional practice or research in this State.

(40) "Prescribe" means to give an order for medication or other therapy by authorized personnel which is dispensed to or for an ultimate user but does not include an order for medication which is dispensed for immediate administration to the ultimate user.

(41) "Prescription drug" means any drug required by federal or state law or regulation to be dispensed only by or on the prescription of a practitioner licensed to prescribe drugs, or which is restricted to use by practitioners only.

(42) "Prescription drug order" means any written, verbal, or electronic order of a practitioner for a prescription drug issued in accordance with regulations promulgated under this chapter.

(43) "Production" includes the manufacturing, planting, cultivating, growing or harvesting of a controlled substance.

(44) "Proof of age" means a document issued by a governmental agency that gives the person's date of birth including a passport, military identification card, or driver's license.

(45) [Repealed.]

(46) "Protected school zone" means either of the following:

a. Any building, structure, athletic playing field, playground, or other land contained on the property of a public or private kindergarten, elementary, secondary, or vocational-technical school.

b. Any area accessible to the public located within 300 feet of the property of a public or private kindergarten, elementary, secondary, or vocational-technical school, or any parked vehicle located within 300 feet of the property of a public or private kindergarten, elementary, secondary, or vocational-technical school.

For the purposes of this section, an "area accessible to the public" includes: sidewalks; streets; parking lots; parks; playgrounds; stores and restaurants; and any other outdoor locations such as front porches or front yards.

(47) "Purported controlled substance" means any substance that is:

a. Expressly or impliedly represented to be a controlled substance; or

b. Expressly or impliedly represented to be of such nature that another person will be able to distribute or use the substance as a controlled substance.

(48) "Researcher" means all persons and firms, not a practitioner, who routinely performs scholarly or scientific investigations or inquiries.

(49) "Secretary" means Secretary of the Department of State or the Secretary's designee in paragraph (22) of this section; §§ 4711; 4713; 4715; 4717; 4718(l); 4719; 4720(c); 4721; 4731; 4732; 4733; 4734(a) and (b); 4735 (b), (c) and (d); 4736(a) and (b); 4737; 4738; 4739(b); 4762(e)(2); 4781(1); 4782; 4783(b); 4785; 4786; 4787(b), (c), (d), (e) and 4791(d) of this title.

"Secretary" means Secretary of the Department of Safety and Homeland Security of the State or the Secretary's designee in §§ 4740; 4781(2), (3) and (4); 4783(a) and (c); 4784; and 4787(a) of this title.

"Secretary" means Secretary of the Department of Health and Social Services or the Secretary's designee in § 4740B of this title.

(50) "State," when applied to a part of the United States, includes any state, district, commonwealth, territory, insular possession thereof and any area subject to the legal authority of the United States of America.

(51) "Ultimate user" means a person who lawfully possesses a controlled substance for the person's own use or for the use of a member of the person's household or for administering to an animal owned by the person or by a member of the person's household.

(52) "Vehicle" shall have the same definition as that set forth in § 101(86) of Title 21.

History.

16 Del. C. 1953, § 4701; 58 Del. Laws, c. 424, § 1; 59 Del. Laws, c. 132, § 1; 60 Del. Laws, c. 583, § 1; 62 Del. Laws, c. 250, § 3; 62 Del. Laws, c. 252, § 1; 65 Del. Laws, c. 287, §§ 1-3; 67 Del. Laws, c. 384, §§ 3-6; 70 Del. Laws, c. 81, § 1; 70 Del. Laws, c. 186, § 1; 71 Del. Laws, c. 288, §§ 1, 12; 73 Del. Laws, c. 329, § 59; 74 Del. Laws, c. 288, § 2; 75 Del. Laws, c. 350, § 193(b); 76 Del. Laws, c. 81, § 35; 77 Del. Laws, c. 155, §§ 1-3; 78 Del. Laws, c. 13, §§ 21-29; 78 Del. Laws, c. 61, § 1; 78 Del. Laws, c. 204, §§ 1, 2[1]; 79 Del. Laws, c. 66, § 1; 79 Del. Laws, c. 164, § 1; 80 Del. Laws, c. 38, § 1; 80 Del. Laws, c. 136, § 1; 80 Del. Laws, c. 168, § 1; 80 Del. Laws, c. 264, § 1; 81 Del. Laws, c. 410, § 1; 82 Del. Laws, c. 93, § 1; 82 Del. Laws, c. 217, § 1; 83 Del. Laws, c. 169, § 1.

Effect of amendments.

83 Del. Laws, c. 169, effective September 15, 2021, in (42), added "or electronic", made related stylist changes, and added "issued in accordance with regulations promulgated under this chapter".

SUBCHAPTER III
REGULATION OF MANUFACTURE, DISTRIBUTION AND DISPENSING OF CONTROLLED SUBSTANCES

§ 4732. Registration requirements; exemptions; inspections.

NOTES TO DECISIONS

Revocation of registration.

Decision revoking a doctor's medical license and controlled substance registration was upheld because: (1) substantial evidence established that the doctor delivered controlled substances to a patient for other than a therapeutic medical purpose; and (2) the doctor's improper behavior over a 4-month period constituted a pattern of negligence in the practice of medicine. Gala v. Bullock, 250 A.3d 52 (Del. 2021).

§ 4735. Investigations; written complaints; grounds for limitation, suspension or revocation of registration.

NOTES TO DECISIONS

Due process.

Decision revoking a doctor's medical license and controlled substance registration was upheld because: (1) substantial evidence established that the doctor delivered controlled substances to a patient for other than a therapeutic medical purpose; and (2) the doctor's improper behavior over a 4-month period constituted a pattern of negligence in the practice of medicine. Gala v. Bullock, 250 A.3d 52 (Del. 2021).

SUBCHAPTER IV
OFFENSES AND PENALTIES

§ 4754. Drug dealing; class D felony.

NOTES TO DECISIONS

Analysis

Evidence.
— Substantial.

Evidence.

— Substantial.

Decision revoking a doctor's medical license and controlled substance registration was upheld because: (1) substantial evidence established that the doctor delivered controlled substances to a patient for other than a therapeutic medical purpose; and (2) the doctor's improper behavior over a 4-month period constituted a pattern of negligence in the practice of medicine. Gala v. Bullock, 250 A.3d 52 (Del. 2021).

§ 4762. Hypodermic syringe or needle; delivering or possessing; disposal; exceptions.

(a) A licensed pharmacist, or pharmacist intern or pharmacy student under the supervision of a pharmacist, may provide hypodermic syringes or hypodermic needles, including pen needles in the State without a prescription, but only to persons who have attained the age of 18 years. When providing hypodermic syringes or hypodermic needles without a prescription, the pharmacist, pharmacist intern or pharmacy student must require proof of identification that validates the individual's age.

(b) Every person who lawfully possesses an instrument described in subsection (a) of this section shall, before disposal, destroy such instrument in such a manner as to render it unfit for reuse in any manner.

(c) [Repealed.]

(d) Nothing in this section shall prohibit the delivery, furnishing, sale, purchase or possession of an instrument commonly known as a hypodermic syringe or an instrument commonly known as a hypodermic needle used or to be used solely and exclusively for treating poultry or livestock and such delivery, furnishing, sale, purchase, possession or use shall be governed by rules and regulations to be prescribed by the Department of Agriculture.

(e) This section does not apply to any of the following:

(1) The sale at wholesale by pharmacies, drug jobbers, drug wholesalers, and drug manufacturers or manufacturers and dealers in surgical instruments to practitioners.

(2) The furnishing or obtaining of hypodermic syringes or hypodermic needles for uses which the Secretary determines are industrial. Notwithstanding the other provisions of this section, a person may obtain such instruments, without a written order or oral order reduced to writing, for such industrial uses.

(3) Any person licensed under the Delaware Board of Nursing or who is otherwise a licensed allied health professional who may provide syringes or hypodermic needles in the course of patient teaching, discharge teaching, or routine patient care to indigent clients in in-patient, out-patient, or community settings.

History.
16 Del. C. 1953, § 4757; 58 Del. Laws, c. 424, § 1; 59 Del. Laws, c. 33, § 1; 59 Del. Laws, c. 291, § 1; 60 Del. Laws, c. 583, §§ 8-12; 67 Del. Laws, c. 130, § 9; 67 Del. Laws, c. 350, §§ 20, 21; 70 Del. Laws, c. 186, § 1; 78 Del. Laws, c. 13, § 50; 79 Del. Laws, c. 66, § 1; 83 Del. Laws, c. 169, § 2.

Effect of amendments.
83 Del. Laws, c. 169, effective Sept. 15, 2021, deleted "penalties" from the end of the section heading; in (a), rewrote the first sentence, and deleted "above-mentioned" following "prescription, the" in the second sentence; repealed (c); added "any of the following" in the introductory paragraph of (e); added a comma following "wholesalers" in (e)(1); substituted a period for a semicolon at the end of (e)(1) and for "; and" in (e)(2); and, in (e)(3), added "or who is otherwise a licensed allied health professional" and substituted "or" for "and/or" preceding "community".

§ 4764. Possession of marijuana; class B misdemeanor, unclassified misdemeanor, or civil violation [For application of this section, see 80 Del. Laws, c. 38, § 6].

(a) [Repealed.]

(b) Any person who knowingly or intentionally uses, consumes, or possesses other than a personal use quantity of a controlled substance or a counterfeit controlled substance classified in § 4714(d)(19) of this title, except as otherwise authorized by this chapter, shall be guilty of an unclassified misdemeanor and be fined not more than $575, imprisoned not more than 3 months, or both.

(c)(1) Any person who knowingly or intentionally possesses a personal use quantity of a controlled substance or a counterfeit controlled substance classified in § 4714(d)(19) of this title, except as otherwise authorized by this chapter, must be assessed a civil penalty of $100 in addition to such routine assessments necessary for the administration of civil violations and the marijuana must be forfeited.

(2) Private use or consumption by a person of a personal use quantity of a controlled substance or a counterfeit controlled substance classified in § 4714(d)(19) of this title is likewise punishable by a civil penalty under this subsection.

(3) Notwithstanding paragraph (c)(1) or (c)(2) of this section, any person under 21 years of age who commits a violation of this subsection must be assessed a civil penalty of $100 for a first violation of this subsection and a civil penalty of not less than $200 nor more than $500 for a second violation of this subsection and is guilty of an unclassified misdemeanor and must be fined $100 for a third or subsequent violation of this subsection. A peace officer having reasonable grounds to believe that a juvenile has committed a violation of paragraph (c)(1) or (c)(2) of this section may issue the juvenile a civil citation in lieu of a civil penalty.

(4) [Repealed.]

(d) Any person who knowingly or intentionally uses or consumes up to a personal use quantity of a controlled substance or a counterfeit controlled substance classified in § 4714(d)(19) of this title in an area accessible to the public or in a moving vehicle, except as otherwise authorized by this chapter, shall be guilty of an unclassified misdemeanor and be fined not more than $200, imprisoned not more than 5 days, or both. For purposes of this section area accessible to the public" means any of the following:

(1) Sidewalks, streets, alleys, parking lots, parks, playgrounds, stores, restaurants, and any other areas to which the general public is invited.

(2) Any outdoor location within a distance of 10 feet from a sidewalk, street, alley, parking lot, park, playground, store, restaurant, or any other area to which the general public is invited.

(3) Any outdoor location within a distance of 10 feet from the entrances, exits, windows that open, or ventilation intakes of any public or private building.

(e) Information concerning a civil offense classified in subsection (c) of this section shall not appear on a person's certified criminal record.

(f) Nothing contained herein shall be construed to repeal or modify any law concerning the medical use of marijuana or tetrahydrocannabinol in any other form, such as Marinol, or the possession of more than 1 ounce of marijuana, or selling, manufacturing, or trafficking in marijuana.

(g) Nothing contained herein shall be construed to repeal or modify existing laws, ordinances or bylaws, regulations, personnel practices, or policies concerning the operation of motor vehicles or other actions taken while under the influence of marijuana.

(h) Nothing contained herein shall be construed to repeal or modify any law or procedure regarding search and seizure.

(i) Any person who was convicted of a single criminal offense under subsection (c) of this section, as it is in effect on or before July 31, 2019, and who was under the age of 21 at the time of the offense may, upon reaching the age of 21, apply for an expungement of the record of the conviction and any indicia of arrest to the court in which the person was convicted. For violations of a criminal offense under subsection (c) of this section, as it is in effect on or before July 31, 2019, an order granting such expungement shall issue upon proof that the person has reached the age of 21, unless the person has failed to comply with the sentencing order or the person has another charge under this section which remains outstanding. Upon issuance of the order of expungement, the records of the conviction and any indicia of arrest shall be dealt with in accordance with the procedures specified in subchapter VII of Chapter 43 of Title 11. Nothing in this section prohibits a court from expunging a record of conviction as otherwise provided by law. The application for or granting of a pardon under §§ 4361 through 4364 of Title 11 does not prohibit an expungement under this section. All sentencing orders for violations of a criminal offense under subsection (c) of this section, as it is in effect on or before July 31, 2019, by persons under the age of 21 at the time of the offense must state that the record of the conviction may be expunged upon reaching the age of 21 and thereafter. The civil filing fee applies to applications for expungement plus a $100 fee payable to the State Bureau of Identification for administrative costs.

(j) Notwithstanding any provision of law to the contrary, any person who prior to December 18, 2015, was convicted of a single offense arising from an original charge under this section or any predecessor statute, law or ordinance prohibiting the possession, use or consumption of marijuana or any controlled substance or counterfeit controlled substance classified in § 4714(d)(19) of this title shall be eligible for mandatory expungement of the records of the conviction and all indicia of arrest pursuant to the provisions of § 4373 of Title 11, provided the applicant is otherwise eligible for mandatory expungement as specified therein. Upon issuance of the order of expungement, the records of the conviction and any indicia of arrest shall be dealt with in accordance with the procedures specified in §§ 4373, 4376, and 4377 of Title 11.

History.
78 Del. Laws, c. 13, § 61; 80 Del. Laws, c. 38, § 2; 81 Del. Laws, c. 394, § 1; 82 Del. Laws, c. 83, § 12; 82 Del. Laws, c. 182, § 1; 82 Del. Laws, c. 217, § 14; 83 Del. Laws, c. 198, § 2.

Effect of amendments.
83 Del. Laws, c. 198, effective Sept. 17, 2021, added the final sentence in (c)(3); and repealed (c)(4).

RESEARCH REFERENCES AND PRACTICE AIDS

Delaware Law Reviews.
First State or Follower?: Marijuana in Delaware, 26 Widener L. Rev. 21 (2020).

§ 4767. First offenders controlled substances diversion program.

(a) Any person who:

(1) Has not previously been convicted of any offense under this chapter or under any statute of the United States or of any state thereof relating to narcotic drugs, marijuana, or stimulant, depressant, hallucinogenic drug or other substance who is charged through information or indictment with possession or consumption of a controlled substance under § 4763, § 4764, or § 4761(a) of this title; and

(2) Has not previously been afforded first offender treatment under this section or its predecessor, may qualify for the first offense election at the time of the person's arraignment, except that no person shall qualify for such first offense election where the offense charged under § 4763, § 4764, or § 4761(a) of this title arises from the same transaction, factual setting or circumstances as those contained in any indictment returned against the defendant alleging violation of any provisions contained within § 4752 or § 4753 of this title.

(b) At time of arraignment any person qualifying under subsection (a) of this section as a first offender and who elects treatment under this section shall admit possession or consumption of a controlled substance by entering a plea of guilty, as a first offender. The court, without entering a judgment of guilt and with the consent of the accused, may defer further proceedings and place the accused on probation for a period of not less than 1½ years, the terms and conditions of which shall include but not be limited to:

(1) Revocation of the person's driver's license and/or privileges within this State for a period of not less than 6 months, restoration of which shall be contingent upon successful completion of all mandatory terms and conditions required of probation to be completed during the term of revocation. Upon entry of a plea of guilty, as a first offender under this section, the clerk of the court or other person designated by the court shall forthwith report that fact to the Division of Motor Vehicles for action consistent with the provisions of this subsection. The Division of Motor Vehicles may issue a conditional license during this period of revocation upon written certification by the person's probation officer that a narrowly drawn conditional license is necessary for the limited purpose of performing the terms and conditions of probation.

(2) Performance of a minimum of 20 hours of community service work monitored by the court or probation office, performance of which shall be accomplished on at least 3 separate days and shall not, in any event consist of segments lasting more than 8 hours in succession. Community service performed pursuant to the terms of this paragraph shall be in addition to all other community service ordered and no community service ordered or performed pursuant to the terms of this section shall be performed or served concurrently with any other court ordered or approved community service.

(3) Completion of a 16-hour first-offender drug rehabilitation program, licensed by the Secretary of the Department of Health and Social Services and paid for by the first offender.

(4) Other such terms and conditions as the court may impose.

(c) If a term or condition of probation is violated, or if the defendant is found to have illegally possessed or consumed any controlled substance within 1½ years of the entry of a plea under this section, the probation officer shall file with the court a written report of same, and the defendant shall be brought before the court and upon determination by the court that the terms have been violated or that the defendant has possessed or consumed any such controlled substance, the court shall enter an adjudication of guilt upon the record and proceed as otherwise provided under this title.

(d) Upon fulfillment of the terms and conditions of probation, including, but not limited to, paying of all costs and fees, and performance of all required community service, the court shall discharge the person and dismiss the proceedings against the person and shall simultaneously therewith submit to the Attorney General a report thereof which shall be retained by the Attorney General for use in future proceedings, if required. Discharge and dismissal under this section shall be without adjudication of guilt and is not a conviction for purposes of this section or for purposes of disqualifications or disabilities imposed by law upon conviction of a crime. Any person who elects to be treated as a first offender under this section shall, by so doing, agree to pay the costs of the person's prosecution as a condition. There may be only 1 discharge and dismissal under this section with respect to any person.

History.
67 Del. Laws, c. 347, § 1; 70 Del. Laws, c. 186, § 1; 74 Del. Laws, c. 110, § 6; 75 Del. Laws, c. 167, § 2; 78 Del. Laws, c. 13, § 60; 82 Del. Laws, c. 217, §§ 12, 16; 83 Del. Laws, c. 37, § 19.

Effect of amendments.
83 Del. Laws, c. 37, effective June 3, 2021, substituted "§ 4763, § 4764, or § 4761(a)" for "§ 4763 or § 4764 or § 4761(a) or (b) [repealed]" in (a)(1).

§ 4768. Medical or psychiatric examination or treatment.

After a conviction and before sentencing for violation of § 4761(a), § 4763, or § 4764 of this title, or before conviction if the defendant consents, the court may order the defendant to submit to a medical or psychiatric examination or treatment. The court may order such examination by the Department of Health and Social Services or by a private physician, hospital, or clinic and the court may make such order regarding the term and conditions of such examination or treatment and the payment therefor by the defendant as a court in its discretion shall determine. The Department of Health and Social Services or the private physician, hospital, or clinic shall report to the court within such time as the court shall order, not more than 90 days from the date of such order. After such report and upon conviction of such violation, the court shall impose sentence or suspend sentence and may impose probation or a requirement of future medical or psychiatric examination or treatment including hospitalization or outpatient care upon such terms and conditions and for such period of time as the court shall order.

History.
16 Del. C. 1953, § 4765; 58 Del. Laws, c. 424, § 1; 78 Del. Laws, c. 13, § 44; 82 Del. Laws, c. 217, § 12; 83 Del. Laws, c. 37, § 20.

Effect of amendments.
83 Del. Laws, c. 37, effective June 3, 2021, substituted "or" for "and/or" twice in the section heading, following "medical" and "examination" in the first sentence, preceding "treatment" in the second sentence, and following "probation", "medical" and "examination" in the final sentence; in the first sentence, substituted "before" for "prior to" in two places and deleted "or (b) [repealed]" following "§ 4761(a)"; and added a comma following "hospital" in the second and third sentences.

§ 4769. Criminal immunity for persons who suffer or report an alcohol or drug overdose or other life threatening medical emergency.

(a) For purposes of this chapter:

(1) "Medical provider" means the person whose professional services are provided to a person experiencing an overdose or other life-threatening medical emergency by a licensed, registered or certified health-care professional who, acting within his or her lawful scope of practice, may provide diagnosis, treatment or emergency services.

(2) "Overdose" means an acute condition including, but not limited to, physical illness, coma, mania, hysteria, or death resulting from the consumption or use of an ethyl alcohol, a controlled substance, another substance with which a controlled substance was combined, a noncontrolled prescription drug, or any combination of these, including any illicit or licit substance; provided that a person's condition shall be deemed to be an overdose if a layperson could reasonably believe that the condition is in fact an overdose and requires medical assistance.

(b) A person who is experiencing an overdose or other life-threatening medical emergency and anyone (including the person experiencing the emergency) seeking medical attention for that person shall not be arrested, charged or prosecuted for an offense for which they have been granted immunity pursuant to subsection (c) and/or (d) of this section, or subject to the revocation or modification of the conditions of probation, if:

(1) The person seeking medical attention reports in good faith the emergency to law enforcement, the 9-1-1 system, a poison control center, or to a medical provider, or if the person in good faith assists someone so reporting; and

(2) The person provides all relevant medical information as to the cause of the overdose or other life-threatening medical emergency that the person possesses at the scene of the event when a medical provider arrives, or when the person is at the facilities of the medical provider.

(c) The immunity granted shall apply to all offenses in this chapter that are not class A, B, or C felonies, including but not limited to the following offenses:

 (1) Miscellaneous drug crimes as described in § 4757(a)(3), (6), and (7) of this title;

 (2) Illegal possession and delivery of noncontrolled prescription drugs as described in § 4761 of this title;

 (3) Possession of controlled substances or counterfeit controlled substances, as described in § 4763 of this title;

 (4) Possession of drug paraphernalia as described in §§ 4762(c) [repealed] and 4771 of this title;

 (5) Possession of marijuana as described in § 4764 of this title.

(d) The immunity granted shall apply to offenses relating to underage drinking as described in § 904(b), (c), (e), and (f) of Title 4.

(e) Nothing in this section shall be interpreted to prohibit the prosecution of a person for an offense other than an offense for which they have been granted immunity pursuant to subsection (c) and/or (d) of this section or to limit the ability of the Attorney General or a law-enforcement officer to obtain or use evidence obtained from a report, recording, or any other statement provided pursuant to subsection (b) of this section to investigate and prosecute an offense other than an offense for which they have been granted immunity pursuant to subsection (c) and/or (d) of this section.

(f) Forfeiture of any alcohol, substance, or paraphernalia referenced in this section shall be allowed pursuant to § 4784 of this title and Chapter 11 of Title 4.

History.
79 Del. Laws, c. 85, § 1; 70 Del. Laws, c. 186, § 1; 83 Del. Laws, c. 169, § 2.

Revisor's note.
Based upon changes contained in 83 Del.

Laws, c. 169, § 2, effective Sept. 15, 2021, "[repealed]" was inserted following "4762(c)" in (c)(4).

SUBCHAPTER V
DRUG PARAPHERNALIA

§ 4773. Exemptions.

This subchapter does not apply to any of the following:

 (1) Any person authorized by local, state, or federal law to manufacture, possess, or distribute such items.

 (2) Any item that in the normal lawful course of business is imported, exported, transported, or sold and traditionally intended for use with tobacco products, including any pipe, paper, or accessory.

 (3) Testing strips to determine the presence of fentanyl or fentanyl-related substances.

History.
73 Del. Laws, c. 359, § 3; 83 Del. Laws, c. 21, § 2.

Effect of amendments.
83 Del. Laws, c. 21, effective June 3, 2021, in the introductory paragraph, substituted "does"

for "will", and added "any of the following"; in (1), added a comma following "state" and following "possess", and substituted a period for "; or"; in (2), added a comma following "transported" and following "paper"; and added (3).

SUBCHAPTER VI
ENFORCEMENT AND ADMINISTRATIVE PROVISIONS

§ 4784. Forfeitures.

(a) The following shall be subject to forfeiture to the State and no property rights shall exist in them:

(1) All controlled substances which have been manufactured, distributed, possessed, dispensed or acquired in violation of this chapter;

(2) All raw materials, products and equipment of any kind which are used, or intended for use, in manufacturing, compounding, processing, delivering, importing or exporting any controlled substance in violation of this chapter;

(3) Any property which is used, or intended for use, as a container for property described in paragraph (a)(1), (2) or (6) of this section;

(4) Any conveyances, including aircraft, vehicles, or vessels which are used, or are intended for use, to transport, or in any manner to facilitate the transportation, sale, or possession with intent to deliver property described in paragraph (a)(1) or (2) of this section except that:

a. No vehicle used by any person as a common carrier in the transaction of business as a common carrier is subject to forfeiture under this section unless the owner or other person in charge of the vehicle is a consenting party or privy to a violation of the Controlled Substances Act;

b. No vehicle is subject to forfeiture under this section by reason of any act or omission established by the owner thereof to have been committed or omitted without the owner's knowledge or consent;

c. A vehicle is not subject to forfeiture for a violation of § 4761(a) or (b) [repealed], § 4763 or § 4764 of this title; and

d. A forfeiture of a vehicle encumbered by a bona fide security interest is subject to the interest of the secured party if the party neither had knowledge of nor consented to the act or omission;

(5) All books, records, and research products and materials including formulas, microfilm, tapes and data which are used or intended for use in violation of this chapter;

(6) All drug paraphernalia as defined in § 4701(18) of this title;

(7) All moneys, negotiable instruments, securities or any other thing of value furnished, or intended to be furnished, in exchange for a controlled substance or drug paraphernalia in violation of this chapter; all profits or proceeds traceable to securities, assets or interest used, or intended to be used, to facilitate any violation of this chapter. However, no property interest or an owner, by reason of any act or omission established by the owner to be committed or omitted without the owner's knowledge or consent shall be forfeited in the items listed in this paragraph:

a. All moneys, negotiable instruments or securities found in close proximity to forfeitable controlled substances, or to forfeitable records of the importation, manufacture or distribution of controlled substances are presumed to be forfeitable under this paragraph. The burden of proof is upon claimant of the property to rebut this presumption.

b. All moneys, negotiable instruments or securities found to have trace amounts of controlled substances on them are presumed to be forfeitable under this paragraph. The burden of proof is upon the claimant of the property to rebut this presumption.

c. To the extent that assets, interests, profits and proceeds forfeitable under this paragraph (i) cannot be located, (ii) have been transferred, sold to or deposited with third parties, or (iii) have been placed beyond the jurisdiction of the State, the court, following conviction of the individual charged, may direct forfeiture of such other assets of the defendant as may be available, limited in value to those assets that would otherwise be forfeited under this paragraph.

Upon petition of the defendant, the court may authorize redemption of assets forfeited under this paragraph, provided the assets described in this paragraph are surrendered or otherwise remitted by such defendant to the jurisdiction of the court; and

(8) Any real property which is used, or is intended for use, to store, grow, manufacture, compound, process, deliver, import, or export any controlled substance in violation of this chapter except that:

a. No real property is subject to forfeiture under this section by reason of any act or omission established by any owner thereof to have been committed or omitted without the owner's knowledge or consent;

b. No real property being leased out by its owner shall be subject to forfeiture under this section unless the owner of the real property is a consenting party or privy to the violation of the Controlled Substances Act;

c. No real property shall be subject to forfeiture for a violation of § 4759, § 4761(a), § 4763 or § 4764 of this title; and

d. A forfeiture of real property encumbered by a bona fide security interest of the secured party if the party neither had knowledge of nor consented to the act or omission.

(b) Notwithstanding any other provisions of the laws of this State or rules of court, the procedures listed in subsections (c)-(j) of this section are applicable to the administrative forfeiture of property subject to forfeiture under this section.

(c) Property subject to forfeiture under this chapter may be seized by the Secretary upon process issued by any Superior Court having jurisdiction over the property. Seizure without process may be made if:

(1) The seizure made is pursuant to subchapter I of Chapter 23 of Title 11 or an inspection under an administrative inspection warrant;

(2) The property subject to seizure has been the subject of a prior judgment in favor of the State in a criminal, injunction or forfeiture proceeding based upon this chapter;

(3) The Secretary has probable cause to believe that the property is directly or indirectly dangerous to health or safety; or

(4) The Secretary has probable cause to believe that the property was used or intended to be used in violation of this chapter.

(d) In the event of seizure pursuant to subsection (c) of this section, proceedings under subsections (e) and (j) of this section shall be instituted promptly.

(e) Property taken or detained under this section shall not be subject to replevin, but is deemed to be in the custody of the Secretary subject only to the orders and decrees of the Superior Court. When property is seized under this chapter, the Secretary may:

(1) Place the property under seal;

(2) Remove the property to a place designated by the Secretary; or

(3) Require the Department of Safety and Homeland Security to take custody of the property and remove it to an appropriate location for disposition in accordance with law.

(f) When property is forfeited under this chapter, the Secretary may:

(1) Retain it for official use;

(2) Sell that which is not required to be destroyed by law and which is not harmful to the public. The proceeds shall be used for payment of all proper expenses of the proceedings for forfeiture and sale, including expenses of seizure, maintenance of custody, advertising and court costs;

(3) Allow the arresting agency or any other law-enforcement division to use the property for the purpose of law enforcement provided that any

proceeds remaining after the payment of expenses and any other money forfeited or realized from forfeited property shall be deposited to the Special Law Enforcement Assistance Fund for the use of the State for the purposes as established by the Attorney General with the concurrence of the Director of the Office of Management and Budget and the Controller General;

(4) Require the Department of Safety and Homeland Security to take custody of the property and remove it for disposition in accordance with law; or

(5) Forward it to the Administration for disposition.

(g) Controlled substances listed in Schedule I that are possessed, transferred, sold or offered for sale in violation of this chapter are contraband and shall be seized and summarily forfeited to the State. Controlled substances listed in Schedule I, the owners of which are unknown, which are seized or come into the possession of the State are contraband and shall be summarily forfeited to the State.

(h) Species of plants from which controlled substances in Schedules I and II may be derived which have been planted or cultivated in violation of this chapter or of which the owners or cultivators are unknown or which are wild growths may be seized and summarily forfeited to the State.

(i) The failure, upon demand by the Secretary or the Secretary's authorized agent, of the person in occupancy or in control of land or premises upon which the species of plants are growing or being stored to produce an appropriate registration or proof that the person is the holder thereof constitutes authority for the seizure and forfeiture of the plants.

(j) Property seized pursuant to this section that is not summarily forfeited pursuant to subsection (f) of this section shall be automatically forfeited to the State upon application to the Superior Court if, within 45 days of notification of seizure to all known parties having possessory interest in the seized property by registered or certified mail to the last known post-office address of the parties in interest and by publication in a newspaper of general circulation in this State, the person or persons claiming title to the seized property do not institute proceedings in the Superior Court to establish:

(1) That they have the lawful possessory interest in the seized property; and

(2) The property was unlawfully seized or not subject to forfeiture pursuant to this section.

History.
16 Del. C. 1953, § 4769; 58 Del. Laws, c. 424, § 1; 62 Del. Laws, c. 250, §§ 2, 4; 64 Del. Laws, c. 246, §§ 2, 3; 67 Del. Laws, c. 260, § 1; 67 Del. Laws, c. 450, § 1; 70 Del. Laws, c. 186, § 1; 71 Del. Laws, c. 288, § 11; 73 Del. Laws, c. 349, § 20; 75 Del. Laws, c. 88, § 21(8); 75 Del. Laws, c. 350, § 193(c); 78 Del. Laws, c. 13, § 65; 81 Del. Laws, c. 410, § 1; 82 Del. Laws, c. 217, § 12; 83 Del. Laws, c. 37, § 21.

Effect of amendments.
83 Del. Laws, c. 37, effective June 3, 2021, added a comma following "import" in the introductory paragraph of (a)(8); and deleted "or (b) [repealed]" following "§ 4761(a)" in (a)(8)c.

SUBCHAPTER VIII
DRUG OVERDOSE FATALITY REVIEW COMMISSION

§ 4799A. Definitions.

For purposes of this subchapter:

(1) "Controlled substance" means a drug, substance or immediate precursor in Schedules I through V of subchapter II of this chapter.

(2) "Fentanyl" means as defined in § 4716(c)(6) of this title.

(3) "Opiate" means any controlled substance having an addiction-forming or addiction-sustaining liability similar to morphine or being

capable of conversion into a drug having addiction-forming or addiction-sustaining liability and is a prescription drug.

(4) "Overdose death" means a death caused, in whole or in part, by the consumption or use of a controlled substance.

(5) "Prescription drug" means as defined in § 4701 of this title.

History.

80 Del. Laws, c. 220, § 1; 83 Del. Laws, c. 49, § 1.

Effect of amendments.

83 Del. Laws, c. 49, effective June 15, 2021, deleted "the following definitions shall apply" from the end of the introductory paragraph; rewrote (2) and (5); and substituted "a controlled substance" for "heroin or theconsumption or use of a opiate, or the consumption or use of fentanyl" in (4).

§ 4799B. Organization and composition.

(a) The following persons, or their designees, shall be members of the Drug Overdose Fatality Review Commission ("the Commission") by virtue of position:

(1) The Delaware Attorney General.

(2) The Secretary of the State Department of Health and Social Services.

(3) The Director of the Delaware Division of Forensic Science.

(4) The Secretary of Safety and Homeland Security.

(5) The Director of the Delaware Division of Public Health.

(6) The Commissioner of the Delaware Department of Correction.

(b) The following persons shall be appointed by the Governor as members of the Commission:

(1) Two representatives of the Medical Society of Delaware.

(2) A representative of the Delaware Nurses Association.

(3) A representative of the Police Chiefs Council of Delaware who is an active law-enforcement officer.

(4) A representative of the Delaware Fraternal Order of Police who is an active law-enforcement officer.

(5) Two advocates from statewide nonprofit organizations.

(6) A representative of the Delaware Healthcare Association.

(c) The chairperson of each regional review team established pursuant to subsection (g) of this section shall also serve as a member of the Commission.

(d) The term of members appointed by the Governor shall be 3 years and shall terminate upon the Governor's appointment of a new member to the Commission. The members of the Commission and regional review teams shall serve without compensation. The Commission shall be staffed by the Delaware Department of Justice.

(e) The Commission shall, by affirmative vote of a majority of all members of the Commission, appoint a chairperson from its membership for a term of 1 year.

(f) Meetings of the Commission and regional review teams shall be closed to the public.

(g) The Commission shall by resolution passed by a majority of its members establish 3 regional review teams authorized to review overdose deaths. Members of the Commission shall appoint representatives to each review team such that the review team reflects the disciplines of the Commission.

History.

80 Del. Laws, c. 220, § 1; 81 Del. Laws, c. 94, § 2; 83 Del. Laws, c. 49, § 2.

Effect of amendments.

83 Del. Laws, c. 49, effective June 15, 2021, deleted "involving opiates, fentanyl and/or heroin" from the end of the first sentence of (g).

§ 4799C. Powers and duties.

(a) The Commission shall investigate and review the facts and circumstances of overdose deaths that occur in Delaware. The review of deaths involving criminal investigations will be delayed until the later of the conclusion of such investigation, or the adjudication of related criminal charges, if any. The Commission shall make recommendations to the Governor and General Assembly, at least annually, regarding those practices or conditions which impact the frequency of overdose deaths and steps that can be taken to reduce the frequency of such overdose deaths. All recommendations made under this subsection must comply with applicable state and federal confidentiality provisions, including those enumerated under § 4799D of this title. Notwithstanding any provision of this subchapter to the contrary, no recommendation may specifically identify any individual or any nongovernmental agency, organization, or entity.

(b) Reviews conducted by the Commission and regional review teams shall in all cases include a review of the medical records of the deceased.

(c) In connection with any review, the Commission and regional review teams shall have the power and authority to:

(1) Administer oaths; and

(2) Compel the attendance of witnesses whose testimony is related to the overdose death under review and the production of any records related to the death or pertinent to the Commission's investigation, through the use of process issued by the Department of Justice pursuant to § 2508 of Title 29.

(d) Notwithstanding any provision of this subchapter to the contrary, no person identified by the Department of Justice as a potential witness in any criminal prosecution arising from an overdose death shall be questioned, deposed or interviewed by or for the Commission in connection with its investigation and review of such death until the completion of such prosecution.

History.
80 Del. Laws, c. 220, § 1; 81 Del. Laws, c. 94, § 2; 83 Del. Laws, c. 49, § 3.

Effect of amendments.
83 Del. Laws, c. 49, effective June 15, 2021, in (a), in the first sentence deleted "all" preceding "overdose" and substituted "that" for "involving opiates, fentanyl or heroin which", deleted "in-volving opiates, fentanyl or heroin" preceding "and steps" in the third sentence, in the fourth sentence substituted the first occurrence of "under" for "pursuant to" and the second occurrence thereof for "in" and "must" for "shall" and deleted "but not limited to" following "includ-ing", and added a comma following "organiza-tion" in the final sentence.

CHAPTER 49
NATURAL FOOD SUBSTANCES

§ 4904. Prescribing or administering of laetrile.

(a) No hospital nor health facility may interfere with the physician-patient relationship by restricting or forbidding the use of laetrile (amygdalin, Vitamin B-17) when prescribed or administered by a physician, surgeon, osteopath or other person engaged in the practice of medicine, as that term is defined in § 1702(11) of Title 24 and/or when requested by a patient, unless the substance as prescribed or administered by the physician or medical practitioner is found to be harmful by the Board of Medical Licensure and Discipline in a public hearing which complies with the Freedom of Information Act [Chapter 100 of Title 29].

(b) No physician, surgeon, osteopath or other person engaged in the practice of medicine, as that term is defined in § 1702(11) of Title 24 shall be subject to disciplinary action solely for the prescribing or administering of laetrile (amygdalin, Vitamin B-17) to a patient under the physician's, surgeon's, osteopath's or other person's care who has requested the substance.

(c) Under this section laetrile shall not be considered a medical drug, but shall be considered a natural food substance.

History.
61 Del. Laws, c. 90, § 2; 70 Del. Laws, c. 186, § 1; 75 Del. Laws, c. 141, § 2; 77 Del. Laws, c. 319, § 1; 80 Del. Laws, c. 80, § 2; 81 Del. Laws, c. 340, § 2; 82 Del. Laws, c. 75, § 3; 83 Del. Laws, c. 52, § 5.

Revisor's note.
Based upon changes contained in 83 Del. Laws, c. 52, § 5, made effective July 1, 2021, by § 21 of that act, "§ 1702(11)" was substituted for "§ 1702(13)" in (a) and for "§ 1702(12)" in (b).

§ 4905. Distribution by pharmacists.

A pharmacist shall not be subject to any penalty for filling a prescription for laetrile (amygdalin, Vitamin B-17) if the prescription is issued to a patient by a physician, surgeon, osteopath or other person engaged in the practice of medicine, as that term is defined in § 1702(11) of Title 24.

History.
61 Del. Laws, c. 90, § 2; 81 Del. Laws, c. 340, § 2; 82 Del. Laws, c. 75, § 3; 83 Del. Laws, c. 52, § 5.

Laws, c. 52, § 5, made effective July 1, 2021, by § 21 of that act, "§ 1702(11)" was substituted for "§ 1702(13)".

Revisor's note.
Based upon changes contained in 83 Del.

CHAPTER 49A
THE DELAWARE MEDICAL MARIJUANA ACT

§ 4901A. Findings.

(a) Marijuana's recorded use as a medicine goes back nearly 5,000 years. Modern medical research has confirmed the beneficial uses for marijuana in treating or alleviating the pain, nausea, and other symptoms associated with a variety of debilitating medical conditions, including cancer, multiple sclerosis, and HIV/AIDS, as found by the National Academy of Sciences' Institute of Medicine in March 1999.

(b) Studies published since the 1999 Institute of Medicine report have continued to show the therapeutic value of marijuana in treating a wide array of debilitating medical conditions. These include relief of the neuropathic pain caused by multiple sclerosis, HIV/AIDS, and other illnesses that often fails to respond to conventional treatments and relief of nausea, vomiting, and other side effects of drugs used to treat HIV/AIDS and hepatitis C, increasing the chances of patients continuing on life-saving treatment regimens. Specifically, in February 2010, the Center for Medicinal Cannabis Research released a lengthy report that summarized 15 recent studies clearly demonstrating marijuana's medical efficacy for a broad range of conditions. These studies, many of which were double blind, placebo-controlled trials, included neuropathic pain trials published in the *Journal of Pain, Neuropsychopharmacology and Neurology*, a study on the analgesic efficacy of smoked marijuana published in *Anesthesiology*, a study on the mechanisms of cannabinoid analgesia in rats published in *Pain*, and a study on vaporization as a "smokeless" marijuana delivery system published in *Clinical Pharmacology & Therapeutics*.

(c) Marijuana has many currently accepted medical uses in the United States, having been recommended by thousands of licensed physicians to at least 350,000 patients in states with medical marijuana laws. Marijuana's medical utility has been recognized by a wide range of medical and public health organizations, including the American Academy of HIV Medicine, the American College of Physicians, the American Nurses Association, the American Public Health Association and the Leukemia and Lymphoma Society.

(d) Data from the Federal Bureau of Investigation's Uniform Crime Reports and the Compendium of Federal Justice Statistics show that approximately 99 out of every 100 marijuana arrests in the U.S. are made under state law, rather than under federal law. Consequently, changing state law will have the practical effect of protecting from arrest the vast majority of seriously ill patients who have a medical need to use marijuana.

(e) Alaska, Arizona, California, Colorado, the District of Columbia, Hawaii, Maine, Michigan, Montana, Nevada, New Mexico, New Jersey, Oregon, Vermont, Rhode Island, and Washington have removed state-level criminal penalties from the medical use of marijuana. Delaware joins in this effort for the health and welfare of its citizens.

(f) States are not required to enforce federal law or prosecute people for engaging in activities prohibited by federal law. Therefore, compliance with this chapter does not put the State of Delaware in violation of federal law.

(g) State law should make a distinction between the medical and nonmedical uses of marijuana. Hence, the purpose of this chapter is to protect patients with debilitating medical conditions, as well as their health-care practitioners and providers, from arrest and prosecution, criminal and other penalties, and property forfeiture if such patients engage in the medical use of marijuana.

History.
78 Del. Laws, c. 23, § 1; 83 Del. Laws, c. 48, § 1.

substituted "health-care practitioners" for "physicians" in the second sentence of (g).

Effect of amendments.
83 Del. Laws, c. 48, effective June 15, 2021,

§ 4902A. Definitions [For application of this section, see 82 Del. Laws, c. 246, § 5].

For purposes of this chapter:

(1) "Cannabidiol-rich medical marijuana" or "CBD-rich" means a marijuana strain or product formulization that has elevated levels of cannabidiol ("CBD") and contains the profile of CBD and tetrahydrocannabinol ("THC") concentrations approved by the Department, based upon the recommendation of the Medical Marijuana Act Oversight Committee.

(2) "Cardholder" means a qualifying patient or a designated caregiver who has been issued and possesses a valid registry identification card.

(3) "Compassion center agent" means a principal officer, board member, employee, or agent of a registered compassion center who is 21 years of age or older and has not been convicted of an excluded felony offense or drug misdemeanor within 5 years.

(4) "Debilitating medical condition" means 1 or more of the following:

a. Terminal illness, cancer, positive status for human immunodeficiency virus, acquired immune deficiency syndrome, decompensated cirrhosis, amyotrophic lateral sclerosis, agitation of Alzheimer's disease, post-traumatic stress disorder, intractable epilepsy, seizure disorder, glaucoma, chronic debilitating migraines, new daily persistent headache, or the treatment of these conditions.

b. A chronic or debilitating disease or medical condition or its treatment that produces 1 or more of the following: cachexia or wasting syndrome; severe, debilitating pain that has not responded to previously prescribed medication or surgical measures for more than 3 months or for which other treatment options produced serious side effects; intractable nausea; seizures; severe and persistent muscle spasms, including those characteristic of multiple sclerosis.

c. Any other medical condition or its treatment added by the Department, as provided for in § 4906A of this title.

(5) "Department" means the Delaware Department of Health and Social Services or its successor agency.

(6) "Designated caregiver" means a person who:

a. Is at least 21 years of age unless the person is the parent or legal guardian of a minor who is a qualifying patient;

b. Has agreed to assist with a patient's medical use of marijuana;

c. Has not been convicted of an excluded felony offense; and

d. Assists no more than 5 qualifying patients with their medical use of marijuana.

(7) "Enclosed, locked facility" means a greenhouse, building, or other enclosed area equipped with locks or other security devices that is on a registered compassion center's property and permits access only the compassion center agents working for the registered compassion center.

(8) "Excluded felony offense" means:

a. A violent crime defined in § 4201(c) of Title 11, that was classified as a felony in the jurisdiction where the person was convicted; or

b. A violation of a state or federal controlled substance law that was classified as a felony in the jurisdiction where the person was convicted, not including:

1. An offense for which the sentence, including any term of probation, incarceration, or supervised release, was completed 10 or more years earlier; or

2. An offense that consisted of conduct for which this chapter would likely have prevented a conviction, but the conduct either occurred prior to July 1, 2011, or was prosecuted by an authority other than the State of Delaware.

(9) "Health-care practitioner" means an individual who is licensed and authorized to write medical orders under Title 24 as a physician, advanced practice registered nurse, or physician assistant, except as otherwise provided in this paragraph. If the qualifying patient is younger than 18 years of age, the health-care practitioner must be a physician who is a pediatric neurologist, pediatric gastroenterologist, pediatric oncologist, pediatric psychiatrist, developmental pediatrician, or pediatric palliative care specialist.

(10) "Intractable epilepsy" means an epileptic seizure disorder for which standard medical treatment does not prevent or significantly ameliorate recurring, uncontrolled seizures or for which standard medical treatment results in harmful side effects.

(11) "Marijuana" has the meaning given that term in § 4701 of this title.

(12) "Medical marijuana oil" means any of the following:

a. Cannabidiol oil" which is a processed Cannabis plant extract that contains at least 15% cannabidiol but no more than 7% tetrahydrocannabinol, or a dilution of the resin of the Cannabis plant that contains at least 50 milligrams of cannabidiol per milliliter but not more than 7% tetrahydrocannabinol.

b. "THC-A oil" which is a processed Cannabis plant extract that contains at least 15% tetrahydrocannabinol acid but not more than 7% tetrahydrocannabinol, or a dilution of the resin of the Cannabis plant that contains at least 50 milligrams of tetrahydrocannabinol acid per milliliter but not more than 7% tetrahydrocannabinol.

c. Any change in the oil formulation which is made by the Department based upon the recommendation of the Medical Marijuana Act Oversight Committee.

(13) "Medical use" means the acquisition; administration; delivery; possession; transportation; transfer; transportation; or use of marijuana or paraphernalia relating to the administration of marijuana to treat or alleviate a registered qualifying patient's debilitating medical condition or symptoms associated with the patient's debilitating medical condition.

(14) "Physician" means a properly licensed physician subject to Chapter 17 of Title 24 except as otherwise provided in this paragraph. If the qualifying patient is younger than 18 years of age, the physician must be a pediatric neurologist, pediatric gastroenterologist, pediatric oncologist or pediatric palliative care specialist.

(15) "Qualifying patient" means an individual who meets the qualifications to receive a registry identification card under this chapter.

(16) "Registered compassion center" means a not-for-profit entity registered pursuant to § 4914A of this title that acquires, possesses, cultivates, manufactures, delivers, transfers, transports, sells, supplies, or dispenses marijuana, paraphernalia, or related supplies and educational materials to registered qualifying patients who have designated the dispenser to cultivate marijuana for their medical use and the registered designated caregivers of these patients.

(17) "Registered safety compliance facility" means a nonprofit entity registered under § 4915A of this title by the Department to provide 1 or more of the following services: testing marijuana produced for medical use for potency and contaminants; and training cardholders and prospective compassion center agents. The training may include, but need not be limited to, information related to 1 or more of the following:

a. The safe and efficient cultivation, harvesting, packaging, labeling, and distribution of marijuana;

b. Security and inventory accountability procedures; and

c. Up-to-date scientific and medical research findings related to medical marijuana.

(18) "Registry identification card" means a document issued by the Department that identifies a person as 1 of the following:

a. A registered qualifying adult patient.

b. A registered designated caregiver for a qualifying adult patient.

c. A registered designated caregiver for a pediatric patient.

d. A registered compassionate use adult patient.

e. A registered designated caregiver for an adult compassionate use patient.

    f. A registered designated caregiver for a pediatric compassionate use patient.

    g. A registered CBD-rich patient.

    h. A registered designated caregiver for a CBD-rich patient.

(19) "Safety compliance facility agent" means a principal officer, board member, employee, or agent of a registered safety compliance facility who is 21 years of age or older and has not been convicted of an excluded felony offense.

(20) "Terminal illness" means any disease, illness or condition sustained by any human being:

    a. For which there is no reasonable medical expectation of recovery;

    b. Which, as a medical probability, will result in the death of such human being regardless of the use or discontinuance of medical treatment implemented for the purpose of sustaining life or the life processes; and

    c. As a result of which, the human being's health-care practitioner would not be surprised if death were to occur within 12 months.

(21) "Usable marijuana" means the dried leaves and flowers of the marijuana plant and any mixture or preparation of those dried leaves and flowers, including but not limited to tinctures, ointments, other preparations including medical marijuana oil, but does not include the seeds, stalks, and roots of the plant. It does not include the weight of any nonmarijuana ingredients combined with marijuana, such as ingredients added to prepare a topical administration, food, or drink.

(22) "Verification system" means a phone or Web-based system that is available to law-enforcement personnel and compassion center agents on a 24-hour basis for verification of registry identification cards.

(23) "Written certification" means a document dated and signed by a health-care practitioner, stating that in the health-care practitioner's professional opinion the patient is likely to receive therapeutic or palliative benefit from the medical use of marijuana to treat or alleviate the patient's debilitating medical condition or symptoms associated with the debilitating medical condition. A written certification shall be made only in the course of a bona fide health-care practitioner-patient relationship where the qualifying patient is under the health-care practitioner's care for the patient's primary care or for the patient's debilitating medical condition after the health-care practitioner has completed an assessment of the qualifying patient's medical history and current medical condition. The bona fide health-care practitioner-patient relationship may not be limited to authorization for the patient to use medical marijuana or consultation for that purpose. The written certification must specify the qualifying patient's debilitating medical condition.

History.

78 Del. Laws, c. 23, § 1; 70 Del. Laws, c. 186, § 1; 80 Del. Laws, c. 39, § 1; 80 Del. Laws, c. 406, § 1; 81 Del. Laws, c. 61, § 1; 81 Del. Laws, c. 383, § 1; 82 Del. Laws, c. 43, § 1; 82 Del. Laws, c. 213, § 1; 82 Del. Laws, c. 246, § 1; 83 Del. Laws, c. 48, § 2.

Effect of amendments.

83 Del. Laws, c. 48, effective June 15, 2021, added present (9) and redesignated the remaining paragraphs accordingly; and, in (23), in the first and second sentences, substituted "health-care practitioner" for "physician" and "health-care practitioner's" for "physicians", in the second and third sentences substituted "health-care practitioner-patient" for "physician-patient", twice substituted "the patient's" for "her or his" in the second sentence, and substituted "must" for "shall" in the final sentence.

RESEARCH REFERENCES AND PRACTICE AIDS

Delaware Law Reviews.
First State or Follower?: Marijuana in Delaware, 26 Widener L. Rev. 21 (2020).

§ 4903A. Protections for the medical use of marijuana.

(a) A registered qualifying patient shall not be subject to arrest, prosecution, or denial of any right or privilege, including but not limited to civil penalty or disciplinary action by a court or occupational or professional licensing board or bureau, for the medical use of marijuana pursuant to this chapter, if the registered qualifying patient does not possess more than 6 ounces of usable marijuana.

(b) A registered designated caregiver shall not be subject to arrest, prosecution, or denial of any right or privilege, including but not limited to civil penalty or disciplinary action by a court or occupational or professional licensing board or bureau:

    (1) For assisting a registered qualifying patient to whom he or she is connected through the Department's registration process with the medical use of marijuana if the designated caregiver does not possess more than 6 ounces of usable marijuana for each qualifying patient to whom he or she is connected through the Department's registration process; and

    (2) For receiving compensation for costs associated with assisting a registered qualifying patient's medical use of marijuana if the registered designated caregiver is connected to the registered qualifying patient through the Department's registration process.

(c) [Repealed.]

(d) A registered qualifying patient or registered designated caregiver shall not be subject to prosecution, or denial of any right or privilege, including but not limited to civil penalty or disciplinary action by a court or occupational or professional licensing board or bureau for possession of seeds and stalks.

(e) A registered qualifying patient or registered designated caregiver shall not be subject to arrest, prosecution, or denial of any right or privilege, including but not limited to civil penalty or disciplinary action by a court or occupational or professional licensing board or bureau for giving marijuana to a registered qualifying patient, a registered compassion center, or a registered designated caregiver for a registered qualifying patient's medical use where nothing of value is transferred in return, or for offering to do the same, if the person giving the marijuana does not knowingly cause the recipient to possess more marijuana than is permitted by this section.

(f)(1) There shall be a presumption that a qualifying patient is engaged in, or a designated caregiver is assisting with, the medical use of marijuana in accordance with this chapter if the qualifying patient or designated caregiver:

    a. Is in possession of a valid registry identification card; and

    b. Is in possession of an amount of marijuana that does not exceed the amount allowed under subsections (a), (b) and (c) [repealed] of this section.

    (2) The presumption may be rebutted by evidence that conduct related to marijuana was not for the purpose of treating or alleviating the qualifying patient's debilitating medical condition or symptoms associated with the debilitating medical condition in compliance with this chapter.

(g) A health-care practitioner may not be subject to arrest, prosecution, or penalty in any manner, or denied any right or privilege, including a civil penalty or disciplinary action by the Delaware Medical Board or by any other occupational or professional licensing board or bureau, solely for providing written certifications or for otherwise stating that, in the health-care practitioner's professional opinion, a patient is likely to receive therapeutic or palliative benefit from the medical use of marijuana to treat or alleviate the patient's serious or debilitating medical condition or symptoms associated with the serious or debilitating medical condition or for refusing to provide such written certifications or statements, provided that nothing in this chapter is deemed to release a health-care practitioner from the duty to exercise a professional standard of care for evaluating or treating a patient's medical condition.

(h) No person may be subject to arrest, prosecution, or denial of any right or privilege, including but not limited to civil penalty or disciplinary action by a court or occupational or professional licensing board or bureau, for:

(1) Selling marijuana paraphernalia to a cardholder upon presentation of an unexpired registry identification card in the recipient's name or to a compassion center agent or safety compliance facility agent upon presentation of an unexpired copy of the entity's registration certificate;

(2) Being in the presence or vicinity of the medical use of marijuana as allowed under this chapter; or

(3) Assisting a registered qualifying patient with using or administering marijuana.

(i) A registered compassion center shall not be subject to prosecution; search or inspection, except by the Department pursuant to § 4919A(u) of this title; seizure; or penalty in any manner, or be denied any right or privilege, including but not limited to civil penalty or disciplinary action by a court or business licensing board or entity, for:

(1) Acting pursuant to this chapter and Department regulations to acquire, possess, cultivate, manufacture, deliver, transfer, transport, supply, sell, or dispense marijuana or related supplies and educational materials to registered qualifying patients who have designated the compassion center to provide for them, to registered designated caregivers on behalf of the registered qualifying patients who have designated the registered compassion center, or to other registered compassion centers;

(2) Selling or transferring marijuana seeds to entities that are licensed or registered in another jurisdiction to dispense marijuana for medical purposes; or

(3) Transferring marijuana to and from a registered safety compliance facility for the purposes of analytical testing.

(j) A compassion center agent shall not be subject to prosecution, search, or penalty in any manner, or be denied any right or privilege, including but not limited to civil penalty or disciplinary action by a court or business licensing board or entity, for working or volunteering for a registered compassion center pursuant to this chapter and Department regulations to perform the actions on behalf of a registered compassion center that are authorized by this chapter.

(k) A Delaware facility which meets FDA-accepted security and operational standards shall not be subject to prosecution; search, except by the Department under § 4919A(u) of this title; seizure; or penalty in any manner, or be denied any right or privilege, including civil penalty or disciplinary action by a court or business licensing board or entity, solely for acting in accordance with this chapter, Department regulations, or federal law for the purposes of conducting research on marijuana under § 4928A of this title and pursuant to all applicable federal law on medical marijuana.

(l) A registered safety compliance facility and safety compliance facility agents acting on behalf of a registered safety compliance facility shall not be subject to prosecution; search, except by the Department pursuant to

§ 4919A(u) of this title; seizure; or penalty in any manner, or be denied any right or privilege, including but not limited to civil penalty or disciplinary action by a court or business licensing board or entity, solely for acting in accordance with this chapter and Department regulations to provide the following services:

(1) Acquiring or possessing marijuana obtained from registered compassion centers;

(2) Returning the marijuana to the same registered compassion centers;

(3) Transporting marijuana that was produced by registered compassion centers to or from those registered compassion centers;

(4) Cultivating, manufacturing, and possessing marijuana for training and analytical testing;

(5) The production or sale of educational materials related to medical marijuana;

(6) The production, sale, or transportation of equipment or materials other than marijuana to registered compassion centers, including lab equipment and packaging materials, that are used by registered compassion centers;

(7) Testing of medical marijuana samples, including for potency and contamination;

(8) Providing training to prospective compassion center agents and compassion center agents, provided that only compassion center agents and safety compliance facility agents may be allowed to possess or cultivate marijuana and any possession or cultivation of marijuana must occur on the location registered with the Department; and

(9) Receiving compensation for actions allowed under this section.

(m) An entity that is registered to dispense marijuana for medical use in other jurisdictions shall not be subject to prosecution; search or inspection, except by the Department pursuant to § 4919A(u) of this title; seizure; or penalty in any manner or be denied any right or privilege, including but not limited to civil penalty or disciplinary action by a court or business licensing board or entity, for providing marijuana seeds to registered compassion centers.

(n) Any marijuana, marijuana paraphernalia, licit property, or interest in licit property that is possessed, owned, or used in connection with the medical use of marijuana as allowed under this chapter, or acts incidental to such use, shall not be seized or forfeited. This chapter shall not prevent the seizure or forfeiture of marijuana exceeding the amounts allowed under this chapter nor shall it prevent seizure or forfeiture if the basis for the action is unrelated to the marijuana that is possessed, manufactured, transferred, or used pursuant to this chapter.

(o) Mere possession of, or application for, a registry identification card or registration certificate shall not constitute probable cause or reasonable suspicion, nor shall it be used to support the search of the person, property, or home of the person possessing or applying for the registry identification card. The possession of, or application for, a registry identification card shall not preclude the existence of probable cause if probable cause exists on other grounds.

(p) For the purposes of Delaware state law, the medical use of marijuana by a cardholder or registered compassion center shall be considered lawful as long as it is in accordance with this chapter.

(q) Where a state-funded or locally funded law-enforcement agency encounters an individual who, during the course of the investigation, credibly asserts that he or she is a registered cardholder, or encounters an entity whose personnel credibly assert that it is a registered compassion center, the law-enforcement agency shall not provide any information from any marijuana-related investigation of the person to any law-enforcement authority that does not recognize the protection of this chapter and any prosecution of the individual, individuals, or entity for a violation of this chapter shall be conducted pursuant to the laws of this State.

History.
78 Del. Laws, c. 23, § 1; 70 Del. Laws, c. 186, § 1; 80 Del. Laws, c. 115, § 1; 80 Del. Laws, c. 406, § 2; 83 Del. Laws, c. 48, § 3.

Effect of amendments.
83 Del. Laws, c. 48, effective June 15, 2021, in

(g), substituted "health-care practitioner may" for "physician shall", "a" for "but not limited to" preceding "civil", "health-care practitioner's" for "physician's", "is" for "shall be" preceding "deemed" and "health-care practitioner" for "physician" near the end.

§ 4905A. Discrimination prohibited.

(a)(1) No school or landlord may refuse to enroll or lease to, or otherwise penalize, a person solely for his or her status as a registered qualifying patient or a registered designated caregiver, unless failing to do so would cause the school or landlord to lose a monetary or licensing-related benefit under federal law or regulations.

(2) For the purposes of medical care, including organ transplants, a registered qualifying patient's authorized use of marijuana under this chapter is considered the equivalent of the authorized use of any other medication used at the direction of a health-care practitioner and does not constitute the use of an illicit substance or otherwise disqualify a qualifying patient from needed medical care.

(3) Unless a failure to do so would cause the employer to lose a monetary or licensing-related benefit under federal law or federal regulations, an employer may not discriminate against a person in hiring, termination, or any term or condition of employment, or otherwise penalize a person, if the discrimination is based upon either of the following:

a. The person's status as a cardholder; or

b. A registered qualifying patient's positive drug test for marijuana components or metabolites, unless the patient used, possessed, or was impaired by marijuana on the premises of the place of employment or during the hours of employment.

(b) A person otherwise entitled to custody of or visitation or parenting time with a minor shall not be denied such a right, and there shall be no presumption of neglect or child endangerment, for conduct allowed under this chapter, unless the person's actions in relation to marijuana were such that they created an unreasonable danger to the safety of the minor as established by clear and convincing evidence.

(c) No school, landlord, or employer may be penalized or denied any benefit under state law for enrolling, leasing to, or employing a cardholder.

History.
78 Del. Laws, c. 23, § 1; 70 Del. Laws, c. 186, § 1; 83 Del. Laws, c. 48, § 4.

Effect of amendments.
83 Del. Laws, c. 48, effective June 15, 2021, in

(a)(2), substituted "under" for "in accordance with", "is" for "shall be" preceding "considered", and "health-care practitioner and does" for "physician and shall".

NOTES TO DECISIONS

Medical records.
Where a hospital made a report of prenatal substance exposure in accordance with 16 Del. C. § 903B, based on the child's positive urine

test on the date of birth, the mother claimed the hospital improperly listed marijuana under substance use for nonmedical purposes and listed the use of medicinal marijuana as a risk factor in the birth mother's records; because the medical records indicated that the patient had a prescription for the marijuana, and that the mother did not lose any parenting time with the child, the hospital properly classified the mother's marijuana use and did not deprive the mother of any right or privilege due to the use of medical marijuana. Coursey v. St. Francis Hosp., Inc., — A.3d —, 2020 Del. Super. LEXIS 2980 (Del. Super. Ct. Dec. 8, 2020).

§ 4907A. Acts not required, acts not prohibited.

(a) Nothing in this chapter requires any of the following:

(1) A government medical assistance program or private health insurer to reimburse a person for costs associated with the medical use of marijuana;

(2) Any person or establishment in lawful possession of property to allow a guest, client, customer, or other visitor to smoke marijuana on or in that property; or

(3) An employer to allow the ingestion of marijuana in any workplace or to allow any employee to work while under the influence of marijuana, except that a registered qualifying patient shall not be considered to be under the influence of marijuana solely because of the presence of metabolites or components of marijuana.

(4) A health-care practitioner to provide a written certification or otherwise recommend marijuana to a patient.

(b) Nothing in this chapter prohibits an employer from disciplining an employee for ingesting marijuana in the workplace or working while under the influence of marijuana.

(c) Nothing in this chapter shall be construed to prevent the arrest or prosecution of a registered qualifying patient for reckless driving or driving under the influence of marijuana where probable cause exists.

History.
78 Del. Laws, c. 23, § 1; 83 Del. Laws, c. 48, § 5.

Effect of amendments.
83 Del. Laws, c. 48, effective June 15, 2021,
added "any of the following" in the introductory paragraph of (a); and substituted "health-care practitioner" for "physician" in (a)(4).

§ 4908A. Registration of qualifying patients and designated caregivers [For application of this section, see 82 Del. Laws, c. 246, § 5].

(a) The Department shall issue registry identification cards to qualifying patients who submit all of the following, in accordance with the Department's final regulations:

(1) A written certification issued by a health-care practitioner within 90 days immediately preceding the date of an application.

(2) The application or renewal fee.

(3) The name, address, and date of birth of the qualifying patient, except that if the applicant is homeless no address is required.

(4) The name, address, and telephone number of the qualifying patient's health-care practitioner.

(5) The name, address, and date of birth of the designated caregiver, if any, chosen by the qualifying patient.

(6) For a compassionate use card, the patient's informed consent and health-care practitioner verification under subsection (c) of this section.

(7) A statement signed by the qualifying patient, pledging not to divert marijuana to anyone who is not allowed to possess marijuana pursuant to this chapter.

(8) A signed statement from the designated caregiver, if any, agreeing to be designated as the patient's designated caregiver and pledging not to

divert marijuana to anyone who is not allowed to possess marijuana pursuant to this chapter.

(b) Registry identification card applications shall be available no later than the day the Department publishes final regulations.

(c) The Department shall issue a compassionate use card to an individual who is eligible for a compassionate use card and who submits all of the following, in accordance with the Department's final regulations, in addition to the requirements under subsection (a) of this section:

(1) A signed statement from the patient's health-care practitioner that includes statements attesting to all of the following:

a. The patient has a severe and debilitating condition.

b. All current standard care practices and treatments have been exhausted and have been ineffective or the side effects are prohibitive with continued use.

c. The health-care practitioner will re-evaluate and document the efficacy of medical marijuana treatment.

d. There are grounds supporting the potential for the patient to benefit from using medical marijuana.

(2)a. If the patient is an adult, a signed statement from the patient acknowledging the patient's informed consent to treatment with medical marijuana and that the patient knows that there is limited or no evidence associated with medical marijuana's effectiveness in treating a condition that is not a debilitating medical condition under this chapter.

b. If the patient is under 18 years of age, a signed statement from the patient's parent or legal guardian acknowledging the patient's informed consent to treatment with medical marijuana and that the patient's parent or legal guardian knows that there is limited or no evidence associated with medical marijuana's effectiveness in treating a condition that is not a debilitating medical condition under this chapter.

(d)(1) An adult is eligible for a CBD-rich card if the individual complies with subsection (a) of this section and the written certification from the patient's health-care practitioner recommends medical marijuana for the treatment of anxiety or other condition approved by the Department for treatment with cannabidiol-rich medical marijuana.

(2) A patient who qualifies for a CBD-rich card may only receive cannabidiol-rich medical marijuana products.

History.
78 Del. Laws, c. 23, § 1; 70 Del. Laws, c. 186, § 1; 80 Del. Laws, c. 406, § 4; 82 Del. Laws, c. 213, § 2; 82 Del. Laws, c. 246, § 2; 83 Del. Laws, c. 48, § 6.

Effect of amendments.
83 Del. Laws, c. 48, effective June 15, 2021, substituted "health-care practitioner" for "physician" in (a)(1), (4) and (6), the introductory paragraph of (c)(1), and in (c)(1)c. and (d)(1).

RESEARCH REFERENCES AND PRACTICE AIDS

Delaware Law Reviews.
First State or Follower?: Marijuana in Delaware, 26 Widener L. Rev. 21 (2020).

§ 4911A. Registry identification cards [For application of this section, see 82 Del. Laws, c. 246, § 5].

(a) Registry identification cards must contain all of the following:

(1) The name of the cardholder.

(2) A designation of whether the cardholder is a designated caregiver or qualifying patient.

(3) That the registered cardholder is 1 of the following:

    a. A qualifying adult patient.

    b. A designated caregiver for a qualifying adult patient.

    c. A designated caregiver for a pediatric patient.

    d. An adult compassionate use patient.

    e. A designated caregiver for an adult compassionate use patient.

    f. A designated caregiver for a pediatric compassionate use patient.

    g. A CBD-rich patient.

    h. A designated caregiver for a CBD-rich patient.

    (4) The date of issuance and expiration date of the registry identification card.

    (5) A random 10-digit alphanumeric identification number, that is unique to the cardholder.

    (6) If the cardholder is a designated caregiver, the random 10-digit alphanumeric identification number of the qualifying patient the designated caregiver is receiving the registry identification card to assist.

  (b)(1) Except as provided in this subsection, the expiration date of a registry identification card is 1 year after the date of issuance.

    (2) If the health-care practitioner stated in the written certification that the qualifying patient would benefit from marijuana until a specified earlier date, then the registry identification card expires on that date.

    (3) If the health-care practitioner stated in the written certification that the compassionate use patient would benefit from a trial period using marijuana until a specified earlier date, then the registry identification card expires on that date.

  (c) The Department may, at its discretion, electronically store in the card all of the information listed in subsection (a) of this section, along with the address and date of birth of the cardholder, to allow it to be read by law-enforcement agents.

History.
  78 Del. Laws, c. 23, § 1; 80 Del. Laws, c. 406, § 7; 82 Del. Laws, c. 213, § 5; 82 Del. Laws, c. 246, § 3; 83 Del. Laws, c. 48, § 7.

Effect of amendments.
  83 Del. Laws, c. 48, effective June 15, 2021, substituted "of a registry identification card is" for "shall be" in (b)(1); substituted "health-care practitioner" for "physician" in (b)(2) and (3); and substituted "expires" for "shall expire" in (b)(2).

§ 4912A. Notifications to Department and responses; civil penalty.

  (a) The following notifications and Department responses are required:

    (1) A registered qualifying patient shall notify the Department of any change in his or her name or address, or if the registered qualifying patient ceases to have his or her debilitating medical condition, within 10 days of the change.

    (2) A registered designated caregiver shall notify the Department of any change in his or her name or address, or if the designated caregiver becomes aware the qualifying patient passed away, within 10 days of the change.

    (3) Before a registered qualifying patient changes his or her designated caregiver, the qualifying patient must notify the Department.

    (4) If a cardholder loses his or her registry identification card, he or she shall notify the Department within 10 days of becoming aware the card has been lost.

  (b) When a cardholder notifies the Department of items listed in subsection (a) of this section, but remains eligible under this chapter, the Department shall issue the cardholder a new registry identification card with a new random 10-digit alphanumeric identification number within 10 days of receiving the updated information and pay a $20 fee. If the person notifying the

Department is a registered qualifying patient, the Department shall also issue his or her registered designated caregiver, if any, a new registry identification card within 10 days of receiving the updated information.

(c) If a registered qualifying patient ceases to be a registered qualifying patient or changes his or her registered designated caregiver, the Department shall promptly notify the designated caregiver. The registered designated caregiver's protections under this chapter as to that qualifying patient shall expire 15 days after notification by the Department.

(d) A cardholder who fails to make a notification to the Department that is required by this section is subject to a civil infraction, punishable by a penalty of no more than $150.

(e) The Department shall administer a real-time statewide patient registry to facilitate patient choice in purchasing medical marijuana from any properly licensed Delaware Compassion Centers. The registry shall track patient purchases to comply with § 4919A(i) of this title.

(f) If the registered qualifying patient's certifying health-care practitioner notifies the Department in writing that either the registered qualifying patient has ceased to suffer from a debilitating medical condition or that the health-care practitioner no longer believes the patient would receive therapeutic or palliative benefit from the medical use of marijuana, the card becomes null and void. However, the registered qualifying patient has 15 days to dispose of their marijuana or give it to a registered compassion center where nothing of value is transferred in return.

History.
78 Del. Laws, c. 23, § 1; 70 Del. Laws, c. 186, § 1; 80 Del. Laws, c. 406, § 8; 83 Del. Laws, c. 48, § 8.

Effect of amendments.
83 Del. Laws, c. 48, effective June 15, 2021, in

(f), in the first sentence substituted "health-care practitioner" for "physician" twice and "becomes" for "shall become", and in the second sentence substituted "has" for "shall have" and "their" for "his or her".

§ 4913A. Affirmative defense and dismissal for medical marijuana.

(a) Except as provided in § 4904A of this title and this section, an individual may assert a medical purpose for using marijuana as a defense to any prosecution of an offense involving marijuana intended for the patient's medical use, and this defense shall be presumed valid and the prosecution shall be dismissed where the evidence shows all of the following:

(1) A health-care practitioner states that, in the health-care practitioner's professional opinion, after having completed a full assessment of the individual's medical history and current medical condition made in the course of a bona fide health-care practitioner-patient relationship, the patient is likely to receive therapeutic or palliative benefit from marijuana to treat or alleviate the individual's serious or debilitating medical condition or symptoms associated with the individual's serious or debilitating medical condition.

(2) The individual was in possession of no more than 6 ounces of usable marijuana.

(3) The individual was engaged in the acquisition, possession, use, or transportation of marijuana, paraphernalia, or both, relating to the administration of marijuana to treat or alleviate the individual's serious or debilitating medical condition or symptoms associated with the individual's serious or debilitating medical condition.

(b) The defense and motion to dismiss shall not prevail if the prosecution proves that

(1) The individual had a registry identification card revoked for misconduct; or

(2) The purposes for the possession of marijuana were not solely for palliative or therapeutic use by the individual with a serious or debilitating medical condition who raised the defense.

(c) An individual is not required to possess a registry identification card to raise the affirmative defense set forth in this section.

(d) If an individual demonstrates the individual's medical purpose for using marijuana pursuant to this section, except as provided in § 4909A of this title, the individual shall not be subject to the following for the individual's use of marijuana for medical purposes:

(1) Disciplinary action by an occupational or professional licensing board or bureau; or

(2) Forfeiture of any interest in or right to nonmarijuana, licit property.

(e)(1) This section shall only apply for arrests made after July 1, 2011, until 75 days after registration for qualified patients is available, and

(2) Thereafter, for arrests made after a valid an application for a qualifying patient has been submitted and before the registry identification card has been received.

History.
78 Del. Laws, c. 23, § 1; 83 Del. Laws, c. 48, § 9.

Effect of amendments.
83 Del. Laws, c. 48, effective June 15, 2021, substituted "all of the following" for "that" at the end of the introductory paragraph; in (a)(1), substituted "health-care practitioner" for "physician" near the beginning, "health-care practitioner's" for "physician's" and "health-care practitioner-patient" for "physician-patient"; and substituted a period for "; and" at the end of (a)(1) and (2).

§ 4914A. Registration of compassion centers.

RESEARCH REFERENCES AND PRACTICE AIDS

Delaware Law Reviews.
First State or Follower?: Marijuana in Delaware, 26 Widener L. Rev. 21 (2020).

§ 4919A. Requirements, prohibitions, penalties.

(a) A registered compassion center shall be operated on a not-for-profit basis. The bylaws of a registered compassion center shall contain such provisions relative to the disposition of revenues to establish and maintain its not-for-profit character. A registered compassion center need not be recognized as tax-exempt by the Internal Revenue Service and is not required to incorporate pursuant to Title 8.

(b) The operating documents of a registered compassion center shall include procedures for the oversight of the registered compassion center and procedures to ensure accurate recordkeeping.

(c) A registered compassion center and a registered safety compliance facility shall implement appropriate security measures to deter and prevent the theft of marijuana and unauthorized entrance into areas containing marijuana.

(d) A registered compassion center and a registered safety compliance facility may not be located within 500 feet of the property line of a preexisting public or private school.

(e) A registered compassion center is prohibited from acquiring, possessing, cultivating, manufacturing, delivering, transferring, transporting, supplying, or dispensing marijuana for any purpose except to assist registered qualifying patients with the medical use of marijuana directly or through the qualifying patients' designated caregivers.

(f) All cultivation of marijuana for registered compassion centers must take place in an enclosed, locked location at the physical address or addresses provided to the Department during the registration process, which can only be accessed by compassion center agents working or volunteering for the registered compassion center.

(g) A registered compassion center may not purchase usable marijuana or mature marijuana plants from any person other than another registered compassion center.

(h) Before marijuana may be dispensed to a designated caregiver or a registered qualifying patient, a compassion center agent must determine that the individual is a current cardholder in the verification system and must verify each of the following:

(1) That the registry identification card presented to the registered compassion center is valid;

(2) That the person presenting the card is the person identified on the registry identification card presented to the compassion center agent; and

(3) That the registered compassion center is the designated compassion center for the registered qualifying patient who is obtaining the marijuana directly or via his or her designated caregiver.

(i) A registered compassion center shall not dispense more than 3 ounces of marijuana to a registered qualifying patient, directly or via a designated caregiver, in any 14-day period. Registered compassion centers shall ensure compliance with this limitation by maintaining internal, confidential records that include records specifying how much marijuana is being dispensed to the registered qualifying patient and whether it was dispensed directly to the registered qualifying patient or to the designated caregiver. Each entry must include the date and time the marijuana was dispensed. These records must be maintained by the compassion centers for a minimum of 3 years.

(j) [Repealed.]

(k) No person may advertise medical marijuana sales in print, broadcast, or by paid in-person solicitation of customers. This shall not prevent appropriate signs on the property of the registered compassion center, listings in business directories including phone books, listings in trade or medical publications, or the sponsorship of health or not-for-profit charity or advocacy events.

(l) A registered compassion center may not share office space with nor refer patients to a health-care practitioner.

(m) A health-care practitioner may not refer patients to a registered compassion center or registered designated caregiver, advertise in a registered compassion center, or, if the health-care practitioner issues written certifications, hold any financial interest in a registered compassion center.

(n) No person who has been convicted of an excluded felony offense or has been convicted of a misdemeanor drug offense, as provided in this title or an equivalent offense from another jurisdiction, within 5 years from the date of application that is not excluded by § 4902A(8)b.2. of this title may be a compassion center agent.

(o) The Department shall issue a civil fine of up to $3,000 for violations of this section.

(p) The Department shall suspend or revoke a registration certificate for serious or multiple violations of this chapter and regulations issued in accordance with this chapter. A registered compassion center may continue to cultivate and possess marijuana plants during a suspension, but it may not dispense, transfer, or sell marijuana.

(q) The suspension or revocation of a certificate is a final Department action, subject to judicial review. Jurisdiction and venue for judicial review are vested in the Superior Court.

(r) Any cardholder who sells marijuana to a person who is not allowed to possess marijuana for medical purposes under this chapter shall have his or her registry identification card revoked and shall be subject to other penalties for the unauthorized sale of marijuana.

(s) Any registered qualifying patient, registered designated caregiver, compassion center agent, or safety compliance facility agent, including a principal owner, board member, employee or volunteer who has access to compassion center or safety compliance facility records, who sells marijuana to someone who is not allowed to use marijuana for medical purposes or who fails to maintain, fraudulently maintains, or fraudulently represents to the Department records required by this chapter or rules promulgated pursuant to this chapter, for the purposes of selling marijuana to someone who is not allowed to use marijuana for medical purposes under this chapter is guilty of a felony punishable by imprisonment for not more than 2 years or a fine of not more than $2,000, or both, in addition to any other penalties for the distribution of marijuana.

(t) The Department shall revoke the registry identification card of any cardholder who knowingly commits multiple or serious violations of this chapter.

(u) Registered compassion centers are subject to random and reasonable inspection by the Department. The Department shall give reasonable notice of an inspection under this paragraph.

(v) Fraudulent representation to a law-enforcement official of any fact or circumstance relating to the medical use of marijuana to avoid arrest or prosecution shall be a class B misdemeanor which may be punishable by up to 6 months incarceration at Level V under § 4204 of Title 11 and a fine of up to $1,150, as the Court deems appropriate which shall be in addition to any other penalties that may apply for making a false statement or for the use of marijuana other than use undertaken pursuant to this chapter and jurisdiction for prosecution shall be exclusively in Superior Court.

(w) Registration cards issued pursuant to § 4909A of this title shall be in the possession of the registrant while in possession of medical marijuana outside the registrant's residence and may be subject to prosecution for failure to do so. If the registrant is unable to produce a valid § 4909A of this title registration card within 2 weeks of the summons, the penalty for a violation of this section shall be an unclassified misdemeanor and jurisdiction shall be exclusively in Superior Court.

(x) For registered qualifying patients and designated caregivers, medical marijuana shall be contained, when not being prepared for ingestion or ingested and outside the registrant's residence, within, sealed, tamperproof containers issued by compassion centers pursuant to Department regulations and may be subject to prosecution for failure to do so. If the registrant is unable to produce a sealed, tamperproof container within 2 weeks of the summons, the penalty for a violation of this section shall be an unclassified misdemeanor.

History.
78 Del. Laws, c. 23, § 1; 70 Del. Laws, c. 186, § 1; 80 Del. Laws, c. 406, § 9; 82 Del. Laws, c. 246, § 1; 83 Del. Laws, c. 48, § 10.

Effect of amendments.
83 Del. Laws, c. 48, effective June 15, 2021,

substituted "may" for "shall" in (l) and (m) and "health-care practitioner" for "physician" once in (l) and twice in (m).

§ 4920A. Confidentiality.

(a) The following information received and records kept by the Department for purposes of administering this chapter are confidential and exempt from the Delaware Freedom of Information Act [Chapter 100 of Title 29], and not subject to disclosure to any individual or public or private entity, except as necessary for authorized employees of the State of Delaware to perform official duties pursuant to this chapter:

(1) Applications and renewals, their contents, and supporting information submitted by qualifying patients and designated caregivers, including information regarding their designated caregivers and health-care practitioners.

(2) Applications and renewals, their contents, and supporting information submitted by or on behalf of compassion centers and safety compliance facilities in compliance with this chapter, including their physical addressees.

(3) The individual names and other information identifying persons to whom the Department has issued registry identification cards.

(4) Any dispensing information required to be kept under § 4919A of this title or Department regulation shall identify cardholders and registered compassion centers by their registry identification numbers and not contain names or other personally identifying information.

(5) Any Department hard drives or other data-recording media that are no longer in use and that contain cardholder information must be destroyed. The Department shall retain a signed statement from a Department employee confirming the destruction.

(b) Nothing in this section precludes the following:

(1) Department employees shall notify law-enforcement about falsified or fraudulent information submitted to the Department if the employee who suspects that falsified or fraudulent information has been submitted.

(2) The Department shall notify state or local law-enforcement about apparent criminal violations of this chapter.

(3) Compassion center agents shall notify the Department of a suspected violation or attempted violation of this chapter or the regulations issued pursuant to it.

(4) The Department shall verify registry identification cards pursuant to 4921A of this title.

(5) The submission of the § 4922A of this title report to the legislature. Information obtained pursuant to this chapter is subject to the same protections and penalties afforded other health information under the Health Insurance Portability and Accountability Act (HIPAA), 45 C.F.R. Part 160, 162 and 164.

History.
78 Del. Laws, c. 23, § 1; 83 Del. Laws, c. 48, § 11.

substituted "health-care practitioners" for "physicians" in (a)(1).

Effect of amendments.
83 Del. Laws, c. 48, effective June 15, 2021,

§ 4922A. Oversight Committee; annual report by Department.

(a) The Medical Marijuana Act Oversight Committee is established to evaluate and make recommendations regarding the implementation of this chapter.

(1) The Oversight Committee shall consist of 9 members who possess the qualifications and are appointed as follows:

a. One member, appointed by the President Pro Tempore of the Senate.

b. One member, appointed by the Speaker of the House.

c. The Secretary of the Department, or a designee appointed by the Secretary.

d. Two medical professionals, each licensed in Delaware, with experience in medical marijuana issues, appointed by the Governor.

    e. One member with experience in policy development or implementation in the field of medical marijuana, appointed by the Governor.

    f. Three members who each shall be a cardholder, as defined in § 4902A of this title, appointed by the Governor.

  (2) The members of the Oversight Committee shall serve at the pleasure of the appointing authority.

  (3) A quorum shall consist of 51% of the membership of the Oversight Committee.

  (4) The Oversight Committee shall select a Chair and Vice Chair from among its members.

  (5) Staff support for the Oversight Committee shall be provided by the Department.

  (6) The Oversight Committee shall meet at least 2 times per year for the purpose of evaluating and making recommendations to the Governor, the General Assembly, and the Department regarding the following:

    a. The ability of qualifying patients in all areas of the State to obtain timely access to high-quality medical marijuana.

    b. The effectiveness of the registered compassion centers, individually and together, in serving the needs of qualifying patients, including the provision of educational and support services, the reasonableness of their fees, whether they are generating any complaints or security problems, and the sufficiency of the number operating to serve the registered qualifying patients of Delaware.

    c. The effectiveness of the registered safety compliance facility or facilities, including whether a sufficient number are operating.

    d. The sufficiency of the regulatory and security safeguards contained in this chapter and adopted by the Department to ensure that access to and use of marijuana cultivated is provided only to cardholders authorized for such purposes.

    e. Any recommended additions or revisions to the Department regulations or this chapter, including relating to security, safe handling, labeling, and nomenclature.

    f. Any research studies regarding health effects of medical marijuana for patients.

 (b) The Department shall submit to the Governor and the General Assembly an annual report that does not disclose any identifying information about cardholders, registered compassion centers, or health-care practitioners, but does contain, at a minimum, all of the following information:

  (1) The number of applications and renewals filed for registry identification cards.

  (2) The number of qualifying patients and designated caregivers approved in each county.

  (3) The nature of the debilitating medical conditions of the qualifying patients.

  (4) The number of registry identification cards revoked for misconduct.

  (5) The number of health-care practitioners providing written certifications for qualifying patients.

  (6) The number of registered compassion centers.

  (7) Specific accounting of fees and costs.

History.

  78 Del. Laws, c. 23, § 1; 80 Del. Laws, c. 11, § 1; 83 Del. Laws, c. 48, § 12.

Effect of amendments.

  83 Del. Laws, c. 48, effective June 15, 2021, substituted "health-care practitioners" for "physicians" in the introductory paragraph of (b) and in (b)(5).

§ 4923A. Department to issue regulations [For application of this section, see 82 Del. Laws, c. 246, § 5].

The Department shall promulgate regulations regarding all of the following:

(1) Governing the manner in which the Department shall consider petitions from the public to add debilitating medical conditions or treatments to the list of debilitating medical conditions under § 4902A(4) of this title, including public notice of and an opportunity to comment in public hearings on the petitions.

(2)a. Establishing the form and content of registration and renewal applications submitted under this chapter.

b. For compassionate use cards, governing the intervals at which a health-care practitioner must re-evaluate the efficacy of medical marijuana treatment and the documentation of the re-evaluations, and may include intervals of different lengths for the conditions for which a patient receives a compassionate use registry identification card.

(3) Governing the manner in which it shall consider applications for and renewals of registry identification cards.

(4) Governing all of the following matters related to registered compassion centers and security compliance facilities, with the goal of protecting against diversion and theft, without imposing an undue burden on the registered compassion centers or compromising the confidentiality of cardholders:

a. Minimum oversight requirements for registered compassion centers.

b. Minimum recordkeeping requirements for registered compassion centers.

c. Minimum security requirements for registered compassion centers, which shall include that each registered compassion center location must be protected by a fully operational security alarm system.

d. The competitive scoring process addressed in §§ 4914A and 4915A of this title.

e. Procedures for suspending or terminating the registration certificates or registry identification cards of cardholders, registered compassion centers, and registered safety compliance facilities that commit multiple or serious violations of the provisions of this chapter or the regulations promulgated pursuant to this section.

f. The design and security features of medical marijuana containers to be provided by the compassion centers.

(5) Requiring application and renewal fees for registry identification cards, and registered compassion center registration certificates, according to all of the following:

a. The total fees collected must generate revenues sufficient to offset all expenses of implementing and administering this chapter, except that fee revenue may be offset or supplemented by private donations.

b. The total amount of revenue from application, renewal, and registration fees for compassion centers and security compliance facilities must be sufficient to implement and administer the compassion center and safety compliance facility provisions of this chapter.

c. The Department may establish a sliding scale of patient application and renewal fees based upon a qualifying patient's household income.

d. The Department may accept donations from private sources to reduce application and renewal fees.

e. The total amount of revenue from application, renewal, and registration fees for compassion centers, security compliance facilities, and registry identification cards will be deposited to a special account within the Department for the operation of the program created by this chapter and shall be used as necessary to support program operations and growth.

(6) Establishing requirements for cannabidiol-rich medical marijuana profile concentrations.

History.
78 Del. Laws, c. 23, § 1; 82 Del. Laws, c. 213, § 6; 82 Del. Laws, c. 246, §§ 1, 4; 83 Del. Laws, c. 48, § 13.

Effect of amendments.
83 Del. Laws, c. 48, effective June 15, 2021, substituted "health-care practitioner" for "physician" in (2)b.

RESEARCH REFERENCES AND PRACTICE AIDS

Delaware Law Reviews.
First State or Follower?: Marijuana in Delaware, 26 Widener L. Rev. 21 (2020).

PART V

MENTAL HEALTH

Chapter
62. The Delaware Suicide Prevention Coalition, §§ 6201 to 6202.

CHAPTER 50
INVOLUNTARY COMMITMENT OF PERSONS WITH MENTAL CONDITIONS; DISCHARGE; PROCEDURE

§ 5002. Determination of mental condition and of procedural compliance as prerequisites to involuntary hospitalization.

NOTES TO DECISIONS

Right to counsel.
Court appointed postconviction counsel under Super. Ct. Crim. R. 61 for a defendant serving a lengthy sentence of total confinement because an alternative highly structured residential setting for long-term effective treatment and supervision of defendant, who had deteriorating mental illness, was unavailable. State v. Thomas, 244 A.3d 197 (Del. Super. Ct. 2020).

§ 5008. Probable cause complaint.

NOTES TO DECISIONS

Firearm ownership.
Where probable cause existed for a gun owner to be involuntarily committed (although later discharged), the Commissioner did not err in entering an order mandating relinquishment of firearms because: (1) there was sufficient evidence the owner had a mental condition and was a danger to that owner's self and others; (2) the relinquishment order was a necessary result of a finding of probable cause; and (3) the State's objective of reducing gun violence and preventing suicide was significant, substantial, important and met an intermediate level of constitutional scrutiny (despite placing a substantial burden on the right to bear arms). State v. Smith, — A.3d —, 2020 Del. Super. LEXIS 2953 (Del. Super. Ct. Aug. 18, 2020).

§ 5009. Probable cause hearing.

NOTES TO DECISIONS

Mental condition.
Where probable cause existed for a gun owner to be involuntarily committed (although later discharged), the Commissioner did not err

in entering an order mandating relinquishment of firearms because: (1) there was sufficient evidence the owner had a mental condition and was a danger to that owner's self and others; (2) the relinquishment order was a necessary result of a finding of probable cause; and (3) the State's objective of reducing gun violence and preventing suicide was significant, substantial, important and met an intermediate level of constitutional scrutiny (despite placing a substantial burden on the right to bear arms). State v. Smith, — A.3d —, 2020 Del. Super. LEXIS 2953 (Del. Super. Ct. Aug. 18, 2020).

§ 5011. Involuntary inpatient commitment hearing and procedure.

NOTES TO DECISIONS

Danger to self or others.

Where probable cause existed for a gun owner to be involuntarily committed (although later discharged), the Commissioner did not err in entering an order mandating relinquishment of firearms because: (1) there was sufficient evidence the owner had a mental condition and was a danger to that owner's self and others; (2) the relinquishment order was a necessary result of a finding of probable cause; and (3) the State's objective of reducing gun violence and preventing suicide was significant, substantial, important and met an intermediate level of constitutional scrutiny (despite placing a substantial burden on the right to bear arms). State v. Smith, — A.3d —, 2020 Del. Super. LEXIS 2953 (Del. Super. Ct. Aug. 18, 2020).

CHAPTER 62
THE DELAWARE SUICIDE PREVENTION COALITION

§ 6201. The Delaware Suicide Prevention Coalition; mission, composition, organization, and reporting.

(a) There is hereby established the Delaware Suicide Prevention Coalition, hereinafter in this chapter referred to as "the Coalition."

(b) The Coalition shall do all of the following:

(1) Review and analyze statistics and patterns related to suicide and suicide attempts.

(2) Consult with the Division of Public Health to determine the prevalence of suicide.

(3) Implement methods to reduce suicide and attempts.

(4) Operate in accordance with the State of Delaware Suicide Prevention Plan.

(5) Manage the Gun Shop Project and comply with § 6202 of this title.

(c) The Coalition shall consist of the following members:

(1) One representative of the Division of Substance Abuse and Mental Health, to be appointed by the Secretary of the Department of Health and Social Services;

(2) One representative of the Division of Prevention and Behavioral Health Services, to be appointed by the Secretary of the Department of Services for Children, Youth and their Families;

(3) One representative of the Division of Public Health, to be appointed by the Secretary of the Department of Health and Social Services;

(4) One representative of the Department of Correction, to be appointed by the Commissioner of the department;

(5) One representative of the Department of Education, to be appointed by the Secretary of the department;

(6) One representative of the Delaware Commission of Veterans Affairs, to be appointed by the Chairman of the Commission;

(7) One representative of the Delaware National Guard, to be appointed by the Adjutant General;

(8) One representative of the Mental Health Association of Delaware, to be appointed by the Executive Director;

(9) One representative of a private psychiatric facility, appointed by the Governor;

(10) One representative to be appointed by the Governor.

(d) The Coalition shall elect a Chairperson from its members.

(e) The Coalition shall meet quarterly, and shall hold additional meetings as deemed necessary by the Chairperson.

(f) The Coalition shall report to the General Assembly and the Governor annually with findings and any pertinent recommendations, including the information required under § 6202(e) of this title.

(g) The Coalition shall be staffed by the Division of Substance Abuse and Mental Health.

History.
80 Del. Laws, c. 410, § 1; 83 Del. Laws, c. 28, § 1.

Effect of amendments.
83 Del. Laws, c. 28, effective June 3, 2021, added "do all of the following" in the introduc-tory paragraph of (b); substituted a period for ", and" at the end of (b)(1) and (b)(2); deleted "shall" preceding "Operate"; added (b)(5); and added "including the information required un-der § 6202(e) of this title" in (f).

§ 6202. The Delaware Gun Shop Project.

(a) The Delaware Gun Shop Project is established, and referred to through-out this chapter as "the Gun Shop Project".

(b) *Definitions.* As used in this chapter:

(1) "Deadly weapon" means as defined under § 222 of Title 11.

(2) "Firearm" means as defined under § 222 of Title 11.

(3) "Gun shop" means a business located in this State that sells firearms, deadly weapons, or related projects, such as ammunition.

(c) The Coalition shall oversee the Gun Shop Project. The Division of Substance Abuse and Mental Health shall provide staff for the Gun Shop Project.

(d) *Educational materials.*

(1) The Gun Shop Project shall develop and create suicide prevention education materials that include all of the following:

a. Information on understanding the various clinical signs, symp-toms, and indicators that might lead an individual to consider suicide.

b. Available suicide prevention resources.

(2) The educational materials under paragraph (d)(1) of this section must be provided through all of the following methods:

a. Written materials, such as a pamphlet, sign, poster, tip sheet, or other medium that meets the requirements of this chapter and the Gun Shop Project determines is appropriate. The Gun Shop Project is not required to provide every type of written material listed in this paragraph.

b. An online training course for deadly weapons dealers licensed under Chapter 9 of Title 24 and other customers.

(3) The Gun Shop Project shall refer to all of the following for guidance in developing and creating the educational materials under this section:

a. Gun shop projects of other states.

b. Industry projects, such as the National Shooting Sports Foun-dation.

c. Other projects or organizations that the Gun Shop Project determines is appropriate.

(4) The Gun Shop Project shall ensure that the written educational materials under paragraph (d)(2)a. of this section are made available for distribution through all of the following:

a. A gun shop, so the gun shop can distribute the materials at the point of purchase to an individual who is purchasing a firearm.

b. Another organization or location that the Gun Shop Project determines is appropriate.

(5) The Gun Shop Project shall ensure that the written educational materials under paragraph (d)(1) of this section are available on the Division of Substance Abuse and Mental Health's website for downloading and access. The Gun Shop Project, the Coalition, or the Division of Substance Abuse and Mental Health are not required to physically deliver the written materials, if the materials are available online for downloading and access.

(e) The Gun Shop Project shall submit a written report as part of the Coalition's annual report under this chapter, with a copy submitted to the Director and the Librarian of the Division of Research of Legislative Council. The annual report must include all of the following:

(1) Progress of the Gun Shop Project.

(2) Number of participating deadly weapons dealers.

(3) Number of training attendees.

History.
83 Del. Laws, c. 28, § 2.

Revisor's note.
This section became effective upon the signature of the Governor on June 3, 2021.

PART VI
SAFETY

CHAPTER 66
FIRE PREVENTION

SUBCHAPTER I
STATE FIRE PREVENTION COMMISSION

§ 6602. State Fire Prevention Commission — Appointment; qualifications; cause for removal; term of office; members to serve without compensation.

(a) The State Fire Prevention Commission shall consist of 7 commissioners as follows: 3 representatives of business and industry to include one from each county to be appointed by the Governor; 3 Delaware volunteer firefighters to include one from each county to be appointed by the Governor; and the immediate past president of the Delaware Volunteer Firefighters' Association.

(b) The Firefighter Commissioners shall be recommended to the Governor by each Delaware Volunteer Firefighters' Association County President of the county in which the expired term or vacancy exists within 60 days prior to the expiration of a Commissioner's term or within 30 days following a vacancy. Each recommendation shall include 3 nominees and any and all necessary information required by the Governor regarding the nominee's qualifications to serve as a Commissioner.

(c) Business and industry Commissioners shall have knowledge in the areas of the Commission's jurisdiction and be employed within an industry regulated by or under the authority of the Commissioner.

(d) Commissioners may be removed by the Governor for continued neglect of the duties required by this chapter, or for refusal to act, misconduct, incompetency, or other sufficient cause. Missing 3 consecutive meetings shall presumptively be neglect of duty for purposes of this section.

(e) Commissioners shall be appointed to serve 4-year terms and shall not serve more than 3 terms to ensure that the terms of no more than 2 Commissioners expire in 1 year.

(f) Commissioners shall serve without compensation but shall be reimbursed for their actual and necessary expenses incurred in the performance of their duties.

(g) No Commissioner, while serving on the State Fire Prevention Commission, shall be an officer of any kind (president/chairperson, president-elect, vice president, secretary, board of directors, or treasurer) of any state or county volunteer firemen's association, including but not limited to, the Delaware Volunteer Firefighter's Association, or any professional board, commission, or trade association, or union representing an industry or service regulated by the State Fire Prevention Commission. No Commissioner shall hold a politically elected or appointed position.

History.

16 Del. C. 1953, § 6601; 49 Del. Laws, c. 335; 52 Del. Laws, c. 5, § 1; 63 Del. Laws, c. 381, § 1; 70 Del. Laws, c. 186, § 1; 77 Del. Laws, c. 444, § 4; 83 Del. Laws, c. 143, § 1.

Effect of amendments.

83 Del. Laws, c. 143, effective Sept. 10, 2021, rewrote (a); added present (b) and (c) and redesignated the remainder of the subsections accordingly; substituted "Commissioners" for "Members" in the first sentence of present (d) and in (f); added the second sentence in present (d); rewrote present (e); and, in present (g), in the first sentence substituted "Commissioner" for "member of the State Fire Prevention Commission", added "of any kind", "board of directors" and "board, commission", and added the final sentence.

§ 6603. State Fire Prevention Commission — Organization and meetings.

(a) The Commission shall elect a Chairperson and Vice Chairperson from among its Commissioners and shall hold regular meetings at least once a month. Special meetings may be called by the Chairperson, by the Vice Chairperson in the absence of the Chairperson, or by 3 Commissioners.

(b) No business shall be transacted by the Commission in the absence of a quorum which shall be 4 Commissioners, 1 of which must be the Chairperson or Vice Chairperson.

History.

16 Del. C. 1953, § 6602; 49 Del. Laws, c. 335; 52 Del. Laws, c. 5, § 1; 63 Del. Laws, c. 381, § 2; 70 Del. Laws, c. 186, § 1; 77 Del. Laws, c. 444, § 4; 83 Del. Laws, c. 143, § 2.

Effect of amendments.

83 Del. Laws, c. 143, effective Sept. 10, 2021, substituted "Commission" for "State Fire Prevention Commission" in the first sentence of (a) and in (b); substituted "elect" for "select" in the first sentence of (a); substituted "Commissioners" for "members" in the first sentence of (a) and in (b) and for "members of the State Fire Prevention Commission" in the second sen-

tence of (a).

§ 6604. State Fire Prevention Commission — Powers and duties.

The State Fire Prevention Commission shall have authority to:

(1) Formulate rules and regulations, with appropriate notice to those affected; all rules and regulations shall be promulgated in accordance with the procedures specified in the Administrative Procedures Act (Chapter 101 of Title 29) of this State.

a. Such regulations shall be in accordance with standard safe practice as embodied in widely recognized standards of good practice for fire prevention and fire protection and shall have the force and effect of law in the several counties, cities and political subdivisions of the State. Whenever such regulations and amendments require the issuance of permits or licenses, the State Fire Prevention Commission is authorized to issue such permits or licenses according to the provisions and schedules in § 6612 of this title. Such regulations and amendments shall not apply to existing installations, plants or equipment unless the State Fire Prevention Commission has duly found that the continuation thereof constitutes a hazard so inimicable to the public welfare and safety as to require correction; nor shall such regulations and amendments limit or prohibit the shipment, transportation, handling or storage incident to transportation of any explosive, combustible or other dangerous article in solid, liquid or gas form by rail, water or highway, when such articles are in conformity with regulations of the Interstate Commerce Commission; nor shall such regulations, insofar as they purport to prohibit the sale, purchase or domestic use of gasoline, kerosene or other fuel burning home appliances for heating or cooking apply to any person whose personal faith or belief prevents the use of any alternative heating or cooking appliance recommended by the State Fire Prevention Commission, the burden of proof is upon the person claiming relief from such regulation. In their interpretation and application the regulations promulgated under this chapter shall be held to be the minimum requirements for the safeguarding of life and property from the hazards of fire and explosion. Whenever the provisions of any other statute or local regulation are more stringent or impose higher standards than are required by any regulations promulgated under this chapter, such statute or local regulation shall govern, provided they are not inconsistent with the state Code and are not contrary to recognized standards and good engineering practices.

b. Promulgate regulations consistent with the following language: The State Fire Marshal shall require that all persons involved in the inspection and testing of water-based fire protection systems maintain current certification in the National Institute for Certification in Engineering Technologies (NICET II) "Inspection and Testing of Water-based Systems" certification program or a substantially similar and equivalent course of instruction, as determined by the State Fire Marshal, as a condition of permit renewal after July 1, 2010.

c. Promulgate regulations consistent with the following language: The State Fire Marshal shall require that persons involved in the inspection and testing of water-based fire protection systems shall complete 16 contact hours of continuing education or similar course of instruction during each biennial period of renewal. Any and all continuing education requirements completed pursuant to paragraph

(1)b. of this section may be used to meet the continuing education requirements as called for under this section.

(2) Create a State Fire Prevention Commission Executive Director. The position will be exempt and will be effective October 10, 2021. The Executive Director shall provide the Commission all of the following:

    a. Reports and data necessary to enable the Commission to perform its duties under this title.

    b. Coordination and implementation of all requirements for Commission meetings, including posting meeting notices and minutes.

    c. Necessary reports and data in conjunction with the Commissions responsibilities.

    d. Support to Commission members in necessary training and preparation to fulfill their roles and responsibilities.

    e. Service as the Commission's point of contact.

    f. Production and posting of minutes for each Commission meeting.

    g. Oversight of the day-to-day operations of the agency.

    h. Management of the support staff of the agency.

(3) Appoint a person qualified by that person's previous training and experience in endeavors similar to those herein prescribed as State Fire Marshal.

(4) Appoint a person qualified by that person's previous training and experience in endeavors similar to those described herein as the State Fire School Director.

(5) Conduct hearings and issue orders in accordance with procedures established pursuant to this chapter and Chapter 101 of Title 29. Where such provisions conflict with this chapter, this chapter shall govern.

(6) Issue subpoenas for named respondents, witnesses, documents, physical evidence or any other source of evidence needed during the investigation of a complaint made under this chapter and/or for a public hearing on the complaint or for an appeal to the State Fire Prevention Commission from an order or decision of the State Fire Marshal. If the party or person subpoenaed fails to comply, the State Fire Prevention Commission may compel compliance with said subpoena by filing a motion to compel in the Superior Court which shall have jurisdiction. The Superior Court may order costs, attorney's fees and/or a civil fine not to exceed $1,000 if the motion to compel is granted.

(7) Acquire any real or personal property by purchase, gift or donation and have water rights.

(8) Make contracts and execute instruments necessary or convenient.

(9) Undertake by contract or contracts, or by its own agent and employees, and otherwise than by contract, any project or projects, and operate and maintain such projects.

(10) Accept grants of money or materials or property of any kind from a federal agency, private agency, county, city, town, corporation, partnership or individual upon such terms and conditions as the grantor may impose.

(11) Impose any civil penalty or fine authorized under this chapter.

(12) Impose reasonable fees for all certifications issued by the Commission under this chapter or Chapter 67 of this title. All fees issued under this section must be based on actual costs, unless otherwise specifically authorized by other provisions of this title.

(13) Perform all acts and do all things necessary or convenient to carry out the power granted herein.

(14) Administer the volunteer firefighter tuition reimbursement program pursuant to § 3467 of Title 14.

History.
16 Del. C. 1953, §§ 6603-6604; 49 Del. Laws, c. 335; 50 Del. Laws, c. 469, § 1; 52 Del. Laws, c. 5, § 1; 57 Del. Laws, c. 672; 57 Del. Laws, c. 727; 63 Del. Laws, c. 381, § 3; 68 Del. Laws, c. 408, § 1; 76 Del. Laws, c. 330, §§ 1-3; 77 Del. Laws, c. 444, § 4; 83 Del. Laws, c. 143, § 3; 83 Del. Laws, c. 181, § 2.

Effect of amendments.
83 Del. Laws, c. 143, effective Sept. 10, 2021, added present (2), (11) and (12) and redesignated the remaining and intervening paragraphs accordingly.
83 Del. Laws, c. 181, effective September 17, 2021, added (a)(14).

§ 6605. State Fire Prevention Commission Advisory Board.

History.
77 Del. Laws, c. 444, § 4; repealed by 83 Del. Laws, c. 143, § 4, effective Sept. 10, 2021.

§ 6607. Power of State Fire Prevention Commission to authorize new fire companies or substations; resolve boundary disputes; and prohibit cessation of necessary fire protection services.

(a) The State Fire Prevention Commission, with the advice of the Advisory Board set forth in § 6605 [repealed] of this title, is empowered to promulgate, amend and repeal regulations related to the exercise of State Fire Prevention Commission powers and responsibilities defined in this section.

(1) Except as provided in subsection (c) of this section, the State Fire Prevention Commission shall determine whether any new fire companies or substations shall be authorized in any part of the State. In making such determination the State Fire Prevention Commission shall consider among other things the ability, financial or otherwise, of the company seeking authorization to maintain an effective fire company and the fire protection needs of the area involved. The State Fire Prevention Commission, however, shall not authorize the establishment of a new fire company main station or substation within 4 miles of an existing fire company's main station or substation unless the State Fire Prevention Commission determines that an existing company is not reasonably equipped, manned, organized, financed or disciplined to deliver, or is not actually delivering, adequate fire protection in accordance with recognized safety standards to the area it serves.

(2) Except as provided in subsection (c) of this section, the State Fire Prevention Commission shall have authority to prohibit the suspension of fire protection services in this State by any fire company or substation thereof when the ability, financial or otherwise, of the company or substation seeking to suspend such service does not warrant such suspension. In making this determination the State Fire Prevention Commission shall consider, among other things, the fire protection needs of the area involved, whether the company or substation seeking to suspend fire protection services is inadequately financed, equipped, manned, organized or disciplined, and whether a new fire company should be authorized to deliver fire protection services to the area.

(3) The State Fire Prevention Commission shall have authority, acting on behalf of the State, to enter into agreements to confirm the established geographical boundaries of areas served by all existing fire companies in the State and to resolve boundary disputes between or among such fire companies.

(4) The State Fire Prevention Commission shall have authority to enter binding orders resolving boundary disputes between fire companies.

(b) The Delaware Volunteer Firefighters' Association shall designate from its members a 9-member advisory board to advise and make recommendations to the State Fire Prevention Commission in connection with the Commission's responsibilities under this section. The Delaware Volunteer Firefighter's Advisory Board shall consist of the President, First Vice-President, Second Vice-President and the 7 members of the Board of Directors, excluding the immediate past President who serves as a Commissioner, of the Delaware Volunteer Firefighters' Association.

(c) Paragraphs (a)(1) and (2) of this section shall not be applied with respect to any fire company in municipalities with a population greater than 50,000 as established in the official 1980 federal census.

History.
16 Del. C. 1953, § 6619; 55 Del. Laws, c. 149; 63 Del. Laws, c. 381, § 4; 68 Del. Laws, c. 437, § 1; 70 Del. Laws, c. 186, § 1; 77 Del. Laws, c. 378, § 1; 77 Del. Laws, c. 444, § 4; 83 Del. Laws, c. 143, § 4.

Revisor's Notes
Based upon changes contained in 83 Del. Laws, c. 143, § 4, effective Sept. 10, 2021, "[repealed]" was inserted following "§ 6605" in the introductory paragraph of (a).

CHAPTER 68
EXEMPTIONS FROM CIVIL LIABILITY

SUBCHAPTER III
IMMUNITY FOR DONATED FOOD

Revisor's note.
83 Del. Laws, c. 196, §§ 2 and 3, effective Sept. 17, 2021, revised this subchapter by substituting "Donated Food" for "Food Donors" in the subchapter heading, repealing former § 6820 of this title and adding §§ 6821 to 6824 of this title.

§ 6820. Food donors exempt from liability.

History.
63 Del. Laws, c. 263, § 1; repealed by 83 Del. Laws, c. 196, § 2, effective Sept. 17, 2021.

§ 6821. Definitions.

For purposes of this subchapter:

(1) "Food" means any raw, cooked, processed, or prepared edible substance, ice, beverage, or ingredient used or intended to be used in whole or part for human consumption that is apparently fit for human consumption. "Food" includes nonperishable food, perishable food, and wild game.

(2) "Gleaner" means a person who gleans an agricultural crop that has been donated by the owner of the agricultural crop.

(3) "Gleans" or "gleaned" means to gather an agricultural crop leftover after a harvest.

(4) "Nonperishable food" means any food that has been commercially processed, prepared, and packaged for human consumption and that is intended to remain fit for human consumption without refrigeration for a reasonable length of time.

(5) "Nonprofit organization" means an incorporated or unincorporated entity that is operating for religious, charitable, or educational purposes and does not provide net earnings to, or operate in any other way that inures to the benefit of, any officer, employee, or shareholder of the entity.

(6) "Perishable food" means any food that may spoil or otherwise

become unfit for human consumption because of its nature, type, or physical condition. "Perishable food" includes all of the following:

    a. Fresh and processed meats, poultry, seafood, dairy products, or bakery products.

    b. Eggs in the shell.

    c. Fresh fruits and vegetables.

(7) "Person" means an individual, corporation, business trust, estate trust, partnership, limited liability company, association, joint venture, or any other legal or commercial entity. "Person" does not include a government; governmental subdivision, agency, or instrumentality; or a public corporation.

(8) "State agency" means any office, department, board, commission, committee, court, school district, board of education, or other instrumentality of the government of this State existing by virtue of an act of the General Assembly or of the Constitution of this State.

(9) "Wild game" means any of the following that are legally taken under the laws of this State:

    a. Game animals under § 701 of Title 7.

    b. Game birds under § 702 of Title 7.

    c. Game fish under § 906 of Title 7.

    d. Shellfish under § 1901 of Title 7.

History.
83 Del. Laws, c. 196, § 3.

§ 6822. Immunity of a person or gleaner from liability.

(a) A person or gleaner who, in good faith, donates food for ultimate distribution without charge by a nonprofit organization or a state agency is not liable for civil damages or criminal penalties resulting from the nature, age, condition, or packaging of the donated food, unless an injury or death is caused by the gross negligence, recklessness, or intentional misconduct of the person or gleaner.

(b) A person who, in good faith, provides services related to the processing of wild game that is donated to a nonprofit organization or a state agency for ultimate distribution without charge by the nonprofit organization or the state agency is not liable for civil damages or criminal penalties resulting from the nature, age, condition, or packaging of the donated food, unless an injury or death is caused by the gross negligence, recklessness, or intentional misconduct of the person.

History.
83 Del. Laws, c. 196, § 3.

§ 6823. Immunity of a nonprofit organization from liability.

A nonprofit organization that, in good faith, accepts donated food for ultimate distribution without charge is not liable for civil damages or criminal penalties resulting from the nature, age, condition, or packaging of the donated food, unless an injury or death is caused by the gross negligence, recklessness, or intentional misconduct of the nonprofit organization.

History.
83 Del. Laws, c. 196, § 3.

§ 6824. Authority of the Division of Public Health and the Department of Agriculture.

This subchapter does not restrict or preempt the authority granted to the Division of Public Health or the Department of Agriculture by other law to inspect, regulate, or ban food.

History.
83 Del. Laws, c. 196, § 3.

CHAPTER 72
LIQUEFIED PETROLEUM GAS CONTAINERS

Sec.
7204. Arrest for violation [Repealed].

§ 7204. Arrest for violation.

History.   70 Del. Laws, c. 186, § 1; repealed by 83 Del.
   16 Del. C. 1953, § 7204; 58 Del. Laws, c. 95;   Laws, c. 202, § 1, effective Sept. 17, 2021.

CHAPTER 74
RADIATION CONTROL

Sec.
7404. Authority on Radiation Protection.

§ 7404. Authority on Radiation Protection.

(a) There is created an Authority on Radiation Protection which shall be governed in accordance with Authority bylaws, established to ensure integrity, accountability, and transparency regarding decisions of the Authority which impact the citizens of Delaware. The Authority shall consist of the following members:

(1) The Secretary of the Department of Health and Social Services or a designee appointed by the Secretary.

(2) The Secretary of the Department of Natural Resources and Environmental Control or a designee appointed by the Secretary.

(3) Thirteen members, appointed by the Governor to include:

a. A Delaware licensed doctor of medicine or osteopathy.

b. A Delaware licensed dentist.

c. A Delaware licensed doctor of medicine or osteopathy specializing in radiology.

d. A Delaware licensed veterinarian.

e. A Delaware certified radiation technologist or technician.

f. A Delaware licensed pharmacist.

g. Two qualified members from the staff or faculty of different Delaware institutions of higher education.

h. Two nonmedical members from industry.

i. Three members of the public, 1 representing each county, who need not fall into any of the other categories for membership on the Authority, but who have an interest in radiation protection. Each public member shall have had training or experience in 1 or more of the following fields: radiology, nuclear medicine, radiation oncology, radiation physics, health physics, or related sciences.

(b) Authority members appointed by the Governor shall be appointed for a term of 3 years. Each Authority member shall hold over after the expiration of the member's term until the member's successor has been appointed and has taken office. Vacancies shall be filled for the unexpired term. The Governor may remove a member for gross inefficiency, misfeasance, nonfeasance, malfeasance, or neglect of duty in office. If an appointed member fails to attend 3 successive meetings of the Authority without just cause, that member's position may be deemed vacant, and the Governor may appoint a replacement.

(c) The Secretary of Health and Social Services or the Secretary's duly authorized designee shall be Secretary of the Authority, and shall provide staffing and facilities required to enable the Office of Radiation Control to deliver core services as defined by the Delaware Radiation Control Regulations, as promulgated or amended by the Authority. The Office of Radiation Control in the Department of Health and Social Services shall be the administrative agent for the Authority. The Office of Radiation Control in the Department of Health and Social Services shall make such inspections, conduct such investigations, collect fees or administrative penalties established or levied by the Authority, administer such revenue through the General Fund, and do such other acts as may be necessary to carry out this chapter within the limits of the appropriation made for this purpose. The administrative agent shall have all of the powers conferred by law upon the Authority except adopting the rules and regulations provided for in this chapter, subject, however, to the general direction of the Authority.

(d) [Repealed.]

(e) The Authority shall elect a Chairperson to serve for at least 1 year from those members appointed by the Governor. The Chairperson shall lead biennial review of the Authority bylaws, chair public hearings and issue approval of regulations amended or promulgated by the Authority. A majority of the Authority shall constitute a quorum to transact its business. Counting for quorum does not include member positions that are vacant.

(f) The Authority shall hold at least 4 regular meetings each calendar year and such special meetings as it deems necessary.

(g) The Authority shall establish and provide biennial review of the Authority bylaws.

(h) The Authority shall review policies and programs relating to control of ionizing radiation and make recommendations thereon to the agencies of the State.

(i) The Authority may aid the Department of Health and Social Services in the employment, training of and prescribing of the power and duties of such individuals as may be necessary to carry out this chapter.

History.
16 Del. C. 1953, § 7404; 56 Del. Laws, c. 266, § 1; 57 Del. Laws, c. 591, §§ 16, 17; 60 Del. Laws, c. 698, § 2; 64 Del. Laws, c. 302, §§ 1, 2; 67 Del. Laws, c. 192, § 5; 69 Del. Laws, c. 67, § 2; 70 Del. Laws, c. 149, § 198; 70 Del. Laws, c. 186, § 1; 76 Del. Laws, c. 249, § 2; 78 Del. Laws, c. 336, § 1; 83 Del. Laws, c. 99, § 1.

Effect of amendments.
83 Del. Laws, c. 99, effective July 30, 2021,
added a comma following "accountability" in the first sentence of the introductory paragraph of (a); substituted "a designee appointed by the Secretary" for "the Secretary's duly authorized designee" in (a)(1) and (2); rewrote (a)(3); added the second and third sentences in (b); and added the final sentence in (e).

PART XI

DELAWARE HEALTH CARE COMMISSION

Chapter
99. Delaware Health Care Commission, §§ 9901 to 9943.

CHAPTER 99

DELAWARE HEALTH CARE COMMISSION

SUBCHAPTER I
FINDINGS, ORGANIZATION AND DUTIES OF COMMISSION

§ 9903. Duties and authority of the Commission.

(a) The Commission shall have the authority to hire staff, contract for consulting services, conduct any technical and/or actuarial studies which it deems to be necessary to support its work, and to publish reports as required in order to accomplish its purposes in accordance with the provisions of this chapter.

(b) As relates to the pilot health access projects, the Commission is expressly authorized to develop such programs in consultation with the appropriate public and private entities; to assign implementation to the appropriate state agency; to monitor and oversee program progress and to ensure that each pilot program is evaluated by an outside, independent evaluator after no more than 2 years of operations.

(c) The Commission shall be responsible for the administration of the Delaware Institute of Medical Education and Research (DIMER), which shall serve as an advisory board to the Commission, and the Chair of the Health Care Commission shall appoint the Chair of DIMER. The Commission shall have such other duties and authorities with respect to DIMER which are necessary to carry out the intent of the General Assembly as expressed in this chapter.

(d) The Commission shall be responsible for the administration of the Delaware Institute for Dental Education and Research (DIDER), which shall serve as an advisory board to the Commission. The Commission shall have such other duties and authorities with respect to DIDER which are necessary to carry out the intent of the General Assembly as expressed in this chapter.

(e) Other functions which the Commission may undertake include:

(1) Serve as the policy body to advise the Governor and General Assembly on strategies to promoting affordable quality health care to all Delawareans and assuring policies are in place to maintain an optimal health-care environment. Analyze all aspects of the health-care landscape, including, but not limited to, population and health outcomes, service delivery infrastructure, quality, costs, accessibility, utilization, insurance coverage and financing;

(2) Convene, as necessary, public and private stakeholders to identify, analyze and address health policy issues and build consensus around workable solutions. Serve as the coordinating entity between the public and private sectors to implement emerging health initiatives at the federal, state and local levels;

(3) Function in such a way that fosters creative thinking and problem solving across state agency lines and across the public and private sectors;

(4) Ensure that data to support the activities of the Commission are available and accessible;

(5) Monitor cost trends in order to recommend methods to reduce and control health-care costs for public programs and in conjunction with the private sector;

(6) Coordinate efforts with the Health Resources Board and any other entities the Commission identifies as essential to carry out its mission;

(7) Review and recommend changes to state health insurance laws and regulations (in conjunction with the Insurance Commissioner) to promote efficiency, equity and affordability in health insurance premiums;

(8) Coordinate and collaborate with the Delaware Health Information Network [DHIN] to assure that the use of health information technology and health information exchange results in cost effective, quality health care for all Delawareans. Consult with DHIN Board of Directors and staff on implementation of health information technology in Delaware and call upon the DHIN to assist in conducting pilot programs, providing technical support, capabilities and expertise, and/or conducting research necessary to achieve the Commission's mission;

(9) Oversee efforts to assure that Delaware has an adequate supply and distribution of health-care professionals to provide quality care to all Delawareans in consultation with DIMER, DIDER and other institutions, bodies or agencies as necessary;

(10) Monitor access to health-care programs and make recommendations for changes where necessary; and

(11) Conduct other activities it considers necessary to carry out the intent of the General Assembly as expressed in this chapter.

(f) The Commission must collaborate with the Primary Care Reform Collaborative to develop annual recommendations that will strengthen the primary care system in Delaware. The scope of the recommendations must include all of the following:

(1) Payment reform.

(2) Value-based care.

(3) Workforce and recruitment.

(4) Directing resources to support and expand primary care access.

(5) Increasing integrated care, including for women's and behavioral health.

(6) Evaluation of system-wide investments into primary care, using claims data obtained from the Delaware Health Care Claims Database.

(g) The Commission shall establish the Delaware Health Insurance Individual Market Stabilization Reinsurance Program & Fund and the Commission shall have all of the following responsibilities.

(1) To provide reinsurance to carriers that offer individual health benefit plans in the State.

(2) Said reinsurance must meet the requirements of a waiver approved under § 1332 of the Affordable Care Act [42 U.S.C. § 18052].

(3) The reinsurance fund must operate under the supervision and control of the Commission, and is funded pursuant to § 8703 of Title 18.

(h) For purposes of funding and administering the reinsurance program outlined in subsection (g) of this section, the fund shall be made up of all of the following:

(1) Any pass-through funds received from the federal government under a waiver approved under § 1332 of the Affordable Care Act [42 U.S.C. § 18052].

(2) Any funds designated by the federal government to provide reinsurance to carriers that offer individual health benefit plans in the State.

(3) Any funds designated by the State pursuant to § 8703 of Title 18 to provide reinsurance to carriers that offer individual health benefit plans in the State.

(i) To carry out its responsibilities in administering the program outlined in subsection (g) of this section and funded pursuant to subsection (h) of this section, the Commission shall promulgate regulations for purposes of all of the following:

(1) Establishing procedures for the handling and accounting of program assets and moneys, as well as for an annual fiscal reporting to the Commission, Insurance Commissioner and General Assembly.

(2) Annually establishing procedures and parameters for reinsuring risks, including all of the following:

    a. An attachment point.

    b. A coinsurance rate.

    c. A coinsurance cap.

(3) Establishing procedures and standards for carriers to submit claims to be reinsured under the program.

(4) Establishing procedures for selecting an administering contractor and setting forth the power and duties of the administering contractor.

(5) Establishing procedures for quarterly reporting or annual reporting, or both, of data under the Affordable Care Act's § 1332 [42 U.S.C. § 18052] waiver to demonstrate that the waiver remains in compliance with the scope of coverage, affordability, comprehensiveness and deficit requirements.

(6) Establishing procedures for providing each year the actual second-lowest cost Silver Plan premium under the Affordable Care Act's § 1332 [42 U.S.C. § 18052] waiver and an estimate of the premium as it would have been without the waiver.

(7) Providing for any additional matters necessary for the implementation and administration of the reinsurance program.

(8) Submitting an annual report to the Governor and General Assembly, in consultation with the Department of Health and Social Services and the Department of Insurance.

(j) The Commission shall be responsible for the administration of a Health Care Provider Loan Repayment Program (HCPLRP). The HCPLRP must be administered consistent with all of the following guidelines:

(1) Subject to the appropriation of sufficient funds, the Commission may award education loan repayment grants to qualifying clinicians of up to $50,000 per year for a maximum of 4 years.

(2) Eligible sites may apply to the Commission on behalf of their affiliated, qualifying clinicians for education loan repayment grants from the HCPLRP. Sites eligible to apply for education loan repayment grants on behalf of their qualifying clinicians include all of the following sites located in underserved areas or areas of need:

    a. Hospital primary care practices.

    b. Private practices.

    c. Federally-qualified health centers.

    d. Community outpatient facilities.

    e. Community mental health facilities.

    f. Free medical clinics.

(3) Health care provider loan repayment grants may only be awarded by the Commission to sites that accept Medicare and Medicaid participants, and may not include concierge practices. To be eligible for a health care provider loan repayment grant, private practice sites must participate in the Voluntary Initiative Program administered by the Department of Health and Social Services' Health Care Connection. Health care provider loan repayment grants to hospital sites must be subject to a dollar-for-dollar match by the applicant hospital.

(4) The award of health care provider loan repayment grants must be limited to the recruitment and retention of new primary care providers in ambulatory and outpatient settings. For purposes of this paragraph, a new primary care provider means any of the following providers who have completed graduate education within 6 months of the application for a health care provider loan repayment grant being submitted:

a. Physicians practicing family medicine (including osteopathic general practice), internal medicine, pediatrics, obstetrics/gynecology, geriatrics, and psychiatry.

b. Nurse practitioners, certified nurse midwives, clinical nurse specialists, and physicians assistants practicing adult medicine, family medicine, pediatrics, psychiatry/mental health, geriatrics, and women's health.

(5) The Commission may grant priority consideration to applications submitted on behalf of primary care clinicians that are DIMER-participating students or participants in Delaware-based residency programs and may annually spend up to $150,000 on marketing and infrastructure to attract clinicians to apply to the HCPLRP.

(6) The Commission shall issue an annual report detailing the number of clinicians applying for and awarded health care provider loan repayment grants, including information regarding the number of applicants and grant recipients by practice area and site location.

History.
67 Del. Laws, c. 334, § 1; 70 Del. Laws, c. 186, § 1; 70 Del. Laws, c. 516, § 2; 73 Del. Laws, c. 4, § 2; 78 Del. Laws, c. 296, § 3; 81 Del. Laws, c. 392, § 1; 82 Del. Laws, c. 61, § 1; 83 Del. Laws, c. 121, § 1.

Revisor's note.
Section 2 of 83 Del. Laws, c. 121, provided: "Notwithstanding any provision of this act or law to the contrary, disbursement of education loan repayment grants from the Health Care Provider Loan Repayment Program shall be contingent upon an initial, one-time contribution to the program, in an amount equal to the Fiscal Year 22 appropriation of State funds up to a maximum of $1 million, from Delaware health insurers."

Effect of amendments.
83 Del. Laws, c. 121, effective Aug. 10, 2021, added (j).

PART XIII

DELAWARE HEALTH INFORMATION NETWORK

CHAPTER 103

DELAWARE HEALTH INFORMATION NETWORK

SUBCHAPTER I

PURPOSE, POWERS, AND DUTIES; OTHER GOVERNING PROVISIONS OF THE DELAWARE HEALTH INFORMATION NETWORK

Revisor's note.

83 Del. Laws, c. 137, § 1, effective Jan. 1, 2022, substituted "Powers, and Duties;" for "Power and Duties, and" in the subchapter heading.

Section 15 of 83 Del. Laws, c. 137, provided: "This act takes effect on January 1 following its enactment into law." This act was signed by the Governor on Sept. 10, 2021, and became effective on Jan. 1, 2022.

§ 10301. Purpose.

(a) The purpose of this chapter is to create the Delaware Health Information Network, a not-for-profit body both politic and corporate, to serve as a public instrumentality that has the right, obligation, privilege, and purpose to promote the design, implementation, operation, and maintenance of facilities for public and private use of health care information in the State. DHIN is the State's sanctioned provider of health information exchange services.

(b) DHIN is a public-private partnership for the benefit of all citizens of this State.

(c) DHIN shall ensure the privacy of patient health-care information.

History.

71 Del. Laws, c. 177, § 1; 77 Del. Laws, c. 368, §§ 1, 16; 80 Del. Laws, c. 329, §§ 1, 2; 83 Del. Laws, c. 137, § 2.

Revisor's note.

Section 15 of 83 Del. Laws, c. 137, provided: "This act takes effect on January 1 following its enactment into law." This act was signed by the Governor on Sept. 10, 2021, and became effective on Jan. 1, 2022.

Effect of amendments.

83 Del. Laws, c. 137, effective Jan. 1, 2022, rewrote the first sentence in (a); substituted "DHIN is" for "The DHIN shall be" in the second sentence of (a) and for "It is intended that the DHIN be" in (b); and deleted "The" from the beginning of (c).

§ 10302. Delaware Health Information Network Board of Directors.

(a) A Board of Directors manages and operates DHIN. Board membership must include individuals with various business, technology, and healthcare industry skills who are committed to managing DHIN in an efficient, effective, and competitive manner. Board membership is comprised as follows:

(1) The Director of the Office of Management and Budget or the Director's designee.

(2) The Chief Information Officer of the Department of Technology and Information or the Chief Information Officer's designee.

(3) The Secretary of the Department of Health and Social Services or the Secretary's designee.

(4) The Controller General or the Controller General's designee.

(5) Fifteen members are appointed by the Governor. The Board, Delaware Healthcare Association, Medical Society of Delaware, Delaware State Chamber of Commerce, and other interested organizations may make nonbinding recommendations to the Governor for appointments to the Board. The Governor's appointments are as follows:

    a. Six general members, including at least 1 individual who represents the interests of medical consumers and at least 3 individuals who have experience or expertise in the health-care industry.

    b. Three members who represent a hospital or health system.

    c. Three members who represent physicians.

    d. One member who represents a business or employer.

    e. Two members who represent a health insurer or health plan.

(6)a. Board members shall elect the Board chair from among its members. The chair serves as chair for a 3-year term.

b. Each member serves a 3-year term, with each member continuing to serve beyond the term until a successor is appointed.

c. The Governor may suspend or remove a member upon the recommendation from the Board or for misfeasance, malfeasance, nonfeasance, or neglect of duty. A member is deemed in neglect of duty if the member is absent from 3 consecutive, regular Board meetings or attends less than 50% of Board meetings in a calendar year. The Governor may consider the member to have resigned and accept the member's resignation.

(b) A state officer or employee appointed to the Board or serving in any other capacity for the Board is not deemed to have resigned from public office or employment by reason of the appointment to or service for the Board.

(c) The number of members needed to be present at a Board meeting to have a quorum and conduct official business is a majority of members. Counting for quorum does not include member positions that are vacant.

History.
71 Del. Laws, c. 177, § 1; 70 Del. Laws, c. 186, § 1; 75 Del. Laws, c. 88, § 21(8); 75 Del. Laws, c. 389, § 1; 77 Del. Laws, c. 368, §§ 2-5, 16; 80 Del. Laws, c. 329, § 1; 83 Del. Laws, c. 137, § 3.

Revisor's note.
Section 15 of 83 Del. Laws, c. 137, provided: "This act takes effect on January 1 following its enactment into law." This act was signed by the Governor on Sept. 10, 2021, and became effective on Jan. 1, 2022.

Effect of amendments.
83 Del. Laws, c. 137, effective Jan. 1, 2022, in the section heading, deleted "Creation of" from the beginning and added "Board of Directors"; and rewrote the section.

§ 10303. Powers and duties.

(a) DHIN has the power and duty to do all of the following:

(1) Develop and maintain a community-based health information network to facilitate communication of patient clinical and financial information, designed to do all of the following:

a. Promote more efficient and effective communication among multiple health care providers, including hospitals, physicians, payers, employers, pharmacies, laboratories, and other health care entities.

b. Create efficiencies in health-care costs by eliminating redundancy in data capture and storage and reducing administrative, billing, and data collection costs.

c. Create the ability to monitor community health status.

d. Provide reliable information to health-care consumers and purchasers regarding the quality and cost-effectiveness of health care, health plans, and health-care providers.

(2) Develop or design other initiatives in furtherance of DHIN's purpose.

(3) Report and make recommendations to the Governor and General Assembly.

(4) Adopt bylaws to govern all of the following:

a. The conduct of DHIN's affairs.

b. The carrying out and discharge of DHIN's powers, duties, and functions functions.

c. Adopt policies as appropriate to carry out and discharge DHIN's powers, duties, and functions; to sue, but not be sued; to enter into contracts and agreements; and to plan, control facilities and DHIN's real and personal property as DHIN may deem necessary, convenient, or desirable without application of Chapters 59, 69, or 70 of Title 29.

(5) All prior regulations and rules promulgated by the Delaware Health Care Commission regarding DHIN remain in full force and effect until DHIN replaces the regulations and rules with bylaws or policies.

(6) A provision pertaining to conflicts of interest and that Board members, staff, committee members, and others conducting business or associated with DHIN are required to sign conflict of interest statements.

(7) To have and exercise all powers available to a corporation organized under Chapter 1 of Title 8, the Delaware General Corporation Law.

(8) To employ personnel and provide benefits necessary to carry out DHIN's functions and to retain by contract engineers, advisors, and other providers of advice, counsel, and services which it deems advisable or necessary in the exercise of DHIN's purposes and powers and upon the terms DHIN deems appropriate.

(9) To exercise power and authority regarding DHIN's operation, development, and maintenance.

(10) To do all acts and things necessary or convenient to carry out DHIN's functions, including having the authority to open and operate separate bank accounts in DHIN's name.

(11) To collect, receive, hold, and disburse funds related to DHIN's operations, including user fees that DHIN sets.

(12) Implement and operate a statewide integrated health information network to enable communication of clinical health, financial health, and other information, and other related functions that the Board deems necessary.

(13) Promote efficient and effective communication among Delaware healthcare providers and stakeholders including hospitals, physicians, state agencies, payers, employers, and laboratories.

(14) Promote efficiencies in the healthcare delivery system.

(15) Provide a reliable health information exchange to authorized users.

(16) Work with governments or other states to integrate into or with DHIN or assist governments or other states in providing regional integrated health information systems.

(17) Work towards improving the quality of health care and the ability to monitor community health status and facilitate health promotions by providing immediate and current outcome, treatment, and cost data and related information so that patients, providers, and payers can make informed and timely decisions about health care.

(18) Submit an annual report to the Governor and the General Assembly setting forth in detail DHIN's operations and transactions, including an annual audit of DHIN's financial books and accounts, to be conducted by a firm of independent certified public accountants that the Auditor of Accounts and the Director of the Office of Management and Budget agree upon.

(19) Develop and maintain a process to enable a hospital to record in the patient's electronic health record contained in DHIN the patient's designation of a lay caregiver and the lay caregiver's contact information, as required by § 3002J(b) of this title, and if the hospital attempted to or did interface with the lay caregiver, as required by § 3004J(b) of this title.

(20) Develop, maintain, and administer the Delaware Health Care Claims Database under subchapter II of this chapter.

(21) Perform any and all other activities in furtherance of this section.

(b) To carry out the duties listed in this section, DHIN is granted all incidental powers, without limitation, including the powers to do all of the following:

(1) Contract with sufficient third parties or employ nonstate employees, without applications of the provisions of Chapter 59, 69, or 70 of Title 29 respectively.

(2) Establish a nonappropriated special funds account in DHIN's budget to receive gifts and donations.

(3) Establish reasonable fees or charges for provision of DHIN's services to nonparticipant third parties.

(4) Sell or license copyrighted or patented intellectual property.

History.
71 Del. Laws, c. 177, § 1; 77 Del. Laws, c. 368, §§ 6-8, 16; 80 Del. Laws, c. 329, §§ 1, 3; 80 Del. Laws, c. 347, § 3; 83 Del. Laws, c. 137, § 4.

Revisor's note.
Section 15 of 83 Del. Laws, c. 137, provided: "This act takes effect on January 1 following its enactment into law." This act was signed by the Governor on Sept. 10, 2021, and became effective on Jan. 1, 2022.

Effect of amendments.
83 Del. Laws, c. 137, effective Jan. 1, 2022, rewrote the introductory paragraph of (a); added "do all of the following" in the introductory paragraph of (a)(1); deleted "but not limited to" following "including" in (a)(1)a.; added a comma following "laboratories" and "pharmacies" in (a)(1)a., following "billing" in (a)(1)b., following "plans" in (a)(1)d., following "committee members" in (a)(6), following "counsel" in (a)(8), following "treatment" and following "providers" in (a)(17); substituted a period for a semicolon at the end of (a)(1)a., (a)(1)b., (a)(1)d., (a)(2), (a)(3), (a)(5)-(a)(8), (a)(15), (a)(17), (a)(19) and (b)(1) and (b)(2) and for "; and" at the end of (a)(1)c., (a)(20) and (b)(3); substituted "DHIN's" for "its" in (a)(2); rewrote (a)(4); in (a)(5), deleted "the" preceding "DHIN" in two places "shall" preceding "remain" and "aforementioned" preceding "regulations", and substituted "or" for "and/or" near the end; in (a)(6), deleted "The bylaws shall include" from the beginning and substituted "are" for "shall be"; in (a)(7), deleted "any and" following "exercise" and substituted "under" for "pursuant to" ; in (a)(8), deleted "such" preceding "personnel" and preceding "benefits", substituted "DHIN's" for "its" in two places, "the" for "such" preceding "terms" and "DHIN" for "as it"; rewrote (a)(9)-(a)(12), (a)(16), (a)(18); in the introductory paragraph of (b), substituted "duties listed in this section" for "above duties the" and added "powers to do all of the"; deleted "To" from the beginning of (b)(1)-(b)(4); substituted "or" for "and/or" in (b)(1); substituted "DHIN's" for "its" in (b)(2) and (b)(3); deleted "in order" following "budget" in (b)(2); and deleted "any" following "license" in (b)(4).

§ 10304. Immunity from suit; limitation of liability.

(a)(1) A Board member, whether temporary or permanent, is not subject to and is immune from claim suit, liability, damages, or other recourse, whether civil or criminal, arising from the member's act, proceeding, decision, or determination performed or reached in good faith and without malice in carrying out the responsibility, authority, duty, power, or privilege of DHIN.

(2) Immunity under this subsection applies to a member acting individually or jointly with another member.

(3) Good faith is presumed under this subsection until proven otherwise. The burden to prove malice is on the complainant.

(4) The immunity from suit provided to state employees under the Delaware Constitution and §§ 4001 through 4005 of Title 10 applies to a DHIN employee or staff member, whether temporary or permanent.

(b) DHIN is not a health-care provider and is not subject to claims under Chapter 68 of Title 18. A person who participates in or subscribes to the services or information that DHIN provides is not liable in an action for damages or costs of any nature, in law or equity, which result solely from that person's use or failure to use DHIN information or data that was imputed or retrieved under DHIN's rules or regulations. A person may not be subject to antitrust or unfair competition liability based on membership or participation in DHIN as the State's sanctioned provider of health information services that are deemed to be essential to governmental function for the public health and safety.

History.

71 Del. Laws, c. 177, § 1; 70 Del. Laws, c. 186, § 1; 77 Del. Laws, c. 368, §§ 9, 10, 16; 80 Del. Laws, c. 329, § 1; 83 Del. Laws, c. 137, § 5.

Revisor's note.

Section 15 of 83 Del. Laws, c. 137, provided: "This act takes effect on January 1 following its enactment into law." This act was signed by the Governor on Sept. 10, 2021, and became effective on Jan. 1, 2022.

Effect of amendments.

83 Del. Laws, c. 137, effective Jan. 1, 2022, rewrote the section.

§ 10305. Property rights.

(a) A person providing information or data to DHIN retains a property right in that information or data, but the provision of information or data grants to the other participant or subscriber a nonexclusive license to retrieve and use that information or data in accordance with the rules or regulation that DHIN promulgates.

(b) Processes or software that DHIN develops, designs, or purchases remains DHIN's property subject to use by a participant or subscriber under the rules or regulations that DHIN promulgates.

History.

71 Del. Laws, c. 177, § 1; 77 Del. Laws, c. 368, §§ 11, 16; 80 Del. Laws, c. 329, § 1; 83 Del. Laws, c. 137, § 6.

Revisor's note.

Section 15 of 83 Del. Laws, c. 137, provided: "This act takes effect on January 1 following its enactment into law." This act was signed by the Governor on Sept. 10, 2021, and became effective on Jan. 1, 2022.

Effect of amendments.

83 Del. Laws, c. 137, effective Jan. 1, 2022, rewrote the section.

§ 10306. Regulations; resolution of disputes.

(a) DHIN may promulgate rules and regulations under subchapter II of Chapter 101 of Title 29 to carry out the objective of this chapter. Regulations and rules that the Delaware Health Care Commission promulgated prior to July 12, 2010, regarding DHIN remain in full force and effect until amended or repealed through DHIN.

(b) DHIN may hear and determine a case decision under subchapter III of Chapter 101 of Title 29 to resolve a dispute among participants, subscribers, or the public under this chapter, or a rule or regulation promulgated under this chapter.

(c) A person may appeal to the Superior Court under subchapter V of Chapter 101 of Title 29 for any of the following:

(1) If the person has been aggrieved by the unlawfulness of a rule or regulation under this chapter.

(2) If a case decision under this chapter has been decided against the person.

History.

71 Del. Laws, c. 177, § 1; 77 Del. Laws, c. 368, §§ 12, 13, 16; 80 Del. Laws, c. 329, §§ 1, 4; 83 Del. Laws, c. 137, § 7.

Revisor's note.

Section 15 of 83 Del. Laws, c. 137, provided: "This act takes effect on January 1 following its enactment into law." This act was signed by the Governor on Sept. 10, 2021, and became effective on Jan. 1, 2022.

Effect of amendments.

83 Del. Laws, c. 137, effective Jan. 1, 2022, rewrote the section.

§ 10307. Privacy; protection and use of information.

(a)(1) DHIN shall by rule or regulation ensure that patient specific health information is disclosed only with the patient's consent or best interest to those having a need to know.

(2) A disclosure that is made in the patient's "best interest to those having a need to know" includes any of the following:

a. Disclosure for treatment, payment and operations purposes, and required disclosures to public health authorities, as "treatment", "payment" , "operations" , and "public health authorities" are defined under the Health Insurance Portability and Accountability Act of 1996 (P.L. 104-191) and associated regulations.

b. Disclosure for other purposes permitted under Health Insurance Portability and Accountability Act of 1996 (P.L. 104-191) and other federal law and regulations addressing the privacy of protected health information.

(b) Health information and data held by DHIN is not subject to the Freedom of Information Act, Chapter 100 of Title 29, or to subpoena by a court. The health information and data may be disclosed only by consent of the patient or under DHIN's rules, regulations, or orders.

(c) DHIN shall by rule or regulation provide a Delaware resident with access to the resident's own health information that is in DHIN's possession, if and to the extent that access is permitted by Health Insurance Portability and Accountability Act of 1996 (P.L. 104-191) and DHIN's contract with a relevant data-sending organization.

(d) DHIN shall by rule or regulation provide a Delaware resident with the ability to direct DHIN to disclose the resident's own health information to a third party that the resident approves, if and to the extent that the disclosure is permitted by Health Insurance Portability and Accountability Act of 1996 (P.L. 104-191) and DHIN's contract with a relevant data-sending organization.

(e) In addition to the disclosures permitted by subsection (a) of this section, DHIN shall by rule or regulation provide a health-care payer, provider, purchaser, or researcher with access to clinical data in DHIN's possession, if and to the extent that the access is permitted by Health Insurance Portability and Accountability Act of 1996 (P.L. 104-191) and DHIN's contract with the relevant data-sending organizations.

(1) The reasons for which access to clinical data is permissible under this subsection include any of the following:

a. The facilitation of data-driven, evidence-based improvements in access to and quality of health care.

b. The improvement of the health of Delawareans generally.

c. Lowering the growth in per capita health-care costs.

d. Providing an enhanced provider experience that promotes patient engagement.

(2) DHIN may not provide patient-specific data to a person under this subsection without first obtaining written consent from the patient authorizing the disclosure.

(3) Clinical data may be provided to a requesting person under this subsection only when a majority of the DHIN Board of Directors, or of a subcommittee established under DHIN's bylaws for purposes of reviewing data requests, determines that the clinical data should be provided to the requesting person to facilitate the purposes of this subsection.

a. If the DHIN Board of Directors or appropriate subcommittee of the Board so determines, DHIN may release fully de-identified data or the analytic evaluation thereof to third parties or the public without obtaining full Board or subcommittee review, for purposes consistent with this subsection.

b. A request for limited data sets or identifiable data must go through Board or subcommittee review.

c. The Board's or subcommittee's determination under this subsection is final and not subject to appeal. A requesting person, data-sending organization, or other party has no private right of action to enforce a requirement under this subsection or otherwise challenge the Board's or subcommittee's determination.

(4)a. DHIN shall promulgate regulations to notify a data-sending organization when clinical data consisting of a limited data set or identifiable data submitted by the data-sending organization may be released for a purpose permitted under this subsection.

b. If DHIN notifies a data-sending organization under paragraph (e)(4)a. of this section, DHIN shall provide the data-sending organization with an opportunity to comment on the data release request prior to releasing the data. DHIN shall review, consider, and respond to the data-sending organization's comments.

(5)a. DHIN shall provide clinical data provided to a requesting person under this subsection under DHIN's existing confidentiality and data security protocols and in compliance with all applicable state and federal laws relating to the privacy and security of protected health information.

b. A person that receives individually-identifiable patient health information under this subsection shall maintain the information by complying with all applicable state and federal laws relating to the confidentiality and security of protected health information, including related regulations promulgated under this chapter.

(f) DHIN may enter a contract under § 10303(a)(11) of this title with a person that requests data or analytic services from DHIN.

(g) A state agency is not required to comply with the State's procurement law under Chapter 69 of Title 29 to procure services from DHIN.

(h) A violation of DHIN's rules or regulations regarding access or misuse of health information or data held by DHIN must be reported to the office of the Attorney General, and is subject to prosecution and penalties under the Delaware Criminal Code or federal law.

History.
71 Del. Laws, c. 177, § 1; 77 Del. Laws, c. 368, §§ 14, 16; 80 Del. Laws, c. 329, § 1; 83 Del. Laws, c. 137, §§ 8, 16; 83 Del. Laws, c. 138, § 1.

Revisor's note.
Section 15 of 83 Del. Laws, c. 137, provided: "This act takes effect on January 1 following its enactment into law." This act was signed by the Governor on Sept. 10, 2021, and became effective on Jan. 1, 2022.

Section 16 of 83 Del. Laws, c. 137, provided: "If Senate Bill No. 88 of the 151st General Assembly is enacted into law before January 1, 2023, Section 8 of this act does not take effect." Senate Bill 88 of the 151st General Assembly became effective as 83 Del. Laws, c. 138, upon

the signature of the Governor on Sept. 10, 2021. As a result, 83 Del. Laws, c. 137, § 8, did not amend this section.

Effect of amendments.
83 Del. Laws, c. 138, effective Sept. 10, 2021, added "and use" in the section heading; in (a)(1), deleted "The" preceding "DHIN", substituted "is" for "be" preceding "disclosed only" and deleted "in accordance" thereafter; added (a)(2); rewrote (b); added present (c)-(g); and redesignated former (c) as present (h) and, in that subsection, substituted "A" for "Any", deleted "the DHIN" preceding "health" and substituted "held by DHIN must" for "shall" and added "is" preceding "subject".

§ 10308. No pledge of state credit; no assumption of liability by State.

DHIN does not have the power, except where expressly granted by separate act of the General Assembly, to pledge the credit or to create any debt or liability of the State, a state agency, or a political subdivision of the State. The State shall not assume or be deemed to have assumed any debt or liability of DHIN as a result of any actions by DHIN.

History.
71 Del. Laws, c. 177, § 1; 77 Del. Laws, c. 368, § 16; 80 Del. Laws, c. 329, § 1; 83 Del. Laws, c. 137, § 9.

Revisor's note.
Section 15 of 83 Del. Laws, c. 137, provided: "This act takes effect on January 1 following its

enactment into law." This act was signed by the Governor on Sept. 10, 2021, and became effective on Jan. 1, 2022.

Effect of amendments.
83 Del. Laws, c. 137, effective Jan. 1, 2022, rewrote the section.

SUBCHAPTER II
THE DELAWARE HEALTH CARE CLAIMS DATABASE

§ 10311. The Delaware Health Care Claims Database — Findings; purpose; creation.

(a) The General Assembly finds that:

(1) The establishment of effective health-care data analysis and reporting initiatives is essential to achieving the "Triple Aim" of the State's ongoing health-care innovation efforts: improved health, health-care quality and experience, and affordability for all Delawareans.

(2) The ongoing work of the Delaware Center for Health Innovation to transform the State's health-care system from a fee-for-service system to a value-based system that rewards health-care providers for quality and efficiency of care is a worthy effort, and, to that end, the General Assembly supports the establishment of a health-care claims database to assist in the State's efforts to achieve the Triple Aim.

(3) Claims data is an important component of population health research and analysis, and that appropriate access to claims data can facilitate the development of value-based health-care purchasing and the study of the prevalence of illness or injury across the broader population of Delaware and in particular communities or neighborhoods.

(4) Providers and other health-care entities accepting financial risk for managing the health-care needs of a population, including the State as a self-insured employer, should have access to claims data as necessary to effectively manage that risk.

(b) The purpose of this subchapter is to create a centralized health-care claims database to enable the State to more effectively understand utilization across the continuum of health care in Delaware and achieve the Triple Aim.

(c) DHIN, assisted by the Department of Health and Social Services and the Delaware Health Care Commission as necessary, shall administer a centralized health-care claims database, known as the "Delaware Health Care Claims Database."

(d) The Delaware Health Care Claims Database is created within DHIN to facilitate data-driven, evidence-based improvements in access, quality, and cost of health care and to promote and improve the public health through increased transparency of accurate health-care claims data and information. DHIN shall collect and maintain claims data under this subchapter.

History.
80 Del. Laws, c. 329, § 5; 83 Del. Laws, c. 137, § 10.

Revisor's note.
Section 15 of 83 Del. Laws, c. 137, provided: "This act takes effect on January 1 following its enactment into law." This act was signed by the Governor on Sept. 10, 2021, and became effective on Jan. 1, 2022.

Effect of amendments.
83 Del. Laws, c. 137, effective Jan. 1, 2022, substituted "to" for "that would" following "database" in (a)(2); deleted "The" from the beginning of (c) and the second sentence of (d); and deleted "the" preceding "DHIN" in the first sentence of (d).

§ 10312. Definitions [Amendments to paragraph (5) of this section by 83 Del. Laws, c. 137, § 11, subject to contingent repeal under § 17 of that act].

As used in this chapter, unless amended, supplemented, or otherwise modified by regulations adopted under this chapter:

(1) "Board" means the Delaware Health Information Network Board of Directors.

(2) "Claims data" includes required claims data and additional health-

care claims information that a voluntary reporting entity may elect, through entry into an appropriate data submission and use agreement under this subchapter, to submit to the Delaware Health Care Claims Database.

(3) "DHIN" means the Delaware Health Information Network.

(4) "Health-care services" means as defined in § 6403 of Title 18.

(5) "Health insurer" means as defined in § 4004 of Title 18. "Health insurer" does not include a provider of any of the following:

a. Casualty insurance, as "casualty insurance" is defined under § 906 of Title 18.

b. Group long-term care insurance, as "group long-term care insurance" is defined in § 7103 of Title 18.

c. A dental plan, as "dental plan" is defined under § 3802 of Title 18.

d. A dental plan organization, as "dental plan organization" defined under § 3802 of Title 18.

(6) "Mandatory reporting entity" means each of the following entities, to the extent permitted under federal law:

a.1. The State Employee Benefits Committee and the Office of Management and Budget, under each entity's respective statutory authority to administer the State Group Health Insurance Program in Chapter 96 of Title 29.

2. A health insurer, third-party administrator, or other entity that receives or collects charges, contributions, or premiums for, or adjusts or settles health claims for, a State employee, or a spouse or dependent of a State employee, participating in the State Group Health Insurance Program. However, a carrier, as defined in § 5290 of Title 29, that the State Group Health Insurance Program has selected to offer supplemental insurance program coverage under Chapter 52C of Title 29 is not included in the definition of "mandatory reporting entity" .

b. The Division of Medicaid and Medical Assistance, with respect to services provided under programs administered under Titles XIX and XXI of the Social Security Act (42 U.S.C. §§ 1396 et seq. and 1397aa et seq.).

c. A health insurer or other entity that is certified as a qualified health plan on the Delaware Health Insurance Marketplace for plan year 2017 or a subsequent plan year. However, a health insurer or other entity that is not otherwise required to provide claims data as a condition of certification as a qualified health plan on the Delaware Health Insurance Marketplace for plan year 2017 or a subsequent plan year is not included in the definition of "mandatory reporting entity" .

d. A federal health insurance plan providing health-care services to a resident of this State, including Medicare and the Federal Employees Health Benefits Plan.

e. A health insurer providing health-care coverage to a resident of this State.

(7) "Pricing information" includes all of the following:

a. The preadjudicated price that a provider or facility charges to a reporting entity for health-care services.

b. The amount a patient or insured individual pays, including copays and deductibles.

c. The postadjudicated price that a reporting entity pays to a provider for health-care services.

(8) "Provider" means a hospital or health-care practitioner that is licensed, certified, or authorized under state law to provide health-care services. "Provider" includes a hospital or health-care practitioner participating in a group arrangement, including an accountable care organization, in which the hospital or health-care practitioner agrees to assume responsibility for the quality and cost of health care for a designed group of beneficiaries.

(9) "Reporting date" means a calendar deadline that is scheduled on a regularly recurring basis, by which a mandatory reporting entity must submit required claims data to the Delaware Health Care Claims Database.

(10) "Required claims data" includes the basic claims information that a mandatory reporting entity must submit to the Delaware Health Care Claims Database by the reporting date, including all of the following:

a. Basic demographic information, including the patient's gender, age, and geographic area of residency.

b. Basic information relating to an individual service, encounter, visit, or episode of care, including all of the following:

1. The date and time of a patient's admission and discharge.

2. The identity of the health-care services provider.

3. The location and type of facility, such as a hospital, office, or clinic, where the service, encounter, visit, or episode of care was provided.

c. Information describing the nature of health-care services provided to the patient in connection with the service, encounter, visit, or episode of care, including diagnosis codes.

d. Health insurance product type, such as HMO or PPO.

e. Pricing information.

(11) "Third-party administrator" means as defined in § 102 of Title 18.

(12) "Voluntary reporting entity" includes, except as prohibited under applicable federal law, any of the following entities, unless the entity is a mandatory reporting entity:

a. A health insurer.

b. A third-party administrator.

c. An entity that is not a health insurer or third-party administrator, if the entity receives or collects charges, contributions, or premiums for, or adjusts or settles health-care claims for, residents of this State.

History.

80 Del. Laws, c. 329, § 5; 81 Del. Laws, c. 79, § 32; 81 Del. Laws, c. 392, § 3; 83 Del. Laws, c. 137, §§ 11, 17.

Revisor's note.

Section 15 of 83 Del. Laws, c. 137, provided: "This act takes effect on January 1 following its enactment into law." This act was signed by the Governor on Sept. 10, 2021, and became effective on Jan. 1, 2022.

Section 17 of 83 Del. Laws, c. 137, provided:

"If Senate Bill No. 119 is enacted into law before January 1, 2023, [former] § 10312(3) [now § 10312(5)], Title 16 of Section 11 of this act does not take effect." Senate Bill 119 of the 151st General Assembly is currently awaiting consideration by the Senate Legislative Oversight and Sunset Committee.

Effect of amendments.

83 Del. Laws, c. 137, effective Jan. 1, 2022, rewrote the section.

§ 10313. Submission of required claims data by mandatory reporting entities; submission of claims data by voluntary reporting entities.

(a) Requirements for submission of required claims data by a mandatory reporting entity.

(1) A mandatory reporting entity shall submit required claims data to the Delaware Health Care Claims Database by the reporting date.

(2) DHIN is subject to the provisions of this subchapter and regulations promulgated under this subchapter, and shall collect the required claims data from mandatory reporting entities by the reporting date.

(3) DHIN shall, under § 10306 of this title, promulgate a template form for a data submission and use agreement for a mandatory reporting entity to use to submit required claims data.

(4) DHIN and each mandatory reporting entity must execute a mutually acceptable data submission and use agreement. The agreement must include procedures for submission, collection, aggregation, and distribution of claims data and must provide for, at a minimum, all of the following:

    a. The protection of patient privacy and data security under this chapter and state and federal privacy laws, including all of the following:

        1. The Health Insurance Portability and Accountability Act (P.L. 104-191).

        2. Titles XIX and XXI of the Social Security Act (42 U.S.C. §§ 1396 et seq. and 1397aa et seq.).

        3. The Health Information Technology for Economic and Clinical Health (HITECH) Act (42 U.S.C. §§ 300jj et seq. and 17901 et seq.).

        4. All other applicable state and federal laws relating to the privacy and security of protected health information.

    b. The identification of claims data that the mandatory reporting entity elects to submit to the Delaware Health Care Claims Database in addition to the required claims data.

    c. A detailed summary of how claims data that the mandatory reporting entity submits may be used for geographic, demographic, economic, and peer group comparisons.

    d. A representation and warranty that DHIN shall, to the fullest extent possible, abide by nationally recognized data collection standards and methods, including the standards promulgated by the APCD Council or successor organization, to establish and maintain the database in a cost-effective manner and facilitate uniformity among various health-care claims databases of other states and specification of data fields included in submitted claims. DHIN may allow for an exemption when a submitting entity does not collect the specified data or pay on a per-claim basis.

(5) Exclusions from required claims data reporting requirement. The required claims data reporting requirements under this subchapter, and rules and regulations promulgated under this chapter, do not apply to required claims data created for an employee welfare benefit plan or other employee health plan that is regulated by the Employee Retirement Income Security Act of 1974 (ERISA), 88 Stat. 829, as amended, 29 U.S.C. § 1001 et seq., unless otherwise permitted by federal law or regulation.

(b) Submission of claims data by a voluntary reporting entity.

(1) DHIN shall collect claims data from a voluntary reporting entity under the terms and conditions of the applicable data submission and use agreement.

(2) DHIN may promulgate regulations to clarify the types of claims data that a voluntary reporting entity may submit.

(3) DHIN and a voluntary reporting entity that elects to submit claims data to the Delaware Health Care Claims Database shall execute a

mutually acceptable data submission and use agreement. DHIN shall publish a template form data submission and use agreement that includes the required data submission and use agreement provisions under paragraph (a)(4) of this section.

(c) Unless modified or supplemented by regulations promulgated under this chapter, if more than 1 entity is involved in the administration of a policy, the health insurer is responsible for submitting the claims data on policies that it has written, and the third-party administrator is responsible for submitting claims data on self-insured plans that it administers.

History.

80 Del. Laws, c. 329, § 5; 83 Del. Laws, c. 137, § 12.

Revisor's note.

Section 15 of 83 Del. Laws, c. 137, provided: "This act takes effect on January 1 following its enactment into law." This act was signed by the Governor on Sept. 10, 2021, and became effective on Jan. 1, 2022.

Effect of amendments.

83 Del. Laws, c. 137, effective Jan. 1, 2022, deleted "The" from the beginning of (a)(1), (a)(2), the introductory paragraph of (a)(4), (b)(1) and (2) and the first and second sentences of (b)(3); in (a)(2), substituted "is" for a semicolon following "DHIN" and added "and" preceding "shall collect"; in (a)(3), deleted "the submission of required claims data by" following "agreement for" and added "to use to submit required claims data"; in the introductory paragraph of (a)(4), substituted "must" for "shall" in the first sentence and twice in the second sentence, and substituted "The" for "Such" in the second sentence; rewrote (a)(4)a.; in (a)(4)b., deleted "any" following "identification" and transferred "in addition to the required claims data" from preceding "that the mandatory" to the end; in (a)(4)c., substituted "that" for "submitted by" preceding "data" and added "submits"; rewrote (a)(4)d.; in the second sentence of (a)(5), deleted "any" preceding "rules" and substituted "an" for "any" preceding "employee"; in (b)(1), added "a" preceding "voluntary" and substituted "entity" for "entities"; in (b)(2), deleted "may be submitted by" following "data that" and added "may submit"; substituted "a" for "any" preceding "voluntary" in the first sentence of (b)(3); and, in (c), substituted "if" for "in instances where" preceding "more", and substituted "the" for "a" following "policy" and "is" for "shall be" preceding "responsible" in two places.

§ 10314. External and public reporting of claims data.

(a) DHIN shall provide Delaware health-care payers, providers, and purchasers with access to the Delaware Health Care Claims Database for the purpose of facilitating the design and evaluation of alternative delivery and payment models, including population health research and provider risk-sharing arrangements.

(1) Claims data provided to the Delaware Health Care Claims Database may be provided to a requesting person only when a majority of the DHIN Board of Directors, or of a subcommittee established under DHIN's bylaws for purposes of administering the Health Care Claims Database, determines that the claims data should be provided to the requesting person to facilitate the purposes of this subchapter or to the Delaware Health Care Commission.

a. A written determination under this paragraph (a)(1) must be provided to the requesting person.

b. A determination under this paragraph (a)(1) is final and not subject to appeal. A requesting person does not have a private right of action against DHIN or another person to enforce this section.

(2) DHIN shall, in consultation with the Delaware Health Care Commission, promulgate rules and regulations regarding the appropriate form and content of an application to receive claims data, providing examples of requests for claims data that will generally be deemed consistent with the purposes of this subchapter.

(b) Claims data provided to a requesting person under this section must be provided under DHIN's existing confidentiality and data security protocols and in compliance with applicable state and federal laws relating to the privacy and security of protected health information, including compliance, to the fullest extent practicable consistent with the purposes under this subchapter, with guidance found in Statement 6 of the Department of Justice and Federal Trade Commission Enforcement Policy regarding the exchange of price and cost information. A provider or purchaser must maintain individually identifiable patient health information under all applicable state and federal laws relating to the confidentiality and security of protected health information, including privacy and security requirements under regulations promulgated under this chapter.

(c)(1) For the purposes of public health improvement research and activities, DHIN shall provide access, at no cost, to all claims data reported by the Delaware Health Care Claims Database under this subchapter to the following state agencies:

  a. Office of Management and Budget.
  b. State Employee Benefits Committee.
  c. Division of Public Health.
  d. State Council for Persons with Disabilities.
  e. Division of Medicaid and Medical Assistance.
  f. Department of Insurance.
  g. Delaware Health Care Commission.

(2) A state agency under paragraph (c)(1) of this section may enter into an appropriate agreement with DHIN to allow DHIN to perform data warehousing and analytics functions that the state agency, or an entity on behalf of the state agency, has performed under the state agency's authority.

(d) DHIN may promulgate regulations to make available to the public certain data extracts and analyses that is not individually identifiable, as DHIN determines is consistent with, and necessary to, achieve the goals and policies of this subchapter. Before the data extracts and analyses, the process under subsection (e) of this section must be completed.

(e)(1) DHIN shall promulgate regulations to notify a mandatory reporting entity or voluntary reporting entity when claims data that the mandatory reporting entity or voluntary reporting entity submitted may be released for a purpose permitted under this subchapter.

(2) DHIN shall provide the mandatory reporting entity or voluntary reporting entity with an opportunity to comment on the data release request prior to its release.

(3) Prior to the data release, DHIN shall review, consider, and respond to comments that a mandatory reporting entity or voluntary reporting entity submits during the comment period.

(4) If a mandatory reporting entity or voluntary reporting entity identifies a party requesting the release of data as a potential competitor of the reporting entity, DHIN shall limit disclosure of pricing information that includes postadjudicated claims data, to the fullest extent practicable and consistent with the purposes of this subchapter, to a summary format that allows for analysis without revealing contracted pricing information.

(5) If a mandatory reporting entity or voluntary reporting entity identifies a person requesting the release of data as a potential competitor of the reporting entity, DHIN shall limit disclosure of pricing information that includes postadjudicated claims data, to the fullest extent practicable and consistent with the purposes of this subchapter, to a summary format that allows for analysis without revealing contracted pricing information.

(f) The DHIN shall promulgate regulations to ensure confidentiality, privacy, and security protections of health-care data and all other information that DHIN collects, stores, or releases, subject to applicable state and federal health-care privacy, confidentiality, and data security laws.

History.

80 Del. Laws, c. 329, § 5; 81 Del. Laws, c. 392, § 4; 82 Del. Laws, c. 156, § 1; 82 Del. Laws, c. 229, § 1; 83 Del. Laws, c. 137, § 13.

Revisor's note.

Section 15 of 83 Del. Laws, c. 137, provided: "This act takes effect on January 1 following its enactment into law." This act was signed by the Governor on Sept. 10, 2021, and became effective on Jan. 1, 2022.

Effect of amendments.

83 Del. Laws, c. 137, effective Jan. 1, 2022, deleted "The" from the beginning of the intro- ductory paragraph of (a) and of (a)(2); in the introductory paragraph of (a)(1), substituted "may" for "shall only", "person only" for "party", and deleted "the" preceding "DHIN's"; substituted "person" for "party" following "requesting" in (a)(1) and the first sentence of (b); rewrote (a)(1)a. and (a)(1)b.; in (b), substituted "must" for "shall" and deleted "all" preceding "applicable" in the first sentence and rewrote the second sentence; rewrote the introductory paragraph of (c)(1) and (c)(2), (d) and (e); and, in (f), substituted "that DHIN collects, stores, or releases" for "collected, stored, or released by DHIN".

§ 10315. Funding the Delaware Health Care Claims Database.

(a) DHIN may not require any mandatory reporting entity, voluntary reporting entity, or provider to pay a cost or fee to submit or verify the accuracy of claims data or otherwise to enable the operation of the Delaware Health Care Claims Database with respect to required claims data submissions.

(b) DHIN may enter a contract under § 10303(a)(11) of this title with a person that voluntarily subscribes to access the database.

(c) DHIN, with the assistance of the Department of Health and Social Services, shall develop short-term and long-term funding strategies for the creation and operation of the Delaware Health Care Claims Database. The strategies may include any of the following:

(1) Public and private grant funding.

(2) Subscriptions for access to data reports, access fees, and revenue for specific data projects, subject to the *l*imitations of this section.

History.

80 Del. Laws, c. 329, § 5; 83 Del. Laws, c. 137, § 14.

Revisor's note.

Section 15 of 83 Del. Laws, c. 137, provided: "This act takes effect on January 1 following its enactment into law." This act was signed by the Governor on Sept. 10, 2021, and became effective on Jan. 1, 2022.

Effect of amendments.

83 Del. Laws, c. 137, effective Jan. 1, 2022, substituted "the" for "of" in the section heading; in (a), deleted "The" from the beginning and substituted "a" for "any" preceding "cost"; and rewrote (b) and (c).

TITLE 17
HIGHWAYS

CHAPTER 1
GENERAL PROVISIONS

SUBCHAPTER III
JURISDICTION, POWERS AND DUTIES OF DEPARTMENT

§ 132. General powers and duties.

(a) The Department shall acquire full information concerning the roads of this State, the nature and improvement thereof, the needs thereof and the character and amount of traffic thereon and such other details as may be necessary or desirable for the Department to have in the performance of its duty of determining upon and laying out, without regard to any personal advantage or disadvantage or bias toward any person or persons, community or political party or organization, consistent and congruous route or routes of state highways with a view to establishing such a consistent, congruous, comprehensive and permanent system of state highways along the route or routes of travel as will accommodate the greatest needs of the people of this State.

(b) The Department shall:

(1) Determine upon, lay out, construct or reconstruct state highways so as to make roads which, with reasonable maintenance, shall be permanent;

(2) Maintain all state highways under its jurisdiction;

(3) Maintain a system of accounting adequate to give in detail the expenditures of the Department and the costs of its works;

(4) Keep full and accurate minutes of all meetings and records of all proceedings of the Department, which minutes and records shall be public records;

(5) Reimburse the owner thereof for the expense (as hereinafter defined) of the relocation of public utility facilities necessitated by any project where the State is to be reimbursed by at least 90% of the cost of such project from federal funds or by the federal government or any agency thereof, such expense to be the amount paid by such owner properly attributable to such relocation after deducting therefrom any increase in the value of the new facilities and any salvage value derived from the old facilities;

(6) Install on state land the tile necessary, in the opinion of the Department, to provide adequate entrances and exits to and from the property of adjoining landowners provided:

a. The tile is supplied by the adjoining landowners;

b. The tile conforms to the specifications established from time to time by the Department; and

c. The property is a single residential lot occupied or to be occupied by the land owners and intended for residential use only; or

d. The property is agricultural use land. "Agricultural use land" shall mean land devoted to the production for sale of plants and animals useful to humans, including but not limited to: Forages and sod crops; grains and feed crops; dairy animals and dairy products; poultry and poultry products; livestock, including beef cattle, sheep, swine, horses, ponies, mules or goats, including the breeding and grazing of any or all of such animals; bees and apiary products; fur animals; trees and forest products; or when devoted to and meeting the requirements and qualifications for payments or other compensation pursuant to soil conversation program under an agreement with an agency of the federal government.

Nothing contained in this subsection shall relieve the Department from the responsibility for replacing tile originally installed by the Department or any governmental agency and subsequently damaged by operations of the Department;

(7) Maintain the Van Buren Street Bridge over the Brandywine Creek;

(8) Provide relocation assistance to persons displaced as a result of the acquisition for highway purposes of real property upon which they live or conduct a business or farm operation in accordance with Chapter 91 of Title 29.

(c) To these ends the Department may do the following:

(1) Determine upon and lay out a system of state highways.

(2) Take over and convert into state highways any public road by whatever name such road or part thereof, or under whatever authority or control such road or part thereof, may have theretofore existed.

(3) Lay out, open, widen, straighten, grade, extend, construct, reconstruct, and maintain any state highway or proposed state highway for the purpose of the improvement of state highways.

(4) Acquire by condemnation or otherwise any land, easement, franchise, material, or property, which, in the judgment of the Department, shall be necessary therefor, provided that the Department may not reconstruct a highway unless there will result a net saving or reconstruction, further provided that § 145 of this title may not be deemed to be inconsistent with the provisions under this paragraph (c)(4).

(5) Have access to and make copies of maps, surveys, data, or information which any state agency may possess concerning any road in the State.

(6) Employ and discharge professional or technical experts, surveyors, agents, assistants, clerks, employees and laborers, skilled and unskilled, and also such advisers and consultants as may be required to accomplish the purposes of the chapter and the other responsibilities of the Department. In the event that the size of the Capital Transportation Program requires overtime to administer in a timely manner, or in the event that: (i) The federal government makes available additional funding for transportation projects which are part of the Department's Capital Transportation Program; and (ii) use of these funds in a particular federal fiscal year is required to access these funds; and (iii) overtime is required to administer the program within that federal fiscal year to assure the use of these funds, then for these purposes the Department may pay overtime moneys to those employed under this subsection, any relevant Delaware law, rule, or regulation to the contrary notwithstanding.

(7) Secure and furnish offices and quarters for the Department.

(8) Exclusively grant franchises and licenses to public service corporations or to corporations furnishing gasoline or petroleum products to the air field installation operated by the federal government in Kent County,

to use the state highways, in whole or in part, for a term not exceeding 50 years; provided, however, that any franchise or license granted to any such corporation furnishing gasoline or petroleum products to said air field installation shall restrict the use of said state highways to the transmission of gasoline or petroleum products to said air field installation. Any franchise or license owned by any public service corporation on April 2, 1917, is not be affected by this chapter.

(9) Make and enter into any and all contracts, agreements or stipulations for the execution of the purposes of this chapter.

(10) Purchase all machinery, tools, supplies, material, and instrumentalities whatsoever which may be necessary for the full performance of its duties.

(11) Call upon the Attorney General for the Attorney General's opinion or advice touching its duties or powers.

(12) Accept lands by easement or lease in the name of the State in areas where it is deemed necessary to establish dumping areas for the use of the public, supervise and control all areas so accepted and provide suitable passageways to the dumping areas and further, police the areas in order to prevent the spread of pests and disease and make such other regulations and rules as shall be deemed necessary for the purpose of carrying out the intent and purpose of this paragraph.

(13) Enter upon the lands or waters of any person for the purpose of surveys, repairs, reconstruction, and operation of publicly financed improvements but subject at all times to responsibility for all and any damages which shall be done to the property of any such person or persons. Water levels to be maintained back of publicly financed sluices, water control structures, dams, and similar structures shall be at a level that will not cause damage to adjoining property, such as seepage of water into basements and wells, and that no lands may be flooded without the owners' full consent.

(14) Place vending machines or other items that will enable drivers to be more rested and refreshed in safety roadside rest areas, unless prohibited by federal laws, rules, or regulations. Any profits derived from such items must be credited to the Department of Transportation Safety Roadside Rest Area Fund.

    a. There is hereby created within the State Treasury a special fund to be designated as the Department of Transportation Safety Roadside Rest Area Fund which must be used in the operation and maintenance of the roadside rest areas under the jurisdiction of the Department.

    b. Any profits realized by the Department from items available at existing roadside rest areas that are for the purpose of enabling drivers to be more rested and refreshed must be deposited in the State Treasury to the credit of said Department of Transportation Safety Roadside Rest Area Fund. Such profits must be used by the Department for the operation and maintenance of the safety roadside rest area facilities within its jurisdiction.

(d) The Department may also do whatever is incidental and germane to the scope of the duties and powers conferred on it by law.

(e) The general powers and duties conferred upon the Department by this section shall be exercised by it by the establishment and supervision of any and all policies pursuant to which such powers and duties shall be carried out.

(f) Whenever the Department of Transportation widens, constructs or reconstructs any major arterial, minor arterial, collector road or proposed road in an urbanized area of this State, the Department shall incorporate within such plans, layout, widening, construction or reconstruction the construction of sidewalks, provided there is a need for sidewalks or that it can be reasonably anticipated that the need for sidewalks will exist. The Department shall have the responsibility for determining whether such need for sidewalks does or will exist for all or any part of any such project and, before arriving at a decision as to the need of such sidewalk construction, shall consult with the county department of planning, the State Planning Office, the Department of Education and the local school district in which the proposed new road construction or road widening construction is to take place. The cost of such sidewalk construction shall be included in the total cost of the new road construction or road widening project. This subsection shall apply only to projects funded pursuant to acts authorizing the State to borrow money and issue bonds and notes for capital improvements, enacted after January 1, 1973.

(g) The Department shall have exclusive original supervision and regulation of all public carriers and also over their property, property rights, equipment, facilities, franchises, rates, fares, tariffs, regulations, practices, measurements and services.

(h) The Department may work in conjunction with any political subdivision of the State and with any private organization to plan and construct such bicycle and pedestrian transportation facilities as may be appropriate. In carrying out this portion of its overall program, the Department may take into consideration in scheduling its projects those in which the affected local community is willing to contribute a matching share (whether in cash, rights of way, or other in-kind services) in order to accomplish the project.

History.

29 Del. Laws, c. 63, § 5; Code 1935, § 5722; 17 Del. C. 1953, § 132; 49 Del. Laws, c. 262; 51 Del. Laws, c. 141, § 1; 51 Del. Laws, c. 328; 52 Del. Laws, c. 295; 53 Del. Laws, c. 39, §§ 5, 6, 13; 54 Del. Laws, c. 251; 55 Del. Laws, c. 14; 56 Del. Laws, c. 101; 57 Del. Laws, c. 327, § 1; 57 Del. Laws, c. 671, § 1F; 57 Del. Laws, c. 754, § 2; 58 Del. Laws, c. 585; 59 Del. Laws, c. 393, § 4; 60 Del. Laws, c. 386, § 1; 60 Del. Laws, c. 503, § 18; 62 Del. Laws, c. 384, § 1; 68 Del. Laws, c. 98, § 1; 68 Del. Laws, c. 156, § 47; 70 Del. Laws, c. 186, § 1; 73 Del. Laws, c. 65, § 19; 73 Del. Laws, c. 351, § 1; 75 Del. Laws, c. 98, § 95; 83 Del. Laws, c. 37, § 33.

Effect of amendments.

83 Del. Laws, c. 37, effective June 3, 2021, added "do the following" in the introductory paragraph of (c); substituted a period for a semicolon at the end of (c)(1)-(12) and for "; and" at the end of (c)(13); added a comma following "reconstruct" in (c)(3), following "material" in (c)(4) and (10), following "data" in (c)(5), following "rule" near the end of (c)(6), following "reconstruction" in the first sentence of (c)(13) and following "dams" in the second sentence of that paragraph and following "rules" in the first sentence of the introductory paragraph of (c)(14); substituted "may" for "shall" in two places in (c)(4) and in the second sentence of (c)(13); substituted "under this paragraph (c)(4)" for "hereof" in (c)(4); in the second sentence of (c)(6), twice substituted "Capital Transportation Program" for "capital improvement program" and substituted "under" for "pursuant to"; in (c)(7), added "and furnish" and deleted "and furnish the same" from the end; substituted "is" for "shall" following "April 2, 1917" in (c)(8); substituted "must" for "shall" in the second sentence of the introductory paragraph of (c)(14), in (c)(14)a. and in the first and second sentences of (c)(14)b.

§ 145. Corridor capacity preservation.

(a) *Application.* — This section is applicable only to transportation routes categorized as corridor capacity preservation projects as described herein.

(b) *Definitions.* — As used in this section:

(1) "Comprehensive development plan" means a comprehensive land use plan, master plan or comprehensive plan as provided in Title 9, 22, or 29.

(2) "Corridor" means a particular route of 1 or more highways of this State, serving predominantly statewide and/or regional travel at a high level of service at the time of the analysis conducted under subsection (d) of this section.

(3) "Corridor capacity" means the ability of a corridor to sustain its level of service for a period of at least 10 years and for up to 20 years.

(4) "Department" means the Department of Transportation.

(5) "Preservation" means to maintain corridor capacity.

(c) *Findings.* — (1) Pursuant to federal and state law, the Department is required to develop long-range plans and principles to consider the various appropriate means of meeting the transportation needs of the State. This work is coordinated with the planning efforts of metropolitan planning organizations pursuant to 23 U.S.C. § 134 et seq. As part of these long-range plans and principles, the Department may identify transportation routes requiring corridor capacity preservation in order to:

a. Focus development toward existing locations;

b. Reduce the need for expansion of the transportation system; and

c. Otherwise advance the quality of life of Delawareans and the development policies adopted by the Cabinet Committee on State Planning Issues.

(2) Pursuant to the Quality of Life Act of 1988, Chapters 26, 49, and 69 of Title 9, as well as the Land Use Planning Act, Chapter 92 of Title 29, each county of this State is required to adopt a comprehensive development plan to guide and control future development. Each plan, which is to have the force and effect of law, includes among its purposes the facilitation of the adequate and efficient provision of transportation. These plans are reviewed by the Cabinet Committee on State Planning Issues to determine their compliance with the State's development policies, including the Department's long-range plans and principles. The State is under no obligation to provide infrastructure improvements to support land use or development actions where a county's comprehensive plans are inconsistent with the State's policies. In addition, pursuant to Chapter 3 of Title 22, municipalities are also required to develop comprehensive development plans, with relief of congestion constituting one of the goals of such plans. As part of this coordinated process, therefore, the comprehensive development plans adopted by the counties and municipalities should incorporate the Department's designation of transportation routes requiring corridor capacity preservation.

(3) This legislation is intended to facilitate the acquisition of property interests sufficient to provide corridor capacity preservation in keeping with these comprehensive development plans and the Department's long-range plans.

(d) *Implementation.* — On or before October 1, 1996, and every 3 years thereafter, under 23 U.S.C. § 134 et seq., the Department's long-range plans shall propose transportation routes requiring corridor capacity preservation, if any. The determination of these routes shall be based upon the following criteria: Level of service analysis; input and comment from the counties and municipalities to the need within growth areas; development trends; traffic growth; additional threats to roadway integrity; safety; support for long range planning goals of the Department and any relevant metropolitan planning organization; deliverability; economic impacts; social or environmental impacts; and air quality. The location of these routes shall be submitted to the local government bodies of the counties and municipalities for review and then presented to the public at a public hearing. The local governing bodies shall have 90 days to review the locations and respond to the Department. The Department shall, after considering public comments and the responses of the local governing bodies of the municipalities and counties, determine those routes requiring corridor capacity preservation. Each county and municipality shall incorporate these determinations into their comprehensive development plans or amendments thereto. Any subsequent Departmental corridor capacity preservation projects shall be subject to the same approval process as other capital projects. When approved by the Council on Transportation and adopted by the General Assembly, the Department may then proceed to pursue these projects as set forth each year in the Department's Capital Transportation Program. Property interests acquired for these projects under this section shall be in fee simple absolute or such lesser interest as the Department may deem appropriate. Acquisition of such property interests may be obtained by gift, devise, purchase, or in the exercise of the power of eminent domain, by condemnation in the manner prescribed in Chapter 61 of Title 10, subject to the provisions of Chapter 95 of Title 29.

(e) *Effect on other powers.* — The powers conveyed to the Department by this section are in addition to and not in derogation of any other powers it may have related to corridor capacity preservation, including but not limited to the power to seek voluntary compliance with its policies, to regulate subdivision streets intended for state maintenance, and the power to regulate access to and from state-maintained highways.

History.

17 Del. C. 1953, § 147; 57 Del. Laws, c. 754, § 1; 70 Del. Laws, c. 523, § 1; 83 Del. Laws, c. 37, § 34.

Effect of amendments.

83 Del. Laws, c. 37, effective June 3, 2021, in (d), substituted "under" for "pursuant to the provisions of" in the first sentence, in the second sentence substituted "any" for "the" preceding "relevant", "organization" for "organization(s)", and "social or environmental" for "social/environmental", and substituted "Transportation" for "Improvement" preceding "Program" in the eighth sentence.

CHAPTER 11
REGULATION OF OUTDOOR ADVERTISING
SUBCHAPTER I
GENERAL PROVISIONS

§ 1114. Signs excepted from provisions of this subchapter.

Revisor's note.

Section 293 of 77 Del. Laws, c. 84, effective July 1, 2009, as amended by 77 Del. Laws, c. 327, § 280, July 1, 2010; 78 Del. Laws, c. 78, § 264, effective July 1, 2011; 78 Del. Laws, c. 290, § 259, effective July 1, 2012; 79 Del. Laws, c. 78, § 256, effective July 1, 2013; 79 Del. Laws, c. 290, § 265, effective July 1, 2014; 80 Del. Laws, c. 79, § 260, effective July 1, 2015; 80 Del. Laws, c. 298, § 258, effective July 1, 2016; 81 Del. Laws, c. 58, § 265, effective July 3, 2017; 81 Del. Laws, c. 280, § 260, effective July 1, 2018; 82 Del. Laws, c. 64, § 259, effective July 1, 2019; 82 Del. Laws, c. 242, § 250, effective July 1, 2020; and 83 Del. Laws, c. 54, § 261, effective June 30, 2021, provided: "Notwithstanding the provisions of 17 Del. C. or any regulation to the contrary, the Department of Transportation shall permit an existing church, school, fire department, or veterans post sign, located on the premises of such church, school, fire department, or veterans post, presently located within 25 feet of the right-of-way line of any public highway to be replaced with a variable message sign or new fixed outdoor advertising display, device or sign structure of equal or smaller dimension than the existing sign, sign structure, display or device, relating to the activities conducted on such property."

TITLE 19
LABOR

Part
I. General Provisions
II. Workers' Compensation
III. Unemployment Compensation
IV. Workplace Fraud Act

PART I
GENERAL PROVISIONS

CHAPTER 2
STATE APPRENTICES

§ 204. Training and apprenticeship programs.

(a) The State Department of Labor shall develop and conduct employee training and registered apprenticeship programs, in cooperation with participating appointing authorities and the Department of Human Resources. The Department of Human Resources shall assist appointing authorities in utilizing such programs, and in developing the apprenticeships which are established pursuant to this section.

(b)(1) The Secretary of the Department of Human Resources, in cooperation with the Department of Labor and other participating appointing authorities, shall develop and annually revise a list of employment classifications in the classified service which are appropriate for apprenticeship training by December 31.

(2) For purposes of the craft training requirement under § 6960A of Title 29, the Department of Labor shall maintain a list of crafts for which there are approved and registered craft training programs in this State as follows:

a. An updated list must be published by January 31 each year.

b. At the time of the annual January update, the list must include all of the following:

1. All of the crafts that had 1 or more active Delaware registered apprentices complete their apprenticeship during the previous 2 years.

2. The amount of the payment that satisfies the craft training requirement under § 6960A of Title 29 for each craft. The Secretary of Labor, with the concurrence of the Director of the Office of Management and Budget and the Controller General, shall establish the amount of the payment which shall be the average annual related technical instruction cost. The annual related technical instruction cost is calculated using the cost or tuition for 1 person to attend training for each craft in each adult education division vocational-technical school district offering training for the craft.

(3) The list of approved programs under paragraph (b)(2) of this section may be updated during the year to add craft training programs after a program is approved and registered.

(4) The amount of the payment under paragraph (b)(2)b.2. of this section must be reviewed at least once every 3 years and the review must consider all of the following:

    a. The amount of moneys collected.

    b. The number of additional programs created.

    c. Changes in the cost or tuition for related technical instruction.

    d. The number of contractors who have complied with the craft training requirement by making payments.

(c) The Apprenticeship and Training Section of the Department of Labor shall establish procedures for the coordination of programs developed under this section, in cooperation with the Secretary of the Department of Human Resources.

(d) Subject to the approval of the Secretary of the Department of Human Resources and the procedures established by the Apprenticeship and Training Section of the Department of Labor, each participating agency shall determine the location and positions in which apprenticeships are to be established.

(e) The Secretary of Labor shall include in the Secretary's annual report the following:

(1) A review of the development and operation of training and apprenticeship programs.

(2) The current list of apprenticeable classifications.

(3) A summary of the agencies and types of positions involved.

(4) A summary of registered apprenticeships.

(5) The number of persons who applied for apprenticeship positions under this section.

(6) The number of persons who were accepted into the apprenticeship programs established under this section.

(7) The number of persons who successfully completed apprenticeships under this section and the number of persons who failed to complete apprenticeships under this section.

(8) The number of persons who remain employed after successfully completing apprenticeships.

(9) A summary of other training programs established.

(10) A summary of characteristics of applicants and participants in the program deemed pertinent by the Secretary of the Department of Human Resources.

(f) Nothing in this section may operate to invalidate or supersede a collective bargaining agreement of an employee organization and the State.

(g) The recruitment, selection, and training of apprentice trainees during their apprenticeship shall be without discrimination because of race, color, religion, national origin, or sex. The State will take affirmative action to provide equal opportunity in apprenticeship programs and will operate the training program as required under the State plan for equal employment in apprenticeship and training. For purposes of this subsection:

(1) "Protective hairstyle" includes braids, locks, and twists.

(2) "Race" includes traits historically associated with race, including hair texture and a protective hairstyle.

(h) The Department of Labor shall file a report on the development of apprenticeship programs in January, 1986.

History.
65 Del. Laws, c. 92, § 1; 70 Del. Laws, c. 186, § 1; 75 Del. Laws, c. 88, § 20(5); 81 Del. Laws, c. 66, § 19; 83 Del. Laws, c. 13, § 13; 83 Del. Laws, c. 129, § 1.

Revisor's note.
Section 6 of 83 Del. Laws, c. 129, provided: "This act is effective immediately and is to be implemented the earlier of the following:
"(1) Notice by the Secretary of Labor published in the Register of Regulations that final regulations to implement this act have been promulgated.

"(2) One year from the date of the act's enactment." The act was signed by the Governor on Sept. 9, 2021.

Effect of amendments.
83 Del. Laws, c. 13, effective April 13, 2021, in the introductory paragraph of (g), added a comma following "selection" and following "national origin" in the first sentence and added "For purposes of this subsection"; and added (g)(1) and (g)(2).
83 Del. Laws, c. 129, effective Sept. 9, 2021, added (b)(2)-(4).

§ 205. Apprenticeship and Training Fund.

(a) A special fund known as the Apprenticeship and Training Fund ("Fund") is established and the State Treasurer shall invest the Fund consistent with the investment policies established by the Cash Management Policy Board. The State Treasurer shall credit interest to the Fund on a monthly basis consistent with the rate established by the Cash Management Policy Board.

(b) The following moneys must be deposited in the Fund:

(1) All payments made under § 6960A of Title 29.

(2) Any other money appropriated or transferred to the Fund by the General Assembly.

(c) The Department of Labor must allocate the money in the Fund at least annually, as follows:

(1) Twenty percent, after administrative costs, to the Apprenticeship and Training Section of the Department of Labor to do any of the following:

a. To promote and increase education and public awareness about registered apprenticeship and other occupational training.

b. To support pre-apprenticeship programs.

(2) Eighty percent, after administrative costs, to the Department of Education to support the related technical instruction of registered apprenticeship programs, including new areas of technical instruction for crafts that are in-demand by employers in this State, and to support pre-apprenticeship programs. The Department of Education shall disperse money from this Fund for the same purposes as other appropriations for adult trade extension and apprenticeship programs.

(3) No more than 15% of the money annually deposited into the Fund may be used for administering this Fund.

(d) Money in the Fund may not be used to supplant existing state funding.

(e) Notwithstanding paragraph (c)(3) of this section, money appropriated by the General Assembly to implement this section may be reimbursed from money received under this section.

History.
83 Del. Laws, c. 129, § 2.

Revisor's note.
Section 6 of 83 Del. Laws, c. 129, provided: "This act is effective immediately and is to be implemented the earlier of the following:
"(1) Notice by the Secretary of Labor published in the Register of Regulations that final regulations to implement this act have been promulgated.
"(2) One year from the date of the act's enactment." The act was signed by the Governor on Sept. 9, 2021.

CHAPTER 7
EMPLOYMENT PRACTICES

SUBCHAPTER II
DISCRIMINATION IN EMPLOYMENT

§ 710. Definitions.

For the purposes of this subchapter:

(1) "Age" as used in this subchapter means the age of 40 or more years of age.

(2) "Charging party" means any individual or the Department who initiates proceedings by the filing of a verified charge of discrimination, and who preserves a cause of action in Superior Court by exhausting the administrative remedies pursuant to the provisions of § 714 of this title.

(3) "Conciliation" for the purposes of this chapter refers to a process which requires the appearance of the parties after a full investigation resulting in a final determination of reasonable cause.

(4) "Delaware Right to Sue Notice" for the purposes of this chapter refers to a final acknowledgement of the charging party's exhaustion of the administrative remedies provided herein and written notification to the charging party of a corresponding right to commence a lawsuit in Superior Court.

(5) "Domestic violence" means the same as defined in § 1041 of Title 10, verified by an official document, such as a court order, or by a reliable third-party professional, including a law-enforcement agency or officer, a domestic violence or domestic abuse service provider, or health-care provider.

(6) "Employee" means an individual employed by an employer, but does not include:

    a. Any individual employed in agriculture or in the domestic service of any person,

    b. Any individual who, as a part of that individual's employment, resides in the personal residence of the employer,

    c. Any individual employed by said individual's parents, spouse or child, or

    d. Any individual elected to public office in the State or political subdivision by the qualified voters thereof, or any person chosen by such officer to be on such officer's personal staff, or an appointee on the policy making level or an immediate advisor with respect to the exercise of the constitutional or legal powers of the office. The exemption set forth in the preceding sentence shall not include employees subject to the merit service rules or civil service rules of the state government or political subdivision.

(7) "Employer" means any person employing 4 or more employees within the State at the time of the alleged violation, including the State or any political subdivision or board, department, commission or school district thereof. The term "employer" with respect to discriminatory practices based upon sexual orientation or gender identity does not include religious corporations, associations or societies whether supported, in whole or in part, by government appropriations, except where

the duties of the employment or employment opportunity pertain solely to activities of the organization that generate unrelated business taxable income subject to taxation under § 511(a) of the Internal Revenue Code of 1986 [26 U.S.C. § 511(a)].

(8) "Employment agency" means any person regularly undertaking with or without compensation to procure employees for an employer or to procure for employees opportunities to work for an employer and includes an agent of such a person.

(9) "Family responsibilities" means the obligations of an employee to care for any family member who would qualify as a covered family member under the Family and Medical Leave Act [26 U.S.C. § 2601 et seq.].

(10) "Gender identity" means a gender-related identity, appearance, expression or behavior of a person, regardless of the person's assigned sex at birth.

(11) "Genetic information" for the purpose of this chapter means the results of a genetic test as defined in § 2317(a)(3) of Title 18.

(12) "Job related and consistent with business necessity" means the condition in question renders the individual unable to perform the essential functions of the position that such individual holds or desires. This includes situations in which the individual poses a direct threat to the health or safety of the individual or others in the workplace.

(13) "Labor organization" includes any organization of any kind, any agency or employee representation committee, group, association or plan so engaged in which employees participate and which exists for the purpose, in whole or in part, of dealing with employers concerning grievances, labor disputes, wages, rates of pay, hours or other terms or conditions of employment, any conference, general committee, joint or system board or joint council so engaged which is subordinate to a national or international labor organization.

(14) "Mediation" for the purposes of this chapter refers to an expedited process for settling employment disputes with the assistance of an impartial third party prior to a full investigation.

(15) "No cause determination" means that the Department has completed its investigation and found that there is no reasonable cause to believe that an unlawful employment practice has occurred or is occurring. A no cause determination is a final determination ending the administrative process and provides the charging party with a corresponding Delaware Right to Sue Notice.

(16) "Person" includes 1 or more individuals, labor unions, partnerships, associations, corporations, legal representatives, mutual companies, joint-stock companies, trusts, unincorporated organizations, trustees, trustees in bankruptcy or receivers.

(17) "Pregnancy" means pregnancy, childbirth, or a related condition, including, but not limited to, lactation.

(18) "Protective hairstyle" includes braids, locks, and twists.

(19) "Public employer" means the State of Delaware, its agencies, or political subdivisions.

(20) "Race" includes traits historically associated with race, including hair texture and a protective hairstyle.

(21) "Reasonable accommodation" has the meaning given this term in § 722 of this title, except that all references to disability shall instead be references to known limitations of a person related to pregnancy, childbirth, or a related condition. Accommodations available under this subchapter may include, but are not limited to, acquisition of equipment for

sitting, more frequent or longer breaks, periodic rest, assistance with manual labor, job restructuring, light duty assignments, modified work schedules, temporary transfers to less strenuous or hazardous work, time off to recover from childbirth, or break time and appropriate facilities for expressing breast milk.

(22) "Reasonable cause determination" means that the Department has completed its investigation and found reasonable cause to believe that an unlawful employment practice has occurred or is occurring. A reasonable cause determination requires the parties' good faith efforts in conciliation.

(23) "Religion" as used in this subchapter includes all aspects of religious observance and practice, as well as belief, unless an employer demonstrates that the employer is unable to reasonably accommodate an employee's or prospective employee's religious observance or practice without undue hardship on the conduct of the employer's business.

(24) "Reproductive health decision" means any decision related to the use or intended use of a particular drug, device, or medical service, including the use or intended use of contraception or fertility control or the planned or intended initiation or termination of a pregnancy.

(25) "Respondent" means any person named in the Charge of Discrimination, including but not limited to employers, employment agencies, labor organizations, joint labor-management committees, controlling apprenticeship or other training programs including on-the-job training programs.

(26) "Secretary" means the Secretary of the Department of Labor or the Secretary's designee.

(27) "Sexual offense" means the same as defined in § 761 of Title 11, verified by an official document, such as a court order, or by a reliable third-party professional, including a law-enforcement agency or officer, a domestic violence or domestic abuse service provider, or health-care provider.

(28) "Sexual orientation" includes heterosexuality, homosexuality, or bisexuality.

(29) "Stalking" means the same as in § 1312 of Title 11, verified by an official document, such as a court order, or by a reliable third-party professional, including a law-enforcement agency or officer, a sexual assault service provider, or health-care provider. It is the sexual assault or stalking victim's responsibility to provide the reliable statement from the reliable third party.

(30) "Undue hardship" means an action requiring significant difficulty or expense when considered in light of factors such as: the nature and cost of the accommodation; the overall financial resources of the employer; the overall size of the business of the employer with respect to the number of employees, and the number, type and location of its facilities; and the effect on expenses and resources or the impact otherwise of such accommodation upon the operation of the employer.

History.

19 Del. C. 1953, § 710; 58 Del. Laws, c. 285; 62 Del. Laws, c. 97, § 1; 70 Del. Laws, c. 186, § 1; 71 Del. Laws, c. 457, § 2; 74 Del. Laws, c. 356; 77 Del. Laws, c. 90, §§ 15, 16; 79 Del. Laws, c. 47, §§ 17, 18; 79 Del. Laws, c. 227, § 1; 79 Del. Laws, c. 429, § 1; 80 Del. Laws, c. 57, § 1; 80 Del. Laws, c. 291, § 1; 80 Del. Laws, c. 292, § 1; 83 Del. Laws, c. 13, § 14; 83 Del. Laws, c. 195, § 5.

Effect of amendments.

83 Del. Laws, c. 13, effective Apr. 13, 2021, added present (18) and (20), redesignating the intervening and remaining paragraphs accordingly.

83 Del. Laws, c. 195, effective Sept. 17, 2021, deleted the final sentence in (10); and substituted "includes" for "exclusively means" in (28).

§ 711. Unlawful employment practices; employer practices.

NOTES TO DECISIONS

Analysis

Prima facie case.
— Not established.

Prima facie case.

— Not established.

Where a former employee alleged retaliation under the Delaware Discrimination in Employment Act (19 Del. C. § 710 et seq.), that employee failed to meet the initial burden of establishing a prima facie causal link between the protected activity of complaints of a hostile work environment and the adverse actions of the employee's suspension without pay and subsequent termination. Bateman v. State, — A.3d —, 2020 Del. Super. LEXIS 2827 (Del. Super. Ct. Oct. 5, 2020), aff'd, 256 A.3d 206 (Del. 2021).

§ 712. Enforcement provisions; powers of the Department; administrative process.

NOTES TO DECISIONS

Judicial review.

A right-to-sue notice, issued by the Department of Labor based on an administrative finding of "reasonable cause," did not act as a determination on the material issues in plaintiff's discrimination case and merely gave plaintiff the right to commence a suit in court; therefore, collateral estoppel and res judicata did not apply with regard to the Department's ruling. Paskins v. Creative Concepts, Inc., — A.3d —, 2020 Del. Super. LEXIS 2834 (Del. Super. Ct. Oct. 12, 2020).

SUBCHAPTER III
PERSONS WITH DISABILITIES EMPLOYMENT PROTECTIONS

§ 722. Definitions.

As used in this subchapter, unless the context otherwise requires:

(1) The terms "person," "employee," "employment agency," "labor organizations," "Secretary" and "review board" are defined in § 710 of this title.

(2) "Disability" means any condition or characteristic that renders a person a person with a disability as defined in this section.

(3) "Employer" means a person qualifying as an employer under § 710 of this title.

(4) "Person with a disability" means any person who satisfies any 1 of the following:

a. Has a physical or mental impairment which substantially limits 1 or more major life activities.

b. Has a record of such an impairment.

c. Is regarded as having such an impairment. As used in this paragraph:

1. "Major life activities" includes caring for oneself, performing manual tasks, seeing, hearing, eating, sleeping, walking, standing, lifting, bending, speaking, breathing, learning, reading, concentrating, thinking, communicating, and working. "Major life activities" also includes the operation of a major bodily function, including functions of the immune system, normal cell growth, digestive, bowel, bladder, neurological brain, respiratory, circulatory, endocrine, and reproductive functions.

2. "Has a record of such impairment" means has a history of, or has been misclassified as having, a mental or physical impairment that substantially limits 1 or more major life activities.

3. "Is regarded as having an impairment" means an individual that establishes that the individual subjected to an action prohibited under this chapter because of an actual or perceived

physical or mental impairment whether or not the impairment limits or is perceived to limit a major life activity. Such impairment does not include impairments that are transitory and minor.

This term is intended to be interpreted in conformity with the federal Rehabilitation Act of 1973 [29 U.S.C. § 701 et seq.], as amended, and, consistent with § 728 of this title, shall be further defined by the Secretary through regulation to clarify and delimit its scope following adequate public notice and comment.

Enforcement of this subchapter by persons qualifying for protection solely under this paragraph (4)c. of this section shall be deferred until the issuance of the Secretary's final regulation.

4. "Substantially limits" means that the impairment so affects a person as to create a likelihood that such person will experience difficulty in securing, retaining or advancing in employment because of a disability.

5. "Person with a disability" shall not include any individual who is an alcoholic or drug abuser whose current use of alcohol or drugs prevents such individual from performing the duties of the job in question or whose employment, by reason of such current alcohol or drug abuse, would constitute a direct threat to property or the safety of others.

6. "Transitory impairment" means an impairment with an actual or expected duration of 6 months or less.

(5) "Qualified person with a disability" means a person with a disability who, with or without reasonable accommodation, can satisfactorily perform the essential functions of the job in question:

a. Provided that the person with a disability shall not be held to standards of performance of essential job functions different from other employees similarly employed; and

b. Further provided that the disability does not create an unreasonable and demonstrable risk to the safety or health of the person with a disability, other employees, the employer's customers or the public.

(6) "Reasonable accommodation" means making reasonable changes in the work place, including, but not limited to, making facilities accessible, modifying equipment and providing mechanical aids to assist in operating equipment, or making reasonable changes in the schedules or duties of the job in question that would accommodate the known disability of a person with a disability by enabling such person to satisfactorily perform the essential duties of the job in question; provided that "reasonable accommodation," unless otherwise prescribed by applicable law, does not require that an employer:

a. Provide accommodations of a personal nature, including, but not limited to, eyeglasses, hearing aids or prostheses, except under the same terms and conditions as such items are provided to the employer's employees generally;

b. Reassign duties of the job in question to other employees without assigning to the employee with a disability duties that would compensate for those reassigned;

c. Reassign duties of the job in question to 1 or more other employees where such reassignment would significantly increase the skill, effort or responsibility required of such other employees from that required prior to the change in duties;

d. Make changes to accommodate a person with a disability where:

    1. For a new employee the cost of such changes would exceed 5 percent of the annual salary or annualized hourly wage of the job in question; or

    2. For an existing employee the total cost of the changes would bring the total cost of changes made to accommodate the employee's disabilities since the employee's initial acceptance of employment with the employer to greater than 5 percent of the employee's current salary or current annualized hourly wage; or

e. Make any changes that would impose on the employer an undue hardship, provided that the costs of less than 5 percent of an employee's salary or annualized wage as determined in paragraph (6)d. of this section shall be presumed not to be an undue hardship.

History.

66 Del. Laws, c. 337, § 2; 70 Del. Laws, c. 572, § 1; 78 Del. Laws, c. 179, §§ 254-260; 79 Del. Laws, c. 381, § 1; 83 Del. Laws, c. 195, § 5.

Effect of amendments.

83 Del. Laws, c. 195, effective Sept. 17, 2021, deleted "paragraph (4) of" in (2); added "satis-fies any 1 of the following" in the introductory paragraph of (4); substituted a period for a semicolon in (4)a. and for "; or" in (4)b.; deleted "the term" from the end of the introductory clause of (4)c.; rewrote (4)c.1. and (4)c.3., including deleting (4)c.3.A. through (4)c.3.B.; added "1 or more" in (4)c.2.; and added (4)c.6.

NOTES TO DECISIONS

Reasonable accommodation.

Post-pregnancy disabled employee did not meet the burden of showing that the employer could have made reasonable accommodations allowing the employee to work at home, because outsourcing those tasks requiring on-site work at the company's office to another employee would have required the employer to incur additional costs of up to 10% of the disabled employee's salary; such a requirement would have placed an undue hardship on the employer. Obilor v. E. I. DuPont De Nemours & Co., — A.3d —, 2021 Del. Super. LEXIS 17 (Del. Super. Ct. Jan. 7, 2021).

CHAPTER 9
MINIMUM WAGE

Sec.
902. Minimum wage rate.

§ 902. Minimum wage rate [For current federal minimum wage, see 29 U.S.C. § 206(a)(1)(A)].

(a) Except as may otherwise be provided under this chapter, every employer shall pay to every employee in any occupation wages of a rate:

    (1) Not less than $9.25 per hour until January 1, 2022;

    (2) Not less than $10.50 per hour effective January 1, 2022;

    (3) Not less than $11.75 per hour effective January 1, 2023;

    (4) Not less than $13.25 per hour effective January 1, 2024;

    (5) Not less than $15.00 per hour effective January 1, 2025.

Upon the establishment of a federal minimum wage in excess of the state minimum wage, the minimum wage in this State shall be equal in amount to the federal minimum wage, except as may otherwise be provided under this chapter.

(b) Gratuities received by employees engaged in occupations in which gratuities customarily constitute part of the remuneration may be considered wages for purposes of this chapter in an amount equal to the tip credit percentage, as set by the federal government as of June 15, 2006, of the minimum rate as set forth in subsection (a) of this section. In no event shall the minimum rate, under this subsection, be less than $2.23 per hour.

(c) For purposes of this section:

    (1) An employee engaged in an occupation in which gratuities customarily constitute part of the remuneration shall be any worker engaged in

an occupation in which workers customarily and regularly receive more than $30 per month in tips or gratuities.

(2) "Gratuities" means monetary contributions received directly or indirectly by an employee from a guest, patron or customer for services rendered where the customer is entirely free to determine whether to make any payment at all and, if so, the amount.

(3) A "primary direct service employee" is one who in a given situation performs the main direct service for a customer and is to be considered the recipient of the gratuity.

(4) A "service charge" is an obligatory sum of money included in the statement of charges. Clear and conspicuous notice must be made on either the menu, placard, the front of the statement of charges or other notice given to the customer indicating that all or part of the service charge is the property of the management. Such notice must be clearly printed, stamped or written in bold type. A service charge assessed to customers, patrons or guests without such notice is the property of the primary direct service employee(s). For the purposes of this section, type which is at least 18 points (¼ inch) on the placard, or 10 points (⅛ inch) or larger on all other notices shall be considered clear and conspicuous.

(d)(1) Any gratuity received by an employee, indicated on any receipt as a gratuity, or deposited in or about a place of business for direct services rendered by an employee is the sole property of the primary direct service employee and may not be taken or retained by the employer except as required by state or federal law.

(2) Employees may establish a system for the sharing or pooling of gratuities among direct service employees, provided that the employer shall not in any fashion require or coerce employees to agree upon such a system. Where more than 1 direct service employee provides personal service to the same customer from whom gratuities are received, the employer may require that such employees establish a tip pooling or sharing system not to exceed 15% of the primary direct service employee's gratuities. The employer shall not, under any circumstances, receive any portion of the gratuities received by the employees.

(3) The Department may require the employer to pay restitution if the employer diverts any gratuities of its employees in the amount of the gratuities diverted. If the records maintained by the employer do not provide sufficient information to determine the exact amount of gratuities diverted, the Department may make a determination of gratuities diverted based on available evidence.

(e)(1) *Training wage.* — In lieu of the minimum wage otherwise required under this section, an employer may pay an employee who is 18 years of age or older, during the first 90 consecutive calendar days after the employee is initially employed by the employer, a wage rate that is not more than $0.50 less than the wage rate prescribed in subsection (a) of this section.

(2) *Youth wage.* — In lieu of the minimum wage otherwise required by this section, an employer may pay an employee who is under 18 years of age a wage rate that is not more than $0.50 less than the wage rate prescribed in subsection (a) of this section.

History.
19 Del. C. 1953, § 902; 55 Del. Laws, c. 18, § 1; 56 Del. Laws, c. 134, § 1; 56 Del. Laws, c. 339; 57 Del. Laws, c. 691; 59 Del. Laws, c. 470, § 1; 64 Del. Laws, c. 84, § 1; 65 Del. Laws, c. 436, § 1; 66 Del. Laws, c. 28, § 1; 67 Del. Laws, c. 141, §§ 1, 3, 4; 70 Del. Laws, c. 319, §§ 1, 2; 72 Del. Laws, c. 16, § 1; 75 Del. Laws, c. 314,

§ 1; 79 Del. Laws, c. 186, § 1; 81 Del. Laws, c. 301, § 1; 81 Del. Laws, c. 302, § 1; 83 Del. Laws, c. 81, § 1.

Effect of amendments.

83 Del. Laws, c. 81, effective July 19, 2021, added present (a)(1) and redesignated the remaining paragraphs in (a) accordingly; in present (a)(2), substituted "$10.50" for "$7.75" and "January 1, 2022" for "June 1, 2014"; in present (a)(3), substituted "$11.75" for "$8.25" and "January 1, 2023" for "June 1, 2015"; in present (a)(4), substituted "$13.25" for "$8.75" and "January 1, 2024" for "January 1, 2019"; and, in present (a)(5), substituted "$15.00" for "$9.25" and "January 1, 2025" for "October 1, 2019".

CHAPTER 11
WAGE PAYMENT AND COLLECTION

§ 1101. Definition of terms.

NOTES TO DECISIONS

Analysis

Employees.
— Contact with Delaware.

Employees.

— Contact with Delaware.

Defendants' motion to dismiss a claim for violation of the Delaware Wage Payment and Collection Act (19 Del. C. § 1101 et seq.) was granted because plaintiffs were not "employees" as defined by the Act; defendants could apply for protection under the Act where none of the plaintiffs physically worked in Delaware during their employment. Servaas v. Ford Smart Mobility Llc & Journey Holding Corp., 2021 Del. Ch. LEXIS 186.

§ 1103. Employees separated from the payroll before regular paydays.

NOTES TO DECISIONS

Analysis

Wages.
— Duty to pay.

Wages.

— Duty to pay.

Defendants' motion to dismiss a claim for violation of the Delaware Wage Payment and Collection Act (19 Del. C. § 1101 et seq.) was granted because plaintiffs were not "employees" as defined by the Act; defendants could apply for protection under the Act where none of the plaintiffs physically worked in Delaware during their employment. Servaas v. Ford Smart Mobility Llc & Journey Holding Corp., 2021 Del. Ch. LEXIS 186.

CHAPTER 13
PUBLIC EMPLOYMENT RELATIONS ACT

§ 1311A. Collective bargaining in the state service.

Revisor's note.

Section 8(a) of 76 Del. Laws, c. 280, effective July 1, 2008; 78 Del. Laws, c. 290, § 8(a), effective July 1, 2012; 79 Del. Laws, c. 78, § 8(a), effective July 1, 2013; 79 Del. Laws, c. 290, § 8(a), effective July 1, 2014; 80 Del. Laws, c. 79, § 8(a), effective July 1, 2015; 80 Del. Laws, c. 298, § 8(a), effective July 1, 2016; 81 Del. Laws, c. 58, § 8(a), effective July 3, 2017; 81 Del. Laws, c. 280, § 8(a), effective July 1, 2018; 82 Del. Laws, c. 26, § 4, effective Jan. 1, 2020; 82 Del. Laws, c. 64, § 8(a), effective July 1, 2019; and as amended by 82 Del. Laws, c. 242, § 8(a), effective July 1, 2020, 82 Del. Laws, c. 243, § 25, effective July 1, 2020; and 83 Del. Laws, c. 54, § 8(a), effective June 30, 2021, provided: "(a) All provisions of subsections (a)(1), (b), (c), and (i) through (*l*) of this section shall not apply to those Merit System employees who are covered by a final collective bargaining agreement under 19 Del. C. § 1311A or 19 Del. C. c. 16. The effective dates of agreements pursuant to 19 Del. C. § 1311A or 19 Del. C. c. 16 shall occur simultaneously with the fiscal year following final agreement between the State of Delaware and ratification of that agreement by the respective certified bargaining unit, provided funds are appropriated in Section 1 of this act for said agreements. All pay changes shall become effective on the first day of a full pay cycle. Section 1 of this act makes no appropriation, and no subsequent appropriation shall be made during the fiscal year, for any compensation items as defined in 19 Del. C. § 1311A reached as a result of negotiations, mediation, or interest arbitration. Should a bargaining agreement not be finalized by December 1 or May 1 of each fiscal year, employees represented by the bargaining unit negotiating said agreement shall receive compensation pursuant to the provisions of this section until such time as an agreement takes effect. A final bargaining agreement shall be defined as an agreement between the State of Delaware and a certified bargaining unit, which is not retroactive and in which the agree-

ment's completion is achieved through ratification by the respective bargaining unit, mediation, or binding interest arbitration."

CHAPTER 16
POLICE OFFICERS' AND FIREFIGHTERS' EMPLOYMENT RELATIONS ACT

Subchapter I. General Provisions

Sec.
1602. Definitions [For application of this sec-
     tion, see 83 Del. Laws, c.146, §§ 2, 3].

SUBCHAPTER I
GENERAL PROVISIONS

§ 1602. Definitions [For application of this section, see 83 Del. Laws, c.146, §§ 2, 3].

As used in this chapter:

(1) "Appropriate bargaining unit" or "bargaining unit" means a group of police officers or firefighters designated by the Public Employment Relations Board as appropriate for representation by an employee organization for purposes of collective bargaining.

(2) "Binding interest arbitration" means the procedure by which the Public Employment Relations Board shall make written findings of fact and a decision for final and binding resolution of an impasse arising out of collective bargaining.

(3) "Board" means the Public Employment Relations Board established by § 4006 of Title 14 and made applicable to this chapter by § 1306 of this title.

(4) "Certification" means official recognition by the Board, following a secret-ballot election, that an employee organization is the exclusive represen-tative for all employees in an appropriate bargaining unit.

(5) "Collective bargaining" means the performance of the mutual obligation of a public employer through its designated representatives and the exclusive bargaining representative to confer and negotiate in good faith with respect to terms and conditions of employment, and to execute a written contract incorporating any agreements reached. However, this obligation does not compel either party to agree to a proposal or require the making of a concession.

(6) "Decertification" means the withdrawal by the Board of an employee organization's official designation as exclusive representative following a decertification election which shows that the exclusive representative no longer has the support of a majority of the members in an appropriate bargaining unit.

(7) "Employee organization" means any organization which admits to mem-bership police officers or firefighters employed by a public employer and which has as a purpose the representation of such employees in collective bargaining, and includes any person acting as an officer, representative or agent of said organization.

(8) "Exclusive bargaining representative" or "exclusive representative" means the employee organization which as a result of certification by the Board has the right and responsibility to be the collective bargaining agent of all employees in that bargaining unit.

(9) "Impasse" means the failure of a public employer and the exclusive

bargaining representative to reach agreement in the course of collective bargaining.

(10) "Mediation" means an effort by an impartial third-party confidentially to assist in reconciling an impasse between the public employer and the exclusive bargaining representative regarding terms and conditions of employment.

(11) "Police officer" means as defined in § 8401 of Title 11 and includes probation and parole officers of the Department of Correction. "Police officer" does not include any of the following:

a. The Department of Correction's Director of Probation and Parole, correctional officers and similar correctional occupations.

b. Correctional supervisors and nonuniformed correctional employees who are employed in a secure facility operated by the Department of Correction or the Department of Services for Children, Youth and their Families, or who have inmate contact which is composed of correctional lieutenants, staff lieutenants, correctional captains, nonuniformed correctional employees who are employed in a secure Department of Correction facility or who have inmate contact and similar occupations.

c. Persons and officers not included pursuant to § 8401(6)b. of Title 11.

d. The Attorney General and the Attorney General's deputies.

e. Any position at a director or executive level whose essential job function and advanced knowledge about the issues involved in collective bargaining would make it unduly burdensome for the employer to negotiate effectively if the employee were a member of an appropriate bargaining unit. This exclusion applies only to those units not already organized upon September 10, 2021, the effective date of this exclusion.

(12) "Public employee" or "employee" means any police officer or firefighter employed by a public employer except those determined by the Board to be inappropriate for inclusion in the bargaining unit; provided, however, that for the purposes of this chapter with respect to any state employee covered under the State Merit System, position classification, health care and other benefit programs established pursuant to Chapters 52 and 96 of Title 29, workers' compensation, disability programs and pension programs shall not be deemed to be compensation.

(13)a. "Public employer" or "employer" means the State or political subdivisions of the State or any agency thereof, any county, or any agency thereof, or any municipal corporation or municipality, city or town located within the State or any agency thereof, which:

1. Upon the affirmative legislative act of its common council or other governing body has elected to come within Chapter 13 of this title;

2. Hereafter elects to come within this chapter; or

3. Employs 25 or more full-time employees. For the purposes of this paragraph, "employees" shall include each and every person employed by the public employer except:

A. Any person elected by popular vote; and

B. Any person appointed to serve on a board or commission.

b. "Public employer" or "employer" includes the Town of Delmar, Delaware.

(14) "Strike" means a public employee's failure, in concerted action with others, to report for duty, or the public employee's wilful absence from the public employee's position, or the public employee's stoppage or deliberate slowing down of work, or the public employee's withholding in whole or in part from the full, faithful and proper performance of the public employee's duties

of employment, or the public employee's involvement in a concerted interruption of operations of a public employer for the purpose of inducing, influencing or coercing a change in the conditions, compensation rights, privileges or obligations of public employment; however, nothing shall limit or impair the right of any public employee to lawfully express or communicate a complaint or opinion on any matter related to terms and conditions of employment.

(15) "Terms and conditions of employment" means matters concerning or related to wages, salaries, hours, grievance procedures and working conditions; provided, however, that such term shall not include those matters determined by this chapter or any other law of the State to be within the exclusive prerogative of the public employer.

History.

65 Del. Laws, c. 477, § 1; 70 Del. Laws, c. 163, § 1; 70 Del. Laws, c. 186, § 1; 70 Del. Laws, c. 466, § 1; 72 Del. Laws, c. 271, §§ 1, 8; 74 Del. Laws, c. 173, § 1; 83 Del. Laws, c. 127, § 1; 83 Del. Laws, c. 146, § 1.

Revisor's note.

Section 2 of 83 Del. Laws, c. 146, provided: "This act applies only to collective bargaining agreements entered into after the enactment of this act. Existing collective bargaining agreements regarding compensation will remain in effect until such time as they, by their terms expire." The act became effective upon the signature of the Governor on Sept. 10, 2021.

Section 3 of 83 Del. Laws, c. 146, provided: "This act applies only to bargaining units not certified pursuant to Chapter 16 of this title as of the effective date of this act, and is not intended and should not be construed to affect the rights of any public employer, police officer, or firefighter already covered by this act." The act became effective upon the signature of the Governor on Sept. 10, 2021.

Effect of amendments.

83 Del. Laws, c. 127, effective Sept. 7, 2021, redesignated *(l)* as present *(l)*(1), former *(l)*(1)-*(l)*(3) as present *(l)*(1)a.-*(l)*(1)c. and former *(l)*(3)a. and *(l)*(3)b. as present *(l)*(1)c.1. and *(l)*(1)c.2.; and added present *(l)*(2).

83 Del. Laws, c. 146, effective Sept. 10, 2021, redesignated the lettered subsections as numbered paragraphs; added the introductory paragraph and present (11), redesignating the remaining paragraphs accordingly; and, in present (12), substituted "with respect to" for "this term shall not include" and added "position classification...deemed to be compensation".

§ 1613. Collective bargaining agreements.

NOTES TO DECISIONS

Residency requirement.

Arbitration award in favor of a police union, regarding a residency requirement for city police officers, was not contrary to law; 22 Del. C. § 841 (imposing residency requirements for municipalities with a population exceeding 50,000) lacked a fixed meaning of residency, leaving room to bargain over the meaning of "residence" under the Police Officers and Firefighters' Employment Relations Act (19 Del. C. § 1601 et seq.). City of Wilmington v. Wilmington FOP Lodge No.1, Inc., — A.3d —, 2020 Del. Ch. LEXIS 389 (Del. Ch. Jan. 22, 2020).

CHAPTER 17
WHISTLEBLOWERS' PROTECTION

§ 1702. Definitions.

NOTES TO DECISIONS

Fund misappropriation.

Former firefighter plaintiff failed to state a claim under the Whistleblowers' Protection Act (19 Del. C. § 1701 et seq.), as plaintiff failed to allege that funds used by the chief of a fire department were under the control of plaintiff's employer; plaintiff's filings actually appeared to state the opposite, alleging that the chief's misconduct was for use of funds related to a third party. Hayman v. City of Wilmington, — A.3d —, 2020 Del. Super. LEXIS 2863 (Del. Super. Ct. Oct. 29, 2020).

PART II
WORKERS' COMPENSATION

CHAPTER 23
WORKERS' COMPENSATION

Subchapter I. General Provisions

Sec.

2301A. Industrial Accident Board.

SUBCHAPTER I
GENERAL PROVISIONS

§ 2301. Definitions.

NOTES TO DECISIONS

Analysis

Causation.

Compensable.

— Physical conditions.

Employment relationships.

— Employer-employee.

Scope of employment.

— Going and coming rule.

Causation.

Industrial Accident Board's decision that an employee had sustained compensable work-related injuries was supported by substantial evidence because the Board did not err when it credited a doctor's opinion that the employee's injuries were, with a high degree of medical probability, caused by the work-related injury; the doctor's ultimate causation opinion, expressed to a reasonable degree of medical probability at least twice, was substantial evidence of causation. Alutech United, Inc. v. Sammons, 2021 Del. Super. LEXIS 545 (Del. Super. Ct. Aug. 12, 2021).

Compensable.

— Physical conditions.

Industrial Accident Board was the appropriate decision-making body to determine in the first instance whether COVID-19 was defined as an "occupational disease" under Delaware Worker's Compensation Act (19 Del. C. § 2301 et seq.); because plaintiff had filed a petition with the Board within the 1-year statute of limitations, and preserved the claim, the case would be returned to the Board in order for it to make that determination. Ingino-Cacchioli v. Infinity Consulting Sols, Inc., 2021 Del. Super. LEXIS 560 (Del. Super. Ct. Aug. 19, 2021).

Employment relationships.

— Employer-employee.

Attempts to link the defendant corporation's refusal to accept an employment application to a workers' compensation retaliation claim were devoid of any merit; as defendants pointed out in their motion to dismiss, plaintiff was not an "employee" as defined in 19 Del. C. § 2301. Tolliver v. Del. Futures, Inc., — A.3d —, 2021 Del. Super. LEXIS 69 (Del. Super. Ct. Jan. 26, 2021), aff'd, 253 A.3d 1048 (Del. 2021).

Scope of employment.

— Going and coming rule.

Decision finding that an employee was not acting in the course and scope of employment when injured, thus making the employee ineligible for workers' compensation benefits, was affirmed; the Board was unable to conclude that the property in question could be considered to be the employer's premises as there was insufficient evidence to support a finding that the employer exercised the requisite control over the street where the employee fell. Browning v. State, — A.3d —, 2021 Del. Super. LEXIS 377 (Del. Super. Ct. May 3, 2021).

§ 2301A. Industrial Accident Board.

(a) The Industrial Accident Board is continued. It shall consist of 10 members, each of whom shall be appointed by the Governor for a term of 6 years and confirmed by the State Senate. The appointments shall be made so that there shall always be on the Board 2 residents of New Castle County outside of the City of Wilmington, 1 resident of the City of Wilmington, 2 residents of Kent County, 2 residents of Sussex County and 3 members-at-large residents of any of the subdivisions of the State, and not more than 6 of said members shall be of the same political party.

(b) Each member of the Board shall receive an annual salary of $24,240, except for the Chairperson, who shall receive an annual salary of $27,270. The members of the Board shall receive from the State their actual and necessary expenses while traveling on the business of the Board, but such expense shall be sworn to by the person who incurred the expense, and any such person falsely making any such report shall be guilty of perjury and punishable accordingly. The salary of the members of the Board shall be paid in the same manner as the salaries of state officers are paid.

(c) A majority of the members of the Board shall constitute a quorum for the exercise of any of the powers or authority conferred on the Board, except for hearings conducted pursuant to this title, in which case, 2 members of the Board shall constitute a quorum and a sufficient panel to decide such hearings. Any disagreement involving a procedural issue arising before or after a hearing may be decided by 1 member of the Board.

(d) The Board, any Board panel or any Board member empowered to decide any matter pursuant to Part II of this title shall act in conformity with applicable provisions of the Administrative Procedures Act set forth in Chapter 101 of Title 29, including, but not limited to, § 10129 of Title 29. Lawyers representing clients before the Board shall act in conformity with applicable provisions of the Delaware Lawyers' Rules of Professional Conduct, including, but not limited to, Rule 3.5 thereof. Disputes regarding prehearing or post-hearing matters shall be presented by written motion and decided by written order.

(e) The Governor shall appoint the Board's Chairperson from among the Board's members and the Chairperson shall serve at the Governor's pleasure in such capacity.

(f) The Administrator of the office of Workers' Compensation shall perform all the administrative duties of the Board, including, but not limited to, scheduling the docket, maintaining the Board's records and providing the liaison between the public and the Board members. The Department may employ such clerical and other staff as it deems necessary.

(g) The Board shall have a seal for authentication of its orders, awards and proceedings, upon which shall be inscribed the words — "Industrial Accident Board — Delaware — Seal."

(h) The Governor may, at any time, after notice and hearing, remove any Board member for gross inefficiency, neglect of duty, malfeasance, misfeasance or nonfeasance in office.

(i) The Board shall have jurisdiction over cases arising under Part II of this title and shall hear disputes as to compensation to be paid under Part II of this title. The Board may promulgate its own rules of procedure for carrying out its duties consistent with Part II of this title and the provisions of the Administrative Procedures Act [§ 10101 et seq. of Title 29]. Such rules shall be for the purpose of securing the just, speedy and inexpensive determination of every petition pursuant to Part II of this title. The rules shall not abridge, enlarge or modify any substantive right of any party and they shall preserve the rights of parties as declared by Part II of this title.

History.

Code 1915, § 3193w; 29 Del. Laws, c. 233; 37 Del. Laws, c. 241, § 1; Code 1935, §§ 373A, 6093; 43 Del. Laws, c. 270, § 1; 48 Del. Laws, c. 150, § 1; 19 Del. C. 1953, §§ 2101-2106, 2121; 51 Del. Laws, c. 285, § 1; 52 Del. Laws, c. 56; 53 Del. Laws, c. 229, § 1; 54 Del. Laws, c. 240; 57 Del. Laws, c. 669, § 12; 58 Del. Laws, c. 531, §§ 1-3; 62 Del. Laws, c. 127, §§ 1, 2; 64 Del. Laws, c. 170, § 1; 65 Del. Laws, c. 469, § 1; 69 Del. Laws, c. 142, §§ 1, 2; 69 Del. Laws, c. 383, § 1; 70 Del. Laws, c. 172, § 2; 70 Del. Laws, c. 186, § 1; 70 Del. Laws, c. 315, § 1; 71 Del. Laws, c. 84, § 2; 75 Del. Laws, c. 89, § 301; 82 Del. Laws, c. 242, § 259; 83 Del. Laws, c. 54, § 271.

Effect of amendments.

83 Del. Laws, c. 54, effective June 30, 2021, substituted "$24,240" for "24,000" and "$27,270" for "$27,000" in the first sentence of (b).

§ 2304. Compensation as exclusive remedy.

NOTES TO DECISIONS

Analysis

Causation.
Compensable injury.
Going and coming rule.
Indemnification.

Causation.

Industrial Accident Board's decision that an employee had sustained compensable work-related injuries was supported by substantial evidence because the Board did not err when it credited a doctor's opinion that the employee's injuries were, with a high degree of medical probability, caused by the work-related injury; the doctor's ultimate causation opinion, expressed to a reasonable degree of medical probability at least twice, was substantial evidence of causation. Alutech United, Inc. v. Sammons, 2021 Del. Super. LEXIS 545 (Del. Super. Ct. Aug. 12, 2021).

Compensable injury.

Industrial Accident Board was the appropriate decision-making body to determine in the first instance whether COVID-19 was defined as an "occupational disease" under Delaware Worker's Compensation Act (19 Del. C. § 2301 et seq.); because plaintiff had filed a petition with the Board within the 1-year statute of limitations, and preserved the claim, the case would be returned to the Board in order for it to make that determination. Ingino-Cacchioli v. Infinity Consulting Sols, Inc., 2021 Del. Super. LEXIS 560 (Del. Super. Ct. Aug. 19, 2021).

Going and coming rule.

Decision finding that an employee was not acting in the course and scope of employment when injured, thus making the employee ineligible for workers' compensation benefits, was affirmed; the Board was unable to conclude that the property in question could be considered to be the employer's premises as there was insufficient evidence to support a finding that the employer exercised the requisite control over the street where the employee fell. Browning v. State, — A.3d —, 2021 Del. Super. LEXIS 377 (Del. Super. Ct. May 3, 2021).

Indemnification.

In an insurance coverage dispute involving a student driver in a State-owned vehicle, the State had a duty to defend and indemnify the driver in the underlying tort action; the workers' compensation exclusivity doctrine did not apply to preclude the State's defense and indemnification of the driver in the underlying tort action brought by the driving instructor because the State was not a defendant in the underlying litigation. State of Def. Ins. Coverage Office v. Perkins-Johnson, — A.3d —, 2021 Del. Super. LEXIS 559 (Del. Super. Ct. Aug. 19, 2021).

SUBCHAPTER II

PAYMENTS FOR INJURIES OR DEATH AND INCIDENTAL BENEFITS

§ 2322. Medical and other services, and supplies as furnished by employer.

NOTES TO DECISIONS

Analysis

Medical expenses.
— Expenses unreasonable.

Medical expenses.

— Expenses unreasonable.

Substantial evidence supported the Industrial Accident Board's decision that claimant's second and third surgeries were unreasonable, and thus not compensable; the conclusion by the employer's expert regarding the unreasonableness of the surgeries was not only based on the expert's opinion, but on various factors including risks associated with multiple surgeries and the claimant's pre-and post-surgical medical condition. Baen v. Urgent Ambulance Serv., 2021 Del. Super. LEXIS 509 (Del. Super. Ct. July 14, 2021).

§ 2322F. Billing and payment for health-care services.

NOTES TO DECISIONS

Analysis

Utilization review.
— Reasonable and necessary.

Utilization review.

— Reasonable and necessary.

Substantial evidence supported the Industrial Accident Board's decision that claimant's fifth surgery was not reasonable and necessary or causally related to a November 2016 work injury because the Board found the testimony by the employer's medical expert persuasive; the expert's examination found that the claimant was neurologically normal and that dependency on opiates was driving the claimant's complaints. Padgett v. R&F Metals, 2021 Del. Super. LEXIS 494 (Del. Super. Ct. June 30, 2021).

§ 2324. Compensation for total disability.

NOTES TO DECISIONS

Analysis

Board authority.
Termination of benefits.
Termination of disability.

Board authority.

Substantial evidence supported the Industrial Accident Board's denial of the claimant's application for total disability benefits because: (1) the employer had physician testimony that questioned whether the claimant's subjective left-side symptoms left the claimant totally incapable of working or capable of working with restrictions; and (2) the Board chose to credit the physician's testimony over the testimony of the claimant's experts. Taylor v. State, 2021 Del. Super. LEXIS 488 (Del. Super. Ct. June 24, 2021).

Termination of benefits.

Where claimant housekeeper experienced an injured lumbar spine in a work accident, the Industrial Accident Board did not err by terminating benefits 1 year later because it: (1) accepted the opinion of the employer's expert and concluded that claimant had reached maximum medical improvement; (2) found that the claimant was able to work in the usual capacity required of the job without restrictions and (3) found that claimant's pain distribution was not consistent with a spinal nerve problem. Davalos v. Allan Indus., — A.3d —, 2021 Del. Super. LEXIS 261 (Del. Super. Ct. Mar. 31, 2021).

Termination of disability.

Decision of the Industrial Accident Board, concluding that claimant's work-related injury resolved on June 25, 2019, was upheld; it was based on the testimony of expert witnesses, as well as physical evidence in the form of surveillance video footage showing the claimant performing acts inconsistent with someone continuing to suffer from the injuries claimed. Peer v. State, — A.3d —, 2020 Del. Super. LEXIS 2860 (Del. Super. Ct. Oct. 29, 2020), aff'd, 251 A.3d 1016 (Del. 2021).

SUBCHAPTER III
DETERMINATION AND PAYMENT OF BENEFITS; PROCEDURE

§ 2350. Jurisdiction, procedure and decision on appeal; review by Board; costs and security.

NOTES TO DECISIONS

Analysis

Attorneys' fees.
Denial of benefits.
Remand hearing.

Attorneys' fees.

Claimant was entitled to an award of attorney's fees because: (1) although the compensation owed to the claimant had not yet been determined by the Industrial Accident Board, the claimant's counsel obtained a favorable result for the claimant; and (2) counsel had shown that the rate charged was commensurate with those customarily charged in Delaware workers' compensation cases, as well as properly reflective of counsel's experience, reputation and ability. Foraker v. Amazon.com, Inc., — A.3d —, 2021 Del. Super. LEXIS 30 (Del. Super. Ct. Jan. 12, 2021).

Denial of benefits.

Substantial evidence did not support the Industrial Accident Board's rejection of the employee's proposed spinal surgery; the Board accepted the opinion of the employer's doctor over the opinion of the employee's surgeon (despite the fact that the doctor offered inconsistent opinions regarding the lumbar injections) and offered contradictory opinions regarding whether the proposed spinal surgery was reasonable and necessary depending merely on which side's physician recommended it. Thompkins v. Reynolds Transp., — A.3d —, 2021 Del. Super. LEXIS 31 (Del. Super. Ct. Jan. 11, 2021).

Remand hearing.

Industrial Accident Board committed legal error on remand due to failure to permit new expert witness testimony on the issue of causation of a worker's injuries because: (1) the record showed that the employer requested permission to call new expert witnesses on the problematic issue of medical causation; and (2) on remand parties are entitled to introduce new evidence and new legal argument with respect to any issue identified as "problematic." Barrett Bus. Serv. v. Edge, — A.3d —, 2020 Del. Super. LEXIS 2855 (Del. Super. Ct. Oct. 29, 2020).

Fairness demanded that denial of workers' compensation benefits, following an employee's injury while latching the bottom shelf of a 2-level dolly, be remanded so that the Industrial Accident Board could consider the impact of evidence of at least 1 other claim of injury caused by the employer's 2-level dollies; such evidence might directly contradict testimony upon which the Board relied and could lead the Board to reject the credibility of the employer's witnesses. Cahall v. Walmart, — A.3d —, 2020 Del. Super. LEXIS 3000 (Del. Super. Ct. Dec. 15, 2020).

§ 2353. Forfeiture or suspension of right to compensation.

NOTES TO DECISIONS

Wilful misconduct.

Appellant forfeited any right to worker's compensation benefits, due to reckless and deliberate indifference to the danger of running in the workplace, because: (1) appellant admitted knowing that running in the plant was a safety violation; and (2) a team leader testified that, prior to the incident, appellant had been repeatedly told in both group settings and individually that running was a safety violation. Pierre v. Perdue Farms, — A.3d —, 2021 Del. Super. LEXIS 544 (Del. Super. Ct. Aug. 12, 2021).

§ 2354. Contribution by 2 or more employers.

NOTES TO DECISIONS

Joint employment.

Industrial Accident Board's erred in finding that a joint employment relationship existed at the time of the employee's injury because: (1) substantial evidence was not provided which suggested the employee (a truck driver) was under contract with both companies (a trucking company and a construction company) when the employee was injured; (2) the testimony from the construction company's vice president (that the employee signed that company's employment paperwork) was contradicted by the employee's statement (that the employee signed the trucking company's paperwork); and (3) the Board did not specify which factors supported its finding that the employee was under the simultaneous control of both companies, that services were simultaneously performed for both companies or that the services performed were closely related. Frederick v. A-Del Constr. Co., — A.3d —, 2020 Del. Super. LEXIS 2951 (Del. Super. Ct. Nov. 30, 2020).

§ 2362. Notice of denial of liability; penalty for delay in payment of compensation.

NOTES TO DECISIONS

Sanctions.

Insurer was not entitled to partial summary judgment on the issue of punitive damages because: (1) once the insurer received confirmation that the insured's employee was in fact electrocuted, it knew or reasonably should have known that the injury occurred in the course of employment; and (2) the extended claims inactivity after the adjuster's initial indifference, along with the insurer's violation of this statute's requirements, would permit a reasonable inference justifying punitive damages. Moyer v. Am. Zurich Ins. Co., — A.3d —, 2021 Del. Super. LEXIS 351 (Del. Super. Ct. Apr. 28, 2021).

§ 2363. Third person liable for injury; right of employee to sue and seek compensation; right of employer and insurer to enforce liability; notice of action; settlement and release of claim and effect thereof; amount of recovery; reimbursement of employer or insurer; expenses of recovery; apportionment; compensation benefits.

NOTES TO DECISIONS

Analysis

Exclusivity provision.
Indemnification.
Liens.

Exclusivity provision.

Superior Court did not err in granting summary judgment in favor of driver and driver's insurer with respect to employer and workers' compensation carrier's action seeking to recover $12,500 lump-sum benefit it paid to employee who was in a work-related accident cause by the driver; there was no evidence of damages that the employee would be able to recover from driver in tort action, as provided by this statute. ACW Corp. v. Maxwell, 242 A.3d 595 (Del. 2020).

Indemnification.

In an insurance coverage dispute involving a student driver in a State-owned vehicle, the State had a duty to defend and indemnify the driver in the underlying tort action; the workers' compensation exclusivity doctrine did not apply to preclude the State's defense and indemnification of the driver in the underlying tort action brought by the driving instructor because the State was not a defendant in the underlying litigation. State of Def. Ins. Coverage Office v. Perkins-Johnson, — A.3d —, 2021 Del. Super. LEXIS 559 (Del. Super. Ct. Aug. 19, 2021).

Liens.

In an appeal from a decision of the Industrial Accident Board, concerning the proper calculation for reimbursement of a workers' compensation lien after a third-party tort suit was resolved, the court concluded that the Board correctly ruled that the workers' compensation lien should be reduced by the entire amount of the recovery (including the full expenses paid in attorneys' fees and costs) to achieve the recovery of policy limits; the Board properly declined to assign any financial responsibility for the third-party litigation to the injured worker. Johnson v. State, — A.3d —, 2020 Del. Super. LEXIS 3035 (Del. Super. Ct. Dec. 31, 2020), aff'd, 257 A.3d 448 (Del. 2021).

PART III

UNEMPLOYMENT COMPENSATION

CHAPTER 31

UNEMPLOYMENT INSURANCE APPEAL BOARD

SUBCHAPTER I

GENERAL PROVISIONS

§ 3105. Compensation of Chairperson and other Board members.

The Chairperson of the Board shall be paid $ $235 for each meeting attended, not to exceed 80 meetings per year. Each of the other members of the Board shall be paid $185 for each meeting attended, not to exceed 80 meetings per year, and shall devote to the duties of their office such time as is necessary for the satisfactory execution thereof. The compensation of the Chairperson and other Board members shall be paid from the Unemployment Compensation Administration Fund provided for in § 3164 of this title, and not from any funds appropriated by the General Assembly.

History.
41 Del. Laws, c. 258, § 10; 44 Del. Laws, c. 208, § 1; 45 Del. Laws, c. 269, § 1; 46 Del. Laws, c. 162, § 13; 47 Del. Laws, c. 198, § 1; 48 Del. Laws, c. 179, § 4; 19 Del. C. 1953, § 3105; 50 Del. Laws, c. 586, § 1; 51 Del. Laws, c. 167; 54 Del. Laws, c. 45; 57 Del. Laws, c. 669, §§ 4B, 4C; 65 Del Laws, c. 417, § 1; 70 Del. Laws, c. 186, § 1; 71 Del. Laws, c. 90, §§ 1, 2; 75 Del. Laws, c. 127, § 1; 75 Del. Laws, c. 350, § 317; 78 Del. Laws, c. 341, § 3; 82 Del. Laws, c. 242, § 260; 82 Del. Laws, c. 284, § 1; 82 Del. Laws, c. 284, § 3; 83 Del. Laws, c. 54, § 272.

Effect of amendments.
83 Del. Laws, c. 54, effective June 30, 2021, substituted "$235" for "$225" in the first sentence and "$185" for "$175" in the second sentence.

CHAPTER 33

UNEMPLOYMENT COMPENSATION

SUBCHAPTER I
GENERAL PROVISIONS

§ 3302. Definitions.

NOTES TO DECISIONS

Unemployed.

Though appellant may have been under the impression that appellant receiving minimum work-hour assignments would be a top priority of the employer's, the record supported the finding that there was no guarantee; thus, there was substantial evidence to support the Unemployment Insurance Appeal Board's decision that appellant was not unemployed. Anderson v. Unemployment Ins. Appeal Bd., 2021 Del. Super. LEXIS 409 (Del. Super. Ct. May 13, 2021).

SUBCHAPTER II
COMPENSATION BENEFITS; DETERMINATION AND PAYMENT

§ 3314. Disqualification for benefits.

NOTES TO DECISIONS

Analysis

Exhaustion of administrative remedies.
Job abandonment.
Warning of discharge.

Exhaustion of administrative remedies.

Substantial evidence supported the Unemployment Insurance Appeal Board's decision that the claimant failed to exhaust all administrative remedies before quitting; while the claimant asserted that the reason for leaving employment was due to safety concerns following a robbery, there was no evidence that the claimant had attempted to raise the issue with management. Morales v. Dollar Tree Stores, Inc., 2021 Del. Super. LEXIS 539 (Del. Super. Ct. Aug. 9, 2021).

Job abandonment.

Where the employee applied for unemployment benefits on April 12, 2020, was unable to work from March 15, 2020, to June 8, 2020 (due to COVID-19 issues) and had declined to sign a statement that work had been offered as of June 8, 2020, the Unemployment Insurance Appeal Board's decision that the employee was terminated for just cause was free from legal error because: (1) the employee did not return to the workplace, or contact the employer, after refusing to sign the statement; (2) the employee was disqualified for unemployment insurance benefits, based upon job abandonment; (3) the Board found the employer's evidence more credible; and (4) the employee did not submit any evidence that could have rebutted the employer's testimony that there were other employees who had not signed the statement and remained employed. Latsch v. Meding & Son, Inc., — A.3d —, 2021 Del. Super. LEXIS 531 (Del. Super. Ct. Aug. 2, 2021).

Warning of discharge.

Lower court did not err in affirming the Unemployment Insurance Appeal Board's conclusion that the claimant was terminated without just cause because: (1) the Board reasonably found that the claimant's conduct did not warrant dismissal without warning; and (2) although no written warning was required, the employer's failure to issue a written warning left it for the Board to weigh the conflicting oral testimony regarding whether any warning was given. Kids & Teens Pediatrics of Dover v. O'Brien, 241 A.3d 218 (Del. 2020).

Employer discharged the claimant for just cause, thereby disqualifying the claimant from receiving unemployment insurance benefits because: (1) the claimant received verbal and written warnings regarding the claimant's absences and tardiness; (2) the written warning was not ambiguous; (3) Delaware law did not require a warning to inform an employee of termination; (4) the warning did put the claimant on notice that the claimant's behavior was in violation of the employer's policy; (5) the claimant's supervisor emailed the claimant that further acts of absenteeism would be considered insubordination and dealt with accordingly; and (6) the claimant engaged in further incidents of unchanged conduct before the employer terminated the claimant. Harris v. Del. Dep't of Labor, — A.3d —, 2020 Del. Super. LEXIS 2948 (Del. Super. Ct. Nov. 30, 2020).

§ 3318. Decision on claim by deputy; notice; appeal.

NOTES TO DECISIONS

Timeliness of appeal.

Unemployment Insurance Appeal Board lacked power to accept a claimant's appeal because the claimant did not file within the 10-day limitation period; the Board did not abuse its discretion in declining to exercise their discretion sua sponte in accepting the claimant's untimely appeal because the claimant had not shown sufficient facts and circumstances to warrant accepting the untimely appeal. Shepherd v. Advanced Home Health Servs., — A.3d —, 2021 Del. Super. LEXIS 164 (Del. Super. Ct. Feb. 26, 2021).

Unemployment Insurance Appeal Board did not err in finding that a former city maintenance worker's appeal was untimely because there was nothing in the record to support a claim that the worker had mailed a timely appeal prior to the deadline; further, the Board did not err in finding that no severe circumstances existed because there was substantial evidence to uphold the denial of benefits on the merits where the worker admitted having smoked marijuana in violation of the city's zero-tolerance drug and alcohol policy. Berry v.

Mayor & Council of Middletown, — A.3d —, 2021 Del. Super. LEXIS 188 (Del. Super. Ct. Mar. 4, 2021).

Unemployment Insurance Appeal Board decision, dismissing the claimant's appeal of an unemployment benefits determination, was supported by substantial evidence where: (1) the referee's decision, finding claimant was in receipt of overpaid benefits, was mailed to claimant's address on file with the Department of Labor on October 25, 2019; (2) the decision included notice that the final day to appeal the decision was November 4, 2019; and (3) although claimant had moved to a new residence at the beginning of November 2019, no updated address or appeal was filed until November 22, 2019. Coster v. Unemployment Ins. Appeal Bd., — A.3d —, 2021 Del. Super. LEXIS 286 (Del. Super. Ct. Apr. 6, 2021).

§ 3320. Review.

NOTES TO DECISIONS

Timeliness of appeal.

Unemployment Insurance Appeal Board lacked power to accept a claimant's appeal because the claimant did not file within the 10-day limitation period; the Board did not abuse its discretion in declining to exercise their discretion sua sponte in accepting the claimant's untimely appeal because the claimant had not shown sufficient facts and circumstances to warrant accepting the untimely appeal. Shepherd v. Advanced Home Health Servs., — A.3d —, 2021 Del. Super. LEXIS 164 (Del. Super. Ct. Feb. 26, 2021).

Unemployment Insurance Appeal Board did not err in finding that a former city maintenance worker's appeal was untimely because there was nothing in the record to support a claim that the worker had mailed a timely appeal prior to the deadline; further, the Board did not err in finding that no severe circumstances existed because there was substantial evidence to uphold the denial of benefits on the merits where the worker admitted having smoked marijuana in violation of the city's zero-tolerance drug and alcohol policy. Berry v. Mayor & Council of Middletown, — A.3d —, 2021 Del. Super. LEXIS 188 (Del. Super. Ct. Mar. 4, 2021).

§ 3322. Finality of Board's decision; duty to exhaust administrative remedies; position of Department in judicial review.

NOTES TO DECISIONS

Analysis

Computation of time.
Exhaustion of administrative remedies.

Computation of time.

Court had jurisdiction to hear claimant's petition because: (1) the Unemployment Insurance Appeal Board mailed its decision on June 30, 2020, specifying that the decision was final on July 10, 2020; (2) the claimant sought judicial review on July 9, 2020; (3) the appeal period began to run before the date that the decision became final; and (4) the petition for appeal to the court was not premature. Pearson

v. Feindt's Plumbing Serv., LLC, — A.3d —, 2021 Del. Super. LEXIS 341 (Del. Super. Ct. Apr. 20, 2021).

Exhaustion of administrative remedies.

Court lacked jurisdiction to hear the claimant's appeal of an unemployment insurance benefit decision because the claimant did not appeal the referee's decision to the Unemployment Insurance Appeal Board; as a result, claimant failed to exhaust all administrative remedies. Cavero v. Unemployment Ins. Bd., — A.3d —, 2020 Del. Super. LEXIS 2818 (Del. Super. Ct. Oct. 2, 2020).

§ 3323. Judicial review; procedure.

NOTES TO DECISIONS

Exhaustion of administrative remedies.

Substantial evidence supported the Unemployment Insurance Appeal Board's decision that the claimant failed to exhaust all administrative remedies before quitting; while the claimant asserted that the reason for leaving

employment was due to safety concerns following a robbery, there was no evidence that the claimant had attempted to raise the issue with management. Morales v. Dollar Tree Stores, Inc., 2021 Del. Super. LEXIS 539 (Del. Super. Ct. Aug. 9, 2021).

§ 3326. Extended benefits.

(a) As used in this section, unless the context clearly requires otherwise:

   (1) "Extended benefit period" means a period which:

    a. Begins with the third week after the first week for which there is a state "on" indicator, and

    b. Ends with either of the following weeks, whichever occurs later:

        1. The third week after the first week for which there is a state "off" indicator, or

        2. The thirteenth consecutive week of such period;

provided, that no extended benefit period may begin the fourteenth week following the end of a prior extended benefit period which was in effect with respect to this State.

   (2)a. There is a state "on" indicator for a week beginning prior to September 25, 1982, if the rate of insured unemployment under the state law for the period consisting of such week and the immediately preceding 12 weeks:

        1. Equaled or exceeded 120 percent of the average of such rates for the corresponding 13-week period ending in each of the preceding 2 calendar years, and

        2. Equaled or exceeded 4 percent.

    b. There is a state "on" indicator for a week beginning after September 25, 1982, if the rate of insured unemployment under the state law for the period consisting of such week and the immediately preceding 12 weeks:

        1. Equaled or exceeded 120 percent of the average of such rates for the corresponding 13-week period ending in each of the preceding 2 calendar years, and

        2. Equaled or exceeded 5 percent.

    c. There is a state "on" indicator for a week beginning after June 6, 2009, if:

        1. The rate of total unemployment (seasonally adjusted), as determined by the United States Secretary of Labor, for the period consisting of the most recent 3 months for which data for all States are published before the close of such week equaled or exceeded 6.5 percent, and

        2. The average rate of total unemployment in the State (seasonally adjusted), as determined by the United States Secretary of Labor, for the 3-month period referred to in paragraph (a)(2)c.1. of this section, equals or exceeds 110 percent of such average for either or both of the corresponding 3-month periods ending in the 2 preceding calendar years; however, for weeks of compensation beginning after December 17, 2010, and ending December 31, 2011, or the expiration date set forth in Public Law 111-312 [Tax Relief, Unemployment Insurance Reauthorization, and Job Creation Act of 2010], whichever is later, the average rate of total unemployment in the State (seasonally adjusted), as determined by the United States Secretary of Labor, for the 3-month period referred to in paragraph (a)(2)c.1. of this section, equals or exceeds 110 percent of such average for any or all of the corresponding 3-month periods ending in the 3 preceding calendar years.

   (3)a. There is a state "off" indicator for a week beginning prior to September 25, 1982, if, for the period consisting of such week and the immediately preceding 12 weeks, either paragraph (a)(2)a.1. or paragraph (a)(2)a.2. of this section was not satisfied.

b. There is a state "off" indicator for a week beginning after September 25, 1982, if, for the period consisting of such week and the immediately preceding 12 weeks, either paragraph (a)(2)b.1. or paragraph (a)(2)b.2. of this section was not satisfied.

c. There is a state "off" indicator for a week beginning after June 6, 2009, if, for the period consisting of such week and the immediately preceding 12 weeks, either paragraph (a)(2)c.1. or paragraph (a)(2)c.2. of this section was not satisfied.

(4) "Rate of insured unemployment," for purposes of paragraphs (a)(2) and (3) of this section, means the percentage derived by dividing:

a. The average weekly number of individuals filing claims for regular benefits in this State for weeks of unemployment with respect to the most recent 13-consecutive-week period, as determined by the Department on the basis of its reports to the United States Secretary of Labor, by

b. The average monthly employment covered under this chapter for the first 4 of the most recent 6 completed calendar quarters ending before the end of such 13-week period.

(5) "Regular benefits" means benefits payable to an individual under this chapter or under any other state law (including benefits payable to federal civilian employees and to ex-servicepersons pursuant to 5 U.S.C. Chapter 85) other than extended benefits.

(6) "Extended benefits" means benefits (including benefits payable to federal civilian employees and to ex-servicepersons pursuant to 5 U.S.C. Chapter 85) payable to an individual under this section for weeks of unemployment in the individual's eligibility period.

(7) "Eligibility period" of an individual means the period consisting of the weeks in the individual's benefit year which begin in an extended benefit period and, if the individual's benefit year ends within such extended benefit period, any weeks thereafter which begin in such period.

(8) "Exhaustee" means an individual who, with respect to any week of unemployment in the individual's eligibility period:

a. Has received, prior to such week, all of the regular benefits that were available to the individual under this chapter or any other state law (including dependents' allowances and benefits payable to federal civilian employees and ex-servicepersons under 5 U.S.C. Chapter 85) in the individual's current benefit year that includes such week; provided, that, for the purposes of this paragraph, an individual shall be deemed to have received all of the regular benefits that were available to the individual although:

1. As a result of a pending appeal with respect to wages that were not considered in the original monetary determination in the individual's benefit year, the individual may subsequently be determined to be entitled to added regular benefits; or

2. The individual's benefit year, having expired prior to such week, the individual has no or insufficient wages on the basis of which the individual could establish a new benefit year that would include such week; and

b. Has no right to unemployment benefits or allowances, as the case may be, under the Railroad Unemployment Insurance Act (45 U.S.C. § 351 et seq.) and such other federal laws as are specified in regulations issued by the United States Secretary of Labor; and

c. Has not received and is not seeking unemployment benefits under the unemployment compensation law of Canada but, if the individual is seeking such benefits and the appropriate agency finally determines that the individual is not entitled to benefits under such law, the individual is considered an exhaustee.

d. Notwithstanding any other provisions of this chapter, if the benefit year of any individual ends within an extended benefit period, the remaining balance of extended benefits that such individual would, but for this section, be entitled to receive in that extended benefit period, with respect to weeks of unemployment beginning after the end of the benefit year, shall be reduced (but not below zero) by the product of the number of weeks for which the individual received any amounts as trade adjustment allowances within that benefit year, multiplied by the individual's weekly benefit amount for extended benefits.

(9) "State law" means the unemployment insurance law of any state, approved by the United States Secretary of Labor under § 3304 of the Internal Revenue Code of 1954 (26 U.S.C. § 3304).

(b) Except when the result would be inconsistent with the other provisions of this section, as provided in the regulations of the Department, the provisions of this part which apply to claims for or the payment of regular benefits shall apply to claims for and the payment of extended benefits.

(c) An individual shall be eligible to receive extended benefits with respect to any week of unemployment in the individual's eligibility period only if the Department finds that with respect to such week:

(1) The individual is an "exhaustee" as defined in paragraph (a)(8) of this section.

(2) The individual has satisfied the requirements of this chapter for the receipt of regular benefits that are applicable to individuals claiming extended benefits, including not being subject to a disqualification for the receipt of benefits.

(3) The individual has, during the individual's base period, been paid wages for employment equal to not less than 40 times the individual's weekly benefit amount and, as used in this paragraph, "wages" means wages for employment by employers for benefit purposes with respect to any benefit year only if such benefit year begins subsequent to the date on which the employment unit by which such wages were paid has satisfied the conditions of § 3302(8) of this title or § 3343 of this title with respect to becoming an employer.

(d) The weekly extended benefit amount payable to an individual for a week of total unemployment in the individual's eligibility period shall be an amount equal to the weekly benefit amount payable to the individual during the individual's applicable benefit year. Provided, that for any week during a period in which federal payments to States under § 204 of the Federal-State Extended Unemployment Compensation Act of 1970 (August 10, 1970, Public Law 91-373) are reduced under an order issued under § 252 of the Balanced Budget and Emergency Deficit Control Act of 1985 (2 U.S.C. § 902), the weekly extended benefit amount payable to an individual for a week of total unemployment in the individual's eligibility period shall be reduced by a percentage equivalent to the percentage of the reduction in the federal payment. Such reduced weekly extended benefit amount, if not a full dollar amount, shall be rounded to the nearest lower dollar amount.

(e) The total extended benefit amount payable to any eligible individual with respect to the individual's applicable benefit year shall be the lesser of the following amounts; provided, however, that during any fiscal year in which federal payments to States under § 204 of the Federal State Extended

Unemployment Compensation Act of 1970 (August 10, 1970, Public Law 91-373) are reduced under an order issued under § 252 of the Balanced Budget and Emergency Deficit Control Act of 1985 (2 U.S.C. § 902), the total extended benefit amount payable to an individual with respect to the individual's applicable benefit year shall be reduced by an amount equal to the aggregate of the reductions under subsection (d) of this section in the weekly amount paid to the individual:

(1) Fifty percent of the total amount of regular benefits which were payable to the individual under this chapter in the individual's applicable benefit year;

(2) Thirteen times the individual's weekly benefit amount which was payable to the individual under this chapter for a week of total unemployment in the applicable benefit year.

(f)(1) Effective with respect to weeks beginning in a high unemployment period, subsection (e) of this section shall be applied by substituting:

a. "Eighty percent" for "fifty percent" in paragraph (e)(1) of this section, and

b. "Twenty" for "thirteen" in paragraph (e)(2) of this section.

(2) For purposes of paragraph (f)(1) of this section, the term "high unemployment period" means any period during which an extended benefit period would be in effect if paragraph (a)(2)c.1. of this section were applied by substituting "8 percent" for "6.5 percent."

(g)(1) Except as provided in paragraph (g)(2) of this section, an individual shall not be eligible for extended benefits for any week if:

a. Extended benefits are payable for such week pursuant to an interstate claim filed in any state under the interstate benefit payment plan; and

b. No extended benefit period is in effect for such week in such state.

(2) Paragraph (g)(1) of this section shall not apply with respect to the first 2 weeks for which extended benefits are payable, (determined without regard to this subsection), pursuant to an interstate claim filed under the interstate benefit payment plan, to the individual from the extended benefit account established for the individual with respect to the benefit year.

(h)(1) Notwithstanding any other provisions of this chapter, payment of extended benefits shall not be made to any individual for any week of unemployment in the individual's eligibility period if the Department finds that during such period:

a. The individual failed to accept any offer of suitable work (as defined in paragraph (h)(3) of this section) or failed to apply for any suitable work to which the individual was referred by the Department; or

b. The individual failed to actively engage in a systematic and sustained effort to obtain work during such week, and/or failed to furnish tangible evidence that the individual did engage in such effort during such week.

(2) Any individual who has been found ineligible for extended benefits for any week by reason of a failure described in paragraph (h)(1) of this section shall also be denied benefits beginning with the first day of the week following the week in which such failure occurred until the individual has been employed in each of 4 subsequent weeks (whether or not consecutive) and has earned remuneration in covered employment equal to not less than 4 times the extended weekly benefit amount.

(3) For purposes of this subsection, the term "suitable work" means, with respect to any individual, any work which is within such individual's capabilities; provided, however, that the gross average weekly remuneration payable for the work must exceed the sum of:

a. The individual's extended weekly benefit amount as determined under subsection (d) of this section, plus the amount, if any, of supplemental unemployment benefits (as defined in § 501(c)(17)(D) of the Internal Revenue Code of 1954 [26 U.S.C. § 501(c)(17)(D)]) payable to such individual for such week; and further,

b. Pays wages not less than the higher of:

1. The minimum wage provided by § 6(a)(1) of the Fair Labor Standards Act of 1938 [29 U.S.C. § 206(a)(1)], without regard to any exemptions; or

2. The applicable state or local minimum wage;

c. Provided, however, that no individual shall be denied extended benefits for failure to accept an offer or to apply for any job which meets the definition of suitability as described in this subsection if:

1. The position was not offered to such individual in writing or was not listed with the employment service.

2. Such failure would not result in a denial of benefits under the definition of suitable work for regular benefit claimants in § 3314 of this title to the extent that the criteria of suitability in that section are not inconsistent with this paragraph.

3. The individual furnishes satisfactory evidence to the Department that the individual's prospects for obtaining work in the individual's customary occupation within a reasonably short period are good. If such evidence is deemed satisfactory for this purpose, the determination of whether any work is suitable with respect to such individual shall be made in accordance with the definition of suitable work for regular benefit claimants in § 3314 of this title without regard to the definition specified by this paragraph.

(4) Notwithstanding subsection (b) of this section to the contrary, no work shall be deemed to be suitable work for an individual which does not accord with the labor standard provisions required by § 3304(a)(5) of the Internal Revenue Code of 1954 [26 U.S.C. § 3304(a)(5)] and set forth herein under § 3314(3)a., b., c. and d. of this title.

(5) The employment service shall refer any claimant entitled to extended benefits under this title to any suitable work which meets the criteria prescribed in paragraph (h)(3) of this section.

(6) The provisions of paragraphs (h)(1), (2), (3) and (5) of this section shall not apply should at any time these provisions be temporarily or permanently suspended by federal law. If these provisions are suspended by federal law, the provisions of state law which apply to claims for or the payment of regular benefits shall apply to claims for and the payment of extended benefits.

(i)(1) Whenever an extended benefit period is to become effective in this State or an extended benefit period is to be terminated in this State, the Department shall make an appropriate public announcement.

(2) Computations required by paragraph (a)(4) of this section shall be made by the Department, in accordance with regulations prescribed by the United States Secretary of Labor.

(j) The provisions of paragraph (a)(2)c. of this section shall be in effect until the week ending December 5, 2009, or until the week ending 4 weeks prior to the last week for which 100 percent federal sharing is authorized by § 2005(a) of Public Law 111-5, whichever is later.

(k) To the extent that the provisions and definitions of terms in the American Recovery and Reinvestment Act of 2009 (Public Law 111-5) are in conflict with, or supplement the provisions and definitions applicable pursuant to this section, the provisions and definitions of the American Recovery and Reinvestment Act of 2009 shall apply to this section.

(*l*) Notwithstanding any other provision of this section, the Governor may, if permitted by federal law, suspend the payment of extended duration benefits under this section, to the extent necessary to ensure that otherwise eligible individuals are not denied, in whole or in part, the receipt of emergency unemployment compensation benefits authorized by the federal Supplemental Appropriations Act of 2008 (Public Law 110-252), the Unemployment Compensation Extension Act of 2008 (Public Law 110-449), and the American Recovery and Reinvestment Act of 2009 (Public Law 111-5), and that the state receives maximum reimbursement from the federal government for the payment of those emergency benefits.

(m) [Repealed.]

(n) With respect to determining whether the State is in an extended benefit period beginning on November 1, 2020, through December 31, 2021, the State shall disregard the requirement in paragraph (a)(1) of this section that no extended benefit period may begin before the fourteenth week following the end of a prior extended benefit period which was in effect with respect to this State.

History.
19 Del. C. 1953, § 3326; 58 Del. Laws, c. 143, § 7; 58 Del. Laws, c. 522, §§ 20, 21; 60 Del. Laws, c. 2, §§ 1-4; 61 Del. Laws, c. 186, §§ 21-24; 63 Del. Laws, c. 192, § 3; 63 Del. Laws, c. 427, §§ 10-14, 20; 65 Del. Laws, c. 414, §§ 1, 2; 65 Del. Laws, c. 514, §§ 6-11; 69 Del. Laws, c. 1, § 1; 70 Del. Laws, c. 186, § 1; 77 Del. Laws, c. 52, § 1; 78 Del. Laws, c. 4, § 1; 82 Del. Laws, c. 284, § 2; 82 Del. Laws, c. 284, § 3; 83 Del. Laws, c. 2, § 1.

Effect of amendments.
83 Del. Laws, c. 2, effective Feb. 8, 2021, added (n).

SUBCHAPTER III
EMPLOYER'S COVERAGE AND ASSESSMENTS

§ 3348. Average employer assessment rate; average industry assessment rate; average construction industry assessment rate; new employer rate; standard rate of assessment.

(a) On or before December 31 of each year, the Secretary of Labor shall establish an average employer assessment rate for the next succeeding calendar year. The average employer assessment rate shall be computed by multiplying total taxable wages paid by each employer, regardless of industrial classification category as listed in the North American Industry Classification System (NAICS) Manual furnished by the federal government, during the 12 consecutive months ending on June 30 by the employer's assessment rate established for the next calendar year and dividing the aggregate product for all employers by the total of taxable wages paid by all employers during the 12 consecutive months ending on June 30.

(b) On or before December 31 of each year, the Secretary of Labor shall establish an average industry assessment rate for the next succeeding calendar year for industrial classification categories (carried to 6 places) 236, 237 and 238 as listed in the North American Industry Classification System (NAICS) Manual furnished by the federal government. The average industry assessment rate for standard industrial classification categories 236, 237, and 238 shall be computed by multiplying total taxable wages paid by each employer in the industrial classification category during the 12 consecutive months ending on June 30 by the employer's assessment rate established for the next calendar year and dividing the aggregate product for all employers in the industrial classification category by the total of taxable wages paid by all employers in the industrial classification category during the 12 consecutive months ending on June 30.

(c) On or before December 31 of each year, the Secretary of Labor shall establish an average construction industry assessment rate for the next succeeding calendar year for industrial classification categories (carried to 3 places) 236, 237 and 238 as listed in the North American Industry Classification System (NAICS) Manual furnished by the federal government. The average construction industry assessment rate shall be computed by multiplying total taxable wages paid by each employer in the construction industry during the 12 consecutive months ending on June 30 by the employer's assessment rate established for the next calendar year and dividing the aggregate product for all employers by the total of taxable wages paid by all construction industry employers during the 12 consecutive months ending on June 30.

(d) For any employer, excluding those employers in NAICS categories 236, 237 and 238, who first becomes subject to this chapter on or after January 1, 2003, the new employer rate shall be the average employer assessment rate.

(e) For any employer in NAICS categories 236, 237 and 238 who first becomes subject to this chapter on or after January 1, 2003, the new employer rate shall be the average industry assessment rate in the employer's particular NAICS category (carried to 6 places) or the average construction industry assessment rate, whichever is the greater.

(f) The NAICS category assigned to any employer shall be as determined by the Secretary of Labor or the Secretary's designee and shall be reviewable only for abuse of discretion.

(g) Each employer subject to the new employer rate shall pay an assessment in an amount equal to the product of the new employer rate times wages paid by the employer during any calendar year, except as may be otherwise prescribed in this chapter.

(h) The standard rate of assessment shall be $2\frac{7}{10}$ percent for calendar years prior to 1985 and $5\frac{4}{10}$ percent for calendar year 1985 and subsequent years.

(i) Notwithstanding the computation of the average employer assessment rate, the average industry assessment rate or the average construction industry assessment rate, no employer assigned an assessment rate under subsection (d) or subsection (e) of this section shall have a rate of less than 1 percent.

(j) Notwithstanding the required computation of the average employer assessment rate, the average industry assessment rate or the average construction industry assessment rate to be established by the Secretary of Labor on or before December 31, 2020 for the next succeeding calendar year pursuant to subsections (a) through (c) of this section, for calendar year 2021, all employers assigned an assessment rate under subsection (d) or (e) of this section shall have the same rate as established by the Secretary of Labor for the calendar year 2020.

History.

41 Del. Laws, c. 258, § 7; 43 Del. Laws, c. 280, § 12; 43 Del. Laws, c. 282, § 3; 19 Del. C. 1953, § 3348; 53 Del Laws, c. 79, § 1; 63 Del. Laws, c. 76, § 9; 63 Del. Laws, c. 192, § 8; 64 Del Laws, c. 427, § 4; 65 Del. Laws, c. 513, § 2; 66 Del. Laws, c. 74, § 1; 66 Del. Laws, c. 115, § 1; 70 Del. Laws, c. 186, § 1; 73 Del. Laws, c. 303, §§ 1-7; 83 Del. Laws, c. 2, § 2.

Effect of amendments.

83 Del. Laws, c. 2, effective Feb. 8, 2021, added (j).

PART IV
WORKPLACE FRAUD ACT

Chapter
35. Workplace Fraud Act, §§ 3501 to 3515.

CHAPTER 35
WORKPLACE FRAUD ACT

§ 3501. Definitions.

(a) As used in this chapter:

(1) "Construction services" includes, without limitation, all building or work on buildings, structures, and improvements of all types such as bridges, dams, plants, highways, parkways, streets, tunnels, sewers, mains, power lines, pumping stations, heaving generators, railways, airports, terminals, docks, piers, wharves, buoys, jetties, breakwaters, levees, canals, dredging, shoring, rehabilitation and reactivation of plants, scaffolding, drilling, blasting, excavating, clearing and landscaping.

(2) "Contractor" means a person, partnership, association, joint stock company, trust, corporation, limited liability company, or other legal business entity or successor or subsidiary thereof that engages in construction services or maintenance under an express or implied contract on behalf of another entity or individual for profit within the State, and includes any subcontractor or lower tier subcontractor of a contractor.

(3) "Debarment" means that no public construction contract in this State shall be bid on, awarded to or received by any employer or any person, firm, partnership or corporation in which such employer has an interest who, within 2 years after entry of a judgment pursuant to this chapter, is adjudicated in violation of this chapter in a subsequent proceeding, until 3 years have elapsed from the date of the subsequent penalty judgment.

(4) "Department" shall have the meaning set forth in § 101(a)(2) of this title.

(5) "Employee" means any person or entity directly hired by, or directly permitted to work by an employer in the State, for work to be performed wholly or partly therein. This chapter does not apply to employees of the United States government, the State or any political subdivision thereof.

(6) "Employer" means any individual, partnership, association, joint stock company, trust, corporation, the administrator or executor of the estate of a deceased individual or the receiver, trustee or successor of any of the same employing any person excepting those provided for in subsection (b) of this section. This chapter does not apply to employees of the United States government, the State or any political subdivision thereof.

(7) "Exempt person" means any individual who:

a. Performs services in a personal capacity and who employs no individuals other than a spouse, child, or immediate family member of the individual;

b. Performs services free from direction and control over the means and manner of providing the services, subject only to the right of the person or entity for whom services are provided to specify the desired result;

 c. Furnishes the tools and equipment necessary to provide the services; and

 d. Operates a business that is considered inseparable from the individual for purposes of taxes, profits, and liabilities, in which the individual:

  1. Owns all of the assets and profits of the business; and

  2. Has sole, unlimited, personal liability for all of the debts and liabilities of the business; or alternatively, if the business is organized as a single-person corporate entity, to which sole, unlimited personal liability does not apply, the individual must be the sole member of said single-person corporate entity; and

  3. For which the individual does not pay taxes for the business separately but reports business income on the individual's personal income tax return; and

 e. Exercises complete control over the management and operations of the business.

(8) "General contractor" and "construction manager" means an entity or individual who has primary responsibility for providing labor and other services necessary for the construction services in a contract. "General contractor" and "construction manager" also means a higher tier contractor of a subcontractor.

(9) "Independent contractor" means an individual or entity who meets all of the following:

 a. Performs the work free from the employer's control and direction over the performance of the employee's services.

 b. Is customarily engaged in an independently established trade, occupation, profession, or business.

 c. Performs work which is either of the following:

  1. Outside of the usual course of business of the employer for whom the work is performed.

  2. Performed by a registered contractor under Chapter 36 of this title outside of any place of business of the employer for whom the work is performed.

(10) "Knowingly" means having actual knowledge of, or acting with deliberate ignorance, or reckless disregard for the prohibition involved.

(11) "Labor broker" means an entity or individual that hires employees and sells the services of the employees to another employer in need of temporary employees.

(12) "Outside of the usual course of business" means work an individual performs for an employer that is any of the following:

 a. At a location that is not the employer's place of business.

 b. Not integrated into the employer's operation.

 c. Unrelated to the employer's business.

(13) "Place of business" means the principal office or headquarters of the employer, but does not mean a work site at which the employer has been contracted to perform services.

(14) "Public body" means:

 a. The State;

 b. A unit of state government or an instrumentality of the State; or

 c. Any political subdivision, agency, person or entity that is a party to a contract for which the State appropriated any part of the funds to be used for payment.

(15) "Secretary" or "Secretary of Labor" shall have the meaning set forth in § 101(a)(5) of this title.

(16) "Stop work order" means written notice from the Secretary to an employer to cease or hold work until the employer is given notice by the Secretary to resume work.

(17) "Subcontractor" means a lower tier contractor of a contractor, including owner operators or independent contractors.

(18) "Violate" or "attempts to violate" includes, but is not limited to, any intent to evade, misrepresent or wilfully nondisclose.

(b) For the purposes of this chapter the officers of a corporation and any agents having the management thereof who knowingly permit the corporation to violate this chapter shall be deemed to be the employers of the employees of the corporation.

History.
77 Del. Laws, c. 192, § 1; 82 Del. Laws, c. 168, § 1; 82 Del. Laws, c. 291, § 1.

Revisor's note.
Section 6 of 82 Del. Laws, c. 168, as amended by 82 Del. Laws, c. 291, § 2, effective Sept. 28, 2020, provided: "This act takes effect upon promulgation of final regulations adopted under this chapter, or on July 1, 2021, whichever occurs first." The act took effect on July 1, 2021.

§ 3503. Acts prohibited.

(a) An employer must not act as a labor broker by improperly classifying an individual who performs work for remuneration provided by an employer as an independent contractor.

(b) An employer has improperly classified an individual when an employer-employee relationship exists, as determined under subsection (c) of this section, but the employer has not classified the individual as an employee.

(c)(1) An "employer-employee" relationship is presumed to exist when work is performed by an individual for remuneration paid by an employer, unless the employer demonstrates, to the satisfaction of the Department, that the individual is an exempt person or independent contractor.

(2) By contract, a general contractor or subcontractor may engage an independent contractor registered under Chapter 36 of this title, to do the same type of work in which the general contractor or subcontractor engages, at the same location where the general contractor or subcontractor is working, without establishing an employer-employee relationship between the multiple contracting parties.

(3) There is a rebuttable presumption that an entity or individual who acts as a labor broker in providing construction services has engaged in a knowing violation of this chapter.

(d) A person must not knowingly incorporate or form, or assist in the incorporation or formation of, a corporation, partnership, limited liability corporation, or other entity, or pay or collect a fee for use of a foreign or domestic corporation, partnership, limited liability corporation, or other entity for the purpose of facilitating, or evading detection of, a violation under this section.

(e) A person must not knowingly conspire with, aid and abet, assist, advise, or facilitate an employer with the intent of violating the provisions of this chapter.

(f) The Department shall adopt regulations to further explain and provide specific examples of subsections (c), (d), and (e) of this section.

History.
77 Del. Laws, c. 192, § 1; 82 Del. Laws, c. 168, § 2; 82 Del. Laws, c. 291, § 2.

Revisor's note.
Section 6 of 82 Del. Laws, c. 168, as amended by 82 Del. Laws, c. 291, § 2, effective Sept. 28, 2020, provided: "This act takes effect upon promulgation of final regulations adopted under this chapter, or on July 1, 2021, whichever occurs first." The act took effect on July 1, 2021.

§ 3505. Penalties.

(a) Any employer who violates or fails to comply with § 3503 of this title or any regulation published thereunder is in violation of § 3503 of this title, and is subject to a civil penalty of not less than $5,000, and not more than $20,000, for each violation. Each employee who is not properly classified in violation of § 3503 of this title is a separate violation under this section.

(b) An employer that fails to produce to the Department the books and records requested pursuant to § 3504(c) of this title within 30 days of the employer's receipt of a written request sent to the employer via federal express or certified mail from the Department, in the course of an investigation to determine whether the employer is in compliance with the provisions of this chapter, may be subject to a stop work order, and may be subject to an administrative penalty, not to exceed $500 per day, for each day that the requested records are not produced after the date on which the employer receives the written request from the Department.

(c) An employer who discharges or in any manner discriminates against a person because that person has made a complaint or has given information to the Department under this chapter, or because the person has caused to be instituted or is about to cause to be instituted any proceedings under this chapter, or has testified or is about to testify in any such proceedings, is subject to a civil penalty of not less than $20,000, and not more than $50,000, for each violation.

(d) A person who knowingly incorporates or forms, or assists in the incorporation or formation of, a corporation, partnership, limited liability corporation, or other entity, or pay or collect a fee for use of a foreign or domestic corporation, partnership, limited liability corporation, or other entity for the purpose of facilitating, or evading detection of, a violation of this chapter, shall be subject to a civil penalty not to exceed $20,000.

(e) A person who knowingly conspires with, aids and abets, assists, advises, or facilitates an employer with the intent of violating this chapter shall be subject to a civil penalty not to exceed $20,000.

(f) In addition to the penalties and procedures enumerated in subsections (a) through (e) of this section, an employer may be subject to a stop-work order, and may be ordered to make restitution, pay any interest due and otherwise comply with all applicable laws and regulations by multiple final determinations of the Department or orders of a courts, including but not limited to, the Division of Unemployment Insurance, the Department of Insurance, the Office of Workers' Compensation, the Division of Revenue, the Office of the Attorney General, or any other agency, department or division of the State.

(g) Notwithstanding subsections (a) through (e) of this section, an employer found by any court or the Department to be in violation of this chapter shall be required, within 30 days of the final order:

(1) To pay restitution to or on behalf of any individual not properly classified; and

(2) To otherwise come into compliance with all applicable labor laws, including those related to income tax withholding, unemployment insurance, wage laws, and workers' compensation.

(h) Notwithstanding subsections (a) through (e) of this section, an employer who has been found by a final order of a court or the Department to have violated this chapter twice in a 2-year period:

(1) Shall be assessed an administrative penalty of $20,000 for each employee that was not properly classified, and may be debarred for 5 years; and

(2) Notwithstanding paragraph (h)(1) of this section, an employer that is fined or debarred in accordance with this section may be ordered to

make restitution, pay any interest due, and otherwise comply with all applicable laws and regulations by orders of a court and all relevant departments, agencies and divisions, including the Division of Unemployment Insurance, the Department of Insurance, the Office of Workers' Compensation, the Division of Revenue, and the Office of the Attorney General.

(i) Any penalty issued under this section against an employer shall be in effect against any successor corporation or business entity that:

(1) Has 1 or more of the same principals or officers as the employer against whom the penalty was assessed; and

(2) Is engaged in the same or equivalent trade or activity, with the intent to violate 1 or more of the provisions of this chapter.

History.

77 Del. Laws, c. 192, § 1; 82 Del. Laws, c. 168, § 3; 82 Del. Laws, c. 291, § 3.

Revisor's note.

Section 6 of 82 Del. Laws, c. 168, as amended by 82 Del. Laws, c. 291, § 2, effective Sept. 28, 2020, provided: "This act takes effect upon promulgation of final regulations adopted under this chapter, or on July 1, 2021, whichever occurs first." The act took effect on July 1, 2021.

TITLE 20
MILITARY AND CIVIL DEFENSE

Part
II. Civil Defense

PART II
CIVIL DEFENSE

Chapter
31. Emergency Management, §§ 3101 to 3156.

CHAPTER 31
EMERGENCY MANAGEMENT

SUBCHAPTER VI

CONTINUATION OF CERTAIN ORDERS ISSUED DURING THE COVID-19 STATE OF EMERGENCY

§ 3156. Notarization.

The provisions of Paragraph B of the Eleventh Modification of the State of Emergency Declaration, dated April 15, 2020, shall continue in full force and effect until June 30, 2022.

History.
82 Del. Laws, c. 255, § 2; 83 Del. Laws, c. 66, § 1.

Effect of amendments.
83 Del. Laws, c. 66, effective June 30, 2021, substituted "2022" for "2021."

TITLE 21
MOTOR VEHICLES

Part
I. General Provisions
II. Registration, Title and Licenses
III. Operation and Equipment
IV. Miscellaneous

PART I
GENERAL PROVISIONS

CHAPTER 3
DEPARTMENT OF PUBLIC TRANSPORTATION AND DEPARTMENT OF SAFETY AND HOMELAND SECURITY

§ 313. Accident statistics and reports; evidence.

(a) The Department of Safety and Homeland Security shall prepare and supply to law-enforcement agencies forms for accident reports that require sufficiently detailed information about the cause, conditions then existing, and the persons and vehicles involved in a highway accident.

(b) Except as provided under this section, accident reports and any data or statistics derived from an accident report are without prejudice, are solely for the information of the Department of Safety and Homeland Security and the Department of Transportation, and are not a public record under the Freedom of Information Act, Chapter 100 of Title 29. The fact that an accident report has been made is admissible in evidence solely to prove compliance with this section but no accident report or any part or statement contained in a report is admissible in evidence for any other purpose in any trial, civil or criminal, arising out of an accident.

(c)(1) An accident report may be disclosed only to the following:

a. A person, or the person's legal representative, who requests a copy of the person's own accident report.

b. An insurer, insurance support organization, or a self-insured entity or its agent, employee, or contractor, in connection with claims investigation activities, anti-fraud activities, rating, or underwriting.

(2)a. The person requesting an accident report under paragraph (c)(1) of this section must submit proof of identity and payment of the fee established by the law-enforcement agency with primary jurisdiction over the accident.

b. A fee under paragraph (c)(2)a. of this section must approximate and reasonably reflect the amount necessary to defray the costs incurred by the law-enforcement agency to provide a copy of the accident report.

(3) Notwithstanding paragraphs (c)(1) through (c)(2) of this section, an accident report associated with a criminal prosecution may be withheld from disclosure until the criminal prosecution has concluded.

(d) Upon written request, the Department of Transportation may prepare a document containing a quantitative analysis of de-identified data if the person requesting the information provides proof of identity and a representation that the data will be strictly used for any of the following purposes:

(1) To comply with federal, state, or local law or regulation.

(2) By any of the following in carrying out official functions:

    a. A municipality or its agents.

    b. A municipal planning organization or its agents.

    c. A member of the General Assembly.

(e) The State shall make some de-identified data public through press releases, publication, or a state-managed website. The Department of Safety and Homeland Security has the sole discretion to determine what data may be disclosed under this subsection, except that the data on the state-managed website must include all of the following:

(1) Accident classification.

(2) Manner of impact.

(3) Alcohol or drug involvement.

(4) Date and time of accident.

(5) Conditions regarding road surface, lighting, and weather.

(6) Seat belt or helmet use.

(7) Geographic location.

(8) Primary contributing circumstances.

(f) Notwithstanding any provision under this section, the Director of the Delaware Criminal Justice Information System (DELJIS) may enter into a contractual agreement for the sale of de-identified data if the contracting party's use of the information is related to public safety. A contract under this subsection may include pricing models based on DELJIS's cost to produce, maintain, and distribute the records containing the information. The Department of Safety and Homeland Security has sole discretion to determine the data that may be disclosed under this subsection.

History.
36 Del. Laws, c. 10, § 109; Code 1935, § 5647; 21 Del. C. 1953, § 318; 57 Del. Laws, c. 670, § 6C; 74 Del. Laws, c. 110, §§ 28, 29; 82 Del. Laws, c. 136, § 1; 83 Del. Laws, c. 148, § 1.

Effect of amendments.
83 Del. Laws, c. 148, effective September 15, 2021, rewrote the section.

CHAPTER 7
ENFORCEMENT; ARREST, BAIL AND APPEAL

Sec.
709. Payment of motor vehicle fines.

§ 709. Payment of motor vehicle fines.

(a) *Applicability.* — Any duly constituted peace officer in the State who charges any person with any of the offenses hereinafter designated "motor vehicle offenses subject to voluntary assessment" may indicate on the Uniform Traffic Complaint and Summons that the fine shall be paid by voluntary assessment unless the driver requests a hearing. When a voluntary assessment is permitted and the Uniform Traffic Complaint and Summons is properly executed by the officer, the driver may dispose of the charge without the necessity of personally appearing in the court to which the Uniform Traffic Complaint and Summons is returnable. The court to which the summons is returnable shall be determined by § 703 of this title unless the summons permits a voluntary assessment, in which case it shall be returnable to either the applicable court or a voluntary assessment center established by the Justice of the Peace Court. Notwithstanding any provision of this section and chapter to the contrary, the City of Wilmington may establish the exclusive voluntary assessment center for parking summonses issued for designated offenses within the boundaries of the City of Wilmington, and the Town of Elsmere may establish a voluntary assessment center for any violation of a town ordinance within the boundaries of the Town of Elsmere.

(b) *Definitions.* — (1) "Payment," as used in this section, shall mean the total amount of the fine and of the costs as herein provided and of the penalty assessment added to the fine pursuant to the Delaware Victim Compensation Law, Chapter 90 of Title 11, and other penalty assessment as provided by law.

(2) "Signature" shall include a written signature or an electronic signature as defined by § 101 of this title.

(3) "Voluntary assessment" means the process set forth in this section by which a driver may voluntarily remit payment of a Title 21 violation without having to appear in a court.

(c) *Places and time of payment.* — Payments made pursuant to this section shall be remitted to the court or voluntary assessment center to which the summons is returnable and shall be disbursed in accordance with § 706 of this title. The court or voluntary assessment center must receive the payment within 30 days of the arrest. Payment to the voluntary assessment center shall be paid only by check, money order or credit card.

(d) *Jurisdiction.* — This section shall apply to any licensed resident of the State; to residents of those jurisdictions with which the State has entered a reciprocal agreement pursuant to Chapter 4 of this title; and to those out-of-state residents who, in the discretion of the arresting peace officer, are deemed to be reliable prospects for a voluntary assessment disposition.

(e) *Offenses designated as "motor vehicle offenses subject to voluntary assessment"; exceptions.* — All offenses as now or hereafter set forth in this title and all motor vehicle offenses falling within the scope of § 5211(a) of Title 30 are hereby designated as motor vehicle offenses subject to voluntary assessment except for the following offenses:

(1) Violation of § 2118 of this title;

(2) Violation of § 2118A of this title;

(3) Violation of § 2701 of this title;

(4) Violation of § 2751 of this title;

(5) Violation of § 2752 of this title;

(6) Violation of § 2756 of this title;

(7) Violation of § 4103 of this title;

(8) Violation of § 4166(d) of this title;

(9) Violation of § 4172 of this title;

(10) Violation of § 4175 of this title;

(11) Violation of § 4175A of this title;

(12) Violation of § 4177 of this title;

(13) Violation of § 4177L of this title;

(14) Violation of § 4201 of this title;

(15) Violation of § 4202 of this title;

(16) Any violation of Chapter 67 of this title; and

(17) Violations of other Title 21 sections which are deemed not appropriate for processing by voluntary assessment.

(f) *Procedure for voluntary assessment.* — (1) At the time of making an arrest for any offense subject to this section, the arresting officer shall determine whether the offense may be handled as a voluntary assessment. If the officer determines that the offense may be so treated, the officer may indicate on the Uniform Traffic Complaint and Summons that payment shall be made by voluntary assessment, unless the driver requests a hearing on the charge or charges. The officer shall inform the arrested person of the court or voluntary assessment center to which payment should be submitted if the person does not request a hearing. No officer shall receive or accept custody of a payment.

(2) A driver who has been given a Uniform Traffic Complaint and Summons which specifies that payment be made by voluntary assessment shall pay the fine, together with costs and penalty assessments, within 30 days from the date of arrest during which time payment must be received by the applicable court or voluntary assessment center.

(3) In lieu of paying the voluntary assessment, a driver who has been given a voluntary assessment may request a hearing by notifying, in writing, the court or the voluntary assessment center to which payment is to be made within 30 days of the date of arrest. If the driver makes a timely request for a hearing, the charge shall be prosecuted as if the voluntary assessment had not been permitted and the officer shall swear to the ticket prior to trial.

(4) If a voluntary assessment is not issued or the driver declines to accept the voluntary assessment, the officer shall follow the procedure for arrest as set forth in Chapter 19 of Title 11.

(g) *Penalty.* — The penalty for offenses for which a voluntary assessment payment is made shall be the minimum fine for each specific offense charged and fines shall be cumulative if more than 1 offense is charged. Provisions of this paragraph as to penalties under voluntary assessment shall not apply if the voluntary assessment payment is not received by the voluntary assessment center or the applicable court within 30 days from the date of arrest.

(h) *Court costs; applicability of Delaware Victim Compensation Law.* — In lieu of any other court costs, and provided the offense is not subject to other proceedings under this section, each fine for an offense under this section shall be subject to court costs for processing a voluntary assessment agreement as prescribed by § 9801 of Title 10. Each fine for an offense under this section shall be subject also to the penalty assessment which is or may be provided for in the Delaware Victim Compensation Law, Chapter 90 of Title 11, and any other penalty assessments as provided by law.

(i) *Effect of payment of fine or signature; repeat offenders.* — (1) Payment of the prescribed fine, costs and penalty assessment is an admission of guilt, a waiver of the right to a hearing, and a complete satisfaction of the violation, except as provided in paragraph (i)(2) of this section. Anything in this section notwithstanding, if an agreement for a voluntary assessment is signed by the driver, the signature of the driver shall constitute an acknowledgment of guilt of the stated offense and an agreement to pay the fine, together with costs and penalty assessment within 30 days from the date of arrest. Payment does not waive any administrative penalty which may be lawfully charged to the violator's driving record by the Department of Safety and Homeland Security.

(2) In the event that, following compliance with the payment provisions of this section, it is determined that within the 2-year period immediately preceding the violation, the violator was convicted of or made a payment pursuant to this section in satisfaction of a violation of the same section of this title, personal appearance before the court to which the summons is returnable or the court which is associated with the applicable voluntary assessment center may be required.

(j) *Failure to pay a voluntary assessment.* — (1)a. The voluntary assessment center shall, pursuant to § 2731 of this title, forward to the

Division of Motor Vehicles the name and address of any driver who was issued a Uniform Traffic Complaint and Summons for which a voluntary assessment could be made and who has failed to do 1 of the following:

    1. Pay the voluntary assessment within 30 days from the date of arrest.

    2. Notify the court or voluntary assessment center within 30 days from the date of arrest, in writing, that the driver is requesting a hearing on the charge stated in the Uniform Traffic Complaint and Summons.

    3. Appear at trial on the charge stated in the Uniform Traffic Complaint and Summons on the date and time required by the court.

    4. Pay the fine on the charge stated in the Uniform Traffic Complaint and Summons in accordance with a deferred payment order.

    b. When the name and address of any driver has been forwarded to the Division of Motor Vehicles under paragraph (j)(1)a. of this section, the Division of Motor Vehicles shall refuse to renew or issue a duplicate of the driver's license of a Delaware resident, in accordance with § 2732(g) of this title.

    c. When the name and address of any driver has been forwarded to the Division of Motor Vehicles under paragraph (j)(1)a. of this section, the Division of Motor Vehicles may suspend the driving privileges in this State of a nonresident of Delaware and immediately advise the Motor Vehicle Administrator of the state in which the person is a resident that the person's license to drive be suspended in accordance with § 2733(m) of this title.

    (2) If a driver pays a voluntary assessment more than 30 days after the date of arrest, the voluntary assessment center or court shall provide the driver with a receipt which shall serve as proof to the Division of Motor Vehicles that the fine has been paid, upon request. The driver shall provide the voluntary assessment center with a self-addressed, stamped envelope in order to receive a copy of the receipt by mail. Such payment shall be an admission of guilt, a waiver of the right to a hearing, and a complete satisfaction of the violation, except as provided in paragraph (i)(2) of this section.

    (3) If a driver who has failed to pay a voluntary assessment or request a hearing within 30 days of the date of arrest appears at court, the charge shall be prosecuted as if the voluntary assessment had not been permitted and the officer shall swear to the Uniform Traffic Complaint and Summons prior to trial. The minimum fine provisions of subsection (g) of this section shall not apply. If the driver who appears pleads not guilty, the court shall provide the driver with a copy of the appearance bond to provide as proof of court appearance to the Division of Motor Vehicles.

    (4) [Repealed.]

(k) *Nonexclusive procedure.* — The procedure prescribed in this section is not exclusive of any other method prescribed by law for the arrest and prosecution of persons violating this title.

History.

60 Del. Laws, c. 509, § 1; 63 Del. Laws, c. 303, § 1; 67 Del. Laws, c. 281, § 27; 70 Del. Laws, c. 157, §§ 1, 2; 70 Del. Laws, c. 186, § 1; 71 Del. Laws, c. 240, § 3; 73 Del. Laws, c. 234, § 2; 74 Del. Laws, c. 110, § 138; 76 Del. Laws, c. 251, § 1; 78 Del. Laws, c. 230, § 1; 80 Del. Laws, c. 137, § 1; 80 Del. Laws, c. 201, § 1; 83 Del. Laws, c. 145, § 2.

Effect of amendments.

83 Del. Laws, c. 145, effective Sept. 10, 2021, added "and the Town of Elsmere may establish

a voluntary assessment center for any violation of a town ordinance within the boundaries of the Town of Elsmere" in the final sentence of (a).

PART II

REGISTRATION, TITLE AND LICENSES

CHAPTER 21

REGISTRATION OF VEHICLES

SUBCHAPTER I

GENERAL PROVISIONS

§ 2118. Requirement of insurance for all motor vehicles required to be registered in this State; penalty [For application of this section, see 82 Del. Laws, c. 160, § 5].

(a) No owner of a motor vehicle required to be registered in this State, other than a self-insurer pursuant to § 2904 of this title, shall operate or authorize any other person to operate such vehicle unless the owner has insurance on such motor vehicle providing the following minimum insurance coverage:

(1) Indemnity from legal liability for bodily injury, death or property damage arising out of ownership, maintenance or use of the vehicle to the limit, exclusive of interest and costs, of at least the limits prescribed by the Financial Responsibility Law of this State.

(2)a. Compensation to injured persons for reasonable and necessary expenses incurred within 2 years from the date of the accident for:

1. Medical, hospital, dental, surgical, medicine, x-ray, ambulance, prosthetic services, professional nursing and funeral services. Compensation for funeral services, including all customary charges and the cost of a burial plot for 1 person, shall not exceed the sum of $5,000. Compensation may include expenses for any nonmedical remedial care and treatment rendered in accordance with a recognized religious method of healing.

2. Net amount of lost earnings. Lost earnings shall include net lost earnings of a self-employed person.

3. Where a qualified medical practitioner shall, within 2 years from the date of an accident, verify in writing that surgical or

dental procedures will be necessary and are then medically ascertainable but impractical or impossible to perform during that 2-year period, the cost of such dental or surgical procedures, including expenses for related medical treatment, and the net amount of lost earnings lost in connection with such dental or surgical procedures shall be payable. Such lost earnings shall be limited to the period of time that is reasonably necessary to recover from such surgical or dental procedures but not to exceed 90 days. The payment of these costs shall be either at the time they are ascertained or at the time they are actually incurred, at the insurer's option.

4. Extra expenses for personal services which would have been performed by the injured person had they not been injured.

5. "Injured person" for the purposes of this section shall include the personal representative of an estate; provided, however, that if a death occurs, the "net amount of lost earnings" shall include only that sum attributable to the period prior to the death of the person so injured.

b. The minimum insurance coverage which will satisfy the requirements of subparagraph a. of this paragraph is a minimum limit for the total of all payments which must be made pursuant to that subparagraph of $15,000 for any 1 person and $30,000 for all persons injured in any 1 accident.

c. The coverage required by this paragraph shall be applicable to each person occupying such motor vehicle and to any other person injured in an accident involving such motor vehicle, other than an occupant of another motor vehicle.

d. The coverage required by this paragraph shall also be applicable to the named insureds and members of their households for accidents which occur through being injured by an accident with any motor vehicle other than a Delaware insured motor vehicle while a pedestrian or while occupying any registered motor vehicle other than a Delaware registered insured motor vehicle, in any state of the United States, its territories or possessions or Canada.

e. The coverage required in this paragraph shall apply to pedestrians only if they are injured by an accident with any motor vehicle within the State except as to named insureds or members of their households to the extent they must be covered pursuant to paragraph (a)(2)d. of this section.

f. The owner of a vehicle may elect to have the coverage described in this paragraph written subject to certain deductibles, waiting periods, sublimits, percentage reductions, excess provisions and similar reductions offered by insurers in accordance with filings made by such insurers with the Department of Insurance; applicable to expenses incurred as a result of injury to the owner of a vehicle or members of the owner's household; provided that the owner of a motorcycle may elect to exclude from such coverage expenses incurred as a result of injury to any person riding such vehicle while not on a highway and in any case of injury when no other vehicle was involved by actual collision or contact. This election must be made in writing and signed by the owner of the vehicle; insurers issuing such policies may not require such reductions. For all policies having a deductible pursuant to this paragraph the insured shall receive in writing as a separate document a full explanation of all deductible options available, and the insured shall sign such written explanation acknowledging receipt of a copy of same. In addition the insured shall sign a separate statement acknowledging the specific deductible the insured is selecting and the related cost for the policies with such deductible. An insured person may not plead and introduce into evidence in an action for damages against a tortfeasor the amount of the deductible; however, insurers shall recover any deductible for their insureds or their household members pursuant to subsection (g) of this section. Any notices or documents required under this section may be delivered in compliance with the provisions of § 107 of Title 18.

g. The coverage required by this paragraph shall be considered excess over any similar insurance for passengers, other than Delaware residents, when the accident occurs outside the State.

h. Insurers shall notify injured persons covered under this section that the coverage is for 2 years from the date of the accident, and that it is only extended for compensation related to surgical or dental procedures that are related to the accident and that were impossible or impractical to perform within the 2-year period. Such surgical or dental procedures must be verified in writing, within 2 years of the accident, by a qualified medical practitioner.

i.1. Expenses under paragraph (a)(2)a. of this section shall be submitted to the insurer as promptly as practical, in no event more than 2 years after they are received by the insured.

2. Payments of expenses under paragraph (a)(2)a. of this section shall be made as soon as practical after they are received during the period of 2 years from the accident. Expenses which are incurred within the 2 years but which have been impractical to present to an insurer within the 2 years shall be paid if presented within 90 days after the end of the 2-year period.

(3) Compensation for damage to property arising as a result of an accident involving the motor vehicle, other than damage to a motor vehicle, aircraft, watercraft, self-propelled mobile equipment and any property in or upon any of the aforementioned, with the minimum limits of $10,000 for any 1 accident.

(4) Compensation for damage to the insured motor vehicle, including loss of use of the motor vehicle, not to exceed the actual cash value of the vehicle at the time of the loss and $10 per day, with a maximum payment of $300, for loss of use of such vehicle.

The owner of the motor vehicle may elect to exclude, in whole or in part, the coverage described in this paragraph by the use of certain deductibles and exclusions in accordance with filings made by the insurer with the Department of Insurance.

(b) No owner of a motor vehicle being operated in this State shall operate in this State, or authorize any other person to operate such vehicle in this State, unless the owner has insurance on such motor vehicle equal to the minimum insurance required by the state or jurisdiction where said vehicle is registered. If the state or jurisdiction of registration requires no minimum insurance coverage, then such owner must have insurance on such motor vehicle equal to the minimum insurance coverage required for motor vehicles registered in this State. However, an owner shall not be convicted under this subsection if, prior to conviction, the owner shall produce to the court in which the offense is to be tried the insurance identification card or in lieu thereof other sufficient proof of insurance showing such insurance to be in full force and effect at all pertinent times when the motor vehicle was being operated in this State. The

Justice of the Peace Court may permit an operator charged under this subsection to provide proof of insurance to the Court by mail or facsimile transmission in lieu of a personal appearance. Proof of insurance shall be as prescribed by the Court and shall be sent to the Court directly from the operator's insurer or the insurer's agent or broker. It shall be the responsibility of the operator to ensure that proof of insurance is received and accepted by the Court. When proof of insurance is sent by mail or fax, the Court may also accept a guilty plea by mail or fax for any accompanying charge for which a voluntary assessment is permitted under § 709(e) of this title. A guilty plea so accepted shall have the same force and effect as if the operator had made the plea in open court. The Justice of the Peace Court shall enact court rules to implement the handling of such cases by mail or facsimile transmission. Where proof of insurance is provided by facsimile, the operator's insurer or the insurer's agent or broker must confirm the information by mail and the Justice of the Peace Court must confirm by telephone that the facsimile was sent by the operator's insurer or the insurer's agent or broker.

(c) Only insurance policies validly issued by companies authorized to write in this State all the kinds of insurance embodied in the required coverages shall satisfy the requirements of this section.

(d) Nothing in this section shall be construed to prohibit the issuance of policies providing coverage more extensive than the minimum coverages required by this section or to require the segregation of such minimum coverages from other coverages in the same policy.

(e) Policies purporting to satisfy the requirements of this section shall contain a provision which states that, notwithstanding any of the other terms and conditions of the policy, the coverage afforded shall be at least as extensive as the minimum coverage required by this section.

(f) The coverage described in paragraphs (a)(1)-(4) of this section may be subject to conditions and exclusions customary to the field of liability, casualty and property insurance and not inconsistent with the requirements of this section, except there shall be no exclusion to any person who sustains bodily injury or death to the extent that benefits therefore are in whole or in part either payable or required to be provided under any workers' compensation law.

(g) Insurers providing benefits described in paragraphs (a)(1)-(4) of this section shall be subrogated to the rights, including claims under any workers' compensation law, of the person for whom benefits are provided, to the extent of the benefits so provided.

(1) Such subrogated rights shall be limited to the maximum amounts of the tortfeasor's liability insurance coverage available for the injured party, after the injured party's claim has been settled or otherwise resolved, except that the insurer providing benefits shall be indemnified by any workers' compensation insurer obligated to make such payments to the injured party.

(2) Any settlement made with an injured party by a liability insurer shall not be challenged or disputed by any insurer having subrogated rights.

(3) Disputes among insurers as to liability or amounts paid pursuant to paragraphs (a)(1)-(4) of this section shall be arbitrated by the Wilmington Auto Accident Reparation Arbitration Committee or its successors. Any disputes arising between an insurer or insurers and a self-insurer or self-insurers shall be submitted to arbitration which shall be conducted by the Commissioner in the same manner as the arbitration of claims provided for in subsection (j) of this section.

(4) No insurer or self-insurer shall join or be joined in an action by an injured party against a tortfeasor for the recovery of damages by the injured party and/or the recovery of benefits paid by the insurer or self-insurer.

(5) Nothing contained herein shall prohibit a liability insurer from paying the subrogated claim of another insurer prior to the settlement or resolution of the injured party's claim. However, should the amount of such settlement or resolution, in addition to the amount of any subrogated claim, exceed the maximum amount for the tortfeasor's liability insurance coverage available for the injured party, then any insurer who has been paid its subrogated claim shall reimburse the tortfeasor's liability insurer that portion of the claim exceeding the maximum amount of the tortfeasor's liability insurance coverage available for the injured party.

(6) Unless specifically excepted by this subsection, this subsection shall also apply to self-insurers.

(h) Any person eligible for benefits described in paragraph (a)(2) or (3) of this section, other than an insurer in an action brought pursuant to subsection (g) of this section, is precluded from pleading or introducing into evidence in an action for damages against a tortfeasor those damages for which compensation is available under paragraph (a)(2) or (3) of this section without regard to any elective reductions in such coverage and whether or not such benefits are actually recoverable.

(i) Nothing in this section shall be construed to require an insurer to insure any particular risk. Nothing herein shall limit the insurer's obligation pursuant to the Delaware Automobile Plan.

(j) Every insurance policy issued under this section shall require the insurer to submit to arbitration, in the manner set forth hereinafter, any claims for losses or damages within the coverages required under paragraph (a)(2) of this section and for damages to a motor vehicle, including the insured motor vehicle, including loss of use of such vehicle, upon request of the party claiming to have suffered a loss or damages within the above-described coverages of paragraph (a)(2) of this section or to such a motor vehicle. Such request shall be in writing and mailed to the Insurance Commissioner.

(1) All arbitration shall be administered by the Insurance Commissioner or the Insurance Commissioner's nominee.

(2) The Insurance Commissioner or the Insurance Commissioner's nominee shall establish a panel of arbitrators consisting of attorneys authorized to practice law in the State and insurance adjusters licensed to act as such in the State.

(3) The Insurance Commissioner, or the Insurance Commissioner's nominee, shall select 3 individuals from the panel of arbitrators, at least 1 of whom shall be an attorney authorized to practice law in the State, to hear each request for arbitration.

(4) The Insurance Commissioner, or the Insurance Commissioner's nominee, shall promulgate all rules and regulations necessary to implement this arbitration program.

(5) The right to require such arbitration shall be purely optional and neither party shall be held to have waived any of its rights by any act relating to arbitration and the losing party shall have a right to appeal de novo to the Superior Court if notice of such appeal is filed with that Court in the manner set forth by its rules within 30 days of the date of the decision being rendered.

(6) The Insurance Commissioner shall establish a schedule of costs of arbitration; provided, however, the arbitrator's fee shall not exceed $25 per arbitrator for any 1 arbitration.

(7) The cost of arbitration shall be payable to the State Department of Insurance, and shall be maintained in a special fund identified as the "Arbitration Fund" which shall be administered by the Insurance Commissioner. These funds under no circumstances shall revert to the General Fund. All costs of arbitration including administrative expenses of the Insurance Department and the arbitrator's fee shall be payable from this Fund.

(8) The applicant may be reimbursed the cost of filing arbitration as a part of the award rendered by the arbitration panel. If an insurer should pay an applicant damages in advance of a hearing, they shall include with those damages the cost to the applicant of filing the arbitration.

(9) This subsection shall also apply to self-insurers.

(k) Every insurance company authorized to transact the business of motor vehicle liability insurance in this State shall file with the Insurance Commissioner as a condition of its continued transaction of such business within this State a form approved by the Insurance Commissioner stating that its motor vehicle liability policies, on Delaware registered vehicles wherever issued, shall be deemed to provide the insurance required by this section. A nonadmitted insurer may file such a form.

(*l*) A motor vehicle registration shall not be issued or renewed for any vehicle not covered by a vehicle insurance policy meeting the requirements of this title. All insurers shall send to the Division of Motor Vehicles notice, in written or electronic form per the direction of the Division, of any cancellations or terminations of private passenger automobile insurance under § 3904(a)(1) of Title 18 for any private passenger automobile policies which are final and occur within the first 6 months after such policies are issued. The Insurance Commissioner may further change the timeframe for notification by regulation. All insurers shall send notice to the named insured when a motor vehicle insurance policy is canceled pursuant to the provisions of § 3905 or § 3920 of Title 18.

(m) A motor vehicle owner shall, upon request of the Division of Motor Vehicles, offer proof of insurance in full force and effect as a condition of registration or continued registration of a motor vehicle. The Division of Motor Vehicles, upon proof from its records or other sufficient evidence that the required insurance has not been provided or maintained or has terminated or otherwise lapsed at any time, shall immediately suspend the registration of the uninsured vehicle. The registration shall remain suspended until:

(1) The required insurance is obtained or replaced and the vehicle owner submits evidence of insurance on a form prescribed by the Division of Motor Vehicles and certified by the insurer or its agent; and

(2) An uninsured motorist penalty fee is paid to the Division of Motor Vehicles.

(n)(1) Except as provided in subsection (p) of this section, within 5 days of the notice of suspension from the Division of Motor Vehicles, the owner will surrender to the Division of Motor Vehicles the vehicle's certificate of registration and the registration plate.

(2) The Division of Motor Vehicles will promulgate rules and/or regulations to cover those circumstances in which there is an allegation of lost or stolen tags.

(3) Each insurer shall report to the Division of Motor Vehicles, within 30 days on a form prescribed by the Division of Motor Vehicles, the name of any person or persons involved in an accident or filing a claim who is alleged to have been operating a Delaware registered motor vehicle without the insurance required under this chapter. At a minimum, the

insurer shall provide the name, address and description of the vehicle alleged to be uninsured. Each insurer shall take reasonable care when reporting potential violations of this section, but in no case shall an insurer, provider or any of its employees or agents incur any liabilities for erroneous reports of a violation.

(4) In addition to any other penalty provided for in the Delaware Motor Vehicle Law, if the required insurance for a vehicle terminates or otherwise lapses during its registration year, the Division of Motor Vehicles shall assess the owner of the vehicle with a penalty of $100 for each vehicle without the required insurance for a period of up to 30 days. When a penalty fee is assessed, beginning on the thirty-first day of the penalty period, the penalty fee shall increase by a rate of $5.00 for each subsequent day until the insurance is replaced, tags are surrendered to the Division of Motor Vehicles, or the registration expires, whichever occurs first. The Division of Motor Vehicles shall also charge a registration reinstatement fee of $50. When the Division of Motor Vehicles assesses a vehicle owner with a penalty under this subsection, the Division shall not reinstate a registration suspended under this section until the penalty is paid, and the owner has also paid a registration reinstatement fee of $50.

(o) "Insurance identification card" shall mean a card issued by or on behalf of an insurance company or bonding company duly authorized to transact business in this State which states in such form as the Insurance Commissioner may prescribe or approve that such company has issued a vehicle insurance policy meeting the requirements of this title. If the insured and insurance company both consent, the insurance identification card may be produced in electronic format. Acceptable electronic formats include display of electronic images on a cellular phone or any other type of portable electronic device. The Insurance Commissioner shall require all insurance companies transacting business within this State to provide with each vehicle insurance policy an insurance identification card describing the vehicle covered. The insurance identification card shall be valid for a period not to exceed 6 months. Notwithstanding this limitation, an insurance identification card may be issued for a period of 12 months if premium has been paid for the 12-month period. If an owner shall have filed a financial security deposit, or shall have qualified as a self-insurer, the term "insurance identification card" shall mean a card issued by the Office of the Insurance Commissioner which evidences that such deposit has been filed or that such owner has so qualified.

(p)(1) The insurance identification card issued for a vehicle required to be registered under this title shall at all times, when the vehicle is being operated upon a highway within this State, be in the possession of the operator thereof or carried in the vehicle and shall be produced upon the request of a police officer or any other party involved in an accident with the insured. If the operator of a motor vehicle is unable to produce an insurance identification card at the time of a traffic stop or an accident the operator shall be issued a summons to appear in court. If the operator is convicted under this subsection and has not provided proof of insurance in effect as of the date of conviction, the court shall, in addition to any other penalties imposed, notify the Division of Motor Vehicles of the lack of insurance. The Division of Motor Vehicles shall promptly suspend the vehicle's registration pursuant to the provisions of subsection (m) of this section.

a. Presentation of proof of insurance in electronic format shall not constitute consent for law enforcement or other state officials to access other contents of the cellular phone or other portable electronic device, and shall not expand or restrict authority to conduct a search or investigation.

b. Law-enforcement officers and other state officials shall not be liable for any damage to a cellular phone or portable electronic device resulting from its use to present satisfactory proof of motor vehicle liability insurance coverage.

c. A police officer may require the operator to electronically forward the proof of insurance to a specified location provided by the officer. The electronic insurance information would then be viewed in a setting which is safe for the officer to verify that all the information is valid and accurate.

(2) An operator shall not be convicted under this subsection if, prior to conviction, the operator shall produce to the court in which the offense is to be tried the insurance identification card or in lieu thereof other sufficient proof, including but not limited to an automobile, garage keeper's or other commercial or personal insurance policy, showing that there was insurance in full force and effect at all pertinent times covering or which would cover the said motor vehicle or the operation of the said motor vehicle by the operator charged under this subsection.

(3) Subject to paragraph (p)(2) of this section above, the Justice of the Peace Court may permit an operator charged under this subsection to provide proof of insurance to the Court by mail or facsimile transmission or other Court approved method in lieu of a personal appearance. Proof of insurance shall be as prescribed by the Court and shall be sent to the Court directly from the operator's insurer or the insurer's agent or broker. It shall be the responsibility of the operator to ensure that proof of insurance is received and accepted by the Court. When proof of insurance is accepted by the court by any means other than personal appearance, the Court may also accept a guilty plea in absentia for any accompanying charge for which a voluntary assessment is permitted under § 709(e) of this title. A guilty plea so accepted shall have the same force and effect as if the operator had made the plea in open court. The Justice of the Peace Court shall enact court rules to implement the handling of such cases by means other than personal appearance of the operator.

(4) Where the individual is charged with violating this section, and at the time of the alleged offense, the individual was operating a vehicle owned or leased by the individual's employer in the course and scope of the individual's employment, the individual shall not be convicted of violating this section unless the individual knew or should have known that the employer's vehicle failed to meet the requirement of this section.

(q)(1) The Division of Motor Vehicles shall annually select for verification on a random sample basis not less than 10% of vehicle registrations subject to the insurance required by this section. This verification will be made through the insurers as reflected in the Division's records.

(2) Any vehicle owner identified by the Division as a possible uninsured shall submit proof of insurance within 30 days of the Division's request for such proof, to the Division of Motor Vehicles on a form prescribed by the Division and certified by an insurer or agent.

(3) The failure of a vehicle owner to submit the required proof under this section within a 30-day period shall be prima facie evidence that the vehicle is uninsured and the owner shall be subject to the penalties as prescribed in subsections (l) and (m) of this section.

(4) With respect to any vehicle which has:

a. Had its registration suspended by the Division of Motor Vehicles pursuant to subsection (m) of this section,

      b. Had transfer of custody of its license plate ordered by the Justice of the Peace Court pursuant to subsection (p) of this section, or

      c. Failed to produce proof of insurance in a timely fashion pursuant to this subsection (q) of this section,

an officer of the Delaware State Police or member of the Department of Insurance's Fraud Prevention Bureau ("the Fraud Bureau") may confiscate the registration plate of that vehicle at any time absent affirmative proof that the vehicle is currently insured. Prior to any confiscation pursuant to this subsection, the registered owner of a vehicle shall receive notice at least 7 days prior to confiscation by regular and certified mail that such confiscation is to occur, and shall be provided a means to prove that the vehicle has current insurance prior to the indicated confiscation date. The Division of Motor Vehicles and the Justice of the Peace Court shall provide information to the Fraud Bureau and Delaware State Police sufficient to allow those organizations to enforce this subsection. Registration plates confiscated pursuant to this subsection shall be turned over to the Division of Motor Vehicles, which shall follow procedures established pursuant to and consistent with subsection (m) of this section for return of said plates. The Fraud Bureau shall provide its members with sufficient training to ensure safe enforcement of this subsection.

(r) In the event of a suspension of a driver's license pursuant to this section, the Department may issue an occupational license during a period of suspension upon application by the applicant upon a form prescribed by the Department and sworn to by the applicant; provided, that the applicant sets forth in said application that the suspension of such license has created an extreme hardship and that no prior occupational license has been issued within the preceding 12 months; provided, however, that no such occupational license shall be issued until the applicant demonstrates proof of liability insurance on all motor vehicles owned by such applicant or spouse. If the suspension of the driver's license resulted from the arrest and conviction of a person stemming from an incident in which property damage or personal injury occurred, an occupational license shall not be issued, the other provisions of this subsection to the contrary notwithstanding.

(s)(1) Whoever violates any subsection of this section shall be fined for the first offense not less than $1,500 nor more than $2,000 and shall have that person's driving license and/or privileges suspended for 6 months. For each subsequent offense occurring within 3 years of a former offense, that person shall be fined not less than $3,000 nor more than $4,000 and shall have that person's driver's license and/or driving privilege suspended for 6 months. The minimum fine levied for a violation of subsection (a), (b), or (p) of this section may be suspended, in whole or in part, by the Court if evidence is presented that the defendant has secured insurance between the date of charge and the date of sentencing.

    (2) Failure of the owner or operator to produce an insurance identification card for insurance which is in full force and effect at the time of the offense shall be presumptive evidence that such person is operating such person's vehicle without having insurance required by this title.

    (3) Notwithstanding the penalties specified above, anyone convicted of driving without minimum insurance as required in this section shall have such person's privileges of driving suspended in this State until such time as such person has furnished proof of insurance to the Division of Motor Vehicles.

(t)(1) The Division of Motor Vehicles shall periodically select for verification of the required insurance all vehicles owned, individually or jointly, by a person who has been previously convicted of violating the provisions of this subchapter.

(2) The Division of Motor Vehicles may determine the accuracy of information relating to the proof of required insurance satisfying the provisions of this section.

(u)(1) The Division of Motor Vehicles may require evidence that any motor vehicle registered in a person's name, individually or jointly, is covered by the insurance required by this chapter, at a conference, hearing or interview:

> a. As a result of point accumulation on the owner's motor vehicle driving record pursuant to the rules and regulations of the Division of Motor Vehicles; or

> b. To show cause why the person's license should not be suspended or revoked pursuant to the laws of this State or the rules and regulations of the Division of Motor Vehicles.

(2) The Division of Motor Vehicles may require evidence that any vehicle registered in a person's name, individually or jointly, is covered by the insurance required by this chapter, at the time of reinstatement of driving privileges.

(3) The evidence of insurance shall be on a form prescribed by the Division of Motor Vehicles and certified by an insurer or its agent.

(4) Failure to submit the required proof under this section shall be prima facie evidence that any vehicle registered in that person's name, either individually or jointly, is uninsured and the owner shall be subject to the penalties as prescribed in subsections (l) and (m) of this section.

(v)(1) If a person has been issued an equipment inspection notice pursuant to § 2144 of this title, the person shall send within 30 days to the Division of Motor Vehicles the evidence of insurance or security required by this chapter on a form prescribed by the Division and certified by an insurer or agent.

(2) A failure to submit the evidence required by paragraph (v)(1) of this section shall result in the suspension of the registration of the vehicle cited and the assessment of the uninsured motorist penalty fee under this section.

(w) The Division of Motor Vehicle shall conduct a study or cause such study to be conducted to assess the feasibility and costs of establishing a direct computer link between the Division of Motor Vehicle's registration files and the insurance companies' data bases for the purposes of allowing the Division to conduct "real time" status reports of uninsured motorists. The Division of Motor Vehicles shall also conduct a study or cause such study to be conducted to analyze the ramifications of implementing an uninsured motorist program in the State similar to that of Virginia's Uninsured Motorist Program.

(x) Notwithstanding any contrary provisions of the Code, there shall be established a special fund of the State to be known as the D.M.V.T. Fund. The Secretary of Finance shall, commencing upon July 18, 1995, and commencing at the beginning of each fiscal year thereafter, cause to be deposited into the D.M.V.T. Fund amounts received as payments of fines and costs assessed by the Justice of the Peace Courts and/or the Court of Common Pleas under this section, until the amount deposited in said fiscal year shall equal $150,000.

(y) The purpose of the D.M.V.T. Fund is to provide for the administrative costs associated with this Act. Any balance in the D.M.V.T. Fund as of the last day of the fiscal year in excess of $15,000 shall be deposited to the General Fund. The Secretary of Finance shall make deposits to the D.M.V.T. Fund as required under this section commencing after August 1, 1995.

(z) The Director of the Division of Motor Vehicles may adopt such rules and regulations, not inconsistent with this title, as are necessary to enforce this section.

History.

21 Del. C. 1953, § 2118; 58 Del. Laws, c. 98, § 1; 58 Del. Laws, c. 353, § 1; 58 Del. Laws, c. 443; 59 Del. Laws, c. 179, §§ 1-3; 59 Del. Laws, c. 574, §§ 1, 3; 60 Del. Laws, c. 337, §§ 1, 2; 60 Del. Laws, c. 433, § 2; 61 Del. Laws, c. 66, § 1; 61 Del. Laws, c. 292, §§ 1-3; 61 Del. Laws, c. 320, § 1; 61 Del. Laws, c. 417, §§ 1, 2; 62 Del. Laws, c. 280, § 1; 63 Del. Laws, c. 149, § 1; 63 Del. Laws, c. 405, § 1; 64 Del. Laws, c. 198, §§ 1, 2; 64 Del. Laws, c. 356, § 1; 65 Del. Laws, c. 177, § 1; 65 Del. Laws, c. 324, § 1; 65 Del. Laws, c. 503, § 4; 67 Del. Laws, c. 177, §§ 1, 2; 68 Del. Laws, c. 331, §§ 1-4; 68 Del. Laws, c. 336, § 1; 69 Del. Laws, c. 116, § 3; 69 Del. Laws, c. 155, §§ 1, 2; 69 Del. Laws, c. 197, § 1; 69 Del. Laws, c. 413, § 1; 70 Del. Laws, c. 186, § 1; 70 Del. Laws, c. 247, §§ 1-3; 72 Del. Laws, c. 20, § 1; 72 Del. Laws, c. 58, §§ 1, 2; 72 Del. Laws, c. 219, § 1; 72 Del. Laws, c. 380, §§ 1, 2; 74 Del. Laws, c. 110, § 139; 74 Del. Laws, c. 400, § 1; 75 Del. Laws, c. 59, § 1; 76 Del. Laws, c. 128, § 1; 77 Del. Laws, c. 419, § 1; 78 Del. Laws, c. 247, § 2; 79 Del. Laws, c. 269, § 1; 82 Del. Laws, c. 16, § 1; 82 Del. Laws, c. 160, § 4; 83 Del. Laws, c. 90, § 1.

Effect of amendments.

83 Del. Laws, c. 90, effective July 30, 2021, rewrote the final sentence of (s)(1).

NOTES TO DECISIONS

Analysis

Active accessory.
Bad faith.
Computerized evaluation of claims.
Government vehicle.
Statute of limitations.

Active accessory.

In a case in which plaintiff sustained injuries while attempting to enter a vehicle owned by the State, Superior Court observed the vehicle did not cause plaintiff's injuries; plaintiff's claim did not meet the threshold to qualify for personal injury protection benefits, because the vehicle was not more than a mere situs to plaintiff's injury. Shaw v. State, — A.3d —, 2021 Del. Super. LEXIS 284 (Del. Super. Ct. Apr. 6, 2021), aff'd, — A.3d —, 2021 Del. LEXIS 347 (Del. 2021).

Bad faith.

Superior Court's determination, that an insurance company's payment practices for medical fees incurred by its personal injury protection (PIP) insureds in connection with covered multi-injection spine procedures contravened this section, was erroneous because the Court erred in assigning the insurance company the burden of proof with regard to determination of reasonable compensation; even in the context of a bad faith claim, the insured bears the burden of proof (rather than the insurance company). State Farm Mut. Auto. Ins. Co. v. Spine Care Del., LLC, 238 A.3d 850 (Del. 2020).

Computerized evaluation of claims.

Defendant's computerized rules used to evaluate personal injury protection claims violated 21 Del. C. §§ 2118(a)(2) and 2118B(c); the inflexible rules excluded benefits without any investigation of the actual claim and ignored relevant factors of a valid claim. Green v. Geico Gen. Ins. Co., — A.3d —, 2021 Del. Super. LEXIS 308 (Del. Super. Ct. Mar. 24, 2021).

Government vehicle.

In an insurance coverage dispute, a student driver was granted summary judgment because the driver was covered by a state agency's insurance policy in the underlying tort litigation; the driver was insured under the policy as a permissive user of a State-owned driver's education vehicle covered under the policy. State of Def. Ins. Coverage Office v. Perkins-Johnson, — A.3d —, 2021 Del. Super. LEXIS 559 (Del. Super. Ct. Aug. 19, 2021).

Statute of limitations.

Insured's failure to file a timely appeal from an insurance arbitration decision precluded the court from reaching the merits of the insured's claim because: (1) the statutory time period for filing an appeal is jurisdictional; (2) no administrative orders had tolled or extended that time period;. and (3) although the insured was a self-represented litigant, the court did not have latitude to extend a jurisdictional deadline. Simpson v. State Farm Ins. Co., — A.3d —, 2021 Del. Super. LEXIS 245 (Del. Super. Ct. Mar. 25, 2021).

§ 2118B. Processing and payment of insurance benefits.

NOTES TO DECISIONS

Analysis

Breach of contract.
Computerized evaluation of claims.

Breach of contract.

In a case where plaintiffs challenged comput-erized rules used by defendant to evaluate personal injury protection (PIP) claims, defendant was entitled to summary judgment on plaintiffs' breach of contract claim because: (1) defendant did not have a common law duty to investigate; and (2) the court could not find a breach of contract under 21 Del. C. § 2118B(d) without a showing that the PIP claims were reasonable and necessary. Green v. Geico Gen. Ins. Co., — A.3d —, 2021 Del. Super. LEXIS 308 (Del. Super. Ct. Mar. 24, 2021).

Computerized evaluation of claims. Defendant's computerized rules used to evaluate personal injury protection claims violated 21 Del. C. §§ 2118(a)(2) and 2118B(c); the inflexible rules excluded benefits without any investigation of the actual claim and ignored relevant factors of a valid claim. Green v. Geico Gen. Ins. Co., — A.3d —, 2021 Del. Super. LEXIS 308 (Del. Super. Ct. Mar. 24, 2021).

SUBCHAPTER II
PLATES

§ 2134. Special license plates for persons with disabilities which limit or impair the ability to walk; parking; penalties.

(a) The owner of a vehicle registered in Delaware and described in subsection (b) of this section may apply to the Department for the issuing to the vehicle a special license plate for persons with disabilities which limit or impair the ability to walk if a licensed physician, a physician assistant who is supervised by a licensed physician, or an advanced practice nurse who is employed by or who has a collaborative agreement with a licensed physician, certifies that the applicant or a household member has 1 or more of the following disabilities that are permanent with no prognosis for improvement:

(1) Cannot walk 200 feet without stopping to rest;

(2) Cannot walk safely without the use of or assistance from a brace, cane, crutch, another person, prosthetic device, wheelchair or other assistive device;

(3) Is restricted by lung disease to such an extent that the applicant's or household member's forced (respiratory) expiratory volume for 1 second, when measured by spirometry, is less than 1 liter or the arterial oxygen tension is less than 60 mm/hg on room air at rest;

(4) Uses portable oxygen;

(5) Has a cardiac condition to the extent that the applicant's or household member's functional limitations are classified in severity as Class III or Class IV according to standards set by the American Heart Association; or

(6) Is severely limited in that person's own ability to walk due to an arthritic, neurological or orthopedic condition.

(b) This section applies only to passenger cars, station wagons, pickup trucks, motorcycles, panel van trucks and other motor vehicles that are reasonably used by persons with disabilities which limit or impair the ability to walk and that have a gross registered weight which does not exceed 14,000 lbs.

(c) A special license plate may be issued under this section only if the applicant submits proof satisfactory to the Department that the applicant or a household member has a disability that is permanent with no prognosis for improvement as described in paragraphs (a)(1)-(6) of this section. Satisfactory proof prior to issuance must include the signature of a licensed physician, a physician assistant who is supervised by a licensed physician, or an advanced practice nurse who is employed by or who has a collaborative agreement with a licensed physician, on a Department special disabled license plate or placard applicant form on which the physician, a physician assistant who is supervised by a licensed physician, or an advanced practice nurse who is employed by or who has a collaborative agreement with a licensed physician, certifies the applicant's or household member's permanent disability. Renewal of the registration for the vehicle to which the special license plate is assigned shall require the applicant to submit a written certification that the applicant continues to require the special license plate for the reason or reasons it was initially issued; a new certification is not required. The issuance of a special license plate does not preclude the issuance of 1 removable windshield placard pursuant to § 2135 of this title.

(d) The fee for the issuance or reissuance of a special license plate may not exceed the fee charged for the issuance or reissuance of a standard license plate for the same class of vehicle.

(e) A special license plate issued pursuant to this section must display the internationally recognized wheelchair symbol of access in the same size as the numbers and/or letters on the plate.

(f)(1) A person for whom a special license plate is issued under this section or under a similar statute of any other state or country may park in parking spaces or zones as follows:

a. Restricted for use by persons with disabilities which limit or impair the ability to walk.

b. For an unlimited period in an unmetered parking space or zone restricted as to the length of parking time permitted.

c. In a metered parking space for no less than 1 hour.

d. If a parking space is assigned to a specific person with a disability as that person's residential or business parking space, that person may use the space without any time restriction.

(2) A person who is driving a vehicle with a special license plate issued under this section or under a similar statute of any other state or country may not park in any of the following places:

a. In a space or zone where stopping, standing, or parking is prohibited to all vehicles.

b. In a space or zone which is reserved for other special types of vehicles.

c. In a space or zone assigned to another person for the other person's residential or business use.

d. Where a local ordinance prohibits parking during heavy traffic periods in morning, afternoon, or evening rush hours.

e. Where parking clearly would present a traffic hazard.

(3) The person for whom a special license plate is issued under this section or under a similar statute of any other state or country must be the driver of or a passenger in the vehicle bearing the special plate whenever the vehicle parks in a parking space or zone restricted for use only by vehicles with a special license plate or placard for persons with disabilities which limit or impair the ability to walk.

(g)(1) A person who intentionally presents false information to a licensed physician, a physician assistant who is supervised by a licensed physician, or an advanced practice nurse who is employed by or who has a collaborative agreement with a licensed physician, or to the Department in an attempt to obtain a special license plate under this section shall be guilty of an unclassified misdemeanor. For the first offense, the person shall receive a mandatory fine of $100. For each subsequent like offense, the person shall receive a mandatory fine of $200 or be imprisoned for not less than 10 nor more than 30 days, or both. Any other violation of this section is a violation. Justices of the peace have jurisdiction over violations of this section.

(2) A summons may be attached to an unattended vehicle found in violation of any of the provisions of this section by any police officer or State Police Academy cadet authorized to issue a summons for a violation of this section. It is prima facie evidence that the person in whose name the unattended vehicle is registered is responsible for the violation.

(h) The Department may adopt rules and regulations that are reasonable or necessary for the implementation of this section.

History.

21 Del. C. 1953, § 2134; 55 Del. Laws, c. 398, § 1; 61 Del. Laws, c. 345, § 1; 63 Del. Laws, c. 341, § 1; 63 Del. Laws, c. 441; 65 Del. Laws, c. 503, § 7; 67 Del. Laws, c. 125, § 1; 70 Del. Laws, c. 186, § 1; 71 Del. Laws, c. 96, § 1; 73 Del. Laws, c. 397, § 1; 76 Del. Laws, c. 210, § 1; 77 Del. Laws, c. 60, § 4; 77 Del. Laws, c. 113, §§ 1-3; 83 Del. Laws, c. 160, § 2.

Effect of amendments.

83 Del. Laws, c. 160, effective September 15, 2021, rewrote (f)(1); added "in any of the following places" in the introductory paragraph of (f)(2); added a comma following "standing" in (f)(2)a. and following "afternoon" in (f)(2)d.; and substituted a period for a semicolon at the end of (f)(2)a.-c. and for "; or" at the end of (f)(2)d.

§ 2135. Parking permits for persons with disabilities which limit or impair the ability to walk; parking; penalties.

(a) A person or a member of the person's household who has a disability that is permanent with no prognosis for improvement as described in § 2134(a)(1)-(6) of this title or who has a physical disability which is not permanent but which substantially limits or impairs the person's or household member's ability to walk for no less than 5 weeks and which is so severe that the person or household member would endure a hardship or be subject to a risk of injury without a temporary parking permit for persons with disabilities, or a person who is age 85 or older, whether or not that person has a disability, or an organization that regularly in its course of business transports persons with disabilities may apply to the Department for a permanent or temporary parking permit, whichever is appropriate, on a form provided by the Department. The form must state:

(1) That a permanent permit for a person with a disability, or for a person 85 or older, or for an organization that regularly in its course of business transports persons with disabilities expires after 3 years and a temporary permit for a person with a disability may not exceed 90 days;

(2) That a licensed physician, a physician assistant who is supervised by a licensed physician, or an advanced practice nurse who is employed by or who has a collaborative agreement with a licensed physician, must certify a disability and indicate whether the applicant or household member needs a permanent parking permit or a temporary parking permit;

(3) That an applicant 85 or older need only submit proof of age that is satisfactory to the Department; and

(4) The possible penalties for intentionally and falsely representing that an applicant or household member is qualified to obtain a permanent or temporary parking permit.

An applicant or a household member who is eligible for a special license plate pursuant to § 2134 of this title may also apply for 1 permanent parking permit under this section. A parking permit is issued in the form of a removable placard capable of hanging from or being attached to the front windshield rearview mirror of a vehicle.

(b) A permanent or temporary parking permit may be issued under this section only if the applicant submits proof satisfactory to the Department that the applicant or household member has a disability that is permanent with no prognosis for improvement as described in § 2134(a)(1)-(6) of this title, or that the applicant or household member has a physical disability which is not permanent but which substantially limits or impairs the applicant's or household member's ability to walk for no less than 5 weeks and which is so severe that the applicant or household member would endure a hardship or be subject to a risk of injury without a temporary parking permit for persons with disabilities, or that the applicant or household member is 85 or older, or that the applicant is an organization that regularly in its course of business transports persons with disabilities. Satisfactory proof of a disability must include the signature of a licensed physician, a physician assistant who is supervised by a licensed physician, or an advanced practice nurse who is employed by or who has a collaborative agreement with a licensed physician, on a Department special license plate or placard application form on which the physician, a physician assistant who is supervised by a licensed physician, or an advanced practice nurse who is employed by or who has a collaborative agreement with a licensed physician, indicates the applicant's or household member's disability.

(c) The Department may not charge a fee for issuing or reissuing a parking placard. However, the Department shall charge a fee to offset the actual replacement cost of replacing a lost or damaged placard.

(d)(1) A permanent permit issued under this section for a person who has a disability stated in § 2134(a) of this title, or for a person 85 or older, or to an organization that regularly in its course of business transports persons with disabilities expires 3 years from the date of issue. However, another permanent permit may be issued upon reapplication.

(2) A temporary permit issued under this section for an applicant who has a physical disability which is not permanent but which substantially limits or impairs the person's ability to walk for no less than 5 weeks and which is so severe that the person would endure a hardship or be subject to a risk of injury without a temporary parking permit for persons with disabilities expires at the discretion of the Department, but may not exceed 90 days from the date of issue. However, another temporary permit may be issued upon reapplication.

(3) There is no limit to the number of times that a person may reapply for a permanent or temporary parking permit issued under this section. However, for each reapplication for a temporary parking permit, the applicant must comply with the requirements for an initial application as set forth in subsection (a) of this section. A new certification is not required for applicants or applicants' household members who have a permanent disability as described in § 2134(a)(1)-(6) of this title; however, the applicant shall submit a written certification that the applicant continues to require the parking permit for the reason or reasons it was initially issued.

(e) A parking permit for a person with a disability which limits or impairs the ability to walk, or for a person 85 or over, or for an organization pursuant to subsection (i) of this section must be in the form of a removable windshield placard of a size and design determined by the Department. A permanent parking placard must be blue; a temporary parking placard must be red; an organization parking placard must be green. The information on the placard must be large enough to be read clearly from outside a motor vehicle when the placard is hanging from the vehicle's front windshield rearview mirror, or if there is no front windshield rearview mirror, the placard must be displayed on the dashboard and be able to be read by a person outside of the vehicle. Both sides of the placard must contain the following: the words "State of Delaware Division of Motor Vehicles" and "Remove placard when vehicle is in motion," the internationally recognized wheelchair symbol of access, an identification number, and the expiration date. The expiration date must appear in letters or numerals at least 1 inch tall. Only 1 placard may be issued initially to an applicant; however, upon written request, the Department shall issue 1 additional placard to an applicant who does not also have a special license plate issued pursuant to § 2134 of this title.

(f)(1) A person or organization for whom a parking placard is issued under this section or under a similar statute of any other state or country may park in parking spaces or zones as follows:

    a. Restricted to use only by persons with disabilities.

    b. For an unlimited period in an unmetered parking space or zone restricted as to the length of parking time permitted.

    c. In a metered parking space for no less than 1 hour.

    d. If a parking space is assigned to a specific person with a disability as that person's residential or business parking space, that person may use the space without any time restriction.

  (2) A person who is driving a vehicle with a parking placard issued under this section or under a similar statute of any other state or country may not park in any of the following places:

    a. In a space or zone where stopping, standing, or parking is prohibited to all vehicles.

    b. In a space or zone which is reserved for other special types of vehicles.

    c. In a space or zone assigned to another person for the other person's residential or business use.

    d. Where a local ordinance prohibits parking during heavy traffic periods in morning, afternoon, or evening rush hours.

    e. Where parking clearly would present a traffic hazard.

  (3) The person for whom a red or blue parking placard is issued under this section or under a similar statute of any other state or country must be the driver of or a passenger in the vehicle displaying the parking placard whenever the vehicle parks in a parking space or zone restricted for use only by vehicles with a special license plate or parking placard for persons with disabilities.

(g) A placard issued under this section is for the exclusive and personal use of the person or organization for whom it is issued and may not be used by any other person or organization.

(h) A parking placard must be returned to the Department:

  (1) When the person or organization for whom it was issued reapplies for a placard;

  (2) When the placard expires;

  (3) When the person or organization for whom it was issued no longer needs it, is no longer disabled, or no longer regularly in its course of business transports persons with disabilities;

  (4) Upon the death of the person for whom it was issued.

(i) Notwithstanding any provisions of this Code to the contrary, the Department may, without the certification of a licensed physician, a physician assistant who is supervised by a licensed physician, or an advanced practice nurse who is employed by or who has a collaborative agreement with a licensed physician, issue a green parking placard upon application by an organization that regularly in its course of business transports persons with disabilities which limit or impair the ability to walk if the organization presents proof satisfactory to the Department that the organization regularly in its course of business transports persons with disabilities. A green parking placard may be used only when at least 1 person who is entitled to obtain a permanent or temporary parking placard pursuant to subsection (a) of this section is being transported and only when an employee or volunteer staff person of the organization is the driver of the vehicle.

(j)(1) A person or organization who intentionally presents false information to a licensed physician, a physician assistant who is supervised by a licensed physician, or an advanced practice nurse who is employed by or who has a collaborative agreement with a licensed physician, or to the Department in an attempt to obtain a parking placard under this section shall be guilty of an unclassified misdemeanor. For the first offense, the person or organization shall receive a mandatory fine of $100. For each subsequent like offense, the person or organization shall receive a mandatory fine of $200 or be imprisoned for not less than 10 nor more than 30 days, or both. Any other violation of this section is a violation. Justices of the peace have jurisdiction over violations of this section.

(2) A summons may be attached to an unattended vehicle found in violation of any of the provisions of this section by any police officer or State Police Academy cadet authorized to issue a summons for a violation of this section. It is prima facie evidence that the person or organization in whose name the unattended vehicle is registered is responsible for the violation.

(k) The Department may adopt rules and regulations that are reasonable or necessary for the implementation of this section.

History.

63 Del. Laws, c. 441, § 2; 64 Del. Laws, c. 88, § 1; 65 Del. Laws, c. 102, §§ 1-3; 65 Del. Laws, c. 503, § 8; 70 Del. Laws, c. 186, § 1; 73 Del. Laws, c. 397, § 2; 76 Del. Laws, c. 210, § 2; 77 Del. Laws, c. 60, § 5; 77 Del. Laws, c. 113, § 4; 83 Del. Laws, c. 160, § 2.

2021, rewrote (f)(1); added "in any of the following places" in the introductory paragraph of (f)(2); added a comma following "standing" in (f)(2)a. and following "afternoon" in (f)(2)d.; and substituted a period for a semicolon at the end of (f)(2)a.-c. and for "; or" at the end of (f)(2)d.

Effect of amendments.

83 Del. Laws, c. 160, effective September 15,

§ 2139M. Law Enforcement Memorial license plate.

(a)(1) The owner of any vehicle described in paragraph (a)(2) of this section may apply to the Department for assignment to that vehicle of a special Law Enforcement Memorial registration number; provided, however, that the owner of the vehicle must possess documentation:

    a. That indicates that such person is a "police officer" as defined in § 8401 of Title 11;

    b. That indicates that such person is an immediate family member of a "police officer" as defined in § 8401 of Title 11 who was killed in the line of duty; or

    c. From the Delaware Police Chiefs' Council that it is appropriate for such person to receive a special Law Enforcement Memorial registration number.

(2) This section applies only to:

    a. A private passenger vehicle; or

    b. A truck or van with a ¾-ton or smaller manufacturer's rated capacity.

(b) No fee in addition to the annual registration fee otherwise required by this title is required for registration under this section; provided, however, that an original application under this section shall be subject to a $35 administrative fee, which shall be deposited into a special fund and used by the Division of Motor Vehicles for the purposes of administering this section and to fund Department projects notwithstanding the provisions of Chapters 13 and 14 of Title 2 to the contrary.

(c) All registration plates issued pursuant to this section shall be of the colors and design as determined by the Law Enforcement Memorial License Plate Committee created pursuant to subsection (d) of this section. The license plate may also include words, a slogan or an emblem supporting the Law Enforcement Memorial. The Committee may at its discretion drop the wording

"The First State" and substitute in lieu thereof "Law Enforcement Memorial". The Division of Motor Vehicles shall have the power to refuse any design which it believes would cause a public safety enforcement problem.

(d) For purposes of this section, the "Law Enforcement Memorial License Plate Committee" shall consist of the following:

(1) The Director of the Division of Motor Vehicles or designee;

(2) The Chairperson of the Delaware Police Chiefs' Foundation or designee;

(3) The Colonel of the Delaware State Police or designee; and

(4) The Chairperson of the Delaware Police Chiefs' Council or designee.

(e) The Department shall reserve sufficient special license plates including the letters "LEM" and numbered consecutively beginning with the numeral "1" as are necessary to implement this section.

(f) The Delaware Police Chiefs' Council shall have the authority to assign the license plate numbers at its discretion.

(g) Upon receipt by the Department of information that the individual to whom the special plate has been issued is no longer affiliated with such organization or has died, whichever is applicable, the Department shall write to such person or the representative of that person's estate, requesting that such plate be returned to the Department within 90 days.

(h) The Division of Motor Vehicles may promulgate rules and regulations as required to administer this section.

History.
78 Del. Laws, c. 153, § 1; 83 Del. Laws, c. 83, § 2.

Revisor's note.
Based upon changes contained in 83 Del.

Laws, c. 83, § 2, effective July 21, 2021, in both (a)(1)a. and (a)(1)b., "police officer" was put in quotes and "(5)" was deleted following "§ 8401".

§ 2139O. Marine Education, Research and Rehabilitation Institute, Inc. special license plates.

(a) The owner of a motor vehicle which is a private passenger vehicle or a truck or trailer with a manufacturer's gross vehicle weight rating (GVWR) of 26,000 pounds or less may apply to the Division of Motor Vehicles for a special Marine Education, Research and Rehabilitation Institute, Inc. license plate.

(b) Upon the initial application for a license plate to be issued pursuant to this section, a 1-time fee of $50, which includes an administrative fee of $15, is required in addition to the annual registration fee required by this title. This additional fee is required for members of nonprofit organizations even if members are exempt from registration fees under § 2159 of this title. A replacement plate may be obtained upon payment of a fee to be set by the Division which shall cover the cost of the plate.

(c) The 1-time administrative fee collected pursuant to subsection (b) of this section shall be deposited into a special fund and used by the Division of Motor Vehicles for the purpose of administering this section and to fund division projects notwithstanding the provisions of Chapters 13 and 14 of Title 2 to the contrary.

(d) All license plates issued pursuant to this section shall be of the colors and design requested by the Marine Education, Research and Rehabilitation Institute, Inc. The numbers and/or letters assigned will be the same as the current license plate assigned to the vehicle. No special numbers or letters will be authorized for these plates. The Division of Motor Vehicles shall have the power to refuse any design which it believes would cause a public safety enforcement problem.

(e) The funds derived by the State from that portion of the 1-time fee of $50 that is not defined as an administrative fee pursuant to subsection (c) of this section shall be deposited by the Division of Motor Vehicles with the State Treasurer and shall be specifically set aside for use by the Marine Education, Research and Rehabilitation Institute, Inc.

(f) The Division of Motor Vehicles may promulgate rules and regulations as required to administer this section.

History.
78 Del. Laws, c. 240, § 1; 78 Del. Laws, c. 385, § 1; 81 Del. Laws, c. 380, § 3; 83 Del. Laws, c. 37, § 23.

Effect of amendments.
83 Del. Laws, c. 37, effective June 3, 2021, added "Research and Rehabilitation Institute, Inc. license plate" in (a).

§ 2139DD. Special license plate to support pollinators.

(a) The owner of a vehicle described in subsection (b) of this section may apply to the Division of Motor Vehicles ("Division") for a special "Support Pollinators" plate. The Division shall issue the plate if it receives at least 50 such applications.

(b) This section applies only to:

(1) A private passenger vehicle.

(2) Subject to paragraph (b)(2)b. of this section, a motor vehicle, including a truck or trailer, with a manufacturer's gross vehicle weight rating ("GVWR") of 26,000 pounds or less.

a. The motor vehicle described in this paragraph (b)(2) may be owned by an individual or an artificial entity, including a corporation, company, association, firm, partnership, society, or joint-stock company.

b. A truck that qualifies to register for the International Registration Plan ("IRP"), individually, or as part of a combination of vehicles, as defined in § 101 of this title, may not be issued a special plate under this section.

(c)(1) On the initial application for a plate to be issued under this section, a 1-time fee of $50, which includes an administrative fee of $15, is required in addition to the annual registration fee required by this title.

(2) The initial application fee under paragraph (c)(1) of this section is required for a person applying for a plate under this section, including a member of a nonprofit organization, even if the member is exempt from registration fees under § 2159 of this title .

(3) A replacement plate may be obtained on payment of a fee to be set by the Division, which must cover the cost of the plate.

(d) The Division shall deposit the 1-time administrative fee collected under subsection (c) of this section into a special fund and use the fund to promote the sale of the plate and for administering this section. Proceeds remaining after the Division has covered the costs of promoting the sale of the plate and administering this section must be applied under subsection (e) of this section.

(e) The Division shall deposit with the Department the funds derived by the State from the portion of the 1-time fee of $50 that is not defined as an administrative fee under subsections (c) and (d) of this section. The Department shall set aside the deposited funds. The Department shall use the set aside deposited funds for pollinator-related work, such as native species and milkweed plantings.

(f)(1) A plate issued under this section must be of the colors and design as determined by the Division and the Department's Environmental Studies Office.

(2) The numbers or letters assigned by the Division must be the same as the plate assigned to an owner's vehicle at the time of the application for the plate.

(3) The Department's Environmental Studies Office may drop the

wording "The First State" and substitute "Support Pollinators, Plant Native Species".

(4) The Division may refuse any design which the Division believes would cause a public safety enforcement problem.

(g) The Division may adopt regulations to administer this section.

History.
83 Del. Laws, c. 23, § 1.

Revisor's note.
This section became effective upon the signature of the Governor on June 3. 2021.

§ 2140. Special registration plates for members of nonprofit organizations.

(a) The owner of a motor vehicle described in subsection (b) of this section who is a member of a nonprofit organization considered eligible by the Division of Motor Vehicles may apply to the Division for the assignment of a special registration plate for such vehicle.

(b) This section applies only to:

(1) A passenger vehicle;

(2) A truck with a ¾-ton or smaller manufacturer's rated capacity; or

(3) A van with a ¾-ton or smaller manufacturer's rated capacity.

(c) The applicant must submit acceptable proof, as required by the Division, that the applicant is a member in good standing or is otherwise eligible for the issuance of such special plate.

(d) No fee in addition to the regular annual registration fee required by this title is required. However, upon the initial application for a special plate issued pursuant to this section, a 1-time administrative fee of $10 shall be assessed.

(e) The 1-time administrative fee collected pursuant to subsection (d) of this section shall be deposited into a special fund and used by the Division of Motor Vehicles for the purpose of administering this section, notwithstanding the provisions of Chapters 13 and 14 of Title 2 to the contrary.

(f) [Repealed.]

(g) At least 200 applications for special plates must be received from a specific organization before the Division of Motor Vehicles will approve the issuance. However, the minimum number of 200 does not apply to any of the following:

(1) Survivors of Pearl Harbor.

(2) Members of university or high school alumni associations, provided that at least 25 applications for special plates must be received from members of a given university or high school alumni association before the Division of Motor Vehicles will approve the issuance of special plates for that particular university or high school alumni association.

(3) Retired Delaware police officers.

(4) Members of Delaware Nur Temple and the Service Alumni Association, provided that at least 100 applications for special plates must be received from members before the Division of Motor Vehicles will approve the issuance of the special plate.

(5) Members of the Marine Corps League and Delaware Veterans of World War 2 Inc. provided that at least 100 applications for special plates must be received from members before the Division of Motor Vehicles will approve the issuance of the special plate.

(6) Members of the Order of Eastern Star, Knights of Columbus, the Telephone Pioneers of America, Lions Club International, and the Senior Olympics, provided that at least 100 applications for special plates must be received from members of any of the said organizations before the

Division of Motor Vehicles will approve the issuance of a special plate for that organization, except for the Telephone Pioneers of America who must have a minimum of 75 applications for special plates before the Division of Motor Vehicles will approve the issuance of a special plate for the organization.

(7) Members of "Fraternal Order of Firemen Wilmington Retired Firefighters," provided that at least 50 applications for special plates must be received from members of such organization before the Division of Motor Vehicles will approve the issuance of the special plate.

(8) Members of the "USSVI, Mid-Atlantic Base," the U.S. Submarine Veterans, Inc., organization, provided that at least 35 applications for special plates be received from members of such organization before the Division of Motor Vehicles will approve the issuance of the special plate.

(9) Members of the "Buffalo Soldiers Motorcycle Club of Delaware," provided that at least 25 applications for special plates must be received from members of such organization before the Division of Motor Vehicles will approve the issuance of the special plate.

(10) Members of "atTAcK addiction," provided that at least 50 applications for special plates must be received from members of the organization before the Division of Motor Vehicles will approve the issuance of the special plate.

(h) The numbers and letters assigned to these special plates must be such that they can be integrated with the Division's computerized vehicle registration records.

(i) The Division of Motor Vehicles may refuse to issue special registration plates when it is deemed not in the best interest of the State.

(j) Upon receipt by the Department of information that the individual to whom the special plate has been issued pursuant to paragraph (g)(1), (g)(5), or (g)(8) of this section is deceased, the surviving spouse may transfer the plate to a vehicle owned by the spouse that meets the requirements of subsection (b) of this section as a valid registration plate. No fee in addition to the annual registration fee otherwise required by this title is required for registration.

(k) The Department upon receipt of any official correspondence from the organization advising that the individual to which a special plate has been issued is no longer affiliated with such organization such special plate shall be forfeited and/or revoked immediately.

(*l*) The Division of Motor Vehicles may promulgate rules and regulations as required to administer this section.

History.

69 Del. Laws, c. 183, § 1; 70 Del. Laws, c. 9, § 1; 70 Del. Laws, c. 12, § 1; 70 Del. Laws, c. 158, § 1; 70 Del. Laws, c. 186, § 1; 70 Del. Laws, c. 200, § 2; 70 Del. Laws, c. 317, § 1; 70 Del. Laws, c. 333, § 1; 70 Del. Laws, c. 417, § 1; 73 Del. Laws, c. 170, §§ 1-4; 76 Del. Laws, c. 204, §§ 4, 6-8; 80 Del. Laws, c. 49, § 1; 83 Del. Laws, c. 24, § 1.

Effect of amendments.

83 Del. Laws, c. 24, effective June 3, 2021, in the first sentence of the introductory paragraph of (g), substituted "does" for "shall" and added "any of"; substituted a period for a semicolon at the end of (g)(1) - (g)(7); in (g)(6), added a comma following "International" and substituted "Division" for "Director" twice; substituted a period for "; and" in (g)(8); and added (g)(10).

§ 2140I. Special registration plates supporting autism awareness and acceptance.

(a) The owner of any vehicle described in subsection (b) of this section may apply to the Division of Motor Vehicles for a special "Autism Awareness and Acceptance" registration plate.

(b) This section applies to:

(1) A private passenger vehicle; or

(2) Subject to paragraph (b)(2)b. of this section, a motor vehicle, including a truck or trailer, with a manufacturer's gross vehicle weight rating (GVWR) of 26,000 pounds or less.

    a. The motor vehicle described in this paragraph may be owned by an individual or an artificial entity, including a corporation, company, association, firm, partnership, society, or joint-stock company.

    b. A truck that qualifies to register for the International Registration Plan (IRP), individually, or as part of a combination of vehicles, as defined § 101 of this title, may not be issued a special plate under this section.

(c) Upon the initial application for a plate to be issued pursuant to this section, a 1-time fee of $50, which includes an administrative fee of $15, is required in addition to the annual registration fee required by this title. This additional fee is required for all persons applying for a special plate pursuant to this section, including members of nonprofit organizations, even if members are exempt from registration fees under § 2159 of this title. A replacement plate may be obtained upon payment of a fee to be set by the Division, which shall cover the cost of the plate.

(d) The 1-time administrative fee collected pursuant to subsection (c) of this section shall be deposited into a special fund and used by the Division of Motor Vehicles for the purpose of promoting the sale of the plate and administering this section. Proceeds remaining after the Division of Motor Vehicles has covered the costs of promoting and administering this section shall be applied pursuant to subsection (e) of this section.

(e) The funds derived by the State from that portion of the 1-time fee of $50 that is not defined as an administrative fee pursuant to subsection (d) of this section shall be deposited by the Division of Motor Vehicles with the State Treasurer and shall be specifically set aside and deposited with the Autism Delaware, Inc. for its deposit in the Autism Awareness and Acceptance Fund.

(f) All registration plates issued pursuant to this section shall be of the colors and design as determined by the Autism Delaware, Inc. The numbers and/or letters assigned will be the same as the current license plate assigned to the vehicle. The committee may, at its discretion, drop the wording "The First State" and substitute in place thereof the wording "Autism Awareness" or "Autism Acceptance". The Division of Motor Vehicles shall have the power to refuse any design which it believes would cause a public safety enforcement problem.

(g) The Division of Motor Vehicles may promulgate rules and regulations as required to administer this section.

History.
83 Del. Laws, c. 192, § 1.

Revisor's note.
This section became effective upon the signature of the Governor on Sept 17, 2021.

CHAPTER 27

DRIVER'S LICENSE

SUBCHAPTER I
GENERAL PROVISIONS

§ 2702. Definitions.

(a) The Division upon issuing a driver's license shall indicate thereon, in a manner prescribed by the Division, the type or general class of vehicles the licensee may drive.

(b) The Division shall establish such qualifications as it believes reasonably necessary for the safe operation of the various types, sizes or combinations of vehicles and shall appropriately examine each applicant according to the type or general class of license applied for.

(c)(1) When the licensee desires to change the type or class of license which the licensee has been issued and such change requires another examination to be administered, a fee of $10 shall be assessed for such change.

(2) When the licensee desires to add an endorsement or endorsements to the licensee's license, and the endorsement requires additional testing, a fee of $5.00 shall be assessed.

(3) These fees shall not be imposed on motorcycle applicants for whom fees are required under § 2703 of this title.

(d) *Vehicles driven by minor permit holders.* — (1) A "Driver Education Learner's Permit" authorizes the holder to operate those vehicles that a holder of a Class D operator's license can operate.

(2) A "Level 1 Learner's Permit" authorizes the holder to operate those vehicles referenced under paragraph (d)(1) of this section.

(e) *Classifications, endorsements and restrictions.* — (1) *Class D operator's license.* — Authorizes the license holder to operate any single vehicle with a GVWR of less than 26,001 pounds or any such vehicle towing a vehicle with a GVWR not in excess of 10,000 pounds. The vehicle must be designed to transport 15 or fewer passengers, including the driver, and they shall not transport hazardous materials which require the vehicle to be placarded under federal law.

(2) *Temporary license.* — A temporary license may be issued to the holder of a valid Class D operator's license or commercial driver's license to extend the expiration date, to replace a lost license or in lieu of the Class D or CDL licensing document. A temporary license or temporary instruction permit may be issued to an unlicensed driver for specialized training.

(3) *Temporary instruction permit.* — Authorizes the holder to operate those vehicles defined under paragraph (e)(1) of this section.

(4) *Commercial driver's license.* — CDL Class A, CDL Class B and CDL Class C licenses are defined in § 2611(b) of this title.

(5) *Conditional license.* — Limited driving privileges granted under § 2607(b) or § 4177C of this title and § 4767 of Title 16.

(6) *Occupational license.* — Limited driving privileges granted under §§ 2118(r), 2607(b) and 2733(g) of this title.

(7) *Hardship license.* — Limited driving privileges granted under § 2751(s) of this title.

(8) *Endorsement and restriction codes.* — The Division is authorized to establish endorsement and restriction codes based upon this title.

(9) *Non-CDL Class A or non-CDL Class B license.* — Authorizes the holder to operate farm vehicles, fire-fighting equipment, and other authorized emergency vehicles under the commercial driver license waivers defined in § 2621 of this title.

(10) *IID license.* — Authorizes the holder to operate a vehicle with full Class D operators driving privileges only when the vehicle is equipped with an ignition interlock device.

History.

36 Del. Laws, c. 10, § 62; Code 1935, § 5600; 21 Del. C. 1953, § 2702; 58 Del. Laws, c. 485; 60 Del. Laws, c. 339, § 1; 67 Del. Laws, c. 157, § 2; 67 Del. Laws, c. 260, § 1; 70 Del. Laws, c. 186, § 1; 71 Del. Laws, c. 282, § 6; 71 Del. Laws, c. 375, § 1; 72 Del. Laws, c. 92, § 3; 73 Del. Laws, c. 414, § 1; 74 Del. Laws, c. 135, § 3; 74 Del. Laws, c. 273, § 1; 76 Del. Laws, c. 233, § 4; 78 Del. Laws, c. 13, §§ 60, 70; 79 Del. Laws, c. 295, § 1; 79 Del. Laws, c. 396, § 2; 82 Del. Laws, c. 91, § 2; 83 Del. Laws, c. 37, § 24.

Effect of amendments.

83 Del. Laws, c. 37, effective June 3, 2021, substituted "§ 2607(b) or § 4177C of this title and § 4767 of Title 16" for "§§ 2607(b), 4177C, 4177E [repealed], § 4177K(c) [repealed] or § 4177K(e) [repealed] of this title; § 4767 of Title 16; and § 1012 of Title 10 [repealed]" in (e)(5).

§ 2707. License qualifications.

(a)(1) No Class D operator's license shall be issued to any person under the age of 16 years. A CDL Class A, CDL Class B or CDL Class C license shall not be issued to any person under 18 years of age nor to any person 18 years of age or older who has not had at least 1 year's experience as an operator of a motor vehicle.

(2) No endorsement for "L", "T", "P" or "N" shall be issued to any person under 18 years of age or to any person 18 years of age or older who has not had at least 1 year's experience as an operator of a motor vehicle. No endorsement of "H" or "X" shall be issued to any person under 21 years of age or to any person 21 years of age or older who has not had at least 1 year's experience as an operator of a motor vehicle.

(b) The Department shall not issue an operator's or chauffeur's license to any:

(1) Person whose license has been suspended, during the period for which license was suspended;

(2) Person whose license has been revoked under this chapter until the expiration of 1 year after such license was revoked;

(3) Person whom it has determined is an habitual drunkard or is addicted to the use of narcotic drugs;

(4) Person when in the opinion of the Department such person is a person with a physical or mental disability or disease as will serve to prevent such person from exercising reasonable and ordinary control over a motor vehicle while operating the same upon the highways;

(5) Person who is unable to understand highway warning or direction signs in the English language;

(6) Person who is subject to loss of consciousness due to disease of the central nervous system, unless such person furnishes the Department with a certificate of the person's treating physician, duly licensed to practice medicine and surgery, which certificate states:

"I (name of treating physician) hereby certify that I am the treating physician for (name of person), that I have been the treating physician for him/her for a period of at least 3 months, that I am aware of his/her medical history, including his/her history with respect to diseases of the central nervous system, and that such person's physical or mental disability under sufficient control to permit him/her to operate a motor vehicle with safety to person and property."

Each person licensed to operate a motor vehicle on the basis of such certificate shall furnish the Department with a new certificate each year not later than the last day of the holder's birth month and not earlier than 45 days before said date. The certificate shall show that on the basis of an examination within said period a physician duly licensed to practice medicine and surgery has determined that the physical or mental disability remains under sufficient control to permit the person to operate a motor vehicle with safety to person and property. Except as provided below, if such certificate is not received by the Department, the Department shall suspend said license and shall notify its holder.

The above provision of this paragraph notwithstanding, if the person's treating physician, duly licensed to practice medicine and surgery, furnishes the Department with a certificate which states:

"(name of treating physician) hereby certify that I am the treating physician for (name of person), that I have been the treating physician for him/her for a period of at least 3 months, that I am aware of his/her medical history, including his/her history with respect to any disease of the central nervous system, that such person's disease no longer requires treatment and that such person can reasonably be expected to suffer no further losses of consciousness on account of such disease.";

the Department may find that the person need no longer submit annual certificates of competence to operate a motor vehicle and shall notify the person accordingly. The Department may at its discretion retain medical consultants to advise it. No physician who examines a person and provides a certificate in good faith in accordance with this paragraph shall be subject to any civil or criminal liability on account of having provided the certificate.

(7) Person who has not reached the person's eighteenth birthday unless such person has either:

    a. Completed a course in driver education in a public or private high school in this State, such course having been approved by the State Board of Education and meeting the standards for such courses described by that Board; or

    b. Been licensed to operate motor vehicles in another state and has completed a course of instruction in driver education and the safe operation of motor vehicles in a public or private high school outside this State.

(8) Person who has not reached the person's eighteenth birthday upon notification by the Family Court of the State pursuant to § 1009 of Title 10, for a time set by the Court in its discretion.

(9) Person who has not reached the person's twenty-first birthday at the time of the offense, who has been convicted of or pleads guilty to, including a conviction or guilty plea pursuant to § 4767 of Title 16 and qualifying for first offender election under § 4177B of this title, any of the offenses listed hereinafter or who has been adjudicated delinquent as a result of acts which would constitute such offense if committed by an adult, for a period of 2 years from the date of sentencing, or until said person's eighteenth birthday, whichever is longer. The following shall constitute offenses under this paragraph:

    a. Any drug offense under Title 16.

    b. Any drug offense under Chapter 5 of Title 11.

    c. Driving under the influence of alcohol or drugs as defined in § 4177 of this title.

    d. Any offense punishable under the laws of the United States or any state of the United States substantially conforming to the provisions of the Delaware Code listed in paragraph (b)(9)a., b. or c. of this section.

Upon entry of conviction or adjudication of delinquency for any offense included in this paragraph, the Clerk of the Court or other person designated by the Court shall forthwith report such conviction or adjudication of delinquency to the Division of Motor Vehicles for action pursuant to the provisions of this paragraph.

(10) Person, other than those persons covered by paragraphs (b)(8) and (9) of this section, who has been convicted of or pleads guilty to any of the offenses listed in paragraph (b)(9)a., b., c. or d. of this section, including a conviction or guilty plea pursuant to § 4767 of Title 16 and qualifying for first offender election under § 4177B of this title, or who has been adjudicated delinquent as a result of acts which would constitute such an offense if committed by an adult, for a period of 6 months after the individual otherwise would have been eligible to have a driver's license issued if the individual does not have a driver's license or reinstated if the driver's license of the person has been suspended at the time the person is so convicted.

(11) Person who is the subject of an outstanding capias or bench warrant issued by the Family Court for failure to appear at any paternity or child support proceeding, or with respect to whom the Department has received notification from the Family Court as provided in § 516(g) of Title 13, or notice from the Director of the Division of Child Support Services as provided in § 2216 of Title 13 regarding the denial or suspension of a license because of such person's child support delinquency.

(12) [Repealed.]

(13) Person deemed "not eligible" by a Family Court Judge or Commissioner pursuant to entry into the Family Court Adjudicated Juvenile Drug Court Program until a further order of the Court permitting licensing.

History.

36 Del. Laws, c. 10, § 54; Code 1935, § 5592; 41 Del. Laws, c. 228, § 1; 43 Del. Laws, c. 246; 45 Del. Laws, c. 289; 21 Del. C. 1953, § 2706; 49 Del. Laws, c. 57, § 1; 55 Del. Laws, c. 361, §§ 1, 2; 56 Del. Laws, c. 390, § 1; 59 Del. Laws, c. 307, § 3; 59 Del. Laws, c. 327, § 1; 62 Del. Laws, c. 237, §§ 12-15; 64 Del. Laws, c. 183, § 1; 67 Del. Laws, c. 108, § 1; 67 Del. Laws, c. 157, § 3; 67 Del. Laws, c. 429, §§ 1, 2; 69 Del. Laws, c. 125, § 1; 70 Del. Laws, c. 18, § 1; 70 Del. Laws, c. 186, § 1; 70 Del. Laws, c. 452, § 3; 70 Del. Laws, c. 471, §§ 1, 2; 71 Del. Laws, c. 107, § 1; 71 Del. Laws, c. 216, § 82; 71 Del. Laws, c. 272, § 3; 72 Del. Laws, c. 57, § 1; 72 Del. Laws, c. 477, § 2; 73 Del. Laws, c. 34, § 3; 73 Del. Laws, c. 408, § 2; 74 Del. Laws, c. 135, § 4; 78 Del. Laws, c. 13, § 69; 78 Del. Laws, c. 179, § 270; 79 Del. Laws, c. 371, §§ 17, 18; 80 Del. Laws, c. 234, § 21; 81 Del. Laws, c. 434, § 2; 82 Del. Laws, c. 91, § 2; 83 Del. Laws, c. 37, § 25.

Effect of amendments.

83 Del. Laws, c. 37, effective June 3, 2021, deleted "Except as provided by § 1012 of Title 10 [repealed], a" from the beginning of the first sentence of (b)(9).

SUBCHAPTER II

SUSPENSION OR REVOCATION

§ 2738. Fee for return of revoked license or driving privileges.

(a) Except as otherwise provided in subsection (b) of this section, an individual whose license or driving privileges have been revoked must pay a fee of $200 at the end of the revocation for the reinstatement of the individual's license or driving privileges. The reinstatement fee described in this subsection does not include the fee for the issuance of a new license.

(b) An individual eligible for reinstatement of the individual's license or driving privileges who applies for reinstatement within 1 year of being released from the custody of the Department of Correction may not be charged the reinstatement fee described in subsection (a) of this section. For purposes of this subsection, "custody of the Department of Correction" has the same meaning as "Accountability Level V sanction" as defined in § 4204(c) of Title 11.

History.

63 Del. Laws, c. 430, § 10; 64 Del. Laws, c. 13, § 10; 67 Del. Laws, c. 260, § 1; 70 Del. Laws, c. 186, § 1; 80 Del. Laws, c. 77, § 8; 83 Del. Laws, c. 18, § 1.

Effect of amendments.

83 Del. Laws, c. 18, effective Apr. 19, 2021, substituted "or" for "and/or" in the section heading and rewrote the section text.

SUBCHAPTER III

SUSPENSION AND REVOCATION OF LICENSE FOR REFUSAL TO SUBMIT TO CHEMICAL TEST

§ 2740. Consent to submit to chemical test; probable cause; test required.

NOTES TO DECISIONS

Probable cause.

Officer had probable cause to believe defendant had been driving under the influence of alcohol and that a blood test to determine defendant's blood alcohol content was appropriate; on arrival at the scene of an accident, the officer observed a damaged pickup truck belonging to defendant, containers of alcohol and beer located in and around the truck and defendant's glassy eyes and odor of alcohol. State v. Binkley, — A.3d —, 2020 Del. Super. LEXIS 3014 (Del. Super. Ct. Dec. 21, 2020).

§ 2742. Revocation; notice; hearing [Effective until fulfillment of the contingency in 81 Del. Laws, c. 155, § 2].

NOTES TO DECISIONS

Probable cause.

Facts relied upon by a Delaware Division of Motor Vehicles hearing officer supported a finding of probable cause that appellant was driving under the influence because: (1) there was undisputed testimony that appellant weaved between the yellow and white lines 9 times and failed to stop completely at a 4–way stop sign; and (2) upon contact with appellant, an officer smelled a strong odor of alcohol on appellant's breath and observed that appellant had bloodshot, glassy eyes. Verde v. Simpler, — A.3d —, 2021 Del. Super. LEXIS 491 (Del. Super. Ct. June 25, 2021).

§ 2742. Revocation; notice; hearing [Effective upon fulfillment of the contingency in 81 Del. Laws, c. 155, § 2].

NOTES TO DECISIONS

Probable cause.

Facts relied upon by a Delaware Division of Motor Vehicles hearing officer supported a finding of probable cause that appellant was driving under the influence because: (1) there was undisputed testimony that appellant weaved between the yellow and white lines 9 times and failed to stop completely at a 4–way stop sign; and (2) upon contact with appellant, an officer smelled a strong odor of alcohol on appellant's breath and observed that appellant had bloodshot, glassy eyes. Verde v. Simpler, — A.3d —, 2021 Del. Super. LEXIS 491 (Del. Super. Ct. June 25, 2021).

CHAPTER 31

NONDRIVER IDENTIFICATION CARDS

Sec.

§ 3103. Issuance fee; renewal; qualifications.

(a) Upon receipt of the application and a fee of $40, the Division shall issue an identification card which shall expire and be renewable on the eighth anniversary date of the birth of the applicant next following the date of its issuance unless the birthdate be February 29, and in which the event the identification card will expire on February 28 every eighth year. A permanent resident foreign national may be issued a full 8-year identification card. However, an identification card issued to a temporary foreign national must be limited to the period of time that the temporary foreign national is authorized to be in the United States.

(b) On or near the date of expiration of an identification card, each holder of such a card desiring renewal of such card shall appear at a Division of Motor Vehicles office in the county in which the holder of the card resides and be photographed by the Department of Transportation.

(c) No identification card shall be issued pursuant to subsection (a) of this section to any nonresident of the State.

(d) An individual who presents a valid, unexpired, Delaware personal credential card, issued under § 8915(d) of Title 29, is exempt from any fee charged under this section for an identification card.

History.
21 Del. C. 1953, § 3103; 58 Del. Laws, c. 516; 65 Del. Laws, c. 37, §§ 2, 3; 70 Del. Laws, c. 186, § 1; 74 Del. Laws, c. 110, § 82; 76 Del. Laws, c. 76, § 26; 76 Del. Laws, c. 126, § 2; 81 Del. Laws, c. 447, § 5; 83 Del. Laws, c. 29, § 1.

Effect of amendments.
83 Del. Laws, c. 29, effective June 3, 2021, in (a), in the first sentence substituted "$40" for "$20" and "eighth" for "fourth" twice, and substituted "8-year" for "4-year" in the second sentence.

CHAPTER 32

LIMITED POWER OF ATTORNEY AND ELECTRONIC SIGNATURES FOR DIVISION OF MOTOR VEHICLES MATTERS

Revisor's Notes
This chapter became effective upon the signature of the Governor on Sept. 15, 2021.

§ 3201. Definitions.

In this chapter:

(1) "Agent" means a person granted authority to act for the benefit of a principal under a limited durable power of attorney for completing all paperwork necessary to accomplish any required action(s) set forth in this title, whether denominated an agent, attorney-in-fact, or otherwise. The term includes an original agent, concurrent agent, joint agent, successor agent, and a person to which an agent's authority is delegated.

(2) "Durable," with respect to a power of attorney, means not terminated by the principal's incapacity, and satisfying the requirements set forth in § 3203 of this title.

(3) "Durable power of attorney" means a power of attorney that is durable, meeting the requirements of § 3203 of this title.

(4) "Electronic" means relating to technology having electrical, digital, magnetic, wireless, optical, electromagnetic, or similar capabilities.

(5) "Electronic signature" shall mean the execution of the document by the identified person after appropriate verification of identity of the person

executing the document using a verification system acceptable to the Department.

(6) "Good faith" means honesty in fact.

(7) "Incapacity" means inability of an individual to manage his or her property or business affairs.

(8) "Limited" means that the power of attorney authorized herein is for the sole purpose of completing all paperwork necessary to accomplish any required action(s) set forth in this title.

(9) "Person" means an individual, corporation, statutory trust, estate, trust, partnership (general or limited), limited liability company, association, joint venture, public corporation, government or governmental subdivision, agency, or instrumentality, or any other legal or commercial entity or association.

(10) "Personal power of attorney" means any limited durable power of attorney executed in this State or, if executed other than in this State, specifying that the laws of this State shall govern such power of attorney.

(11) "Power of attorney" means a grant of authority to an agent to act in the place of the principal, whether or not the term power of attorney is used.

(12) "Principal" means an individual who grants authority to an agent in a power of attorney acting for himself or herself and not as a fiduciary, officer, employee, representative, agent or official of any legal, governmental, or commercial entity or association.

(13) "Record" means information that is inscribed on a tangible medium or that is stored in an electronic or other medium and is retrievable in perceivable form.

(14) "Sign" means, with present intent to authenticate or adopt a record:

    a. To execute or adopt a tangible symbol; or

    b. To attach to or logically associate with the record an electronic sound, symbol, or process using an electronic program acceptable to the Department.

(15) "State" means a state of the United States, the District of Columbia, Puerto Rico, the United States Virgin Islands, or any territory or insular possession subject to the jurisdiction of the United States.

History.
83 Del. Laws, c. 149, § 1; 70 Del. Laws, c. 186, § 1.

§ 3202. Applicability.

(a)(1) This chapter shall only apply to limited durable powers of attorney which are executed for the sole purpose of completing documentation required and allowable by the Department to accomplish certain actions set forth in this title.

(2) The provisions of this chapter shall not apply to any business or individual who is specifically required by statute or regulation to identify persons who have authority to sign on behalf of the business or individual. In those instances, all documentation must still be executed by an individual who has been previously identified in writing to the Department.

(b) A power of attorney that was granted in compliance with the laws of the jurisdiction governing such power of attorney will be recognized and enforceable under the laws of the State of Delaware in accordance with its terms.

History.
83 Del. Laws, c. 149, § 1.

§ 3203. Power of attorney is durable.

A power of attorney is durable if it contains the words:"This power of attorney shall not be affected by the subsequent incapacity of the principal," or similar words showing the intent of the principal that the authority conferred shall be exercisable notwithstanding the principal's subsequent incapacity.

History.
83 Del. Laws, c. 149, § 1.

§ 3204. Execution of personal power of attorney.

(a) A personal power of attorney must be:

(1) In writing;

(2) Signed by the principal or by another person subscribing the principal's name in the principal's presence and at the principal's express direction;

(3) Dated; and

(4) Signed in the presence of a notarial officer or contain an electronic signature acceptable to the Department.

(b) A personal power of attorney may be accompanied by a notice in the following form, signed by the principal and placed at the beginning of the personal power of attorney. In the absence of a signed notice, upon a challenge to the authority of an agent to act under the personal power of attorney, the agent shall have the burden of demonstrating that the personal power of attorney is valid.

NOTICE

As the person signing this limited durable power of attorney you are the Principal.

The purpose of this power of attorney is to give the person you designate (your "Agent") broad powers to complete all paperwork necessary to accomplish any required actions set forth in this title without advance notice to you or approval by you.

This power of attorney does not authorize your Agent to make health-care decisions for you.

Unless you specify otherwise, your Agent's authority will continue even if you become incapacitated, or until you die or revoke the power of attorney, or until your Agent resigns or is unable to act for you. You should select someone you trust to serve as your Agent.

This power of attorney does not impose a duty on your Agent to exercise granted powers, but when powers are exercised, your Agent must use due care to act for your benefit and in accordance with this power of attorney.

Your Agent must keep your funds and other property separate from your Agent's funds and other property.

A court can take away the powers of your Agent if it finds your Agent is not acting properly.

A court can take away the powers of your Agent if it finds your Agent is not acting properly.

If there is anything about this form that you do not understand, you should ask a lawyer of your own choosing to explain it to you.

I have read or had explained to me this notice and I understand its contents.

_____Principal_____Date

(c) Regardless of the method by which a person accepts appointment as an agent under a personal power of attorney (pursuant to § 3211 of Title 21 of the

Delaware Code), such agent shall have no authority to act as agent under the personal power of attorney unless the agent has first executed and affixed to the personal power of attorney a certification in substantially the following form:

AGENT'S CERTIFICATION

I, _____ (Name of Agent), have read the attached limited durable personal power of attorney and I am the person identified as the Agent or identified as the Agent for the Principal. To the best of my knowledge this power has not been revoked. I hereby acknowledge that, when I act as Agent, I shall:

Act in good faith;

Act only within the scope of authority granted in the personal power of attorney; and

To the extent reasonably practicable under the circumstances, keep in regular contact with the principal and communicate with the principal.

In addition, in the absence of a specific provision to the contrary in the limited durable personal power of attorney, when I act as Agent, I shall:

Keep the assets of the Principal separate from my assets;

Exercise reasonable caution and prudence; and

Keep a full and accurate record of all actions, receipts and disbursements on behalf of the Principal.

_____Agent_____Date

History.
83 Del. Laws, c. 149, § 1.

§ 3205. Execution of personal power of attorney.

(a) A personal power of attorney is validly executed if it complies with § 3204 of this title, unless such personal power of attorney provides that it is governed by the laws of another jurisdiction, in which case, such personal power of attorney is validly executed if such execution complies with the laws of such other jurisdiction.

(b) A limited durable power of attorney (other than a personal power of attorney) will be deemed to be validly executed under the laws of this State if, when the power of attorney was executed, the execution complied with:

(1) The law of the jurisdiction that determines the meaning and effect of the power of attorney; or

(2) The requirements for a military power of attorney pursuant to 10 U.S.C. § 1044b, as amended.

(c) Except as otherwise provided by statute other than this chapter, a photocopy or electronically transmitted copy of an original power of attorney has the same effect as the original.

History.
83 Del. Laws, c. 149, § 1.

§ 3206. Nomination of guardian of person or property; relation of agent to court-appointed fiduciary.

(a) The appointment by a court of a guardian or other fiduciary charged with the management of the principal's property or the care of the principal's person shall terminate all personal powers of attorney.

(b) After the appointment of a guardian or other fiduciary charged with the management of the principal's property or the care of the principal's person, the agent is accountable to such guardian or other fiduciary as well as to the principal as to any personal powers of attorney which the agent continues to hold. A guardian or other fiduciary shall only have such powers to revoke or amend the powers of the agent as shall be given to such guardian or other fiduciary by the court.

History.
83 Del. Laws, c. 149, § 1.

§ 3207. When the personal power of attorney is effective.

A personal power of attorney is effective when executed.

History.
83 Del. Laws, c. 149, § 1.

§ 3208. Termination of personal power of attorney or agent's authority.

(a) A personal power of attorney terminates when:

(1) The principal dies;

(2) The principal revokes the personal power of attorney;

(3) A terminating event set forth in the personal power of attorney occurs;

(4) The purpose of the personal power of attorney is accomplished;

(5) The principal revokes the agent's authority or the agent dies, becomes incapacitated, or resigns, and the personal power of attorney does not provide for another agent to act; or

(6) The personal power of attorney is revoked by order of the Court of Chancery pursuant to § 3214 of this title or otherwise.

(b) An agent's authority terminates when:

(1) The principal revokes the authority;

(2) The agent dies, becomes incapacitated, or resigns;

(3) An action is filed for the dissolution or annulment of the agent's marriage to the principal, unless the personal power of attorney otherwise provides;

(4) All documentation has been submitted, accepted, processed and acted upon by the Department;

(5) One year from the date of execution of the power of attorney; or

(6) The personal power of attorney terminates.

(c) Unless the personal power of attorney otherwise provides, an agent's authority is exercisable until the authority terminates under subsection (b) of this section, notwithstanding a lapse of time since the execution of the personal power of attorney.

(d) Termination of an agent's authority or of a personal power of attorney is not effective as to the agent or another person that, without actual knowledge of the termination, acts in good faith under the personal power of attorney. An act so performed, unless otherwise invalid or unenforceable, binds the principal and the principal's successors in interest.

(e) The execution of a personal power of attorney does not revoke a personal power of attorney previously executed by the principal unless the subsequent personal power of attorney provides that the previous personal power of attorney is revoked or that all other personal powers of attorney are revoked.

History.
83 Del. Laws, c. 149, § 1.

§ 3209. Concurrent agents, joint agents, and successor agents.

(a) A principal may designate 2 or more persons to act as concurrent agents. Each concurrent agent may exercise its authority independently.

(b) A principal may designate 2 or more persons to act as joint agents. No joint agent shall have the power to act without the agreement of all other joint agents and shall have no power to act independent of the other agent.

(c) If the principal designates more than 1 agent and does not specify that they are concurrent agents or joint agents, such agents shall be considered concurrent agents.

(d) A principal may designate 1 or more successor agents to act if an agent resigns, dies, becomes incapacitated, is not qualified to serve, or declines to serve. Unless the personal power of attorney otherwise provides, a successor agent:

(1) Has the same authority as that granted to the original agent; and

(2) May not act until all predecessor agents have resigned, died, become incapacitated, are no longer qualified to serve, or have declined to serve.

(e) A principal may give an appointed agent or another person designated by name, office or function the authority to designate by a writing executed by such person, 1 or more concurrent, joint, or successor agents in addition to those designated in the personal power of attorney. Unless the personal power of attorney authorizing the appointment of such further agents otherwise provides, a concurrent, joint, or successor agent appointed by this method:

(1) Has the same authority as that granted to the original agent; and

(2) May not act until the predecessor designee has resigned, died, become incapacitated, is no longer qualified to serve, or has declined to serve.

(f) Except as otherwise provided in the personal power of attorney and subsection (g) of this section, an acting agent that does not participate in or conceal a breach of fiduciary duty committed by another agent, including a predecessor agent, is not liable for the actions of the other agent.

(g) An acting agent that has actual knowledge of a breach or imminent breach of fiduciary duty by another agent shall notify the principal and, if the principal is incapacitated, take any action reasonably appropriate in the circumstances to safeguard the principal's best interest. An agent that fails to notify the principal or take action as required by this subsection is liable for the reasonably foreseeable damages that could have been avoided if the agent had notified the principal or taken such action.

History.
83 Del. Laws, c. 149, § 1.

§ 3210. Reimbursement and compensation of agent.

(a) An agent is entitled to reimbursement of expenses reasonably incurred on behalf of the principal.

(b) An agent shall not be entitled to compensation unless:

(1) The personal power of attorney so provides; and

(2) The compensation is reasonable under the circumstances.

History.
83 Del. Laws, c. 149, § 1.

§ 3211. Agent's acceptance.

Except as otherwise provided in the personal power of attorney, a person accepts appointment as an agent under a personal power of attorney by signing the agent's certification (pursuant to § 3204 of this title) or by exercising authority or performing duties as an agent or by any other assertion or conduct indicating acceptance.

History.
83 Del. Laws, c. 149, § 1.

§ 3212. Agent's duties.

(a) Notwithstanding provisions in the personal power of attorney, an agent that has accepted appointment pursuant to a personal power of attorney shall, in connection with exercising the authority granted to such agent therein:

(1) Act in accordance with the principal's reasonable expectations to the extent actually known by the agent and, otherwise, in the principal's best interest;

(2) Act in good faith;

(3) Act only within the scope of authority granted in the personal power of attorney; and

(4) To the extent reasonably practicable under the circumstances, keep in regular contact with the principal and communicate with the principal.

(b) Except as otherwise provided in the personal power of attorney, an agent that has accepted appointment shall:

(1) Act loyally for the principal's benefit;

(2) Act so as not to create a conflict of interest that impairs the agent's ability to act impartially in the principal's best interest;

(3) Act with the care, competence, and diligence ordinarily exercised by agents in similar circumstances; and

(4) Keep a record of all receipts, disbursements, and transactions made on behalf of the principal.

(c) An agent that acts with care, competence, and diligence for the best interest of the principal is not liable solely because the agent also benefits from the act or has an individual or conflicting interest in relation to the property or affairs of the principal.

(d) If an agent has special skills or expertise the special skills or expertise must be considered in determining whether the agent has acted with care, competence, and diligence under the circumstances.

(e) An agent that engages another person on behalf of the principal is not liable for an act, error of judgment, or default of that person if the agent exercises care, competence, and diligence in selecting and monitoring the person.

(f) Except as otherwise provided in the personal power of attorney and by § 3206 of this title, an agent is not required to disclose receipts, disbursements, or transactions conducted on behalf of the principal unless ordered by a court or requested by the principal, a guardian, a conservator, another fiduciary acting for the principal, a governmental agency having authority to protect the welfare of the principal, or, upon the death of the principal, by the personal representative or successor in interest of the principal's estate. If so requested the agent shall comply with the request within a reasonable period of time.

History.
83 Del. Laws, c. 149, § 1.

§ 3213. Exoneration of agent.

A provision in a personal power of attorney relieving an agent of liability for breach of duty is binding on the principal and the principal's successors in interest except to the extent the provision:

(1) Relieves the agent of liability for breach of duty committed in bad faith or with reckless indifference to the purposes of the personal power of attorney or the best interest of the principal; or

(2) Was inserted as a result of undue influence upon the principal.

History.
83 Del. Laws, c. 149, § 1.

§ 3214. Judicial relief.

(a) A person designated in subsection (b) of this section may petition the Court of Chancery requesting that the Court:

(1) Determine whether the personal power of attorney or the authority of an agent is in effect or has terminated pursuant to § 3208 of this title or otherwise;

(2) Compel the agent to exercise or refrain from exercising authority in a particular manner or for a particular purpose;

(3) Compel the agent to account for transactions conducted on the principal's behalf pursuant to § 3212(f) of this title;

(4) Modify, suspend, or revoke the powers of the agent to act under a personal power of attorney, and, if the principal has not designated another agent or successor agent in the personal power of attorney, appoint another agent to act in place of the agent whose powers are modified, suspended, or revoked;

(5) Determine an agent's liability for violation of his or her duties pursuant to § 3212 of this title.

(b) Any of the following persons may file a petition seeking appropriate relief under this section:

(1) The principal or the agent;

(2) The spouse, child, or parent of the principal;

(3) A guardian, trustee, or other fiduciary acting for the principal;

(4) The personal representative, trustee, or a beneficiary of the principal's estate;

(5) Any other interested person, as long as the person demonstrates to the Court's satisfaction that the person is interested in the welfare of the principal and has a good faith belief that:

a. The Court's intervention is necessary; and

b. The principal is incapacitated at the time of filing the petition or otherwise unable to protect that principal's own interests; or

(6) A person asked to accept a personal power of attorney.

(c) Upon motion by the principal, who shall be presumed to have legal capacity, the Court shall dismiss a petition filed under this section, unless the Court finds that the principal lacks capacity to revoke the agent's authority or the personal power of attorney.

(d) Nothing in this section shall preclude or diminish the Court's authority to appoint a guardian or other fiduciary pursuant to Chapter 39 of Title 12, or to order other judicial relief, in order to grant appropriate relief upon review of a personal power of attorney or an agent's conduct with respect to a personal power of attorney.

(e) Nothing in this section shall preclude the Department of Health and Social Services, the Public Guardian, or other governmental agency having authority to protect the welfare of the principal from petitioning the Court for access to the principal or to records necessary to determine, or terminate, possible abuse, neglect, exploitation or abandonment of the principal.

History.

83 Del. Laws, c. 149, § 1; 70 Del. Laws, c. 186, § 1.

§ 3215. Agent's resignation; notice.

Unless the personal power of attorney provides a different method for an agent's resignation, an agent may resign by giving written notice to the principal and, if the principal is incapacitated:

(1) To the guardian, if 1 has been appointed for the principal, and a concurrent agent or successor agent; or

(2) If there is no person described in paragraph (1) of this section, to:

    a. The principal's primary caregiver;

    b. Another person reasonably believed by the agent to have sufficient interest in the principal's welfare; or

    c. A governmental agency having authority to protect the welfare of the principal.

History.
83 Del. Laws, c. 149, § 1.

§ 3216. Acceptance of and reliance upon acknowledged personal power of attorney.

(a) For purposes of this section, "acknowledged" means purportedly verified before a notarial officer or contain an electronic signature acceptable to the Department.

(b) A person that in good faith accepts an acknowledged personal power of attorney without actual knowledge that the signature is not genuine may rely upon a presumption that the signature is genuine.

(c) A person that in good faith accepts an acknowledged personal power of attorney without actual knowledge that the personal power of attorney is void, invalid, or terminated, that the purported agent's authority is void, invalid, or terminated, or that the agent is exceeding or improperly exercising the agent's authority may rely upon the personal power of attorney as if the personal power of attorney were genuine, valid and still in effect, the agent's authority were genuine, valid and still in effect, and the agent had not exceeded and had properly exercised the authority.

(d) A person that is asked to accept an acknowledged personal power of attorney may request, and rely upon, without further investigation, an English translation, under oath of the translator, of the personal power of attorney if it contains, in whole or in part, language other than English.

(e) For purposes of this section, a person that conducts activities through employees is without actual knowledge of a fact relating to a personal power of attorney, a principal, or an agent if the employee conducting the transaction involving the personal power of attorney is without actual knowledge of the fact. Notification of revocation of a personal power of attorney by a principal or agent to an officer of a bank or other financial institution shall constitute actual notice to all employees.

History.
83 Del. Laws, c. 149, § 1.

§ 3217. Acceptance of electronic signatures.

The Department may accept electronic signatures on any documents required to be submitted pursuant to this title.

History.
83 Del. Laws, c. 149, § 1.

PART III

OPERATION AND EQUIPMENT

CHAPTER 41
RULES OF THE ROAD

SUBCHAPTER I
OBEDIENCE TO AND EFFECT OF
TRAFFIC LAWS

§ 4101. Provisions refer to vehicles upon highways; exceptions; powers of local authorities.

Revisor's note.

Section 142 of 83 Del. Laws, c. 56, effective June 30, 2021 (by virtue of § 178 of that act), provided: "I-95 Restore the Corridor Work Zone Safety. The Delaware Department of Transportation is authorized to enter into an agreement with an existing vendor for the installation of temporary mobile speed enforcement devices along the work zone of the I-95 Restore the Corridor project to reduce speeding, crashes and increase safety. Civil Speeding violations will be issued pursuant to 21 Del. C. §4169 and §4105 and will be reviewed and issued by Delaware State Police. The procedures for issuance of violations and appeals of the issuance of a civil violation shall be pursuant to the provisions set forth in 21 Del. C. §4101(d). This technology can only be used within the work zone limits and during construction of the project. Once construction is complete, the devices will be removed. The Department will provide the Joint Committee on Capital Improvements a report at the conclusion of the project."

§ 4105. Persons and vehicles working on highways and utilities; exceptions.

Revisor's note.

Section 142 of 83 Del. Laws, c. 56, effective June 30, 2021 (by virtue of § 178 of that act), provided: "I-95 Restore the Corridor Work Zone Safety. The Delaware Department of Transportation is authorized to enter into an agreement with an existing vendor for the installation of temporary mobile speed enforcement devices along the work zone of the I-95 Restore the Corridor project to reduce speeding, crashes and increase safety. Civil Speeding violations will be issued pursuant to 21 Del. C. §4169 and §4105 and will be reviewed and issued by Delaware State Police. The procedures for issuance of violations and appeals of the issuance of a civil violation shall be pursuant to the provisions set forth in 21 Del. C. §4101(d). This technology can only be used within the work zone limits and during construction of the project. Once construction is complete, the devices will be removed. The Department will provide the Joint Committee on Capital Improvements a report at the conclusion of the project."

SUBCHAPTER II
TRAFFIC SIGNS, SIGNALS AND MARKINGS

§ 4106. Authorized emergency vehicles.

NOTES TO DECISIONS

Pleading.

In an action arising from a no-contact motorcycle accident in which an ambulance allegedly forced plaintiff's motorcycle off the road, causing significant injuries to plaintiff, plaintiff's claims against the ambulance company and plaintiff's uninsured motorist insurer failed; defendants were entitled to summary judgment because plaintiff failed to plead gross negligence or wilful conduct on the part of the

ambulance driver. Naughton v. GEM Ambulance, LLC, — A.3d —, 2021 Del. Super. LEXIS
356 (Del. Super. Ct. Apr. 29, 2021).

SUBCHAPTER IV
RIGHT-OF-WAY

§ 4134. Operation of vehicles on approach of authorized emergency vehicles.

NOTES TO DECISIONS

Duty of driver.
It was clear that plaintiff failed to yield the right-of-way, when continuing through an intersection after seeing an emergency vehicle with its lights on, and failed to comply with this statute. Naughton v. GEM Ambulance, LLC, — A.3d —, 2021 Del. Super. LEXIS 356 (Del. Super. Ct. Apr. 29, 2021).

SUBCHAPTER VIII
SPEED RESTRICTIONS

§ 4169. Specific speed limits; penalty.

Revisor's note.
Section 142 of 83 Del. Laws, c. 56, effective June 30, 2021 (by virtue of § 178 of that act), provided: "I-95 Restore the Corridor Work Zone Safety. The Delaware Department of Transportation is authorized to enter into an agreement with an existing vendor for the installation of temporary mobile speed enforcement devices along the work zone of the I-95 Restore the Corridor project to reduce speeding, crashes and increase safety. Civil Speeding violations will be issued pursuant to 21 Del. C. §4169 and §4105 and will be reviewed and issued by Delaware State Police. The procedures for issuance of violations and appeals of the issuance of a civil violation shall be pursuant to the provisions set forth in 21 Del. C. §4101(d). This technology can only be used within the work zone limits and during construction of the project. Once construction is complete, the devices will be removed. The Department will provide the Joint Committee on Capital Improvements a report at the conclusion of the project."

SUBCHAPTER IX
RECKLESS DRIVING; DRIVING
WHILE INTOXICATED

§ 4177. Driving a vehicle while under the influence or with a prohibited alcohol or drug content; evidence; arrests; and penalties.

(a) No person shall drive a vehicle:

(1) When the person is under the influence of alcohol;

(2) When the person is under the influence of any drug;

(3) When the person is under the influence of a combination of alcohol and any drug;

(4) When the person's alcohol concentration is .08 or more; or

(5) When the person's alcohol concentration is, within 4 hours after the time of driving .08 or more. Notwithstanding any other provision of the law to the contrary, a person is guilty under this subsection, without regard to the person's alcohol concentration at the time of driving, if the person's alcohol concentration is, within 4 hours after the time of driving .08 or more and that alcohol concentration is the result of an amount of alcohol present in, or consumed by the person when that person was driving;

(6) When the person's blood contains, within 4 hours of driving, any amount of an illicit or recreational drug that is the result of the unlawful use or consumption of such illicit or recreational drug or any amount of a substance or compound that is the result of the unlawful use or consumption of an illicit or recreational drug prior to or during driving.

(b) In a prosecution for a violation of subsection (a) of this section:

(1) Except as provided in paragraph (b)(3)b. of this section, the fact that any person charged with violating this section is, or has been, legally entitled to use alcohol or a drug shall not constitute a defense.

(2)a. No person shall be guilty under paragraph (a)(5) of this section when the person has not consumed alcohol prior to or during driving but has only consumed alcohol after the person has ceased driving and only such consumption after driving caused the person to have an alcohol concentration of .08 or more within 4 hours after the time of driving.

b. No person shall be guilty under paragraph (a)(5) of this section when the person's alcohol concentration was .08 or more at the time of testing only as a result of the consumption of a sufficient quantity of alcohol that occurred after the person ceased driving and before any sampling which raised the person's alcohol concentration to .08 or more within 4 hours after the time of driving.

(3)a. No person shall be guilty under paragraph (a)(6) of this section when the person has not used or consumed an illicit or recreational drug prior to or during driving but has only used or consumed such drug after the person has ceased driving and only such use or consumption after driving caused the person's blood to contain an amount of the drug or an amount of a substance or compound that is the result of the use or consumption of the drug within 4 hours after the time of driving.

b. No person shall be guilty under paragraph (a)(6) of this section when the person has used or consumed the drug or drugs detected according to the directions and terms of a lawfully obtained prescription for such drug or drugs.

c. Nothing in this subsection nor any other provision of this chapter shall be deemed to preclude prosecution under paragraph (a)(2) or (a)(3) of this section.

(4) The charging document may allege a violation of subsection (a) of this section without specifying any particular paragraph of subsection (a) of this section and the prosecution may seek conviction under any of the paragraphs of subsection (a) of this section.

(c) For purposes of subchapter III of Chapter 27 of this title and this subchapter, the following definitions shall apply:

(1) "Alcohol concentration of .08 or more" shall mean:

a. An amount of alcohol in a sample of a person's blood equivalent to .08 or more grams of alcohol per 100 milliliters of blood; or

b. An amount of alcohol in a sample of a person's breath equivalent to .08 or more grams per 210 liters of breath.

(2) "Alcohol concentration of .15 or more" shall mean:

a. An amount of alcohol in a sample of a person's blood equivalent to .15 or more grams of alcohol per 100 milliliters of blood; or

b. An amount of alcohol in a sample of a person's breath equivalent to .15 or more grams per 210 liters of breath.

(3) "Alcohol concentration of .20 or more" shall mean:

a. An amount of alcohol in a sample of a person's blood equivalent to .20 or more grams of alcohol per 100 milliliters of blood; or

b. An amount of alcohol in a sample of a person's breath equivalent to .20 or more grams per 210 liters of breath.

(4) "Chemical test" or "test" shall include any form or method of analysis of a person's blood, breath or urine for the purposes of determin-

ing alcohol concentration or the presence of drugs which is approved for use by the Forensic Sciences Laboratory, Division of Forensic Science, the Delaware State Police Crime Laboratory, any state or federal law-enforcement agency, or any hospital or medical laboratory. It shall not, however, include a preliminary screening test of breath performed in order to estimate the alcohol concentration of a person at the scene of a stop or other initial encounter between an officer and the person.

(5) "Drive" shall include driving, operating, or having actual physical control of a vehicle.

(6) "Drug" shall include any substance or preparation defined as such by Title 11 or Title 16 or which has been placed in the schedules of controlled substances pursuant to Chapter 47 of Title 16. "Drug" shall also include any substance or preparation having the property of releasing vapors or fumes which may be used for the purpose of producing a condition of intoxication, inebriation, exhilaration, stupefaction or lethargy or for the purpose of dulling the brain or nervous system.

(7) "Illicit or recreational drug" as that phrase is used in paragraph (a)(6) of this section means any substance or preparation that is:

a. Any material, compound, combination, mixture, synthetic substitute or preparation which is enumerated as a Schedule I controlled substance under § 4714 of Title 16; or

b. Cocaine or of any mixture containing cocaine, as described in § 4716(b)(4) of Title 16; or

c. Amphetamine, including its salts, optical isomers and salt of its optical isomers, or of any mixture containing any such substance, as described in § 4716(d)(1) of Title 16; or

d. Methamphetamine, including its salt, isomer or salt of an isomer thereof, or of any mixture containing any such substance, as described in § 4716(d)(3) of Title 16; or

e. Phencyclidine, or of any mixture containing any such substance, as described in § 4716(e)(5) of Title 16; or

f. A designer drug as defined in § 4701 of Title 16; or

g. A substance or preparation having the property of releasing vapors or fumes which may be used for the purpose of producing a condition of intoxication, inebriation, stupefaction or lethargy or for the purpose of dulling the brain or nervous system.

(8) "Unlawful use or consumption" as that phrase is used in paragraph (a)(6) of this section means that the person used or consumed a drug without legal authority to do so as provided by Delaware law. This Code describes the procedure by which a person may lawfully obtain, use or consume certain drugs. In a prosecution brought under paragraph (a)(6) of this section, the State need not present evidence of a lack of such legal authority. In a prosecution brought under paragraph (a)(6) of this section, if a person claims that such person lawfully used or consumed a drug, it is that person's burden to show that person has complied with and satisfied the provisions of this Code regarding obtaining, using or consumption of the drug detected.

(9) "Substance or compound that is the result of the unlawful use or consumption of an illicit or recreational drug" as that phrase is used in paragraph (a)(6) of this section shall not include any substance or compound that is solely an inactive ingredient or inactive metabolite of such drug.

(10) "Vehicle" shall include any vehicle as defined in § 101(86) of this title, any off-highway vehicle as defined in § 101(45) of this title and any moped as defined in § 101(36) of this title.

(11) "While under the influence" shall mean that the person is, because of alcohol or drugs or a combination of both, less able than the person would ordinarily have been, either mentally or physically, to exercise clear judgment, sufficient physical control, or due care in the driving of a vehicle.

(d) Whoever is convicted of a violation of subsection (a) of this section shall:

(1) For the first offense, be fined not less than $500 nor more than $1,500 or imprisoned not more than 12 months or both. Any period of imprisonment imposed under this paragraph may be suspended.

(2) For a second offense occurring at any time within 10 years of a prior offense, be fined not less than $750 nor more than $2,500 and imprisoned not less than 60 days nor more than 18 months. The minimum sentence for a person sentenced under this paragraph may not be suspended. The sentencing Court may suspend the minimum sentence set forth in this subsection upon the condition that the offender shall successfully complete the Court of Common Pleas Driving Under the Influence Treatment Program in which the offender shall complete a minimum of 30 days of community service.

(3) For a third offense occurring at any time after 2 prior offenses, be guilty of a class G felony, be fined not more than $5,000 and be imprisoned not less than 1 year nor more than 2 years. The provisions of § 4205(b)(7) or § 4217 of Title 11 or any other statute to the contrary notwithstanding, the first 3 months of the sentence shall not be suspended, but shall be served at Level V and shall not be subject to any early release, furlough or reduction of any kind. The sentencing court may suspend up to 9 months of any minimum sentence set forth in this paragraph provided, however, that any portion of a sentence suspended pursuant to this paragraph shall include participation in both a drug and alcohol abstinence program and a drug and alcohol treatment program as set forth in paragraph (d)(9) of this section.

(4) For a fourth offense occurring any time after 3 prior offenses, be guilty of a class E felony, be fined not more than $7,000, and imprisoned not less than 2 years nor more than 5 years. The provisions of § 4205(b)(5) or § 4217 of Title 11 or any other statute to the contrary notwithstanding, the first 6 months of the sentence shall not be suspended, but shall be served at Level V and shall not be subject to any early release, furlough or reduction of any kind. The sentencing court may suspend up to 18 months of any minimum sentence set forth in this paragraph provided, however, that any portion of a sentence suspended pursuant to this paragraph shall include participation in both a drug and alcohol abstinence program and a drug and alcohol treatment program as set forth in paragraph (d)(9) of this section.

(5) For a fifth offense occurring any time after 4 prior offenses, be guilty of a class E felony, be fined not more than $10,000 and imprisoned not less than 3 years nor more than 5 years.

(6) For a sixth offense occurring any time after 5 prior offenses, be guilty of a class D felony, be fined not more than $10,000 and imprisoned not less than 4 years nor more than 8 years.

(7) For a seventh offense occurring any time after 6 prior offenses, or for any subsequent offense, be guilty of a class C felony, be fined not more than $15,000 and imprisoned not less than 5 years nor greater than 15 years.

(8) For the fifth, sixth, seventh offense or greater, the provisions of § 4205(b) or § 4217 of Title 11 or any other statute to the contrary notwithstanding, at least ½ of any minimum sentence shall be served at

Level V and shall not be subject to any early release, furlough or reduction of any kind. The sentencing court may suspend up to ½ of any minimum sentence set forth in this section provided, however, that any portion of a sentence suspended pursuant to this paragraph shall include participation in both a drug and alcohol abstinence program and a drug and alcohol treatment program as set forth in paragraph (d)(9) of this section. No conviction for a violation of this section, for which a sentence is imposed pursuant to this paragraph or paragraph (d)(3) or (d)(4) of this section, shall be considered a predicate felony for conviction or sentencing pursuant to § 4214 of Title 11. No offense for which sentencing pursuant to this paragraph or paragraph (d)(3) or (d)(4) of this section is applicable shall be considered an underlying felony for a murder in the first degree charge pursuant to § 636(a)(2) of Title 11.

(9) Any minimum sentence suspended pursuant to paragraph (d)(3), (d)(4), or (d)(8) of this section shall be upon the condition that the offender shall complete a program of supervision which shall include:

a. A drug and alcohol abstinence program requiring that the offender maintain a period of not less than 90 consecutive days of sobriety as measured by a transdermal continuous alcohol monitoring device or through periodic breath or urine analysis. In addition to such monitoring, the offender shall participate in periodic, random breath or urine analysis during the entire period of supervision.

b. An intensive inpatient or outpatient drug and alcohol treatment program for a period of not less than 3 months as approved by the Court or the Department of Correction.

1. Such treatment and counseling may be completed either while an offender is serving any level of supervision as defined by § 4204(c)(2) through (5) of Title 11 or after arrest but before adjudication of the offense.

2. Notwithstanding paragraph (d)(9)b.1. of this section, the offender must complete the required drug and alcohol treatment program within 9 months from the date the offender is sentenced or from the date of release following a Level V or Level IV sentence.

3. If an offender fails to complete the required drug and alcohol treatment program as required under paragraph (d)(9)b.2. of this section, the court shall impose the portion of the minimum sentence suspended by the court under paragraphs (d)(3), (d)(4), or (d)(8) of this section for the offender's participation in the program.

4. On petition by the offender, or the Department of Correction, filed before the expiration of the 9-month period under paragraph (d)(9)b.2. of this section, the court may, for good cause shown, extend the 9-month period to accommodate the completion of the required drug and alcohol treatment program.

c. Any other terms or provisions deemed appropriate by the sentencing court or the Department of Correction.

(10) In addition to the penalties otherwise authorized by this subsection, any person convicted of a violation of subsection (a) of this section, committed while a person who has not yet reached the person's seventeenth birthday is on or within the vehicle shall:

a. For the first offense, be fined an additional minimum of $500 and not more than an additional $1,500 and sentenced to perform a minimum of 40 hours of community service in a program benefiting children.

b. For each subsequent like offense, be fined an additional minimum of $750 and not more than an additional $2,500 and sentenced to perform a minimum of 80 hours of community service in a program benefiting children.

c. Violation of this paragraph shall be considered as an aggravating circumstance for sentencing purposes for a person convicted of a violation of subsection (a) of this section. Nothing in this paragraph shall prevent conviction for a violation of both subsection (a) of this section and any offense as defined elsewhere by the laws of this State.

d. Violation of or sentencing pursuant to this paragraph shall not be considered as evidence of either comparative or contributory negligence in any civil suit or insurance claim, nor shall a violation of or sentencing pursuant to this paragraph be admissible as evidence in the trial of any civil action.

(11) A person who has been convicted of prior or previous offenses of this section, as defined in § 4177B(e) of this title, need not be charged as a subsequent offender in the complaint, information or indictment against the person in order to render the person liable for the punishment imposed by this section on a person with prior or previous offenses under this section. However, if at any time after conviction and before sentence, it shall appear to the Attorney General or to the sentencing court that by reason of such conviction and prior or previous convictions, a person should be subjected to paragraph (d)(3), (d)(4), (d)(5), (d)(6) or (d)(7) of this section, the Attorney General shall file a motion to have the defendant sentenced pursuant to those provisions. If it shall appear to the satisfaction of the court at a hearing on the motion that the defendant falls within paragraph (d)(3), (d)(4), (d)(5), (d)(6) or (d)(7) of this section, the court shall enter an order declaring the offense for which the defendant is being sentenced to be a felony and shall impose a sentence accordingly.

(12) The Court of Common Pleas and Justice of the Peace Courts shall not have jurisdiction over offenses which must be sentenced pursuant to paragraph (d)(3), (d)(4), (d)(5), (d)(6), (d)(7), (d)(8) or (d)(9) of this section.

(13) The Justice of the Peace Court shall have jurisdiction to accept pleas of guilt and to impose sentence for violations of this section that are not subject to sentencing pursuant to paragraphs (d)(3) through (d)(9) of this section and to enter conditional adjudications of guilt requiring or permitting a person to enter a first offender election pursuant to § 4177B of this title. The Justice of the Peace Court shall not have jurisdiction to try any violations of this section. If an offense or criminal case within the exclusive jurisdiction of a justice of the peace or alderman or mayor of any incorporated city or town, except the City of Newark, is or may be joined properly with a violation of this section, such offense or criminal case shall remain joined with any violation of this section for the purpose of trial.

(14) If a person enters a guilty plea in a court of competent jurisdiction to a violation of subsection (a) of this section, such action shall constitute a waiver of the right to an administrative hearing as provided for in § 2742 of this title and shall act to withdraw any request previously made therefor.

(15) Notwithstanding any law to the contrary, the phrase "all crimes" as used in the Truth in Sentencing Act of 1989 shall include felonies under this section, and any amendments thereto.

(e) In addition to any penalty for a violation of subsection (a) of this section, the court shall prohibit the person convicted from operating any motor vehicle unless such motor vehicle is equipped with a functioning ignition interlock device; the terms of installation of the device and licensing of the individual to drive shall be as set forth in § 4177C and § 4177G of this title. A person who is prohibited from operating any motor vehicle unless such motor vehicle is equipped with a functioning ignition interlock device under this title at the time of an offense under subsection (a) of this section shall, in addition to any other penalties provided under law, pay a fine of $2,000 and be imprisoned for 60 days.

(f) In addition to any penalty for a violation of subsection (a) of this section, the court shall order the person to complete an alcohol evaluation and to complete a program of education or rehabilitation pursuant to § 4177D of this title which may include inpatient treatment and be followed by such other programs as established by the treatment facility, not to exceed a total of 15 months and to pay a fee not to exceed the maximum fine; provided however, that successful completion of the Court of Common Pleas Driving Under the Influence Treatment Program shall satisfy this requirement.

(g) For purposes of a conviction premised upon subsection (a) of this section, or any proceeding pursuant to this Code in which an issue is whether a person was driving a vehicle while under the influence, evidence establishing the presence and concentration of alcohol or drugs in the person's blood, breath or urine shall be relevant and admissible. Such evidence may include the results from tests of samples of the person's blood, breath or urine taken within 4 hours after the time of driving or at some later time. In any proceeding, the resulting alcohol or drug concentration reported when a test, as defined in paragraph (c)(3) of this section, is performed shall be deemed to be the actual alcohol or drug concentration in the person's blood, breath or urine without regard to any margin of error or tolerance factor inherent in such tests.

(1) Evidence obtained through a preliminary screening test of a person's breath in order to estimate the alcohol concentration of the person at the scene of a stop or other initial encounter between a law-enforcement officer and the person shall be admissible in any proceeding to determine whether probable cause existed to believe that a violation of this Code has occurred. However, such evidence may only be admissible in proceedings for the determination of guilt when evidence or argument by the defendant is admitted or made relating to the alcohol concentration of the person at the time of driving.

(2) Nothing in this section shall preclude conviction of an offense defined in this Code based solely on admissible evidence other than the results of a chemical test of a person's blood, breath or urine to determine the concentration or presence of alcohol or drugs.

(3) A jury shall be instructed by the court in accordance with the applicable provisions of this subsection in any proceeding pursuant to this Code in which an issue is whether a person was driving a vehicle while under the influence of alcohol or drugs or a combination of both.

(h)(1) For the purpose of introducing evidence of a person's alcohol concentration or the presence or concentration of any drug pursuant to this section, a report signed by the Forensic Toxicologist, Forensic Chemist or State Police Forensic Analytical Chemist who performed the test or tests as to its nature is prima facie evidence, without the necessity of the Forensic Toxicologist, Forensic Chemist or State Police Forensic Analytical Chemist personally appearing in court:

a. That the blood delivered was properly tested under procedures approved by the Division of Forensic Science, or the Delaware State Police Crime Laboratory;

b. That those procedures are legally reliable;

    c. That the blood was delivered by the officer or persons stated in the report; and,

    d. That the blood contained the alcohol, drugs or both therein stated.

  (2) Any report introduced under paragraph (h)(1) of this section must:

    a. Identify the Forensic Toxicologist, Forensic Chemist or State Police Forensic Analytical Chemist as an individual certified by the Division of Forensic Science, the Delaware State Police Crime Laboratory or any county or municipal police department employing scientific analysis of blood, as qualified under standards approved by the Division of Forensic Science, or the Delaware State Police Crime Laboratory to analyze the blood;

    b. State that the person made an analysis of the blood under the procedures approved by the Division of Forensic Science or the Delaware State Police Crime Laboratory; and,

    c. State that the blood, in that person's opinion, contains the resulting alcohol concentration or the presence or concentration of any drug within the meaning of this section.

Nothing in this subsection precludes the right of any party to introduce any evidence supporting or contradicting the evidence contained in the report entered pursuant to paragraphs (h)(1) and (2) of this section.

  (3) For purposes of establishing the chain of physical custody or control of evidence defined in this section which is necessary to admit such evidence in any proceeding, a statement signed by each successive person in the chain of custody that the person delivered it to the other person indicated on or about the date stated is prima facie evidence that the person had custody and made the delivery stated, without the necessity of a personal appearance in court by the person signing the statement, in accordance with the same procedures outlined in § 4331(3) of Title 10.

  (4) In a criminal proceeding, the prosecution shall, upon written demand of a defendant filed in the proceedings at least 15 days prior to the trial, require the presence of the Forensic Toxicologist, Forensic Chemist, State Police Forensic Analytical Chemist, or any person necessary to establish the chain of custody as a witness in the proceeding. The chain of custody or control of evidence defined in this section is established when there is evidence sufficient to eliminate any reasonable probability that such evidence has been tampered with, altered or misidentified.

  (i) In addition to any other powers of arrest, any law-enforcement officer is hereby authorized to arrest without a warrant any person who the officer has probable cause to believe has violated the provisions of this section, regardless of whether the alleged violation was committed in the presence of such officer. This authority to arrest extends to any hospital or other medical treatment facility located beyond the territorial limits of the officer's jurisdiction provided there is probable cause to believe that the violation of this section occurred within the officer's jurisdiction. This authority to arrest also extends to any place where the person is found within 4 hours of the alleged driving of a vehicle if there is reason to believe the person has fled the scene of an accident in which that person was involved, and provided there is probable cause to believe that the violation of this section occurred within the officer's jurisdiction.

  (j) Any court in which a conviction of or guilty plea to a driving under the influence offense shall include the blood alcohol concentration of the defendant (if any is on record) when forwarding notice of said conviction or guilty plea to the Division of Motor Vehicles.

History.

21 Del. C. 1953, § 4176; 54 Del. Laws, c. 160, § 1; 57 Del. Laws, c. 71, §§ 1-3; 57 Del. Laws, c. 526, §§ 1, 2; 57 Del. Laws, c. 613, § 1; 57 Del. Laws, c. 670, § 13B; 58 Del. Laws, c. 80, § 3; 59 Del. Laws, c. 46, §§ 1, 2; 60 Del. Laws, c. 701, §§ 48, 49; 60 Del. Laws, c. 702, § 2; 61 Del. Laws, c. 474, § 2; 64 Del. Laws, c. 13, § 13; 67 Del. Laws, c. 437, §§ 1, 2; 68 Del. Laws, c. 9, § 32; 68 Del. Laws, c. 125, § 1; 69 Del. Laws, c. 325, §§ 2, 3; 70 Del. Laws, c. 26, §§ 1-8; 70 Del. Laws, c. 34, § 1; 70 Del. Laws, c. 62, §§ 1-8; 70 Del. Laws, c. 186, § 1; 70 Del. Laws, c. 265, § 2; 70 Del. Laws, c. 474, § 1; 70 Del. Laws, c. 553, § 2; 71 Del. Laws, c. 209, §§ 1, 2; 71 Del. Laws, c. 222, §§ 2, 3; 72 Del. Laws, c. 36, §§ 1-3, 5, 6; 73 Del. Laws, c. 352, §§ 1, 11; 73 Del. Laws, c. 432, § 4; 74 Del. Laws, c. 182, §§ 1-3; 74 Del. Laws, c. 285, § 4; 74 Del. Laws, c. 333, §§ 1, 2; 75 Del. Laws, c. 315, §§ 1-5; 75 Del. Laws, c. 397, § 15; 77 Del. Laws, c. 162, §§ 1-6; 78 Del. Laws, c. 167, §§ 1-18; 78 Del. Laws, c. 349, § 1; 79 Del. Laws, c. 265, § 16; 79 Del. Laws, c. 378, §§ 3, 5; 79 Del. Laws, c. 396, § 2; 80 Del. Laws, c. 75, § 2; 80 Del. Laws, c. 120, § 1; 80 Del. Laws, c. 136, § 1; 80 Del. Laws, c. 168, § 1; 80 Del. Laws, c. 289, § 1; 81 Del. Laws, c. 51, § 1; 82 Del. Laws, c. 93, § 1; 83 Del. Laws, c. 17, § 1.

Effect of amendments.

83 Del. Laws, c. 17, effective Apr. 13, 2021, added "as approved by the Court or the Department of Correction" in the introductory paragraph of (d)(9)b.; substituted "any level of supervision as defined by § 4204(c)(2) through (5) of Title 11 or after arrest but before adjudication of the offense" for "a Level V or Level IV sentence" in (d)(9)b.1.; and added (d)(9)b.2.-(d)(9)b.4.

NOTES TO DECISIONS

Analysis

Evidence.
— Sufficient.
Offenses.
— Foreign.
Traffic stop.

Evidence.

— Sufficient.

Finding that defendant was under the influence of alcohol was supported by overwhelming testamentary and video evidence where: (1) both a passenger in another vehicle and a trooper contemporaneously perceived defendant as intoxicated and remarked upon it; (2) the other passenger corroborated the trooper's perception about the odor of alcohol; and (3) a recording showed that defendant changing replies to concede defendant's alcohol consumption when confronted about it. Trala v. State, 244 A.3d 989 (Del. 2020).

Offenses.

— Foreign.

In a DUI case, the sentencing court erred by counting defendant's New Jersey conviction under N.J. Stat. Ann. § 39:4-50(a) (prohibiting driving a vehicle while under the influence) as a prior offense because: (1) the New Jersey statute was not sufficiently similar to 21 Del. C. § 4177, in that it has a broader reach than the Delaware statute; (2) the New Jersey statute imposes penalties on persons who permit another person who is under the influence of intoxicating liquor or drugs to operate a motor vehicle the person owns or which is in the person's custody or control; and (3) the Delaware statute has no corresponding permissive use provision. Daniels v. State, 246 A.3d 557 (Del. 2021).

Traffic stop.

Facts relied upon by a Delaware Division of Motor Vehicles hearing officer supported a finding of probable cause that appellant was driving under the influence because: (1) there was undisputed testimony that appellant weaved between the yellow and white lines 9 times and failed to stop completely at a 4-way stop sign; and (2) upon contact with appellant, an officer smelled a strong odor of alcohol on appellant's breath and observed that appellant had bloodshot, glassy eyes. Verde v. Simpler, — A.3d —, 2021 Del. Super. LEXIS 491 (Del. Super. Ct. June 25, 2021).

SUBCHAPTER XII

OPERATION OF BICYCLES AND OTHER HUMAN-POWERED VEHICLES; OPERATION OF ELECTRIC PERSONAL ASSISTIVE MOBILITY DEVICES

§ 4196A. Bicycle approaching or entering intersection.

(a) A bicycle operator approaching a stop sign at an intersection with a roadway having 3 or more lanes for moving traffic shall come to a complete stop before entering the intersection.

(b) A bicycle operator approaching a stop sign at an intersection where a vehicle is stopped in the roadway at the same stop sign shall come to a complete stop before entering the intersection.

(c) A bicycle operator approaching a stop sign at an intersection with a roadway having 2 or fewer lanes for moving traffic shall reduce speed and, if required for safety, stop before entering the intersection. After slowing to a reasonable speed or stopping, the person shall yield the right-of-way to any vehicle in the intersection or approaching on another roadway so closely as to constitute an immediate hazard during the time the person is moving across or within the intersection, except that a person, after slowing to a reasonable speed and yielding the right-of-way if required, may cautiously make a turn or proceed through the intersection without stopping.

(d) A bicycle operator approaching an intersection shall always yield the right-of-way to any vehicle which has already entered the intersection.

(e) When a bicycle and a vehicle enter an intersection from different roadways at approximately the same time, the operator of the vehicle or bicycle on the left shall yield the right-of-way to the vehicle or bicycle on the right.

History.

81 Del. Laws, c. 196, § 1; 83 Del. Laws, c. 206, § 1.

Revisor's note.

Section 2 of 81 Del. Laws, c. 196, provided: "Section 4196A(c) of this act expires 4 years after the enactment of this Act into law, unless otherwise provided by a subsequent act of the General Assembly." The act was signed by the Governor on Oct. 5, 2017, setting an expiration date of Oct. 5, 2021, for subsection (c) of this section. That provision was repealed by 83 Del. Laws, c. 206, § 1, effective Sept. 17, 2021.

CHAPTER 43
EQUIPMENT AND CONSTRUCTION OF VEHICLES

SUBCHAPTER I
EQUIPMENT REQUIREMENTS

§ 4313. Safety glass — Federal safety standards applicable to windshield, front side windows and side wings; window tinting.

(a) No person shall operate any motor vehicle on any public highway, road or street with the front windshield, the side windows to the immediate right and left of the driver and/or side wings forward of and to the left and right of the driver that do not meet the requirements of Federal Motor Vehicle Safety Standard 205 in effect at the time of its manufacture.

(b) Nothing in this section shall prohibit the use of any products or materials along the top edge of the windshield so long as such products or materials are transparent and do not encroach upon the AS-1 portion of the windshield as provided by FMVSS 205 and [former] FMVSS 128.

(c) No person shall operate any motor vehicle on any public highway, road or street which does not conspicuously display a certificate by the manufacturer of any "after manufacture" window tinting material which may have been installed that such window tinting material meets the requirements of FMVSS 205 in effect at the time of the vehicle's manufacture. It shall be a valid defense to any charge under this subsection if the person so charged produces in court a validated mandatory inspection notice showing that the Division of Motor Vehicles has examined the motor vehicle since the date of offense and certifies compliance with FMVSS 205.

(d) No person shall be convicted under this section if that person possesses a statement signed by a licensed practitioner of medicine and surgery or osteopathic medicine or optometry verifying that tinted windows are medically necessary for the owner or usual operator of said vehicle.

(e) This section shall not apply to anodized glass which is correctly installed in the windshield and windows of an antique motor vehicle or street rod, as such are defined in §§ 2196 and 2197 of this title or of a motor vehicle validly insured under an antique, classic or street rod designated motor vehicle insurance policy that covers the motor vehicle, pursuant to § 2118 of this title.

(f) This section shall not apply to any police K-9 unit vehicles, or any surveillance vehicles operated by a "police officer," as defined under § 8401 of Title 11. This exception shall not apply to marked vehicles, except for police K-9 unit vehicles, or those unmarked vehicles used primarily for regular duty patrols.

History.
40 Del. Laws, c. 35, § 4; Code 1935, § 5717; 46 Del. Laws, c. 63; 21 Del. C. 1953, § 4313; 57 Del. Laws, c. 670, § 15B; 64 Del. Laws, c. 33, § 1; 67 Del. Laws, c. 227, § 1; 68 Del. Laws, c. 210, § 1; 70 Del. Laws, c. 357, § 1; 71 Del. Laws, c. 396, § 1; 74 Del. Laws, c. 393, § 1; 79 Del. Laws, c. 230, § 1; 83 Del. Laws, c. 83, § 2.

Revisor's note.
Based upon changes contained in 83 Del. Laws, c. 83, § 2, effective July 21, 2021, in the first sentence of (f), "police officer" was put in quotes and "(5)" was deleted following "§ 8401".

§ 4315. Penalties for §§ 4301-4316.

(a) Whoever violates §§ 4301-4305 of this title shall for the first offense be fined not less than $25 nor more than $115. For each subsequent like offense, the person shall be fined not less than $57.50 nor more than $230, or imprisoned not less than 10 nor more than 30 days, or both.

(b) Whoever violates §§ 4306-4311 of this title, except for § 4306(c) of this title, shall for the first offense be fined not less than $10 nor more than $28.75. For each subsequent like offense, the person shall be fined not less than $28.75 nor more than $100. Whoever violates § 4306(c) of this title shall be subject to a fine of at least $50 and not to exceed $250. For each subsequent offense such person shall be subject to a fine of at least $125 and not to exceed $500.

(c) Whoever violates § 4311A of this title shall be fined $500.

(d) Whoever being the operator, owner or custodian of any motor vehicle which is operated in violation of §§ 4312-4316 of this title shall be fined not less than $28.75 nor more than $100.

(e) In case of any violation of §§ 4301-4316 of this title by any common carrier or person operating under a permit or certificate issued by any public authority, in addition to the penalties prescribed in this section, such permit or certificate shall be revoked or, in the discretion of the issuing authority suspended until such sections are satisfactorily complied with.

(f) A violation of § 4303(c) of this title shall also constitute a moving violation which shall be part of the person's driving record.

(g) In cases where no collision has occurred, violation of § 4306, § 4308, or § 4313 of this title may be dismissed before trial if the defendant establishes that repairs have been made so that the vehicle is in compliance.

History.
36 Del. Laws, c. 10, §§ 141, 142; 37 Del. Laws, c. 10, § 34; 38 Del. Laws, c. 30; 40 Del. Laws, c. 35, § 6; 40 Del. Laws, c. 37, § 1; Code 1935, §§ 5679, 5680, 5719; 45 Del. Laws, c. 292, § 2; 46 Del. Laws, c. 61; 21 Del. C. 1953, § 4315; 65 Del. Laws, c. 503, § 22; 68 Del. Laws, c. 9, §§ 41-43; 70 Del. Laws, c. 186, § 1; 74 Del. Laws, c. 399, §§ 2, 3; 75 Del. Laws, c. 164, § 2; 80 Del. Laws, c. 277, § 1; 83 Del. Laws, c. 204, § 1.

Effect of amendments.
83 Del. Laws, c. 204, effective Sept. 17, 2021, added (g).

SUBCHAPTER II
LIGHTS

§ 4358. Penalties.

Whoever violates this subchapter shall for the first offense be fined not less than $10 nor more than $28.75. For each subsequent like offense, the person shall be fined not less than $28.75 nor more than $100. A violation of § 4333, § 4334, § 4336, § 4337, or § 4351 of this title may be dismissed before trial if the defendant establishes that repairs have been made so that the vehicle is in compliance.

History.
21 Del. C. 1953, § 4356; 50 Del. Laws, c. 292, § 1; 65 Del. Laws, c. 503, § 24; 68 Del. Laws, c. 9, § 46; 70 Del. Laws, c. 186, § 1; 83 Del. Laws, c. 204, § 2.

Effect of amendments.
83 Del. Laws, c. 204, effective Sept. 17, 2021, added the final sentence.

CHAPTER 44
ABANDONED VEHICLES

§ 4404. Sale of abandoned vehicles; disposition of proceeds.

The Department of Safety and Homeland Security shall have a possessory lien against said abandoned vehicles and shall have a right to sell said abandoned vehicles after complying with the notice and sale provisions outlined in Chapter 39 of Title 25, with the exception that the proceeds of the sale shall be applied first to the costs of the sale, then to the costs of removing, towing, preserving and storing and then to the payment of any liens to which said motor vehicle, trailer or part thereof may be subject in order of their priority, then to the State Treasurer who shall create a special fund thereof and who shall pay to the owner the moneys held if a claim is made within 1 year of the removal or deposit the moneys in the General Fund if no claim is made within 1 year of removal. Any possessory lien created under this section shall not extend to any personal property that is not attached to or considered necessary for the proper operation of any motor vehicle, and such property shall be returned to the owner of the motor vehicle if the owner of the motor vehicle claims the items prior to the sale of such motor vehicle.

History.
21 Del. C. 1953, § 4404; 55 Del. Laws, c. 173; 57 Del. Laws, c. 670, § 16B; 57 Del. Laws, c. 713, § 6; 61 Del. Laws, c. 367, § 2; 74 Del. Laws, c. 110, § 94; 83 Del. Laws, c. 125, § 1.

Effect of amendments.
83 Del. Laws, c. 125, effective Aug. 10, 2021, added the final sentence.

CHAPTER 45

SIZE AND WEIGHT OF VEHICLES AND LOADS

§ 4505. Traffic control devices.

(a) For purposes of this section:

(1) "Commercial vehicle" means as defined under § 101 of this title and includes a truck.

(2) "Local service" means an origin, destination, or service located

directly on a restricted roadway segment or at a location that can only be accessed by a restricted roadway segment.

    (3) "Residential service" means an origin, destination, or service located at a building that is used as a residence.

    (4) "Service" means a stop at any of the following:

        a. A point where freight originates, terminates, or is handled.

        b. A facility for food, fuel, repair, or rest.

        c. A location where commercial motor carriers maintain an operating facility.

        d. A location where labor is performed.

(b) The Secretary of the Department may implement this chapter and §§ 134 and 141 of Title 17 by erecting traffic control devices.

(c) The Secretary of the Department may do all of the following:

    (1) Order traffic control devices erected on any highway establishing the maximum permitted weight or height of any vehicle including load that may be driven on the highway.

    (2) Order traffic control devices erected on any highway prohibiting the operation of commercial vehicles on the highway, with exceptions for local service or residential service.

(d)(1) The Secretary of the Department shall submit an order issued under subsection (c) of this section to the Registrar of Regulations for publication in the Register of Regulations. The Secretary shall also publish the order on the Department's website with other similar orders.

    (2) An incorporated municipality exercising its authority under § 134(e) of Title 17 shall submit notice of the municipality's action to the Registrar of Regulations for publication in the Register of Regulations. For a state-maintained highway, the notice must include a certification from the Department that the notice has been approved by the Department. The Secretary shall publish the notice on the Department's website with orders issued by the Department under paragraph (d)(1) of this section.

(e) It is unlawful for a person to drive or move or, being the owner, cause or knowingly permit to be driven or moved, a vehicle or combination of vehicles in violation of a traffic control device erected under subsection (c) of this section.

(f)(1) For purposes of this subsection:

        a. "First offense" means a person has not, before the date of this offense, previously been convicted of violating the traffic control device at the location of the offense.

        b. "Subsequent like offense" means a person has, before the date of this offense, been convicted of violating the traffic control device at the location of the offense.

    (2) Section 4508 of this title does not apply to a violation of subsection (e) of this section.

    (3) A violation of paragraph (c)(1) of this section is punishable as follows:

        a. For a first offense, by both of the following:

            1. A fine of not less than $250 nor more than $450 or by a term of imprisonment of not more than 30 days or both.

            2. A fine for all excess weight up to and including 5,000 pounds in the amount of 2.3 cents per pound and a fine for all excess weight over 5,000 pounds in the amount of 5.75 cents per pound or by a term of imprisonment not to exceed 30 days or both.

        b. For a subsequent like offense, by both of the following:

            1. A fine of not less than $500 nor more than $650 or by a term of imprisonment of not more than 60 days or both.

2. A fine for all excess weight up to and including 5,000 pounds in the amount of 5.75 cents per pound and a fine for all excess weight over 5,000 pounds in the amount of 11.5 cents per pound or by a term of imprisonment not to exceed 60 days or both.

(4) A violation of paragraph (c)(2) of this section is punishable as follows:

a. For a first offense, by a fine of not less than $250 nor more than $450 or by a term of imprisonment of not more than 30 days or both.

b. For a subsequent like offense, by a fine of not less than $450 nor more than $650 or by a term of imprisonment of not more than 60 days or both.

(5) A subsequent like offense under this subsection constitutes a moving violation.

History.

36 Del. Laws, c. 10, § 120; Code 1935, § 5658; 46 Del. Laws, c. 124; 21 Del. C. 1953, § 4505; 58 Del. Laws, c. 550; 60 Del. Laws, c. 503, § 24; 60 Del. Laws, c. 700, § 9; 60 Del. Laws, c. 701, § 64; 64 Del. Laws, c. 207, § 5; 83 Del. Laws, c. 68, § 1.

Effect of amendments.

83 Del. Laws, c. 68, effective June 30, 2021, rewrote former section as (b) and (c) and added (a) and (d)-(f).

§ 4513. Truck monitoring system.

(a) *Definitions.* — As used in this section:

(1) "County" means the 3 counties of this State: New Castle, Kent, and Sussex.

(2) "County law" means any legislative, administrative, or other law or policy implemented by the governing body of a county.

(3) "Driver" does not include an employee of the owner of a motor vehicle.

(4) "Municipality" includes all cities, towns, and villages created under any general or special law of this State for general governmental purpose and which possesses legislative, administrative, or police powers for the general exercise of municipal functions and carry on the functions through a set of elected and other officials.

(5) "Municipal law" means any legislative, administrative, or other law or policy implemented by a municipality.

(6) "Recorded image" means an image recorded by a truck monitoring system and includes any of the following:

a. A photograph.

b. A microphotograph.

c. A digital image.

d. A video.

e. Any other medium used to store images or sounds to be seen or heard later.

(7) "Road" means an open way for motor vehicles, and includes all of the following:

a. A Delaware byway, express highway, road, highway, or state highway, as those terms are defined under § 101 of this title.

b. A road, street, highway, roadway, or any similar term, as defined under a county or municipal law.

(8) "Truck monitoring system" means a device that is capable of producing a recorded image of a motor vehicle for identification of the vehicle type.

(b) *Purpose.* — This section establishes the authority for the State or its counties or municipalities to use a truck monitoring system to assist in the enforcement of Chapter 45 and § 4505 of this title. This section does not establish a new violation.

(c) *Applicability.* — (1) This section does not apply to any of the following:

a. An emergency vehicle.

b. An authorized state vehicle or snow plow.

c. A school bus.

d. A vehicle for which an owner, an employee of an owner, or a driver provides proof of lawful use of a restricted roadway.

e. A recreational vehicle.

(2) An employer, not the employer's employee, is liable under this section if a violation under this section occurs while an employee is using, for the purposes of employment, a vehicle that the employer owns.

(d) *Initial implementation; responsible authority.* — A truck monitoring system may be installed or used to record images of a motor vehicle traveling on a road in this State after the requirements of paragraph (d)(1) of this section and, if applicable, paragraph (d)(3) of this section, have been met.

(1) By August 15, 2020, the Department of Transportation shall do both of the following:

a. Identify roads in this State as potential candidates for the placement of truck monitoring systems.

b. Conduct an analysis to determine the appropriateness of each location.

(2) After the requirements of paragraph (d)(1) of this section have been met, the Secretary of the Department of Safety and Homeland Security may approve and install a truck monitoring system. The Secretary of the Department of Safety and Homeland Security may consult with the Department of Transportation for best practices in installing a truck monitoring system.

(3) A county or municipality may install and use a truck monitoring system after all of the following requirements have been met:

a. Paragraph (d)(1) of this section.

b. The county or municipality adopts an ordinance authorizing the use of a truck monitoring system at a location identified as a potential candidate under paragraph (d)(1) of this section.

c. The county or municipality publishes notice of each truck monitoring system location in a newspaper of general circulation in the area in which the truck monitoring system will be installed or used.

d. All signs stating restrictions on the presence of certain motor vehicles during certain times approaching and within the segment of road on which the truck monitoring system is located meet all of the following criteria:

1. Are in accordance with the Delaware Manual on Uniform Traffic Control Devices.

2. Indicate that a truck monitoring system is in use.

(4) The county or municipality that adopts an ordinance to authorize the use of a truck monitoring system is responsible for paying or obtaining funds for payment of the installation, use, maintenance, or other costs associated with the truck monitoring system that the county or municipality authorized. The Community Transportation Fund may be used to pay for a truck monitoring system.

(e) *Vendor selection.* — The Department of Safety and Homeland Security shall utilize a supporting vendor to provide truck monitoring systems for the State, counties, and municipalities. The system vendor must be selected through an open competitive procurement process which allows for the government and taxpayer to benefit from improved quality at lower pricing. To assure integrity and propriety, a person involved in the administration or enforcement of the truck monitoring system may not own any interest or equity in the vendor used.

(f) *Truck monitoring system requirements and maintenance; daily set-up log.* — (1) [Repealed.]

(2) A daily log must be maintained for each truck monitoring system. A county or municipality that has adopted an ordinance to install a truck monitoring system shall designate a truck monitoring system technician to fulfill the requirements of paragraph (f)(3)a. of this section for a truck monitoring system.

(3) A truck monitoring system technician shall do all of the following:

a. Fill out and sign a daily set-up log for each truck monitoring system to which the truck monitoring system technician is assigned. The log must do all of the following:

1. Include a statement that the technician successfully performed the manufacturer-specified self-test of the truck monitoring system before producing a recorded image.

2. Be kept on file.

3. Be admitted as evidence in any court proceeding for the violation that the recorded image captured.

b. With the approval of a law-enforcement officer of the applicable jurisdiction, issue a violation notice and send the notice to the registered owner of the motor vehicle.

(g) [Repealed.]

(h) *Civil penalty.* — Unless a law-enforcement officer issued a citation to the owner or driver of the motor vehicle at the time of the violation, the owner or driver is subject to a civil penalty if a truck monitoring system captures the owner's motor vehicle while violating state, county, or municipal law restricting the presence of certain vehicles at certain times. A civil penalty under this subsection may not exceed any of the following:

(1) For a first violation by the owner, an employee of the owner, or the driver of the motor vehicle, a mailed warning notice instead of a civil penalty. For purposes of this section, "first violation" means the owner, an employee of the owner, or the driver of the motor vehicle has not previously violated a state, county, or municipal law restricting the presence of certain motor vehicles at certain times within 24 months before the date of the violation.

(2) For a second violation by the owner, an employee of the owner, or the driver of the motor vehicle, $250.

(3) For third or subsequent violation by the owner, an employee of the owner, or the driver of the motor vehicle, $500.

(i) *Issuance of citation; contents; duty of recipient.* — The State, county, or municipality, whichever applies, shall, within 30 days of the violation, mail a notice of violation to the owner of a motor vehicle that was captured on a truck monitoring system while violating a state, county, or municipal law restricting the presence of certain vehicles at certain times. The notice of violation must include all of the following:

(1) The name and address of the registered owner of the motor vehicle.

(2) The registration number of the motor vehicle involved in the violation.

(3) The violation charged.

(4) The location at which the violation occurred.

(5) The date and time of the violation.

(6) A copy of the recorded image of the motor vehicle.

(7) The amount of the civil penalty imposed and the date by which the civil penalty must be paid.

(8) A signed statement by a law-enforcement officer of the applicable jurisdiction that, based on inspection of the recorded image, the motor vehicle was being operated in violation of a state, county, or municipal law restricting the presence of certain vehicles at certain times.

(9) A statement that the recorded image is evidence of the violation.

(10) Information advising the owner of the manner, time, and place by which liability as alleged in the notice may be contested.

(11 Information warning the owner that failure to pay the civil penalty or contest liability in a timely manner is an admission of liability and may result in a judgment being entered against the owner or the denial of the registration or renewal of any of the owner's motor vehicles.

(12) Notice that the owner's ability to rebut the presumption that the owner or an employee of the owner was the operator of the motor vehicle at the time of the alleged violation and the means for rebutting the presumption.

(j) *Evidence; witnesses.* — (1) A certificate alleging that a violation of a state, county, or municipal law restricting the presence of a certain motor vehicle during a certain time occurred and that the requirements under subsections (d) and (f) of this section have been met and affirmed by a duly authorized law-enforcement officer based on inspection of a recorded image produced by a truck monitoring system is both of the following:

   a. Evidence of the facts contained in the certificate.

   b. Admissible in a proceeding alleging a violation under this section without the presence or testimony of the truck monitoring system technician.

(2) A recorded image from a truck monitoring system is evidence of a violation only if the image shows all of the following:

   a. The front or side of a motor vehicle.

   b. At least 2 time-stamped recorded images of the motor vehicle that include the same stationary object near the motor vehicle.

   c. On at least 1 recorded image, a clear and legible identification of the entire registration plate number of the motor vehicle.

(3) If an owner or driver who received a notice of violation under this section desires the truck monitoring system technician to be present and testify at trial, the owner or driver shall notify the court and the State, county, or municipality, whichever issued the notice of violation, in writing no later than 20 days before trial.

(4) Adjudication of liability is based on a preponderance of the evidence.

(k) *Defenses.* — (1) The court may consider in defense of a violation either of the following:

   a. Subject to paragraph (k)(2) of this section, that the motor vehicle or the registration plates of the motor vehicle were stolen before the violation occurred and were not under the control or possession of the owner, an employee of the owner, or the driver at the time of the violation.

   b. Subject to paragraph (k)(2) of this section, presence on the road was required to complete a local service, including trash removal. It is the driver's or owner's burden to prove that presence on the road was required to complete a local service.

   c. Any other issue or evidence that the court deems pertinent.

(2) To demonstrate a defense under paragraph (k)(1) of this section, the owner or driver must submit proof that a police report regarding the stolen motor vehicle or registration plates was filed in a timely manner.

(*l*) *Status of violation.* — A violation for which a civil penalty is imposed under this section is not a moving violation for the purpose of assessing points under 2 DE Admin. Code § 2208, and may not be any of the following:

(1) Recorded on the driving record of the owner, an employee of the owner, or driver of the motor vehicle.

(2) Treated as a parking violation under state, county, or municipal law.

(3) Considered in the provision of motor vehicle insurance coverage.

(m) *Adoption of procedures for issuance of citations.* — The Justice of the Peace Court, upon approval by the Chief Justice, may develop court rules, administrative directives, or other forms of policies for handling violations under this section.

(n) *Administration and processing of citations.* — (1) The county or municipality that installed the truck monitoring system, or a contractor designated by the county or municipality, shall administer and process civil citations issued under this section in coordination with the court.

(2) If a contractor operates a truck monitoring system on behalf of a county or municipality, the contractor's fee may not be contingent on the number of citations issued or paid.

History.
82 Del. Laws, c. 203, § 1; 83 Del. Laws, c. 155, § 1.

Effect of amendments.
83 Del. Laws, c. 155, effective Sept. 15, 2021, substituted "truck" for "vehicle height" in the section heading, (a)(6), the introductory paragraph of (d), in (d)(1)a., (d)(3)b., twice in (d)(3)c., once each in (d)(3)d., the introductory paragraph of (d)(3)d., in (d)(3)d.2., the first and final sentences of (e), in the first sentence of the introductory paragraphs of (h) and (i), wherever it appeared in (j), and once in (n)(2); deleted "As used in this section" from the beginning of (a)(7); rewrote (a)(8) and the first sentence of (b); substituted "of lawful use of a restricted roadway" for "that it is being used to make a delivery" in (c)(1)d.; rewrote (d)(2) and the introductory paragraph of (d)(3); added (d)(4); rewrote (f); repealed (g); added present (k)(1)b. and redesignated former (k)(1)b. as present (k)(1)c.; substituted "demonstrate" for "demonstration" in (k)(2); deleted "State or a" preceding "county" in two places in (n)(1) and once in (n)(2); and added "that installed the truck monitoring system" in (n)(1).

PART IV

MISCELLANEOUS

CHAPTER 63

SALE OF MOTOR VEHICLES

§ 6314A. Effect of suspension, revocation, or renewal refusal on licensee.

(a) Dealers who have their dealer license suspended, revoked, or renewal refused pursuant to this title are prohibited from being employed at any dealership licensed pursuant to this title in any of the following positions:

(1) Manager.

(2) Sales person in any capacity.

(3) Authorized signer.

(4) Any other position in which the individual would interact with

customers, handle financial transactions, or complete any paperwork required to be submitted to the Division.

(b) Dealers who have their dealer license suspended, revoked, or renewal refused pursuant to this title are prohibited from being employed in any of the capacities listed in this section for the following time periods:

(1) If a license is revoked, for 5 years from the effective date of the revocation.

(2) If a license is suspended, for the length of the suspension from the effective date of the suspension.

(3) If renewal is refused, for 12 months from the date that the dealer received the certified letter sent pursuant to § 6314(a) of this title or any time period set forth in a decision issued by the Division on appeal. If the certified letter is unable to be delivered, the 12-month period will start 30 days after the Division mails the certified letter required by § 6314(a) of this title.

(4) If the dealer receives a notice pursuant to § 6314 of this title that its license will be suspended, or renewal refused, and the dealer chooses not to request a hearing pursuant to § 6314(a) of this title, for 12 months from the date that the dealer received the certified letter sent pursuant to § 6314(a) of this title. If the certified letter is unable to be delivered, the 12-month period will start 30 days after the Division mails the certified letter required by § 6314(a)(4) of this title.

(5) If the dealer receives a notice pursuant to § 6314 of this title that its license will be revoked and the dealer chooses not to request a hearing pursuant to § 6314(a) of this title, for 5 years from the date that the dealer received the certified letter sent pursuant to § 6314(a) of this title. If the certified letter is unable to be delivered, the 5-year period will start 30 days after the Division mails the certified letter required by § 6314(a)(4) of this title.

(c) The Division shall notify any dealer subject to the restrictions set forth in this section by certified mail, return receipt requested, addressed to the last known address as shown on the license or dealership application or other record of information in possession of the Division, to turn in all documentation required by § 6316 of this title. If the dealer does not return the documentation required by § 6316 of this title within 10 days from the date that the dealer receives the certified letter, the time periods set forth above will be extended out by 1 day for every day past day 10 the § 6316 of this title documentation is outstanding. If the certified letter is unable to be delivered, the counting for the purposes of the extension period will start 30 days after the Division mails the certified letter. The Division shall notify the dealer in writing on a monthly basis of any extensions for failure to turn in documentation required by § 6316 of this title. If the documentation required by § 6316 of this title is not turned in within 6 months from the date required in this section, the time periods set forth above will be extended indefinitely. A dealer may turn in documentation at any time after the 6-month period and the prohibited employment time period will end 12 months after the date the documentation is turned in, or when the extended time period was set to end, whichever is longer.

(d) The prohibitions set forth in this section apply to any individual licensee, or if the licensee is a partnership, each individual partner listed on the application submitted pursuant to § 6302 of this title, or if the licensee is a corporation, the individual or individuals who signed the application submitted pursuant to § 6302 of this title on behalf of the corporation.

(e) Should the Division learn that a dealer has been employed in violation of the section, the period of time set forth in this section shall be extended by 6 months for every month the dealer is employed in violation of this section. The Division shall notify the dealer of any violation in writing by certified mail, return receipt requested, addressed to the last known address as shown on the license or dealership application or other record of information in possession of the Division. The written notice shall inform the dealer of the following:

(1) This Division's intention to extend the suspension, revocation, or other time period set forth in this section.

(2) The nature of the violations by the dealer.

(3) The notice shall inform the dealer of its right to request a hearing to dispute the violation. The hearing must be requested within 10 days from earlier of the dates that the dealer received the certified letter or the Division received the return receipt on the certified letter.

(4) The notice shall inform the dealer of its right to present evidence, to be represented by counsel and to appear personally or by other representative at the hearing.

(f) Any hearings requested by a dealer under this section shall follow the procedures set forth in §§ 6314(b) and 6315 of this title.

History.
83 Del. Laws, c. 163, § 1.

Revisor's note.
This section became effective upon the signature of the Governor on Sept. 15, 2021.

CHAPTER 64
ODOMETERS

Sec.
6408. Exemptions.

§ 6408. Exemptions.

Notwithstanding the requirements of § 6407 of this title:

(1) A transferor or lessee of any of the following motor vehicles need not disclose the vehicle's odometer mileage:

a. A vehicle having a gross vehicle weight rating of more than 16,000 pounds.

b. A vehicle that is not self-propelled.

c. A vehicle manufactured in or before the 2010 model year that is transferred at least 10 years after January 1 of the calendar year corresponding to its designated model year.

d. A vehicle manufactured in or after the 2011 model year that is transferred at least 20 years after January 1 of the calendar year corresponding to its designated model year.

e A vehicle sold directly by the manufacturer to any agency of the United States in conformity with contractual specifications.

(2) A transferor of a new vehicle prior to its first transfer for purposes other than resale need not disclose the vehicle's odometer mileage.

(3) A lessor of any of the vehicles listed in paragraph (1) of this section need not notify the lessee of these vehicles of the disclosure requirements of § 6409 of this title.

History.
69 Del. Laws, c. 113, § 4; 83 Del. Laws, c. 161, § 1.

Revisor's note.
Section 2 of 83 Del. Laws, c. 161, provided: "This act is effective retroactive to January 1, 2021."

Effect of amendments.
83 Del. Laws, c. 161, effective Jan. 1, 2021, substituted a period for a semicolon at the end of (1)a. and (1)b.; rewrote (1)c.; added present (1)d.; and redesignated former (1)d. as present (1)e.

CHAPTER 69

REMOVAL OF MOTOR VEHICLES FROM PUBLIC HIGHWAYS BY POLICE

§ 6901. Removal of motor vehicles from public highways by police; sale of vehicles; towers.

(a) Any police officer of this State, or a county or municipality therein, while in the performance of duty, may remove, store or cause to be removed or stored from any public highway, highway right-of-way, street or alley, at the owner's or operator's expense, any motor vehicle, trailer or part thereof which:

(1) Is unregistered or has an expired registration; or

(2) Is parked or left standing in such manner as to create a hazard by interfering with the normal movement of traffic:

a. By preventing the exit from or entrance to any public highway, private road or driveway;

b. By interfering with emergency firefighting equipment;

c. By being involved in a collision and rendered incapable of being moved under its own power, when the owner or operator has been arrested and detained; or

d. When the owner or operator is unable, unwilling or not available to do so immediately.

Anyone so removing any motor vehicle, trailer or part thereof shall have a possessory lien against said motor vehicle, trailer or part thereof for the costs of removing, towing, preserving and storing said motor vehicle, trailer or part thereof and shall have the right to sell said motor vehicle, trailer or part thereof after complying with the notice and sale provisions outlined in Chapter 39 of Title 25, with the exception that the proceeds of the sale shall be applied first to the costs of the sale, then to the costs of removing, towing, preserving and storing and then to the payment of any liens to which said motor vehicle, trailer or part thereof may be subject in order of their priority, then to the State Treasurer who shall create a special fund thereof and who shall pay to the owner the moneys held if a claim is made within 1 year of the removal or deposit the moneys in the General Fund if no claim is made within 1 year of removal. Any possessory lien created under this section shall not extend to any personal property that is not attached to or considered necessary for the proper operation of any motor vehicle, and such property shall be returned to the owner of the motor vehicle if the owner of the motor vehicle claims the items prior to the sale of such motor vehicle.

There shall be no liability incurred by any police officer of this State or a county or municipality therein, or agents directed by them, whether or not they are also police officers, while in the performance of duty, for damages incurred to immobilized motor vehicle or vehicles moved under this subsection, or to the vehicle's contents or surrounding area caused by the emergency measures employed by the officer or employee to move the vehicle or vehicles for the purpose of clearing the lane or lanes to remove any threat to public safety, unless the circumstances meet the conditions for liability established in § 4001(2) or (3) or § 4011(c) of Title 10.

(b) In effecting the removal and subsequent storage of such vehicles, any police officer of this State, or a county or municipality therein, may select and engage the services, vehicles, equipment or facilities of another person, hereinafter called the "tower", who shall be compensated at the expense of the owner or operator. Such selection shall be made pursuant to the regulations promulgated under subsection (c) of this section.

(c) The Department of Safety and Homeland Security shall promulgate regulations governing the selection of towers by State Police officers. Such regulations shall prescribe qualifications for eligibility of towers to be selected by police officers under this section, shall describe the method to be used by police officers in selecting from eligible towers, and may make such other provisions as the Department of Safety and Homeland Security deems fit; provided, however, that there shall be no prohibitions against the owner of a vehicle from choosing the tower of that person's choice if no emergency exists. All eligible towers shall file with the Superintendent of the Delaware State Police a schedule of towing charges of such towers and other incidental charges of such tower customarily incurred in connection with the towing and storage of vehicles under the section.

History.

21 Del. C. 1953, § 6901; 55 Del. Laws, c. 340; 61 Del. Laws, c. 247, § 1; 61 Del. Laws, c. 367, § 3; 63 Del. Laws, c. 173, § 1; 63 Del. Laws, c. 355, § 1; 66 Del. Laws, c. 313, § 1; 70 Del. Laws, c. 186, § 1; 74 Del. Laws, c. 110, §§ 115, 138; 76 Del. Laws, c. 401, § 16; 83 Del. Laws, c. 125, § 2.

Effect of amendments.

83 Del. Laws, c. 125, effective Aug. 10, 2021, added the final sentence in the first concluding paragraph of (a).

TITLE 22
MUNICIPALITIES

Chapter
1. General Provisions, §§ 101 to 118.

CHAPTER 1
GENERAL PROVISIONS

Sec.
114. Public advertising and notices.

§ 114. Public advertising and notices.

Notwithstanding any provision to the contrary, public advertising and notices by any municipality in the State of any nature may include use of the State's electronic procurement advertising system required by § 6902(10) of Title 29 or other website allowing for the electronic posting of local government bid opportunities, and the website designed pursuant to §§ 10004(e)(5), 10115(b) and 10124(1) of Title 29.

History.
78 Del. Laws, c. 288, § 10; 82 Del. Laws, c. 36, § 1; 83 Del. Laws, c. 65, § 2.

Laws, c. 65, § 1, effective June 30, 2021, "§§ 10004(e)(5)" was substituted for "§§ 10004(e)(4)".

Revisor's note.
Based upon changes contained in 83 Del.

CHAPTER 8
HOME RULE
SUBCHAPTER VII
RESIDENCY REQUIREMENTS

§ 841. Residency requirements.

NOTES TO DECISIONS

Arbitration.
Arbitration award in favor of a police union, regarding a residency requirement for city police officers, was not contrary to law; 22 Del. C. § 841 lacked a fixed meaning of residency, leaving room to bargain over the meaning of "residence" under the Police Officers and Firefighters' Employment Relations Act (19 Del. C. § 1601 et seq.). City of Wilmington v. Wilmington FOP Lodge No.1, Inc., 2020 Del. Ch. LEXIS 389.

TITLE 24
PROFESSIONS AND OCCUPATIONS

CHAPTER 5
PODIATRY

SUBCHAPTER I
BOARD OF PODIATRY

§ 502. Definitions.

The following words, terms and phrases, when used in this chapter, shall have the meanings ascribed to them under this section, except where the context clearly indicates a different meaning:

(1) "Board" shall mean the State Board of Podiatry established in this chapter.

(2) "Diagnosis" shall mean the ascertainment of a disease or ailment by its general symptoms.

(3) "Division" shall mean the State Division of Professional Regulation.

(4) "Electrical treatment" shall mean the administration of electricity to the foot and ankle by means of electrodes, machinery, rays and the like.

(5) "Electronic prescription" means a prescription that is generated on an electronic application and transmitted as an electronic data file.

(6) "Excessive use or abuse of drugs" shall mean any use of narcotics, controlled substances or illegal drugs without a prescription from a licensed physician or the abuse of alcoholic beverages such that it impairs a person's ability to perform the work of a podiatrist.

(7) "Manipulative treatment" shall mean the use of the hand or machinery in the operation of or working upon the foot and its articulations.

(8) "Mechanical treatment" shall mean the application of any mechani-

cal appliance made of steel, leather, felt or any material to the foot or the shoe for the purpose of treating any disease, deformity or ailment.

(9) "Medical treatment" shall mean the application to or prescription for the foot and ankle of medicine, pads, adhesives, felt, plasters or any medicinal agency.

(10) "Podiatrist" shall mean a person who is qualified to practice podiatry and is licensed under this chapter.

(11) "Practice of podiatry" shall mean the diagnosis and the medical, surgical, mechanical, manipulative and electrical treatment of all ailments of the foot and ankle. As appropriate in regulation, these services may be performed with the use of telemedicine. Podiatry may also include participation in telehealth, as further defined in regulation. Amputation of the foot shall be restricted to state-licensed podiatrists who have completed an American Podiatric Medical Association accredited surgical residency program acceptable to the Board and have current amputation privileges, or have fulfilled the credentialing criteria of the surgical committee of the Joint Committee on Accreditation of Hospitals accredited hospital where the amputation is to be performed.

(12) "Protective hairstyle" includes braids, locks, and twists.

(13) "Race" includes traits historically associated with race, including hair texture and a protective hairstyle.

(14) "State" shall mean the State of Delaware.

(15) "Substantially related" means the nature of the criminal conduct, for which the person was convicted, has a direct bearing on the fitness or ability to perform 1 or more of the duties or responsibilities necessarily related to podiatry.

(16) "Surgical treatment" shall mean the use of any cutting instrument to treat a disease, ailment or condition.

History.
33 Del. Laws, c. 66, § 2; 40 Del. Laws, c. 108, § 2; Code 1935, § 5385; 24 Del. C. 1953, § 501; 53 Del. Laws, c. 315, § 1; 61 Del. Laws, c. 356, § 1; 64 Del. Laws, c. 39, § 1; 70 Del. Laws, c. 186, § 1; 72 Del. Laws, c. 213, § 1; 74 Del. Laws, c. 262, § 12; 80 Del. Laws, c. 80, § 7; 82 Del. Laws, c. 75, § 1; 82 Del. Laws, c. 261, §§ 5, 16; 83 Del. Laws, c. 13, §§ 15, 16; 83 Del. Laws, c. 52, § 7.

Revisor's note.
Section 1 of 83 Del. Laws, c. 52, provided: "This Act shall be known as the 'Telehealth Access Preservation and Modernization Act of 2021'."

Section 21 of 83 Del. Laws, c. 52, provided: "Sections 1-19 of this act take effect on July 1, 2021. Nothing in this act shall be interpreted as affecting or invalidating any health-care services provided through telehealth or telemedicine prior to effective date of this act."

Effect of amendments.
83 Del. Laws, c. 13, effective April 13, 2021, added present (14) and (15) and redesignated the remaining paragraphs accordingly.

83 Del. Laws, c. 52, effective July 1, 2021, deleted former (3), (11), (17), (20) and (21) and redesignated the remaining and intervening paragraphs accordingly.

§ 503. Board of Podiatry; appointments; composition; qualifications; term; vacancies; suspension or removal; unexcused absences; compensation.

(a) There is created a State Board of Podiatry that shall administer and enforce this chapter.

(b) The Board shall consist of 5 members, appointed by the Governor, who are residents of this State: 3 shall be podiatrists licensed under this chapter and 2 shall be public members. The public members shall not be, nor ever have been, podiatrists, nor members of the immediate family of a podiatrist; shall not have been employed by a podiatrist or a company engaged in the practice of podiatry; shall not have a material interest in the providing of goods and services to podiatrists; nor have been engaged in an activity directly related to podiatry. The public members shall be accessible to inquiries, comments and suggestions from the general public.

(c) Except as provided in subsection (d) of this section, each member shall serve a term of 3 years, and may serve 1 additional term in succession. Each term of office shall expire on the date specified in the appointment; however, the Board member shall remain eligible to participate in Board proceedings unless or until replaced by the Governor. Persons who are members of the Board on July 20, 1999, shall complete their terms.

(d) A person who has never served on the Board may be appointed to the Board for 2 consecutive terms, but no such person shall thereafter be eligible for 2 consecutive appointments. No person who has been twice appointed to the Board or who has served on the Board for 6 years within any 9-year period shall again be appointed to the Board until an interim period of at least 1 term has expired since such person last served.

(e) Any act or vote by a person appointed in violation of this section shall be invalid. An amendment or revision of this chapter is not sufficient cause for any appointment or attempted appointment in violation of subsection (d) of this section, unless such an amendment or revision amends this section to permit such an appointment.

(f) A member of the Board shall be suspended or removed by the Governor for misfeasance, nonfeasance, malfeasance, misconduct, incompetency or neglect of duty. A member subject to disciplinary hearing shall be disqualified from Board business until the charge is adjudicated or the matter is otherwise concluded. A Board member may appeal any suspension or removal to the Superior Court.

(g) No member of the Board, while serving on the Board, shall hold elective office in any professional association of podiatrists; this includes a prohibition against serving as head of the professional association's Political Action Committee (PAC).

(h) The provisions set forth in Chapter 58 of Title 29 shall apply to all members of the Board.

(i) Any member who is absent without adequate reason for 3 consecutive meetings or fails to attend at least ½ of all regular business meetings during any calendar year shall be guilty of neglect of duty.

(j) Each member of the Board shall be reimbursed for all expenses involved in each meeting, including travel, and in addition, shall receive compensation per meeting attended in an amount determined by the Division in accordance with Del. Const. art. III, § 9.

History.
33 Del. Laws, c. 66, §§ 3, 14; 40 Del. Laws, c. 108, §§ 3, 17; Code 1935, §§ 5386, 5398; 42 Del. Laws, c. 159, § 1; 24 Del. C. 1953, §§ 502, 503; 53 Del. Laws, c. 315, § 1; 61 Del. Laws, c. 356, § 1; 64 Del. Laws, c. 39, § 1; 67 Del. Laws, c. 368, § 4; 70 Del. Laws, c. 186, § 1; 72 Del. Laws, c. 213, § 1; 81 Del. Laws, c. 85, § 3; 83 Del. Laws, c. 193, § 1.

Effect of amendments.
83 Del. Laws, c. 193, effective September 17, 2021, in (c), rewrote the first sentence, and deleted the former second sentence.

§ 504. Organization; meetings; officers; quorum.

(a) The Board shall hold a regularly scheduled business meeting at least once in each calendar year and at such times as the President deems necessary, or at the request of a majority of the Board members.

(b) The Board annually shall elect a president and secretary. Each officer shall serve for 1 year, and shall not succeed himself or herself for more than 2 consecutive terms.

(c) A majority of the members shall constitute a quorum for the purpose of transacting business, and no disciplinary action shall be taken without the affirmative vote of at least 3 members.

(d) Minutes of all meetings shall be recorded, and the Division of Professional Regulation shall maintain copies. At any hearing where evidence is presented, a record from which a verbatim transcript can be prepared shall be made. The expense of preparing any transcript shall be incurred by the person requesting it.

History.

33 Del. Laws, c. 66, § 3; 40 Del. Laws, c. 108, § 3; Code 1935, § 5386; 42 Del. Laws, c. 159, § 1; 24 Del. C. 1953, § 502; 53 Del. Laws, c. 315, § 1; 61 Del. Laws, c. 356, § 1; 64 Del. Laws, c. 39, § 1; 65 Del. Laws, c. 355, § 1; 70 Del. Laws, c. 186, § 1; 72 Del. Laws, c. 213, § 1; 83 Del. Laws, c. 193, § 2.

Effect of amendments.

83 Del. Laws, c. 193, effective September 17, 2021, in (a), inserted "a" following "hold", substituted "meeting" for "meetings" and deleted "quarter of a" preceding "calendar".

CHAPTER 7

BOARD OF CHIROPRACTIC

§ 701. Chiropractic defined; limitation of chiropractic license.

(a) As used in this chapter:

(1) "Chiropractic" means a drugless system of health care based on the principle that interference with the transmission of nerve impulses may cause disease.

(2) "Protective hairstyle" includes braids, locks, and twists.

(3) "Race" includes traits historically associated with race, including hair texture and a protective hairstyle.

(b) The practice of chiropractic includes the diagnosing and locating of misaligned or displaced vertebrae (subluxation complex), using x-rays and other diagnostic test procedures. Practice of chiropractic includes the treatment through manipulation/adjustment of the spine and other skeletal structures and the use of adjunctive procedures not otherwise prohibited by this chapter.

(c) Except as otherwise provided in this chapter, the practice of chiropractic does not include the use of drugs, surgery or obstetrical or gynecological examinations or treatment.

(d) All examinations performed by chiropractors shall be in accordance with the protocol and procedures as taught in the majority of accredited chiropractic colleges.

History.

41 Del. Laws, c. 261, § 8; 24 Del. C. 1953, § 701; 70 Del. Laws, c. 514, § 2; 80 Del. Laws, c. 80, § 8; 82 Del. Laws, c. 261, §§ 6, 16; 83 Del. Laws, c. 13, §§ 17, 18; 83 Del. Laws, c. 52, § 8.

Revisor's note.

Section 1 of 83 Del. Laws, c. 52, provided: "This Act shall be known as the 'Telehealth Access Preservation and Modernization Act of 2021'."

Section 21 of 83 Del. Laws, c. 52, provided: "Sections 1-19 of this act take effect on July 1, 2021. Nothing in this act shall be interpreted as affecting or invalidating any health-care services provided through telehealth or telemedicine prior to effective date of this act."

Effect of amendments.

83 Del. Laws, c. 13, effective April 13, 2021, added "As used in this chapter" to (a); added present (a)(4) and (a)(5) and redesignated the remaining paragraphs accordingly.

83 Del. Laws, c. 52, effective July 1, 2021, deleted former (a)(2), (3), (6), (7) and (8) and redesignated the remaining and intervening paragraphs in (a) accordingly; and, in (b), deleted "but is not limited to" in the first sentence and deleted the former second sentence.

§ 716. Chiropractic practitioners eligible for compensation from insurance; reimbursement at Medicare rate or comparable.

(a) For purposes of disability insurance, standard health and accident, sickness, and all other such insurance plans, whether or not they be considered insurance policies, and contracts issued by health service corporations and health maintenance organizations, if the chiropractor is authorized by law to perform a particular service, the chiropractor is entitled to compensation for that chiropractor's services under such plans and contracts, and such plans and contracts may not have annual or lifetime numerical limits on chiropractic visits for the treatment of back pain.

(b) Nothing in this section shall prevent the operation of reasonable and nondiscriminatory cost containment or managed care provisions, including but not limited to, deductibles, coinsurance, allowable charge limitations, coordination of benefits and utilization review. Any copayment or coinsurance amount shall be equal to or less than 25% of the fee due or to be paid to the doctor of chiropractic under the policy, contract, or certificate for the treatment, therapy, or service provided.

(c) The Insurance Commissioner shall issue and administer regulations to aid the administration, effectuation, investigation, and enforcement of this section.

(d)(1) For purposes of this subsection:

    a.1. "Carrier" means any entity that provides health insurance in this State.

    2. "Carrier" includes an insurance company, health service corporation, health maintenance organization, and any other entity providing a plan of health insurance or health benefits subject to state insurance regulation under Title 18.

    3. "Carrier" also includes any third-party administrator, as defined under § 102 of Title 18, or other entity that adjusts, administers, or settles claims in connection with health benefit plans.

    4. "Carrier" does not mean a plan of health insurance or health benefits designed for issuance to persons eligible for coverage under Titles XVIII, XIX, and XXI of the Social Security Act (42 U.S.C. §§ 1395 et seq., 1396 et seq. and 1397aa et seq.), known as Medicare, Medicaid, or any other similar coverage under state or federal governmental plans.

    b. "Medicare" means the federal Medicare Program (U.S. Public Law 89-97, as amended) (42 U.S.C. § 1395 et seq.).

(2) A carrier shall reimburse services provided by a chiropractor at a reimbursement rate that is not less than the Medicare reimbursement rate for comparable services.

(3) If a comparable Medicare reimbursement rate is not available, a carrier shall reimburse for services provided by a chiropractor at the rates generally available under Medicare for services such as office visits or prolonged preventive services.

(4) The Medicare reimbursement rate provisions under paragraphs (d)(2) and (d)(3) of this section do not apply to accident-only, specified disease, hospital indemnity, Medicare supplement, long-term care, disability income, or other limited benefit health insurance policies.

(5) This subsection may not be waived by contract. A contractual arrangement in conflict with this subsection or that purports to waive any requirements of this subsection is void.

(6) This subsection applies to an individual or group health insurance

policy, plan, or contract that is delivered, issued for delivery, or renewed by a carrier on or after January 1, 2022.

History.

24 Del. C. 1953, § 717; 54 Del. Laws, c. 147, § 2; 69 Del. Laws, c. 168, § 1; 69 Del. Laws, c. 393, § 1; 70 Del. Laws, c. 186, § 1; 70 Del. Laws, c. 514, § 40; 72 Del. Laws, c. 125, § 6; 77 Del. Laws, c. 462, § 3; 78 Del. Laws, c. 165, § 1; 81 Del. Laws, c. 430, § 2; 83 Del. Laws, c. 136, § 1.

Revisor's note.

Section 2 of 83 Del. Laws, c. 136, provided: "This act takes effect on January 1, 2022."

Effect of amendments.

83 Del. Laws, c. 136, effective Jan. 1, 2022, added "reimbursement at Medicare rate or comparable" in the section heading; added a comma following "investigation" in (c); and added (d).

CHAPTER 11
DENTISTRY AND DENTAL HYGIENE

SUBCHAPTER I
STATE BOARD OF DENTISTRY AND DENTAL HYGIENE

§ 1101. Definitions.

The following words, terms and phrases, when used in this chapter, shall have the meanings ascribed to them under this section except where the context clearly indicates a different meaning:

(1) "Academic license" means a license issued under § 1132A of this title to a full-time director, chairperson, or attending faculty member of a hospital based dental, oral and maxillofacial surgery or other specialty dental residency program for the purposes of teaching.

(2) "Board" shall mean the State Board of Dentistry and Dental Hygiene established in this chapter.

(3) "Dental assistant" shall mean any person not licensed to practice dentistry and/or dental hygiene in this State, who aids a dentist in the performance of generalized tasks, including chair-side aid, clerical work, reception, radiography, dental laboratory work, and any other such tasks delegated by the dentist.

(4) "Dental auxiliary personnel" shall mean any person not licensed to practice dentistry in this State, who works in a dental office as either a dental assistant, dental hygienist, dental technician, or otherwise.

(5) "Dental hygienist" shall mean a person who is qualified to practice dental hygiene as prescribed in this chapter.

(6) "Dental technician" shall mean any person not licensed to practice dentistry in this State, engaged in the business of constructing, altering, repairing or duplicating full dentures ("plates"), partial dentures, splints, orthodontic appliances, fixed bridges or any other prosthetic appliances.

(7) "Dentist" shall mean a person who is qualified to practice dentistry as prescribed in the chapter.

(8) "Division" shall mean the State Division of Professional Regulation.

(9) "Electronic prescription" means a prescription that is generated on an electronic application and transmitted as an electronic data file.

(10) "Excessive use or abuse of drugs" shall mean any use of narcotics, controlled substances or illegal drugs without a prescription from a

licensed individual with valid prescriptive authority or the abuse of alcoholic beverage or prescription or nonprescription drugs, such that it impairs a person's ability to perform the work of a dentist or dental hygienist.

(11) "Person" shall mean a corporation, company, association or partnership, as well as an individual.

(12) "Practice of dental hygiene" shall mean the removal of calculus deposits, plaque and stains from all surfaces of the teeth, and making instrumental examinations of the oral cavity, and assembling all necessary information for use by the dentist in diagnosis and treatment planning, and the performance of such prophylactic or preventive measures in the case of teeth, including the application of chemicals to the teeth and periodontal tissues, designed and approved for the prevention of dental caries and/or periodontal disease, as the Board may authorize; but the "practice of dental hygiene" shall not include any other operation on the teeth or tissues of the mouth.

(13) "Practice of dentistry" is defined as the evaluation, diagnosis, prevention and treatment (nonsurgical, surgical or related procedures) of diseases, disorders and conditions of the oral cavity, maxillofacial area and the adjacent and associated structures and their impact on the human body provided by a dentist within the scope of the dentist's education, training and experience, in accordance with the ethics of the profession and applicable law. A person shall be construed to practice dentistry who by verbal claim, sign, advertisement, opening of an office, or in any other way, including use of the words "dentist," "dental surgeon," the letters "D.D.S.," "D.M.D.," or other letters or titles, represents the person to be a dentist or who holds himself or herself out as able to perform, or who does perform, dental services or work. A person shall be regarded as practicing dentistry who is a manager, proprietor, operator or conductor of a place for performing dental operations or who for a fee, salary or other reward paid, or to be paid either to himself or herself or to another person, performs or advertises to perform dental operations of any kind.

(14) "State" shall mean the State of Delaware.

(15) "Substantially related" means the nature of the criminal conduct, for which the person was convicted, has a direct bearing on the fitness or ability to perform 1 or more of the duties or responsibilities necessarily related to the practice of dentistry or dental hygiene.

History.

73 Del. Laws, c. 332, § 3; 70 Del. Laws, c. 186, § 1; 74 Del. Laws, c. 262, § 20; 75 Del. Laws, c. 436, § 8; 77 Del. Laws, c. 463, §§ 1, 2, 3; 79 Del. Laws, c. 261, § 1; 80 Del. Laws, c. 80, § 9; 81 Del. Laws, c. 79, § 37; 82 Del. Laws, c. 75, § 2; 82 Del. Laws, c. 261, §§ 7, 16; 83 Del. Laws, c. 52, § 9.

Revisor's note.

Section 1 of 83 Del. Laws, c. 52, provided: "This Act shall be known as the 'Telehealth Access Preservation and Modernization Act of 2021'."

Section 21 of 83 Del. Laws, c. 52, provided:

"Sections 1-19 of this act take effect on July 1, 2021. Nothing in this act shall be interpreted as affecting or invalidating any health-care services provided through telehealth or telemedicine prior to effective date of this act."

Effect of amendments.

83 Del. Laws, c. 52, effective July 1, 2021, deleted former (8), (12), (17), (19) and (20) and redesignated the remaining and intervening paragraphs accordingly; and, in present (13), in the first sentence, substituted "and" for "and/or" following "prevention", "disorders" for "area", and deleted the former second sentence.

§ 1105. Dental Hygiene Advisory Committee.

(a) There is created a State Dental Hygiene Advisory Committee which shall serve the Board on matters pertaining to the policy and practice of dental hygiene.

(b) The Committee shall consist of 3 licensed dental hygienists, appointed by the Governor, who are residents of this State and who have been actively practicing dental hygiene in this State for 2 years immediately preceding appointment to the Committee.

(1) No person shall be eligible for appointment to the Committee who is in any manner connected with or who has an interest in any dental hygiene college or the dental hygiene department of any college or university or any commercial dental enterprise.

(2) Each member shall serve a term of 3 years and remain eligible to participate in proceedings unless and until replaced by the Governor.

(3) All terms shall be staggered so that 1 new member is added and 1 member is retired each year.

(4) A member of the Committee shall be suspended or removed by the Governor for misfeasance, nonfeasance, malfeasance, misconduct, incompetency or neglect of duty.

(5) No member of the Committee shall hold elective office in any professional association of dental hygienists.

(6) Each member of the Committee shall be reimbursed, according to the policy of the Division of Professional Regulation, for all expenses involved in each meeting, including travel; and in addition, shall receive $50 for each meeting attended but not more than $500 in any calendar year. After 10 meetings have been attended, the member shall not be compensated for any subsequent meetings attended in that year.

(7) No 2 dental hygienists from the same practice may serve on the Advisory Committee at the same time.

(c) The Committee shall participate with members of the Board in:

(1) Voting on the qualifications of candidates who apply for licensure to practice dental hygiene;

(2) Voting on the composition of the state dental hygiene clinical/practical examination;

(3) Voting on the requirements for renewal of dental hygiene licenses;

(4) Voting on disciplinary actions involving hygienists; and

(5) Voting on other matters involving the policy and practice of dental hygiene as defined in § 1101(12) of this title and further defined in the Board's rules and regulations. The Committee shall not vote on matters involving changing the scope of practice as defined in § 1101(12) of this title.

History.
65 Del. Laws, c. 210, § 16; 71 Del. Laws, c. 31, § 1; 73 Del. Laws, c. 332, § 3; 77 Del. Laws, c. 463, §§ 6-8; 79 Del. Laws, c. 261, § 1; 80 Del. Laws, c. 80, § 9; 82 Del. Laws, c. 75, § 2; 83 Del. Laws, c. 52, § 9.

Revisor's note.
Based upon changes contained in 83 Del. Laws, c. 52, § 9, made effective July 1, 2021, by § 21 of that act, "§ 1101(12)" was substituted for "§ 1101(14)" in the first and second sentences of (c)(5).

CHAPTER 17

MEDICAL PRACTICE ACT

SUBCHAPTER I
GENERAL PROVISIONS

§ 1702. Definitions.

The following definitions apply to this chapter unless otherwise expressly stated or implied by the context:

(1) "Board" means the Board of Medical Licensure and Discipline.

(2) "Certificate to practice medicine" means the authorization awarded by the Board to a person who has been qualified to practice medicine in this State by meeting the requirements of this chapter.

(3) "Conversion therapy" means any practice or treatment that seeks to change an individual's sexual orientation or gender identity, as "sexual orientation" and "gender identity" are defined in § 710 of Title 19, including any effort to change behaviors or gender expressions or to eliminate or reduce sexual or romantic attractions or feelings toward individuals of the same gender. "Conversion therapy" does not mean any of the following:

a. Counseling that provides assistance to an individual who is seeking to undergo a gender transition or who is in the process of undergoing gender transition.

b. Counseling that provides an individual with acceptance, support, and understanding without seeking to change an individual's sexual orientation or gender identity.

c. Counseling that facilitates an individual's coping, social support, and identity exploration and development, including counseling in the form of sexual orientation-neutral interventions or gender identity-neutral interventions provided for the purpose of preventing or addressing unlawful conduct or unsafe sexual practices, without seeking to change an individual's sexual orientation or gender identity.

(4) "Division" means the Division of Professional Regulation.

(5) "Electronic prescription" means a prescription that is generated on an electronic application and transmitted as an electronic data file.

(6) "Executive Director" means the Executive Director of the Board of Medical Licensure and Discipline.

(7) "Healthcare institution" means a facility or agency licensed, certified, or otherwise authorized by law to provide, in the ordinary course of business, treatments, services, or procedures to maintain, diagnose, or otherwise affect a person's physical or mental condition.

(8) "Medical group" means 1 or more physicians or other health-care practitioners who work together under the name of a professional corporation, a limited liability partnership, or other legal entity.

(9) "Medicine" means the science of restoring or preserving health and includes allopathic medicine and surgery, osteopathic medicine and surgery, and all the respective branches of the foregoing.

(10) "Physician" means an allopathic doctor of medicine and surgery or a doctor of osteopathic medicine and surgery who is registered and certified to practice medicine pursuant to this chapter.

(11) "Practice of medicine" or "practice medicine" includes:

a. Advertising, holding out to the public, or representing in any manner that one is authorized to practice medicine in this State;

b. Offering or undertaking to prescribe, order, give, or administer any drug or medicine for the use of another person;

c. Offering or undertaking to prevent or to diagnose, correct, and/or treat in any manner or by any means, methods, or devices a disease, illness, pain, wound, fracture, infirmity, defect, or abnormal physical or mental condition of another person, including the management of pregnancy and parturition;

d. Offering or undertaking to perform a surgical operation upon another person;

e. Rendering a written or otherwise documented medical opinion concerning the diagnosis or treatment of a person or the actual rendering of treatment to a person within the State by a physician located outside the State as a result of transmission of the person's medical data by electronic or other means from within the State to the physician or to the physician's agent;

f. Rendering a determination of medical necessity or a decision affecting or modifying the diagnosis and/or treatment of a person;

g. Using the designation Doctor, Doctor of Medicine, Doctor of Osteopathy, physician, surgeon, physician and surgeon, Dr., M.D., or D.O., or a similar designation, or any combination thereof, in the conduct of an occupation or profession pertaining to the prevention, diagnosis, or treatment of human disease or condition, unless the designation additionally contains the description of another branch of the healing arts for which one holds a valid license in the State.

For the purposes of this chapter, in order that the full resources of the State are available for the protection of persons using the services of physicians, the act of the practice of medicine occurs where a person is located at the time a physician practices medicine upon the person.

(12) "Protective hairstyle" includes braids, locks, and twists.

(13) "Race" includes traits historically associated with race, including hair texture and a protective hairstyle.

(14) "Registration" means the entry of a certificate to practice medicine into the records of the Board of Medical Licensure and Discipline pursuant to the regulations of the Board.

(15) "Store and forward transfer" means the transmission of a patient's medical information either to or from an originating site or to or from the provider at the distant site, but does not require the patient being present nor must it be in real time.

(16) "Substantially related" means the nature of criminal conduct for which a person was convicted has a direct bearing on the person's fitness or ability to perform 1 or more of the duties or responsibilities necessarily related to the practice of medicine, the work of a physician assistant, of the practice of respiratory care.

(17) "Unauthorized practice of medicine" means the practice of medicine as defined in paragraph (11) of this section by a person not authorized under this chapter to perform an act set forth in that subsection, unless excepted by § 1703 of this title.

(18) "Viability" means the point in a pregnancy when, in a physician's good faith medical judgment based on the factors of a patient's case, there is a reasonable likelihood of the fetus's sustained survival outside the uterus without the application of extraordinary medical measures.

History.

60 Del. Laws, c. 462, § 1; 61 Del. Laws, c. 68, §§ 2, 3; 62 Del. Laws, c. 90, § 1; 62 Del. Laws, c. 112, § 1; 63 Del. Laws, c. 62, § 1; 65 Del. Laws, c. 490, § 1; 67 Del. Laws, c. 5, § 1; 67 Del. Laws, c. 434, § 1; 68 Del. Laws, c. 147, § 1; 68 Del. Laws, c. 152, § 1; 69 Del. Laws, c. 355, §§ 1, 2, 6; 70 Del. Laws, c. 186, § 1; 71 Del. Laws, c. 283, § 1; 74 Del. Laws, c. 262, § 27; 75 Del. Laws, c. 141, § 1; 77 Del. Laws, c. 319, § 1; 80 Del. Laws, c. 80, § 2; 81 Del. Laws, c. 35, § 1; 81 Del. Laws, c. 340, § 2; 82 Del. Laws, c. 75, § 3; 82 Del. Laws, c. 261, §§ 4, 16; 83 Del. Laws, c. 13, §§ 19, 20; 83 Del. Laws, c. 52, § 5.

Revisor's note.

Section 1 of 83 Del. Laws, c. 52, provided: "This Act shall be known as the 'Telehealth Access Preservation and Modernization Act of 2021'."

Section 21 of 83 Del. Laws, c. 52, provided: "Sections 1-19 of this act take effect on July 1, 2021. Nothing in this act shall be interpreted as affecting or invalidating any health-care services provided through telehealth or telemedicine prior to effective date of this act."

Effect of amendments.

83 Del. Laws, c. 13, effective April 13, 2021, added present (14) and (15) and redesignated the remaining paragraphs accordingly.

83 Del. Laws, c. 52, effective July 1, 2021, deleted former (4), (11), (19) and (20) and redesignated the remaining and intervening paragraphs accordingly; and in present (17), substituted "(11)" for "(12)".

§ 1703. Nonapplicability of certain provisions.

Provisions of this chapter pertaining to the practice of medicine do not apply to:

(1) A person providing service in an emergency, where no fee or other consideration is contemplated, charged, or received;

(2) Physicians of any civilian or military branch of the United States government in the discharge of their official duties;

(3) Advanced practice nurses, chiropodists, chiropractors, dental hygienists, dentists, emergency medical technicians, optometrists, pharmacists, physical therapists, physician assistants, podiatrists, practical nurses, professional nurses, psychologists, respiratory care practitioners, veterinarians, or persons engaged in other professions or occupations who are certified, licensed, or registered according to law and are acting within the scope of the activity for which they are certified, licensed, or registered;

(4) A person administering a lawful domestic or family remedy to a member of that person's family;

(5) A person fully certified, licensed, or otherwise authorized to practice medicine in another state of the United States who briefly renders emergency medical treatment or briefly provides critical medical service at the specific lawful direction of a medical institution or federal agency that assumes full responsibility for the treatment or service;

(6) A person who has earned a doctorate degree from a recognized college or university and who uses the designation of "Dr." in connection with that person's name or calls himself or herself "Doctor", except in matters related to medicine or health, in which case the type of doctorate held must be specified;

(7) The mechanical application of glasses;

(8) The practice of massage;

(9) The business of barbering, cosmetology, and manicuring;

(10) The practice of ritual circumcision performed pursuant to the requirements or tenets of a religion; provided, however, that a person certified and registered to practice medicine in this State certifies in writing to the Board that, in the person's opinion, the circumcision practitioner has sufficient knowledge and competence to perform a ritual circumcision according to accepted medical standards;

(11) The practice of healing by spiritual means in accordance with the tenets and practice of a religion by an accredited practitioner of the religion. In the practice of healing by spiritual means, an accredited practitioner may not use medical titles or other designations which imply

or designate that the practitioner is certified to practice medicine in this State. A person engaged in the practice of healing by spiritual means may not perform surgical operations or prescribe medications, nor may a pharmacist or pharmacy honor a prescription drawn by the person. A person engaged in the practice of healing by spiritual means must observe all state and federal public health laws;

(12) A physician from another state or jurisdiction who is in this State to testify in a judicial or quasi judicial proceeding;

(13) The performing of delegated medical acts pursuant to subchapter VI of this chapter by a person who is licensed by the Board as a physician assistant;

(14) A person rendering medical, surgical, or other health services who is functioning as a member of an organized emergency program which has been approved by the Board of Medical Licensure and Discipline; who has successfully completed an emergency medical course; and who is acting under the supervision and control of a person certified and registered to practice medicine in this State or in a state contiguous to this State;

(15) A licensed registered nurse making a pronouncement of death and signing all forms or certificates registering the death as permitted or required by the State, but only if the nurse is an attending nurse caring for a terminally ill patient:

    a. In the patient's home or place of residence as part of a hospice program or a certified home healthcare agency program;

    b. In a skilled nursing facility;

    c. In a residential community associated with a skilled nursing facility;

    d. In an extended care facility; or

    e. In a hospice;

and only if the attending physician of record has agreed in writing to permit the attending licensed registered nurse to make a pronouncement of death in that case;

(16) The provisions of subchapter II, Chapter 27 of Title 16, the Uniform Anatomical Gift Act;

(17) A medical student who is engaged in training;

(18) A person performing health care acts pursuant to Chapter 94 of Title 16 and § 1921(a) of this title;

(19) Notwithstanding the provisions of § 1702(11)e. of this title, a physician licensed in another state or the District of Columbia may render a written or otherwise documented medical opinion to a person covered by the State Group Health Insurance Program pursuant to any second opinion or diagnosis evaluation program offered by the State Group Health Insurance Program without obtaining a certificate to practice medicine in this State.

History.
75 Del. Laws, c. 141, § 1; 70 Del. Laws, c. 186, § 1; 76 Del. Laws, c. 378, § 1; 77 Del. Laws, c. 319, § 1; 80 Del. Laws, c. 80, § 2; 81 Del. Laws, c. 340, § 2; 82 Del. Laws, c. 75, § 3; 83 Del. Laws, c. 52, § 5.

Revisor's note.
Based upon changes contained in 83 Del. Laws, c. 52, § 5, made effective July 1, 2021, by § 21 of that act, "§ 1702(11)" was substituted for "§ 1702(13)".

SUBCHAPTER II
THE BOARD OF MEDICAL LICENSURE AND DISCIPLINE

§ 1710. Composition.

(a) The Board of Medical Licensure and Discipline has the sole authority in this State to issue certificates to practice medicine and is the State's supervisory, regulatory, and disciplinary body for the practice of medicine. The Board also has the sole authority in this State to issue authorizing documents to practice other specified professions or occupations regulated by this chapter, and to supervise, regulate, and discipline members of those professions and occupations.

(b) The Board consists of 16 voting members appointed by the Governor, which shall be composed of the following members:

(1) Eight persons certified and registered to practice medicine in this State, at least 1 of whom is an osteopathic physician, as follows:

a. Four have their primary place of practicing medicine in New Castle County;

b. Two shall have their primary place of practicing medicine in Kent County;

c. Two shall have their primary place of practicing medicine in Sussex County.

(2) Five public members.

(3) Two physician assistants recommended by the Regulatory Council for Physician Assistants.

(4) The Director of the Division of Public Health.

(c) A public member, except a physician assistant, may not be nor may ever have been certified, licensed, or registered pursuant to this chapter; may not be the spouse of someone certified, licensed, or registered pursuant to this chapter; at the time of appointment may not be a member of the immediate family of someone certified, licensed, or registered pursuant to this chapter.

(d) The Medical Society of Delaware and the Delaware State Osteopathic Medical Society may submit lists of their resident members and any recommendations to the Governor by January 1 of each year under the seal of and signed by the Secretary of the Society to aid the Governor in the appointment of new members to the Board.

(e) An appointment to the Board to succeed a member whose term has expired shall be for a 3-year term. Vacancies occurring for any cause other than expiration of term shall be filled by the Governor for the unexpired term as provided in this subsection.

(f) A physician-appointee to the Board must be a certified and registered physician in good standing, and must have practiced medicine under the laws of this State for a period of not less than 5 years prior to the physician-appointee's appointment to the Board.

(g) The Governor shall fill vacancies on the Board and, after a hearing, may remove a member of the Board for cause due to the member's neglect of the duties required by this chapter, or on the recommendation of the Board, after a hearing, due to the member's unprofessional or dishonorable conduct.

(h) A member of the Board may not serve more than 3 full, consecutive 3-year terms, which is not diminished by serving an unexpired term. Upon serving 3 full, consecutive 3-year terms, a former member is eligible for reappointment to the Board no earlier than 1 year after the expiration of the last term served on the Board by the former member.

(i)(1) While serving on the Board, a member may not be an officer of any state or local allopathic or osteopathic medical society.

(2) While serving on the Board, a member of the Board may not be a member of the board of directors of a professional review organization.

(j) Each member of the Board shall be compensated at an appropriate and reasonable level as determined by the Division of Professional Regulation not more than $100 for each meeting attended, and not more than a total of $1,500 for meetings attended in a calendar year, and may be reimbursed for all expenses involved in each meeting, including travel, according to Division policy.

History.
60 Del. Laws, c. 462, § 1; 63 Del. Laws, c. 270, § 1; 64 Del. Laws, c. 327, § 5; 64 Del. Laws, c. 477, § 1; 67 Del. Laws, c. 226, §§ 1-4; 67 Del. Laws, c. 368, § 9; 70 Del. Laws, c. 186, § 1; 71 Del. Laws, c. 102, § 1; 71 Del. Laws, c. 105, § 1; 75 Del. Laws, c. 141, § 1; 75 Del. Laws, c. 358, § 1; 77 Del. Laws, c. 319, §§ 1-4, 12, 13; 81 Del. Laws, c. 97, § 1; 83 Del. Laws, c. 16, § 1.

Effect of amendments.
83 Del. Laws, c. 16, effective Apr. 13, 2021, rewrote the former first sentence of (b) as the present introductory paragraph containing designations for present paragraphs (b)(1)-(3); redesignated the former second sentence of (b) as present (b)(4) and deleted "shall serve as a voting member of the Board" from the end thereof; redesignated the former final sentence of (b) as present (c), adding "except a physician assistant" therein; and redesignated former (c)-(i) as present (d)-(j).

§ 1713. Powers and duties of the Board.

NOTES TO DECISIONS

Discipline.
Decision revoking a doctor's medical license and controlled substance registration was upheld because: (1) substantial evidence established that the doctor delivered controlled substances to a patient for other than a therapeutic medical purpose; and (2) the doctor's improper behavior over a 4-month period constituted a pattern of negligence in the practice of medicine. Gala v. Bullock, 250 A.3d 52 (Del. 2021).

SUBCHAPTER IV
DISCIPLINARY REGULATION; PROCEEDINGS OF THE BOARD

§ 1731. Unprofessional conduct and inability to practice medicine.

NOTES TO DECISIONS

Substantial evidence.
Decision revoking a doctor's medical license and controlled substance registration was upheld because: (1) substantial evidence established that the doctor delivered controlled substances to a patient for other than a therapeutic medical purpose; and (2) the doctor's improper behavior over a 4-month period constituted a pattern of negligence in the practice of medicine. Gala v. Bullock, 250 A.3d 52 (Del. 2021).

SUBCHAPTER V
MISCELLANEOUS PROVISIONS

§ 1768. Immunity of boards of review; confidentiality of review board record.

NOTES TO DECISIONS

Analysis

Privilege.
— Boards of review.

Privilege.

— Boards of review.
Court denied plaintiff's motion to compel discovery of a hospital-conducted peer review consideration of the outcome of a surgery because: (1) the medical peer review statute, 24 Del. C. § 1768, is directed at protecting the exchange of ideas, criticisms and comments; (2) the members of a review committee need to feel free to contribute in order to ensure that the committee's analysis is candid, rigorous and can assist the medical community in reviewing and improving the quality of its services; (3) a peer committee review is the essence of the peer

review privilege; and (4) peer review committee work should not be the commencement point for discovery. Palmer v. Christiana Care Health Servs., — A.3d —, 2021 Del. Super. LEXIS 153 (Del. Super. Ct. Feb. 22, 2021).

§ 1769D. Telemedicine and telehealth.

History.
80 Del. Laws, c. 80, § 3; 81 Del. Laws, c. 65, § 1; 82 Del. Laws, c. 261, §§ 4, 16; repealed by 83 Del. Laws, c. 52, § 6, effective July 1, 2021.

Revisor's note.
Section 1 of 83 Del. Laws, c. 52, provided: "This Act shall be known as the 'Telehealth Access Preservation and Modernization Act of 2021'."

Section 21 of 83 Del. Laws, c. 52, provided: "Sections 1-19 of this act take effect on July 1, 2021. Nothing in this act shall be interpreted as affecting or invalidating any health-care services provided through telehealth or telemedicine prior to effective date of this act."

SUBCHAPTER VI
PHYSICIAN ASSISTANTS

§ 1770. The Regulatory Council for Physician Assistants.

(a) The Regulatory Council for Physician Assistants (Council) shall consist of 7 voting members, 1 of whom is a physician member appointed by the Board, 1 of whom is a physician who regularly collaborates with physician assistants appointed by the Board, and 1 of whom is a pharmacist appointed by the Board of Pharmacy. The remaining 4 members, recommended by the Council and appointed by the Board, must be practicing physician assistants, subject to the same causes for removal as a physician member of the Board except that the requirement for certification and registration to practice medicine is replaced by licensure to practice medicine as a physician assistant. The Council may elect officers as necessary and recommend Council members to the Governor for appointment to the Board.

(b) Each Council member shall be appointed for a term of 3 years and may succeed himself or herself for 1 additional 3-year term. A person appointed to fill a vacancy on the Council is entitled to hold office for the remainder of the unexpired term of the former member. Each term of office expires on the date specified in the appointment; however, a member whose term of office has expired remains eligible to serve until replaced by the Board. A person who has never served on the Council may be appointed for 2 consecutive terms, but that person is thereafter ineligible for appointment to the Council except as hereinafter provided. A person who has twice been appointed to the Council or who has served on the Council for 6 years within any 9-year period may not again be appointed until an interim period of at least 1 year has expired since the person last served. The members of the Council are to be compensated at an appropriate and reasonable level as determined by the Division of Professional Regulation and may be reimbursed for meeting-related travel expenses at the State's approved rate. A member serving on the Council may not be an elected officer or a member of the board of directors of any professional association of physician assistants.

(c) The Council, in accordance with the Administrative Procedures Act [Chapter 101 of Title 29], shall promulgate rules and regulations governing the practice of physician assistants, subject to approval of the Board. The Board must approve or disapprove any proposed rule or regulation within 60 days of submission by the Council. If the Board fails to approve or disapprove the proposed rules or regulations within 60 days, the proposed rule or regulation is deemed approved by the Board.

(d) The Council shall meet at least on a quarterly basis and at other such times as license applications are pending. The Council shall evaluate the credentials of all applications for licensure as a physician assistant in this State, in order to determine whether the applicant meets the qualifications for licensure set forth in this chapter. The Council shall present to the Board the names of individuals qualified for licensing, shall review and consider disciplinary complaints and recommend disciplinary action against licensees as necessary, and shall suggest changes in operations or regulations.

(e) The Regulatory Council for Physicians Assistants, by the affirmative vote of 4 of its members and with the approval of the Board within 30 days of the vote, may waive the quarterly meeting requirements of this subchapter.

History.

75 Del. Laws, c. 141, § 1; 70 Del. Laws, c. 186, § 1; 77 Del. Laws, c. 319, § 1; 78 Del. Laws, c. 387, § 2; 81 Del. Laws, c. 97, § 7; 83 Del. Laws, c. 16, § 2.

Effect of amendments.

83 Del. Laws, c. 16, effective Apr. 13, 2021, in (a), substituted "collaborates with" for "supervises" in the first sentence, in the second sentence added "recommended by the Council and" and the second occurrence of "to practice medicine", and added "and recommend Council members to the Governor for appointment to the Board" in the final sentence.

§ 1770A. Physician assistants; definitions.

As used in this subchapter:

(1) "Collaborating physician" means physicians licensed by the Board who practices with a physician assistant using a Collaborative Agreement.

(2) "Collaboration" or "collaborating" means a process in which the physician who oversees patient services and the physician assistant jointly contribute to the healthcare and medical evaluation and treatment or management of patients with each performing actions he or she is individually licensed for and has the education, training, and experience to perform. The collaborating physician must be available for consultation with the physician assistant during the time of the patient encounter with the physician assistant, if necessary to provide advice on the ongoing care of the patient. The constant physical presence of the collaborating physician is not required on-site in the practice setting, provided that the collaborating physician is readily accessible by some form of electronic communication.

(3) "Collaborative agreement" means a written document expressing an arrangement of collaboration between a licensed physician and a physician assistant.

(4) "Physician assistant" or "PA" means an individual who:

a. Has graduated from a physician assistant or surgeon assistant program which is accredited by the Accreditation Review Commission on Education for the Physician Assistant (ARC-PA) or, prior to 2001, by the Committee on Allied Health Education and Accreditation (CAHEA) of the American Medical Association (AMA), or a successor agency acceptable to and approved by the Board, or has passed the Physician Assistant National Certifying Examination administered by the National Commission on Certification of Physician Assistants prior to 1986;

b. Has a baccalaureate degree or the equivalent education to a baccalaureate degree, as determined by the Council and the Board;

c. Has passed a national certifying examination acceptable to the Regulatory Council for Physician Assistants and approved by the Board;

d. Is licensed under this chapter to practice medicine as a physician assistant;

e. Has completed any continuing education credits required by rules and regulations developed under this chapter; and

f. Completes a collaborative agreement with the collaborating physician.

History.
68 Del. Laws, c. 147, § 2; 68 Del. Laws, c. 345, § 1; 69 Del. Laws, c. 355, §§ 3-5; 71 Del. Laws, c. 102, § 26; 74 Del. Laws, c. 262, § 30A; 75 Del. Laws, c. 141, § 1; 78 Del. Laws, c. 387, § 2; 83 Del. Laws, c. 16, § 2.

Effect of amendments.
83 Del. Laws, c. 16, effective Apr. 13, 2021,

repealed former (1), added present (1) and (3), and redesignated former (2) and (3) as present (4) and (2), respectively; rewrote present (2); added "medicine" in present (4)d.; added (4)f. and made related stylistic changes.

§ 1771. Physician's role in collaborating with a physician assistant.

(a) A physician who collaborates with a physician assistant must be available for consultation with the physician assistant. It is the obligation of each team of physician(s) and physician assistant(s) to ensure that the physician assistant's scope of practice is identified, and is appropriate to the physician assistant's level of education, training, and experience, that the relationship of, and access to, the collaborating physician is defined, and that a process for evaluation of the physician assistant's performance is established.

(b) Each physician-physician assistant team, hospital, clinic, medical group, or other healthcare facility shall be responsible for creating a written collaborative agreement, which shall be kept on file at the primary location where the physician assistant provides care, describing the information required by subsection (a) of this section. The written collaborative agreement shall be made available to the Board or the Council upon request.

(c) [Repealed.]

(d) A collaborating physician may not be involved in patient care in name only and must be involved in active patient care on a regular basis.

(e) A collaborating physician may not assign medical acts to a physician assistant that exceed the physician's license.

(f) A collaborating physician may not at any given time collaborate with more than 4 physician assistants, unless a regulation of the Board increases or decreases the number. This limit does not apply to physicians and physician assistants who practice in the same physical office or facility building, such as an emergency department so long as there is active, physician coverage.

(g) A physician who collaborates with a physician assistant in violation of the provisions of this subchapter or of regulations adopted pursuant to this subchapter is subject to disciplinary action by the Board of Medical Licensure and Discipline for permitting the unauthorized practice of medicine.

(h) Hospitals, clinics, medical groups and other healthcare facilities may employ physician assistants subject to subsection (f) of this section.

(i) If the collaborating physician is not routinely present the physician must assure that the means and methods of collaboration are adequate to assure appropriate patient care. This may include telecommunication, chart review, or other methods of communication and oversight that are appropriate to the care setting and the education, training and experience of the physician assistant.

History.
75 Del. Laws, c. 141, § 1; 70 Del. Laws, c. 186, § 1; 77 Del. Laws, c. 319, § 1; 78 Del. Laws, c. 387, § 2; 83 Del. Laws, c. 16, § 2.

Effect of amendments.
83 Del. Laws, c. 16, effective Apr. 13, 2021, in the section heading, substituted "role in collaborating with" for "duties in supervision of"; rewrote (a); added "collaborative" in the first and second sentences of (b); repealed (c); and, in

(d), substituted "A collaborating" for "Supervising" and added "and must be involved in active patient care on a regular basis"; substituted "collaborating" for "supervising" in (e) and in the first sentence of (f); in (e), substituted "assign" for "delegate" and "license" for "scope of practice"; in (f), substituted "collaborate with" for "supervise" in the first sentence and added the second sentence; substituted "collaborates with" for "supervises" in (g); rewrote (h); and, in (i), in the first sentence substituted "the collaborating" for "the supervising physician delegates the authority to a physician assistant to treat patients in a setting where the supervising" and "collaboration" for "supervision", and deleted the former third and fourth sentences.

§ 1772. Prohibited acts by a physician assistant.

(a) A physician assistant may not maintain or manage a location that does not have oversight by the physician assistant's collaborating physician.

(b)-(d) [Repealed.]

(e) Nothing in this chapter may be construed to authorize a physician assistant to practice independent of a collaborating physician.

(f) Except as otherwise provided in this chapter or in a medical emergency, a physician assistant may not perform any medical act without a collaborative agreement.

(g) A physician assistant may not practice as a member of any other health profession regulated under this code unless the physician assistant is certified, licensed, registered, or otherwise authorized to practice the other profession.

History.

75 Del. Laws, c. 141, § 1; 70 Del. Laws, c. 186, § 1; 78 Del. Laws, c. 387, § 2; 83 Del. Laws, c. 16, § 2.

Effect of amendments.

83 Del. Laws, c. 16, effective Apr. 13, 2021, substituted "collaborating" for "supervising" in (a) and (e); substituted "a location that does not have oversight by the" for "an office separate and apart from the office of the" in (a); repealed (b)-(d); and substituted "without a collaborative agreement" for "which has not been delegated by a supervising physician" in (f).

§ 1773. Regulation of physician assistants.

(a) The Council shall adopt rules and regulations which address the following:

    (1) The licensing of physician assistants to allow:

        a. The practice of medicine within the education, training, and experience of physician assistants; and

        b. The performance of medical services customary to the practice of the collaborating physician;

    (2) Medical acts provided by physician assistants to include:

        a. The performance of complete patient histories and physical examinations;

        b. The recording of patient progress notes in an in-patient or out-patient setting;

        c. The ordering, relaying, transcribing, or executing of specific diagnostic or therapeutic orders or procedures;

        d. Medical acts of diagnosis and prescription of therapeutic drugs and treatments; and referral of patients to specialists as needed;

        e. Prescriptive authority for therapeutic drugs and treatments within the scope of physician assistant practice. The physician assistant's prescriptive authority and authority to practice as a physician assistant are subject to biennial renewal upon application to the Physician Assistant Regulatory Council; and

        f. The use of telemedicine as defined in this chapter and, as further described in regulation, the use of and participation in telehealth.

    (b)(1) The Board, in conjunction with the Regulatory Council for Physician Assistants, shall suspend, revoke, or restrict the license of a physician assistant or take disciplinary action or other action against a physician assistant for engaging in unprofessional conduct as defined in § 1731(b) of this title; or for the inability to render medical acts with reasonable skill or safety to patients because of the physician assistant's physical, mental, or emotional illness or incompetence, including but not limited to: deterioration through the aging process, or loss of motor skills, or excessive use of drugs, including alcohol; or for representing himself or herself as a physician, or for knowingly allowing himself or herself to be represented as a physician; for failing to report in writing to the Board within 30 days of becoming aware of any physician, physician assistant, or healthcare provider who the licensee reasonably believes has engaged in unprofessional conduct as defined in § 1731(b) of this title or is unable to act with reasonable skill or safety to patients because of the physician's, physician assistant's, or other healthcare provider's physical, mental, or emotional illness or incompetence, including but not limited to deterioration through the aging process, or loss of motor skills, or excessive use of drugs, including alcohol for failing to report child abuse and neglect as required by § 903 of Title 16. The license of any physician assistant who is convicted of a felony sexual offense shall be revoked. Disciplinary action or other action undertaken against a physician assistant must be in accordance with the procedures, including appeal procedures, applicable to disciplinary actions against physicians pursuant to subchapter IV of this chapter, except that a hearing panel for a complaint against a physician assistant consists of 3 unbiased members of the Regulatory Council, the 3 members being 2 physician assistant members and 1 physician or pharmacist member if practicable.

A person reporting or testifying in any proceeding as a result of making a report pursuant to this section is immune from claim, suit, liability, damages, or any other recourse, civil or criminal, so long as the person acted in good faith and without gross or wanton negligence; good faith being presumed until proven otherwise, and gross or wanton negligence required to be shown by the complainant.

(2)a. If the Board or the Regulatory Council for Physician Assistants receives a formal or informal complaint concerning the activity of a physician assistant and the Regulatory Council members reasonably believe that the activity presents a clear and immediate danger to the public health, the Regulatory Council may issue an order temporarily suspending the physician assistant's license to practice pending a hearing upon the written order of the Secretary of State or the Secretary's designee, with the concurrence of the Council Chair or the Chair's designee. An order temporarily suspending a license to practice may not be issued by the Council unless the physician assistant or the physician assistant's attorney received at least 24 hours' written or oral notice prior to the temporary suspension so that the physician assistant or the physician assistant's attorney can be heard in opposition to the proposed suspension. An order of temporary suspension pending a hearing may remain in effect for no longer than 60 days from the date of the issuance of the order unless the temporarily suspended physician assistant requests a continuance of the hearing date. If the physician assistant requests a continuance, the order of temporary suspension remains in effect until the hearing panel convenes and a decision is rendered.

b. A physician assistant whose license to practice has been temporarily suspended pursuant to this section must be notified of the temporary suspension immediately and in writing. Notification consists of a copy of the complaint and the order of temporary suspension pending a hearing personally served upon the physician assistant or sent by certified mail, return receipt requested, to the physician assistant's last known address.

c. A physician assistant whose license to practice has been temporarily suspended pursuant to this section may request an expedited hearing. The Council shall schedule the hearing on an expedited basis, provided that the Council receives the request within 5 calendar days from the date on which the physician assistant received notification of the decision of the Council, with the approval of the Board, to temporarily suspend the physician assistant's license to practice.

d. As soon as possible after the issuance of an order temporarily suspending a physician assistant's license to practice pending a hearing, the Executive Director shall appoint a 3-member hearing panel. After notice to the physician assistant pursuant to subsection (b) of this section, the hearing panel shall convene within 60 days of the date of the issuance of the order of temporary suspension to consider the evidence regarding the matters alleged in the complaint. If the physician assistant requests in a timely manner an expedited hearing, the hearing panel shall convene within 15 days of the receipt of the request by the Council. The 3-member panel shall proceed to a hearing and shall render a decision within 30 days of the hearing.

e. In addition to making findings of fact, the hearing panel shall also determine whether the facts found by it constitute a clear and immediate danger to public health. If the hearing panel determines that the facts found constitute a clear and immediate danger to public health, the order of temporary suspension must remain in effect until the Board deliberates and reaches conclusions of law based upon the findings of fact made by the hearing panel. An order of temporary suspension may not remain in effect for longer than 60 days from the date of the decision rendered by the hearing panel unless the suspended physician assistant requests an extension of the order pending a final decision of the Board. Upon the final decision of the Board, an order of temporary suspension is vacated as a matter of law and is replaced by the disciplinary action, if any, ordered by the Board.

History.

75 Del. Laws, c. 141, § 1; 70 Del. Laws, c. 186, § 1; 77 Del. Laws, c. 319, § 1; 77 Del. Laws, c. 325, § 19; 78 Del. Laws, c. 149; 78 Del. Laws, c. 387, § 2; 80 Del. Laws, c. 80, § 4; 81 Del. Laws, c. 97, § 8; 83 Del. Laws, c. 16, § 2.

Effect of amendments.

83 Del. Laws, c. 16, effective Apr. 13, 2021, substituted "practice of medicine" for "performance of delegated medical acts" in (a)(1)a.; in (a)(1)b., added "medical" and substituted "collaborating" for "supervising"; in the introductory paragraph of (a)(2), deleted "Delegated" from the beginning and "but not limited to" from the end; substituted "in-patient or outpatient" for "outpatient" in (a)(2)b.; in (a)(2)c., added "ordering" and "or procedures"; substituted "and referral of patients to specialists as needed" for "which have been delegated by the supervising physician" in (a)(2)d.; deleted "as delegated by the supervising physician" from the end of the first sentence in (a)(2)e.; and deleted "delegated" following "render" in the first sentence of the first paragraph of (b)(1).

§ 1773A. Participation in disaster or emergency care.

(a) A physician assistant licensed in this State or licensed or authorized to practice in any other U.S. jurisdiction or credentialed as a physician assistant by a federal employer who is responding to a need for medical care created by an emergency or a state or local disaster (excluding an emergency which occurs in that person's place of employment or practice) may render such care that the physician assistant is able to provide without collaboration pursuant to § 1770A of this title or with such collaboration as is available.

(b) Any physician who collaborates with a physician assistant providing medical care in response to such an emergency or state or local disaster shall not be required to meet the requirements set forth in this subchapter for a collaborating physician.

(c) A person licensed as a physician assistant under this chapter who, in good faith and without gross or wanton negligence, renders emergency care at the scene of an emergency, excluding an emergency which occurs in that person's place of employment or practice, shall not be liable for civil damages as a result of any acts or omissions in rendering the emergency care.

History.
78 Del. Laws, c. 387, § 2; 70 Del. Laws, c. 186, § 1; 83 Del. Laws, c. 16, § 2.

Effect of amendments.
83 Del. Laws, c. 16, effective Apr. 13, 2021, in (a), substituted "the physician assistant" for "he or she" and "collaboration" for "supervision" in two places; and, in (b), substituted "collaborates with" for "supervises" and "collaborating" for "supervising".

§ 1774. Temporary licensing of physician assistants.

(a) Notwithstanding any provision of this subchapter to the contrary, the Executive Director, with the approval of a Council member, may grant a temporary license to an individual who has graduated from a physician or surgeon assistant program which has been accredited by the Accreditation Review Commission on Education for the Physician Assistant (ARC-PA) or, prior to 2001, by the Committee on Allied Health Education and Accreditation (CAHEA) of the American Medical Association (AMA) or a successor agency and who otherwise meets the qualifications for licensure but who has not yet taken a national certifying examination, provided that the individual is registered to take and takes the next scheduled national certifying examination. A temporary license granted pursuant to this subsection is valid until the results of the examination are available from the certifying agency. If the individual fails to pass the national certifying examination, the temporary license granted pursuant to this subsection must be immediately rescinded until the individual successfully qualifies for licensure pursuant to this subchapter.

(b) An individual who is temporarily licensed pursuant to this section may not have a prescriptive practice and may not perform medical acts except in the physical presence of the individual's collaborating physician.

History.
75 Del. Laws, c. 141, § 1; 70 Del. Laws, c. 186, § 1; 78 Del. Laws, c. 387, § 2; 81 Del. Laws, c. 97, § 9; 83 Del. Laws, c. 16, § 2.

Effect of amendments.
83 Del. Laws, c. 16, effective Apr. 13, 2021, in (b), deleted "delegated" following "perform" and substituted "collaborating" for "supervising".

§ 1774D. Inactive license; return to clinical practice.

(a) Any physician assistant who notifies the Board in writing on forms prescribed by the Board may elect to place his or her license on inactive status. A physician assistant whose license is inactive shall be excused from payment of renewal fees and shall not practice as a physician assistant. Any licensee who engages in practice while his or her license is inactive shall be considered to be practicing without a license, which shall be grounds for discipline under § 1774B of this title. A physician assistant whose license has been inactive for 3 years or less may reactivate the license by paying the renewal fee pursuant to § 1774A of this title and meeting the requirements for ordinary license renewal as determined by the Board.

(b) If a physician assistant whose license has been on inactive status for in excess of 3 years and who has not practiced as a physician assistant in any jurisdiction of the United States for over 3 years requests to reactivate the license, the Board may grant a re-entry license and may, after consultation with the Council, impose additional practice and collaboration requirements for the re-entry license. A re-entry license granted under this subsection shall be valid for no longer than 6 months and may be renewed only once at the

Board's discretion. In the month immediately preceding the month during which the re-entry license will expire, a physician assistant may apply to the Board for a full license as a physician assistant. The Board shall grant a full license to a physician assistant who meets all qualifications for licensure and whom the Board determines is qualified to practice. If the Board determines that a physician assistant is still not qualified to receive a full license at the conclusion of the re-entry license period, the Board may only once renew the re-entry license. If the Board elects to renew a re-entry license instead of issuing a full license, the Board shall provide to the physician assistant a written explanation for that decision when issuing the renewed re-entry license.

Additional practice requirements that the Board may choose to impose as a condition of a re-entry license may include:

(1) Requiring the collaborating physician to be physically on-site while the physician assistant is practicing;

(2) Requiring the collaborating physician to review and countersign a portion of patient charts for patients seen by the physician assistant;

(3) Requiring the physician assistant to possess current certification from the NCCPA;

(4) Requiring the physician assistant to take a review course or to complete a specified amount of Category 1 CME, as determined by the Council and agreed upon by the Board as appropriate; and

(5) Requiring documentation of a specific minimum number of clinical practice hours performed under the re-entry license.

(c) The above subsection (b) of this section shall also apply to a physician assistant who has not placed his or her license on inactive status in this State but who has previously practiced as a physician assistant in another jurisdiction of the United States and has not actively engaged in clinical practice for a period in excess of 3 years immediately prior to applying for a license under this subchapter.

History.
78 Del. Laws, c. 387, § 2; 70 Del. Laws, c. 186, § 1; 83 Del. Laws, c. 16, § 2.

Effect of amendments.
83 Del. Laws, c. 16, effective Apr. 13, 2021, in (b), in the first sentence of the first paragraph substituted "the" for "his or her" following "reactivate" and "collaboration" for "supervision" and, transferred the former second paragraph to be the third through sixth sentences of the first paragraph; and substituted "collaborating" for "supervising" in (b)(1) and (2).

§ 1774E. Participation in charitable and voluntary care.

A physician assistant licensed in this State, or licensed or authorized to practice in any other U.S. jurisdiction, or who is credentialed by a federal employer or meets the licensure requirements of their requisite federal agency as a physician assistant may volunteer to render such medical care the physician assistant is able to provide at public or community events and facilities without a collaborating physician as defined in this chapter or with such collaborating physicians as may be available. Such medical care must be rendered without compensation or remuneration.

History.
83 Del. Laws, c. 16, § 2.

Revisor's note.
This section became effective upon the signature of the Governor on Apr. 13, 2021.

CHAPTER 17A

INTERSTATE MEDICAL LICENSURE COMPACT [EFFECTIVE JULY 1, 2022].

Revisor's note.

Section 1 of 83 Del. Laws, c. 52, provided: "This Act shall be known as the 'Telehealth Access Preservation and Modernization Act of 2021'."

Section 21 of 83 Del. Laws, c. 52, provided: "Section 20 of this act, entering the State of Delaware into the Interstate Medical Licensure Compact, shall take effect on July 1, 2022. Nothing in this act shall be interpreted as affecting or invalidating any health-care services provided through telehealth or telemedicine prior to effective date of this act."

§ 1701A. Interstate Medical Licensure Compact; findings and declaration of purpose [Effective July 1, 2022].

(a) The State hereby enters into the Interstate Medical Licensure Compact (IMLC) the text of which is as set forth in this chapter.

(b) In order to strengthen access to health care, and in recognition of the advances in the delivery of health care, the member states of the Interstate Medical Licensure Compact have allied in common purpose to develop a comprehensive process that complements the existing licensing and regulatory authority of state medical boards, provides a streamlined process that allows physicians to become licensed in multiple states, thereby enhancing the portability of a medical license and ensuring the safety of patients. The Compact creates another pathway for licensure and does not otherwise change a state's existing Medical Practice Act. The Compact also adopts the prevailing standard for licensure and affirms that the practice of medicine occurs where the patient is located at the time of the physician-patient encounter, and therefore, requires the physician to be under the jurisdiction of the state medical board where the patient is located. State medical boards that participate in the Compact retain the jurisdiction to impose an adverse action against a license to practice medicine in that state issued to a physician through the procedures in the Compact.

History.
83 Del. Laws, c. 52, § 20.

§ 1702A. Definitions [Effective July 1, 2022].

In this compact:

(a) "Bylaws" means those bylaws established by the Interstate Commission pursuant to § 1714A.

(b) "Commissioner" means the voting representative appointed by each member board pursuant to § 1711A.

(c) "Conviction" means a finding by a court that an individual is guilty of a criminal offense through adjudication, or entry of a plea of guilt or no contest to the charge by the offender. Evidence of an entry of a conviction of a criminal offense by the court shall be considered final for purposes of disciplinary action by a member board.

(d) "Expedited license" means a full and unrestricted medical license granted by a member state to an eligible physician through the process set forth in the Compact.

(e) "Interstate Commission" means the interstate commission created pursuant to § 1711A of this title.

(f) "License" means authorization by a member state for a physician to engage in the practice of medicine, which would be unlawful without authorization.

(g) "Medical Practice Act" [Chapter 17 of this title in Delaware] means laws and regulations governing the practice of allopathic and osteopathic medicine within a member state.

(h) "Member board" means a state agency in a member state that acts in the sovereign interests of the state by protecting the public through licensure, regulation, and education of physicians as directed by the state government.

(i) "Member state" means a state that has enacted the Compact.

(j) "Practice of medicine" means that clinical prevention, diagnosis, or treatment of human disease, injury, or condition requiring a physician to obtain and maintain a license in compliance with the Medical Practice Act of a member state.

(k) "Physician" means any person who:

(1) Is a graduate of a medical school accredited by the Liaison Committee on Medical Education, the Commission on Osteopathic College Accreditation, or a medical school listed in the International Medical Education Directory or its equivalent.

(2) Passed each component of the United State Medical Licensing Examination (USMLE) or the Comprehensive Osteopathic Medical Licensing Examination (COMLEX-USA) within 3 attempts, or any of its predecessor examinations accepted by a state medical board as an equivalent examination for licensure purposes.

(3) Successfully completed graduate medical education approved by the Accreditation Council for Graduate Medical Education or the American Osteopathic Association.

(4) Holds specialty certification or a time-unlimited specialty certificate recognized by the American Board of Medical Specialties or the American Osteopathic Association's Bureau of Osteopathic Specialists.

(5) Possesses a full and unrestricted license to engage in the practice of medicine issued by a member board.

(6) Has never been convicted, received adjudication, deferred adjudication, community supervision, or deferred disposition for any offense by a court of appropriate jurisdiction.

(7) Has never held a license authorizing the practice of medicine subjected to discipline by a licensing agency in any state, federal, or

foreign jurisdiction, excluding any action related to nonpayment of fees related to a license.

(8) Has never had a controlled substance license or permit suspended or revoked by a state or the United States Drug Enforcement Administration.

(9) Is not under active investigation by a licensing agency or law-enforcement authority in any state, federal, or foreign jurisdiction.

(*l*) "Offense" means a felony, gross misdemeanor, or crime of moral turpitude.

(m) "Rule" means a written statement by the Interstate Commission promulgated pursuant to § 1712A of this title that is of general applicability, implements, interprets, or prescribes a policy or provision of the Compact, or an organizational, procedural, or practice requirement of the Interstate Commission, and has the force and effect of statutory law in a member state, and includes the amendment, repeal, or suspension of an existing rule.

(n) "State" means any state, commonwealth, district, or territory of the United States.

(o) "State of principal license" means a member state where a physician holds a license to practice medicine and which has been designated as such by the physician for purposes of registration and participation in the Compact.

History.
83 Del. Laws, c. 52, § 20.

§ 1703A. Eligibility [Effective July 1, 2022].

(a) A physician must meet the eligibility requirements as defined in § 1702A(k) of this title to receive an expedited license under the terms and provisions of the Compact.

(b) A physician who does not meet the requirements of § 1702A(k) of this title may obtain a license to practice medicine in a member state if the individual complies with all laws and requirements, other than the Compact, relating to the issuance of a license to practice medicine in that state.

History.
83 Del. Laws, c. 52, § 20.

§ 1704A. Designation of state of principal license [Effective July 1, 2022].

(a) A physician shall designate a member state as the state of principal license for purposes of registration for expedited licensure through the Compact if the physician possesses a full and unrestricted license to practice medicine in that state, and the state is any of the following:

(1) The state of principal residence for the physician.

(2) The state where at least 25% of the practice of medicine occurs.

(3) The location of the physician's employer.

(4) If no state qualifies under paragraph (a)(1), (a)(2), or (a)(3) of this section the state designated as state of residence for purpose of federal income tax.

(b) A physician may re-designate a member state as state of principal license at any time, as long as the state meets the requirements of subsection (a) of this section.

(c) The Interstate Commission is authorized to develop rules to facilitate re-designation of another member state as the state of principal license.

History.
83 Del. Laws, c. 52, § 20.

§ 1705A. Application and issuance of expedited licensure [Effective July 1, 2022].

(a) A physician seeking licensure through the Compact shall file an application for an expedited license with the member board of the state selected by the physician as the state of principal license.

(b) Upon receipt of an application for an expedited license, the member board within the state selected as the state of principal license shall evaluate whether the physician is eligible for expedited licensure and issue a letter of qualification, verifying or denying the physician's eligibility, to the Interstate Commission.

(1) Static qualifications, which include verification of medical education, graduate medical education, results of any medical or licensing examination, and other qualifications as determined by the Interstate Commission through rule, shall not be subject to additional primary source verification where already primary source verified by the state of principal license.

(2) The member board within the state selected as the state of principal license shall, in the course of verifying eligibility, perform a criminal background check of an applicant, including the use of the results of fingerprint or other biometric data checks compliant with the requirements of the Federal Bureau of Investigation, with the exception of federal employees who have suitability determination in accordance with 5 C.F.R. § 731.202.

(3) Appeal on the determination of eligibility shall be made to the member state where the application was filed and shall be subject to the law of that state.

(c) Upon verification in subsection (b) of this section, physicians eligible for an expedited license shall complete the registration process established by the Interstate Commission to receive a license in a member state selected pursuant to subsection (a) of this section, including the payment of any applicable fees.

(d) After receiving verification of eligibility under subsection (b) of this section and any fees under subsection (c) of this section, a member board shall issue an expedited license to the physician. This license shall authorize the physician to practice medicine in the issuing state consistent with the Medical Practice Act and all applicable laws and regulations of the issuing member board and member state.

(e) An expedited license shall be valid for a period consistent with the licensure period in the member state and in the same manner as required for other physicians holding a full and unrestricted license within the member state.

(f) An expedited license obtained through the Compact shall be terminated if a physician fails to maintain a license in the state of principal licensure for a non-disciplinary reason, without re-designation of a new state of principal licensure.

(g) The Interstate Commission is authorized to develop rules regarding the application process, including payment of any applicable fees, and the issuance of an expedited license.

History.
83 Del. Laws, c. 52, § 20.

§ 1706A. Fees for expedited licensure [Effective July 1, 2022].

(a) A member state issuing an expedited license authorizing the practice of medicine in that state may impose a fee for a license issued or renewed through the Compact.

(b) The Interstate Commission is authorized to develop rules regarding fees for expedited licenses.

History.
83 Del. Laws, c. 52, § 20.

§ 1707A. Renewal and continued participation [Effective July 1, 2022].

(a) A physician seeking to renew an expedited license granted in a member state shall complete a renewal process with the Interstate Commission if the physician:

(1) Maintains a full and unrestricted license in a state of principal license.

(2) Has not been convicted, received adjudication, deferred adjudication, community supervision, or deferred disposition for any offense by a court of appropriate jurisdiction.

(3) Has not had a license authorizing the practice of medicine subject to discipline by a licensing agency in any state, federal, or foreign jurisdiction, excluding any action related to non-payment of fees related to a license.

(4) Has not had a controlled substance license or permit suspended or revoked by a state or the United States Drug Enforcement Administration.

(b) Physicians shall comply with all continuing professional development or continuing medical education requirements for renewal of a license issued by a member state.

(c) The Interstate Commission shall collect any renewal fees charged for the renewal of a license and distribute the fees to the applicable member board.

(d) Upon receipt of any renewal fees collected in subsection (c) of this section, a member board shall renew the physician's license.

(e) Physician information collected by the Interstate Commission during the renewal process will be distributed to all member boards.

(f) The Interstate Commission is authorized to develop rules to address renewal of licenses obtained through the Compact.

History.
83 Del. Laws, c. 52, § 20.

§ 1708A. Coordinated information system [Effective July 1, 2022].

(a) The Interstate Commission shall establish a database of all physicians licensed, or who have applied for licensure, under § 1705A of this title.

(b) Notwithstanding any other provision of law, member boards shall report to the Interstate Commission any public action or complaints against a licensed physician who has applied or received an expedited license through the Compact.

(c) Member boards shall report disciplinary or investigatory information determined as necessary and proper by rule of the Interstate Commission.

(d) Member boards may report any nonpublic complaint, disciplinary, or investigatory information not required by subsection (c) to the Interstate Commission.

(e) Member boards shall share complaint or disciplinary information about a physician upon request of another member board.

(f) All information provided to the Interstate Commission or distributed by member boards shall be confidential, filed under seal, and used only for investigatory or disciplinary matters.

(g) The Interstate Commission is authorized to develop rules for mandated or discretionary sharing of information by member boards.

History.
83 Del. Laws, c. 52, § 20.

§ 1709A. Joint investigations [Effective July 1, 2022].

(a) Licensure and disciplinary records of physicians are deemed investigative.

(b) In addition to the authority granted to a member board by its respective Medical Practice Act or other applicable state law, a member board may participate with other member boards in joint investigations of physicians licensed by the member boards.

(c) A subpoena issued by a member state shall be enforceable in other member states.

(d) Member boards may share any investigative, litigation, or compliance materials in furtherance of any joint or individual investigation initiated under the Compact.

(e) Any member state may investigate actual or alleged violations of the statutes authorizing the practice of medicine in any other member state in which a physician holds a license to practice medicine.

History.
83 Del. Laws, c. 52, § 20.

§ 1710A. Disciplinary actions [Effective July 1, 2022].

(a) Any disciplinary action taken by any member board against a physician licensed through the Compact shall be deemed unprofessional conduct which may be subject to discipline by other member boards, in addition to any violation of the Medical Practice Act or regulations in that state.

(b) If a license granted to a physician by the member board in the state of principal license is revoked, surrendered or relinquished in lieu of discipline, or suspended, then all licenses issued to the physician by member boards shall automatically be placed, without further action necessary by any member board, on the same status. If the member board in the state of principal license subsequently reinstates the physician's license, a license issued to the physician by any other member board shall remain encumbered until that respective member board takes action to reinstate the license in a manner consistent with the Medical Practice Act of that state.

(c) If disciplinary action is taken against a physician by a member board not in the state of principal license, any other member board may deem the action conclusive as to matter of law and fact decided, and may:

(1) Impose the same or lesser sanction(s) against the physician so long as such sanctions are consistent with the Medical Practice Act of that state.

(2) Pursue separate disciplinary action against the physician under its respective Medical Practice Act, regardless of the action taken in other member states.

(d) If a license granted to a physician by a member board is revoked, surrendered or relinquished in lieu of discipline, or suspended, then any license issued to the physician by any other member board shall be suspended, automatically and immediately without further action necessary by the other member board, for 90 days upon entry of the order by the disciplining board, to permit the member board to investigate the basis for the action under the Medical Practice Act of that state. A member board may terminate the automatic suspension of the license it issued prior to the completion of the 90 day suspension period in a manner consistent with the Medical Practice Act of that state.

History.
  83 Del. Laws, c. 52, § 20.

§ 1711A. Interstate Medical Licensure Compact Commission [Effective July 1, 2022].

(a) The member states hereby create the "Interstate Medical Licensure Compact Commission".

(b) The purpose of the Interstate Commission is the administration of the Interstate Medical Licensure Compact, which is a discretionary state function.

(c) The Interstate Commission shall be a body corporate and joint agency of the member states and shall have all the responsibilities, powers, and duties set forth in the Compact, and such additional powers as may be conferred upon it by a subsequent concurrent action of the respective legislatures of the member states in accordance with the terms of the Compact.

(d) The Interstate Commission shall consist of 2 voting representatives appointed by each member state who shall serve as Commissioners. In states where allopathic and osteopathic physicians are regulated by separate member boards, or if the licensing and disciplinary authority is split between separate member boards, or if the licensing and disciplinary authority is split between multiple member boards within a member state, the member state shall appoint 1 representative from each member board. A Commissioner shall be any of the following:

  (1) An allopathic or osteopathic physician appointed to a member board.

  (2) An executive director, executive secretary, or similar executive of a member board.

  (3) A member of the public appointed to a member board.

(e) The Interstate Commission shall meet at least once each calendar year. A portion of this meeting shall be a business meeting to address such matters as may properly come before the Commission, including the election of officers. The chairperson may call additional meetings and shall call for a meeting upon the request of a majority of the member states.

(f) The bylaws may provide for meetings of the Interstate Commission to be conducted by telecommunication or electronic communication.

(g) Each Commissioner participating at a meeting of the Interstate Commission is entitled to 1 vote. A majority of Commissioners shall constitute a quorum for the transaction of business, unless a larger quorum is required by the bylaws of the Interstate Commission. A Commission shall not delegate a vote to another Commissioner. In the absence of its Commissioner, a member state may delegate voting authority for a specified meeting to another person from that state who shall meet the requirements of subsection (d) of this section.

(h) The Interstate Commission shall provide public notice of all meetings and all meetings shall be open to the public. The Interstate Commission may close a meeting, in full or in portion, where it determines by a ⅔ vote of the Commissioners present that an open meeting would be likely to:

  (1) Relate solely to the internal personnel practice and procedures of the Interstate Commission.

  (2) Discuss matters specifically exempted from disclosure by federal statute.

  (3) Discuss trade secrets, commercial, or financial information that is privileged or confidential.

(4) Involve accusing a person of a crime, or formally censuring a person.

(5) Discuss information of a personal nature where disclosure would constitute a clearly unwarranted invasion of personal privacy.

(6) Discuss investigative records compiled for law-enforcement purposes.

(7) Specifically relate to the participation in a civil action or other legal proceeding.

(i) The Interstate Commission shall keep minutes which shall fully describe all matters discussed in a meeting and shall provide a full and accurate summary of actions taken, including record of any roll call votes.

(j) The Interstate Commission shall make its information and official records, to the extent not otherwise designated in the Compact or by its rules, available to the public for inspection.

(k) The Interstate Commission shall establish an executive committee, which shall include officers, members, and others as determined by the bylaws. The executive committee shall have the power to act on behalf of the Interstate Commission, with the exception of rulemaking, during periods when the Interstate Commission is not in session. When acting on behalf of the Interstate Commission, the executive committee shall oversee the administration of the Compact including enforcement and compliance with the provisions of the Compact, its bylaws and rules, and other such duties as necessary.

(*l*) The Interstate Commission shall establish other committees for governance and administration of the Compact.

History.
83 Del. Laws, c. 52, § 20.

§ 1712A. Powers and duties of the Interstate Commission [Effective July 1, 2022].

The Interstate Commission shall have the following powers and duties:

(a) Oversee and maintain the administration of the Compact.

(b) Promulgate rules which shall be binding to the extent and in the manner provided for in the Compact.

(c) Issue, upon the request of a member state or member board, advisory opinions concerning the meaning or interpretation of the Compact, its bylaws, rules, and actions.

(d) Enforce compliance with Compact provisions, the rules promulgated by the Interstate Commission, and the bylaws, using all necessary and proper means, including but not limited to the use of judicial process.

(e) Establish and appoint committees including an executive committee as required by § 1711A(k) of this title, which shall have the power to act on behalf of the Interstate Commission in carrying out its powers and duties.

(f) Pay, or provide for the payment of the expenses related to the establishment, organization, and ongoing activities of the Interstate Commission.

(g) Establish and maintain one or more offices.

(h) Borrow, accept, hire, or contract for services of personnel.

(i) Purchase and maintain insurance and bonds.

(j) Employ an executive director who shall have such powers to employ, select or appoint employees, agents, or consultants, and to determine their qualifications, define their duties, and fix their compensation.

(k) Establish personnel policies and programs relating to conflicts of interest, rates of compensation, and qualifications of personnel.

(*l*) Accept donations and grants of money, equipment, supplies, materials, and services and to receive, utilize, and dispose of it in a manner consistent with the conflict of interest policies established by the Interstate Commission.

(m) Lease, purchase, accept contributions or donations of, or otherwise to own, hold, improve or use, any property, real, personal, or mixed.

(n) Sell, convey, mortgage, pledge, lease, exchange, abandon, or otherwise dispose of any property, real, personal, or mixed.

(o) Establish a budget and make expenditures.

(p) Adopt a seal and bylaws governing the management and operation of the Interstate Commission.

(q) Report annually to the legislatures and governors of the member states concerning the activities of the Interstate Commission during the preceding year. Such reports shall also include reports of financial audits and any recommendations that may have been adopted by the Interstate Commission.

(r) Coordinate education, training, and public awareness regarding the Compact, its implementation, and its operation.

(s) Maintain records in accordance with the bylaws.

(t) Seek and obtain trademarks, copyrights, and patents.

(u) Perform such functions as may be necessary or appropriate to achieve the purpose of the Compact.

History.
83 Del. Laws, c. 52, § 20.

§ 1713A. Finance powers [Effective July 1, 2022].

(a) The Interstate Commission may levy on and collect an annual assessment from each member state to cover the cost of the operations and activities of the Interstate Commission and its staff. The total assessment must be sufficient to cover the annual budget approved each year for which revenue is not provided by other sources.

(b) The aggregate annual assessment amount shall be allocated upon a formula to be determined by the Interstate Commission, which shall promulgate a rule binding upon all member states.

(c) The Interstate Commission shall not pledge the credit of any of the member states, except by, and with the authority of, the member state.

(d) The Interstate Commission shall be subject to a yearly financial audit conducted by a certified or licensed accountant and the report of the audit shall be included in the annual report of the Interstate Commission.

History.
83 Del. Laws, c. 52, § 20.

§ 1714A. Organization and operation of the Interstate Commission [Effective July 1, 2022].

(a) The Interstate Commission shall, by a majority of Commissioners present and voting, adopt bylaws to govern its conduct as may be necessary or appropriate to carry out the purposes of the Compact within 12 months of the first Interstate Commission meeting.

(b) The Interstate Commission shall elect or appoint annually from among its Commissioners a chairperson, a vice-chairperson, and a treasurer, each of whom shall have such authority and duties as may be specified in the bylaws. The chairperson, or in the chairperson's absence or disability, the vice-chairperson, shall preside at all meetings of the Interstate Commission.

(c) Officers selected under subsection (b) of this section shall serve without remuneration from the Interstate Commission. The officers and employees of the Interstate Commission shall be immune from suit and liability, either personally or in their official capacity, for a claim for damage to or loss of property or personal injury or other civil liability caused or arising out of, or relating to, an actual or alleged act, error, or omission that occurred, or that such person had a reasonable basis for believing occurred, within the scope of Interstate Commission employment, duties, or responsibilities; provided that such person shall not be protected from suit or liability for damage, loss, injury, or liability caused by the intentional or willful and wanton misconduct of such person.

(d) The liability of the executive director and employees of the Interstate Commission or representatives of the Interstate Commission, acting within the scope of such person's employment or duties for acts, errors, or omissions occurring within such person's state, may not exceed the limits of liability set forth under the constitution and laws of that state for state officials, employees, and agents. The Interstate Commission is considered to be an instrumentality of the states for the purpose of any such action.

(e) Nothing in this subsection shall be construed to protect such person from suit or liability for damage, loss, injury, or liability caused by the intentional or willful and wanton misconduct of such person.

(f) The Interstate Commission shall defend the executive director, its employees, and subject to the approval of the attorney general or other appropriate legal counsel of the member state represented by an Interstate Commission representative, shall defend such Interstate Commission representative in any civil action seeking to impose liability arising out of an actual or alleged act, error or omission that occurred within the scope of Interstate Commission employment, duties or responsibilities, or that the defendant had a reasonable basis for believing occurred within the scope of Interstate Commission employment, duties, or responsibilities, provided that the actual or alleged act, error, or omission did not result from intentional or willful and wanton misconduct on the part of such person.

(g) To the extent not covered by the state involved, member state, or the Interstate Commission, the representatives or employees of the Interstate Commission shall be held harmless in the amount of a settlement or judgement, including attorney's fees and costs, obtained against such persons arising out of an actual or alleged act, error, or omission that occurred within the scope of the Interstate Commission employment, duties, or responsibilities, or that such persons had a reasonable basis for believing occurred within the scope of Interstate Commission employment, duties, or responsibilities, provided that the actual or alleged act, error, or omission did not result from intentional or willful and wanton misconduct on the part of such person.

History.
83 Del. Laws, c. 52, § 20.

§ 1715A. Rulemaking functions of the Interstate Commission [Effective July 1, 2022].

(a) The Interstate Commission shall promulgate reasonable rules in order to effectively and efficiently achieve the purpose of the Compact. Notwithstanding the foregoing, in the event the Interstate Commission exercises its rulemaking authority in a manner that is beyond the scope of the purposes of the Compact, or the powers granted hereunder, then such an action by the Interstate Commission shall be invalid and have no force or effect.

(b) Rules deemed appropriate for the operations of the Interstate Commission shall be made pursuant to a rulemaking process that substantially conforms to the "Model State Administrative Procedure Act" of 2010 [MSAPA, 15 U.L.A. (2010)], and subsequent amendments thereto.

(c) Not later than 30 days after a rule is promulgated, any person may file a petition for judicial review of the rule in the United States District Court for the District of Columbia or the federal district where the Interstate Commission has its principal offices, provided that the filing of such a petition shall not stay or otherwise prevent the rule from becoming effective unless the court finds that the petitioner has a substantial likelihood of success. The court shall give deference to the actions of the Interstate Commission consistent with applicable law and shall not find the rule to be unlawful if the rule represents a reasonable exercise of the authority granted to the Interstate Commission.

History.
83 Del. Laws, c. 52, § 20.

§ 1716A. Oversight of the Interstate Compact [Effective July 1, 2022].

(a) The executive, legislative, and judicial branches of state government in each member state shall enforce the Compact and shall take all actions necessary and appropriate to effectuate the Compact's purposes and intent. The provisions of the Compact and the rules promulgated hereunder shall have standing as statutory law but shall not override existing state authority to regulate the practice of medicine.

(b) All courts shall take judicial notice of the Compact and the rules in any judicial or administrative proceeding in a member state pertaining to the subject matter of the Compact which may affect the powers, responsibilities or actions of the Interstate Commission.

(c) The Interstate Commission shall be entitled to receive all service of process in any such proceeding, and shall have standing to intervene in the proceeding for all purposes. Failure to provide service of process to the Interstate Commission shall render a judgment or order void as to the Interstate Commission, the Compact, or promulgated rules.

History.
83 Del. Laws, c. 52, § 20.

§ 1717A. Enforcement of Interstate Compact [Effective July 1, 2022].

(a) The Interstate Commission, in the reasonable exercise of its discretion, shall enforce the provisions and rules of the Compact.

(b) The Interstate Commission may, by majority vote of the Commissioners, initiate legal action in the United States Court for the District of Columbia, or, at the discretion of the Interstate Commission, in the federal district where the Interstate Commission has its principal offices, to enforce compliance with the provisions of the Compact, and its promulgated rules and bylaws, against a member state in default. The relief sought may include both injunctive relief and damages. In the event judicial enforcement is necessary, the prevailing party shall be awarded all costs of such litigation including reasonable attorney's fees.

(c) The remedies herein shall not be the exclusive remedies of the Interstate Commission. The Interstate Commission may avail itself of any other remedies available under state law or regulation of a profession.

History.
83 Del. Laws, c. 52, § 20.

§ 1718A. Default procedures [Effective July 1, 2022].

(a) The grounds for default include failure of a member state to perform such obligations or responsibilities imposed upon it by the Compact, or the rules and bylaws of the Interstate Commission promulgated under the Compact.

(b) If the Interstate Commission determines that a member state has defaulted in the performance of its obligations or responsibilities under the Compact, or the bylaws or promulgated rules, the Interstate Commission shall:

(1) Provide written notice to the defaulting state and other member states of the nature of the default, the means of curing the default, and any action taken by the Interstate Commission. The Interstate Commission shall specify the conditions by which the defaulting state must cure its default.

(2) Provide remedial training and specific technical assistance regarding the default.

(c) If the defaulting state fails to cure the default, the defaulting state shall be terminated from the Compact upon an affirmative vote of a majority of the Commissioners and all rights, privileges, and benefits conferred by the Compact shall terminate on the effective date of termination. A cure of the default does not relieve the offending state of obligations or liabilities incurred during the period of the default.

(d) Termination of membership in the Compact shall be imposed only after all other means of securing compliance have been exhausted. Notice of intent to terminate shall be given by the Interstate Commission to the governor, the majority and minority leaders of the defaulting state's legislature, and each of the member states.

(e) The Interstate Commission shall establish rules and procedures to address licenses and physicians that are materially impacted by the termination of a member state, or the withdrawal of a member state.

(f) The member state which has been terminated is responsible for all dues, obligations, and liabilities incurred through the effective date of termination including obligations, the performance of which extends beyond the effective date of termination.

(g) The Interstate Commission shall not bear any costs relating to any state that has been found to be in default, or which has been terminated from the Compact, unless otherwise mutually agreed upon in writing between the Interstate Commission and the defaulting state.

(h) The defaulting state may appeal the action of the Interstate Commission by petitioning the United States District Court for the District of Columbia or the federal district where the Interstate Commission has its principal offices. The prevailing party shall be awarded all costs of such litigation including reasonable attorney's fees.

History.
83 Del. Laws, c. 52, § 20.

§ 1719A. Dispute resolution [Effective July 1, 2022].

(a) The Interstate Commission shall attempt, upon the request of a member state, to resolve disputes which are subject to the Compact and which may arise among member states or member boards.

(b) The Interstate Commission shall promulgate rules providing for both mediation and binding dispute resolution as appropriate.

History.
83 Del. Laws, c. 52, § 20.

§ 1720A. Member states, effective date and amendment [Effective July 1, 2022].

(a) Any state is eligible to become a member of the Compact.

(b) The Compact shall become effective and binding upon legislative enactment of the Compact into law by no less than 7 states. Thereafter, it shall become effective and binding on a state upon enactment of the Compact into law by that state.

(c) The governors of non-member states, or their designees, shall be invited to participate in the activities of the Interstate Commission on a nonvoting basis prior to adoption of the Compact by all states.

(d) The Interstate Commission may propose amendments to the Compact for enactment by the member states. No amendment shall become effective and binding upon the Interstate Commission and the member states until it is enacted into law by unanimous consent of the member states.

History.
83 Del. Laws, c. 52, § 20.

Revisor's note.
The minimum state adoption requirement set by subsection (b) of this section has been met.

§ 1721A. Withdrawal [Effective July 1, 2022].

(a) Once effective, the Compact shall continue in force and remain binding upon every member state, provided that a member state may withdraw from the Compact by specifically repealing the statute which enacted the Compact into law.

(b) Withdrawal from the Compact shall be by the enactment of a statute repealing the same, but shall not take effect until 1 year after the effective date of such statute and until written notice of the withdrawal has been given by the withdrawing state to the governor of each other member state.

(c) The withdrawing state shall immediately notify the chairperson of the Interstate Commission in writing upon the introduction of legislation repealing the Compact in the withdrawing state.

(d) The Interstate Commission shall notify the other member states of the withdrawing state's intent to withdraw within 60 days of its receipt of notice provided under subsection (c) of this section.

(e) The withdrawing state is responsible for all dues, obligations and liabilities incurred through the effective date of withdrawal, including obligations, the performance of which extend beyond the effective date of withdrawal.

(f) Reinstatement following withdrawal of a member state shall occur upon the withdrawing date reenacting the Compact or upon such later date as determined by the Interstate Commission.

(g) The Interstate Commission is authorized to develop rules to address the impact of the withdrawal of a member state on licenses granted in other member states to physicians who designated the withdrawing member state as the state of principal license.

History.
83 Del. Laws, c. 52, § 20.

§ 1722A. Dissolution [Effective July 1, 2022].

(a) The Compact shall dissolve effective upon the date of the withdrawal or default of the member state which reduces the membership of the Compact to 1 member state.

(b) Upon the dissolution of the Compact, the Compact becomes void and has no further effect. The business and affairs of the Interstate Commission shall be concluded, and surplus funds shall be distributed in accordance with the bylaws.

History.
83 Del. Laws, c. 52, § 20.

§ 1723A. Severability and construction [Effective July 1, 2022].

(a) The provisions of the Compact shall be severable, and if any phrase, clause, sentence, or provision is deemed unenforceable, the remaining provisions of the Compact shall be enforceable.

(b) The provisions of the Compact shall be liberally construed to effectuate its purposes.

(c) Nothing in the Compact shall be construed to prohibit the applicability of other interstate compacts to which the member states are members.

History.
83 Del. Laws, c. 52, § 20.

§ 1724A. Binding effect of Compact and other laws [Effective July 1, 2022].

(a) Nothing in this chapter prevents the enforcement of any other law of a member state that is not inconsistent with the Compact.

(b) All laws in a member state in conflict with the Compact are superseded to the extent of the conflict. All lawful actions of the Interstate Commission, including all rules and bylaws promulgated by the Commission, are binding upon the member states.

(c) All agreements between the Interstate Commission and the member states are binding in accordance with their terms.

(d) In the event any provision of the Compact exceeds the constitutional limits imposed on the legislature of any member state, such provision shall be ineffective to the extent of the conflict with the constitutional provision in question in that member state.

History.
83 Del. Laws, c. 52, § 20.

CHAPTER 19
NURSING

§ 1902. Definitions.

(a) "Administration of medications" means a process whereby a single dose of a prescribed drug or biological is given to a patient by an authorized licensed person by 1 of several routes, oral, inhalation, topical, or parenteral. The person verifies the properly prescribed drug order, removes the individual dose from a previously dispensed, properly labeled container (including a unit dose container), assesses the patient's status to assure that the drug is given as prescribed to the patient for whom it is prescribed and that there are no known contraindications to the use of the drug or the dosage that has been prescribed, gives the individual dose to the proper patient, records the time and dose given, and assesses the patient following the administration of medication for possible untoward side effects.

(b) "Advanced practice registered nurse" ("APRN") means an individual with knowledge and skills in basic nursing education; licensure as a registered nurse ("RN"); and graduation from or completion of a graduate-level APRN program accredited by a national accrediting body and current certification by a national certifying body in the appropriate APRN role and at least 1 population focus. "Advanced practice registered nurse" includes certified nurse practitioners, certified registered nurse anesthetists, certified nurse midwives, or clinical nurse specialist. Advanced practice nursing is an expanded scope of nursing licensed as an independent licensed practitioner in a role and population focus approved by the Board of Nursing, with or without compensation or personal profit, and includes the RN scope of practice. The scope of an APRN includes performing acts of advanced assessment, diagnosing, prescribing, and ordering. Advanced practice nursing is the application of nursing principles, including those described in subsection (r) of this section.

(c) "Compact Administrator" means the Executive Director of the Delaware Board of Nursing who is designated as the Compact Administrator under Chapter 19A and 19B of this title.

(d) "Compact Administrator" means the Executive Director of the Delaware Board of Nursing who is designated as the compact Administrator under Chapters 19A and 19B of this title.

(e) "Conversion therapy" means any practice or treatment that seeks to change an individual's sexual orientation or gender identity, as "sexual orientation" and "gender identity" are defined in § 710 of Title 19, including any effort to change behaviors or gender expressions or to eliminate or reduce sexual or romantic attractions or feelings toward individuals of the same gender. "Conversion therapy" does not mean any of the following:

(1) Counseling that provides assistance to an individual who is seeking to undergo a gender transition or who is in the process of undergoing gender transition.

(2) Counseling that provides an individual with acceptance, support, and understanding without seeking to change an individual's sexual orientation or gender identity.

(3) Counseling that facilitates an individual's coping, social support, and identity exploration and development, including counseling in the form of sexual orientation-neutral interventions or gender identity-neutral interventions provided for the purpose of preventing or addressing unlawful conduct or unsafe sexual practices, without seeking to change an individual's sexual orientation or gender identity.

(f) "Dispensing" means providing medication according to an order of a practitioner duly licensed to prescribe medication. The term includes both the repackaging and labeling of medications from bulk to individual dosages.

(g) "Electronic prescription" means a prescription that is generated on an electronic application and transmitted as an electronic data file.

(h) "Full-practice authority," as granted to an advanced practice registered nurse, means the collection of state practice and licensure laws that allow APRNs to evaluate patients, diagnose, order and interpret diagnostic tests, initiate and manage treatments, including prescribing medications, under exclusive licensure authority of the Delaware Board of Nursing and includes:

(1) Practicing within standards established or recognized by the Board of Nursing.

(2) Being accountable to patients, the nursing profession, and the Board of Nursing for complying with the requirements of this chapter and the quality of advanced nursing care rendered.

(3) Recognizing limits of knowledge and experience.

(4) Planning for the management of situations beyond the APRN's expertise.

(5) Consultation with or referring patients to other health-care providers as appropriate.

(i) "Head of the Nursing Licensing Board" means the President of the Delaware Board of Nursing.

(j) "Licensure" means the authorization to practice nursing within this State granted by the Delaware Board of Nursing and includes the authorization to practice in Delaware under the Interstate Nurse Licensure Compact [Chapter 19A of this title].

(k) "Limited lay administration of medications (LLAM)" means a process by which LLAM trained unlicensed assistive personnel, functioning in a setting authorized by § 1932 of this title, give a prescribed medication to clients, patients, residents, or students as ordered by a licensed practitioner authorized to prescribe medications or gives a nonprescription medication pursuant to the Delacare regulations.

(*l*) "LLAM trained unlicensed assistive personnel (UAP)" means an individual who has successfully completed the Board of Nursing approved LLAM course, including the core course and any program specific specialized training modules required.

(m) "Nurse educator" means a registered nurse who is a faculty member or director of a Delaware board-approved nursing education program preparing individuals at the registered nurse entry level.

(n) "Nursing diagnosis" means the description of the individual's actual or potential health needs which are identified through a nursing assessment and are amenable to nursing intervention. The focus of the nursing diagnosis is on the individual's response to illness or other factors that may adversely affect the attainment or maintenance of wellness. These diagnostic acts are distinct from medical, osteopathic, and dental diagnosis.

(o) "Nursing education program" means a course of instruction offered and conducted to prepare persons for licensure as a registered or licensed practical nurse, or a course of instruction offered and conducted to increase the knowledge and skills of the nurse and leads to an academic degree in nursing, or refresher courses in nursing.

(p) "Standards of nursing practice" means those standards of practice adopted by the Board that interpret the legal definitions of nursing, as well as provide criteria against which violations of the law can be determined. Such standards of nursing practice may not be used to directly or indirectly affect the employment practices and deployment of personnel by duly licensed or accredited hospitals and other duly licensed or accredited health-care facilities and organizations. In addition, such standards may not be assumed the only evidence in civil malpractice litigation, nor may they be given a different weight than any other evidence.

(q) "Substantially related" means the nature of the criminal conduct, for which the person was convicted, has a direct bearing on the fitness or ability to perform 1 or more of the duties or responsibilities necessarily related to the practice of nursing.

(r) "The practice of practical nursing" as a licensed practical nurse means the performance for compensation of nursing services by a person who holds a valid license pursuant to the terms of this chapter and who bears accountability for nursing practices which require basic knowledge of physical, social, and nursing sciences. These services, at the direction of a registered nurse or a person licensed to practice medicine, surgery, or dentistry, include:

(1) Observation;

(2) Assessment;

(3) Planning and giving of nursing care to the ill, injured and infirm;

(4) The maintenance of health and well-being;

(5) The administration of medications and treatments prescribed by a licensed physician, dentist, podiatrist, or advanced practice registered nurse; and

(6) Additional nursing services and supervision commensurate with the licensed practical nurse's continuing education and demonstrated competencies;

(7) Dispensing activities only as permitted in the Board's Rules and Regulations. Nothing contained in this chapter shall be deemed to permit

acts of surgery or medical diagnosis; nor shall it be deemed to permit dispensing of drugs, medications, or therapeutics independent of the supervision of a physician who is licensed to practice medicine and surgery, or those licensed to practice dentistry or podiatry; and

(8) [Repealed.]

(s) "The practice of professional nursing" as a registered nurse means the performance of professional nursing services by a person who holds a valid license pursuant to the terms of this chapter, and who bears primary responsibility and accountability for nursing practices based on specialized knowledge, judgment, and skill derived from the principles of biological, physical, and behavioral sciences. The registered nurse practices in the profession of nursing by the performance of activities, among which are:

(1) Assessing human responses to actual or potential health conditions;

(2) Identifying the needs of the individual or family by developing a nursing diagnosis;

(3) Implementing nursing interventions based on the nursing diagnosis;

(4) Teaching health-care practices. Nothing contained in this subsection limits other qualified persons or agencies from teaching health-care practices without being licensed under this chapter;

(5) Advocating the provision of health-care services through collaboration with other health service personnel;

(6) Executing regimens, as prescribed by a licensed physician, dentist, podiatrist, or advanced practice registered nurse, including the dispensing or administration of medications and treatments;

(7) Administering, supervising, delegating, and evaluating nursing activities;

(8) [Repealed.]

(9) Nothing contained in this chapter shall be deemed to permit acts of surgery or medical diagnosis; nor shall it be deemed to permit dispensing of drugs, medications, or therapeutics independent of the supervision of a physician who is licensed to practice medicine and surgery, or those licensed to practice dentistry or podiatry.

A registered nurse shall have the authority, as part of the practice of professional nursing, to make a pronouncement of death; provided, however, that this provision shall only apply to attending nurses caring for terminally ill patients or patients who have "do not resuscitate" orders in the home or place of residence of the deceased as a part of a hospice program or a certified home health-care agency program; in a skilled nursing facility; in a residential community associated with a skilled nursing facility; any licensed assisted living community; in an extended care facility; or in a hospice; and provided that the attending physician of record has agreed in writing to permit the attending registered nurse to make a pronouncement of death in that case.

(t) "The profession of nursing" is an art and process based on a scientific body of knowledge. The practitioner of nursing assists patients in the maintenance of health; the management of illness, injury, or infirmity; or the achievement of a dignified death.

History.

24 Del. C. 1953, § 1902; 54 Del. Laws, c. 153; 64 Del. Laws, c. 26, § 1; 67 Del. Laws, c. 5, § 2; 67 Del. Laws, c. 434, § 2; 68 Del. Laws, c. 152, § 2; 68 Del. Laws, c. 161, § 2; 69 Del. Laws, c. 319, §§ 3-7, 13; 71 Del. Laws, c. 283, § 2; 71 Del. Laws, c. 478, § 1; 72 Del. Laws, c. 334, § 2; 73 Del. Laws, c. 285, §§ 1, 2; 73 Del. Laws, c. 316, §§ 1, 2; 74 Del. Laws, c. 262, § 34; 77 Del. Laws, c. 319, § 1; 77 Del. Laws, c. 420, § 2; 80 Del. Laws, c. 80, § 10; 80 Del. Laws, c. 171; 80 Del. Laws, c. 172, § 1; 81 Del. Laws, c. 80, § 1; 81 Del. Laws, c. 340, § 4; 82 Del. Laws, c. 75, § 4; 82 Del. Laws, c. 261, §§ 8, 16; 83 Del. Laws, c. 52, § 10; 83 Del. Laws, c. 111, § 1.

Revisor's note.

Section 1 of 83 Del. Laws, c. 52, provided: "This Act shall be known as the 'Telehealth

Access Preservation and Modernization Act of 2021'."

Section 21 of 83 Del. Laws, c. 52, provided: "Sections 1-19 of this act take effect on July 1, 2021. Nothing in this act shall be interpreted as affecting or invalidating any health-care services provided through telehealth or telemedicine prior to effective date of this act."

Effect of amendments.

83 Del. Laws, c. 52, effective July 1, 2021, substituted "(t)" for "(y)" in the final sentence of (b); deleted former (i), (t), (v), (x) and (y) and redesignated the remaining and intervening paragraphs accordingly; and repealed present (t)(8) and (u)(8).

83 Del. Laws, c. 111, effective Aug. 4, 2021, in the third sentence of (b), substituted "is" for "means" preceding "an expanded", added "as an independent licensed practitioner" and substituted "(r)" for "(t)" in the final sentence; deleted former (c) and (j) and redesignated the remaining and intervening paragraphs accordingly; in present (c), added "and 19B" and deleted "by the President of the Board" from the end; and deleted "all of the following" following "means" in the introductory paragraph of present (h).

§ 1922. Disciplinary proceedings; appeal.

(a) *Grounds.* — The Board may impose any of the following sanctions (subsection (b) of this section) singly or in combination when it finds a licensee or former licensee is guilty of any offense described herein, except that the license of any licensee who is convicted of a felony sexual offense shall be permanently revoked:

(1) Is guilty of fraud or deceit in procuring or attempting to procure a license to practice nursing; or

(2) Has been convicted of a crime that is substantially related to the practice of nursing; or

(3) Is unfit or incompetent by reason of negligence, habits, or other causes; or

(4) Is habitually intemperate or is addicted to the use of habit-forming drugs; or

(5) Is mentally incompetent; or

(6) Has a physical condition such that the performance of nursing service is or may be injurious or prejudicial to patients or to the public; or

(7) Has had a license to practice as a registered nurse or licensed practical nurse suspended or revoked in any jurisdiction; or

(8) Is guilty of unprofessional conduct or the wilful neglect of a patient; or

(9) Has wilfully or negligently violated this chapter; or

(10) Has failed to report child abuse or neglect as required by § 903 of Title 16, or any successor thereto; or

(11) Has failed to report to the Division of Professional Regulation as required by §§ 1930 and 1930A of this title; or

(12) Has engaged in conversion therapy with a child; or

(13) Has referred a child to a provider in another jurisdiction to receive conversion therapy.

(b) *Disciplinary sanctions.* — (1) Permanently revoke a license to practice.

(2) Suspend a license.

(3) Censure a licensee.

(4) Issue a letter of reprimand.

(5) Place a licensee on probationary status and require the licensee to do 1 or more of the following:

a. Report regularly to the Board upon the matters which are the basis of probation.

b. Limit practice to those areas prescribed by the Board.

c. Continue or renew professional education until satisfactory degree of skill has been attained in those areas which are the basis of the probation.

(6) Refuse a license.

(7) Refuse to renew a license.

(8) Impose a monetary penalty not to exceed $500 for each violation.

(9) Take any other disciplinary action.

(c) *Procedure.* — (1) When a complaint is filed pursuant to § 8735 of Title 29, alleging a violation of this chapter, the complaint shall be received and investigated by the Division of Professional Regulation and the Division shall be responsible for issuing a final written report at the conclusion of its investigation.

(2) The Board shall cause a copy of the complaint, together with a notice of the time and place fixed for the hearing to be served upon the practitioner at least 20 days before the date fixed for the hearing. In cases where the practitioner cannot be located or where the personal service cannot be effectuated, substitute service shall be effected in the same manner as with civil litigation.

(3) In all proceedings under this chapter:

a. The accused may be represented by counsel who shall have the right of examination and cross-examination.

b. The accused and the Board may subpoena witnesses. Subpoenas shall be issued by the President or the Vice-President of the Board upon written request and shall be served as provided by the rules of the Superior Court and shall have like effect as a subpoena issued by said Court.

c. Testimony before the Board shall be under oath. Any member of the Board shall have power to administer oaths for this purpose.

d. A stenographic record of the hearing shall be made by a qualified court reporter. At the request and expense of any party such record shall be transcribed with a copy to the other party.

e. The decision of the Board shall be based upon sufficient legal evidence. If the charges are supported by such evidence, the Board may refuse to issue, or revoke or suspend a license, or otherwise discipline a licensee. A suspended license may be reissued upon a further hearing initiated at the request of the suspended licensee by written application in accordance with the rules of the Board.

f. All decisions of the Board shall be final and conclusive. Where the practitioner is in disagreement with the action of the Board, the practitioner may appeal the Board's decision to the Superior Court within 30 days of service or of the postmarked date of the copy of the decision mailed to the practitioner. The appeal shall be on the record to the Superior Court and shall be as provided in §§ 10142-10145 of Title 29.

g. Upon reaching its conclusion of law and determining an appropriate disciplinary action, if any, the Board shall issue a written decision and order in accordance with § 10128 of Title 29. The order must restate the factual findings, but need not summarize the evidence presented. However, notwithstanding the provisions of § 10128(c) of Title 29, the decision and order, including an order issued pursuant to § 1923 of this title, may be issued over the signature of only the President or other officer of the Board. The decision and order must be sent by certified mail, return receipt requested, to the person complained about, with a copy to the Executive Director.

History.
24 Del. C. 1953, § 1921; 54 Del. Laws, c. 153; 64 Del. Laws, c. 26, § 1; 65 Del. Laws, c. 221, § 1; 70 Del. Laws, c. 186, § 1; 70 Del. Laws, c. 482, §§ 21, 22, 29; 74 Del. Laws, c. 262, § 36; 77 Del. Laws, c. 420, § 3; 78 Del. Laws, c. 35, §§ 5, 6; 81 Del. Laws, c. 80, § 10; 81 Del. Laws, c. 340, § 5; 83 Del. Laws, c. 111, § 2.

Effect of amendments.

83 Del. Laws, c. 111, effective Aug. 4, 2021, in (c)(2), substituted "20" for "30" in the first sentence and "effectuated" for "effected" in the second sentence.

NOTES TO DECISIONS

Analysis

Hearing record.
Standard of review.

Hearing record.

Delaware Board of Nursing did not abuse its discretion through failure to include conclusions of law in their decision when the Board rejected 2 of the hearing officer's conclusions and implicitly adopted the third conclusion; the Board modified and reduced the proposed sanction of a nurse found to have violated the board regulation regarding unprofessional conduct by failing to competently and safely turn obese patient in bed. Cooper v. Del. Bd. of Nursing, — A.3d —, 2021 Del. Super. LEXIS 169 (Del. Super. Ct. Feb. 26, 2021), aff'd, — A.3d —, 2021 Del. LEXIS 332 (Del. 2021).

Standard of review.

Substantial evidence supported the Delaware Board of Nursing's finding that a nurse violated the board regulation regarding unprofessional conduct by failing to competently and safely turn an obese patient in bed because: (1) the nurse roughly roused the patient and began turning the patient without any advanced notice or warning; and (2) the patient cried out in pain and questioned the nurse as to the rough treatment, to which the nurse did not respond and left the room. Cooper v. Del. Bd. of Nursing, — A.3d —, 2021 Del. Super. LEXIS 169 (Del. Super. Ct. Feb. 26, 2021), aff'd, — A.3d —, 2021 Del. LEXIS 332 (Del. 2021).

§ 1924. Unlawful practices.

(a) No person shall practice or offer to practice professional, practical, or advanced practice registered nursing or shall represent himself or herself as a registered nurse, practical nurse, or advanced practice registered nurse in this State, or shall use any title, abbreviation, sign, card or device to indicate that such person is a registered nurse, licensed practical nurse, or advanced practice registered nurse, unless such person is licensed under this chapter.

(b) No person, hospital or institution shall conduct or shall offer to conduct a professional or practical nursing education program unless such person, hospital or institution is approved under this chapter.

History.

24 Del. C. 1953, § 1923; 54 Del. Laws, c. 153; 64 Del. Laws, c. 26, § 1; 70 Del. Laws, c. 186, § 1; 83 Del. Laws, c. 111, § 2.

Effect of amendments.

83 Del. Laws, c. 111, effective Aug. 4, 2021, in (a), substituted "practical, or advanced practice registered" for "or practical" following "professional", deleted "or" preceding the each of two occurrences of "practical nurse" and added "or advanced practice registered nurse" thereafter.

§ 1930. Duty to report conduct that constitutes grounds for discipline or inability to practice.

NOTES TO DECISIONS

Defamation.

Plaintiff's defamation claims against a nursing home, arising out of employees' accusation that plaintiff committed abuse against a resident, were dismissed because: (1) the employees were required to report suspected abuse by 16 Del. C. § 1132(a)(1); (2) employees were protected from defamation claims by 16 Del. C. § 1135(a); and under 24 Del. C. § 1930, nurses were protected from any liability in exercising their duty to report abuse so long as they acted in good faith. Cooper v. Cadia Pike Creek, — A.3d —, 2021 Del. Super. LEXIS 105 (Del. Super. Ct. Feb. 4, 2021).

§ 1933. Telemedicine.

History.

80 Del. Laws, c. 80, § 22; 82 Del. Laws, c. 261, §§ 8, 16; repealed by 83 Del. Laws, c. 52, § 11, effective July 1, 2021.

Revisor's note.

Section 1 of 83 Del. Laws, c. 52, provided: "This Act shall be known as the 'Telehealth Access Preservation and Modernization Act of 2021'."

Section 21 of 83 Del. Laws, c. 52, provided: "Sections 1-19 of this act take effect on July 1, 2021. Nothing in this act shall be interpreted as

affecting or invalidating any health-care services provided through telehealth or telemedicine prior to effective date of this act."

§ 1934. Advanced Practice Registered Nurse Committee.

(a) The Advanced Practice Registered Nurse Committee's ("Committee")
purpose is to:

　　(1) Recommend and draft regulations regarding the practice of advance
　　practice registered nurses.

　　(2)-(4) [Repealed.]

(b) The Committee shall have 9 members, appointed by the Board of
Nursing, and consist of the following: 9 advanced practice registered nurses,
including 2 certified nurse practitioners, 2 certified registered nurse anesthe-
tists, 2 certified nurse midwives, 2 clinical nurse the specialists, and 1 at-large
member from any of the 4 APRN roles. The Committee Chair must be 1 of the
APRN members of the Board of Nursing and shall serve a term of 1 year.
Subsequent terms may be served as long as the Chair remains a member of the
Board of Nursing.

　　(1)-(4) [Repealed.]

(c) Appointments shall be for 3-year terms, provided that the terms of
newly-appointed members will be staggered so that no more than 5 appointments shall expire annually. Members may be appointed for less than 3 years
to ensure that members' terms expire on a staggered basis.

(d) A majority of members appointed to the Committee shall constitute a
quorum to conduct official business.

(e) A Committee member may be removed at any time for gross inefficiency,
neglect of duty, malfeasance, misfeasance, or nonfeasance in office. A member
who is absent from 3 consecutive committee meetings without good cause or
who attends less than 50% of committee meetings in a calendar year shall be
deemed in neglect of duty.

(f) The Committee shall:

　　(1) Draft rules and regulations regarding the practice of advance
　　practice registered nurses.

　　(2) Review emerging practices and advise the Board of Nursing on
　　APRN licensure, the APRN Compact, and practice standards, including
　　prescribing trends, and provide recommendations to the Board of Nursing
　　regarding APRN practice.

　　(3), (4) [Repealed.]

History.
　80 Del. Laws, c. 172, § 3; 70 Del. Laws, c.
186, § 1; 81 Del. Laws, c. 80, § 11; 83 Del.
Laws, c. 111, § 2.

Effect of amendments.
　83 Del. Laws, c. 111, effective Aug. 4, 2021,
substituted a period for "; and" in (a)(1); repealed (a)(2)-(4), (b)(1)-(4), (f)(3) and (f)(4); rewrote the introductory paragraph of (b) and
(f)(1); and added "the APRN Compact" in (f)(2).

§ 1935. Advanced Practice Registered Nurse (APRN) — Authority and duties.

(a)(1) The board of nursing grants full-practice and prescriptive authority
　　upon the issuance of an APRN license.

　　(2) The Board may, by endorsement, license as an advanced practice
　registered nurse an applicant who is duly licensed as an advanced practice
　registered nurse or is entitled to perform similar services under a different
　title under the laws of another state or a territory of the United States or
　a foreign country if, in the opinion of the Board, the applicant meets the
　qualifications specified by its regulations for advanced practice registered
　nurses in this State.

(b) An APRN licensed by the Board of Nursing with full-practice authority is authorized within the APRN's role and population foci to:

(1) Prescribe, procure, administer, store, dispense, and furnish over the counter, legend and controlled substances pursuant to applicable state and federal laws and within the APRN's role and population foci.

(2) Plan and initiate a therapeutic regimen within the APRN's role and population foci that includes ordering and prescribing nonpharmacological interventions, including:

a. Medical devices and durable medical equipment, nutrition, blood, and blood products.

b. Diagnostic and supportive services including home health care, hospice, and physical and occupational therapy.

(3) Diagnose, prescribe and institute therapy or referrals of patients within the APRN's role and population foci to health-care agencies, health-care providers and community resources.

(4) Sign death certificates.

(c) APRNs with full-practice authority shall seek consultation regarding treatment and care of patients as appropriate to patient needs and the APRN's level of expertise and scope of practice.

(d) An APRN may be designated as the primary care provider by an insurer or health-care services corporation.

(e) An APRN shall not be held to any lesser standard of care than that of a physician providing care to a specific patient condition or population.

(f) Any APRN rendering services in person or by electronic means in Delaware must hold an active Delaware RN and APRN license.

(g) [Repealed.]

History.
80 Del. Laws, c. 172, § 3; 81 Del. Laws, c. 80, § 12; 83 Del. Laws, c. 111, § 2.

Effect of amendments.
83 Del. Laws, c. 111, effective Aug. 4, 2021, deleted the second sentence in (a)(1); deleted "in all circumstances, subject to the restrictions set forth in the definition of the term 'practice of professional nursing' as provided in this chapter" from the end of (b)(4); deleted "granted independent practice" following "APRN" in (e); and repealed (g).

§ 1936. Collaborative agreements.

History.
80 Del. Laws, c. 172, § 3; 81 Del. Laws, c. 80, § 13; repealed by 83 Del. Laws, c. 111, § 2, effective Aug. 4, 2021.

CHAPTER 19B

ADVANCED PRACTICE REGISTERED NURSE COMPACT [EFFECTIVE UPON FULFILLMENT OF 83 DEL. LAWS, C. 110, § 2]

Revisor's note.
Section 2 of 83 Del. Laws, c. 110, provided: "This act takes effect on the date on which the Commission [of APRN Compact Administrators] adopts the APRN uniform licensure requirements as defined in § 1903B of this title, notice of which the Director of the Division of Professional Regulation must provide to the Registrar of Regulations."

§ 1901B. Advanced Practice Registered Nurse Compact [Effective upon fulfillment of 83 Del. Laws, c. 110, § 2].

The State hereby enters into the Advanced Practice Registered Nurse Compact (Compact) as set forth in this chapter. The text of the Compact is as set forth in this chapter.

History.
83 Del. Laws, c. 110, § 1.

§ 1902B. Findings and declaration of purpose [Effective upon fulfillment of 83 Del. Laws, c. 110, § 2].

(a) The party states find the following:

(1) The health and safety of the public are affected by the degree of compliance with advanced practice registered nurse licensure requirements and the effectiveness of enforcement activities related to state APRN licensure laws.

(2) Violations of APRN licensure and other laws regulating the practice of nursing may result in injury or harm to the public.

(3) The expanded mobility of APRNs and the use of advanced communication and intervention technologies as part of our nation's healthcare delivery system require greater coordination and cooperation among states in the areas of APRN licensure and regulation.

(4) New practice modalities and technology make compliance with individual state APRN licensure laws difficult and complex.

(5) The current system of duplicative APRN licensure for APRNs practicing in multiple states is cumbersome and redundant for healthcare delivery systems, payors, state licensing boards, regulators and APRNs.

(6) Uniformity of APRN licensure requirements throughout the states promotes public safety and public health benefits as well as provides a mechanism to increase access to care.

(b) The general purposes of this Compact are to do the following:

(1) Facilitate the states' responsibility to protect the public's health and safety.

(2) Ensure and encourage the cooperation of party states in the areas of APRN licensure and regulation, including promotion of uniform licensure requirements.

(3) Facilitate the exchange of information between party states in the areas of APRN regulation, investigation and adverse actions.

(4) Promote compliance with the laws governing APRN practice in each jurisdiction.

(5) Invest all party states with the authority to hold an APRN accountable for meeting all state practice laws in the state in which the patient is located at the time care is rendered through the mutual recognition of party state privileges to practice.

(6) Decrease redundancies in the consideration and issuance of APRN licenses.

(7) Provide opportunities for interstate practice by APRNs who meet uniform licensure requirements.

History.
83 Del. Laws, c. 110, § 1.

§ 1903B. Definitions [Effective upon fulfillment of 83 Del. Laws, c. 110, § 2].

As used in this Compact:

(a) "Advanced practice registered nurse" or "APRN" means a registered nurse who has gained additional specialized knowledge, skills and experience through a program of study recognized or defined by the Interstate Commission of APRN Compact Administrators ("Commission"), and who is licensed to perform advanced nursing practice. An advanced practice registered nurse is licensed in an APRN role that is congruent with an APRN educational program, certification, and Commission rules.

(b) "Adverse action" means any administrative, civil, equitable or criminal action permitted by a state's laws which is imposed by a licensing board or other authority against an APRN, including actions against an individual's license or multistate licensure privilege such as revocation, suspension, probation, monitoring of the licensee, limitation on the licensee's practice, or any other encumbrance on licensure affecting an APRN's authorization to practice, including the issuance of a cease and desist action.

(c) "Alternative program" means a non-disciplinary monitoring program approved by a licensing board.

(d) "APRN licensure" means the regulatory mechanism used by a party state to grant legal authority to practice as an APRN.

(e) "APRN uniform licensure requirements" means the minimum uniform licensure, education and examination requirements set forth in § 1904B(b) of this title.

(f) "Coordinated licensure information system" means an integrated process for collecting, storing and sharing information on APRN licensure and enforcement activities related to APRN licensure laws that is administered by a nonprofit organization composed of and controlled by licensing boards.

(g) "Current significant investigatory information" means:

(1) Investigative information that a licensing board, after a preliminary inquiry that includes notification and an opportunity for the APRN to respond, if required by state law, has reason to believe is not groundless and, if proved true, would indicate more than a minor infraction; or

(2) Investigative information that indicates that the APRN represents an immediate threat to public health and safety regardless of whether the APRN has been notified and has had an opportunity to respond.

(h) "Encumbrance" means a revocation or suspension of, or any limitation on, the full and unrestricted practice of nursing imposed by a licensing board in connection with a disciplinary proceeding.

(i) "Home state" means the party state that is the APRN's primary state of residence.

(j) "Licensing board" means a party state's regulatory body responsible for regulating the practice of advanced practice registered nursing.

(k) "Multistate license" means an APRN license to practice as an APRN issued by a home state licensing board that authorizes the APRN to practice as an APRN in all party states under a multistate licensure privilege, in the same role and population focus as the APRN is licensed in the home state.

(l) "Multistate licensure privilege" means a legal authorization associated with an APRN multistate license that permits an APRN to practice as an APRN in a remote state, in the same role and population focus as the APRN is licensed in the home state.

(m) "Non-controlled prescription drug" means a device or drug that is not a controlled substance and is prohibited under state or federal law from being dispensed without a prescription. The term includes a device or drug that bears or is required to bear the legend "Caution: federal law prohibits dispensing without prescription" or "prescription only" or other legend that complies with federal law.

(n) "Party state" means any state that has adopted this Compact.

(o) "Population focus" means 1 of the 6 population foci of family/individual across the lifespan, adult-gerontology, pediatrics, neonatal, women's health/gender-related, and psych/mental health.

(p) "Prescriptive authority" means the legal authority to prescribe medications and devices as defined by party state laws.

(q) "Remote state" means a party state that is not the home state.

(r) "Role" means 1 of the 4 recognized roles of certified registered nurse anesthetists (CRNA), certified nurse-midwives (CNM), clinical nurse specialists (CNS), and certified nurse practitioners (CNP).

(s) "Single-state license" means an APRN license issued by a party state that authorizes practice only within the issuing state and does not include a multistate licensure privilege to practice in any other party state.

(t) "State" means a state, territory or possession of the United States and the District of Columbia.

(u) "State practice laws" means a party state's laws, rules, and regulations that govern APRN practice, define the scope of advanced nursing practice and create the methods and grounds for imposing discipline except that prescriptive authority shall be treated in accordance with § 1904B(f) and (g) of this title. "State practice laws" does not include:

(1) A party state's laws, rules, and regulations requiring supervision or collaboration with a healthcare professional, except for laws, rules, and regulations regarding prescribing controlled substances.

(2) The requirements necessary to obtain and retain an APRN license, except for qualifications or requirements of the home state.

History.
83 Del. Laws, c. 110, § 1.

§ 1904B. General provisions and jurisdiction [Effective upon fulfillment of 83 Del. Laws, c. 110, § 2].

(a) A state must implement procedures for considering the criminal history records of applicants for initial APRN licensure or APRN licensure by endorsement. Such procedures shall include the submission of fingerprints or other biometric-based information by APRN applicants for the purpose of obtaining an applicant's criminal history record information from the Federal Bureau of Investigation and the agency responsible for retaining that state's criminal records.

(b) Each party state shall require all of the following for an applicant to satisfy the APRN uniform licensure requirements to obtain or retain a multistate license in the home state:

(1) Meets the home state's qualifications for licensure or renewal of licensure, as well as all other applicable state laws.

(2) Has (a) completed an accredited graduate-level education program that prepares the applicant for 1 of the 4 recognized roles and population foci; or (b) has completed a foreign APRN education program for 1 of the 4 recognized roles and population foci that has been (a) approved by the authorized accrediting body in the applicable country and (b) verified by an independent credentials review agency to be comparable to a licensing board approved APRN education program.

(3) Has, if a graduate of a foreign APRN education program not taught in English or if English is not the individual's native language, successfully passed an English proficiency examination that includes the components of reading, speaking, writing and listening.

(4) Has successfully passed a national certification examination that measures APRN, role and population-focused competencies and maintains continued competence as evidenced by recertification in the role and population focus through the national certification program.

(5) Holds an active, unencumbered license as a registered nurse and an active, unencumbered authorization to practice as an APRN.

(6) Has successfully passed an NCLEX-RN® examination or recognized predecessor, as applicable.

(7) Has practiced for at least 2,080 hours as an APRN in a role and population focus congruent with the applicant's education and training. For purposes of this section, practice shall not include hours obtained as part of enrollment in an APRN education program.

(8) Has submitted, in connection with an application for initial licensure or licensure by endorsement, fingerprints or other biometric data for the purpose of obtaining criminal history record information from the Federal Bureau of Investigation and the agency responsible for retaining that state or, if applicable, foreign country's criminal records.

(9) Has not been convicted or found guilty, or has entered into an agreed disposition, of a felony offense under applicable state, federal or foreign criminal law.

(10) Has not been convicted or found guilty, or has entered into an agreed disposition, of a misdemeanor offense related to the practice of nursing as determined by factors set forth in rules adopted by the Commission.

(11) Is not currently enrolled in an alternative program.

(12) Is subject to self-disclosure requirements regarding current participation in an alternative program.

(13) Has a valid United States Social Security number.

(c) An APRN issued a multistate license shall be licensed in an approved role and at least 1 approved population focus.

(d) An APRN multistate license issued by a home state to a resident in that state will be recognized by each party state as authorizing the APRN to practice as an APRN in each party state, under a multistate licensure privilege, in the same role and population focus as the APRN is licensed in the home state.

(e) Nothing in this Compact shall affect the requirements established by a party state for the issuance of a single-state license, except that an individual may apply for a single-state license, instead of a multistate license, even if otherwise qualified for the multistate license. However, the failure of such an individual to affirmatively opt for a single-state license may result in the issuance of a multistate license.

(f) Issuance of an APRN multistate license shall include prescriptive authority for non-controlled prescription drugs.

(g) For each state in which an APRN seeks authority to prescribe controlled substances, the APRN shall satisfy all requirements imposed by such state in granting and/or renewing such authority.

(h) An APRN issued a multistate license is authorized to assume responsibility and accountability for patient care independent of any supervisory or collaborative relationship. This authority may be exercised in the home state and in any remote state in which the APRN exercises a multistate licensure privilege.

(i) All party states shall be authorized, in accordance with state due process laws, to take adverse action against an APRN's multistate licensure privilege such as revocation, suspension, probation or any other action that affects an APRN's authorization to practice under a multistate licensure privilege, including cease and desist actions. If a party state takes such action, it shall promptly notify the administrator of the coordinated licensure information system. The administrator of the coordinated licensure information system shall promptly notify the home state of any such actions by remote states.

(j) Except as otherwise expressly provided in this Compact, an APRN practicing in a party state must comply with the state practice laws of the state in which the client is located at the time service is provided. APRN practice is not limited to patient care but shall include all advanced nursing practice as defined by the state practice laws of the party state in which the client is located. APRN practice in a party state under a multistate licensure privilege will subject the APRN to the jurisdiction of the licensing board, the courts, and the laws of the party state in which the client is located at the time service is provided.

(k) Except as otherwise expressly provided in this Compact, this Compact does not affect additional requirements imposed by states for advanced practice registered nursing. However, a multistate licensure privilege to practice registered nursing granted by a party state shall be recognized by other party states as satisfying any state law requirement for registered nurse licensure as a precondition for authorization to practice as an APRN in that state.

(l) Individuals not residing in a party state shall continue to be able to apply for a party state's single-state APRN license as provided under the laws of each party state. However, the single-state license granted to these individuals will not be recognized as granting the privilege to practice as an APRN in any other party state.

History.
83 Del. Laws, c. 110, § 1.

§ 1905B. Applications for APRN licensure in a party state [Effective upon fulfillment of 83 Del. Laws, c. 110, § 2].

(a) Upon application for an APRN multistate license, the licensing board in the issuing party state shall ascertain, through the coordinated licensure information system, whether the applicant has ever held or is the holder of a licensed practical/vocational nursing license, a registered nursing license or an advanced practice registered nurse license issued by any other state, whether there are any encumbrances on any license or multistate licensure privilege held by the applicant, whether any adverse action has been taken against any license or multistate licensure privilege held by the applicant and whether the applicant is currently participating in an alternative program.

(b) An APRN may hold a multistate APRN license, issued by the home state, in only 1 party state at a time.

(c) If an APRN changes primary state of residence by moving between 2 party states, the APRN must apply for APRN licensure in the new home state, and the multistate license issued by the prior home state shall be deactivated in accordance with applicable Commission rules.

(1) The APRN may apply for licensure in advance of a change in primary state of residence.

(2) A multistate APRN license shall not be issued by the new home state until the APRN provides satisfactory evidence of a change in primary state of residence to the new home state and satisfies all applicable requirements to obtain a multistate APRN license from the new home state.

(d) If an APRN changes primary state of residence by moving from a party state to a non-party state, the APRN multistate license issued by the prior home state will convert to a single-state license, valid only in the former home state.

History.
83 Del. Laws, c. 110, § 1.

§ 1906B. Additional authorities invested in party state licensing boards [Effective upon fulfillment of 83 Del. Laws, c. 110, § 2].

(a) In addition to the other powers conferred by state law, a licensing board shall have the authority to:

(1) Take adverse action against an APRN's multistate licensure privilege to practice within that party state.

a. Only the home state shall have power to take adverse action against an APRN's license issued by the home state.

b. For purposes of taking adverse action, the home state licensing board shall give the same priority and effect to reported conduct that occurred outside of the home state as it would if such conduct had occurred within the home state. In so doing, the home state shall apply its own state laws to determine appropriate action.

(2) Issue cease and desist orders or impose an encumbrance on an APRN's authority to practice within that party state.

(3) Complete any pending investigations of an APRN who changes primary state of residence during the course of such investigations. The licensing board shall also have the authority to take appropriate action(s) and shall promptly report the conclusions of such investigations to the administrator of the coordinated licensure information system. The administrator of the coordinated licensure information system shall promptly notify the new home state of any such actions.

(4) Issue subpoenas for both hearings and investigations that require the attendance and testimony of witnesses, as well as the production of evidence. Subpoenas issued by a party state licensing board for the attendance and testimony of witnesses and/or the production of evidence from another party state shall be enforced in the latter state by any court of competent jurisdiction, according to that court's practice and procedure in considering subpoenas issued in its own proceedings. The issuing licensing board shall pay any witness fees, travel expenses, mileage, and other fees required by the service statutes of the state in which the witnesses and/or evidence are located.

(5) Obtain and submit, for an APRN licensure applicant, fingerprints or other biometric-based information to the Federal Bureau of Investigation for criminal background checks, receive the results of the Federal Bureau of Investigation record search on criminal background checks and use the results in making licensure decisions.

(6) If otherwise permitted by state law, recover from the affected APRN the costs of investigations and disposition of cases resulting from any adverse action taken against that APRN.

(7) Take adverse action based on the factual findings of another party state, provided that the licensing board follows its own procedures for taking such adverse action.

(b) If adverse action is taken by a home state against an APRN's multistate licensure, the privilege to practice in all other party states under a multistate licensure privilege shall be deactivated until all encumbrances have been removed from the APRN's multistate license. All home state disciplinary orders that impose adverse action against an APRN's multistate license shall include a statement that the APRN's multistate licensure privilege is deactivated in all party states during the pendency of the order.

(c) Nothing in this Compact shall override a party state's decision that participation in an alternative program may be used in lieu of adverse action. The home state licensing board shall deactivate the multistate licensure privilege under the multistate license of any APRN for the duration of the APRN's participation in an alternative program.

History.
83 Del. Laws, c. 110, § 1.

§ 1907B. Coordinated licensure information system and exchange of information [Effective upon fulfillment of 83 Del. Laws, c. 110, § 2].

(a) All party states shall participate in a coordinated licensure information system of all APRNs, licensed registered nurses, and licensed practical/vocational nurses. This system will include information on the licensure and disciplinary history of each APRN, as submitted by party states, to assist in the coordinated administration of APRN licensure and enforcement efforts.

(b) The Commission, in consultation with the administrator of the coordinated licensure information system, shall formulate necessary and proper procedures for the identification, collection and exchange of information under this Compact.

(c) All licensing boards shall promptly report to the coordinated licensure information system any adverse action, any current significant investigative information, denials of applications (with the reasons for such denials) and APRN participation in alternative programs known to the licensing board regardless of whether such participation is deemed nonpublic and/or confidential under state law.

(d) Notwithstanding any other provision of law, all party state licensing boards contributing information to the coordinated licensure information system may designate information that may not be shared with non-party states or disclosed to other entities or individuals without the express permission of the contributing state.

(e) Any personally identifiable information obtained from the coordinated licensure information system by a party state licensing board shall not be shared with non-party states or disclosed to other entities or individuals except to the extent permitted by the laws of the party state contributing the information.

(f) Any information contributed to the coordinated licensure information system that is subsequently required to be expunged by the laws of the party state contributing the information shall be removed from the coordinated licensure information system.

(g) The Compact administrator of each party state shall furnish a uniform data set to the Compact administrator of each other party state, which shall include, at a minimum all of the following:

(1) Identifying information.

(2) Licensure data.

(3) Information related to alternative program participation information.

(4) Other information that may facilitate the administration of this Compact, as determined by Commission rules.

(h) The Compact administrator of a party state shall provide all investigative documents and information requested by another party state.

History.
83 Del. Laws, c. 110, § 1.

§ 1908B. Establishment of the Interstate Commission of APRN Compact Administrators [Effective upon fulfillment of 83 Del. Laws, c. 110, § 2].

(a) The party states hereby create and establish a joint public agency known as the Interstate Commission of APRN Compact Administrators.

(1) The Commission is an instrumentality of the party states.

(2) Venue is proper, and judicial proceedings by or against the Commission shall be brought solely and exclusively, in a court of competent jurisdiction where the principal office of the Commission is located. The Commission may waive venue and jurisdictional defenses to the extent it adopts or consents to participate in alternative dispute resolution proceedings.

(3) Nothing in this Compact shall be construed to be a waiver of sovereign immunity.

(b) *Membership, voting and meetings.* —

(1) Each party state shall have and be limited to 1 administrator. The head of the state licensing board or designee shall be the administrator of this Compact for each party state. Any administrator may be removed or suspended from office as provided by the law of the state from which the Administrator is appointed. Any vacancy occurring in the Commission shall be filled in accordance with the laws of the party state in which the vacancy exists.

(2) Each administrator shall be entitled to 1 vote with regard to the promulgation of rules and creation of bylaws and shall otherwise have an opportunity to participate in the business and affairs of the Commission. An administrator shall vote in person or by such other means as provided in the bylaws. The bylaws may provide for an administrator's participation in meetings by telephone or other means of communication.

(3) The Commission shall meet at least once during each calendar year. Additional meetings shall be held as set forth in the bylaws or rules of the Commission.

(4) All meetings shall be open to the public, and public notice of meetings shall be given in the same manner as required under the rulemaking provisions in § 1909B of this title.

(5) The Commission may convene in a closed, nonpublic meeting if the Commission must discuss any of the following:

a. Noncompliance of a party state with its obligations under this Compact.

b. The employment, compensation, discipline or other personnel matters, practices or procedures related to specific employees or other matters related to the Commission's internal personnel practices and procedures.

    c. Current, threatened, or reasonably anticipated litigation.

    d. Negotiation of contracts for the purchase or sale of goods, services or real estate.

    e. Accusing any person of a crime or formally censuring any person.

    f. Disclosure of trade secrets or commercial or financial information that is privileged or confidential.

    g. Disclosure of information of a personal nature where disclosure would constitute a clearly unwarranted invasion of personal privacy.

    h. Disclosure of investigatory records compiled for law enforcement purposes;

    i. Disclosure of information related to any reports prepared by or on behalf of the Commission for the purpose of investigation of compliance with this Compact.

    j. Matters specifically exempted from disclosure by federal or state statute.

    (6) If a meeting, or portion of a meeting, is closed pursuant to this provision, the Commission's legal counsel or designee shall certify that the meeting may be closed and shall reference each relevant exempting provision. The Commission shall keep minutes that fully and clearly describe all matters discussed in a meeting and shall provide a full and accurate summary of actions taken, and the reasons therefor, including a description of the views expressed. All documents considered in connection with an action shall be identified in such minutes. All minutes and documents of a closed meeting shall remain under seal, subject to release by a majority vote of the Commission or order of a court of competent jurisdiction.

(c) The Commission shall, by a majority vote of the administrators, prescribe bylaws or rules to govern its conduct as may be necessary or appropriate to carry out the purposes and exercise the powers of this Compact, including all of the following:

    (1) Establishing the fiscal year of the Commission.

    (2) Providing reasonable standards and procedures for the following:

      a. The establishment and meetings of other committees.

      b. Governing any general or specific delegation of any authority or function of the Commission.

    (3) Providing reasonable procedures for calling and conducting meetings of the Commission, ensuring reasonable advance notice of all meetings and providing an opportunity for attendance of such meetings by interested parties, with enumerated exceptions designed to protect the public's interest, the privacy of individuals, and proprietary information, including trade secrets. The Commission may meet in closed session only after a majority of the administrators vote to close a meeting in whole or in part. As soon as practicable, the Commission must make public a copy of the vote to close the meeting revealing the vote of each administrator, with no proxy votes allowed.

    (4) Establishing the titles, duties and authority and reasonable procedures for the election of the officers of the Commission.

    (5) Providing reasonable standards and procedures for the establishment of the personnel policies and programs of the Commission. Notwithstanding any civil service or other similar laws of any party state, the bylaws shall exclusively govern the personnel policies and programs of the Commission.

    (6) Providing a mechanism for winding up the operations of the Commission and the equitable disposition of any surplus funds that may exist

after the termination of this Compact after the payment and/or reserving of all of its debts and obligations.

(d) The Commission shall publish its bylaws and rules, and any amendments thereto, in a convenient form on the website of the Commission.

(e) The Commission shall maintain its financial records in accordance with the bylaws.

(f) The Commission shall meet and take such actions as are consistent with the provisions of this Compact and the bylaws.

(g) The Commission shall have the following powers:

(1) To promulgate uniform rules to facilitate and coordinate implementation and administration of this Compact. The rules shall have the force and effect of law and shall be binding in all party states.

(2) To bring and prosecute legal proceedings or actions in the name of the Commission, provided that the standing of any licensing board to sue or be sued under applicable law shall not be affected.

(3) To purchase and maintain insurance and bonds.

(4) To borrow, accept or contract for services of personnel, including but not limited to employees of a party state or nonprofit organizations.

(5) To cooperate with other organizations that administer state compacts related to the regulation of nursing, including but not limited to sharing administrative or staff expenses, office space or other resources.

(6) To hire employees, elect or appoint officers, fix compensation, define duties, grant such individuals appropriate authority to carry out the purposes of this Compact, and to establish the Commission's personnel policies and programs relating to conflicts of interest, qualifications of personnel and other related personnel matters.

(7) To accept any and all appropriate donations, grants and gifts of money, equipment, supplies, materials and services, and to receive, utilize and dispose of the same; provided that at all times the Commission shall strive to avoid any appearance of impropriety and/or conflict of interest.

(8) To lease, purchase, accept appropriate gifts or donations of, or otherwise to own, hold, improve or use, any property, whether real, personal or mixed; provided that at all times the Commission shall strive to avoid any appearance of impropriety.

(9) To sell convey, mortgage, pledge, lease, exchange, abandon or otherwise dispose of any property, whether real, personal or mixed.

(10) To establish a budget and make expenditures.

(11) To borrow money.

(12) To appoint committees, including advisory committees comprised of administrators, state nursing regulators, state legislators or their representatives, and consumer representatives, and other such interested persons.

(13) To issue advisory opinions.

(14) To provide and receive information from, and to cooperate with, law enforcement agencies.

(15) To adopt and use an official seal.

(16) To perform such other functions as may be necessary or appropriate to achieve the purposes of this Compact consistent with the state regulation of APRN licensure and practice.

(h) *Financing of the Commission.* —

(1) The Commission shall pay, or provide for the payment of, the reasonable expenses of its establishment, organization and ongoing activities.

(2) The Commission may also levy on and collect an annual assessment from each party state to cover the cost of its operations, activities and staff

in its annual budget as approved each year. The aggregate annual assessment amount, if any, shall be allocated based upon a formula to be determined by the Commission, which shall promulgate a rule that is binding upon all party states.

(3) The Commission shall not incur obligations of any kind prior to securing the funds adequate to meet the same; nor shall the Commission pledge the credit of any of the party states, except by, and with the authority of, such party state.

(4) The Commission shall keep accurate accounts of all receipts and disbursements. The receipts and disbursements of the Commission shall be subject to the audit and accounting procedures established under its bylaws. However, all receipts and disbursements of funds handled by the Commission shall by audited yearly by a certified or licensed public accountant, and the report of the audit shall be included in and become part of the annual report of the Commission.

(i) *Qualified immunity, defense, and indemnification.* —

(1) The administrators, officers, executive director, employees and representatives of the Commission shall be immune from suit and liability, either personally or in their official capacity, for any claim for damage to or loss of property or personal injury or other civil liability caused by or arising out of any actual or alleged act, error or omission that occurred, or that the person against whom the claim is made had a reasonable basis for believing occurred, within the scope of Commission employment, duties or responsibilities; provided that nothing in this paragraph shall be construed to protect any such person from suit and/or liability for any damage, loss, injury or liability caused by the intentional, willful or wanton misconduct of that person.

(2) The Commission shall defend any administrator, officer, executive director, employee or representative of the Commission in any civil action seeking to impose liability arising out of any actual or alleged act, error or omission that occurred within the scope of Commission employment, duties or responsibilities, or that the person against whom the claim is made had a reasonable basis for believing occurred within the scope of Commission employment, duties or responsibilities; provided that nothing herein shall be construed to prohibit that person from retaining his or her own counsel; and provided further that the actual or alleged act, error or omission did not result from that person's intentional, willful or wanton misconduct.

(3) The Commission shall indemnify and hold harmless any administrator, officer, executive director, employee or representative of the Commission for the amount of any settlement or judgment obtained against that person arising out of any actual or alleged act, error or omission that occurred within the scope of Commission employment, duties or responsibilities, or that such person had a reasonable basis for believing occurred within the scope of Commission employment, duties or responsibilities, provided that the actual or alleged act, error or omission did not result from the intentional, willful or wanton misconduct of that person.

History.
83 Del. Laws, c. 110, § 1; 70 Del. Laws, c. 186, § 1.

§ 1909B. Rulemaking [Effective upon fulfillment of 83 Del. Laws, c. 110, § 2].

(a) The Commission shall exercise its rulemaking powers pursuant to the criteria set forth in this section and the rules adopted thereunder. Rules and amendments shall become binding as of the date specified in each rule or amendment and shall have the same force and effect as provisions of this Compact.

(b) Rules or amendments to the rules shall be adopted at a regular or special meeting of the Commission.

(c) Prior to promulgation and adoption of a final rule or rules by the Commission, and at least 60 days in advance of the meeting at which the rule will be considered and voted upon, the Commission shall file a notice of proposed rulemaking as follows:

(1) On the website of the Commission.

(2) On the website of each licensing board or the publication in which each state would otherwise publish proposed rules.

(d) The notice of proposed rulemaking shall include the following:

(1) The proposed time, date and location of the meeting in which the rule will be considered and voted upon.

(2) The text of the proposed rule or amendment, and the reason for the proposed rule.

(3) A request for comments on the proposed rule from any interested person.

(4) The manner in which interested persons may submit notice to the Commission of their intention to attend the public hearing and any written comments.

(e) Prior to adoption of a proposed rule, the Commission shall allow persons to submit written data, facts, opinions and arguments, which shall be made available to the public.

(f) The Commission shall grant an opportunity for a public hearing before it adopts a rule or amendment.

(g) The Commission shall publish the place, time, and date of the scheduled public hearing.

(1) Hearings shall be conducted in a manner providing each person who wishes to comment a fair and reasonable opportunity to comment orally or in writing. All hearings will be recorded, and a copy will be made available upon request.

(2) Nothing in this section shall be construed as requiring a separate hearing on each rule. Rules may be grouped for the convenience of the Commission at hearings required by this section.

(h) If no one appears at the public hearing, the Commission may proceed with promulgation of the proposed rule.

(i) Following the scheduled hearing date, or by the close of business on the scheduled hearing date if the hearing was not held, the Commission shall consider all written and oral comments received.

(j) The Commission shall, by majority vote of all administrators, take final action on the proposed rule and shall determine the effective date of the rule, if any, based on the rulemaking record and the full text of the rule.

(k) Upon determination that an emergency exists, the Commission may consider and adopt an emergency rule without prior notice, opportunity for comment, or hearing, provided that the usual rulemaking procedures provided in this Compact and in this section shall be retroactively applied to the rule as soon as reasonably possible, in no event later than 90 days after the effective date of the rule. For the purposes of this provision, an emergency rule is one that must be adopted immediately in order to do any of the following:

(1) Meet an imminent threat to public health, safety or welfare.

(2) Prevent a loss of Commission or party state funds.

(3) Meet a deadline for the promulgation of an administrative rule that is established by federal law or rule.

(*l*) The Commission may direct revisions to a previously adopted rule or amendment for purposes of correcting typographical errors, errors in format, errors in consistency or grammatical errors. Public notice of any revisions shall be posted on the website of the Commission. The revision shall be subject to challenge by any person for a period of 30 days after posting. The revision may be challenged only on grounds that the revision results in a material change to a rule. A challenge shall be made in writing, and delivered to the Commission, prior to the end of the notice period. If no challenge is made, the revision will take effect without further action. If the revision is challenged, the revision may not take effect without the approval of the Commission.

History.
83 Del. Laws, c. 110, § 1.

§ 1910B. Oversight, dispute resolution and enforcement [Effective upon fulfillment of 83 Del. Laws, c. 110, § 2].

(a) *Oversight.* —

(1) Each party state shall enforce this Compact and take all actions necessary and appropriate to effectuate this Compact's purposes and intent.

(2) The Commission shall be entitled to receive service of process in any proceeding that may affect the powers, responsibilities or actions of the Commission, and shall have standing to intervene in such a proceeding for all purposes. Failure to provide service of process to the Commission shall render a judgment or order void as to the Commission, this Compact or promulgated rules.

(b) *Default, technical assistance and termination.* —

(1) If the Commission determines that a party state has defaulted in the performance of its obligations or responsibilities under this Compact or the promulgated rules, the Commission shall do all of the following:

a. Provide written notice to the defaulting state and other party states of the nature of the default, the proposed means of curing the default, or any other action to be taken by the Commission.

b. Provide remedial training and specific technical assistance regarding the default.

(2) If a state in default fails to cure the default, the defaulting state's membership in this Compact may be terminated upon an affirmative vote of a majority of the administrators, and all rights, privileges and benefits conferred by this Compact may be terminated on the effective date of termination. A cure of the default does not relieve the offending state of obligations or liabilities incurred during the period of default.

(3) Termination of membership in this Compact shall be imposed only after all other means of securing compliance have been exhausted. Notice of intent to suspend or terminate shall be given by the Commission to the governor of the defaulting state and to the executive officer of the defaulting state's licensing board, the defaulting state's licensing board, and each of the party states.

(4) A state whose membership in this Compact has been terminated is responsible for all assessments, obligations and liabilities incurred through the effective date of termination, including obligations that extend beyond the effective date of termination.

(5) The Commission shall not bear any costs related to a state that is found to be in default or whose membership in this Compact has been terminated, unless agreed upon in writing between the Commission and the defaulting state.

(6) The defaulting state may appeal the action of the Commission by petitioning the U.S. District Court for the District of Columbia or the federal district in which the Commission has its principal offices. The prevailing party shall be awarded all costs of such litigation, including reasonable attorneys' fees.

(c) *Dispute resolution.* —

(1) Upon request by a party state, the Commission shall attempt to resolve disputes related to the Compact that arise among party states and between party and non-party states.

(2) The Commission shall promulgate a rule providing for both mediation and binding dispute resolution for disputes, as appropriate.

(3) In the event the Commission cannot resolve disputes among party states arising under this Compact:

> a. The party states may submit the issues in dispute to an arbitration panel, which will be comprised of individuals appointed by the Compact administrator in each of the affected party states and an individual mutually agreed upon by the Compact administrators of all the party states involved in the dispute.

> b. The decision of a majority of the arbitrators shall be final and binding.

(d) *Enforcement.* —

(1) The Commission, in the reasonable exercise of its discretion, shall enforce the provisions and rules of this Compact.

(2) By majority vote, the Commission may initiate legal action in the United States District Court for the District of Columbia or the federal district in which the Commission has its principal offices against a party state that is in default to enforce compliance with the provisions of this Compact and its promulgated rules and bylaws. The relief sought may include both injunctive relief and damages. In the event judicial enforcement is necessary, the prevailing party shall be awarded all costs of such litigation, including reasonable attorneys' fees.

(3) The remedies herein shall not be the exclusive remedies of the Commission. The Commission may pursue any other remedies available under federal or state law.

History.
83 Del. Laws, c. 110, § 1.

§ 1911B. Effective date, withdrawal and amendment [Effective upon fulfillment of 83 Del. Laws, c. 110, § 2].

(a) This Compact shall come into limited effect at such time as this Compact has been enacted into law in 7 party states for the sole purpose of establishing and convening the Commission to adopt rules relating to its operation.

(b) Any state that joins this Compact subsequent to the Commission's initial adoption of the APRN uniform licensure requirements shall be subject to all rules that have been previously adopted by the Commission.

(c) Any party state may withdraw from this Compact by enacting a statute repealing the same. A party state's withdrawal shall not take effect until 6 months after enactment of the repealing statute.

(d) A party state's withdrawal or termination shall not affect the continuing requirement of the withdrawing or terminated state's licensing board to report adverse actions and significant investigations occurring prior to the effective date of such withdrawal or termination.

(e) Nothing contained in this Compact shall be construed to invalidate or prevent any APRN licensure agreement or other cooperative arrangement between a party state and a non-party state that does not conflict with the provisions of this Compact.

(f) This Compact may be amended by the party states. No amendment to this Compact shall become effective and binding upon any party state until it is enacted into the laws of all party states.

(g) Representatives of non-party states to this Compact shall be invited to participate in the activities of the Commission, on a nonvoting basis, prior to the adoption of this Compact by all states.

History.
83 Del. Laws, c. 110, § 1.

§ 1912B. Construction and severability [Effective upon fulfillment of 83 Del. Laws, c. 110, § 2].

This Compact shall be liberally construed so as to effectuate the purposes thereof. The provisions of this Compact shall be severable, and if any phrase, clause, sentence or provision of this Compact is declared to be contrary to the constitution of any party state or of the United States, or if the applicability thereof to any government, agency, person or circumstance is held invalid, the validity of the remainder of this Compact and the applicability thereof to any government, agency, person or circumstance shall not be affected thereby. If this Compact shall be held to be contrary to the constitution of any party state, this Compact shall remain in full force and effect as to the remaining party states and in full force and effect as to the party state affected as to all severable matters.

History.
83 Del. Laws, c. 110, § 1.

CHAPTER 20
OCCUPATIONAL THERAPY

Subchapter I. Board of Occupational
     Therapy Practice
Sec.
2002. Definitions.

SUBCHAPTER I
BOARD OF OCCUPATIONAL THERAPY PRACTICE

§ 2002. Definitions.

As used in this chapter:

(1) "Applicant" means an individual who applies to be licensed under this chapter.

(2) "Board" means the Board of Occupational Therapy Practice established in this chapter.

(3) "Division" means the Division of Professional Regulation.

(4) "Excessive use or abuse of drugs or alcohol" or "excessively uses or abuses drugs or alcohol" means any use of narcotics, controlled substances, or illegal drugs without a prescription from a licensed physician, or the abuse of alcoholic beverage such that it impairs a person's ability to perform the work of an occupational therapist or occupational therapy assistant.

(5) "Licensee" means an individual licensed under this chapter to practice occupational therapy services.

(6) "Occupational therapist" means a person who is licensed to practice occupational therapy under this chapter and offers such services to the public under any title incorporating the words "occupational therapy,"

"occupational therapist," or any similar title or description of occupational therapy services.

(7) "Occupational therapy assistant" means a person licensed to assist in the practice of occupational therapy under the supervision of an occupational therapist.

(8)a. "Occupational therapy services" includes any of the following:

1. The assessment, treatment, and education of or consultation with an individual, family, or other persons.

2. Interventions directed toward developing, improving, or restoring daily living skills, work readiness or work performance, play skills, or leisure capacities, or enhancing educational performance skills.

3. Providing for the development, improvement, or restoration of sensorimotor, oralmotor, perceptual or neuromuscular functioning, or emotional, motivational, cognitive, or psychosocial components of performance.

b. "Occupational therapy services" or "practice of occupational therapy" may require assessment of the need for use of interventions such as the design, development, adaptation, application, or training in the use of assistive technology devices; the design, fabrication, or application of rehabilitative technology such as selected orthotic devices; training in the use of assistive technology, orthotic or prosthetic devices; the application of thermal agent modalities, including paraffin, hot and cold packs, and fluido therapy, as an adjunct to, or in preparation for, purposeful activity; the use of ergonomic principles; the adaptation of environments and processes to enhance functional performance; or the promotion of health and wellness.

c. [Repealed.]

(9) "Person" means a corporation, company, association, or partnership, or an individual.

(10) "Practice of occupational therapy" means the use of goal-directed activities with individuals who are limited by physical limitations due to injury or illness, psychiatric and emotional disorders, developmental or learning disabilities, poverty and cultural differences, or the aging process, in order to maximize independence, prevent disability, and maintain health.

(11) "Substantially related" means the nature of the criminal conduct for which a person was convicted has a direct bearing on the fitness or ability to perform 1 or more of the duties or responsibilities necessarily related to the practice of occupational therapy.

(12) "Supervision" means the interactive process between a licensed occupational therapist and an occupational therapy assistant, and requires more than a paper review or cosignature. "Supervision" means that the supervising occupational therapist is responsible for insuring the extent, kind, and quality of the services that the occupational therapy assistant renders.

History.
65 Del. Laws, c. 172, § 1; 70 Del. Laws, c. 186, § 1; 71 Del. Laws, c. 293, § 1; 74 Del. Laws, c. 262, § 37; 80 Del. Laws, c. 80, § 11; 81 Del. Laws, c. 424, § 2; 82 Del. Laws, c. 261, §§ 9, 16; 83 Del. Laws, c. 52, § 12.

Revisor's note.
Section 1 of 83 Del. Laws, c. 52, provided: "This

Act shall be known as the 'Telehealth Access Preservation and Modernization Act of 2021'."

Section 21 of 83 Del. Laws, c. 52, provided: "Sections 1-19 of this act take effect on July 1, 2021. Nothing in this act shall be interpreted as affecting or invalidating any health-care services provided through telehealth or telemedicine prior to effective date of this act."

Effect of amendments.

83 Del. Laws, c. 52, effective July 1, 2021, repealed former (3), (10), (13), (16) and (17), and redesignated the remaining paragraphs accordingly; and repealed present (8)c.

CHAPTER 21

OPTOMETRY

Sec.
2101. Definition of practice of optometry.

§ 2101. Definition of practice of optometry.

(a) "Practice of optometry" means the examination or measurement by any subjective or objective means including automated or testing devices for the diagnosis, treatment, and prevention of conditions of the human eye, lid, adnexa, and visual system as outlined below.

(1) "Practice of optometry" includes all of the following:

a. Use, adapting, and fitting of all types of lenses or devices except as provided in paragraph (a)(2) of this section.

b. Dispensing of any type of contact lenses that must be dispensed in accordance with a written, current contact lens prescription from a licensed physician or optometrist, including information that the Board may specify by rule or regulation.

c. Determination of refractive error or visual, muscular, or anatomical anomalies of the eye.

d. Provision or prescription of vision therapy, low-vision rehabilitation, or developmental or perceptual therapy.

(2) A license to practice optometry includes the utilization of any method or means which the optometrist is educationally qualified to provide, as established by the Delaware State Board of Examiners in Optometry and:

a. Includes performance of minor procedures on the surface of the skin of the ocular adnexa, of the cornea and conjunctiva of the globe and lid that can be performed safely with topical anesthesia and that would not require the use of injections or penetration of the globe, and the cutting or closure of human tissue by suture or staple, glue, adhesive, soldering, or cauterization. Also excludes anterior corneal stromal puncture, collagen cross-linking, postsurgical pterygium or conjuctival graft gluing of amniotic membranes, mechanical polishing of the corneal basement membrane, or any procedure that requires full- or partial-thickness incision of the sclera or cornea. Such minor procedures include: removal of superficial foreign body of the external eye conjunctiva; removal of conjunctival nonperforating foreign bodies; removal of a foreign body with or without slit lamp; superficial corneal scraping for diagnostic purposes; epilation of trichiasis by forceps; expression of conjunctival follicles; closure of lacrimal punctum by plug; intense pulsed light therapy; thermal treatment of eyelid margin for dry eye and blepharitis such as Lipiflow; and dilation of lacrimal punctum, with or without irrigation except on infant and toddler patients.

b. Prohibits surgery.

c. Prohibits the use of ophthalmic lasers or other modalities in which tissue is burned, vaporized, cut, or otherwise irreversibly altered by thermal, light-based, electromagnetic, radiation, chemical, ultrasound, infusion, cryotherapy, or similar means, excluding the use of pharmaceutical agents described in paragraph (a)(3) of this section.

d. Procedures must meet the standard of care as if performed by a physician.

(3) "Practice of optometry," as it relates to pharmaceutical agents, means as follows:

a. Includes the use of pharmaceutical agents for the diagnosis and treatment of diseases, disorders, and conditions of the eye and adnexa based on the licensing requirement that satisfies the requirement for graduate level coursework that includes general and ocular pharmacology as follows:

1. Prescription for controlled substances.

A. Schedule II controlled substances containing Hydrocodone, with a limitation on maximum 72-hour supply.

B. Schedules III, IV, and V controlled substances, with a limitation on maximum 72-hour supply.

2. Prescription for the use of an oral steroid with a limitation not to exceed a single 6-day methylprednisolone dose pack.

b. Includes the use of an epinephrine auto-injector to counteract anaphylaxis.

c. Excludes prescription for oral immuno-suppressives except for the use of oral steroids under § 2101(a)(3)a.2. of this title.

d. Excludes the prescription of oral antifungals.

e. Excludes the prescription of oral antimetabolites.

f. Excludes the prescription of any substance delivered intravenously or by injection.

g. Excludes any medication used solely for the treatment of systemic conditions outside the scope of an optometrist.

(b) For purposes of this chapter, the term "diagnostically certified optometrists" applies only to those currently licensed in the category and if that license lapses, the licensee could only relicense by meeting current licensing requirements in § 2107 of this title. The duties of a nondiagnostically certified optometrist are limited to those that do not utilize therapeutic pharmaceutical agents or perform procedures that require subsequent treatment with therapeutic pharmaceutical agents.

(c) In administering this chapter, the State Board shall, by rule or regulation, specify those acts, services, procedures and practices which constitute the "practice of optometry" within the definitions of this section and consistent with having submitted proof of graduate level coursework that includes general and ocular pharmacology.

(d) For purposes of disability insurance, workers' compensation, standard health and accident, sickness and other insurance policies, programs and plans, if the optometrist is authorized by law to perform the particular services, the optometrist shall be entitled to compensation for services under the said programs. Individuals entitled to such services shall have freedom to choose between any optometrist and any physician skilled in diseases of the eye.

(e) [Repealed.]

History.

25 Del. Laws, c. 113, § 1; Code 1915, § 894; 37 Del. Laws, c. 69, § 1; 38 Del. Laws, c. 49, § 1; Code 1935, § 1003; 47 Del. Laws, c. 106, § 1; 24 Del. C. 1953, § 2101; 54 Del. Laws, c. 30; 59 Del. Laws, c. 250, §§ 1, 2, 13; 66 Del. Laws, c. 1, § 1; 69 Del. Laws, c. 288, § 1; 70 Del. Laws, c. 186, § 1; 72 Del. Laws, c. 172, §§ 1-3; 80 Del. Laws, c. 80, § 12; 80 Del. Laws, c. 356, § 1; 81 Del. Laws, c. 78, § 11; 82 Del. Laws, c. 261, §§ 10, 16; 83 Del. Laws, c. 52, § 13.

Revisor's note.

Section 1 of 83 Del. Laws, c. 52, provided: "This Act shall be known as the 'Telehealth Access Preservation and Modernization Act of 2021'."

Section 21 of 83 Del. Laws, c. 52, provided: "Sections 1-19 of this act take effect on July 1, 2021. Nothing in this act shall be interpreted as affecting or invalidating any health-care services provided through telehealth or telemedicine prior to effective date of this act."

Effect of amendments.

83 Del. Laws, c. 52, effective July 1, 2021, repealed (e).

CHAPTER 25
PHARMACY

SUBCHAPTER I
OBJECTIVES; DEFINITIONS; BOARD OF PHARMACY

§ 2502. Definitions.

The following words, terms, and phrases when used in this chapter have the meanings ascribed to them in this section, except where the context clearly indicates a different meaning.

(1) "Biological product" means a biological product as defined in § 351 of the Public Health Service Act (42 U.S.C. § 262).

(2) "Board," "Board of Pharmacy," or "State Board of Pharmacy" means the Delaware State Board of Pharmacy.

(3) "Certified pharmacy technician" means a person who is certified by the Pharmacy Technician Certification Board (PTCB) or other entity approved by the Board of Pharmacy.

(4) "Direct supervision" means oversight and control by a licensed pharmacist who remains on the premises and is responsible for the work performed by a subordinate.

(5) "Dispense" means to furnish or deliver a drug to an ultimate user by or pursuant to the lawful prescription of a practitioner. Dispense includes the preparation, packaging, labeling, or compounding necessary to prepare a drug for furnishing or delivery.

(6) "Division" means the Division of Professional Regulation.

(7) "Drug" means:

a. A substance recognized as a drug in the Official United States Pharmacopoeia/National Formulary;

b. A substance intended for use in the diagnosis, cure, mitigation, treatment, or prevention of any illness, condition, or disease in humans or animals;

c. A substance, other than food, intended to affect the structure or any function of the body of a human or an animal; or

d. A substance intended for use as a component of any substance specified in paragraph (8)a., b. or c. of this section.

"Drug" does not include devices or their components, parts, or accessories.

(8) "Drug outlet" means a pharmacy, an in-state or out-of-state drug wholesaler, a drug manufacturer, a drug distributor, or a nonpharmacy veterinary drug seller.

(9) "Executive Secretary" means the executive secretary of the Delaware State Board of Pharmacy who shall be a pharmacist.

(10) "Federal Food and Drug Administration (FDA) Approved Drug

Products with Therapeutic Equivalence Evaluations" means the publication with that title containing a list of prescription drugs by generic name.

(11) "Interchangeable" means a biological product licensed by the Federal Food and Drug Administration pursuant to 42 U.S.C. § 262(k)(4).

(12) "Intern" means a person who is registered by the Board of Pharmacy and supervised by an approved preceptor and who is completing the practical experience requirement of the Board prior to that person's licensure as a pharmacist.

(13) "Internship" or "externship" means a period of practical experience established by Board of Pharmacy regulation that must be completed by an applicant for a license to practice pharmacy in this State.

(14) "Manufacturer" means a person who is engaged in manufacturing, preparing, propagating, compounding, processing, packaging, repackaging, or labeling of a drug, but does not include a person who is engaged in the preparation and dispensing of a drug pursuant to a prescription.

(15) "Monitoring drug therapy" means interpreting and analyzing information needed to evaluate the safety and efficacy of drug therapy.

(16) "Over-the-counter product" or "OTC" means a substance which may be sold without a prescription and which is packaged for use by the consumer and labeled in accordance with the requirements of state and federal statutes and regulations.

(17) "Person" means a natural person or an entity.

(18) "Pharmacist" or "licensee" means an individual licensed by the State pursuant to this chapter to engage in the practice of pharmacy.

(19) "Pharmacy" means a place where drugs are compounded or dispensed.

(20) "Pharmacy technician" means an individual who is not registered as an intern with the Board of Pharmacy or a certified pharmacy technician.

(21) "Practice of pharmacy" means the interpreting, evaluating, and dispensing of a practitioner's or prescriber's order. The practice of pharmacy includes the proper compounding, labeling, packaging, and dispensing of a drug to a patient or the patient's agent, and administering a drug to a patient. The practice of pharmacy includes the application of the pharmacist's knowledge of pharmaceutics, pharmacology, pharmacokinetics, drug and food interactions, drug product selection, and patient counseling. It also includes:

    a. Participation in drug utilization and/or drug regimen reviews;

    b. Participation in therapeutic drug selection, substitution of therapeutically equivalent drug products;

    c. Advising practitioners and other health-care professionals, as well as patients, regarding the total scope of drug therapy, so as to deliver the best care possible;

    d. Monitoring drug therapy;

    e. Performing and interpreting capillary blood tests to screen and monitor disease risk factors or facilitate patient education, the results of which must be reported to the patient's health-care practitioner; screening results to be reported only if outside normal limits;

    f. Conducting or managing a pharmacy or other business establishment where drugs are compounded or dispensed;

    g. [Repealed.]

    h. Administration of injectable medications, biologicals and adult immunizations pursuant to a valid prescription or physician-approved protocol approved by a physician duly licensed in the State under subchapter III of Chapter 17 of this title. Pharmacists shall request which physician or physicians and notify the physician or physicians as designated by the patient of such administration within 24 hours. The notice shall include the patient's name, the name of the immunizations, inoculations or vaccinations administered, and the date of administration and may be submitted by phone, fax, post or electronically. Upon request a copy of the protocol will be made available to the designated physician or physicians without costs.

(22) "Practitioner" or "prescriber" means an individual who is authorized by law to prescribe drugs in the course of professional practice or research in any state.

(23) "Preceptor" means a licensed pharmacist who is approved by the Board to supervise an intern.

(24) "Prescription drug" or "legend drug" means a drug required by federal or state law or regulation to be dispensed only by a prescription, including finished dosage forms and active ingredients, subject to § 503(b) of the Federal Food, Drug and Cosmetic Act (21 U.S.C. § 353(b)).

(25) "Prescription drug order" or "prescription" means the lawful written or verbal order of a practitioner for a drug.

(26) "Reference product" means a product as defined by the Federal Food and Drug Administration pursuant to 42 U.S.C. § 262.

(27) "State" means the State of Delaware.

(28) "Substantially related" means the nature of the criminal conduct, for which the person was convicted, has a direct bearing on the fitness or ability to perform 1 or more of the duties or responsibilities necessarily related to the practice of pharmacy.

(29) "Substitution" or "substitute" means pharmacist's selection of prescriber authorized generic or therapeutically equivalent prescription medications or, in the case of biologicals, pharmacist selection of an interchangeable biological product in place of the prescribed product. Generic substitution means a drug that is the same active ingredient, equivalent in strength to the strength written on the prescription and which is classified as being therapeutically equivalent to another drug in the latest edition or supplement of the Federal Food and Drug Administration (FDA) Approved Drug Products with Therapeutic Equivalence Evaluations, sometimes referred to as the "Orange Book."

(30) "Therapeutically equivalent drug" means a drug which contains the same active ingredient or ingredients and is identical in strength or concentration, dosage form, and route of administration and which is classified as being therapeutically equivalent to another drug in the latest edition or supplement of the Federal Food and Drug Administration (FDA) Approved Drug Products with Therapeutic Equivalence Evaluations, Evaluations, sometimes referred to as the Orange Book.

(31) "Use or abuse of drugs" means:

    a. The use of illegal drugs;

    b. The use of prescription drugs without a prescription; or

    c. The excessive use or abuse of alcoholic beverage or drugs to the extent that it impairs a pharmacist's ability to perform the work of a pharmacist.

(32) "Wholesale distribution" means the distribution of drugs to a person other than a consumer or patient. Wholesale distribution does not include:

    a. The distribution of drugs within a healthcare group-purchasing organization;

    b. The transfer of prescription drugs by a pharmacy to another pharmacy to alleviate a temporary shortage;

    c. The dispensing of a drug pursuant to a prescription; or

    d. The sale, purchase, or trade of a drug or an offer to sell, purchase, or trade a drug:

        1. By a charitable organization described in § 501(c)(3) of the Internal Revenue Code of 1954 (26 U.S.C. § 501(c)(3)) to a nonprofit affiliate of the charitable organization to the extent permitted by law;

        2. Among hospitals or other health care entities which are under common control;

        3. For emergency medical reasons.

    (33) "Wholesale distributor" means a person engaged in the wholesale distribution of drugs, including, but not limited to, a manufacturer's or distributor's warehouse, a chain drug warehouse or wholesale drug warehouse, an independent wholesale drug trader, and a pharmacy that engages in the wholesale distribution of drugs.

History.

    68 Del. Laws, c. 206, § 1; 70 Del. Laws, c. 186, § 1; 71 Del. Laws, c. 412, § 1; 74 Del. Laws, c. 262, § 42; 76 Del. Laws, c. 167, § 1; 79 Del. Laws, c. 238, § 1; 80 Del. Laws, c. 80, § 13; 82 Del. Laws, c. 261, § 11; 82 Del. Laws, c. 261, § 16; 83 Del. Laws, c. 52, § 14.

Revisor's note.

    Section 1 of 83 Del. Laws, c. 52, provided: "This Act shall be known as the 'Telehealth Access Preservation and Modernization Act of 2021'."

    Section 21 of 83 Del. Laws, c. 52, provided:

"Sections 1-19 of this act take effect on July 1, 2021. Nothing in this act shall be interpreted as affecting or invalidating any health-care services provided through telehealth or telemedicine prior to effective date of this act."

Effect of amendments.

    83 Del. Laws, c. 52, effective July 1, 2021, repealed former (6), (17), (30), (33) and (34) and redesignated the remaining and intervening paragraphs accordingly; and, in present (21) deleted "but is not limited to" following "includes" in the second sentence of the introductory paragraph and repealed (21)g.

§ 2503. Board of Pharmacy; appointments; composition; qualifications; terms; vacancies; suspension or removal; unexcused absences; compensation.

    (a) The Delaware State Board of Pharmacy shall administer and enforce this chapter.

    (b) The Board consists of 9 members who are appointed by the Governor and who are residents of the State. Six members are pharmacists who have been engaged in the practice of pharmacy in Delaware for at least 5 years and who are representative of the various practice settings in the field of pharmacy. Three members are public members, 1 from each county. A public member may not be, nor ever have been, a pharmacist or a member of the immediate family of a pharmacist; may not be, nor ever have been, employed by a pharmacy; may not have a material interest in the providing of goods or services to a pharmacy; and may not be, nor ever have been, engaged in an activity directly related to the practice of pharmacy. A public member must be accessible to inquiries, comments, and suggestions from the general public.

    (c) Except as provided in subsection (d) of this section, each Board member serves a term of 3 years, and may succeed himself or herself for 1 additional term; provided, however, that where a member was initially appointed to fill a vacancy, the member may succeed himself or herself for only 1 additional full term. A person appointed to fill a vacancy on the Board holds office for the remainder of the unexpired term of the vacating member. Each term of office expires on the date specified in the appointment; however, a Board member whose appointment has expired remains eligible to participate in Board proceedings unless or until replaced by the Governor. Members must be appointed so that the terms of no more than 3 members expire in any 1 year. A person who is a member of the Board on July 24, 2007, may complete that person's own term.

(d) A person who has never served on the Board may be appointed to the Board for 2 consecutive terms; but that person is thereafter ineligible to serve for 2 consecutive appointments. A person who has been twice appointed to the Board or who has served on the Board for 6 years within any 9-year period may not again be appointed to the Board until an interim period of at least 1 term has expired since the person last served.

(e) An act or vote on Board business by a person appointed to the Board in violation of this section is invalid.

(f) The Governor shall suspend or remove a member of the Board for the member's misfeasance, nonfeasance, malfeasance, misconduct, incompetency, or neglect of duty. A member subject to a disciplinary hearing must be disqualified from Board business until the charge is adjudicated or the matter is otherwise concluded. A Board member may appeal to the Superior Court a suspension or removal initiated pursuant to this subsection.

(g) A member of the Board, while serving on the Board, may not hold elective office in any professional association of pharmacists or serve as an officer of a professional association's political action committee (PAC).

(h) The provisions of the State Employees', Officers' and Officials' Code of Conduct set forth in Chapter 58 of Title 29 apply to the members of the Board.

(i) A member who is absent without adequate reason for 3 consecutive regular business meetings or who fails to attend at least ½ of all regular business meetings during any calendar year is guilty of neglect of duty.

(j) Each member of the Board shall be reimbursed for all expenses involved in each meeting, including travel, and in addition shall receive compensation per meeting attended in an amount determined by the Division in accordance with Del. Const. art. III, § 9.

(k) The Pharmacy Regulatory Council shall fall under the authority of the Board of Medical Licensure and Discipline and shall consist of 4 pharmacists and 1 member of the public appointed by the Board of Pharmacy, and 2 physicians appointed by the Board of Medical Licensure and Discipline. One of the physicians shall serve as chairperson of the Council. Regulations applicable to activities described in § 2502(21)h. of this title must be approved by the Council.

History.

24 Del. Laws, c. 140, §§ 7, 10; Code 1915, §§ 856, 859; 36 Del. Laws, c. 103, § 1; Code 1935, § 936; 45 Del. Laws, c. 90, § 2; 24 Del. C. 1953, §§ 2501, 2505; 53 Del. Laws, c. 90, §§ 1, 3; 59 Del. Laws, c. 318, § 1; 60 Del. Laws, c. 586, §§ 1, 2; 62 Del. Laws, c. 251, §§ 2, 3; 65 Del. Laws, c. 378, § 1; 67 Del. Laws, c. 366, § 7; 67 Del. Laws, c. 368, § 13; 68 Del. Laws, c. 206, § 1; 70 Del. Laws, c. 186, § 1; 76 Del. Laws, c. 167, § 1; 77 Del. Laws, c. 319, § 1; 79 Del. Laws, c. 238, § 1; 80 Del. Laws, c. 80, § 13; 81 Del. Laws, c. 85, § 12; 83 Del. Laws, c. 52, § 14.

Revisor's note.

Based upon changes contained in 83 Del. Laws, c. 52, § 14, made effective July 1, 2021, by § 21 of that act, "§ 2502(21)h." was substituted for "§ 2502(23)h." in the final sentence of (k).

SUBCHAPTER II
LICENSURE

§ 2515. Grounds for discipline.

(a) A pharmacist licensed under this chapter is subject to disciplinary sanctions set forth in § 2516 of this title if, after a hearing, the Board finds that the pharmacist:

(1) Has employed or knowingly cooperated in fraud or material deception in order to acquire a license to practice pharmacy, has impersonated

another person holding a license, has allowed another person to use the pharmacist's license, or has aided or abetted a person not licensed to practice pharmacy to represent himself or herself as a pharmacist;

(2) Has illegally, incompetently, or negligently practiced pharmacy;

(3) Has been convicted of a crime that is substantially related to the practice of pharmacy; a copy of the record of conviction certified by the clerk of the court entering the conviction is conclusive evidence of conviction;

(4) Has used or abused drugs, as defined in § 2502(31) of this title, in the past 2 years;

(5) Has engaged in an act of consumer fraud or deception, engaged in the restrain of competition, or participated in price-fixing activities;

(6) Has violated a lawful provision of this chapter or any lawful regulation established hereunder;

(7) Has had that pharmacist's own license to practice pharmacy suspended or revoked or has been subjected to other disciplinary action taken by the appropriate licensing authority in another jurisdiction; provided, however, that the underlying grounds for the suspension, revocation, or other action in another jurisdiction have been presented to the Board by certified record and the Board has determined that the facts found by the appropriate licensing authority in the other jurisdiction constitute 1 or more of the acts listed in this subsection. Every person licensed to practice pharmacy in this State is deemed to have given consent to the release of information regarding license suspension or revocation or other disciplinary action by the Board of Pharmacy or by other comparable agencies in other jurisdictions and to have waived all objections to the admissibility of previously adjudicated evidence of the acts or offenses which underlie license suspension or revocation or other disciplinary action;

(8) Has failed to notify the Board that the pharmacist's license to practice pharmacy in another jurisdiction has been subject to discipline, or has been surrendered, suspended, or revoked; or that the licensee has been convicted of a crime that is substantially related to the practice of pharmacy. A certified copy of the record of disciplinary action, or of the surrender, suspension, or revocation of the license is conclusive evidence thereof. A copy of the record of conviction certified by the clerk of the court entering the conviction is conclusive evidence of conviction; or

(9) Has a physical or mental impairment that prevents the pharmacist from engaging in the practice of pharmacy with reasonable skill, competence, and safety to the public.

(b) Subject to the provisions of this chapter and subchapter IV of Chapter 101 of Title 29, the Board shall not restrict, suspend, or revoke a license to practice pharmacy or limit a licensee's right to engage in the practice of pharmacy until the Board gives to the licensee proper notice and opportunity to be heard.

History.

24 Del. Laws, c. 140, § 4; Code 1915, § 865; 32 Del. Laws, c. 45, § 1; Code 1935, § 945; 24 Del. C. 1953, § 2527; 53 Del. Laws, c. 90, § 10; 53 Del. Laws, c. 267; 54 Del. Laws, c. 253; 55 Del. Laws, c. 316, § 2; 59 Del. Laws, c. 318, § 4; 62 Del. Laws, c. 251, § 11; 65 Del. Laws, c. 355, § 1; 65 Del. Laws, c. 378, § 4; 68 Del. Laws, c. 206, § 1; 70 Del. Laws, c. 186, § 1; 74 Del. Laws, c. 262, §§ 44, 45; 75 Del. Laws, c. 436, §§ 24-26; 76 Del. Laws, c. 167, § 1; 79 Del. Laws, c. 238, § 1; 80 Del. Laws, c. 80, § 13; 83 Del. Laws, c. 52, § 14.

Revisor's note.

Based upon changes contained in 83 Del. Laws, c. 52, § 14, made effective July 1, 2021, by § 21 of that act, "§ 2502(31)" was substituted for "§ 2502(36)" in (a)(4).

CHAPTER 28
PROFESSIONAL ENGINEERS

§ 2803. Definitions.

The following words, terms and phrases, when used in this chapter, shall have the meaning ascribed to them, except where the context clearly indicates a different meaning;

(1) "Active roster" shall mean the record of members, associate members, permittees and holders of a certificate of authorization.

(2) "Adjunct member" shall mean an adjunct member of the Association, as defined in § 2806(d) of this title.

(3) "Administrative order" means an order issued by an investigating committee, with the prior approval of the Council pursuant to § 2824(b)(1)g.1. of this title, which attempts to resolve a complaint of a violation under § 2823 of this title. Administrative orders become final 14 days from the day the order is received by the accused but only if there is positive proof of service, such as a signed return receipt or an affidavit of personal service.

(4) "Affiliate member" shall mean an affiliate member of the Association, as defined in § 2806(c) of this title.

(5) "Applicant" shall mean a person who applies to become licensed as a professional engineer, applies to become certified as engineer intern, applies to become an adjunct member of the association, or applies for a certificate of authorization or permit.

(6) "Associate member" shall mean an associate member of the Association, as defined in § 2806(b) of this title.

(7) "Association" shall mean the Delaware Association of Professional Engineers.

(8) "Bylaw" shall mean a bylaw of the Association.

(9) "Certificate of authorization" shall mean an authorization issued by the Council to engage in the practice of engineering.

(10) "Committee" shall mean a committee appointed by the Council.

(11) "Consent order" means a voluntary agreement between parties attempting resolution of a complaint of a violation under § 2823 of this title or a complaint of unlicensed practice under § 2825 of this title. To become a final order, a consent order must be approved by Council pursuant to § 2824(b)(1)g.2. of this title.

(12) "Continuing professional competency" shall mean and refer to compliance with or satisfaction of a published set of guidelines and requirements for the maintenance of professional competency in the practice of engineering.

(13) "Council" shall mean the Council of the Association.

(14) "Engineer" shall mean a person who, by reason of special knowledge and use of the mathematical, physical, and engineering sciences and the principles and methods of engineering analysis and design acquired by an engineering education, through graduation with a baccalaureate degree from a Council-approved 4-year educational program in engineering, in engineering technology or in science related to engineering, is qualified to begin the path to licensure.

(15) "Engineering corporations or partnerships" are corporations or partnerships who practice engineering to provide engineering services to the public.

(16) "Engineer intern" shall mean a person certified as an engineer intern by the Council.

(17) "Examination" shall mean any qualifying examination or examinations required by this chapter.

(18) "Hearing committee" means a committee of Council members to which the Council has delegated authority to adjudicate a complaint of a violation under § 2823 of this title or allegations of unlicensed practice under § 2825 of this title.

(19) "Investigating committee" means a committee of the Council to which the Council has delegated authority to investigate a complaint of a violation under § 2823 of this title or allegations of unlicensed practice under § 2825 of this title.

(20) "Licensed" means licensure as a professional engineer under this chapter.

(21) "Licensee" shall mean a person licensed as a professional engineer under this chapter.

(22) "Member" shall mean a member of the Association, as defined in § 2806(a) of this title.

(23) "Practice of engineering" or "to practice engineering" includes any professional service performed for the general public such as consultation, investigation, evaluation, planning, design, or responsible supervision of construction or operation in connection with any public or private buildings, structures, utilities, machines, equipment, processes, works, or projects wherein the public welfare or the safeguarding of life, health or property is concerned or involved when such professional service requires the application of engineering principles and data, but it does not include the work ordinarily performed by persons who operate or maintain machinery or equipment, neither does it include engineering services performed by an employee of a firm or corporation that does not offer professional engineering services to the general public.

(24) "Professional engineer" shall mean a person who has been duly licensed as a professional engineer by the Council.

(25) "Responsible charge" means a professional engineer's supervision of, control over, and possession of detailed professional knowledge of an engineering work. A professional engineer is only considered to be in responsible charge of an engineering work if the professional engineer makes independent professional decisions regarding the engineering work without requiring instruction or approval from another authority and maintains control over those decisions by the professional engineer's physical presence at the location where the engineering work is performed or by electronic communication with the individual executing the engineering work.

(26) "Retired member" shall mean a person who has elected to claim retired status as defined in § 2806(g) of this title.

(27) "Substantially related" shall mean the nature of the criminal conduct, for which the person was convicted, has a direct bearing on the fitness or ability to perform 1 or more of the duties or responsibilities necessarily related to the practice of engineering.

History.

24 Del. C. 1953, § 2803; 58 Del. Laws, c. 501, § 1; 61 Del. Laws, c. 124, § 1; 65 Del. Laws, c. 336, § 1; 69 Del. Laws, c. 43, § 1; 69 Del. Laws, c. 412, § 1; 70 Del. Laws, c. 186, § 1; 71 Del. Laws, c. 51, § 4; 74 Del. Laws, c. 267, § 1; 76 Del. Laws, c. 291, §§ 1-6; 79 Del. Laws, c. 112, § 1; 83 Del. Laws, c. 190, § 1.

Effect of amendments.
83 Del. Laws, c. 190, effective Sept. 17, 2021,   repealed former (23) and (24) and redesignated
the remaining paragraphs accordingly.

§ 2817. Requirements for licensure.

The following requirements for the 3 essential components of education, experience, and examination shall be considered as the minimum satisfactory evidence that an applicant is qualified for licensure as a professional engineer:

(1) Graduates from an engineering educational program approved by the Engineering Accreditation Commission (EAC) of ABET, Inc. (formerly the Accreditation Board for Engineering and Technology), or from an ABET recognized foreign accreditation agency approved educational program, or an engineering educational program approved by an accrediting agency that is a signatory to the Washington Accord.

a. Graduation with a baccalaureate degree from an engineering educational program accredited by the EAC of ABET, Inc., or by a foreign educational program accreditation agency adjudged by ABET to use substantially equivalent accreditation; procedures or by an accrediting agency that is a signatory to the Washington Accord; and

b. Professional experience in engineering work of a character satisfactory to the Council in the amount of 4 years or more, such experience indicating that the applicant is competent to practice as a professional engineer; and

c. Successful passing of an examination approved by the Council; and

d. Meeting the additional requirements of paragraph (7) of this section.

(2) Graduates from non-EAC of ABET accredited engineering programs, from engineering technology programs or from science programs related to engineering.

a. Graduation with a baccalaureate degree from a Council approved 4-year educational program in engineering that is not EAC of ABET accredited, in engineering technology or in science related to engineering; and

b. Professional experience in engineering work of a character satisfactory to the Council in the amount of 8 years or more, such experience indicating that the applicant is competent to practice as a professional engineer; and

c. Successful passing of an examination approved by the Council; and

d. Meeting the additional requirements of paragraph (7) of this section.

(3) Graduates from non-EAC of ABET accredited engineering programs, from engineering technology programs or from science programs related to engineering who hold master's degrees in engineering from institutions that offer EAC of ABET-accredited engineering programs, or the equivalent:

a. Graduation with a baccalaureate degree from a Council approved 4-year educational program in engineering that is not EAC of ABET accredited, in engineering technology or in science related to engineering; and

b. Professional experience in engineering work of a character satisfactory to the Council in the amount of 5 years or more, such experience indicating that the applicant is competent to practice as a professional engineer; and

c. Successful passing of an examination approved by the Council; and

d. Meeting the additional requirements of paragraph (7) of this section.

(4) Graduates from non-EAC of ABET accredited engineering programs, from engineering technology programs or from science programs related to engineering who hold doctoral degrees in engineering from institutions that offer EAC of ABET-accredited engineering programs, or the equivalent:

a. Graduation with a baccalaureate degree from a Council approved 4-year educational program in engineering that is not EAC of ABET accredited, in engineering technology or in science related to engineering; and

b. Professional experience in engineering work of a character satisfactory to the Council in the amount of 4 years or more, such experience indicating that the applicant is competent to practice as a professional engineer; and

c. Successful passing of an examination approved by the Council; and

d. Meeting the additional requirements of paragraph (7) of this section.

(5) *Engineering experience and examination.* — a. Professional experience in engineering work of a character satisfactory to the Council, consisting of 15 years or more of lawful practice and indicating that the applicant is competent to practice as a professional engineer; and

b. Successful passing of an examination approved by the Council; and

c. Meeting the additional requirements of paragraph (7) of this section.

(6) *Comity.* — a. The Council may, upon application and payment of the required fee and without further examination, issue a license as a professional engineer to any person holding a current, valid certificate of registration or a license as a professional engineer issued to that person by a proper authority of a state, territory, or possession of the United States, the District of Columbia, or a province or territory of Canada, provided the applicant's certificate or license is in good standing as defined in paragraph (9) of this section, and the applicant's qualifications meet at least 1 of the following:

1. The professional engineering qualifications of the applicant on the effective date of such certificate of registration or a license would have satisfied the requirements for licensure in this State on that date.

2. The professional engineering qualifications of the applicant at any time subsequent to the effective date of such certificate of registration or a license would have satisfied the requirements for licensure in this State in effect at that time. A personal interview may be required by Council to ascertain the facts in the case.

3. [Repealed.]

4. The professional engineering qualifications of the applicant include a minimum of 5 years of continuous and verifiable experience as a professional engineer. The applicant must meet the additional requirements of paragraph (7)a. of this section.

5. An applicant holding a valid NCEES council record issued by the National Council of Examiners for Engineering and Surveying, whose qualifications meet the requirements of this chapter, may be registered by Council as a professional engineer

upon receipt from the National Council of Examiners for Engineering and Surveying of a certified copy of such registration record.

6. An applicant who has been designated as a "model law engineer" by the National Council of Examiners for Engineering and Surveying. Such person may be issued a license administratively without Council review.

b. The Council may, upon application and payment of the required fee, issue a license as a professional engineer to an applicant who is an International Professional Engineer (IntPE) registrant under the International Engineering Alliance (IEA) International Professional Engineers Agreement (IPEA). The applicant's IntPE registration must be current and in good standing as defined in paragraph (9) of this section. Such applicant must also have 5 years of experience obtained after receipt of the initial license.

c. If the person who has been licensed in Delaware pursuant to paragraph (6)a. or b. of this section has that person's license to practice revoked in the state in which the person was registered or licensed at the time licensure in Delaware through comity was sought, then the authorization issued in Delaware shall be automatically revoked followed 30 days' written notice from the Council unless the person makes application to the Council for consideration for retaining the Delaware authorization and the Council acts favorably on such application.

(7) *Additional requirements.* — a. Every applicant shall give not less than 5 references, people who state that in their opinion and by their personal knowledge the applicant is qualified to practice as a professional engineer. At least 3 such references shall be registered or licensed professional engineers in this or any other state or territory or possession of the United States, the District of Columbia, or the province or territory of Canada or an IntPE registrant under the IEA.

b. An applicant, otherwise qualified, shall not be required to be actively practicing the applicant's profession at the time of the applicant's application.

c. Every applicant must demonstrate knowledge of the Delaware Professional Engineers Act and the code of ethics to the satisfaction of the Council.

d. The required examination shall consist of a Fundamentals of Engineering examination and a Principles and Practice of Engineering examination furnished by, and scored by, the National Council of Examiners for Engineering and Surveying, or other nationally normed examinations which are approved by the Council.

e. The examination in the Fundamentals of Engineering shall be taken after graduation, except it may be taken by a college or university senior in good academic standing in an educational program leading to a baccalaureate degree in engineering, related science or engineering technology. The Council may permit other students in such programs to take the Fundamentals of Engineering examination prior to graduation.

f. The examination in Principles and Practice of Engineering shall not be taken until after the satisfactory completion of the educational requirements as outlined in paragraphs (1)-(4) of this section or the experience requirements of paragraph (5) of this section. The order in which examinations are taken relative to when an applicant's professional experience under paragraphs (1)-(4) of this section is acquired shall not be considered.

g. Applicants with 4 failures of the Principles and Practice of Engineering examination may only apply to retake the examination after completing the following:

1. Present 3 new references to the Council, at least 2 of whom must be registered or licensed professional engineers in this or any other state or territory or possession of the United States, the District of Columbia, or any province or territory of Canada, pursuant to paragraph (7)a. of this section; and

2.A. Successful completion of 6 college-level semester credit hours that are preapproved by Council to assure that the courses adequately address the subject matter weaknesses outlined in the diagnostic report resulting from the preceding failure of the Principles and Practice of Engineering Examination. Applicants must provide official transcripts of the courses that were taken demonstrating that a grade of "C minus" or higher was achieved; or

B. Submit such documentation to Council that demonstrates, to Council's satisfaction, that the applicant has acquired at least 2 years of additional engineering experience, including a brief summary explaining how that experience has better prepared the applicant to pass the examination; or

C. submit such documentation to Council that demonstrates, to Council's satisfaction, that the applicant has acquired sufficient educational and engineering experience, including a brief summary explaining how that educational and engineering experience has better prepared the applicant to pass the examination.

3. On the fifth and all subsequent attempts, applicants must reapply and meet the requirement stipulated in paragraphs (7)g.1. and 2. of this section above.

(8) Applicants for licensure as a professional engineer shall be exempt from the requirement to pass the Fundamentals of Engineering Examination, if they are qualified as follows:

a. An individual holding an earned doctoral degree in engineering from a university, which has an undergraduate program, accredited by ABET or by an accrediting agency that is a signatory to the Washington Accord, in that discipline at the time that individual earned the doctoral degree, providing that doctoral degree required the passing of a Ph.D. qualifying examination from that university; or,

b. An individual holding a baccalaureate degree from a Council-approved 4-year engineering educational program, who has at least 15 years of professional experience in the lawful practice of engineering of a character satisfactory to the Council, and which indicates that the applicant is competent to practice as a professional engineer.

(9) The Council may refuse an applicant for licensure if the Council finds that the applicant has:

a. Been convicted of a crime that is substantially related to the practice of engineering; or

b. Misstated or misrepresented a fact in connection with the applicant's application; or

c. Been found guilty of a violation of this chapter or of the Delaware Association of Professional Engineers' Code of Ethics; or

d. Engaged in the practice of engineering in this State without being licensed as a professional engineer. Notwithstanding such a finding, the Council may allow licensure of such applicant if the applicant presents to the Council suitable evidence of reform; or

e. Used improper means to gain information usable by the applicant on or in connection with an examination taken by the applicant to obtain licensure as a professional engineer or certification as an engineer intern; or

f. Been disciplined by another jurisdiction, state, territory, or possession of the United States, the District of Columbia, foreign country, the United States government, or any other governmental entity, if at least 1 of the grounds for discipline is the same or substantially equivalent to those contained in § 2823 of this title; or

g. Voluntarily surrendered an engineering license in order to avoid disciplinary action by another jurisdiction, state, territory, or possession of the United States, the District of Columbia, foreign country, the United States government, or any other governmental entity, if at least 1 of the grounds for discipline is the same or substantially equivalent to those contained in § 2823 of this title.

(10) Where an application of a person has been refused or rejected, and such applicant feels that the Council has acted without justification, has imposed higher or different standards for that person than for other applicants, or has in some other manner contributed to or caused the failure of such application, the applicant may appeal to the Superior Court.

History.

24 Del. C. 1953, § 2817; 58 Del. Laws, c. 501, § 1; 61 Del. Laws, c. 467, §§ 5, 6; 66 Del. Laws, c. 56, §§ 1-8; 67 Del. Laws, c. 6, §§ 1-4; 68 Del. Laws, c. 24, § 4; 68 Del. Laws, c. 321, §§ 1-4; 69 Del. Laws, c. 43, §§ 9-11; 69 Del. Laws, c. 412, §§ 4, 13-15; 70 Del. Laws, c. 186, § 1; 71 Del. Laws, c. 259, §§ 1-3; 74 Del. Laws, c. 267, § 1; 75 Del. Laws, c. 304, §§ 1, 2; 76 Del. Laws, c. 291, § 11; 77 Del. Laws, c. 50, §§ 1, 2; 78 Del. Laws, c. 162, § 3; 79 Del. Laws, c. 112, § 1; 82 Del. Laws, c. 116, §§ 1-3; 83 Del. Laws, c. 190, § 2.

Effect of amendments.

83 Del. Laws, c. 190, effective Sept. 17, 2021, added a comma following "Technology)" in the introductory paragraph of (1), following "Inc." in (1)a. and following "program" in (8)a.; added "or an engineering educational program approved by an accrediting agency that is a signatory to the Washington Accord" in the introductory paragraph of (1); added "procedures or by an accrediting agency that is a signatory to the Washington Accord" in (1)a.; in the introductory paragraph of (6)a., added "current" and "certificate or license...and the applicant's"; repealed (6)a.3.; rewrote the second second sentence of (6)a.4.; added (6)a.5. and (6)a.6.; rewrote (a)(6)b.; added "or an IntPE registrant under the IEA" in (7)a.; in (8)a., deleted "ABET accredited" preceding "undergraduate" and added "accredited by ABET or by an accrediting agency that is a signatory to the Washington Accord"; and added (9)f. and (9)g. and made related stylistic changes.

§ 2820. Qualifications for a temporary permit.

History.

24 Del. C. 1953, § 2820; 58 Del. Laws, c. 501, § 1; 61 Del. Laws, c. 124, § 3; 61 Del. Laws, c. 467, §§ 9, 10; 67 Del. Laws, c. 6, § 7; 74 Del. Laws, c. 267, § 1; 81 Del. Laws, c. 193, § 3; repealed by 83 Del. Laws, c. 190, § 3, effective Sept. 17, 2021.

§ 2828. Applicability of Freedom of Information Act.

(a) The Association, the Council, and its committees shall each be deemed a "public body" as that term is used in the Freedom of Information Act, Chapter 100 of Title 29, and for purposes of this section only, all references to "the Council" shall be understood as referring to the Association and committees as well.

(b) In addition to the records which are not deemed public by reason of

§ 10002 of Title 29, the following records shall not be deemed to be public records:

(1) The application of any person to practice engineering in the State together with all records relating thereto;

(2) Records, reports, correspondence and other documents received by the Council relating to charges against any person that could lead to disciplinary action by the Council; and

(3) All examination materials and related documents.

(c) In addition to the purpose for which a public body may go into executive session pursuant to the Freedom of Information Act, the Council may conduct an executive session for the following purposes:

(1) Consideration of the application of any person for authorization to practice engineering in the State which consideration involves matters of qualification, recommendations, education, experience or testing of the applicant.

(2) Consideration of any charges which could result in disciplinary action by the Council.

(d) For purposes of this section, the term "application" shall mean any application or filing with the Council for the purpose of obtaining authorization to use the term "engineer," licensure, a certification of authorization, or certification as an engineer intern.

History.
62 Del. Laws, c. 167, § 1; 74 Del. Laws, c. 267, § 1; 78 Del. Laws, c. 162, §§ 7, 8; 78 Del. Laws, c. 382, § 1; 83 Del. Laws, c. 190, § 4.

Effect of amendments.
83 Del. Laws, c. 190, effective September 17, 2021, deleted "a temporary permit" following "authorization" in (d).

§ 2829. Seals, stamps, and signature.

(a) Each licensee shall obtain a seal of the design authorized by the Council, bearing the licensee's name, license number and the legend "professional engineer." The seal format may be embossing, rubber stamp or digital. All new licensees must submit proof of their Delaware seal to the Council office no later than 6 months after the licensee's application approval date, and failure to do so will result in the licensee being placed by the Council in delinquent status.

(b) In addition to the embossing seal required by the foregoing provisions of this section:

(1) Licensees may procure and use a stamp containing the same data as the embossing seal, or

(2) Licensees may use a seal, signature, and date that can be created or transmitted electronically.

History.
68 Del. Laws, c. 24, § 8; 74 Del. Laws, c. 267, § 1; 81 Del. Laws, c. 193, § 4; 83 Del. Laws, c. 190, § 5.

Effect of amendments.
83 Del. Laws, c. 190, effective September 17,

2021, in (a), substituted "a" for "an embossing" following "obtain" in the first sentence, added the second sentence, and rewrote the final sentence.

§ 2830. Dating, signing and sealing.

(a) All final drawings, specifications and documents involving the practice of engineering as defined in this chapter when issued or filed for public record shall be dated and bear the signature and seal of the licensee or licensees who prepared or approved them.

(b) If original tracings are sealed or stamped, the date of sealing or stamping must appear under the signature.

(c) [Repealed.]

History.

68 Del. Laws, c. 24, § 9; 70 Del. Laws, c. 186, § 1; 74 Del. Laws, c. 267, § 1; 83 Del. Laws, c. 190, § 6.

Effect of amendments.

83 Del. Laws, c. 190, effective September 17, 2021, repealed (c).

CHAPTER 30
MENTAL HEALTH AND CHEMICAL DEPENDENCY PROFESSIONALS

SUBCHAPTER I
BOARD OF MENTAL HEALTH AND CHEMICAL DEPENDENCY PROFESSIONALS

§ 3002. Definitions.

The following words, terms and phrases, when used in this chapter, shall have the meanings ascribed to them under this section, except where the context clearly indicates a different meaning:

(1) "Board" means the Board of Mental Health and Chemical Dependency Professionals.

(2) "Conversion therapy" means any practice or treatment that seeks to change an individual's sexual orientation or gender identity, as "sexual orientation" and "gender identity" are defined in § 710 of Title 19, including any effort to change behaviors or gender expressions or to eliminate or reduce sexual or romantic attractions or feelings toward individuals of the same gender. "Conversion therapy" does not mean any of the following:

a. Counseling that provides assistance to an individual who is seeking to undergo a gender transition or who is in the process of undergoing gender transition.

b. Counseling that provides an individual with acceptance, support, and understanding without seeking to change an individual's sexual orientation or gender identity.

c. Counseling that facilitates an individual's coping, social support, and identity exploration and development, including counseling in the form of sexual orientation-neutral interventions or gender identity-neutral interventions provided for the purpose of preventing or addressing unlawful conduct or unsafe sexual practices, without seeking to change an individual's sexual orientation or gender identity.

(3) "Division" means the Division of Professional Regulation of the State of Delaware.

(4) "Excessive use or abuse of drugs" means any use of narcotics, controlled substances or illegal drugs without a prescription from a licensed physician, or the abuse of alcoholic beverage such that it impairs a licensee's ability to perform the work of a licensed mental health or chemical dependency professional.

(5) "Person" means a corporation, company, association and partnership, as well as an individual.

(6) "Store and forward transfer" means the transmission of a patient's medical information either to or from an originating site or to or from the provider at the distant site, but does not require the patient being present nor must it be in real time.

(7) "Substantially related" means the nature of the criminal conduct, for which a person was convicted, has a direct bearing on the fitness or ability of the person to perform 1 or more of the duties or responsibilities of a licensed mental health or chemical dependency professional.

History.

66 Del. Laws, c. 128, § 1; 68 Del. Laws, c. 52, § 1; 70 Del. Laws, c. 186, § 1; 72 Del. Laws, c. 267, § 1; 74 Del. Laws, c. 262, § 59; 74 Del. Laws, c. 355, §§ 3, 4; 75 Del. Laws, c. 83, § 1; 80 Del. Laws, c. 80, § 14; 81 Del. Laws, c. 340, § 6; 82 Del. Laws, c. 261, §§ 12, 16; 83 Del. Laws, c. 52, § 15.

Revisor's note.

Section 1 of 83 Del. Laws, c. 52, provided: "This Act shall be known as the 'Telehealth Access Preservation and Modernization Act of 2021'."

Section 21 of 83 Del. Laws, c. 52, provided: "Sections 1-19 of this act take effect on July 1, 2021. Nothing in this act shall be interpreted as affecting or invalidating any health-care services provided through telehealth or telemedicine prior to effective date of this act."

Effect of amendments.

83 Del. Laws, c. 52, effective July 1, 2021, deleted former (3), (6), (8), (10) and (11) and redesignated the remaining and intervening paragraphs accordingly.

§ 3011. Disciplinary sanctions.

NOTES TO DECISIONS

License revocation.

Delaware Board of Mental Health and Chemical Dependency Professionals Board's decision to revoke a counselor's license had a substantial and rational basis, was supported by substantial evidence, and was well within the Board's discretion because: (1) the Board found that the counselor's long-standing pattern of unethical actions and conduct was clearly outside of the bounds of appropriate behavior; (2) there was substantial evidence that the counselor violated ethics code directives by sexually harassing a client; (3) the counselor breached the duty of confidentiality when revealing a second client's issues to an unauthorized person; and (4) the counselor's text message exchange to a client's caregiver was offensive and discomforting. Brousell v. Del. Bd. of Mental Health & Chem. Dependency Professionals, — A.3d —, 2021 Del. Super. LEXIS 306 (Del. Super. Ct. Apr. 14, 2021).

§ 3012. Hearing procedures.

NOTES TO DECISIONS

Due process.

Delaware Board of Mental Health and Chemical Dependency Professionals Board's reliance on a hearing officer's discretion to admit a text message exchange was not a violation of due process because: (1) the board-licensed professional mental health counselor was on notice of the contents of the exchange; (2) the exchange was relevant; (3) the exchange was professionally inappropriate; and (4) the hearing officer did not abuse discretion by admitting it into evidence. Brousell v. Del. Bd. of Mental Health & Chem. Dependency Professionals, — A.3d —, 2021 Del. Super. LEXIS 306 (Del. Super. Ct. Apr. 14, 2021).

SUBCHAPTER III

CHEMICAL DEPENDENCY PROFESSIONALS

§ 3041. Definitions.

As used in this subchapter:

(1) "Chemical dependency professional" is a person who uses addiction counseling methods to assist an individual or group to develop an understanding of alcohol and drug dependency problems, define goals, and plan action reflecting the individual's or group's interest, abilities and needs as affected by addiction problems.

(2) "Counseling experience" is a formal, systematic process that focuses on skill development and integration of knowledge related to addiction counseling and reflects the accumulation of hours spent providing substance abuse counseling services while under the supervision of an approved clinical supervisor.

(3) "Licensed chemical dependency professional" is a person who holds a current, valid license issued pursuant to this chapter.

(4) "Professional counseling experience" is the accumulation of hours spent providing chemical dependency counseling services in a substance abuse counseling setting, including face to face interaction with clients and other services directly related to the treatment of clients.

(5) "Supervised counseling experience" is the overseeing of a supervisee's application of chemical dependency counseling principles, methods or procedures to assist clients in achieving more effective personal and social adjustment.

(6) "Uncompensated addictions services" are services offered to chemical dependent individuals free of charge.

History.

74 Del. Laws, c. 355, § 12; 75 Del. Laws, c. 83, § 1; 80 Del. Laws, c. 80, § 16; 82 Del. Laws, c. 261, §§ 12, 16; 83 Del. Laws, c. 52, § 16.

Revisor's note.

Section 1 of 83 Del. Laws, c. 52, provided: "This Act shall be known as the 'Telehealth Access Preservation and Modernization Act of 2021'."

Section 21 of 83 Del. Laws, c. 52, provided: "Sections 1-19 of this act take effect on July 1, 2021. Nothing in this act shall be interpreted as affecting or invalidating any health-care services provided through telehealth or telemedicine prior to effective date of this act."

Effect of amendments.

83 Del. Laws, c. 52, effective July 1, 2021, deleted the former final sentence in (1).

CHAPTER 31
FUNERAL SERVICES

SUBCHAPTER I
BOARD OF FUNERAL SERVICES

§ 3101. Definitions.

The following words, terms and phrases, when used in this chapter shall have the meanings ascribed to them under this section, except where the context clearly indicates a different meaning:

(1) "Board" shall mean the State Board of Funeral Services established in this chapter.

(2) "Burial" shall mean the interment of human remains.

(3) "Cremation" shall mean the process of burning human remains to ashes.

(4) "Division" shall mean the State Division of Professional Regulation.

(5) "Embalming" shall mean the disinfecting or preservation of a dead human body, entirely or in part, by the use of chemical substances, fluids, or gases in the body, or by the introduction of the same into the body by vascular or hypodermic injection, or by the direct application of the same into the organs or cavities.

(6) "Embalming room assistant" shall mean a person who has met all of the requirements, including all necessary training in blood borne pathogens standards, and who has received all necessary vaccinations related to the industry, to be able to perform their duties in the embalming or dressing room areas for the preparation of a deceased human remains. Such individual shall not possess the ability to embalm a decedent.

(7) "Funeral director" shall mean a person engaged in the care of human remains or in the disinfecting and preparing by embalming of human remains for the funeral service, transportation, burial, entomb-

ment or cremation, and who shall file all death certificates or permits as required by Chapter 31 of Title 16.

(8) "Funeral establishment" shall mean any place used in the care and preparation of human remains for funeral service, burial, entombment or cremation; said place shall also include areas for embalming, the convenience of the bereaved for viewing and other services associated with human remains. A funeral establishment shall also include a place or office in which the business matters associated with funeral services are conducted. Satellite funeral establishments existing as of May 12, 1988, shall not be required to include an area for embalming.

(9) "Funeral services" shall mean those services rendered for the disinfecting, embalming, burial, entombment or cremation of human remains, including the sale of those goods and services usual to arranging and directing funeral services.

(10) "Intern" shall mean a person, duly registered with the Board, engaged in training to become a licensed funeral director in this State under the direction and personal supervision of a state-licensed funeral director.

(11) "Nonresident funeral director" shall mean a funeral director licensed in another state, district, territory or foreign country.

(12) "Person" shall mean a corporation, company, association and partnership, as well as an individual.

(13) "Practitioner" shall mean a funeral director.

(14) "Protective hairstyle" includes braids, locks, and twists.

(15) "Race" includes traits historically associated with race, including hair texture and a protective hairstyle.

(16) "Student of mortuary science" shall mean a person registered in an official accredited Institution of Mortuary Science program.

(17) "Substantially related" means the nature of the criminal conduct, for which the person was convicted, has a direct bearing on the fitness or ability to perform 1 or more of the duties or responsibilities necessarily related to the provision of funeral services.

History.
  66 Del. Laws, c. 225, § 1; 69 Del. Laws, c. 147, § 1; 71 Del. Laws, c. 460, § 1; 74 Del. Laws, c. 262, § 64; 80 Del. Laws, c. 194, § 1; 83 Del. Laws, c. 13, § 21.

Effect of amendments.
  83 Del. Laws, c. 13, effective April 13, 2021, added present (14) and (15) and redesignated the remaining paragraphs accordingly.

CHAPTER 35
PSYCHOLOGY

SUBCHAPTER I
BOARD OF EXAMINERS OF PSYCHOLOGISTS

§ 3502. Definitions.

The following words, terms and phrases, when used in this chapter shall have the meanings ascribed to them under this section, except where the context clearly indicates a different meaning:

(1) "Board" shall mean the State Board of Examiners of Psychologists established in this chapter.

(2) "Conversion therapy" means any practice or treatment that seeks to

change an individual's sexual orientation or gender identity, as "sexual orientation" and "gender identity" are defined in § 710 of Title 19, including any effort to change behaviors or gender expressions or to eliminate or reduce sexual or romantic attractions or feelings toward individuals of the same gender. "Conversion therapy" does not mean any of the following:

a. Counseling that provides assistance to an individual who is seeking to undergo a gender transition or who is in the process of undergoing gender transition.

b. Counseling that provides an individual with acceptance, support, and understanding without seeking to change an individual's sexual orientation or gender identity.

c. Counseling that facilitates an individual's coping, social support, and identity exploration and development, including counseling in the form of sexual orientation-neutral interventions or gender identity-neutral interventions provided for the purpose of preventing or addressing unlawful conduct or unsafe sexual practices, without seeking to change an individual's sexual orientation or gender identity.

(3) "Excessive use or abuse of drugs" shall mean any use of narcotics, controlled substances or illegal drugs without a prescription from a licensed physician, or the abuse of alcoholic beverage such that it impairs the person's ability to perform the work of a psychologist.

(4) "Person" shall mean a corporation, company, association and partnership, as well as an individual.

(5) "Practice of psychology" shall mean the observation, description, evaluation, interpretation and modification of human behavior by the application of psychological principles, methods, and/or procedures, for the purpose of preventing or eliminating symptomatic, maladaptive or undesired behavior, and of enhancing interpersonal relationships, work and life adjustment, personal effectiveness, behavioral health and mental health. The practice of psychology includes psychological testing and the evaluation or assessment of personal characteristics, such as intelligence, personality, abilities, interests, aptitudes and neuropsychological function; counseling, psychoanalysis, psychotherapy, hypnosis, biofeedback, and behavior analysis and therapy; diagnosis and treatment of mental and emotional disorder or disability, alcoholism and substance abuse, disorders of habit or conduct, as well as the psychological aspects of physical illness, accident, injury or disability; and psychoeducational evaluation, therapy, remediation, and consultation. Psychological services may be rendered to individuals, families, groups, organizations, institutions and the public.

The practice of psychology shall be construed within the meaning of this definition without regard to whether or not payment is received for services rendered.

a. "Psychological testing" shall mean, but not be limited to: Administration and interpretation of standardized intelligence and neuropsychological tests which yield an intelligence quotient and/or are the basis for a diagnosis of organic brain syndromes for the purposes of classification and/or disability determination; and

b. The administration and interpretation of psychological tests which are the basis of a diagnosis of mental or emotional disorder.

(6) "Psychological assistant" shall mean a person who is registered with the Board to perform certain functions within the practice of psychology,

only under the direct supervision of a supervising psychologist, and who is authorized by the Board to use the title "psychological assistant." The Board in its rules and regulations will specify the arrangements for supervision by the licensed psychologist.

(7) "Psychologist" shall mean a person who makes representations to the public by any title or description of services incorporating the words "psychology," "psychological," "psychologist," or who engages in the practice of psychology.

(8) "Substantially related" means the nature of the criminal conduct, for which the person was convicted, has a direct bearing on the fitness or ability to perform 1 or more of the duties or responsibilities necessarily related to the practice of psychology.

(9) "Supervising psychologist" shall mean a psychologist licensed in this State who has practiced as a licensed psychologist for 2 years in this or any other jurisdiction and who applies to the Board for the registration of a psychological assistant.

(10) "Supervision" shall mean the face-to-face consultation between the registered psychological assistant and the supervising psychologist as required by the nature of the work of the psychological assistant. The supervising psychologist is responsible for insuring that the extent, kind and quality of the services rendered by the psychological assistant are consistent with the person's education, training and experience.

History.

24 Del. C. 1953, § 3501; 58 Del. Laws, c. 380; 62 Del. Laws, c. 314, § 1; 70 Del. Laws, c. 57, § 1; 70 Del. Laws, c. 186, § 1; 74 Del. Laws, c. 262, § 72; 80 Del. Laws, c. 80, § 18; 81 Del. Laws, c. 340, § 8; 82 Del. Laws, c. 261, §§ 13, 16; 83 Del. Laws, c. 52, § 17.

Revisor's note.

Section 1 of 83 Del. Laws, c. 52, provided: "This Act shall be known as the 'Telehealth Access Preservation and Modernization Act of 2021'."

Section 21 of 83 Del. Laws, c. 52, provided: "Sections 1-19 of this act take effect on July 1, 2021. Nothing in this act shall be interpreted as affecting or invalidating any health-care services provided through telehealth or telemedicine prior to effective date of this act."

Effect of amendments.

83 Del. Laws, c. 52, effective July 1, 2021, repealed former (3), (5), (10), (14) and (15) and redesignated the remaining and intervening paragraphs accordingly; and in present (7), substituted "and" for "and/or" following "interpretation" in the first paragraph, deleted "but is not limited to" following "includes" in the first sentence of the second paragraph, designated the former final sentence of the second paragraph as the third paragraph and deleted the former final paragraph.

SUBCHAPTER II
LICENSE AND REGISTRATION

§ 3508. Qualifications of applicant; report to Attorney General; judicial review.

Revisor's note.

Section 325 of 78 Del. Laws, c. 78, effective July 1, 2011; and 78 Del. Laws, c. 290, § 322, effective July 1, 2012, as amended by 79 Del. Laws, c. 78, § 301, effective July 1, 2013; 79 Del. Laws, c. 290, § 333, effective July 1, 2014; 80 Del. Laws, c. 79, § 328, effective July 1, 2015; 80 Del. Laws, c. 298, § 323, effective July 1, 2016; 81 Del. Laws, c. 58, § 328, effective July 3, 2017; 81 Del. Laws, c. 280, § 323, effective July 1, 2018; 82 Del. Laws, c. 64, § 323, effective July 1, 2019; 82 Del. Laws, c. 242, § 316, effective July 1, 2020; and 83 Del. Laws, c. 54, § 330, effective June 30, 2021, provided: "For the purpose of participating in CSCRP, provisions of the Delaware Code to the contrary notwithstanding, school psychologists certified or otherwise licensed by the Department of Education in accordance with the provisions 14 Del. C. § 1092, shall be considered in compliance with qualification standards equivalent to state licensure to practice psychology as set forth in 24 Del. C. § 3508. Such equivalent state licensure status shall be limited to the delivery of services related to the Department of Education or local school district approved school programs conducted within the course of the regular school day at a Department of Education or local school district approved school site or least restrictive environment location. The provisions of this section shall in no way be construed as entitling a person not otherwise qualified to do so to represent himself to the public by any title or description of services incorporating the words "psychology," "psychological" and/or "psycholo- gist" within the meaning of 24 Del. C. § 3502, except as may be herein specifically provided."

§ 3511. Reciprocity.

(a) Where an applicant is already licensed or certified as a doctoral-level psychologist in another jurisdiction and has practiced continually for 2 years in that jurisdiction, the Board shall require:

(1) A certificate or other evidence that the applicant is currently licensed or certified.

(2) Evidence that the psychologist has practiced continually for 2 years.

(3) Evidence that the psychologist has achieved the passing score set by the Board on the written standardized Examination for Professional Practice of Psychology (EPPP) developed by the Association of State and Provincial Psychology Boards (ASPPB) or its successor as approved by the Board.

(4) Evidence that the candidate has received a doctoral degree in psychology from a recognized educational institution, or in lieu of such degree, a doctoral degree in a closely-allied field if it is the opinion of the board that the training required therefor is substantially similar, or has otherwise had training in psychology deemed equivalent by the board. Graduates of foreign programs will be required to have their credentials evaluated by a credential evaluation service approved by the National Association of Credential Evaluation Services to determine equivalency to the accreditation requirements of § 3508 of this title.

(b) Upon receipt of an application from an applicant who has been or who currently is licensed, certified or registered as a psychologist, or is registered as a psychological assistant, in another jurisdiction, the Board shall contact the licensing authority, or comparable agency, in such other jurisdiction or jurisdictions and request a certified statement to determine whether or not there are disciplinary proceedings or unresolved complaints pending against the applicant or whether the applicant has engaged in any of the acts or offenses that would be grounds for disciplinary action under this chapter. In the event that a disciplinary proceeding or unresolved complaint is pending, the applicant shall not be licensed until the proceeding or complaint has been resolved. Applicants for licensure under this section shall be deemed to have given consent to the release of such information and to waive all objections to the admissibility of such evidence.

(c) In lieu of the documentation required by subsections (a) and (b) of this section above, the applicant may submit a certificate of professional qualification in psychology from a credential bank approved by the Board. The Board shall identify acceptable credentialing organizations in its rules and regulations. In addition, the Board may require the applicant to submit such supplemental information as it deems necessary to assure that the applicant meets the qualifications for licensure.

History.

70 Del. Laws, c. 57, § 1; 70 Del. Laws, c. 186, § 1; 75 Del. Laws, c. 337, § 1; 79 Del. Laws, c. 364, § 1; 83 Del. Laws, c. 197, § 1.

Effect of amendments.

83 Del. Laws, c. 197, effective September 17, 2021, rewrote the first sentence of (a)(4).

CHAPTER 36

GEOLOGY

Subchapter I. Board of Geologists

SUBCHAPTER I
BOARD OF GEOLOGISTS

§ 3602. Definitions.

The following words, terms and phrases, when used in this chapter shall have the meanings ascribed to them under this section, except where the context clearly indicates a different meaning:

(1) "Board" shall mean the State Board of Geologists established in this chapter.

(2) "Excessive use or abuse of drugs" shall mean any use of narcotics, controlled substances or illegal drugs without a prescription from a licensed physician, or the abuse of alcoholic beverage such that it impairs a person's ability to perform the work of a geologist.

(3) "Geologist" shall mean a person who is qualified to practice professional geology including specialists in its various subdisciplines.

(4) "Person" shall mean a corporation, company, association and partnership, as well as an individual.

(5) "Practice of geology" shall mean any service or creative work, the adequate performance of which requires geologic education, training and experience in the application of the principles, theories, laws and body of knowledge encompassed in the science of geology. This may take the form of, but is not limited to, consultation, research, investigation, evaluations, mapping, sampling, planning of geologic projects and embracing such geological services or work in connection with any public or private utilities, structures, roads, building, processes, works or projects. A person shall be construed to practice geology, who by verbal claim, sign, advertisement or in any other way represents himself or herself to be a geologist, or who holds himself or herself out as able to perform or who does perform geologic services or work.

(6) "Responsible charge" shall mean the individual control and direction, by the use of initiative, skill and individual judgment, of the practice of geology.

(7) "Substantially related" means the nature of the criminal conduct, for which the person was convicted, has a direct bearing on the fitness or ability to perform 1 or more of the duties or responsibilities necessarily related to the practice of geology.

History.
24 Del. C. 1953, § 3601; 58 Del. Laws, c. 477; 61 Del. Laws, c. 477, § 1; 70 Del. Laws, c. 186, § 1; 71 Del. Laws, c. 298, § 1; 74 Del. Laws, c. 262, § 75; 83 Del. Laws, c. 153, § 1.

Effect of amendments.
83 Del. Laws, c. 153, effective Sept. 15, 2021, deleted the concluding paragraph.

CHAPTER 37

SPEECH/LANGUAGE PATHOLOGISTS, AUDIOLOGISTS, AND HEARING AID DISPENSERS

SUBCHAPTER II
LICENSE

§ 3708. Qualifications of applicant; report to Attorney General; judicial review.

(a) An applicant who is applying for licensure under this chapter shall submit evidence, verified by oath and satisfactory to the Board, that such person:

    (1) For licensure as a speech/language pathologist, has met the national requirements for certification of clinical competence issued by the American Speech/Language and Hearing Association (ASHA). The requirements include:

        a. Possession of a master's degree or its equivalent from an accredited college or university in accordance with the Board's rules and regulations.

        b. A supervised clinical practicum in accordance with the Board's rules and regulations.

        c. Completion of 9-months' full-time or 18-months' part-time supervised clinical fellowship year, begun after fulfilling academic and clinical practicum requirements.

        d. Successful completion of a national examination in the area of applicant's specialty prepared by a national testing service and approved by the Division.

    (2) For licensure as an audiologist, has met the national requirements for certification of clinical competence issued by the American Speech/Language Hearing Association, or has been issued board certification from the American Board of Audiology, or its successors. The requirements include:

        a. Possession of a doctoral degree in audiology from an accredited college or university.

        b. Successful completion of a national examination in the area of the applicant's specialty prepared by a national testing service approved by the Division.

        c. Audiologists licensed prior to July 10, 2009, shall be exempted from the educational requirement set forth in paragraph (a)(2)a. of this section.

    (3) For licensure as a hearing aid dispenser, shall submit evidence, verified by oath and satisfactory to the Board, that such person has met the current standards promulgated by the National Institute for Hearing Instrument Studies or its successor; in addition, the applicant shall:

        a. Provide verification of a high school diploma or its equivalent.

        b. Provide proof of successful completion of a national examination prepared by a national testing service and approved by the Division.

        c. An applicant shall complete 6 months of training prior to taking the examination. The Board in its rules and regulations shall establish the frequency of direct supervision during the training period.

        d. [Repealed.]

        e. Paragraphs (a)(3)a. and c. of this section do not apply to applicants who are licensed audiologists.

(b) All applicants shall meet the following conditions:

    (1) Shall not have been the recipient of any administrative penalties regarding their practice of speech/language pathology, audiology or dispensing of hearing aids, including but not limited to fines, formal reprimands, license suspensions or revocation (except for license revocations

for nonpayment of license renewal fees), probationary limitations, and/or has not entered into any "consent agreements" which contain conditions placed by a Board on that applicant's professional conduct and practice, including any voluntary surrender of a license. The Board, after a hearing, may determine whether such administrative penalty is grounds to deny licensure.

(2) Shall not have any impairment related to drugs, alcohol or a finding of mental incompetence by a physician that would limit the applicant's ability to undertake that applicant's practice in a manner consistent with the safety of the public.

(3) Shall not have a criminal conviction record, nor pending criminal charge relating to an offense the circumstances of which substantially relate to their licensed practice. Applicants who have criminal conviction records or pending criminal charges shall request appropriate authorities to provide information about the conviction or charge directly to the Board in sufficient specificity to enable the Board to make a determination whether the conviction or charge is substantially related to the applicant's area of practice. However, after a hearing or review of documentation demonstrating that the applicant meets the specified criteria for a waiver, the Board, by an affirmative vote of a majority of the quorum, may waive this paragraph (b)(3), if it finds all of the following:

a. For waiver of a felony conviction, more than 5 years have elapsed since the date of the conviction. At the time of the application the applicant may not be incarcerated, on work release, on probation, on parole or serving any part of a suspended sentence and must be in substantial compliance with all court orders pertaining to fines, restitution and community service.

b. For waiver of a misdemeanor conviction or violation, at the time of the application the applicant may not be incarcerated, on work release, on probation, on parole or serving any part of a suspended sentence and must be in substantial compliance with all court orders pertaining to fines, restitution and community service.

c. The applicant is capable of practicing speech/language pathology, audiology or the dispensing of hearing aids in a competent and professional manner.

d. The granting of the waiver will not endanger the public health, safety or welfare.

(4) Shall not have been convicted of a felony sexual offense.

(5) Shall submit, at the applicant's expense, fingerprints and other necessary information in order to obtain the following:

a. A report of the applicant's entire criminal history record from the State Bureau of Identification or a statement from the State Bureau of Identification that the State Central Repository contains no such information relating to that person.

b. A report of the applicant's entire federal criminal history record pursuant to the Federal Bureau of Investigation appropriation of Title II of Public Law 92-544 (28 U.S.C. § 534). The State Bureau of Identification shall be the intermediary for purposes of this section and the Board of Speech/Language Pathologists, Audiologists and Hearing Aid Dispensers shall be the screening point for the receipt of said federal criminal history records.

c. An applicant may not be licensed as a speech/language pathologist, audiologist or hearing aid dispenser until the applicant's criminal history reports have been produced. An applicant whose record shows a prior criminal conviction may not be licensed by the Board unless a waiver is granted pursuant to paragraph (b)(3) of this section.

(c) Where the Board has found to its satisfaction that an applicant has been intentionally fraudulent or that false information has been intentionally supplied, it shall report its findings to the Attorney General for further action.

(d) Where the application of a person has been refused or rejected and such applicant feels that the Board has acted without justification, has imposed higher or different standards for that person than for other applicants or licensees, or has in some other manner contributed to or caused the failure of such application, the applicant may appeal to the Superior Court.

(e) All individuals licensed to practice speech/language pathology, audiology or hearing aid dispensing in this State shall be required to be fingerprinted by the State Bureau of Identification, at the licensee's expense, for the purposes of performing subsequent criminal background checks. Licensees shall submit by January 1, 2016, at the applicant's expense, fingerprints and other necessary information in order to obtain a criminal background check.

History.

24 Del. C. 1953, § 3605; 59 Del. Laws, c. 206, § 1; 63 Del. Laws, c. 151, § 6; 65 Del. Laws, c. 224, § 1; 70 Del. Laws, c. 186, § 1; 72 Del. Laws, c. 266, § 1; 74 Del. Laws, c. 262, § 82; 75 Del. Laws, c. 359, §§ 1, 2; 75 Del. Laws, c. 436, § 42; 77 Del. Laws, c. 154, §§ 3-11; 77 Del. Laws, c. 199, § 31; 78 Del. Laws, c. 44, §§ 60, 61; 79 Del. Laws, c. 277, § 12; 82 Del. Laws, c. 9, § 2; 83 Del. Laws, c. 37, § 26.

Effect of amendments.

83 Del. Laws, c. 37, effective June 3, 2021, in (a)(3)e., substituted "(a)(3)a. and c." for "(a)(3)a., c. and d. [repealed]" and "do" for "herein shall".

CHAPTER 38

DIETITIAN/NUTRITIONIST LICENSURE ACT

Sec.
3802. Definitions.

§ 3802. Definitions.

The following words, terms and phrases, when used in this chapter, shall have the meanings ascribed to them in this chapter, except where the context clearly indicates a different meaning:

(1) "Board" shall mean the State Board of Dietetics/Nutrition.

(2) "Dietetic and nutrition therapy" shall mean the scope of services utilized in the delivery of preventive nutrition services and nutrition therapy. It involves an assessment of the individual's specific nutritional needs and the development and implementation of an intervention plan. The intervention plan can include nutrition education, counseling, administration and monitoring of specialized nutrition support and referrals for additional services. This application and practice of "dietetic and nutrition therapy" shall include the following Scope of Practice:

Scope of Practice:

(a) Nutrition assessment to include the establishment of nutritional care plans, including the development of nutritional related priorities, goals and objectives.

(b) Provision of nutrition counseling or education as components of preventive, and restorative health care.

(c) Evaluation and maintenance of appropriate standards of quality in food and nutrition.

(d) Evaluation and education of nutrient-drug interactions.

(e) Interpreting and recommending interventions to meet nutrient needs relative to individual health status, including but not limited to medically prescribed diets, tube feedings and specialized intravenous solutions.

(f) Development, administration, evaluation and consultation regarding nutritional care standards.

(g) Conduct independent research or collaborate in research areas including, but not limited to food and pharmaceutical companies, universities and hospitals by directing or conducting experiments to answer critical nutrition and food science questions and develop nutrition recommendations for the public.

(h) Direct supervision of registered dietetic technicians.

(3) "Dietetics/nutrition" shall mean the integration and application of principles derived from the sciences of food, nutrition, biochemistry, physiology and behavior as an integral part of health-care delivery to achieve and maintain a person's health throughout the life cycle. Its application to health care is both preventive and in response to an illness, injury or condition. The application of dietetics/nutrition to health care shall be called "dietetic and nutrition therapy." The terms "dietetics" and "nutrition" are used interchangeably in this chapter.

(4) "Dietitian" and/or "nutritionist" shall mean a person who engages in the provision of nutrition services. The terms "nutritionist" and "dietitian" are used interchangeably in this chapter.

(5) "L.D.N." shall be the abbreviation for the title "licensed dietitian/nutritionist".

(6) "License" shall mean any document which indicates that a person is currently licensed by the Board of Dietetics/Nutrition.

(7) "Licensed dietitian/nutritionist" shall mean a person holding a current license under this chapter.

(8) "Substantially related" means the nature of the criminal conduct, for which the person was convicted, has a direct bearing on the fitness or ability to perform 1 or more of the duties or responsibilities necessarily related to the provision of dietetics/nutrition therapy services.

History.

69 Del. Laws, c. 306, § 1; 70 Del. Laws, c. 186, § 1; 74 Del. Laws, c. 262, § 85; 76 Del. Laws, c. 49, § 1; 80 Del. Laws, c. 80, § 19; 82 Del. Laws, c. 261, §§ 14, 16; 83 Del. Laws, c. 52, § 18.

Revisor's note.

Section 1 of 83 Del. Laws, c. 52, provided: "This Act shall be known as the 'Telehealth Access Preservation and Modernization Act of 2021'."

Section 21 of 83 Del. Laws, c. 52, provided: "Sections 1-19 of this act take effect on July 1, 2021. Nothing in this act shall be interpreted as affecting or invalidating any health-care services provided through telehealth or telemedicine prior to effective date of this act."

Effect of amendments.

83 Del. Laws, c. 52, effective July 1, 2021, in (2), substituted "and" for "and/or" following "services" in the first sentence and following "support" in the second sentence and deleted (i) under the "Scope of Practice"; and deleted former (5), (9), (10), (12) and (13) and redesignated the remaining and intervening paragraphs accordingly.

CHAPTER 39
BOARD OF SOCIAL WORK EXAMINERS

§ 3902. Definitions.

As used in this chapter:

(1) "Advanced practice" means the specialized professional application of social work theory, knowledge, methods, principles, values, and ethics, and the professional use of self to community and organizational systems, meaning systemic and macrocosm issues, and other indirect, nonclinical

services. "Advanced practice" includes activities such as community organization and development; social planning and policy development; administration of social work policies, programs, and activities; outcome evaluation; client education; research; nonclinical supervision of employees; nonclinical consultation; nonclinical assessment and referral; mediation; expert testimony; and advocacy.

(2) "Another jurisdiction" means another state of the United States, the District of Columbia, a territory of the United States, or a country outside of the United States or its territories.

(3) "Applicant" means an individual seeking licensure under this chapter.

(4) "Baccalaureate social work" is the entry level of social work and means the application of social work theory, knowledge, methods, ethics, and the professional use of self to restore or enhance social, psychosocial, or biopsychosocial functioning of individuals, couples, families, groups, organizations, and communities. "Baccalaureate social work" is generalist practice.

(5) "Baccalaureate social worker" means an individual licensed to practice baccalaureate social work.

(6) "Board" means the Board of Social Work Examiners.

(7) "Case management" means a method to plan, provide, evaluate, and monitor services from a variety of resources on behalf of and in collaboration with a client.

(8) "Client" means an individual, couple, family, group, organization, or community that seeks or receives social work services from a social worker or an organization whether those services are free or for a fee.

(9) "Clinical supervisor" means a licensed clinical social worker who has met the qualifications as determined by the Board.

(10) "Consultation" means an advisory professional relationship between a social worker and other professionals, with the social worker ethically maintaining responsibility for all judgments and decisions regarding service to a client.

(11) "Conversion therapy" means any practice or treatment that seeks to change an individual's sexual orientation or gender identity, as "sexual orientation" and "gender identity" are defined in § 710 of Title 19, including any effort to change behaviors or gender expressions or to eliminate or reduce sexual or romantic attractions or feelings toward individuals of the same gender. "Conversion therapy" does not mean any of the following:

    a. Counseling that provides assistance to an individual who is seeking to undergo a gender transition or who is in the process of undergoing gender transition.

    b. Counseling that provides an individual with acceptance, support, and understanding without seeking to change an individual's sexual orientation or gender identity.

    c. Counseling that facilitates an individual's coping, social support, and identity exploration and development, including counseling in the form of sexual orientation-neutral interventions or gender identity-neutral interventions provided for the purpose of preventing or addressing unlawful conduct or unsafe sexual practices, without seeking to change an individual's sexual orientation or gender identity.

(12) "Counseling" means a method, in addition to psychotherapy, advocacy, research, and consultation, used by social workers to assist individu-

als, couples, families, and groups in learning how to solve problems and make decisions about personal, health, social, educational, vocational, financial, and other interpersonal concerns.

(13) "Division" means the Division of Professional Regulation.

(14) "Excessive use or abuse of drugs" means the use of narcotics, controlled substances, or illegal drugs without a prescription from a licensed physician or other professional licensed to prescribe, or the abuse of alcoholic beverages such that it impairs an individual's ability to perform social work.

(15) "Generalist practice" means a professional problem process that includes engagement, assessment, treatment planning, intervention, and evaluation. Methods of generalist practice include case management, information and referral, counseling, consultation, education, advocacy, community organization, research, and the development, implementation, and administrations of policies, programs, or activities.

(16) "Good standing" means meeting the standards of § 3907(a) of this title.

(17) "Licensed clinical social work" means the specialty within the practice of master's social work, that requires the application of specialized clinical knowledge and advanced clinical skills of social work theory, knowledge, methods, and ethics, as applied to a clinical, therapeutic relationship which may include the person-in-environment perspective, to the assessment, diagnosis, prevention, and treatment of biopsychosocial dysfunction, disability, and impairment, including mental and emotional disorders, developmental disabilities, and substance abuse. "Licensed clinical social work" includes the provision of individual, marital, couple, family and group counseling, and psychotherapy, as they are related to clinical, therapeutic relationship. "Licensed clinical social work" also includes private practice and supervision. "Licensed clinical social work" does not include the administration of psychological tests, which are reserved exclusively for use by licensed psychologists under Chapter 35 of this title.

(18) "Licensed clinical social worker" means an individual licensed to practice licensed clinical social work.

(19) "Licensee" means an individual licensed under this chapter.

(20) "Master's social work" means the application of social work theory, knowledge, methods, ethics, and the professional use of self to restore or enhance social, psychosocial, or biopsychosocial functioning of individuals, couples, families, groups, organizations, and communities. "Master's social work" is the application of generalist practice, specialized knowledge, and advanced practice skills, and includes supervision.

(21) "Master's social worker" means an individual licensed to practice master's social work.

(22) "Person-in-environment perspective" means observing human behavior, development, and function in the context of the environment, social functioning, mental health, physical health, or any combination thereof.

(23) "Social work" means baccalaureate social work, master's social work, and licensed clinical social work, collectively or, if context demands, individually.

(24) "Social worker" means baccalaureate social worker, master's social worker, and licensed clinical social worker, collectively or, if context demands, individually.

(25) "Substantially related" means the nature of the criminal conduct for which the individual was convicted has a direct bearing on the fitness

or ability to perform 1 or more of the duties or responsibilities necessarily related to social work.

(26) "Supervision" means the professional relationship between a clinical supervisor and a social worker that provides evaluation and direction over the services that the social worker provides and promotes continued development of the social worker's knowledge, skills, and abilities to provide social work services in an ethical and competent manner.

History.
63 Del. Laws, c. 462, § 2; 70 Del. Laws, c. 143, § 1; 70 Del. Laws, c. 186, § 1; 71 Del. Laws, c. 106, §§ 1, 2; 74 Del. Laws, c. 262, § 88; 77 Del. Laws, c. 224, §§ 2, 3; 80 Del. Laws, c. 80, § 20; 81 Del. Laws, c. 340, § 11; 81 Del. Laws, c. 263, § 3; 82 Del. Laws, c. 261, §§ 15, 16; 83 Del. Laws, c. 52, § 19.

Revisor's note.
Section 1 of 83 Del. Laws, c. 52, provided: "This Act shall be known as the 'Telehealth Access Preservation and Modernization Act of 2021'."

Section 21 of 83 Del. Laws, c. 52, provided: "Sections 1-19 of this act take effect on July 1, 2021. Nothing in this act shall be interpreted as affecting or invalidating any health-care services provided through telehealth or telemedicine prior to effective date of this act."

Effect of amendments.
83 Del. Laws, c. 52, effective July 1, 2021, deleted former (13), (23), (27), (30) and (31) and redesignated the remaining and intervening paragraphs accordingly.

CHAPTER 51
COSMETOLOGY AND BARBERING AND LICENSURE OF AESTHETICIANS

SUBCHAPTER I
BOARD OF COSMETOLOGY AND BARBERING

§ 5101. Definitions.

As used in this chapter:

(1) "Aesthetician" is an individual who practices any of the following:

a. Cleansing, stimulating, manipulating and beautifying skin by hand or mechanical or electric apparatus or appliance.

b. Application of lash extensions, additions or enhancements, including permanent waving and tinting.

c. Removal of superfluous hair.

d. Gives treatments to keep skin healthy and attractive.

An aesthetician is not authorized to prescribe medication or provide medical treatment in the same manner as a dermatologist.

(2) "Apprentice" means any person who is engaged in the learning of any or all the practices of cosmetology, barbering, nail technology or electrology from a practitioner licensed in the profession the apprentice is studying. The apprentice may perform or assist the licensed practitioner in any of the functions which the practitioner is licensed to perform.

(3) "Barber" means any person licensed under this chapter who, for a monetary consideration, shaves or trims beards, cuts or dresses hair, gives facial or scalp massages, or treats beards or scalps with preparations made for this purpose.

(4) "Board" means the state Board of Cosmetology and Barbering under this chapter.

(5) "Classroom hour" means 50 minutes of each 60-minute hour.

(6) "Cosmetologist" means any person licensed under this chapter who is not an apprentice or student practicing cosmetology, who shall have the qualifications provided for by this chapter.

(7) "Cosmetology" means performing any of the following services for compensation:

    a. The embellishment, cleansing and beautification of human hair, such as arranging, dressing, curling, permanent waving, cutting, singeing, pressing, chemically bleaching or coloring, chemically straightening, or similar services.

    b. Applying lash extensions, additions or enhancements, including permanent waving and tinting.

    c. The temporary removal of superfluous hair.

    d. Nail technology.

    e. Massaging, stimulating, beautifying, or similar services, of the scalp, face, arms, hands or the upper body.

Any service performed under the definition of "cosmetology" may be performed by hand or mechanical or electrical devices and may include the use of cosmetic preparations, tonics, lotions or creams.

(8) "Cosmetology shop" means any place or part thereof wherein cosmetology, barbering, electrology, nail technology, aesthetics, or any of their practices, are performed for compensation, whether or not the establishment holds itself out as a cosmetology shop.

(9) "Division" means the Delaware Division of Professional Regulation.

(10) "Electrologist" means any person licensed under this chapter who, for a monetary consideration, engages in the removal of superfluous hair by use of specially designed electric needles.

(11) "Instructor" means any person who teaches cosmetology, barbering, electrology or nail technology.

(12) "Master barber" means any person licensed under this chapter who, for a monetary consideration, shaves or trims beards, gives facial or scalp massages, treats beards or scalps with preparations made for this purpose, or embellishes, cleans or beautifies human hair, which includes arranging, dressing, curling, permanent waving, cutting, singeing, pressing, chemically bleaching or coloring, chemically straightening, or similar work.

(13) "Nail technician" means any person licensed under this chapter who engages only in the practice of manicuring, pedicuring or sculpting nails, including acrylic nails, of any person.

(14) "Person" means a corporation, company, association or partnership, as well as an individual.

(15) "Professional-in-charge" means a licensee who is responsible for the operation of a cosmetology shop, including ensuring that all employees are licensed, where required by law.

(16) "School of cosmetology," "school of electrology," "school of nail technology," "school of barbering" means any place or part thereof where cosmetology, barbering, electrology, nail technology or any of the practices are taught, whether or not such place holds itself out as such.

(17) "State" means the State of Delaware.

(18) "Substantially related" means the nature of the criminal conduct, for which the person was convicted, has a direct bearing on the fitness or ability to perform 1 or more of the duties or responsibilities necessarily

related to cosmetology, barbering, electrology, nail technology or aesthetics.

History.

69 Del. Laws, c. 178, § 1; 70 Del. Laws, c. 186, § 1; 73 Del. Laws, c. 158, § 1; 74 Del. Laws, c. 262, § 91; 75 Del. Laws, c. 169, § 1; 77 Del. Laws, c. 65, § 1; 79 Del. Laws, c. 170, § 1; 80 Del. Laws, c. 317, §§ 1, 2; 82 Del. Laws, c. 77, § 1; 83 Del. Laws, c. 76, § 1.

Effect of amendments.

83 Del. Laws, c. 76, effective June 30, 2021, rewrote (1) and (7); in (4), deleted "and refers to" following "means" and substituted "under" for "as provided for in"; and substituted "means" for "is defined as" in (5).

§ 5104. Board of Cosmetology and Barbering; appointment; composition; qualifications; term of office; suspension or removal; compensation; continuation of former Board.

(a) The Board of Cosmetology and Barbering shall consist of 13 members appointed by the Governor and shall be composed of the following:

(1) Two cosmetologists.

(2) One nail technician.

(3) One barber.

(4) One aesthetician.

(5) One cosmetology instructor.

(6) One owner or operator of a shop licensed under this chapter.

(7) One owner or administrator of a school licensed under this chapter.

(8) Five public members. A public member may not be any of the following:

a. At any time, a cosmetologist, barber, electrologist, nail technician or aesthetician.

b. A member of the immediate family of a cosmetologist, barber, electrologist, nail technician or aesthetician.

c. Employed by a cosmetologist, barber, electrologist, nail technician or aesthetician.

d. At any time have a material or financial interest in the providing of goods or services to a cosmetologist, barber, electrologist, nail technician or aesthetician.

e. At any time engaged in an activity directly related to cosmetology, barbering, electrology, nail technology or aesthetics.

A public member shall be accessible to inquiries, comments and suggestions from the general public.

(b) Each member shall serve for a term of 3 years, and may successively serve for 1 additional term; provided, however, that where a member was initially appointed to fill a vacancy, such member may successively serve for only 1 additional full term. Any person appointed to fill a vacancy on the Board shall hold office for the remainder of the unexpired term of the former member.

(c) A person who has never served on the Board may be appointed to serve on the Board for 2 consecutive terms, but no such person shall thereafter be eligible for 2 consecutive appointments. No person who has been twice appointed to the Board, or who has served on the Board for 6 years within any 9-year period, shall again be appointed to the Board until an interim period of at least 1 term has expired since such person last served.

(d) Any act or vote by a person appointed in violation of subsection (c) of this section shall be invalid. An amendment or revision of this chapter is not sufficient cause for any appointment or attempted appointment in violation of subsection (c) of this section, unless such amendment or revision amends this section to permit such an appointment.

(e) A member of the Board shall be suspended or removed by the Governor for misfeasance, nonfeasance or malfeasance. A member subject to disciplinary proceedings shall be disqualified from Board business until the charge is adjudicated or the matter is otherwise concluded.

(f) Any member who fails to attend 3 consecutive regular business meetings, or who fails to attend at least ½ of all regular business meetings during any calendar year, shall automatically upon such occurrence be deemed to have resigned from office and a replacement shall be appointed by the Governor.

(g) No member of the Board of Cosmetology and Barbering, while serving on the Board, shall be a president, chairperson or other official of a professional cosmetology, barbering, nail technology, electrology or aesthetics association.

(h) The provisions set forth in Chapter 58 of Title 29 shall apply to all members of the Board.

(i) Each member of the Board shall be reimbursed for all expenses involved in each meeting, including travel, and in addition shall receive compensation per meeting attended in an amount determined by the Division in accordance with Del. Const. art. III, § 9.

History.
63 Del. Laws, c. 146, § 3; 64 Del. Laws, c. 8, § 1; 67 Del. Laws, c. 368, § 26; 69 Del. Laws, c. 178, § 1; 70 Del. Laws, c. 186, § 1; 72 Del. Laws, c. 177, § 1; 73 Del. Laws, c. 158, §§ 2, 3; 77 Del. Laws, c. 65, § 1; 80 Del. Laws, c. 317, § 4; 81 Del. Laws, c. 85, § 26; 83 Del. Laws, c. 76, § 2.

Effect of amendments.
83 Del. Laws, c. 76, effective June 30, 2021, rewrote (a).

§ 5107. Qualifications of applicant; judicial review; report to Attorney General.

(a) All persons applying for a license to practice under this chapter:

(1) Shall have successfully completed an education equivalent to a tenth grade education. Instructors shall have successfully completed an education equivalent to completion of a twelfth grade education. Proof of the required education shall be a certified high school transcript or any other document or affidavit which constitutes reliable proof of educational attainment as determined by the Board.

(2) Shall have passed a written and practical examination to the satisfaction of the Board as set forth in board rules and regulations.

(3) Shall have paid the appropriate fee as established by the Division of Professional Regulation. In addition, except as otherwise provided for in this chapter, no individual shall be permitted to sit for an examination or shall be granted a license to practice in any of the professions regulated by this chapter, unless the individual meets the following education requirements, or has successfully completed an apprenticeship. The requirements are for:

a. *Cosmetologists.* — The successful completion of a minimum of 1,500 classroom hours of continuous training for a complete course in cosmetology. School owners shall have the option of the amount of hours of training per day and shall be able to choose which days of the week the student works provided the hours accumulated do not exceed 40 hours per week, excluding make-up hours. The Board shall establish by regulation the portion of the 1,500 classroom hours that may be credited to an applicant who previously obtained classroom hours while studying to become an aesthetician, nail technician or electrologist. A cosmetologist may obtain a shaving certification in connection with the cosmetologist's license upon successful completion of a course in shaving consisting of at least 35 hours of instruction from a licensed barbering instructor.

b. *Apprentice cosmetologists.* — The completion of 3,000 hours in an apprenticeship to a licensed cosmetologist with the total number of hours worked not to exceed 40 hours per week. The Board shall establish by regulation the portion of the 3,000 apprenticeship hours that may be credited to an applicant who previously obtained apprenticeship hours while studying to become an aesthetician, nail technician or electrologist.

c. *Transfer of apprentice hours to a cosmetology program.* — An apprentice cosmetologist may transfer up to 1,800 apprentice hours at a rate of 2 apprentice hours to 1 transfer hour to a cosmetology program totaling 1,500 hours. A minimum of 600 hours of course work must be completed at school. The Board must provide documentation of the apprentice hours to the school prior to transfer.

d. *Master barbers.* — For a licensed barber, the successful completion of an additional 600 hour apprenticeship for chemicals, as set forth in the Board's rules and regulations, and the passing of the master barber's examination.

For all other applicants, the successful completion of a minimum of 1,500 classroom hours of continuous training for a complete course in master barbering and the passing of the master barber's examination, or the completion of 3,000 hours in a master barber apprenticeship, as set forth in the Board's rules and regulations, and the passing of the master barber's examination. School owners shall have the option of the amount of hours of training per day and shall be able to choose which days of the week the student works provided the hours accumulated do not exceed 40 hours per week, excluding make-up hours. Any barber who was issued a barber's license by the Division prior to April 28, 2008, shall be deemed a master barber. A master barber may obtain a skin and nails certification in connection with a master barber's license upon completion of at least 250 hours of instruction in a licensed cosmetology school or a 500 hour apprenticeship in skin and nails in accordance with the Board's rules and regulations.

e. *Barbers.* — The successful completion of a minimum of 1,250 classroom hours of continuous training for a complete course in barbering, or the completion of 3,000 hours in an apprenticeship to a licensed barber with the total number of hours worked not to exceed 40 hours per week.

f. *Transfer of apprentice hours to a barbering program.* — An apprentice barber may transfer up to 1,800 apprentice hours at a rate of 2 apprentice hours to 1 transfer hour to a barbering program totaling 1,500 hours. A minimum of 600 hours of course work must be completed at school. The Board must provide documentation of the apprentice hours to the school prior to transfer.

g. *Nail technicians.* — The successful completion of a course of training in nail technology of not less than 300 hours in a school of nail technology or cosmetology; or successful completion of 600 hours as an apprentice under the supervision of a licensed nail technician. In either case, training is not to exceed 40 hours per week, excluding make-up hours.

h. *Electrologists.* — The successful completion of a course of training in electrology of not less than 300 hours in a school of electrology or cosmetology, or successful completion of 600 hours as an apprentice under the supervision of a licensed electrologist. In either case, training is not to exceed 40 hours per week, excluding make-up hours.

i. [Repealed.]

j. *Cosmetology and barbering instructors.* — For cosmetology and barbering, an instructor must have a license in the respective field of cosmetology or barbering and the successful completion of a teacher training course, consisting of at least 500 hours of instruction in a registered school of cosmetology or barbering, or at least 2 years' experience as an active licensed, practicing cosmetologist or barber, supplemented by at least 250 hours of instruction in a teacher training course. In addition, the applicant shall have successfully passed an instructor examination designated by the Board in its rules and regulations. A person licensed as a cosmetology instructor may also provide instruction in nail technology and aesthetics. A person licensed as a cosmetology instructor may obtain a certification to instruct barbering upon successful completion of a course in shaving consisting of at least 35 hours of instruction from a licensed barbering instructor.

k. *Electrology instructor.* — An instructor must have a license in electrology and the successful completion of a teacher training course, consisting of at least 500 hours of instruction in a registered school of electrology or cosmetology; or at least 2 years' experience as an active licensed, practicing electrologist, supplemented by at least 250 hours' instruction in a teacher training course. In addition, the applicant shall have successfully passed an examination designated by the Board in its rules and regulations.

l. *Nail technician instructor.* — An instructor must have a license in nail technology and the successful completion of a teacher training course, consisting of at least 500 hours of instruction in a registered school of cosmetology or nail technology; or at least 2 years' experience as an active licensed, practicing nail technician, supplemented by at least 250 hours of instruction in a teacher training course. Proof of education or experience shall be provided to the satisfaction of the Board. In addition, the applicant shall have successfully passed an examination designated by the Board in its rules and regulations.

(4) Shall not have been the recipient of any administrative penalties regarding that person's licensed practice, including but not limited to fines, formal reprimands, license suspensions or revocation (except for license revocations for nonpayment of license renewal fees), probationary limitations, and/or have not entered into any agreements which contain conditions placed by a board on that person's professional conduct and practice, including any voluntary surrender of a license. The Board may, after a hearing, determine whether such administrative penalty is grounds to deny licensure;

(5) Shall not have any impairment related to drugs or alcohol that would limit the applicant's ability to undertake that applicant's licensed practice in a manner consistent with the safety of the public;

(6) Shall not have been convicted of a crime substantially related to the practice of cosmetology, barbering, electrology or nail technology, unless the applicant was previously so licensed or was enrolled in a training program to be so licensed while an offender under the supervision of the Department of Correction prior to July 10, 2001. In determining whether a crime is substantially related to the professions regulated by this chapter, the Board shall not consider a conviction where more than 10 years have elapsed since the date of conviction, if there have been no other criminal convictions in the intervening time. After a hearing or review of documentation demonstrating that the applicant meets the specified

criteria for a waiver, the Board, by an affirmative vote of a majority of the quorum, or, during the time period between Board meetings, the Board President or his or her designee, may waive this paragraph (a)(6), if it finds all of the following:

    a. For waiver of a felony conviction where the crime was committed against a person, more than 3 years have elapsed since the date of the conviction and for all other felonies, more than 2 years have elapsed since the date of conviction. At the time of the application the applicant may not be incarcerated, on work release, on probationor parole at Level III Supervision or higher, or serving any part of a suspended sentence and must be in substantial compliance with all court orders pertaining to fines, restitution and community service.

    b. For waiver of a misdemeanor conviction or violation, at the time of the application the applicant may not be incarcerated, on work release, on probation or parole at Level III Supervision or higher, or serving any part of a suspended sentence and must be in substantial compliance with all court orders pertaining to fines, restitution and community service.

    c. The applicant is capable of practicing cosmetology, barbering, electrology or nail technology in a competent and professional manner.

    d. The granting of the waiver will not endanger the public health, safety or welfare.

    (7) Shall not have a pending criminal charge relating to an offense the circumstances of which substantially relate to the practice of cosmetology, barbering, electrology or nail technology. Applicants who have criminal conviction records or pending criminal charges shall require appropriate authorities to provide information about the record or charge directly to the Board in sufficient specificity to enable the Board to make a determination whether the applicant can carry out that applicant's own professional services with due regard for the health and safety of the recipients of those services and the public.

    (8) Shall not have any disciplinary proceedings or unresolved complaints pending against that person in any jurisdiction where the applicant previously has been, or currently is, licensed to practice cosmetology, barbering, electrology or nail technology.

(b) As set forth in board rules and regulations, foreign-trained applicants shall provide evidence satisfactory to the Board of training equivalent to that required in paragraph (a)(3) of this section, in addition to meeting all other requirements of this section.

(c) When a person who feels the Board has refused or rejected an application without justification; has imposed higher or different conditions for the person than for other applicants or persons now licensed; or has in some other manner contributed to or caused the failure of such person's application, the applicant may appeal to Superior Court.

(d) Where the Board has found to its satisfaction that an application has been intentionally fraudulent, or that false information has been intentionally supplied, it shall report its findings to the Attorney General for further action.

History.
    64 Del. Laws, c. 8, § 1; 69 Del. Laws, c. 178, § 1; 70 Del. Laws, c. 186, § 1; 73 Del. Laws, c. 158, §§ 11-13; 74 Del. Laws, c. 150, §§ 1, 2; 75 Del. Laws, c. 169, § 3; 75 Del. Laws, c. 436, § 49; 77 Del. Laws, c. 65, § 1; 77 Del. Laws, c. 199, § 37; 78 Del. Laws, c. 44, §§ 72, 73; 79 Del. Laws, c. 170, § 1; 79 Del. Laws, c. 418, § 1; 81 Del. Laws, c. 214, § 1; 82 Del. Laws, c. 77, § 2; 83 Del. Laws, c. 76, § 3.

Effect of amendments.
    83 Del. Laws, c. 76, effective June 30, 2021, substituted a period for a semicolon at the end of (a)(1), (a)(2), (a)(3)a., (a)(3)e., (a)(3)g., the final paragraph of (a)(3)d.; in (a)(3)a. and the

second paragraph of (a)(3)d., added "excluding make-up hours" in the second sentence and added the final sentence; rewrote (a)(3)c. and (a)(3)f.; deleted the last sentence in the first paragraph of (a)(3)d.; substituted "1250" for "1,500" in (a)(3)e.; added "excluding make-up hours" in (a)(3)g. and (a)(3)h.; and rewrote the third and fourth sentences in (a)(3)j.

SUBCHAPTER II
AESTHETICIAN LICENSE

§ 5124. Definitions.

For the purpose of this subchapter:

(1) "Aesthetician" is person who practices any of the following:

a. Cleansing, stimulating, manipulating and beautifying skin by hand or mechanical or electric apparatus or appliance.

b. Application of lash extensions, additions or enhancements, including permanent waving and tinting.

c. Removal of superfluous hair.

d. Gives treatments to keep skin healthy and attractive.

An aesthetician is not authorized to prescribe medication or provide medical treatment in the same manner as a dermatologist.

(2) "Aesthetics shop" means any place or part thereof wherein aesthetics are performed for compensation, whether or not the establishment holds itself out as an aesthetic shop. This definition shall not apply to places where aesthetics are performed by licensed health care professionals acting within the scope of their licensed profession.

(3) "Apprentice in aesthetics" means any person who is engaged in the learning of any or all the practices of aesthetics from a practitioner licensed in the profession the apprentice is studying. The apprentice may perform or assist the licensed practitioner in any of the functions which the practitioner is certified to perform.

(4) "Board" means the Board of Cosmetology and Barbering.

(5) "School of aesthetics" shall mean any place or part thereof where aesthetics or any of the practices are taught, whether or not such place holds itself out as such.

History.
69 Del. Laws, c. 178, § 1; 73 Del. Laws, c. 158, § 32; 77 Del. Laws, c. 65, § 1; 83 Del. Laws, c. 76, § 4.

Effect of amendments.
83 Del. Laws, c. 76, effective June 30, 2021, rewrote (1).

§ 5127. Qualifications.

(a) No person shall be licensed under this subchapter unless the person has done all of the following:

(1) Successfully completed an education equivalent to a tenth grade education. Proof of the required education shall be a certified high school transcript or any other document or affidavit which constitutes reliable proof of educational attainment as determined by the Board.

(2) Completed a course of study of not less than 600 hours in the principles pertaining to the practice of aesthetics; or completed 1200 hours in an apprenticeship to a licensed aesthetician, with the total number of hours worked per day not to exceed 10, nor to exceed 40 per week, excluding make-up hours. An apprenticeship must be completed within 2 years.

(3) Passed the national examination required in § 5128 of this title.

(4) Paid the appropriate fee as established by the Division of Professional Regulation.

(5) Shall not have any impairment related to drugs or alcohol that

would limit the applicant's ability to undertake that applicant's licensed practice in a manner consistent with the safety of the public.

(6) Shall not have been convicted of a crime substantially related to the practice of aesthetics. In determining whether a crime is substantially related to the practice of aesthetics, the Board shall not consider a conviction where more than 10 years have elapsed since the date of conviction, if there have been no other criminal convictions in the intervening time. After a hearing or review of documentation demonstrating that the applicant meets the specified criteria for a waiver, the Board, by an affirmative vote of a majority of the quorum, or, during the time period between Board meetings, the Board President or his or her designee, may waive this paragraph (a)(6), if it finds all of the following:

a. For waiver of a felony conviction where the crime was committed against a person, more than 3 years have elapsed since the date of the conviction and for all other felonies, more than 2 years have elapsed since the date of conviction. At the time of the application the applicant may not be incarcerated, on work release, on probation or parole at Level III Supervision or higher, or serving any part of a suspended sentence and must be in substantial compliance with all court orders pertaining to fines, restitution and community service.

b. For waiver of a misdemeanor conviction or violation, at the time of the application the applicant may not be incarcerated, on work release, on probation or parole at Level III Supervision or higher, or serving any part of a suspended sentence and must be in substantial compliance with all court orders pertaining to fines, restitution and community service.

c. The applicant is capable of performing as a licensed aesthetician in a competent and professional manner.

d. The granting of the waiver will not endanger the public health, safety or welfare.

(7) Shall not have been the recipient of any administrative penalties regarding that person's licensed practice, including but not limited to fines, formal reprimands, license suspensions or revocation (except for license revocations for nonpayment of license renewal fees), probationary limitations, and/or have not entered into any "agreements" which contain conditions placed by a Board on that person's professional conduct and practice, including any voluntary surrender of a license. The Board may, after a hearing, determine whether such administrative penalty is grounds to deny licensure.

(8) Shall not have any disciplinary proceedings or unresolved complaints pending against that person in any jurisdiction where the applicant previously has been, or currently is, licensed to practice aesthetics.

(b) As set forth in Board rules and regulations, foreign-trained applicants shall provide evidence satisfactory to the Board of training equivalent to that required in paragraph (a)(2) of this section, in addition to meeting all other requirements of this section.

(c) When a person who feels the Board has refused or rejected an application without justification; has imposed higher or different conditions for the person than for other applicants or persons now licensed; or has in some other manner contributed to or caused the failure of such person's application, the applicant may appeal to the Superior Court.

(d) Where the Board has found to its satisfaction that an application has been intentionally fraudulent, or that false information has been intentionally supplied, it shall report its findings to the Attorney General for further action.

History.
  67 Del. Laws, c. 299, § 1; 69 Del. Laws, c. 178, § 1; 70 Del. Laws, c. 186, § 1; 73 Del. Laws, c. 158, § 32; 75 Del. Laws, c. 169, § 6; 75 Del. Laws, c. 436, § 50; 77 Del. Laws, c. 65, § 1; 77 Del. Laws, c. 199, § 38; 78 Del. Laws, c. 44, §§ 74, 75; 79 Del. Laws, c. 170, § 1; 81 Del. Laws, c. 214, § 2; 83 Del. Laws, c. 76, § 5.

Effect of amendments.
  83 Del. Laws, c. 76, effective June 30, 2021, added "done all of the following" in the introductory paragraph of (a); substituted a period for a semicolon at the end of (a)(1)-(5); and added "excluding make-up hours" in the first sentence of (a)(2).

CHAPTER 52
NURSING HOME ADMINISTRATORS
SUBCHAPTER II
LICENSE

§ 5210. Criteria for registration as a nursing home administrator-in-training; preceptors; requirements of supervision.

NOTES TO DECISIONS

Progress reports..
  Substantial evidence did not support the finding by the Board of Examiners of Nursing Home Administrators that the applicant failed to submit progress reports in a timely manner; there was no competent evidence disproving that the applicant was told by a representative of the Division of Professional Regulation in March 2018 that the applicant could wait to submit the final set of progress reports until after completing a required 120-hour course. Brown v. Del. Bd. of Examiners of Nursing Home Adm'rs, — A.3d —, 2021 Del. Super. LEXIS 37 (Del. Super. Ct. Jan. 15, 2021).

CHAPTER 60
PROVISIONS APPLICABLE TO TELEHEALTH AND TELEMEDICINE

Sec.
6001. Definitions.
6002. Authorization to practice by telehealth and telemedicine.
6003. Scope of practice; provider-patient relationship required.

Sec.
6004. Practice requirements.
6005. Exceptions.

Revisor's note.
  Section 1 of 83 Del. Laws, c. 52, provided: "This Act shall be known as the 'Telehealth Access Preservation and Modernization Act of 2021'."
  Section 21 of 83 Del. Laws, c. 52, provided:

"Sections 1-19 of this act take effect on July 1, 2021. Nothing in this act shall be interpreted as affecting or invalidating any health-care services provided through telehealth or telemedicine prior to effective date of this act."

§ 6001. Definitions.

As used in this chapter:

  (1) "Distant site" means a site at which a health-care provider legally allowed to practice in the state is located while providing health-care services by means of telemedicine.

  (2) "Health-care provider" means any person authorized to deliver clinical health-care services by telemedicine and participate in telehealth pursuant to this chapter and regulations promulgated by the respective professional boards listed in § 6002 of this title.

  (3) "Originating site" means a site in Delaware at which a patient is located at the time health-care services are provided to the patient by means of telemedicine or telehealth. Notwithstanding any other provision of law, insurers and providers may agree to alternative siting arrangements deemed appropriate by the parties.

  (4) "Store and forward transfer" means the synchronous or asynchronous transmission of a patient's medical information either to or from an

originating site or to or from the provider at the distant site, but does not require the patient being present nor must it be in real time.

(5) "Telehealth" means the use of information and communications technologies consisting of telephones, remote patient monitoring devices or other electronic means which support clinical health care, provider consultation, patient and professional health-related education, public health, health administration, and other services as described in regulation.

(6) "Telemedicine" means a form, or subset, of telehealth, which includes the delivery of clinical health-care services by means of real time 2-way audio (including audio-only conversations, if the patient is not able to access the appropriate broadband service or other technology necessary to establish an audio and visual connection), visual, or other telecommunications or electronic communications, including the application of secure video conferencing or store and forward transfer technology to provide or support health-care delivery, which facilitates the assessment, diagnosis, consultation, treatment, education, care management and self-management of a patient's health care.

History.
83 Del. Laws, c. 52, § 4.

§ 6002. Authorization to practice by telehealth and telemedicine.

(a) Health-care providers licensed by the following professional boards existing under this title are authorized to deliver health-care services by telehealth and telemedicine subject to the provisions of this chapter:

(1) The Board of Podiatry created pursuant to Chapter 5 of this title.

(2) The Board of Chiropractic created pursuant to Chapter 7 of this title.

(3) The Board of Medical Licensure and Discipline created pursuant Chapter 17 of this title.

(4) The State Board of Dentistry and Dental Hygiene created pursuant to Chapter 11 of this title.

(5) The Delaware Board of Nursing created pursuant to Chapter 19 of this title.

(6) The Board of Occupational Therapy Practice created pursuant to Chapter 20 of this title.

(7) The Board of Examiners in Optometry created pursuant to Chapter 21 of this title.

(8) The Board of Pharmacy created pursuant to Chapter 25 of this title.

(9) The Board of Mental Health and Chemical Dependency Professionals created pursuant to Chapter 30 of this title.

(10) The Board of Examiners of Psychologists created pursuant to Chapter 35 of this title.

(11) The State Board of Dietetics/Nutrition created pursuant to Chapter 38 of this title.

(12) The Board of Social Work Examiners created pursuant to Chapter 39 of this title.

(b) A professional board listed in subsection (a) of this section may promulgate or revise regulations and establish or revise rules applicable to health-care providers under the professional board's jurisdiction in order to facilitate the provision of telehealth and telemedicine services consistent with this chapter.

History.
83 Del. Laws, c. 52, § 4.

§ 6003. Scope of practice; provider-patient relationship required.

(a) Except for the instances listed in this chapter, health-care providers may not deliver health-care services by telehealth and telemedicine in the absence of a health-care provider-patient relationship. A health-care provider-patient relationship may be established either in-person or through telehealth and telemedicine but must include the following:

(1) Thorough verification and authentication of the location and, to the extent possible, identity of the patient.

(2) Disclosure and validation of the provider's identity and credentials.

(3) Receipt of appropriate consent from a patient after disclosure regarding the delivery model and treatment method or limitations, including informed consent regarding the use of telemedicine technologies as required by paragraph (a)(5) of this section.

(4) Establishment of a diagnosis through the use of acceptable medical practices, such as patient history, mental status examination, physical examination (unless not warranted by the patient's mental condition), and appropriate diagnostic and laboratory testing to establish diagnoses, as well as identification of underlying conditions or contraindications, or both, for treatment recommended or provided.

(5) Discussion with the patient of any diagnosis and supporting evidence as well as risks and benefits of various treatment options.

(6) The availability of a distant site provider or other coverage of the patient for appropriate follow-up care.

(7) A written visit summary provided to the patient.

(b) Health-care services delivered by telehealth and telemedicine may be synchronous or asynchronous using store-and-forward technology. Telehealth and telemedicine services may be used to establish a provider-patient relationship only if the provider determines that the provider is able to meet the same standard of care as if the health-care services were being provided in-person.

(c) Treatment and consultation recommendations delivered by telehealth and telemedicine shall be subject to the same standards of appropriate practice as those in traditional (in-person encounter) settings. In the absence of a proper health-care provider-patient relationship, health-care providers are prohibited from issuing prescriptions solely in response to an internet questionnaire, an internet consult, or a telephone consult.

History.
83 Del. Laws, c. 52, § 4.

§ 6004. Practice requirements.

(a) A health-care provider using telemedicine and telehealth technologies to deliver health-care services to a patient must, prior to diagnosis and treatment, do at least 1 of the following:

(1) Provide an appropriate examination in-person.

(2) Require another Delaware-licensed health-care provider be present at the originating site with the patient at the time of the diagnosis.

(3) Make a diagnosis using audio or visual communication.

(4) Meet the standard of service required by applicable professional societies in guidelines developed for establishing a health-care provider-patient relationship as part of an evidenced-based clinical practice in telemedicine.

(b) After a health-care provider-patient relationship is properly established in accordance with this section, subsequent treatment of the same patient by the same health-care provider need not satisfy the limitations of this section.

(c) A health-care provider treating a patient through telemedicine and telehealth must maintain complete records of the patient's care and follow all applicable state and federal statutes and regulations for recordkeeping, confidentiality, and disclosure to the patient.

(d) Telehealth and telemedicine services shall include, if required by the applicable professional board listed in § 6002(a) of this title, use of the Delaware Health Information Network (DHIN) in connection with the practice.

(e) Nothing in this section shall be construed to limit the practice of radiology or pathology.

History.
83 Del. Laws, c. 52, § 4.

§ 6005. Exceptions.

(a) Telehealth and telemedicine may be practiced without a health-care provider-patient relationship during:

(1) Informal consultation performed by a health-care provider outside the context of a contractual relationship and on an irregular or infrequent basis without the expectation or exchange of direct or indirect compensation.

(2) Furnishing of assistance by a health-care provider in case of an emergency or disaster when circumstances do not permit the establishment of a health-care provider-patient relationship prior to the provision of care if no charge is made for the medical assistance.

(3) Episodic consultation by a specialist located in another jurisdiction who provides such consultation services at the request of a licensed health-care professional.

(4) Circumstances which make it impractical for a patient to consult with the health-care provider in-person prior to the delivery of telemedicine services.

(b) A mental health provider, behavioral health provider, or social worker licensed in another jurisdiction who would be authorized to deliver health-care services by telehealth or telemedicine under this chapter if licensed in this State pursuant to Chapter 30 (Mental Health and Chemical Dependency Professionals), Chapter 35 (Psychologists), or Chapter 38 (Social Workers) of this title may provide treatment to Delaware residents through telehealth and telemedicine services. The Division of Professional Regulation shall require any out-of-state health-care provider practicing in this State pursuant to this section to complete a Medical Request Form and comply with any other registration requirements the Division of Professional Regulation may establish.

History.
83 Del. Laws, c. 52, § 4.

TITLE 25
PROPERTY

PART I
GENERAL PROVISIONS

CHAPTER 3
TITLES AND CONVEYANCES

§ 301. Fines and common recoveries.

RESEARCH REFERENCES AND PRACTICE AIDS

Delaware Law Reviews.
Is It Time to Modernize the Laws of Old England?: Arguments for Statutory Adjust- ments to the Rule in Shelley's Case and the Rule Against Perpetuities, 17 Del. L. Rev. 25 (2021).

§ 302. Bar of estate tail by deed.

RESEARCH REFERENCES AND PRACTICE AIDS

Delaware Law Reviews.
Is It Time to Modernize the Laws of Old England?: Arguments for Statutory Adjust- ments to the Rule in Shelley's Case and the Rule Against Perpetuities, 17 Del. L. Rev. 25 (2021).

CHAPTER 5
RULE AGAINST PERPETUITIES; POWERS OF APPOINTMENT; RULE AGAINST ACCUMULATIONS

§ 501. Powers of appointment; effect of rule against perpetuities.

RESEARCH REFERENCES AND PRACTICE AIDS

Delaware Law Reviews.
Is It Time to Modernize the Laws of Old England?: Arguments for Statutory Adjust- ments to the Rule in Shelley's Case and the Rule Against Perpetuities, 17 Del. L. Rev. 25 (2021).

§ 503. Rule against perpetuities.

RESEARCH REFERENCES AND PRACTICE AIDS

Delaware Law Reviews.
Is It Time to Modernize the Laws of Old England?: Arguments for Statutory Adjust- ments to the Rule in Shelley's Case and the Rule Against Perpetuities, 17 Del. L. Rev. 25 (2021).

CHAPTER 16
LIS PENDENS

§ 1601. Written notice of pendency of action.

NOTES TO DECISIONS

Attorneys' fees. — Plaintiff improperly re- corded a lis pendens against defendant's per- sonal residence, thereby entitling defendant to an award of attorneys' fees; the lis pendens had no relation to plaintiff's claim, which involved a dispute over a contract between 2 businesses and alleged a single claim for breach of per- sonal guaranty. KMI Grp., Inc. v. Comer, — A.3d —, 2021 Del. Super. LEXIS 90 (Del. Super. Ct. Feb. 1, 2021).

§ 1606. Mandatory cancellation.

NOTES TO DECISIONS

Attorneys' fees. — Plaintiff improperly recorded a lis pendens against defendant's personal residence, thereby entitling defendant to an award of attorneys' fees; the lis pendens had no relation to plaintiff's claim, which involved a dispute over a contract between 2 businesses and alleged a single claim for breach of personal guaranty. KMI Grp., Inc. v. Comer, — A.3d —, 2021 Del. Super. LEXIS 90 (Del. Super. Ct. Feb. 1, 2021).

§ 1611. Costs and attorneys' fees.

NOTES TO DECISIONS

Improper recordation. — Plaintiff improperly recorded a lis pendens against defendant's personal residence, thereby entitling defendant to an award of attorneys' fees; the lis pendens had no relation to plaintiff's claim, which involved a dispute over a contract between 2 businesses and alleged a single claim for breach of personal guaranty. KMI Grp., Inc. v. Comer, — A.3d —, 2021 Del. Super. LEXIS 90 (Del. Super. Ct. Feb. 1, 2021).

PART II

MORTGAGES AND OTHER LIENS

Chapter
22. Unit Properties, §§ 2201 to 2246.
39. Liens of Garage Owners, Livery and Stable Keepers; Replevin by Owner, §§ 3901 to 3910.
40. Rights and Title to Abandoned Personal Property, §§ 4001 to 4008.

CHAPTER 22

UNIT PROPERTIES

Subchapter VIII. Miscellaneous

Sec.
2246. Exceptions for nonresidential condominiums.

SUBCHAPTER VIII

MISCELLANEOUS

§ 2246. Exceptions for nonresidential condominiums.

A nonresidential condominium may elect to be exempt from the requirement for creating and maintaining a repair and replacement reserve pursuant to § 2211 of this title if the declaration so provides or otherwise by the vote of a majority of the unit owners. A condominium that contains units restricted exclusively to nonresidential purposes and other units that may be used for residential purposes is not subject to this section (and therefore is not required to maintain a repair and replacement reserve) unless the units that may be used for residential purposes would comprise a condominium in the absence of the nonresidential units or the declaration provides that this section applies. Nothing herein shall prevent the establishment of a condominium for residential purposes and a nonresidential condominium for the same real estate.

History.
77 Del. Laws, c. 92, § 11; 83 Del. Laws, c. 173, § 1.

Revisor's note.
Section 15 of 83 Del. Laws, c. 173, provided: "This act takes effect 30 days after its enactment into law." The act was signed by the Governor on Sept. 15, 2021, and became effective on Oct. 15, 2021.

Effect of amendments.
83 Del. Laws, c. 173, effective October 15, 2021, added "not" preceding "required" in the parenthetical in the second sentence.

CHAPTER 27
MECHANICS' LIENS
SUBCHAPTER II
ENFORCEMENT IN SUPERIOR COURT

§ 2712. Requirements of complaint or statement of claim.

NOTES TO DECISIONS

II. COMPLAINT AND/OR STATEMENT OF CLAIM.

Strict compliance with statute required. — Documents submitted by a subcontractor in support of its bill of particulars were insufficient to meet the standard required to impose a mechanic's lien on an owner's property and failed to provide a precise calculation of the amount demanded or how that amount was calculated; plaintiff simply stated a total of $610,633 and attached a trade contractor agreement with invoices. Drywall v. V., — A.3d —, 2021 Del. Super. LEXIS 573 (Del. Super. Ct. Aug. 3, 2021).

CHAPTER 29
LIENS OF THE STATE AND/OR ITS POLITICAL SUBDIVISIONS

§ 2901. Lien of taxes and other charges; Notice of Lien.

NOTES TO DECISIONS

Standing. — Application of 25 Del. C. § 2901(a)(1) does not turn on the identity of the owner of the property that incurred fees and penalties; if it did, owners could simply evade tax liens by conveying the property. Baldwin v. New Castle Cty., — A.3d —, 2021 Del. Super. LEXIS 589 (Del. Super. Ct. Sept. 14, 2021).

Plaintiff lacked standing to challenge the transfer of fees and penalties to tax bills where: (1) plaintiff had no legal interest in the property tax liens arising from the fees and penalties; (2) plaintiff did not own the property at the time of transfer; (3) property tax liens were owed by the current owner of the property; (4) plaintiff forfeited standing to challenge the property tax liens upon plaintiff's conveyance of the property; and (5) the automatic transfer of the challenged fees and penalties to the property tax bills was statutorily authorized pursuant to 25 Del. C. § 2901(a)(1). Baldwin v. New Castle Cty., — A.3d —, 2021 Del. Super. LEXIS 589 (Del. Super. Ct. Sept. 14, 2021).

CHAPTER 39
LIENS OF GARAGE OWNERS, LIVERY AND STABLE KEEPERS; REPLEVIN BY OWNER

Sec.
3906. Motor vehicles.

§ 3906. Motor vehicles.

(a) In the case of motor vehicles required to be registered under the motor vehicle laws of this or any other state, notice containing the information required in § 3903(b) of this title shall be given to the registered owners and known lienholders at their addresses of record with the Division of Motor Vehicles or similar agency and the return receipt, signed or unsigned, shall be held and considered as prima facie evidence of service of such notice. The lienholder shall notify the appropriate Delaware auto theft unit.

(b) Any lien created under this chapter shall not extend to any personal property that is not attached to or considered necessary for the proper operation of any motor vehicle and such property shall be returned to the owner of the motor vehicle if the owner of the motor vehicle claims the items prior to the sale of such motor vehicle.

History.
61 Del. Laws, c. 367, § 1; 83 Del. Laws, c. 125, § 3.

Effect of amendments.
83 Del. Laws, c. 125, effective Aug. 10, 2021, added (b).

CHAPTER 40

RIGHTS AND TITLE TO ABANDONED PERSONAL PROPERTY

Sec.
4001. Definition of abandoned personal property.

§ 4001. Definition of abandoned personal property.

(a) For the purposes of this chapter "abandoned personal property" shall be deemed to be tangible personal property which the rightful owner has left in the care or custody of another person and has failed to maintain, pay for the storage of, exercise dominion or control over, and has failed to otherwise assert or declare the ownership rights to the tangible personal property for a period of 1 year.

(b) The following personal property shall not be deemed to be "abandoned personal property":

(1) Marital property subject to division in a proceeding for divorce or annulment under § 1513 of Title 13;

(2) Personal property which has been stolen or otherwise taken from its rightful owner in violation of Title 11;

(3) Personal property which has been taken from the rightful owner by conversion;

(4) Personal property of a person who dies intestate subject to subchapter I of Chapter 11 of Title 12;

(5) Unclaimed property held by banking organizations as defined by subchapter II of Chapter 11 of Title 12;

(6) Any intangible personal property and the tangible evidence thereof under Chapter 11 of Title 12; or

(7) Personal property in a motor vehicle that is not attached to or considered necessary for the proper operation of the motor vehicle if the owner of the personal property files an answer to the petition pursuant to § 4003 of this title.

History.
72 Del. Laws, c. 192, § 1; 78 Del. Laws, c. 21, § 1; 83 Del. Laws, c. 125, § 4.

Effect of amendments.
83 Del. Laws, c. 125, effective Aug. 10, 2021,

added (b)(7) and made other related stylistic changes.

RESEARCH REFERENCES AND PRACTICE AIDS

Delaware Law Reviews.
Rights to Tenant Property Upon Termination of a Commercial Lease, 17 Del. L. Rev. 39 (2021).

PART III
RESIDENTIAL LANDLORD-TENANT CODE

Chapter
51. General Provisions, §§ 5101 to 5141.
55. Tenant Obligations and Landlord Remedies, §§ 5501 to 5518.

CHAPTER 51
GENERAL PROVISIONS

SUBCHAPTER I
RIGHTS, OBLIGATIONS AND PROCEDURES, GENERALLY

§ 5106. Rental agreement; term and termination of rental agreement.

(a) No rental agreement, unless in writing, shall be effective for a longer term than 1 year.

(b) Where no term is expressly provided, a rental agreement for premises shall be deemed and construed to be for a month-to-month term.

(c) Subject to the provisions of § 5512 of this title, the landlord may terminate any rental agreement, other than month-to-month agreements, by giving a minimum of 60 days' written notice to the tenant prior to the expiration of the term of the rental agreement. The notice shall indicate that the agreement shall terminate upon its expiration date. A tenant may terminate a rental agreement by giving a minimum of 60 days' written notice prior to the expiration of the term of the rental agreement that the agreement shall terminate upon its expiration date.

(d) Where the term of the rental agreement is month-to-month, the landlord or tenant may terminate the rental agreement by giving the other party a minimum of 60 days' written notice, which 60-day period shall begin on the first day of the month following the day of actual notice.

(e) With regard to a tenant occupying a federally-subsidized housing unit, in the event of any conflict between the terms of this Code and the terms of any federal law, regulations or guidelines, the terms of the federal law, regulations or guidelines shall control.

History.
70 Del. Laws, c. 513, § 1; 83 Del. Laws, c. 203, § 1.

Effect of amendments.
83 Del. Laws, c. 203, effective Sept. 17, 2021,

added "Subject to the provisions of § 5512 of this title" in the first sentence of (c).

SUBCHAPTER II
DEFINITIONS

§ 5141. Definitions.

The following words, terms and phrases, when used in this part, shall have the meanings ascribed to them in this section, except where the context clearly indicates a different meaning:

(1) "Action" shall mean any claim advanced in a court proceeding in which rights are determined.

(2) "Building and housing codes" shall include any law, ordinance or governmental regulation concerning fitness for habitation or the construction, maintenance, operation, occupancy, use or appearance of any premises or dwelling unit.

(3) "Certificate of mailing" shall mean United States Postal Form No. 3817, or its successor.

(4) "Commercial rental unit" shall mean any lot, structure or portion thereof, which is occupied or rented solely or primarily for commercial or industrial purposes.

(5) "Deceased sole tenant" shall mean the sole leaseholder under a residential rental agreement entitled to occupy a residential rental unit to the exclusion of all others who has died. The right of nonleaseholder authorized occupant(s) of the residential rental unit, if any, to occupy the residential rental unit at the sole discretion of the deceased sole tenant while that tenant was alive shall immediately terminate upon the death of the sole tenant. The deceased sole tenant is also referred to as the "decedent" pursuant to § 2306(c)(3) of Title 12.

(6) "Disabled or handicapped" person shall have the same meaning as found in the Americans with Disabilities Act (1992) [42 U.S.C. § 12101 et seq.] as amended.

(7) "Domestic abuse" shall mean any act or threat against a victim of domestic abuse or violence that either constitutes a crime under Delaware law or any act or threat that constitutes domestic violence or domestic abuse as defined anywhere in the Delaware Code. Domestic abuse can be verified by an official document, such as a court order, or by a reliable third-party professional, including a law-enforcement agency or officer, a domestic violence or domestic abuse service provider, or health care provider. It is the domestic violence or abuse victim's responsibility to provide the reliable statement from the reliable third party.

(8) "Equivalent substitute housing" shall mean a rental unit of like or similar location, size, facilities and rent.

(9) "Extended absence" shall mean any absence of more than 7 days.

(10) "Forthwith summons" shall mean any summons requiring the personal appearance of a party or person or persons at the earliest convenience of the court.

(11) "Gender identity" means a gender-related identity, appearance, expression or behavior of a person, regardless of the person's assigned sex at birth.

(12) "Good faith dispute" shall mean the manifestation of an honest difference of opinion relating to the rights of the parties to a rental agreement pursuant to such agreement, or pursuant to this Code.

(13) "Holdover" or "holdover tenant" shall mean a tenant who wrongfully retains possession or who wrongfully exercises control of the rental unit after the expiration or termination of the rental agreement.

(14) "Injunction" shall mean a court order prohibiting a party from doing an act or restraining a party from continuing an act.

(15) "Landlord" shall mean:

    a. The owner, lessor or sublessor of the rental unit or the property of which it is a part and, in addition, shall mean any person authorized to exercise any aspect of the management of the premises, including any person who, directly or indirectly, receives rents or any part thereof other than as a bona fide purchaser and who has no obligation to deliver the whole of such receipts to another person; or

b. Any person held out by any landlord as the appropriate party to accept performance, whether such person is a landlord or not; or

c. Any person with whom the tenant normally deals as a landlord; or

d. Any person to whom the person specified in paragraphs (15)b. and c. of this section is directly or ultimately responsible.

(16) "Legal holiday" shall mean any date designated as a legal holiday under § 501 of Title 1.

(17) "Local government unit" shall mean a political subdivision of this State, including, but not limited to, a county, city, town or other incorporated community or subdivision of the subdivision providing local government service for residents in a geographically limited area of the State as its primary purpose, and has the power to act primarily on behalf of the area.

(18) "Month to month" shall mean a renewable term of 1 month.

(19) "Normal wear and tear" shall mean the deterioration in the condition of a property or premises by the ordinary and reasonable use of such property or premises.

(20)a. "Owner" shall mean 1 or more persons, jointly or severally, in whom is vested:

1. All or part of the legal title to property; or

2. All or part of the beneficial ownership, usufruct and a right to present use and enjoyment of the premises.

b. The word "owner" shall include a mortgagee in possession.

(21) "Person" shall include an individual, artificial entity pursuant to Supreme Court Rule 57, government or governmental agency, statutory trust, business trust, 2 or more persons having a joint or common trust or any other legal or commercial entity.

(22) "Pet deposit" shall mean any deposit made to a landlord by a tenant to be held for the term of the rental agreement, or any part thereof, for the presence of an animal in a rental unit.

(23) "Premises" shall mean a rental unit and the structure of which it is a part, and the facilities and appurtenances therein, grounds, areas and facilities held out for the use of tenants generally, or whose use is contracted for between the landlord and the tenant.

(24) "Protective hairstyle" includes braids, locks, and twists.

(25) "Race" includes traits historically associated with race, including hair texture and a protective hairstyle.

(26) "Rental agreement" shall mean and include all agreements, written or oral, which establish or modify the terms, conditions, rules, regulations or any other provisions concerning the use and occupancy of a rental unit.

(27) "Rental unit," "dwelling unit" or "dwelling place" shall mean any house, building, structure, or portion thereof, which is occupied, rented or leased as the home or residence of 1 or more persons.

(28) "Security deposit" shall mean any deposit, exclusive of a pet deposit, given to the landlord which is to be held for the term of the rental agreement or for any part thereof.

(29) "Senior citizen" shall mean any person, 62 years of age or older, regardless of the age of such person's spouse.

(30) The terms "sexual offenses" and "stalking" shall here have the same meanings as in Title 11. Sexual offenses and stalking can be verified by an official document, such as a court order, or by a reliable third party professional, including a law-enforcement agency or officer, a sexual

assault service provider, or health care provider. It is the sexual assault or stalking victim's responsibility to provide the reliable statement from the reliable third party.

(31) "Sexual orientation" includes heterosexuality, homosexuality, or bisexuality.

(32) "Source of income" shall have the meaning given in § 4602 of Title 6.

(33) "Support animal" shall mean any animal individually trained to do work or perform tasks to meet the requirements of a disabled person, including, but not limited to, minimal protection work, rescue work, pulling a wheelchair or retrieving dropped items.

(34) "Surety bond fee or premium" shall mean the amount of money the tenant pays to the surety for enrollment in a surety bond program in lieu of posting a security deposit.

(35) "Tenant" shall mean a person entitled under a rental agreement to occupy a rental unit to the exclusion of others, and the word "tenant" shall include an occupant of any premises pursuant to a conditional sales agreement which has been converted to a landlord/tenant agreement pursuant to § 314(d)(3) of this title.

(36) "Utility services" shall mean water, sewer, electricity or fuel.

History.

70 Del. Laws, c. 513, § 1; 73 Del. Laws, c. 329, § 70; 75 Del. Laws, c. 293, § 1; 76 Del. Laws, c. 311, § 6; 77 Del. Laws, c. 90, § 20; 79 Del. Laws, c. 47, §§ 22, 23; 79 Del. Laws, c. 57, § 1; 79 Del. Laws, c. 65, § 2; 80 Del. Laws, c. 355, § 9; 83 Del. Laws, c. 13, § 22; 83 Del. Laws, c. 195, § 6.

Effect of amendments.

83 Del. Laws, c. 13, effective April 13, 2021, added present (24) and (25) and redesignated the remaining paragraphs accordingly.

83 Del. Laws, c. 195, effective September 17, 2021, deleted the final sentence in (11); and substituted "includes" for "exclusively means" in (31).

NOTES TO DECISIONS

"Tenant." — Plaintiffs' unlawful ouster claim failed because: (1) they did not prove by a preponderance of the evidence that they were entitled to occupy a unit to the exclusion of others where, according to a lease agreement entered into between defendant landlord and an autistic adult, only individuals approved by the Delaware State Housing Authority (DSHA) and the landlord could reside in the unit; (2) the lease agreement restricted subleasing; and (3) plaintiffs were never approved by DSHA or the landlord to occupy the unit. Johnson v. Gandy, 2021 Del. C.P. LEXIS 10 (Del. C.P. May 13, 2021).

CHAPTER 53

LANDLORD OBLIGATIONS AND TENANT REMEDIES

§ 5313. Unlawful ouster or exclusion of tenant.

NOTES TO DECISIONS

"Tenant." —

Plaintiffs' unlawful ouster claim failed because: (1) they did not prove by a preponderance of the evidence that they were entitled to occupy a unit to the exclusion of others where, according to a lease agreement entered into between defendant landlord and an autistic adult, only individuals approved by the Delaware State Housing Authority (DSHA) and the landlord could reside in the unit; (2) the lease agreement restricted subleasing; and (3) plaintiffs were never approved by DSHA or the landlord to occupy the unit. Johnson v. Gandy, 2021 Del. C.P. LEXIS 10 (Del. C.P. May 13, 2021).

CHAPTER 55

TENANT OBLIGATIONS AND LANDLORD REMEDIES

§ 5512. Rules and regulations relating to certain buildings; landlord remedies.

Any provision of the Landlord-Tenant Code (Chapters 51 through 59 of this title) to the contrary notwithstanding, written rental agreements for the rental of single rooms in certain buildings may be terminated immediately upon notice to the tenant for a tenant's material violation of a regulation which has been given to a tenant at the time of contract or lease, and in cases where there is no written lease, either 15 days after written notice to the tenant of a breach of the covenant of quiet enjoyment of similar conduct, or 30 days after written notice for any other reason, and the landlord shall be entitled to bring a proceeding for possession where:

(1) The building is the primary residence of the landlord; and

(2) No more than 3 rooms in the building are rented to tenants; and

(3) No more than 3 tenants occupy such building.

History.
70 Del. Laws, c. 513, § 3; 83 Del. Laws, c. 203, § 2.

Effect of amendments.
83 Del. Laws, c. 203, effective Sept. 17, 2021,

substituted parentheses for brackets, and added "written" following "notwithstanding" and "and in cases ... any other reason" in the introductory paragraph.

CHAPTER 57
SUMMARY POSSESSION

§ 5715. Execution of judgment; writ of possession.

RESEARCH REFERENCES AND PRACTICE AIDS

Delaware Law Reviews.
Rights to Tenant Property Upon Termination of a Commercial Lease, 17 Del. L. Rev. 39 (2021).

PART VI
MANUFACTURED HOME COMMUNITIES

Chapter

CHAPTER 70
MANUFACTURED HOMES AND MANUFACTURED HOME COMMUNITIES ACT

SUBCHAPTER V
DELAWARE MANUFACTURED HOME RELOCATION TRUST FUND

§ 7041. Delaware Manufactured Home Relocation Authority [For application of this section, see 79 Del. Laws, c. 304, § 7].

NOTES TO DECISIONS

Discovery. — Superior Court did not err in dismissing a manufactured home community owner's petition for a writ of prohibition because, based on a plain reading of the Rent Increase Justification Act (25 Del. C. § 7050 et seq.), an arbitrator appointed by the Manufactured Home Relocation Authority possessed the authority to compel the production of documents; the arbitrator was authorized to compel the owner to produce business records to afford the homeowners' association a chance to test the owner's justifications for its rent increase. Wild Meadows MHC, LLC v. Weidman, 250 A.3d 751 (Del. 2021).

SUBCHAPTER VI

RENT INCREASE JUSTIFICATION

§ 7050. Purpose [For application of this section, see 79 Del. Laws, c. 304, § 7].

NOTES TO DECISIONS

Burden of proof. — Arbitrator correctly compelled the discovery of a manufactured home community owner's relevant financial information because the arbitrator acted within its authority by compelling the owner to produce business records to afford the homeowners' association a chance to fairly test its justi-

fications for its rent increase; imposing an asymmetric burden on the homeowners was contrary to the statute's purpose of accommodating the conflicting interests of homeowners and landowners. Wild Meadows MHC, LLC v. Weidman, 250 A.3d 751 (Del. 2021).

§ 7052. Rent justification [For application of this section, see 79 Del. Laws, c. 304, § 7].

NOTES TO DECISIONS

Burden of proof. — Superior Court did not err in dismissing a manufactured home community owner's petition for a writ of prohibition because, based on a plain reading of the Rent Increase Justification Act (25 Del. C. § 7050 et seq.), an arbitrator appointed by the Manufactured Home Relocation Authority possessed the authority to compel the production of documents; the arbitrator was authorized to compel the owner to produce business records to afford the homeowners' association a chance to test the owner's justifications for its rent increase. Wild Meadows MHC, LLC v. Weidman, 250 A.3d 751 (Del. 2021).

The Rent Increase Justification Act (25 Del. C. § 7050 et seq.) did not permit a community owner to incorporate a capital improvement component of the 2017 and 2018 rent increases into a lot's base rent for succeeding years after recovering that lot's full, proportionate share of

those costs in those years; the justification for a rent increase expired when the costs were fully recovered. Rehoboth Bay Homeowners' Ass'n v. Hometown Rehoboth Bay, LLC, 252 A.3d 434 (Del. 2021).

Factors supporting rent increase. — Trial court correctly ruled that a bulkhead stabilization project was a capital improvement or rehabilitation work warranting an increased lot rent under the Rent Increase Justification Act (25 Del. C. § 7050 et seq.), and not ordinary repair, replacement and maintenance, because: (1) the old bulkhead did not have riprap protecting the shoreline; (2) the project was massive and required work completed over multiple years at significant expense; and (3) riprap, consisting of large rocks added onto the bulkhead, was better technology. Rehoboth Bay Homeowners' Ass'n v. Hometown Rehoboth Bay, LLC, 252 A.3d 434 (Del. 2021).

§ 7053. Rent increase dispute resolution [For application of this section, see 79 Del. Laws, c. 304, § 7, and 80 Del. Laws, c. 229, § 3].

(a)(1) A community owner shall give written notice to each affected homeowner and to the homeowners' association, if one exists, and to the Delaware Manufactured Home Relocation Authority ("Authority"), at least 90 days prior to any increase in rent. The notice shall identify all affected homeowners by lot number, name, group, or phase. If the affected homeowners are not identified by name, the community owner shall make the names and addresses available to any affected homeowner, homeowners' association, and the Authority, upon request.

(2) The Authority must maintain a form final meeting notice that includes all of the following:

a. The deadline to request arbitration under subsection (f) of this section.

      b. A statement that an informal meeting under subsection (e) of this section does not affect, in any way, the date by which arbitration must be requested under subsection (f) of this section.

    (3) The written notice under this subsection (a) must contain all of the following:

      a. The approved date, time, and place for the final meeting required under subsection (b) of this section.

      b. The form language maintained by the Authority under paragraph (a)(2) of this section.

(b) If the proposed rent increase exceeds the CPI-U, the Authority shall approve a final meeting between the community owner and the affected homeowners, and the homeowners' association, if one exists, to discuss the reasons for the proposed increase. The final meeting must be held within 30 days from the mailing of the notice of the rent increase.

    (1) The community owner proposing the rent increase shall recommend to the Authority, in writing, a date, time, and place of the final meeting and provide a copy of this recommendation to the homeowner's association, if one exists.

    (2) The Authority shall approve the community owner's recommendation if it determines that the date, time, and place are reasonable.

    (3) The community owner shall include the approved date, time, and place for the final meeting in the notice required under subsection (a) of this section.

(c) At or before the final meeting the community owner shall, in good faith, disclose in writing all of the material factors resulting in the decision to increase the rent. When market rent is a factor used by the community owner, the community owner shall provide a range of rental rates from low to high, and when relevant the mean and median; this disclosure must include all of the following:

    (1) Whether comparable rents were determined at arm's length, each case in which the community owner or related party has an ownership interest in the comparable lot/community.

    (2) The time relevance of the data.

    (3) The community owner shall disclose financial and other pertinent documents and information supporting the reasons for the rent increase.

(d) The community owner and at least 1 affected homeowner or the homeowners' association may agree to extend or continue the final meeting required under this section by doing all of the following:

    (1) The community owner and the homeowner or homeowner's association must sign a written document containing a specific date for the rescheduled final meeting.

    (2) Within 2 business days of signing the agreement to continue or extend, the community owner shall notify the Authority of the agreement by forwarding the signed agreement to the Authority.

(e) At the community owner's election, the community owner may schedule 1 or more informal meetings, before or after the final meeting, to discuss the proposed rent increase.

(f) After the final meeting, any affected homeowner who has not already accepted the proposed increase, or the homeowners' association on the behalf of 1 or more affected homeowners who have not already accepted the proposed increase may, within 30 days from the conclusion of the final meeting, petition the Authority to appoint a qualified arbitrator to conduct nonbinding arbitration proceedings. If the thirtieth day is a Saturday, Sunday, legal holiday, or other day on which the office of the Authority is closed, the 30-day period shall run until the end of the next day on which the office of the Authority is open. Only if a petition is timely filed, the Authority shall select an arbitrator who is a member of the Delaware Bar with appropriate training in alternative dispute resolution. The Authority may select an arbitrator from the list of arbitrators maintained by the Superior Court of the State, or by soliciting applicants for a list maintained by the Authority, or through another method which the Authority, in its discretion, has determined will be sufficient to result in the selection of an appropriate arbitrator. The tenants and the landlord must each pay $250 to the Delaware Manufactured Home Relocation Trust Fund to be applied to the arbitrator's fee. The Authority shall pay all direct arbitration costs in excess of the $500 collected from the homeowners and community owner. All other costs shall be the responsibility of the respective parties. The arbitration must be held within 60 days from the date of the petition.

(g) The Delaware Uniform Rules of Evidence shall be used as a guide by the arbitrator for admissibility of evidence submitted at the arbitration hearing.

(h) Unless waived by all parties, testimony will be under oath or affirmation, administered by the arbitrator.

(i) Testimony shall be transcribed and shall be considered a written record.

(j) The arbitrator will render a decision employing the standards under § 7052 of this title.

(k) The arbitrator will render a written decision within 15 days of the conclusion of the arbitration hearing.

(*l*) The homeowners will be subject to the rent increase as notified; however, if the rent increase is not approved through the process provided in this section, the community owners shall rebate the increase.

(m) Notwithstanding any other law or regulation to the contrary, all of the following may attend a final meeting as described in subsection (b) of this section:

(1) The homeowner's designee.

(2) The homeowner's attorney.

(3) The homeowners' association's attorney.

(4) A representative from The Delaware Manufactured Home Owners Association (DMHOA) or its successor.

(5) Elected Delaware officials, including officials holding a federal office.

(6) A representative from the Delaware Manufactured Home Relocation Authority Board.

History.
79 Del. Laws, c. 63, § 1; 79 Del. Laws, c. 304, §§ 2-4; 80 Del. Laws, c. 229, § 1; 82 Del. Laws, c. 38, § 43; 83 Del. Laws, c. 175, § 1.

Effect of amendments.
83 Del. Laws, c. 175, effective September 15, 2021, added (m).

NOTES TO DECISIONS

Required disclosures. — Superior Court did not err in dismissing a manufactured home community owner's petition for a writ of prohibition because, based on a plain reading of the Rent Increase Justification Act (25 Del. C. § 7050 et seq.), an arbitrator appointed by the Manufactured Home Relocation Authority possessed the authority to compel the production of documents; the arbitrator was authorized to compel the owner to produce business records to afford the homeowners' association a chance to test the owner's justifications for its rent increase. Wild Meadows MHC, LLC v. Weidman, 250 A.3d 751 (Del. 2021)

Arbitrator appointed by the Manufactured Home Relocation Authority had the authority to impose a confidentiality agreement on a manufactured home community owner and a homeowners' association (HOA) because the arbitrator carefully balanced the owner's concerns in order to reasonably protect its sensitive information; the arbitrator crafted a confidentiality agreement that balanced legitimate business interests of the owner against the HOA's interest in fairly testing the owner's rent increase justifications. Wild Meadows MHC, LLC v. Weidman, 250 A.3d 751 (Del. 2021).

§ 7054. Appeal [For application of this section, see 79 Del. Laws, c. 304, § 7 and 80 Del. Laws, c. 229, § 3]

NOTES TO DECISIONS

Discovery. — Superior Court did not err in dismissing a manufactured home community owner's petition for a writ of prohibition because, based on a plain reading of the Rent Increase Justification Act (25 Del. C. § 7050 et seq.), an arbitrator appointed by the Manufactured Home Relocation Authority possessed the authority to compel the production of documents; the arbitrator was authorized to compel the owner to produce business records to afford the homeowners' association a chance to test the owner's justifications for its rent increase. Wild Meadows MHC, LLC v. Weidman, 250 A.3d 751 (Del. 2021).

PART VII

COMMON INTERESTS AND OWNERSHIP OF REAL ESTATE

CHAPTER 81

DELAWARE UNIFORM COMMON INTEREST OWNERSHIP ACT

SUBCHAPTER I

GENERAL PROVISIONS

PART 1

DEFINITIONS AND OTHER GENERAL PROVISIONS

§ 81-103. Definitions.

NOTES TO DECISIONS

Common interest communities. — In an action by a partygoer against a condominium unit owner association for injuries suffered when cutting across the property at night, the claim could proceed against the association because it could defend litigation in its own name on matters, including torts on the common areas, which affected the common interest community; summary judgment on the issue of liability was not warranted because there were genuine issues of material fact as to whether the predicates for the imposition of a duty were satisfied, including whether the association should have expected that a business invitee would not discover or be able to avoid the danger presented by an unlit and unmarked ditch. Rawls v. Commons at Stones Throw, — A.3d —, 2021 Del. Super. LEXIS 80 (Del. Super. Ct. Jan. 29, 2021).

In an action by a condominium owner against a condominium association that retaliated by publicizing the owner's appeal from a fine, the owner was entitled to recover litigation expenses pursuant to the Delaware Uniform Common Interest Ownership Act (DUCIOA, 25 Del. C. § 81-101 et seq.) because: (1) the association declarations did not conflict with the DUCIOA enforcement provision; (2) the owner established the association breached the declaration and the DUCIOA; (3) the owner was adversely affected by actions of the association; and (4) the court considered fee reasonableness

factors set out in Law. Prof. Conduct R. 1.5.
Bragdon v. Bayshore Prop. Owners Ass'n, 251
A.3d 661 (Del. Ch. 2021).

§ 81-108. Supplemental general principles of law applicable.

NOTES TO DECISIONS

Attorneys' fees. — In an action by a condominium owner against a condominium association that retaliated by publicizing the owner's
appeal from a fine, the owner was entitled to
recover litigation expenses pursuant to the
Delaware Uniform Common Interest Ownership Act (DUCIOA, 25 Del. C. § 81-101 et seq.)
because: (1) the association declarations did not
conflict with the DUCIOA enforcement provision; (2) the owner established the association
breached the declaration and the DUCIOA; (3)
the owner was adversely affected by actions of
the association; and (4) the court considered fee
reasonableness factors set out in Law. Prof.
Conduct R. 1.5. Bragdon v. Bayshore Prop.
Owners Ass'n, 251 A.3d 661 (Del. Ch. 2021).

§ 81-110. Uniformity of application and construction.

NOTES TO DECISIONS

Attorneys' fees. — In an action by a condominium owner against a condominium association that retaliated by publicizing the owner's
appeal from a fine, the owner was entitled to
recover litigation expenses pursuant to the
Delaware Uniform Common Interest Ownership Act (DUCIOA, 25 Del. C. § 81-101 et seq.)
because: (1) the association declarations did not
conflict with the DUCIOA enforcement provision; (2) the owner established the association
breached the declaration and the DUCIOA; (3)
the owner was adversely affected by actions of
the association; and (4) the court considered fee
reasonableness factors set out in Law. Prof.
Conduct R. 1.5. Bragdon v. Bayshore Prop.
Owners Ass'n, 251 A.3d 661 (Del. Ch. 2021).

PART 2
APPLICABILITY

§ 81-116. Applicability to new common interest communities; effective date.

(a) Except as provided in this subchapter, this chapter applies to all common
interest communities created within this State after the effective date that are
not excepted from this chapter by the provisions of this chapter. The provisions
of the Unit Property Act (Chapter 22 of this title) do not apply to common
interest communities created after the effective date except for those governed
by §§ 81-117 and 81-118 of this title and those others that are otherwise
excepted from this chapter by the provisions of this chapter including nonresidential common interest communities. Amendments to this chapter apply to
all common interest communities created after the effective date, or subjected
to this chapter, regardless of when the amendment is adopted.

(b) The effective date of this chapter shall be September 30, 2009. All
references in this Chapter 81 to the date of October 31, 2008, were deleted and
replaced with the aforementioned effective date, except as provided in this
section.

(c) Actions taken in reliance upon DUCIOA as effective on October 31, 2008,
shall not be invalidated by the amendment of the effective date to September
30, 2009.

(d) Anything to the contrary in this chapter notwithstanding, compliance
with DUCIOA was not intended to be required, and shall not be required, until
September 30, 2009, subject to the provisions of subsection (c) of this section
above.

(e) Any amendment or amendment and restatement of the declaration of a
preexisting common interest community does not affect the status of that
preexisting common interest community as excepted from some or all of this
chapter as provided in this chapter.

History.

76 Del. Laws, c. 422, § 2; 77 Del. Laws, c. 4, § 8; 77 Del. Laws, c. 91, §§ 14, 82; 77 Del. Laws, c. 364, §§ 1, 2; 83 Del. Laws, c. 173, § 2.

Revisor's note.

Section 15 of 83 Del. Laws, c. 173, provided: "This act takes effect 30 days after its enactment into law." The act was signed by the

Governor on Sept. 15, 2021, and became effective on Oct. 15, 2021.

Effect of amendments.

83 Del. Laws, c. 173, effective October 15, 2021, added "including nonresidential common interest communities" in the second sentence of (a)

§ 81-119. Applicability to preexisting common interest communities and approved common interest communities.

Except as provided in § 81-120 (Exception for small preexisting cooperatives and planned communities), and § 81-124 and except as limited by § 81-122 of this title hereof, §§ 81-105, 81-106, 81-107, 81-127, 81-203, 81-204, 81-217(i), 81-221, 81-301, 81-302(a)(1) through (6) and (11) through (17), 81-302(f), 81-302(g), 81-303, 81-306, 81-307(a), 81-308A, 81-309(a), 81-310, 81-311, 81-314, 81-315, 81-316, 81-318, 81-321, 81-322 [repealed], 81-323, 81-324, 81-409, and 81-417 of this title, and § 81-103 of this title to the extent any definitions are necessary in construing any of the foregoing sections to the extent the definitions do not conflict with the declaration, apply to all common interest communities and approved common interest communities created in this State before the effective date; but those sections apply only with respect to events and circumstances occurring after the effective date, and do not invalidate existing provisions of the declaration, bylaws, code of regulations, declaration plan, or plats or plans of those preexisting common interest communities and approved common interest communities that do not conflict with this chapter. With respect to all common interest communities, such existing provisions of those declarations, bylaws, codes of regulations, declaration plans, plats or plans, and subsequent amendments thereto adopted subsequent to the effective date of this chapter in strict accordance with those existing provisions, and not in conflict with the Unit Property Act (Chapter 22 of this title), shall be controlling in the event of any express conflict between those existing provisions (as duly amended) and the provisions of this chapter.

In matters and as to issues where neither such existing provisions of the declaration, bylaws, code of regulations, declaration plan, or plats or plans (as duly amended) of preexisting common interest communities or approved common interest communities nor the Unit Property Act (Chapter 22 of this title) expressly addresses the matter or issue, the provisions of this chapter shall control. As to any such preexisting common interest community or approved common interest community prior to the effective date: (i) this chapter shall not operate to terminate or allow the termination of existing contractual obligations created prior to the effective date, including, but not limited to contracts for units for preexisting common interest communities or approved common interest community projects; (ii) this chapter shall not invalidate the declaration, code of regulations, bylaws, declaration plan, or plats or plans of such common interest community that do not conflict with this chapter; (iii) the Unit Property Act (Chapter 22 of this title), and not this chapter shall govern all obligations of a declarant created under the Unit Property Act (Chapter 22 of this title); (iv) unless the declarant or other person with the right to do so elects to conform the requirements of this chapter in exercising any development right or special declarant rights, this chapter is not applicable to the procedures for the exercise of any such development rights or special declarant rights; (v) this chapter does not require that the preexisting declaration, code of regulations, bylaws, declaration plans, or plats or plans or other governing documents, including, but not limited to certificates or articles of incorporation, formation or otherwise of any preexisting common interest community or approved common interest community be amended to, or otherwise to comply with, the requirements of this chapter; and (vi) except for §§ 81-409 and 81-417 of this title, subchapter IV of this chapter is not applicable to any such preexisting common interest community or approved interest community. Without limiting the generality of any other provision of this chapter, and notwithstanding any other provision of this chapter, any condominium created under the Unit Property Act for which future expansions are provided under its declaration made pursuant to the Unit Property Act shall remain governed by the Unit Property Act and not this chapter with respect to all of such future sections, phases or other expansion rights.

Any preexisting common interest community or approved common interest community has the right to amend its declaration, code of regulations, bylaws, declaration plans, or plats or plans or other governing documents, including, but not limited to certificates or articles of incorporation, formation or otherwise to comply with any or all of the requirements of this chapter, or a preexisting common interest community or approved common interest community may select particular additional sections of this chapter to apply to that community without adopting the entire chapter.

History.

76 Del. Laws, c. 422, § 2; 77 Del. Laws, c. 4, § 9; 77 Del. Laws, c. 91, §§ 18, 82; 77 Del. Laws, c. 364, § 5; 80 Del. Laws, c. 160, § 1; 83 Del. Laws, c. 173, § 3.

Revisor's note.

Section 15 of 83 Del. Laws, c. 173, provided: "This act takes effect 30 days after its enactment into law." The act was signed by the Governor on Sept. 15, 2021, and became effective on Oct. 15, 2021.

Effect of amendments.

83 Del. Laws, c. 173, effective October 15, 2021, in the first paragraph, added "81-217(i)", "81-306", "81-308A", "81-310" and "81-314" in the first sentence, and substituted "all common interest communities" for "condominiums and cooperatives" in the second sentence.

NOTES TO DECISIONS

Governance documents control over statute. — In an action by a condominium owner against a condominium association that retaliated by publicizing the owner's appeal from a fine, the owner was entitled to recover litigation expenses pursuant to the Delaware Uniform Common Interest Ownership Act (DUCIOA, 25 Del. C. § 81-101 et seq.) because: (1) the association declarations did not conflict with the DUCIOA enforcement provision; (2) the owner established the association breached the declaration and the DUCIOA; (3) the owner was adversely affected by actions of the association; and (4) the court considered fee reasonableness factors set out in Law. Prof. Conduct R. 1.5. Bragdon v. Bayshore Prop. Owners Ass'n, 251 A.3d 661 (Del. Ch. 2021).

In a dispute between a developer and the unit owners' association as to who had the right to control the common interest community association, as determined by whether the developer should have been required to relinquish control of the association, the court found that the community was a master-planned community because its charter described itself as such; because the community fell within the master-planned community statutory exception, the community's charter (along with its higher and unmet 90% occupancy threshold) controlled the timing of relinquishment of control of the common interest community association from developer to the unit owners, rather than the 75% threshold for control relinquishment in 25 Del. C. § 81-803. Green v. Carl M. Freeman Cmtys. L.L.C., — A.3d —, 2021 Del. Ch. LEXIS 96 (Del. Ch. May 19, 2021).

SUBCHAPTER II
CREATION, ALTERATION, AND TERMINATION OF COMMON INTEREST

§ 81-217. Amendment of declaration.

(a) Except in cases of amendments that may be executed by a declarant under § 81-209(f) or § 81-210 of this title, or by the association under § 81-107, § 81-206(d), § 81-208(c), § 81-212(a), or § 81-213 of this title, or by certain unit owners under § 81-208(b), § 81-212(a), § 81-213(b), or § 81-218(b) of this title, or by secured lenders pursuant to § 81-219 of this title, and except as limited by subsection (d) of this section or as otherwise provided in this § 81-217 of this title, the declaration, including any plats and plans, may be amended only by vote or agreement of unit owners of units to which at least 67 percent of the votes in the association are allocated, unless the declaration specifies a different percentage for all amendments or for specific subjects of amendment. If the declaration requires the approval of another person as a condition of its effectiveness, the amendment is not valid without the approval.

(b) No action to challenge the validity of an amendment adopted by the association pursuant to this section may be brought more than 1 year after the amendment is recorded.

(c) Every amendment to the declaration must be recorded in every county in which any portion of the common interest community is located and is effective only upon recordation. An amendment, except an amendment pursuant to § 81-212(a) of this title, must be indexed in the grantee's index in the name of the common interest community and the association and in the grantor's index in the name of the parties executing the amendment.

(d) Except to the extent expressly permitted or required by other provisions of this chapter, or in a nonresidential common interest community, except as provided in the declaration, no amendment may create or increase special declarant rights, increase the number of units, change the boundaries of any unit or the allocated interests of a unit, in the absence of unanimous consent of the unit owners.

(e) Amendments to the declaration required by the chapter to be recorded by the association must be prepared, executed, recorded, and certified on behalf of the association by any officer of the association designated for that purpose or, in the absence of designation, by the president of the association.

(f) By vote or agreement of unit owners of units to which at least 80 percent of the votes in the association are allocated, or any larger percentage specified in the declaration, an amendment to the declaration may prohibit or materially restrict the permitted uses of or behavior in a unit or the number or other qualifications of persons who may occupy units. The amendment must provide reasonable protection for a use or occupancy permitted at the time the amendment was adopted.

(g) The time limits specified in the declaration pursuant to § 81-205(a)(8) of this title within which reserved development rights must be exercised may be extended, and additional development rights may be created, if persons entitled to cast at least 80 percent of the votes in the association, including 80 percent of the votes allocated to units not owned by the declarant, agree to that action. The agreement is effective 30 days after an amendment to the declaration reflecting the terms of the agreement is recorded unless all the persons holding the affected special declarant rights, or security interests in those rights, record a written objection within the 30-day period, in which case the amendment is void, or consent in writing at the time the amendment is recorded, in which case the amendment is effective when recorded.

(h) Provisions in the declaration creating special declarant rights which have not expired may not be amended without the consent of the declarant.

(i) Notwithstanding any provision of the declaration or bylaws to the contrary, any provision of this chapter or of the declaration of any common interest community subject to this chapter requires the consent of a person holding a security interest in a unit as a condition to the effectiveness of any amendment to the declaration, that consent shall be deemed granted if no written refusal to consent is received by the association within 45 days after the association delivers notice of the proposed amendment to the holder of the interest or mails the notice to the holder of the interest by certified mail, return receipt requested. The association may rely on the last recorded security interest of record in delivering or mailing notice to the holder of that interest. Notwithstanding this section, no amendment to the declaration that affects the priority of a holder's security interest or the ability of that holder to foreclose its security interest may be adopted without that holder's consent in a record if the declaration requires that consent as a condition to the effectiveness of the amendment.

(j) Unless the declaration or bylaws provide otherwise and subject to paragraphs (j)(ii) and (j)(iii) of this section:

(i) The executive board may execute and record an amendment to the declaration bylaws, or plat, to conform the declaration or bylaws to be consistent with the provisions of this chapter or to correct:

(1) A typographical error or other error in the percentage interests or number of votes appurtenant to any unit;

(2) A typographical error or other incorrect reference to another prior recorded document; or

(3) A typographical error or other incorrect unit designation or assignment of limited common elements if the affected unit owners and their mortgagees consent in writing to the amendment, and the consent documents are recorded with the amendment.

(ii) If the executive board executes and records an amendment under paragraph (j)(i) of this section, the executive board shall also record with the amendment:

(1) During the time that the declarant has an interest:

(A) The consent of the declarant; or

(B) An affidavit by the executive board that any declarant who has an interest in the condominium has been provided a copy of the amendment and a notice that the declarant may object in writing to the amendment within 30 days of receipt of the amendment and notice, that 30 days have passed since delivery of the amendment and notice, and that the declarant has made no written objection; and

(2) An affidavit by the executive board that at least 30 days before recordation of the amendment a copy of the amendment was sent with a notice of the amendment sent to each unit owner as required for notices pursuant to this chapter.

(iii) An amendment under this section is entitled to be recorded and is effective upon recordation if accompanied by the supporting documents required by this section.

(k) During the time that the declarant has an interest, the declaration, bylaws or plat may be amended by declarant in order to achieve compliance with the requirements of Federal National Mortgage Association, Federal Home Loan Mortgage Corporation, Federal Housing Authority, Veterans Administration or other governmental agency or their successors.

(l) During the time that the declarant has an interest, the declaration, bylaws or plat may be amended by declarant to conform the same to be consistent with the provisions required or allowed by this chapter.

(m) During the time that the declarant has an interest, the declaration, bylaws, or plat may be amended by declarant to correct any clerical or typographical errors or other errors, ambiguities, title questions, or defects or conflicts with or to comply with applicable laws.

History.
76 Del. Laws, c. 422, § 2; 77 Del. Laws, c. 91, §§ 33-36, 82; 83 Del. Laws, c. 173, §§ 4, 5.

Revisor's note.
Section 15 of 83 Del. Laws, c. 173, provided: "This act takes effect 30 days after its enact-

ment into law." The act was signed by the Governor on Sept. 15, 2021, and became effective on Oct. 15, 2021.

Effect of amendments.
83 Del. Laws, c. 173, effective October 15,

2021, substituted "Notwithstanding any provision of the declaration or bylaws to the contrary" for "If" in the first sentence of (i); and added (m).

§ 81-223. Master planned communities.

NOTES TO DECISIONS

Common interest community associations. —
In a dispute between a developer and the unit owners' association as to who had the right to control the common interest community association, as determined by whether the developer should have been required to relinquish control of the association, the court found that the community was a master-planned community because its charter described itself as such; because the community fell within the master-

planned community statutory exception, the community's charter (along with its higher and unmet 90% occupancy threshold) controlled the timing of relinquishment of control of the common interest community association from developer to the unit owners, rather than the 75% threshold for control relinquishment in 25 Del. C. § 81-803. Green v. Carl M. Freeman Cmtys. L.L.C., — A.3d —, 2021 Del. Ch. LEXIS 96 (Del. Ch. May 19, 2021).

SUBCHAPTER III
MANAGEMENT OF THE COMMON INTEREST COMMUNITY

§ 81-302. Powers of unit owners' association.

NOTES TO DECISIONS

Tort liability. — In an action by a partygoer against a condominium unit owner association for injuries suffered when cutting across the property at night, the claim could proceed against the association because it could defend litigation in its own name on matters, including torts on the common areas, which affected the common interest community; summary judgment on the issue of liability was not warranted because there were genuine issues of material fact as to whether the predicates for the imposition of a duty were satisfied, including whether the association should have expected that a business invitee would not discover or be able to avoid the danger presented by an unlit and unmarked ditch. Bragdon v. Bayshore Prop. Owners Ass'n, 251 A.3d 661 (Del. Ch. 2021).

In an action by a condominium owner against a condominium association that retaliated by publicizing the owner's appeal from a fine, the owner was entitled to recover litigation expenses pursuant to the Delaware Uniform Common Interest Ownership Act (DUCIOA, 25 Del. C. § 81-101 et seq.) because: (1) the association declarations did not conflict with the DUCIOA enforcement provision; (2) the owner established the association breached the declaration and the DUCIOA; (3) the owner was adversely affected by actions of the association; and (4) the court considered fee reasonableness factors set out in Law. Prof. Conduct R. 1.5. Bragdon v. Bayshore Prop. Owners Ass'n, 251 A.3d 661 (Del. Ch. 2021).

§ 81-303. Executive board members and officers.

(a) The declaration must create an executive board. Except as provided in the declaration, the bylaws, subsection (b) of this section, or other provisions of this chapter, the executive board may act in all instances on behalf of the association. In the performance of their duties, officers and members of the executive board shall exercise the degree of care and loyalty to the association required of an officer or director of a corporation organized under Delaware law. The standards of care and loyalty described in this section apply regardless of the form of legal entity in which the association is organized.

(b) The executive board may not act on behalf of the association to amend the declaration or the bylaws, to terminate the common interest community, or to elect members of the executive board or determine the qualifications, powers and duties, or terms of office of executive board members, but the executive board may fill vacancies in its membership for the unexpired portion of any term.

(c) Subject to subsection (d) of this section, the declaration may provide for a period of declarant control of the association, during which a declarant, or persons designated by the declarant, may appoint and remove the officers and members of the executive board. Regardless of the period provided in the declaration, and except as provided in § 81-223(g) of this title, a period of declarant control terminates no later than the earlier of: (i) except as to a nonresidential common interest community, 60 days after conveyance of 75 percent of the units that may be created to unit owners other than a declarant; (ii) as to units for residential purposes, 2 years after all declarants have ceased to offer units for residential purposes for sale in the ordinary course of business; (iii) as to units for residential purposes, 2 years after any right to add new units for residential purposes was last exercised; (iv) as to a common interest community other than a condominium or cooperative, at such time as may be required by other applicable laws; or (v) as to nonresidential units in a common interest community that is subject to this chapter, 7 years after all declarants have ceased to offer nonresidential units for sale in the ordinary course of business; (vi) as to nonresidential units in a common interest community that is subject to this chapter, 7 years after any right to add new nonresidential units was last exercised; or (vii) the day the declarant, after giving written notice to unit owners, records an instrument voluntarily surrendering all rights to control activities of the association; or (viii) as to a condominium or cooperative created before September 30, 2009, as provided in the declaration. A declarant may voluntarily surrender the right to appoint and remove officers and members of the executive board before termination of that period, but in that event the declarant may require, for the duration of the period of declarant control, that specified actions of the association or executive board, as described in a recorded instrument executed by the declarant, be approved by the declarant before they become effective.

(d) Not later than 60 days after conveyance of 25 percent of the units that may be created to unit owners other than a declarant, at least one member and not less than 25 percent of the members of the executive board must be elected by unit owners other than the declarant. Not later than 60 days after conveyance of 50 percent of the units that may be created to unit owners other than a declarant, not less than 33⅓ percent of the members of the executive board must be elected by unit owners other than the declarant.

(e) Except as otherwise provided in §§ 81-220(e) and 81-303(f) of this title, not later than the termination of any period of declarant control, the unit owners must elect an executive board of at least 3 members, at least a majority of whom must be unit owners. Unless the declaration provides for the election of officers by the unit owners, the executive board shall appoint the officers. The executive board members and officers shall take office upon election or appointment.

(f) The declaration may provide for the appointment of members of the executive board before or after the period of declarant control and the method of filling vacancies in appointed memberships, rather than election of those members by the unit owners. After the period of declarant control, such appointed members:

    (i) Shall not be appointed by the declarant or an affiliate of the declarant;

    (ii) Shall not comprise more than 33 percent of the entire board; and

    (iii) Have no greater authority than any other member of the executive board.

(g) Not later than the termination of any period of declarant control, the declarant shall provide at its sole expense an audit of all expenditures made with funds collected from unit owners not affiliated with the declarant together with a list of all items paid for out of association funds that specifically benefited only the units owned by declarant and not the units generally. The audit shall be conducted by a certified public accountant that is not an affiliate of declarant.

History.

76 Del. Laws, c. 422, § 2; 77 Del. Laws, c. 91, §§ 41-43, 82; 83 Del. Laws, c. 173, §§ 6, 7.

Revisor's note.

Section 15 of 83 Del. Laws, c. 173, provided: "This act takes effect 30 days after its enactment into law." The act was signed by the Governor on Sept. 15, 2021, and became effective on Oct. 15, 2021.

Effect of amendments.

83 Del. Laws, c. 173, effective October 15, 2021, in (a), deleted "appointed by the declarant" preceding "shall exercise" in the third sentence and deleted the former fourth sentence; and added clause (viii) in the second sentence of (c).

NOTES TO DECISIONS

Control of property-owners' association. — In a dispute between a developer and the unit owners' association as to who had the right to control the common interest community association, as determined by whether the developer should have been required to relinquish control of the association, the court found that the community was a master-planned community because its charter described itself as such; because the community fell within the master-

planned community statutory exception, the community's charter (along with its higher and unmet 90% occupancy threshold) controlled the timing of relinquishment of control of the common interest community association from developer to the unit owners, rather than the 75% threshold for control relinquishment in 25 Del. C. § 81-803. Green v. Carl M. Freeman Cmtys. L.L.C., — A.3d —, 2021 Del. Ch. LEXIS 96 (Del. Ch. May 19, 2021).

§ 81-306. Bylaws.

NOTES TO DECISIONS

Attorneys' fees. — In an action by a condominium owner against a condominium association that retaliated by publicizing the owner's appeal from a fine, the owner was entitled to recover litigation expenses pursuant to the Delaware Uniform Common Interest Ownership Act (DUCIOA, 25 Del. C. § 81-101 et seq.) because: (1) the association declarations did not

conflict with the DUCIOA enforcement provision; (2) the owner established the association breached the declaration and the DUCIOA; (3) the owner was adversely affected by actions of the association; and (4) the court considered fee reasonableness factors set out in Law. Prof. Conduct R. 1.5. Bragdon v. Bayshore Prop. Owners Ass'n, 251 A.3d 661 (Del. Ch. 2021).

§ 81-310. Voting; proxies.

(a) If only 1 of several owners of a unit is present at a meeting of the association, that owner is entitled to cast all the votes allocated to that unit. If more than 1 of the owners is present, the votes allocated to that unit may be cast only in accordance with the agreement of a majority in interest of the owners, unless the declaration expressly provides otherwise. There is majority agreement if any 1 of the owners casts the votes allocated to that unit without protest being made promptly to the person presiding over the meeting by any of the other owners of the unit. The vote may be expressed by (i) an in-person vote at a meeting, (ii) a proxy vote if the governing documents or law allow for proxy voting, (iii) voting electronically from a source known to the community such as an email address registered with the association, (iv) voting by electronic voting software, (v) signing a petition calling for the amendment, or (vi) signing an amendment to the governing document. A signature may be in ink or electronic. For purposes of this subsection (a) of this section, an entity or trust owning a unit may designate a person to vote for the entity or trust.

(b) Votes allocated to a unit may be cast pursuant to a proxy duly executed by a unit owner. If a unit is owned by more than 1 person, each owner of the unit may vote or register protest to the casting of votes by the other owners of the unit through a duly executed proxy. A unit owner may revoke a proxy given pursuant to this section only by actual notice of revocation to the person presiding over a meeting of the association. A proxy is void if it is not dated or purports to be revocable without notice. A proxy terminates 1 year after its date, unless it specifies a shorter term.

(c) If the declaration requires that votes on specified matters affecting the common interest community be cast by lessees rather than unit owners of leased units: (i) the provisions of subsections (a) and (b) of this section apply to lessees as if they were unit owners; (ii) unit owners who have leased their units to other persons may not cast votes on those specified matters; and (iii) lessees are entitled to notice of meetings, access to records, and other rights respecting those matters as if they were unit owners. Unit owners must also be given notice, in the manner provided in § 81-308 of this title, of all meetings at which lessees are entitled to vote.

(d) Votes allocated to a unit owned by the association may not be cast and shall not be calculated either in a quorum or in any percentage of unit votes needed for any action by the unit owners.

(e) Except in cases where a greater percentage of unit votes in the association is required by this chapter or the declaration, a majority of the votes cast in person, by proxy or by ballot at a meeting of unit owners where a quorum is present shall determine the outcome of any action of the association where a vote is taken so long as the number of votes cast in favor comprise at least a majority of the number of votes required for a quorum for that meeting.

(f) Action may be taken by ballot without a meeting as follows:

(1) Unless prohibited or limited by the declaration or bylaws, any action that the association may take at any meeting of members may be taken without a meeting if the association delivers a written or electronic ballot to every member entitled to vote on the matter. A ballot shall set forth each proposed action and provide an opportunity to vote for or against each proposed action.

(2) All solicitations for votes by ballot must: (A) indicate the number of responses needed to meet the quorum requirements; (B) state the percentage of approvals necessary to approve each matter other than election of directors; (C) specify the time by which a ballot must be delivered to the association in order to be counted, which time shall not be less than 3 days after the date that the association delivers the ballot; and (D) describe procedures (including time and size and manner) by when unit owners wishing to deliver information to all unit owners regarding the subject of the vote may do so.

(3) Approval by the ballot pursuant to this section is valid only if: (A) the number of votes cast by ballot equals or exceeds the quorum required to be present at a meeting authorizing the action; and (B) the number of approvals equals or exceeds the number of votes that would be required to approve the matter at a meeting at which the total number of votes cast was the same as the number of votes by ballot.

(4) Except as otherwise provided in the declaration or bylaws, a ballot shall not be revoked after delivery to the association by death, disability or revocation by the person who cast that vote.

History.
76 Del. Laws, c. 422, § 2; 77 Del. Laws, c. 91, § 82; 83 Del. Laws, c. 173, § 8.

Revisor's note.
Section 15 of 83 Del. Laws, c. 173, provided: "This act takes effect 30 days after its enactment into law." The act was signed by the Governor on Sept. 15, 2021, and became effective on Oct. 15, 2021.

Effect of amendments.
83 Del. Laws, c. 173, effective October 15, 2021, added the fourth through sixth sentences in (a).

§ 81-315. Assessments for common expenses.

Process to approve assessment. — Decision which recommended approving bylaws of corporation was affirmed; the new bylaws' procedure for increasing an annual assessment without a vote did not conflict with the Delaware Uniform Common Interest Ownership Act (25 Del. C. § 81-101 et seq.), because the Act did not require a separate vote to set the annual assessment. Beck v. Greim, — A.3d —, 2020 Del. Ch. LEXIS 343 (Del. Ch. Nov. 17, 2020).

§ 81-316. Lien for assessments.

(a) The association has a statutory lien on a unit for any assessment levied against that unit or fines imposed against its unit owner. Unless the declaration otherwise provides, fees, charges, late charges, fines, and interest charged pursuant to § 81-302(a)(10), (11), and (12) of this title, and any other sums due the association under the declaration, this chapter or as a result of an administrative or judicial decision, together with court costs and reasonable attorneys' fees incurred in attempting collection of the same, are enforceable in the same manner as unpaid assessments under this section. If an assessment is payable in installments, the lien is for the full amount of the assessment from the time the first installment thereof becomes due. Unless the declaration provides for a different rate of interest, interest on unpaid assessments shall accrue at the rate of the lesser of 18% per annum or the highest rate permitted by law.

(b) Except as otherwise provided in the declaration, a lien under this section is prior to all other liens and encumbrances on a unit except (i) liens and encumbrances recorded before the recordation of the declaration and, in a cooperative, liens and encumbrances which the association creates, assumes, or takes subject to, (ii) a first or second security interest on the unit recorded before the date on which the assessment sought to be enforced became delinquent, or, in a cooperative, the first or second security interest encumbering only the unit owner's interest and perfected before the date on which the assessment sought to be enforced became delinquent, and (iii) liens for real estate taxes and other governmental assessments or charges against the unit or cooperative. The lien shall have priority over the security interests described in paragraph (ii) above for an amount not to exceed the aggregate customary common expense assessment against such unit for 6 months as determined by the periodic budget adopted by the association pursuant to § 81-315(a) of this title; provided that for the lien to have priority over the security interests described in paragraph (ii) above, an association with assessments shall have recorded in the county or counties in which the common interest community is located a document which contains the name of the association, the address, a contact telephone number, a contact e-mail address and a web-site address, if any. In addition, the association shall have recorded at any time, but not less than 30 days prior to the sheriff's sale of a unit in its common interest community for which common expense assessments are due, a statement of lien which shall include a description of such unit, the name of the record owner, the amount due and the date due, the amount paid for recording the statement of lien and the amount required to be paid for filing a termination thereof upon payment, and the signature and notarized statement of an officer of the association that the amount described in the statement of lien is correct and due and owing. Upon payment of the amount due in paragraph (ii) above, the payer shall be entitled to a recordable termination of lien for the amount paid. The liens recorded pursuant to this subparagraph shall expire on the first day of the sixtieth month after recording. This subsection does not affect the priority of mechanics' or materialmen's liens, nor the priority of liens for other assessments made by the association. The lien under this subsection is not subject to the provisions of homestead or other exemptions.

(c) Unless the declaration otherwise provides, if 2 or more associations have liens for assessments created at any time on the same property, those liens have equal priority.

(d) Recording of the declaration constitutes record notice and perfection of the lien. No further recordation of any claim of lien for assessment under this section is required.

(e) A lien for unpaid assessments is extinguished unless proceedings to enforce the lien are instituted within 3 years after the full amount of the assessments becomes due; provided, that if an owner of a unit subject to a lien under this section files a petition for relief under the United States Bankruptcy Code [11 U.S.C. § 101 et seq.], the period of time for instituting proceedings to enforce the association's lien shall be tolled until 30 days after the automatic stay of proceedings under § 362 of the Bankruptcy Code [11 U.S.C. § 362] is lifted.

(f) This section does not prohibit actions against unit owners to recover sums for which subsection (a) of this section creates a lien or prohibit an association from taking a deed in lieu of foreclosure.

(g) A judgment or decree in any action brought under this section must include costs and reasonable attorney's fees for the prevailing party.

(h) The association upon written request shall furnish to a unit owner a statement setting forth the amount of unpaid assessments against the unit. If the unit owner's interest is real estate, the statement must be in recordable form. The statement must be furnished within 10 business days after receipt of the request and is binding on the association, the executive board, and every unit owner. The association may impose a charge as a condition to providing that statement. The charge for such statement shall not exceed $25, except in cases where an account has been referred to the association's legal counsel. Except if the result of fraud or gross negligence, any liability of the association for an error or omission in the statement is limited to the amount of any fees paid the association for that statement. The foregoing limitation shall not apply to the liability of a managing agent acting on behalf of the association.

(i) In a cooperative, upon nonpayment of an assessment on a unit, the unit owner may be evicted in the same manner as provided by law in the case of an unlawful holdover by a commercial tenant, and the lien may be foreclosed as provided by this section.

(j) The association's lien may be foreclosed or executed upon as provided in this subsection and subsection (m) of this section:

(1) In a condominium or planned community, the association's lien must be foreclosed in like manner as a mortgage on real estate, by equitable foreclosure or executed upon by other lawful procedures provided for in the declaration;

(2) In a cooperative whose unit owners' interests in the units are real estate, the association's lien must be foreclosed in like manner as a mortgage on real estate; or

(3) In a cooperative whose unit owners' interests in the units are personal property, the association's lien must be foreclosed in like manner as a security interest under Article 9 of the Uniform Commercial Code [§ 9-101 et seq. of Title 6].

(4) In the case of foreclosure, the association shall give reasonable notice of its action to all lien holders of the unit whose interest would be affected and to all other persons as would be required under applicable law for the foreclosure of a mortgage on real estate.

(k) In a cooperative, if the unit owner's interest in a unit is real estate:

(1) The association, upon nonpayment of assessments and compliance with this subsection, may sell that unit at a public sale or by private negotiation, and at any time and place. Every aspect of the sale, including the method, advertising, time, place, and terms must be reasonable. The association shall give to the unit owner and any lessees of the unit owner reasonable written notice of the time and place of any public sale or, if a private sale is intended, or the intention of entering into a contract to sell and of the time after which a private disposition may be made. The same notice must also be sent to any other person who has a recorded interest in the unit which would be cut off by the sale, but only if the recorded interest was on record 7 weeks before the date specified in the notice as the date of any public sale or 7 weeks before the date specified in the notice as the date after which a private sale may be made. The notices required by this subsection may be sent to any address reasonable in the circumstances. Sale may not be held until 5 weeks after the sending of the notice. The association may buy at any public sale and, if the sale is conducted by a fiduciary or other person not related to the association, at a private sale.

(2) Unless otherwise agreed, the unit owner is liable for any deficiency in a foreclosure sale.

(3) The proceeds of a foreclosure sale must be applied in the following order:

(i) The reasonable expenses of sale;

(ii) The reasonable expenses of securing possession before sale, holding, maintaining, and preparing the unit for sale, including payment of taxes and other governmental charges, premiums on hazard and liability insurance, and, to the extent provided for by agreement between the association and the unit owner, reasonable attorneys' fees and other legal expenses incurred by the association;

(iii) Satisfaction of the association's lien;

(iv) Satisfaction in the order of priority of any subordinate claim of record; and

(v) Remittance of any excess to the unit owner.

(4) A good faith purchaser for value acquires the unit free of the association's debt that gave rise to the lien under which the foreclosure sale occurred and any subordinate interest, even though the association or other person conducting the sale failed to comply with this section. The person conducting the sale shall execute a conveyance to the purchaser sufficient to convey the unit and stating that it is executed by the person after a foreclosure of the association's lien by power of sale and that the person was empowered to make the sale. Signature and title or authority of the person signing the conveyance as grantor and a recital of the facts of nonpayment of the assessment and of the giving of the notices required by this subsection are sufficient proof of the facts recited and of the authority to sign. Further proof of authority is not required even though the association is named as grantee in the conveyance.

(5) At any time before the association has disposed of a unit in a cooperative or entered into a contract for its disposition under the power of sale, the unit owners or the holder of any subordinate security interest may cure the unit owner's default and prevent sale or other disposition by tendering the performance due under the security agreement, including any amounts due because of exercise of a right to accelerate, plus the reasonable expenses of proceeding to foreclosure incurred to the time of tender, including reasonable attorneys' fees of the creditor.

(l) In an action by an association to collect assessments or to foreclose a lien on a unit under this section, the court may appoint a receiver to collect all sums alleged to be due and owing to a unit owner before commencement or during pendency of the action. The court may order the receiver to pay any sums held by the receiver to the association during pendency of the action to the extent of the association's common expense assessments based on a periodic budget adopted by the association pursuant to § 81-315 of this title.

(m) The following restrictions apply to any action by the association to foreclose its lien under this section:

(1) No foreclosure action may be commenced unless: (A) the unit owner, at the time the action is commenced, owes a sum equal to at least 3 months of common expense assessments based on the periodic budget last adopted by the association pursuant to § 81-315(a) of this title; and (B) the executive board expressly votes to commence a foreclosure action against that specific unit.

(2) The association shall apply any sums paid by unit owners who are delinquent in paying assessments as follows: (i) first, to unpaid assessments; (ii) then to late charges; (iii) then to attorney's fees and other reasonable collection charges and costs; and (iv) finally, to all other unpaid fees, charges, penalties, interest and late charges.

(3) If the only sums due with respect to a unit consist of fines and related sums levied against that unit, a foreclosure action may not be commenced against that unit unless the association has first secured a judgment against the unit owner with respect to those fines and has perfected a judgment lien against the unit under state law.

History.

76 Del. Laws, c. 422, § 2; 77 Del. Laws, c. 91, §§ 51, 52, 82; 83 Del. Laws, c. 173, §§ 9, 10.

Revisor's note.

Section 15 of 83 Del. Laws, c. 173, provided: "This act takes effect 30 days after its enactment into law." The act was signed by the Governor on Sept. 15, 2021, and became effective on Oct. 15, 2021.

Effect of amendments.

83 Del. Laws, c. 173, effective October 15, 2021, added the fourth through sixth sentences in (h); and added a comma following "estate" in (j)(1).

§ 81-318. Association records.

(a) The association shall maintain the following records in written form or in another form capable of conversion into written form within a reasonable time:

(1) Detailed records of receipts and expenditures affecting the operation and administration of the association and other appropriate accounting records, including those for the repair and replacement reserve. All financial records shall be kept in accordance with generally accepted accounting practices.

(2) Minutes of all meetings of its members and executive board, a record of all actions taken by the members or executive board without a meeting, and a record of all actions taken by a committee of the executive board in place of the board or directors on behalf of the association.

(3) A record of its members in a form that permits preparation of a list of the names and addresses of all members, in alphabetical order by class, showing the number of votes each member is entitled to cast and the members' class of membership, if any; and

(4) In addition, the association shall keep a copy of the following records at its principal office: (1) its original or restated certificate of incorporation and bylaws and all amendments to them currently in effect; (2) the minutes of all members' meetings and records of all action taken by members without a meeting for the past 3 years; (3) any financial statements and tax returns of the association prepared for the past 3

years, together with the report of the auditors of the financial records; (4) a list of the names and business addresses of its current directors and officers; (5) its most recent annual report delivered to the Secretary of the State; (6) in the case of a condominium or cooperative, the association's most recent reserve study; and (7) financial and other records sufficiently detailed to enable the association to comply with § 81-409 of this title.

(b) Subject to the provisions of subsection (c) of this section, all records kept by the association, including the association's membership list and address, and aggregate salary information of employees of the association, shall be available for examination and copying by a unit owner or the unit owner's authorized agent so long as the request is made in good faith and for a proper purpose related to the owner's membership in the association. This right of examination may be exercised: (i) only during reasonable business hours or at a mutually convenient time and location, and (ii) upon 5-days' written notice reasonably identifying the purpose for the request and the specific records of the association requested.

(c) Records kept by an association may be withheld from inspection and copying to the extent that they concern:

(1) Personnel matters relating to specific persons or a person's medical records;

(2) Contracts, leases, and other commercial transactions to purchase or provide goods or services, currently in or under negotiation;

(3) Pending or threatened litigation, arbitration, mediation or other administrative proceedings;

(4) Matters involving federal, state or local administrative or other formal proceedings before a government tribunal for enforcement of the declaration, bylaws or rules;

(5) Communications with legal counsel which are otherwise protected by the attorney-client privilege or the attorney work product doctrine;

(6) Disclosure of information in violation of law;

(7) Meeting minutes or other confidential records of an executive session of the executive board; or

(8) Individual unit owner files other than those of the requesting owner.

(d) An attorney's files and records relating to the association are not records of the association and are not subject to inspection by owners or production in a legal proceeding for examination by owners.

(e) The association may charge a fee, in advance, to the unit owner for converting records into written form, for permitting inspection, and for providing copies of any records under this section, but that fee may not exceed the actual cost of the materials and labor incurred by the association.

(f) The right to copy records under this section includes the right to receive copies by xerographic or other means, including copies through an electronic transmission if available and so requested by the unit owner.

(g) An association is not obligated to compile or synthesize information.

(h) Information provided pursuant to this section may not be used for commercial purposes.

History.
76 Del. Laws, c. 422, § 2; 77 Del. Laws, c. 91, §§ 54-56, 82; 83 Del. Laws, c. 173, § 11.

Revisor's note.
Section 15 of 83 Del. Laws, c. 173, provided: "This act takes effect 30 days after its enactment into law." The act was signed by the Governor on Sept. 15, 2021, and became effective on Oct. 15, 2021.

Effect of amendments.
83 Del. Laws, c. 173, effective October 15, 2021, added "in advance, to the unit owner for converting records into written form, for permitting inspection, and" in (e).

§ 81-324. Adoption of budget.

(a) The executive board shall, at least annually, prepare a proposed budget for the common interest community. In a condominium or cooperative, the proposed budget shall include a line item for any required funding of a repair and replacement reserve. Within 30 days after adoption of any proposed budget after the period of declarant control, the executive board shall provide to all unit owners a summary of the budget, including any reserves and a statement of the basis on which any reserves are calculated and funded. Simultaneously, the executive board shall set a date for a meeting of the unit owners to consider ratification of the budget not less than 14 nor more than 60 days after providing the summary. Unless at that meeting a majority of all unit owners or any larger vote specified in the declaration, voting in person or by proxy, reject the budget, the budget is ratified, whether or not a quorum is present. If a proposed periodic budget is rejected, the periodic budget last ratified by the unit owners must be continued until such time as the unit owners ratify a subsequent budget proposed by the executive board.

(b) In addition to adoption of its regular periodic budget, the executive board may at any time propose a budget which would require a special assessment against all the units. Except as provided in subsection (c) of this section, the special assessment is effective only if the executive board follows the procedures for ratification of a budget described in subsection (a) of this section and the unit owners do not reject that proposed special assessment.

(c) If the executive board determines by unanimous vote that the special assessment is necessary in order to respond to an emergency, then: (i) the special assessment shall become effective immediately in accordance with the terms of the vote; (ii) notice of the emergency assessment shall be promptly provided to all unit owners; and (iii) the executive board shall spend the funds paid on account of the emergency assessment solely for the purposes described in the vote.

History.

76 Del. Laws, c. 422, § 2; 77 Del. Laws, c. 91, §§ 59, 60, 82; 83 Del. Laws, c. 173, § 12.

Revisor's note.

Section 15 of 83 Del. Laws, c. 173, provided: "This act takes effect 30 days after its enactment into law." The act was signed by the Governor on Sept. 15, 2021, and became effective on Oct. 15, 2021.

Effect of amendments.

83 Del. Laws, c. 173, effective October 15, 2021, added "voting in person or by proxy" in the fourth sentence of (a).

SUBCHAPTER IV
PROTECTION OF PURCHASERS

§ 81-408. Purchaser's right to cancel.

(a) A person required to deliver a public offering statement pursuant to § 81-402(c) of this title shall provide a purchaser with a copy of the public offering statement and all amendments thereto before conveyance of the unit, and not later than the date of any contract of sale. Unless such a purchaser is given the public offering statement more than 5 days before execution of a contract for the purchase of a unit, the purchaser, before conveyance, may cancel the contract within 5 days after first receiving the public offering statement.

(b) If a purchaser elects to cancel a contract pursuant to subsection (a) of this section, the purchaser may do so by notice to the offeror. Cancellation is without penalty, and all payments made by the purchaser before cancellation must be refunded promptly.

(c) Anything to the contrary in this chapter notwithstanding, any declarant, dealer, or unit owner who entered into a contract with a purchaser for a unit on or before the effective date shall not be subject to any of the provisions of this section and no such purchaser shall be entitled to exercise any of the rights and remedies against such declarant, dealer or unit owner under this section.

History.

76 Del. Laws, c. 422, § 2; 77 Del. Laws, c. 4, § 15; 77 Del. Laws, c. 91, §§ 68-70, 82; 83 Del. Laws, c. 173, § 13.

Revisor's note.

Section 15 of 83 Del. Laws, c. 173, provided: "This act takes effect 30 days after its enactment into law." The act was signed by the Governor on Sept. 15, 2021, and became effective on Oct. 15, 2021.

Effect of amendments.

83 Del. Laws, c. 173, effective October 15, 2021, in (a), deleted "for a condominium or cooperative" following "of this title" in the first sentence, and in the second sentence added "more than 5 days" and substituted "5" for "15" following "within".

§ 81-409. Resales of units.

(a) Except in the case of a sale in which delivery of a public offering statement is required, or unless exempt under § 81-401(b) of this title, a unit owner shall furnish to a purchaser not later than the time of the signing of the contract to purchase, a copy of the declaration (other than any plats and plans), all amendments to the declaration, the bylaws, and the rules of the association (including all amendments to the rules), and a certificate containing or attaching the following, to be correct to within 120 days prior to the date the certificate of the unit owner is furnished to the purchaser:

(1) A statement disclosing the effect on the proposed disposition of any right of first refusal or other restraint on the free alienability of the unit held by the association;

(2) A statement setting forth the amount of the periodic common expense assessment and any unpaid common expense or special assessment currently due and payable from the selling unit owner;

(3) A statement of any other fees payable by the owner of the unit being sold;

(4) In a condominium or cooperative, a statement of the current number of unit owners delinquent in the payment of common expense assessments and the aggregate amount of such delinquency;

(5) In a condominium or cooperative, a statement of the current balance in the repair and replacement reserve;

(6) A statement of any capital expenditures approved by the association for the current and succeeding fiscal years, including a statement of the amount of such capital expenditures to be taken from the repair and replacement reserve;

(7) In a condominium or cooperative, a copy of the most recent reserve study;

(8) The most recent regularly prepared balance sheet and income and expense statement, if any, of the association;

(9) The most recent report of auditors (if required by § 81-306(a)(6) of this title) on the association balance sheet and income and expense statement or any accountant's report on any unaudited association balance sheet and income and expense statement;

(10) The current operating budget of the association;

(11) A statement of any unsatisfied judgments against the association and the status of any pending suits in which the association is a defendant;

(12) A statement describing any insurance coverage provided for the benefit of unit owners;

(13) In a condominium or cooperative, a statement as to whether the executive board has given or received written notice that any existing

uses, occupancies, alterations, or improvements in or to the unit or to the limited common elements assigned thereto violate any provision of the declaration;

(14) In a condominium or cooperative, a statement as to whether the executive board has received written notice from a governmental agency of any violation of environmental, health, or building codes with respect to the unit, the limited common elements assigned thereto, or any other portion of the common interest community which has not been cured;

(15) In a condominium or cooperative, a statement of the remaining term of any leasehold estate affecting the common interest community and the provisions governing any extension or renewal thereof;

(16) In a cooperative, an accountant's statement, if any was prepared, as to the deductibility for federal income tax purposes by the unit owner of real estate taxes and interest paid by the association;

(17) A statement describing any pending sale or encumbrance of common elements;

(18) A statement of any fees payable by the purchaser of the unit to the association at settlement; and

(19) Copies of the minutes for the executive board meeting for the preceding 6 months or, if none, for the most recent executive board meeting for which minutes are available.

(b) The association, within 10 days after a request by a unit owner, shall furnish a certificate containing the information necessary to enable the unit owner to comply with this section. If the unit owner has requested the information from the association and the association fails to provide any portion of the requested information or if the unit owner, after reasonable investigation, has no information on any particular item to be included in the certificate, or if the requested information does not exist, the unit owner shall include a statement to that effect in the certificate from the unit owner. A unit owner providing a certificate pursuant to subsection (a) of this section is not liable to the purchaser for any erroneous information provided by the association and included in the certificate and is not liable to the purchaser under this section if the owner had, after reasonable investigation, reasonable grounds to believe, and did believe, at the time the information was provided to the purchaser, that the statements were true and there was no omission to state a material fact necessary to make the statements made not misleading, in light of the circumstances under which the statements were made. The association may require that such certificate and information be furnished in an electronic format. Except as provided in this subsection, the association may charge a fee for providing such certificate and related information. Such fee shall not exceed $200 for each certificate, except that if the association agrees to furnish a certificate and related information in a paper copy format, it may charge an additional cost not to exceed $50 for each such certificate. If the association fails to provide the requested certificate within the 10-day period, the association may not charge any fee for providing that certificate. Unless the purchaser is given the resale certificate before execution of a contract for the purchase of a unit, the purchaser, before conveyance, may cancel the contract within 5 calendar days after first receiving the resale certificate. Unless the result of fraud, gross negligence, recklessness or willful misconduct, any liability of the association for an error or omission in the certificate provided by the association is limited to any fees paid the association for that certificate. The foregoing limitation shall not apply to the liability of a managing agent acting on behalf of the association.

(c) In the event that a unit for which a certificate is required pursuant to subsection (a) of this section is subject to more than one association, the unit owner must include in the certificate the information required by subsection (a) of this section for each association governing that unit, but the unit owner does not have to duplicate the information for any particular association if it is already included with respect to any one of the associations.

(d) A purchaser is not liable for any unpaid assessment or fee greater than the amount set forth in the certificate prepared by the association.

History.

76 Del. Laws, c. 422, § 2; 77 Del. Laws, c. 91, §§ 71-75, 82; 77 Del. Laws, c. 364, §§ 8-10; 83 Del. Laws, c. 173, § 14.

Revisor's note.

Section 15 of 83 Del. Laws, c. 173, provided: "This act takes effect 30 days after its enact-

ment into law." The act was signed by the Governor on Sept. 15, 2021, and became effective on Oct. 15, 2021.

Effect of amendments.

83 Del. Laws, c. 173, effective October 15, 2021, added the ninth and tenth sentences in (b).

§ 81-417. Effect of violations on rights of action; attorneys' fees.

NOTES TO DECISIONS

Application. — In an action by a condominium owner against a condominium association that retaliated by publicizing the owner's appeal from a fine, the owner was entitled to recover litigation expenses pursuant to the Delaware Uniform Common Interest Ownership Act (DUCIOA, 25 Del. C. § 81-101 et seq.) because: (1) the association declarations did not conflict with the DUCIOA enforcement provision; (2) the owner established the association breached the declaration and the DUCIOA; (3) the owner was adversely affected by actions of the association; and (4) the court considered fee reasonableness factors set out in Law. Prof. Conduct R. 1.5. Bragdon v. Bayshore Prop. Owners Ass'n, 251 A.3d 661 (Del. Ch. 2021).

TITLE 26
PUBLIC UTILITIES

Chapter
1. Public Service Commission, §§ 101 to 711.
10. Electric Utility Restructuring, §§ 1001 to 1020.

CHAPTER 1
PUBLIC SERVICE COMMISSION

SUBCHAPTER III
RATES

§ 315. Electric and natural gas utility distribution system improvement charge [Effective June 14, 2025].

(a) The following definitions shall apply in this section:

(1) "Eligible utility facility relocations" means new, used and useful utility plant or facilities of an electric or natural gas utility that:

a. Do not include that portion of any plant or facilities used to increase capacity of or connect to the transmission or distribution system to serve new or additional load;

b. Are in service; and

c. Were not included in the utility's rate base in its most recent general rate case; and which

d. Relocate, as required or necessitated by Department of Transportation or other government agency projects, without reimbursement existing facilities, including but not limited to, mains, lines and services, whether underground or aerial. For purposes of this subparagraph (1)d. of this section, "existing facilities" and "relocate" include the physical relocation of existing facilities and also include removal, abandonment or retirement of existing facilities and the construction of new facilities in a relocated location.

(2) "Pretax return" means the revenues necessary to:

a. Produce net operating income equal to the electric or natural gas utility's weighted cost of capital as established in the most recent general rate proceeding for that utility multiplied by the net original cost of eligible utility facility relocations. At any time the Commission by its own motion, or by motion of the electric or natural gas utility, Commission staff or the Public Advocate, may determine to revisit and, after hearing without the necessity of a general rate filing reset the UFRC rate to reflect the affected utility's current cost of capital. The UFRC rate shall be adjusted back to the date of the motion to reflect any change in the cost of capital determined by the Commission through this process;

b. Provide for the tax deductibility of the debt interest component of the cost of capital; and

c. Pay state and federal income taxes applicable to such income.

(3) "UFRC costs" means depreciation expenses and pretax return associated with eligible utility facility relocations.

(4) "UFRC rate" refers to utility facility relocation charge.

(5) "UFRC revenues" means revenues produced through a UFRC exclusive of revenues from all other rates and charges.

(b) Notwithstanding other sections of this subchapter, electric and natural gas utilities subject to the regulation of the Public Service Commission under this title may file with the Commission rate schedules establishing a UFRC rate that will allow for the automatic adjustment of the electric or natural gas utility's basic rates and charges to provide recovery of UFRC costs on an annual basis.

(c) Any electric or natural gas utility that files under subsection (b) of this section will be subject to the same statutory requirements of a public water utility seeking to implement or change a DSIC rate found under § 314(b)(1) et seq. of this title, except that such statutory requirements will apply to the UFRC rate and that the level of increase permitted under § 314(b)(7) of this title is limited to the portion of the customer's charge related to the delivery or distribution of natural gas or electricity.

(d) The UFRC rate shall not be available for application to the electric rates of Delmarva Power & Light Company or its successors until July 1, 2006, and shall also not be available for application to the electric rates of Delaware Electric Cooperative or its successors until July 1, 2005.

(e) This section applies only to regulated natural gas and electric utilities that file general rate cases with the Public Service Commission. With respect to a telecommunications service provider electing to be governed under subchapter VII-A of this chapter, upon application by such service provider, utility facility relocation costs not otherwise reimbursed under § 143 of Title 17 shall be considered by the Commission.

(f) The Commission may adopt rules and regulations, not inconsistent with this title, that the Commission finds reasonable or necessary to administer a UFRC.

(g) [Expired.]

History.
75 Del. Laws, c. 170, § 2; 81 Del. Laws, c. 268, § 1; 82 Del. Laws, c. 11, § 8; 83 Del. Laws, c. 37, § 27.

deleted "under § 707(c)(6) of this title [repealed]" from the end of the final sentence of (e).

Effect of amendments.
83 Del. Laws, c. 37, effective June 3, 2021,

SUBCHAPTER III-A
RENEWABLE ENERGY PORTFOLIO STANDARDS

§ 352. Definitions.

As used in this subchapter:

(1) "Alternative compliance payment" means a payment of a certain dollar amount per megawatt hour, which a retail electricity supplier or municipal electric company may submit in lieu of supplying the minimum percentage from Eligible Energy Resources required under Schedule I in § 354 of this title.

(2) "Commission" means the Delaware Public Service Commission.

(3) "Community-owned energy generating facility" has the meaning given in § 1001 of this title.

(4) "Compliance year" means the calendar year beginning with June 1 and ending with May 31 of the following year, for which a retail electricity

supplier or municipal electric company must demonstrate that it has met the requirements of this subchapter.

(5) "Customer-sited generation" means a generation unit that is interconnected on the end-use customer's side of the retail electricity meter in such a manner that it displaces all or part of the metered consumption of the end-use customer.

(6) "DNREC" means Delaware Department of Natural Resources and Environmental Control.

(7) "Eligible energy resources" include the following energy sources located within or imported into the PJM region:

    a. Solar photovoltaic or solar thermal energy technologies that employ solar radiation to produce electricity or to displace electricity use;

    b. Electricity derived from wind energy;

    c. Electricity derived from ocean energy including wave or tidal action, currents, or thermal differences;

    d. Geothermal energy technologies that generate electricity with a steam turbine, driven by hot water or steam extracted from geothermal reservoirs in the earth's crust;

    e. Electricity generated by a fuel cell powered by renewable fuels;

    f. Electricity generated by the combustion of gas from the anaerobic digestion of organic material;

    g. Electricity generated by a hydroelectric facility that has a maximum design capacity of 30 megawatts or less from all generating units combined that meet appropriate environmental standards as determined by DNREC;

    h. Electricity generated from the combustion of biomass that has been cultivated and harvested in a sustainable manner as determined by DNREC, and is not combusted to produce energy in a waste to energy facility or in an incinerator, as that term is defined in Title 7;

    i. Electricity generated by the combustion of methane gas captured from a landfill gas recovery system; provided however, that:

        1. Increased production of landfill gas from production facilities in operation prior to January 1, 2004, demonstrates a net reduction in total air emissions compared to flaring and leakage;

        2. Increased utilization of landfill gas at electric generating facilities in operation prior to January 1, 2004;

            A. Is used to offset the consumption of coal, oil, or natural gas at those facilities;

            B. Does not result in a reduction in the percentage of landfill gas in the facility's average annual fuel mix when calculated using fuel mix measurements for 12 out of any continuous 15-month period during which the electricity is generated; and

            C. Causes no net increase in air emissions from the facility; and

        3. Facilities installed on or after January 1, 2004, meet or exceed 2004 federal and state air emission standards, or the federal and state air emission standards in place on the day the facilities are first put into operation, whichever is higher.

(8) "End-use customer" means a person or entity in Delaware that purchases electrical energy at retail prices from a retail electricity supplier or municipal electric company.

(9) "Fund" means the Delaware Green Energy Fund.

(10) "GATS" means the generation attribute tracking system developed by PJM.

(11) "Generation attribute" means a nonprice characteristic of the electrical energy output of a generation unit including, but not limited to, the unit's fuel type, geographic location, emissions, vintage and RPS eligibility.

(12) "Generation unit" means a facility that converts a fuel or an energy resource into electrical energy.

(13) "Municipal electric company" means a public corporation created by contract between 2 or more municipalities pursuant to provisions of Chapter 13 of Title 22 and the electric utilities that are municipally owned within the State of Delaware.

(14) "New renewable generation resources" means eligible energy resources first going into commercial operation after December 31, 1997.

(15) "PJM" or "PJM interconnection" means the regional transmission organization (RTO) that coordinates the movement of wholesale electricity in the PJM region, or its successors at law.

(16) "PJM region" means the area within which the movement of wholesale electricity is coordinated by PJM Interconnection. The PJM region is as described in the Amended and Restated Operating Agreement of PJM.

(17) "Qualified fuel cell provider" means an entity that:

    a. By no later than the commencement date of commercial operation of the full nameplate capacity of a fuel cell project, manufactures fuel cells in Delaware that are capable of being powered by renewable fuels; and

    b. Prior to approval of required tariff provisions, is designated by the Director of the Division of Small Business and the Secretary of DNREC as an economic development opportunity.

(18) "Qualified fuel cell provider project" means a fuel cell power generation project located in Delaware owned and/or operated by a qualified fuel cell provider under a tariff approved by the Commission pursuant to § 364(d) of this title.

(19) "Renewable energy credit" ("REC") means a tradable instrument that is equal to 1 megawatt-hour of retail electricity sales in the State that is derived from eligible energy resources and that is used to track and verify compliance with the provisions of this subchapter.

(20) "Renewable energy portfolio standard" and "RPS" means the percentage of electricity sales at retail in the state that is to be derived from eligible energy resources.

(21) "Renewable fuel" means a fuel that is derived from eligible energy resources. This term does not include a fossil fuel or a waste product from a fossil fuel source.

(22) "Retail electricity product" means an electrical energy offering that is distinguished by its generation attributes and that is offered for sale by a retail electricity supplier or municipal electric company to end-use customers.

(23) "Retail electricity supplier" means a person or entity that sells electrical energy to end-use customers in Delaware, including but not limited to nonregulated power producers, electric utility distribution companies supplying standard offer, default service, or any successor service to end-use customers. A retail electricity supplier does not include a municipal electric company for the purposes of this subchapter.

(24) "Rural electric cooperative" means a nonstock, nonprofit, membership corporation organized pursuant to the federal Rural Electrification

Act of 1936 [7 U.S.C § 901 et seq.] and operated under the cooperative form of ownership.

(25) "Solar Alternative Compliance Payment" means a payment of a certain dollar amount per megawatt-hour, which a retail electricity supplier or municipal electric supplier may submit in lieu of supplying the minimum percentage from solar photovoltaics required under Schedule I in § 354 of this title.

(26) "Solar Renewable Energy Credit" ("SREC") means a tradable instrument that is equal to 1 megawatt-hour of retail electricity sales in the State that is derived from solar photovoltaic energy resources and that is used to track and verify compliance with the provisions of this subchapter.

(27) "Total retail sales" means retail sales of electricity within the State of Delaware exclusive of sales to any industrial customer with a peak demand in excess of 1,500 kilowatts.

(28) "Unsubscribed energy" means any community-owned energy generating facility percentage of 6 output that is not allocated to any customer.

History.
75 Del. Laws, c. 205, § 1; 76 Del. Laws, c. 165, §§ 1-3; 78 Del. Laws, c. 99, § 1; 81 Del. Laws, c. 49, § 18; 81 Del. Laws, c. 374, § 47; 83 Del. Laws, c. 178, § 1.

Effect of amendments.
83 Del. Laws, c. 178, effective September 17, 2021, added present (3) and (28) and redesignated the intervening paragraphs accordingly.

§ 354. Renewable energy portfolio standards, eligible energy resources and industrial exemption.

(a) The total retail sales of each Retail Electricity Product delivered to Delaware end-use customers by a commission-regulated utility or municipal electric company during any given compliance year shall include a minimum percentage of electrical energy sales with eligible energy resources and solar photovoltaics as follows:

SCHEDULE I		
Compliance Year (beginning June 1st)	Minimum Cumulative Percentage from Eligible Energy Resources	Minimum Cumulative Percentage from Solar Photovoltaics*
2018	17.50%	1.75%
2019	19.00%	2.00%
2020	20.00%	2.25%
2021	21.00%	2.50%
2022	22.00%	2.75%
2023	23.00%	3.00%
2024	24.00%	3.25%
2025	25.00%	3.50%
2026	25.50%	3.75%
2027	26.00%	4.00%
2028	26.50%	4.25%
2029	27.00%	4.50%
2030	28.00%	5.00%
2031	30.00%	5.80%
2032	32.00%	6.60%

SCHEDULE I		
Compliance Year (beginning June 1st)	Minimum Cumulative Percentage from Eligible Energy Resources	Minimum Cumulative Percentage from Solar Photovoltaics*
2033	34.00%	7.40%
2034	37.00%	8.40%
2035	40.00%	10.00%
* Minimum Percentage from Eligible Energy Resources Includes the Minimum Percentage from Solar Photovoltaics.		

(b) Cumulative minimum percentage requirements of eligible energy resources and solar photovoltaics shall be established by Commission rules for compliance year 2036 and each subsequent year. The minimum percentages established by Commission rules may not be lower than those required for compliance year 2035 in Schedule I, subsection (a) of this section. Each of the rules setting such minimum percentage must be adopted at least 2 years before the minimum percentage being required.

(c), (d) [Repealed.]

(e) Beginning with compliance year 2012, commission-regulated electric companies shall be responsible for procuring RECs, SRECs and any other attributes needed to comply with subsection (a) of this section with respect to all energy delivered to such companies' end use customers.

(f) For each commission-regulated electric company, retail electricity supplier with existing contractual electric supply obligation or municipal electric company, no more than 1% of each year's total retail sales may be met from eligible energy resources that are not new renewable generation resources. In compliance year 2026, and for each compliance year thereafter, all eligible energy resources used to meet cumulative minimum percentage requirements set by the Commission rules shall be new renewable generation resources.

(g) A retail electricity supplier or municipal electric company shall not use energy used to satisfy another state's renewable energy portfolio requirements for compliance with Schedule I of subsection (a) of this section.

(h) An applicant's compliance with Schedule I of subsection (a) of this section shall be based on historical data, collected in a manner consistent with industry standard and, with respect to retail electricity suppliers, Commission regulations. A retail electricity supplier or municipal electric company shall meet the renewable energy portfolio standards by accumulating the equivalent amount of renewable energy credits and solar renewable energy credits that equal the percentage required under this section.

(i), (j) [Repealed.]

History.

75 Del. Laws, c. 205, § 1; 76 Del. Laws, c. 165, §§ 4(a), (b), 5; 77 Del. Laws, c. 451, §§ 1, 2, 4-11; 78 Del. Laws, c. 99, §§ 3-6; 83 Del. Laws, c. 3, § 1.

Effect of amendments.

83 Del. Laws, c. 3, effective Feb. 10, 2021, in (a), substituted "commission-regulated utility" for "retail electricity supplier" in the introductory paragraph, in the table for Schedule I deleted the entries for 2010 through 2017 and added the entries for 2026 through 2035, and deleted the paragraph following Schedule I and table for "Schedule I (Revised)"; in (b), substituted "2036" for "2026" in the first sentence, in the second sentence deleted "In no case shall" from the beginning, added "may not" and substituted "2035" for "2025", and in the final sentence substituted "must" for "shall" and "before" for "prior to"; repealed (c), (d), (i) and (j).

§ 358. Issuance of renewable energy credits; reporting requirement; alternative compliance payment.

(a) The Commission shall establish by regulation the mechanisms under which a REC and SREC shall be created and recorded with respect to the entity generating electricity using eligible energy resources for use in complying with the renewable energy portfolio standards of this subchapter. Once the GATS system is operational and the PJM Interconnection, or a related organization currently known as PJM Environmental Services, Inc. (PJM-ESI), begins issuing RECs and SRECs, the Commission may issue an order approving the use of RECs and SRECs issued by the PJM Interconnection or PJM-ESI for compliance with the renewable energy portfolio Standards of this subchapter.

(b) Beginning June 1, 2007, each retail electricity supplier shall submit an annual report to the Commission, on a form and by a date specified by the Commission, that:

(1) Demonstrates that the retail electricity supplier has complied with the renewable energy portfolio standards established pursuant to this subchapter and includes the submission of the required amount of renewable energy credits; or

(2) Demonstrates the amount of electricity sales for the compliance year by which the retail electricity supplier failed to meet the renewable energy portfolio standard.

(c) Beginning June 1, 2007, each municipal electric company shall submit an annual report to the Delaware Energy Office and the Controller General that:

(1) Demonstrates that the municipal electric company has complied with the RPS established pursuant to this subchapter and includes the submission of the required amount of renewable energy credits; or

(2) Demonstrates the amount of electricity sales for the compliance year by which the municipal electric company failed to meet the RPS.

(d) In lieu of standard means of compliance with this subchapter, any commission-regulated utility may pay into the Fund an alternative compliance payment of $25 for each megawatt-hour deficiency between the credits available and used by a commission-regulated utility in a given compliance year for eligible nonsolar renewable energy resources and the credits necessary for such commission-regulated utility to meet the year's renewable energy portfolio standard. A municipal electric company may pay the alternative compliance payment into a fund established by its municipal members. If alternative compliance payments representing 15% or more of the total number of RECs for eligible nonsolar renewable energy resources are paid into the Fund for each of 2 consecutive compliance years, the minimum cumulative percentage from eligible energy resources specified in Schedule I of § 354(a) of this title remains at the percentage specified for the immediately preceding year and does not increase from that percentage until a year passes during which less than 15% of the REC obligation is satisfied by alternative compliance payments. After the year in which less than 15% of the REC obligation is satisfied by alternative compliance payments, the annual increases in Schedule I of § 354(a) of this title resume, starting from the percentage specified for the year immediately before the current compliance year. A freeze of the minimum cumulative percentage from eligible nonsolar technology does not permit a freeze of the minimum cumulative percentage from eligible solar energy resources.

(1)-(4) [Repealed.]

(e) In lieu of standard means of compliance with this subchapter, a commission-regulated utility may pay into the Fund a Solar Alternative Compliance

Payment of $150 for each megawatt-hour deficiency between the credits available and used by a commission-regulated utility in a given compliance year and the credits necessary for such commission-regulated utility to meet the year's Renewable Energy Portfolio Standard. A municipal electric company may pay the solar alternative compliance payment into a fund established by its municipal members. If solar alternative compliance payments representing 15% or more of the total number of SRECs are paid into the Fund for each of 2 consecutive compliance years, the minimum cumulative percentage from solar technology specified in Schedule I of § 354(a) of this title remains at the percentage specified for the immediately preceding year and does not increase from that percentage until a year passes during which less than 15% of the SREC obligation is satisfied by solar alternative compliance payments. After the year in which less than 15% of the total SREC obligation is satisfied by solar alternative compliance payments, the annual increases set forth in Schedule I of § 354(a) of this title resume, starting from the percentage specified for the year immediately before the current compliance year. A freeze of the minimum cumulative percentage from solar technology does not freeze the minimum cumulative percentage from eligible energy resources.

    (1)-(3) [Repealed.]

  (f)(1) *Recovery of costs.* — A retail electricity supplier or municipal electric company may recover, through a nonbypassable surcharge, actual dollar for dollar costs incurred in complying with a state mandated renewable energy portfolio standard, except that any compliance fee assessed pursuant to subsection (d) of this section shall be recoverable only to the extent authorized by paragraph (f)(2) of this section.

    (2) A retail electricity supplier or municipal electric company may recover any alternative compliance payment if:

      a. The payment of an alternative compliance payment is the least cost measure to ratepayers as compared to the purchase of eligible energy resources to comply with a renewable energy portfolio standard; or

      b. There are insufficient eligible energy resources available for the electric supplier to comply with a renewable energy portfolio standard.

    (3) Any cost recovered under this section shall be disclosed to customers at least annually on inserts accompanying customer bills.

History.
75 Del. Laws, c. 205, § 1; 76 Del. Laws, c. 165, §§ 7-9; 77 Del. Laws, c. 451, §§ 3, 13-19; 83 Del. Laws, c. 3, § 2.

Effect of amendments.
83 Del. Laws, c. 3, effective Feb. 10, 2021, rewrote (d) and (e).

§ 360. Renewable energy trading.

(a) A retail electricity supplier or municipal electric company may use accumulated renewable energy credits or solar renewable energy credits to meet the renewable energy portfolio standard established pursuant to this subchapter, and may sell or transfer any renewable energy credit or solar renewable energy credit not needed to meet said standards.

(b) An unused renewable energy credit or solar renewable energy credit shall exist for 3 years from the date created.

(c) The 3-year period referred in subsection (b) of this section above shall be tolled during any period that a renewable energy credit or solar renewable energy credit is held by the SEU as defined in § 8059 of Title 29.

(d) The Renewable Energy Taskforce shall be formed for the purpose of making recommendations about the establishment of trading mechanisms and other structures to support the growth of renewable energy markets in Delaware.

(1) The Taskforce shall comprise the following appointments:

a. Four appointments by the Secretary of DNREC, which shall include 1 representative from the renewable energy research and development industry, 1 representative from the local renewable energy manufacturing industry, and 1 representative from an environmental advocacy organization;

b. One appointment by the Commission;

c. One appointment by Delmarva Power & Light;

d. One appointment by the Delaware Electric Cooperative;

e. One appointment by municipal electric companies;

f. One appointment by the Sustainable Energy Utility;

g. One appointment by the Delaware Public Advocate; and

h. One appointment by the Delaware Solar Energy Coalition.

(2) The Taskforce shall be charged with making recommendations about and reporting on the following and matters related thereto:

a. Establishing balanced markets mechanisms for REC and SREC trading;

b. Establishing REC and SREC aggregation mechanisms and other devices to encourage the deployment of renewable, distributed renewable, and solar energy technologies, including community-owned energy generating facilities, in Delaware with the least impact on retail electricity suppliers, municipal electric companies and rural electric cooperatives;

c. After an analysis by the Taskforce, the annual progress towards achieving the minimum cumulative percentages for all renewable energy resources including, but not limited to, solar and other eligible energy resources and making appropriate recommendations based upon deliberate and factual analysis and study;

d. Minimizing the cost for complying with any portion of this subchapter based upon deliberate and factual analysis and study;

e. Establishing revenue certainty for appropriate investment in renewable energy technologies, including, but not limited to, consideration of long-term contracts and auction mechanisms;

f. Establishing mechanisms to maximize in-state renewable energy generation and local manufacturing; and

g. Ensuring that residential, commercial, and utility scale photovoltaic and solar thermal systems of various sizes, including community-owned energy generating facilities, are financially viable and cost-effective investments in Delaware.

(3) The Taskforce shall be formed by October 26, 2010, and be staffed by the Delaware Energy Office. The Taskforce shall make recommendations to the Commission, the Secretary of DNREC, the Board of Directors for rural electric cooperatives, and the pertinent local regulatory authorities on the abovementioned subjects for their consideration. Upon making these recommendations, the Commission, DNREC, the Board of Directors for rural electric cooperatives, or the pertinent local regulatory authorities, as appropriate, shall promulgate rules and regulations, or adopt policies, based on the Taskforce findings.

History.
75 Del. Laws, c. 205, § 1; 77 Del. Laws, c. 131, §§ 6-8; 77 Del. Laws, c. 451, § 22; 83 Del. Laws, c. 178, § 2.

Effect of amendments.
83 Del. Laws, c. 178, effective September 17, 2021, added "including community-owned energy generating facilities" in (d)(2)b. and (d)(2)g.

§ 362. Rules and regulations.

(a) The Commission shall adopt rules and regulations necessary to implement the provisions of this subchapter as it applies to retail electricity suppliers. The Commission shall make its regulations as consistent as possible with those of other states in the region with similar requirements in order to minimize the compliance burdens imposed by this subchapter and in order to avoid duplication of effort.

(b) [Repealed.]

History.
75 Del. Laws, c. 205, § 1; 77 Del. Laws, c. 451, § 20; 83 Del. Laws, c. 3, § 3.

Effect of amendments.
83 Del. Laws, c. 3, effective Feb. 10, 2021, substituted "subchapter" for "statute" in the final sentence of (a); and repealed (b).

§ 363. Special provisions for municipal electric companies and rural electric cooperatives.

(a) Any municipal electric company and any rural electric cooperative may elect to exempt itself from the requirements of this subchapter, if it develops and implements a comparable program to the renewable energy portfolio standards for its ratepayers beginning in 2022.

(b) In the event that a municipal electric company or rural electric cooperative elects to exempt itself from the requirements of this subchapter, it shall submit a plan at the beginning of 2022 to its local regulatory authority, the Delaware General Assembly, and the Department of Natural Resources and Environmental Control detailing its approach to achieve a level of renewable energy penetration in its service territory, and shall submit an annual compliance report to its local regulatory authority, the Delaware General Assembly, and the Department of Natural Resources and Environmental Control detailing its progress toward yearly targets.

(c) The Board of Directors for a rural electric cooperative or local regulatory authority of a municipal electric company shall base renewable energy portfolio standard decisions on the need, value and feasibility of the renewable energy resources pertaining to the economic and environmental well being of their members. The Board of Directors for a rural electric cooperative or local regulatory authority of a municipal electric company shall continue to evaluate all renewable energy resources including but not limited to: wind, biomass, hydroelectric and solar and submit an annual report to the General Assembly and their membership as to their determination.

(d) In the event that a municipal electric company or rural electric cooperative elects to exempt itself, it shall either contribute to the Green Energy Fund at levels commensurate with other retail electricity suppliers or create an independent, self-administered fund separate from the Green Energy Fund to be used in support of energy efficiency technologies, renewable energy technologies, or demand side management programs, into which it shall make payments of at least $0.178 for each megawatt-hour it sells, transmits, or distributes in this State.

(e)-(i) [Repealed.]

(j) In pursuit of their renewable energy goals, a municipal electric company or rural electric cooperative shall receive all appropriate multiple credits for specific energy sources, as established under §§ 356 and 357 of this title and sited in Delaware for the life of contracts for renewable energy credits.

History.
75 Del. Laws, c. 205, § 1; 77 Del. Laws, c. 451, § 21; 83 Del. Laws, c. 3, § 4.
Effect of amendments.
83 Del. Laws, c. 3, effective Feb. 10, 2021, substituted "2022" for "2013" in (a) and (b); substituted "Department of Natural Resources and Environmental Control" for "Delaware Energy Office" twice in (b); and repealed (e)-(i).

CHAPTER 10
ELECTRIC UTILITY RESTRUCTURING

§ 1001. Definitions.

As used in this chapter, unless the context otherwise requires:

(1) "Aggregator" means any person or entity who contracts with an electric distribution company, electric supplier or PJM Interconnection (or its successor) to provide energy services, which facilitate battery storage systems for grid-integrated electric vehicles and related technologies.

(2) "Ancillary services" means services that are necessary for the transmission and distribution of electricity from supply sources to loads and for maintaining reliable operation of the transmission and distribution system.

(3) "Broker" means a person or entity that acts as an agent or intermediary in the sale or purchase of, but that does not take title to, electricity for sale to retail electric customers.

(4) "Commission" means the Delaware Public Service Commission.

(5) "Community-owned energy generating facility" means a renewable energy generating facility, located in the service area of a utility under the regulation of the Public Service Commission, that has multiple owners or customers who share the output of the generator, which may be located either as a stand-alone facility or behind the meter of a participating owner or customer. The facility shall be interconnected to the distribution system and operated in parallel with an electric distribution company's transmission and distribution facilities.

(6) "DEC" means the Delaware Electric Cooperative and its successors.

(7) "Demand-side management" means cost effective energy efficiency programs that are designed to reduce customers' electricity consumption, especially during peak periods.

(8) "Direct access" means the right of electric suppliers and their customers to use an electric distribution company's transmission and distribution system on a nondiscriminatory basis at rates, terms and conditions of service comparable to the electric distribution company's own use of the system to transmit or distribute electricity from any electric supplier to any customer.

(9) "Distribution facilities" means electric facilities located in Delaware that are owned by a public utility that operate at voltages of 34,500 volts or below and that are used to deliver electricity to customers, up through and including the point of physical connection with electric facilities owned by the customer.

(10) "Distribution services" means those services, including metering, relating to the delivery of electricity to a customer through distribution facilities.

(11) "DP&L" means Delmarva Power & Light Company and its successors.

(12) "Electric distribution company" means a public utility owning and/or operating transmission and/or distribution facilities in this State.

(13) "Electricity demand response" has the same definition set forth in § 1501 of this title.

(14) "Electric supplier" means a person or entity certified by the Commission that sells electricity to retail electric customers utilizing the transmission and/or distribution facilities of a nonaffiliated electric utility, including:

    a. Municipal corporations which choose to provide electricity outside their municipal limits (except to the extent provided prior to February 1, 1999);

    b. Electric cooperatives which, having exempted themselves from the Commission's jurisdiction pursuant to §§ 202(g) and 223 of this title, choose to provide electricity outside their assigned service territories; and

    c. Any broker, marketer or other entity (including public utilities and their affiliates).

(15) "Electric supply service" means the provision of electricity and related services to customers.

(16) "Fuel cell" means an electric generating facility that:

    a. Includes integrated power plant systems containing a stack, tubular array, or other functionally similar configuration used to electrochemically convert fuel to electric energy, and

    b. May include an inverter and fuel processing system or other plant equipment to support the plant's operation or its energy conversion, including heat recovery equipment.

(17) "Grid-integrated electric vehicle" means a battery-run motor vehicle that has the ability for 2-way power flow between the vehicle and the electric grid and the communications hardware and software that allow for the external control of battery charging and discharging by an electric distribution company, electric supplier, PJM Interconnection, or an aggregator.

(18) "Integrated resource planning" means the planning process of an electric distribution company that systematically evaluates all available supply options, including but not limited to: generation, transmission and demand-side management programs, during the planning period to ensure that the electric distribution company acquires sufficient and reliable resources over time that meet its customers' needs at a minimal cost.

(19) "Marketer" means a person or entity that purchases and takes title to electricity for sale to customers in this State.

(20) "Retail competition" means the right of a customer to purchase electricity from an electric supplier.

(21) "Retail electric customer" or "customer" means a purchaser of electricity for ultimate consumption and not for resale in this State, including the owner/operator of any building or facility, but not the occupants thereof, that purchases and supplies electricity to the occupants of such building or facility.

(22) "Returning customer service" means the electric supply service offered to customers with a peak monthly load of 1000 kW or more, which have left standard offer service as of April 30, 2007, and later decide to receive electric supply service from their electric distribution company. For purposes of determining customers eligible for returning customer service, peak monthly load shall be measured by the electric distribution company's separate customer account, not by facility or service location or by customer, in aggregate or otherwise.

(23) "Standard offer service" means the provision of electric supply service after the transition period by a standard offer service supplier to customers who do not otherwise receive electric supply service from an electric supplier.

(24) "Standard offer service supplier" means the electric distribution company serving within its certificated service territory.

(25) "Transition period" means the period of time beginning with the implementation of retail competition and ending on the dates specified in § 1004 of this title.

(26) "Transmission facilities" means electric facilities located in Delaware, including those in offshore waters and integrated with onshore electric facilities, and owned by a public utility that operate at voltages above 34,500 volts and that are used to transmit and deliver electricity to customers (including any customers taking electric service under interruptible rate schedules as of December 31, 1998) up through and including the point of physical connection with electric facilities owned by the customer.

(27) "Transmission services" means the delivery of electricity from supply sources through transmission facilities.

History.
72 Del. Laws, c. 10, § 3; 73 Del. Laws, c. 157, § 4; 75 Del. Laws, c. 242, § 2; 77 Del. Laws, c. 188, § 3; 77 Del. Laws, c. 212, § 1; 77 Del. Laws, c. 453, § 1; 81 Del. Laws, c. 205, § 3; 83 Del. Laws, c. 178, § 3.

Effect of amendments.
83 Del. Laws, c. 178, effective September 17, 2021, added "located in the service area of a utility under the regulation of the Public Service Commission" in the first sentence of (5).

§ 1014. Public purpose programs and consumer education.

(a) In separating the rates or prices for DP&L's services under § 1005(a) of this title, the Commission shall reassign to the separate transmission and distribution rates of each rate class from the total base rates $0.000356 per kilowatt-hour to be deposited each month by DP&L into an environmental incentive fund effective on October 1, 1999. Such fund shall be known as the "Green Energy Fund" and all moneys deposited into the Green Energy Fund shall be transferred in their entirety on the July 1 of each year to the State Energy Office to fund environmental incentive programs for conservation and energy efficiency in the State. The State Energy Office shall submit to the General Assembly by May 30 of each year a written accounting of moneys received from the fund during the previous year and how those moneys were used or disbursed during that year.

(b) The Commission shall further reassign to the separate transmission and distribution rates of each rate class from the total base rates $0.000095 per kilowatt-hour to be deposited each month by DP&L into a low-income program fund effective on October 1, 1999. Such fund shall be administered by the Department of Health and Social Services, Division of State Service Centers and shall be used to fund low-income fuel assistance and weatherization programs within DP&L's service territory.

(c) The Commission shall establish a working group by June 1, 1999, comprised of representatives of the Commission, electric utilities, electric suppliers, the Division of the Public Advocate, environmental community, consumers, a member of the House of Representatives appointed by the Speaker of the House, a member of the House of Representatives appointed by the Minority Leader of the House, a member of the Senate appointed by the President Pro Tempore of the Senate, a member of the Senate appointed by the Minority Leader of the Senate and other interested parties to design and implement a consumer education program, including "Green Power" options, to prepare the citizens of Delaware for retail competition. The Commission shall direct the payment of up to a total of $250,000 from DP&L and DEC (apportioned on the 1998 kw Delaware retail sales of each entity) for the purpose of providing customer education materials to citizens of Delaware in connection with retail competition.

(d) The Commission, municipal electric companies, and electric cooperatives during any period of exemption under § 223 of this title shall each promulgate rules and regulations that provide for net energy metering for customers who own and operate, lease and operate, or contract with a third party that owns and operates an electric generation facility that:

(1) Has a capacity that:

a. For residential customers of DP&L, DEC, and municipal electric companies, has a capacity of not more than 25 kW;

b. For farm customers as described in § 902(3) of Title 3 who are customers of DP&L, DEC, or municipal electric companies that receive distribution service under a residential tariff or service offering, does not exceed more than 100 kW. On a case by case basis the Delaware Energy Office shall review a farm's application for a system above 100 kW by comparing the output of the system to the energy requirements of the farm and may grant a waiver to increase the size of the system above the 100 kW limit. The Delaware Energy Office shall promulgate rules and regulations for such waivers in consultation with DP&L and municipal electric companies. Such waivers for DEC customers shall be approved by DEC;

c. For nonresidential customers, is not more than 2 megawatts per DP&L meter, and 500 kW per DEC or municipal electric company meter. DEC and municipal electric companies are encouraged to provide for net metering up to a capacity of not more than 2 megawatts for nonresidential customers.

d. [Repealed.]

(2) Uses as its primary source of fuel solar, wind, hydro, a fuel cell, or gas from the anaerobic digestion of organic material;

(3) Is located on the customer's premises;

(4) Is interconnected and operated in parallel with an electric distribution company's transmission and distribution facilities; and

(5) Is designed to produce no more than 110% of the host customer's expected aggregate electrical consumption, calculated on the average of the 2 previous 12-month periods of actual electrical usage at the time of installation of energy generating equipment. For new building construction, electrical consumption will be estimated at 110% of the consumption of units of similar size and characteristics at the time of installation of energy generating equipment.

(e) The rules and regulations promulgated for net energy metering by the Commission, municipal electric companies, and electric cooperatives during any period of exemption under § 223 of this title shall:

(1) Provide for customers to be credited in kilowatt-hours (kWh), valued at an amount per kilowatt-hour equal to the sum of delivery service charges and supply service charges for residential customers and the sum of the volumetric energy (kWh) components of the delivery service charges and supply service charges for nonresidential customers for any excess production of their generating facility that exceeds the customer's on-site consumption of kWh in a billing period. Excess kWh credits shall be credited to subsequent billing periods to offset a customer's consumption in those billing periods. At the end of the annualized billing period, a customer may request a payment from the electric supplier for any excess

kWh credits. The payment shall be calculated by multiplying the excess kWh credits by the customer's supply service rate. Such payment if less than $25 may be credited to the customer's account through monthly billing. Any excess kWh credits shall not reduce any fixed monthly customer charges imposed by the electric supplier. The customer-generator retains ownership of all renewable energy credits (RECs) associated with electric energy produced unless the customer has relinquished such ownership by contractual agreement with a third party.

(2), (3) [Repealed.]

(4) Ensure that electric suppliers provide net-metered customers electric service at nondiscriminatory rates that are identical, with respect to rate structure and monthly charges, to the rates that a customer who is not net-metering would be charged. electric suppliers shall not charge a net-metering customer any stand-by fees or similar charges, with the exception that the Delaware Energy Office shall promulgate rules that allow DEC and municipal electric companies to request to assess nonresidential net-metering customers a fee or charge if the electric utility's direct costs of interconnection and administration of net-metering for these customer classes outweigh the distribution system, environmental, and public policy benefits of allocating the costs among the electric supplier's entire customer base.

(5) Require that all generating systems and grid-integrated electric vehicles used by eligible customers meet all applicable safety and performance standards established by the National Electrical Code, and those of the Institute of Electrical and Electronic Engineers, UL, or the Society of Automotive Engineers, to ensure that net metering customers meet applicable safety and performance standards and comply with the electric supplier's interconnection tariffs and operating guidelines. An electric supplier's interconnection rules must be developed by using as a guide the Interstate Renewable Energy Council's Model Interconnection Rules and best practices identified by the U.S. Department of Energy. Municipal electric companies shall establish interconnection rules no later than July 24, 2008. An electric supplier may not require eligible net-metering customers who meet all applicable safety and performance standards to install excessive controls, perform or pay for unnecessary tests, or purchase excessive liability insurance.

(6) Net energy metering shall be accomplished using a single meter capable of registering the flow of electricity in 2 directions. An additional meter or meters to monitor the flow of electricity in each direction may be installed with the consent of the net-metering customer, at the expense of the electric supplier, and the additional metering shall be used only to provide the information necessary to accurately bill or credit the customer pursuant to paragraph (e)(1) of this section, or to collect system performance information on the eligible technology for research purposes. If the existing electrical meter of an eligible net-metering customer is incapable of measuring the flow of electricity in 2 directions through no fault of the customer, the electric supplier shall be responsible for all expenses involved in purchasing and installing a meter that is able to measure the flow of electricity in 2 directions. However, where a larger capacity meter is required to serve the customer, or a larger capacity meter is requested by the customer, the customer shall pay the electric supplier the difference between the larger capacity meter investment and the metering investment normally provided under the customer's service classification. If an additional meter or meters are installed, the net energy metering calculation shall yield a result identical to that of a single meter.

(7) If the total generating capacity of all customer-generation using net metering systems served by an electric utility exceeds 5% of the capacity necessary to meet the electric utility's aggregated customer monthly peak demand for a particular calendar year, the electric utility may elect not to provide net metering services to any additional customer-generators.

(8) In instances where 1 customer has multiple meters under the same account or different accounts, regardless of the physical location and rate class, the customer may aggregate meters for the purpose of net energy metering regardless of which individual meter receives energy from the energy generating facility, provided that:

    a. Electric suppliers, DEC, DP&L, and municipal electric companies shall only allow meter aggregation for customer accounts of which they provide electric supply service; and

    b. The customer's energy generating facility is designed to produce no more than 110% of the customer's aggregate electrical consumption of the individual meters or accounts that the customer wishes to aggregate under this paragraph (e)(8) of this section, calculated on the average of the 2 previous 12-month periods of actual electrical usage at the time of installation of energy generating equipment. For new building construction, electrical consumption will be estimated at 110% of the consumption of units of similar size and characteristics at the time of installation of energy generating equipment; and

    c. The customer's energy generating facility shall not exceed a capacity as defined under paragraph (d)(1) of this section; and

    d. At least 90 days before a customer commences construction of an energy generating facility or a customer desires to aggregate multiple meters, the customer shall file with the electric supplier, DP&L, DEC, or the appropriate municipal electric company the following information:

        1. A list of individual meters the customer desires to aggregate, identified by name, address, and account number, and ranked according to the order in which the customer desires to apply credit;

        2. A description of the energy generating facility, including the facility's location, capacity, and fuel type or generating technology; and

        3. A complete interconnection application to facilitate a transmission and distribution analysis, including an evaluation of potential reliability, safety and stability impacts and determination of whether infrastructure upgrades are necessary and appropriate allocation of applicable interconnection costs;

    e. The customer may change its list of aggregated meters no more than once annually by providing 90 days' written notice; and

    f. Credit shall be applied first to the meter through which the energy generating facility supplies electricity, then through the remaining meters for the customer's accounts according to the rank order as specified in accordance with paragraph (e)(8)d. of this section; and

    g. Credit in kWh shall be valued according to each account's rate schedule and the rules and regulations promulgated for net energy metering under paragraph (e)(1) of this section; and

    h. An electric supplier, DP&L, DEC, or the appropriate municipal electric company may require that a customer's aggregated meters be read on the same billing cycle; and

      i. The rules and regulations promulgated for net energy metering under this section shall also apply to net energy metering aggregation.

    (9) [Repealed.]

(f) Individual customers may aggregate their individual meters in conjunction with a community-owned energy generating facility provided that:

    (1) The Commission promulgates rules and regulations that provide for customers participating in a community-owned energy generating facility to be credited for the customers' subscribed percentage of generation valued at the sum of the volumetric (kWh) components of the distribution service charges and supply service charges for residential customers and the sum of the volumetric energy (kWh) components of the distribution service charges and supply service charges for nonresidential customers according to each participating customer account's rate schedule. At the end of the annualized billing period, a customer may request a refund from the electric distribution company.

    (2) A customer may not receive credit for more than 110% of the customer's expected aggregate electrical consumption, calculated on the average of the 2 previous 12-month periods of actual electrical usage at the time of subscription with the community-owned energy generating facility. For new building construction, electrical consumption will be estimated at 110% of the consumption of units of similar size and characteristics. On an annual basis, an electric distribution company shall be permitted to audit individual customer's subscribed amounts to ensure the associated usage does not exceed 110% of the customer's annual usage. The community-owned energy generating facility shall provide updated individual customer's subscribed percentage as required. In the event the community-owned energy generating facility does not provide the required update within 30 days after notification by the electric distribution company, the electric distribution company shall be permitted to set the customer's percentage to zero. Customers of a community-owned energy generating facility shall only pay for credits received. A community-owned energy generating facility may update customer allocation percentages on a monthly basis.

    (3) Any unsubscribed energy that constitutes 10% or less of the community-owned energy generating facility shall be compensated using the average annual locational marginal price of energy in the DPL Zone based on the prior calendar year. Any unsubscribed energy that is greater than 10% of the community-owned energy generating facility not allocated shall not be compensated by the electric distribution company.

    (4) An electric distribution company shall use energy generated from a community-owned energy generating facility to offset purchases from wholesale electricity suppliers for standard offer service.

    (5) Excess credits shall be credited to subsequent billing periods to offset the customers' charges in those billing periods.

    (6) The community-owned energy generating facility shall ensure that the net-metering credits from the community-owned energy generating facility are accurate. The amount of electricity generated each month available for allocation as subscribed or unsubscribed energy shall be determined by a revenue quality production meter installed and paid for by the owner of the community-owned energy generating facility. Further, the community-owned energy generating facility shall be responsible for any additional costs incurred by the electric distribution company, including billing-related costs associated with community-owned energy generating facility customers.

(7) The community-owned energy generating facility will retain ownership of all RECs and SRECs associated with the electric energy it produces unless it has relinquished such ownership by contractual agreement with a third party or its customers.

(8) The community-owned energy generating facility shall not have subscriptions larger than 200 kilowatts constituting more than 60% of its capacity. The community-owned energy generating facility host's self-consumption is not included in this calculation.

(9) The electric distribution company shall only allow meter aggregation for customer accounts for which they provide electric distribution service.

(10) A community-owned energy generating facility shall not exceed a capacity of 4 megawatts and all costs associated with the interconnection are the responsibility of the community-owned energy generating facility.

(11) Community-owned energy generating facilities may include technologies defined under § 352(7)a.-h. of this title.

(12) A community-owned energy generating facility seeking to provide service to customers must apply for and obtain a certificate to operate from the Commission, and pay an application fee of $750. Community-owned energy generating facilities are not required to obtain a certificate of public convenience and necessity from the Commission. To obtain a certificate to operate, a community-owned energy generating facility must provide the following:

 a. A completed interconnection study or signed interconnection agreement with the electric distribution company.

 b. Proof of site control.

 c. Evidence that it possesses the financial, operational, and managerial capacity to comply with all state and federal regulations.

(13) If a community-owned energy generating facility fails to comply with orders, rules, or regulations promulgated or issued by the Commission governing such a facility, or any other laws, rules, or regulations that apply to such a facility, the Commission may impose penalties, including monetary assessments, and may suspend or revoke the certificate to operate, and impose other sanctions permitted by law.

(14) Every 3 years, the community-owned energy generating facility must certify to the Public Service Commission in writing that it meets the low-income eligibility criteria provided in this chapter.

(15) Community-owned energy generating facilities are subject to the fees and charges in § 114 of this title. In addition, community-owned energy generating facilities are required to pay the annual gross revenue assessment in § 115 of this title, and the "gross operating revenue" shall equal the sum of the net-metering credits produced by the community-owned energy generating facility and the revenue derived from unsubscribed energy.

(16) Before a community-owned energy generating facility receives permission to operate pursuant to the interconnection process from the electric distribution company, a community-owned energy generating facility shall provide the electric distribution company with the following information:

 a. A list of individual meters the community-owned energy generating facility desires to aggregate identified by name, address, and account number.

 b. A description of the energy generating facility, including the facility's host location, capacity, and fuel type or generating technology.

     c. The subscribed percentage of generation attributed to each customer, which the electric distribution company shall true-up at the end of the annualized billing period.

     d. Certification that the subscription level of each customer does not exceed 110% of that customer's expected aggregate electrical consumption calculated on the average of the 2 previous 12-month periods of actual electrical usage at the time of subscription with the community-owned energy generating facility.

     e. Before a community-owned energy generating facility receives permission to interconnect with an electric distribution company, the community-owned energy generating facility must certify to the electric distribution company and the Commission that participants in the community-owned energy generating facility include at least 15% low income customers whose gross annual income, by family size, is at or below 200% of the federal poverty guidelines, or 60% of the state median household income published by the United States Census Bureau, whichever is greater.

    (17) A community-owned energy generating facility may change its list of aggregated meters no more than monthly by providing 30 days written notice to the electric distribution company.

    (18) An electric distribution company may require that customers participating in a community-owned energy generating facility have their meters read on the same billing cycle.

    (19) Neither customers nor owners of community-owned energy generating facilities shall be subject to regulation as either public utilities or an electric supplier, except as set forth in this section.

    (20) Community-owned energy generating facilities shall be subject to regulation under the purview of the Commission, and the Commission will engage in rule-making in consultation with the Consumer Protection Unit of the Delaware Department of Justice. In addition to the promulgation of rules and regulations pursuant to this section relating to net energy metering, the Commission may promulgate rules and regulations with respect to community-owned energy generating facilities and this section to protect customers, including provisions related to standardized customer information billing, service terms and conditions, dispute procedures, and portability and transferability of contracts. Community-owned energy generating facilities shall not solicit customers by means of telemarketing where such telemarketing is prohibited by applicable laws and regulations.

    (21) All community-owned energy generating facilities shall consent to the jurisdiction of the Delaware courts for acts or omissions arising from their activities in the State.

    (22) Community-owned energy generating facilities must adhere to state and the Federal Energy Regulatory Commission rules.

    (23) The Commission shall open a rule-making docket to promulgate the rules and regulations for community-owned energy generating facilities called for in this section by August 1, 2021, and the rules and regulations must be promulgated no later than March 11, 2022, unless the deadline is extended by law.

    (24) A violation of any provision of this chapter related to community-owned energy generating facilities, and any rules or regulations promulgated pursuant to this section shall be deemed an unlawful practice under § 2513 of Title 6 and a violation of subchapter II of Chapter 25 of Title 6.

 (g) The Commission shall periodically review the impact of net-metering rules in this section and recommend changes or adjustments necessary for the economic health of utilities.

(h) A retail electric customer having on its premises 1 or more grid-integrated electric vehicles shall be credited in kilowatt-hours (kWh) for energy discharged to the grid from the vehicle's battery at the same kWh rate that customer pays to charge the battery from the grid, as defined in paragraph (e)(1) of this section. Excess kWh credits shall be handled in the same manner as net metering as described in paragraph (e)(1) of this section. To qualify under this subsection, the grid-integrated electric vehicle must meet the requirements in paragraphs (d)(1)a., (d)(1)b. and (d)(4) of this section. Connection and metering of grid integrated vehicles shall be subject to the rules and regulations found in paragraphs (e)(4), (5), and (6) of this section.

(i) The Commission may adopt tariffs for regulated electric utilities that are not inconsistent with subsection (h) of this section. Such tariffs may include rate and credit structures that vary from those set forth in subsection (h) of this section, as long as alternative rate and credit structures are not inconsistent with the development of grid-integrated electric vehicles.

(j) Nothing in this section is intended in any way to limit eligibility for net energy metering services based upon direct ownership, joint ownership, or third-party ownership or financing agreement related to an electric generation facility, where net energy metering would otherwise be available.

(k) Disputes shall be resolved by the Commission or appropriate governing body.

(*l*) Rules, regulations and programs for paragraphs (e)(8) and (9) [repealed] of this section shall be promulgated by the Commission or the appropriate local regulatory authority not later than July 1, 2011.

History.

72 Del. Laws, c. 10, § 3; 74 Del. Laws, c. 38, § 2; 76 Del. Laws, c. 164, §§ 1-4; 76 Del. Laws, c. 166, § 1; 76 Del. Laws, c. 200, § 2; 77 Del. Laws, c. 146, §§ 1-3; 77 Del. Laws, c. 212, §§ 2, 3; 77 Del. Laws, c. 453, §§ 2-11; 82 Del. Laws, c. 24, § 1; 83 Del. Laws, c. 178, § 4.

Effect of amendments.

83 Del. Laws, c. 178, effective September 17, 2021, repealed (e)(2), (3) and (9); added present (f) and redesignated the remaining subsections accordingly; and twice substituted "subsection (h)" for "subsection (g)" in present (i).

TITLE 29
STATE GOVERNMENT

PART I
GENERAL PROVISIONS

CHAPTER 4
BUILDINGS AND GROUNDS

SUBCHAPTER I
GENERAL PROVISIONS

§ 408. Display of POW/MIA flag.

A state agency, including a public school, shall cause a POW/MIA flag to be displayed out-of-doors on its installation, grounds, or campus at each location on each day the flag of the United States is so displayed.

History.
78 Del. Laws, c. 408, § 1; 83 Del. Laws, c. 30, § 1.

Effect of amendments.
83 Del. Laws, c. 30, effective June 3, 2021, substituted "A state agency, including a public school" for "State agencies, including all public schools", deleted "(weather permitting)" following "out-of-doors", substituted "each day the flag of the United States is so displayed" for "National POW/MIA Recognition Day", and deleted the final sentence.

PART II
THE GENERAL ASSEMBLY

CHAPTER 8
COMPOSITION OF AND REAPPORTIONMENT OF THE GENERAL ASSEMBLY

SUBCHAPTER I
GENERAL PROVISIONS

§ 804A. Criteria for counting incarcerated individuals for redistricting purposes.

(a) The General Assembly, in determining the reapportionment and redistricting for the State, applying the criteria set forth in § 804 of this title, and using the official reporting of the federal decennial census as set forth in § 805 of this title, may not count as part of the population in a given district boundary an incarcerated individual who meets both of the following:

(1) Was incarcerated in a state correctional facility in this State or federal correctional facility, as determined by the decennial census.

(2) Was not a resident of the State before the individual's incarceration.

(b)(1) The General Assembly, in determining the reapportionment and redistricting for the State as provided in this subchapter, shall count as part of the population in a given district boundary an individual incarcerated in a state correctional facility in this State or federal correctional facility, as determined by the decennial census, if the individual was a resident of the State before incarceration.

(2) The General Assembly shall count the individual for reapportionment and redistricting purposes at the individual's last known residence before incarceration.

(c) This section does not apply to the redistricting of the State following the 2010 federal decennial census. This section applies to the redistricting of the State following each federal decennial census thereafter.

(d) The Department of Elections shall geocode the last known residence of an incarcerated individual that is provided by the Department of Correction or the Federal Bureau of Prisons and is required to be counted under section (b) of this section.

(1) On or before September 15 of the year of a federal decennial census, the Department of Correction shall provide to the Department of Elections information in the Department of Correction's possession regarding the last known residence of an incarcerated individual required to be counted under subsection (b) of this section.

(2) The Department of Elections shall make reasonable efforts to correct a last known residence of an incarcerated individual that is not able to be geocoded, including by doing the following:

a. Verifying and correcting zip codes against the United States Postal Service zip code locator.

b. Correcting misspellings of city and street names.

c. Correcting or adding street suffixes against the United State Postal Service zip code locator.

d. Correcting street direction using the United States Postal Service zip code locator.

e. Removing extra information from the address field.

f. Removing an apartment number.

g. Removing a decimal point.

(3) The Department of Elections may request from a state or federal agency information necessary to geocode the last known residence of an incarcerated individual required to be counted under section (b) of this section.

(4) If, after making reasonable efforts under paragraph (d)(2) of this section, the Department of Elections is not able to geocode the last known residence of an incarcerated individual, the Department shall establish

the last known residence of the incarcerated individual as the state correctional facility where the individual is incarcerated.

(5) The Department of Elections shall provide to the General Assembly the geocoded last known residence data for incarcerated individuals required to be counted under subsection (b) of this section on or before January 15 of the year following a federal decennial census.

(6) The Department of Elections may adopt regulations to implement this section.

History.
77 Del. Laws, c. 472, § 1; 78 Del. Laws, c. 24, § 1; 83 Del. Laws, c. 128, § 1.

Revisor's note.
Section 2 of 83 Del. Laws, c. 128, provided: "For purposes of redistricting the State for the general election of 2022, the following applies: "(1) The Department of Correction shall, as soon as practicable after the enactment of this act, provide to the Department of Elections information in the Department of Correction's possession regarding the last known residence of an incarcerated individual required to be counted under § 804A of Title 29 of the Delaware Code.

"(2) The Department of Elections shall, as soon as practicable after the Department of Correction provides the information under paragraph (1) of this Section, provide to the General Assembly the geocoded last known residence data for incarcerated individuals as required under this act." The act was signed by the Governor on Sept. 8, 2021.

Effect of amendments.
83 Del. Laws, c. 128, effective Sept. 8, 2021, substituted "Criteria for counting incarcerated individuals for redistricting purposes" for "Determining district boundaries for incarcerated individuals; criteria" in the section heading and rewrote the section.

§ 805. Redistricting after federal decennial census.

The apportionment provided for by this chapter shall continue in effect until the official reporting by the President of the United States of the next federal decennial census. Within 120 calendar days following the receipt, by the entity designated by the Governor, of the federal decennial census data for redistricting pursuant to Public Law 94-171, the General Assembly shall reapportion and redistrict the State, wherever necessary, for the general election of 2022 and thereafter in such a manner that the several representative and senatorial districts shall comply, insofar as possible, with the criteria set forth in § 804(1)-(4) of this title. Such apportionment shall thence continue in effect until the next succeeding federal decennial census.

History.
29 Del. C. 1953, §§ 605, 607; 54 Del. Laws, c. 360; 56 Del. Laws, c. 243; 58 Del. Laws, c. 280, §§ 14-18; 63 Del. Laws, c. 183, § 1; 68 Del. Laws, c. 73, § 1; 68 Del. Laws, c. 188, § 1; 73 Del. Laws, c. 243, § 1; 78 Del. Laws, c. 105, § 2; 83 Del. Laws, c. 162, § 1.

Effect of amendments.
83 Del. Laws, c. 162, effective September 15,

2021, in the second sentence, substituted "Within 120 ... Public Law 94-171" for "After the official reporting of the 2020 federal decennial census by the President to Congress" and deleted "not later than June 30, 2021" preceding "reapportion".

PART III

STATE OFFICES CREATED BY CONSTITUTION

Chapter
25. State Department of Justice, §§ 2501 to 2553.

CHAPTER 25

STATE DEPARTMENT OF JUSTICE

SUBCHAPTER I
GENERAL POWERS

§ 2512A. False Claims and Affirmative Litigation Fund.

(a) All money received by the State as a result of civil actions brought by the Attorney General (or in the name of the State) pursuant to Chapter 12 of Title 6, Chapter 71 of Title 10, and Chapter 15 of Title 11, or pursuant to a written agreement by the Attorney General in settlement of the State's claims under Chapter 12 of Title 6, Chapter 71 of Title 10, and Chapter 15 of Title 11, shall be credited by the State Treasurer to a fund to be known as the "False Claims and Affirmative Litigation Fund."

(b) Money in the False Claims and Affirmative Litigation Fund shall be used for the payment of expenses incurred by the Department of Justice in connection with activities under Chapter 12 of Title 6, Chapter 71 of Title 10, § 1505 of Title 11 or, if approved by the Director of the Office of Management and Budget and the Controller General, for other Department of Justice expenses resulting from General Fund deficits. At the end of any fiscal year, if the balance in the False Claims Fund exceeds $3,000,000, the excess shall be withdrawn from the False Claims and Affirmative Litigation Fund and deposited in the General Fund.

(c) The Attorney General is authorized to expend from the False Claims and Affirmative Litigation Fund such moneys as are necessary for the payment of salaries, costs, expenses, and charges incurred in the investigation, preparation, institution, and maintenance of false claims and other affirmative civil actions brought on behalf of the State, and the maintaining of electronic discovery resources for the Department of Justice or other state agencies. The State Solicitor shall have the authority, under the direction of the Attorney General, to maintain and supervise the deposits and expenditures into and out of the False Claims and Affirmative Litigation Fund.

(d) When the State or agencies thereof, public bodies or subdivisions of the State, or qui tam plaintiffs are due a portion of the funds in the False Claims and Affirmative Litigation Fund as a result of a right to restitution, a right to reimbursement, or the operation of § 1205 of Title 6, the Attorney General is authorized to approve release of such funds to the appropriate fund, entity, or recipient.

History.
83 Del. Laws, c. 54, § 99.

Revisor's note.
This section became effective upon signature of the Governor on June 30, 2021.

SUBCHAPTER II
CONSUMER PROTECTION

§ 2520. Enforcement authority.

(a) Among other powers, the Director shall have the authority to:

(1) Investigate matters that may reveal violations of Chapter 25 of Title 6 or other unlawful conduct;

(2) Issue cease and desist orders, either summarily or after a hearing;

(3) Seek administrative remedies for violations of the statutes the Division of Consumer Protection is charged to enforce;

(4) Initiate and prosecute civil or criminal actions related to the purposes of this chapter in any court of competent jurisdiction;

(5) Seek restitution, rescission, reformation of contract, recoupment, disgorgement of profits or any moneys improperly obtained, or otherwise prevent unjust enrichment against violators of this chapter and on behalf of consumers;

(6) Promulgate rules and regulations;

(7) Under the direction of the Attorney General, maintain and supervise the deposits and expenditures into and out of the Consumer Protection Fund;

(8) Hold fact-finding, rulemaking or adjudicative hearings and issue opinions, orders or reports based thereon; and

(9) Take any other lawful action to enforce the consumer protection statutes and to carry out their purposes.

(b) The scope of authority of the Director to initiate administrative proceedings or take civil enforcement action does not extend to matters within the jurisdiction of the Public Service Commission or of the Insurance Commissioner of the State, except for matters covered by § 1014 of Title 26, but only as they relate to community-owned energy generating facilities.

History.
77 Del. Laws, c. 282, § 2; 83 Del. Laws, c. 178, § 6.

Effect of amendments.
83 Del. Laws, c. 178, effective September 17, 2021, added the exception in (b).

PART IV

STATE AGENCIES AND OFFICES NOT CREATED BY CONSTITUTION

Chapter
48. Lotteries, §§ 4801 to 4873.

CHAPTER 48
LOTTERIES

SUBCHAPTER I
STATE LOTTERY

§ 4805. Director — Powers and duties.

(a) The Director shall have the power and the duty to operate and administer the state lottery and to promulgate such rules and regulations governing the establishment and operation of the lottery as the Director deems necessary and desirable in order that the lottery be initiated at the earliest feasible time and in order that the system shall produce the maximum amount of net revenues consonant with the dignity of the State and the general welfare of the people. The rules shall provide for all matters necessary or desirable for the efficient and economical operation and administration of the system and for the convenience of the purchasers of lottery tickets and the holders of winning tickets, and the players of all state lottery games including, the following:

(1) Type and number of games to be conducted;

(2) Price or prices of tickets for any game;

(3) Numbers and sizes of the prizes on the winning tickets;

(4) Manner of selecting the winning tickets;

(5) Manner of payment of prizes to the holders of winning tickets;

(6) Frequency of the drawings or selections of winning tickets;

(7) Number and types of locations at which tickets may be sold and the sports lottery and keno may be conducted;

(8) Method to be used in selling tickets;

(9) Licensing of agents to sell tickets or host keno; provided, that, no person under the age of 18 shall be licensed as an agent;

(10) Manner and amount of compensation, if any, to be paid to licensed agents, other than video lottery agents, necessary to provide for the adequate availability of games to prospective buyers and for the convenience of the public;

(11) Apportionment of the total revenues accruing from the sale of tickets among:

    a. Payment of prizes to the holders of winning tickets;

    b. Payment of costs incurred in the operation and administration of the state lottery system, including the expenses of the office and the costs resulting from any contract or contracts entered into for promotional, advertising or operational services or for the purchase or lease of gaming equipment and materials;

    c. Repayment of the moneys appropriated to the State Lottery Fund pursuant to § 3 of 59 Del. Laws, c. 348; and

    d. Payment of earnings to the General Fund of the State.

(12) Such other matters necessary or desirable for the efficient and economical operation and administration of the game and for the convenience of the purchasers of tickets and the holders of winning tickets and the players of the video lottery, the sports lottery, Internet lottery, keno, and table games;

(13) Value of bills, coins or tokens needed to play the video lottery machines, sports lottery machines and table games;

(14) Licensing of agents for video lotteries;

(15) Payout from video lottery machines, provided that such payouts shall not be less than 87% on an average annual basis, and further provided that video lottery agents may return a payout greater than 87% but not greater than 95% upon 10 days written notice to the Director, and further provided that video lottery agents may, with the approval of the Lottery Director, return a greater payout percentage than 95%;

(16) A licensure requirement and enforcement procedure for officers, directors, key employees, gaming employees, gaming room service employees, sports lottery operations employees, and persons who own directly or indirectly 10% or more of such agent, in accordance with § 4828 of this title;

(17) A licensure requirement and enforcement procedure for service companies in accordance with § 4829 of this title;

(18) Standards for advertising, marketing and promotional materials used by video lottery agents;

(19) Regulations and procedures for the accounting and reporting of the payments required under §§ 4815 and 4819 of this title;

(20) The registration, kind, type, number and location of video lottery machines, sports lottery machines and table games on the licensee's premises, subject to the Director's obligations set forth in § 4820(b) of this title;

(21) The on-site security arrangements for video lottery agents and sports lottery agents;

(22) Requiring the reporting of information about video lottery agents, sports lottery agents, their employees, vendors and finances necessary or desirable to ensure the security of the lottery system. None of the information disclosed pursuant to this subsection shall be subject to disclosure under the Freedom of Information Act, § 10001 et seq. of this title;

(23) The reporting and auditing of financial information of licensees including, but not limited to, the reporting of profits or losses incurred by licensees and the reporting by licensees of such employment and payroll information as is necessary for the Director to determine compliance with § 10148(1) of Title 3 or § 100048 of Title 3 as the case may be. None of the information disclosed pursuant to this subsection shall be subject to disclosure under the Freedom of Information Act, § 10001 et seq. of this title;

(24)a. A registration requirement and enforcement procedure for any employee organization representing or seeking to represent employees who are employed by a Delaware video lottery agent. Any employee organization may at any time file with the office an application for registration as an employee organization. However, an employee organization shall be required to file such registration application within 10 business days after it secures a signed authorization card from any employee who is employed by a Delaware video lottery agent.

Any registration statement filed by an employee organization after the signature of an authorization card but prior to the employee organization's petition for election shall not be subject to disclosure by the Lottery Office to any video lottery agent;

b. Every key employee of an employee organization shall be required to register with the office at the same time as the application for registration is filed under paragraph (24)a. of this section or within 30 days after the date on which such individual is elected, appointed or hired, whichever is later;

c. The application for registration by an employee organization or key employee of such employee organization may be denied or registration revoked under the following circumstances:

1. If such employee organization or key employee of such employee organization is in violation of standards established

under the Labor-Management Reporting and Disclosure Procedure Prohibition Against Certain Persons Holding Office, 29 U.S.C § 504(a);

2. The applicant's competence, honesty or integrity pose a threat to the public interest of the State or to the reputation of or effective regulation and control of the lottery based on the applicant's associations or by virtue of the fact that the applicant has been convicted of a felony crime of moral turpitude or has been arrested for an act constituting racketeering under § 1502(9)a., b.2. or b.4. through 10. of Title 11 within 10 years prior to applying for registration hereunder or at any time thereafter. Any employee or employee organization denied registration based on an arrest for an act constituting racketeering under § 1502(9)a., b.2. or b.4. through 10. of Title 11 may apply for reconsideration of registration if subsequently acquitted or a nolle prosequi is entered or the charge is otherwise dismissed. In such instances, the Lottery Office shall reconsider the applicant's registration based on the criteria previously set forth in this subsection;

3. The organization or individual has knowingly made or caused to be made any written statement to any representative of the office or the Delaware State Police or any oral response to an official inquiry by the office, its employees or agents which was at the time and in light of circumstances under which it was made false or misleading;

4. The organization or key employee thereof holds or obtains a direct financial interest in any video lottery agent, provided the employee organization is provided a 30-day period to divest of any such direct financial interest.

The Division of Gaming Enforcement shall conduct the background checks required by this paragraph. The failure of any key employee to satisfy the requirements of paragraphs (a)(24)c.1. through 4. of this section may constitute grounds for suspension of the registration of the employee organization if the organization does not remove the key employee from the key employee's duties as defined in § 4803(o) of this title. The employee organization will be given a reasonable opportunity to remove or replace any key employee found to be in violation of paragraphs (a)(24)c.1. through 4. of this section;

d. The entity or individual filing a registration form is under a continuing duty to promptly notify the Director of any changes in disclosed information;

e. The Secretary of Finance shall, within a reasonable time, if requested by the Director, appoint a hearing officer to determine whether the application for registration shall be denied or the registration suspended or revoked. The hearing officer shall be required to hold a hearing in conformance with the requirements of § 10131 of this title. In any hearing, the Delaware Uniform Rules of Evidence shall be in effect. The denial of an application of registration or the suspension or revocation of a registration shall be bound by the provisions of §§ 10133 and 10134 of this title. The hearing officer's decision to deny an application of registration or to suspend or revoke a registration shall be appealable to the Superior Court under the Delaware Administrative Procedures Act (Chapter 101 of this title). All applications for registration shall be deemed approved unless the

Director notifies the applicant within 60 days of his or her decision not to approve and to appoint a hearing officer under this paragraph, or unless extenuating circumstances require a longer period, in which case the Director shall act with all deliberate speed to complete the process. Any employee organization may continue to provide services to employees of a Delaware video lottery agent during the review of the application process and the appeal process, except where the employee organization is found in violation of paragraph (a)(24)c.4. of this section or there has been a previous violation of paragraphs (a)(24)c.1. through 3. of this section by the employee organization within the previous 10 years;

f. Information requested in the application of registration provided for under this paragraph shall be adopted as part of the office's official rules and regulations upon notice and opportunity for a hearing under the Delaware Administrative Procedures Act [Chapter 101 of this title];

(25) The Director shall adopt procedures under the Delaware Administrative Procedures Act (Chapter 101 of this title) for employment investigations of the honesty, integrity, reputation and associations of office employees in order to determine that the employee's employment does not pose a threat to the public interest of the State or the integrity of the office. The procedures and any rules and regulations shall require any person seeking employment for compensation with the office for a position which has direct access to lottery ticket sales agents, video lottery agents, sports lottery agents, or vendors to submit his or her fingerprints and other relevant information in order to obtain the individual's entire federal and state criminal history record. Upon the Director's request, the Division of Gaming Enforcement shall conduct the investigations required under such rules and regulations. The rules and regulations shall require new employees to submit fingerprints for purposes of the state and federal criminal history checks;

(26) Type and number of sports lottery games to be conducted, the location and licensure of facilities where the sports lottery be conducted pursuant to § 4825 of this title, the price or prices for any sports lottery games, the rules for any sports lottery games, and the payout and manner of compensation to be paid to winners of sports lottery games;

(27) Type and number of table games to be conducted, the price or prices for any table games, the rules for any table games, the payout and manner of compensation to be paid to winners of table games, and the minimum and maximum wagers for any table games;

(28) The licensure and location of facilities where keno games may be conducted, the price or prices for any keno games, the rules for any keno games, and the payout and manner of compensation to be paid to winners of keno games;

(29) The regulations and procedures for the display and presentation of messages concerning responsible gaming and the regulations, procedures and training for identification of and assistance to compulsive gamblers;

(30) The provision of complimentary services, gifts, transportation, cash, food, nonalcoholic beverages, entertainment or any other thing of value by a video lottery agent to a guest;

(31) The procedures for the review and evaluation of licensing applications, including the forms of applications, procedures for fingerprinting and other means of identification, procedures for hearings, and grounds and procedures for the approval, denial, revocation or suspension of a license;

(32) Procedures relating to internal management controls of video lottery agents, including accounting controls and employee and supervisory organizational charts and responsibilities;

(33) Standards for the manufacture, sale, distribution, maintenance, repair, and servicing of video lottery machines and table game equipment; and

(34) Standards for the conduct of the Internet lottery in accordance with this chapter.

(b) The Director shall also have the power and it shall be the Director's duty to:

(1) Appoint such deputy directors as may be required to carry out the functions and duties of the office. Each deputy director shall have had 3 years' management experience in areas pertinent to the prospective responsibilities and an additional 3 years of experience in the same field.

(2) Within the limit of the funds made available in § 3 of 59 Del. Laws, c. 348, and proceeding from the sale of lottery tickets and generated by the operations of video lottery agents, appoint such professional, technical, and clerical assistants and employees as may be necessary to perform the duties imposed upon the office by this subchapter.

(3) In accordance with this subchapter, license as agents to sell lottery tickets persons who will best serve, by location or accessibility, the public convenience and promote the sale of lottery tickets. The Director may require a bond from every agent so licensed in such amount as the Director deems necessary. Every licensed agent shall prominently display the agent's license or a copy thereof.

(4) Enter into contracts for the operation of any game or part thereof and into contracts for the promotion of the game or games. This authorization is to be construed to include, but not be limited to, contracting with any racing or other sporting association to conduct sporting events within any racetrack or sports field in the State, the outcome of which shall determine the winners of a state game or, as an alternative, to affiliate the determination of the winners of a game with any racing or sporting event held within or without the State, and, including agreements with other state, provincial or international lotteries for participation in lottery games. All contracts for other than professional services in an amount greater than $2,000 shall be awarded to the lowest responsible bidder in the manner prescribed by state bidding laws. No contract awarded or entered into by the Director may be assigned by the holder thereof except by specific approval of the Director.

(5) Make arrangements for any person or organization, including banks, to perform such functions, activities or services in connection with the operation of the system as the Director may deem advisable.

(6) Suspend or revoke any license issued pursuant to this subchapter or the rules and regulations promulgated hereunder.

(7) Certify and report monthly to the State Treasurer the total lottery revenues, prize disbursements and other expenses for the preceding month, and to make an annual report to the Governor and the General Assembly, which report shall include a full and complete statement of revenues, prize disbursements and other expenses and recommendations for such changes in this subchapter as the Director deems necessary or desirable.

(8) Report immediately to the Governor and members of the General Assembly any matters which shall require immediate changes in the laws of the State in order to prevent abuses and evasions of this subchapter or

the rules and regulations promulgated hereunder or to rectify undesirable conditions in connection with the administration or operation of the gaming system. Such a report shall be disclosed to the public immediately upon issuance.

(9) Carry on a continuous study and investigation of the system:

a. For the purpose of ascertaining any defects in this subchapter or in the rules and regulations issued hereunder by reason whereof any abuses in the administration and operation of the lottery or any evasion of this subchapter or the rules and regulations may arise or be practiced;

b. For the purpose of formulating recommendations for changes in this subchapter and the rules and regulations promulgated hereunder to prevent such abuses and evasions;

c. To guard against the use of this subchapter to benefit organized gambling and crime or criminals in any manner whatsoever; and

d. To insure that this law and the rules and regulations shall be in such form and be so administered as to serve the true purpose of this subchapter.

(10) Make a continuous study and investigation of:

a. The operation and administration of similar laws which may be in effect in other states and countries;

b. Any literature on the subject which from time to time may be published or available;

c. Any federal laws which may affect the operation of the lottery; and

d. The reaction of Delaware citizens to existing and potential features of the games with a view to recommending or effecting changes that will tend to serve the purposes of this subchapter.

(11) Make available to the State Auditor or the State Auditor's representative such information as may be required to perform an annual audit as prescribed in Chapter 29 of this title.

(12) Establish state-operated sales offices, without limit as to number or location, as the Director shall deem suitable and economical in order to make lottery tickets more available to the public, which offices shall be operated solely from funds generated by the lotteries permitted by this subchapter.

(13) License as video lottery agents each person, corporation or association which, in 1993, held either a horse racing meet pursuant to Title 3 or Title 28 or a harness horse racing meet pursuant to Title 3 and who satisfies such fitness and background standards as the Director may promulgate pursuant to paragraph (a)(16) of this section. In the event that there shall have been or shall be a change of ownership or such person, corporation or association after the close of the 1993 racing meet then the issuance by the Director of a license to serve as a video lottery agent shall be conditioned upon the Director's determination that such person, corporation or association shall have met the requirements of § 4806(a)(1)-(4) and (b) of this title and satisfies such fitness and background standards as the Director may promulgate pursuant to paragraph (a)(16) of this section. Change of ownership occurring after the Director has issued a license shall automatically terminate the license 90 days thereafter unless the Director has determined after application to issue a license to the new owner(s) because the new owner(s) have met the requirements of § 4806(a)(1)-(4) and (b) of this title and satisfied such fitness and background standards as the Director may promulgate pursu-

ant to paragraph (a)(16) of this section. Any license granted pursuant to this subsection is a privilege personal to the video lottery agent and is not a legal right. A license granted or renewed pursuant to this subsection may not be transferred or assigned to another person, nor may a license be pledged as collateral. For purposes of this subsection, "a change of ownership" shall have occurred if more than 20 percent of the legal or beneficial interests in such person, corporation or association shall be transferred, whether by direct or indirect means.

(14) Whenever the Director deems necessary, examine all accounts, bank accounts, financial statements and records of the licensee in a licensee's possession or under its control in which it has an interest and the licensee must authorize all third parties, including parents, subsidiaries or related entities, in possession or control of the accounts or records of the licensee to allow examination of any of those accounts or records by the Director. None of the information disclosed pursuant to this subsection shall be subject to disclosure under the Freedom of Information Act, § 10001 et seq. of this title.

(15) Subpoena witnesses and compel the production of books, papers and documents of a licensee in connection with any hearings of the Director and may administer oaths or affirmations to the witnesses whenever, in the judgment of the Director, it may be necessary for the effectual discharge of duties.

If any person refuses to obey any subpoena or to testify or to produce any books, papers or documents, then the Director may apply to the Superior Court of the county in which the Director may be sitting and, thereupon, the Court shall issue its subpoena requiring the person to appear and testify or to produce the books, papers and documents before the Director. Whoever fails to obey or refuses to obey a subpoena of the Superior Court shall be guilty of contempt of court and shall be punished accordingly. False swearing on the part of any witness shall be deemed perjury and shall be punished as such.

(16) Bar, pursuant to §§ 4834 and 4835 of this title, any person from entering the premises of a video lottery agent or from participating in any capacity in the play of any table game, sports lottery game, video lottery game, or Internet lottery game, and, as applicable, procure such assistance from video lottery agents as is appropriate to enforce any such bar.

(17) Impose reasonable fees, as set by the Director and payable to the Office, upon applicants for licenses pursuant to §§ 4828 and 4829 of this title for the conduct of the review and investigation of the applicant, such fees to approximate and reasonably reflect all costs necessary to defray the expenses of the lottery and Division of Gaming Enforcement.

(18) Require video lottery agents to submit regular internal control submissions, which shall contain a narrative description of the internal control system to be utilized by the video lottery facility, including, but not limited to:

a. Accounting controls, including the standardization of forms and definition of terms to be utilized in the gaming;

b. Procedures, forms and, where appropriate, formulas covering the calculation of hold percentages; revenue drop; expense and overhead schedules; complimentary services;

c. Job descriptions and the system of personnel and chain-of-command, establishing a diversity of responsibility among employees engaged in gaming operations and identifying primary and secondary supervisory oversight responsibilities; and personnel practices;

d. Procedures within the cashier's cage for the receipt, storage and disbursal of chips, cash, and other cash equivalents used in wagering; the cashing of checks; the redemption of chips and other cash equivalents used in gaming;

e. Procedures for the collection and security of moneys at the gaming tables;

f. Procedures for the transfer and recordation of chips between the gaming tables and the cashier's cage and the transfer and recordation of moneys within the facility;

g. Procedures for the transfer of moneys from the gaming tables to the counting process and the transfer of moneys within the facility for the counting process;

h. Procedures and security for the counting and recordation of table game revenue;

i. Procedures and security standards for the handling and storage of gaming apparatus, including cards, dice, machines, wheels and all other gaming equipment;

j. Procedures and rules governing the conduct of particular games and the responsibility of casino personnel in respect thereto;

k. Procedures for the security, storage and recording of cash, chips, and cash equivalents utilized in gaming operations.

(19) Make Internet lottery games available at such websites and in such a manner as determined by the Office in accordance with this chapter, and utilizing technology to ensure that players are legally eligible to engage in such gaming.

(c)(1) The licenses granted pursuant to paragraph (b)(13) of this section or § 4825 of this title may be revoked or suspended for cause upon 30 days' written notice to the licensee or due to a change in ownership as set forth in those provisions, but shall otherwise not be subject to expiration or termination. "Cause" shall by way of example and not by limitation include falsifying any application for license or report required by the rules and regulations, the failure to report any information required by the rules and regulations, the material violation of any rules and regulations promulgated by the Director or any conduct by the licensee which undermines the public confidence in the video lottery system or serves the interest of organized gambling or crime and criminals in any manner. A license may be revoked for an unintentional violation of any federal, state or local law, rule or regulation provided that the violation is not cured within a reasonable time as determined by the Director; or a longer period where the video lottery agent has made diligent efforts to cure. Notwithstanding the foregoing, nothing in this subsection shall otherwise prohibit the termination or revocation of a license in accordance with the rules and regulations adopted hereunder.

(2) Within 30 days after an adverse determination by the Director, the licensee seeking to appeal the revocation or suspension for cause may demand a hearing before the Lottery Commission and show cause why the Director's determination was in error. Failure to demand a hearing within the time allotted in this paragraph precludes the person from having an administrative hearing, but in no way affects his or her right to petition for judicial review.

(3) Upon receipt of a licensee's demand for a hearing under this subsection, the Lottery Commission shall set a time and place for the hearing. This hearing must not be held later than 30 days after receipt of the demand for the hearing, unless the time of the hearing is changed by

the Lottery Commission with the agreement of the Director and the licensee. At the hearing, the licensee shall have the affirmative obligation to demonstrate by clear and convincing evidence that the Director's determination was in error under the criteria for cause established by this subsection and any regulations hereunder.

(4) If, upon completion of the hearing, the Lottery Commission determines that the licensee has met its burden of proof, an order to that effect shall be entered and the license shall be reinstated. If, upon completion of the hearing, the Lottery Commission finds that the licensee has not met its burden of proof, an order shall be entered to that effect. This order is subject to review in the Superior Court pursuant to the Administrative Procedures Act (Chapter 101 of this title).

(5) Any decision of the Director relating to the business plan or the number of video lottery machines to be awarded to licensees under § 4820(b) of this title shall be appealable under the Administrative Procedures Act (Chapter 101 of this title) in the manner of a case decision.

History.

59 Del. Laws, c. 348, § 1; 61 Del. Laws, c. 189, § 1; 69 Del. Laws, c. 446, §§ 4-8, 10-13; 70 Del. Laws, c. 167, § 1; 70 Del. Laws, c. 186, § 1; 71 Del. Laws, c. 184, § 2; 71 Del. Laws, c. 253, §§ 3-5; 74 Del. Laws, c. 53, § 1; 77 Del. Laws, c. 28, §§ 3-9; 77 Del. Laws, c. 219, §§ 5-11; 78 Del. Laws, c. 285, § 4; 79 Del. Laws, c. 1, §§ 1, 4; 79 Del. Laws, c. 77, § 5; 82 Del. Laws, c. 158, § 1; 83 Del. Laws, c. 70, § 1.

Revisor's note.

Section 9 of 83 Del. Laws, c. 70, provided: "This act takes effect 30 days after its enactment into law." The act was signed by the Governor on June 30, 2021, and became effective on July 30, 2021.

Effect of amendments.

83 Del. Laws, c. 70, effective July 30, 2021, deleted "but not limited to" preceding "following" in the last sentence of the introductory paragraph of (a); in (a)(11), substituted a period for the semicolon at the end of (a)(11)d. and deleted the former concluding paragraph; substituted "Division of Gaming Enforcement" for "Delaware State Police" in the first sentence of the final paragraph of (a)(24)c.; in (a)(24)d., deleted the former first sentence, and substituted "a registration" for "such" in the remaining sentence; substituted "Upon the Director's request, the Division of Gaming Enforcement" for "The Delaware State Police" in the second sentence of (a)(25); deleted the former fourth through sixth sentences in (c)(1); and added (c)(2)-(5).

§ 4807A. Fingerprinting procedure required.

(a) Any person seeking a license from the State Lottery Office shall be required to submit fingerprints and other necessary information in order to obtain the following:

(1) A report of the individual's entire criminal history record from the State Bureau of Identification or a statement from the State Bureau of Identification that the State Bureau of Identification Central Repository contains no such information relating to that person; and

(2) A report of the individual's entire federal criminal history record pursuant to the Federal Bureau of Investigation appropriation of Title II of Public Law 92-544. The Division of Gaming Enforcement shall be the intermediary for the purposes of this section and the State Lottery Office shall be the screening point for the receipt of said federal criminal history records.

(b) All information obtained pursuant to subsection (a) of this section shall be forwarded to the Division of Gaming Enforcement, which shall access the information and make a recommendation to the Director of suitability for licensure. The person seeking licensure shall be provided with a copy of all information forwarded to the State Lottery Office pursuant to this subsection. Information obtained under this subsection is confidential and may only be disclosed to the Director and Deputy Director of the State Lottery Office. The State Bureau of Identification may release any subsequent criminal history to the Division of Gaming Enforcement.

(c) Costs associated with obtaining criminal history information shall be paid by the person seeking licensure.

(d) A person seeking licensure shall have an opportunity to respond to the State Lottery Office regarding any information obtained pursuant to subsection (b) of this section prior to a determination of suitability for licensure. The grounds upon which a person seeking licensure may be denied consideration for a license include, but are not limited to:

(1) A conviction of a felony in this State or any other jurisdiction; or

(2) A conviction of any crime involving gambling or a crime of moral turpitude within 10 years prior to applying for a license or at any time subsequent to the granting of a license.

(e) Upon making its determination of suitability for licensure, the State Lottery Office shall forward the determination to the person seeking a license.

(f) Any person seeking a license with the State Lottery Office who has submitted to a criminal background check in this or any other state within the previous 12 months shall not be required to submit to another criminal background check; provided, however, that the person submits:

(1) the results of such previous criminal background check, including any previous federal criminal background check; and

(2) a reference from the person's most recent employer, if any, covering the previous 12 months.

(g) The State Lottery Office shall, in the manner provided by law, promulgate regulations necessary to implement this subchapter. These regulations shall include, but are not limited to:

(1) Establishment, in conjunction with the State Bureau of Identification, of a procedure for fingerprinting persons seeking licensure with the State Lottery Office and providing the reports obtained pursuant to subsection (a) of this section;

(2) Establishment of a procedure to provide confidentiality of information obtained pursuant to subsection (a) of this section and of the determination of suitability for licensure.

History.
70 Del. Laws, c. 167, § 2; 70 Del. Laws, c. 186, § 1; 83 Del. Laws, c. 70, § 2.

Revisor's note.
Section 9 of 83 Del. Laws, c. 70, provided: "This act takes effect 30 days after its enactment into law." The act was signed by the Governor on June 30, 2021, and became effective on July 30, 2021.

Effect of amendments.
83 Del. Laws, c. 70, effective July 30, 2021, substituted "Division of Gaming Enforcement" for "State Bureau of Identification" in (a)(2) and for "State Lottery Office" in the first and final sentences of (b); and substituted "recommendation to the Director" for "determination" in the first sentence of (b).

§ 4809. Restrictions on ticket sales; penalties.

(a) No person shall sell a ticket for any type of lottery game at a price greater than that fixed by rule or regulation of the Director. No person other than a licensed lottery sales agent or a licensed sports lottery agent shall sell lottery tickets or shares, except that nothing in this section shall be construed to prevent any person from giving lottery tickets to another as a gift or bonus.

(b) Any person convicted of violating this section shall pay a fine not exceeding $500.

History.
59 Del. Laws, c. 348, § 1; 83 Del. Laws, c. 70, § 3.

Revisor's note.
Section 9 of 83 Del. Laws, c. 70, provided: "This act takes effect 30 days after its enactment into law." The act was signed by the

Governor on June 30, 2021, and became effective on July 30, 2021.

Effect of amendments.
83 Del. Laws, c. 70, effective July 30, 2021, in (a), added "for any type of lottery game" in the first sentence and "or a licensed sports lottery agent" in the second sentence.

§ 4811. Jurisdiction in Superior Court.

The Superior Court has exclusive jurisdiction over offenses under this subchapter, except for offenses under §§ 4810(a) and 4836(a) and (b) of this title.

History.
59 Del. Laws, c. 348, § 1; 61 Del. Laws, c. 189, § 1; 70 Del. Laws, c. 186, § 1; 77 Del. Laws, c. 221, § 11; 78 Del. Laws, c. 285, § 26; 81 Del. Laws, c. 250, § 2; 83 Del. Laws, c. 47, § 1.

Effect of amendments.
83 Del. Laws, c. 47, effective June 15, 2021, substituted "§§ 4810(a) and 4836(a) and (b)" for "§ 4810(a)".

§ 4815. State Lottery Fund.

(a) All moneys received from the sale of lottery tickets, keno, and from Internet ticket games, shall be accounted for to the State Treasurer and all net moneys shall be placed into a special account known as the State Lottery Fund. From the Fund, the Director shall first pay for the operation and administration of the lottery as authorized in this subchapter and thereafter shall pay as prizes not less than 45% on the average of the total amount of tickets which have been sold and are scheduled for sale throughout the games, which percentage shall include prizes already awarded or to be awarded. The total of payments for operations and administration of the lottery shall not exceed 20% of the gross amount received from the sales of such games. The remaining moneys shall accumulate in the State Lottery Fund for the payments of operations and administration costs and on a monthly basis, or more frequently if required by the Director, the lottery shall undertake to provide into the General Fund of the State a payment of earnings of 30% of the total revenues accruing from the sales of such games or shares shall be so dedicated. In the event that the percentage allocated for operations (including prize payments) generates a surplus, said surplus shall be allowed to accumulate to an amount not to exceed $1,000,000. On a quarterly basis, the Director shall report to the Secretary of Finance any surplus in excess of $1,000,000 and remit to the General Fund of the State the entire amount of those surplus funds in excess of $1,000,000.

(b) All proceeds, net of proceeds returned to players pursuant to paragraph (b)(1) of this section, from the operation of the video lottery shall be electronically transferred daily or weekly at the discretion of the Lottery Director into a designated State Lottery account by the agent, and transferred to the State Lottery Fund by the Lottery on a daily or weekly basis and shall be applied as follows:

(1) *Proceeds returned to players.* — A portion of such proceeds, but not less than 87% of the total proceeds on an average annual basis received from the operation of a video lottery, shall be retained by and returned to the players under rules prescribed by the Director. Proceeds returned to players in excess of the payout authorized pursuant to § 4805(a)(15) of this title shall be the sole responsibility of the video lottery agent and the State Lottery's proceeds shall not be reduced on account of such excess payment. Subject to the recommendations of the Lottery Director, and approval of the Secretary of Finance, a video lottery agent may choose to offer free promotional play to players. The amount of free promotional play permitted shall be recommended by the Lottery Director and approved by the Secretary of Finance. The amount of money given away as free promotional play and used by players shall not be included in the amounts remaining after all payments to players. If the amount of money given away as free promotional play by a video lottery agent and used by players exceeds the amount authorized by the Lottery Director and the Secretary

of Finance authorized during a fiscal year, the video lottery agent shall reimburse net proceeds the amount of the overage which will be distributed as outlined in paragraphs (b)(3) and (b)(4) of this section.

(2) *Certain administrative and vendor costs.* — The State shall retain a portion of such proceeds in an amount equal to 75% of all costs of equipment (both video lottery machines and related equipment), including video lottery machine license and proprietary fees, whether leased or owned by the State, used or under the control of such agent, the cost of the central computer used to monitor the equipment used by the agent, and related vendor fees, and from these proceeds, and the proceeds provided pursuant to paragraph (b)(4)a. of this section, remit these amounts to vendors.

(3)a. *Proceeds returned to the State.* — Except as otherwise provided by this paragraph, of amounts remaining after all payments under paragraphs (b)(1) and (b)(2) of this section, there shall be returned to the State 42½%, less any qualified capital expenditure adjustment provided for in this paragraph. For licensees which conducted 40 or fewer (but at least 1) days of live harness horse races during 1992, should such licensees' video lottery proceeds, net of proceeds returned to players, at the end of any fiscal year fall below $107,500,000, then, in the subsequent fiscal year, there shall be returned to the State 41½% of amounts remaining after all payments under paragraphs (b)(1) and (b)(2) of this section, less any qualified capital expenditure adjustment provided for in this paragraph.

1. Beginning in fiscal year 2020, for each video lottery agent, the percentage of proceeds returned to the State shall be decreased by 2% if such video lottery agent's qualified capital expenditures equal or exceed 3% of video lottery agent net proceeds remaining after payments made under paragraph (b)(1) of this section for the calendar year ending the immediately preceding December 31. Notwithstanding the first sentence of this paragraph (b)(3)a.1. of this section, for calendar year ending December 31, 2018, only, qualified capital expenditures must equal or exceed 2.8%.

2. For purposes of this paragraph (b)(3)a. of this section, "qualified capital expenditures" means amounts properly characterized as capital expenditures under generally accepted accounting principles during each calendar year ending December 31 and apply to any facilities used by the video lottery agent in connection with its operations. "Qualified capital expenditures" does not include payments made for debt service.

3. Any amounts incurred or paid in any single year which exceed the 3% required for the adjustment under paragraph (b)(3)a.1. of this section may be carried forward for no more than 2 years.

b. The State shall also receive the funds on each credit slip that has not been presented for redemption within 1 year from the date the slip is issued.

c. *Application of funds retained by the state lottery.*— The funds retained by the state lottery shall be applied as follows: first, to the administrative costs and expenses in respect of the video lottery including, but not limited to, administrative expenses including payroll and other employment costs attributable to the operation of the video lottery by the State Lottery Office, law-enforcement and security expenses, including payroll and other employment costs of the state lottery, the Office of the Attorney General and the Division of Gaming Enforcement, attributable to the operation by the state lottery of a video lottery; second, $1,000,000 or 1%, whichever is greater, of the proceeds returned to the State under this paragraph (b)(3), to the Division of Substance Abuse and Mental Health of the Department of Health and Social Services for funding programs for the treatment, education and assistance of compulsive gamblers and their families; third, costs of the Administrator of Racing and racing inspectors referenced in Chapters 100 and 101 of Title 3; fourth, the State's contribution to the Delaware Standardbred Breeder's Program and Delaware Certified Thoroughbred Program (DCTP); and fifth, the remainder shall be paid into the State's General Fund.

d. The State's contribution to the Delaware Standardbred Breeder's Program pursuant to this subsection shall be $1,250,000, and said amount is to be allocated equally as of January 1 of the calendar year among existing licensees which conduct live harness horse racing, but moneys shall not be expended for the program until such time as a plan has been approved pursuant to paragraph (b)(4)b.2. of this section. The State's contribution to the Delaware Certified Thoroughbred Program (DCTP) pursuant to this subsection shall be $500,000, and said amount shall be allocated as of January 1 of each calendar year to the existing licensee which conducts live thoroughbred horse racing, but moneys shall not be expended for the program until such time as a plan has been approved pursuant to paragraph (b)(4)b.1. of this section.

(4) *Application of remaining proceeds.* — The proceeds remaining after payments as set forth in paragraphs (b)(1), (2) and (3) of this section shall be applied as follows:

a. *Balance of administrative and vendor costs.* — The State shall receive an amount equal to 25% of all costs of equipment (both video lottery machines and related equipment), including video lottery machine license and proprietary fees, whether leased or owned by the State, used or under the control of such agent, the cost of the central computer used to monitor the equipment used by the agent, and related vendor fees to be applied pursuant to paragraph (b)(2) of this section.

b. *Purses.* — 1. For video lottery agents licensed only to conduct horse racing meets under Chapter 101 of Title 3 or Chapter 4 of Title 28, such agents shall be paid and shall pay additional purses (and related administrative expenses of the horse racing association) to be applied under the direction of the Delaware Thoroughbred Racing Commission, for races conducted at such agent's racetrack in accordance with § 10148 of Title 3 or § 427 of Title 28 as appropriate, in an amount calculated as follows: 9.6% of the proceeds remaining after payments made under paragraph (b)(1) of this section. Seven hundred fifty thousand dollars of those proceeds, which would otherwise fund purses, on an annual basis, shall fund a Delaware Certified Thoroughbred Program (DCTP) to enhance the quantity of thoroughbred foals and/or yearlings stabled within Delaware for a period meeting the Delaware minimum residency requirement. The DCTP shall be administered by a Board comprised of the following:

A. Four members of the Delaware Thoroughbred Horseman's Association;

B. One member designated by the video lottery agent licensed to conduct live thoroughbred horse racing meets under Chapter 101 of Title 3;

C. One member appointed by the Speaker of the House of the General Assembly;

D. One member appointed by the President Pro Tempore of the Senate of the General Assembly;

E. The Secretary of Agriculture or the Secretary's designee; and

F. The Secretary of Finance or the Secretary's designee. Members shall be chosen by the organizations they represent, and shall serve 4-year terms, except the 4 initial Board members selected by the Delaware Thoroughbred Horseman's Association shall serve an initial term of 2 years, and 4 years thereafter. The Board created hereunder must develop and present a plan for the administration of the DCTP no later than December 31, 2005. This plan and all subsequent plans amending the DCTP shall be subject to the written approval of the Secretary of Agriculture or the Secretary's designee, the Secretary of Finance or the Secretary's designee, and the Chairperson of the Thoroughbred Racing Commission or the Chairperson's designee. The Board shall transmit minutes and actions from all meetings to the Chairperson of the Delaware Thoroughbred Racing Commission within 10 days of the meeting. The Board shall submit an annual report detailing the allocation of such funds of the DCTP to the Commission and make available to the State Auditor such information as may be required to perform an annual audit of funds allocated from the DCTP. The Board may also, at its discretion, use funds from the DCTP for advertising, promotion, education and administrative purposes directly related to the program, however, the total amount for these purposes cannot exceed 5% of the total allocation. Funds dedicated to the DCTP shall not be subject to a 1-year payout requirement, but payouts may be dispersed throughout the year.

2. For video lottery agents licensed only to conduct harness racing meets under Chapter 100 of Title 3, such agents shall be paid and shall pay additional purses (and related administrative expenses of the horse racing association) to be applied under the direction of the Delaware Harness Racing Commission to purses for races conducted at such agent's racetrack in accordance with § 10048 of Title 3, in an amount calculated as follows: 11.35% of the proceeds remaining after payments made under paragraph (b)(1) of this section.

Two million dollars of those proceeds, which would otherwise fund purses, on an annual basis ($1,000,000 to come from each licensee which conducts live harness horse racing) to be set aside for purses under this paragraph (b)(4)b.2. shall be used to fund a Delaware Standardbred Breeder's Program which shall be administered by a board comprised of 4 members from the Delaware Standardbred Owners Association, 1 member from the Standardbred Breeders and Owners of Delaware, Inc., 1 member from each video lottery agent licensed to conduct harness racing meets under Chapter 100 of Title 3, 1 member appointed by the Speaker of House of the General Assembly, 1 member appointed by the

President Pro Tempore of the Senate of the General Assembly, the Secretary of Agriculture or the Secretary's designee, and the Secretary of Finance or the Secretary's designee. Members shall be chosen by the organizations they represent, and shall serve 4-year terms except that 4 of the initial board selected by the members of the Delaware Standardbred Owners Association shall serve an initial term of 2 years, and 4 years thereafter. The board created hereunder will present a plan for the administration of the Program to the General Assembly no later than May 15, 1999. This plan, and all subsequent amendments to the plan, shall be subject to the written approval of the Secretary of Agriculture or the Secretary's designee, the Chairperson of the Delaware Harness Racing Commission or the Chairperson's designee, and the Secretary of Finance or the Secretary's designee. The board shall transmit minutes of all meetings and any proposed actions to the Delaware Harness Racing Commission within 10 days after each meeting. The board shall transmit an annual report detailing the allocation of proceeds from the fund and make available to the State Auditor or the State Auditor's representative such information as may be required to perform an annual audit of funds allocated from the Delaware Standardbred Breeder's Program. In addition to funding special purses for Delaware standardbred horses, the board created hereby may also use the funds dedicated to this Program for advertising, promotion, educational and administrative purposes. Funds dedicated to the Delaware Standardbred Breeder's Program shall not be subject to the 1-year payout requirement of § 10048 of Title 3.

3. For video lottery agents licensed to conduct harness horse racing meets under Chapter 100 of Title 3 on January 1, 1993, such agents, which in the future also conduct horse racing meets under Chapter 101 of Title 3 or Chapter 4 of Title 28, shall be paid and shall pay additional purses (and related administrative expenses of the horse racing association) administered by either the Delaware Thoroughbred Racing Commission or the Delaware Harness Racing Commission, as appropriate, in accordance with the formula set forth in paragraph (b)(4)b.2. of this section, for races conducted at such agent's racetrack based on the ratio of live horse racing days to total live racing days and live harness horse racing days to total live racing days.

4. For video lottery agents licensed to conduct horse racing meets under Chapter 101 of Title 3 on January 1, 1993, such agents, which in the future also conduct harness horse racing meets under Chapter 100 of Title 3, shall be paid and shall pay additional purses (and related administrative expenses of the horse racing association) administered by either the Delaware Thoroughbred Racing Commission or the Delaware Harness Racing Commission, as appropriate, in accordance with the formula set forth in paragraph (b)(4)b.1. of this section, for races conducted at such agent's racetrack based on the ratio of live horse racing days to total live racing days and live harness racing days to total live racing days.

c. *Jockey health and other welfare benefits.* — For video lottery agents which are licensed only to conduct thoroughbred horse racing meetings under Chapter 101 of Title 3 or Chapter 4 of Title 28, such agents annually shall be paid and shall pay the sum of $175,000 plus an additional $175,000 (which shall be subtracted from the amount such agent is paid and shall pay as additional purses under paragraph (b)(4)b.1. of this section) for a total payment of $350,000 annually, adjusted for inflation by the Delaware Thoroughbred Racing Commission, which shall be payable to fund a Delaware Jockeys Health and Welfare Benefit Fund on July 20 of each year. The Fund shall be used to provide, for jockeys who regularly ride in Delaware, health and other welfare benefits for active, disabled and retired jockeys pursuant to reasonable criteria for benefit eligibility. The Jockeys Health and Welfare Benefit Fund shall be administered by a Board, known as the Jockeys Health and Welfare Benefit Board, comprised of 1 member of the Delaware Thoroughbred Racing Commission, 1 member from the licensed agent under Chapter 101 of Title 3 or Chapter 4 of Title 28, 1 member of the Delaware Horsemen's Association, and 1 representative from the organization that represents the majority of the jockeys who are licensed and ride regularly in Delaware, 1 jockey who is licensed and rides regularly in Delaware, and 1 retired Delaware jockey who is participating in the benefit program. The Chairperson of the Commission shall serve as an ex officio member and vote on matters in the event of a tie vote on any issue. Members shall be appointed by the Commission and shall serve 2-year terms. In addition to providing funding for jockey health and other welfare benefits, the fund may expend reasonable expenses for administrative purposes.

d. *Commissions to agents.* — The portion of such proceeds remaining after the payments required by paragraphs (b)(4)a., b. and c. of this section shall be paid to such video lottery agent as commission.

For video lottery agents licensed only to conduct horse racing meets under Chapter 101 of Title 3 or Chapter 4 of Title 28, such agents shall pay $250,000 of the proceeds received under this section to fund the video lottery agent's contribution to the Delaware Certified Thoroughbred Program (DCTP) annually. Said amount shall be allocated as of January 1 of each calendar year.

For video lottery agents licensed only to conduct harness racing meets under Chapter 100 of Title 3, each agent shall pay $375,000 of the proceeds received under this section to fund the video lottery agent's contribution to the Delaware Standardbred Breeder's Program annually. Said amount shall be allocated as of January 1 of each calendar year.

(c)(1) All proceeds, net of proceeds returned to players, from the operation of the sports lottery at video lottery agents shall be electronically transferred daily or weekly at the discretion of the Lottery Director into a designated state lottery account by the agent, and transferred to the State Lottery Fund by the lottery on a daily or weekly basis. Proceeds from the sports lottery at video lottery agents, less the amounts returned to winning players and vendor fees, shall be returned to the State at a rate of 50% of the total win so experienced. Purses shall be paid from the proceeds from the sports lottery conducted at video lottery agents, less amounts returned to winning players and vendor fees, at the rate of 10.2% for video lottery agents licensed only to conduct harness racing meets and at the rate of 9.6% for video lottery agents licensed only to conduct thoroughbred racing meets. The Director, by regulation shall adopt accounting procedures for the sports lottery in order to accommodate the differences between the sports lottery and the video lottery. Administrative costs and expenses incurred by the video lottery agent for the initiation of the sports lottery and the costs of the equipment shall be solely the responsibility of the video lottery agent. The provisions of subsection (b) of this section shall not apply to the proceeds from the operation of the sports lottery.

(2) All proceeds, net of proceeds returned to players, from the operation of the sports lottery at sports lottery agents other than video lottery agents shall be held by the State Lottery Fund and such sports lottery agents shall be compensated pursuant to rules adopted under § 4805(a) of this title. Purses shall be paid from the proceeds from the sports lottery conducted at such sports lottery agents, less amounts returned to winning players and fees for sports lottery agents and vendors, to video lottery agents as follows:

a. For video lottery agents licensed only to conduct horse racing meets under Chapter 101 of Title 3 or Chapter 4 of Title 28, such agents shall be paid and shall pay additional purses at the rate of 9.6% of the proportion of all sports lottery proceeds in the prior fiscal year generated by video lottery agents that is generated by that video lottery agent.

b. For video lottery agents licensed only to conduct harness racing meets under Chapter 100 of Title 3, such agents shall be paid and shall pay additional purses at the rate of 10.2% of the proportion of all sports lottery proceeds in the prior fiscal year generated by video lottery agents that is generated by that video lottery agent.

c. For video lottery agents licensed to conduct both horse racing meets under Chapter 101 of Title 3 or Chapter 4 of Title 28 and Chapter 100 of Title 3, such agents shall be paid and shall pay additional purses at a rate between 9.6% and 10.2% determined by the Office to reflect the ratio of live horse racing days to live harness racing days.

(d) Gross table game revenue shall be electronically transferred daily or weekly at the direction of the Lottery Director into a designated state lottery account by the agent, and transferred to the State Lottery Fund by the lottery on a daily or weekly basis. Gross table game revenue shall be applied as follows:

(1) *Proceeds returned to the State.* — a. Except as otherwise provided by this paragraph, of gross table game revenue, there shall be returned to the State 15.5%.

b. The funds retained by the State shall be applied as follows: first, to the administrative costs and expenses of the Office, including, but not limited to, administrative expenses including payroll and other employment costs, and law-enforcement and security expenses, including payroll and other employment costs of the state lottery, the Office of the Attorney General, and the Division of Gaming Enforcement; second, $250,000 or 1%, whichever is greater, of the proceeds returned to the State under this paragraph, to the Division of Substance Abuse and Mental Health of the Department of Health and Social Services to be used exclusively for funding programs for the treatment, education and assistance of compulsive gamblers and their families; third, costs of the Administrator of Racing and racing inspectors referenced in Chapters 100 and 101 of Title 3; and fourth, the remainder shall be paid into the State's General Fund.

(2) *Purses.* — Of gross table game revenue, such agent shall be paid and shall pay additional purses in the amount of 4.5% of such proceeds.

a. For video lottery agents licensed only to conduct horse racing meets under Chapter 101 of Title 3 or Chapter 4 of Title 28, such purses shall be applied under the direction of the Delaware Thoroughbred Racing Commission for races conducted at such agent's racetrack in accordance with § 10148 of Title 3 or § 427 of Title 28, as appropriate.

b. For video lottery agents licensed only to conduct harness racing meets under Chapter 100 of Title 3, such purses shall be applied under the direction of the Delaware Harness Racing Commission to races conducted at such agent's racetrack in accordance with § 10048 of Title 3.

c. For video lottery agents licensed to conduct both harness racing meets under Chapter 100 of Title 3 and horse racing meets under Chapter 101 of Title 3 or Chapter 4 of Title 28, such purses shall be applied pursuant to the formulae set forth in paragraphs (b)(3)b.3. and (b)(3)b.4. of this section.

(3) The proceeds remaining after the payments in paragraphs (d)(1) and (2) of this section above shall be paid to video lottery agents as their commission.

(4) The administrative costs incurred by the Office shall be an administrative cost of the State.

(e) Gross revenue from the Internet video lottery and Internet table games shall be accounted for to the State Treasurer and all proceeds, net of moneys returned to players, shall be placed into a special account known as the State Internet Lottery Fund. From the Fund, the Director shall first pay for the operation and administration of the Internet video lottery and Internet table games. Thereafter, the first $3,750,000 of proceeds in each fiscal year shall be transferred to the State Lottery Fund for the benefit of the State. After $3,750,000 of proceeds has been transferred to the State each fiscal year, the remaining proceeds shall be distributed as follows:

(1) The proceeds from the sales of Internet video lottery games shall be distributed pursuant to paragraphs (b)(3) and (b)(4)b.1 - (b)(4)b.4 of this section, provided that the calculations for such distribution shall be done after netting out the proceeds returned to players and administrative and vendor costs; and

(2) The proceeds from the sales of Internet table games shall be distributed pursuant to subsection (d) of this section, net of proceeds returned to players, provided that the calculations for such distribution shall be done after netting out the proceeds returned to players and administrative and vendor costs.

History.

59 Del. Laws, c. 348, § 1; 60 Del. Laws, c. 9, §§ 2, 3; 60 Del. Laws, c. 91, § 1; 60 Del. Laws, c. 92, § 1; 60 Del. Laws, c. 539, § 6; 61 Del. Laws, c. 189, § 1; 66 Del. Laws, c. 367, § 1; 69 Del. Laws, c. 446, § 16; 70 Del. Laws, c. 186, § 1; 71 Del. Laws, c. 253, §§ 6-9; 71 Del. Laws, c. 414, § 8; 73 Del. Laws, c. 41, § 1; 74 Del. Laws, c. 53, §§ 2, 3; 74 Del. Laws, c. 222, §§ 1-3; 74 Del. Laws, c. 424, § 1; 75 Del. Laws, c. 98, §§ 131, 132; 75 Del. Laws, c. 229, §§ 2-4; 76 Del. Laws, c. 19, §§ 1, 2; 76 Del. Laws, c. 283, §§ 1-4, 6, 7; 77 Del. Laws, c. 28, §§ 10-15; 77 Del. Laws, c. 186, §§ 1, 2; 77 Del. Laws, c. 219, § 12; 78 Del. Laws, c. 285, §§ 7-9; 79 Del. Laws, c. 134, § 1; 79 Del. Laws, c. 311, § 1; 81 Del. Laws, c. 287, §§ 1-7; 83 Del. Laws, c. 70, § 4; 83 Del. Laws, c. 88, § 1.

Revisor's note.

Section 9 of 83 Del. Laws, c. 70, provided: "This act takes effect 30 days after its enactment into law." The act was signed by the Governor on June 30, 2021, and became effective on July 30, 2021.

Section 2 of 83 Del. Laws, c. 88, provided: "This act take effect on July 1 of the year of its enactment." The act was signed by the Governor on July 29, 2021, and became effective July 1, 2021.

Effect of amendments.

83 Del. Laws, c. 70, effective July 30, 2021, substituted "Division of Gaming Enforcement" for "Delaware State Police" in (b)(3)c.; in (d)(1)b., deleted "and" preceding "the Division of Gaming Enforcement" and "and the Dela-

ware State Police" thereafter; and substituted "(b)(3) and (b)(4)b.1.–(b)(4)b.4." for "(b)(2) and (b)(3)" in (e)(1).

83 Del. Laws, c. 88, effective July 1, 2021, in (b)(3)d., substituted "$1,250,000" for "$750,000" in the first sentence and "$500,000" for "$250,000" in the final sentence; substituted

"Seven hundred fifty thousand" for "Five hundred thousand" in the second sentence of the introductory paragraph of (b)(4)b.1.; and, in the first sentence of the final paragraph of (b)(4)b.2., substituted "Two million" for "One million five hundred thousand" and "$1,000,000" for "$750,000".

§ 4822. Annual crime report.

29 Del. C. § 4822 Annual crime report.

The State Lottery Office, with the assistance of the Attorney General's Office and the Division of Gaming Enforcement, shall annually provide to the General Assembly a report detailing the crimes that occur within the communities surrounding each racetrack property, including an analysis of crimes relating to table gaming, whether in or outside the property of a video lottery facility.

History.
69 Del. Laws, c. 446, § 28; 77 Del. Laws, c. 219, § 19; 83 Del. Laws, c. 70, § 5.

Revisor's note.
Section 9 of 83 Del. Laws, c. 70, provided: "This act takes effect 30 days after its enactment into law." The act was signed by the

Governor on June 30, 2021, and became effective on July 30, 2021.

Effect of amendments.
83 Del. Laws, c. 70, effective July 30, 2021, substituted "Division of Gaming Enforcement" for "State Bureau of Identification".

§ 4828. Licensing of video lottery agent directors, officers, and employees.

(a) The Director shall have the power and duty to license those persons required by this chapter to be licensed and to promulgate rules and regulations for such purpose. The licensure procedure shall include the satisfaction of such security, fitness and background standards as determined necessary relating to competence, honesty and integrity, such that a person's reputation, habits and associations do not pose a threat to the public interest of the State or to the reputation of or effective regulation and control of the lottery.

(b) It shall be the obligation of the video lottery agent to notify the Director on a continuing basis of any change in officers, directors, key employees, gaming employees, gaming room service employees, sports lottery operations employees and persons who own, directly or indirectly, 10% or more of such entity. Persons holding key employee licenses on January 28, 2010, shall remain licensed as key employees and shall not be required to seek licensure under this section until the license is to be renewed. Persons holding video lottery operations employee licenses shall remain licensed as a gaming employee, but shall be required to seek renewal of their licenses no later than July 28, 2010.

(c) [Repealed.]

History.
77 Del. Laws, c. 219, § 20; 83 Del. Laws, c. 70, § 6.

Revisor's note.
Section 9 of 83 Del. Laws, c. 70, provided: "This act takes effect 30 days after its enact-

ment into law." The act was signed by the Governor on June 30, 2021, and became effective on July 30, 2021.

Effect of amendments.
83 Del. Laws, c. 70, effective July 30, 2021, repealed (c).

§ 4829. Licensing of service companies.

(a) "Service company" shall mean:

(1) Any vendor offering goods or services relating to the manufacture, operation, maintenance, security, distribution, service or repair of video lottery machines, sports lottery machines or table game equipment directly to the State;

(2) Any vendor offering goods or services to a video lottery agent on a regular and continuing basis, as defined in regulations promulgated hereunder; or

(3) Any person providing gaming excursion services to a video lottery agent.

(b) The Director shall have the power and duty to license those service companies meeting this definition as the Director determines to be necessary to the integrity of the operations of the lottery, and to promulgate rules and regulations for such purpose. The licensure procedure shall include the satisfaction of such security, fitness and background standards as determined necessary relating to competence, honesty and integrity, such that a service company's reputation, habits and associations do not pose a threat to the public interest of the State or to the reputation of, or effective regulation and control of, the lottery. Vendors holding licenses as technology providers or other service provider shall remain licensed as a service company and shall not be required to seek licensure under this section until the license is to be renewed. Vendors licensed or approved by the Harness Racing Commission or the Thoroughbred Racing Commission to provide services to a video lottery agent need not secure a service company license pursuant to this section unless such vendor seeks to provide services other than those already authorized.

(c) Each service company identified in this section shall be licensed in accordance with the standards of a key employee. The owners, management, and supervisory personnel of each such service company shall be qualified to the standards of and for the term of a key employee. The employees of each such service company whose duties and responsibilities involve the security, maintenance, servicing, repair, or operation of video lottery machines or table game equipment shall be licensed to the standards of and for the term of a gaming employee.

(d) Each service company identified in paragraph (a)(2) of this section shall be licensed in accordance with the standards of a key employee except as to the requirement to establish financial stability, integrity and responsibility. The owners, management, and supervisory personnel of each such service company shall be qualified to the standards of a key employee, except as to the requirement to establish financial stability integrity and responsibility.

(e) Each service company identified in paragraph (a)(3) of this section shall be licensed in accordance with the standards of a key employee except as to the requirement to establish financial stability, integrity and responsibility. The employees of each such service company whose duties and responsibilities include arranging, procuring or selecting participants in a gaming excursion shall be qualified to the standards of a key employee, except as to the requirement to establish financial stability integrity and responsibility.

(f) For purposes of this section, an owner of a corporation shall be defined as "any person who owns directly or indirectly more than 10% of the equity securities of the corporation."

(g)(1) Each service company identified in paragraph (a)(1) of this section shall be licensed as a service company prior to conducting any business whatsoever, provided, however, that upon a finding of good cause by the Director for each business transaction, the Director may permit an applicant for such service company license to conduct business transactions prior to the licensure of that company.

(2) Each service company identified in paragraph (a)(2) of this section, may transact business with a video lottery agent prior to obtaining a service company license upon the filing of a vendor registration form by a video lottery agent for such service company pursuant to regulations promulgated hereunder.

(h) [Repealed.]

(i) The risk manager of the sports lottery must be a bookmaker currently licensed to operate, and operating, sports books in the United States and the sports lottery technology system provider must be licensed to operate lotteries in the United States. The Director may determine whether the licensing standards of another state are comprehensive, thorough and provide similar adequate safeguards and, if so, may, in the Director's discretion, license an application already licensed in such state without the necessity of a full application and background check.

History.
77 Del. Laws, c. 219, § 20; 70 Del. Laws, c. 186, § 1; 83 Del. Laws, c. 70, § 7.

Revisor's note.
Section 9 of 83 Del. Laws, c. 70, provided: "This act takes effect 30 days after its enact-

ment into law." The act was signed by the Governor on June 30, 2021, and became effective on July 30, 2021.

Effect of amendments.
83 Del. Laws, c. 70, effective July 30, 2021, repealed (h).

§ 4831. Prohibition on employment of persons or service companies without a license.

(a) It shall be unlawful for any licensed agent to employ or continue to employ an individual or service company that is required to possess a license under the provisions of this chapter, but that is not licensed. A licensed agent who violates the provisions of this section shall pay a fine imposed by the Director of not less than $1,000 and not more than $5,000. A licensed person who knowingly violates the provisions of this section is guilty of a class A misdemeanor.

(b) Any individual or service company that works or is employed in a position whose duties require licensing under the provisions of this chapter, without holding the requisite license, is guilty of a class A misdemeanor.

History.
77 Del. Laws, c. 219, § 20; 83 Del. Laws, c. 70, § 8.

Revisor's note.
Section 9 of 83 Del. Laws, c. 70, provided: "This act takes effect 30 days after its enactment into law." The act was signed by the

Governor on June 30, 2021, and became effective on July 30, 2021.

Effect of amendments.
83 Del. Laws, c. 70, effective July 30, 2021, substituted "Director" for "Office" in the second sentence of (a).

PART V

PUBLIC OFFICERS AND EMPLOYEES

CHAPTER 52

HEALTH CARE INSURANCE

§ 5207. Temporary employees.

Revisor's note.
Section 28 of 76 Del. Laws, c. 80, effective July 1, 2007; 77 Del. Laws, c. 84, § 24, effective July 1, 2009; 77 Del. Laws, c. 327, § 24, effective July 1, 2010; 78 Del. Laws, c. 78, § 26, effective July 1, 2011; 78 Del. Laws, c. 290,

§ 21, effective July 1, 2012; 79 Del. Laws, c. 78, effective July 1, 2013; 79 Del. Laws, c. 290, § 20, effective July 1, 2014; and 80 Del. Laws, c. 79, § 19, effective July 1, 2015; 80 Del. Laws, c. 298, § 20, effective July 1, 2016; 81 Del. Laws, c. 58, § 26, effective July 3, 2017; 82 Del.

Laws, c. 64, § 21, effective July 1, 2019; 82 Del. Laws, c. 242, § 21, effective July 1, 2020; and 83 Del. Laws, c. 54, § 21, effective June 30, 2021, provided: "Notwithstanding any provision of the Delaware Code to the contrary, 29 Del. C. § 5207 shall not apply to individuals employed in accordance with 29 Del. C. § 5903(17)."

§ 5213. Coverage for epinephrine autoinjectors.

(a) For purposes of this section, "epinephrine autoinjector" means a single-use device used for the automatic injection of a premeasured dose of epinephrine into the human body.

(b) The plan shall provide coverage for medically-necessary epinephrine autoinjectors for individuals who are 18 years of age or under by including at least 1 formulation of epinephrine autoinjectors on the lowest tier of the drug formulary developed and maintained by the carrier.

History.
83 Del. Laws, c. 42, § 3.

Revisor's note.
This section became effective upon the signature of the Governor on June 15, 2021.

CHAPTER 55
STATE EMPLOYEES' PENSION PLAN

SUBCHAPTER I
GENERAL PROVISIONS

§ 5501. Definitions.

Revisor's note.
Section 2g. of 83 Del. Laws, c. 55, effective June 30, 2021, provided: "This supplement [a one-time salary supplement of $1,000.00 for state employees] shall be considered within the pension definitions stated in 29 Del. C. § 5501 (c), §5501(d), §5501 (e), §5600 (3), and 11 Del. C. §8351 (2)."

SUBCHAPTER II
ELIGIBILITY REQUIREMENTS AND BENEFITS

§ 5522. Eligibility for service pension.

(a) An employee shall become eligible to receive a service pension, beginning with the month after the employee has terminated employment, if:

(1) The employee has 5 years of credited service, exclusive of service credited under § 5501(e)(4), (5) and (12) of this title, and has attained age 62;

(2) The employee has 15 years of credited service, exclusive of service credited under § 5501(e)(4), (5) and (12) of this title, and has attained age 60;

(3) The employee has 30 years of credited service;

(4) The employee has 25 years of credited service, exclusive of service credited under § 5501(e)(4), (5) and (12) of this title, regardless of age;

(5) The employee has 25 years of credited service, exclusive of service credited under § 5501(e)(4), (5) and (12) of this title, regardless of age, and is a Department of Correction employee or a specified peace officer. The

employee must have 20 years of credited service as a correction officer or specified peace officer; or

(6) The employee has 25 years of credited service, exclusive of service credited under § 5501(e)(4), (5), and (12) of this title, regardless of age, and is a 9-1-1 operator. The employee must have 25 years of credit service as a 9-1-1 operator.

(b) A former employee with a vested right to a service pension shall become eligible to receive such pension, computed in accordance with this chapter beginning with the first month after his or her attainment of:

(1) Age 60 if credited service is equal to or greater than 20 years and includes service prior to July 1, 1976; or

(2) Age 62 if credited service is equal to or greater than 5 years.

(c) An employee shall become eligible to receive a reduced service pension, beginning with the month after he or she has terminated employment, if he or she has 15 years of credited service, exclusive of service credited under § 5501(e)(4), (5) and (12) of this title, and has attained age 55; the amount of the service pension payable to such an employee shall be reduced by $2/10$ percent of each month the employee is under age 60.

(d) The amount of the service pension payable to an employee who becomes eligible to receive a service pension pursuant to paragraph (a)(4) of this section shall be reduced by $2/10$ percent for each month of credited service the employee has less than 30 years.

(e) A post-2011 employee shall become eligible to receive a service pension, beginning with the month after the employee has terminated employment, if:

(1) The employee has 10 years of credited service, exclusive of service credited under § 5501(e)(12) of this title, and has attained age 65;

(2) The employee has 20 years of credited service, exclusive of service credited under § 5501(e)(12) of this title, and has attained age 60; or

(3) The employee has 30 years of credited service.

(f) A post-2011 employee shall become eligible to receive a reduced service pension, beginning with the month after he or she has terminated employment, if:

(1) He or she has 15 years of credited service, exclusive of service credited under § 5501(e)(12) of this title, and has attained age 55; the amount of the service pension payable to such an employee shall be reduced by $4/10$ percent of each month the employee is under age 60; or

(2) He or she has 25 years of credited service, exclusive of service credited under § 5501(e)(12) of this title, regardless of age; the amount of the service pension payable to such an employee shall be reduced by $4/10$ percent of each month the employee has less than 30 years.

(g) A former post-2011 employee with a vested right to a service pension shall become eligible to receive such pension, computed in accordance with this chapter beginning with the first month after his or her attainment of age 65 if credited service is equal to or greater than 10 years.

History.

29 Del. C. 1953, § 5522; 57 Del. Laws, c. 592, § 1; 57 Del. Laws, c. 702; 58 Del. Laws, c. 180, § 3; 60 Del. Laws, c. 483, §§ 15, 16; 62 Del. Laws, c. 392, §§ 1, 2; 63 Del. Laws, c. 423, § 2; 67 Del. Laws, c. 124, §§ 2, 3; 70 Del. Laws, c. 186, § 1; 70 Del. Laws, c. 524, §§ 7, 10; 72 Del. Laws, c. 253, § 1; 78 Del. Laws, c. 14, § 11; 79

Del. Laws, c. 174, §§ 1, 3, 5; 80 Del. Laws, c. 403, § 2; 81 Del. Laws, c. 154, § 2; 81 Del. Laws, c. 445, § 3; 83 Del. Laws, c. 141, § 1.

Effect of amendments.

83 Del. Laws, c. 141, effective Sept. 10, 2021, substituted "§ 5501(e)(4), (5), and (12)" for "§ 5501(d)(4), (5), and (12)" in the first sentence of (a)(6).

§ 5526. Payment of disability pension.

(a) Disability pension payments shall be made to a retired employee for each month beginning with the month in which the retired employee becomes eligible to receive such pension and ending with the month in which the retired employee ceases to be eligible or dies.

(b) Any disability pensioner who has not attained age 60 shall report to the Board by April 30 each year, beginning in 1972, in a form prescribed by the Board, the total earnings from any gainful occupation or business in the preceding calendar year. The excess of such earnings over ½ of the annual rate of compensation, adjusted annually for any increase in the total "Median Usual Weekly Earnings" as published by the U.S. Department of Labor, received before the pensioner developed a disability shall be deducted from the disability pension during the 12 months beginning in July of the year following the calendar year for which earnings are reported, in a manner determined by the Board. If any person received a disability pension for less than 12 months in the calendar year for which earnings are reported, the deduction, if any, shall be determined on a pro rata basis.

(c) Any disability pensioner who was employed as a "police officer" as defined in § 8401 of Title 11 or employed as an officer of the Capitol Police who has not attained age 60 shall report to the Board by April 30 each year, in a form prescribed by the Board, their total earnings from any gainful occupation or business in the preceding calendar year. The excess of such earnings over the annual rate of compensation, adjusted annually for any increase in the total "Median Usual Weekly Earnings" as published by the U.S. Department of Labor, received at the time of the disability shall be deducted from their disability pension during the 12 months beginning in July of the year following the calendar year for which the earnings are reported, in a manner determined by the Board. If any person received a disability pension for less than 12 months in the calendar year for which earnings are reported, the deduction, if any, shall be determined on a pro-rata basis.

(d) Termination of a disability pension on account of recovery from disability shall not prejudice the right of the pensioner to qualify subsequently for a service pension or another disability pension.

History.
29 Del. C. 1953, § 5526; 57 Del. Laws, c. 592, § 1; 58 Del. Laws, c. 180, § 2G; 63 Del. Laws, c. 310, §§ 1, 2; 68 Del. Laws, c. 364, § 1; 70 Del. Laws, c. 186, § 1; 74 Del. Laws, c. 46, § 1; 78 Del. Laws, c. 179, § 286; 83 Del. Laws, c. 83, § 2.

Revisor's note.
Based upon changes contained in 83 Del. Laws, c. 83 § 2, effective July 21, 2021, "(5)" was deleted following "§ 8401" in the first sentence of (c).

§ 5527. Amount of ordinary service or disability pension [For application of this section, see 79 Del. Laws, c. 315, § 10].

(a) The amount of the monthly service or disability pension payable to an employee or former employee shall be the sum of 2.0% of the employee's final average compensation multiplied by the number of years, taken to the nearest twelfth of a year, in the employee's period of credited service prior to January 1, 1997, plus 1.85% of the employee's final average compensation multiplied by the number of years, taken to the nearest twelfth of a year, in the employee's period of credited service after December 31, 1996. If the employee is a correction officer or specified peace officer then the amount of pension would also include 2.45% of the employee's final average compensation multiplied by years of service above 25 years. If the employee is a 9-1-1 operator, then the amount of pension would also include 2.45% of the employee's final average compensation multiplied by years of service above 25 years. The amount payable to a participant who does not make the additional contribution provided in § 5501(j) of this title for years of credited service before 1977 shall be the sum of 2.0% of the employee's final average compensation multiplied by the number of years, taken to the nearest twelfth of a year, in the employee's period of credited service between January 1, 1977, and December 31, 1996, plus 2.0% of the employee's final average compensation multiplied by the number of years, taken to the nearest twelfth of a year, in the employee's period of credited service prior to January 1, 1977, provided that the maximum amount based on the service before 1977 is $1,000, plus 1.85% of the employee's final average compensation multiplied by the number of years, taken to the nearest twelfth of a year, in the employee's period of credited service after December 31, 1996.

(b) In the case of an employee or former employee whose credited service under § 5501(e)(1), (2) and (3) of this title includes service before June 1970, the minimum amount payable shall be:

(1) If he or she has 15 years of such credited service, the lesser of $150 or his or her final average compensation; or

(2) If he or she does not have 15 years of such credited service, the minimum amount payable under subsection (c) of this section, subject to the limitation specified in subsection (c) of this section.

(c) In the case of an employee or former employee whose credited service under § 5501(e)(1), (2) and (3) of this title does not include service before June 1970, but does include service prior to July 1, 1976, the minimum amount payable shall be $5.00 multiplied by the number of years, taken to the nearest twelfth of a year, in his or her period of credited service, but not more than 30 such years.

(d)(1) Notwithstanding provisions of this chapter to the contrary, an elected official shall receive a pension computed in accordance with this subsection. The service or disability pension payable to the elected official and the survivor's pension payable to the eligible survivor of such individuals shall be computed on the basis of compensation to the elected official as an elected official irrespective of other credited service, with contribution to be determined based upon compensation as an elected official. The minimum amount of pension payable to an elected member of the General Assembly or a retired elected member of the General Assembly shall be computed by multiplying his or her years of service as an elected member of the General Assembly times the highest rate of payment being paid to any retired member of the General Assembly, such rate to be computed by dividing the monthly pension being paid to such retired member by his or her years of service as an elected member of the General Assembly. An elected official elected prior to January 1, 2012, shall be eligible to receive a pension beginning with the first month after the attainment of age 60, provided that he or she shall have served at least 5 years at the time of his or her termination of service as an elected official, or beginning with the first month after attainment of age 55, provided that he or she shall have served at least 10 years at the time of his or her termination of service as an elected official. An elected official elected on or after January 1, 2012, shall be eligible to receive a pension beginning with the first month after the attainment of age 60, provided that he or she shall have served at least 20 years at the time of his or her termination of service as an elected official, or beginning with the first month after attainment of age 65, provided that he or she shall have served at least 10 years at the time of his or her termination of service as an elected official. Any pension for credited service other than as an elected official shall be determined under the remainder of this chapter as a separate pension.

(2)a. The minimum amount of pension payable to a statewide elected official shall be computed by multiplying his or her years of service as an elected official times the highest rate of payment being paid to any retired member of the General Assembly. The employee must elect to receive the minimum pension provided for in this subsection prior to the issuance of his or her first benefit check. This election must be made in a form approved by the Board and shall be irrevocable.

b. A statewide elected official receiving a service or disability pension which was effective prior to July 1, 1996, may elect to receive the minimum provisions of subsection (a) of this section. This election must be made in a form approved by the Board, filed prior to July 31, 1996, to be effective August 1, 1995, for statewide elected officials receiving a service or disability pension on July 1, 1996.

(e) Any section of this chapter to the contrary notwithstanding, the amount of the monthly service or disability pension payable to any regular part-time employee who is not employed on a full-time or annual basis, as the term full-time or annual basis is defined in rules and regulations adopted by the Board, shall be determined in accordance with subsection (a) of this section, provided that no minimum amount shall be payable to any such regular part-time employee. However, for any public school cafeteria employee who entered state service on or before July 1, 1971, and who accrues 15 years of credited service as an employee under § 5501(e)(1) of this title by the date of the employee's retirement eligibility, shall receive, beginning at age 62, a minimum amount which, when combined with the social security benefit, shall not be less than $ 200 per month.

(f) Notwithstanding provisions of this chapter to the contrary, the minimum amount of monthly service, including vested, or disability pension payable to any full-time or regular part-time employee shall be $1.00 multiplied by each year of service taken to the nearest $\frac{1}{12}$ of a year. In the case of a regular part-time cafeteria worker also eligible for a minimum pension under subsection (e) of this section, the minimum shall be the greater of subsection (e) or this subsection. The minimums specified in this subsection shall not apply to members of boards or commissions.

(g)(1) Notwithstanding provisions of this chapter to the contrary, an employee may elect to have his or her service or disability pension computed under this chapter reduced by 2% thereby providing a survivor's pension equal to $\frac{2}{3}$ of such reduced amount to the employee's eligible survivor or survivors at the time of the employee's death. This election must be made in a form approved by the Board, filed prior to the issuance of the employee's first benefit check and shall be irrevocable.

(2) Notwithstanding provisions of this section to the contrary, an employee may elect to have his or her service or disability pension, computed under this section, reduced by 3% thereby providing a survivor's pension equal to 75% of such reduced amount to the employee's eligible survivor or survivors at the time of the employee's death. This election must be made in a form approved by the Board, filed prior to the issuance of his or her first benefit check and shall be irrevocable.

(3) Notwithstanding the provisions of this section to the contrary, an individual receiving a service or disability pension which was effective prior to July 1, 1989, or an individual with a vested right to a service pension may elect to have his or her service or disability pension reduced by 3%, thereby providing a survivor's pension equal to 75% of such reduced amount to his or her eligible survivor or survivors at the time of his or her death. This election must be made in a form approved by the Board, filed prior to December 15, 1989, to be effective January 1, 1990, for individuals receiving a service or disability pension on July 1, 1989, or, in the case of an individual with a vested right to a service pension, filed prior to the issuance of his or her first pension check.

(4) Notwithstanding provisions of this chapter to the contrary, an employee may elect to have his or her service or disability pension computed under this chapter reduced by 6% thereby providing a survivor's pension equal to 100% of such reduced amount to the employee's eligible survivor or survivors at the time of the employee's death. This election must be made in a form approved by the Board, filed prior to the issuance of the employee's first benefit check and shall be irrevocable.

History.

29 Del. C. 1953, § 5527; 57 Del. Laws, c. 592, § 1; 58 Del. Laws, c. 180, §§ 2H, 2I; 58 Del. Laws, c. 527, § 1F; 60 Del. Laws, c. 214, § 1; 60 Del. Laws, c. 483, §§ 19-22; 61 Del. Laws, c. 409, § 96; 61 Del. Laws, c. 454, §§ 5-9, 12; 61 Del. Laws, c. 455, § 8; 61 Del. Laws, c. 519, § 29; 63 Del. Laws, c. 199, § 1; 63 Del. Laws, c. 244, § 1; 66 Del. Laws, c. 172, § 1; 66 Del. Laws, c. 422, § 1; 67 Del. Laws, c. 47, §§ 66, 69; 67 Del. Laws, c. 86, § 13; 70 Del. Laws, c. 186, § 1; 70 Del. Laws, c. 425, § 75; 70 Del. Laws, c. 524, §§ 1-3; 72 Del. Laws, c. 438, § 1; 73 Del. Laws, c. 146, § 1; 78 Del. Laws, c. 14, §§ 10, 13; 79 Del. Laws, c. 174, §§ 1, 4, 5; 79 Del. Laws, c. 315, § 1; 80 Del. Laws, c. 403, § 3; 83 Del. Laws, c. 141, § 2.

Revisor's note.

Section 32(b) of 83 Del. Laws, c. 54, effective June 30, 2021, provided: "The increases provided by this act [in § 5532 of this title] shall not apply to pensions awarded under §5527(d)(1), Chapter 55, Title 29, Delaware Code."

Effect of amendments.

83 Del. Laws, c. 141, effective Sept. 10, 2021, in (a), substituted "the employee's" for "his or her" wherever it appeared in the first, second and final sentences and inserted the present third sentence.

§ 5532. Increases in pensions.

(a) Any monthly service or disability pension which became effective on or before January 1, 1993, and is payable on the date this subsection is enacted into law and any survivor pension based on a former service or disability pension that was effective on or prior to January 1, 1993, and is payable on the date this subsection is enacted into law shall be increased effective January 1, 1994, by 1% plus an additional 2% for pensions effective prior to January 1, 1991, up to a maximum of 3% plus .15% for each full month of retirement preceding January 1, 1981, up to a maximum of 9%. These increases shall continue to be paid through June 30, 1994, and every fiscal year thereafter provided that funds are appropriated in accordance with § 5544 of this title.

(b) Any monthly service or disability pension which became effective on or before December 1, 1990, and is payable on July 21, 1994, and any survivor pension based on a former service or disability pension that was effective on or prior to December 1, 1990, and is payable on the date this subsection is enacted into law shall be increased effective April 1, 1995, by 2% plus .10% for each full month of retirement preceding January 1, 1981, up to a maximum of 15%. These increases shall continue to be paid through June 30, 1995, and every fiscal year thereafter provided that funds are appropriated in accordance with § 5544 of this title.

(c) Any monthly service or disability pension which became effective on or before July 1, 1995, and is payable on July 18, 1996, and any survivor pension based on a former service or disability pension that was effective on or before July 1, 1995, and is payable on July 18, 1996, shall be increased effective July 1, 1996, by 2% plus 1% for pensions that were effective prior to January 1, 1980. These increases shall continue to be paid through June 30, 1997, and every fiscal year thereafter; provided that funds are appropriated in accordance with § 5544 of this title.

(d) Any monthly service or disability pension which became effective on or after July 1, 1976, and is payable on July 18, 1996, and any survivor pension based on a former service or disability pension which became effective on or after July 1, 1976 and is payable on the date this subsection is enacted into law shall also be increased effective July 1, 1996, by the amount of difference between the pensioner's computed benefit under § 5527(a) of this title, as effective July 1, 1996, less the benefit previously awarded under § 5527(a)(1) and (2) of this title [repealed].

(e) Any monthly service or disability pension which became effective on or before July 1, 1996, and is payable on July 9, 1997, and any survivor pension based on a former service or disability pension that was effective on or before July 1, 1996, and is payable on July 9, 1997, shall be increased effective July 1, 1997, in accordance with the following schedule:

Year Pension Became Effective	Percent Increase
Prior to 1974	9%
1974	8%
1975	7%
1976	6%
1977	5%
1978	4%
After 1978	2%

These increases shall continue to be paid through June 30, 1998, and every fiscal year thereafter provided that funds are appropriated by the General Assembly in accordance with § 5544 of this title.

(f) Any monthly service, disability and survivor pension based on a former service or disability pension that was effective on or before July 1, 1997, but after December 31, 1985, and is payable on the effective date of this subsection shall be increased effective July 1, 1998, by 2%. Any monthly service, disability, or survivor pension based on a former service or disability pension that was effective prior to January 1, 1986, shall be increased effective July 1, 1998, by 3% or $20 per month, whichever is greater. These increases shall continue to be paid through June 30, 1999, and every fiscal year thereafter provided that funds are appropriated by the General Assembly in accordance with § 5544 of this title.

(g) Any monthly service, disability and survivor pension based on a former service or disability pension that was effective on or before July 1, 1998, but after December 31, 1979, and is payable on July 9, 1999, shall be increased effective July 1, 1999 by 2%. Any monthly service, disability or survivor pension based on a former service or disability pension that was effective prior to January 1, 1980. Shall be increased effective July 1, 1999 by 3% or $25 per month, whichever is greater. These increases shall continue to be paid through June 30, 2000, and every fiscal year thereafter provided that funds are appropriated by the General Assembly in accordance with § 5544 of this title.

(h) Any monthly service, disability and survivor pension based on a former service or disability pension that was effective on or before June 30, 2000, but after December 31, 1979, and is payable on July 21, 2000, shall be increased effective July 1, 2000, by 2%. Any monthly service, disability, or survivor pension based on a former service or disability pension that was effective prior to January 1, 1980, shall be increased effective July 1, 2000, by 3% or $25 per month, whichever is greater. These increases shall continue to be paid through June 30, 2001, and every fiscal year thereafter provided that funds are appropriated by the General Assembly in accordance with § 5544 of this title.

(i)(1) Any monthly service, disability and survivor pension based on a former service or disability pension that was effective prior to July 1, 2001, and is payable on July 1, 2001, shall be increased effective July 1, 2001, by 1.5%. These increases shall continue to be paid through June 30, 2002, and every fiscal year thereafter provided that funds are appropriated by the General Assembly in accordance with § 5544 of this title.

(2) Any monthly service, disability and survivor pension based on a former service or disability pension that was effective prior to July 1, 2001, and is payable on July 1, 2001, shall be increased effective July 1, 2001, by 0.5%. These increases shall continue to be paid through June 30, 2002, and every fiscal year thereafter provided that funds are appropriated by the General Assembly in accordance with § 5544 of this title.

(j) Any monthly service, disability and survivor pension based on a former service or disability pension that was effective on or before June 30, 2001, but after December 31, 1975, and is payable on September 1, 2003, shall be increased effective September 1, 2003, by 2% or $25 per month, whichever is greater. Any monthly service, disability and survivor pension based on a former service or disability pension that was effective before January 1, 1976, and is payable on September 1, 2003, shall be increased effective September 1, 2003, by 2% or $35 per month, whichever is greater. These increases shall continue to be paid through June 30, 2004, and every fiscal year thereafter provided that funds are appropriated by the General Assembly in accordance with § 5544 of this title.

(k)(1) Any monthly service, disability, and survivor pension based on a former service or disability pension that was effective on or before June 30, 2001, but after December 31, 1975, and is payable on July 1, 2004, shall be increased effective July 1, 2004, by 2%. Any monthly service, disability, and survivor pension based on a former service or disability pension that was effective before January 1, 1976, and is payable on July 1, 2004, shall be increased effective July 1, 2004, by 2% or $35 per month, whichever is greater. These increases shall continue to be paid through June 30, 2005, and every fiscal year thereafter provided that funds are appropriated by the General Assembly in accordance with § 5544 of this title.

(2) Any monthly service, disability, and survivor pension based on a former service or disability pension that was effective on or before June 30, 2003, but after June 30, 2001, and is payable on July 1, 2004, shall be increased effective July 1, 2004, by 2%. These increases shall continue to be paid through June 30, 2005, and every fiscal year thereafter provided that funds are appropriated by the General Assembly in accordance with § 5544 of this title.

(3) Any monthly service, disability, and survivor pension based on a former service or disability pension that was effective on or before May 31, 2004, but after June 30, 2003, and is payable on July 1, 2004, shall be increased effective July 1, 2004, by 2%. These increases shall continue to be paid through June 30, 2005, and every fiscal year thereafter provided that funds are appropriated by the General Assembly in accordance with § 5544 of this title.

(l) Any monthly service, disability, and survivor pension based on a former service or disability pension that was effective on or before June 30, 2004, but after December 31, 1980, and is payable on July 1, 2005, shall be increased effective July 1, 2005, by 2%. Any monthly service, disability, and survivor pension based on a former service or disability pension that was effective before January 1, 1981, and is payable on July 1, 2005, shall be increased effective July 1, 2005, by 2% plus $50 per month. These increases shall continue to be paid through June 30, 2006, and every fiscal year thereafter provided that funds are appropriated by the General Assembly in accordance with § 5544 of this title.

(m) Any monthly service, disability, and survivor pension based on a former service or disability pension that was effective on or before June 30, 2005, but after December 31, 1980, and is payable on July 1, 2006, shall be increased effective July 1, 2006, by 2%. Any monthly service, disability, and survivor pension based on a former service or disability pension that was effective before January 1, 1981, and is payable on July 1, 2006, shall be increased effective July 1, 2006, by 2% or $25 per month, whichever is greater. These increases shall continue to be paid through June 30, 2007, and every fiscal year thereafter provided that funds are appropriated by the General Assembly in accordance with § 5544 of this title.

(n) Any monthly service, disability, and survivor pension based on a former service or disability pension that was effective on or before June 30, 2010, and is payable on January 1, 2012, shall be increased effective January 1, 2012, by 2%. These increases shall continue to be paid through June 30, 2012, and every fiscal year thereafter provided that funds are appropriated by the General Assembly in accordance with § 5544 of this title.

(o) Any monthly service, disability, and survivor pension based on a former service or disability pension that was effective on or before June 30, 2011, and is payable on July 1, 2012, shall be increased effective July 1, 2012, by 1%. These increases shall continue to be paid through June 30, 2013, and every fiscal year thereafter provided that funds are appropriated by the General Assembly in accordance with § 5544 of this title.

(p) Any monthly service, disability, and survivor pension based on a former service or disability pension that was effective on or before June 30, 2013, and is payable on January 1, 2015, shall be increased effective January 1, 2015, by 1%. These increases shall continue to be paid through June 30, 2015, and every fiscal year thereafter provided that funds are appropriated by the General Assembly in accordance with § 5544 of this title.

(q) Any monthly service, disability, and survivor pension based on a former service or disability pension that was effective on or before June 30, 1991, and is payable on July 1, 2021, shall be increased effective July 1, 2021, by 3%. Any monthly service, disability, and survivor pension based on a former service or disability pension that was effective on or before June 30, 2001, but after June 30, 1991, and is payable on July 1, 2021, shall be increased effective July 1, 2021, by 2%. Any monthly service, disability, and survivor pension based on a former service or disability pension that was effective on or before June 30, 2016, but after July 1, 2001, and is payable on July 1, 2021, shall be increased effective July 1, 2021, by 1%. These increases shall continue to be paid through June 30, 2022, and every fiscal year thereafter provided that funds are appropriated by the General Assembly in accordance with § 5544 of this title.

History.
29 Del. C. 1953, § 5532; 57 Del. Laws, c. 592, § 1; 60 Del. Laws, c. 483, §§ 28, 29; 61 Del. Laws, c. 36, § 1; 61 Del. Laws, c. 455, § 3; 62 Del. Laws, c. 6, § 1; 62 Del. Laws, c. 103, § 1; 64 Del. Laws, c. 249, § 1; 65 Del. Laws, c. 489, § 1; 66 Del. Laws, c. 363, § 1; 67 Del. Laws, c. 422, § 1; 69 Del. Laws, c. 105, § 1; 69 Del. Laws, c. 174, § 1; 69 Del. Laws, c. 450, §§ 1,2; 70 Del. Laws, c. 525, §§ 1, 3; 71 Del. Laws, c. 165, § 1; 71 Del. Laws, c. 397, § 1; 72 Del. Laws, c. 152, § 1; 72 Del. Laws, c. 438, §§ 2, 4; 72 Del. Laws, c. 447, § 1; 73 Del. Laws, c. 146, § 2; 74 Del. Laws, c. 183, § 1; 74 Del. Laws, c. 398, § 1; 75 Del. Laws, c. 136, § 1; 75 Del. Laws, c. 403, § 1; 78 Del. Laws, c. 116, § 1; 78 Del. Laws, c. 289, § 1; 79 Del. Laws, c. 343, § 1; 83 Del. Laws, c. 54, § 32(a).

Revisor's note.
Section 32(b) of 83 Del. Laws, c. 54, effective June 30, 2021, provided: "The increases provided by this act shall not apply to pensions awarded under §5527(d)(1), Chapter 55, Title 29, Delaware Code."

Effect of amendments.
83 Del. Laws, c. 54, effective June 30, 2021, added (q).

SUBCHAPTER III
FINANCING AND ADMINISTRATION

§ 5544. Actuarial valuations and appropriations.

(a) The actuary shall prepare an actuarial valuation of the assets and liabilities of the funds as of June 30, each year. On the basis of reasonable actuarial assumptions and tables approved by the Board, the actuary shall determine the normal cost required to meet the actuarial cost of current service and the unfunded actuarial accrued liability.

(b) The State's appropriation to the funds for Fiscal Year 2008, and for each fiscal year thereafter, shall be the percentage of covered payroll approved by the Board on the basis of the most recent actuarial valuation, and shall equal the sum of the normal cost plus the payment required to implement the provisions of subsection (c) of this section plus the payment required to amortize the unfunded actuarial accrued liability using an open amortization period of 20 years. For plan amendments effective after Fiscal Year 2007 the unfunded actuarial accrued liability for such amendments shall be amortized over an open amortization period of 20 years. The amortization payment shall be an amount computed as a level percentage of the prospective total covered payroll over the remainder of the amortization period, with such prospective total covered payroll to be determined on the basis of a growth rate, as determined by the Board, compounded annually. Except as provided in subsection (c) of this section, all funds appropriated pursuant to this subsection shall be deposited into the fund established by § 5541 of this title.

(c)(1) In order to provide a fund for post retirement increases, the State shall include in its annual appropriation payments equal to 2.33% of covered payroll, subject to the limitations contained in § 5548(a)(2) of this title. Beginning with the Fiscal Year 1994 budget, .70% of covered payroll shall be appropriated; in Fiscal Year 1995, 1.11% of covered payroll shall be appropriated; in Fiscal Year 1996, 1.52% of covered payroll shall be appropriated; in Fiscal Year 1997, 1.93% of covered payroll shall be appropriated; in Fiscal Year 1998 and each fiscal year thereafter 2.33% of covered payroll shall be appropriated. Funds appropriated to implement this subsection shall be deposited into the Post Retirement Fund established by § 5548 of this title.

(2) In order to provide a fund for post retirement health insurance premiums, the State shall include in its annual appropriation payments the sum of the anticipated cost of the State's post retirement health insurance premiums for that year, plus the greater of 5.00% of the normal cost or the difference of 2.00% of covered payroll less the amount appropriated for the normal cost and unfunded actuarial accrued liability in subsection (b) of this section. Funds appropriated to implement this subsection shall be deposited into the OPEB Fund as established by § 5281 of this title.

(d)(1) The State's obligation to the State Employees' Pension Trust Fund, the State Judiciary Retirement Fund and the State Police Retirement Fund to implement the provisions of § 5532(a) of this title shall be the payment required to amortize the unfunded accrued liability over 5 years from January 1, 1994.

(2) The State's obligation to the Special Pension Fund authorized by 61 Del. Laws, c. 455, to implement the provisions of § 5532(a) of this title in Fiscal Year 1994, shall be the lump sum actuarial liability of the benefits granted.

(e)(1) The State's obligation to the State Employees' Pension Trust Fund, the State Judiciary Retirement Fund and the State Police Retirement Fund to implement the provisions of § 5532(b) of this title shall be the payment required to amortize the unfunded accrued liability over 5 years from April 1, 1995.

(2) The State's obligation to the Special Pension Fund authorized by 61 Del. Laws, c. 455, to implement the provision of § 5532(b) of this title in

Fiscal Year 1995, shall be the lump sum actuarial liability of the benefits granted.

(f)(1) The State's obligation to the State Employees' Pension Trust Fund, the State Judiciary Retirement Fund and the State Police Retirement Fund to implement the provisions of § 5532(c) and (d) of this title shall be the payment required to amortize the unfunded accrued liability over 5 years from July 1, 1996.

(2) The State's obligation to the Special Pension Fund authorized by 61 Del. Laws, c. 455, to implement the provisions of § 5532(c) of this title in Fiscal Year 1997 shall be the lump sum actuarial liability of the benefits granted.

(g)(1) The State's obligation to the State Employees' Pension Trust Fund, the State Judiciary Retirement Fund and the State Police Retirement Fund to implement the provisions of § 5532(e) of this title shall be the payment required to amortize the unfunded accrued liability over 5 years from July 1, 1997.

(2) The State's obligation to the Special Pension Fund authorized by Volume 61, Chapter 455, Laws of Delaware, to implement the provisions of § 5532(c) of this title in Fiscal Year 1998 shall be the lump sum actuarial liability of the benefits granted.

(h)(1) The State's obligation to the State Employees' Pension Plan, the State Judiciary Retirement Fund, and the New State Police Retirement Fund to implement § 5532(f) of this title shall be the payment required to amortize the unfunded accrued liability over 5 years from July 1, 1998.

(2) The State's obligation to the Special Pension Fund authorized by Volume 61, Chapter 455, Laws of Delaware, to implement § 5532(f) of this title in Fiscal Year 1999 shall be the lump sum actuarial liability of the benefits granted.

(i)(1) The State's obligation to the State Employees' Pension Plan, the State Judiciary Retirement Fund, and the New State Police Retirement Fund to implement the provisions of § 5532(g) of this title shall be the payment required to amortize the unfunded accrued liability over 5 years from July 1, 1999.

(2) The State's obligation to the Special Pension Fund authorized by Volume 61, Chapter 455, Laws of Delaware, to implement the provisions of § 5532(g) of this title in Fiscal Year 2000 shall be the lump sum actuarial liability of the benefits granted.

(j)(1) The State's obligation to the State Employees' Pension Plan, the State Judiciary Retirement Fund and the New State Police Retirement Fund to implement the provisions of § 5532(h) of this title shall be the payment required to amortize the unfunded accrued liability over 5 years from July 1, 2000.

(2) The State's obligation to the Special Pension Fund authorized by Volume 61, Chapter 455, Laws of Delaware, to implement the provisions of § 5532(g) of this title in Fiscal Year 2001 shall be the lump sum actuarial liability of the benefits granted.

(k)(1) The State's obligation to the State Employees' Pension Plan, the State Judiciary Retirement Fund and the New State Police Retirement Fund to implement the provisions of § 5532(i)(1) of this title shall be the payment required to amortize the unfunded accrued liability over 5 years from July 1, 2001, pursuant to § 5548 of this title.

(2) The State's obligation to the State Employees' Pension Plan to implement the provisions of § 5532(i)(2) of this title shall be treated as an actuarial loss during the next actuarial valuation process.

(3) The State's obligation to the Special Pension Fund authorized by 61 Del. Laws, c. 455, to implement the provisions of § 5532(i) of this title shall be treated as an actuarial loss during the next actuarial valuation process of the Special Pension Fund.

(*l*)(1) The State's obligation to the State Employees' Pension Plan, the State Judiciary Retirement Fund, and the New State Police Retirement Fund to implement the provisions of § 5532(j) of this title shall be the payment required to amortize the unfunded accrued liability over 5 years from September 1, 2003, pursuant to § 5548 of this title.

(2) The State's obligation to the Special Pension Fund authorized by 61 Del. Laws, c. 455, to implement the provisions of § 5532(j) of this title shall be treated as an actuarial loss during the next actuarial valuation process of the Special Pension Fund.

(m)(1) The State's obligation to the State Employees' Pension Plan, the State Judiciary Retirement Fund, and the New State Police Retirement Fund to implement the provisions of § 5532(k) of this title shall be the payment required to amortize the unfunded accrued liability over 5 years from July 1, 2004, pursuant to § 5548 of this title.

(2) The State's obligation to the Special Pension Fund authorized by Volume 61, Chapter 455, Laws of Delaware, to implement the provisions of § 5532(k) of this title shall be treated as an actuarial loss during the next actuarial valuation process of the Special Pension Fund.

(n)(1) The State's obligation to the State Employees' Pension Plan, the State Judiciary Retirement Fund, and the New State Police Retirement Fund to implement the provisions of § 5532(*l*) of this title shall be the payment required to amortize the unfunded accrued liability over 5 years from July 1, 2005, pursuant to § 5548 of this title.

(2) The State's obligation to the Special Pension Fund authorized by 61 Del. Laws, c. 455, to implement the provisions of § 5532(*l*) of this title shall be treated as an actuarial loss during the next actuarial valuation process of the Special Pension Fund.

(o)(1) The State's obligation to the State Employees' Pension Plan, the State Judiciary Retirement Fund, and the New State Police Retirement Fund to implement the provisions of § 5532(m) of this title shall be the payment required to amortize the unfunded accrued liability over 5 years from July 1, 2006, pursuant to § 5548 of this title.

(2) The State's obligation to the Special Pension Fund authorized by 61 Del. Laws, c. 455, to implement the provisions of § 5532(m) of this title shall be treated as an actuarial loss during the next actuarial valuation process of the Special Pension Fund.

(p)(1) The State's obligation to the State Employees' Pension Plan, the State Judiciary Retirement Fund, and the New State Police Retirement Fund to implement the provisions of § 5532(n) of this title shall be the payment required to amortize the unfunded accrued liability over 5 years from January 1, 2012, pursuant to § 5548 of this title.

(2) The State's obligation to the Special Pension Fund authorized by Volume 61, Chapter 455, Laws of Delaware, to implement the provisions of § 5532(n) of this title shall be treated as an actuarial loss during the next actuarial valuation process of the Special Pension Fund.

(q)(1) The State's obligation to the State Employees' Pension Plan, the State Judiciary Retirement Fund, and the New State Police Retirement Fund to implement the provisions of § 5532(o) of this title shall be the payment required to amortize the unfunded accrued liability over 5 years from July 1, 2012, pursuant to § 5548 of this title.

(2) The State's obligation to the Special Pension Fund authorized by 61 Del. Laws, c. 455, to implement the provisions of § 5532(o) of this title shall be treated as an actuarial loss during the next actuarial valuation process of the Special Pension Fund.

(r)(1) The State's obligation to the State Employees' Pension Plan, the State Judiciary Retirement Fund, and the New State Police Retirement Fund to implement the provisions of § 5532(p) of this title shall be the payment required to amortize the unfunded accrued liability over 5 years from January 1, 2015, pursuant to 5548 of this title.

(2) The State's obligation to the Special Pension Fund authorized by 61 Del. Laws, c. 455, to implement the provisions of § 5532(p) of this title shall be treated as an actuarial loss during the next actuarial valuation process of the Special Pension Fund.

(s)(1) The State's obligation to the State Employees' Pension Plan, the State Judiciary Retirement Fund, and the New State Police Retirement Fund to implement the provisions of § 5532(q) of this title shall be the payment required to amortize the unfunded accrued liability over 5 years from July 1, 2021, pursuant to § 5548 of this title.

(2) The State's obligation to the Special Pension Fund authorized by 61 Del. Laws, c. 455, to implement the provisions of § 5532(q) of this title shall be treated as an actuarial loss during the next actuarial valuation process of the Special Pension Fund.

History.
69 Del. Laws, c. 104, § 2; 69 Del. Laws, c. 105, § 3; 70 Del. Laws, c. 525, § 4; 71 Del. Laws, c. 165, § 3; 71 Del. Laws, c. 397, § 3; 72 Del. Laws, c. 152, § 3; 72 Del. Laws, c. 438, § 2; 72 Del. Laws, c. 447, § 3; 73 Del. Laws, c. 146, § 6; 74 Del. Laws, c. 183, § 3; 74 Del. Laws, c. 398, § 3; 75 Del. Laws, c. 136, § 3; 75 Del. Laws, c. 403, § 3; 76 Del. Laws, c. 70, § 7; 76 Del. Laws, c. 80, § 68; 78 Del. Laws, c. 116, §§ 3, 4; 78 Del. Laws, c. 289, § 2; 79 Del. Laws, c. 343, § 3; 83 Del. Laws, c. 54, § 32(c).

Effect of amendments.
83 Del. Laws, c. 54, effective June 30, 2021, added (s).

CHAPTER 56
PENSIONS FOR MEMBERS OF THE STATE JUDICIARY

§ 5600. Definitions.

Revisor's note.
Section 2g. of 83 Del. Laws, c. 55, effective June 30, 2021, provided: "This supplement [a one-time salary supplement of $1,000.00 for state employees] shall be considered within the pension definitions stated in 29 Del. C. § 5501 (c), §5501(d), §5501 (e), §5600 (3), and 11 Del. C. §8351 (2)."

CHAPTER 59
MERIT SYSTEM OF PERSONNEL ADMINISTRATION

Subchapter V. Miscellaneous
Sec.
5953. Discrimination prohibited.

SUBCHAPTER I
DEFINITIONS AND EXCLUSIONS

§ 5903. Classified service and exemptions.

Revisor's note.
Section 6 of 74 Del. Laws, c. 68; 78 Del. Laws, c. 78, § 6, effective July 1, 2011; 78 Del. Laws, c. 290, § 6, effective July 1, 2012; 79 Del. Laws, c. 78, § 6, effective July 1, 2013; 79 Del. Laws, c. 290, § 6, effective July 1, 2014; 80 Del. Laws, c. 79, § 6, effective July 1, 2015; 80 Del. Laws, c. 298, § 6, effective July 1, 2016; 81 Del. Laws, c. 58, § 6, effective July 3, 2017; 81 Del. Laws, c. 280, § 6, effective July 1, 2018; 82 Del. Laws, c. 64, § 6, effective July 1, 2019; 82 Del. Laws, c. 242, § 6, effective July 1, 2020; and 83 Del. Laws, c. 54, § 6, effective June 30, 2021, provided: "Due to the budget format, the restruc-

turing of divisions into programs within divisions has created more exempt positions per division than allowed by law for the participating departments; therefore, all exempt positions authorized by 29 Del. C. § 5903, prior to July 1, 1987, shall remain exempt for this current fiscal year, except as otherwise specified in this act."

Section 28 of 76 Del. Laws, c. 80, effective July 1, 2007; 77 Del. Laws, c. 84, § 24, effective July 1, 2009; 77 Del. Laws, c. 327, § 24, effective July 1, 2010; 78 Del. Laws, c. 78, § 26, effective July 1, 2011; 78 Del. Laws, c. 290, § 21, effective July 1, 2012; 79 Del. Laws, c. 78,

effective July 1, 2013; 79 Del. Laws, c. 290, § 20, effective July 1, 2014; and 80 Del. Laws, c. 79, § 19, effective July 1, 2015; 80 Del. Laws, c. 298, § 20, effective July 1, 2016; 81 Del. Laws, c. 58, § 26, effective July 3, 2017; 81 Del. Laws, c. 280, § 21, effective July 1, 2018; 82 Del. Laws, c. 64, § 21, effective July 1, 2019; 82 Del. Laws, c. 242, § 21, effective July 1, 2020; and 83 Del. Laws, c. 54, § 21, effective June 30, 2021, provided: "Notwithstanding any provision of the Delaware Code to the contrary, 29 Del. C. § 5207 shall not apply to individuals employed in accordance with 29 Del. C. § 5903(17)."

SUBCHAPTER III

RULES

§ 5915. Classification; uniformity; appeal of classification.

Revisor's note.

Section 8(d)(1) of 78 Del. Laws, c. 78, effective July 1, 2011; as amended by 78 Del. Laws, c. 290, § 8(d)(1), effective July 1, 2012; 79 Del. Laws, c. 78, § 8(d)(1), effective July 1, 2013; 79 Del. Laws, c. 290, § 8(d)(1), effective July 1, 2014; 80 Del. Laws, c. 79, § 8(d)(1), effective July 1, 2015; 80 Del. Laws, c. 298, § 8(d)(1), effective July 1, 2016; 81 Del. Laws, c. 58, § 8(d)(1), effective July 3, 2017; 81 Del. Laws, c. 280, § 8(d)(1), effective July 1, 2018; 82 Del. Laws, c. 64, § 8(d)(1), effective July 1, 2019; 82 Del. Laws, c. 242, § 8(d)(1), effective July 1, 2020; 82 Del. Laws, c. 243, § 25, effective July 1, 2020; and as amended by 83 Del. Laws, c. 54, § 8(d)(1), effective June 30, 2021, provided: "(d) MAINTENANCE REVIEWS. (1) Any such re-

classifications/regrades that the Secretary of the Department of Human Resources determines to be warranted as a result of the classification maintenance reviews regularly scheduled by the Department of Human Resources shall be designated to become effective the first day of the first full pay cycle following approval, provided that such reclassifications/regrades have been processed as part of the regular budgetary process and the funds for such reclassifications/regrades have been appropriated. Maintenance review classification determinations may be appealed to the Merit Employee Relations Board in accordance with 29 Del. C. § 5915. Pay grade determinations shall not be appealed."

SUBCHAPTER V

MISCELLANEOUS

§ 5953. Discrimination prohibited.

(a) For purposes of this section:

(1) "Protective hairstyle" includes braids, locks, and twists.

(2) "Race" includes traits historically associated with race, including hair texture and a protective hairstyle.

(b) A person may not be appointed or promoted to, or demoted or dismissed from, any position in the classified service, or be in any way favored or discriminated against with respect to employment in the classified service, because of political or religious opinions or affiliations, sexual orientation, gender identity, sex, or race.

History.

29 Del. C. 1953, § 5953; 55 Del. Laws, c. 443, § 1; 70 Del. Laws, c. 186, § 1; 77 Del. Laws, c. 90, § 22; 79 Del. Laws, c. 47, § 25; 83 Del. Laws, c. 13, § 23.

Effect of amendments.

83 Del. Laws, c. 13, effective April 13, 2021, added (a); and in (b), substituted "A person may not" for "No person shall" and added a comma following "service" and following "sex".

CHAPTER 60A

DEFERRED COMPENSATION FOR PUBLIC OFFICERS AND EMPLOYEES OF THE STATE

§ 6055. Payroll deductions.

Revisor's note.

Section 7(d) of 77 Del. Laws, c. 84, effective July 1, 2009; 77 Del. Laws, c. 327, effective July 1, 2010; 78 Del. Laws, c. 78, § 7(d), effective July 1, 2011; as amended by 78 Del. Laws, c. 290, § 7(e), effective July 1, 2012; 79 Del. Laws, c. 78, § 7(e) effective July 1, 2013; 79 Del. Laws, c. 290, § 7(e), effective July 1, 2014; 80 Del. Laws, c. 79, § 7(e), effective July 1, 2015; 80 Del. Laws, c. 298, § 7(e), effective July 1, 2016; 81 Del. Laws, c. 58, § 7(e), effective July 3, 2017; 81 Del. Laws, c. 280, § 7(e), effective July 1, 2018; 82 Del. Laws, c. 64, § 7(e), effec-tive July 1, 2019; 82 Del. Laws, c. 242, § 7(e), effective July 1, 2020; and 83 Del. Laws, c. 54, § 7(e), effective June 30, 2021, provided: "Not-withstanding 29 Del. C. c. 60A or any other provision of the Delaware Code or this act to the contrary, the employer contribution from state agencies and non-state entities to quali-fied participants of the Deferred Compensation Program shall be suspended beginning July 1, 2008. It is the intent of the General Assembly that this program be reinstated when funding becomes available."

§ 6061. Employer contribution to qualified participants [Suspended effective July 1, 2008; see 83 Del. Laws, c. 54, § 7(e)].

Revisor's note.

Section 7(d) of 77 Del. Laws, c. 84, effective July 1, 2009; 77 Del. Laws, c. 327, effective July 1, 2010; 78 Del. Laws, c. 78, § 7(d), effective July 1, 2011; as amended by 78 Del. Laws, c. 290, § 7(e), effective July 1, 2012; 79 Del. Laws, c. 78, § 7(e) effective July 1, 2013; 79 Del. Laws, c. 290, § 7(e), effective July 1, 2014; 80 Del. Laws, c. 79, § 7(e), effective July 1, 2015; 80 Del. Laws, c. 298, § 7(e), effective July 1, 2016; 81 Del. Laws, c. 58, § 7(e), effective July 3, 2017; 81 Del. Laws, c. 280, § 7(e), effective July 1, 2018; 82 Del. Laws, c. 64, § 7(e), effec-tive July 1, 2019; 82 Del. Laws, c. 242, § 7(e), effective July 1, 2020; and 83 Del. Laws, c. 54, § 7(e), effective June 30, 2021, provided: "Not-withstanding 29 Del. C. c. 60A or any other provision of the Delaware Code or this act to the contrary, the employer contribution from state agencies and non-state entities to quali-fied participants of the Deferred Compensation Program shall be suspended beginning July 1, 2008. It is the intent of the General Assembly that this program be reinstated when funding becomes available."

PART VI

BUDGET, FISCAL, PROCUREMENT AND CONTRACTING REGULATIONS

CHAPTER 61

GENERAL FUND

§ 6102. Composition of General Fund; Delaware Higher Education Loan Program Fund.

(a) Except as otherwise specifically provided by law, all receipts and moneys of this State shall be deposited by or to the credit of the State Treasurer in 1 General Fund. The General Fund shall include all moneys derived from taxes, fees, permits, licenses, fines, forfeitures or from any other sources or of other receipts of any kind or from any other source including the sale or disposition of surplus or other property of the State and of every agency thereof including receipts heretofore authorized as funds for specific use of any agency by the authority of any law of this State, but not including funds specified by the Constitution of the State to the extent thereof only and not including funds derived from the sale of bonds for the specific purposes named therein, and not including funds or receipts or grants made for a particular purpose pursuant to an act of Congress of the United States, and not including any endowment fund or gift made for particular purposes and not including any sinking fund authorized by the laws of this State. This section shall be construed to include moneys formerly credited to the School Fund except that all sums required to be credited to such School Fund by the Constitution of this State shall continue to be credited to the School Fund to the extent thereof only.

(b) Nothing in this chapter shall be construed to deprive any agency of the right to receive and expend, for the purpose for which they were collected, any proceeds collected for board, tuition or hospital treatment and from the sale of farm products, and this chapter shall have no application to any money or other property received by the University of Delaware, Delaware State University or Delaware Technical and Community College from any source except money appropriated to it, or for its use, by the General Assembly of the State.

(c) If an agency, in the process of replacing an item of state-owned equipment, should sell such equipment, the proceeds of the sale may be credited to the appropriate General Fund appropriation account of the agency and applied toward the cost of the replacement in accordance with regulations established by the Director of the Office of Management and Budget.

(d) This section notwithstanding, the State Board of Education shall be authorized to charge a rental rate for portable classrooms owned by the State and to use the proceeds for necessary repairs or lease purchase of additional portable classrooms.

(e) All money which has been appropriated by the General Assembly now deposited in a special fund account, as well as all money hereafter appropriated by the General Assembly to Delaware Higher Education Loan Program, hereinafter called the agency, established by Executive Order 40, dated August 27, 1970, for the use in and purpose of carrying out the function of the Delaware Higher Education Loan Program established under the provisions of the United States Higher Education Act of 1965 (20 U.S.C. § 1001 et seq.), shall be deposited by or to the credit of the State Treasurer in 1 special fund account to be known as the Delaware Higher Education Loan Program Fund. In addition, the following money or receipts shall be deposited by or to the credit of the State Treasurer in the Delaware Higher Education Loan Program Fund:

(1) Money or receipts advanced by the federal government for carrying out the program of the agency;

(2) Money or receipts received by the agency as loan insurance premiums;

(3) Money or receipts received by the agency through gift, grant or by other means from other sources;

(4) Money or receipts collected on defaulted loans by the agency after expenses of collection; or

(5) Money or receipts in the nature of interest or other earnings derived from the investment by the State Treasurer thereof.

The money or receipts deposited in or credited to the Delaware Higher Education Loan Program Fund shall not be part of the General Fund of the State and shall not be commingled with the money or receipts of the General Fund or of any other special fund of the State.

(f) All moneys collected pursuant to Chapter 73 of Title 6, other than those which are to be deposited in or transferred to the Investor Protection Fund pursuant to § 73-703 of Title 6, shall be part of the General Fund. The Attorney General shall specifically include in the Attorney General's annual operational budget the salaries, including, but not limited to, the salary of the Deputy Attorney General appointed Securities Commissioner, and other expenses of administering Chapter 73 of Title 6 which are not met by the Investor Protection Fund.

(g) All revenue collected by the Division of Child Support Services, as established under the Social Services Amendments of 1974 (P.L. 93-647, 42 U.S.C. § 651 et seq.) pursuant to its functions under the Division of Child Support Services and Paternity Program, except for an amount to be specified annually in the budget act as an appropriated special fund which shall be considered an incentive payment to enable the Division to increase child support collections, shall be deposited into a special fund account known as the Division of Child Support Services Account. The revenue deposited into the Division of Child Support Services Account shall not be a part of the General Fund of the State and shall only be handled in accordance with § 457 of the Social Services Amendments of 1974 (42 U.S.C. § 657). Further, such portions of these funds deposited to the credit of the Division of Child Support Services Account, as shall be periodically determined to belong to the State, shall be deposited to the credit of the General Fund of the State.

(h) Nothing in this chapter shall be construed to deprive the Delaware State Housing Authority of the right to receive and expend, for operating costs, replacements and maintenance, rental and operating income from housing managed by said Authority and to maintain separate internal funds accounts and reserve accounts for such purposes; provided, further, that any interest or other earnings which accrue on balances in any accounts managed by the Delaware State Housing Authority shall not be deposited in the General Fund except on General Fund appropriations.

(i) Provisions of this chapter to the contrary notwithstanding, the Delaware Emergency Management Agency shall have the right to apply for, receive and expend funds or grants, pursuant to contracts or otherwise, from public or private sources, for operating expenses associated with the Delaware radiological emergency plan, and to have such funds maintained in a special fund account for such purposes.

(j) Other provisions of this section notwithstanding, certain funds deposited by a reorganized school district shall be credited to the local fund account of that district. Funds so credited shall include:

    (1) Library funds;

    (2) Payments for lost or damaged equipment, books, supplies and materials of the school;

    (3) Payment for damaged real property of the school district;

    (4) Parking permits;

    (5) Any other income derived from fees, permits, licenses, fines or forfeitures.

    (k)(1) Provisions of this chapter to the contrary notwithstanding, the Office of Management and Budget is authorized to establish and maintain a special fund for the purposes of improving statewide, departmental, and divisional indirect cost recoveries from programs financed in whole or in part with federal funds. The Director of the Office of Management and Budget, with the approval of the Controller General, may enter into such contracts and employ such people or services as the Director deems necessary to increase the amounts of and monitor the receipt of indirect cost recoveries to the State. Specifically, this fund may reimburse the State Auditor's office for federal audits performed if the audited agency has deposited sufficient federal funds to compensate the Auditor of Accounts for services rendered. Federal reimbursements deposited in such special fund, and not required to carry out the purposes described in this section, shall be transferred to the General Fund. The Director of the Office of Management and Budget will make periodic reports of progress toward increased indirect cost reimbursements to the Delaware State Clearinghouse Committee at such time as the chairperson may determine.

(2) The Indirect Cost Recovery Program is authorized to recover indirect costs from nonfederal special funded regulatory and service agencies. Costs that are allocated to a state agency under this authority shall be billed to the state agency, and the cost is payable to the Office of Management and Budget. The source of payment for the billed indirect cost shall be any revenue source except the General Fund. If the billed agency is authorized to bill and recover direct expenses, the agency shall recover indirect costs in the same manner.

(*l*) Provisions of this chapter to the contrary notwithstanding, the Business Enterprise Program, operated by the Division for the Visually Impaired within the Department of Health and Social Services under the authority of 20 U.S.C. § 107 et seq., shall be authorized to expend receipts from the vending stands in the Program for operating costs, maintenance and overhead.

(m)(1) A Revenue Management Unit shall be established, within the Division of Business Administration and General Services, for the administration of all responsibilities and duties related to the revenue collection function of the institutions and agencies operated by the Department, including all policies and procedures pertaining to the administration of subchapter III of Chapter 79 of this title.

(2) An appropriated special fund (ASF) is to be designated as the Department of Health and Social Services Revenue Management Fund, which shall be used for the operation of the Revenue Management Unit, to be funded through the Department revenues which the Unit collects. On or about July 1 of each fiscal year, the total amount of the ASF appropriation for this Unit for the fiscal year shall be deposited in the aforementioned holding account. At the close of the fiscal year, the unspent and unencumbered balance in said line shall revert to the General Fund.

(n) Notwithstanding any other provision of law to the contrary, every fee or other charge for a license or permit (whether the revenue generated has been deposited in the General Fund or in an appropriated special fund account) which is in effect and was imposed before July 2, 1990, by any authority, department, agency, instrumentality, commission, officer, board or other unit of state government which is authorized by law to issue such license or permit is hereby approved and ratified by the General Assembly retroactive to the date each such fee or other charge was imposed or increased.

(o)(1) Notwithstanding other provisions of this chapter, there shall be established a special fund of the State to be known as the "Inspection and Maintenance Fund" (referred to in this subsection as "the I & M Fund").

(2) The Secretary of Finance shall, commencing at the beginning of each fiscal year, cause to be deposited into the I & M Fund amounts received as payments of costs assessed by the Justice of the Peace Courts relating to traffic and criminal cases under § 9801(2) of Title 10 [repealed], until the amount deposited in said fiscal year shall equal $2,800,000.

(3) The purpose of the I & M Fund is to provide operating expenses associated with the Delaware Motor Vehicle Enhanced Inspection and

Maintenance Program. Any balance in the I & M Fund as of the last day of the fiscal year in excess of $250,000 shall be deposited into the General Fund.

(4) The Secretary of Finance shall make deposits into the I & M Fund as required under this section commencing after June 30, 1995.

(p) [Transferred.]

(q)(1) A special fund of the State is created in the Department of Finance to be known as the "Elderly Property Tax Relief and Education Expense Fund," to which shall be deposited $13,000,000 received in any revenue source not otherwise committed to a special fund and from which shall be paid claims made under this subsection and § 1919(d) of Title 14. Should such claims exceed $13,000,000 during any fiscal year, the Secretary of Finance, with the approval of the Director of the Office of Management and Budget and Controller General, may transfer from the general contingency line in the Department of Education to the Elderly Property Tax Relief and Education Expense Fund the amount of such reasonably foreseen additional claims. Any balance remaining in the Elderly Property Tax Relief and Education Expense Fund at the conclusion of any fiscal year shall revert to the General Fund.

(2) Sums appropriated pursuant to this subsection shall be allocated to school districts using a method that recognizes factors including, but not limited to, the number of primary residential households owned by persons 65 or over who meet the durational residency requirement of § 1917(c) of Title 14 in each school district, the relative value of residential property owned by persons 65 and over, the relative property values of each school district, the school tax rates of each school district, and the average rate of application for tax relief pursuant to this subsection. The final method and allocation of these moneys shall be approved by the Secretary of Finance in consultation with the Controller General.

(3) Local school boards shall decide through majority vote of the whole school board whether to authorize a credit against taxation imposed pursuant to Chapter 19 of Title 14 on the valuation of any qualified property, as defined in § 1917(c) of Title 14. The maximum such credit shall be the lesser of 50% of such tax remaining after taking into account any exemption pursuant to Title 9 and Title 22, or $500. The receiver of taxes and county treasurer shall apply such credit after any change to the current expense tax rate pursuant to this section. Should the local school board decide to authorize less than the maximum amount of credit against taxation, the local school board shall develop a plan for using moneys received pursuant to this subsection, provide appropriate and reasonable public notice and comment on the proposed plan, and approve the plan through majority vote of the local school board. Local school boards shall submit the approved plan to the Secretary of Finance, the Secretary of Education, the Director of the Office of Management and Budget and the Controller General. In the event that local school boards choose not to authorize the aforementioned credit against taxation, the sums appropriated herein will result in increased state funding for education-related expenses of the school districts. Education-related expenses for the purposes of this subsection shall be defined as including, but not being limited to, computer hardware and software, library resources and other instructional materials, and minor capital improvements to school facilities. Local school boards and all other responsible parties under this paragraph are hereby directed to cause such conditions to be met as soon as practicable after the enactment of this section, but in no event later than

October 30, 1999, and shall notify the Secretary of Finance and the Controller General as soon as such conditions are met. Notwithstanding any of the foregoing to the contrary, funds received pursuant to this section shall not be used for major capital improvements or debt service.

(r)(1) A special fund of the State is created in the Department of Finance to be known as the "Disabled Veterans Property Tax Relief and Education Expense Fund," to which shall be deposited $1,000,000 received in any revenue source not otherwise committed to a special fund and from which shall be paid claims made under this subsection and § 1919(e) of Title 14. Should such claims exceed $1,000,000 during any fiscal year, the Secretary of Finance, with the approval of the Director of the Office of Management and Budget and Controller General, may transfer from the general contingency line in the Department of Education to the Disabled Veterans Property Tax Relief and Education Expense Fund the amount of such reasonably foreseen additional claims. Any balance remaining in the Disabled Veterans Fund at the conclusion of any fiscal year shall revert to the General Fund.

(2) Sums appropriated pursuant to this subsection shall be allocated to school districts using a method that recognizes factors including, but not limited to, the number of primary residential households owned by disabled veterans in each school district, the relative value of residential property owned by disabled veterans, the relative property values of each school district, the school tax rates of each school district, and the average rate of application for tax relief pursuant to this subsection. The final method and allocation of these moneys shall be approved by the Secretary of Finance in consultation with the Controller General.

(3) Local school boards shall decide through majority vote of the whole school board whether to authorize a credit against taxation imposed pursuant to Chapter 19 of Title 14 on the valuation of any qualified property, as defined in § 1917(d) of Title 14. The credit shall be for the full amount of tax remaining after taking into account any exemption pursuant to Title 9 and Title 22. The receiver of taxes and county treasurer shall apply such credit after any change to the current expense tax rate pursuant to this subsection. In the event that local school boards choose not to authorize the aforementioned credit against taxation, the sums appropriated herein will revert to the General Fund. In the first year after a school board authorizes a credit, the Secretary of Finance, in consultation with the receiver of taxes or county treasurer, shall determine the effective date of such credit based upon reasonable implementation requirements and operational capacity.

(s) Receipts received under Chapter 11 of Title 12, shall be deposited into the General Fund provided; however, that in no fiscal year shall such General Fund deposits exceed $554,000,000.

(t)(1) An appropriated special fund of the State to be known as the "Federal Fiscal Relief Fund" is hereby created in the Office of Management and Budget. The State Treasurer shall deposit all state assistance funds received under Title VI of the federal Social Security Act [42 U.S.C. § 801 (repealed)] to the Federal Fiscal Relief Fund.

(2) Moneys from the Federal Fiscal Relief Fund must be expended for Delaware's citizens in the following areas:

a. To provide essential government services;

b. To cover the costs to the State of complying with any federal intergovernmental mandate to the extent that the mandate applies to the State and the federal government has not provided funds to cover the costs; and

c. To make investments in those areas of highest priority of the General Assembly to the benefit of all Delawareans.

(3) The Federal Fiscal Relief Fund is an interest earning account. All interest earned must be reinvested in the Federal Fiscal Relief Fund.

(4) Money may not be expended from the Federal Fiscal Relief Fund except pursuant to an appropriation within the State's Bond and Capital Improvement Act or the annual Appropriations Act, or otherwise enacted by the General Assembly.

(u) All debt service payments collected by the State from local school districts with respect to the school districts' obligations issued to the State pursuant to § 7506 of this title, for the local share of school district capital projects shall be deposited in a special fund account to be known as the "School District Local Share Special Account." The amounts are to be deposited in said account to pay the debt service payable by the State with respect to general obligation bonds issued by the State. The holders of the general obligation bonds which are paid, in whole or in part, from the special account created pursuant to this subsection shall continue to have all the rights and remedies to which they are entitled under § 10, article VIII of the Constitution of this State and under Chapter 74 of this title.

Should the amount in said special fund account prove insufficient relative to the debt service obligations at any time during the fiscal year, the State Treasurer is hereby authorized to pay the obligation from any debt service account. Any interfund transaction so required shall be reversed when funding becomes available.

(v) Notwithstanding any other provision in law to the contrary, the Division of Medicaid and Medical Assistance shall be allowed to deposit the applicable state share of any drug rebate funds, drug settlement proceeds, including qui tam cases, third-party collections and other collections related to the provision of health care (minus retention amounts specified in state or federal law), as well as any fines, restitution or punitive damages related thereto into the appropriate Medicaid and Medical Assistance account and use them to meet program costs.

History.

42 Del. Laws, c. 77, § 1; 43 Del. Laws, c. 12; 29 Del. C. 1953, § 6102; 50 Del. Laws, c. 46, § 1; 50 Del. Laws, c. 406, § 1; 55 Del. Laws, c. 325; 57 Del. Laws, c. 196; 58 Del. Laws, c. 367; 59 Del. Laws, c. 208, § 3; 59 Del. Laws, c. 311, § 1; 60 Del. Laws, c. 281, § 1; 60 Del. Laws, c. 408, § 1; 60 Del. Laws, c. 444, § 1; 61 Del. Laws, c. 468, § 4; 62 Del. Laws, c. 172, § 1; 63 Del. Laws, c. 254, § 2; 64 Del. Laws, c. 50, § 1; 64 Del. Laws, c. 99, § 1; 64 Del. Laws, c. 334, § 165(a)-(c); 65 Del. Laws, c. 181, § 1; 66 Del. Laws, c. 190, § 15; 66 Del. Laws, c. 303, §§ 118, 175, 210; 67 Del. Laws, c. 259, § 1; 67 Del. Laws, c. 274, § 14; 69 Del. Laws, c. 67, § 2; 69 Del. Laws, c. 78, § 4; 69 Del. Laws, c. 172, § 1; 69 Del. Laws, c. 222, § 1; 70 Del. Laws, c. 186, § 1; 70 Del. Laws, c. 210, § 21; 72 Del. Laws, c. 251, § 1; 72 Del. Laws, c. 252, § 1; 72 Del. Laws, c. 256, § 1; 73 Del. Laws, c. 9, § 4; 73 Del. Laws, c. 310, § 3; 74 Del. Laws, c. 49, § 1; 75 Del. Laws, c. 88, § 21(13); 75 Del. Laws, c. 89, § 145; 75 Del. Laws, c. 350, § 165; 76 Del. Laws, c. 205, § 5; 76 Del. Laws, c. 288, § 11; 77 Del. Laws, c. 84, § 160; 78 Del. Laws, c. 76, § 15; 78 Del. Laws, c. 77, § 33(a); 78 Del. Laws, c. 78, § 108; 78 Del. Laws, c. 175, § 113; 79 Del. Laws, c. 79, § 29; 80 Del. Laws, c. 78, § 15; 80 Del. Laws, c. 234, § 24; 81 Del. Laws, c. 71, § 2; 81 Del. Laws, c. 78, § 12; 83 Del. Laws, c. 124, § 3.

Revisor's note.

Section 4 of 83 Del. Laws, c. 124, provided: "This act takes effect upon enactment." The act became effective upon the signature of the Governor on Aug. 10, 2021.

Section 5 of 83 Del. Laws, c. 124, provided: "In FY 2022, the Secretary of Finance may use up to 5% of the amount appropriated for the Disabled Veterans Property Tax Relief and Education Expense Fund established pursuant to this act to offset administrative expenses. The Secretary of Finance shall pay over to each receiver of taxes and county treasurer an amount equal to 2% of the amount appropriated for the Disabled Veterans Property Tax Relief and Education Expense Fund established pursuant to this act to offset administrative expenses." The act became effective upon the signature of the Governor on Aug. 10, 2021."

Effect of amendments.

83 Del. Laws, c. 124, effective Aug. 10, 2021, substituted "§ 1919(d)" for "§ 1919" in the first

sentence of (q)(1); substituted "subsection" for "section" in two places in the first sentence of (q)(2); substituted "§1917(c)" for "§ 1917" in the first sentence of (q)(2) and (3); and added (r).

CHAPTER 63
BUDGET COMMISSION AND APPROPRIATIONS
SUBCHAPTER III
BUDGET APPROPRIATION BILL

§ 6341. Grants-in-aid.

Revisor's note.

82 Del. Laws, c. 243, § 7, effective July 1, 2020; and 83 Del. Laws, c. 57, § 7, effective June 30, 2021, provided: "Beginning with the Fiscal Year 2023 application period, an agency must not request funding for a Grant-in-Aid appropriation through a fiscal agent. Organiza- tions already receiving Grant-in-Aid funding who use fiscal agents will continue to receive funding but must be in compliance by the application period for the Fiscal Year 2023 to be considered for an appropriation in future fiscal years."

CHAPTER 64
BUDGET APPROPRIATION BILL POLICIES AND PROCEDURES

§ 6404. General provisions.

Revisor's note.

Section 122 of 77 Del. Laws, c. 84, effective July 1, 2009, as amended by 77 Del. Laws, c. 327, § 115, effective July 1, 2010; 78 Del. Laws, c. 78, § 112, effective July 1, 2011; 78 Del. Laws, c. 290, § 104, effective July 1, 2012; 79 Del. Laws, c. 78, § 102, effective July 1, 2013; 79 Del. Laws, c. 290, § 106, effective July 1, 2014; 80 Del. Laws, c. 79, § 107, effective July 1, 2015; 80 Del. Laws, c. 298, § 110, effective July 1, 2016; 81 Del. Laws, c. 58, § 111, effective July 3, 2017; 81 Del. Laws, c. 280, § 94, effective July 1, 2018; 82 Del. Laws, c. 64, § 91, effective July 1, 2019; as amended by 82 Del. Laws, c. 242, § 89, effective July 1, 2020; and 83 Del. Laws, c. 54, § 92, effective June 30, 2021, provided: "Notwithstanding the provisions of 29 Del. C. § 6404(h)(1) and (2), the Department of Justice shall be allowed to retain the federal reimbursement of direct costs in an ASF account to pay the ASF share of operating expenses associated with the Child Support Services function.

"The Department of Justice shall also be allowed to retain up to a maximum of $30.0 of the departmental portion of indirect cost recoveries for this function to support the agency's overhead and $16.3 to be applied to the State's share for four clerical positions. The statewide portion of indirect cost recoveries will be deposited into the indirect cost account in the Office of Management and Budget. The remainder of the indirect cost recoveries and any unused portion of indirect cost funds in the Department of Justice will be deposited into a separate account and retained to support the General Fund portion of the budget for this function in subsequent years.

Adjustments to ASF spending authority for the Department of Justice may be made upon the concurrence and approval of the Director of the Office of Management and Budget and the Controller General."

CHAPTER 64A
BOND AND CAPITAL IMPROVEMENT ACT POLICIES AND PROCEDURES

Sec.
6405A. Department of Transportation.

§ 6405A. Department of Transportation.

(a) Any funds appropriated from any source to the Department of Transportation shall be accounted for by program category as specified in the Section 1 Addendum of the Annual Bond and Capital Improvement Act. Amounts indicated for individual projects in the "Supplemental Information for Transportation Projects" are the Department's best estimates of cost, but may vary depending on bid results and project designs. The descriptions and limits are general in nature and are to be used only for project identification purposes. It is the intent of the General Assembly that the Department of Transportation make all reasonable efforts to ensure the timely completion of projects subject to the limitation of the total funds available in each program.

(b) The Department is directed to continue inspecting the condition of bridges and pavements in the State and to use the Road System Program funds made available by the Annual Bond and Capital Improvement Acts and the Bridge Program, the Rehabilitation and Reconstruction Program, and the Pave and Rehabilitation Program funds made available by previous acts to ensure the bridge repairs and replacements and pavement resurfacings and rehabilitations are carried out in an expeditious manner based on the Department's priority and management systems.

(c) It is the intent of the General Assembly that the Co-Chairs of the Joint Legislative Committee on the Capital Improvement Program shall be delegated the responsibility of approving modifications to the list of paving and rehabilitation projects in the "Road System" portion of the "Supplemental Information for Transportation Projects" when the Department of Transportation needs such modifications. These changes may be made subject to the Co-Chairs' approval, when:

(1) The Department has completed or determined that it has sufficient funds on hand to complete projects in the program category; or

(2) When projects so listed cannot be constructed in the construction season covered by the Annual Bond and Capital Improvement Act because of conflicting public works projects in progress or scheduled, or for other compelling reasons; and

(3) Funds appropriated to the Road System program category are available for use on additional or other projects fitting within that category.

In modifying the list, the Department must substitute the next suitable paving and rehabilitation project or projects from the most recently approved Department of Transportation Capital Transportation Program or based on the Department's Road System priority and management systems. A copy of the changes should be forwarded to the Director of the Office of Management and Budget and Controller General.

(d) Any funds appropriated from the Community Transportation Fund (XX/00) of the "Supplemental Information For Transportation Projects" attached hereto may be designated for Greenways having a transportation component as long as those Greenways will be dedicated to public use. Legislators may designate moneys to be appropriated into a general pooled account to be used statewide, or may reserve moneys for Greenways projects to be designated at a later time, or may designate specific sums of moneys to specific Greenways projects. For the purposes of this section, a project shall be deemed to have a "transportation component" whenever it involves walkways, pathways, bikeways, trails or other routes for the movement of people or goods. Project estimates shall be prepared by the Department of Natural Resources and Environmental Control (DNREC) and processed through the Department of Transportation's (DOT) Community Transportation Fund procedure for inclusion in the Capital Improvement Act by the General Assembly. Funds appropriated through an Annual Bond and Capital Improvement Act will be funded from the Transportation Trust Fund and transferred to DNREC by DOT. DNREC will be responsible for the design, rights-of-way purchasing, construction and maintenance of such Greenways and establishing a process similar to DOT's process for administering the Community Transportation Fund. The Delaware Transportation Authority shall have the authority to use its powers granted under Chapter 13 of Title 2 to acquire property for

Greenways projects having a transportation component dedicated to public use, and to transfer the property so acquired to the Department of Natural Resources and Environmental Control or to a local government accepting responsibility for the projects' development, ownership and operation.

(e) The Department of Transportation is hereby authorized to explore and/or construct feasible alternatives to traffic signals, including, but not limited to, geometric design changes to intersections or crossovers, in the vicinity of those locations where traffic signals may currently exist or otherwise be considered as warranted.

(f) The Delaware Transit Corporation ("DTC") administers a program to provide assistance to certain qualifying agencies for the transportation of the elderly, persons with disabilities, and thereafter for others needing transportation services, under the provisions of 49 U.S.C. § 5310 ("5310 Program"). The 5310 Program requires the qualifying agencies to agree to comply with the program's rules and regulations, and the agencies compete for funding in an annual certification/approval process. The normal match of federal funds to other funds is on an 80/20 funds basis. The following provisions shall apply in the DTC's administration of the 5310 Program.

(1) In ranking applicants for the 5310 Program, enhanced scoring of the applications will be given first to those qualifying applicants emphasizing the replacement of their existing fleet, and second to those qualifying applicants who provide a contributing share commitment larger than the normal nonfederal ratio, thus expanding the leverage provided by the federal funds available for the 5310 Program. These additional funds shall not be used as a replacement for Transit System funds or federal funds for this program, but shall be applied to this program in addition to the amount authorized in the Annual Bond and Capital Improvement Act.

(2) In administering the 5310 Program, the DTC shall take steps to assure that the qualifying applicant agencies use these vehicles first for program related needs, then to meet the transportation needs of elderly persons and persons with disabilities who do not participate in the agencies' programs, and finally for other local transportation needs, as required by federal regulations. In keeping these commitments and providing DTC-originated trips beyond the qualifying agencies program needs, those agencies receiving funds from the Kent/Sussex reimbursable line (55-06-01-85-83) Kent and Sussex Transportation shall be reimbursed at a rate of twice the applicable DTC fare. All other agencies providing such DTC-originated trips shall be reimbursed at a rate of 3 times the applicable DTC fare. Agencies providing such trips will be responsible for collection of and accounting for fares in accordance with DTC guidelines. Receipt of such fares and reimbursement to the qualifying agencies shall occur on a monthly basis between DTC and the agencies.

History.
72 Del. Laws, c. 489, § 25; 73 Del. Laws, c. 95, §§ 84(e)(2)-(4); 75 Del. Laws, c. 88, § 21(13); 83 Del. Laws, c. 37, § 29.

Effect of amendments.
83 Del. Laws, c. 37, effective June 3, 2021,

substituted "Transportation" for "Improvement" preceding "Program" in the first sentence of the concluding paragraph of (c).

CHAPTER 65
BUDGET AND FISCAL REGULATIONS FOR STATE AGENCIES

§ 6529. Control of agency expenditures.

Revisor's note.

Section 56 of 74 Del. Laws, c. 307, as amended by 77 Del. Laws, c. 327, effective July 1, 2010, § 63; 78 Del. Laws, c. 78, § 63, effective July 1, 2011; 78 Del. Laws, c. 290, § 59, effective July 1, 2012; 79 Del. Laws, c. 78, § 57, effective July 1, 2013; 79 Del. Laws, c. 290, § 60, effective July 1, 2014; 80 Del. Laws, c. 79, § 59, effective July 1, 2015; 80 Del. Laws, c. 298, § 63, effective July 1, 2016; 81 Del. Laws, c. 58, § 65, effective July 3, 2017; 81 Del. Laws, c. 280, § 61, effective July 1, 2018; 82 Del. Laws, c. 64, § 56, effective July 1, 2019; 82 Del. Laws, c. 242, § 55, effective July 1, 2020; and 83 Del. Laws, c. 54, § 56, effective June 30, 2021, provided:

"(a) For the current fiscal year, 29 Del. C. § 6529 is interpreted to include the ability to implement a hiring review process. All state agencies with the exception of Legislative, Judicial, Higher Education and school districts shall be subject to the provisions of 29 Del. C. § 6529 as interpreted by this section. Imple-

mentation of a hiring review process shall require all positions to be reviewed and approved by the Secretary of the Department of Human Resources and the Director of the Office of Management and Budget prior to filling. All non-cabinet agency hiring requests shall also require the review and approval of the Controller General prior to filling.

"(b) In the event the authority granted in subsection (a) of this section is implemented, Chapters 3.0 and 13.0 of the Merit Rules notwithstanding, the Secretary of the Department of Human Resources and the Director of the Office of Management and Budget shall have the authority to extend temporary promotions based on agency need until the hiring review process has ended. At the time the hiring review process has ended, those temporary promotions granted during the hiring review process shall be subject to the limitations identified in the Merit Rules governing the duration of temporary promotions."

CHAPTER 69
STATE PROCUREMENT

Revisor's note.

Section 30(a) of 78 Del. Laws, c. 78, effective July 1, 2011; 78 Del. Laws, c. 290, § 24(a), effective July 1, 2012; 79 Del. Laws, c. 78, § 24(a), effective July 1, 2013; 79 Del. Laws, c. 290, § 24(a), effective July 1, 2014; 80 Del. Laws, c. 79, § 22(a), effective July 1, 2015; 80 Del. Laws, c. 298, § 24(a), effective July 1, 2016; 81 Del. Laws, c. 58, § 29(a), effective July 3, 2017; 81 Del. Laws, c. 280, § 24(a), effective July 1, 2018; 82 Del. Laws, c. 64, § 24(a),

effective July 1, 2019; 82 Del. Laws, c. 242, § 24(a), effective July 1, 2020; and 83 Del. Laws, c. 54, § 24(a), effective June 30, 2021, provided: "(a) For the purposes of meeting the public notice and advertising requirements of 29 Del. C. c. 69, the announcement of bid solicitations and associated notices for the required duration on www.bids.delaware.gov shall satisfy the public notice and advertisement requirements under this chapter."

SUBCHAPTER I
GENERAL PROVISIONS

§ 6902. Definitions [For application of this section, see 82 Del. Laws, c. 36, § 3].

For purposes of this chapter:

(1) "Agency" means every board, department, bureau, commission, person or group of persons or other authority which directly receives moneys under any budget appropriation act or supplemental appropriation act and which was created and now exists or hereafter is created to:

    a. Execute, supervise, control and/or administer governmental functions under the laws of this State; and/or

    b. To perform such governmental functions under the laws of this State, or to perform such other duties as may be prescribed; and/or

    c. To collect and/or use any taxes, fees, licenses, permits or other receipts for service or otherwise for the performance of any function or related to or supported in whole or in part by the laws of this State; and/or

    d. To administer any laws providing for the collection of taxes, fees, permits, licenses or other forms of receipts from any sources whatsoever for the use of the State or any agency of the State.

"Agency" shall include Delaware Technical and Community College and the Delaware State University but shall not include any local government unit or agency receiving only grants-in-aid appropriations from the State and no other appropriations, as described herein, the University of Delaware, volunteer ambulance/rescue companies, volunteer fire departments and the Delaware Transit Corporation. Nothing in this paragraph shall be deemed to exempt any entity that is otherwise required to comply with § 6960 of this title.

(2) "Agency head" means the top official in an agency whether elected, appointed or otherwise. The agency head may delegate duties under this chapter to a designee within the agency.

(3) "Agency official" means any employee, consultant, person in the category of other personal service or any other person receiving compensation from the State, its agencies, municipalities, political subdivisions or school boards.

(4) "Compensation" means the total amount paid by an agency for professional services, including reimbursed expenses, unless otherwise stated in the contract.

(5) "Contractor" means any person, partnership, firm, corporation, nonprofit agency or other business association who has a contract with an agency.

(6) "Covered agency" means any agency except school districts, Delaware Technical & Community College, the Delaware State University and the Legislative Branch of State government.

(7) "Craft training program" means an apprenticeship program approved by and registered with any state apprenticeship agency or the United States Department of Labor.

(8) "Director" means, for the purposes of this chapter, the Director of the Office of Management and Budget, except as provided by § 6960 of this title, in which case it shall mean the Secretary of the Department of Labor.

(9) "Electronic bid" means the bidder, in response to an advertised invitation to bid, submits all documentation, except for information and documents specified in the invitation to bid, only through an electronic process to an identified secure electronic mail account that will not be opened by the Office or an agency until the close of the bidding period. In this process, no hard copy documentation shall be submitted to the Office or an agency prior to the award of the contract.

(10) "Electronic procurement advertising system" means the advertising system on which all state agencies must submit public notice of contracts subject to the public advertising requirements of this chapter.

(11) "Electronic submission" means the vendor, in response to an advertised request for proposal, submits all documentation, unless specified in the request for proposal, only through an electronic process to an identified secure electronic mail account that will not be opened by the Office or an agency until the close of the request for proposal submittal period. In this process, no hard copy is to be submitted to the Office or an agency after the close of the request for proposal submittal period unless specifically requested by the Office or agency.

(12) "Firm" means a person, organization, partnership, limited partnership, corporation, association, nonprofit agency or other business association.

(13) "Internet" means the international computer network of both federal and nonfederal interoperable packet switched data networks, including the graphical subnetwork called the world wide web.

(14) "Labor supply ratio" means the number of skilled crafts persons per unskilled workers employed on a public works project. Any person who has completed a federal apprenticeship program, an apprenticeship program approved by the Delaware Department of Labor under Chapter 2 of Title 19, or has otherwise documented 8 years of experience in a particular craft, is deemed to be a skilled crafts person for the purposes of this definition.

(15) "Lifecycle costing analysis" means the contracting agency's evaluation of costs associated with the cost of acquisition, the cost of energy consumption required for operation, the cost of maintenance and the cost of consumables that affect the State's overall cost of ownership of equipment or public works projects. Such evaluation is used by the contracting agency or project architect or project engineer for the development of contract specifications.

(16) "Local government unit" means any municipality incorporated in this State under the authority of the General Assembly and any of the 3 counties.

(17) "Materiel" means materials, equipment, tools, supplies, or any other personal property, but does not include real property or electric, gas, water, telephone or similar utilities.

(18) "Office" means the Office of Management and Budget; as provided in § 6960 of this title, "Department" shall mean the Department of Labor.

(19) "On-line bidding method" means a procurement process in which the Office or an agency receives vendors' bids electronically over the Internet as either a substitute for a hard copy bid submission or in a real-time, competitive bidding event.

(20) "Professional services" means services which generally require specialized education, training or knowledge and involve intellectual skills. Examples of professional services include, but are not limited to, engineering, environmental engineering, environmental monitoring, land surveying, landscape architecture, geology, architectural, archaeologists, architectural historians, historians, educational consultants, management, medical, teaching, planning, computer information management, financial, accounting, auditing, construction management and arbitration services. Professional services subject to the provisions of § 2507 of this title or which require compliance with Delaware Supreme Court Rule 52 or a substantially similar rule of another state shall not be included in this definition and shall not be subject to this chapter.

(21) "Public building" means any edifice or building which is or is to be constructed, reconstructed, altered or repaired pursuant to a public works

contract. It does not mean the act or process itself of constructing, reconstructing, altering or repairing.

(22) "Public funds" means funds of the State, of any agency within the State, of any public school district, of or from the United States government or of or from any department or representative body thereof.

(23) "Public works contract" means construction, reconstruction, demolition, alteration and repair work and maintenance work paid for, in whole or in part, with public funds.

(24) "Reverse auctioning" means an on-line procurement method wherein bidders bid on specified goods and nonprofessional services through real-time electronic competitive bidding, with the award being made to the lowest responsive and responsible bidder. During the bidding process, bidders' prices are public and are revealed electronically, and bidders shall have the opportunity to modify their bid prices for the duration of the time period established for the auction.

(25) "Section" means the Section of Government Support Services in the Office of Management and Budget.

(26) "Third tier contractor" means a firm that has contracted with a subcontractor to provide services and/or materiel in connection with a public works contract.

(27) "User group" means 2 or more agency or nonagency representatives, one of whom shall be an agency representative who provides technical advice to the Government Support Services concerning the requirements of certain materiel and nonprofessional services contracts. Nonagency representatives shall be limited to expected users of the materiel and/or services being procured and/or persons having technical expertise deemed necessary by the agency. In no event shall nonagency representatives be affiliated with a vendor or prospective vendor of the contract.

(28) "Volunteer ambulance/rescue companies" means a volunteer ambulance or rescue company certified as such by the State Fire Prevention Commission.

(29) "Volunteer fire department" means a volunteer fire department recognized as such by the State Fire Prevention Commission.

(30) "Z score" means a calculation used to assess a bidder's fiscal health. The calculation is based on the following weighted ratios: return on total assets, sales to total assets, equity to debt, working capital to total assets, and retained earnings to total assets.

History.

29 Del. C. 1953, § 6901; 54 Del. Laws, c. 106, § 2; 61 Del. Laws, c. 386, § 1; 62 Del. Laws, c. 306, § 1; 66 Del. Laws, c. 298, § 1; 70 Del. Laws, c. 601, § 3; 71 Del. Laws, c. 4, § 1; 71 Del. Laws, c. 309, §§ 1-3; 72 Del. Laws, c. 133, § 2; 73 Del. Laws, c. 143, § 5; 73 Del. Laws, c. 416, §§ 1-3; 73 Del. Laws, c. 438, § 1; 74 Del. Laws, c. 359, § 1; 74 Del. Laws, c. 373, § 1; 74 Del. Laws, c. 419, §§ 1, 2; 75 Del. Laws, c. 88, §§ 16(5), 22(4); 78 Del. Laws, c. 288, § 1; 81 Del. Laws, c. 298, § 1; 82 Del. Laws, c. 36, § 1; 83 Del. Laws, c. 129, § 3.

Revisor's note.

Section 6 of 83 Del. Laws, c. 129, provided:

"This act is effective immediately and is to be implemented the earlier of the following:

"(1) Notice by the Secretary of Labor published in the Register of Regulations that final regulations to implement this act have been promulgated.

"(2) One year from the date of the act's enactment." The act was signed by the Governor on Sept. 9, 2021.

Effect of amendments.

83 Del. Laws, c. 129, effective Sept. 9, 2021, substituted "For purposes" for "As used in" in the introductory paragraph; and, in (7), deleted the second sentence, and in the remaining sentence added "program" in the defined phrase, and substituted "state" for "Delaware".

§ 6904. Exceptions.

(a) If any provision of this chapter conflicts or is inconsistent with any statute, rule or regulation of the federal government applicable to a project or activity, the cost of which is to be paid or reimbursed in whole or in part by the federal government, and due to such conflict or inconsistency the availability of federal funds may be jeopardized, such provision shall not apply to such project or activity. If any provisions of this chapter conflict or are inconsistent with Chapter 40 of Title 31, the provisions of Chapter 40 of Title 31 shall prevail and govern.

(b) This chapter shall not apply to any purchase of materials or services from the federal government or from the government of the State including any agency of the State, as defined in § 6902 of this title.

(c) This chapter shall not apply to contracts for the transportation of school children. Such contracts shall be submitted to the Secretary of Education through the Department of Education Transportation Office for approval.

(d) This chapter shall not apply to any purchase of library materials such as books, periodicals, subscriptions and software by libraries of any agency, nor shall this chapter apply to the purchase of services by libraries of any agency pursuant to Chapter 66 of this title.

(e) If no state contract exists for a certain good or service, covered agencies may procure that certain good or service under another agency's contract so long as the arrangement is agreeable to all parties. Agencies, other than covered agencies, may also procure such goods or services under another agency's contract when the arrangement is agreeable to all parties.

(f) Where, because of changed situations, unforeseen conditions, strikes or acts of God, a change order is determined to be necessary and is requested by the agency and not specified in the agency's solicitation or advertisement for bids and in the contract, as awarded, the awarding agency may issue a change order setting forth the change, addition or extra work required to be undertaken by the contractor on a contract, which shall not:

(1) Be subject to the competitive bidding requirements of this chapter; or

(2) Invalidate the contract; provided, that such change is within the scope of the contract as set forth in the standard specifications, special provisions or similar publication of the agency.

(g) All material required by any agency shall be purchased, except where hereinafter provided, and all work of a nonprofessional nature, except as hereinafter provided, which is not to be performed by employees of the agency shall be performed under a contract entered into pursuant to this subchapter and after competitive bidding as provided for in this section except that an agency may purchase material or contract for work to be performed without competitive bidding in the following instances:

(1) When the purchased material will be used by the Delaware Industries for the Blind within the Department of Health and Social Services as raw material for goods and services which the program manufactures and provides for resale or the purchased material will be used by the Business Enterprise Program of the Division for the Visually Impaired as supplies to operate the vending stands in the program;

(2) When material or services are on the procurement list published by the commission for the purchase of products and services of the blind and other severely disabled individuals those materiel or services shall be purchased in accordance with the procedure described in § 9605 of Title 16; or

(3) Where the purchased material or work which is the subject of the contract is necessary to enable the Department of Natural Resources and Environmental Control to engage in the preservation of the beaches of the

Atlantic Ocean and Delaware Bay shoreline of Delaware in accordance with the Beach Preservation Act, Chapter 68 of Title 7. Notwithstanding the foregoing, any such purchase must be approved by the Budget Commission prior to the commencement of any purchase of material or work.

(h) This chapter shall not apply to purchases of historical artifacts or art for the purpose of public display.

(i) A contract may be awarded without competition if the agency head, prior to the procurement, determines in writing that there is only 1 source for the required contract. Sole source procurement shall not be used unless there is sufficient evidence that there is only 1 source for the required contract and no other type of goods or service will satisfy the requirements of the agency. The agency shall examine cost or pricing data prior to an award under this subsection. Sole source procurement shall be avoided, except when no reasonable alternative sources exist. A written determination by the agency for the sole source procurement shall be included in the agency's contract file.

(j) This chapter shall not apply to any purchase of educational materials and supplies by post-secondary educational institutions participating in and benefiting from special educational discount and cooperative programs.

(k) This chapter shall not apply to the Wilmington Housing Authority in the procurement of goods and/or services when such goods and/or services are provided by primarily Wilmington Housing Authority resident-owned businesses.

(l) This chapter shall not apply to the office of the Commissioner of Elections or the several departments of elections in the purchase of material or work which is the subject of the contract and which is necessary to enable the Department of Elections to conduct a primary, general, special election or voter registration pursuant to Title 15.

(m) This chapter shall not apply to the Department of Education in the procurement of goods and/or services from the Data Service Center, University of Delaware, Delaware State University and Delaware Technical and Community College.

(n) This chapter shall not apply to contracts entered into by the Board of Pension Trustees, authorized pursuant to § 8308(c)(5) of this title, with respect to the procurement of financial services, including advisory, management and investment services relating to any fund administered by the Delaware Public Employees' Retirement System.

(o) [Repealed.]

History.
70 Del. Laws, c. 601, § 4; 71 Del. Laws, c. 4, § 5; 71 Del. Laws, c. 132, § 368; 71 Del. Laws, c. 378, § 112; 73 Del. Laws, c. 310, § 23; 76 Del. Laws, c. 80, § 67; 82 Del. Laws, c. 248, § 2; 82 Del. Laws, c. 248, § 3; 83 Del. Laws, c. 54, § 378.

Effect of amendments.
83 Del. Laws, c. 54, effective June 30, 2021, added "Data Service Center" in (m).

SUBCHAPTER II
CENTRAL CONTRACTING

§ 6913. Contracting and purchasing advisory council.

(a) There is established a Contracting and Purchasing Advisory Council to consist of all covered agency heads or their designee and 1 additional member representing all public school districts. The Administrator of the Section shall be a nonvoting member of the Council.

(b) The Director of the Office shall be the Council Chair.

(c) The purpose of the Council is to advise as to the effectiveness of and make recommendations for changes to the State's procurement laws, policies and practices to the Director of the Office and the Administrator of the Section.

(d) The Council shall be responsible for:

(1) Recommending procurement policy and administrative procedures to the Director. The Director shall elicit the Council's comments before issuing policy statements, policy changes, administrative procedures or administrative changes regarding this chapter;

(2) Reporting annually to the Governor by December 31 of each year concerning the effectiveness of the State's procurement processes. This report shall include recommended changes to the State's procurement laws as may be necessary to improve the State's overall effectiveness;

(3) Reviewing vendor concerns regarding the overall procurement process and recommending appropriate action relating to these concerns; and

(4) Setting the dollar amount thresholds required in this chapter. When setting these dollar amount thresholds, the Council shall take into consideration operational issues and inflation. Nothing in this subsection shall affect the amounts set in § 6960 of this title.

(e) A Contracting and Purchasing Committee shall also be established. The Section Administrator shall appoint representatives to the Committee, with the approval of the Council. The Section Administrator shall chair the Committee. The Committee shall staff the Council, monitor the effectiveness of the State's procurement process, recommend changes to the procurement process, policies and procedures and any other duties deemed necessary by the Council.

History.

70 Del. Laws, c. 601, § 7; 74 Del. Laws, c. 419, § 3; 75 Del. Laws, c. 88, §§ 16(5), 22; 83 Del. Laws, c. 56, § 33(b).

Revisor's note.

Section 78 of 83 Del. Laws, c. 56, provided: "This act shall take effect in accordance with the provisions of state law." The act became effective upon the signature of the Governor on June 30, 2021.

Effect of amendments.

83 Del. Laws, c. 56, effective June 30, 2021, added "or their designee" in the first sentence of (a).

SUBCHAPTER IV
PUBLIC WORKS CONTRACTING

§ 6960. Prevailing wage requirements.

(a) The specifications for every contract or aggregate of contracts relating to a public works project in excess of $500,000 for new construction (including painting and decorating) or $45,000 for alteration, repair, renovation, rehabilitation, demolition or reconstruction (including painting and decorating of buildings or works) to which this State or any subdivision thereof is a party and for which the State appropriated any part of the funds and which requires or involves the employment of mechanics and/or laborers shall contain a provision stating the minimum wages to be paid various classes of laborers and mechanics which shall be based upon the wages that will be determined by the Delaware Department of Labor, Division of Industrial Affairs, to be prevailing in the county in which the work is to be performed. As of January 1, 2016, the Delaware Department of Labor, Division of Industrial Affairs shall establish the prevailing wage for each respective craft or class of laborers and mechanics at the same rates established in collective bargaining agreements between labor organizations and their employers, or when collective bargaining agreement rates do not prevail, that govern work of a similar nature and similar crafts or classes of laborers and mechanics for the county where the public works contract will be performed if that particular labor organization's collective bargaining rate prevailed and they participated in the survey, for that particular trade or craft in that particular county for 4 consecutive years. When collective bargaining rates do not apply, the prevailing wage shall be the highest rate of the 4 years. If the agreed rate of pay is designated to be the craft's collective bargaining agreement, the annual rate adjustment will be determined by the collective bargaining agreement rate for each craft and county, each year. When collective bargaining rates do not prevail, the annual rate adjustment shall be the Consumer Price Index-Construction. If the prevailing wage cannot be reasonably and fairly determined in any locality because no such agreements exists or the collective bargaining rate has not prevailed for 4 consecutive years the Department shall use the prevailing wage as established by the Department's annual prevailing wage survey. There will be a 1-time challenge of the prevailing wage rate per cycle as in the Department regulations.

For each respective craft or class of laborers or mechanics, the craft or class whose collectively bargained wages as of January 1, 2015, for that particular labor organization's collective bargaining rate prevailed for that particular trade or craft in that particular county is the prevailing wage rate and whose rate has prevailed for 4 of the last 5 years, or will prevail in the future for 4 consecutive years, shall have their collective bargaining agreement adopted as the prevailing wage rate negotiated by industry standards between workers and employers and the raise be determined by the collective bargaining agreement rate as of September 1 for that craft, county, and year.

All other provisions of this law are to remain unchanged.

(b) Every contract based upon these specifications shall contain a stipulation that the employer shall pay all mechanics and laborers employed directly upon the site of the work, unconditionally and not less often than once a week and without subsequent deduction or rebate on any account, the full amounts accrued at time of payment, computed at wage rates not less than those stated in the specifications, regardless of any contractual relationship which may be alleged to exist between the employer and such laborers and mechanics. The specifications shall further stipulate that the scale of wages to be paid shall be posted by the employer in a prominent and easily accessible place at the site of the work, and that there may be withheld from the employer so much of accrued payments as may be considered necessary by the Department of Labor to pay to laborers and mechanics employed by the employer the difference between the rates of wages required by the contract to be paid laborers and mechanics on the work and rates of wages received by such laborers and mechanics to be remitted to the Department of Labor for distribution upon resolution of any claims.

(c) Every contract based upon these specifications shall contain a stipulation that sworn payroll information, as required by the Department of Labor, be furnished weekly. The Department of Labor shall keep and maintain the sworn payroll information for a period of 6 months from the last day of the work week covered by the payroll.

(d) The Department of Labor shall investigate all claims that the prevailing wage rates as provided for under this section are not being or have not been paid. Upon finding that an employer has not paid or is not paying the prevailing wage rates, the Department of Labor shall notify the employer of the violations by certified mail and make an effort to obtain compliance. Upon failure to obtain compliance within 15 days of receipt of said certified mail, the Secretary may terminate all rights of the employer to proceed with the work under the public construction contract, and the employer shall be responsible for all damages resulting therefrom.

(e) Any employer who knowingly fails or refuses to pay the prevailing wage rates provided for under this section, or who fails to submit payroll reports or post notice of the wage rates which apply to the project shall, for each such violation, be subject to a civil penalty of not less than $1,000 nor more than $5,000 for each violation. No public construction contract in this State shall be bid on, awarded to or received by any contractor or subcontractor or any person, firm, partnership or corporation in which such employer has an interest who, within 2 years after entry of a judgment pursuant to this chapter, is adjudicated in violation of this chapter in a subsequent proceeding until 3 years have elapsed from the date of the subsequent penalty judgment. A civil penalty claim may be filed in any court of competent jurisdiction.

(f) Any laborer or mechanic employed by any employer, or the Department of Labor on behalf of any laborer or mechanic employed by any employer, who is paid in a sum less than the prevailing wage rates provided for under this section shall have a right of action against the employer in any court of competent jurisdiction to recover treble the difference between the amount so paid and the prevailing wage rate. Such action may be brought by the Department of Labor in the name and for the benefit of the laborer or mechanic with or without an assignment of the claim from the employee and upon notice to the aggrieved employee, the Department of Labor shall have the power to settle and adjust any such claim to the same extent as would the aggrieved employee. It shall not be a defense to such action that the underpayment was received by the laborer or mechanic without protest. Upon the filing of an action under this section, the employer shall post suitable bond approved by the court for the damages which may be recoverable thereunder. Any judgment entered for plaintiff shall include an award for reasonable attorney's fees and costs of prosecution. The Department of Labor shall not be required to pay the filing fee or other costs of the action or fees of any nature to file bond or other security of any nature in connection with such action or with proceedings supplementary thereto or as a condition precedent to the availability to the Department of any process in aid of such action or proceedings. The Department shall have the authority to join various claimants in 1 preferred claim lien and, in case of suit, to join them in 1 cause of action.

(g) Any wages collected under this chapter, but not claimed by the employee within 1 year from the date of collection, shall be retained by the Department of Labor for enforcement purposes.

(h) No action to recover wages and damages under this section shall be brought after the expiration of 2 years from the accruing of the cause of action.

(i) Whenever any person shall contract with another for the performance of any work which the contracting person has undertaken to perform, he or she shall become civilly liable to employees engaged in the performance of work under such contract for the payment of wages, exclusive of treble damages, as required under this section, whenever and to the extent that the employer of such employees fails to pay such wages, and the employer of such employees shall be liable to such person for any wages paid by the employer under this section. If pursuant to this subsection a person becomes civilly liable to employees of another, such liability shall not constitute a violation of this section for purposes of the termination, civil penalty and debarment provisions of subsections (d) and (e) of this section.

(j) A contract manager shall be responsible for monitoring compliance with this section, but shall not become civilly liable to the same extent as the contracting person. For purposes of this section, "contract manager" means any person who performs the function of the contracting person without becoming a party to the contract of performance, but rather contracts with the recipient of the goods or services to act as his or her agent. A contract manager who knowingly fails or refuses to monitor compliance with this section shall, for each such failure or refusal, be subject to a civil penalty of not less than $100 nor more than $500. A civil penalty claim under this subsection may be filed in any court of competent jurisdiction. A contract manager's liability for a civil penalty pursuant to this subsection shall not constitute a violation of this section for purposes of the termination, civil penalty and debarment provisions of subsections (d) and (e) of this section.

(k) Any employer who discharges or in any manner discriminates against an employee because that employee has made a complaint or has given information to the Department pursuant to this chapter, or because that employee has caused to be instituted or is about to cause to be instituted any proceedings under this chapter, or has testified or is about to testify in any such proceedings, shall be deemed in violation of this chapter and shall be subject to a civil penalty of not less than $1,000 nor more than $5,000 for each violation.

(*l*) The Committee shall have its first meeting no later than September 1, 2015. The Committee will sunset after 4 years unless extended by law.

(m) None of the specifications of this section shall apply to a project of the Department of Transportation wholly funded by Community Transportation Funds. None of the specifications of this section shall apply to a project wholly funded by the Municipal Street Aid Program authorized pursuant to Chapter 51 of Title 30.

History.

29 Del. C. 1953, § 6913; 53 Del. Laws, c. 380, § 1; 57 Del. Laws, c. 454, § 17; 58 Del. Laws, c. 408; 63 Del. Laws, c. 80, § 69; 65 Del. Laws, c. 368, § 1; 67 Del. Laws, c. 260, § 1; 69 Del. Laws, c. 64, § 28; 69 Del. Laws, c. 295, § 1; 70 Del. Laws, c. 99, § 1; 70 Del. Laws, c. 186, § 1; 70 Del. Laws, c. 601, §§ 6, 8; 71 Del. Laws, c. 310, § 1; 71 Del. Laws, c. 312, § 1; 72 Del. Laws, c. 170, § 1; 73 Del. Laws, c. 129, § 1; 74 Del. Laws, c. 279, §§ 1, 3; 76 Del. Laws, c. 185, § 1; 80 Del. Laws, c. 105, §§ 1-3; 83 Del. Laws, c. 37, § 36.

Effect of amendments.

83 Del. Laws, c. 37, effective June 3, 2021, in (*l*), repealed the introductory paragraph and (*l*)(1)-(5).

NOTES TO DECISIONS

Jurisdiction.

Interlocutory review was not warranted on a summary judgment order in a wage dispute because: (1) although the decision involved a matter of first impression relating to the construction of this statute, which had not been contested in the 25 years of its existence, the trial court merely applied plain meaning to it; (2) the issue at hand was meaning of "the employer" as used in the this statute and the affirmed authority of the Delaware Department of Labor to order withholding from a primary contractor for the wage deficiencies of a subcontractor; and (3) the application for interlocutory review did not meet the strict standards for certification where exceptional circumstances were lacking. In re Port of Wilmington Gantry Crane Litig., 241 A.3d 221 (Del. 2020).

§ 6960A. Craft training requirement.

(a)(1) A contract relating to a public works project under § 6962 of this title must include a craft training program for each craft in the project if at the time the contractor executes a public works contract, all of the following apply:

a. A project meets the prevailing wage requirement under § 6960 of this title.

b. The contractor employs 10 or more total employees.

c. The project is not a federal highway project, except for the project under § 6962(c)(11) of this title.

d. There is an apprenticeship program for a craft in the project on the list of crafts under § 204(b)(2) of Title 19.

(2) A contractor must commit that all subcontractors provide craft training if paragraph (a)(1) of this section apply to the subcontractor.

(b)(1) If a contract requires a craft training program under subsection (a) of this section, the contractor must satisfy the craft training requirement before the contract is executed. A contractor or subcontractor may satisfy the craft training requirement under this section by doing any of the following for each craft under subsection (a) of this section:

    a. Having at least 1 active apprentice in a craft training program for the craft.

    b. Having at least 1 active apprentice who completes a craft training program for the craft within the 6 months before the date the contract was executed.

    c. Being a member of a consortium that provides craft training for the craft and all of the following apply to the craft training program for the craft:

        1. The consortium requires a regular financial contribution.

        2. The contractor or subcontractor has access to the craft training program.

        3. There is at least 1 active apprentice in the craft training program.

    d. Making a payment under subsection (c) of this section.

    (2) The craft training program under paragraphs (b)(1)a. through (b)(1)b. of this section may be provided by the contractor or subcontractor or through agreement with another entity.

    (3) The active apprentice under paragraphs (b)(1)a. through (b)(1)b. of this section does not have to work on the contract being executed under paragraph (b)(1) of this section.

(c)(1) For contracts executed after [the implementation date under 83 Del. Laws, c. 129, § 6], a contractor or subcontractor may satisfy the craft training requirement under this section by making a payment in the amount established under § 204(b)(2)b.2. of Title 19, for the craft into the Apprenticeship and Training Fund of the Department Labor.

    (2) For each calendar year, a contractor or subcontractor satisfies the craft training requirement for all contracts executed during that year when payments made under paragraph (c)(1) of this section after January 1 equal the following amounts:

    a. For employers with 10 through 25 employees, payments that total $10,000.

    b. For employers with more than 25 employees, payments that total $20,000.

(d)(1) All contracts that require a craft training program under subsection (a) of this section must contain a penalty provision against the successful bidder for the failure to comply with the requirements under this section. The penalty provision must require all of the following:

    a. The contractor must pay the amount of the payment required under subsection (c) of this section to the Apprenticeship and Training Fund.

    b. An amount that does not exceed 10 percent of the payment under paragraph (d)(1)a. of this section.

    (2) A penalty assessed under paragraph (d)(1) of this section may be fully or partially remitted or refunded by the agency awarding the contract only if the contractor establishes compliance within 60 days of the notice of the penalty. A claim for remission or refund of a penalty may only be granted if an application for the remission or refund is filed within 1 year of the notice of the penalty.

    (3) All money received from penalties under paragraph (d)(1)b. of this section, that is not remitted or refunded, reverts to the government entity under the contract for which the penalty was imposed.

History.
83 Del. Laws, c. 129, § 4.

Revisor's note.
Section 6 of 83 Del. Laws, c. 129, provided: "This act is effective immediately and is to be implemented the earlier of the following:
"(1) Notice by the Secretary of Labor pub-

lished in the Register of Regulations that final regulations to implement this act have been promulgated.
"(2) One year from the date of the act's enactment." The act was signed by the Governor on Sept. 9, 2021.

§ 6962. Large public works contract procedures [For application of this section, see 82 Del. Laws, c. 36, § 3].

(a) *Applicability.* — Any state contract for which an agency is a party and for which the probable cost is greater than the amount set by the Contracting and Purchasing Advisory Council pursuant to § 6913 of this title for small public works contracts shall be subject to the provisions of this section.

(b) *Advertising requirements.* — Each agency shall publicly announce, not less than once a week for 2 consecutive weeks in a newspaper published or circulated in each county of the State, each public works contract. Public advertising shall require electronic publication accessible to the public in a manner prescribed pursuant to § 6902(10) of this title for 2 consecutive weeks. An agency may also maintain a register of prospective bidders which may be used to provide direct notification of contracts to be bid. This register shall not be used in a manner which will limit the competitiveness of the bidding process described in this subchapter. No agency shall be subject to a cause of action or be otherwise liable for any errors or omissions in administering a bid registry. The public announcement shall also state the nature of the contract under the following conditions:

(1) If the agency requires all bidders to be registered or prequalified in order to receive bidding documents for the proposed contract, the announcement shall state in general terms the character and location of the work and bid and performance bond requirements. If the agency requires prequalification of subcontractors in its invitation to bid, no contractor shall list a subcontractor in its subcontractor listing who has not already been prequalified by the agency.

(2) If the agency does not require bidder registration or prequalification for the proposed contract, the announcement shall state with reasonable accuracy the character, quantity and location of the work as well as bid and performance bond requirements. The public announcement shall also state that the agency may extend the time and place for the opening of bids from that described in the announcement. Such extension shall not take place unless at least 2 calendar days' notice, by certified delivery, facsimile transmission or by other verifiable electronic means, is sent to those bidders who obtained copies of the plans and specifications or contract descriptions.

(c) *Bidder prequalification requirements.* — (1) The Office shall establish a 2-step process for the prequalification of contractors and subcontractors that desire to bid on large public works contracts for which prequalification is specified by the contracting agency. A contractor shall not be permitted to bid on a contract that requires prequalification unless the contractor has been prequalified pursuant to this subsection. A prequalified and classified contractor shall not be permitted to submit a bid on a specific contract unless the contractor completes a questionnaire and submits supplemental information at the option of the contracting agency or per paragraph (c)(9)a. of this section to the Office pertaining to that contract. The supplemental request for information shall not include any information requested during the first step of the prequalification process, but may require the contractor to affirm that no material changes have occurred since the application for the first step of the prequalification process was submitted to the Office. The prequalification process shall apply to general contractors and subcontractors in the areas that are deemed necessary by the Office.

(2) The prequalification classification issued by the Office as part 1 of the prequalification process shall be valid for 12 months. A contractor or subcontractor subject to prequalification shall request to be reclassified by the Office after the 12-month period in order to remain eligible to bid on public works contracts that require prequalification. A contractor or subcontractor who holds a valid prequalification classification shall report any material changes which could adversely affect the prequalification, as established in paragraph (c)(3) of this section, to the Office in writing within 10 days of the material change. A contractor or subcontractor may report to the Office in writing material changes which could positively affect the prequalification, as established in paragraph (c)(3) of this section. Based on the information provided, the Office may change the classification or revoke prequalification at the sole discretion of the Director.

(3) The prequalification process shall include a requirement that the contractor or subcontractor submit a statement under oath on a form designated by the Office. The form shall fully describe and establish the financial ability, responsibility, plant and equipment, organization, ownership, relationships, and prior experience of the contractor or subcontractor and any other pertinent and material facts as may be deemed necessary by the Office. At the discretion of the Office, the submission shall include part or all of the following:

    a. The most recent audited financial statement and/or financial statement review containing a complete statement of the proposing contractor's or subcontractor's financial status. Such statement shall include the contractor's Z score;

    b. The proposing contractor's or subcontractor's experience on other public works or private sector projects, including but not limited to the size, complexity and scope of the firm's prior projects;

    c. Performance reviews of the proposing contractor or subcontractor on previously awarded public works or private sector construction projects within the last 5 years;

    d. Civil judgments and/or criminal history of the proposing contractor's or subcontractor's principals;

    e. Any debarment or suspension by any government agency;

    f. Any revocation or suspension of a license;

    g. Any bankruptcy filings or proceedings; and

    h. A statement as to organization, which shall demonstrate the adequacy of such organization to undertake a public works contract. This statement shall include the resumes of the management and professional staff.

(4) After the receipt of the submission provided for in paragraph (c)(3) of this section, the Office may verify all information provided in the contractor's or subcontractor's submission, including applicable license and certificate requirements, federal or state debarments, and violations of law. The Office may also conduct inquiries or surveys of the contractor's or subcontractor's prior customers.

(5)a. Based upon the submission provided for in paragraphs (c)(3) and (4) of this section, the Office Review Committee, which shall include at least 2 Office employees, shall assign a contractor or subcontractor the following classification or classifications and limits for the purpose of determining the types of projects for which a contractor or subcontractor is entitled to bid:

    1. A trade(s) or work classification(s); and

    2. The maximum contract dollar value for which the contractor or subcontractor may submit a bid.

To effectuate these requirements of the prequalification process, the Office shall develop rules and regulations for assigning classifications and maximum dollar limits.

    b. The classification shall be made, or prequalification may be denied, and notice thereof shall be sent to the contractor or subcontractor within 5 days of the determination made pursuant to paragraph (c)(5)a. of this section by registered or certified mail or other legally valid methods. Notice of prequalification classification or denial shall also be sent to the contracting agency if said agency is not the Office.

  (6) Based upon the proposing contractor's or subcontractor's answers to the step-1 or step-2 prequalification questionnaire, the Office may deny prequalification for any 1 of the following specified reasons:

    a. Insufficient financial ability to perform a public works contract;

    b. Inadequate experience to undertake a public works contract;

    c. Documented failure to perform on prior public or private construction contracts, including but not limited to final adjudication or admission of violations of prevailing wage laws in Delaware or any other state;

    d. Prior judgments for breach of contract that indicate the proposing contractor or subcontractor may not be capable of performing the work or completing a large public works contract;

    e. Criminal convictions for fraud, misrepresentation or theft relating to contract procurement;

    f. Previous debarment or suspension of the contractor or subcontractor by any government agency that indicates the proposing contractor or subcontractor may not be capable of performing the work or completing a large public works contract;

    g. Previous revocation or suspension of a license that indicates the proposing contractor or subcontractor may not be capable of performing the work or completing a public works contract;

    h. Previous bankruptcy proceedings that indicate the proposing contractor or subcontractor may not be capable of performing the work or completing a public works contract; or

    i. Failure to provide accurate prequalification information on past or current prequalification questionnaires.

Reason or reasons for the denial of prequalification shall be in writing, and shall be sent to the contractor or subcontractor within 5 working days of such decision. An agency may refuse to provide any contractor or subcontractor disqualified under this paragraph plans and specifications for a contract. An agency receiving a bid from a contractor or subcontractor disqualified under this paragraph shall not consider such bid.

  (7) Any contractor or subcontractor disqualified pursuant to paragraph (c)(6) of this section may request a review of such decisions with the Director within 5 working days of the receipt of the agency's notification of the prequalification decision. Such request shall be made in writing. No action in law or equity shall lie against any agency or its employees if the contractor or subcontractor does not first review the decision with the

Director. To the extent the contractor or subcontractor brings an action challenging a decision made pursuant to paragraph (c)(6) of this section after such review by the Director, the court shall afford great weight to the decision of the Office head and shall not overturn such decision unless the contractor or subcontractor proves by clear and convincing evidence that such decision was arbitrary and capricious.

(8) The Office shall maintain a registry of all contractors and subcontractors prequalified to bid on public works projects. The registry shall include the classification or classifications of the contractor or subcontractor and the maximum contract dollar value for which the contractor or subcontractor may submit a bid.

(9)a. In addition to the prequalification required herein, any agency shall require a contractor or subcontractor to provide supplemental information that is specifically relevant to the public works contract to be bid. Such additional information shall be considered supplemental certification and shall not duplicate in any way the information required by the Office in its prequalification process except for labor supply available to complete the project in a timely manner.

b. Based upon the proposing contractor's or subcontractor's answers to the agency's supplemental prequalification questionnaire, the Director, or in the case of school projects, the school district may deny the prequalification for any 1 of the following specified reasons:

1. Inadequate experience to undertake the specific project that requires supplemental prequalification;

2. Inadequate expertise to undertake the specific project that requires supplemental prequalification;

3. Failure to provide supplemental prequalification information for the specific project that requires supplemental prequalification; or

4. Inadequate labor supply available to complete the project in a timely manner.

Denial of supplemental prequalification by the Office, or in the case of school projects, the school district shall be in writing no later than 2 weeks before the close of the project bid and shall be sent to the contractor or subcontractor within 5 working days of such decision. An agency may refuse to provide any contractor or subcontractor disqualified under this paragraph plans and specifications for the contract. An agency receiving a bid from a contractor or subcontractor disqualified under this paragraph shall not consider such bid.

(10) Any contractor or subcontractor disqualified pursuant to paragraph (c)(9) of this section may request in writing within 5 working days of the receipt of the Office's or, in the case of school projects, the school district's, supplemental prequalification a review of such decisions with the Director or the Director's designee or, in the case of school projects, the school district. No action in law or equity shall lie against any agency or its employees if the contractor or subcontractor does not first review the decision with the Director or, in the case of school projects, the school district within 5 working days after the decision is rendered by the Office or, in the case of school projects, the school district. To the extent the contractor or subcontractor brings an action challenging a decision made pursuant to paragraph (c)(9) of this section after such review by the Director or, in the case of school projects, the school district, the court shall afford great weight to the decision of the Director or, in the case of school projects, the school district and shall not overturn such decision unless the

contractor or subcontractor proves by clear and convincing evidence that such decision was "arbitrary and capricious."

(11) In addition, for the US 301 project from the Maryland-Delaware state line to its termination at Delaware Route 1, all contractors and subcontractors are required, independently or through agreement with other organizations, to provide craft training for journeyman and apprentice levels through a bona fide program approved by and registered with the State of Delaware and/or United States Department of Labor.

(12)a. A Department of Transportation project, excluding a municipal street aid contract, must include a performance-based rating system.

b. The Department of Transportation's performance-based rating system must be defined in regulations promulgated by the Secretary of the Department of Transportation.

c. A contractor is eligible to bid as follows:

1. A contractor meeting or exceeding the minimum contractor's performance rating at the time of bid, as determined by the Department's performance-based contractor evaluation system, is eligible to bid.

2.A. A contractor who does not meet or exceed the minimum contractor's performance rating at the time of bid is eligible to bid if the contractor agrees to allow the Department to retain 5% of the payments to be made to the contractor for work performed under the contract under the procedures provided in paragraph (d)(5)a.1. of this section.

B. A contract under paragraph (c)(12)c.2. of this section must contain all of the following provisions:

I. A variable retainage in an amount that does not exceed 5%, that is established at the discretion of the Secretary.

II. When the project is at 50% completion, the contractor may request that the retainage be reduced to 2% after an interim evaluation of the current project.

III. The project completion percentage will be based on the actual work completed, excluding money paid for stored materials.

(13)a. If there is a craft training requirement for a craft in the project under § 6960A of this title, a contractor must commit that the contractor and all subcontractors will provide craft training for journeyman and apprentice levels at the time the contractor executes the public works contract.

1.–3. [Repealed.]

b., c. [Repealed.]

d. The Secretary of the Department of Labor may promulgate and adopt regulations to implement this paragraph (c)(13) of this section.

(d) *Bid specifications and plans requirements.* — (1) *Preparation of plans and specifications and approvals.* — The contracting agency shall cause suitable plans and specifications to be prepared for all contracts pursuant to this section. All plans and specifications shall be prepared by registered and licensed architects and/or engineers who shall sign the plans and specifications and affix their seals thereto. This requirement may be waived if:

a. The work to be covered by the public works contract is to be performed in accordance with identical plans and specifications similarly signed and sealed pursuant to which previous public works contracts have been awarded under this subchapter. Any architect and/or engineer who signed and sealed the original of such identical plan(s) will have no liability arising from the use of those plans other than the use contemplated by the contract pursuant to which the original copies of such plans was created, unless such architect and/or engineer reviews and approves such different use; or

b. The project does not require architectural and engineering services and the agency head waives in writing the use of such services.

(2) *Agency assistance.* — An agency may retain, in accordance with subchapter V of this chapter, the professional services of a general contractor or other qualified firm to assist in cost estimation, economic design analysis and construction.

(3) *Prohibition of brand specification.* — The description of work and/or materiel and the plans and specifications shall not use a brand or trade name, except as an indication of the type or quality of materiel and in all such limited cases shall contain the words "or approved equal."

(4) *Special provisions.* — a. *Anti-pollution, conservation, environmental measures or Energy Star equipment not covered by contract specifications.* — 1. The description of the materiel and the plans and specifications for the work issued by the agency shall set forth those provisions of federal, state and local statutes, ordinances, rules and regulations respecting anti-pollution, conservation and environmental protection which affect the project or projects for which such solicitations or bids are sought.

2. If the successful bidder must undertake anti-pollution, conservation or environmental protection work not specified in the agency's plans and specifications or descriptions of materiel, including measures required by the enactment of new or the amendment of existing statutes, ordinances, rules or regulations occurring after the submission of the successful bid or quotation, the awarding agency shall issue a change order, as provided for in § 6963 of this title, setting forth the additional measures that must be undertaken.

3. *Cost.* — The cost of such a change order to the awarding agency shall be determined in accordance with the contract for change orders or force accounts. If no such provision is set forth in the contract, then the cost to the awarding agency shall be the contractor's costs for wages, labor costs other than wages, wage taxes, materiel, equipment rentals, insurance and subcontracts attributable to the additional activity plus a reasonable sum for overhead and profit.

4. *Authorization.* — Written authorization by the agency is to be given to the successful bidder prior to the bidder undertaking such additional activity. Costs incurred by the successful bidder for additional work performed without prior approval shall not be approved for payment by the agency.

5. *Energy Star equipment.* — Prior to finalizing specifications for equipment to be purchased as part of a large public works contract, the agency or its architect and/or engineer shall review all equipment to determine whether Energy Star rated products are available. For each piece of equipment, if an Energy Star product is available, the specifications and bid documents shall require the use of an Energy Star product unless the agency can

demonstrate, in writing, to the satisfaction of the Director, that a product with an Energy Star rating meets at least 1 of the following criteria:

A. The Energy Star rated equipment is not available competitively,

B. The Energy Star rated equipment is not available within a reasonable time frame, or

C. The Energy Star rated equipment does not meet appropriate performance standards.

The agency may include non-Energy Star rated equipment as an alternate in the bid documents to enable lifecycle costing analysis to be performed as part of the analysis of responsive bids. The agency shall be required to award a contract that includes the procurement of Energy Star rated equipment unless the agency can demonstrate, in writing, to the satisfaction of the Director, that the interests of the state would be better served by procuring non-Energy Star rated equipment.

b. *Preference for Delaware labor.* — In the construction of all public works for the State or any political subdivision thereof or by firms contracting with the State or any political subdivision thereof, preference in employment of laborers, workers or mechanics shall be given to bona fide legal citizens of the State who have established citizenship by residence of at least 90 days in the State. Each public works contract for the construction of public works for the State or any political subdivision thereof shall contain a stipulation that any person, company or corporation who violates this section shall pay a penalty to the Secretary of Finance equal to the amount of compensation paid to any person in violation of this section.

(5) *Retainages and substitution of securities.* — a. *Authority to withhold contract retainage.* — 1. Agencies may retain a portion of the payments to be made to a contractor for work performed pursuant to a public works contract. The percentage of the value of work performed which may be retained shall be established for each particular contract in the contract bidding documents and shall be incorporated into the contract. The percentage retained shall be 5% of the value of the work completed by the contractor under the contract. Upon completion of the work under the contract, the agency may release 60% of the amount then retained. The balance of the amount retained will be held until:

A. All reports required of the contract are received;

B. All subcontractors in trades listed on the bid form are paid by the contractor, unless the amount owed to the subcontractor is disputed, in which case the agency may withhold 150% of the amount withheld by the contractor in its dispute with the subcontractor; and

C. Final payment is authorized by the agency.

2. The agency may, at its option, retain, temporarily or permanently, a small amount and may cause the contractor to be paid, temporarily or permanently, from time to time, such portion of the amount retained as it deems equitable. The contractor shall be paid for all work that is due to the contractor under the contract except for the amount retained.

3. The agency may at the beginning of each public works contract establish a time schedule for the completion of the

project. If the project is delayed beyond the completion date due to the contractor's failure to meet his or her responsibilities, the agency may forfeit all or part of retainage at its discretion.

b. *Procedures requirement.* — Agencies shall establish standard procedures and regulations for the administration of contract retainages prior to entering into contracts which require retainages. All agency procedures shall provide for contract retainage and substitution of securities for retainage.

c. *Substitution of securities.* — 1. The contractor under a public works contract, with the approval of the agency, may deposit securities as authorized by this section in substitution for moneys being withheld from the contractor as retainage. Securities allowable for substitution of retainage shall be: United States Treasury Bonds, United States Treasury Notes, United States Treasury Certificates of Indebtedness or United States Treasury Bills; bonds or notes of the State; bonds of any political subdivision of the State; or certificates of deposit from state or national banks located in this State; or any letter of credit or other security approved by the agency.

2. The contractor shall have the right to withdraw and take all or portions of the moneys being retained from the contractor under the contract by depositing securities in substitution for such moneys. The contractor may do so only in accordance with the agency's standard procedures and mechanisms. Such substitution shall be approved by the agency only if the aggregate market value of the securities are at least as great as the contract retainages being withdrawn.

3. A contractor may substitute cash for and receive back all or part of the securities on deposit from the contractor. The cash must at least have the same value as the market value of the securities received back from the agency.

4. The contractor shall be entitled to receive, in all events, all interest and income earned on the securities deposited by the contractor in substitution for contract retainage. If the securities deposited are in the form of coupon bonds, the agency or the escrow agent designated by it and holding the deposited securities shall deliver each coupon to the contractor as it matures.

5. All securities shall be released, delivered and paid over to the contractor at such time as cash moneys being retained from the contractor would have been released, delivered and paid over to the contractor under the public works contract if there had been no substitution for the cash moneys.

6. All costs of depositing and maintaining securities as provided for in this section shall be borne by the contractor.

7. No agency shall have any duty to invest moneys being retained by it from a contractor under a public works contract in any interest bearing account or to establish any procedures or mechanisms for any such investment.

8. Notwithstanding any other provisions of this section, any contracting agency may deny the contractor on any public works contract permission to substitute securities for moneys being held as retainages. This action shall be taken only for good cause and when the agency deems it to be in the best interest of the contracting agency. Written notice shall be given to the contractor

and a hearing shall be held by the agency showing cause for such denial if requested in writing by the contractor. Denial of such substitution shall be for a stated period of time, not to exceed a period of 3 years, and shall continue until the end of the stated time period, or until the contractor has successfully completed all outstanding public works contracts without forfeiting any part of the retainage held by the agency, whichever occurs first.

(6) *Partial payments.* — Any public works contract executed by any agency may provide for partial payments with respect to materials placed along or upon the sites or stored at secured locations, which are suitable for use in the performance of the contract. When approved by the agency, partial payments may include the values of tested and acceptable materials of a nonperishable or noncontaminative nature which have been produced or furnished for incorporation as a permanent part of work yet to be completed, provided acceptable provisions have been made for storage. Any allowance made for materials on hand will not exceed the delivered cost of the materials as verified by invoices furnished by the contractor, nor will it exceed the contract bid price for the material complete in place.

(7) *Equality of employment opportunity and equal pay on public works.* — a. As a condition of the awarding of any contract for public works financed in whole or in part by state appropriation, such contracts shall include the following provisions:

During the performance of this contract, the contractor agrees as follows:

1. The contractor will not discriminate against any employee or applicant for employment because of race, creed, color, sex, sexual orientation, gender identity or national origin. The contractor will take positive steps to ensure that applicants are employed and that employees are treated during employment without regard to their race, creed, color, sex, sexual orientation, gender identity or national origin. Such action shall include, but not be limited to, the following: employment, upgrading, demotion or transfer; recruitment or recruitment advertising; layoff or termination; rates of pay or other forms of compensation; and selection for training, including apprenticeship. The contractor agrees to post in conspicuous places available to employees and applicants for employment notices to be provided by the contracting agency setting forth this nondiscrimination clause.

2. The contractor will, in all solicitations or advertisements for employees placed by or on behalf of the contractor, state that all qualified applicants will receive consideration for employment without regard to race, creed, color, sex, sexual orientation, gender identity or national origin.

3. The contractor will ensure employees receive equal pay for equal work, without regard to sex. Employee pay differential is acceptable if pursuant to a seniority system, a merit system, a system which measures earnings by quantity or quality of production, or if the differential is based on any other factor other than sex.

b. The Secretary of the Department of Labor shall be responsible for the administration of this provision and shall adopt such rules and regulations and issue such orders as deemed necessary to achieve the purposes thereof; provided, that no requirement established hereby shall be in conflict with § 6904 of this title.

    c. For the purposes of this section:

       1. "Protective hairstyle" includes braids, locks, and twists.

       2. "Race" includes traits historically associated with race, including hair texture and a protective hairstyle.

(8) *Bid bonding requirements.* — a. All bids shall be accompanied by a deposit of either a good and sufficient bond to the agency for the benefit of the agency, with corporate surety authorized to do business in this State, the form of the bond and the surety to be approved by the agency, and the bond form used shall be the standard form issued by the Office of Management and Budget for this purpose or a security of the bidder assigned to the agency, for a sum equal to at least 10% of the bid. The bid bond need not be for a specific sum, but may be stated to be for a sum equal to 10% of the bid to which it relates and not to exceed a certain stated sum, if said sum is equal to at least 10% of the bid. Any bid which, at the time it is submitted, is not accompanied by a bid bond or sufficient security as required by this paragraph shall not be opened or read, and shall be rejected.

    b. Upon the execution of a formal contract and performance bond, the bid bond or security shall be returned to the successful bidder. The security of the unsuccessful bidders shall be returned to them immediately upon the awarding of the contract or the rejection of all bids, but in no event later than 30 days after the opening of bids with the exception of school districts and the Department of Public Instruction, which shall be no more than 60 days unless the contracting agency or school district extends the bid evaluation period by 5 working days per the requirements of paragraph (d)(13)a. of this section. If the bid evaluation period is extended by 5 working days, then the security of each unsuccessful bidder shall be returned to them on the first working day after the end of the extended bid evaluation period.

    c. *Loss of bid bond as damages.* — In the event of any successful bidder refusing or neglecting to execute a formal contract and bond within 20 days of the awarding of the contract, the bid bond or security deposited by the successful bidder shall be taken and become the absolute property of the State for the benefit of the agency as liquidated damages. Such damages shall neither constitute a forfeiture nor a penalty and shall be deposited with the Secretary of Finance. Such moneys pertaining to Department of Transportation contracts shall be deposited in the Transportation Trust Fund. The contracting agency may award the contract to the next lowest responsible bidder or re-advertise for new bids.

    d. In the case of bids submitted to agencies other than any county of this State and other than any public school district, wherever security is required under this section, the vendor shall also supply with its bid its taxpayer identification number (i.e., federal employer identification number or social security number) or a Delaware business license number and, should the vendor be awarded a contract, such vendor shall provide to the agency the taxpayer identification or Delaware business license numbers of such subcontractors. Such numbers shall be provided on the later of the date on which such subcontractor is required to be identified or the time the contract is executed. The agency shall report to the Division of Revenue each vendor selected for award within 15 days of execution of the contract and each subcontractor within 15 days of such contractor having been identified to the agency or on the date of execution of the contract, whichever is later, unless the Director of the Division of Revenue has notified the agency of criteria according to which, in the Director's discretion, reporting is not required and the contract meets such criteria.

(9) *Performance bonding requirements.* — a. Simultaneous with the execution of the formal contract, the successful bidder shall also execute a good and sufficient bond to the contracting agency for the benefit of the agency, with corporate surety authorized to do business in this State, in a sum equal to 100% of the contract price and the bond form used shall be the standard form issued by the Office of Management and Budget.

b. The bond shall be conditioned upon the faithful compliance and performance by the successful bidder of each and every term and condition of the contract and the proposal and plans and specifications thereof, at the time and in the manner prescribed by the contract and the plans and specifications, including the payment in full, to every firm furnishing materiel or performing labor in the performance of the contract, of all sums of money due it for such labor or materiel. The bond shall also contain the successful bidder's guarantee to indemnify and save harmless the agency from all costs, damages and expenses growing out of or by reason of the successful bidder's failure to comply and perform the work and complete the contract in accordance with the contract.

c. The agency may, when it considers that the interests of the agency so require, cause judgment to be confessed upon the bond. All sums received through confession of judgment shall be paid for the credit of the agency to the Secretary of Finance or to the chief financial officer of the agency if it is not a state agency.

d. Every firm furnishing materiel or performing labor under the contract for which the successful bidder is liable may maintain an action on the bond for its own use in the name of the agency in any court of competent jurisdiction for the recovery of such sum or sums as may be due such firm from the successful bidder, but if the bond so provides, no suit shall be commenced after the expiration of 1 year following the date on which the successful bidder ceased work on the contract. Otherwise, suits may be commenced at any time within 3 years following the date the last work was done on the contract.

e. No firm or surety, in any action brought under this section, or on the bond required by this section, shall assert as a defense to such action the claim that the bond given pursuant to this section contained a limitation or restriction not provided for by this section.

f. In the event of defaults of its contracts, the money collected on the performance bonds shall be utilized by the contracting agency for the projects for which the performance bonds were issued. All performance bond proceeds received shall be deposited with the Secretary of Finance for the credit of the agency. Such moneys pertaining to Department of Transportation contracts shall be deposited in the Transportation Trust Fund.

g. In addition to the bond, letter of credit or other financial security posted by the successful bidder in conjunction with the execution of the formal contract, each successful bidder, regardless of the type of the security posted or waived, as the case may be, must purchase adequate insurance for the performance of the contract and, by submission of a bid, does agree to indemnify and save harmless and to defend all legal or equitable actions brought against the agency or officer or employee of the agency for and from all claims of liability which is or may be the result of the successful bidder's actions during the performance of the contract. The purchase or nonpurchase of such insurance or the involvement of the successful bidder in any legal or equitable defense of any action brought against the successful bidder based upon work performed pursuant to the contract shall not waive any defense which the agency and its officers and employees might otherwise have to such claims, specifically including the defense of sovereign immunity, where applicable, and by the terms of this section, the agency and its officers and employees shall not be financially responsible for the consequences of work performed, pursuant to said contract.

h. Contracts may contain a waiver of the bond requirement; provided however, that the successful bidder post with the contracting agency an irrevocable letter of credit or other suitable or readily collectible financial security for the project. Such security shall be subject to the terms and conditions of the contracting agency.

(10) *Public buildings; special requirements.* — a. *Pre-bid meeting requirement.* — In the case of any public works contract for the construction, reconstruction, alteration or repair of any public building (not a road, street or highway) the agency shall call a meeting of all prospective bidders upon reasonable notice and at a place and time stated in the notice. The meeting shall be at least 15 days before the date for the submission of bids.

At the meeting, all the participants, including the agency, shall attempt to agree upon a listing of all subcontractor categories to be included in the bids for performing the work as required by paragraph (d)(10)b. of this section and any such agreed listing shall be final and binding upon all bidders and upon the agency. If all of the participants do not agree on such a listing at the meeting, then the agency itself, at least 10 days before the due date for the submission of bids, shall determine the subcontractor categories to be included in the listing. The listing, whether agreed to by all of the participants at the meeting or determined by the agency itself in the absence of the unanimous agreement of the participants at the meeting, shall be published by the agency at least 10 days before the due date for the submission of bids by mailing and listing to all of the participants at the meeting. The listing, as so published, shall be final and binding upon all bidders and the agency and it shall be filled out completely, in full, without any abbreviations. If the agency required prequalification of subcontractors pursuant to this section in its invitation to bid, no contractor shall list a subcontractor in its subcontractor listing required by this subsection who has not already been prequalified by the agency.

b. *Subcontracting requirements.* — All contracts for the construction, reconstruction, alteration or repair of any public building (not a road, street or highway) shall be subject to the following provisions:

1. Such contract shall be awarded only to a bidder whose bid is accompanied by a statement containing, for each subcontractor category set forth in the listing as provided in paragraph (d)(10)a. of this section the name and address (city or town and State only — street number and P.O. Box addresses not required) of the subcontractor whose services the bidder intends to use in performing the work and providing the materiel for such subcontrac-

tor category. Where any services and/or materiel are to be provided by or through a third-tier contractor, the bidder shall also supply the name and address of the third-tier contractor. If a bidder intends to perform the work or provide the materiel for any subcontractor category specifically established by the agency and as set forth in the listing provided for in paragraph (d)(10)a. of this section, the bidder must list itself as the subcontractor for that category. If at the time it is submitted a bid is not accompanied by the subcontractor statement required by this subparagraph, or if a bidder fails to list itself as the subcontractor for any category for which it intends to perform the work or provide the materiel, the bid shall not be opened or read, and shall be rejected.

2. The contracting agency shall neither accept any bid nor award any contract to any bidder which, as the prime contractor, has listed itself as the subcontractor for any subcontractor category on the listing as provided in paragraph (d)(10)a. of this section, unless:

A. It has been established to the satisfaction of the awarding agency that the bidder has customarily performed the specialty work of such subcontractor category by artisans regularly employed by the bidder's firm;

B. That the bidder is duly licensed by the State to engage in such specialty work, if the State requires such licenses; and

C. That the bidder is recognized in the industry as a bona fide subcontractor or contractor in such specialty work and subcontractor category.

The typical subcontractor categories involving specialty work includes, by way of illustration and not limited to, plumbing, electrical wiring, heating, roofing, insulating, weather stripping, masonry, bricklaying and plastering. The decision of the awarding agency as to whether a bidder who lists itself as the subcontractor for a subcontractor category set forth in the listing as provided in paragraph (d)(10)a. of this section shall be final and binding upon all bidders, and no action of any nature shall lie against any awarding agency or its employees or officers because of its decision in this regard.

3. After such a contract has been awarded, the successful bidder shall not substitute another subcontractor for any subcontractor whose name was set forth in the statement which accompanied the bid without the written consent of the awarding agency. No agency shall consent to any substitution of subcontractors unless the agency is satisfied that the subcontractor whose name is on the bidders accompanying statement:

A. Is unqualified to perform the work required;

B. Has failed to execute a timely reasonable subcontract;

C. Has defaulted in the performance on the portion of the work covered by the subcontract; or

D. Is no longer engaged in such business.

4. All such contracts shall contain a provision for a penalty against the successful bidder for its failure to utilize any or all the subcontractors in the successful bidder's accompanying statement in the performance of the work on the public building

contemplated by the contract. The penalty amount shall be set by the agency. The agency will also determine if the amount is to be deducted from payments to the bidder for contract performance or if the amount is to be paid directly to the agency by the bidder. Any penalty amount assessed against the contractor may be remitted or refunded, in whole or in part, by the agency awarding the contract, only if it is established to the satisfaction of the agency that the subcontractor in question has defaulted or is no longer engaged in such business. No claim for the remission or refund of any penalty shall be granted under this section unless an application is filed within 1 year after the liability of the successful bidder accrues. All penalty amounts assessed and not refunded or remitted to the contractor shall be reverted to the State, municipality or other agency as the case may be.

5. If awarded, not to a general contractor, but to a prime contractor which contracts directly with agency awarding and/or administering the contract, such contract may include a provision in its contract specifications that the successful bidder perform a fixed percentage of the work of said public works contract up to 50% of the total contract bid. Factors to be considered by the agency awarding the contract in setting the required percentage of amount of work the successful bidder must perform may include the degree of difficulty involved in the agency's administration of the work covered under the terms of the public works contract; the degree of specialty work contemplated in the contract including, but not limited to, the amount of plumbing, electrical wiring, heating, roofing, insulation, weather-stripping, masonry, bricklaying or plastering work under the contract; and the time period required in which to complete the public works project. The terms of the contract shall so specify reasons for the stated percentage in its general terms and conditions. The decision of the agency setting the required percentage shall not be set aside by any court of competent jurisdiction as long as there is a rational basis for setting the required fixed percentage to be performed by the contractor. If the successful bidder fails to perform pursuant to the terms of this provision, the agency awarding and/or administering the contract may invoke the provisions of § 6964 of this title.

6. No construction manager contract for public school projects may be signed unless approved by the Director.

(11) *Other contracting requirements.* — a. *Asbestos abatement.* — The selection of any contractor to perform asbestos abatement for State-funded projects shall be approved by the Office of Management and Budget pursuant to Chapter 78 of Title 16.

b. *Standards of construction; protection of physically handicapped.* — All contracts shall conform with the standards established by the Delaware Architectural Accessibility Board as authorized by Chapter 73 of this title, unless otherwise exempted by the Board.

(12) *Public bid opening requirements.* — a. Bids shall be opened publicly and the contractor and total bid price or the contractor, base bid, and alternate price should be read aloud at the time and place designated in the plans and specifications.

b. Bids shall be unconditionally accepted without alteration. After the bid opening, no corrections in bid prices or other provisions of bids prejudicial to the interests of the State or fair competition shall be permitted.

(13) *Bid evaluation, contract award and execution procedure.* — a. The contracting agency shall award any public works contract within 30 days of the bid opening to the lowest responsive and responsible bidder, unless the agency elects to award on the basis of best value, in which case the election to award on the basis of best value shall be stated in the invitation to bid. Any public school district and its board shall award public works contracts in accordance with this section's requirements except it shall award the contract within 60 days of the bid opening. A contracting agency shall extend the 30-day bid evaluation period by a total of 5 working days and a school district shall extend the 60-day bid evaluation period by a total of 5 working days if a bid is nonresponsive or a bidder is judged to be not responsible, and the bidder cannot be notified in writing a minimum of 5 days prior to the end of the 30-day bid evaluation period in the case of an agency, or the 60-day bid evaluation period in the case of a school district. Written notification to the bidder or bidders whose bid is nonresponsive or who have been determined to be not responsible shall be received at least 5 working days prior to the end of the original or the extended evaluation period and shall specify the reason or reasons why the bid is nonresponsive or the bidder determined to be not responsible. If the bid evaluation period is extended by 5 working days, the contracting agency or school district shall notify each bidder in writing prior to the end of the 30-day bid evaluation period in the case of an agency, or the 60-day bid evaluation period in the case of a school district, that the bid evaluation period is being extended by 5 working days. The written notification to all bidders shall include the calendar date by which the agency or school district shall award a contract or reject all bids.

1. Each bid on any public works contract must be deemed responsive by the agency to be considered for award. A responsive bid shall conform in all material respects to the requirements and criteria set forth in the contract plans and specifications.

2. An agency shall determine that each bidder on any public works contract is responsible before awarding the contract. Factors to be considered in determining the responsibility of a bidder include:

A. The bidder's financial, physical, personnel or other resources including subcontracts;

B. The bidder's record of performance on past public or private construction projects, including, but not limited to, defaults and/or final adjudication or admission of violations of prevailing wage laws in Delaware or any other state;

C. The bidder's written safety plan;

D. Whether the bidder is qualified legally to contract with the State;

E. Whether the bidder supplied all necessary information concerning its responsibility; and,

F. Any other specific criteria for a particular procurement, which an agency may establish; provided however, that, the criteria shall be set forth in the invitation to bid and is otherwise in conformity with state and/or federal law.

3. If an agency determines that a bidder is nonresponsive and/or nonresponsible, the determination shall be in writing and

set forth the basis for the determination. A copy of the determination shall be sent to the affected bidder within 5 working days of said determination. The final determination shall be made part of the procurement file.

    4.A. If the agency elects to award on the basis of best value, the agency must determine that the successful bidder is responsive and responsible, as defined in this subsection. The determination of best value shall be based upon objective criteria that have been communicated to the bidders in the invitation to bid. The following objective criteria shall be assigned a weight consistent with all of the following:

       I. Price — must be at least 70% but no more than 90%.

       II. Schedule — must be at least 10% but no more than 20%.

       III. Performance — must be at least 10% but no more than 20%.

    B. Performance criterion must be based on a contractor's performance rating as determined by the agency's performance-based rating system. The agency's performance-based rating system must be based on previous contracting performance and may not be based on a set of prescriptive rules favoring a particular business model or business procedure. The performance-based rating system must be defined in regulations promulgated by the Secretary of the agency and must include a procedure for a contractor to appeal a performance-based rating.

    C. A weighted average stated in the invitation to bid shall be applied to each criterion according to its importance to each project. The agency shall rank the bidder according to the established criteria and award to the highest ranked bidder. Every state agency and school district shall, on a yearly basis, file a report with every member of the General Assembly and the Governor that states which projects were bid under best value and what contractor was awarded each contract.

  b. A contract may be awarded to a bidder other than the lowest responsible and responsive bidder if, in the opinion of the contracting agency, the interest of the agency shall be better served by awarding the contract to another bidder. Such award shall be made only if the contracting agency makes a written determination of the award describing the reason or reasons why such award better serves the interest of the agency. The reason or reasons for making such award may include, but are not limited to, unsatisfactory performance on any previously awarded contract by the bidder being rejected.

  c. The successful bidder shall execute a formal contract within 20 days after the award of the contract. The contract shall be in a form with terms and conditions approved by the contracting agency. The successful bidder shall also provide a bond as required in paragraph (d)(8) of this section within 20 days after the award of the contract.

  d. If the successful bidder refuses or neglects to execute a formal contract and bond as required in this subchapter, the bidder's bid bond or security deposit shall be taken and become the absolute property of the agency for the benefit of the agency as liquidated damages, and not as a forfeiture or as a penalty. Such moneys shall be deposited with the Secretary of Finance or the chief financial officer of the agency if the agency is not a state agency.

e. If 2 or more responsible and responsive bidders shall bid an equal amount and such amount shall be the lowest bid, the contracting agency may award the contract to any 1 of them or may reject all bids.

f. A contracting agency may reject all bids on any contract prior to the award of the contract for any reason it believes to be in the best interest of the agency.

g. *Electronic bid or electronic submission.* — 1. If the Office or an agency determines that an electronic bid or electronic submission is beneficial, the Office or the agency may use the selected method to obtain bids for public works contracts.

2. The solicitation must designate that the procurement method will be an electronic bid or electronic submission, a schedule of bid activities, and an electronic mail account to which the response must be sent.

3. The Office's or the agency's representative and a witness shall open the electronic mail account immediately after the closing date and time; record the names of the vendors that responded, the date and time submitted, and the bids or associated prices; and prepare a tabulation of all responsive vendors for review.

h. *On-line bidding method.* — If the Office or an agency determines that an on-line bidding method is beneficial, the Office or the agency may use an on-line bidding method to obtain and evaluate bids for public works contracts. The Office or agency must indicate the method in the solicitation.

i. [Repealed.]

(14) *Suspension and debarment.* — a.1. Any contractor who fails to perform a public works contract or complete a public works project within the time schedule established by the agency in the invitation to bid, may be subject to suspension or debarment for 1 or more of the following reasons:

A. Failure to supply the adequate labor supply ratio for the project.

B. Inadequate financial resources.

C. Poor performance on the project.

D. Failure to provide required craft training under § 6960A of this title.

2. Any subcontractor who fails to provide required craft training under § 6960A of this title may be subject to suspension or debarment.

b. If a contractor fails to perform a public works contract or complete a public works project under paragraph (d)(14)a. of this section or a subcontractor fails to provide required craft training under § 6960A of this title, the agency that contracted for the public works project may petition the Director of the Office of Management and Budget for suspension or debarment of the contractor. The agency shall send a copy of the petition to the contractor within 3 working days of filing with the Director. If the Director concludes that the petition has merit, the Director shall schedule and hold a hearing to determine whether to suspend the contractor, debar the contractor or deny the petition. The agency shall have the burden of proving, by a preponderance of the evidence, that either the subcontractor failed to provide required craft training under § 6960A of this title or the contractor failed to perform or complete the public works project within the time schedule established by the agency by failing to do so for 1 or more of the following reasons:

1. Failure to supply the adequate labor supply ratio for the project.

2. Inadequate financial resources.

3. Poor performance on the project.

4. Failure to provide required craft training under § 6960A of this title.

c.1. Upon a finding in favor of the agency under paragraph (d)(14)b. of this section because a contractor failed to perform a public works contract or complete a public works project, the Director may suspend a contractor from bidding on any project funded, in whole or in part, with public funds for up to 1 year for a first offense, up to 3 years for a second offense and permanently debar the contractor for a third offense.

2. Notwithstanding the penalties under paragraph (d)(14)c.1, of this section, upon a finding in favor of the agency that a contractor or subcontractor failed to perform the requirements under § 6960A of this title, the Director shall suspend a contractor or subcontractor who fails to perform the requirements under § 6960A of this title and shall debar the contractor or subcontractor from bidding on any project funded, in whole or in part, with public funds for up to 5 years.

d. The Director shall issue a written decision and shall send a copy to the contractor and the agency. Such decision may be appealed to the Superior Court within 30 days for a review on the record.

History.

70 Del. Laws, c. 601, § 9; 70 Del. Laws, c. 186, § 1; 72 Del. Laws, c. 133, §§ 3-6; 72 Del. Laws, c. 258, § 77; 73 Del. Laws, c. 289, § 1; 73 Del. Laws, c. 300, § 1; 73 Del. Laws, c. 364, § 4; 73 Del. Laws, c. 428, §§ 3, 4; 73 Del. Laws, c. 438, § 2; 74 Del. Laws, c. 373, §§ 2-4; 74 Del. Laws, c. 416, §§ 2, 3; 75 Del. Laws, c. 88, § 16(5); 77 Del. Laws, c. 90, § 23; 77 Del. Laws, c. 329, § 116; 78 Del. Laws, c. 288, § 3; 79 Del. Laws, c. 47, § 26; 80 Del. Laws, c. 56, § 1; 81 Del. Laws, c. 298, § 4; 81 Del. Laws, c. 365, § 1; 82 Del. Laws, c. 36, § 2; 83 Del. Laws, c. 13, § 24; 83 Del. Laws, c. 129, § 5; 83 Del. Laws, c. 188, § 1.

Revisor's note.

Section 6 of 83 Del. Laws, c. 129, provided: "This act is effective immediately and is to be implemented the earlier of the following:

"(1) Notice by the Secretary of Labor published in the Register of Regulations that final regulations to implement this act have been promulgated.

"(2) One year from the date of the act's enactment." The act was signed by the Governor on Sept. 9, 2021.

Effect of amendments.

83 Del. Laws, c. 13, effective April 13, 2021, added (d)(7)c.

83 Del. Laws, c. 129, effective Sept. 9, 2021, rewrote (c)(13); repealed (d)(13)i.; transferred the "a." designation formerly appearing preceding the (d)(14) heading to appear in direct association with the paragraph designated as "1." thereunder; substituted "6960A of this title" for "paragraph (d)(13)i. of this section" in present (14)a.1.D., (14)a.2., the first and final sentences of the introductory paragraph of (14)b., in (14)b.4. and in two places in (14)c.2.

83 Del. Laws, c. 188, effective September 17, 2021, deleted "Community Transportation Fund or" preceding "municipal" in (c)(12)a.

§ 6968. Requirement of certificate of registration.

(a) After a bid proposal for a public works contract is submitted, but before the award of a public works contract, a 259 contractor must provide the agency to which it is contracting a copy of the certificate of registration under Chapter 36 of 260 Title 19 for each subcontractor listed in the bid proposal.

(b) An agency shall provide contractors and subcontractors the opportunity to register under Chapter 36 of Title 19 262 before the award of a contract.

History.
82 Del. Laws, c. 168, §§ 5, 6; 82 Del. Laws, c. 291, § 2.

Revisor's note.
Section 6 of 82 Del. Laws, c. 168, as amended by 82 Del. Laws, c. 291, § 2, effective Sept. 28,

2020, provided: "This act takes effect upon promulgation of final regulations adopted under this chapter, or on July 1, 2021, whichever occurs first." The act became effective on July 1, 2021.

§ 6969. [Reserved].

History.
82 Del. Laws, c. 168, §§ 5, 6; 82 Del. Laws, c. 291, § 2.

SUBCHAPTER VI
PROFESSIONAL SERVICES

§ 6981. Large professional service procurement process.

(a) Any state contract for which an agency is a party with probable fees, including reimbursable expenses and amendments, greater than the threshold amount or amounts established by the Contracting and Purchasing Advisory Council pursuant to § 6913 of this title for the completed job will be subject to the provisions of this subchapter. Agencies may, alternately, at their discretion, procure services which include materiel other than professional services in accordance with § 6924 of this title.

(b) Each agency shall publicly announce, not less than once a week for 2 consecutive weeks in a newspaper published or circulated in each county of the State, when professional services are required except:

(1) In case of critical needs so certified pursuant to § 6907 of this title; or

(2) Where professional services are determined by the agency to be necessary during the course of completion of a previously awarded contract and:

a. The agency determines that it would be in the best interest of the State to procure such additional or supplemental professional services from a firm already under contract for which the supplemental and additional professional services are required; and

b. Such additional or supplemental professional services are within the scope of the contract.

(c) Subject to the exceptions of subsection (b) of this section, each agency shall publicly announce each professional services contract subject to subsection (a) of this section by electronic publication accessible to the public in a manner prescribed pursuant to § 6902(10) of this title for 2 consecutive weeks.

(d) Such announcement shall include:

(1) The project identification;

(2) General description and scope of the project;

(3) Location;

(4) Deadline for submission of brief letters of interest;

(5) Criteria for selection of professionals including any special criteria required for any particular project;

(6) Indication of how interested professionals can apply for consideration;

(7) The agency's intention to award to more than 1 firm, if applicable; and

(8) A description of the selection process to be used, as defined in § 6982 of this title.

(e) Additional advertising shall be at the discretion of the agency.

(f) Each agency shall establish written administrative procedures for the evaluation of applicants. These administrative procedures shall be adopted and made available to the public by each agency before publicly announcing an occasion when professional services are required. One or more of the following criteria may be utilized in ranking the applicants under consideration:

    (1) Experience and reputation;

    (2) Expertise (for the particular project under consideration);

    (3) Capacity to meet requirements (size, financial condition, etc.);

    (4) Location (geographical);

    (5) Demonstrated ability;

    (6) Familiarity with public work and its requirements; or

    (7) Distribution of work to individuals and firms or economic considerations.

(g) In addition to the above, other criteria necessary for a quality, cost-effective project may be utilized.

(h) Each project shall be given individual attention, and a weighted average may be applied to criteria according to its importance to each project.

(i) For the selection process described in § 6982(b) of this title, price may be a criteria used to rank applicants under consideration.

(j) If the Office or an agency determines that an electronic submission is beneficial, the Office or the agency may use this method to obtain proposals for professional services contracts.

    (1) The solicitation must designate that the procurement method will be an electronic submission, a schedule of bid activities, and an electronic mail account to which the responses must be sent.

    (2) The Office's or the agency's representative and a witness shall open the electronic mail account immediately after the closing date and time; record the names of the vendors that responded and the date and time submitted; and prepare a tabulation of all responsive vendors for review.

History.

    70 Del. Laws, c. 601, § 9; 78 Del. Laws, c. 288, § 4; 81 Del. Laws, c. 298, § 5; 82 Del. Laws, c. 36, § 1; 83 Del. Laws, c. 56, § 37.

Revisor's note.

    Section 78 of 83 Del. Laws, c. 56, provided: "This act shall take effect in accordance with the provisions of state law." The act became effective upon the signature of the Governor on June 30, 2021.

Effect of amendments.

    83 Del. Laws, c. 56, effective June 30, 2021, deleted "large" preceding "professional" in (j).

PART VIII

DEPARTMENTS OF GOVERNMENT

CHAPTER 79

DEPARTMENT OF HEALTH AND SOCIAL SERVICES

SUBCHAPTER I

ESTABLISHMENT AND ORGANIZATION OF DEPARTMENT

§ 7910. Advisory Council to the Division of Developmental Disabilities Services.

(a) There is established the Advisory Council to the Division of Developmental Disabilities Services.

(b) The Advisory Council to the Division of Developmental Disabilities Services serves in an advisory capacity to the Director of the Division of Developmental Disabilities Services, to consider matters relating to individuals diagnosed with intellectual disabilities or specific developmental disabilities in this State and other matters that the Governor, Secretary of the Department, or Director of the Division of Developmental Disabilities Services may refer to it. The Council may study, research, plan, and advise the Director, the Secretary, and the Governor on matters it deems appropriate to enable the Division to function in the best possible manner.

(c) The Advisory Council to the Division of Developmental Disabilities Services is composed of 17 members who are appointed by the Governor. Membership is comprised as follows:

(1) Seven members who represent families, service recipients, and self-advocates in the developmental disabilities community and currently receive services from the Division of Developmental Disabilities Services. An Advisory Council member appointed to represent a family member who received services may continue to serve the appointed term if the family member dies before the term expires.

(2) Five members who represent a cross section of service providers in the developmental disabilities community and currently operate in the Division of Developmental Disabilities Services system, including from any of the following:

a. Residential service providers.

b. Day habilitation service providers.

c. Employment service providers.

d. Clinical service providers.

e. Behavioral or mental health service providers.

(3) Five members who are professional advocates representing individuals with disabilities and represent each of the following:

a. Delaware Developmental Disabilities Council.

b. State Council for Persons with Disabilities.

c. Disabilities Law Program at Delaware Community Legal Aid Society, Inc.

d. The Arc of Delaware.

e. Center for Disabilities Studies at University of Delaware.

(d) [Repealed.]

(e) Members of the Council receive no compensation, but may be reimbursed for reasonable and necessary expenses incident to their duties as members of the Council.

(f) The Council shall annually elect a chair from among its members. The chair or vice chair must be an individual with a developmental disability.

(g) The Governor may appoint a member for a term of up to 3 years to ensure that no more than 3 members' terms expire in a year.

(h) The number of members who must be present at a Council meeting in order to have a quorum and conduct official business is a majority of the appointed members. Counting for quorum does not include member positions that are vacant.

(i) The Governor may remove a member for gross inefficiency, misfeasance, nonfeasance, malfeasance, or neglect of duty in office. A member is deemed in neglect of duty if the member is absent from 3 consecutive, regular Council meetings or attends less than 50% of Council meetings in a calendar year. The Governor may consider the member to have resigned, and may accept the member's resignation.

History.
29 Del. C. 1953, § 7910; 57 Del. Laws, c. 301, § 1; 57 Del. Laws, c. 591, § 64; 70 Del. Laws, c. 186, § 1; 73 Del. Laws, c. 97, § 7[6]; 78 Del. Laws, c. 179, § 316; 82 Del. Laws, c. 130, § 1; 83 Del. Laws, c. 101, § 1.

Effect of amendments.
83 Del. Laws, c. 101, effective July 30, 2021, in (c), substituted "17" for "7" in the first sentence and added the second sentence, including (c)(1)-(3); and added the second sentence of (f).

CHAPTER 80
DEPARTMENT OF NATURAL RESOURCES AND ENVIRONMENTAL CONTROL

SUBCHAPTER I
NATURAL RESOURCES AND ENVIRONMENTAL CONTROL

§ 8003. Powers, duties and functions of the Secretary.

NOTES TO DECISIONS

Regulatory authority.
Hunters could use semi-automatic rifles for deer hunting, pursuant to 7 Del. C. § 704(g), so long as they followed all statutory restrictions regarding the types of sights, ammunition and number of cartridges allowed; the Department of Natural Resources and Environmental Control exceeded its statutory authority by prohibiting semi-automatic rifles within its hunting guide. Del. State Sportsmen's Ass'n v. Garvin, — A.3d —, 2020 Del. Super. LEXIS 2927 (Del. Super. Ct. Nov. 18, 2020).

§ 8011. Water Infrastructure Advisory Council.

(a) There is hereby established a Water Infrastructure Advisory Council.

(b) *Definition.* — "Wastewater facility" shall mean any property, easement, equipment, pipe, pump, plant or appurtenance used in any way to collect, transport, store, handle, treat or dispose of wastewater. "Surface water management" shall mean a strategy for the integration of drainage, flood control and stormwater management through habitat protection, restoration, and other green infrastructure. "Drinking water supply or water supply" facilities shall mean any property, equipment, pipe or other conveyance, pump, tower, tank or other storage device, well, filter and any other appurtenances used to collect, treat, store, and distribute the best quality water available to address strategies to correct, present or prevent future violations of health-based drinking water standards.

(c) The Water Infrastructure Advisory Council (the "Council") shall serve in an advisory capacity to the Secretaries of the Departments of Natural Resources and Environmental Control ("DNREC"), Agriculture ("DDA"), Health and Social Services ("DHSS"), Transportation ("DelDOT"), and Finance ("DOF") and collectively the ("Secretaries"). The Council shall be composed of 16 members appointed by the Governor with the advice and consent of the Senate. The Governor shall appoint a chairperson. Members of the Council shall serve for up to 3 years excluding the Chairperson who shall serve at the pleasure of the Governor. Members shall be appointed for staggered terms so that no more than 4 members' terms expire in any calendar year. There shall be at least 1 member who is a resident of New Castle County, 1 member who is a resident of Kent County, 1 member who is a resident of Sussex County, and 1 member who is a resident of the City of Wilmington. Members of the Council shall represent interest and possess expertise in the areas of wastewater, stormwater, agricultural water use, and drinking water infrastructure. Members may include, but not be limited to representatives from local government, public health, agriculture, and financial management, and 3 members representing nonprofit environmental organizations, 1 of whom may represent an environmental justice organization. No more than 9 members shall be affiliated with any 1 major political party. The Governor shall appoint a member representing the water utilities, the president of 1 of the conservation districts, and a member of the Farm Bureau, all of whom shall serve as nonvoting members of the Council, and at the pleasure of the Governor. The nonvoting members may provide annual recommendations to the Council relating to stormwater, drainage, flood protection, resource and conservation development projects, agricultural and conservation cost share, cover crops, conservation reserve enhancement, and tax ditches.

(d) Members of the Council shall serve without compensation except that they shall be reimbursed for reasonable and necessary expenses incidental to their duties as members of the Council.

(e) The Council's duties and responsibilities shall include the following:

(1) To evaluate, establish, recommend, and adopt a long-term plan for the public funding of drinking water supply and wastewater facility infrastructure projects that shall cover a period of not less than 6 years. The plan shall be updated and prioritized on an annual basis and incorporated in DNREC's and DHSS's annual capital budget requests to the Governor. A copy of the adopted plan shall be submitted to members of the General Assembly on or before November 15 of each year. Additionally, the Council shall submit to the Clean Water Trust Fund Oversight Committee annual advisory recommendations related to wastewater, stormwater and drinking water infrastructure addressing those elements required for inclusion in the strategic plan for clean water as required in § 8082(a) of this title on or before September 15 of each year.

(2) To establish standards and procedures for persons to submit requests for funding the construction, repair, renovation or expansion of water supply and wastewater facilities and to recommend specific grants or loans, or both, in accordance with such standards and procedures using funds authorized for such purposes by act of the General Assembly or funds approved by the Delaware State Clearinghouse Committee. The Council shall develop and recommend projects for the planning, construction, repair, renovation or expansion of water supply and wastewater facilities to be funded in whole or in part by the Delaware Water Pollution Control Revolving Fund, the Drinking Water State Revolving Loan Fund (the "Funds") and any other source of funding authorized by the General Assembly;

(3) To develop and periodically update a nonbinding comprehensive, statewide water supply and wastewater facilities assessment to be presented in 3 sections, 1 for each county. The Council may retain the services of necessary professionals and may enter into agreements in order to prepare such an assessment. Each of the counties may, at its option, designate a county agency responsible for preparing the assessment for such county, provided however, that the assessments shall be prepared in a uniform manner pursuant to criteria established by the Council. In the absence of such a designation, the DNREC and DHSS shall be the lead agencies in coordinating preparation of the assessment. The assessment shall include, but not be limited to, a description of the status of existing water supply and wastewater facilities, the current usage thereof, the adequacy of existing water supply and wastewater facilities, projected long range requirements for such facilities, the compatibility of existing land use plans with existing and long range requirements of water supply and wastewater facilities, and recommendations for improvements to existing facilities;

(4) To recommend affordability standards for water supply and wastewater facility infrastructure projects. Such recommendations shall reflect the goals of establishing fair rates that equitably distribute the costs of water supply and wastewater facilities using public funds based upon usage and relying upon private firms to provide services if it is economical and in the public interest to do so; and

(5) The Council shall review and recommend the payment of administrative and operating expenses of the Council to the DNREC and DHSS.

(6) The Council shall make funding recommendations to the Secretaries of the DNREC and DHSS of drinking water and wastewater infrastructure projects that are "ready to proceed."

(f) The Council shall adopt all motions and approve the 6-year water supply and wastewater infrastructure plan, the assessment, and recommendations for loans or grants only by a majority vote of the entire voting membership of the Council. All voting shall be done in person and at regular or special meetings of the Council. The Council shall conduct a public meeting in each county prior to annual adoption of the 6-year water supply and wastewater infrastructure plan. The Council is subject to the applicable provisions of the Administrative Procedures Act (Chapter 101 of this title).

(g) The Council shall work in concert with the DNREC, DHSS, the Department of Transportation, the Department of Agriculture, Conservation Districts, the Delaware Geological Survey, the Public Service Commission, the DOF, the Cabinet Committee on State Planning Issues and any other appropriate department, agency or committee focusing on statewide planning issues and each shall provide reasonable staff time and resources as may be required by the Council to fulfill its duties and responsibilities. The Council shall also work in concert with the Water Resources Agency of New Castle County and any other appropriate agency designated by the counties. The DNREC and DHSS shall be the lead agencies in coordinating support for the Council.

(h) The Council shall provide guidance and policy advice to the Governor and Secretaries and assistance in the statewide effort to develop infrastructure programs related to water supply, drainage, stormwater management and flood control. This guidance shall include State level direction to the DNREC and DHSS, and local agencies and operating units in the development of standardized processes and procedures for identifying and prioritizing problems and development of watershed-based solutions. The Council also shall provide guidance to the State in improving the quality of customer service and reviewing annual localized work plans.

(i) The Council shall provide assistance in defining areas of responsibility between the State and local agencies, and coordinating implementation and operations.

(j) The Council shall provide assistance to the State in the establishment of a central response unit coordinated by the DNREC to handle public calls relating to drainage, stormwater and flood control.

(k) The Council shall provide assistance in the statewide effort for the development of sustainable program funding options.

(*l*) The Council shall provide assistance in the development and evaluation of criteria for watershed-based plans for surface water management. The Council shall also provide assistance developing the priority needs for watershed plans. The Council shall assist in developing a strategy for long term planning for future growth as it relates to surface water management. This strategy may include options for private-public partnerships for infrastructure improvement and regional solutions.

History.

69 Del. Laws, c. 303, § 1; 70 Del. Laws, c. 186, § 1; 75 Del. Laws, c. 219, §§ 1-5; 75 Del. Laws, c. 353, § 81(c)-(e); 77 Del. Laws, c. 430, § 66; 79 Del. Laws, c. 48, § 1; 81 Del. Laws, c. 49, § 3; 81 Del. Laws, c. 374, § 21; 83 Del. Laws, c. 84, §§ 2, 3.

Effect of amendments.

83 Del. Laws, c. 84, effective July 22, 2021, in (c), added "Agriculture ('DDA')" in the first sentence, substituted "16" for "13" in the second sentence, added "agricultural water use" in the sixth sentence and "and 3 members representing" and "1 of whom may represent and environmental justice organization" in the seventh sentence, substituted "9" for "7" in the eighth sentence and added the ninth and tenth sentences; in (e)(1), deleted "beginning in calendar year 1995" from the end of the third sentence and added the final sentence; and added "voting" in the first sentence of (f).

SUBCHAPTER II
THE DELAWARE ENERGY ACT

§ 8059. Sustainable Energy Utility.

(a) *Definitions.* — As used in this section:

(1) "Affected electric energy provider" means an electric distribution company, rural electric cooperative, or municipal electric company serving energy customers in Delaware.

(2) "Affected energy provider" means an affected electric energy provider or affected natural gas distribution company.

(3) "Affected natural gas distribution company" means a natural gas distribution company serving energy customers in Delaware.

(4) "Agency" means any state agency, authority, or any political subdivision of the State or local government, including, but not limited to, county, city, township, village or municipal government, local school districts, and institutions of higher education, any state-supported institution, or a joint action agency composed of political subdivisions.

(5) "Commission" means the Delaware Public Service Commission.

(6) "Energy efficiency" means a decrease in consumption of electric energy or natural gas on a per unit of production basis which does not cause a reduction in the quality or level of service provided to the energy customer, achieved through measures or programs that target consumer behavior, or replace or improve the performance of equipment, processes, or devices. Energy efficiency can also mean the reduction in transmission and distribution losses associated with the design and operation of the electrical system.

(7) "Energy savings" means reductions in electricity consumption, reductions in natural gas consumption, electricity peak demand response programs resulting in reduced electricity consumption, or measurable

efficiency gains from the transition to lower-emission fuels, as determined by the Secretary through regulations pursuant to paragraph (h)(3) of this section.

(8) "Secretary" means the Secretary of the Department of Natural Resources and Environmental Control.

(9) "SEU Oversight Board" ("the Board") means the board created pursuant to this section.

(10) "Sustainable Energy Utility" ("SEU") is the nonprofit entity created pursuant to the provisions of this section to develop and coordinate programs for energy end-users in Delaware for the purpose of promoting the sustainable use of energy in Delaware.

(b) *Intent of legislation.* — The General Assembly finds that there remain in Delaware significant, cost-effective opportunities to acquire end-user energy efficiency savings that can lower customers' bills and reduce the environmental impacts of energy production, delivery, and use. Delaware has an opportunity to create new markets for customer-sited renewable energy generation that will help build jobs in Delaware, improve our national security, keep value within the local economy, improve energy reliability, and protect Delawareans from the damaging effects of recurrent energy price spikes.

(c) *Sustainable Energy Utility administrative organization.* — (1) This section creates the "Sustainable Energy Utility" ("SEU"). The SEU shall design and deliver comprehensive end-user energy efficiency and customer-sited renewable energy services to Delaware's households and businesses. The SEU shall be unaffiliated with any of the State's electric or gas utilities, public or private.

(2) Routine administration of the SEU shall be managed by an executive director selected by the Board through an open and competitive selection process.

(d) *SEU Oversight Board.* — (1)a. The business and affairs of the SEU shall be managed by or under the direction of the SEU Oversight Board. The SEU Oversight Board shall consist of 11 members and shall include the Secretary of the Department of Natural Resources and Environmental Control ("DNREC") or the Secretary's designee, and the Public Advocate or the Public Advocate's designee. The Board shall include representation from each county. Seven members of the SEU Oversight Board shall be appointed by and serve at the pleasure of the Governor, and may include, but not be limited to, representatives from the nonprofit environmental community, the nonprofit energy community, the nonprofit community servicing the low and moderate income community, the financing/accounting community, business, labor, and education. One member of the SEU Oversight Board shall be appointed by and serve at the pleasure of the President Pro Tempore, and 1 member shall be appointed by and serve at the pleasure of the Speaker of the House. The Board shall elect 1 of its members to serve as a chairperson by a majority vote. The Director of the Division of Energy and Climate of DNREC, or the Director's designee, shall serve on the Board in an ex officio nonvoting capacity. The terms of the board members shall typically be 4 years, and shall be staggered. The Governor may appoint members for terms of less than 4 years to ensure that the terms are staggered. The Governor may, at any time, remove any gubernatorial appointee to the SEU Oversight Board for gross inefficiency, malfeasance, misfeasance or nonfeasance, in office. A gubernatorial appointee may be deemed to have resigned their position if they are absent from 3 consecutive board meetings without good cause.

      b. The SEU Oversight Board shall be governed by and subject to the Delaware Freedom of Information Act (Chapter 100 of this title).

      c. The SEU Oversight Board shall include a provision in its bylaws pertaining to conflicts of interest and Board members shall be required to sign conflict of interest statements.

  (2) The SEU Oversight Board may, from time to time, appoint 1 or more advisory committees. An advisory committee may include representatives of organizations which represent low and moderate income energy consumers, low and moderate income housing consumers, civic organizations, environmental organizations, the energy industry, the energy efficiency and energy conservation community, the renewable energy community, marketing and public relations, small business, agriculture, accounting, business management, banking, finance, nonprofit communities, the general public, and the academic community. The Board shall decide the number of advisory committee members (including ex officio members).

      a. Among other things, the advisory committee may provide advice to the Board on issues of public policy and public education which may enhance the performance and quality of service of the SEU.

      b. A candidate for an advisory committee shall require a ⅔ vote of Board members in order to serve. Criteria for the advisory committee members shall include professional experience, community service, reputation, significance to Delaware, a diversified representation of the Delaware community and geographical representation of the State.

      c. Nominations for the advisory committee may be submitted by Board members and public solicitation.

  (3) Board members shall serve without compensation.

  (4) No board member shall receive financial gain from service on the Board.

  (5) Board members shall not be employed by any organization directly or indirectly affiliated with the SEU or its contractors for a period of not less than 2 years after the end of their service on the Board.

  (6) The Board shall adopt by-laws, by September 28, 2007, to govern itself.

  (7) The Board shall have the following responsibilities, among others permitted by law:

      a. Review and approve the contract-term and performance targets recommended by the executive director.

      b. Review and approve any proposed modifications to SEU performance targets or program designs.

(e) *SEU executive director responsibilities.* — The SEU executive director is responsible for the day-to-day functions and responsibilities of the SEU. The executive director's chief responsibilities include oversight of program management, and setting and compliance with appropriate performance and budgetary targets.

  (1) *Program research and design.* — a. The executive director shall develop a comprehensive suite of program designs. Each program design must specify, at minimum, program goals, performance targets, an estimated budget, an implementation strategy, and an evaluation strategy. The executive director is not required to design or initiate all programs at once, but he or she must demonstrate how each program fits within the SEU's overall strategy to meet the SEU's long-term performance targets.

      b. The executive director is expected to fulfill the following responsibilities through program designs, RFPs, and program implementation:

1. To be responsive to customers and market forces in implementing and redesigning the programs;

2. To design a portfolio of programs to allow all energy end-users, regardless of electricity or gas retail providers, and regardless of market segment or end-use fuel, to participate in the SEU programs;

3. To promote program initiatives and market strategies that address the needs of persons or businesses facing the most significant barriers to participation;

4. To promote coordinated program delivery, including coordination with low income programs, other efficiency programs, and utility programs;

5. To coordinate with relevant regional and national energy efforts and markets, including markets for pollution emissions offsets and credits, and renewable energy credits;

6. To consider innovative approaches to delivering sustainable energy services, including strategies to encourage third-party financing and leveraged customer contributions to the cost of program measures, as consistent with principles of sound program design;

7. To offer "one-stop shopping" and be the point-of-contact for sustainable energy services in Delaware;

8. To create a comprehensive website that provides easy access to SEU programs and information for all Delawareans, allowing them to participate in SEU programs electronically;

9. To emphasize "lost opportunity" markets, which are sustainable energy measures that can only be cost-effectively captured at particular times, such as during new construction or extensive remodeling; and

10. To emphasize market strategies to deliver services.

(2) *Administration of contracts.* — The SEU shall propose and adopt rules to guide the bidding process and criteria to guide bid selection. The RFPs shall specify a contract term not to exceed the limitation set forth in The Energy Performance Contracting Act set forth in subchapter V of Chapter 69 of this title.

(3) *Oversight and reporting.* — a. The SEU Oversight Board shall develop a 3- to 5-year strategic plan, with input provided by board members, stakeholder groups across the State, and the public at large. The strategic plan shall be made available to the public on the SEU's website. The SEU's strategic plan shall include an educational component for the general public with a continued focus on residential energy efficiency projects.

b. The SEU shall publish a comprehensive annual report which shall be submitted to the Governor and the General Assembly and made available to the public on the SEU's website.

c. The SEU shall have certified financial statements prepared at the end of each fiscal year and make them available to the public on the SEU's website.

d. The SEU's financial statements shall be audited every other year by an independent certified public accounting firm qualified to perform such an audit, and the audit results shall be made available to the public on the SEU's website.

(f) *Funding for the SEU.* — (1) DNREC may partner with the SEU to assist in the administration of some or all of the Green Energy Fund in accordance with § 8057 of this title.

(2) *Bonds of the SEU.* — a. The SEU may from time to time issue bonds for any corporate purpose and all such bonds, notes, bond anticipation notes or other obligations of the SEU issued pursuant to this section shall be and are hereby declared to be negotiable for all purposes notwithstanding their payment from a limited source and without regard to any other law or laws. In anticipation of the sale of such bonds, the SEU may issue negotiable bond anticipation notes and may renew the same from time to time, but the maximum maturity of any such note, including renewals thereof, shall not exceed 5 years from the date of issue of the original note. Such notes shall be paid from any revenues of the SEU available therefor and not otherwise pledged, or from the proceeds of sale of the bonds of the SEU in anticipation of which they were issued. The notes shall be issued in the same manner as the bonds. Such notes and the resolution or resolutions authorizing the same may contain any provisions, conditions or limitations which a bond resolution of the SEU may contain.

b. The bonds and notes of every issue shall be payable solely out of the revenues of the SEU, subject only to any agreements with the holders of particular bonds or notes pledging any particular revenues and subject to any agreements with any participating facility. Notwithstanding that bonds and notes may be payable from a special fund, they shall be and be deemed to be, for all purposes, negotiable instruments subject only to the provisions of the bonds and notes for registration.

c. The bonds may be issued as serial bonds or as term bonds, or the SEU, in its discretion may issue bonds of both types. The bonds shall be authorized by resolution of the members of the SEU Oversight Board and shall bear such date or dates, mature at such time or times, not exceeding 50 years from their respective dates, bear interest at such rate or rates, payable at such time or times, be in such denominations, be in such form, either coupon or registered, carry such registration privileges, be executed in such manner, be payable in lawful money of the United States of America at such place or places, and be subject to such terms of redemption, as such resolution or resolutions may provide. Such resolution or resolutions may delegate to any combination of 3 of the members of the SEU Oversight Board, the power to determine any of the matters set forth in this paragraph (f)(2) and the power to award the bonds to a purchaser or purchasers at public sale or to negotiate a sale to a purchaser or purchasers. The bonds or notes may be sold at public or private sale for such price or prices as the SEU shall determine. Pending preparation of the definitive bonds, the SEU may issue interim receipts or certificates which shall be exchanged for such definitive bonds.

d. Neither the members of the SEU Oversight Board nor any person executing the bonds or notes shall be liable personally on the bonds or notes or be subject to any personal liability or accountability by reason of the issuance thereof.

e. The SEU shall have power, out of any funds available therefor, to purchase its bonds or notes. The SEU may hold, pledge, cancel or resell such bonds or notes subject to and in accordance with agreements with bondholders or participating facilities. The SEU may elect to have bonds issued by a conduit issuer and borrow the proceeds thereof.

f. Bonds or notes issued under this section shall not be deemed to constitute a debt or liability of the State or of any political subdivisions thereof or a pledge of the faith and credit of the State or of any such political subdivision, but shall be payable solely from the funds herein provided therefor. All such bonds or notes shall contain on the face thereof a statement to the effect that neither the State nor any political subdivision thereof shall be obligated to pay the same or the interest thereon and that neither the faith and credit nor the taxing power of the State or of any political subdivision thereof is pledged to the payment of the principal of or the interest on such bonds. The issuance of bonds under this section shall not directly or indirectly or contingently obligate the State or any political subdivision thereof to levy or to pledge any form of taxation whatever therefor, or to make any appropriation for their payment. Nothing contained in this section shall prevent or be construed to prevent the SEU from pledging its full faith and credit or the full faith and credit of a participating facility to the payment of bonds or issue of bonds authorized pursuant to this section.

g. Interest on bonds or notes issued under this section shall be exempt from income taxation by this State or any political subdivision thereof.

(3) Revenue sources contributing to the SEU for the purpose of paying bond debt may include but not be limited to funds from shared savings agreements with SEU participants and partial proceeds from the sale of Renewable Energy Credits or Solar Renewable Energy Credits in local and regional markets. The Green Energy Fund shall provide equity leverage for the SEU.

(4) Incentives provided through the SEU or proceeds from the Regional Greenhouse Gas Initiative shall be exempt from taxation by the State and by the counties and municipalities of the State.

(g) *Contracts with the State or agencies.* — The State or any agency may enter into contracts with the SEU or a qualified provider (as defined in § 6972(5) of this title) for the purpose of acquiring, constructing, operating, or providing a project, including arrangements for paying the costs of such project, which costs may include debt service requirements of the SEU relating to that project. If the SEU procures a contract in accordance with subsection (e) of this section, a contract between the SEU and the State or an agency that provides the benefit of the contract to the State or agency may be entered into by the State or agency without additional competitive procurement.

No obligation of the State or an agency under an installment payment agreement, a guaranteed energy performance contract or any other agreement entered into in connection with a project under this Chapter 80 or Chapter 69 of this title shall constitute or create a debt of the State or agency. No such obligation of the State or an agency shall constitute a tax supported obligation or a bond or a note of the State as provided in Chapter 74 of this title.

(h) *Expansion of cost-effective energy efficiency programs.* — Notwithstanding progress towards the achievement of the energy savings targets in § 1502(a) of Title 26, each affected energy provider shall implement energy efficiency, energy conservation, and peak demand reduction programs that are cost-effective, reliable, and feasible as determined through regulations promulgated pursuant to paragraph (h)(3) of this section and delivered in collaboration with the Sustainable Energy Utility as described herein.

(1) *Development and delivery of programs.* — a. An advisory council consisting of 13 members shall be established by the Secretary and shall include 2 representatives of the Sustainable Energy Utility, and 1 representative of each of the following sectors:

1. Affected energy providers;
2. Manufacturing;
3. Agriculture;
4. Environmental;
5. Commercial;
6. Residential; and
7. Low-income sectors.

The advisory council will assist affected energy providers in the development of energy efficiency, peak demand reduction, and emission-reducing fuel switching programs to meet the requirements of this section and in evaluation, measurement and verification of energy savings. Programs shall be designed to maximize the cost-savings benefits for ratepayers by utilizing private financing and allowance proceeds from the Regional Greenhouse Gas Initiative to the maximum extent practicable and consistent with this section, as the preferred sources of program financing prior to expenditures that would otherwise be eligible for rate recovery. The advisory council shall also recommend adoption of financing mechanisms, including, but not limited to, on-bill financing, property assessed clean energy ("PACE") models, and other innovative financing tools.

b. The advisory council, in collaboration with the Public Service Commission staff, and the Public Advocate, shall recommend candidate energy efficiency, and reduction, and emission-reducing fuel-switching program elements that are cost-effective, reliable, and feasible, including financing mechanisms. Such programs shall prioritize the use of energy audits to identify comprehensive energy efficiency measures that maximize cost-effective savings. The advisory council shall recommend 3-year program portfolios and define associated savings targets for the consideration of each affected energy provider.

c. Unless otherwise provided, affected energy providers shall prepare and submit to the advisory council 3-year program plans, schedules, and budgets designed to reflect the recommended program portfolios, including the defined energy savings targets. On a 3-year cycle, the advisory council shall review energy efficiency, peak demand reduction, and fuel switching program plans for each affected energy provider and recommend them for approval by the appropriate regulatory authority, if it finds them to be cost-effective through a net-cost-benefit analysis that quantifies expected cost savings when considered in their entirety pursuant to regulations required by paragraph (h)(3) of this section. Such programs must reduce overall utility bills.

d. Evaluation, measurement, and verification costs incurred by the advisory council and affected energy providers shall be included as costs in the cost-effectiveness test for the program portfolios. Costs shall be reimbursed first by any direct revenues from the programs, including but not limited to revenues from wholesale capacity markets. If such revenues are greater than program costs, the additional revenues shall be applied towards reducing the costs of future energy efficiency programs. If such revenues are less than program costs, the remaining costs shall be allocated to affected energy providers on the basis of total annual sales of energy and reimbursed by affected energy providers as part of energy efficiency and peak demand response program operation costs.

e. The Commission shall review the programs and portfolios recommended by the advisory council, including evaluating the projected net-cost savings, in determining whether to approve such programs for implementation by Commission-regulated affected energy providers. Notwithstanding any provision in Title 26, the Commission shall approve the recovery of appropriate costs incurred by Commission-regulated affected energy providers for approved programs and portfolios on an annual basis, in the same manner as other supply resources, including allocated costs pursuant to this paragraph (h)(1). The Commission shall approve cost recovery for cost-effective energy savings resulting from cost-effective programs and portfolios of commission-regulated affected energy providers that are verified through procedures established in regulations promulgated pursuant to paragraph (h)(3) of this section and determined not to increase overall utility bills. Recovery of appropriate costs shall be through a rate-recovery mechanism that is consistent with the goals and objectives of this section and recommended by the advisory council, filed by the affected energy providers, and approved by the Commission.

1. For the portion of efficiency programs not financed through SEU-secured private financing or Regional Greenhouse Gas Initiative allowance proceeds, or other SEU resources, the Commission shall utilize a process that achieves the efficient and timely recovery on an annual basis by commission-regulated affected energy providers of appropriate costs and associated rates of return related to implementing activities and programs recommended by the advisory council.

2. For commission-regulated affected energy providers, appropriate costs incurred arising out of activities and programs recommended by the advisory council that are not subject to contemporaneous recovery shall be subject to deferred accounting treatment to ensure that program costs are less than expected savings. Program costs may not be placed in the permanent rate base, nor exceed the amortization schedule of the deferred accounting treatment.

3. Peak demand reduction programs of commission-regulated affected energy providers that are currently under review or already have been approved by the Commission, including dynamic pricing and direct load control, shall not be subject to review and approval by the advisory council.

f. Affected energy providers that are not regulated by the Commission may elect to develop, implement and fund programs for energy efficiency and peak demand reduction recommended for approval by the boards of directors for rural electric cooperatives or the pertinent local regulatory authorities for municipal electric companies. For purposes of any comparable plan implemented pursuant to the requirements of § 363 of Title 26, energy efficiency resulting in a reduction in overall energy consumption that exceeds 10% of the electricity provider's 2007 electric consumption shall constitute an "eligible energy resource" under § 352 of Title 26, provided such energy provider has first achieved the 15% energy savings goal as required by § 1502(a)(1) of Title 26 and determined pursuant to paragraph (h)(3) of this section. Such energy efficiency shall be measured and verified as provided in paragraph (h)(3) of this section.

g. The affected energy providers and the Sustainable Energy Utility shall collaborate to promote available energy efficiency and peak demand reduction programs through a common marketing platform provided by the SEU, which shall serve as an easily accessible resource for all residents of Delaware seeking to save money through energy efficiency.

h. Nothing in this section shall reduce the authority of the Sustainable Energy Utility as defined in this title. The Sustainable Energy Utility, at its discretion, may provide private financing, allowance proceeds from the Regional Greenhouse Gas Initiative, or other financial resources to reduce implementation costs of energy efficiency programs in coordination with the affected energy providers and may collaborate with affected energy providers to provide efficiency programs.

(2) *Annual reporting.* — DNREC shall annually publish a report on statewide electricity and natural gas consumption and electricity peak energy demand and make the report available to the general public by December 31 of each calendar year. All affected energy providers shall provide actual and projected electric and natural gas consumption and peak usage data to DNREC on an annual basis as specified in regulations promulgated pursuant to paragraph (h)(3) of this section. The report shall identify progress toward the energy and peak savings targets of § 1502(a) of Title 26. In determining compliance with the applicable energy savings requirements, the Secretary shall exclude reported electricity savings or natural gas savings that are not adequately demonstrated and documented, in accordance with the regulations promulgated under paragraph (h)(3) of this section.

(3) *Evaluation, measurement, and verification of energy efficiency.* — a. Not later than June 30, 2015, the Secretary of the Department of Natural Resources and Environmental Control, with the cooperation of affected energy providers, shall, by regulation, establish the requirements of this subsection, including, but not limited to:

1. Evaluation, measurement and verification procedures and standards, including impact evaluation, environmental outcomes, process evaluation, market effects, and cost-effectiveness evaluation;

2. Requirements under which affected energy providers shall demonstrate, document, and report compliance with the energy savings targets established under § 1502(a) of Title 26; and

3. Procedures and standards for defining and measuring electricity savings and natural gas savings that can be counted towards the energy savings targets established under § 1502(a) and (b) of Title 26.

b. All regulations promulgated under this chapter shall be adopted under the Administrative Procedures Act, Chapter 101 of Title 29. Regulations promulgated by the Secretary shall not differ significantly among affected natural gas distribution companies or among affected electric energy providers. Regulations promulgated pursuant to this chapter and case decisions issued under the auspices of this chapter by the Secretary shall be subject to direct appeal to the Superior Court pursuant to the provisions of the Administrative Procedures Act, Chapter 101 of Title 29. The Environmental Appeals Board shall not have jurisdiction over any such appeal.

History.
76 Del. Laws, c. 54, § 1; 70 Del. Laws, c. 186, § 1; 76 Del. Laws, c. 235, §§ 1, 2; 76 Del. Laws, c. 296, § 1; 77 Del. Laws, c. 131, §§ 1-5; 77 Del. Laws, c. 222, §§ 3, 4; 77 Del. Laws, c. 452, § 8; 78 Del. Laws, c. 85, § 1; 79 Del. Laws, c. 395, § 1; 81 Del. Laws, c. 79, § 44; 83 Del. Laws, c. 178, § 1.

Revisor's note.
Based upon changes contained in 83 Del. Laws, c. 178, § 1, effective Sept. 17, 2021, in the second sentence of (h)(1)f., "eligible energy resource" was placed within quotation marks and "(6)" was deleted following "§ 352".

§ 8061. Delaware Voluntary Clean Energy Financing Program based on property assessments (D-PACE) or other local assessments.

(a) The General Assembly finds and declares that:

(1) The production and efficient use of energy will continue to play a central role in the economic future and environmental sustainability of Delaware and the nation as a whole; and

(2) The development, production, and efficient use of clean energy will strengthen the economy, improve the public and environmental health of this State, and contribute to the energy security of our nation; and

(3) The financing of clean energy systems and energy efficient technologies, and the powers conferred and expenditures made pursuant to this statute, will serve a valid public purpose and that the enactment of this section is expressly declared to be in the public interest.

(b) It is the purpose and intent of the General Assembly:

(1) To establish a voluntary commercial property assessed clean energy program in the State to provide access to financing for clean energy systems and energy efficient technologies with free and willing commercial property owners of both existing properties and new construction within the State.

(2) To utilize the Sustainable Energy Utility and the unique capabilities and qualities inherent within its structure and finances to launch a commercial voluntary assessed clean energy program that ensures the private capital markets can participate in this program.

(c) *Definitions.* — (1) "Benefit assessment" means a voluntary property assessment or other government service fee assessment, as authorized by this section, which is the mechanism through which a commercial property owner repays the financing for the qualifying energy improvements;

(2) "Benefited property owner" means an owner of qualifying commercial real property who desires to install qualifying energy improvements and provides free and willing consent to the benefit assessment against the qualifying commercial real property;

(3) "Clean energy systems" means renewable energy power generation including solar photovoltaic and thermal, wind, biomass, or geothermal and including waste heat recovery and other zero or net-zero emission energy sources available with advancing technology;

(4) "Commercial property" means any real property other than a residential dwelling containing less than 5 dwelling units;

(5) "County" means any county as defined in Title 9, and as authorized by this legislation or the SEU to issue benefit assessments;

(6) "Delaware Voluntary Property Assessed Clean Energy Program" or "D-PACE Program" means a program that facilitates reductions in energy production and consumption and utilizes the benefit assessments authorized by this section as security for the financing of these qualifying energy improvements;

(7) "Energy efficient technologies" means any device or piece of equipment, used in conjunction with existing infrastructure and appliances or as a replacement, that reduces energy consumption, but does not itself generate energy;

(8) "Energy utilities" means Delmarva Power and Light, Chesapeake Utilities, Delaware Electric Co-operative, Delaware Municipal Electric Corporation, or their successors as defined in Chapter 10 of Title 26;

(9) "Participating county" means a county that has entered into a written agreement, as approved by its legislative body, with the D-PACE Program pursuant to which the county has agreed to levy benefit assessments for qualifying energy improvements for benefited commercial property owners within such county and costs reasonably incurred in performing such duties;

(10) "Qualifying commercial real property" means any commercial property located in the State, regardless of ownership, that meets the qualifications established for the D-PACE Program;

(11) "Qualifying energy improvements" means any construction, renovation or retrofitting of energy efficient technology, clean energy systems, or qualifying waste heat recovery technologies that are permanently fixed to qualifying commercial real property;

(12) "Qualifying waste heat recovery technologies" means equipment and processes that capture the waste thermal energy from electric generation and other waste heat sources for use in nonpower generating commercial/industrial processes, including but not limited to space and water heating, in qualifying commercial real estate where fossil fuel power generation is not the principal business;

(13) "SEU" means the Sustainable Energy Utility as defined in this chapter; and

(14) "Third-party capital provider" means 1 or more entities, other than the SEU, that provides financing to benefited property owners for energy improvements.

(d) The SEU shall establish a D-PACE Program in the State to fund qualifying energy improvements to commercial real property, such that the improvements, property, and owner or owners fulfill the requirements enumerated herein, and those established by the SEU as part of the administration of the program.

(1) If a benefited property owner requests D-PACE financing from the SEU or a third-party capital provider for qualifying energy improvements under this section, the SEU shall:

a. Require performance of an SEU approved energy audit or feasibility analysis of such qualifying energy improvements on the qualifying commercial real property that assesses the expected energy cost savings over the useful life of such improvements unless a qualifying energy improvement is deemed automatically qualified by the SEU;

b. Require an evaluation of the property owner's credit, history, and other financial obligations, before approving such financing;

c. If financing is approved, either by the SEU or the third-party capital provider, require the participating county to levy a benefit assessment on the qualifying commercial real property with the property owner in a principal amount sufficient to pay the costs of the improvements and any associated costs covered by the D-PACE Program that will benefit the qualifying commercial real property;

d. Impose requirements and criteria to ensure that the proposed improvements are consistent with the purpose of the D-PACE Program;

e. Impose requirements and conditions on the financing to ensure timely repayment, including, but not limited to, procedures for placing a lien on a property as security for the repayment of the benefit assessment;

f. Require that written consent for a superior lien from all existing properly recorded lien holders be obtained before any improvements are financed or made; and

g. Allow the property owner to rescind any D-PACE financing agreement entered into, with either the SEU or a third-party capital provider, not later than 3 business days after such an agreement.

(2) SEU shall collect fees to offset costs associated with executing the program, including but not limited to, administrative costs, conducting feasibility studies, and monitoring and verifying project results.

(3) The SEU may serve as an aggregating entity for the purpose of securing public, foundation, or private third-party financing for qualifying energy improvements pursuant to this section.

(4) The SEU may use the services of 1 or more private, public or quasi-public third-party administrators to administer, provide support, or obtain financing for the D-PACE Program.

(5) The benefit assessment:

a. May cover up to 100% of project costs, including but not limited to, application fees, audits, equipment, maintenance, labor, and other costs directly related to the project over the project's life;

b. May also cover a portion of the D-PACE Program costs;

c. May be neither extinguished nor accelerated in the event of default or bankruptcy; and

d. Shall be levied and collected as to assessment payments currently and past due in the same manner as the property assessments of the participating county government on real property.

(6) The benefit assessment shall constitute a lien against the qualifying commercial real property on which the qualifying energy improvements are made. This lien shall:

a. Be superior to any other liens except the lien for other property taxes and other governmental service assessments of the participating county and other municipalities and share the same senior lien as other property taxes and governmental service assessments to the extent only of the amount of the DPACE assessments, penalties and fees currently due and/or in arrears;

b. Remain with the real property upon sale, including sale or transfer by operation of a tax monition sale or mortgage foreclosure, regardless of method; and

c. In the event of default or delinquency, be pursued in the same manner as with other property assessments, with respect to any penalties, fees and remedies and lien priorities; provided that notwithstanding any other provision of law including without limitation the provisions regarding the discharge of liens contained in §§ 8761 and 8773 of Title 9, in any event a tax sale or other foreclosure sale brought by the SEU or a third-party capital provider with respect to D-PACE assessments shall not have the effect of extinguishing any subordinate mortgage liens against the qualifying commercial real property. Notwithstanding the foregoing or any other provision of law:

1. The SEU and third-party capital providers shall not have the authority to pursue a foreclosure of benefit assessment liens by the monition method established pursuant to § 8721 et seq. of Title 9 but shall have the authority to pursue a foreclosure of benefit assessment liens by attachment methods pursuant to § 8771 et seq. of Title 9 and § 8741 et seq. of Title 9.

2. The tax collecting authority in a monition sale may collect in such sale, in addition to taxes, D-PACE assessments but to the extent only of the D-PACE assessments, penalties, and fees currently due or in arrears.

3. The provisions above with respect to not extinguishing subordinate mortgage liens shall not apply in the case of a sale by monition method brought by a tax collecting authority, regardless of whether D-PACE assessments are collected at such sale.

4. The SEU and third-party capital providers shall not be required to, nor shall they have the authority to, unless so directed by the applicable tax collecting authority, foreclose liens for property taxes and other governmental service assessments or collect such taxes and assessments in a sale with respect to D-PACE assessments.

5. The SEU and third-party capital providers shall not be required to pay proceeds upon a tax or other sale to collect D-PACE assessments to holders of subordinate mortgage liens.

(7) The liens created by benefit assessments may be assigned as follows:

a. Any participating county may assign to the SEU any and all liens filed by the tax collector, as provided in the written D-PACE agreement between participating county and the SEU;

b. The SEU may sell or assign, for consideration, any and all liens received from the participating county;

c. The assignee or assignees of such liens shall have and possess the same powers and rights at law or in equity as the participating county and its tax collector with regard to the precedence and priority of such lien, the accrual of interest, the fees and expenses of collection, and lien enforcement including, but not limited to, foreclosure and a suit on the debt; and

d. Costs and reasonable attorneys' fees incurred by the assignee as a result of any foreclosure action or other legal proceeding brought pursuant to this section and directly related to the proceeding shall be assessed in any such proceeding against each person having title to any property subject to the proceedings. Such costs and fees may be collected by the assignee at any time after demand for payment has been made by the assignee.

(8) The SEU shall allow third-party capital providers to provide loans directly to benefited property owners in lieu of, or in addition to, the SEU providing such loans.

(9) Pursuant to the purpose and objectives outlined herein, and with respect to the responsibilities of administering the D-PACE Program, the SEU shall develop program guidelines governing the terms and conditions under which financing may be made available to the D-PACE Program, in consultation with the Department of Natural Resources and Environmental Control, Division of Energy and Climate, energy utilities, the banking industry, local governments, and commercial property owners;

The program guidelines document shall include:

a. Underwriting criteria, which at a minimum must include verification of ownership, an assessment of property debt and value, an ability to pay evaluation, and for all financing arrangements by the SEU and third-party capital providers a savings to investment ratio evaluation;

b. A requirement that the life of the improvements is greater than the term of the financing;

c. Qualifications for improvements, including but not limited to: minimum project life for cost-effective, permanent application; minimum project value, consistent with ensuring the recapture of applicable administrative costs; maximum project value and project value relative to property value, consistent with local and national renewable and energy efficiency credit/funding programs and ensuring mortgage lender support; and maximum renewable energy project size consistent with local and national credit/funding programs, and with local energy service company (utility) regulations;

d. Recommended energy efficiency improvements to qualified commercial property owners seeking financing for clean energy generation systems;

e. Criteria for approving energy audits and auditors, selecting engineering reports for feasibility analyses, and determining the appropriate method of analyzing expected energy performance for D-PACE projects;

f. Standards for the processes of approval, financing, construction, repayment, including optional repayment at the time of sale of the property and SEU, third-party capital provider, and/or participating county actions of recourse in the event of default;

g. Standards for monitoring and verifying the energy and cost savings and other relevant outcomes of D-PACE funded projects, consistent with the project scale and scope, as well as the goals of the D-PACE Program;

h. A requirement to educate the property owner about the costs and risks associated with participating in the D-PACE Program established by this section, including but not limited to, the effective interest rate of the benefit assessment, fees charged by the SEU to administer the program, and the risks related to the failure of the property owner to pay the benefit assessment; and

i. Greater detail on all program specifications, processes, and party duties as assigned to the SEU in this section, as well as all necessary program guidelines and other specifications consistent with the administration of a statewide D-PACE Program not listed herein.

(e) The SEU shall have the authority to:

(1) Use principal and interest payments from existing benefit assessments to fund other projects;

(2) Use other legally available funds for project financing, including but not limited to, existing revenues, federal, state, local, or philanthropic grants, or private financing, notes, or other obligations;

(3) Impose fees to offset costs associated with executing the financing, including but not limited to, administrative costs, attorneys' fees, conducting feasibility studies, and monitoring and verifying project results;

(4) Specify whether these fees are to be collected at certain steps or intervals, or added into the project financing;

(5) Set a fixed or variable rate of interest for the repayment of the financing amount at the time the financing is arranged, or allow a third-party capital provider to set the interest rate, provided that party is financing the improvements;

(6) Enter into a financing agreement with the owner of qualifying commercial real property, to include billing and receiving payments from the participants (in the same manner property and government service assessments are collected); with approval of the participating county, transfer the rights and authorities of the financing agreement, including but not limited to billing and receiving payments, to a third-party capital provider, such that the party is directly financing the qualified energy improvement.

(7) Establish a D-PACE loss reserve.

(f) The D-PACE Program shall not be operational and available for commercial property owner participation/financing until a comprehensive program guideline document is adopted by the SEU Board of Directors. Prior to submission to the Board of Directors for adoption, the SEU shall:

(1) Organize a public hearing regarding the program guidelines document;

(2) Publish a notice to include the time, date, place of the public hearing, and a summary of the nature of the guidelines in at least 2 Delaware newspapers of general circulation, and by electronic posting on the SEU website, a minimum of 20 days prior to such hearing; and

(3) Provide the SEU Board of Directors minutes of the public hearing with the submission of the program guidelines.

History.
81 Del. Laws, c. 402, § 1; 83 Del. Laws, c. 91, § 1.

Effect of amendments.
83 Del. Laws, c. 91, effective July 30, 2021, in

(d)(6)b., added "sale or transfer by operation of a tax monition sale or mortgage" and "regardless of method"; and rewrote (d)(6)c.

§ 8062. State electric vehicle charging infrastructure.

(a) As used in this section:

(1) "Agency" means as defined in § 6301 of Title 29.

(2) "All-electric vehicle" means an electric vehicle that operates solely from an internal electric battery.

(3) "Costs" means the costs associated with electricity used by the agency's EVSEs, installation of the agency's EVSEs, and maintenance of the infrastructure and equipment of the agency's EVSEs.

(4) "Electric vehicle supply equipment" or "EVSE" means equipment that connects an electric vehicle to an external source of electricity to recharge the electric vehicle's internal battery.

(5) "Electric Vehicle" or "EV" includes plug-in hybrid vehicles and all-electric vehicles, and means a motor vehicle, as defined in § 101 of Title 21, that satisfies both of the following:

a. Uses 1 or more electric motors for propulsion.

b. Is powered through an internal battery that is charged using an external electricity source.

(6) "Plug-in hybrid vehicle" means an electric vehicle that operates with an internal combustion engine and an electric motor that can be plugged into an external electric power source to charge the internal battery.

(b) An agency that has installed EVSE may make the EVSE available for use, at the agency's discretion, by the public or employees, or both.

(c) If an agency provides access to its EVSE for charging to an electric vehicle not owned by the State, it may charge a fee for the use of its EVSE that does not exceed the agency's costs. The agency shall use the fees collected for the payment of the electricity used by the EVSE and for the maintenance of the EVSE infrastructure and equipment.

(d) Agency EVSE must be located on state-owned or state-leased real property used for state offices, service centers, maintenance facilities, correctional facilities, visitor centers, research centers, health-care facilities, recreational facilities, or other state-owned or state-leased real property where state employees work or receive visitors conducting business with state agencies.

History.
83 Del. Laws, c. 179, § 1.

Revisor's note.
This section became effective upon the signa-

ture of the Governor on Sept. 17, 2021.

SUBCHAPTER IV
CLEAN WATER FOR DELAWARE ACT

Revisor's note.
This subchapter became effective upon the
signature of the Governor on July 22, 2021.

§ 8080. Short title.

This act shall be known and may be cited as the "Clean Water for Delaware
Act."

History.
83 Del. Laws, c. 84, § 1.

§ 8081. Legislative findings.

(a) The General Assembly finds all of the following:

(1) The waters of this State are among Delaware's most basic and
valuable resources and should be conserved and protected in a manner to
realize their full benefits.

(2) Delaware's continued economic vitality is dependent upon: maintaining and improving the State's water and wastewater systems; and
protecting and enhancing the State's water resources and natural infrastructure as the foundation for a healthy population and environment to
sustain a high quality of life for residents, healthy habitats, as well as an
attraction for tourism, employers and workers.

(3) Many Delaware homes, farms, agricultural lands, and businesses
are at risk from flooding and drainage hazards, which have environmental, public safety, health, and economic impacts, and some Delawareans
lack access to potable drinking water or basic wastewater disposal in their
homes.

(4) Delaware's list of impaired waters includes 377 bodies of water that
suffer from excess nutrients, low dissolved oxygen, toxins and bacteria
that negatively impact human and aquatic life.

(5) It is important that priorities for clean water projects in this State
be given to projects that utilize green infrastructure and enhancement of
natural systems to provide ecological benefits that improve water quality,
demonstrate a high ratio of nutrient or pollution reduction to the amount
of funding, and improve of community resilience to extreme weather, sea
level rise, and other climate impacts.

(6) Existing federal and state funding resources alone are inadequate to
meeting the State's current and future demand for clean water projects.

(7) It is fitting and proper for the State to encourage local governments,
private entities and farmers to undertake clean water projects that
effectively and efficiently reduce pollution in the waters of the State by
establishing mechanisms to assist planning and financing of such projects
at the lowest reasonable costs.

(b) Based on its findings in subsection (a) of this section, the General
Assembly determines that it is in the public interest to designate a Delaware
Clean Water Trust account to ensure the greatest environmental return on
investment through the management and coordination of financial resources
available to the State for drinking water, wastewater, drainage, stormwater,
and other eligible clean water projects to be funded from the following sources:

(1) Appropriations, including supplemental funds in the bond bill,
intended to satisfy all of the following purposes:

a. Section 7903(14) of this title related to the Delaware Safe Drinking Water Revolving Fund.

b. Section 8003(12) of this title related to the Delaware Water Pollution Control Revolving Fund.

c. Section 3923 of Title 7 related to resource conservation and development projects undertaken by the County Conservation Districts in Kent, New Castle and Sussex Counties.

(2) Moneys received as repayments of principal and interest on loans, interest received on invested funds, and other funding made available for the programs and purposes in paragraph (b)(1) of this section.

History.
83 Del. Laws, c. 84, § 1.

§ 8082. Clean Water Trust oversight.

(a) To ensure coordination of the management of resources available for Clean Water Trust projects and other programs that impact the quality of the State's water resources, the Clean Water Trust Oversight Committee ("Committee") is established and shall serve in an advisory capacity to the Governor and the General Assembly.

(b) The Committee shall be comprised of 7 members to include all of the following:

(1) The Secretary of the Department of Natural Resources who shall serve as its Chair.

(2) The Secretary of the Department of Health and Social Services.

(3) The Secretary of the Department of Finance.

(4) The Secretary of the Department of Agriculture.

(5) The Secretary of the Department of Transportation.

(6) The Chair and Co-Chair of the Joint Capital Improvement Committee of the Delaware General Assembly.

(c) Members who serve by virtue of their position may designate a designee to serve on the Committee.

(d) The Committee shall be responsible for oversight of the Clean Water Trust account and shall produce and publish an annual report and strategic plan for clean water that shall include all of the following:

(1) An annual report, titled "The Mulrooney Report," accounting for the sources, benefits, and uses of the Clean Water Trust account and other water quality programs funded with state or federal resources including wastewater, stormwater and drinking water infrastructure and programs for drainage, beach preservation, waterway management, cover crop, the conservation reserve enhancement program, tax ditches and conservation cost-sharing that shall include a list of all funded projects.

(2) An annually updated strategic plan that shall include all of the following:

a. Multi-year water quality goals and progress toward meeting those goals.

b. Challenges facing the achievement of such water quality goals.

c. A prioritized list of proposed projects to attain such goals, including increased accessibility to low-income and traditionally underserved communities.

d. Drinking water testing priorities of the State.

e. Recommendations on minimum funding levels for wastewater and drinking water projects benefitting low-income and traditionally underserved communities through low interest loans and affordability grants.

    f. Recommendations on strategies that support low-income consumer affordability.

    g. An annual work plan report on the implementation of the strategic plan for the previous fiscal year addressing success indicators, deliverables and milestones.

  (e) Prior to the publication of the initial annual report and strategic plan, the Committee shall hold at least 3 publicly noticed meetings in Dover to seek input and allow public comment. Thereafter, the Committee shall hold at least 1 publicly noticed meeting prior to publication of the annual report and annually updated strategic plan. All meetings under this subsection shall comply with § 10004 of this title.

  (f) The Water Infrastructure Advisory Council and the conservation districts shall provide outside, technical assistance and advice to the Committee.

History.
83 Del. Laws, c. 84, § 1.

CHAPTER 84
DEPARTMENT OF TRANSPORTATION

§ 8409. Council on Transportation.

  (a) There is hereby established a Council on Transportation.

  (b) The Council shall serve in an advisory capacity, except as otherwise provided, to the Secretary, the Deputy Secretary, the Transportation Directors and the Governor, and shall do all of the following:

    (1) Consider matters relating to transportation in the State and other matters such as the budget and Capital Transportation Program which may be referred to it by the Governor or the Secretary of the Department.

    (2) Study, research, plan and advise on matters it deems appropriate to enable the Department to function in the best possible manner.

    (3) Have final approval of and adopt the Department of Transportation Capital Transportation Program which shall be submitted biennially to the Council by the Department.

      a. The Council shall review the updated Department Capital Transportation Program prepared by the Department of Transportation, and established under § 8419 of this title, as amended. The updated Capital Transportation Program shall cover a period of not less than 6 years. The draft Capital Transportation Program shall be available to the public and the Council shall publish notices in a newspaper of general circulation in each county. The notices shall specify dates and places at which public meetings will be held, by the Council, 1 in each county, at which time the program will be reviewed and publicly explained and objections or comments may be made by an individual or group. Public meetings shall be held at least 2 weeks after the draft Capital Transportation Program is made available to the public. The notices shall also specify the name and address of the person to whom written comments may be sent. The written comments must be received by the person within 10 days after the last public meeting, which must be scheduled no later than September 30 of the program year. Following the written comment period, the Council may make priority changes to the proposed Capital Transportation Program in an open meeting by documenting the reasons and justifications for changes, using the priority formula-based processes described in § 8419 of this title, and shall adopt the program by March 1 of the program year. The Capital Transportation Program as prepared by the Department and as adopted by vote of the Council shall become the adopted Capital Transportation Program for the upcoming fiscal years. The adopted program shall be submitted to the agency charged with preparation of the State Capital Improvement Program and members of the General Assembly on or before March 15 of the program year for inclusion in the State Capital Improvement Program for the following fiscal year.

b. The Department Capital Transportation Program, as recommended to the agency charged with preparation of the State Capital Improvement Program, shall set forth estimated expenditures by project or program for engineering, rights-of-way, and construction of any major capital transportation project or program when applicable. The Program shall include detailed information by project as to location, description of improvement, areas of deficiency, and priority rating.

(4) Have final approval of and adopt all corridor route projects in connection with new road alignments, which project shall be submitted to the Council by the Department.

(5) Have final approval on matters relating to highway transportation priority planning under § 8419 of this title.

(6) Review and comment on the issuance, suspension, revocation, or reinstatement of all certificates of public convenience and necessity issued under Chapter 18 of Title 2.

(c) The Council shall adopt all motions and approve all projects only by a majority vote of the entire membership of the Council. All voting shall be done in person and at regular or special meetings of the Council. If the Council, for any reason, shall fail to approve and adopt in writing within a reasonable period of time after receipt of the programs or projects referred to it, the Secretary of the Department may, with the approval of the Governor, upon 15 days prior written notice to the Chairperson of the Council, give final approval to said programs or projects notwithstanding the absence of the Council's written comments or approval.

(d) The Council shall consist of 9 members, with the members of no 1 political party holding a number of seats greater than one in excess of that held by the members of any other political party. This provision shall be applied only as existing Council members complete their present terms and all appointments made after July 18, 1990, shall be made in a manner sufficient to implement the political balance sought by this section, upon completion of the terms of the existing council members, at the earliest possible date.

(e) The Governor shall appoint the members of the Council, all of whom shall reside in the State, with a minimum of 2 members residing in any 1 county. A Chairperson of the Council shall be appointed by the Governor from the membership of the Council to serve at the Governor's pleasure.

(f) No person shall be eligible for appointment to the Council on Transportation who is a director, officer or employee of any public carrier, as defined by Chapter 18 of Title 2, as amended, or who owns or directly or indirectly controls more than 1 percent of the stock of any public carrier.

(g) No member of the Council shall hold any office or position or be engaged in any business, employment or vocation, the duties of which are incompatible with the duties of their membership on the Council.

(h) Members of the Council shall serve for a term of 3 years, provided however, that after the expiration of 3 years such members shall continue to serve until such time as the Governor appoints a replacement. Members of the Council on Transportation existing prior to January 1, 1990, shall be permitted to complete the existing term of their membership, subject to the other provisions of this section as amended. As the terms of their existing members of the Council expire, each of the first 3 appointments of members of the Council shall be for a term of 1 year, and the next 3 such appointments shall be each for a term of 2 years. Thereafter, all appointments shall be made for 3 year terms such that three members of the Council are appointed each year.

(i) Members of the Council shall serve without compensation, except that they may be reimbursed for reasonable and necessary expenses incident to their duties as members of the Council.

(j)(1) Failure to attend 3 consecutive regular meetings of the Council shall be construed as a request by that member to resign from the Council and a replacement may thereafter be appointed in the member's stead.

(2) Members may be removed only for just cause, except as otherwise provided herein. Prior to removal, members shall be entitled to notice of the reason for removal and shall be entitled to a hearing before the Governor or the Governor's designee.

(k) Any replacement appointment to the Council to fill a vacancy prior to the expiration of the term shall be filled for the remainder of the term.

History.

29 Del. C. 1953, § 8409; 57 Del. Laws, c. 514, § 1; 57 Del. Laws, c. 671, § 16; 60 Del. Laws, c. 503, § 7; 61 Del. Laws, c. 520, § 3; 62 Del. Laws, c. 164, § 3; 67 Del. Laws, c. 394, § 1; 69 Del. Laws, c. 362, §§ 1-3; 70 Del. Laws, c. 186, § 1; 82 Del. Laws, c. 13, § 2; 83 Del. Laws, c. 37, § 28.

Effect of amendments.

83 Del. Laws, c. 37, effective June 3, 2021, added "do all of the following" in the introductory paragraph of (a); substituted a period for a semicolon in (b)(1), (b)(2), the introductory paragraph of (b)(3), and in the final sentence of (b)(3)b., in (b)(4) and (b)(5); made changes in capitalization in (b)(3)a. and (b)(3)b.; in (b)(3)a., substituted "under" for "pursuant to" in the first sentence, and in the final sentence substituted "Improvement" for "Transportation" and "on or" for "on/or"; added a comma following "rights-of-way" in the first sentence and following "deficiency" in the second sentence of (b)(3)b. and following "revocation" in (b)(6); in the first sentence of (b)(3)b., substituted "State" for "State's", "or" for "and/or" following the first occurrence of "project" and "project or program" for "project/program" preceding "when"; substituted "under" for "as set forth in" in (b)(5) and for "pursuant to" in (b)(6) and deleted "as amended" from the end of both paragraphs.

§ 8419. Transportation priority planning.

The Department of Transportation, with Council approval, shall:

(1) Establish a method of determining current needs and costs of the entire multi-modal transportation requirements in the State which will be utilized in allocating capital funds for the Capital Transportation Program. The costs will be updated annually.

(2)a. Establish a formula-based process which shall be used for setting priorities on all Department transportation projects and which shall consider, but not be limited to the following: Safety, service and condition factors; social, economic and environmental factors; long range transportation plans and comprehensive land use plans; and continuity of improvement.

b. The formula based process shall not be utilized for setting priorities for dirt roads, suburban street aid projects, municipal street aid projects or system preservation projects. System preservation projects will be prioritized based upon performance measures established in the Department for pavement management, bridge management and safety management projects.

(3) Review and approve the Long Range Transportation Plan, to be used in connection with the Department's internal review process for transportation projects. Department programs or projects utilizing other than

state, Transportation Trust Fund or federal funds shall be indicated within the Capital Transportation Program with their priority rating as specified in paragraph (2)a. of this section, but the costs shall not be added to the total estimated cost of the overall program. An annual written report including this data shall accompany the Department recommendations.

(4) Update and prepare biennially a statewide Capital Transportation Program for submission to the Council on Transportation. The current year of the Program shall consist of transportation programs and projects to be advanced in that year based upon the prioritization ranking process specified in paragraph (2) of this section. No program or project will be funded for implementation except those that can with reasonable certainty be advertised for bid that year. Proposed projects or programs for the remaining years of the 6-year Capital Transportation Program shall be pursued in accordance with the prioritization ranking process specified in paragraph (2) of this section. The estimated cost of the Program for each year shall not exceed the estimated federal and state funds available for transportation purposes during that year. The estimated federal and state fund availability will be developed annually by the Department of Transportation based upon the dollar amount of funds available and the ability to use the funds for a specific program or project.

(5) Review any priority changes that would result in the introduction of new projects or programs to a proposed or adopted Department Capital Transportation Program and make recommendations on such priority changes or introduction of new projects or programs based on the criteria and formula-based process which establish the priorities or projects and programs. The Department shall fully document its recommendations in a written report to the Council on Transportation.

History.
61 Del. Laws, c. 520, § 2; 63 Del. Laws, c. 191, § 5; 67 Del. Laws, c. 394, § 2; 72 Del. Laws, c. 229, §§ 1-8; 82 Del. Laws, c. 13, § 3; 83 Del. Laws, c. 37, § 30.

Effect of amendments.
83 Del. Laws, c. 37, effective June 3, 2021, substituted "Transportation" for "Improvements" in the first sentence of (5).

CHAPTER 85
DEPARTMENT OF LABOR

§ 8503. Powers, duties and functions of the Secretary [Effective until Mar. 31, 2022].

The Secretary shall have the following powers, duties and functions:

(1) To supervise, direct and account for the administration and operation of the Department, its divisions, subdivisions, offices, functions and employees;

(2) To appoint, and fix the salary of, with the written approval of the Governor, the following division directors and office heads, who may be removed from office by the Secretary with the written approval of the Governor, and who shall have such powers, duties and functions in the administration and operation of the Department as may be assigned by the Secretary:

a. An administrator and head of the Office of Administration, who shall be known as the Chief of Administration and who shall be qualified by training and experience to perform the duties of the office;

b. An administrator and head of the Office of Planning, Research and Evaluation, who shall be known as the Chief of Planning, Research and Evaluation, and who shall be qualified by training and experience to perform the duties of the office;

c. A Director of the Division of Employment Services, who shall be known as the Director of Employment Services, and who shall be qualified by training and experience to perform the duties of the office;

d. A Director of the Division of Unemployment Insurance, who shall be known as the Director of Unemployment Insurance, and who shall be qualified by training and experience to perform the duties of the office;

e. A Director of the Division of Industrial Affairs, who shall be known as the Director of Industrial Affairs, and who shall be qualified by training and experience to perform the duties of the office;

f. A Director of the Division of Vocational Rehabilitation, who shall be known as the Director of Vocational Rehabilitation, and who shall be qualified by training and experience to perform the duties of the office;

(3) To appoint such additional personnel as may be necessary for the administration and operation of the Department within such limitations as may be imposed by law;

(4) To establish, consolidate or abolish such divisions, subdivisions and offices within the Department or transfer or combine the powers, duties and functions of the divisions, subdivisions and offices within the Department as the Secretary, with the written approval of the Governor, may deem necessary, provided that all powers, duties and functions required by law shall be provided for and maintained;

(5) To make and enter into any and all contracts, agreements or stipulations, and to retain, employ and contract for the services of private and public consultants, research and technical personnel, and to procure by contract, consulting, research, technical and other services and facilities, whenever the same shall be deemed by the Secretary necessary or desirable in the performance of the functions of the Department and whenever funds shall be available for such purpose. All necessary legal services shall be provided pursuant to Chapter 25 of this title;

(6) To delegate any of the Secretary's powers, duties or functions to a director of a division, except the power to remove employees of the Department or to fix their compensation;

(7) To establish and to promulgate such rules and regulations governing the operation of the Department as may be deemed necessary by the Secretary and which are not inconsistent with the laws of this State. The Secretary is authorized to develop emergency rules amending the Delaware Unemployment Insurance Code which enhance the flexibility of the unemployment insurance program in response to COVID-19 and alleviate some of the burden of temporary layoffs, isolation and quarantine by ensuring unemployment benefits are available to individuals whose employment has been impacted directly by COVID-19.

(8) To maintain such facilities throughout the State as may be required for the effective and efficient operation of the Department;

(9) To adopt an official seal or seals for the Department.

History.
29 Del. C. 1953, § 8503; 57 Del. Laws, c. 571, § 1; 70 Del. Laws, c. 186, § 1; 82 Del. Laws, c. 249, § 2; 83 Del. Laws, c. 2, §§ 3, 5.

Effect of amendments.
83 Del. Laws, c. 2, effective Feb. 8, 2021, added the second sentence in (7). The amendment expired under the terms of 83 Del. Laws,

c. 2, § 5, effective March 22, 2022.

§ 8503. Powers, duties and functions of the Secretary [Effective Mar. 31, 2022].

The Secretary shall have the following powers, duties and functions:

(1) To supervise, direct and account for the administration and operation of the Department, its divisions, subdivisions, offices, functions and employees;

(2) To appoint, and fix the salary of, with the written approval of the Governor, the following division directors and office heads, who may be removed from office by the Secretary with the written approval of the Governor, and who shall have such powers, duties and functions in the administration and operation of the Department as may be assigned by the Secretary:

a. An administrator and head of the Office of Administration, who shall be known as the Chief of Administration and who shall be qualified by training and experience to perform the duties of the office;

b. An administrator and head of the Office of Planning, Research and Evaluation, who shall be known as the Chief of Planning, Research and Evaluation, and who shall be qualified by training and experience to perform the duties of the office;

c. A Director of the Division of Employment Services, who shall be known as the Director of Employment Services, and who shall be qualified by training and experience to perform the duties of the office;

d. A Director of the Division of Unemployment Insurance, who shall be known as the Director of Unemployment Insurance, and who shall be qualified by training and experience to perform the duties of the office;

e. A Director of the Division of Industrial Affairs, who shall be known as the Director of Industrial Affairs, and who shall be qualified by training and experience to perform the duties of the office;

f. A Director of the Division of Vocational Rehabilitation, who shall be known as the Director of Vocational Rehabilitation, and who shall be qualified by training and experience to perform the duties of the office;

(3) To appoint such additional personnel as may be necessary for the administration and operation of the Department within such limitations as may be imposed by law;

(4) To establish, consolidate or abolish such divisions, subdivisions and offices within the Department or transfer or combine the powers, duties and functions of the divisions, subdivisions and offices within the Department as the Secretary, with the written approval of the Governor, may deem necessary, provided that all powers, duties and functions required by law shall be provided for and maintained;

(5) To make and enter into any and all contracts, agreements or stipulations, and to retain, employ and contract for the services of private and public consultants, research and technical personnel, and to procure by contract, consulting, research, technical and other services and facilities, whenever the same shall be deemed by the Secretary necessary or desirable in the performance of the functions of the Department and whenever funds shall be available for such purpose. All necessary legal services shall be provided pursuant to Chapter 25 of this title;

(6) To delegate any of the Secretary's powers, duties or functions to a director of a division, except the power to remove employees of the Department or to fix their compensation;

(7) To establish and to promulgate such rules and regulations governing the administration and operation of the Department as may be deemed necessary by the Secretary and which are not inconsistent with the laws of this State;

(8) To maintain such facilities throughout the State as may be required for the effective and efficient operation of the Department;

(9) To adopt an official seal or seals for the Department.

History.
29 Del. C. 1953, § 8503; 57 Del. Laws, c. 571, § 1; 70 Del. Laws, c. 186, § 1; 82 Del. Laws, c. 249, § 2; 83 Del. Laws, c. 2, §§ 3, 5; 82 Del. Laws, c. 249, § 3.

Effect of amendments.
83 Del. Laws, c. 2, effective Feb. 8, 2021, added the second sentence in (7). The amendment expired under the terms of 83 Del. Laws, c. 2, § 5, effective March 22, 2022.

§ 8511. Industrial Accident Board.

NOTES TO DECISIONS

Appeals.
Industrial Accident Board was the appropriate decision-making body to determine in the first instance whether COVID-19 was defined as an "occupational disease" under Delaware Worker's Compensation Act (19 Del. C. § 2301 et seq.); because plaintiff had filed a petition with the Board within the 1-year statute of limitations, and preserved the claim, the case would be returned to the Board in order for it to make that determination. Ingino-Cacchioli v. Infinity Consulting Sols, Inc., 2021 Del. Super. LEXIS 560 (Del. Super. Ct. Aug. 19, 2021).

CHAPTER 87
DEPARTMENT OF STATE

SUBCHAPTER I
GENERAL PROVISIONS

§ 8707. Delaware Government Information Center.

(a) The Government Information Center shall have the following functions and duties:

(1) To publish, maintain and continuously update content on the State's Internet portal to facilitate convenient and comprehensive access to government information;

(2) To provide convenient access to a complete collection of on-line information and resources published by state government and a comprehensive and current collection of online information and resources published by local, state and federal agencies of interest to the public;

(3) To provide information and resource materials related to Internet content management and online publishing services to state agencies, state and local governmental units and their subdivisions and, at the Department's discretion, to not-for-profit and other organizations to ensure every Delaware citizen easy access to online government information;

(4) To promote increased usage of Delaware's diverse collection of online resources and encourage community input in identifying and assessing areas for improvement;

(5) To recommend statewide web publishing standards and projects consistent with information technology standards articulated by the Department of Technology and Information;

(6) To promote adherence to statewide standards that improve citizen access to information and to institute and maintain a training and

information program on Internet publishing and content management to bring approved and current practices, methods, procedures and devices for the efficient and economical management of Internet content to the attention of all agencies and political subdivisions;

(7) To coordinate efforts to ensure that content on state websites is readily accessible to individuals with disabilities;

(8) To receive, accept, administer and expend any money, materials or other aid granted, appropriated or otherwise provided by local, state or federal governments, or by any source, public or private, in accordance with the terms thereof, and for the purposes provided hereinafter;

(9) To recommend legislation in concert with affected state agencies to ensure that citizens achieve convenient and meaningful access to state-wide Internet content;

(10) To enter into contracts or agreements to provide or to obtain services and materials; provided that such contracts or agreements relating to information technology will follow the business policies and procedures established by the Department of Technology and Information;

(11) To perform all other activities pertinent to the organizational function of the Government Information Center; and

(12) To set reasonable fees for and make available for all political subdivisions in this State either the electronic procurement advertising system, required by § 6902(10) of this title if practicable or in lieu thereof another website allowing for the public posting of local government bid opportunities, and the website designed pursuant to §§ 10004(e)(5), 10115(b) and 10124(1) of this title. The fees establish pursuant to this paragraph shall approximately and reasonably reflect all costs necessary to defray the expenses of the Government Information Center's activities required in providing such websites for political subdivisions in this State.

(b) In lieu of the requirements of § 8731(b) of this title, state agencies that publish on-line copies of publications, reports, forms and other materials may provide the Department with electronic addresses to access such materials for the purpose of making accessible to Delaware and other citizens resource materials published electronically at the expense of the State. The Administrator of the Government Information Center shall disseminate policies and procedures for providing such access and shall publish a comprehensive online directory of all government forms, publications and other such information available to the public through the State's websites.

History.
75 Del. Laws, c. 89, § 131; 78 Del. Laws, c. 288, § 8; 82 Del. Laws, c. 36, § 1; 83 Del. Laws, c. 65, § 2.

Laws, c. 65, § 2, effective June 30, 2021, "§§ 10004(e)(5)" was substituted for "§§ 10004(e)(4)" in the first sentence of (a)(12).

Revisor's note.
Based upon changes contained in 83 Del.

§ 8721. Delaware Commission of Veterans' Affairs — Duties and responsibilities.

(a) [Repealed.]

(b)(1) The Commission shall hire, through the State Merit System employment process, and employ an Executive Director, a clerical assistant, and other personnel necessary to perform the duties prescribed by the Commission. All employees of the Commission, including the Executive Director, must be veterans as defined in § 8720(b) of this title.

(2) The Executive Director is authorized to use the designation "Delaware Office of Veterans' Services" when promoting, performing, or furthering the work of the Commission.

(3) The Executive Director and staff shall report to the Secretary of State on all administrative matters and shall report to the Commission on all substantive matters.

(c) The Commission shall have the power of oversight in the administration of the Delaware State Veterans' Home and shall have the authority to promulgate such rules, regulations and policy as is necessary to the operation of a veterans' home provided, however, such rules, regulations and policy are not inconsistent with the other provisions of this chapter.

(d) The Commission shall have the power to operate and/or administer a Delaware Veterans' Memorial Cemetery in the State and shall have the authority to promulgate such rules and regulations governing the operation of a cemetery as it deems necessary; provided, however, such rules and regulations are not inconsistent with the provisions of this chapter.

(e) The Commission shall establish a repository for all veterans' "Statement of Service" or similar documentary verification of active armed service.

(f) The Commission shall establish and administer the "Delaware Veterans Trust Fund" which will provide financial assistance or grants to veterans with a minimum discharge of general discharge under honorable conditions to cover costs associated with medical and dental needs; medical transportation; homelessness support; home repairs and safety modifications; household utilities; and educational or retraining programs.

(g) The Commission shall represent the State in concert with other states' veterans' agencies and the U.S. Veterans' Administration on matters of mutual interest and concern.

(h) The Commission shall coordinate with and advise all departments and agencies of the State on all matters pertaining to education, training, employment, medical and financial benefit programs for veterans, their dependents and survivors.

(i) The Commission shall initiate, review, and/or sponsor state legislation pertaining to veterans.

(j) The Commission and/or its Executive Director shall augment, not replace nor infringe upon, the functions of the service officers (representatives) of veterans' organizations; provided, however, the Commission may appoint a service officer in each county, such service officer to be accountable and responsible to the Commission.

(k) The Commission shall submit to the Governor and to the General Assembly an annual report of the Commission's activities and recommendations.

History.
65 Del. Laws, c. 232, § 1; 67 Del. Laws, c. 42, §§ 1, 2; 69 Del. Laws, c. 225, § 1; 69 Del. Laws, c. 228, § 3; 70 Del. Laws, c. 358, §§ 1, 2; 75 Del. Laws, c. 288, § 1; 79 Del. Laws, c. 183, § 1; 82 Del. Laws, c. 18, § 1; 82 Del. Laws, c. 70, § 1; 83 Del. Laws, c. 37, § 37.

Effect of amendments.
83 Del. Laws, c. 37, effective June 3, 2021, rewrote (b).

CHAPTER 87A

ECONOMIC DEVELOPMENT

Subchapter I. General Provisions

SUBCHAPTER I
GENERAL PROVISIONS

§ 8711A. Site Readiness Fund.

(a) The Site Readiness Fund ("Fund") is established to provide economic assistance for renovation, construction, or other improvements to infrastructure to attract new businesses to this State, or expand existing businesses in this State, when such an economic development opportunity would create a significant number of direct, quality, full-time jobs within the State.

(b) The purpose of the Fund is to cultivate a resource of commercial, industrial sites that are readily available to new businesses, established businesses that are considering moving to the State, or existing businesses within the State that need additional sites to remain or expand within the State. To expand and sustain economic growth within the State, it is critical to consistently maintain readily available commercial, industrial sites to attract new business, or expand existing businesses. Without a stable inventory of sites that are ready or able to be developed in a timely manner for business use, the delay in converting undeveloped sites capable of conducting business in compliance with applicable regulations and ordinances may cause the State to lose significant business opportunities that would benefit the economic well-being of its citizens.

(c) The applicant must meet all of the following criteria for projects to be eligible for funding under this section:

    (1) Be sponsored by at least 1 public entity. For purposes of this section, a public entity is ether a county or a municipality. The sponsoring public entity must identify any regulations, zoning requirements, or local ordinances that apply to the project.

    (2) Establish that the proposed improvement will create a significant number of direct, quality, full-time jobs.

    (3) Demonstrate financial stability.

    (4) Serve a public purpose.

(d) In addition to the criteria established in subsection (c) of this section, an applicant to the Fund must establish all of the following business organizational requirements:

    (1) Validly exist as a corporation, public entity, limited liability company, or other regulated entity.

    (2) Be in good standing under the laws of this State, duly qualified to do business.

    (3) Be in good standing in each other jurisdiction in which its conduct of business requires such qualification.

    (4) Possess any business and professional licenses required under Titles 24 and 30.

(e) Applications to the Fund shall be administered by the Division of Small Business within the Department of State in accordance with 1 Del. Admin. Code § 402 that governs the administration of projects under the Delaware Strategic Fund.

(f) The Council on Development Finance shall review projects and make recommendations to the Director of the Division of Small Business, as chairperson of the Delaware Economic Development Authority, pursuant to § 8707A of this title.

(g) The Director may consider recommendations of the Council made under subsection (f) of this section. The Director is authorized to determine whether the applicant and the improvements are eligible under the requirements of this section.

(h) The Director is further authorized to approve projects and make grants, loans, or other economic assistance from the Fund to qualified applicants.

(i) The administration of funding approved under this section shall be administered pursuant to the requirements of this chapter and 1 Del. Admin. Code § 402.

(j) To ensure that Fund assets are expended in the public interest, the Director may require recapture provisions in any contract agreements for grants, loans, or other economic assistance from the Fund to recover for any substantial or complete cessation of operations by the applicant, or failure to reach any employment or other project benchmarks. The Director may impose the recapture provisions for the number of years necessary to realize the purpose of the Fund.

(k) The Director may require the applicant to report financial statements, progress reports on the status of the project, including, the number of direct, quality, full-time jobs created or saved as a result of the project, any economic impact of the funding, and any other information required to assess the project. The reporting period for each project is within the discretion of the Director to determine that the purpose of the Fund is realized.

History.
83 Del. Laws, c. 86, § 1.

Revisor's note.
This section became effective upon the signature of the Governor on July 27, 2021.

CHAPTER 89
DEPARTMENT OF CORRECTION

SUBCHAPTER I
GENERAL PROVISIONS

§ 8902. Appointment, qualifications, etc., of Commissioner; Deputy Commissioner; bureau chiefs; Acting Commissioner.

(a) The administrator and head of the Department shall be the Commissioner of the Department of Correction, who shall be a person qualified by training and experience to perform the duties of the office. The Commissioner shall be appointed by the Governor, with the advice and consent of the Senate, and shall serve at the pleasure of the Governor. The Commissioner shall be paid an annual salary as approved by the General Assembly. The Commissioner of the Department of Correction shall become a bona fide resident of the State within 6 months after his or her appointment; provided, however, that upon good cause shown, the Governor may grant an additional extension of 6 months. After becoming a resident of the State, the Commissioner of the Department of Correction shall continuously be a resident of the State as long as he or she retains the office. Failure to obtain or retain such residency shall serve to terminate said office.

(b) In the event the position of Commissioner is vacant, the Governor, by appointment, shall have the power to fill the position or positions of Deputy

Commissioner and bureau chief as are vacant. Deputy Commissioner and chiefs so appointed shall serve at the pleasure of the Governor, and, upon the position of Commissioner being filled, such Deputy Commissioner and chiefs may be removed from office by the Commissioner with the written approval of the Governor.

(c) In the event of death, resignation, temporary incapacity or removal of the Commissioner and prior to the appointment of a successor, the Governor may appoint the Deputy Commissioner or chief of any bureau of the Department to serve as Acting Commissioner. The Governor may during the Commissioner's absence from the State appoint the Deputy Commissioner or chief of any bureau of the Department to serve as Acting Commissioner during such absence. In either case, the Acting Commissioner shall have all the powers and perform all the duties and functions of the Commissioner during such absence or incapacity or until the successor is duly qualified and appointed.

History.

60 Del. Laws, c. 251, § 14; 70 Del. Laws, c. 186, § 1; 72 Del. Laws, c. 140, § 9; 78 Del. Laws, c. 305, § 4; 83 Del. Laws, c. 31, § 1.

Effect of amendments.

83 Del. Laws, c. 31, effective June 3, 2021,

added "Deputy Commissioner" in the section heading; added "Deputy Commissioner and" three times in (b); and added "Deputy Commissioner or" two times in (c).

§ 8903. Powers, duties and functions — Commissioner.

The Commissioner shall:

(1) Supervise, direct and account for the administration and operation of the Department, its bureaus, subbureaus, offices, functions and employees;

(2) Appoint and fix the salary, with the written approval of the Governor, of the Deputy Commissioner and chiefs of the Department's Bureaus and other office heads, who may be removed from office by the Commissioner with the written approval of the Governor, and who shall have such powers, duties and functions in the administration and operation of the Department as may be assigned by the Commissioner.

(3) Appoint such additional personnel as may be necessary for the administration and operation of the Department within such limitations as may be imposed by law;

(4) Establish, consolidate, abolish, transfer or combine the powers, duties and functions of the bureaus, subbureaus and offices within the Department as the Commissioner, with the written approval of the Governor, may deem necessary, providing that all powers, duties and functions required by law shall be provided for and maintained;

(5) Make and enter into any and all contracts, agreements or stipulations, and retain, employ and contract for the services of private and public consultants, research and technical personnel and to procure by contract, consulting, research, technical and other services and facilities, whenever the same shall be deemed by the Commission necessary or desirable, in the performance of the functions of the Department, and whenever funds shall be available for such purpose. All necessary legal services shall be provided pursuant to Chapter 25 of this title;

(6) Delegate any of the Commissioner's powers, duties or functions to the Deputy Commissioner or a chief of a bureau, except the power to remove employees of the Department or to fix their compensation;

(7) Establish and promulgate such rules and regulations governing the administration and operation of the Department as may be deemed necessary by the Commissioner and which are not inconsistent with the laws of this State;

(8) Maintain such facilities throughout the State as may be required for the effective and efficient operation of the Department;

(9) Adopt an official seal or seals for the Department;

(10) Adopt a plan for use of personnel within the correctional system;

(11) Adopt a plan to identify and classify very low risk inmates convicted of misdemeanors and sentenced to serve no more than 24 months of incarceration and to provide an ongoing list of such inmates eligible for release to alternative programs of punishment which do not include incarceration. Such plan shall include a provision that all inmates sentenced to serve no more than 24 months of incarceration shall be so identified and classified within 90 days of their commitment to an institution supervised by the Department;

(12) Devise and adopt a plan to provide weapons training to all probation and parole officers. Such plan shall include an option for each such officer to carry a firearm, after successful completion of a course in weapons, during work in the field. Said course of training shall meet or exceed the standards established by the Council on Police Training. Such plan shall be in operation no later than September 15, 1992;

(13) Upon an order of the court directing the Department to debit moneys in an inmate account in accordance with Chapter 88 of Title 10, the Department shall, to the extent adequate funds are available, transfer such moneys to the court. To the extent an inmate's account does not have adequate funds to comply with the court's order, the Department shall debit the inmate's account for future payment to the court. The Department shall retain records of an inmate's account upon the release of the prisoner from the custody of the Department if such account has a negative balance pursuant to a court order under Chapter 88 of Title 10. The outstanding balance of such an account shall be reinstated should that person be committed to the custody of the Department at some future time. Notwithstanding the above, no court order pursuant to Chapter 88 of Title 10, shall have priority over charges or debits pursuant to § 6536(b) or (c) of Title 11; and

(14) Provide feminine hygiene products to inmates at no cost in facilities maintained by the Department. For purposes of this paragraph, "feminine hygiene products" means tampons and sanitary napkins, for use in connection with the menstrual cycle.

History.

60 Del. Laws, c. 251, § 14; 61 Del. Laws, c. 15, §§ 1, 2; 62 Del. Laws, c. 283, § 1; 64 Del. Laws, c. 108, § 15; 64 Del. Laws, c. 304, § 1; 68 Del. Laws, c. 414, § 1; 70 Del. Laws, c. 186, § 1; 70 Del. Laws, c. 411, § 2; 78 Del. Laws, c. 305, § 4; 81 Del. Laws, c. 436, § 1; 83 Del. Laws, c. 31, § 1.

Effect of amendments.

83 Del. Laws, c. 31, effective June 3, 2021, added "Deputy Commissioner and" in (2); and added "Deputy Commissioner or" in (6).

§ 8905. Council on Correction [Effective until Sept. 17, 2026].

(a) *Purpose.* — The Council on Correction, referred throughout this section as "Council," is established to serve in an advisory capacity to the Commissioner of the Department of Correction. Council's purpose is to collect and evaluate the best available data to make recommendations to the Commissioner of the Department of Correction to further the following goals:

(1) Enhance the safe and orderly operation of Department of Correction facilities, for both employees and offenders.

(2) Enhance the efficiency of Department of Correction policies.

(3) Ensure system and offender accountability.

(4) Foster a constructive and respectful relationship between the Department of Correction and the public.

(b) Council shall consider matters relating to the development and progress of the adult correctional system of this State, including all of the following:

(1) Correctional facilities.

(2) Services provided to an adult offender.

(3) The care and supervision of an individual released on probation or parole.

(4) Another matter that the Governor, the Commissioner of the Department of Correction, or a chief of a bureau or division within the Department of Correction may refer to Council.

(c) Council may study, research, plan, and advise the Governor, the Commissioner of the Department of Correction, or the chiefs of the bureaus or divisions within the Department of Correction on matters that Council identifies as appropriate to enable the Department to function in the best manner.

(d) *Council membership.* — (1) Council is comprised of 7 members who are appointed by the Governor. Council may submit names for the Governor to consider when making an appointment.

(2) Each member is appointed for a period of 3 years. Each term of office expires on the date specified in the appointment; however, a member remains eligible to participate in Council proceedings until the Governor replaces that member. The Governor may appoint a member for a term of less than 3 years to ensure that members' terms expire on a staggered basis.

(3) Council shall annually elect a chair and a vice chair from among its members.

(4)a. The Governor may remove a member for gross inefficiency, misfeasance, nonfoeasance, or neglect of duty in office.

b. A member is deemed in neglect of duty if the member is absent from 3 consecutive, regular Council meetings without good cause or attends less than 50% of Council meetings in a calendar year.

c. The Governor may consider a member who is deemed in neglect of duty as having resigned, and may accept the member's resignation.

(5) A member does not receive compensation but may be reimbursed for actual and necessary expenses incurred in the performance of official duties.

(e) *Meetings and quorum.* — (1) Council shall meet at least 6 times per year.

(2) Council shall conduct at least 1 meeting in each county per calendar year.

(3) The number of Council members who must be present at a meeting to have quorum and conduct official business is the majority of appointed members. A member vacancy is not counted for quorum.

(f) Council may adopt bylaws or other procedural rules to carry out its functions under this section.

(g) Council must conduct its meetings and other business under Chapter 100 of this title (Freedom of Information Act).

(h) Council shall submit an annual report no later than December 1 to the Governor, General Assembly, Commissioner of the Department of Correction, chiefs of the bureaus and divisions under the Department of Correction, Executive Director of the Criminal Justice Council, and Director and Librarian of the Division of Research of Legislative Council. The annual report must include at least all of the following:

(1) Meeting agendas and minutes.

(2) Training programs Council members completed.

(3) Council's priorities and activities, including participation in legislative matters.

(4) Correspondence with the Commissioner of the Department of Correction and the Department of Correction in general. The correspondence must be redacted to remove any information that is not deemed a public record under § 10002 of this title.

(5) Council's goals, priorities, and planned activities for the next calendar year.

(i) Council is a Department of Correction entity, but the Criminal Justice Council, through its Executive Director, shall provide reasonable and necessary staff support and materials to assist Council in performing its duties under this section.

History.

60 Del. Laws, c. 251, § 14; 64 Del. Laws, c. 108, §§ 16, 17; 70 Del. Laws, c. 186, § 1; 79 Del. Laws, c. 379, § 1; 83 Del. Laws, c. 186, § 1.

Revisor's note.

Section 2 of 83 Del. Laws, c. 186, provided: "Section 8905(i) of Title 29 under this act expires 5 years after its enactment into law, unless otherwise provided by a subsequent act

of the General Assembly." The act became effective upon the signature of the Governor on Sept. 17, 2021. Subsection (i) of this section expired on Sept. 17, 2026.

Effect of amendments.

83 Del. Laws, c. 186, § 1, effective September 17, 2021, rewrote the section. Subsection (i), as added by § 1 of the act, expired by operation of § 2 of the act, effective September 17, 2026.

§ 8905. Council on Correction [Effective Sept. 17, 2026].

(a) *Purpose.* — The Council on Correction, referred throughout this section as "Council," is established to serve in an advisory capacity to the Commissioner of the Department of Correction. Council's purpose is to collect and evaluate the best available data to make recommendations to the Commissioner of the Department of Correction to further the following goals:

(1) Enhance the safe and orderly operation of Department of Correction facilities, for both employees and offenders.

(2) Enhance the efficiency of Department of Correction policies.

(3) Ensure system and offender accountability.

(4) Foster a constructive and respectful relationship between the Department of Correction and the public.

(b) Council shall consider matters relating to the development and progress of the adult correctional system of this State, including all of the following:

(1) Correctional facilities.

(2) Services provided to an adult offender.

(3) The care and supervision of an individual released on probation or parole.

(4) Another matter that the Governor, the Commissioner of the Department of Correction, or a chief of a bureau or division within the Department of Correction may refer to Council.

(c) Council may study, research, plan, and advise the Governor, the Commissioner of the Department of Correction, or the chiefs of the bureaus or divisions within the Department of Correction on matters that Council identifies as appropriate to enable the Department to function in the best manner.

(d) *Council membership.* — (1) Council is comprised of 7 members who are appointed by the Governor. Council may submit names for the Governor to consider when making an appointment.

(2) Each member is appointed for a period of 3 years. Each term of office expires on the date specified in the appointment; however, a member remains eligible to participate in Council proceedings until the Governor replaces that member. The Governor may appoint a member for a term of

less than 3 years to ensure that members' terms expire on a staggered basis.

(3) Council shall annually elect a chair and a vice chair from among its members.

(4)a. The Governor may remove a member for gross inefficiency, misfeasance, nonfoeasance, or neglect of duty in office.

b. A member is deemed in neglect of duty if the member is absent from 3 consecutive, regular Council meetings without good cause or attends less than 50% of Council meetings in a calendar year.

c. The Governor may consider a member who is deemed in neglect of duty as having resigned, and may accept the member's resignation.

(5) A member does not receive compensation but may be reimbursed for actual and necessary expenses incurred in the performance of official duties.

(e) *Meetings and quorum.* — (1) Council shall meet at least 6 times per year.

(2) Council shall conduct at least 1 meeting in each county per calendar year.

(3) The number of Council members who must be present at a meeting to have quorum and conduct official business is the majority of appointed members. A member vacancy is not counted for quorum.

(f) Council may adopt bylaws or other procedural rules to carry out its functions under this section.

(g) Council must conduct its meetings and other business under Chapter 100 of this title (Freedom of Information Act).

(h) Council shall submit an annual report no later than December 1 to the Governor, General Assembly, Commissioner of the Department of Correction, chiefs of the bureaus and divisions under the Department of Correction, Executive Director of the Criminal Justice Council, and Director and Librarian of the Division of Research of Legislative Council. The annual report must include at least all of the following:

(1) Meeting agendas and minutes.

(2) Training programs Council members completed.

(3) Council's priorities and activities, including participation in legislative matters.

(4) Correspondence with the Commissioner of the Department of Correction and the Department of Correction in general. The correspondence must be redacted to remove any information that is not deemed a public record under § 10002 of this title.

(5) Council's goals, priorities, and planned activities for the next calendar year.

(i) [Expired.]

History.

60 Del. Laws, c. 251, § 14; 64 Del. Laws, c. 108, §§ 16, 17; 70 Del. Laws, c. 186, § 1; 79 Del. Laws, c. 379, § 1; 83 Del. Laws, c. 186, § 1.

Revisor's note.

Section 2 of 83 Del. Laws, c. 186, provided: "Section 8905(i) of Title 29 under this act expires 5 years after its enactment into law, unless otherwise provided by a subsequent act

of the General Assembly." The act became effective upon the signature of the Governor on Sept. 17, 2021. Subsection (i) of this section expired on Sept. 17, 2026.

Effect of amendments.

83 Del. Laws, c. 186, § 1, effective September 17, 2021, rewrote the section. Subsection (i), as added by § 1 of the act, expired by operation of § 2 of the act, effective September 17, 2026.

§ 8906. Exemptions from merit system.

All of the following positions set forth in this section shall specifically be exempt from Chapter 59 of this title, as well as any others allowed by Chapter 59 of this title:

(1) Commissioner of Correction.

(2) Deputy Commissioner of Correction.

(3) Chiefs as established by this chapter, as well as any hereafter established, by the Commissioner, with the approval of the Governor.

History.
60 Del. Laws, c. 251, § 14; 83 Del. Laws, c. 31, § 1.

Effect of amendments.
83 Del. Laws, c. 31, effective June 3, 2021,

substituted "All of the" for "The" in the introductory paragraph; substituted a period for "; and" in (1); added (2) and renumbered former (2) as present (3).

SUBCHAPTER III
DEPARTMENT EMPLOYEES

Revisor's note.
This subchapter heading was added by 83 Del. Laws, c. 185, § 1, and became effective,

upon the signature of the Governor on Sept. 17, 2021.

§ 8926. Department Employee Education Assistance Fund.

(a) Any employee of the Department holding a position classified at paygrade 15 or below may avail themselves of the provisions of this section to prepay the tuition costs for higher education related to their position.

(b) The classes will be 100% prepaid by the Department upon application to the Human Resources Director of the Department prior to commencement of classes at a college or university within the State for classes related to corrections, public safety, criminal justice, psychology, or sociology or related fields. Related fields include any courses necessary to complete a degree program in criminal justice, corrections, public safety, psychology, or sociology. Department employees who work in the food service, mechanical, or building trades and maintenance area are eligible for prepayment for classes that relate to their field or trade. The employee must maintain a C average or better in the classes taken to remain eligible for this program.

(c)(1) The Department shall take the funds appropriated for this section in each fiscal year and allocate them as follows:

    a. 40% for the fall semester.

    b. 40% for the spring semester.

    c. 20% for the summer semester.

  (2) The Department shall establish a deadline date for applying for said funds. If there are more applications than funds for any semester, then the funds shall be prorated between the applications. If there are fewer funding applications than funds available, the Department shall roll excess funds over to the next semester.

(d) An employee who has received funding under this section but who is terminated from the Department for cause prior to completion of current vouchered courses or who otherwise fails to comply with any requirement of this section immediately becomes ineligible to receive education benefits under this section and shall repay the Department for all tuition and fee funding previously extended to the employee, including interest, on a pro rata basis from the time of termination or noncompliance. The Commissioner shall adopt appropriate procedures to determine the amount of repayment and the method of collection due by the employee under this subsection. If an employee voluntarily leaves the Department prior to completion of funded courses, the employee will not be required to repay previously funded tuition but will have to repay the current quarter or semester's tuition.

History.
72 Del. Laws, c. 273, § 1; 73 Del. Laws, c. 102, §§ 1, 2; 73 Del. Laws, c. 175, §§ 1-6; 83 Del. Laws, c. 185, §§ 1, 2.

Effect of amendments.
83 Del. Laws, c. 185, effective September 17, 2021, substituted "Department Employee" for "Correctional Officer" in the section heading;

rewrote (a); in (b), added a comma following "psychology" in the first and second sentences and following "mechanical" in the third sentence, made minor stylistic changes in the second sentence, and in the third sentence substituted "Department employees" for "Correctional officers" and "are" for "shall be" preceding "eligible", and substituted "employee" for "officer" in the final sentence; deleted "shall" preceding "include" in the second sentence of (b) and preceding "immediately" in the first sentence of (d); added the designations for (c)(1), (c)(1)a., (c)(1)b., (c)(1)c. and (c)(2); substituted a period for a semicolon at the end of (c)(1)a. and for "; and" in (c)(1)b.; in the final sentence of (c)(2), substituted "fewer" for "less", added "the Department shall roll" and deleted "shall be rolled" preceding "over"; and, in (d), substituted "employee" for "officer" in two places in the first sentence and preceding "will not" in the final sentence, "under" for "pursuant to" and "becomes" for "become" in the first sentence and "employee under" for "officer pursuant to" in the penultimate sentence.

CHAPTER 90
DEPARTMENT OF SERVICES FOR CHILDREN, YOUTH AND THEIR FAMILIES

Sec.
9003. Powers, duties and functions.

§ 9001. Intent and purpose.

NOTES TO DECISIONS

Safeguard the well-being of children.

Child was removed from the foster home because the Department of Services for Children, Youth and Their Families failed to meet the emotional needs of the child placed in its care where the child was placed in an austere home without emotional support while grieving and experiencing significant trauma; the Department failed to use reasonable efforts to meet the child's emotional needs because it did not reasonably address his mental health, particularly in light of the devastating effect of his father's rejection of him and the effect of his return to the Department's physical care. In re Redding, — A.3d —, 2020 Del. Fam. Ct. LEXIS 27 (Del. Fam. Ct. July 13, 2020).

§ 9003. Powers, duties and functions.

(a) The Department of Services for Children, Youth and Their Families shall have the following powers, duties and functions:

(1) To provide to children, youth and their families a comprehensive and effective statewide program of services for children and youth who have been committed to the Department or placed in the care of the Department by the Court, referred to the Department by parents, agencies or other individuals, or who have otherwise voluntarily applied to the Department for services;

(2) To provide services to children, youth and their families to prevent children and youth from becoming abused, neglected, dependent and delinquent, as defined under existing law, and to prevent mental illness and emotional disorders among children and youth;

(3)a. To provide for a variety of facilities and services to children, youth and their families which shall include, but not be limited to the following:

    1. Protective services;

    2. Preplacement, preventive services and reunification services;

    3. Home-based services;

    4. Mental health outpatient services;

    5. Drug and alcohol outpatient services;

    6. Residential and institutional facilities;

    7. Probation, aftercare and follow-up services;

    8. Adoption and permanent placement services;

    9. Evaluation, diagnostic and treatment services;

    10. Foster care services;

    11. Independent living services;

12. A continuum of residential mental health services, which shall include, but not be limited to, inpatient psychiatric hospitalization for all children requiring such care, mental health residential treatment centers and specialized mental health treatment services in other group-care facilities and foster homes;

b. The Division of Family Services will provide family preservation services to those families whose children are at imminent risk of out-of-home placement when it has determined that out-of-home placement can be avoided; provided, however, that the Division's highest priority in cases of abuse and neglect where an investigation is required pursuant to § 906 of Title 16 shall be the health and safety of the child and nothing herein will prevent the Division from removing a child from the child's home when it has determined that the child's safety and well-being may be jeopardized by remaining in the family home;

(4) To prepare and maintain a written case plan for each child under its supervision or custody, which shall include but not be limited to a description of the child's problems, the care and treatment of the child, and any other services to be provided to the child and the child's family; each case plan must be designed to achieve any placement of the child outside of the child's home in the least restrictive setting available and in close proximity to the child's home, consistent with the best interests and special needs of the child;

(5) To conduct a written review at least every 6 months of the case plan for each child under its supervision or custody for the purpose of determining whether the plan is appropriate;

(6) To develop a central case management system which will provide coordinated information on client progress, including the client's entry and exit from the system, assessment of the client's needs, development and review of the case plan and evaluation and monitoring of the client's progress;

(7) To license, register and monitor all residential and nonresidential child care facilities, including but not limited to institutions, child placement and adoption agencies, day care centers, family day care homes, group day care homes, group homes and foster homes unless otherwise exempted by law; provided however, that no license for a residential or nonresidential child care facility to be operated within the corporate limits of the City of Wilmington shall be granted until the applicant has provided the Department with verification of licensure by the City of Wilmington to operate a childcare facility;

(8) To supervise the provision of education in all facilities operated by the Department, with the Education Unit of the Department being considered a local education agency only for purposes of:

a. Any federal, state, or private loan forgiveness programs available to educators;

b. Any federal, state, or private competitive grant made available to, and awarded directly to, local education agencies, provided that any specific qualifying requirements are met;

c. Credits issued for youth who complete the requirements for credit-bearing courses provided through the Education Unit in the Department and credits for youth returning from placement by the Department;

(9) To monitor and evaluate all aspects of its service delivery system and document the need for or degree of compliance with standards, policies and procedures adopted by the Department;

(10) To administer the Interstate Compact on Juveniles and the Interstate Compact on Child Placement;

(11) To establish, implement and follow procedures and standards compatible with due process of law with respect to the removal of a child from the child's home, a change in the placement of a child who is under the supervision or custody of the Department, and any other actions by the Department that may affect the legal rights of a child and the child's family;

(12) To provide or contract with public and private agencies in this State and other states for facilities and services necessary to achieve the purposes of this chapter;

(13) To provide or contract for services designed to maintain or provide permanent homes for children who are in out-of-home care, through the provision of adoption services or, whenever feasible, reunification services for children and their families;

(14) To develop, administer, implement, and provide or contract a developmentally appropriate, comprehensive program that fully integrates independent living services such as financial stability, housing supports, medical, employment and training, education, and connection to resources and individuals, until age 21 and that will assist youth with their successful transition to adulthood, subject to appropriation;

(15) To develop and implement rules, regulations, standards and policies governing the internal operation and administration of the Department and provision of services;

(16) To exercise the authority and power to administer protective, mental health, correctional and probation services to children presently delegated by law to the Department of Health and Social Services, Division of Mental Health; Department of Correction, Bureau of Juvenile Correction; Family Court; and previously delegated by law to the Department of Health and Social Services, Division of Child Protective Services;

(17) To certify annually on January 31 to the Governor and the General Assembly that the mixing of adjudicated and nonadjudicated youths shall not take place in the Ferris School;

(18) Provide feminine hygiene products to youth at no cost in facilities maintained by the Department. For purposes of this paragraph, "feminine hygiene products" means tampons and sanitary napkins, for use in connection with the menstrual cycle;

(19) To exercise all other powers necessary and proper for the discharge of its duties.

(20) Shall devise and adopt a body-worn camera policy that shall meet or exceed the standards established by the Council on Police Training by regulation.

(b)(1) For purposes of this subsection, "conversion therapy" means any practice or treatment that seeks to change an individual's sexual orientation or gender identity, as "sexual orientation" and "gender identity" are defined in § 710 of Title 19, including any effort to change behaviors or gender expressions or to eliminate or reduce sexual or romantic attractions or feelings toward individuals of the same gender. For purposes of this subsection, "conversion therapy" does not mean any of the following:

 a. Counseling that provides assistance to an individual who is seeking to undergo a gender transition or who is in the process of undergoing gender transition.

 b. Counseling that provides an individual with acceptance, support, and understanding without seeking to change an individual's sexual orientation or gender identity.

    c. Counseling that facilitates an individual's coping, social support, and identity exploration and development, including counseling in the form of sexual orientation-neutral interventions or gender identity-neutral interventions provided for the purpose of preventing or addressing unlawful conduct or unsafe sexual practices, without seeking to change an individual's sexual orientation or gender identity.

    (2) The Department may not engage in conversion therapy with a child or recommend that a child receive conversion therapy.

History.
    64 Del. Laws, c. 108, §§ 1, 14; 65 Del. Laws, c. 211, §§ 1, 2; 69 Del. Laws, c. 352, § 1; 70 Del. Laws, c. 186, § 1; 70 Del. Laws, c. 198, § 1; 71 Del. Laws, c. 199, § 10; 71 Del. Laws, c. 301, § 1; 73 Del. Laws, c. 310, § 19; 79 Del. Laws, c. 185, § 3; 80 Del. Laws, c. 64, § 1; 81 Del. Laws, c. 340, § 13; 81 Del. Laws, c. 436, § 2; 83 Del. Laws, c. 83, § 4.

Effect of amendments.
    83 Del. Laws, c. 83, effective July 21, 2021, added (a)(20).

PART X

GENERAL REGULATIONS FOR STATE AGENCIES

Chapter
100. Freedom of Information Act, §§ 10001 to 10007.

CHAPTER 100
FREEDOM OF INFORMATION ACT

§ 10002. Definitions.

    (a) "Agenda" shall include but is not limited to a general statement of the major issues expected to be discussed at a public meeting, as well as a statement of intent to hold an executive session and the specific ground or grounds therefor under § 10004(b) of this title.

    (b) "Anchor location" means the physical location within the geographic jurisdiction of the public body that is open to the public and at which 1 or more members of a public body attend a virtual meeting.

    (c) "Caucus" means members of the House of Representatives or Senate, of the same political party, who assemble to discuss matters of public business.

    (d) "Disability" means as defined in § 4502 of Title 6.

    (e) "Electronic" means as defined in § 12A-102 of Title 6.

    (f) "FOIA" means the Freedom of Information Act under this chapter.

    (g) "FOIA coordinator" shall mean the person designated by the Cabinet Secretary, school district superintendent, local government head, Chair, or equivalent executive officer of the public body to receive and process FOIA requests.

    (h) "FOIA request" or "request" means a request to inspect or copy public records pursuant to § 10003 of this title.

    (i) "FOIA Request Form" means the form promulgated by the Office of the Attorney General upon which requests for public records may be made.

    (j) "Meeting" means the formal or informal gathering of a quorum of the members of any public body for the purpose of discussing or taking action on public business.

(k) "Public body" means, unless specifically excluded, any regulatory, administrative, advisory, executive, appointive or legislative body of the State, or of any political subdivision of the State, including, but not limited to, any board, bureau, commission, department, agency, committee, ad hoc committee, special committee, temporary committee, advisory board and committee, subcommittee, legislative committee, association, group, panel, council or any other entity or body established by an act of the General Assembly of the State, or established by any body established by the General Assembly of the State, or appointed by any body or public official of the State or otherwise empowered by any state governmental entity, which:

(1) Is supported in whole or in part by any public funds; or

(2) Expends or disburses any public funds, including grants, gifts or other similar disbursals and distributions; or

(3) Is impliedly or specifically charged by any other public official, body, or agency to advise or to make reports, investigations or recommendations.

"Public body" shall not include any caucus of the House of Representatives or Senate of the State. "Public body" shall include any authority created under Chapter 14 of Title 16.

(*l*) "Public body," "public record" and "meeting" shall not include activities of the University of Delaware and Delaware State University, except that the Board of Trustees of both universities shall be "public bodies," university documents relating to the expenditure of public funds shall be "public records," and each meeting of the full Board of Trustees of either institution shall be a "meeting." Additionally, any university request for proposal, request for quotation, or other such document soliciting competitive bids for any contract, agreement, capital improvement, capital acquisition or other expenditure proposed to involve any amount or percentage of public funds by or on behalf of the university shall indicate on the request for proposal or other such document that it relates to the expenditure of public funds.

(m) "Public business" means any matter over which the public body has supervision, control, jurisdiction or advisory power.

(n) "Public funds" are those funds derived from the State or any political subdivision of the State.

(o) "Public record" is information of any kind, owned, made, used, retained, received, produced, composed, drafted or otherwise compiled or collected, by any public body, relating in any way to public business, or in any way of public interest, or in any way related to public purposes, regardless of the physical form or characteristic by which such information is stored, recorded or reproduced. For purposes of this chapter, the following records shall not be deemed public:

(1) Any personnel, medical or pupil file, the disclosure of which would constitute an invasion of personal privacy, under this legislation or under any State or federal law as it relates to personal privacy;

(2) Trade secrets and commercial or financial information obtained from a person which is of a privileged or confidential nature;

(3) Investigatory files compiled for civil or criminal law-enforcement purposes including pending investigative files, pretrial and presentence investigations and child custody and adoption files where there is no criminal complaint at issue;

(4) Criminal files and criminal records, the disclosure of which would constitute an invasion of personal privacy. Any person may, upon proof of identity, obtain a copy of the person's personal criminal record. All other criminal records and files are closed to public scrutiny. Agencies holding

such criminal records may delete any information, before release, which would disclose the names of witnesses, intelligence personnel and aids or any other information of a privileged and confidential nature;

(5) Intelligence files compiled for law-enforcement purposes, the disclosure of which could constitute an endangerment to the local, state or national welfare and security;

(6) Any records specifically exempted from public disclosure by statute or common law;

(7) Any records which disclose the identity of the contributor of a bona fide and lawful charitable contribution to the public body whenever public anonymity has been requested of the public body with respect to said contribution by the contributor;

(8) Any records involving labor negotiations or collective bargaining;

(9) Any records pertaining to pending or potential litigation which are not records of any court;

(10) Subject to § 10004(f) of this title with respect to release of minutes of executive sessions, any record of discussions held in executive session pursuant to § 10004(b) and (c) of this title;

(11) Any records which disclose the identity or address of any person holding a permit to carry a concealed deadly weapon; provided, however, all records relating to such permits shall be available to all bona fide law-enforcement officers;

(12) Any records of a public library which contain the identity of a user and the books, documents, films, recordings or other property of the library which a patron has used;

(13) Any records in the possession of the Department of Correction where disclosure is sought by an inmate in the Department's custody;

(14) Investigative files compiled or maintained by the Victims' Compensation Assistance Program;

(15) Any photographs, video recordings or audio recordings of a postmortem examination in the possession of the Division of Forensic Science;

(16) Emails received or sent by members of the Delaware General Assembly or their staff;

(17)a. The following records, which, if copied or inspected, could jeopardize the security of any structure owned by the State or any of its political subdivisions, or could facilitate the planning of a terrorist attack, or could endanger the life or physical safety of an individual:

    1. Response procedures or plans prepared to prevent or respond to emergency situations, the disclosure of which would reveal vulnerability assessments, specific tactics, specific emergency procedures or specific security procedures.

    2. Building plans, blueprints, schematic drawings, diagrams, operational manuals or other records of mass transit facilities, bridges, tunnels, emergency response facilities or structures, buildings where hazardous materials are used or stored, arenas, stadiums, waste and water systems, electric transmission lines and substations, high-pressure natural gas pipelines and compressor stations, and telecommunications networks facilities and switching equipment, the disclosure of which would reveal the building's or structure's internal layout, specific location, life, safety and support systems, structural elements, surveillance techniques, alarm or security systems or technologies, operational and transportation plans or protocols, or personnel deployments. Records that disclose the substances being used or stored

on a given piece of property are public records; however, records which disclose the specific location on that property of the substances being used or stored may be disclosed only if the chief administrative officer of the agency from which the record is requested determines that disclosure will not jeopardize the security of any structure owned by the State or any of its political subdivisions, or will not facilitate the planning of a terrorist attack, or will not endanger the life or physical safety of an individual.

3. Records of any building or structure operated by the State or any of its political subdivisions, the disclosure of which would reveal the building's or structure's life, safety and support systems, surveillance techniques, alarm or security systems or technologies, operational and evacuation plans or protocols, or personnel deployments.

4. Records prepared to prevent or respond to emergency situations identifying or describing the name, location, pharmaceutical cache, contents, capacity, equipment, physical features or capabilities of individual medical facilities, storage facilities, or laboratories established, maintained or regulated by the State or any of its political subdivisions.

5. Those portions of records assembled, prepared or maintained to prevent, mitigate or respond to criminal acts, the public disclosure of which would have a substantial likelihood of threatening public safety. The only items that are protected from disclosure by this paragraph are:

    A. Specific and unique vulnerability assessments or specific and unique response or deployment plans, including compiled underlying data collected in preparation of or essential to the assessments or to the response or deployment plans; and

    B. Records not subject to public disclosure under federal law that are shared by federal or international agencies and information prepared from national security briefings provided to state or local government officials related to domestic preparedness for criminal acts against United States citizens or targets.

6. Nothing in this subsection shall be deemed to prohibit the disclosure of information necessary to comply with the requirements of Chapter 8 of Title 26, the Underground Utility Damage Prevention and Safety Act.

7. Information technology (IT) infrastructure details, source code, logical and physical design of IT systems and interfaces, detailed hardware and software inventories, network architecture and schematics, vulnerability reports, and any other information that, if disclosed, could jeopardize the security or integrity of an information and technology system owned, operated or maintained by the State or any public body subject to the requirements of this chapter.

b. Nothing in this paragraph shall interfere with the right of any committee of the General Assembly to hear information in the committee at the request of the committee chair or, if appropriate, to hear information in an executive session of the committee, or to subpoena information pursuant to § 705 of this title;

(18)a. Any military service discharge document or documents, a discharge, separation notice, certificate of service, report of transfer or discharge, or any other notice or document which is evidence of severance or transfer from military service and which contains a service record from the armed forces of the United States, or any document that purports to represent a notice of separation from or service in any armed forces of the United States including but not limited to the United States Department of Defense, DD Form 214, of a veteran of the armed forces of the United States, which has been heretofore recorded at a county recorder of deeds. Such document or documents may only be disclosed in accordance with the provisions of paragraph (o)(17)b. of this section.

b. *Access to authorized persons.* — The following persons are permitted to view or reproduce recorded military service discharge documents:

1. The veteran subject of the discharge;

2. The spouse or child of a veteran, with consent of the veteran;

3. If the veteran is deceased, a survivor or heir of the veteran who may be eligible to claim any type of benefit by virtue of the veteran's service in the military;

4. A person with a signed and notarized authorization from the veteran;

5. A county, state or federal officer assisting the veteran or veteran's family with a veteran's benefit application;

6. Anyone authorized by an order from a Delaware court, to view or copy the document; or

7. Government agencies, including courts, that have an interest in assisting the veteran subject to the military service discharge record or in assisting the beneficiaries of the deceased veteran subject to the military service discharge record in obtaining a benefit.

c. Any document referenced in paragraph (o)(18)a. of this section shall be deemed a public record upon the passage of 70 years from the date of the subject veteran's separation or discharge from service; or

(19) Any communications between a member of the General Assembly and that General Assembly member's constituent, or communications by a member of the General Assembly on behalf of that General Assembly member's constituent, or communications between members of the General Assembly.

(p) "Requesting party" shall mean the person filing the FOIA request.

(q) "State of emergency" means as defined in § 3102 of Title 20.

(r) "Virtual meeting" means a meeting of a public body that 1 or more members attend through the use of an electronic means of communication.

History.

60 Del. Laws, c. 641, § 1; 61 Del. Laws, c. 55, § 1; 63 Del. Laws, c. 424, § 1; 64 Del. Laws, c. 113, § 1; 65 Del. Laws, c. 191, §§ 2-6; 66 Del. Laws, c. 143, § 1; 67 Del. Laws, c. 281, § 194; 69 Del. Laws, c. 67, § 2; 69 Del. Laws, c. 250, § 2; 70 Del. Laws, c. 186, § 1; 73 Del. Laws, c. 260, §§ 1, 2, 3; 73 Del. Laws, c. 354, § 1; 75 Del. Laws, c. 235, §§ 3-5; 77 Del. Laws, c. 38, §§ 1-5, 8; 77 Del. Laws, c. 211, §§ 1, 2; 78 Del. Laws, c. 12, § 1; 78 Del. Laws, c. 382, § 1; 79 Del. Laws, c. 265, § 19; 79 Del. Laws, c. 272, § 1; 79 Del. Laws, c. 307, § 1; 79 Del. Laws, c. 334, § 1; 80 Del. Laws, c. 296, § 1; 82 Del. Laws, c. 265, § 2; 82 Del. Laws, c. 265, § 5; 83 Del. Laws, c. 65, § 1.

Revisor's note.

Section 5 of 82 Del. Laws, c. 265, as amended by 83 Del. Laws, c. 65, § 5 provided: "This act expires upon the enactment of Senate Bill No. 94 of the 151st General Assembly." Senate bill 94 of the 151st General Assembly was signed by the Governor on June 30, 2021, and became effective on that date as 83 Del. Laws, c. 65.

Effect of amendments.

83 Del. Laws, c. 65, effective June 30, 2021, added (b), (d), (e), (q), and (r); redesignated the

remaining and intervening paragraphs accordingly; substituted "under this chapter" for "[this chapter]" in present (f); deleted "either in person or by video conference" from the end of

present (j); deleted the definition of "video conferencing", and substituted "(o)(17)b." for "(*l*)(17)b." in present (o)(18)a. and "(o)(18)a." for "(*l*)(18)a." in present (o)(18)c.

NOTES TO DECISIONS

Analysis

Public funds.

Record.

— Public library.

Public funds.

Denial of a request for documents donated to the University of Delaware by the President-Elect while a Senator did not violate Delaware's Freedom of Information Act (29 Del. C. § 10001 et seq.); because the President-Elect had never been an employee of the university, there was no reason to believe that any information contained in the papers would relate to the university's financial expenditures. Judicial Watch Inc. v. Del. DOJ, — A.3d —, 2021 Del. Super. LEXIS 4 (Del. Super. Ct. Jan. 4, 2021).

Record.

— Public library.

University of Delaware was not required to produce log-in sheets, recording individuals who had visited the special collections department where records from the President-Elect's Senate career were stored, because those documents were exempted from disclosure; the log-in sheets were records of a public library which contained the identity of a user and would identify the documents of the library which a patron had used. Judicial Watch Inc. v. Del. DOJ, — A.3d —, 2021 Del. Super. LEXIS 4 (Del. Super. Ct. Jan. 4, 2021).

Opinions of the Attorney General

FOIA Petition Regarding the Finance/Employee Compensation & Benefits/Facilities Committee of the Delaware Association of Professional Engineers, see No. 20-IB31, December 11, 2020.

FOIA Petition Regarding the Delaware Department of Corrections, see No. 21-IB01, January 14, 2021.

FOIA Petition Regarding Village of Arden, see No. 21-IB02, January 21, 2021.

FOIA Petition Regarding the City of Wilmington, see No. 21-IB06, March 8, 2021.

FOIA Petition Regarding the Delaware State Police, see No. 21-IB07, March, 24, 2021.

FOIA Petition Regarding the Delaware Department of Insurance, see No. 21-IB09, April 22, 2021.

FOIA Petition Regarding the Delaware Department of Corrections, see No. 21-IB10, May 4, 2021.

FOIA Petition Regarding the Delaware Department of Agriculture, see No. 21-IB12, May 18, 2021.

FOIA Petition Regarding the Delaware Department of Health and Social Services, see No. 21-IB13, June 23, 2021.

FOIA Petition Regarding the Delaware Department of Transportation, see No. 21-IB15, July 2, 2021.

FOIA Petition Regarding the Delaware Department of Transportation, see No. 21-IB18, August 6, 2021.

§ 10003. Examination and copying of public records.

NOTES TO DECISIONS

Opinions of the Attorney General.

FOIA Petition Regarding the City of Rehoboth Beach, see No. 20-IB25, October 28, 2020.

FOIA Petition Regarding the Delaware Department of Safety and Homeland Security, see No. 20-IB33, December 18, 2020.

FOIA Petition Regarding the City of Wilmington, see No. 21-IB08, April 21, 2021.

FOIA Petition Regarding the Delaware De-

partment of Agriculture, see No. 21-IB12, May 18, 2021.

FOIA Petition Regarding the Delaware Department of Transportation, see No. 21-IB15, July 2, 2021.

FOIA Petition Regarding the Delaware Department of Transportation, see No. 21-IB18, August 6, 2021.

§ 10004. Open meetings.

(a) Every meeting of all public bodies shall be open to the public except those closed pursuant to subsections (b), (c), (d) and (h) of this section.

(b) A public body may call for an executive session closed to the public pursuant to subsections (c) and (e) of this section, but only for the following purposes:

(1) Discussion of an individual citizen's qualifications to hold a job or pursue training unless the citizen requests that such a meeting be open. This provision shall not apply to the discussion by a licensing board or commission which is subject to the provisions of § 8735 of this title, of an individual citizen's qualifications to pursue any profession or occupation

for which a license must be issued by the public body in accordance with Delaware law;

(2) Preliminary discussions on site acquisitions for any publicly funded capital improvements, or sales or leases of real property;

(3) Activities of any law-enforcement agency in its efforts to collect information leading to criminal apprehension;

(4) Strategy sessions, including those involving legal advice or opinion from an attorney-at-law, with respect to collective bargaining or pending or potential litigation, but only when an open meeting would have an adverse effect on the bargaining or litigation position of the public body;

(5) Discussions which would disclose the identity of the contributor of a bona fide and lawful charitable contribution to the public body whenever public anonymity has been requested of the public body with respect to said contribution by the contributor;

(6) Discussion of the content of documents, excluded from the definition of "public record" in § 10002 of this title where such discussion may disclose the contents of such documents;

(7) The hearing of student disciplinary cases unless the student requests a public hearing;

(8) The hearing of employee disciplinary or dismissal cases unless the employee requests a public hearing;

(9) Personnel matters in which the names, competency and abilities of individual employees or students are discussed, unless the employee or student requests that such a meeting be open.

(c) A public body may hold an executive session closed to the public upon affirmative vote of a majority of members present at a meeting of the public body. The vote on the question of holding an executive session shall take place at a meeting of the public body which shall be open to the public, and the results of the vote shall be made public and shall be recorded in the minutes. The purpose of such executive sessions shall be set forth in the agenda and shall be limited to the purposes listed in subsection (b) of this section. Executive sessions may be held only for the discussion of public business, and all voting on public business must take place at a public meeting and the results of the vote made public.

(d) This section shall not prohibit the removal of any person from a public meeting who is wilfully and seriously disruptive of the conduct of such meeting.

(e)(1) This subsection concerning notice of meetings does not apply to any emergency meeting which is necessary for the immediate preservation of the public peace, health, or safety, or to the General Assembly.

(2) All public bodies shall give public notice of their regular meetings and of their intent to hold an executive session closed to the public, at least 7 days in advance of the meeting. The notice must include all of the following:

a. The agenda, if the agenda has been determined.

b. The date, time, and place of a meeting, including whether the meeting will be conducted under § 10006A of this title.

(3) An agenda provided under paragraph (e)(2) of this section is subject to change. Changes to an agenda may include any of the following:

a. Additional items, including an executive session, which arise at the time of the public body's meeting.

b. The deletion of items, including an executive session.

(4) All public bodies shall give public notice of the type set forth in paragraph (e)(2) of this section of any special or rescheduled meeting as

soon as reasonably possible, but in any event no later than 24 hours before such meeting. A special or rescheduled meeting shall be defined as one to be held less than 7 days after the scheduling decision is made. The public notice of a special or rescheduled meeting shall include an explanation as to why the notice required by paragraph (e)(2) of this section could not be given.

(5) Public notice required by this subsection shall include, but not be limited to, conspicuous posting of said notice at the principal office of the public body holding the meeting, or if no such office exists at the place where meetings of the public body are regularly held, and making a reasonable number of such notices available. In addition, for all noncounty and nonmunicipal public bodies, public notice required by this subsection shall include, but not be limited to, electronic posting on a designated State of Delaware website, approved by the Registrar of Regulations by May 1, 2013, which shall be accessible to the public. In addition, all public bodies in the executive branch of state government that are subject to the provisions of this chapter shall electronically post said notice to the designated State of Delaware website approved by the Secretary of State.

(6) When the agenda is not available as of the time of the initial posting of the public notice it shall be added to the notice at least 6 hours in advance of said meeting, and the reasons for the delay in posting shall be briefly set forth on the agenda.

(f) Each public body shall maintain minutes of all meetings, including executive sessions, conducted pursuant to this section, and shall make such minutes available for public inspection and copying as a public record. Such minutes shall include a record of those members present and a record, by individual members (except where the public body is a town assembly where all citizens are entitled to vote), of each vote taken and action agreed upon. Such minutes or portions thereof, and any public records pertaining to executive sessions conducted pursuant to this section, may be withheld from public disclosure so long as public disclosure would defeat the lawful purpose for the executive session, but no longer. All public bodies in the executive branch of state government that are subject to the provisions of this chapter and meet 4 or fewer times per year shall electronically post draft minutes of open public meetings, identified as "draft minutes," to the designated State website approved by the Secretary of State within 20 working days after the conclusion of the meeting. Prior to being posted, draft minutes may be distributed to members of the public body who were present at the open public meeting. Draft minutes may continue to be revised and corrected up until final minutes are approved by the public body at an open meeting. All public bodies in the executive branch of state government that are subject to the provisions of this chapter shall electronically post final approved minutes of open public meetings to the designated State of Delaware website approved by the Secretary of State within 5 working days of final approval of said minutes.

(g) Every regularly scheduled meeting of a public body shall be held within the geographic jurisdiction of that public body. All such other meetings shall be held as follows:

(1) A public body serving any political subdivision of the State, including, but not limited to, any city, town or school district, shall hold all such other meetings within its jurisdiction or the county in which its principal office is located, unless it is school board training that has been approved by the Secretary of Education as beneficial to school board development activities.

(2) For the purposes of this subsection, a "regularly scheduled meeting" shall mean any meeting of a public body held on a periodic basis.

(3) The provisions of this subsection, insofar as they are not practicable, shall not apply to any emergency meeting which is necessary for the immediate preservation of the public peace, health or safety, or to a meeting held by a public body outside of its jurisdiction which is necessary for the immediate preservation of the public financial welfare.

(h) This section shall not apply to the proceedings of:

(1) Grand juries;

(2) Petit juries;

(3) Special juries;

(4) The deliberations of any court;

(5) The Board of Pardons and Parole;

(6) Public bodies having only 1 member;

(7) Public bodies within the legislative branch of the state government other than the House of Representatives, the Senate, the Joint Finance Committee, the Joint Committee on Capital Improvement, the Joint Legislative Oversight and Sunset Committee, Legislative Council, committees, excluding ethics committees, specifically enumerated and created by Resolution of the House of Representatives or Senate or task forces specifically enumerated and created by Resolution of the House of Representatives or Senate;

(8)a. The Victims' Compensation Assistance Program Appeals Board may close any meeting to the public where:

1. The claim to be considered derives from any sexual offense within the definitions of a crime in § 9002 of Title 11.

2. The claim to be considered derives from any offense by or against a child, as defined in this section, unless such child has been deemed amenable to the jurisdiction of a criminal court as to the matter before the Board.

3. The claim to be considered derives from any matter not yet adjudicated.

4. The claim to be considered involves a "victim" who is a "child" as those terms are defined in Chapter 90 of Title 11.

b. The Board shall produce a complete record of any proceedings closed to the public which record may be denied to anyone seeking access for good cause shown; and

(9) The deliberations of the following agencies for any case decision governed by the Administrative Procedures Act in Chapter 101 of this title:

a. State Human Relations Commission;

b. Industrial Accident Board;

c. Tax Appeals Board; and

d. Victims' Compensation Assistance Program Appeals Board.

(i) In an enforcement action pursuant to § 10005 of this title, a citizen or the Attorney General, as the case may be, may seek the forfeiture of all or part of the compensation of members of a board, commission or other public body for any closed meeting which such board, commission or other public body closed knowing that such action violated this chapter. Such forfeiture may only be ordered by the Court if the Court makes a specific finding that the board, commission or public body had no good faith basis to believe that the meeting could be closed. It shall be an absolute defense that an individual never voted in favor of the closed meeting. If the board, commission or public body also met validity for other purposes on the same day as the meeting which violated the act, such valid action shall be considered by the Court in determining the extent of any forfeiture award.

History.

60 Del. Laws, c. 641, § 1; 63 Del. Laws, c. 269, § 1; 65 Del. Laws, c. 191, §§ 7-12; 66 Del. Laws, c. 419, § 1; 67 Del. Laws, c. 367, §§ 1, 2; 71 Del. Laws, c. 38, § 1; 71 Del. Laws, c. 117, § 1; 71 Del. Laws, c. 191, § 1; 71 Del. Laws, c. 193, § 1; 72 Del. Laws, c. 459, § 1; 72 Del. Laws, c. 460, § 18; 75 Del. Laws, c. 178, §§ 1, 2; 77 Del. Laws, c. 38, §§ 6, 7; 77 Del. Laws, c. 211, § 3; 78 Del. Laws, c. 288, § 5; 79 Del. Laws, c. 125, § 4; 79 Del. Laws, c. 271, § 1; 79 Del. Laws, c. 393, § 1; 80 Del. Laws, c. 260, § 5; 82 Del. Laws, c. 265, § 3; 82 Del. Laws, c. 265, § 5; 83 Del. Laws, c. 65, § 2.

Revisor's note.

Section 5 of 82 Del. Laws, c. 265, as amended by 83 Del. Laws, c. 65, § 5 provided: "This act expires upon the enactment of Senate Bill No. 94 of the 151st General Assembly." Senate bill 94 of the 151st General Assembly was signed by the Governor on June 30, 2021, and became effective on that date as 83 Del. Laws, c. 65.

Effect of amendments.

83 Del. Laws, c. 65, effective June 30, 2021, in (e)(1), substituted "does" for "shall" and added a comma following "health"; and rewrote former (e)(2) as present (e)(2) and (e)(3) and redesignated the remaining paragraphs in (e) accordingly.

NOTES TO DECISIONS

Opinions of the Attorney General

FOIA Petition Regarding the Finance/Employee Compensation & Benefits/Facilities Committee of the Delaware Association of Professional Engineers, see No. 20-IB31, December 11, 2020.

FOIA Petition Regarding Village of Arden, see No. 21-IB02, January 21, 2021.

FOIA Petition Regarding Sussex County, see No. 21-IB14, June 30, 2021.

FOIA Petition Regarding the Governor's Council on Agriculture and the Delaware Council on Food and Farm Policy, see No. 21-IB16, July 5, 2021.

§ 10005. Enforcement.

NOTES TO DECISIONS

Burden of proof.

Statements by the University of Delaware's general counsel, that no public funds were used to support documents donated to the University by the President-Elect while a Senator, were sufficient to justify denial of access to the documents (given the duty of candor imposed upon every lawyer licensed in Delaware and the requesters' failure to provide anything other than unsupported speculation in opposition). Judicial Watch Inc. v. Del. DOJ, — A.3d —, 2021 Del. Super. LEXIS 4 (Del. Super. Ct. Jan. 4, 2021).

Opinions of the Attorney General

FOIA Petition Regarding the City of Wilmington, see No. 20-IB22, October 6, 2020.

FOIA Petition Regarding the Environmental Appeals Board, see No. 20-IB23, October 13, 2020.

FOIA Petition Regarding Wilmington Neighborhood Conservancy Land Bank Corporation, see No. 20-IB24, October 21, 2020.

FOIA Petition Regarding the City of Rehoboth Beach, see No. 20-IB25, October 28, 2020.

Two FOIA Petitions Regarding the City of Rehoboth Beach, see No. 20-IB26, October 28, 2020.

FOIA Petition Regarding the Christina School District Board of Education, see No. 20-IB29, December 2, 2020.

FOIA Petition Regarding New Castle County, see No. 20-IB30, December 7, 2020.

FOIA Petition Regarding the Finance/Employee Compensation & Benefits/Facilities Committee of the Delaware Association of Professional Engineers, see No. 20-IB31, December 11, 2020.

FOIA Petition Regarding the Delaware Department of Transportation, see No. 20-IB32, December 14, 2020.

FOIA Petition Regarding the Delaware Department of Safety and Homeland Security, see No. 20-IB33, December 18, 2020.

FOIA Petition Regarding the Delaware Department of Corrections, see No. 21-IB01, January 14, 2021.

FOIA Petition Regarding Village of Arden, see No. 21-IB02, January 21, 2021.

FOIA Petition Regarding the Sussex Technical School District Board of Education, see No. 21-IB03, February 25, 2021.

Two FOIA Petitions Regarding the City of Delaware City, see No. 21-IB04, March 1, 2021.

FOIA Petition Regarding the Delaware Department of State, see No. 21-IB05, March, 5, 2021.

FOIA Petition Regarding the City of Wilmington, see No. 21-IB06, March 8, 2021.

FOIA Petition Regarding the Delaware State Police, see No. 21-IB07, March, 24, 2021.

FOIA Petition Regarding the City of Wilmington, see No. 21-IB08, April 21, 2021.

FOIA Petition Regarding the Delaware Department of Insurance, see No. 21-IB09, April 22, 2021.

FOIA Petition Regarding the Delaware Department of Corrections, see No. 21-IB10, May 4, 2021.

FOIA Petition Regarding the Delaware Department of Insurance, see No. 21-IB11, May 12, 2021.

FOIA Petition Regarding the Delaware Department of Agriculture, see No. 21-IB12, May 18, 2021.

FOIA Petition Regarding the Delaware Department of Health and Social Services, see No. 21-IB13, June 23, 2021.

FOIA Petition Regarding Sussex County, see No. 21-IB14, June 30, 2021.

FOIA Petition Regarding the Delaware Department of Transportation, see No. 21-IB15, July 2, 2021.

FOIA Petition Regarding the Governor's Council on Agriculture and the Delaware Council on Food and Farm Policy, see No. 21-IB16, July 5, 2021.

FOIA Petition Regarding the Town of Georgetown, see No. 21-IB17, July 23, 2021.

FOIA Petition Regarding the Delaware Department of Transportation, see No. 21-IB18, August 6, 2021.

§ 10006. Video-conferencing participation in open meetings.

History.
77 Del. Laws, c. 211, § 4; repealed by 83 Del. Laws, c. 65, § 3, effective June 30, 2021.

§ 10006A. Open meetings; virtual meetings; reasonable accommodations for members with a disability.

(a) A public body shall allow a member of the public body with a disability to attend a meeting of the public body through the use of an electronic means of communication, instead of being required to attend in-person at a physical location, as a reasonable accommodation under § 4504 of Title 6, unless it imposes an undue burden. A member attending a meeting through the use of an electronic means of communication as a reasonable accommodation is considered present for all purposes as if the member is physically attending, including for quorum and voting.

(b) At the discretion of the chair or presiding officer, a public body may allow the public to monitor or provide public comment through the use of an electronic means of communication at any meeting.

(c) A public body may hold a virtual meeting if all of the following occur:

(1) The meeting notice under § 10004 of this title includes information regarding how the public can monitor or participate in the meeting under paragraph (c)(6) of this section.

(2) The meeting has an anchor location.

(3) The identity of a member or witness is verified, and the actions of a member are authenticated, in a manner satisfactory to the presiding officer or chair.

(4) All participating members and witnesses can simultaneously do 1 of the following regarding each member or witness who is recognized by the presiding officer or chair:

a. Hear the comments of each member or witness.

b. Hear the comments of and view each member or witness.

(5) A document used during the meeting by a member or witness, and that is accepted by the presiding officer or chair, is immediately provided to each member or witness participating in the meeting and made available to the public under § 10003 of this title.

(6) Except during an executive session under § 10004 of this title, the public is able to do all of the following through an electronic means of communication:

a. Monitor the meeting.

b. Provide public comment, if the public body is required to accept, or provides an opportunity for, public comment.

(7) Minutes of the virtual meeting are maintained under § 10004 of this title.

(d)(1) All actions taken during a virtual meeting conducted under this section have the same legal effect as if the members were physically present at the same location.

(2) For the purposes of determining quorum for a virtual meeting, a

member participating in a virtual meeting is considered present as if the member were physically present at the meeting.

(3) For the purposes of voting during a virtual meeting, a member participating in a virtual meeting is able to vote as if the member were physically present at the meeting.

(4) A technological problem that prevents or limits public access otherwise required under this chapter does not invalidate a virtual meeting or an action taken at a virtual meeting.

(e) During a state of emergency, a public body may hold a virtual meeting at which members participate through the use of an electronic means of communication without an anchor location if, in addition to the requirements under subsection (c) of this section, all of the following occur:

(1) The virtual meeting is preceded by the same public notice as required under § 10004 of this title, except that notice of the public meeting does not need to be conspicuously posted at the principal office of the public body holding the meeting or where meetings of the public body are regularly held.

(2) If all of the members of the public body are elected by the public to serve on the public body, all of the following must occur:

a. A document that is used during the meeting by a member or witness, and that is accepted by the presiding officer or chair, is immediately transmitted to each member or witness participating in the meeting.

b. The public is able to review a recording of the meeting within a reasonable time after the meeting concludes.

(f) If necessary to prevent a public health emergency, as defined in § 3132 of Title 20, the Governor may issue an executive order allowing public bodies to hold virtual meetings at which all members may participate through the use of an electronic means of communication without an anchor location. A virtual meeting held under this subsection must comply with the requirements under subsection (e) of this section.

History.
82 Del. Laws, c. 265, §§ 4, 5; 83 Del. Laws, c. 65, § 4.

Revisor's note.
Section 5 of 82 Del. Laws, c. 265, as amended by 83 Del. Laws, c. 65, § 5 provided: "This act expires upon the enactment of Senate Bill No. 94 of the 151st General Assembly." Senate bill 94 of the 151st General Assembly was signed by the Governor on June 30, 2021, and became effective on that date as 83 Del. Laws, c. 65.

Effect of amendments.
83 Del. Laws, c. 65, effective June 30, 2021, rewrote the section.

CHAPTER 101

ADMINISTRATIVE PROCEDURES

SUBCHAPTER III

CASE DECISIONS

§ 10125. Conduct of public hearings; burden of proof; record.

NOTES TO DECISIONS

Due process.
Delaware Board of Mental Health and Chemical Dependency Professionals Board's reliance on a hearing officer's discretion to admit a text message exchange was not a violation of due process because: (1) the board-licensed professional mental health counselor was on notice of the contents of the exchange; (2) the exchange was relevant; (3) the exchange was professionally inappropriate; and (4) the hearing officer did not abuse discretion by admitting it into evidence. Brousell v. Del. Bd. of Mental Health & Chem. Dependency Professionals, — A.3d —, 2021 Del. Super. LEXIS 306 (Del. Super. Ct. Apr. 14, 2021).

SUBCHAPTER VII
APPLICATION OF CHAPTER

§ 10161. State agencies affected.

NOTES TO DECISIONS

Industrial Accident Board.

Employer was not entitled to reargue the court's reversal and remand of a decision by the Industrial Accident Board (IAB) for reconsideration because: (1) the employer failed to establish that the court overlooked a legal principal or misapprehended a fact; (2) the employer's motion was a repetitive submission focused on whether the IAB could have considered an exhibit, a doctor's log of an injured employee's treatments and a handwritten note indicating that a doctor's bill remained outstanding, during the hearing; (3) it remained unclear whether the doctor's bill in question had been paid in full by the employer; and (4) the exhibit appeared to be a part of the correspondence between the IAB and the parties. Bristor v. Dover Downs, Inc., — A.3d —, 2021 Del. Super. LEXIS 12 (Del. Super. Ct. Jan. 4, 2021).

TITLE 30
STATE TAXES

PART I

GENERAL PROVISIONS; STATE TAX AGENCIES; PROCEDURE AND ENFORCEMENT

CHAPTER 5
PROCEDURE, ADMINISTRATION AND ENFORCEMENT

**Subchapter III. Procedure and
Administration**

SUBCHAPTER III
PROCEDURE AND ADMINISTRATION

§ 534. Failure to file tax return or to pay tax.

(a) In case of failure to file any return required under authority of this title or Title 4 on or before the date prescribed therefor (determined with regard to any extension of time for filing), unless it is shown that such failure is due to reasonable cause and not due to wilful neglect, there shall be added to the amount required to be shown as tax on such return 5% of the amount of such tax if the failure is for not more than 1 month, with an additional 5% for each additional month or fraction thereof during which such failure continues, not exceeding 50% in the aggregate. For purposes of this subsection, the amount of tax required to be shown on the return shall be reduced by the amount of any part of the tax which is paid on or before the date prescribed for payment of the tax and by the amount of any credit against the tax which may be claimed on the return.

(b)(1) In case of failure to pay the amount shown as tax on any return specified in subsection (a) of this section on or before the date prescribed for payment of such tax (determined with regard to any extension of time for payment), unless it is shown that such failure is due to reasonable cause and not due to wilful neglect, there shall be added to the amount shown as tax on such return 1% of the amount of such tax if the failure is for not more than 1 month, with an additional 1% for each additional month or fraction thereof during which such failure continues, not exceeding 25% in the aggregate. For purposes of computing such addition for any month, the amount of tax shown on the return shall be reduced by the amount of any part of the tax which is paid on or before the beginning of such month and by the amount of any credit against the tax which may be claimed on the return. If the amount required to be shown as tax on the return is less than the amount shown as tax on the return, this paragraph shall be applied by substituting such lower amount.

(2) In the case of failure to pay any amount in respect of any tax required to be shown on a return specified in subsection (a) of this section which is not so shown (including an assessment made pursuant to § 528(a) of this title) within 10 days after any assessment thereof becoming final, unless it is shown that such failure is due to reasonable cause and not due to wilful neglect, there shall be added to the amount of tax stated in the notice of proposed assessment 1% of the amount of such tax if the failure is for not more than 1 month, with an additional 1% for each additional month or fraction thereof during which such failure continues, not exceeding 25% in the aggregate. For purposes of computing such addition for any month, the amount of tax stated in the notice of proposed assessment shall be reduced by the amount of any part of the tax which is paid before the beginning of such month.

(c)(1) For tax periods beginning after December 31, 1999, if any pass-through entity required to file a return under § 1605(a)(1) of this title for any taxable year fails to file such return by the date prescribed therefor (determined with regard to any extension of time for filing) or files a return which fails to show the information required under § 1605(a)(1) of this title, such pass-through entity shall be liable for a penalty determined under paragraph (c)(2) of this section for each month, or fraction thereof, during which such failure continues (but not to exceed 5 months), unless it is shown that such failure was due to reasonable cause.

(2) For purposes of paragraph (c)(1) of this section, the amount of penalty for any month is the product of $25, multiplied by the number of persons who were members in the pass-through entity during any part of the taxable year; provided, however, that the maximum penalty for any taxable year shall not exceed $10,000.

(3) The penalty prescribed by this subsection shall be assessed against and shall be payable by the pass-through entity, and the deficiency and appeal procedures provided in §§ 521-526 of this title shall not apply; provided, however, that the Director shall mail written notice of such penalty to the pass-through entity, which may, within 60 days from the date of the mailing of such notice, institute a protest of such penalty to the Director, whose determination shall be final.

(d)(1) For tax periods beginning after December 31, 1999, if any pass-through entity fails to comply with the provisions of § 1605(a)(2) of this title, such pass-through entity shall be liable for a penalty determined under paragraph (d)(2) of this section for each month, or fraction thereof, during which such failure continues (but not to exceed 5 months), unless it is shown that such failure was due to reasonable cause.

(2) For purposes of paragraph (d)(1) of this section, the amount of penalty for any month is $25, multiplied by the number of persons who were members of the pass-through entity at any time during the tax year, provided, however, that the maximum penalty for any taxable year shall not exceed $10,000.

(3) The penalty prescribed by this subsection shall be assessed against and shall be payable by the pass-through entity and the deficiency and appeal procedures provided in §§ 521-526 of this title shall not apply; provided, however, that the Director shall mail written notice of such penalty to the pass-through entity, which may, within 60 days from the date of the mailing of such notice, institute a protest of such penalty to the Director, whose determination shall be final.

(e) This section shall not apply to any failure to file a declaration of estimated tax or to pay any estimated tax.

(f)(1) In case of each failure to file a statement of payment to another person required under the authority of this title, including the duplicate statement of tax withheld on wages, by the date prescribed therefor (determined with regard to any extension of time for filing), unless it is shown that such failure is due to reasonable cause and not due to wilful neglect, there shall be paid by the person so failing to file such statement, in the same manner as tax, a penalty of $2.00 for each such failure, but the total amount imposed on the delinquent person for all such failures during any calendar year shall not exceed $2,000.

(2) Any person required to file an information return pursuant to § 1154(i) of this title who fails to file such return on or before the date prescribed for its filing or who fails to include all the information required to be shown on the return or who includes incorrect information on the return or who fails to file in the required manner, shall unless it is shown that such failure is due to reasonable cause and not due to wilful neglect, pay a penalty in an amount equal to one half the amount specified in the Internal Revenue Code, as it may be amended from time to time, for such failure.

(g) The Director shall assess a penalty of $500 against any individual who files what purports to be a return of any tax imposed by this title or Title 4 but which:

(1) Does not contain information on which the substantial correctness of the self-assessment may be judged or contains information that on its face indicates that the self-assessment is substantially incorrect; and

(2) Evidences a position that is frivolous or a desire to delay or impede the administration of the revenue laws of this State.

(h) In the case of failure of an employer required to deposit taxes by electronic funds transfer under the provisions of § 1154(g) of this title to make transfer by such means, unless it is shown that such failure is due to reasonable cause and not due to wilful neglect, there shall be added to the amount shown as tax required to have been electronically transferred 5% of the amount or $500 per required payment, whichever is less.

(i) For tax periods beginning after December 31, 1994, with respect to any return, the amount of the addition to the tax under subsection (a) of this section shall be reduced by the amount of the addition to the tax under subsection (b) of this section for any month (or fraction thereof) to which an addition to the tax is applied under both subsections (a) and (b) of this section.

(j) If any failure to file any return is fraudulent, subsection (a) of this section shall be applied by substituting "15" for "5%" each place it appears and by substituting "75%" for "50%."

(k) For purposes of subsection (a) of this section, reasonable cause shall be deemed established in the case of failure to file a return in the time prescribed by Part III of this title, where the taxpayer filed within the time prescribed in a written notification by the Director that the taxpayer is eligible to file returns on a basis less frequent than is actually the case.

(l) In the case of failure of any person to obtain or renew a business license required under the provisions of Part III of this title, unless it is shown that such failure is due to reasonable cause and not due to wilful neglect, there shall be added to the amount of the business license fee required to be paid a penalty in the amount of $200. Whenever a penalty has been proposed for assessment under this subsection, the Director shall not be required to issue a business license to the taxpayer to whom such assessment has been proposed unless and until the taxpayer has paid any license fee necessary for issuance of such license and has either:

(1) Paid the assessment provided under this subsection (subject to any claim for refund); or

(2) Filed a written protest regarding such assessment of penalty pursuant to § 523 of this title.

The penalty described in this subsection shall not be assessed in the instance of self-disclosure by a taxpayer of delinquency in meeting the licensing requirements of Part III. The penalty described in this subsection shall, only with respect to the same failure to obtain or renew a license and not with respect to failure to pay taxes on gross receipts or any other acts or omissions, be in lieu of the penalty described in subsection (a) of this section, except where such penalty determined under subsection (a) of this section shall exceed the penalty determined under this subsection, in which event subsection (a) of this section shall apply, and this subsection shall not apply.

(m) Any person who fails to file any return in the manner prescribed by law and required under authority of this title or Title 4 on or before the date prescribed therefor (determined with regard to any extension of time for filing), unless it is shown that such failure is due to reasonable cause and not due to wilful neglect, shall be liable for a penalty of not more than $50, in addition to any other amounts prescribed under this title that shall be assessed and collected by the Director.

History.

68 Del. Laws, c. 187, § 1; 69 Del. Laws, c. 289, § 13; 70 Del. Laws, c. 117, § 3; 71 Del. Laws, c. 314, § 7; 72 Del. Laws, c. 220, § 1; 73 Del. Laws, c. 131, § 3; 75 Del. Laws, c. 411, § 3; 77 Del. Laws, c. 79, §§ 2, 3; 79 Del. Laws, c. 120, §§ 1, 2; 79 Del. Laws, c. 142, §§ 2-4; 81 Del. Laws, c. 103, § 4; 83 Del. Laws, c. 107, § 2.

Revisor's note.

Based upon changes made necessary by 83 Del. Laws, c. 107, § 2, effective July 30, 2021, "(i)" was substituted for "(h)" following "§ 1154" in (f)(2); and "(g)" was substituted for "(f)" following "§ 1154" in (h).

PART II

INCOME, INHERITANCE AND ESTATE TAXES

CHAPTER 11
PERSONAL INCOME TAX

SUBCHAPTER II
RESIDENT INDIVIDUALS

§ 1106. Modifications.

(a) *Additions.* — There shall be added to federal adjusted gross income:

(1)a. Interest qualifying under § 103 of the United States Internal
Revenue Code of 1986 [26 U.S.C. § 103] or any similar statute, other
than interest on obligations and securities of this State and its
political subdivisions and authorities; and

b. Dividends paid by a regulated investment company (sometimes
referred to as a mutual fund) qualifying under § 852(b)(5) of the
United States Internal Revenue Code of 1986 [26 U.S.C. § 852(b)(5)]
or any similar statute;

provided, that dividends attributable to interest on obligations and
securities of this State and its political subdivisions and authorities may
be excluded from such addition if the amount of interest attributable
thereto is reported in writing to the holder or owner of the shares or units
of the regulated investment company by or on behalf of the manager of the
regulated investment company, and such report states the dollar amount
or percentage of Delaware and non-Delaware dividends pertaining to the
taxpayer;

(2) The amount of any deduction for depletion of oil and gas wells
allowed under § 611 of the Federal Internal Revenue Code of 1986 [26
U.S.C. § 611] to the extent such deduction is determined by reference to
§ 613 of the Federal Internal Revenue Code [26 U.S.C. § 613] (relating to
percentage depletion);

(3) Any deduction, to the extent such deduction exceeds $30,000, for a
net operating loss carryback as provided for in § 172 of the Internal
Revenue Code or successor provisions.

(b) *Subtractions.* — There shall be subtracted from federal adjusted gross
income:

(1)a. Interest on obligations of the United States and its territories and
possessions, or of any authority, commission or instrumentality of the
United States, to the extent includable in gross income for federal
income tax purposes, but exempt from state income taxes under the
laws of the United States; and

b. Dividends paid by a regulated investment company (as defined
in § 851 of the United States Internal Revenue Code of 1986 [26
U.S.C. § 851], or any similar statute, sometimes referred to as a
mutual fund) to the extent such dividends are attributable to interest
paid on obligations of the United States and its territories and
possessions, or of any authority, commission or instrumentality of the
United States, which interest would be subject to subtraction from
federal adjusted gross income under paragraph (b)(1)a. of this section
if such obligations were owned directly by an individual and the
interest on them were paid to such individual. The portion of the
dividends of a regulated investment company which represents
United States government interest which is exempt from state income
taxes under this subparagraph shall be as reported in writing to the
holder or owner of the share or units of the regulated investment
company by or on behalf of the manager of the regulated investment
company, and such report shall state the dollar amount or percentage
of exempt and nonexempt dividends pertaining to the taxpayer;

(2) The amount of $2,000 by any person who has a total and permanent
disability or by a person who is over 60 years of age, and (i) whose earned
income in the taxable year is less than $2,500 and (ii) whose adjusted gross
income (without reduction by this exclusion) does not exceed $10,000.

For purposes of this paragraph, in the case of spouses filing a joint
return, the amount of the exclusion shall be $4,000 if (i) both are either

over 60 years of age or have total and permanent disabilities or 1 is over 60 years of age and the other has a total and permanent disability and (ii) their total earned income in the taxable year is less than $5,000 and their adjusted gross income does not exceed $20,000;

(3)a. Amounts received as pensions by persons under age 60 from employers, the United States, the State or any subdivision thereof, not to exceed $2,000. For taxable years beginning on or after January 1, 1987, amounts received as pensions by persons age 60 or older from employers, the United States, the State or any subdivision thereof, not to exceed $3,000;

b.1. Amounts not to exceed $2,000 received by persons under age 60 as pensions from employers, the United States, the State or any subdivision, or

2.(A) Amounts not to exceed $12,500 received by persons age 60 or older as pensions from employers, the United States, the State or any subdivision or as eligible retirement income.

(B) For the purposes of this paragraph, "eligible retirement income" shall include distributions received from qualified retirement plans defined in § 4974 of the federal Internal Revenue Code ("IRC") [26 U.S.C. § 4974] or a successor provision, cash or deferred arrangements described in IRC § 401(k) [26 U.S.C. § 401(k)] or a successor provision, government deferred compensation plans described in IRC § 457 [26 U.S.C. § 457] or a successor provision, dividends, capital gains, interest and rental income from real property less deductible rental expenses. For purposes of this paragraph, eligible retirement income received by spouses as joint tenants with right of survivorship or as tenants by the entirety shall be deemed to have been received one-half by each;

(4) Social Security benefits paid by the United States and all payments received under the Railroad Retirement Act of 1974 [45 U.S.C. §§ 231-231[v] to the extent included in federal adjusted gross income;

(5) An amount equal to the portion of the wages paid or incurred for the taxable year which is disallowed as a deduction for federal tax purposes under § 280C, Internal Revenue Code [26 U.S.C. § 280C], relating to portion of wages for which the new jobs tax credit is claimed;

(6) Benefits received by a resident individual through participation in a travelink program certified by the Delaware Department of Transportation to the extent such benefits are included in the federal adjusted gross income of the taxpayer;

(7) Any deduction, consistent with the operation of § 172 of the Internal Revenue Code [26 U.S.C. § 172] or successor provision, to carry forward losses which were carried back in calculating federal taxable income but which were prevented from being carried back under paragraph (a)(3) of this section;

(8)a. Distributions received from qualified retirement plans as defined in § 4974 of the Internal Revenue Code (I.R.C.) [26 U.S.C. § 4974], cash or deferred arrangements described in § 401(k) of the I.R.C. [26 U.S.C. § 401(k)], and governmental deferred compensation plans described in § 457 of the I.R.C. [26 U.S.C. § 457], to the extent such distributions are applied within the tax year of the distributions for books, tuition or fees at an institution of higher education attended by the person or by any of the person's dependents who have not attained the age of 26, so long as such amounts received have been included in the person's federal adjusted gross income.

　b. For the purposes of this section, an institution of higher education is a school which:

　　1. Admits as regular students only individuals having a certificate of graduation from a high school or the recognized equivalent of such a certificate;

　　2. Is legally authorized in this or another state to provide a program of education beyond high school; and

　　3. Provides an educational program for which it awards a bachelor's or higher degree or provides a program which is acceptable for full credit toward such a degree, a program of postgraduate or postdoctoral studies or a program of training to prepare students for gainful employment in a recognized occupation.

　(9) The amount of any refund of Delaware State income taxes imposed under this chapter, to the extent included in federal adjusted gross income for the tax period.

　(10) The amount of any unemployment benefits received in calendar year 2020, to the extent included in federal adjusted gross income.

(c) *Fiduciary adjustment.* — There shall be added to, or subtracted from, federal adjusted gross income, as the case may be, the taxpayer's share of the fiduciary adjustment determined under § 1634 of this title.

History.
30 Del. C. 1953, § 1106; 57 Del. Laws, c. 737, § 1; 58 Del. Laws, c. 318; 58 Del. Laws, c. 342, § 1; 58 Del. Laws, c. 551, § 1; 59 Del. Laws, c. 151, § 1; 60 Del. Laws, c. 18, § 1; 60 Del. Laws, c. 269, § 1; 60 Del. Laws, c. 270, § 1; 60 Del. Laws, c. 639, § 1; 61 Del. Laws, c. 202, § 1; 61 Del. Laws, c. 298, § 1; 62 Del. Laws, c. 353, § 2; 64 Del. Laws, c. 224, § 1; 64 Del. Laws, c. 470, § 1; 65 Del. Laws, c. 203, § 1; 67 Del. Laws, c. 160, § 2; 67 Del. Laws, c. 263, §§ 3, 4; 67 Del. Laws, c. 399, §§ 1, 2; 67 Del. Laws, c. 408, § 2; 70 Del. Laws, c. 186, § 1; 70 Del. Laws, c. 495, § 1; 71 Del. Laws, c. 131, § 1; 71 Del. Laws, c. 352, §§ 1, 2; 72 Del. Laws, 1st Sp. Sess., c. 243, § 1; 72 Del. Laws, 1st Sp. Sess., c. 246, § 1; 74 Del. Laws, c. 138, § 1; 78 Del. Laws, c. 179, §§ 320-322; 83 Del. Laws, c. 2, § 4.

Effect of amendments.
83 Del. Laws, c. 2, effective Feb. 8, 2021, added (b)(10).

§ 1117. Earned income tax credit [Effective upon fulfillment of 83 Del. Laws, c. 118, § 2].

(a)(1) For any tax year beginning before January 1, [of the year in which the contingency under 83 Del. Laws, c. 118, § 2, is fulfilled] an individual who is a resident of this State may receive a nonrefundable credit against the individual's tax otherwise due under this chapter in the amount of 20% of the corresponding federal earned income credit allowed under § 32 or successor provision of the Internal Revenue Code (26 U.S.C. § 32).

　(2) For any tax year beginning on or after January 1, [of the year in which the contingency under 83 Del. Laws, c. 118, § 2, is fulfilled], an individual who is a resident of this State may receive a credit against the individual's tax under this chapter in an amount based on a percentage of the corresponding federal earned income credit allowed under § 32 or successor provision of the Internal Revenue Code (26 U.S.C. § 32). The individual may claim either of the following amounts:

　　a. 20% of the corresponding federal earned income tax credit, not to exceed the tax otherwise due under this chapter.

　　b. 4.5% of the corresponding federal earned income tax credit, of which the amount that exceeds the tax otherwise due under this chapter is refundable.

(b) In the case of spouses who file a joint federal return but who elect to determine their Delaware taxes separately, the credit allowed under subsection (a) of this section may only be used by the spouse with the greater tax otherwise due, computed without regard to this credit.

(c) The credit allowed under paragraph (a)(1) of this section may not exceed the tax otherwise due under this chapter.

History.

75 Del. Laws, c. 221, § 1; 83 Del. Laws, c. 118, § 1.

Revisor's note.

Section 2 of 83 Del. Laws, c. 118, provided: "This act takes effect on the date of the last of the following to occur:

"(1) The Division of Revenue has implemented the personal income tax release of the Integrated Revenue Administration System.

"(2) The Secretary of Finance provides a written notice to the Registrar of Regulations that the contingency in paragraph (1) of this section has been fulfilled."

Effect of amendments.

83 Del. Laws, c. 118, effective upon fulfillment of § 2 of the act, rewrote (a); and, in (c), deleted "In no event shall" from the beginning and substituted "paragraph (a)(1)" for "subsection (a)".

SUBCHAPTER III
NONRESIDENT INDIVIDUALS

§ 1126. Withholding of income tax on sale or exchange of real estate by nonresident individuals.

(a) *Definitions.* — (1) "Director" means the Director of the Division of Revenue or the Secretary of Finance of the State.

(2) "Nonresident individual" means, for purposes of this section, an individual who is not a resident individual of this State for the individual's entire tax year.

(3) "Recorder" means the official with the duty to record deeds and similar instruments.

(4) "Transfer under a deed in lieu of foreclosure" includes all of the following:

    a. A transfer by the owner of the property to the following:

        1. With respect to a deed in lieu of foreclosure of a mortgage, the mortgagee, the assignee of the mortgage, or any designee or nominee of the mortgagee or assignee of the mortgage.

        2. With respect to a deed in lieu of foreclosure of any other lien instrument, the holder of the debt or other obligation secured by the lien instrument or any designee, nominee, or assignee of the holder of the debt secured by the lien instrument.

    b. A transfer by any of the persons described in paragraph (a)(4)a. of this section to a subsequent purchaser for value.

(5) "Transfer under a foreclosure of a mortgage or other lien instrument" includes the following:

    a. With respect to the foreclosure of a mortgage, all of the following:

        1. A transfer by the sheriff or other party authorized to conduct the foreclosure sale under the mortgage to 1 of the following:

            A. The mortgagee or the assignee of the mortgage.

            B. Any designee, nominee, or assignee of the mortgagee or assignee of the mortgage.

            C. Any purchaser, substituted purchaser, or assignee of any purchaser or substituted purchaser of the foreclosed property.

        2. A transfer by any of the persons described in paragraphs (a)(5)a.1.A. and (a)(5)a.1.B. of this section to a subsequent purchaser for value.

    b. With respect to the foreclosure of any other lien instrument, all of the following:

1. A transfer by the party authorized to make the sale to 1 of the following:

A. The holder of the debt or other obligation secured by the lien instrument.

B. Any designee, nominee, or assignee of the holder of the debt secured by the lien instrument.

C. Any purchaser, substituted purchaser, or assignee of any purchaser or substituted purchaser of the foreclosed property.

2. A transfer by any of the persons described in paragraphs (a)(5)b.1.A. and (a)(5)b.1.B. of this section to a subsequent purchaser for value.

(b) *Estimated tax return; alternative forms.* — Every nonresident individual who sells or exchanges Delaware real estate shall file with the Recorder 1 of the following:

(1) A "Declaration of Estimated Income Tax" for the quarter in which the sale or exchange is settled, applying the highest marginal rate under § 1102 of this title to an estimate of the gain recognized on the sale or exchange.

(2) An alternative form prepared by the Director to calculate income tax at the highest marginal rate under § 1102 of this title, applied to the difference between the total amount realized by the transferor and the net balance due at the time of settlement of all recorded liens encumbering the real estate.

(3)a. An alternative form prepared by the Director to declare under penalties of perjury 1 of the following:

1. That the sale or exchange of real estate is exempt from recognition of capital gain with respect to the tax year of the sale or exchange.

2. That all or a part of the gain realized that may be excluded from income with respect to the tax year of the sale or exchange.

3. That the sale or exchange of real estate is 1 of the following:

A. A transfer under a foreclosure of a mortgage or other lien instrument.

B. A transfer under a deed in lieu of foreclosure.

b. With respect to a claim of exemption or exclusion under paragraph (b)(3)a.1. or (b)(3)a.2. of this section, a statement of the facts and a citation to the provision of the Internal Revenue Code (Title 26, U.S.C.) relied upon for such exemption or exclusion must also be included in the declaration.

(c) *Due date of estimated tax return, payment.* — The return or form provided for in subsection (b) of this section, and the estimated tax reported due on such return or form, shall be remitted with the deed to the Recorder before the deed shall be recorded. Such payment shall be withheld from the net proceeds of the sale. To the extent that the sale does not result in net proceeds being available for the payment of the estimated tax, the Recorder may accept the form without payment, upon receipt of confirmation from the closing attorney that no funds are available for payment of the tax and that no funds were distributed to the seller.

(d) *Payment credited to transferor.* — The estimated tax remitted under subsection (c) of this section shall be deemed to have been paid to the Director on behalf of the nonresident transferor and the nonresident transferor shall be credited for purposes of §§ 1169 and 1170 of this title as a payment made on the date remitted to the Recorder.

(e) *Persons or entities not liable for payments.* — Neither the transferee, title insurance producer, title insurer, settlement agent, closing attorney, lending institution, nor the real estate agent or broker in a transaction subject to this section shall be liable for any amounts required to be collected and paid over to the Recorder or Director under this section.

(f) *Tax not imposed; lawful collection of taxes not prohibited.* — This section does not:

(1) Impose any tax on a transferor or affect any liability of the transferor for any tax; or

(2) Prohibit the Director from collecting any taxes due from a transferor in any other manner authorized by law.

History.

77 Del. Laws, c. 291, § 1; 81 Del. Laws, c. 363, § 1; 83 Del. Laws, c. 107, § 1.

Effect of amendments.

83 Del. Laws, c. 107, effective July 30, 2021,

in (c), added "on such return or form" in the first sentence, and added the second sentence.

SUBCHAPTER VII
WITHHOLDING OF TAX

§ 1154. Information returns and payment of tax withheld.

(a) Every employer required to deduct and withhold tax under this chapter shall file a withholding return as prescribed by the Division of Revenue and pay over such tax to the Division of Revenue, or to a depository designated by the Division of Revenue, at a frequency to be determined as follows:

(1) An employer whose aggregate amount of taxes required by this subchapter to be deducted and withheld during the lookback period did not exceed the applicable threshold of $4,500 shall be a quarterly filer;

(2) An employer whose aggregate amount of taxes required by this subchapter to be deducted and withheld during the lookback period exceeded the applicable threshold of $4,500 but did not exceed the applicable threshold of $25,000 or which had no employees within Delaware during the lookback period shall be a monthly filer; and

(3) An employer whose aggregate amount of taxes required by this subchapter to be deducted and withheld during the lookback period exceeded the applicable threshold of $25,000 shall be an eighth-monthly filer.

The levels of the applicable thresholds in this subsection are subject to annual adjustment as more fully set forth in § 515 of this title.

(b) The Division of Revenue may modify the filing frequency defined in paragraphs (a)(1)-(3) of this section for any taxpayer, in response to a request from the taxpayer, upon a showing by the taxpayer that they would suffer a hardship if required to comply with the statutory filing frequency.

(c) A quarterly filer shall file a return and pay over taxes required to be deducted and withheld under this chapter not later than the last day of the month following the close of each calendar quarter.

(d) A monthly filer shall, for each month, file a return and pay over taxes required to be deducted and withheld during such month on or before the fifteenth day of the month following the end of such month.

(e) An eighth-monthly filer shall file a return and pay over taxes required to be deducted and withheld under this chapter not later than 3 working days following the end of any deposit or return period during which an employer made any payment subject to a requirement to withhold tax under this chapter. For purposes of this subsection, each month shall be divided into 8 deposit or return periods. These deposit or return periods end on the third, seventh, eleventh, fifteenth, nineteenth, twenty-second, twenty-fifth and last day of every month.

(f) For purposes of this subchapter, the term "lookback period" shall refer to the 12-month period between July 1 and June 30 immediately preceding the calendar year for which the filing frequency is determined by reference to the lookback period.

(g) Any employer required under the provisions of § 6302 (or successor provision) of the Internal Revenue Code [26 U.S.C. § 6302] to deposit federal employment taxes by electronic funds transfer shall be required to deposit taxes withheld under this subchapter by electronic funds transfer, except that, for purposes of this subsection, 1 year shall be added to the "applicable effective date" on which deposit by electronic funds transfer is required of a particular employer under regulations promulgated pursuant to the provisions of § 6302 (or successor provision) of the Internal Revenue Code [26 U.S.C. § 6302]. The Director of Revenue shall prescribe such regulations as may be necessary for the development and implementation of an electronic funds transfer system which is required to be used for the collection of taxes withheld under this chapter. Such system shall be designed in such manner as may be necessary to ensure that such taxes will be credited to an account maintained by the State Treasurer on the date on which the return and taxes would otherwise have been required to be filed under this subchapter.

(h) Any employer that demonstrates it filed and paid over withholding taxes under this chapter on or before the date on which it was required to deposit federal employment taxes shall be deemed to have established reasonable cause for late filing and payment of withheld taxes for purposes of Chapter 5 of this title.

(i) *Information returns.* — Any person:

(1) Required to withhold, account for, and pay over taxes under this chapter for which federal information return form W-2 is required;

(2) Making any payment of salary, fee, commission or other compensation for services to any Delaware resident individual or to any individual nonresident for work done or services performed or rendered within Delaware for which federal information returns form 1099 MISC or successor form is required;

(3) Otherwise withholding Delaware taxes from payment of any wage, pension, distribution or other remuneration; or

(4) Making any payment of any other remuneration to any Delaware resident individual for which any other federal information return is required,

shall also file with the Division of Revenue information returns with respect to each such individual to whom such federal forms are required to be issued. If a person is required to make and return such information reports to the Internal Revenue Service on magnetic media or in other machine-readable form under Internal Revenue Code § 6011 (26 U.S.C. § 6011) and regulations thereunder or successor provision, then the information returns required to be made under this section shall, unless excepted by the Director, also be made on magnetic media or in other machine-readable form. All returns required to be filed under this section shall be filed with the Division of Revenue on or before the date on which such returns are required to be filed with the Internal Revenue Service.

History.

30 Del. C. 1953, § 1154; 57 Del. Laws, c. 737, § 1; 58 Del. Laws, c. 56, § 1; 60 Del. Laws, c. 17, § 1; 60 Del. Laws, c. 276, §§ 1, 2; 62 Del. Laws, c. 56, § 2; 64 Del. Laws, c. 6, §§ 1-3; 65 Del. Laws, c. 402, §§ 1, 2; 70 Del. Laws, c. 186, § 1; 70 Del. Laws, c. 371, §§ 1, 2; 73 Del. Laws, c. 131, § 2; 80 Del. Laws, c. 195, § 6; 81 Del.

Laws, c. 19, § 3; 83 Del. Laws, c. 107, § 2.

Effect of amendments.

83 Del. Laws, c. 107, effective July 30, 2021, substituted "Information returns" for "Employer's return" in the section heading; added pres-ent (b) and redesignated the remaining subsections accordingly; added (i)(4) and "or in other machine-readable form" twice in the penultimate sentence of the final paragraph of (i).

SUBCHAPTER IX
MISCELLANEOUS

§ 1186. Delaware Combined Campaign for Justice Fund.

(a) There is hereby established a Delaware Combined Campaign for Justice Fund for individuals who claim an overpayment of taxes to designate a portion of the overpayment to be paid to the Fund, or individuals who have an income tax liability to designate an amount to be paid to the Fund, according to subsections (b) and (c) of this section.

(b) An individual who claims an overpayment of taxes on an income tax return may designate that $1.00 or more shall be deducted from the refund that would otherwise be payable to the individual and paid to the Delaware Combined Campaign for Justice Fund.

(c) An individual who has an income tax liability may, in addition to the obligation, include a donation of $1.00 or more to be paid to the Delaware Combined Campaign for Justice Fund.

(d) The Division of Revenue shall provide a space on the Delaware income tax return form or schedule by which an individual may voluntarily designate a contribution of an amount of $1.00 or more to the Delaware Combined Campaign for Justice Fund.

(e) The Division of Revenue shall determine the total amount designated under to this section and shall transfer the amount designated to the Delaware Combined Campaign for Justice to advance its efforts to fund civil legal services for disadvantaged Delawareans.

(f) On a schedule to be determined by the Delaware State Clearinghouse Committee, the Delaware Combined Campaign for Justice shall submit a detailed report to members of the Committee of revenues, expenditures, and program measures for the fiscal period in question. The report must be descriptive, but concise and informative. The Committee may require any person employed by or associated with the Delaware Combined Campaign for Justice to appear before the Committee and to answer questions as the Committee may raise.

History.
83 Del. Laws, c. 109, § 1.

Revisor's note.
This section became effective upon the signature of the Governor on July 30, 2021.

A former version of this section, concerning the Delaware Children's Trust Fund, was repealed by 77 Del. Laws, c. 351, effective July 12, 2010.

§ 1192. The Delaware Ovarian Cancer Foundation.

(a) To honor and memorialize the lives of Cynthia Waterman and Sidney DeSmyter and all other women who have fought valiantly against the ravages of ovarian cancer, but lost, the Delaware Ovarian Cancer Foundation is hereby established. Individuals who claim an overpayment of taxes may designate an amount to be deposited in the Delaware Ovarian Cancer Foundation, and individuals who have an income tax liability may designate an amount to be paid to the Delaware Ovarian Cancer Foundation, pursuant to subsections (b) and (c) of this section.

(b) An individual who claims an overpayment of taxes on an income tax return may designate that $1.00 or more be deducted from the refund that would otherwise be payable to the individual, and, instead, be paid to the

Delaware Ovarian Cancer Foundation. The Division of Revenue shall forward the designated amounts to the Delaware Ovarian Cancer Foundation to be used for ovarian cancer research, with emphasis on early detection, education, and awareness.

(c) An individual who has an income tax liability may, in addition to the liability, include a donation of $1.00 or more to be paid to the Delaware Ovarian Cancer Foundation. The Division of Revenue shall forward the designated amounts to the Delaware Ovarian Cancer Foundation to be used for ovarian cancer research, with emphasis on early detection, education and awareness.

(d) The Division of Revenue shall provide a space on the Delaware income tax return form or schedule where an individual may voluntarily designate a contribution of an amount of $1.00 or more to the Delaware Ovarian Cancer Foundation.

(e) An amount designated for the Delaware Ovarian Cancer Foundation on the income tax return form must be deducted from the tax refund to which the individual is entitled, or an amount designated may be added to the individual's payment of taxes due. In neither case may those amounts be included in the general revenue of the State.

(f) From time to time as determined by the Delaware State Clearinghouse Committee, the custodians of the Delaware Ovarian Cancer Foundation shall submit a detailed report to members of the Committee of revenues, expenditures, and program measures for the fiscal period in question. The report must be descriptive in nature, as well as concise and informative. The Committee may cause any person employed by or associated with the Delaware Ovarian Cancer Foundation to appear before the Committee and answer questions that the Committee may require.

History.

77 Del. Laws, c. 209, § 1; 83 Del. Laws, c. 107, § 3.

Effect of amendments.

83 Del. Laws, c. 107, effective July 30, 2021, deleted "Fund at the Delaware Community Foundation" following "Cancer Foundation" in the section heading, wherever it appeared in (a), in the first sentence of (b) and (c), in (d) and (e) and in the first and final sentences of (f); and deleted "Fund at the Delaware Community Foundation who, in turn, shall deposit them to the credit of the Delaware Ovarian Cancer Foundation Fund" preceding "to be used" in the second sentence of (b) and (c).

CHAPTER 16
PASS-THROUGH ENTITIES, ESTATES AND TRUSTS

SUBCHAPTER I
IN GENERAL

§ 1606. Withholding of income tax on sale or exchange of real estate by nonresident pass-through entities.

(a) *Definitions.* — (1) "Director" means the Director of the Division of Revenue or the Secretary of Finance of the State.

(2) "Nonresident pass-through entity" means, for purposes of this section, a pass-through entity having 1 or more members who are nonresident individuals or nonresident corporations.

(3) "Recorder" means the official with duty to record deeds and similar instruments.

(4) "Transfer under a deed in lieu of foreclosure" includes all of the following:

    a. A transfer by the owner of the property to the following:

        1. With respect to a deed in lieu of foreclosure of a mortgage, the mortgagee, the assignee of the mortgage, or any designee or nominee of the mortgagee or assignee of the mortgage.

        2. With respect to a deed in lieu of foreclosure of any other lien instrument, the holder of the debt or other obligation secured by the lien instrument or any designee, nominee, or assignee of the holder of the debt secured by the lien instrument.

    b. A transfer by any of the persons described in paragraph (a)(4)a. of this section to a subsequent purchaser for value.

(5) "Transfer under a foreclosure of a mortgage or other lien instrument" includes the following:

    a. With respect to the foreclosure of a mortgage, all of the following:

        1. A transfer by the sheriff or other party authorized to conduct the foreclosure sale under the mortgage to 1 of the following:

        A. The mortgagee or the assignee of the mortgage.

        B. Any designee, nominee, or assignee of the mortgagee or assignee of the mortgage.

        C. Any purchaser, substituted purchaser, or assignee of any purchaser or substituted purchaser of the foreclosed property.

        2. A transfer by any of the persons described in paragraphs (a)(5)a.1.A. and (a)(5)a.1.B. of this section to a subsequent purchaser for value.

    b. With respect to the foreclosure of any other lien instrument, all of the following:

        1. A transfer by the party authorized to make the sale to 1 of the following:

        A. The holder of the debt or other obligation secured by the lien instrument.

        B. Any designee, nominee, or assignee of the holder of the debt secured by the lien instrument.

        C. Any purchaser, substituted purchaser, or assignee of any purchaser or substituted purchaser of the foreclosed property.

        2. A transfer by any of the persons described in paragraphs (a)(5)b.1.A. and (a)(5)b.1.B. of this section to a subsequent purchaser for value.

(b) *Estimated tax return; alternative forms.* — Every nonresident pass-through entity that sells or exchanges Delaware real estate shall file with the Recorder for and on behalf of each of its nonresident members 1 of the following:

(1) A "Declaration of Estimated Income Tax" or a "Delaware Corporate Tentative Tax Return" for the quarter in which the sale or exchange is settled, applying the highest marginal rate of each of its nonresident members under § 1102 or § 1902 of this title, as the case may be, to an estimate of the nonresident member's distributive share of the gain recognized on the sale or exchange.

(2) An alternative form prepared by the Director to calculate income tax at the highest marginal rate under § 1102 or § 1902 of this title, applied to the nonresident member's distributive share of the difference between the total amount realized by the transferor and the net balance due at the time of settlement of all recorded liens encumbering the real estate.

(3) An alternative form prepared by the Director to declare under penalties of perjury that the sale or exchange of real estate is exempt from recognition of capital gain with respect to the tax year of the sale or exchange, with a statement of the facts and a citation to the provision or provisions of the Internal Revenue Code (Title 26, U.S.C.) relied upon.

(4) An alternative form prepared by the Director to declare under penalties of perjury that the sale or exchange of real estate is 1 of the following:

    a. A transfer under a foreclosure of a mortgage or other lien instrument.

    b. A transfer under a deed in lieu of foreclosure.

(5) An alternative form prepared by the Director to declare under penalties of perjury that the nonresident pass-through entity that is selling or exchanging Delaware real estate is exempt from the requirements of subsection (d) of this section and is not required to remit any tax due with the deed to the Recorder before the deed shall be recorded.

(c) *Exemption.* — (1) The Director will create an application process through which a nonresident pass-through entity involved in the sale or exchange of an average of 5 or more residential homes or residential lots in Delaware per quarter can apply for an exemption from the requirements of subsection (d) of this section.

(2) Subject to paragraph (c)(3) of this section, if an exemption is granted in accordance with paragraph (c)(1) of this section, such nonresident pass-through entity will be exempt from the requirements of subsection (d) of this section and will not be required to remit any tax due with the deed to the Recorder before the deed shall be recorded.

(3) If an exemption is granted in accordance with paragraph (c)(1) of this section and the Director subsequently determines that such nonresident pass-through entity or any member of such nonresident pass-through entity has failed to comply with its tax filing and payment obligations, the Director may revoke the exemption granted to such nonresident pass-through entity in accordance with paragraph (c)(1) of this section by providing written notice of such revocation to such nonresident pass-through entity.

(4) Within 60 days after the date of the mailing of a notice of revocation under paragraph (c)(3) of this section, the nonresident pass-through entity may file with the Director a written protest challenging the proposed revocation, in which the nonresident pass-through entity shall set forth the grounds upon which the protest is based. If such protest is filed, the Director will reconsider the proposed revocation and, if requested, may grant the taxpayer or the taxpayer's authorized representative an oral hearing.

(5) Except to the extent inconsistent with the specific provisions of this section, the provisions of Chapter 5 of this title shall govern the review and appeal of such proposed revocation.

(d) *Due date of estimated tax return, payment.* — The return or form provided for in subsection (b) of this section and, unless the taxpayer is exempt as provided in subsection (c) of this section, the estimated tax reported due on such return or form, shall be remitted with the deed to the Recorder before the deed shall be recorded. Such payment shall be withheld from the net proceeds of the sale. To the extent that the sale does not result in net proceeds being available for the payment of the estimated tax, the Recorder may accept the form without payment, upon receipt of confirmation from the closing attorney that no funds are available for payment of the tax and that no funds were distributed to the seller.

(e) *Payment credited to transferor.* — The estimated tax remitted under subsection (d) of this section shall be deemed to have been paid to the Director on behalf of the nonresident members of the pass-through entity and the nonresident members shall be credited for purposes of §§ 1169 and 1170 or § 1905 of this title as a payment made on the date remitted to the Recorder.

(f) *Persons or entities not liable for payments.* — Neither the transferee, title insurance producer, title insurer, settlement agent, closing attorney, lending institution, nor the real estate agent or broker in a transaction subject to this section shall be liable for any amounts required to be collected and paid over to the Recorder or Director under this section.

(g) *Tax not imposed; lawful collection of taxes not prohibited.* — This section does not:

(1) Impose any tax on a transferor or affect any liability of the transferor for any tax; or

(2) Prohibit the Director from collecting any taxes due from a transferor in any other manner authorized by law.

History.
77 Del. Laws, c. 291, § 2; 81 Del. Laws, c. 363, § 2; 82 Del. Laws, c. 194, § 1; 83 Del. Laws, c. 37, § 38; 83 Del. Laws, c. 107, § 4.

Effect of amendments.
83 Del. Laws, c. 37, effective June 3, 2021, in (d), deleted a comma following "subsection (b) of this section" and following "due" and added a comma following "subsection (c) of this section".

83 Del. Laws, c. 107, effective July 30, 2021, in (d), added "on such return or form" in the first sentence and added the second and third sentences.

CHAPTER 18
LAND AND HISTORIC RESOURCE TAX CREDIT

SUBCHAPTER II
HISTORIC PRESERVATION AND REPAIR

Revisor's note.
Section 2 of 77 Del. Laws, c. 413, effective July 19, 2010, provided: "The Historic Preservation Tax Credit Act shall be effective for approvals granted in fiscal years ending before June 30, 2020." That provision was repealed by 83 Del. Laws, c. 154 § 1, effective Sept. 15, 2021.

§ 1813. Preservation and repair of historic structures; tax credits; sunset.

(a) Any person incurring qualified expenditures pursuant to this subchapter in the substantial rehabilitation of any certified historic property shall be entitled to a credit against bank franchise or income taxes imposed under Title 5, or under Chapter 11 or Chapter 19 of this title, respectively, subject to limitations set forth in this section and up to a maximum of:

(1) Twenty percent of qualified expenditures made in the rehabilitation of any certified historic property which is eligible for a federal tax credit under § 47 of the Internal Revenue Code [26 U.S.C. § 47];

(2) Thirty percent of the qualified expenditures made in the rehabilitation of any certified historic property which is not eligible for a federal tax credit under § 47 of the Internal Revenue Code [26 U.S.C. § 47];

(3) One hundred percent of the qualified expenditures made in the rehabilitation of a certified historic property qualifying for credit award as a resident curatorship property regardless of eligibility for a federal tax credit under § 47 of the Internal Revenue Code [26 U.S.C. § 47].

(4) In no event shall the credit claimed pursuant to this section exceed the credit award.

(b) Any person, in order to receive a Certificate of Completion from the Delaware State Historic Preservation Officer that would entitle said person to a tax credit under this section, shall submit documentation of those qualified expenditures and project plans that would be required in order to qualify for tax credit under § 47 of the Internal Revenue Code [26 U.S.C. § 47], whether or not such project would be eligible for such federal tax credit.

(c) Any person eligible for credits under this chapter may transfer, sell or assign any or all unused credits. If a certified historic property for which a certified rehabilitation has been completed is sold or transferred, the amount of any credit not used by the time of such sale or transfer may be transferred to the person to which the structure is sold or transferred.

(d) Except as otherwise provided, if the amount of credit allowed pursuant to this subchapter exceeds that total tax liability of the taxpayer for the tax year for which the credit is claimed, the amount of the credit not used as an offset against income or franchise taxes in said tax year shall not be refunded, but may be carried forward as a credit against subsequent years' income or franchise tax liability for a period not exceeding 10 years, and shall be applied first to the earliest tax years possible.

(e) With respect to the tax credits awarded under paragraph (a)(2) of this section, no single certified rehabilitation of owner-occupied historic property may receive a tax credit in excess of $30,000. Owner-occupied historic properties may be eligible for multiple certified rehabilitations representing separate phases of rehabilitation of a certified historic property; provided, however, that following an initial credit award, any subsequent credit award shall be made not less than 24 months after any preceding credit award. With respect to tax credits awarded for qualifying expenditures by a resident curator, no single certified rehabilitation may receive a tax credit in excess of $5,000.

(f) Whenever any part of the certified rehabilitation of a residential property is determined under regulations promulgated by the State Office to be committed to low-income housing, subsection (a) of this section shall be applied with respect to such part by substituting "30%" for "20%" and "40%" for "30%" in said subsection.

(g) The Historic Preservation Tax Credit Act [73 Del. Laws, c. 6] is effective for an approval granted in a fiscal year that ends before June 30, 2030.

History.
73 Del. Laws, c. 6, § 3; 73 Del. Laws, c. 240, §§ 2, 3; 74 Del. Laws, c. 68, §§ 107(D), 107(E); 81 Del. Laws, c. 390, § 1; 83 Del. Laws, c. 154, § 2.

Effect of amendments.
83 Del. Laws, c. 154, effective September 15, 2021, added "sunset" in the section heading; and added (g).

CHAPTER 19

CORPORATION INCOME TAX

§ 1903. Computation of taxable income.

(a) The "entire net income" of a corporation for any income year means the amount of its federal taxable income for such year as computed for purposes of the federal income tax increased by:

(1) Any interest income (including discount) on obligations issued by

states of the United States or political subdivisions thereof other than this State and its subdivisions, and

(2) The amount of any deduction allowed for purposes of the federal income tax pursuant to § 164 of the Internal Revenue Code (26 U.S.C. § 164) for taxes paid on, or according to or measured by, in whole or in part, such corporation's net income or profits, to any state (including this State), territory, county or political subdivision thereof, or any tax paid in lieu of such income tax, and its federal taxable income shall be further adjusted by eliminating:

a. Dividends received on shares of stock or voting trust certificates of foreign corporations or interest income or royalty income, on which a foreign tax is paid, deemed paid or accrued under the applicable provisions of the United States Internal Revenue Code [26 U.S.C. § 1 et seq.];

b. Interest income (including discount) from securities issued by the United States or agencies or instrumentalities thereof and interest income (including discount) arising from obligations representing advances, loans or contractual transactions between corporations which are eligible to file a consolidated return for federal income tax purposes and which are subject to taxation under this chapter, if the paying corporation eliminates such interest (including discount) in determining its entire net income; provided, however, that the expenses allocable to interest income from securities issued by the United States or agencies or instrumentalities thereof shall not be allowed as a deduction;

c. Gains and losses from the sale or other disposition of securities issued by the United States or agencies or instrumentalities thereof or by this State or political subdivisions thereof. Expenses incurred in connection with such gains and losses shall not be considered in computing the entire net income of the corporation;

d. Any deduction allowed for depletion of oil and gas wells under § 611 of the federal Internal Revenue Code [26 U.S.C. § 611] to the extent such deduction is determined by reference to § 613 of the federal Internal Revenue Code [26 U.S.C. § 613] (relating to percentage depletion);

e. An amount equal to the portion of the wages paid or incurred for the taxable year which is disallowed as a deduction for federal purposes under § 280C, Internal Revenue Code [26 U.S.C. § 280C], relating to the portion of wages for which the new jobs tax credit is claimed;

f. The cost, not to exceed $5,000, of a renovation project to remove physical design features in a building that restrict the full use of the building by physically handicapped persons. The modification shall be allowed for the taxable year in which the renovation project is completed and is in addition to any depreciation or amortization of the cost of the renovation project. "Building" means a building or structure or that part of a building or structure and its related sidewalks, curbing, driveways and entrances that are located in Delaware and open to the general public;

g. The "eligible net income" of an Edge Act corporation organized pursuant to § 25(a) of the Federal Reserve Act, 12 U.S.C. § 611 et seq. The eligible net income of an Edge Act corporation shall be the net income from any international banking facility of such corporation each computed as described in § 1101(a)(1)d. and e. of Title 5;

h. Any deduction, to the extent such deduction exceeds $30,000, for a net operating loss carryback as provided for in Internal Revenue Code § 172 [26 U.S.C. § 172] or successor provisions; provided, however, that the taxpayer may increase deductions in any year, consistent with the operation of § 172, to carry forward losses which were carried back in calculating federal taxable income but which were prevented from being carried back under this paragraph;

i. Any deduction for a net operating loss carryforward calculated in accordance with the provisions of the Internal Revenue Code, provided however that the deduction may not exceed the amount claimed on the federal return filed for the taxable year in which the taxpayer was included as a party.

(b) "Taxable income" subject to taxation under this chapter means the portion of the entire net income of a corporation which is allocated and apportioned to this State in accordance with the following provisions:

(1) Rents and royalties (less applicable or related expenses) from tangible property shall be allocated to the state in which the property is physically located;

(2) Patent and copyright royalties (less applicable or related expenses) shall be allocated proportionately to the states in which the product or process protected by the patent is manufactured or used or in which the publication protected by the copyright is produced or printed;

(3) Gains and losses from the sale or other disposition of real property shall be allocated to the state in which the property, and expenses incurred in connection with dispositions resulting in such gains and losses, is physically located;

(4) Gains and losses from the sale or other disposition of tangible property for which an allowance for depreciation is permitted for federal income tax purposes, and expenses incurred in connection with dispositions resulting in such gains and losses, shall be allocated to the state where the property is physically located or is normally used in the taxpayer's business;

(5) Interest (including discount) to the extent included in determining entire net income under subsection (a) of this section, less related or applicable expenses, shall be allocated to the state where the transaction took place which resulted in the creation of the obligation with respect to which the interest was earned;

(6)a. If the entire business of the corporation is transacted or conducted within this State, the remainder of its entire net income shall be allocated to this State. If the business of the corporation is transacted or conducted in part without this State, such remainder, whether income or loss, shall be apportioned to this State:

1. For taxable periods beginning before January 1, 2017, by multiplying such remainder by the arithmetical average of the 3 factors set forth in paragraphs (b)(6)b.1.,2., and 3. of this section;

2. For taxable periods beginning after December 31, 2016, and before January 1, 2018, by multiplying such remainder by a fraction, the numerator of which is the sum of the property factor set forth in paragraph (b)(6)b.1. of this section plus the payroll factor set forth in paragraph (b)(6)b.2. of this section plus double the sales factor set forth in paragraph (b)(6)b.3. of this section, and the denominator of which is 4;

3. For taxable periods beginning after December 31, 2017, and before January 1, 2019, by multiplying such remainder by a fraction,

the numerator of which is the sum of the property factor set forth in paragraph (b)(6)b.1. of this section plus the payroll factor set forth in paragraph (b)(6)b.2. of this section plus triple the sales factor set forth in paragraph (b)(6)b.3. of this section, and the denominator of which is 5;

4. For taxable periods beginning after December 31, 2018, and before January 1, 2020, by multiplying such remainder by a fraction, the numerator of which is the sum of the property factor set forth in paragraph (b)(6)b.1. of this section plus the payroll factor set forth in paragraph (b)(6)b.2. of this section plus 6 times the sales factor set forth in paragraph (b)(6)b.3. of this section, and the denominator of which is 8; and

5. For taxable periods beginning after December 31, 2019, by multiplying such remainder by the sales factor set forth in paragraph (b)(6)b.3. of this section.

b. The factors shall be calculated as follows:

1. The property factor shall equal the average of the value, at the beginning and end of the income year, of all the real and tangible personal property, owned or rented, in this State by the taxpayer, expressed as a percentage of the average of the value at the beginning and end of the income year of all such property of the taxpayer both within and without this State; provided, that any property, the income from which is separately allocated under paragraph (b)(1) of this section or which is not used in the taxpayer's business, shall be disregarded, and provided further, that in the case of a non-U.S. corporation, property without this State shall include only property located without this State, but also within the United States. For the purposes of this paragraph, property owned by the taxpayer shall be valued at its original cost to the taxpayer, and property rented by the taxpayer shall be valued at 8 times the annual rental;

2. The payroll factor shall equal the wages, salaries and other compensation paid by the taxpayer to employees within this State, except general executive officers, during the income year expressed as a percentage of all such wages, salaries and other compensation paid within and without this State during the income year to all employees of the taxpayer, except general executive officers; provided, that in the case of a non-U.S. corporation, wages, salaries and other compensation paid without this State during the income year shall include only wages, salaries and other compensation paid during the income year to employees of the taxpayer, except general executive officers, that are deductible under § 882 of the Internal Revenue Code of 1986 (26 U.S.C. § 882), as amended, in determining federal taxable income which is effectively connected with the conduct of a trade or business within the United States;

3. The sales factor shall equal the gross receipts from sales of tangible personal property physically delivered within this State to the purchaser or the purchaser's agent (but not including delivery to the United States mail or to a common or contract carrier for shipment to a place outside this State) and gross income from other sources within this State for the income year expressed as a percentage of all such gross receipts from sales of tangible personal property and gross income from other sources

both within and without the State for the income year; provided, that any receipts or items of income that are excluded in determining the taxpayer's entire net income or are directly allocated under paragraphs (b)(1) to (5) of this section shall be disregarded.

    c. This paragraph (b)(6) shall not apply in the case of:

      1. An asset management corporation;

      2. A telecommunications corporation; or

      3. A worldwide headquarters corporation.

(7) The remainder of the entire net income of an asset management corporation shall be apportioned to this State on the basis of the ratio of gross receipts from asset management services from sources within this State for the income year expressed as a percentage of all such gross receipts from asset management services both within and without the State for the income year; provided, that any receipts or items of income that are excluded in determining the taxpayer's entire net income or are directly allocated under paragraphs (b)(1) to (5) of this section shall be disregarded. The source of gross receipts from asset management services shall be determined as follows:

    a. In the case of asset management services provided directly or indirectly to an individual, gross receipts with respect to such services shall be sourced to the State of the individual's domicile.

    b. In the case of asset management services provided directly or indirectly to an institutional investor holding investments for the benefit of others, such as a pension plan, retirement account or pool of intangible investments, including a fund (other than an investment company under the Investment Company Act of 1940 (15 U.S.C. § 80a-1 et seq.)), or to an institutional investor organized as a pass-through entity (as defined in § 1601(6)a. of this title), gross receipts with respect to such services shall be sourced according to the following rules in the following order:

      1. If information regarding domicile of beneficiaries, owners or members is available to the asset management corporation providing asset management services to a pension plan, retirement account or pool of intangible investments, including a fund (other than an investment company under the Investment Company Act of 1940 (15 U.S.C. § 80a-1 et seq.)), or to an institutional investor organized as a pass-through entity (as defined in § 1601(6)a. of this title) through the exercise of reasonable diligence in ascertaining such information, gross receipts with respect to such services shall be sourced to the domicile of such beneficiaries, owners or members;

      2. If information regarding domicile of beneficiaries, owners or members is not available to the asset management corporation providing asset management services to a pension plan, retirement account or pool of intangible investments, including a fund (other than an investment company under the Investment Company Act of 1940 (15 U.S.C. § 80a-1 et seq.)), or to an institutional investor organized as a pass-through entity (as defined in § 1601(6)a. of this title) through the exercise of reasonable diligence in ascertaining such information, a reasonable alternative method based on information readily available to the asset management corporation may be used to determine the source of gross receipts with respect to such services, and such reasonable alternative method shall be disclosed and explained in the return

in which the method is used. The burden of demonstrating the reasonableness of the method rests on the taxpayer. Based on facts and circumstances in specific cases, reasonable alternative methods used to determine the source of gross receipts from asset management services may take into account the latest population census data available from the United States Census Bureau, the domicile of the sponsor of a pension plan or retirement account or an account or pool of intangible investments (other than an investment company under the Investment Company Act of 1940 (15 U.S.C. § 80a-1 et seq.)) or the domicile of an institutional investor organized as a pass-through entity (as defined in § 1601(6)a. of this title); or,

    3. If

       A. The domicile of beneficiaries, owners or members is not ascertained under paragraph (b)(7)b.1. of this section; or,

       B. No reasonable alternative sourcing method exists under paragraph (b)(7)b.2. of this section, gross receipts with respect to such services shall be sourced to the domicile of the institutional investor or the domicile of the sponsor of a pension plan or retirement account or an account or pool of intangible investments, including a fund (other than an investment company under the Investment Company Act of 1940 (15 U.S.C. § 80a-1 et seq.)), to which asset management services are provided.

    c. In the case of asset management services provided directly or indirectly to an investment company under the Investment Company Act of 1940 (15 U.S.C. § 80a-1 et seq.), gross receipts with respect to such services shall be sourced to the domicile of the shareholders of such investment company in accordance with the following procedure: the portion of the gross receipts with respect to such services that are sourced to this State shall be determined by multiplying the total of such gross receipts by a fraction, the numerator of which is the average of the sum of the beginning of year and the end of year balance of shares owned by the investment company shareholders domiciled in this State for the investment company's taxable year for federal income tax purposes and the denominator of which is the average of the sum of the beginning of year and the end of year balance of shares owned by all investment company shareholders. A separate computation shall be made with respect to gross receipts for asset management services provided directly or indirectly to each investment company.

    d. In the case of asset management services provided directly or indirectly to a person other than those persons described in paragraph (b)(7)a. through c. of this section, to the domicile of such person.

(8) If the entire business of a telecommunications corporation or a worldwide headquarters corporation is transacted or conducted within this State, the remainder of its entire net income shall be allocated to this State. If the business of a telecommunications corporation or a worldwide headquarters corporation is transacted or conducted in part without this State, such remainder, whether income or loss, shall be apportioned to this State:

    a. For taxable periods beginning before January 1, 2017, by multiplying such remainder by the arithmetical average of the 3 factors set forth in paragraphs (b)(6)b.1., 2., and 3.of this section; and

　　b. For taxable periods beginning after December 31, 2016, by electing, on an annual basis, either to:

　　　　1. Multiply such remainder by the sales factor set forth in paragraph (b)(6)b.3. of this section; or

　　　　2. Multiply such remainder by the arithmetical average of the 3 factors set forth in paragraphs (b)(6)b.1., 2., and 3. of this section.

　(c) If, in the discretion of the Secretary of Finance, the application of the allocation or apportionment provisions of this section result in an unfair or inequitable proportion of the taxpayer's entire net income being assigned to this State, then the Secretary of Finance or the Secretary's delegate may permit or require the exclusion or alteration of the weight to be given to 1 or more of the factors in the formula specified above or the use of separate accounting or other method to produce a fair and equitable result.

　(d) In determining the taxable income of a fiscal year taxpayer for that portion of its fiscal year ending within 1977 which falls within the calendar year 1977, the taxpayer may, at its election, treat such period as though it were the entire fiscal year, or it may compute its taxable income for the entire fiscal year and pay the tax herein imposed on that portion of the taxable income so determined which the number of days from January 1, 1977, to the close of the fiscal year in 1977 bears to 365.

History.

30 Del. C. 1953, § 1903; 51 Del. Laws, c. 298; 51 Del. Laws, c. 315, § 4; 57 Del. Laws, c. 136, §§ 2, 3; 57 Del. Laws, c. 188, §§ 19, 41; 57 Del. Laws, c. 533; 57 Del. Laws, c. 741, § 8B; 58 Del. Laws, c. 320; 59 Del. Laws, c. 113, §§ 1, 2; 60 Del. Laws, c. 18, § 3; 61 Del. Laws, c. 76, § 2; 61 Del. Laws, c. 297, § 1; 62 Del. Laws, c. 56, § 3; 63 Del. Laws, c. 295, § 2; 64 Del. Laws, c. 43, § 8; 67 Del. Laws, c. 263, §§ 1, 2; 68 Del. Laws, c. 82, §§ 9, 10; 70 Del. Laws, c. 186, § 1; 71 Del. Laws, c. 19, § 80; 71 Del. Laws, c. 217, §§ 3-6; 76 Del. Laws, c. 234, §§ 5, 6; 80 Del. Laws, c. 195, §§ 8, 9; 83 Del. Laws, c. 107, § 5.

Effect of amendments.

83 Del. Laws, c. 107, effective July 30, 2021, added (a)(2)i. and made a minor related stylistic change.

NOTES TO DECISIONS

Constitutionality. — Delaware Division of Revenue's policy of limiting separate-company net operating loss (NOL) to the consolidated NOL deduction of the federal consolidated group of which the taxpayer was a member was consistent with this section, but violated the state uniformity clause, Del. Const. art. VIII, § 1; it treated Delaware corporate taxpayers differently depending upon whether they filed their federal returns as consolidated groups or separate corporations. Verisign, Inc. v. Dir. of Revenue, — A.3d —, 2020 Del. Super. LEXIS 3011 (Del. Super. Ct. Dec. 17, 2020).

§ 1909. Withholding of income tax on sale or exchange of real estate by nonresident corporations.

　(a) *Definitions.* — (1) "Director" means the Director of the Division of Revenue or the Secretary of Finance of the State.

　　(2) "Nonresident corporation" means, for purposes of this section, a corporation that:

　　　a. Is not organized under the laws of this State, and

　　　b. Is not qualified or registered with the Secretary of State to do business in this State.

　　(3) "Recorder" means the official with the duty to record deeds and similar instruments.

　　(4) "Transfer under a deed in lieu of foreclosure" includes all of the following:

　　　a. A transfer by the owner of the property to the following:

　　　　1. With respect to a deed in lieu of foreclosure of a mortgage, the mortgagee, the assignee of the mortgage, or any designee or nominee of the mortgagee or assignee of the mortgage.

2. With respect to a deed in lieu of foreclosure of any other lien instrument, the holder of the debt or other obligation secured by the lien instrument or any designee, nominee, or assignee of the holder of the debt secured by the lien instrument.

b. A transfer by any of the persons described in paragraph (a)(4)a. of this section to a subsequent purchaser for value.

(5) "Transfer under a foreclosure of a mortgage or other lien instrument" includes the following:

a. With respect to the foreclosure of a mortgage, all of the following:

1. A transfer by the sheriff or other party authorized to conduct the foreclosure sale under the mortgage to 1 of the following:

A. The mortgagee or the assignee of the mortgage.

B. Any designee, nominee, or assignee of the mortgagee or assignee of the mortgage.

C. Any purchaser, substituted purchaser, or assignee of any purchaser or substituted purchaser of the foreclosed property.

2. A transfer by any of the persons described in paragraphs (a)(5)a.1.A. and (a)(5)a.1.B. of this section to a subsequent purchaser for value.

b. With respect to the foreclosure of any other lien instrument, all of the following:

1. A transfer by the party authorized to make the sale to 1 of the following:

A. The holder of the debt or other obligation secured by the lien instrument.

B. Any designee, nominee, or assignee of the holder of the debt secured by the lien instrument.

C. Any purchaser, substituted purchaser, or assignee of any purchaser or substituted purchaser of the foreclosed property.

2. A transfer by any of the persons described in paragraphs (a)(5)b.1.A. and (a)(5)b.1.B. of this section to a subsequent purchaser for value.

(b) *Estimated tax return; alternative forms.* — Every nonresident corporation that sells or exchanges Delaware real estate shall file with the Recorder 1 of the following:

(1) A "Delaware Corporate Tentative Tax Return" due for the quarter in which the sale or exchange is settled, applying the tax rate provided under § 1902 of this title to an estimate of the gain recognized on the sale or exchange.

(2) An alternative form prepared by the Director to calculate income tax at the tax rate provided under § 1902 of this title, applied to the difference between the total amount realized by the transferor and the net balance due at the time of settlement of all recorded liens encumbering the real estate.

(3) An alternative form prepared by the Director to declare under penalties of perjury that the sale or exchange of real estate is exempt from recognition of capital gain with respect to the tax year of the sale or exchange, with a statement of the facts and a citation to the provision or provisions of the Internal Revenue Code (Title 26, U.S.C.) relied upon.

(4) An alternative form prepared by the Director to declare under penalties of perjury that the sale or exchange of real estate is 1 of the following:

a. A transfer under a foreclosure of a mortgage or other lien instrument.

b. A transfer under a deed in lieu of foreclosure.

(c) *Due date of estimated tax return; payment.* — The return or form provided for in subsection (b) of this section, and the estimated tax reported due on such return or form, shall be remitted with the deed to the Recorder before the deed shall be recorded. Such payment shall be withheld from the net proceeds of the sale. To the extent that the sale does not result in net proceeds being available for the payment of the estimated tax, the Recorder may accept the form without payment, upon receipt of confirmation from the closing attorney that no funds are available for payment of the tax and that no funds were distributed to the seller.

(d) *Payment credited to transferor.* — The estimated tax remitted under subsection (c) of this section shall be deemed to have been paid to the Director on behalf of the nonresident transferor and the nonresident transferor shall be credited for purposes of § 1905 of this title as a payment made on the date remitted to the Recorder.

(e) *Persons or entities not liable for payments.* — Neither the transferee, title insurance producer, title insurer, settlement agent, closing attorney, lending institution, nor the real estate agent or broker in a transaction subject to this section shall be liable for any amounts required to be collected and paid over to the Recorder or Director under this section.

(f) *Tax not imposed; lawful collection of taxes not prohibited.* — This section does not:

(1) Impose any tax on a transferor or affect any liability of the transferor for any tax; or

(2) Prohibit the Director from collecting any taxes due from a transferor in any other manner authorized by law.

History.
77 Del. Laws, c. 291, § 3; 81 Del. Laws, c. 363, § 3; 83 Del. Laws, c. 107, § 6.

in (c), added "on such return or form" in the first sentence, and added the second and third sentences.

Effect of amendments.
83 Del. Laws, c. 107, effective July 30, 2021,

CHAPTER 20

BUSINESS TAX CREDITS AND DEDUCTIONS

SUBCHAPTER VI
COMMUTER BENEFITS FOR STATE EMPLOYEES [SUSPENDED BEGINNING FISCAL YEAR 2013; SEE 83 DEL. LAWS, C. 54, § 264].

Revisor's note.

Section 268 of 78 Del. Laws, c. 290, effective July 1, 2012; as amended by 79 Del. Laws, c. 78, § 259, effective July 1, 2013; 79 Del. Laws, c. 290, § 268, effective July 1, 2014; 80 Del. Laws, c. 79, § 263, effective July 1, 2015; and 80 Del. Laws, c. 298, § 261, effective July 1, 2016; 81 Del. Laws, c. 58, § 268, effective July 3, 2017;

81 Del. Laws, c. 280, § 263, effective July 1, 2018; 82 Del. Laws, c. 64, § 262, effective July 1, 2019; 82 Del. Laws, c. 242, § 253, effective July 1, 2020; and 83 Del. Laws, c. 54, § 264, effective June 30, 2021, provided: "Beginning in Fiscal Year 2013, provisions of 30 Del. C. § 2051- 2057 shall be suspended."

§ 2051. Declaration of purpose [Suspended beginning in Fiscal Year 2013; see 83 Del. Laws, c. 54, § 264].

The purpose of this subchapter shall be to mitigate traffic congestion associated with state employees' commuting to and from the work place, and to facilitate compliance with the requirements of the Clean Air Act [42 U.S.C. § 7401 et seq.] as amended in 1990.

History.

68 Del. Laws, c. 426, § 2; 78 Del. Laws, c. 290, § 262; 79 Del. Laws, c. 78, § 259; 79 Del. Laws, c. 290, § 268; 80 Del. Laws, c. 79, § 263;

80 Del. Laws, c. 298, § 261; ; 81 Del. Laws, c. 58, § 268; 81 Del. Laws, c. 280, § 263; 82 Del. Laws, c. 64, § 262; 82 Del. Laws, c. 242, § 253; 83 Del. Laws, c. 54, § 264.

§ 2052. Definitions [Suspended beginning Fiscal Year 2013; see 83 Del. Laws, c. 54, § 264].

(a) "Commuter benefits" means incentives including monetary incentives, provided by the employer to the employee in conjunction with an approved traffic plan.

(b) "Department" shall mean the Department of Transportation and its several divisions, agencies, authorities and administrations as appropriate.

(c) "Employee" shall mean an individual employed by a state agency.

(d) "Employer" shall mean a state agency.

(e) "Secretary" shall mean the Secretary of the Department of Transportation or the Secretary's delegate.

(f) "State" means the State of Delaware.

(g) "State agency" shall mean any office, department, board, commission, committee, court, school district, board of education and all public bodies existing by virtue of an act of the General Assembly or the Constitution of the State, excepting only political subdivisions of the State, their agencies and other public agencies not specifically included in this definition and which exist by virtue of state law and whose jurisdiction:

(1) Is limited to a political subdivision of the State or to a portion thereof; or

(2) Extends beyond the ordinance of the State.

History.

68 Del. Laws, c. 426, § 2; 70 Del. Laws, c. 186, § 1; 78 Del. Laws, c. 290, § 262; 79 Del. Laws, c. 78, § 259; 79 Del. Laws, c. 290, § 268;

80 Del. Laws, c. 79, § 263; 80 Del. Laws, c. 298, § 261; 81 Del. Laws, c. 58, § 268; 81 Del. Laws, c. 280, § 263; 82 Del. Laws, c. 64, § 262; 82 Del. Laws, c. 242, § 253; 83 Del. Laws, c. 54, § 264.

§ 2053. Agency plans [Suspended beginning Fiscal Year 2013; see 83 Del. Laws, c. 54, § 264].

Each state agency shall develop and submit for review by the Department a plan to reduce work-related vehicle trips and miles traveled by employees. If submitting an individual plan is not practical because of the state agency's location or number of employees, a state agency may join with another state agency in submitting a plan for review.

History.
68 Del. Laws, c. 426, § 2; 78 Del. Laws, c. 290, § 262; 79 Del. Laws, c. 78, § 259; 79 Del. Laws, c. 290, § 268; 80 Del. Laws, c. 79, § 263; 80 Del. Laws, c. 298, § 261; 81 Del. Laws, c. 58, § 268; 81 Del. Laws, c. 280, § 263; 82 Del. Laws, c. 64, § 262; 82 Del. Laws, c. 242, § 253; 83 Del. Laws, c. 54, § 264.

§ 2054. Department review of plans [Suspended beginning in Fiscal Year 2013; see 83 Del. Laws, c. 54, § 264].

The Department shall review plans required by § 2053 of this title and submitted by state agencies for conformity with the rules and regulations promulgated by the Secretary pursuant to § 2055 of this title and any plan required to be submitted by the State to the federal government for purposes of the Clean Air Act [42 U.S.C. § 7401 et seq.] as amended in 1990.

History.
68 Del. Laws, c. 426, § 2; 78 Del. Laws, c. 290, § 262; 79 Del. Laws, c. 78, § 259; 79 Del. Laws, c. 290, § 268; 80 Del. Laws, c. 79, § 263; 80 Del. Laws, c. 298, § 261; 81 Del. Laws, c. 58, § 268; 81 Del. Laws, c. 280, § 263; 82 Del. Laws, c. 64, § 262; 82 Del. Laws, c. 242, § 253; 83 Del. Laws, c. 54, § 264.

§ 2055. Rules and regulations [Suspended beginning in Fiscal Year 2013; see 83 Del. Laws, c. 54, § 264].

The Secretary shall prescribe such rules and regulations as the Secretary may deem necessary to carry out the purpose of this subchapter including but not limited to regulations concerning the submittal of plans, guidelines for reviewing plans by the Department and the amount and nature of commuter benefits not to exceed the amount established in the Internal Revenue Code or Internal Revenue Service Regulations and which qualifies as a tax free benefit to employees.

History.
68 Del. Laws, c. 426, § 2; 70 Del. Laws, c. 186, § 1; 78 Del. Laws, c. 290, § 262; 79 Del. Laws, c. 78, § 259; 79 Del. Laws, c. 290, § 268; 80 Del. Laws, c. 79, § 263; 80 Del. Laws, c. 298, § 261; 81 Del. Laws, c. 58, § 268; 81 Del. Laws, c. 280, § 263; 82 Del. Laws, c. 64, § 262; 82 Del. Laws, c. 242, § 253; 83 Del. Laws, c. 54, § 264.

§ 2056. Agency provision of commuter benefits [Suspended beginning in Fiscal Year 2013; see 83 Del. Laws, c. 54, § 264].

A state agency is authorized to grant commuter benefits to agency employees in conjunction with any plan submitted and approved by the Department pursuant to §§ 2053 and 2054 of this title. The state agency shall request each year as part of the budget process, a specific appropriation request sufficient to fund the commuter benefits included in the plan submitted to the Department for review.

History.
68 Del. Laws, c. 426, § 2; 78 Del. Laws, c. 290, § 262; 79 Del. Laws, c. 78, § 259; 79 Del. Laws, c. 290, § 268; 80 Del. Laws, c. 79, § 263; 80 Del. Laws, c. 298, § 261; 81 Del. Laws, c. 58, § 268; 81 Del. Laws, c. 280, § 263; 82 Del. Laws, c. 64, § 262; 82 Del. Laws, c. 242, § 253; 83 Del. Laws, c. 54, § 264.

§ 2057. Preemption [Suspended beginning in Fiscal Year 2013; see 83 Del. Laws, c. 54, § 264].

Any other provision of the Code notwithstanding, a Department-approved traffic reduction plan may provide commuter benefits to state employees.

History.
68 Del. Laws, c. 426, § 2; 78 Del. Laws, c. 290, § 262; 79 Del. Laws, c. 78, § 259; 79 Del. Laws, c. 290, § 268; 80 Del. Laws, c. 79, § 263; 80 Del. Laws, c. 298, § 261; 81 Del. Laws, c. 58, § 268; 81 Del. Laws, c. 280, § 263; 82 Del. Laws, c. 64, § 262; 82 Del. Laws, c. 242, § 253; 83 Del. Laws, c. 54, § 264.

PART III

OCCUPATIONAL AND BUSINESS LICENSES AND TAXES

CHAPTER 21

GENERAL PROVISIONS CONCERNING LICENSES

§ 2102. Term of licenses.

(a) *In general.* — All licenses issued under this title shall be for a term of 1 year, expiring on December 31, or on the date prescribed pursuant to the provision of the Delaware Code under which it was issued. Lost or stolen license certificates may be replaced for their unexpired terms upon payment of a $15 fee to the Department of Finance.

(b) *Optional 3-year renewal.* — Persons licensed under this section may, but are not required to, renew their licenses for a term of 3 years upon payment of a license fee equal to 3 times the fee in effect for said license at the time of renewal. Holders of 3-year licenses which add locations or units separately licensable under this section shall pro-rate the license fee for additional units or locations to the expiration date of their current licenses.

(c) [Repealed.]

History.
Code 1852, § 1226; 25 Del. Laws, c. 14, § 3; 27 Del. Laws, c. 30; Code 1915, §§ 187, 212; 28 Del. Laws, c. 13; 40 Del. Laws, c. 27, § 1; Code 1935, §§ 198, 240; 41 Del. Laws, c. 14, §§ 8, 9; 30 Del. C. 1953, § 2102; 57 Del. Laws, c. 136, § 4; 60 Del. Laws, c. 24, § 20; 71 Del. Laws, c. 314, § 2; 74 Del. Laws, c. 108, § 1; 83 Del. Laws, c. 107, § 7.

Effect of amendments.
83 Del. Laws, c. 107, effective July 30, 2021, repealed (c).

CHAPTER 23

COST OF OCCUPATIONAL LICENSES AND FEES

§ 2301. Occupations requiring licenses; definitions; fees; exemptions.

(a) "Persons" as defined in § 2701 of this title engaged in the occupations listed and defined in this section shall pay annual license taxes at the rates specified below. In addition to the license fee indicated below, each such person shall pay a fee of $25 for each additional branch or business location, except that a finance or small loan agency as defined in this section shall pay the basic annual fee for each place of business.

(1) *Advertising agency,* $75. "Advertising agency" includes every person engaged in the business of displaying advertising matter by billboards, posters or circulars, signs or window display, or of undertaking the writing or composition of advertisements for other persons on a commission, rental or flat fee basis.

(2) *Amusement conductor,* $75. "Amusement conductor" includes every person engaged in the business of conducting or maintaining or furnishing

on a commission or other basis mechanical or electronic devices for entertainment of the general public, for which a charge is made for the use thereof; provided further than an owner of certain of such mechanical or electrical devices operated automatically by insertion of a coin or token shall pay an additional license fee for the business as defined and at the rates prescribed as follows:

"Amusement machine owner" embracing every person engaged in the business of owning and operating either on the person's own account or by an agent, or by lease to another from such person or the agent, certain of the mechanical or electronic devices referred to in this section for furnishing to the public, music by the playing of records or transcriptions or which constitute a game or other device designed for public amusement, a fee for a license at the rate of $75 for each machine so owned and operated, provided the coin or token necessary to operate such machine is worth 5 cents or more.

(3) *Auctioneer,* $ 75. "Auctioneer" includes every person engaged in the business of crying sales of real or personal property on behalf of other persons for profit, except as otherwise provided by the provisions of this chapter. Any auctioneer not a citizen of this State shall be required to pay $ 225 for each county in which the person acts as auctioneer. No auctioneer shall be authorized by virtue of the license granted to employ any other person to act as auctioneer in the auctioneer's behalf, except in the auctioneer's own store or warehouse or in the auctioneer's presence, nor shall the term "auctioneer" apply or extend to a judicial or executive officer making sales in pursuance of any execution, judgment, or decree of any court nor to public sales made by executors or administrators.

(4) *Broker,* $75. "Broker" includes every person operating a business of buying and selling for the account of other persons for a commission or for profit, stocks, bonds, currency, negotiable paper, securities and any other intangible personal property.

(5) *Circus exhibitor,* $750. "Circus exhibitor" includes every person engaged in the business of exhibiting in a tent, arena, or other open space equestrian stunts, acrobatic stunts, freaks, trained or wild animals, and other forms of entertainment commonly known as a circus. This paragraph shall not be construed to include any circus or carnival for private profit sponsored by or in which any fire company of the State, or any fraternal, veteran's or religious organization shall share in the profits. The license fee for such circus or carnival shall be $300.

(6) *Commercial lessor,* $75. "Commercial lessor" includes every person who, as lessor or sublessor, receives rental income pursuant to any agreement transferring a title interest or possessory interest in real property located in this State under a lease of a commercial unit for any term. For this purpose, "commercial unit " means a structure or that part of a structure which is used for purposes other than a dwelling unit or farm unit.

(7) *Drayperson or mover,* $75. "Drayperson or mover" includes every person operating a business of transporting for profit tangible personal property of other persons.

(8) *Finance or small loan agency,* $450. "Finance or small loan agency" includes every person engaged in the business of lending money, with or without security, to other persons, with repayments of the loans to be made by installments or otherwise, but shall not include, either in reference to future or past transactions, banks or trust companies authorized to do banking business in the State under Title 5.

(9) *Hotel,* $25 for each room and $30 for each suite. "Hotel" includes every person engaged in the business of operating a place where the public may, for a consideration, obtain sleeping accommodations and meals and which, in an incorporated town, has at least 10 and in any other place at least 6 permanent bedrooms for the use of guests.

(10) *Manufacturer's agent or representative,* $75. "Manufacturer's agent" or "representative" includes every independent contractor in the business of representing 1 or more manufacturers for purposes of promoting the sale of the goods, product, or line of goods or products of such manufacturer or manufacturers within the State.

(11) *Mercantile agency or collection agency,* $75. "Mercantile agency" or "collection agency" includes every person operating a business of investigation of financial ratings and credit and/or the collection of commercial or consumer accounts for other persons, except attorneys-at-law having a license to practice such profession in this State.

(12) *Motel,* $25 for each room. "Motel" includes every person engaged in the business of furnishing for a consideration, transient guests with sleeping accommodations, private bath and toilet facilities, linen service and a place to park an automobile and who is not in the business of operating a hotel or tourist home as defined in this section.

(13) *Outdoor musical festival promoter,* $750. "Outdoor musical festival promoter" includes every person engaged in the business of organizing, operating, producing or staging musical entertainment in open spaces and not in a permanent structure for a gathering of 1,000 or more persons who pay a consideration or admission charge to view or hear such musical entertainment.

(14) *Parking lot or garage operator,* $75 for the first lot or garage facility and $35 for each additional facility. "Parking lot" or "garage operator" includes every person engaged in the business of operating any motor vehicle parking facility, whether open or enclosed, with space for 10 or more vehicles.

(15) *Photographer,* $75. "Photographer" includes every person operating a business of taking, making and/or developing photographs or pictures by action of light for profit or reward. Transient photographers without a regular and established place of business within the State shall pay an additional license tax of $25 for each day of operation within the State.

(16) *Real estate broker,* $75. "Real estate broker" includes every person certified as such by the Delaware Real Estate Commission and engaged in the real estate business. It includes those among such persons who deal exclusively or partly with rental property.

(17) *Sales representative,* $75. "Sales representative" includes every person who works in excess of 80 hours in any calendar month in the year selling goods or merchandise door to door. It includes soliciting orders and home demonstrations.

(18) *Security alarm business,* $115. "Security alarm business" includes every security alarm business defined in § 1201 of Title 24.

(19) *Showperson,* $375. "Showperson" includes every person engaged in the business of conducting or operating for profit a public theater, house or other enclosed place for the exhibition of stage shows or musical presentations, animal shows, carnivals for private profit and all other amusements of like character.

(20) *Taxicab or bus operator,* $45, for the first motor vehicle; $30, for each additional motor vehicle. "Taxicab" or "bus operator" includes every person engaged in the business of the operation of motor vehicles in

transporting persons for hire in the accommodation of the general public. A public carrier holding a certificate of public convenience and necessity issued by the Delaware Transportation Authority of the Department of Transportation authorizing it to operate a taxicab business, which actually operates such taxicab business through the leasing of its taxicab vehicles to independent contractor lessee drivers, shall be construed to be a "person" under this paragraph "engaged in the business of the operation of motor vehicles in transporting persons for hire in the accommodation of the general public" and shall pay the above-specified annual fees for its taxicab motor vehicles which are subject to such leasing for the year involved, and none of the independent contractor lessee drivers of such vehicles shall be construed to be a "person engaged in the business of the operation of motor vehicles in transporting persons for hire in the accommodation of the general public" within the meaning of this paragraph. This tax shall not apply however, to the operation of school buses used solely in the transportation of children to and from kindergarten, grade school, vocational school and high school.

(21) *Tourist home,* $15 for each room. "Tourist home" includes every person who operates a place where tourists or transient guests, for a consideration, may obtain sleeping accommodations and which has at least 5 permanent bedrooms for the use of tourists or transient guests and who is not in the hotel or motel business as defined in this section.

(22) *Trailer park,* $10 for each space as specified on a plot plan or as designated by the owner. "Trailer park", which may also be identified as a recreational vehicle park, or a tenting recreation park, includes any person engaged in the business of operating any place where space is furnished for units to park and hook up to or use sanitary and/or electrical facilities. This paragraph shall not apply to mobile home parks.

(23) *Transportation agent,* $75. "Transportation agent" includes every person operating a business of selling tickets on behalf of other persons, for transportation by common carriers on a commission basis or for profit.

(24) *Travel agency,* $225. "Travel agency" includes every person in the business of operating a full service travel bureau or department which assists in the planning and acquisition of tickets for contemplated trips of its customers by land, sea or air and for related accommodations.

(25) *Headquarters Management Corporation,* $5,000; provided, however, that in the case of any affiliated group, as defined in § 6401(1) of this title, only 1 member of such affiliated group that is a Headquarters Management Corporation shall be liable for a $5,000 annual license tax under this paragraph, and each other member of such affiliated group that is a Headquarters Management Corporation shall pay a license tax of $500. For purposes of this paragraph, "Headquarters Management Corporation " has the meaning set forth in § 6401(5) of this title.

(26) *Direct care worker,* $75. "Direct care worker" means, for purposes of this title, an individual (aide, assistant, caregiver, technician or other designation used) under contract to, but not employed by, a personal assistance services agency to provide personal care services, companion services, homemaker services, transportation services and those services as permitted in § 1921(a)(15) of Title 24 to consumers. The direct care worker provides these services to an individual primarily in the individual's place of residence.

(27) *Interactive fantasy sports registrant,* $50,000. "Interactive fantasy sports registrant" shall have the same meaning as set forth in § 4862 of Title 29.

(b) Upon every person engaging or continuing to engage in any service industry, business, calling or profession not otherwise specifically licensed and taxed under subsection (a) of this section, there is hereby levied and there shall be collected an annual general service license fee of $75.

(c)(1) Any person licensed under subsection (a) or (b) of this section whose business activity or operation is not limited to the rendition of services for other persons but also involves the sale or exchange of goods or personal property shall also be subject to the license fees imposed by Chapter 29 of this title.

(2) Paragraph (c)(1) of this section shall not apply to any case in which the sale or exchange of goods or personal property is incidental to the business activity licensed under subsection (a) or (b) of this section. For the purposes of this subsection, such sales or exchanges shall be deemed to be incidental if the gross receipts from such sales or exchanges do not exceed $8,500. In such case, Chapter 29 of this title shall not apply, but such incidental sales shall be included in gross receipts subject to tax under Chapter 23 of this title.

(3) The purchase of debt obligations of "affiliated corporations" shall not cause a person to be subject to tax under this chapter; provided, that the foregoing provision shall not apply to an "affiliated finance company" as defined in § 6301(2) of this title. For purposes of the foregoing sentence "affiliated corporations" shall have the same meaning as in § 6301(1) of this title.

(d)(1) In addition to the license fee required by subsections (a) and (b) of this section, every person shall also pay a license fee at the rate of 0.3983% of the aggregate gross receipts paid to such person attributable to activities licensable under this chapter, which fee shall be payable monthly on or before the twentieth day of each month with respect to the aggregate gross receipts for the immediately preceding month. In computing the fee due on such aggregate gross receipts for each month, there shall be allowed a deduction of $100,000. For purposes of this subsection, all branches or entities comprising an enterprise with common ownership or common direction and control shall be allowed only 1 monthly deduction from the aggregate gross receipts of the entire enterprise. The monthly returns shall be accompanied by a certified statement on such forms as the Department of Finance shall require in computing this fee due.

(2) Notwithstanding paragraph (d)(1) of this section, if the taxable gross receipts prescribed by paragraph (d)(1) of this section during the lookback period as defined in § 2122 of this title do not exceed the applicable threshold of $1,500,000, the return and payment of the additional license fee imposed for such month shall be due on or before the last day of the first month following the close of the quarter. (The applicable threshold in this paragraph is subject to annual adjustment as more fully set forth in § 515 of this title.) In the case of such return, in computing the fee due on such aggregate gross receipts for each quarter, there shall be allowed a deduction of $300,000. For purposes of this paragraph, all branches or entities comprising an enterprise with common ownership or common direction and control shall be allowed only 1 quarterly deduction from the aggregate gross receipts of the entire enterprise. The quarterly return shall be accompanied by a certified statement on such forms as the Department of Finance shall require in computing this fee due.

(3)a. For persons described in paragraph (a)(27) of this section, for the privilege of conducting interactive fantasy sports contests in the State, interactive fantasy sports registrants shall also pay a license fee at a rate equal to 15.5% of their aggregate interactive fantasy sports gross receipts generated within the State. For purposes of this section, "interactive fantasy sports gross receipts" means an amount equal to the total of all entry fees that the registrant collects from all authorized players, less the total of all sums paid out as winnings to all authorized players, multiplied by the "resident percentage," as defined in § 4862 of Title 29.

b. The fees provided by this section shall be remitted to the Division of Revenue on forms issued by the Director of Revenue and subject to such regulations and requirements as shall be prescribed by the Director of Revenue. The Director of Revenue shall deposit the license fees imposed by paragraphs (a)(27) and (d)(3) of this section on interactive fantasy sports registrants to the credit of the general fund, net of administrative expenses incurred by the Division of Revenue in enforcing this subsection and the Division of Gaming Enforcement in enforcing Chapter 48 of Title 29.

c. [Repealed.]

(4) [Repealed.]

(e) "Gross receipts" is defined as total consideration for services rendered, goods sold, or other-income producing transaction within this State, including fees and commissions.

(1) For persons described in paragraphs (a)(4) and (16) of this section the tax imposed under subsection (d) of this section shall be imposed on the broker. Salespersons operating in the broker's office shall be exempt from the taxes and fees imposed by subsections (b) and (d) of this section with respect to services performed in connection with the broker's business; provided, however, that commissions and fees paid to such salespersons shall be subject to tax under subsection (d) of this section as though such fees or commissions were received by the broker.

(2) Any person functioning in an "employee" relationship as defined in the Federal Insurance Contribution Act [26 U.S.C. § 3101 et seq.] shall be exempt from this chapter with respect to activities as an employee.

(3) In the case of partnerships, professional corporations or associations, the tax imposed under subsection (d) of this section shall be imposed on the aggregate gross receipts of such partnerships, professional corporation or association.

(4) Any person functioning as a "partner" shall be exempt from this chapter with respect to activities solely as a "partner".

(5) Gross receipts for businesses described in paragraphs (a)(1), (3), (4), (10), (11) and (16) of this section shall consist of commissions and fees earned.

(6) Gross receipts for commercial lessors as defined in paragraph (a)(6) of this section shall consist of the rental payment received for a commercial unit located in this State; provided, however, that:

a. Nothing in this section shall be interpreted to impair a commercial lessor's right under an existing or future lease to require the lessee therein to pay or to reimburse the lessor for the license fees herein imposed as part of the lessee's specified or general obligation to pay or reimburse lessor for gross receipts tax, real estate taxes or other governmental assessments, charges or fees;

b. Every commercial lessor, who is also a sublessor, shall exclude from gross receipts the amount said lessor pays to another lessor as rent for the same commercial unit; and

c. Any rental income received by a commercial lessor who has paid the transfer tax pursuant to § 5402(d) of this title shall not be included as gross receipts received by the commercial lessor.

(7) For licenses covered under subsection (b) of this section, any exception from the gross receipts definition as set forth in this subsection is subject to the rules and regulations as promulgated by the Secretary of Finance.

(f) Paragraphs (a)(5), (8), (9), (12), (13), (17) and (19)-(25) of this section shall be exempt from the additional license fee imposed by subsection (d) of this section.

(g) The additional license fee imposed by subsection (d) of this section shall not apply to those receipts of draypersons or movers if such receipts are derived from interstate transports, nor shall this section be applicable to receipts received during the time in which said section was enacted into law.

(h) – (n) [Repealed.]

(o) Banks, corporations described in § 1902(b)(8) of this title, insurance companies, including, general agents, agents, brokers and employees licensed under Title 18, pension plans and/or profit-sharing plans whether or not regulated under § 401 of the Internal Revenue Code of 1986 [26 U.S.C. § 401], as amended, public utilities as defined in Chapter 1 of Title 26 (but only with respect to gross receipts or the sale price of services and commodities taxable under, or with respect to which taxes are imposed by Chapter 55 of this title), distributors of direct-to-home satellite services (but only with respect to gross receipts or the sale price of services and commodities upon which taxes are imposed by Chapter 55 of this title), public utility holding companies regulated under the Public Utility Holding Company Act of 1935 [former 15 U.S.C. § 79 et seq., now repealed; see Energy Policy Act of 2005 (42 U.S.C. § 15801 et seq.)], savings and loan associations or building and loan associations licensed under Chapter 17 of Title 5, and similar or related financial institutions licensed or otherwise regulated under the Delaware law or the United States Code are exempt from payment of fees as set forth in subsections (b) and (d) of this section; provided, however, this exemption shall not apply to those activities of the foregoing persons which are required to be licensed under paragraph (6) of subsection (a) of this section.

(p) Nonprofit organizations exempted from federal income taxation under § 501 of the Internal Revenue Code of 1986 [26 U.S.C. § 501], as amended, shall be exempt from payment of fees as set forth in subsections (a), (b) and (d) of this section.

(q), (r) [Repealed.]

(s) Real estate mortgage investment conduits (as defined in § 860D of the Internal Revenue Code of 1986 [26 U.S.C. § 860D], as amended), are exempt from payment of fees as set forth in subsections (b) and (d) of this section.

(t) Chapter 12 of Title 24 notwithstanding, the term of new licenses and renewals issued to security alarm businesses shall be governed exclusively by this part; provided, however, that the Division shall not issue a license to a security alarm business without the approval of the Superintendent of the Delaware State Police under Chapter 12 of Title 24. Two-year security business licenses expiring between June 27, 1989, and June 27, 1991, shall be renewed for a period no greater than 1 year at an annual fee of $75, and such license shall expire the following December 31. The fee shall be reduced according to the number of full calendar months remaining in the year.

(u) Statutory trusts formed under the laws of this State which are registered as investment companies under the Investment Company Act of 1940, as amended (15 U.S.C. § 80a-1 et seq.), are exempt from payment of fees as set forth in subsections (b) and (d) of this section.

(v) Corporations registered as investment advisors under the Investment Advisors Act of 1940, as amended (15 U.S.C. § 80b-1 et seq.), corporations registered as transfer agents under § 17A of the Securities Exchange Act of 1934, as amended (15 U.S.C. § 78q-1) and corporations acting as principal underwriters as defined in § 2(a)(29) of the Investment Company Act of 1940, as amended (15 U.S.C. § 80a-2(a)(29)), are exempt from the payment of fees as set forth in subsection (b) of this section and from fees as set forth in subsection (d) of this section upon gross receipts received from statutory trusts described in subsection (u) of this section.

(w) Licensees to conduct horse racing meetings and licensees to conduct pari-mutuel or totalizator wagering or betting licensed under Chapter 101 of Title 3 or Chapter 4 of Title 28 shall be exempt from any license or license fees under this chapter, to the extent activities under this chapter are related to the conduct of horse racing meets.

(x) For tax periods beginning after December 31, 2002, and ending on or before December 31, 2005, individuals who contract with the State Fire Prevention Commission to provide instructional services to the Delaware State Fire School pursuant to § 6619 of Title 16 are exempt from the license requirement and fees imposed by this section, but only to the extent that the license and fees relate to receipts from and services provided to the Delaware State Fire School.

History.

11 Del. Laws, c. 646, § 1; 12 Del. Laws, c. 123, § 1; 17 Del. Laws, c. 503, §§ 1, 2; 18 Del. Laws, c. 555, §§ 2, 4; 22 Del. Laws, c. 22; 26 Del. Laws, c. 15, §§ 2, 6; 27 Del. Laws, c. 30; 28 Del. Laws, c. 16; Code 1915, §§ 181, 183-185, 214, 226A, 232, 258, 261; 40 Del. Laws, c. 27, § 1; 40 Del. Laws, c. 29, § 1; 40 Del. Laws, c. 30, § 1; Code 1935, §§ 189, 193, 195-197, 202, 204, 205, 232; 41 Del. Laws, c. 14, §§ 3, 5; 41 Del. Laws, c. 16; 41 Del. Laws, c. 17, §§ 1, 2; 42 Del. Laws, c. 67, §§ 1-6; 42 Del. Laws, c. 69, §§ 1, 2; 42 Del. Laws, c. 71, § 1; 45 Del. Laws, c. 11, §§ 1, 2; 45 Del. Laws, c. 12; 45 Del. Laws, c. 13, §§ 1, 2; 45 Del. Laws, c. 14, § 1; 47 Del. Laws, c. 341, § 1; 48 Del. Laws, c. 17; 48 Del. Laws, c. 324; 30 Del. C. 1953, § 2301; 49 Del. Laws, c. 346, § 2; 50 Del. Laws, c. 241, § 1; 53 Del. Laws, c. 107, §§ 2, 3; 54 Del. Laws, c. 5; 54 Del. Laws, c. 62; 54 Del. Laws, c. 321; 54 Del. Laws, c. 357, §§ 1-3; 55 Del. Laws, c. 65; 55 Del. Laws, c. 268, §§ 1, 2; 55 Del. Laws, c. 330; 57 Del. Laws, c. 136, §§ 11, 12; 57 Del. Laws, c. 188, §§ 2-4, 6-12, 20-22, 40, 48; 57 Del. Laws, c. 466, § 2; 57 Del. Laws, c. 575, § 1; 58 Del. Laws, c. 37; 58 Del. Laws, c. 71; 58 Del. Laws, c. 155; 60 Del. Laws, c. 24, §§ 1-4, 22; 60 Del. Laws, c. 223, § 1; 60 Del. Laws, c. 296, §§ 1-5; 60 Del. Laws, c. 507, §§ 1, 2; 60 Del. Laws, c. 545, § 1; 60 Del. Laws, c. 546, §§ 1, 2; 61 Del. Laws, c. 117, § 1; 61 Del. Laws, c. 126, § 1; 61 Del. Laws, c. 143, § 1; 61 Del. Laws, c. 442, § 1; 62 Del. Laws, c. 329, §§ 1, 2; 63 Del. Laws, c. 12, § 1; 63 Del. Laws, c. 246, § 1; 63 Del. Laws, c. 314, § 1; 63 Del. Laws, c. 417, §§ 1, 4; 64 Del. Laws, c. 281, § 2; 64 Del. Laws, c. 287, § 1; 64 Del. Laws, c. 461, §§ 11, 12; 65 Del. Laws, c. 29, §§ 1-6; 65 Del. Laws, c. 155, §§ 3-5; 65 Del. Laws, c. 160, § 5; 65 Del. Laws, c. 172, § 4; 65 Del. Laws, c. 392, §§ 1, 2; 65 Del. Laws, c. 402, § 3; 66 Del. Laws, c. 128, § 4; 66 Del. Laws, c. 267, § 3; 66 Del. Laws, c. 381, § 10; 67 Del. Laws, c. 40, §§ 17, 20-24; 67 Del. Laws, c. 261, §§ 1-4, 6; 67 Del. Laws, c. 296, § 1; 67 Del. Laws, c. 408, §§ 7, 8; 68 Del. Laws, c. 80, § 3; 69 Del. Laws, c. 83, § 1; 69 Del. Laws, c. 289, §§ 2, 3; 70 Del. Laws, c. 142, § 4; 70 Del. Laws, c. 186, § 1; 70 Del. Laws, c. 484, § 4; 70 Del. Laws, c. 489, §§ 3, 4; 71 Del. Laws, c. 217, §§ 9, 10; 71 Del. Laws, c. 314, § 3; 71 Del. Laws, c. 351, §§ 1, 18; 72 Del. Laws, c. 104, § 1; 73 Del. Laws, c. 329, § 73; 74 Del. Laws, c. 256, § 2[2]; 75 Del. Laws, c. 171, § 2; 75 Del. Laws, c. 199, §§ 4, 14, 23; 75 Del. Laws, c. 311, § 1; 75 Del. Laws, c. 412, §§ 2, 3; 76 Del. Laws, c. 282, §§ 1, 16; 77 Del. Laws, c. 81, §§ 1, 2; 77 Del. Laws, c. 82, § 1; 77 Del. Laws, c. 83, §§ 1-4, 25; 77 Del. Laws, c. 444, § 4; 78 Del. Laws, c. 73, §§ 4-9, 31; 78 Del. Laws, c. 104, § 2; 78 Del. Laws, c. 218, §§ 1, 2; 79 Del. Laws, c. 13, § 1; 80 Del. Laws, c. 83, § 2; 80 Del. Laws, c. 195, § 11; 81 Del. Laws, c. 73, § 1; 81 Del. Laws, c. 371, §§ 2, 3; 81 Del. Laws, c. 425, § 24; 82 Del. Laws, c. 69, § 2; 83 Del. Laws, c. 107, § 8.

Effect of amendments.

83 Del. Laws, c. 107, effective July 30, 2021, added "or consumer" in (a)(11).

PART IV

COMMODITY TAXES

CHAPTER 51

MOTOR FUEL TAX

SUBCHAPTER III

STATE AID TO MUNICIPALITIES FOR STREETS

§ 5162. Appropriations paid through State Treasurer.

(a) There shall be appropriated annually to municipalities within the State beginning in the State's 1998 fiscal year and each subsequent year thereafter in conjunction with, under, and as a portion of, the Delaware Transportation Trust Fund within the Capital Transportation Program, a sum in the amount as appropriated in the annual Bond and Capital Improvement Act. The sum so appropriated shall be transferred to the Municipal Street Aid Fund by the State Treasurer and distributed to municipalities as provided in this subchapter.

(b) When deemed in full compliance with the provisions of § 5165(b) of this title, including the annual submission of an affidavit that will certify the municipality's boundary, mileage and population totals, the State Treasurer is authorized to process payments to municipalities in the following manner:

(1) Recipients of municipal street aid whose total fiscal year share is $50,000 or less shall be paid 1 lump-sum in August.

(2) Recipients of municipal street aid whose total fiscal year share is greater than $50,000 but not more than $200,000 shall be paid in 2 equal installments, 1 in August and the other in January.

(3) Recipients of municipal street aid whose total fiscal year share exceeds $200,000 shall be paid in 4 equal installments, 1 each in August, October, January and April of each year.

(c) Disbursements can be accrued for up to 3 years for larger construction projects.

History.
30 Del. C. 1953, § 5162; 51 Del. Laws, c. 55, § 1; 55 Del. Laws, c. 106; 59 Del. Laws, c. 216, § 2; 61 Del. Laws, c. 414, § 1; 64 Del. Laws, c. 415, § 1; 66 Del. Laws, c. 87, § 3; 66 Del. Laws, c. 360, § 52; 67 Del. Laws, c. 285, § 53(a); 71 Del. Laws, c. 150, § 73; 81 Del. Laws, c. 336, § 1; 83 Del. Laws, c. 37, § 35.

Effect of amendments.
83 Del. Laws, c. 37, effective June 3, 2021, in the first sentence of (a), substituted "under" for "pursuant to" and "Transportation" for "Improvement" preceding "Program".

CHAPTER 54

REALTY TRANSFER TAX

SUBCHAPTER I
REALTY TRANSFER TAX

§ 5401. Definitions [For application of this section, see 81 Del. c. 384, § 3].

As used in this subchapter, except where the context clearly indicates a different meaning:

(1) "Document" means any deed, instrument or writing whereby any real estate within this State, or any interest therein, shall be quitclaimed, granted, bargained, sold, or otherwise conveyed to the grantee, but shall not include the following:

a. Any will;

b. Any lease other than those described or defined in paragraph (5) of this section below;

c. Any mortgage;

d. Any conveyance between corporations operating housing projects pursuant to Chapter 45 of Title 31 and the shareholders thereof;

e. Any conveyance between nonprofit industrial development agencies and industrial corporations purchasing from them;

f. Any conveyance to nonprofit industrial development agencies;

g. Any conveyance between husband and wife;

h. Any conveyance between persons who were previously husband and wife, but who have since been divorced; provided such conveyance is made after the granting of the final decree in divorce and the real estate or interest therein subject to such conveyance was acquired by the husband and wife, or husband or wife, prior to the granting of the final decree in divorce;

i. Any conveyance between parent and child or the spouse of such a child;

j. Any conveyance:

1. To a trustee, nominee or straw party for the grantor as beneficial owner,

2. For the beneficial ownership of a person other than the grantor where, if such person were the grantee, no tax would be imposed upon the conveyance pursuant to this chapter, or

3. From a trustee, nominee or straw party to the beneficial owner;

k. Any conveyance between a parent entity and a wholly-owned subsidiary entity; provided such conveyance is without actual consideration;

l. Correctional deeds without actual consideration;

m. Any conveyance to or from the United States or this State, or to or from any of their instrumentalities, agencies or political subdivisions and the University of Delaware and Delaware State University;

n. Any conveyance to or from an entity, where the grantor or grantee owns an equity interest in the entity in the same proportion as the grantor's or grantee's interest in, or ownership of, the real estate being conveyed; provided, however, that this paragraph shall not apply to any distribution in liquidation or other conveyance resulting from the partial or complete liquidation of an entity, unless the equity interest of the entity being liquidated has been held by the grantor or grantee for more than 3 years;

o. Any conveyance by the owner of previously occupied residential premises to a builder of new residential premises when such previously occupied residential premises are taken in trade by such builder as a part of the consideration from the purchaser of new, previously unoccupied premises;

p. Any conveyance to the lender holding a bona fide mortgage, which is genuinely in default, either by a sheriff conducting a foreclosure sale or by the mortgagor in lieu of foreclosure;

q. Any conveyance to a religious organization or other body or person holding title to real estate for a religious organization, if such real estate will not be used following such transfer by the grantee, or by any privy of the grantee, for any commercial purpose; provided, however, that only that portion of the tax which is attributable to and payable by the religious organization or other body or person holding title to real estate for a religious organization under § 5402 of this title shall be exempt;

r. Any conveyance to or from a volunteer fire company, organized under the laws of this State; provided, however, that only that portion of the tax which is attributable to and payable by the volunteer fire company under § 5402 of this title shall be exempt;

s. Any conveyance of a "manufactured home" as defined in § 7003 of Title 25, provided tax on said conveyance has been paid under § 3002 of this title;

t. Any conveyance without consideration to an organization exempt from tax under § 501(c)(3) of the federal Internal Revenue Code [26 U.S.C. § 501(c)(3)];

u. Any conveyance to a nonprofit conservation organization when the property is purchased for open space preservation purposes;

v. Any conveyance to or from an organization exempt from tax under § 501(c)(3) of the federal Internal Revenue Code when the purpose of said conveyance is to provide owner-occupied housing to low and moderate income households by rehabilitating residential properties and reselling said properties without profit;

w. Any conveyance between siblings, half siblings, or step siblings;

x. Any conveyance to or from a land bank formed under Chapter 47 of Title 31.

(2) "First-time home buyer" means any 1 of the following:

a. A natural person who has at no time held any direct legal interest in residential real estate, wherever located, and who intends to occupy the property being conveyed as his or her principal residence within 90 days following the transaction.

b. Spouses purchasing as joint tenants or tenants by the entirety, when neither spouse has ever held any direct legal interest in residential real estate, wherever located, and both of whom intend to occupy the property being conveyed as their principal residence within 90 days following the transaction.

c. Individuals purchasing as joint tenants or cotenants, when none of the individuals has ever held any direct legal interest in residential real estate, wherever located, and both of whom intend to occupy the property being conveyed as their principal residence within 90 days following the transaction.

(3) "Transaction" means the making, executing, delivering, accepting or presenting for recording of a document.

(4) "Value" means, in the case of any document granting, bargaining, selling or otherwise conveying any real estate or interest or leasehold interest therein, the amount of the actual consideration thereof, including

liens or other encumbrances thereon and ground rents, or a commensurate part of the liens or other encumbrances and ground rents which encumber the interest in real estate and any other interest in real estate conveyed; provided, that in the case of a transfer for an amount less than the highest appraised full value of said property for local real property tax purposes, "value" shall mean the highest such appraised value unless the parties or one of them can demonstrate that fair market value is less than the highest appraised value, in which case "value" shall mean fair market value, or actual consideration, whichever is greater.A demonstration that the transaction was at arm's length between unrelated parties shall be sufficient to demonstrate that the transaction was at fair market value.

(5) The term "document" defined in paragraph (1) of this section shall include the following:

a. Any writing purporting to transfer a title interest or possessory interest for a term of more than 5 years in a condominium unit or any unit properties subject to the Unit Property Act;

b. Any writing purporting to transfer a title interest or possessory interest of any lessee or other person in possession of real estate owned by the State or other political subdivision thereof;

c. Any writing purporting to assign or transfer a leasehold interest or possessory interest in residential property under a lease for a term of more than 5 years. For this purpose, the term "residential property" means any structure or part of structure which is intended for residential use, and excluding any commercial unit subject to tax under § 2301(a)(6) of this title, relating to commercial lessors.

(6) In determining the term of a lease under paragraph (5) of this section above, it shall be presumed for the purpose of computing the lease term that any rights or options to renew or extend will be exercised.

(7) For purposes of paragraph (4) of this section, in the case of a document described in paragraph (5) of this section under which the consideration is based in whole or in part on a percentage of the income or receipts to be received in the future, actual consideration shall include the amounts actually received under such percentage of income or receipts provision; provided, however, and notwithstanding any other provisions of this chapter, that the tax imposed by this chapter shall be due and payable to the Division of Revenue within 30 days after the date such amounts become due and payable under the agreement.

(8)a. Except as provided in paragraphs (8)b. and c. of this section, where beneficial ownership in real estate in this State is transferred through a conveyance or series of conveyances of intangible interests including mergers and all other indirect exchanges, in a corporation, limited liability company, partnership, trust, pass-through entity or other entity, such conveyance shall be taxable under this chapter as if such property were conveyed through a duly recorded "document" as defined in paragraph (1) of this section, and subject to the exemptions contained therein, except those exemptions contained in paragraphs (1)j. and n. of this section.

b. No bona fide pledge of stock or limited liability membership interest, or partnership interests as loan collateral nor any transfer of publicly traded stock; publicly traded limited liability company member interest or publicly traded partnership interest shall be deemed subject to taxation under this paragraph.

c. Where the beneficial owners of real property prior to the conveyance or series of conveyances referred to in this paragraph own 80% or more of the beneficial interest in the real estate following said conveyance or conveyances, such transfers shall not be subject to tax under this paragraph. Where the beneficial owners of real property prior to the conveyance or series of conveyances referred to in this paragraph own less than 80% of the beneficial interest in the real estate following said conveyance or conveyances, such transfers shall not be subject to tax under this paragraph, unless, under regulations promulgated by the Secretary of Finance, such transfer or transfers are properly characterized as a sale of real property. Such characterization shall take into account the timing of the transaction, beneficial ownership prior to and subsequent to the conveyance or conveyances; the business purpose of the corporation, limited liability company, partnership, trust, pass-through entity or other entity, and such other factors as may be relevant.

(9)a. Notwithstanding paragraph (1) of this section, there shall be included in the definition of "document" for purposes of this chapter any contract or other agreement or undertaking for the construction of all or a part of any building all or a portion of which contract, agreement or undertaking (or any amendment to the foregoing) is entered into, or labor or materials are supplied, either prior to the date of the transfer of the land on which the building is to be constructed or within 1 year from the date of the transfer to the grantee.

b. No jurisdiction in this State shall issue a building permit for any such building unless and until the person or persons (including corporations or other associations) requesting such permit shall demonstrate in whatever form may be specified by the Director of Revenue, including at the Director's discretion, a form of affidavit, that:

1. No transfer as described in this section has occurred within the preceding year;

2. No portion of the contract for construction for which the permit is being requested was entered into and no materials or labor with respect to the building have been provided within 1 year of the date on which the property was transferred; or

3. There has been paid a realty transfer tax on the document as defined in this paragraph.

c. In addition, no jurisdiction in this State shall issue a certificate of occupancy relative to any building on which a tax is provided by this subsection unless and until the owner recertifies the actual cost of the building and pays any additional tax due as a result of such recertification.

d. A "building" for purposes of this paragraph shall mean any structure having a roof supported by columns or walls which structure is intended for supporting or sheltering any use or occupancy but shall not include any alteration of or addition to an existing building where the cost of said alteration or addition is less than 50% of the value of the property transferred.

e. A "transfer" for purposes of this paragraph shall include any transfer made by a "document" as described in this section, other than this paragraph, and shall not include any transaction excluded from the definition of "document" under the provisions of paragraphs (1)a.-u. of this section.

History.

30 Del. C. 1953, § 5401; 55 Del. Laws, c. 109, § 1; 55 Del. Laws, c. 413, § 1; 59 Del. Laws, c. 153, §§ 1-4; 60 Del. Laws, c. 507, § 3; 62 Del. Laws, c. 316, § 1; 64 Del. Laws, c. 182, §§ 1, 2; 65 Del. Laws, c. 118, § 3; 65 Del. Laws, c. 426, § 1; 67 Del. Laws, c. 40, §§ 8, 9; 67 Del. Laws, c. 262, § 1; 68 Del. Laws, c. 165, § 1; 69 Del. Laws, c. 188, § 4; 70 Del. Laws, c. 186, § 1; 72 Del. Laws, c. 217, § 1; 72 Del. Laws, c. 372, § 1; 75 Del. Laws, c. 225, §§ 1-3, 5-7; 80 Del. Laws, c. 155, § 3; 81 Del. Laws, c. 384, § 1; 83 Del. Laws, c. 56, § 72; 83 Del. Laws, c. 107, § 9.

Revisor's note.

Section 78 of 83 Del. Laws, c. 56, provided:

"This act shall take effect in accordance with the provisions of state law." The act became effective upon the signature of the Governor on June 30, 2021.

83 Del. Laws, c. 56, § 178, provided: "This act shall take effect in accordance with the provisions of state law." The act became effective upon the signature of the Governor on June 30, 2021.

Effect of amendments.

83 Del. Laws, c. 56, effective June 30, 2021, added "and Delaware State University" in (1)m.

83 Del. Laws, c. 107, effective July 30, 2021, substituted "entity" for "corporation" twice in (1)k.; and rewrote (1)n.

TITLE 31
WELFARE

Part
I. In General

PART I
IN GENERAL

CHAPTER 3
CHILD WELFARE

SUBCHAPTER I
GENERAL PROVISIONS

§ 309. Background checks for child-serving entities and other organizations.

(a) A background check for employees or volunteers of child-serving entities and members of school boards shall consist of a fingerprinted Delaware and national background check completed by the State Bureau of Identification (SBI) and the Federal Bureau of Investigation (FBI) as well as a Child Protection Registry check completed by the Department of Services for Children, Youth and Their Families (DSCYF).

(b) *Definitions.* — For purposes of this section:

(1) "Administrator of educator preparation program" means the individual identified by the higher education institution as being responsible for overseeing the placement of candidates into student teaching placements in a Delaware public school.

(2) "Adult who is impaired" shall have the meaning as defined in § 3902 of this title.

(3) "Child Protection Registry" as used in this section, shall have the meaning as defined in § 921 of Title 16.

(4) "Child-serving entity" as used in this section shall mean:

a. The DSCYF; which includes any employee or volunteer of DSCYF or 1 of its contractors who have regular direct access to children and/or adolescents under the age of 18, but who do not provide child-care services at a facility as referred to in paragraph (b)(4)b. of this section;

b. Residential child-care facilities in Delaware which are under contract with or operated directly by DSCYF;

c. Public and private schools, including employees of the Department of Education;

d. Child-care providers as defined in § 3002A of Title 14; or

e. Youth camps or summer schools that are exempt from child-care licensing requirements;

f. Facilities and individuals registered and eligible for Federal Child Care Development Block Grant funds through the Delaware Department of Health and Social Services.

(5) "Contractor" means a person, not an employee, providing services within a child-serving entity and who:

a. Has regular direct access to children, or

b. Provides services directly to a child or children.

(6) "Conviction" or "convicted" shall have the same meaning as defined in § 902 of Title 16.

(7) "Direct access" means the opportunity to have personal, unsupervised contact with persons receiving care or education during the course of one's assigned duties.

(8) "Elderly person" shall have the meaning as defined in § 222 of Title 11.

(9) "Employee" means any person seeking employment for compensation with a child-serving entity, or any person who for any reason has regular direct access to children at a child-serving entity. This definition shall also include applicants wishing to become adoptive, foster, or respite parents and their adult household members and any person seeking a student teaching placement in a public school.

(10) "Felony convictions involving physical or sexual assault crimes" shall include: §§ 604-607, 612-613, 626, 629-636, 645, 651, 768-780, 782-783A, 785, 787, 802, 803,1100A-1102, 1103A-1103B, 1105, 1108-1112B of Title 11, felony convictions of § 1136 of Title 16, and felony convictions of § 3913(c) of Title 31.

(11) "Higher education institution" means a Delaware college or university that has a teacher preparation program that places candidates into student teaching placements in a Delaware public school.

(12) "Member of a school board" means a candidate, prospective, or current member of the State Board of Education, or the board of a public school district, vocational-technical school district, or charter school.

(13) "Misdemeanor convictions against children" shall include: §§601-603, 611, 621, 625-628A,763, 764, 765, 766, 767, 781, 785, 1102, 1103, 1106, 1107 of Title 11, and misdemeanor convictions of § 1136 of Title 16.

(14) "Private school" means a school having any or all of grades kindergarten through 12, operating under a board of trustees and maintaining a faculty and plant which are properly supervised.

(15) "Public school" means any public school and includes any board of education, school district, reorganized school district, special school district, charter school or charter school board and any person acting as an agent thereof.

(16) "Student teacher" means an individual participating in a student teaching placement.

(17) "Student teaching placement" means a structured, supervised classroom teaching, internship, clinical or field experience in a teacher education program in which the student teacher practices the skills being learned in the teacher education program and gradually assumes increased responsibility for instruction, classroom management, and other related duties for a class of students in a local school district or charter school. These skills are practiced under the direct supervision of the certified teacher who has official responsibility for the class. Successful

completion of a student teaching placement may be used to meet the requirements for an initial license set forth in § 1210 of Title 14.

(18) "Volunteer" means a person providing volunteer services within a child-serving entity and who has regular direct access to children.

(19) "Youth camp" means a child-serving entity having custody or control of 1 or more school-age children, unattended by parent or guardian, for the purpose of providing a program of recreational, athletic, educational and/or religious instruction or guidance and operates for up to 12 weeks for 3 or more hours per day, during the months of May through September or some portion thereof, or during holiday breaks in the course of a school year and is operated in a space or at a location other than a space or location subject to licensing pursuant to§ 3004A of Title 14.

(c) Except as provided in paragraph (c)(4) of this section, all child-serving entities are required to obtain criminal and Child Protection Registry checks for prospective employees, volunteers, and contractors. Members of school boards must obtain criminal and Child Protection Registry checks under § 209 or § 511 of Title 14.

(1) The SBI shall furnish information pertaining to the identification and criminal history record of prospective employees, volunteers, and contractors of child-serving entities, and members of school boards, except as otherwise allowed or required, provided that the prospective board member, employee, volunteer, or contractor submits to a reasonable procedure established by standards set forth by the Superintendent of State Police to identify the person whose record is sought. Such procedure shall include the fingerprinting of the individual subject to a criminal background check and the provision of such other information as may be necessary to obtain a report of the individual's entire criminal history record from SBI and a report of the individual's entire federal criminal history record under the FBI appropriation of Title II of Public Law 92-544. Notwithstanding any provision to the contrary, the information to be furnished by SBI shall include child sex abuser information. The Division of State Police shall be the intermediary for purposes of this section.

(2) Any person who is required to request a Child Protection Registry check under this section shall obtain a statement signed by the prospective board member, employee, volunteer, or contractor wherein the individual authorizes a full release for the person to obtain the information provided as a result of a check. The DSCYF will process a Child Protection Registry check of the individual upon receipt of the above-mentioned statement which shall be attached to the request from the person for the Child Protection Registry check.

(3) Notwithstanding paragraph (c)(1) of this section, private schools and youth camps may choose to perform a name-based Delaware criminal background check for prospective employees, volunteers and contractors through the Delaware Justice Information System (DELJIS) and an out-of-state criminal record check using private, third-party providers of such checks, provided that any out-of-state criminal record check shall include a Social Security trace search and county-based criminal record search in the counties in which the individual has resided within the past 10 years. Such check shall be valid for a 5-year period.

(4) Any private school, including youth camps directly operated by a private school, may choose not to perform the background checks and Child Protection Registry checks described in paragraphs (c)(1) and (c)(2) of this section, provided that the private school or youth camp that is

directly operated by the private school informs parents or guardians of the youth in attendance that the school or youth camp is not meeting minimum background check safety requirements for its staff members. The school or camp must obtain and retain for at least 1 year a signed acknowledgement of same from the parents or guardians.

(5) Costs associated with obtaining said criminal history information and Child Protection Registry information shall be borne by the applicant, except for those designated in paragraph (b)(4)d. of this section, whose costs shall be borne by the State. Notwithstanding the foregoing:

a. Public schools may use funds other than state funds to pay for criminal background check costs and may enter into consortia of school districts to pay such costs for persons covered by this act who work in more than 1 school district during the course of a year.

b. A candidate for election to a school board may use campaign funds to pay for background check costs under § 1075 of Title 14.

(6) All employees, volunteers and contractors shall inform their employer of any criminal conviction or entry on the Child Protection Registry which would lead to a prohibition pursuant to subsection (d) of this section.

(7) Child-serving entities may conditionally hire an employee or volunteer or place a child, pending the determination of suitability for employment. If the information obtained from the background checks indicates that the individual is prohibited from employment pursuant to subsection (d) of this section, the person may not continue in employment and is subject to termination.

(8) Any persons or organization whose primary concern is that of child welfare and care, which is not otherwise required to do so under the provisions of this section may voluntarily submit to the provisions of this subchapter at such person's or organization's expense pursuant to procedures established by the Superintendent of State Police.

(d) *Prohibitions.* — (1) The following criminal convictions or entries on the Child Protection Registry shall prohibit an individual from being an employee, volunteer, or contractor for a child-serving entity for the amount of time indicated:

a. Felony convictions involving physical or sexual assault crimes against a child, an adult who is impaired, or elderly person. Such convictions shall require a lifetime prohibition.

b. Felony convictions involving physical or sexual assault crimes against another adult. Such prohibition shall last for 10 years following the date of conviction.

c. Any other convictions for a violent felony as defined in § 4201(c) of Title 11 not already included within the convictions subject to a lifetime or 10 year prohibition under paragraphs (d)(1)a. and b. of this section shall prohibit the individual for 7 years following the date of conviction, unless the felony is included within the crimes that can lead to entry on the Child Protection Registry pursuant to § 923 of Title 16, in which case the length of time for the prohibition shall be as provided in the Child Protection Registry regulations.

d. Misdemeanor convictions against children. Such prohibitions shall last for 7 years following the date of conviction, unless the misdemeanor is included within the crimes that can lead to entry on the Child Protection Registry pursuant to § 923 of Title 16, in which case the length of time for the prohibition shall be as provided for in the Child Protection Registry regulations.

(2) If an individual has more than 1 prohibition, the higher level prohibition shall apply.

(3) For any other criminal conviction that does not prohibit employment according to paragraph (d)(1) of this section, the child-serving entity may set forth job-related prohibitions for employees, contractors, and volunteers considering number and types of offenses, their recency, the individual's criminal record since the offenses, and the responsibilities of the position which the individual has obtained or is seeking to obtain, provided that such prohibitions are not otherwise prohibited by law.

(4) The child-serving entity may prohibit employment for longer than that set out in paragraph (d)(1) of this section for those crimes that are prohibited and are job-related. The prohibition must not be shorter than the time proscribed in paragraph (d)(1) of this section, provided such time restrictions are not otherwise prohibited by law.

(e) Upon completion of the criminal background and Child Protection Registry checks:

(1) Where the child-serving entity is a public or private school:

a. The SBI shall provide the criminal background information and DSCYF shall provide the Child Protection Registry check information to the individual and the employing school or district, which shall determine whether the individual is prohibited from being employed by the school or district, pursuant to subsection (d) of this section. If the individual is not prohibited from employment by subsection (d) of this section but the individual has a criminal conviction or is on the Child Protection Registry, the school or district shall make a determination regarding suitability for employment using the factors in paragraph (d)(3) of this section. Information obtained under this subsection is confidential and may only be disclosed to the chief school officer or head of school and the chief personnel officer of the school and 1 person in each school who shall be designated to assist in the processing of criminal background checks, receive training in confidentiality and be required to sign an agreement to keep such information confidential.

b. Upon making its determination of suitability, the public school shall forward the determination to the person seeking employment. If a determination is made to deny the person from employment based on the criminal history of the person, the person shall have an opportunity to appeal to the chief school officer and/or head of school or designee for reconsideration.

c. In the case of a student teacher:

1. The SBI shall provide the criminal background information and DSCYF shall provide the Child Protection Registry check information to the individual and to the Higher Education Institution identified by the individual, through the Administrator of Educator Preparation Program. The Higher Education Institution shall determine whether the individual is prohibited from being employed pursuant to subsection (d) of this section and shall send a copy of the complete criminal background check and Child Protection Registry check information to the district superintendent or charter school director of the Delaware school district or charter school considering the person as a candidate for a student teaching position. If the individual is not prohibited from employment by subsection (d) of this section but the individual has a criminal conviction or is or has been on the Child

Protection Registry, the school or district shall make a determination regarding suitability for employment using the factors in paragraph (d)(3) of this section. Information obtained under this subsection is confidential and may only be disclosed to the chief school officer or head of school and the chief personnel officer of the school, and 1 person in each school who shall be designated to assist in the processing of criminal background checks, receive training in confidentiality and be required to sign an agreement to keep such information confidential.

2. Upon making its determination of suitability, the public school shall forward the determination to the administrator of educator preparation program of the designated higher education institution.

(2) Where the child-serving entity is DSCYF, a residential child-care facility under contract to or operated directly by DSCYF, or where the individual is applying to become an adoptive, foster or respite parent, SBI shall provide the criminal background information to DSCYF and DSCYF shall perform the Child Protection Registry check. DSCYF shall determine whether or not the individual is prohibited based on the results of the criminal background and Child Protection Registry checks. DSCYF may, by regulation, set forth criteria for unsuitability for its employees, contractors, volunteers, residential child-care employees, individuals applying to become an adoptive, foster or respite parent. These criteria shall relate to criminal history information and other information in addition to that set forth above. Such criteria and information shall be reasonably related to the prevention of child abuse. Upon making its determination, the DSCYF shall forward the determination to the applicant and the employer. Any adverse judgment affecting the applicant may be reviewed subject to regulations promulgated by DSCYF. The State Bureau of Identification may release all subsequent criminal history to DSCYF.

(3) Where the child-serving entity is a child-care provider, facility receiving Federal Child Care Development Block Grant funds, or a Youth Camp, SBI shall provide the criminal background information to DSCYF, and DSCYF shall perform the Child Protection Registry check. DSCYF shall determine whether or not the individual is prohibited by subsection (d) of this section based on the results of the criminal background and Child Protection Registry checks. If the applicant has a criminal conviction or is on the Child Protection Registry but is not prohibited from employment pursuant to paragraph (d)(1) of this section, DSCYF will assess the background check information and make a determination of suitability based upon factors set forth by DSCYF regulation consistent with paragraph (d)(3) of this section. If an applicant is determined unsuitable by DSCYF, the employer shall be informed. The employer shall make the final determination of whether or not to employ the individual. Notwithstanding the above, if the employer is a family child-care provider, DSCYF shall make the final decision based on the criteria established by regulations. If an applicant is determined unsuitable by DSCYF, the applicant and employer shall be informed. Any adverse judgment affecting the applicant shall be reviewed subject to regulations promulgated by the DSCYF. SBI may release all subsequent criminal history to DSCYF.

(4) Where the child-serving entity is a private school or youth camp that chooses to perform background checks using the method permitted in paragraph (c)(3) of this section, DELJIS shall perform a name-based criminal check based on the identifying information provided by the

private school or youth camp. If the individual is found to have a criminal background that would make them prohibited for employment, DELJIS shall so inform the employer. If the individual's background would not make them prohibited from employment, then DELJIS shall forward the information to DSCYF, which shall perform a check of the Child Protection Registry. DSCYF shall determine whether or not the individual is prohibited based on the results of the Child Protection Registry check.

(5)a. When the background checks are for a member of a school board, the SBI shall provide the criminal background information and DSCYF shall provide the Child Protection Registry check information pertaining to members and prospective members within 15 days of a request under subsection (c) of this section as follows:

1. To the Governor, for an individual seeking appointment to or serving on the State Board of Education or a vocational-technical school district.

2. To the Commissioner of Elections, for an individual seeking to be a candidate for election to a school board.

3. To the superintendent of a school district, for an individual serving as a member of the school district board.

4. To the board of a charter school, for an individual seeking to serve or serving on the charter school board.

b. Information provided under paragraph (e)(5)a. of this section is confidential and is not a public record under Chapter 100 of Title 29.

(f) The DSCYF shall, in the manner provided by law, promulgate regulations necessary to implement this section.

(g) The State Department of Education shall, in the manner provided by law, promulgate regulations necessary to implement this section. These regulations shall include:

(1) Establishment, in conjunction with SBI, of a procedure for fingerprinting persons seeking employment with a public school and providing the reports and certificate obtained pursuant to subsection (c) of this section;

(2) Establishment of a procedure to provide confidentiality of information obtained pursuant to subsection (c) of this section.

(3) Establishment of a procedure for determining other job-related prohibitions for employees, volunteers and contractors, pursuant to paragraph (d)(3) of this section.

History.

67 Del. Laws, c. 409, § 1; 79 Del. Laws, c. 290, § 202; 80 Del. Laws, c. 154, § 1; 80 Del. Laws, c. 211, §§ 1, 2; 81 Del. Laws, c. 433, § 1; 82 Del. Laws, c. 184, §§ 2, 3; 83 Del. Laws, c. 187, § 7.

Effect of amendments.

83 Del. Laws, c. 187, effective Sept. 17, 2021, added "and other organizations" in the section heading; added "and members of school boards" in (a); rewrote the introductory paragraph of (b); added present (b)(12) and redesignated the remaining paragraphs in (b) accordingly; added a comma following "volunteers" in the first sentence of (c) and in two places in the first sentence of (c)(1); added the second sentence in the introductory paragraph of (c); in (c)(1), in the first sentence added "and members of school boards" and "board member", and in the second sentence substituted "individual subject to a criminal background check" for "prospective employee", "individual's" for "person's" twice and "under" for "pursuant to"; in (c)(2), substituted "person" for "employer" in two places in the first sentence and once in the final sentence, in the first sentence added "board member", and substituted "individual" for "person" and "as a result of" for "pursuant to such"; restructured the former second sentence of (c)(5) by substituting a colon for a comma following "foregoing", designating the language beginning with "Public schools" as (c)(5)a. and adding (c)(5)b.; and added (e)(5).

SUBCHAPTER VIII
PARENTS RIGHT TO KNOW ACT

§ 398. Inspection of child care facility records.

History.
71 Del. Laws, c. 468, § 1; repealed by 83 Del. Laws, c. 194, § 2, effective Sept. 17, 2021.

CHAPTER 5
STATE PUBLIC ASSISTANCE CODE

Sec.
528. Coverage for epinephrine autoinjectors.

§ 520. Judicial review.

Any applicant for or recipient of public assistance benefits under this chapter or Chapter 6 of this title against whom an administrative hearing decision has been decided may appeal such decision to the Superior Court if the decision would result in financial harm to the appellant. The appeal shall be filed within 30 days of the day of the final administrative decision. The appeal shall be on the record without a trial de novo. The Court shall decide all relevant questions and all other matters involved, and shall sustain any factual findings of the administrative hearing decision that are supported by substantial evidence on the record as a whole. The Court may remand the matter for further factual findings or other proceedings consistent with the Court's order. The notice of appeal and all other matters regulating the appeal shall be in the form and according to the procedure as shall be provided by the rules of the Superior Court.

History.
64 Del. Laws, c. 482, § 1; 83 Del. Laws, c. 134, § 1.

Effect of amendments.
83 Del. Laws, c. 134, effective Sept. 10, 2021, added the penultimate sentence.

§ 528. Coverage for epinephrine autoinjectors.

(a) For purposes of this section, "epinephrine autoinjector" means a single-use device used for the automatic injection of a premeasured dose of epinephrine into the human body.

(b) Carriers shall provide coverage for medically-necessary epinephrine autoinjectors for individuals who are 18 years of age or under.

History.
83 Del. Laws, c. 42, § 4.

Revisor's note.
This section became effective upon the signature of the Governor on June 15, 2021.

DISTRIBUTION TABLE I

This table, in conjunction with the table in the bound volume and the 2020 Cumulative Supplement, shows the original disposition of general and permanent acts passed since the Code of 1974.

83 DELAWARE LAWS
151st Gen. Assem. 2021

Ch.	Sec.	Title	Del. Code Ann. Sec.
1	1	Const.	Art. I, § 21
2	1	19	3326
2	2	19	3348
2	3	29	8503
2	4	30	1106
2	5	29	8503; 8503, note
3	1	26	354
3	2	26	358
3	3	26	362
3	4	26	363
5	1	14	1270
6	1	14	Pt. V, Ch. 89E; 8901E; 8902E; 8903E; 8904E; 8905E; 8906E; 8907E
7	1	9	1101A
7	2	9	Pt. II, Ch. 11, Subch. III, Subpt. I
7	3	9	1125; 1126; 1128
7	4	9	Pt. II, Ch. 11, Subch. III, Subpt. II; 1131; 1132; 1133; 1134; 1135; 1136; 1137; 1138
7	5	9	1131; 1133; 1134
7	6	9	1155; 1158; 1159; 1160R
7	7	9	2515
7	8	9	2910
7	9	9	1129
7	10	9	1101A; 1102; 1125; 1126; 1127; 1128
7	11	9	1101A, note; Pt. II, Ch. 11, Subch. III, Subpt. I, note; Pt. II, Ch. 11, Subch. III, Subpt. II, note
7	12	9	1131, note; 1133, note; 1134, note; 1155, note; 1158, note; 1159, note; 1160, note; 2515, note; 2910, note; 1129, note
7	13	9	1101A, note;

83 DELAWARE LAWS
151st Gen. Assem. 2021

Ch.	Sec.	Title	Del. Code Ann. Sec.
7	13	9	1102, note; 1125, note; 1126, note; 1127, note; 1128, note
8	1	3	Pt. II, Ch. 29; 2901; 2902; 2903; 2904; 2905; 2906; 2907
8	2	3	Pt. II, Ch. 29, note
9	2	4	512; 512
9	3	4	512; 524; 543
9	4	4	561; 562
9	5	4	512, note; 524, note; 543, note; 561, note; 562, note
10	1	16	3123; 3123R
11	1	14	4142
12	1	11	4218
13	1	2	1901
13	2	6	4502
13	3	6	4602
13	4	9	1183
13	5	9	9605
13	6	10	4503
13	7	11	1213
13	8	11	1304
13	9	14	506
13	10	14	4161
13	11	14	8501
13	12	18	2304
13	13	19	204
13	14	19	710
13	15	24	502
13	16	24	502
13	17	24	701
13	18	24	701
13	19	24	1702
13	20	24	1702
13	21	24	3101
13	22	25	5141
13	23	29	5953
13	24	29	6962
14	1	14	2601
14	2	14	2602
14	3	14	2605
16	1	24	1710
16	2	24	1770; 1770A; 1771; 1772; 1773;

83 DELAWARE LAWS
151st Gen. Assem. 2021

83 DELAWARE LAWS
151st Gen. Assem. 2021

Ch.	Sec.	Title	Del. Code Ann. Sec.
48	8	16	4912A
48	9	16	4913A
48	10	16	4919A
48	11	16	4920A
48	12	16	4922A
48	13	16	4923A
49	1	16	4799A
49	2	16	4799B
49	3	16	4799C
50	1	18	6902
50	2	18	6903
50	3	18	6906
50	4	18	6916
51	1	14	4143
51	2	14	4143, note
52	1	18	3370, note; 3571R, note
52	1	24	Ch. 60, note; 1702, note; 1769D, note; 502, note; 701, note; 1101, note; 1902, note; 1933, note; 2002, note; 2101, note; 2502, note; 3002, note; 3041, note; 3502, note; 3802, note; 3902, note; Ch. 17A, note
52	2	18	3370
52	3	18	3571R
52	4	24	Ch. 60; 6001; 6002; 6003; 6004; 6005
52	5	24	1702
52	5	16	4904; 4904, note; 4905; 4905, note
52	5	24	1703; 1703, note
52	6	24	1769DR
52	7	24	502
52	8	24	701
52	9	24	1101; 1105; 1105, note
52	10	24	1902
52	10	16	3123; 3123, note
52	11	24	1933R
52	12	24	2002
52	13	24	2101
52	14	24	2502; 2503; 2503, note; 2515; 2515, note
52	15	24	3002
52	16	24	3041
52	17	24	3502
52	18	24	3802
52	19	24	3902

83 DELAWARE LAWS
151st Gen. Assem. 2021

Ch.	Sec.	Title	Del. Code Ann. Sec.
52	20	24	Ch. 17A; 1701A; 1702A; 1703A; 1704A; 1705A; 1706A; 1707A; 1708A; 1709A; 1710A; 1711A; 1712A; 1713A; 1714A; 1715A; 1716A; 1717A; 1718A; 1719A; 1720A; 1720A, note; 1721A; 1722A; 1723A; 1724A
52	21	18	3370, note; 3571R, note
52	21	24	Ch. 60, note; 1702, note; 1769D, note; 502, note; 701, note; 1101, note; 1902, note; 1933, note; 2002, note; 2101, note; 2502, note; 3002, note; 3041, note; 3502, note; 3802, note; 3902, note; Ch. 17A, note
53	1	14	1726
53	2	14	1726
53	3	14	1726, note
54	6	29	5903, note
54	7(e)	29	6055, note; 6061, note
54	8(a) intro	19	1311A, note
54	8(d)(1)	29	5915, note
54	8(g)	14	1305, note
54	8(m)(1)-(m)(3)	14	1322, note
54	8(m)(6) intro	14	1305, note; 1308, note; 1311, note; 1322, note; 1324, note
54	8(m)(6)(i)	14	1305
54	8(m)(6)(iii)	14	1308
54	8(m)(6)(iv)	14	1311
54	8(m)(6)(v)	14	1322
54	8(m)(6)(vi)	14	1324
54	8(n)	14	9219
54	21	29	5207, note; 5903, note
54	24(a)	29	Pt. VI, Ch. 69, note
54	25	18	3206, note
54	32(a)	29	5532

83 DELAWARE LAWS
151st Gen. Assem. 2021

Ch.	Sec.	Title	Del. Code Ann. Sec.
63	2	6	17-220
63	3	6	17-305
63	4	6	17-403
63	5	6	17-1201
63	6	6	17-1202
63	7	6	17-1203R
63	8	6	17-1204
63	9	6	17-1205
63	10	6	17-106, note; 17-220, note; 17-305, note; 17-403, note; 17-1201, note; 17-1202, note; 17-1203, note; 17-1204, note; 17-1205, note
65	1	29	10002
65	1	18	8309; 8309, note
65	1	16	197; 197, note
65	1	18	1133; 1133, note
65	1	14	1703A; 1703A, note
65	1	10	7123; 7123, note
65	2	29	10004
65	2	9	349; 349, note
65	2	22	114; 114, note
65	2	29	8707; 8707, note
65	3	29	10006R
65	4	29	10006A
65	5	29	10002, note; 10004, note; 10006A, note
66	1	20	3156
67	1	14	8001; 8002; 8003
68	1	21	4505
69	1	6	12A-103
69	2	12	3315; 3326; 3327; 3331; 3339; 3342; 3344
69	3	12	3536
69	29	12	3545
69	3	12	3550
70	1	29	4805
70	2	29	4807A
70	3	29	4809
70	4	29	4815
70	5	29	4822
70	6	29	4828
70	7	29	4829
70	8	29	4831
70	9	29	4805, note; 4807A, note; 4809, note; 4815, note; 4822, note; 4828, note; 4829, note; 4831, note
71	1	15	2050
71	2	15	2050A
71	3	15	3161
71	4	15	1701

83 DELAWARE LAWS
151st Gen. Assem. 2021

Ch.	Sec.	Title	Del. Code Ann. Sec.
71	5	15	2050, note; 2050A, note; 3161, note; 1701, note
72	1	11	2107
72	2	11	2107, note
72	3	11	2107; 2107, note
73	1	11	464
73	2	11	465
73	3	11	466
73	4	11	467
73	5	11	468
73	6	11	470
73	7	11	471
74	1	6	4501
74	2	6	4502
74	3	6	4503
74	4	6	4504
74	5	6	4501, note; 4502, note; 4503, note; 4504, note
75	1	16	2601
75	2	16	2602
75	3	16	2603
75	4	16	2604
75	5	16	2606
75	6	18	3337
75	7	18	3554
75	9	18	3337, note; 3554, note
76	1	24	5101
76	2	24	5104
76	3	24	5107
76	4	24	5124
76	5	24	5127
77	1	14	2702
77	2	14	2702, note
78	2	14	2707
79	1	14	1210
79	2	14	1211
79	3	14	1212
79	4	14	1252
79	5	14	1260
79	6	14	1262
79	7	14	1263
79	8	14	1266
79	9	14	1280
80	1	14	1280
81	1	19	902
82	1	11	6532
82	2	11	4381
83	1	11	4321
83	2	11	8401
83	2	21	4313; 4313, note; 2139M; 2139M, note
83	2	29	5526; 5526, note
83	2	11	8402; 8403; 8404
83	3	11	Pt. V, Ch. 84A; 8401A; 8402A
83	4	29	9003

83 DELAWARE LAWS
151st Gen. Assem. 2021

Ch.	Sec.	Title	Del. Code Ann. Sec.
122	3	16	Pt. II, Ch. 30E, Subch. II; 3011E; 3012E; 3013E; 3014E; 3015E; 3016E; 3017E
122	4	16	Pt. II, Ch. 30E, note
123	1	18	Pt. I, Ch. 67B
123	1	18	Pt. I, Ch. 67B, note
123	1	18	6701B; 6702B; 6703B; 6704B; 6705B; 6706B; 6707B; 6708B; 6709B
123	2	18	705
124	1	14	1917
124	2	14	1919
124	3	29	6102
124	4	14	1917, note; 1919, note
124	4	29	6102, note
124	5	14	1917, note; 1919, note
124	5	29	6102, note
125	1	21	4404
125	2	21	6901
125	3	25	3906
125	4	25	4001
126	1	14	1716E
126	1	14	1716E, note
127	1	19	1602
128	1	29	804A
128	2	29	804A, note
129	1	19	204
129	2	19	205
129	3	29	6902
129	4	29	6960A
129	5	29	6962
129	6	19	204, note; 205, note
129	6	29	6902, note; 6960A, note; 6962, note
130	1	14	5106
132	1	9	1120
132	2	9	1392
133	1	9	Pt. II, Ch. 34; 3401; 3402; 3403; 3404; 3405; 3406; 3407; 3408; 3409; 3410
133	2	9	Pt. II, Ch. 34, note
134	1	31	520
135	1	14	8609
136	1	24	716
136	2	24	716, note

83 DELAWARE LAWS
151st Gen. Assem. 2021

Ch.	Sec.	Title	Del. Code Ann. Sec.
137	1	16	Pt. XIII, Ch. 103, Subch. I; Pt. XIII, Ch. 103, Subch. I, note
137	2	16	10301
137	3	16	10302
137	4	16	10303
137	5	16	10304
137	6	16	10305
137	7	16	10306
137	8	16	10307
137	9	16	10308
137	10	16	10311
137	11	16	10312
137	12	16	10313
137	13	16	10314
137	14	16	10315
137	15	16	Pt. XIII, Ch. 103, Subch. I, note; 10301, note; 10302, note; 10303, note; 10304, note; 10305, note; 10306, note; 10307, note; 10308, note; 10311, note; 10312, note; 10313, note; 10314, note; 10315, note
137	16	16	10307, note; 10307
137	17	16	10312, note; 10312
138	1	16	10307
139	1	16	2721
140	1	3	Pt. II, Ch. 21; Pt. II, Ch. 21, note; 2101; 2102; 2103; 2104; 2105; 2106; 2107; 2108; 2109; 2110; 2111; 2112; 2113; 2114; 2115; 2116; 2117; 2118; 2119; 2120; 2121; 2122; 2123
141	1	29	5522
141	2	29	5527
142	1	7	Pt. VI, Ch. 54; Pt. VI, Ch. 54, note; 5401; 5402; 5403; 5403; 5404; 5404; 5405; 5405; 5406; 5406; 5407; 5407; 5408; 5408; 5409; 5409; 5410; 5410; 5411
143	1	16	6602
143	2	16	6603
143	3	16	6604

83 DELAWARE LAWS
151st Gen. Assem. 2021

Ch.	Sec.	Title	Del. Code Ann. Sec.
185	1	29	8926
185	2	29	8926
186	1	29	8905
186	2	29	8905; 8905, note
187	1	14	209; 209, note
187	2	14	104
187	3	14	511
187	4	14	1052
187	5	14	1064
187	6	14	1075
187	7	31	309
187	8	14	209, note
188	1	29	6962
190	1	24	2803
190	2	24	2817
190	3	24	2820R
190	4	24	2828
190	5	24	2829
190	6	24	2830
191	1	7	521
191	2	7	521, note
192	1	21	2140I; 2140I, note
193	1	24	503
193	2	24	504
194	1	14	Pt. I, Ch. 30B
194	1	14	Pt. I, Ch. 30B, note
194	1	14	3001B; 3002B; 3003B
194	2	31	398R
195	1	6	4502
195	2	6	4602
195	3	11	1304
195	4	18	2304

83 DELAWARE LAWS
151st Gen. Assem. 2021

Ch.	Sec.	Title	Del. Code Ann. Sec.
195	5	19	710; 722
195	6	25	5141
196	1	10	8130R
196	2	16	Pt. VI, Ch. 68, Subch. III
196	2	16	Pt. VI, Ch. 68, Subch. III, note
196	2	16	6820R
196	3	16	6821; 6822; 6823; 6824
197	1	24	3511
198	1	4	904
198	2	16	4764
198	3	10	1004A
199	1	11	6518
200	1	11	632; Pt. I, Ch. 5, Subch. II, Subpt. CR; 651R; 652R; 653R; 654R; 2702; 2702, note
201	1	18	1707
202	1	16	7204R
203	1	25	5106
203	2	25	5512
204	1	21	4315
204	2	21	4358
205	1	6	4902A
205	2	6	4903A; 4907A; 4907A, note
206	1	21	4196A; 4196A, note
207	1	4	101
207	2	4	513